# ESSENTIAL READINGS IN CANADIAN CONSTITUTIONAL POLITICS

# Essential Readings in Canadian Constitutional Politics

Edited by Christian Leuprecht and Peter H. Russell

UNIVERSITY OF TORONTO PRESS

Library and Archives Canada Cataloguing in Publication

Essential readings in Canadian constitutional politics / Christian Leuprecht and Peter H. Russell.

Includes bibliographical references.
ISBN 978-1-4426-0368-4

1. Constitutional history—Canada. 2. Constitutional law—Canada. 3. Canada—Politics and government.
I. Russell, Peter H. II. Leuprecht, Christian, 1973–

KE4199.E87 2011          342.7102'9          C2011-903364-X
KF4482.E87 2011

We welcome comments and suggestions regarding any aspect of our publications—please feel free to contact us at news@utphighereducation.com or visit our Internet site at www.utppublishing.com.

*North America*
5201 Dufferin Street
North York, Ontario, Canada, M3H 5T8

2250 Military Road
Tonawanda, New York, USA, 14150

*UK, Ireland, and continental Europe*
Plymbridge Distributors Ltd.
Estover Road, Plymouth, PL6 7PY, UK
TEL: 44 (0) 1752 202301
FAX ORDER LINE: 44 (0) 1752 202333
enquiries@nbninternational.com

ORDERS PHONE: 1-800-565-9523
ORDERS FAX: 1-800-221-9985
ORDERS E-MAIL: utpbooks@utpress.utoronto.ca

The University of Toronto Press acknowledges the financial support for its publishing activities of the Government of Canada through the Canada Book Fund.

Cover design and interior by Em Dash Design

Printed in Canada

In memory of

## PETER LESLIE

Professor of Political Studies, Queen's University
Director of the Institute of Intergovernmental Relations

# Contents

# Acknowledgements

PEOPLE TEND TO think of Queen's University as a provincial university and the Royal Military College of Canada (RMC) as a federal one. Federal–provincial relations are not quite that straightforward, though. When Queen's sought to amend its charter in the 1880s, it approached the provincial government at Queen's Park, figuring that education was an area of provincial jurisdiction. The federal government, looking to assert its sovereignty, challenged Ontario's jurisdiction over the University. The dispute ended up before the Judicial Committee of the Privy Council (JCPC), then the highest court of the land. Since Queen's University had been chartered before Confederation, and since Quebec and Ontario were both represented when the Charter was granted, albeit *ex officio*, the JCPC sided with the federal government. Queen's thus became the country's only federally chartered university. To this day the University has to seek approval from the federal parliament to amend its Charter. Upon its founding in 1876, by contrast, RMC, notwithstanding its status as a federally funded military university, had to be chartered by the Province of Ontario.

I have come to develop an interest in the arcane minutiae of federal–provincial relations, in part because I hold a primary faculty appointment at RMC while also cross-appointed to Queen's University. Why would an immigrant such as me take an interest in studying Canada's constitution? Actually, several of the authors in this compendium were not born in Canada. My interest in the Canadian constitution was honed as a result of a second-year course in which I enrolled while reading for my undergraduate degree

at the University of Toronto with the same professor with whom I am now co-editing this anthology, Peter H. Russell. To be candid, I had little interest in the constitution; it sounded like a pretty dry topic. I was wrong. And in the process, I confirmed the rule by which I was told to enrol in this course in the first place: Choose courses by professor rather than topic.

Ten years on I had just finished my Ph.D. at Queen's and the department was looking for someone to teach its third-year course on the principles of the Canadian constitution. I had always felt that no student should graduate from a program in political science without having some understanding of the country's constitution. But political science and its students have become so enthralled with results, such as the benefits claimed or the values expressed in politics, that they no longer pay much attention to form and formalities. Political scientists qualified to teach such a course are on their way to becoming an endangered species. Many professors have at least a basic understanding of Canada's mega-constitutional negotiations from the mid-1960s through the Charlottetown Accord in the early 1990s; the temptation thus is to teach it as a course in political history. Alternatively, the constitutional-law and judicial-politics approach to teaching such a course consists largely of reading seminal Supreme Court cases. Of course, there is plenty of interest in the Charter of Rights and Freedoms, on which there is a proliferation of scholarship.

For the purpose of a course on the Canadian constitution, these approaches miss the mark. While the constitutional rounds from Victoria through Charlottetown remain relevant, much of it is, by now, political history that hardly warrants taking up the bulk of a course on the constitution. Similarly, I had found that undergraduate students are not all that fond of reading reams of court cases. They enjoy taking in court cases in moderation only. The Charter, finally, is but one aspect of the constitutional whole. There are suitable books that can serve as supporting course texts for all these approaches.

When I design my courses, I begin by identifying the core material that I would expect a student with a course by that title on her/his transcript to have covered. Once I had charted out this course on the Canadian constitution, however, and much to my surprise, I discovered that there was no current textbook to support such a course. I was left with little choice but to assemble a reader of relevant material. Over the years I refined the reader that has proven quite popular with students—but it became ever more expensive! The first year I taught the course, Guy Laforest came to town. He kindly agreed to give a guest lecture to my students. Perusing the reader, he encouraged me to turn it into a textbook. At about the same time, a major publisher approached me about authoring a textbook on the constitution. Having neither the competence nor the time to spare, I respectfully declined. Still, it was evident that the material I was using stood to benefit from greater exposure. Publishing it as a reader would make the material more accessible and less costly to disseminate to students.

The anthology has not been easy to assemble. Peter and I tried diligently to balance differing perspectives. In tune with Canadian constitutional politics, the result is bound to be controversial. We would have liked to include (or should have included) more material. Most publishers were accommodating. Many believed in the project to such an extent that they made their material available free of charge. The remainder settled for a nominal fee. Some, however, insisted on fees that vastly exceeded a modest Canadian publishing budget. Others yet imposed unreasonable limits on the material we would be permitted to reproduce from that source. We would have liked to include more material by women and younger scholars, and more on the West, cities, the North, and so forth. Balancing those imperatives against budgetary constraints, the overall size of the final product, and keeping the final book affordably priced was agonizing. At the same

time, we wanted to optimize the number of pieces that, in consultation with others, we deemed integral to a project such as this.

Many authors in this volume have passed on and their contributions risk collecting dust in a library; half of the readings in this volume had never before been digitized, which added an additional layer of complexity to the project. This reader is thus meant to do its part in paying homage to pioneering scholars and their legacy. Many of them laid the groundwork for the discipline; many are giants on whose shoulders we stand today. Other authors are obscure yet their contributions included here stand out. Others still are well known but their selections included here may be unfamiliar to many of the audience.

One of the objectives of this book is for English Canada to gain a better understanding not only of Quebec's claims for autonomy but also of the rationale that informs these claims. To this end, we have made a point of including francophone scholars who, although they may not be widely read outside of Quebec, have shaped constitutional thinking in Quebec. Part of the challenge here is that many of these figures have written little in English. This volume tries to make some of these writings more accessible to an English-language audience.

Another objective is to reinvigorate and innovate the way the constitution is taught at the undergraduate level. This collection offers a good overview of the key figures and debates in a way that is accessible and interesting for students. This book also stands apart as a resource for graduate students in Canadian politics, making readily accessible core material with which anyone who professes to have a teaching and research competency in Canadian government and politics should have at least some familiarity. Students in constitutional law also stand to benefit from taking a more contextual approach to the cases they are reading. Indeed, a good deal of material in this anthology has been written by legal scholars, first appeared in law journals, and, directly or indirectly, has weighed in on key legal debates. The volume also hopes to draw in public and civil servants. Much of the vernacular discussion involving constitutional principles is wrought with ignorance or misunderstanding, especially insofar as principles such as responsible government and ministerial responsibility are concerned. Similarly, when working with officials at the federal, provincial, and municipal levels of government, I find disconcerting their limited knowledge of the source of their authority as well as the constraints the constitution imposes upon that authority.

Finally, much of the world looks at Canada for the way it has managed its constitutional affairs, its federal system and concomitant intergovernmental relations, and the way it has endeavoured to accommodate competing rights and autonomy claims in a deeply diverse society. There is much to be learned from the Canadian experience, not all of it necessarily positive: If nothing else, we can always serve as a bad example of how not to do it. Lest we forget that what is interpreted as a successful constitutional regime in much of English Canada is rather inchoate in the eyes of many of the country's geographic, ethnic, or linguistic minorities. Still, even the critics largely agree on at least one successful aspect of Canada's constitutional regime: It has proven sufficiently robust to offer a strong disincentive against resorting to violence as a way to resolve deeply divisive political disputes in a society as diverse as Canada.

Given such disparate objectives, determining the content of the reader relied on input and feedback from many people who suggested a particular piece or author be included here, or pointed out an omission there. Special mention must go to my co-editor, to whom I am infinitely grateful for his immediate enthusiasm and input. Nothing like an island in the midst of Georgian Bay to hatch a quintessentially Canadian venture such as this! I am also grateful to David Elder and Sean Conway for their inspiration and advice. We were lucky to have our pick of publishers and I am grateful to the University of Toronto Press, Higher Education Division and, especially, to Anne Brackenbury for taking on the project. Anne's patience with me saw the project through despite my many competing commitments and often tardy delivery of materials. Beate Schwirtlich coordinated having the manuscript copyedited, laid out, and printed, and many long additional hours were put in by Beth McAuley and her team at The Editing Company who assembled the final electronic files and made sure each and every note in each and every reading was correctly in place!

Obtaining permissions to reproduce material is not always easy, especially when the material is older

and it is not immediately apparent who, if anyone, may still retain copyright. I am deeply indebted to a former student of my course on the Canadian constitution, Meaghan McClurg, for her dedication to this part of the project and for digitizing large parts of the material. Spencer Baker meticulously edited Pierre Trudeau's chapter, which, perhaps not without irony, proved exceptionally stubborn to digitize. As difficult as it may seem for a younger generation to imagine, most of the selections in this book were written on a typewriter and typeset manually, which means that we had to create electronic copies of these pieces in order to use them. We discovered that even material published as recently as the late 1990s was not available digitally! In the case of Richard Sigurdson's article from the *Journal of Canadian Studies*, his secretary, Tobi Hawkins, actually agreed to retype the entire article so as to make it available to us in digital format.

In the case of publishers who granted permission to use their materials, honourable mention goes to Brittany Lavery of the University of Toronto Press for generously facilitating reproduction of excerpts from several books to which the press holds the rights. Adrian Galwin at McGill-Queen's University Press helped to secure material by Samuel LaSelva and Guy Laforest. Susan Ostiguy McIntyre and the Institute for Research on Public Policy graciously let us reproduce a chapter from Gordon Robertson's book. I am also grateful to Ronald L. Watts and the Institute of Intergovernmental Relations; Springer Press; Wendy Stephens at the University of Calgary Press, and F.L. (Ted) Morton as well as his assistants Jodi-Lyn McCaw and Robert Whittaker; and Adam Hirschberg at Cambridge University Press for their cooperation. The many journals from which material is reproduced deserve particular mention for their kind support: Marilyn MacFarlane and Dr. Jennifer Philips at the Osgoode Society for Canadian Legal Studies; Stephen Hanson at the *Canadian Bar Review*; Olivier Lebert at *Canadian Public Policy*; Nancy Jacobson at the *Alberta Law Review*; Guy Leclair at the *Journal of Canadian Studies*; Annette Gregory at the *American Journal of Comparative Law*; Dr. Richard Bronaugh at the *Canadian Journal of Law and Jurisprudence*; and Colin Trehearne at the *U.B.C. Law Review*. In several cases we had to seek permission from the authors or their estates, for which I want to thank Mary Rawlyk (and

Anna Kate at Newfoundland's Breakwater Books); Ruth L. Stanley and her daughter Della; Alan Cairns; Peter Hogg; and Brian Slattery. I also want to thank the authors who took it upon themselves to write introductions to their pieces. These introductions provide an indispensable backdrop to each of the selections.

A bit closer to home, I want to thank my employer, the Royal Military College of Canada, and several of my colleagues: Principal Joel Sokolsky for his unwavering support; Dean Jane Errington for liaising with Mary Rawlyk; and my department head, David Last, for his encouragement. Finally, my family deserves special mention. I want to thank my wife and three children for their patience with me. Having an academic for a husband or father is not always easy, no matter how hard I try to balance work and family. Who knows, were it not for my son playing rep hockey and the time I found during practices and on the many bus trips to games across the province, this manuscript may never have never seen the light of day. After all, what could be more Canadian than to begin and finish a book about Canadian government and politics at a hockey rink!

The book is dedicated to my colleague and friend Peter Leslie (1939–2010) who passed away from pancreatic cancer during its completion. The 1982 *Constitution Act* had produced a constitutional stalemate of sorts: No one was quite sure how to move forward, how to bring Quebec back into the fold. In 1985, Peter, then director of the Institute of Intergovernmental Relations, organized a conference at Mont Gabriel. On its occasion, then Quebec minister of justice Gil Rémillard, whose reaction to the *Constitution Act, 1982* is found in this reader, presented what would become known as Quebec's five minimum requests, which ended up forming the basis for the Meech Lake Accord. I tell this story for a reason: Many of the authors in this book are not just scholars; they are patriots, nationalists, and political activists. They were not standing on the sidelines; they rolled up their sleeves and got their hands dirty, so to speak. Their scholarship was meant to inform and inspire debate. They invested preciously scarce time—time many young scholars today would rather spend on writing another article or another book—advising governments in cumbersome negotiations; or they went a step further and ran for public office. They stand apart for their scholarship, their citizenship, and their dedication to Canada. We are in their debt for bolstering the boisterous yet robust and civilized democracy that Canada is.

Canada's constitutional regime is worthwhile studying, not only for its institutions but also for the civic culture it has fostered that makes possible public debate of a sort that in many other countries would be taboo: The mere possibility of having a separatist party in Parliament remains an anathema to so many democracies. Measured as a function of the substance, quality, and civility of constitutional debate relative to the country's longevity, Canada's constitutional regime is second to none. This makes Canada intriguing: institutions that have fostered a constitutional society whose democracy is so robust that, unlike so many of its democratic homologues, it does not shy away from even the most potentially divisive of political debates.

Christian Leuprecht
Kingston, Ontario

# Introduction

## CANADA'S CONSTITUTIONAL INGENUITY

### Christian Leuprecht

AND IT CAME to pass that a democratic people lived together happily ever after in the magic Peaceable Kingdom. Thus starts the Disneyland version of Canada's constitutional regime. In fact, constitutional democracy in Canada had a difficult birth. Parliament passed the Rebellion Losses Bill in 1849 to compensate the damages suffered in the Rebellion led by Papineau. Governor General Lord Elgin sanctioned the measure; the bill had been recommended by the first responsible ministry, the Reform cabinet of Lafontaine and Baldwin, and then passed by the parliamentary majority in the legislature. The Tory-Conservative opposition expected that Lord Elgin would side with them and refuse his assent, but he did not. By assenting to the Act, he solidified the convention that the Governor General would hitherto act on the advice of the executive government responsible to the legislative branch. Protestors, instigated by the opposition, promptly reacted by torching Parliament, mobbing the Governor General and stoning his carriage (had the crowds laid hands on Elgin, they would have lynched him). And within the first year of Confederation Thomas D'Arcy McGee, a prominent father of Confederation and Member of Parliament, was assassinated in an act of blatant politically motivated violence. All this to say that it is far from obvious that Canadian constitutional democracy would turn out the way it did. Nor is everyone necessarily pleased about the outcome. As Canadians know all too well, many francophone Quebeckers have reservations about the constitutional

status quo, as do other provinces. Yet no group may pose as vexing a challenge to Canada's constitutional ingenuity as its Aboriginal nations. Thus Canada's constitutional odyssey continues apace.

The rationale behind this reader is to capture essential issues and debates that have animated Canada's constitutional politics since its founding in 1867. These issues are divided into seven sections: institutions, federalism, intergovernmental relations, the judiciary, bilingualism and biculturalism, the Charter of Rights and Freedoms, and minority rights and constitutional renewal. To give readers a better sense of what is at stake, the overview provided in this introduction is supplemented by additional introductions within each section of the collection and prefacing each of the readings. Many of the readings and their authors are mainstays of Canadian constitutional politics and governance. They were chosen not only with a domestic audience in mind but also with a view to reaching people around the world who share an interest in the dynamics of Canada's constitutional system—its background and outcomes. It is precisely the distinctive factors underlying Canada's constitutional structure that produce its distinctive outputs. The nature of the conflict about political community that bedevils this country is not unique to Canada. Many nation-states face the challenge of reconciling differing societal values within the community and differing understandings of how best to organize the community. It is this challenge that has given rise to the ingenuity of Canada's constitutional system. In the prescient words of George Brown, a Father of Confederation who was notorious for his virulent anti-Catholicism:

> Here is a people composed of two distinct races, speaking different languages, with religious and social and municipal and education institutions totally different; with sectional hostilities of such a character as to render government for many years well-nigh impossible; with a Constitution so unjust in the view of one section as to justify any resort to enforce a remedy. And yet, sir, here we sit, patiently and temperately discussing how over the course of a hundred years these great evils and hostilities may justly and amicably be swept away forever. We are endeavouring to adjust harmoniously greater difficulties than have plunged other countries into all the horrors of civil war.[1]

## NATURE OF THE CONSTITUTION

The Fathers of Confederation bore witness to the tragic turmoil of civil war that had beset the great failed experiment in democratic governance to the south. As George Brown observed: "We are striving to settle forever issues hardly less momentous than those that have rent the neighbouring republic and are now exposing it to all the horrors of civil war. Have we not then, Mr. Speaker, great cause for thankfulness that we have found a better way for the solution of our troubles than that which has entailed on other countries such deplorable results?"[2] However inchoate, Canada's constitutional system has enabled it to become one of the longest-enduring constitutional democracies in the world. Still, in a country of Canada's complexity, as Canada's constitutional odyssey shows, it is virtually impossible to "settle" divisive issues once and for all. For a political system to persist, it has to balance two functions: pattern maintenance and adaptation. Canada's constitution[3] is exemplary in the way

it reconciles rigidity and flexibility, a model of democratic practices in which people acquire, exercise, question, negotiate, and modify their identities as national and multinational citizens.

On the one hand, a constitution modifies human behaviour and influences the political process and is, therefore, an independent variable. On the other hand, a constitution is the product of societal forces. Insofar as it reflects its environment and a country's political culture, the constitution is a dependent variable. Lest one forget, 1867 was Canada's fifth attempt over the course of a hundred years at finding a workable constitutional arrangement. The *Royal Proclamation* (1763), the *Quebec Act* (1774), the *Constitution Act* (1791), and the *Act of Union* (1840) had all proven unsustainable. Although these first four constitutional arrangements contained some of Canada's enduring constitutional principles, they could not serve as the constitution for the complex and democratic society Canada was to become.

As a statement about the values of the community, a Constitution ideally provides a focus for the loyalty of the members of the political community—a unifying symbol that binds citizens together. However, Canada's formal Constitution, the *British North America Act, 1867* was largely concerned with providing politically stable institutions of government and setting out the new country's federal structure. Aside from a preamble that says that Canada will have "a Constitution similar in Principle to that of the United Kingdom" and that its federal Union will "conduce to the Welfare of the Provinces and the Interests of the British Empire," it is largely silent on the way of life the Constitution is meant to foster.

But Canada's Constitution, as the reading by MacGregor Dawson explains, is not limited to a single document. The elements of the Canadian Constitution are based on multiple sources and take various forms. They include the following:

- Landmark documents in British constitutional history encompassing agreements between the monarch and the British people, such as the *Magna Carta* (1215), the *Bill of Rights*

---

1   P.B. Waite, *The Confederation Debates in the Province of Canada, 1865,* Carleton Library Series No. 206, rev. ed. (1965; reprint, Montreal: McGill-Queen's University Press, 2006), 35.

2   Ibid.

3   In this volume, "constitution" in the lower case refers to all the components of the constitutional system, while "Constitution" in

the upper case refers to the formal written Constitution, the *British North America Act, 1867* (since renamed the *Constitution Act, 1867*) and its amendments.

(1689), the *Act of Settlement* (1701), and the *Petition of Right* (1628) that form the basis for constitutional monarchy.

- British legal instruments such as the *Royal Proclamation* (1763), the *Statute of Westminster* (1931), and the Letters Patent (1947).
- Treaties made by the imperial government in London and the Canadian government, such as those establishing international boundaries and with Aboriginal peoples in Canada.
- Decisions by the British and Canadian courts serving as precedents in matters not dealt with by laws passed by Parliament or in the *Constitution Act, 1867*.
- Judicial decisions interpreting the provisions of the *Constitution Act, 1867* and its amendments, such as those concerning the allocation of powers to the federal and provincial governments and the interpretation of the Canadian Charter of Rights and Freedoms.
- Constitutional conventions—agreed upon practices that have evolved through political history and incorporate principles such as responsible government and whose main purpose "is to ensure that the legal framework of the Constitution will be operated in accordance with the prevailing constitutional values or principles of the period."[4]
- Organic laws of Parliament and the provincial legislatures—legislation and parliamentary rules dealing with fundamental matters such as the conditions of citizenship, the conduct of elections and the rights of the opposition in Parliament.

In its decision in the 1998 *Reference re Secession of Quebec*, the Supreme Court of Canada acknowledged the complex structure of Canada's Constitution: "These supporting principles and rules, which include constitutional conventions and the workings of Parliament, are a necessary part of our Constitution…. The Constitution is more than a written text. It embraces the entire global system of rules and principles which

govern the exercise of constitutional authority."[5] In a similar vein, James Tully speaks of "the publicly recognized and accepted rules and procedures by which the members of the society recognize each other and coordinate their cooperation."[6] Together, they give rise to obligations, responsibilities, and constraints on decision-making by members of parliament *and* the public service upon which they confer a constitutional identity and the public service's loyalty to the Crown (as opposed to the party in power). These are the effective elements of the constitution.

The distinction between the formal and the effective constitution, that is, the actual *modus operandi* of Canada's political system, matters. A founding father and the new Confederation's first prime minister, John A. Macdonald, clung tenaciously to a British Conservative bias against contrivances more specific and rigid than what appeared necessary for the immediate occasion: "We should keep before us the principles of the British constitution. It [our constitution] should be a mere skeleton and framework that would not bind us down. We now have all the elasticity which has kept England together."[7] Since the United Kingdom does not have a written Constitution, that meant Canada would be importing British conventions such as responsible government and party discipline, and consolidating extant Canadian practice in these respects. Unlike the United Kingdom, however, Canada would have a written Constitution.

Macdonald and other framers of Canada's founding Constitution were happy to minimize written elements, fearing that anything more might create deadlock or restrict flexibility.

They were primarily concerned with codifying the constitutional framework for unification. They did not think it necessary to make explicit the principles of governance within that framework. Westminster-style parliamentary systems such as Canada's are generally lacking in a comprehensive statement of their fundamental law as is found in the constitutions of civil law

---

5   Supreme Court of Canada, *Quebec Secession Reference* 2 [S.C.R] 217, 1998.
6   James Tully, *Multinational Democracies*, ed. Alain-G. Gagnon and James Tully (Cambridge: Cambridge University Press, 2001), 1–34.
7   Quoted in Alexander Brady, "Background to the Constitutional Controversy and Settlement," in *Politics: Canada*, ed. Paul W. Fox (Toronto: McGraw Hill Ryerson, 1982), 49.

---

4   Supreme Court of Canada, *Attorney General of Manitoba et al. v. Attorney General of Canada et al.*, 28 September 1981.

countries. Canada's constitution was not in its inception "government by the people, with the people, for the people." Canada was brought into existence by a legislative enactment of the British parliament—the *British North America Act* (1867)—which was thus the foundation of the Canadian constitution.

## PART 1: INSTITUTIONS

Canada's founding Constitution does hint at the nature of Canada's political regime. Instead of "life, liberty, and the pursuit of happiness" as fundamental constitutional ideals, Canada's Constitution refers in less lofty terms to "peace, order and good government." The principle of institutional design that governs the United States is "checks and balances," which are manifest in the "separation of powers" between the executive and legislative branches of government. The Constitution of the United States resonates with a sense of profound mistrust of government and the need to guard against it. Given America's revolutionary past, perhaps that is not surprising. In contrast to a separation of powers, Canada's Constitution establishes a parliamentary system of government that fuses executive and legislative power by drawing the heads of government from Parliament and requiring that government command the confidence of the elected chamber of the Parliament.

FIGURE 1: Responsible Government in Canadian Parliamentary Democracy

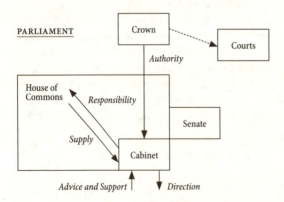

The principle of responsible government gives effect to democratic control of the executive branch of government. It requires that the Crown (in which all executive power is formally vested) act only on the advice from a prime minister and ministers who have the support of a majority in the House of Commons. Yet other than the one reference to it as "a Constitution similar in principle to that of the United Kingdom," the *Constitution Act, 1867*, makes no express provisions for the operation of responsible government in the new Dominion of Canada, but left the composition of the executive council and its relations with the Governor General and Parliament to be determined by the usages already established in the several provinces: the ministry, that is, the prime minister and ministers, is responsible to Parliament; the need for the prime minister and ministers to maintain confidence, that is, to continue only as the government as long as they have the support of a majority in the House of Commons; the office of the prime minister or its powers; the establishment and operation of cabinet—although it makes the bulk of decisions of government—and the positions of the ministers.

As James Mallory decried decades ago in an article on responsive and responsible government (reproduced in this first section of the reader), a growing number of Canadians, including students of political science, public servants, and even politicians, exhibit a frustrating ignorance about this part of Canada's constitution. To some extent, this is understandable. Cohesive, disciplined political parties have come to dominate parliamentary life, while a diverse, populist, and less deferential population does not readily imbibe principles of government that derive from nineteenth-century constitutional history. For better or for worse, though, and the cacophony of proposals for reform notwithstanding, these remain Canada's governing principles and institutions. It is imperative that Canadians come to understand them better—that is certainly the sentiment left by David Smith in his book on the Senate, the chamber of "sober second thought" of the Canadian Parliament, an excerpt of which is included here.

Section 17 of the Constitution provides for "One Parliament for Canada, consisting of the Queen, and Upper House styled the Senate, and a House of Commons." Representation is thus operationalized in a bicameral Parliament of Canada. No aspect of Canada's constitutional system has fallen into as much disrepute as the Senate. David Smith, however, is an articulate defender of the status quo, a defence mounted in part on the premise that the critics fail to understand the institution and its place in Canada's parliamentary system. Smith should be read not as an apologist but as an introduction to matters arising from the constitutional system Canada has—as opposed to the one that critics might wish it had.

## PART 2: FEDERALISM

The Constitution of the United States of America was bedevilled by differences of opinion among its principal negotiators as to what exactly had been agreed upon at Philadelphia. It was no different in Canada. Was Confederation meant to divide powers between a strong central government and subordinate provinces? Or was it a genuine confederation where the constituent units had, at their discretion, delegated powers upwards to a federal government? Was Confederation an agreement among two founding nations? If so, how do Canada's Aboriginal nations factor into that calculus? Or was Confederation a compact among four founding provinces? Were these provinces equal? Or was one of them special by virtue of the majority of its population being linguistically and culturally distinct? The readings in the second section of this volume problematize the nature of federalism in Canada and its role as a constitutional instrument in defining the nature of Canada's constitutional regime and political community.

As George Stanley makes clear, a quasi-federal dualism had entrenched itself functionally during the course of the Union parliament. John A. Macdonald's genius had long realized that successful government in Canada hinged on the accommodation of English and French: "Treat them as a faction, they will act as a faction." A possible inference to draw is that powers not ceded were retained by the provincial legislatures, which continued to act within their own sphere. From this vantage point, Quebeckers deem the division of power "a compromise allowing them to dominate those institutions that were ancillary to Quebec."[8]

Far from having been conferred upon them by the federal government, the powers of the provinces were the residue of their former colonial powers. The following quote by Alain-G. Gagnon typifies this view which nowadays is especially prominent among francophone Quebeckers:

> Only federalism as a political system permits two cultures to live and develop side by side within a single state: that was the real reason for the Canadian state's federative form.... There can be no federalism without autonomy of the state's constituent parts, and no sovereignty of the various governments without fiscal and financial autonomy.[9]

As A.I. Silver explains, historically Quebec has been striving to have its understanding of Confederation respected—rather like an estranged spouse trying to get a former partner to live up to his/her original agreement of separation. George A. Rawlyk's reading on the Maritime perspective on Confederation shows that there are other competing interpretations of, motives behind, and concerns about the 1867 arrangements.

Is the federal government, then, a creation of the provinces, the result of their association and of their compact? Or were both the provinces and the federal government created by the Constitution? By convention, the *Constitution Act, 1867* is also thought to provide both the federal and provincial governments with exclusive jurisdiction in those domains that were essential to their particular interests.

Or are the provinces simply the appendages of the federal government and, therefore, subservient to it? After all, pursuant to the reading in which Donald Creighton depicts Sir John A. Macdonald's vision of Confederation, the provinces were no more than a "decentralized system of minor legislatures for local purposes," given the centralized power manifest in the national executive's nomination of senators for life, its appointment of lieutenant-governors, the selection

---

8    Alain-G. Gagnon, "Quebec's Constitutional Odyssey," in *Canadian Politics*, 3rd ed., ed. James Bickerton and Alain-G. Gagnon

(Peterborough, ON: Broadview Press, 1999), 281.

9    Royal Commission of Inquiry on Constitutional Problems, *The Tremblay Report*, Carleton University Library Series No. 64, ed. and trans. David Kwavnick (Toronto: McClelland and Stewart, 1973), 209, 215.

of judges holding office during good behaviour, the location of residual legislative power in the national Parliament, and provision for the exercise of federal reservation and disallowance over provincial enactments (ss. 56, 57, 90).[10] The reading by Samuel LaSelva, however, calls this perspective into question, contending that federal theory was far more incipient among the Fathers of Confederation than is commonly assumed. Is Canada constituted of competing regional/national communities with provincial governments as their principal representatives? Or is the federal/central government obligated to protect all Canadians and confer similar rights and status on them? In epitomizing different takes on the nature and purpose of Canada's federal regime, the readings in this section are meant to convey a greater appreciation as to why the Constitution remains a flashpoint for discord among the peoples and governments of the Canadian federation.

## PART 3: INTERGOVERNMENTAL RELATIONS

Formally, Canada appears to start out as a highly centralized federation; over the course of a century, it ends up as a highly decentralized one. This development was not effected through changes to the formal Constitution but through intergovernmental relations and the politics that drive them. The shift that intergovernmental relations have undergone in Canada is of both substantive and methodological interest, not only for the purpose of studying Canadian constitutional governance but also for the field of comparative politics more broadly. The reading by Donald Smiley exemplifies the approach that dominates the literature on federalism and that has traditionally dominated much of the political-science scholarship in and on Canada: the way institutional changes emerge from and are embedded in temporal processes. This approach contrasts with the reading by Richard Simeon who uses the rational-choice paradigm that has come to define a growing part of political science in recent years. From this perspective, institutions are viewed as coordination mechanisms that generate

and sustain equilibria. Intergovernmental relations in Canada is a critical case study (using the terminology of comparative politics) because its *modus operandi* would be impossible to infer from a simple reading of the formal Constitution.

Gaps and abeyances, tacit or deliberate, are at the crux of ambiguities and evasions that make constitutions sustainable. Constitutions can, in fact, serve a social function not by settling ambiguities but by avoiding them. The "great silences," as US Supreme Court Associate Justice Robert Jackson has called them, are no less significant for the purposes of Canadian constitutional politics than the actual constitutional text. The readings by Smiley and Peter H. Russell on the division of powers and the subsequent evolution of federal-provincial relations and provincial autonomy make this abundantly clear. As a "fuzzy set" (in game-theoretic parlance), the BNA Act, 1867 actually steers clear of a host of fundamental issues thereby enlarging the potential for creative ambiguity. That includes the contemporary intergovernmental infrastructure which, although it is connected to the governments created by that constitution and to the concentration of power within those governments brought about by the conventions of responsible government, is not anchored in the 1867 Constitution.

On this last point, conventional wisdom holds out Quebec as the impetus behind much of the political tension in Canadian federalism. Christopher Armstrong, by contrast, points to the critical role of other political actors as alternative forces shaping the federal dynamic. In the aftermath of Confederation, Ontario Premier Oliver Mowat pioneered the political use of legal resources in Canada. This gave rise to a strong Canadian intergovernmental practice that persists to this day. In fact, a significant amount of Canada's high court's time has been and continues to be spent adjudicating jurisdictional disputes between the federal government and the provinces.

## PART 4: THE JUDICIARY

The readings in the section on intergovernmental relations clearly show that the principle of legislative supremacy does not prevail in Canada. Rather, Canada combines parliamentary government with American

10   Quoted in Brady, "Background to the Constitutional Controversy and Settlement," 50.

constitutionalism. Canada's constitution is a system in which constitutional supremacy trumps legislative supremacy. Constitutional supremacy is manifest in the education and language rights that are entrenched in the Constitution. Moreover, a genuine federal system is unthinkable without a definitive division of powers of which an independent judiciary is the final arbiter. This dimension of federalism is pivotal. There can be no constitutional supremacy without judicial independence. Thus this section includes William Lederman's classic piece on this subject from a Canadian perspective.

Judicial review was implicitly incorporated in the Canadian constitution by the assignment of separate federal and provincial jurisdictions. The practice of judicial review though, as Jennifer Smith explains, is not prescribed in the formal Constitution. Although judicial review by the Judicial Committee of the Privy Council, the British Empire's highest court, rested on the premises of imperialism, it emerged as a principal mechanism for mediating federal–provincial conflict. As discussed by Alan Cairns in his first reading in this section, it often fell to the courts to determine whether a particular law was within the jurisdiction of the legislature that passed it. As Cairns details in his second reading in this section, the Canadian constitution turned out to be an organic and living organism; rather than buckling, it proved adept at adapting to changing demands over time. Frank R. Scott's contribution to this section tells us in poetic terms that nobody could have imagined the impact the courts would have. Yet, as John Saywell reminds us in his piece, both the decisions and the rationale have, at times, left people scratching their heads. Should so powerful a judiciary that is nowadays appointed at the discretion of the federal government be cause for concern? Peter Hogg examines whether there is any evidence of bias by the Supreme Court in constitutional cases dealing with the division of powers.

## PART 5: BILINGUALISM AND BICULTURALISM

The *Constitution Act, 1867* protected the language and education rights of the French Catholic minority outside Quebec and of the English Protestant minority

inside Quebec. It is in these provisions of the founding Constitution that the vision of a bilingual and bicultural Canada is most evident. Yet the first major test of the strength of those minority education and language protections came not in Ontario or Quebec but in Manitoba and showed how weak these protections were for the French Catholic minority in an expanding Canada. A.I. Silver's reading on the Manitoba School Crisis is an account of a turning point with respect to language and education rights as well as a turning point with respect to federal and provincial jurisdiction in relation to these highly charged issues. Moreover, as the excerpt from J.W. Dafoe illustrates, education and language have a long history of making or breaking political careers in Canada. Indeed, the Manitoba School Crisis was instrumental in propelling Wilfrid Laurier to become the country's first French-Canadian prime minister.

Although the federal government's approach vis-à-vis the provinces became less heavy-handed under Laurier, the interlude was a short-lived one as the emergencies of two world wars and the economic exigencies of the interbellum period caused the role of the federal government to expand. Quebec jurist Louis-Philippe Pigeon wrote a highly insightful piece from the vantage point of Quebec as a culturally distinct and autonomous province as to why this expansion was not as benign as it may have seemed. Quebec recoiled from the expanded role of the federal government in building up the Canadian welfare state; a visceral reaction that was manifested in the *Tremblay Report*. Alexander Brady's piece provides a perceptive reflection on this classic expression of Quebec's view of its place in Confederation. The opening round of the constitutional negotiations that followed was the Confederation of Tomorrow Conference convened by Ontario Premier John Robarts on the occasion of Canada's centennial in 1967. Robarts's conference was the background to one of the classic political exchanges in Canadian constitutional politics between Daniel Johnson, Quebec's premier at the time, and then Minister of Justice Pierre-Elliott Trudeau. Given Trudeau's eventual impact on Canadian constitutional politics, a reader on this topic would be lacking without his take on Quebec and the constitutional problem. Trudeau's piece is intentionally paired with an exceptional account by Guy Laforest that shows how

Trudeau and his constitutional vision have been such irritants to many francophone Quebeckers. In short, this section strives to convey an understanding of the competing constitutional visions that arise in dealing with the perspectives of French Canada and French Quebec and which continue to feature prominently in Canada's constitutional debates.


## PART 6: THE CHARTER

Given the voluminous literature on the Canadian Charter of Rights and Freedoms, this reader confines itself to the Charter in terms of the national unity challenges facing Canada and the Constitution's diffuse and fragmented nature that made it largely ineffective as an instrument for building loyalty to the political community. As noted earlier, the *Constitution Act, 1867* provided neither a clear and enduring declaration of national purpose, nor a clear statement of the fundamental values on which the political community was based. The *Constitution Act, 1982* was partially intended to remedy these shortcomings. As the excerpt from Alan Cairns in this section argues, the Charter was a thoroughly political means to achieve specific political ends.

The *Canada Act* and the *Constitution Act, 1982*, which contained the Charter, conferred full constitutional autonomy on Canada. The *Canada Act* patriated Canada's founding Constitution and its amendments, while the *Constitution Act, 1982* established procedures for amending the Constitution that required only the consent of Canadian legislative assemblies and not the British Parliament (sections 38 to 49). The *Constitution Act, 1982* provided the first explicit constitutional acknowledgement of Aboriginal rights since the *Royal Proclamation, 1763* a commitment to fiscal equalization among the provinces, and recognition of intergovernmental relations (through its mention of the First Ministers' Conferences). The act incorporated the Canadian Charter of Rights and Freedoms, which is among the most comprehensive entrenchments of rights and freedoms found in a constitutional democracy.

In the Charter's detailed regulation of relations between citizens and the state, the 1982 additions to Canada's Constitution clarified the basis and

extended considerably the scope of judicial review. First, the binding nature of the Constitution, including the Charter, on the federal and provincial legislatures is formalized in section 52(1), which declares that "any law that is inconsistent with the provisions of the Constitution is, to the extent of the inconsistency, of no force or effect." Second, section 24(1) of the Charter of Rights and Freedoms allows anyone whose Charter rights have been infringed or denied to apply to the courts "to obtain such remedy as the court considers appropriate and just in the circumstances." Together, these two sections "explicitly establish a political regime of constitutional (as opposed to legislative) supremacy in which constitutional limits of political power are enforced through judicial review of statutes, regulations and official conduct."[11] The courts could henceforth strike down federal or provincial legislation on grounds other than a violation of the federal–provincial division of powers of the traditional language and education rights.

This "Charter revolution" raised the specter of emboldened judges asserting themselves ideologically or the Charter as an ideological instrument whose benefits might accrue disproportionately to one side of the ideological spectrum or another. From a political science perspective, these sorts of debates are especially interesting as they can be subjected to empirical scrutiny. One of the earliest such assessments, by Richard Sigurdson, is included in this reader.

Although the Constitution offers protection to the rights of citizens comparable to that found in the American Bill of Rights and upholds the rule of law by empowering the courts to invalidate acts of government that contravene the provisions of the Charter, the Canadian constitution is not an example of "pure constitutionalism." Some provincial governments were unwilling to accept the further limitation on their legislative powers that an entrenched Charter of Rights would inevitably impose. To secure provincial agreement and to counterbalance the courts, the so-called notwithstanding clause, section 33 was ultimately inserted in the Charter. This clause gives both the federal Parliament and the provincial legislatures

11   Christopher P. Manfredi, *Judicial Power and the Charter: Canada and the Paradox of Liberal Constitutionalism*, 2nd ed. (Toronto: Oxford University Press, 2001), 21.

the right to declare any law they pass exempt for five years from section 2 (fundamental rights) and sections 7 to 15 (legal and equality rights). As the exchange between John Whyte and Peter H. Russell demonstrates, an enabling mechanism that allows legislation to operate even where it violates rights and freedoms that are otherwise constitutionally guaranteed, makes the "notwithstanding clause" a real bone of contention.

## PART 7: MINORITY RIGHTS AND CONSTITUTIONAL RENEWAL

Akin to Canadian democracy, the Canadian constitution remains a work in progress. Many of the grievances from 1867 persist today. From Antoine Aimé Dorion to Christopher Duncan, the Confederation debates are littered with reservations about what would become the BNA Act (1867). On the one hand, as Roderick A. Macdonald does in this section, one might argue that a high tolerance of criticism and an open discussion about constitutional renewal is indicative of the strength and resilience of Canadian democracy. Some countries worship their Constitution almost as if it were a holy book. Critique is almost tantamount to heresy. On the other hand, Canada's Constitution and its concomitant commitment to constitutionalism and constitutional supremacy afford sufficient protection to secure a fairly broad consensus among minority and dissenting groups about the legitimacy of Canada's Constitution. That is evidenced by the fact that they prefer working for change within the constitutional framework at hand rather than resorting to extra-constitutional means or political violence to have their grievances addressed. The mere recognition of collective rights already sets Canada's Constitution apart. In affording recognition and protection for all three of the different minority types found in modern states—national minorities, Aboriginal peoples, and immigrant minorities—it is unique among constitutional democracies the world over. Moreover, many of these protections were part and parcel of Canadian political culture long before Confederation.

This section offers a tour of salient controversies that have thus far received scant attention in this reader but which are likely to influence the trajectory of Canadian constitutional politics henceforth.

In some ways, the major issues showcased in this section set Canadian constitutional politics apart from those in other countries, such as the United States and the United Kingdom. In other ways, they foreshadow constitutional politics around the world.

An excerpt from a book by Roger Gibbins and Loleen Berdahl introduces the reader to the constitutional significance of the rise of both Canada's West and Canada's urban areas—three of the largest five of which are now located in the West. The compound effect of environmental change and domestic politics has been increasing the prominence of the North. This is an area of the country where constitutional governance has been highly innovative, forging groundbreaking treaties with the Inuit and some of the North's Aboriginal nations, and carving out a new self-governing territory, Nunavut, in which the Inuit of the Eastern Arctic will be the dominant people. So, why does the North consist of three territories rather than three provinces? To answer that question, a chapter of Gordon Robertson's treatise is included in this section. Robertson is one of the country's most renowned civil servants who spent considerable time in the North during his career.

Compared to Quebec, the West and the North are relative newcomers to Canadian constitutional politics. The national unity question is bound to continue to ravage the country, in part because of the ire stirred up by the Constitution Act (1982). In a rare English reflection, Gil Rémillard, one of Quebec's foremost intellectuals and politicians offers an insider's perspective as to why Quebec considered 1982 an "unfinished compromise" that would, almost necessarily, give rise to further rounds of constitutional negotiations. The courts are bound to continue to be thrust into the political fray with respect to adjudicating controversies that are inherently political, rather than legal, in nature. In their essay, Sujit Choudhry and Robert Howse expound on the challenges and competing pressures the courts face in doing so while preserving their legitimacy with the parties involved.

The reader closes by acknowledging the Aboriginal element that has been rapidly emerging as the most challenging part of Canada's ongoing constitutional odyssey, one that is bound to test Canadian constitutional ingenuity in unprecedented ways. This final section contains two excerpts on this matter: one is by John Borrows, one of Canada's leading Aboriginal legal scholars, and the other is by Brian Slattery. Both authors elucidate what has proven to be among the most explosive matters in contemporary Canadian constitutional politics: Aboriginal and treaty rights.

Peter H. Russell's essay concludes this reader. There is widespread recognition that Canada's formal and effective constitutions are far from perfect. Canada seems to have fared well with the functional balance it has struck between pattern maintenance and adaptation. This is not to deny the great injustices that have been committed under its system nor the cacophony of discontent with its constitutional arrangements. But the country has been spared civil war or other large-scale protracted forms of political violence. That is no small feat given Canada's deep societal diversity that in many other countries has led to political tensions that have culminated in intercommunal violence. Elsewhere, because of unmet grievances, people have become all too familiar with constitutional rules and their applications. Canadians, by contrast, seem to suffer from a degree of constitutional malaise of the sort one might expect to find only in a system that, all its faults notwithstanding, enjoys an exceptionally high degree of legitimacy. Yet history has shown repeatedly that democracy, constitutions, and constitutionalism are not to be taken for granted: they need to be defended. As the extent of ethno-social, geographic, demographic, and urban-rural differentiation in Canada reaches proportions unprecedented both in Canada and the democratic world, the greatest challenges to Canada's constitutional ingenuity may yet be lurking. Failure is not an option, not merely for the sake of the country but also for much of the rest of the world that takes constitutional cues from Canada. A democratic constitutional system and the safeguards built into it are premised on the fact that the people are reasonably familiar with the rules that govern them. However imperfect Canada's constitutional system is and however incomplete the selection of readings, this anthology is meant to make Canadians less complacent about their Constitution and to arm Canadian society for the constitutional odyssey that lies ahead. At the same time, it is meant to offer inspiration and hope to those around the world embroiled in constitutional struggles, especially those involving the accommodation of many competing claims to which diversity gives rise.

There is no time for Canada to rest on its constitutional laurels.

## RESOURCES FOR FURTHER READING

Aucoin, Peter, Jennifer Smith, and Geoff Dinsdale. 2004. *Responsible Government: Clarifying Essentials, Dispelling Myths and Exploring Change*. Ottawa: Canadian Centre for Management Development. http://www.myschool-monecole.gc.ca/Research/publications/html/resgov/rg2_e.html

Browne, G.P. 1867. *The Judicial Committee and the British North America Act: An Analysis of the Interpretive Scheme for the Distribution of Legislative Powers*. Toronto: University of Toronto Press.

Bzdera, André. 1993. "Comparative Analysis of Federal High Courts: A Political Theory of Judicial Review." *Canadian Journal of Political Science* 26: 3–29.

Franks, C.E.S. 1987. *The Parliament of Canada*. Toronto: University of Toronto Press.

Forsey, Eugene. 1974. *Freedom and Order: Collected Essays*. Toronto: McClelland and Stewart.

Forsey, Eugene. 2010 [1980]. *How Canadians Govern Themselves*. 7th ed. Ottawa: Ministry of Public Works and Government Services. http://www2.parl.gc.ca/sites/lop/aboutparliament/forsey/index-e.asp

Heard, Andrew. 1991. *Canadian Constitutional Conventions: The Marriage of Law and Politics*. Toronto: Oxford University Press.

Hogg, Peter W. 2007. "Responsible Government." In *Constitutional Law of Canada*. 5th ed. Toronto: Carswell.

*Journal of Canadian Studies*. 1979. Special Issue on Responsible Government.

Leeson, Howard. 2000. "Section 33, the Notwithstanding Clause: A Paper Tiger?" *Choices* 6(4).

Responsibility in the Constitution. 1993. Ottawa: Minister of Supply and Services Canada. http://www.pco-bcp.gc.ca/index.asp?lang=eng&page=information&sub=publications&doc=constitution/table-eng.htm

Rogers, Norman McL. 1933. "The Introduction of Cabinet Government in Canada." *Canadian Bar Review* 11(1): 1–17.

Vipond, Robert. 1991. *Liberty and Community: Canadian Federalism and the Failure of the Constitution*. Albany: State University of New York Press.

*Part One*

# Institutions

A CONSTITUTION IS, at its heart, a statement about the nature of a political community. It is meant to provide stability. It is meant to bring continuity, certainty, and predictability to a polis that might otherwise be subject to the vagaries of its expediency and leadership. Aside from establishing inviolable rules of the game, defining and limiting the power of government, a core function of any constitution is to establish the institutions of government: the executive, the legislature, and the judiciary. Yet Canada's constitutional system is far more comprehensive than might seem at first glance. As Robert MacGregor Dawson points out at the outset of his piece, there is a lot more to the constitution than a few dozen pages in an old book. It is not limited to the acts that make up the text of Canada's formal Constitution. Additionally, it encompasses unwritten rules of constitutional practice, which are commonly referred to as conventions, acts of Parliament, and judicial decisions. This abridged version of MacGregor Dawson's original chapter also points to the need to change the formal constitution. The BNA *Act, 1867,* did not include any provisions to change it, attesting to the hubris of framers to whom it never appears to have occurred that their document might be imperfect. With the advent of the *Constitution Act, 1982,* there are now five different ways to amend the constitution, depending on what it is that needs changing.

The chapter from James Mallory's *The Structure of Canadian Government* explores the sources and evolution of Canada's constitution. He recounts its basic elements—a system of law, the right to representative institutions, and the principle of religious tolerance—and how they combine to make for stable government. The other fundamental patterns of Canadian government he details include representative, parliamentary, and cabinet government as well as the legislative autonomy that is part and parcel of a system of governance that combines the self-rule of its constituent units with the shared-rule of a central government.

Another piece of Mallory's follows. *Responsive and Responsible Government* was born out of challenges not unlike the ones we face today: the shortcoming in realizing Canada's most fundamental constitutional principle. Realizing here denotes both a failure to know the principle of responsible government, to understand it, and to live up to it. Mallory's piece is important insofar as he contextualizes concerns about the democratic efficacy that underlies this fundamental constitutional principle. In the process, he deconstructs some of the myths that surround it, myths that are no less widespread today as they were when Mallory wrote it. Many of the resulting pitfalls that are thought to ail democratic representative government in Canada could be avoided if the principle were fully grasped.

The following piece by Eugene Forsey and G.C. Eglinton expounds on responsible government as the principle governing the executive–legislative relationship in Canada. They mount an eloquent defence of the theory that underlies Canada's constitutional system. In the process, they lay out the principles that underlie responsible government, including a ministry's responsibility to the Sovereign and a minister's responsibility to the House.

A chapter from David E. Smith's book on the Senate follows. The Senate may well be the most debated yet least understood institution of parliamentary government in Canada. The first major treatise on its reform dates back almost a century to Robert MacKay's *The Unreformed Senate of Canada*. Proposals for reform are as long as misunderstandings about the institution and its purpose. Reformers of the Senate are many, apologists few. Smith is one of the Senate's most knowledgeable defenders. Rather than musing about what could or should be, in this selection Smith explains the Senate's place, purpose, and rationale within the framework of Canadian parliamentary and constitutional government.

This first part closes with a reflection by one of the world's foremost scholars of comparative federalism. Why is it that 1867 is referred to as Confederation while we talk today only of federalism? Ronald L. Watts explains this important distinction and its implications for constitutional governance. He then proceeds to situate federalism as a guiding constitutional principle of governance in Canada.

1

*Editors' Introduction*

A study of Canada's constitution, and especially the constitution's impact on Canadian government would be incomplete without an excerpt from Robert MacGregor Dawson's monumental textbook *Democratic Government in Canada*. It was the first comprehensive textbook on the subject and remains a milestone in the study of Canadian political institutions. It first appeared in 1947 and remained in print for forty years, distinguishing itself as the standard introductory text for a generation of students. The book is a classic example of the legal-formal approach to institutions that dominated the early decades of Canadian political science. An author of major studies of Canada's civil service, its constitution, and on the status of the Dominion, Dawson's chapter included here prevails as an authoritative synthesis by one of the greats of Canada's founding generation of political scientists.

Source: Robert MacGregor Dawson, "The Constitution," in *Democratic Government in Canada*, 6th ed., rev. Norman Ward (Toronto: University of Toronto Press, 1989), 86–94.

Robert MacGregor Dawson

# The Constitution

THE CONSTITUTION OF CANADA is not confined, as some people think, to the thirty-odd pages of the original British North America Act (since 1982, it must be remembered, given a new title, the Constitution Act, 1867), or even to the act and its amendments. Although a large section of the constitution is set forth in the act and its amendments, other parts are found elsewhere and under a variety of forms: some written, some unwritten; some explicit, some extremely intangible and at times even uncertain. The chief categories into which the constitution may be divided are as follows: the Constitution Act (and its amendments); custom or usage; acts of the Canadian Parliament; acts of the British Parliament; judicial decision; other forms.

## 1 / The Constitution Act (and its amendments)

This act not only marked the beginning of the Canadian federation, it also stated many of the essential rules under which the new government was to function. The powers of the federal government; the powers of the provinces; the broad features of the executive, the judiciary, the Senate, and the House of Commons; general provisions regarding the provincial governments and special provisions concerning Ontario and Quebec (which started them on their new provincial existence)—all these appear in the written clauses of the Constitution Act. Amendments (which in some instances were formally passed by the British Parliament and in others by the Canadian Parliament) occupy the same basic constitutional position as the original act.

A special variation of the normal amendment is composed of what might be called "constitutional statutes," which are acts passed by the Canadian Parliament that have substantially modified the Constitution Act in accordance with powers granted by its own clauses. Thus the Saskatchewan Act and the Alberta Act (which in 1905 created these provinces and admitted them to the federation), while nominally statutes of the Canadian Parliament, come very close to being in effect amendments to the constitution itself. Moreover, once the Canadian Parliament has enacted one of these statutes creating or admitting a province, it has no legal power to change it. Curiously enough, solemn treaties with Indians, although they have often involved jurisdiction over large tracts of land, have not been considered parts of the Canadian constitution. The constitutional amendments of 1982 declare that "the existing aboriginal and treaty rights of the aboriginal peoples of Canada are hereby recognized and affirmed"; but they do not give constitutional definition to "existing" rights.

## 2 / Custom or usage

This is scarcely less essential than the provisions of the British North America Act. The government of

Canada, like those of the colonies before federation, has always rested to a remarkable degree upon custom; that is, certain things have tended to be done in a certain way because they have been done in that way before. [O]ne of these customs ... [is] the introduction of responsible government by the simple expedient of instructing a governor to select his cabinet from the members of the legislature who would be able to secure the support of the elected lower house. This was, of course, simply an adoption of the British custom under which the sovereign chose the British cabinet according to the same unwritten understanding; and the custom which was thus reproduced in Nova Scotia in 1848 has been consistently followed since then by both federal and provincial governments. This practice is not even mentioned in the Constitution Act of 1867, nor does it occur in any Canadian statute. Yet every knowledgeable Canadian knows that if the cabinet ceases to enjoy the support of the House of Commons it must either resign or hold a general election. In the latter alternative, it must still resign (again by custom) if it is unable to command a majority of votes in the newly elected House. No part of the written constitution is more firmly established than this cardinal principle, which rests on nothing more substantial than a generally accepted usage. It is, none the less, the most important single fact about the government of Canada.

There are many other customary parts of the constitution, several of which have already been discussed: those which are concerned with the exercise of the powers of the governor general; the position and functions of the prime minister and the cabinet and their relations to Parliament; the system of political parties and the place they occupy in the government; and many of the relations between English- and French-speaking Canadians. As time goes on, customs may help produce laws, and there are now laws relating (for example) to some activities of political parties, and to the recognition of French and English as official languages; but custom still governs large areas of the activities of the people involved with these subjects.

## 3 / Acts of the Canadian Parliament

Many aspects of Canadian government are covered by the ordinary statutes which are enacted by Parliament from time to time. Some of these are of outstanding importance, such as the statute which created the Supreme Court of Canada, that which decides how elections will be held, and the statutes that establish new departments or reorganize the cabinet; others deal with constitutional matters of relatively minor consequences. All of those which remain statutes may be altered by Parliament; but just as customs may help produce laws, laws themselves can get promoted into the constitution. It is now the constitution, not an electoral law, which says who may vote in elections.

## 4 / Acts of the British Parliament

Historically these occupied a prominent place, but decades ago a constitutional usage developed whereby the British Parliament became careful not to enact any laws which might be interpreted as an interference in Canadian affairs. Three exceptions, however, should be noted. Before the Statute of Westminster in 1931, British statutes were made applicable to Canada in a few fields where it was desirable to have common legislation for the whole empire; for example, the regulation of merchant shipping. Secondly, there was the Constitution Act itself (and its amendments) which was, of course, an act of the British Parliament. Thirdly, the Constitution Act of 1982 was also a British statute, whose own terms make it the last that will have any application to Canada.

The Statute of Westminster not only confirmed and emphasized the general policy of the British Parliament to abstain from legislating on Canadian matters; it also provided explicitly that no future British statutes would apply to Canada unless Canada so desired. Past acts remained applicable to Canada, but these could be modified or repealed (so far as Canada was concerned) by the Canadian Parliament. The Constitution Act of 1867, however, remained in its dominant position until 1982, and before that year could not be amended by the Canadian Parliament acting alone: since it was a British statute, the co-operation of the British Parliament was needed for changes to its text. The text itself remains a fundamental element in Canada's constitution, but the act has become a Canadian law. This development is discussed below.

## 5 / Judicial decision

The courts make a notable contribution to the Canadian constitution through their interpretation of the law in cases which are brought before them for decision. One aspect of this function involves the pronouncement by the courts on the validity of federal and provincial legislation which is enacted under the constitution. If the courts decide that a statute of either the federal or provincial legislature has gone beyond the powers given that body by the supreme law, the Constitution Acts from 1867, they declare the statute void or *ultra vires* (beyond the powers of) that legislature; if the courts consider it is within the powers so granted, the statute is declared valid or *intra vires*. This is no more than the application of the simple principle that no body can legally do any act which it has not been empowered legally to do. Inasmuch as the Constitution Acts are the source of all legislative power in Canada, both dominion and province are necessarily limited by the power so given. The courts of law thus stand as an arbiter between rival federal and provincial authorities and they prevent encroachment on rival fields of jurisdiction, a most valuable function under a federal system where such conflicts are inevitable and unending. As already noted, the role of the courts has recently been considerably enlarged by the establishment in 1982 of the Charter of Rights and Freedoms. Where before 1982 the courts' chief role in constitutional disputes was generally to decide whether particular items fell under federal or provincial jurisdiction, a new test has been added: is the item acceptable under the Charter?

Questions of jurisdiction may arise in regard to the legal powers of bodies other than Parliament and the legislatures. The Governor-General-in-Council may exceed the statutory powers which have been vested in it by Parliament, or a municipal authority may pass a by-law which exceeds the powers granted it by provincial statute, or either may transgress a section of the Constitution Acts, including now the Charter. If the courts are satisfied that such a body has stepped outside the powers legally conferred on it, they will declare the order-in-council, by-law, or whatever it may be, to be *ultra vires*. All these constitutional interpretations, whether of jurisdiction or of the meaning to be placed on the words and phrases of a statute, are clearly almost as significant as the actual provisions of the Constitution Acts.

## 6 / Other forms

The constitution takes other forms which need not be set down in detail here. The English common law which came to Canada (except Quebec) with the early settlement is an essential part of the constitution, especially as it affects the fundamental rights of the citizen, such as freedom of speech, freedom of assembly, the right to trial by jury. For historical reasons, British orders-in-council comprise a small part of Canada's foundations (British Columbia, for example, was created a province by a British order-in-council), and Canadian orders-in-council a much larger part of the constitution. The rules and privileges of Parliament make up another section; it is not generally known, for example, that the House of Commons can even order a citizen to be imprisoned, and once did so. There are many other forms.

## CONSTITUTIONAL DEVELOPMENT

This complex constitution is, moreover, never stationary: it is always in process of change; and its composite nature suggests the variety of methods through which it is constantly developing. Customs will inevitably alter from time to time; Parliament will enact new or amending statutes; the courts of law never cease to pass judgment on disputes which come before them. Thus year by year, and almost day by day, the constitution grows and takes on new characteristics which in large measure spring out of the needs of the time. A few of these adaptations—especially the customary ones—may be almost unsuspected until they have become established and rooted by repetition; Canada, for example, is cited in the preamble to the Constitution Act of 1867 as a "Dominion" but the use of the word had been quietly declining for years before MPs began to notice it and complain about it. Even the specific terms of the Constitution Act of 1867 are subject to quiet transformation by judicial decision or by custom. The act, for example, vests the executive power in the queen, and the governor general acts in her name; but the building up of many precedents has had the effect of transferring the real exercise of power to the cabinet. The governor thus continues to perform his constitutional functions according to the law, but he does so while acting on the advice of his cabinet, who assume the responsibility for what he does and defend it as their own act in the House of Commons. A most conscientious reading of the Constitution Act [...] does not necessarily give an accurate picture of how Canadian government actually works. That knowledge must be extended and even substantially modified by an understanding of the other parts of the constitution.

## FORMAL AMENDMENT

Until 1949 the Constitution Act could be *formally* amended or altered only by an act of the British Parliament; in that year Parliament, by amendment, received the power to amend the act with certain major exceptions, the chief of which were "provincial matters and subjects" and constitutional guarantees governing the use of English or French. (The importance of those "provincial matters" became apparent when in the late 1970s the Supreme Court was asked if Parliament could unilaterally alter the form of the Senate and the Court, holding that each province had a stake in the Senate, ruled "No.") Even before 1949, custom had become of vital importance in the amendment of the constitution; by long-established precedent the British Parliament would not pass any amendment on its own initiative, but only after it has received a joint address passed by the Canadian Senate and House of Commons requesting that the desired amendment should be enacted. Could the Canadian Parliament, then, ask for any amendment it wished? It frequently did so without reference to any other body; and there was no legal provision which prevented such procedure. But mere legal provisions, as the above pages have indicated, are not necessarily decisive. The provinces are frequently deeply concerned in constitutional amendment, and have views which they will wish to have considered. One school of thought, indeed, insists that the original federation embodied a compact or agreement which cannot be altered except with the unanimous consent of all the provinces, and that the Canadian Parliament is therefore bound to obtain this consent before forwarding its request to Westminster. This "compact theory" has little legal or historical justification, though it was generally admitted that Parliament did not and should not have an unfettered right of demanding any amendment it desires without regard for provincial opinion.

One fact concerning the system of making amendments was indisputable: it was extremely unsatisfactory that Canada should have to request the Parliament of another country to amend major parts of the Canadian constitution. Yet the obstacles in the path of removing this condition baffled Canadian statesmen for decades. Ideally, the long-sought amending process needed to be both elastic and inelastic: elastic for relatively simple parts of the constitution such as the qualifications of senators; inelastic for those parts involving the fundamental rights of some or all citizens. Despite many attempts to solve the problem, the ideal continued to elude Canadians, although over the years a consensus developed for the idea that different parts of the constitution required different amending procedures. In the event, to cut a long and involved story short, that is the kind of amending process finally chosen.

The Constitution Act of 1982 includes several major sections apart from the Charter of Rights and Freedoms, and one of them provides clearly for "Procedure for Amending Constitution of Canada." The procedure then described reserves certain subjects for the unanimous consent of Parliament and all ten provincial legislatures. Mention has already been made of the monarchy and the composition of the Supreme Court; other topics in the list include the governor general and the lieutenant governors; the right of a province to be guaranteed at least as many MPs as it has senators; the use (under stated circumstances) of English or French; and this particular amending clause itself.

The general amending power, which applies (with modifications stated in the relevant section) to all ordinary circumstances, requires:

(a) resolutions of the Senate and House of Commons; and
(b) resolutions of the legislative assemblies of at least two-thirds of the provinces that have, in the aggregate, according to the then latest general census, at least fifty per cent of the population of all the provinces.

That sounds straightforward, and it is. But given the huge variations in the populations of the provinces, the largest provinces plainly carry a weight in the amending procedure not shared by the smallest.

And quite apart from that, it should be emphasized that the Constitution Act of 1982 gives Canada an extremely rigid amending process. Still, it *is* an amending process, a goal sought over several generations of statesmen.

2

## Editors' Introduction

James Mallory is a fixture in the study of Canadian government. *The Structure of Canadian Government* includes an incisive overview of the patterns and context that facilitate constitutional governance in Canada. Both the book and the selection will be familiar to the informed reader. By contrast, the second selection, taken from *Responsive Responsible Government*, deals with responsible government and has largely been forgotten. It is included here because of its outstanding explanation of responsive and responsible government as the crux of Canadian constitutional governance.

Sources: James R. Mallory, "The Pattern of the Constitution," from *The Structure of Canadian Government*, rev. ed. (Toronto: Gage Publishing, 1984), 1–26; "Responsive and Responsible Government," *Transactions of the Royal Society of Canada* 12 (1974): 210; Mallory, James R., "Responsive and Responsible Government," *Transactions of the Royal Society of Canada* 12 (1974), 210. Public domain.

James Mallory

# The Pattern of the Constitution

MOST COUNTRIES OF the world today claim to be democracies. Canada is one of the much smaller number that can be called constitutional democracies. The difference is important. From at least the time of the ancient Romans the question has been asked *quis custodiet ipsos custodies*? Or, who controls the controllers? There is a constitutional order if the polity has effective means of preventing the abuse of power, and ensures that those in authority cannot take away the ultimate right of the governed to remove them or reject their policies. How is this to be done? The usual method is to enshrine basic values in the fundamental law of the constitution, which governments and legislatures cannot readily change, but which may be modified by a special and difficult procedure. This was the method pursued by the founders of the American republic, who lavished their considerable learning and experience in producing the constitution of the United States, which defines the powers of government and subjects them to the restraints of fundamental law. They could justly describe the system which they had created as "a government of laws and not of men."

Initially the Canadian solution was different. It derived from the "unwritten" British constitution, where there is no single document which sets down the overriding principles of constitutional government, and where the basic rights of the citizen are protected by the benevolent interpretation of the law by the courts. Through more than a century after Confederation the basic document of the Canadian constitution was the British North America Act, the most important provisions of which confined the two levels of government—federal and provincial—to their own proper spheres. But the Act did little to protect the rights of the citizen. Nevertheless the courts have managed to recognize and protect a number of the basic rights of the citizen even though these rights were not spelled out in the British North America Act.[1] Since the introduction into the Canadian constitution of the Charter of Rights and Freedoms in 1982, this constitutional gap has largely been filled and the constitution of Canada is now much more a "written" one like that of the United States.

Canada has been nourished by the same stream of constitutional ideas, and in many respects the same

---

1    For example, while the law was never completely clear on the extent that the constitution protected the free discussion and debate which must underlie the process of free government, the Supreme Court nevertheless found a legal basis for protecting them as part of an "unwritten constitution." It is doubtful, however, if the courts would have gone as far as Mr. Justice Abbott, in an *obiter dictum* in the *Padlock* case, and hold that "as our constitutional Act stands, Parliament itself could not abrogate this right of discussion and debate." *Switzman v. Elbling and A.G. for Quebec* [1957] S.C.R. 285. However, these rights are now protected in the Charter of Rights and Freedoms.

constitutional atmosphere, as the United States. Both countries have a common tradition of liberty, equality and respect for law. Both have grown out of heterogeneous communities with differences among them so great that a federal form of government was necessary to bring them together.

The similarities end on a point of emphasis. The American constitution was born of war, revolution and the fear of counter-revolution. It has about it the air of leaving nothing to chance. The Canadian constitution was a product of bargaining, of a feeling that the practical operation is more important than the letter of the *law,* and that the spirit supersedes the letter of the agreement. This has made our constitutional law harder to discover and apply than the American, for it shares the ambiguities of the British constitution. The difference between American and British constitutionalism is essentially this: for the Americans, anything unconstitutional is illegal, however right and necessary it may seem; for the British, anything unconstitutional is wrong, however legal it may be.

To the extent that a constitution is a "written" one, the courts must play an important role as the final guardians and interpreters of the constitution. In the United States, this role of the courts is an omnipresent one since the courts must not only interpret the boundaries between the powers of the national and state governments, but also enforce the restraints which the Bill of Rights imposes on all governments. In Canada, the role of the courts has been more limited. Whereas in the United States the powers of government derive from the people and are expressed and limited in the constitution, Canada inherited the British constitutional idea of the unlimited sovereignty of the legislature, so that the only role of the courts was to define the boundary between federal and provincial powers. Thus the Canadian courts inherited a more deferential attitude towards legislatures and have been more reluctant to substitute their own judgment of what is constitutionally proper for that of Parliament or a provincial legislature unless there is a clear conflict between them which must be resolved. This judicial attitude is deeply embedded and the inclusion of a Charter of Rights and Freedoms in the constitution may constitute a difficult challenge to the courts when they are confronted with a larger and different role in interpreting the constitution.

The purpose of a constitution is simply to lay down the rules for the operation of the organs of government in relation to one another and in relation to the citizen. The constitution of Canada is not easy either to describe or to discover, for it does not exist in any single document. It is customary to speak of the British North America Act, 1867, together with its various amendments, as "the Canadian constitution," but in fact only a part of the important provisions of the constitution are contained therein.

Our system of government took for granted, and continued in force, an elaborate system of government which had grown up for over a century in the provinces of British North America before Confederation. The BNA Act hardly concerns itself at all, for example, with the organization and powers of the courts of law, or with the structure of the executive or its relationship to Parliament. It does not mention either the Prime Minister or the Cabinet.

Some of these matters are not regulated by law but by "conventions of the constitution." These are rules which are well known and clearly stated, but are not legally enforceable. A breach of these rules is not a breach of the law, though it may be contrary to the spirit of the constitution. A breach of these conventions is unconstitutional but not illegal. The most important areas of the Canadian constitution established by convention rather than by law have been Canada's changing relationship to the United Kingdom—from colony to member of the Commonwealth—and the operation of Cabinet government.

These two areas are closely interrelated and it is the gradual change in them which comprehends the evolution from a number of dependent colonies to an independent and sovereign state. Unlike most other modern states, Canada has never experienced a revolutionary break with the past or an abrupt transfer of sovereignty which laid the foundation for a completely new constitution.

## THE BASIC ELEMENTS OF CONSTITUTIONALISM

The three basic elements of the Canadian constitution were all found in the British North American colonies in the eighteenth century. These elements were (1) a system of law, (2) the right to representative institutions and (3) the principle of religious toleration. With them, the firm basis of a constitutional order was laid nearly a century before the frontiers of local self-government began to expand in the nineteenth century.

Under the common law of England, the rights of Englishmen accompanied them overseas. The consequence was that in "settled territories"[2] the common law itself and such of the statute law of England, in general character, accompanied the settlers. Thus, they brought with them their traditional rights, including the legal rights of action which safeguarded English liberty, such as habeas corpus. The case was different for "conquered territories," that is, territories acquired by cession from another European power, for they already had an established system of European law. The abrogation of a system of civilized law by mere conquest could only result in complete confusion and serious damage to the property rights of the inhabitants. It was customary, therefore, to leave the existing system of law undisturbed. This was done when Canada passed from French to British control in 1763. Subsequently, by the Quebec Act, 1774, the colony was made subject to English criminal law, but the civil law was left unchanged. Consequently, although nine Canadian provinces have legal systems based on English common law, the province of Quebec has a system based, in common with the countries of continental Europe, on the Roman civil law.

The right to representative institutions, regarded as inherent in the settled territories, was also necessarily accorded to ceded territory where there were sufficient inhabitants to justify it. Otherwise such territories would naturally be unattractive to English settlers. In practice, the machinery by which local bodies were given legislative powers was the same in both cases.[3]

Territories in aboriginal hands which were acquired by settlement were initially governed under the provisions of a charter or letters patent issued under the prerogative. They had no inherent right to elect representatives, to make local laws, or to approve taxes for the cost of local government. What political institutions they might have were those which the Crown, under the prerogative, chose to give them. Since it was impossible to govern territories inhabited by Europeans without some form of local government, the difference in practice between settled and conquered territories became slight. But the constitutional position was not the same. However, once the Crown had granted some form of local representative institutions, this could not be taken away, and the Crown could not revive its right to raise taxes and legislate.[4] This limitation applied, of course, only to the prerogative. When constitutional provisions were made by the Parliament of the United Kingdom, as in the Quebec Act, the right to make new arrangements by a further act of Parliament was not affected.

By the end of the eighteenth century the overseas colonies of the "old British Empire" where there were European settlers, conformed, with minor exceptions, to a standard pattern. The executive power was vested in a Governor. In the exercise of his function he was aided and advised by a Council, whose members he nominated. Legislation was enacted by the passage of bills through an elected Assembly, as well as through the Council (acting as a second legislative chamber), and with the assent of the Governor.[5] Thus the colonial constitutions were similar in outline to the British constitution as it existed in the early years of the eighteenth century. The Council performed the dual function of the House of Lords and the Privy Council.

2 Of the British North American colonies, only Nova Scotia and Newfoundland were regarded as "settled" territories. Nova Scotia was originally claimed by the British Crown in the seventeenth century, and although it changed hands more than once, the courts regarded it as "settled." All of the western provinces of Canada are regarded as acquired by settlement. Cf. Arthur Berriedale Keith, *The Dominions as Sovereign States* (London, 1938), pp. 154–5.

3 In English constitutional law there are two sources of legislative power, *statute* and *prerogative*. Statute law is made by the Sovereign in Parliament in the form of an act of Parliament. The Sovereign may also legislate without the participation of Parliament by proclamation, letters patent, or some other prerogative instrument. Since the time of the Stuarts the prerogative power to legislate

has been steadily shrinking, and the general rule is that once Parliament has dealt with a legislative field the prerogative power to legislate has gone. Nevertheless, there are a few areas in which it is still possible to legislate under the prerogative. Thus, while the British North America Act provides that there shall be a Governor General, the constitution of his office and powers are provided for in a prerogative instrument, the royal letters patent.

4 This was settled in a famous judgment of Lord Mansfield in the case of *Campbell v. Hall* in 1774. The case dealt with a dispute which had arisen in Grenada, but the rule laid down has been universally applied ever since.

5 Martin Wight, *The Development of the Legislative Council, 1606–1945* (London, 1946), pp. 29–33.

The English constitution under the early Stuarts was inherently unstable. A clash of interest between King and Parliament grew into a conflict of constitutional principle which led to civil war. Similarly, in North America, a cleavage in interest and outlook between the Governor and the Assembly was bound to emerge when the Governor lay under the control of a distant British government and local interests were focussed in the Assembly. A British constitution of similar design worked only because the Whig magnates, who supported the Crown and dominated the House of Lords after 1688, were also able to control the House of Commons.

The British constitution, which was taken as a model in the government of British colonies overseas, was, except when some powerful interest could hold King, Lords, and Commons together, essentially unstable. Its dangers were revealed when George III, in the early years of his reign, was able to assert considerable dominance over the executive, and the threat appeared of the emergence of a party of "King's friends" who might control the House of Commons and thus undo the established balance of the constitution. The Americans, in their struggle for self-government, perceived the analogy between their own constitutional difficulties and those brought about in Britain by George III. Thus, in drafting the constitutions of the states and in constructing the government of the Union, they sought by a rigid separation of powers to curb the influence of the executive over the legislature.

Perhaps unfortunately, the Americans did not see that an alternative solution to the problem was already being worked out in Britain with the emergence of a Cabinet of Ministers, responsible to the House of Commons. When the time came, at a later date, for the other British North American colonies to gain greater control over their own affairs, it was possible to weigh the merits of the two very different products of the seventeenth-century English constitution.

The third basic constitutional decision which was reached in British North America in the eighteenth century was the principle of religious toleration. In England, Protestantism had been part of the constitution since the sixteenth century. After the expulsion of James II, a Protestant monarchy reinforced a system in which political office was in effect restricted to adherents of the Church of England. This, when applied in Canada and Nova Scotia, imposed a serious obstacle to the participation by French Canadians and Acadians in their own government. The Treaty of Paris contained guarantees of freedom of worship in Canada, and this right was confirmed and amplified in the Quebec Act of 1774.[6] In the same act a special form of oath was provided so that Catholics could hold office in Canada.

## REPRESENTATIVE GOVERNMENT

The Quebec Act had asserted that a legislative assembly was unsuited to the circumstances of the colony, and had provided that such legislative power as was required should be exercised by the Governor acting with an appointed Council. The normal state of constitutional deadlock in the older American colonies, which had resulted from the dependence of the Governor on a recalcitrant Assembly for supply, had decided the British authorities to strengthen the executive. When legislative assemblies were granted to the northern provinces, the British Parliament provided revenues for the Governor to support the costs of government and reduce his dependence on the legislature.

Meanwhile, the northern provinces gradually acquired representative legislatures. The first Assembly in Nova Scotia was summoned in 1758, and in Prince Edward Island in 1773. The end of the American War of Independence led to a substantial wave of immigration into the northern provinces. The Loyalists who fought for the British connection against their fellow-Americans disapproved of revolution, but they were determined to retain their rights to representative institutions. The settlers who had come to that part of Nova Scotia lying north of the Bay of Fundy were given a separate provincial government in 1784. This legislation, which set up the province of New Brunswick, included in it the normal representative assembly. Finally, in 1791, representative government was extended to Canada.

The constitutions of the Maritime provinces conformed to the old colonial pattern. They were

---

6    Similar guarantees for the exercise of the Catholic religion in Nova Scotia were contained in the Treaty of Utrecht in 1713.

grants from the Crown under the royal prerogative. Each province possessed, in addition to the elected Assembly, an undifferentiated Council which performed the dual function of advising the Governor and of acting as a legislative second chamber.

The constitutional provisions for the colony of Canada differed from the older constitutions in two respects. In the first place, they were created by a different constituent power—the Parliament of the United Kingdom. With the passage of the Quebec Act in 1774, the power of the Crown to legislate for Canada under the prerogative lapsed. Henceforth the constitution of that province lay in the gift of the British Parliament. The act of 1791, commonly referred to in Canada as the Constitutional Act, departed somewhat from the old colonial model, producing a constitution superficially similar to that of Great Britain. The Governor was to be advised by a small Executive Council, while a separate and larger body, the Legislative Council, together with the Legislative Assembly, made up the legislature. At the same time the colony was divided into two, each province with its own legislature. Lower Canada included all of the colony east of the Ottawa River, while Upper Canada took in the new settlements lying to the west along the upper St. Lawrence and the Great Lakes. Since almost all of the French Canadians lived in Lower Canada, it alone retained the French civil law. Upper Canada, with its English-speaking settlers, joined the ranks of the common-law provinces.

## PARLIAMENTARY GOVERNMENT

John Graves Simcoe, the first Lieutenant-Governor of Upper Canada, claimed that the system of government over which he presided was indeed a facsimile of the British constitution, adapted to suit the needs of a backwoods colony. There was more truth in this claim than either the early reformers or the later historians have ever been prepared to admit. It requires an effort of imagination to grasp the context of the politics of another age. The fact that there did not exist in Canada, at the beginning of the nineteenth century, a constitution which was the same as the British constitution at the time of Mr. Gladstone's first ministry (1868–74) is less cause for complaint if

we remember that such a constitution also did not exist in the United Kingdom in 1791. Similarly, there is as much difference between the position of Lord Dufferin and Mr. Michener as Governor General as there is between the position of Queen Victoria and Queen Elizabeth II.

In theory the eighteenth-century English constitution was one in which the King was the head of an autonomous executive, the Lords represented the great landed interests and the Commons represented a smaller but substantial property interest in the community. As described by Sir William Blackstone, the system depended in part on a legal separation of power between the executive and the legislature. It also depended on the fact that the King operated as a check on the power of the legislature, and Parliament acted as a check on the power of the Crown, to produce a system of countervailing power which resulted in constitutional government. But the overriding veto of the Crown in legislation was too closely associated with the memory of the Stuarts to be an effective check on the power of Parliament. The Crown's power was still real, but becoming more subtle and indirect. No sovereign after Queen Anne refused to assent to legislation. It was to be a long time before anyone noticed that by the last half of the eighteenth century the underlying reality was changing.

The change taking place was the emergence of Cabinet government, though it was not a part of the literary theory of the constitution until the days of Walter Bagehot. Before the accession of Queen Victoria it meant that the Crown's business was conducted by ministers who retained office through their ability to control and manage the House of Commons. Thus emerged a government continuously responsive to the majority in the House. This was not the separation of powers in the classic sense, but Bagehot's "close union, the nearly complete fusion of the executive and the legislative powers."[7] We may say, in short, that the British constitution in the last half of the eighteenth century worked in spite of, rather than because of, the separation of power. The real reason why the models of the British constitution broke down first in the old American colonies and later in British North

7  Walter Bagehot, *The English Constitution*, World's Classics Edition (London, 1928), p. 9.

America was that they failed to represent the realities of political and economic power in North America. In Great Britain the system worked, not because the interests of King, Lords and Commons were different, but because they were the same. The great landed families were not only an agricultural interest, for their wealth had been invested in trade and transportation. They controlled the rotten borough seats in the House of Commons, and a complex system of party management left them a decisive voice in the executive. The British system, in its turn, was to approach the brink of collapse before the Reform Bill of 1832 admitted the rising middle classes to a share in political power appropriate to their stake in the country.

The North American counterpart of this system provided no such neat behind-the-scenes combination of interests. The local elected Assemblies, with a wider franchise and a wider distribution of property, came to be the voices of the agrarian frontier. The Legislative Council in the Canadas represented a combination of large-scale wealth in land and trade. The Governor became the focus of a serious conflict of interest between the local communities and his imperial masters. Under such conditions harmony was only achieved by astute political management by the Governor. He, in his turn, suffered under the double disadvantage of strict control from Downing Street and (in most cases) a military background from which the arts of compromise and political management were notably absent. The result was collision without compromise, stiff-necked and unimaginative administration confronted with extremist and irresponsible legislative leadership.

Responsible government was finally achieved in the eighteen-forties. As H.A. Innis suggested, it was necessary to have responsible local politicians managing the administration of the provinces in order that the combined resources of the community be mobilized to underwrite the great developmental undertakings on which growth and prosperity of the colonies depended.[8] The repeal of the Corn Laws and the Navigation Acts, and the revolution in British commercial policy from mercantilism to free trade weakened the vested interests in the old colonial system and removed one

of the major obstacles to responsible government as a means of local autonomy.[9]

The question of colonial responsible government had been debated many times. In Canada, prominent members of the Reform Party like the Baldwins, had urged it. Lord Durham had seen it as the one vital principle of British constitutionalism whose lack had turned the whole system of colonial government sour. A dispatch from Lord John Russell is the classic statement of the old Colonial Office view that no Governor could be put in the position of acknowledging two masters.[10] The Colonial Office was unimpressed by Durham's breezy assertion that there was no real difficulty since it was perfectly possible to separate things imperial from things local, that the Governor could render unto his ministers the things that were the colonies' and render unto the Queen's ministers the things that were the Queen's. Perhaps the Colonial Office was right, but it is the genius of the British constitution to avoid logical dilemmas.

For years colonial reformers had argued that the only way to ensure harmony between the executive and the legislature was for the Governor to appoint to his Executive Council those who had the confidence of, and were responsible to, the Assembly. This was how constitutional government worked in Great Britain, and this was how it must work in British North America. But this was a practice which the British government, impaled on the horns of its logic, could not accept. Nothing could arrest the drift to a constitutional crisis in all of the British North American provinces. The outbreak of armed rebellion in the Canadas in 1837 galvanized Whitehall into action.

The constitutions of the two Canadian provinces were suspended and Lord Durham was sent out to investigate and deal with the situation in the whole of British North America. In what was to live as one of the great state papers in British colonial policy, Durham made two major recommendations. He had found in Lower Canada a constitutional struggle which was also a struggle for mastery between two races. He therefore recommended a union of the two colonies to submerge

8    H.A. Innis, *Political Economy in the Modern State* (Toronto, 1946), p. 188.

9    Ibid., p. 222.

10   Russell to Thomson, October 11, 1839. Quoted in Arthur Berriedale Keith, ed., *Selected Speeches and Documents on British Colonial Policy, 1763–1917*, Vol. 1 (London, 1918), pp. 173–8.

the racial conflict. Secondly, he recommended the granting of responsible government.

But on this issue the British government was not prepared to yield. In 1840 the two provinces were reunited but the old framework remained. However, the pattern thereafter was very different, for the first Governor of the new united colony was to be the real founder of Cabinet government in Canada. It was Lord Sydenham who, as Adam Shortt said,

> boldly introduced the British parliamentary system into Canada, thus completely revolutionizing the previous system of colonial government. This he accomplished by personally undertaking its introduction, directly combining in himself the duties of governor-general, prime minister and party leader. He initiated his personally selected cabinet into the mysteries of cabinet government, dependent for its life upon retaining the support of the majority of the legislature including the assembly and the council. To accomplish this, he organized and maintained for the first time in Canada a government party, of which he was the recognized leader and upon which he depended for getting his numerous and important bills through the legislature, for voting the necessary supplies, and supporting his executive government.[11]

Neither Sydenham nor his successors were able to make this system work effectively, and it led within a decade to the granting of responsible government. But we should recognize that the Sydenham system was not such a constitutional monstrosity as it has appeared to some later historians. It was a necessary stage for which there are historical parallels. For the British constitution in the eighteenth century passed through just such a phase—a "mixed" form of government in which ministers were dependent on the King, and also on their ability to manage Parliament. It was, in both British and Canadian constitutional history, a period of "essentially unstable equilibrium." "It would be difficult to think," wrote Professor Butterfield of the early years of the reign of George III, "of a situation

which could have been more burdened with tensions, more clouded with ambiguities, more pregnant with the varied possibilities of development."[12] The result in both cases was Cabinet government.

## CABINET GOVERNMENT

The emergence of Cabinet government in Canada illustrates the flexibility of the British constitutional system. Far more than any other single stage in Canadian constitutional development, it constituted the "great leap forward" which brought about genuine self-government by conferring initiative and power on the Canadian elite operating through the Canadian party system. This was not the result of a change in the formal constitution, but of a gradual change in the arrangements of the executive government.

Two important steps by Lord Sydenham were essential prerequisites to the granting of responsible government. He put into practice Lord Durham's recommendations for improving the organization of the executive by creating departments, placing each under a single political head, and making his Executive Council a genuine policy-making body of ministers. Without this, as Professor Hodgetts says, "any grant of responsible government would be dangerous," because there could be no effective and coherent executive leadership.[13]

Sydenham's second step was equally important. He created a government party to sustain his ministers in the legislature. He was the head of the executive, presiding over his Council and using his powers and patronage to ensure support in the legislature for his ministry.

To the modern eye this may have a somewhat unseemly look, yet it should be remembered that it did not differ significantly from the Cabinet system in England under George III. But by the middle of the nineteenth century Cabinet government in England had changed considerably, and the incongruity of Sydenham's system was apparent to any well-informed observer. A change of government in England in 1846

11  Adam Shortt, "The Relations between the Legislative and Executive Branches of the Canadian Government," *American Political Science Review* VII, No. 2 (May 1913), p. 187.

12  Herbert Butterfield, *George III and the Historians* (London, 1957), p. 254.

13  J.E. Hodgetts, *Pioneer Public Service: An Administrative History of the United Canadas, 1841–1867* (Toronto, 1956), p. 26.

made it possible to grant the concession of responsible government which had been so adamantly refused five years before. The new Colonial Secretary, Lord Grey, made it plain to the two new Governors appointed in 1847—Sir John Harvey in Nova Scotia and Lord Elgin in Canada—that in future they should choose their Councils from the leaders of the majority party in the Assembly.

The first test of this principle came early in 1848, when a non-confidence vote was carried against the government in Nova Scotia on January 25. Two days later the ministry resigned and Harvey called upon the leader of the majority to form a new government. Within a few weeks similar changes of government had taken place in Canada and in New Brunswick, and thus the principle of responsible government was firmly established in British North America. Henceforth the government was to be constituted from the group able to gain the support of a majority of the elected legislature, and the principle of ultimate control of the government by the electorate was established.

This fundamental change in constitutional practice was based on no formal alteration in constitutional documents. It did not even require a change in the Governor's official instructions. All that was necessary was a dispatch from the Colonial Secretary to the Governor. As the great Nova Scotian reformer Joseph Howe had written: "You have no Act of Parliament to define the duty of the Sovereign when ministers are in a minority; we want none to enable us to suggest to a Governor when his advisers have lost the confidence of our colonial Assemblies. But what we do want, my Lord, is a rigid enforcement of British practice, by the imperial authorities, on every Governor; the intelligence and public spirit of the people will supply the rest."[14]

The development of Cabinet government in Canada took place in three distinct stages, each of which was necessary to create the conditions favourable to the one that followed. Lord Sydenham's system of ministerial government, in which the Governor was still the effective leader of the administration, proved to be unworkable, but it did create the administrative foundations of Cabinet government. When responsible government came in 1848, Canadian politicians had had over six years' experience as ministers, there

was an administrative system accustomed to ministerial direction and a two-party system accustomed to the responsibility of power. This second stage required that the Governor should retain his advisers only so long as they, as a group, were able to maintain a majority in the lower house of the legislature. As long as a ministry remained in office the Governor must, except where imperial interests were at stake, adhere to its advice. There followed a third stage—the introduction of true Cabinet government—which required the withdrawal of the Governor from direct participation in the deliberations of his constitutional advisers. This did not come about until at least six years after the introduction of responsible government. What happened in effect was the separation of the Cabinet from the Executive Council. What Sir William Anson had called the deliberative and the executive functions were already quite clearly divided between two different bodies, the Committee of Council and the Governor-in-Council. "The Council," wrote Sir Edmund Head in 1858, "... discuss in committee, the Governor not being present, the various measures or questions with which they have to deal."[15] The Committee of Council was simply the ministers meeting in the absence of the Governor. Its conclusions were given legal sanction by becoming formal actions of the Governor-in-Council. If the submissions were routine they were usually transmitted to the Governor for his signature at leisure in his office. But the Governor reserved the right to go into Council to discuss measures and to approve them in formal Council. For the Governor to attend regularly at meetings of ministers would, as Head wrote to the Colonial Secretary in 1853, "check all freedom of debate and embarrass himself as well as his advisers."[16]

The third stage, in which the Governor did not normally participate in the discussion which led to

14  *Novascotian*, January 4 and 11, 1847.

15  Quoted in D.G.G. Kerr, *Sir Edmund Head: A Scholarly Governor* (Toronto, 1954), pp. 174–6.
16  Public Archives of Canada, *Secret and Confidential Despatches, Colonial Secretary 1856–1866*, Series G 10, Vol. II, and *Guide to Canadian Ministries since Confederation*, Ottawa, 1957. On the development of the Cabinet out of the Governor's council see J.R. Mallory, "Cabinet Government in Canada," *Political Studies II*, No. 2, pp. 142–53; "Cabinets and Councils in Canada," *Public Law*, Autumn, 1957, pp. 231–51; W.E.D. Halliday, "The Privy Council Office and Cabinet Secretariat in Relation to the Development of Cabinet Government," *Canada Year Book*, 1956.

decision-making, created a shift in the balance of power in the executive from the Governor to the political leaders of the Cabinet, and this contributed to the distinctive position of the First Minister. The union of the two parts of the Province of Canada as a result of the Act of Union of 1840 did not completely fuse the politics of its constituent parts, and there was indeed a de facto federalism which made coalitions essential. As a result there were always two Premiers (or First Ministers, as they were called), one from each part of the province. Only after Confederation did a single First Minister emerge. This had the effect of further diminishing the role of the Governor. As long as there were two First Ministers, he retained a degree of initiative by being able to hold the balance between them. But after Confederation, the single Prime Minister left the political head of the executive in a dominant position and the Governor General in the increasingly passive role of a constitutional head of state.

By 1867, the transformation of the Governor General from Colonial Governor to personal representative to the Sovereign had gone more than halfway. But the Governor General still possessed far more formidable powers than the Sovereign. In addition, the normal prerogatives were enhanced by the prestige of his position as an imperial officer. In those early years the Governor General consciously engaged in presiding over the birth of constitutional government in Canada. As Lord Dufferin somewhat grandly put it in a letter to Sir John A. Macdonald, "my great desire is to enhance the prestige and authority of Canadian statesmen, and teach the Canadian people to believe in and to be proud of their public men."[17] In an age when party leaders were not selected by any regular process of intra-party democracy, the choice by the Governor General of a Prime Minister was much more important than it is today. His ability to resist policy decisions of which he did not approve was far greater in the nineteenth century than it is today, and the correspondence of Prime Ministers with the Governor General in that period shows that on many issues there was a battle of wills between the Governor General and his ministers. In the end, of course, he had to yield because he could not afford to force their resignation,

for "he would do so with the full knowledge that he would be compelled to find successors who would be prepared to take constitutional responsibility for his action."[18] In fact, no Governor General was ever driven to the actual dismissal of his ministers.

An open refusal of advice always endangers the political neutrality of a constitutional ruler. Thus Lord Aberdeen, in 1896, was successful in refusing to approve a number of appointments by the Tupper ministry after it had been decisively defeated at the polls, because in this case the Governor General was protecting the rights of the newly elected majority. On the other hand, Lord Dufferin apparently did not feel justified in demanding the resignation of Sir John A. Macdonald over the Pacific Railway scandal in 1873, though the subsequent resignation of the government relieved him of further embarrassment.[19]

Even where imperial interests appeared to be at stake it was not always possible for the Governor General to prevail over an intransigent ministry with a strong majority. For example, in 1900 there developed a difference of view between Lord Minto and the Laurier administration. Differences had arisen between ministers and the Officer Commanding the Canadian Militia (an officer then appointed by the government of the United Kingdom). The Cabinet submitted an order-in-council demanding that the United Kingdom should recall the offending officer, General Hutton. Lord Minto felt that this constituted political interference in purely military matters, and submitted a lengthy memorandum to the Cabinet arguing against the recommendation for dismissal. However, the Cabinet persisted in its recommendation, and Minto signed the order because he had become convinced that a refusal would lead to the resignation of the Prime Minister, and in due course to a general election on the issue.[20]

17  Sir Joseph Pope, *Correspondence of Sir John Macdonald* (Toronto, n.d.), p. 203.

18  W.P.M. Kennedy, *The Constitution of Canada, 1534–1937*, 2nd ed. (London, 1937), p. 382.

19  Sir Charles Tupper claims that Lord Dufferin did in fact ask Macdonald to resign, but that he (Tupper) dissuaded him. Sir Charles Tupper, *Recollections of Sixty Years* (London, 1914), pp. 156–7. This incident is not corroborated in any contemporary document.

20  John Buchan, *Lord Minto* (London, 1924), pp. 144–52. A better account of this issue is in H. Pearson Gundy, "Sir Wilfrid Laurier and Lord Minto," *Canadian Historical Association, Annual Report*, 1952, p. 28.

As an imperial officer the Governor General possessed a number of specific powers which could be employed to protect imperial interests against the actions of the government and Parliament of Canada. Some of these powers were statutory. Section 55 of the British North America Act empowered him to withhold royal assent, or to reserve the bill for consideration by the government of the United Kingdom. This power was discretionary, but subject to the provisions of the act and to his instructions. In 1867 the powers of the Governor General were largely contained in the instructions issued to each Governor General on his appointment. In 1878 the powers of the Governor General were put on a more permanent basis by the issue of letters patent constituting the office. The instructions had enumerated classes of bills which should automatically be reserved.[21] There were also some doubts in the early years after Confederation about whether the prerogative of pardon should be exercised by the Governor General in his discretion or whether it should be based on ministerial advice and responsibility. The ambiguities which had emerged in practice were made more serious by proposals from the Colonial Office which would have had the effect of requiring the Governor General to preside in person over all meetings of his Council and which would have enabled him to act in certain circumstances without consulting his ministers or even against their advice. As a result of representation by Edward Blake, Minister of Justice, the Colonial Office proposals for the new letters patent were considerably modified. The enumerated list of bills on which assent was to be reserved was dropped, and it was provided that the prerogative of pardon was to be exercised on ministerial advice.[22]

Blake's memorandum made it clear that the limits within which the Governor General's reserve powers could be brought to bear in defence of imperial interests were too narrow to be based on a form of words:

> As a rule the Governor does and must act through the agency of Ministers, and Ministers must be responsible for such action—Upon the argument that there are certain conceivable circumstances in which, owing to the existence of substantial imperial interests, it may be considered that full freedom of action is not vested in the Canadian people, it appears to me that any such cases must, pending a solution of the great problem of Imperial Government, be dealt with as they arise…. The effort to reconcile by any form of words the responsibility of Ministers under the Canadian Constitution with a power to the Governor to take even a negative line independently of advice, cannot I think, succeed. The truth is, that Imperial interests are, under our present system of Government to be secured in matters of Canadian executive policy, not by any such clause in the Governor's instructions (which would be mischievous); but by mutual good feeling and by proper consideration of Imperial interests on the part of His [sic] Majesty's Canadian advisers; the Crown necessarily retaining all its constitutional rights and powers, which would be exercisable in any emergency in which the indicated securities might be found to fail.[23]

Blake's memorandum served to emphasize how far the facts of constitutional government in Canada had already outrun the forms of the constitution, even at that time. For while it was true that the Governor General retained the reserve powers so jealously guarded by the United Kingdom government, these powers were no longer of substantial importance. It

---

21  Under his instructions the Governor General should not give royal assent to certain kinds of bills, but reserve them for final decision by the Queen-in-Council, that is, by the British government. Under the instructions before 1878 the following bills had to be reserved: bills (a) for divorce; (b) for granting land or money gratuity to the Governor General; (c) for making paper or other currency legal tender; (d) for imposing differential duties; (e) contrary to treaty obligations; (f) interfering with discipline or control of H.M. forces in Canada; (g) interfering with the royal prerogative, the property of British subjects outside Canada, or the trade or shipping of Great Britain or her dependencies; (h) containing provisions to which royal assent had already been refused or disallowed. As a consequence of these instructions, twenty-one bills had been reserved. W.P.M. Kennedy, ed., *Statutes, Treaties and Documents of the Canadian Constitution, 1713–1929* (Toronto, 1930), p. 672 (hereafter cited as *Constitutional Documents*).

22  The proposed letters patent had originally been circulated to the Canadian government. Edward Blake, then Minister of Justice, presented a memorandum in August 1876, objecting strongly to a number of proposals. In the result they were considerably revised. The letters patent, together with the new instructions, are in Kennedy, *Constitutional Documents*, pp. 672–5.

23  Ibid., pp. 669–70.

was no longer possible to contemplate an open clash in which the advice of Canadian ministers could be rudely overridden on the grounds of imperial interest. If imperial interest were to be protected through the Governor General's office, it must be through influence rather than overt action. For in the last analysis a Canadian government could make a constitutional issue of the matter. In such a case a Governor General would find it difficult, if not impossible, to find an alternative government, and if he did so he would certainly bring his office into politics—a situation above all to be avoided.

Blake had objected to the Governor General's reserve powers as an imperial officer. He correctly pointed out that the normal reserve powers of the Crown were in themselves a powerful means of restricting hasty, unfair, or undesirable measures by Canadian governments. However, over the years the Governor General's reserve powers had come to be so closely identified with his function as an imperial officer that it finally became doubtful how far he could exercise discretionary powers appropriate to the Sovereign in the constitution of the United Kingdom without arousing undue and misinformed controversy. Such was the case with Lord Byng's refusal of a dissolution of Parliament to Mackenzie King in 1926. We now know that the Sovereign is not bound automatically to grant a dissolution when it is requested by a Prime Minister, though there was some reason to be less certain in 1926 that any such discretion existed.[24] In the event, what was essentially a problem of the relationship between the head of state and the Prime Minister was perceived by a great many Canadians at the time as a struggle between a Canadian government and an arm of the British government.

At the height of the crisis Mackenzie King had demanded that the Governor General seek direction from the Secretary of State for the Dominions before refusing to grant the dissolution. Whether or not King knew that his request was constitutionally outrageous, it was a shrewd political move. But Lord Byng sensibly kept his own counsel. As L.S. Amery, who was Secretary of State for the Dominions at the time, said:

This was a pretty obvious trap. If I took Mackenzie King's view Byng would be held clearly in the wrong,

and would have to give way. If I supported Byng, I should provide all the ammunition required for raising the issue of Downing Street interference. Byng refused, on the sound constitutional ground that this was a matter for his own personal judgment of his duty to the people of Canada, and no concern of anyone outside—the answer I should certainly have given if I had been consulted.[25]

The outcome of this incident was that it strengthened King's resolve to join with some of the other Dominion governments in pressing to strip the Governor General of his functions as an imperial officer. The question was raised at the Imperial Conference of 1926, and circumstances were propitious for the change. The great military contributions of the Dominions in the First World War, and the recognition of a greater degree of autonomy in their external as well as their internal affairs after the war, indicated that the constitutional structure of the British Empire was due for an overhaul. Canada was not the only Dominion anxious to modify the position of the Governor General, and the British government was sympathetic to such a modification. As a consequence the Governor General ceased to be in any sense an imperial officer and, necessarily, ceased to be the channel of communication between the United Kingdom and Canadian governments. What advantages this method of communication had possessed were, by this time, outweighed by its disadvantages. In the period of transition from purely local self-government to full nationhood it had been a useful method of transmitting the decisions of the imperial government on matters of imperial policy, and had served as a means of keeping the two governments in reasonably close touch with one another.[26]

25 L.S. Amery, *My Political Life*, Vol. II (London, 1953), p. 378. Reprinted by permission of Hutchinson and Co.

26 "In more recent years it had still served, more informally, to keep Dominion Ministers to some extent in touch with general Imperial policy. At the same time the Governor-General in his private letters could give the Colonial Secretary an intimate and detached view of the political affairs of his Dominion. But the practice was inconsistent with the theoretical conception of equal status, according to which the Governor-General had ceased to be in any respect an agent of the British Government, but was an integral part of the Dominion constitution with an undivided responsibility to the nation concerned. What is more, as the issue between Byng and Mackenzie King had just shown, it could lend itself to serious misrepresentation." Ibid., pp. 386–7.

24 See below, Chapter II.

The dual status of the Governor General had been outmoded by events, and the Imperial Conference of 1926 resolved to end the ambiguity in its declaration that

It is an essential consequence of the equality status … that the Governor General of a Dominion is the representative of the Crown, holding in all essential respects the same position in relation to the administration of public affairs as is held by His Majesty the King in Great Britain, and that he is not the representative or agent of His Majesty's Government in Great Britain or of any Department of that Government.

It followed as a necessary consequence that the Governor General's documents, which (apart from a minor revision in 1905) were still in the form in which they had been made in 1878, should be amended to reflect his altered status. New letters patent and instructions were issued on March 23, 1931, at the request of the Canadian government. These removed the most obvious anomalies, including the clause empowering the King to give instructions to the Governor General by imperial order-in-council or through a United Kingdom Secretary of State, and required that leave of absence to a Governor General should in future be on the authority of his own Prime Minister rather than that of the Secretary of State.[27] A number of anomalies remained. The instructions, for example, still required the Governor General to transmit to the United Kingdom copies of all acts of Parliament and of all bills reserved by him, although the power of reservation had been formally declared to be obsolete by the Imperial Conference of 1930.[28] In certain other respects, the Governor General was not in the same position as the Sovereign since substantial parts of the royal prerogative were not exercised by the Governor General but remained with

the Sovereign acting on the advice of the Canadian ministers.

These incongruities, and others, were finally removed by the issue on September 8, 1947, of new letters patent under the Great Seal of Canada, replacing the old letters patent and instructions.[29] This instrument empowered the Governor General to exercise, on the advice of his Canadian ministers, all of the powers of the Sovereign in relation to Canada; and the portions of the superseded instruments which were inappropriate to current constitutional practice were omitted. The effect of these changes is that the Governor General is now governed by wholly Canadian instruments in regard to his office, and may exercise, on the advice of Canadian ministers, all of the powers of the Sovereign in relation to Canada. The effect of the letters patent of 1947, as regards the exercise of those matters which normally are submitted to the Sovereign (such as the appointment and issue of letters of credence to ambassadors), is more apparent than real. There seems to have been an understanding at the time that the letters patent were approved that no change in existing practice was contemplated, and the Governor General has not in fact dealt with any of the submissions which are normally laid before the Sovereign.

Thus there has been a full emancipation from the United Kingdom in the Canadian executive. This has developed first through the gradual erosion of the power, and the constitutional right, of the British government to interfere in any way with Canadian matters. Secondly, it has been brought about by the disappearance of the Governor General's functions as an imperial officer, and by the wasting away of his influence in the process of government. Thirdly, it has come about by the development of a direct constitutional relationship between Canadian ministers and the Sovereign; so that in Canadian matters they are dealing with the Queen of Canada and not the Queen of the United Kingdom.

27  Cf. Keith, *The Dominions as Sovereign States*, p. 210.
28  The practice of transmitting copies of all acts of Parliament to the United Kingdom was quietly dropped in 1942. Canada, *House of Commons Debates*, April 5, 1943, p. 1829. In 1947, the Canadian statute requiring transmission of copies of all acts of Parliament to the Governor General for transmission to the United Kingdom was amended (11 Geo. VI C.44).
29  Instead of assimilating the relevant part of the instructions to the letters patent, the Union of South Africa followed the rather incongruous course of issuing new letters patent and instructions over the signature of the Prime Minister of the Union as submitting officer. The Governor General of South Africa thus became bound by instructions emanating from his own Prime Minister. See Nicholas Mansergh, *Documents and Speeches on Commonwealth Affairs, 1931–1952* (London, 1953), pp. 71–6.

## LEGISLATIVE AUTONOMY

The British North American colonies were given the power to legislate in local matters when they were granted legislatures. These powers of local legislation were subject, however, to a number of limitations. In the first place, they could not make laws having effect outside their own territories. In the second place, colonial legislatures could not make laws which contravened the law of England. But what was the law of England? If it meant the whole statute and common law applicable in England, then the things a colonial legislature could do were restricted indeed. This question gave rise to serious difficulties in the nineteenth century, and it was only settled by the Colonial Laws Validity Act, 1865. By virtue of this act, it was declared that the only laws of England which stood in the way of colonial legislation were those statutes which specifically or by implication applied to the colony. In the context of its time, then, the Colonial Laws Validity Act was a liberating statute, since it reduced the number of colonial laws which could be held null and void to those which were repugnant to such English statute law as applied to the colonies. This act marks a stage in the gradual rise of local colonial institutions to ultimate full equality with those of the United Kingdom. The British North America Act of 1867 did not increase the powers of self-government of British North America, but it did widen the area covered by a single colonial Parliament, and subtly enhanced the status of the new Dominion by describing its legislature as a Parliament and its lower house as a House of Commons.

In addition to the above, the legislative restraints on Canada were the following: matters reserved exclusively for the British Parliament (such as legislation having extra-territorial effect, legislation respecting the constitution, and legislation dealing with other reserved topics, such as copyright).[30] If the Governor General had doubts about colonial legislation he could reserve it for consideration by the British government, which could then give assent to it by imperial order-in-council if it had no objection to the bill's becoming law. In addition, the British government could disallow any act of the Canadian Parliament within two years of its enactment. There was no limit in law whatever on this last power; it could be used to nullify any act whatsoever. An act which was disallowed became null and void from the date of its first passage.

The powers of reservation and disallowance of Canadian legislation still remain, superficially unimpaired, in sections 55 and 56 of the British North America Act. However, both are constitutionally obsolete: reservation because the Governor General is no longer an imperial officer and therefore has no constitutional right to reserve a bill; and disallowance because the Queen-in-Council in the United Kingdom has lost the constitutional right to deal with Canadian matters.[31] In any event the powers of disallowance and reservation, except as theoretical limitations of Canadian sovereignty, had ceased to be of any practical importance long before they were declared to be obsolete by the Imperial Conference of 1930. Most of the bills reserved had been dealt with in accordance with the detailed instructions to the Governor General regarding numerous classes of bills which had been superseded by the letters patent of 1878. Thereafter reservation was no longer important. The last Canadian act to be disallowed had been in 1873. The true safeguard of British imperial interests had turned out to be, as Edward Blake had argued in 1876, not the exercise of imperial veto in Canadian affairs, but mutual respect and consideration.

The restraints on Canadian self-government which depended on the positive exercise of British powers of veto disappeared by a process of constitutional evolution. The restraints which flowed from the limited powers which the Canadian Parliament possessed in constitutional law presented greater difficulty, because they could not be modified by changes in the conventions of the constitution but only through a change in the substance of British constitutional law.

The right to legislate beyond the limits laid down by the Colonial Laws Validity Act and the British North America Act was conferred by the Statute of

---

30  The Governor General was required in his instructions to reserve bills in a number of enumerated categories for consideration by the British government. Cf. fn. 21, *ante*.

31  Cf. statement of the Prime Minister, Mr. St. Laurent, in Canada, *House of Commons Debates*, 1949, p. 287.

Westminster, 1931. This step had been agreed to in principle at the Imperial Conference of 1926, but the technical problems involved in the transfer of power were considerable. A great deal of merchant shipping and similar legislation had to be carefully scrutinized to prepare the way for Canadian enactments to repair the gaps which would be opened in the law. A committee reported on the question in 1929, and its report was accepted by the Imperial Conference of 1930. Agreement was there reached on the outstanding questions of detail, and the Statute of Westminster was passed in the following year.

In effect the Statute of Westminster was a declaratory act that removed the previous limits on the legislative power of the Parliaments of the Dominions. At the same time, it laid down that the Parliament of the United Kingdom could not in future legislate with regard to the Dominions, except at the request and with the consent, of the Dominion concerned. It further declared that in future all laws relating to the succession to the throne and the royal style and titles would be enacted only with the assent of all Parliaments of the Dominions as well as the Parliament of the United Kingdom. Of course, theoretically, it would be possible for the United Kingdom Parliament to repeal the Statute of Westminster, since no Parliament has, in English constitutional law the power to bind a subsequent Parliament. However, this is a sufficiently unlikely contingency that it need not be a cause of serious apprehension. As Professor Wheare argues, "section 4 [which restricts the application of future United Kingdom acts to the Dominions save with their consent] ... is not a rule restricting power; it is a rule of construction. It is not directed to the United Kingdom Parliament; it is directed to the Courts.... But it does not render it legally impossible for the United Kingdom Parliament to legislate for a Dominion without the request and consent of the Dominion."[32] The important thing is that, as far as the constitutional law of Canada is concerned, the power of Parliament is no longer restricted to the areas it occupied before the passage of the Statute of Westminster. It might be neater, in a thorough attempt to domesticate the entire Canadian constitution, if

Canada, following the practice of South Africa, re-enacted the Statute of Westminster as part of an act of the Canadian Parliament. However, nothing would be gained in practice by this and in any event our constitutional law would still depend on a large body of English constitutional law which no one has seen fit to touch for centuries.

There was one question regarding the new powers of the Dominions which could not be resolved in 1930. This was the question of amending procedure for the British North America Act itself, so that it was excepted (by section 7) from the general operation of the Statute of Westminster. The reason for the difficulty was that no agreement could be reached in Canada on a method of amending the Canadian constitution, and so it was still necessary to secure certain constitutional amendments by recourse to amending acts passed by the United Kingdom Parliament at the request of the Parliament of Canada.

It may seem odd that in providing Canada with a constitution in 1867 the British Parliament did not insert in the British North America Act some machinery for its amendment. However, in this we have paid the price for having the first Dominion constitution. In the nineteenth century the British Parliament was jealous of delegating its legislative powers to subordinate bodies. It still regarded itself as the supreme constituent power in the British Empire and it would not lightly have been persuaded to grant an entirely Canadian procedure of amendment. The Quebec Resolutions of 1866, upon which the B.N.A. Act was based, made no mention at all of a general amending procedure for the constitution of Canada. The act did enable the provinces to amend their own constitutions, but this was significantly safeguarded by the protection of the office of Lieutenant-Governor as well as by the existence of the federal power of disallowance.

The most significant fact is that it did not seem to the Fathers of Confederation that the inclusion of an amending power was either desirable or necessary. Dr. Gerin-Lajoie was led to the conclusion that the amending provisions were deliberately left out to avoid dissention in the negotiations, and more important, "because the Imperial authority [was] thus considered as the ultimate safeguard of the rights granted to the provinces and to minorities by the

32  K.C. Wheare, *The Statute of Westminster and Dominion Status*, 5th ed. (London, 1953), p. 153.

constitution."[33] Whatever the original reason for the omission, the system of seeking amendments through the United Kingdom Parliament was to remain until the final achievement of patriation in 1982, as successive efforts after the passage of the Statute of Westminster in 1931 failed to achieve general agreement. However, a partial patriation of the amending power, relating to the institutions of the central government, was achieved in 1949, so that relatively few matters, notably those relating to the distribution of legislative power between the two levels of government, still required the old procedure.

33  Paul Gerin-Lajoie, *Constitutional Amendment in Canada* (Toronto, 1950) p. 38. Alexander Brady's view is that the omission of the amending power was "conscious and deliberate, and so grounded in conviction that the Founding Fathers hardly took pains to explain it." They assumed that the Canadian Government and Parliament could get on request any needed amendment from Westminster, and that a more formalized amending procedure "might only detract from the unitary nature of the federation." "Constitutional Amendment and the Federation," *Canadian Journal of Economics and Political Science.* XXIX:4 (November, 1963) pp. 486–7. In the absence of conclusive evidence, Professor Brady's views must be regarded as authoritative.

# 3

James Mallory

# Responsive and Responsible Government

IT USED TO BE that every Canadian child not only understood the term "responsible government," but was taught that it was a system marvellously contrived both to achieve democratic control over the executive and to adapt ingeniously to deal with whatever perils might threaten us. At the beginning of the present century the British system was so universally admired that it could be found in modified form in most of civilized Europe, and there were many Americans willing to consider that this system might well be superior to their own. Similarly, colonial territories aspiring to self-government wished as a matter of course to develop—as we in British North America had done—a constitution "similar in principle to that of the United Kingdom."

Today it would be hard to find anywhere unqualified acceptance of the virtues of the British parliamentary and cabinet system. Where it exists in newly emerging countries it is perverted from the Victorian model by the existence of one-party states or at best by situations where—as in India—there seems to be only one "party of government" permanently in power. From there the easy and natural route is to dictatorship. Thus, as Gerald Graham points out, "by exercising in perfectly legal fashion the unrestricted powers of parliament over an illiterate electorate that had

voted away its freedom, Kwame Nkrumah was able to set up his dictatorship in Ghana. In the words of Tanzania's President Julius Nyerere, the Westminster model, depending for its effectiveness on the two-party system, was 'a positive invitation to tyranny.'" And, he concludes, "in retrospect it would seem likely that most emerging Asian and African states would have found a presidential form of government with strong executive powers more appropriate."[1]

Even in Canada there have been mounting doubts. In a curious way these doubts have become mixed with the surviving rhetoric of anti-colonialism. It may well have been that the best we could hope for in colonial times was the "Westminster model," but surely, it is said, we no longer have to design a constitution which has to be approved in Downing Street. By taking thought we should be able to do much better now. Something of this feeling seems to have risen to confront the recent Joint Parliamentary Committee on the Constitution, as evidence of widespread sentiment that we need a constitution phrased in appropriate democratic rhetoric.

It is, of course, important to recognize what kind of constitution we have. The Westminster model is a

1   *Tides of Empire* (Montreal and London, 1972), 105.

product of nineteenth-century England, and as such it is not a democratic constitution, but an oligarchic one. The centre of authority in the system was not the people, but the legislature, and a government which was able to control the legislature could govern without serious interference between elections. This was so because of a party system which provided little or no opportunity for popular participation in government, and it should be recognized that representative government tends to be elitist. In spite of universal suffrage, the mass of citizenry is perhaps as far away from the real decisions of government as they were two hundred years ago, and the cabinet system provides strong institutional barriers to the development of more democratic ways of doing things. This being so, what should be the desired path of constitutional reform?

It is argued by some that to retain a system which was designed for the very different conditions of nineteenth-century Britain is a mere vestige of colonialism. Furthermore, in Canada the power of the executive has become excessive because of the weakness of parliament and the failure of the public to understand how the system should work. At the same time there persists a distrust of the legitimacy of "third" parties as an obstacle to a yearned-for "strong" government. The fact that in five out of the last seven general elections there have been minority governments is often thought to be a symptom of some profound malaise.[2]

Another cause of dismay has been the apparent personalization of politics around a cult of the leader rather than a concern with issues—though one would have thought that this phenomenon is not as new as it seems. Nevertheless, television, as well as reinforcing American images of politics, tends to emphasize personalities, while being weak in conveying policies. As a result, the public sees politics only as a contest between leaders (that is, as *presidential* politics) and is generally impatient with what seems to be parliamentary obstruction because the role of the opposition is not understood. Furthermore we have the worst of both worlds by having presidential politics without a presidential system—the written constitution, the

separation of powers, and the other restraints which exist in the United States.[3]

I mention these various cries of alarm to demonstrate that questioning the assumptions of "responsible government, Canadian style" has some of the characteristics of a growth industry. Except in passing I shall not consider them in detail. It is my purpose rather to raise a few questions of my own. Some of the arguments I have mentioned seem to me to be misconceived, for responsible government is foreign neither to our habits nor our traditions. In fact the term is a Canadian invention, and our cabinet system was developed here at about the same time that the modern cabinet was emerging in Britain. We built it out of our own experience—as much in French Canada as in English Canada. Whatever the trouble with the system, it stems from our own political culture.

One of the problems with cabinet government is that it is based on certain conventional myths which do not seem to have much relevance in actual situations. Thus, as Richard Crossman argued, the very terms "executive" and "legislature" mean such utterly different things in British (as well as Canadian) and American usage that they are bound to cause misunderstanding. What Walter Bagehot called the fusion of the executive and the legislature in cabinet government makes nonsense of the idea of two separate, coordinate, and distinct bodies.[4] In "normal" circumstances of majority government, once a parliament is elected it is no longer independent, but a groaning beast of burden for the government's legislative program. It may complain and drag its feet, but it cannot have an effective choice of the right road. So effective is the control which a majority government has over the operations of the House of Commons that it can hardly be said to be a separate branch of the government at all in the American sense. Yet most members of parliament think of themselves as a part of a distinct entity called "parliament" and most ministers of the Crown pay lip service to the idea. Judged by their actions very few prime ministers—federal or provincial—ever took it seriously. Certainly not Mackenzie

2   A.C. Cairns, "The Electoral System and the Party System in Canada, 1921–1965," *Canadian Journal of Political Science*, I, no. 1 (March, 1968), 55–80.

3   See, for example, Denis Smith, "President and Parliament: the Transformation of Parliamentary Government in Canada," in Thomas Hockin (ed.), *Apex of Power* (Toronto, 1971), 224 ff.

4   *Inside View: Three Lectures on Prime Ministerial Government* (London, 1972), 34.

King, Bennett, Aberhart, Hepburn, or Duplessis. Of course, minority governments are different. Ministers suddenly realize that every vote counts and adjust their behaviour accordingly. And if Crossman were writing today he might have to qualify his claim that the British House of Commons has become one of the "dignified" parts of the constitution.

Another cause of difficulty is the notion of ministerial responsibility. In the theory of the constitution a minister whose department is in trouble may be compelled to resign—for that is what political accountability means. But in fact no prime minister will drop a minister in these circumstances, for that will be construed as a sign of weakness. Instead he will wait for a time of comparative peace and then quietly shift the minister when the House is not in session and the press (he hopes) is not paying much attention, As Brian Chapman says: "A minister resigns, or is effectively dismissed, if he really becomes too embarrassing to have on the front bench, or if he manages to earn the overwhelming hostility of his own party's backbenchers and has the jib of a scapegoat, or if he becomes too closely associated with a policy which events prove either disastrously wrong or likely to lead to electoral suicide."[5]

Why then do writers on the constitution seek to perpetuate these myths? The reason is that they have a homiletic value. We all know that most people who show outward signs of religious observance are nevertheless sinners, but it is generally felt that one of the roles of the professional clergy is to engage in weekly reminders of the sinfulness of man. So also the eloquent fulminations of Eugene Forsey were a necessary corrective to Mackenzie King's belief that he embodied the divine will—a belief that his most intimate associates were liable to share. The myths of the constitution in a civil polity may be a large part of the necessary apparatus of restraining those whose power is great.

THE VIRTUES OF cabinet government flow in part from the unique structure of the cabinet. However that structure is subject to severe internal and self-generated pressures which force constant adaptation and change. The most obvious fault of cabinet government in this century has been the difficulty of making complex decisions quickly, of being able to do first things first, and the need to plan effectively so that all decisions are not just some form of crisis management.

The great advantage of cabinet government is that it operates as a small group of more-or-less equals who reach decisions by uninhibited secret discussion. They can do this because, while they represent a variety of views and interests, they have an over-riding interest in joint survival. But how are such discussions to be managed so that good decisions are reached quickly and time is not wasted in futile bickering? Rigid rules which accomplish this purpose in open debating chambers will not work, for they destroy the informality and flexibility which is the heart of the process. The answer to a considerable extent has come from the development of the cabinet secretariat which enables a prime minister to guide a cabinet to clear-cut conclusions and to ensure that these decisions are carried out.

Cabinets seem to suffer from an endemic disease which forces their numbers up above the point where efficiency begins to fall rapidly. Clearly a cabinet of thirty is absurdly large, but what should the proper size be and how is it to be achieved?[6] The causes of growth are various, and stem from the numerous and in part incompatible roles of a minister of the Crown. New responsibilities of government lead to the creation of new departments. A department needs a minister, not only to assume responsible authority for its operations and planning, but also to represent it in the cabinet so that its requirements are made a part of the totality of government policy. However, ministers not only represent fragmented chunks of policy: they also represent sections of opinion in the party and sectional interests in the country. The calculus of representation in a country of ten provinces, two major cultures, and a variety of other sectional interests has always made it difficult to resist the claims for representation in the cabinet.

More hands do not make lighter work. While a minister must find some time to keep abreast of his department, much of his time will inevitably be taken

---

5  *British Government Observed* (London, 1963), 34.

6  For example, Mr Pearson once foresaw the development in Canada of the British system, by which the cabinet is made up of a relatively small number of senior ministers while the rest are outside the cabinet. For this the time is not yet ripe in Canada. Canada. *House of Commons Debates.* 24 May 1966, 5429.

up by his representative role in the cabinet and its committees. During the parliamentary session the minister's day must be expanded outwards at both ends to the limits of endurance. Since every day seems to bring its own crisis, ministers seldom have time for either effective coordination or long-range planning. One possible response to this difficulty is to develop a specialization of function among ministers.

A solution repeatedly urged over the last fifty years has been to reduce the burden on a few senior ministers so that they can devote the bulk of their energies to a steady and systematic overview of the major problems of government in the manner of Lloyd George's war cabinet. In other words they become policy ministers, and the exhausting business of departmental supervision and parliamentary accountability falls to a larger number of lesser "departmental" ministers.[7]

Attractive as this sounds, it has not worked well in practice. It is hard to exercise effective control over others unless one is directly responsible and closely in touch. Furthermore, ministers are nearly all ambitious politicians who cherish a high profile which comes from the capacity to spend a big budget, conferring gratifying benefits on a large electoral group, and thus enhancing their leadership aspirations. The "policy minister," whose work is hidden from view in a cabinet committee, does not hold an office which is attractive to an ambitious politician. But even if this difficulty did not exist, there is the further problem in Canada that the possible emergence of an "inner" or "policy" cabinet will seriously reduce the representativeness which enables a cabinet consensus to coincide with a policy likely to be acceptable to the country as a whole.

Recent Canadian attempts to deal with these problems have consisted, first, of removing from the full cabinet the hard-choice decisions arising from the need to plan ahead and to identify priorities, and placing these in the hands of a cabinet committee on priorities and planning. The second expedient has been to experiment with giving ministers specific policy-planning roles.

The need for some such instrument had become clearly apparent near the end of the Pearson era. While it is too soon to evaluate the effectiveness of this mechanism, it does seem clear that greater rationality in decision-making may go too far in creating insensitivity to strongly felt political demands. This insensitivity may have contributed to the electoral rebuff suffered by the Liberals in the 1972 general election.

In addition to the functions described in its title, the Committee on Priorities and Planning has a further, and possibly more important, role in the long run, since the prime minister's control over the cabinet is thereby subtly and effectively strengthened. All new proposals must go to this committee before being considered by the cabinet or its other committees. Thus the prime minister and a handful of senior colleagues can speed up or slow down a proposal, or ensure its modification in a certain direction, simply by deciding which of the functional committees of the cabinet to send the proposal to. Is the matter, for example, essentially one of economic policy, or is it social policy?

A further and potentially significant change has been to create two new classes of ministers under the new title of minister of state. This further complicates any attempt to define cabinet ministers in terms of parity. If the prime minister is *primus inter pares*, he is now the first among at least four different kinds of equals. Of course, there have been visible differences among ministers for a long time. Until 1966, when he was given important statutory responsibilities and a department to go with them, the solicitor general was little more than a second and junior minister in the Department of Justice. There also existed, from time to time, an associate minister of national defence. And there were ministers without portfolio, either aspiring politicians on the way up or elder statesmen on the way out.

The Ministers and Ministries of State Act, which was an important part of the Government Reorganization Act of 1971, has produced two more types. This change was deliberately played down by the Honourable C.M. Drury when he introduced the bill, emphasizing that this was not a radical reorganization of the ministerial system which would create distinct classes of ministers, playing functionally separate roles of departmental administration, policy-initiation, and

---

7   L.S. Amery, *Thoughts on the Constitution* (London, 1953), 90 ff. See also James D. Fleck, "Restructuring the Ontario Government," *Canadian Public Administration*, XVI, no. 1 (Spring, 1973), 55, and J.R. Mallory, "Restructuring the Government of Ontario: A Comment," *Ibid.*, 69.

control. The blurring of distinctions of this sort, he said, was a product of history and "reason" and was worth retaining, since decision-making is a political as well as an administrative process.[8]

The most striking category of new ministers consists of those who head the new ministries of state, which are not to exceed five at any one time and which are created by proclamation subject to parliamentary approval. Their function is to develop new policies, so that when their mission is accomplished they will either be wound up or merged into the departmental structure. It may be significant that the two which have so far been created—Urban Affairs and Science and Technology—are both in areas of shared jurisdiction with the provinces.

One is still left a little puzzled about these new agencies. If their role is one of seriously generating and coordinating policy in areas which involve several strong and well-established departments, two things would seem to be necessary. They should be headed by strong senior ministers and backed by knowledgeable and influential teams of civil servants. Common observation suggests that neither condition holds. As Volume Three of the Lamontagne Report points out, the effectiveness of the Ministry of State for Science and Technology can only be assured if it has some authority to coordinate science budgets and if the minister is both chairman of the relevant cabinet committee and a member of both the Committee on Priorities and Planning and the Treasury Board.[9] As things are, the minister of state for science and technology is in fact the most junior member of the cabinet and in the nature of things a feeble voice even in the one cabinet committee most relevant to the work of the ministry.

As for the other category of minister of state, little needs to be said. In the past there has been an occasional need for an extra minister in large departments for the nourishment of a particular program, or at least the public appearance of such. Usually such tasks have somewhat illogically been given to ministers without portfolio. All that has been changed is a title than can hardly be said to confer enhanced status.

What are we to make of these changes? The most significant is clearly the growing role of the Cabinet Committee on Priorities and Planning in making visible an identifiable core of power in the cabinet. As Parkinson has reminded us, any body which exceeds about twenty in number has already lost effective power to some smaller body within it. It may well be, as Gordon Robertson argues, that Priorities and Planning is not a true "inner cabinet" as defined by Patrick Gordon Walker.[10] I do not think that this disposes of the question. Ministers in intimate and frequent contact with the prime minister, who are a party to the major allocative decisions which affect the needs and aspirations of their colleagues, are in positions of real and unique power. Perhaps to reduce the appearance of centralized power, the prime minister has so far refrained from the ultimate step of making the Committee into a committee of committee chairmen. It might be better for the efficiency of the whole operation if he did.

The other changes, unless they are part of a series of mutations in an evolutionary chain, may turn out to mean very little. What can one say of MOSST, except that it is certainly an administrative improvement over both a science secretariat in the Privy Council Office—whose head had little or no contact with the prime minister, or indeed anyone else "up there"—or the Science Council, which seems to do little except exhort the government and all the rest of us from a lonely eminence altogether outside the process of decision-making?

Perhaps the next step in the evolution of the Canadian cabinet system is the already visible but little-noticed tendency to group as many related functions together as possible under a single minister, as in the case of the new Department of the Environment or the growing cluster of culture-related agencies now covered by the umbrella of the Department of the Secretary of State. There was even an abortive name for this agglomeration. At about the same time that the ministries of state were being planned for, there was also in operation a large-scale review of the

8  Canada. *House of Commons Debates.* 26 January 1971, 2772. And see G. Bruce Doern, "Horizontal and Vertical Portfolios in Government: Implications for Cabinet Reform and Cabinet Behaviour in Canada," in G. Bruce Doern and V. Seymour Wilson, *Issues in Canadian Public Policy* (Toronto, 1974), 310–36.

9  *A Science Policy for Canada: Report of the Senate Special Committee on Science Policy, Volume III: A Government Organization for the Seventies,* 656–67.

10  "The Changing Role of the Privy Council Office," *Canadian Public Administration,* XIV, no. 4 (Winter, 1971), 495.

Department of Transport, whose minister is responsible for a variety of Crown agencies dealing with air, surface, and water transportation. There were plans to bring these agencies under effective coordination and control in the Department, since it was felt that insufficient coordination was being achieved by the simple requirement that the transport corporations reported to parliament through the minister. To indicate the integration of all transport modes under a single policy unit the minister's enlarged "parish" was to be called the Ministry of Transport. The planners in Transport seemed to have been unaware that their new term was already being planned for the ministries of state.[11] Nevertheless, the "ministry" concept is already visible in the case of some large departments. It only remains to reinforce it with the addition, where necessary, of subsidiary ministers to occupy posts of limited responsibility under the over-all authority of a senior minister. One such, in fact, already exists in the form of a minister of state attached to the Department of the Secretary of State.

Beyond this point difficulties will emerge. It would clearly make more sense if this lesser breed of minister were outside the cabinet altogether, though playing a necessary role in cabinet committees. The objection to this step is that it ignores the requirement for balancing the representation of the vital interests of a plural society—a need which makes the present size of the cabinet difficult to reduce.

It is possible that the root of the problem lies not so much in the size of the cabinet as in the method of doing business. The real debate on most decisions of government policy now takes place in the "functional" committees of the cabinet. These committees are constructed to represent departmental interests in policy areas. Thus the influence of a minister outside the field of interest of his department is negligible, no matter how urgent the policy issue may be to his sectional constituents. Consequently, the growing rationalization of cabinet decision-making has profoundly altered the old representation-model cabinet, so that it has lost much of its sensitivity to sectional interests. If the composition of cabinet committees were modified to take serious account of the sectional and policy interests of ministers, rather than departmental interests, some of the essential representative quality of the cabinet might be restored. If this were done, it might be possible to reconsider the possibility of a smaller cabinet with a number of ministers outside the cabinet but still able to play a significant role in committees.

THE PROCESS OF government comprehends much more than the operation of the cabinet. For most decisions are made somewhere within an official hierarchy of civil servants. It is therefore important to consider the interrelationship of ministers and their officials if a true picture of the process of government decision-making is to be understood.

Democratic representative government is by its very nature government by amateurs. Over a century ago it was still possible to extend this idea to cover almost the whole of the activities of government. The fact was that almost all public employment involved tasks so simple that any man could perform them, and so it was easy to accept the idea of the "spoils system." We know that the prospect of opening up government jobs to party supporters in place of the friends and relations of the various "family compacts" was one of the strongest motives behind the campaign to achieve responsible government in British North America.

With the growing complexity of government business, administration became more and more the preserve of career professionals. The great object of civil service reform, which began nearly a century ago in this country, was to ensure that the public departments were no longer staffed by political hacks but by competent administrators. Thus there has developed the clear distinction between political officers on the one hand and the public service on the other. These two groups combined to bring about government which was both responsive and effective. The professionals were responsible for the continuity of government, since problems do not change just because ministries have been replaced. The politicians were there to inject new ideas into the system and to tell the civil servants how far the policies which appeared to be necessary could be made acceptable to the public. Thus cabinet government involves, as Walter Bagehot pointed out, that due mixture of lay and specialized minds which is the true art of business.

---

11  John Langford, "The Reorganization of the Federal Transport Portfolio: the Application of a Ministry System," Ph.D. thesis, McGill University, 1973.

Hence the ideal relationship between ministers and officials has been one of creative tension. The experts can usually tell the minister what needs to be done and what is administratively possible. But if a policy cannot be made convincing to a minister, there is something lacking. Ministers, who have to face the House of Commons, their own back-benchers, and the public, are the brokers between the process of government and the people.

However, because "knowledge is power" in the daily contest between the busy minister and the more single-minded senior civil servant, policy innovation has come more and more from the "within-puts" generated inside the higher civil service. While we are still taught to believe that new policies are the result of public discussion, party policy, and the innovative role of the member of parliament, the facts seem to be otherwise. Nevertheless, it was perhaps not surprising that such a large proportion of back-benchers in the Hoffman and Ward study of the House of Commons—who are in fact mostly tongue-tied slaves of the division bells—thought of their prime function as "legislators."[12]

The fact of the matter is that the optimal relationship between the politicians on the top and the civil servants can become—in democratic terms—seriously out of balance. Senior civil servants can deploy vast knowledge and skill in "capturing" ministers so that the politicians are all too easily overcome by the official line that nothing can be done or that what is done is right and should not be altered. It is even possible that the unique Canadian system of cabinet committees in which ministers and senior officials argue policy questions as equals is seriously dysfunctional in the sense that the minister in these conditions has small chance of winning the argument against the superior knowledge and experience of the official. If there is creative innovation at lower levels in the departments it is equally easy for senior officials, reluctant to re-think policies of their own original creation, to provide equally effective delay and obstruction. This may be the reason for a significant number of middle-level civil servants to leave in frustration in recent years.

In spite of all of the recognized virtues of a civil service based on the merit system and animated by a dedicated professionalism which gives them something of the character of a "guardian" class, it must be recognized that they themselves are a vested interest, While it would be naive to pretend that they do not in fact advise ministers of whichever party may be in office to adopt policies which are politically advantageous, nevertheless the nature of their lives makes them somewhat remote from politics. The fact that they work in the dominant industry in a one-industry town which does not share many of the visible concerns of most of the electorate contributes to their isolation. This is further strengthened by their social homogeneity, so that they tend to become over-persuaded of the uniqueness of their wisdom.

John Porter has shown, in *The Vertical Mosaic*, how the higher managerial groups in government and business are still dominated by the traditional Canadian elite groups, WASP in outlook and largely the products of the older and more prestigious parts of the university system.[13] How far this is as true now as it was when Porter's research was under way is far from certain. But to the extent that it is true we lack one of the necessary ingredients of a fully effective bureaucracy—that it should be representative of the diversity of the country in order to be responsive. Within the last few years heroic efforts have been made to redress one aspect of the imbalance by increasing the role of French Canadians in the higher bureaucracy. But what of the more general problem? Can it be that one explanation of the "alienation of the West" is the failure of the federal bureaucracy to absorb an adequate number of convinced and unrepentant westerners?

One of the first things that a newly elected government with novel policies discovers is that the bureaucracy has both an inertia and a momentum of its own. The first obstacle to policy innovation is the deputy head of a department. While deputy heads are order-in-council appointments, and are not protected by the Public Service Employment Act in the same way as their lesser colleagues, an unconscious extension of civil service tenure under the merit system has made them at least as difficult to remove as other members of

12  *Bilingualism and Biculturalism in the Canadian House of Commons. Documents of the Royal Commission on Bilingualism and Biculturalism* (Ottawa, 1970).

13  Toronto, 1965.

the public service. Possibly more so, for the powerful cadre of mandarins can and does protect its own.

As we know from the experience of the CCF in Saskatchewan in the forties, and the later experience of the NDP in Manitoba, it may be too dangerous politically to remove a body of unsympathetic and unimaginative senior civil servants lest one be accused of the worst kind of political patronage. In Ottawa the recent tendency has been to strengthen the position of the top civil servants as a class. The present operation of the system of appointments of deputy heads, by which the prime minister is advised by a small group of senior officials, in effect enables the recognized senior members of the "club" to control the process of promotion and selection. The appointment of deputy heads has been recognized from time immemorial as one of the "prerogatives" of the prime minister. Different prime ministers have used the power lightly or firmly, depending on temperament, but the present incumbent seems to have been the first to bureaucratize the process.

If, as one former cabinet minister has alleged,[14] the Trudeau government was getting bad advice from senior officials and should get rid of the source of it, would this violate either the merit system or the conventions of the constitution? It is too easy to say that it would. After the 1957 election many of us congratulated ourselves that the top civil servants (or most of them) had survived to serve their new masters, and that this was a good thing. It may have been the best thing at the time, but I now think that it was an exaggeration to elevate it into a constitutional principle. It is time that we thought about it again.

It seems to have been his misgivings about the inflexibility and insensitivity of the senior public service to new ideas from the party and other "outside" sources that led Mr Trudeau to enlarge and expand the policy-innovative role of the Prime Minister's Office. Now whether the Prime Minister's Office was conceived as a "counter-bureaucracy" or operated as such is not clear. It does seem from Marc Lalonde's description of the work of the office in his time that the PMO tried scrupulously to avoid the "operational and administrative" jurisdictions of the public service,

just as the regular public service sought to avoid entanglement in "partisan" political advice.[15] What may have happened is that instead of the Prime Minister's Office becoming a major power centre in its own right, it served—in close and intimate cohabitation with the other tenant of the East Block, the Privy Council Office—as a means of strengthening the central control mechanisms at the expense of the departments. Furthermore, its activities did not range across the whole area of government policy but were mainly limited to a few selected targets. Thus the entirely different rhetoric surrounding Canadian foreign policy seems to have come from this source.

If, as I suspect, the final result of the growth of the Prime Minister's Office has been merely to add another element to the same mix of like-minded men, then the problem remains. And the problem is real. The need to make our system of government receptive to new ideas is as great as ever. Neither the PMO nor ministers' private office staffs seem to have done the job. Indeed, the latter have been successfully confined to running the minister's political life for him, but I think in general have been excluded from any significant impact on the work of the departments.[16]

I turn now to the question of numerous breaches of official secrecy, which is thought to be at least in degree a new and growing problem. Gordon Robertson has this to say about it: "While one cannot be completely sure of the circumstances or the motivations that produce them, there is reason to believe that many are the result of attitudes and values held by people with access to classified information who reject any sense of obligation, let alone any overriding duty, to maintain the confidentiality of government information in their charge. If that is so, I think the implications may indeed be serious, however well-meaning individual intentions may be."[17]

What clearly gave him the most pain was the fact that "No member of parliament except the prime minister suggested that there was a moral issue involved,

14 Eric Kierans, "The Day the Cabinet was Misled," *The Canadian Forum* (March, 1974).

15 "The Changing Role of the Prime Minister's Office," *Canadian Public Administration*, XIV, no. 4. (Winter, 1971), 509.

16 J.R. Mallory, "The Minister's Office Staff: An Unreformed Part of the Public Service," *Ibid.*, X, no. 1 (March, 1967), 25.

17 "Responsibility, Conscience, and Public Information," *Transactions of the Royal Society of Canada*, Fourth Series, X (1972), 149.

or considered the implications of the disclosures for the operations of government."[18]

Mr Robertson admits that there are difficult problems about the limits of government secrecy in a democracy, since the public which has to make political judgments at the end of the day needs to know as much as possible about the issues involved. Nevertheless he argues that secrecy in government is essential, in order that both ministers and officials can freely explore all possible courses of action before taking decisions, without the threat that they may be publicly branded at a later date for adopting a particular line of argument. He then deploys the familiar argument in support of administrative secrecy. A lack of secrecy undermines the whole notion of ministerial responsibility; in particular instances it may be fatal to ongoing international or intergovernmental relationships, or to national security. He admits that there is too much secrecy and that both practice and regulations should be modified to minimize it. Nevertheless the general interest requires that the private and personal conscience of those with special knowledge should not be permitted to lead to breaches of security lest the process of government be rendered ineffective. He is alarmed at what he perceives to be a new system of values, chiefly among the young, which rejects authority and puts a premium on individual decision. Such tendencies, which lead to extra-legal attempts to influence policy, are no different in kind than that other phenomenon of the sixties—the use of social violence as a form of protest.

This argument has some force, but it seems to me that it goes too far. He fails to admit that administrative secrecy has always been, and no doubt always will be, abused to protect administrators from the consequences of their own mistakes.[19] One need only mention the belated recognition that there needs to be some kind of ombudsman, privy to administrative secrecy, to provide some reasonable check on administrative abuse of power. There is all the more reason

for this because in the past an extreme use of the doctrine of Crown privilege in the courts has often stood in the way of the rights of the citizen.[20] Furthermore, Robertson leaves the situation of the troubled civil servant without any answer, even though in practice there has always been a way out. If one follows the Robertson argument as stated, an official has no choice but to put the "public good" as interpreted by the government above his own conscience. But surely there have been cases where officials, unable to win the argument within the administration, have resigned in order to campaign publicly against what they regard as a serious wrong. Ministers at odds with their colleagues have likewise resigned. In both cases their position may be somewhat hampered by the legal requirement to respect confidentiality, but the publicity surrounding the resignation itself can be a very powerful argument. Of course, one does not resign lightly, and covert action instead of resignation can, by the standards by which we have grown up, look both underhand and cowardly.

Nor can we neglect the fact that both the press and the average MP can take a hint as well as anyone else, and that the whole history of the relationship between government, parliament, and the press has been based on a healthy osmosis of information outward from the central executive. Otherwise the political system could hardly work at all in a democratic and responsive way. I suspect that it is dangerously easy to be panicked into a black-and-white, either-or, view of official secrecy which is both naive and unnecessary. Political intelligence-gathering, to give it a high-sounding name, may have been somewhat altered since the xerox machine has made whole documents readily violable. And governments now produce documents in such profusion that there is no way of protecting them all by some kind of chastity belt of security. Good government, as always, rests on a balance of considerations. The case for cutting down on administrative secrecy is one that needs to be made. Certainly it is not likely to be made by those for whom it is normal protective clothing.

---

18  *Ibid.*, 151.

19  Cf. Chapman: "This mania for secrecy and for shielding the activities of the Executive from profane eyes also seriously impedes the possibility of effective a posteriori control. At this stage the public at large begins to suffer directly." *British Government Observed*, 44.

20  The abuse of Crown privilege in Britain has been greatly curtailed since the decision of the House of Lords in *Conway* v. *Rimmer* [1968] A.C. 910, while the provision of the Federal Court Act of 1971 which empowered that court to decide on the validity of the claim of Crown privilege may have a comparable effect in Canada.

It has been argued that excessive secrecy in government may often be used as a cover for administrative mistakes or possibly worse. As such it does much to undermine ministerial accountability, to the point that ministerial responsibility has become not only a myth but a myth that nobody believes anyway.[21] If ministers are not really responsible in the classic sense, what does the doctrine mean in practice? In the main it protects the anonymity and the secrecy of the policy-making process, so that one never knows how or why a decision was taken. It becomes impossible to identify the source of wrong advice and thus removes any effective check on the performance of the bureaucracy. Unless, of course, there are leaks or the quarrel between a minister and the officials becomes loud and open. In sum, the effect of the doctrine of ministerial responsibility is often to inhibit public debate of serious issues of policy.

AT THE HEART of the difficulty is the state of balance between the government of the day and the House of Commons. We have come a long way since the days when governments were seriously accountable to the House. Perhaps that golden age never did exist, but it is one of the myths of the constitution that it did. What is clear is that the balance has been steadily shifting in the direction of the government. We are now being told, from the somewhat suspect source of ministers themselves, that the balance has shifted strongly the other way. The Honourable Donald S. Macdonald has asserted that the House of Commons, which had drifted along for a hundred years with the rules and procedures inherited from the pre-Confederation legislature of the province of Canada, suddenly in 1968 and 1969 "took giant steps forward from its colonial origins and to bring itself into step not only with the Mother of Parliaments, but, what is more important, with the needs of our country as it enters upon its second century."[22] How far can we believe this piece of good news?

There were not many major changes in parliamentary procedure in the century after 1867, but some of them were in fact important. The House of Commons moved gradually to the point where practically all business is government business, and the times allotted to matters initiated by private members has become so restricted that they have little chance of even being voted upon. On the other hand, the gradual emergence of the question period has provided one new and important method of bringing ministers to account. Also, there have been changes which reduced futile debate and made procedure more businesslike through the imposition of time limits on the throne speech and budget debates and on supply motions. In one sense these changes were good, in another they took away important opportunities for the opposition to use the weapon of delay. And lastly, the committee system, which still flourished in 1867, had become almost moribund by the end of the 1950s. In Macdonald's words, "the mills of Parliament ground exceedingly slow, and also exceedingly coarse." What effective control there was to secure honest and efficient administration was in the hands of ministers and the bureaucracy.

The first important change of the nineteen-sixties was the emergence of the speaker as a genuinely impartial presiding officer, above the claims of party. This owed as much to the exceptional quality of three distinguished speakers (Michener, MacNaughton, and Lamoureux) as it did to a change in standing orders which prevented a majority of members from overturning a speaker's ruling. It is clear now that the office of speaker is no longer, as it so often was in the past, a consolation prize for a government supporter disappointed in the allocation of places in the cabinet.

The most important change in procedure relates to the handling of financial business. In essence what has been done is to abolish the old committees of Supply and Ways and Means and remove the discussion of the estimates into smaller standing committees, from which they must emerge at a date certain on the calendar. Thus the opposition has been deprived of two powerful weapons at one stroke. The discussion of the estimates in committee gets only modest press coverage, so that the serious discussion of departmental policy (which is what debate on the estimates is all about) now takes place in an almost invisible forum. The second loss is equally serious. No longer can the opposition threaten to withhold supply in order to force a government either to give way or to dissolve parliament.

---

21   Chapman, *British Government Observed*, 38–9.

22   "Change in the House of Commons—New Rules," *Canadian Public Administration*, XIII, no. 1 (Spring, 1970), 39.

The compensatory provisions have been bought at a high price. Scrutiny of the estimates in smaller committees *may* be more effective and knowledgeable, but this is partly offset by the reduction in the number of money votes as a consequence of program budgeting. The twenty-five allotted days which enable the opposition parties to initiate debates of their choice, and bring about a no-confidence vote on six of these occasions, is useful and necessary. However, even this gain is somewhat offset by the fact that the actual designation of an allotted day is still in the hands of the government house leader, who controls the allocation of parliamentary time.

The other changes of importance are also based on the theory that the real business of the House is to act as a legislative sausage-machine. There are three new methods of limiting debate, in addition to the old and unpopular closure rule. One of these rules makes it possible for the house leaders of the parties themselves to agree to a limit of debate, without the danger of being sabotaged by their own followers. The second makes it possible for a majority of the house leaders to over-ride one recalcitrant opposition party. The third permits the government alone, after a short debate, to impose time allocation on a bill. It may be significant that none of these provisions has been much used. Perhaps their existence alone may have some deterrent effect.

The reform which has done most to alter the lives of members has undoubtedly been the change by which, with the exception of financial bills, all committee debate on legislation is in small committees instead of in the time-hallowed committee of the whole. This has of course increased the amount of legislation in the pipeline. It has also provided a better and more effective forum of the party experts to bring about constructive changes in legislation. It enlarges the possibility that legislation will be improved by the amendments it may get on the way from all sides of the House. This is bound to happen when there are minority governments. It may even happen when the government has a majority, but the experience of the twenty-eighth parliament, in which the government had a huge majority, is not encouraging. Liberal committee members, under explicit instruction or not, behaved in a way which must have afforded great satisfaction to the whips. They were defensive-minded.

They understood that their prime duty was to ensure the preservation of the government majority on the committee, to vote when required, and not to delay business by the expression of unwanted opinions. Thus the committee system opened up debate only on the opposition side of the House.

One of the consequences of increased committee activity has been to decrease the visibility of debate on the floor of the House. If the twenty-eighth Parliament was dull, it was partly because attendance in the House much of the time was very small. Members cannot be in two places at once, and frequently committees drew them away from the floor unless they were required to return by the ringing of the division bells. We were getting perilously close to the situation in Washington, with the important exception that nothing important was happening in committees either.

The cumulative effect of the recent reforms has been to make parliament into a much more efficient legislative machine. This is not unimportant, because there is never enough parliamentary time to get through all essential legislation. But it has been bought at a high price. For legislation is only one part of the business of the House of Commons, and not necessarily the most important part. In the first place there is what Bernard Crick has called "the continuous election campaign"—the constant confrontation of contending political parties which will shape the issues in the next election. Secondly, there is the point that not all policy is new policy (that is, legislation), but much of the stuff of life in the House of Commons is criticism, evaluation, continuous oversight of administration—what Crick calls "control."[23] And there is the further role of inquiry and investigation—a sort of pre-policy-formulation, such as the discussion of the White Paper on Taxation in the Committee on Finance and Economic Affairs, the Joint Committee on the Constitution, the Special Committee on Statutory Instruments, and others. Therefore the needs of legislation have to be balanced against these other functions in order to get the "best" (not necessarily the most efficient) machinery.

How far is the present difficulty one of committee overload? There are still not enough committee rooms; delays are caused by shortage of translation

---

23  *The Reform of Parliament* (London, 1964).

and "table" staffs; and when committees need research staffs there may be delays before they can be authorized or employed. The present state of the parties inhibits the efficiency of the committee system. It would work much better if there were only two parties, one of which had a small but workable majority, but do we want this on other grounds? Furthermore the House is too small to sustain an elaborate committee system, particularly since the number of ministerial appointments is still rising. The need to increase the size of the House for other reasons connected with a change in the constitutional provisions for redistribution may help to solve this problem. None of these difficulties exist in the United States Senate, because it has few debates on the floor and does most of its business in committee. Similarly the British House of Commons avoids the problem with a membership nearly two and a half times as large as ours.

The business of a parliamentary body is not merely managerial. It is essentially political. The party struggle for power is the major strategic contest. So committees are at best subordinate to the perceived political necessities. While "small group" situations and good chairmanship can achieve better "control," the committee rooms are not major theatres of war, and there is seldom great political advantage to be gained in the committee room. Occasionally, in such all-out punishing battles as occurred in the Agriculture Committee on the Grain Stabilization Bill in 1971, some hint of the action may reach the ears of the public, but even there the final confrontation took place on the floor of the House at the Report stage.

With the present degree of committee overload, we may have to choose between estimates and legislation as the main area of committee activities. Under the new Standing Orders the House may, and sometimes does, take the committee stage of a major bill in Committee of the Whole, as was done with the Public Order Temporary Measures bill in 1970. When a bill is very technical, as well as not a serious partisan issue, there are strong reasons for using the smaller committees where expert witnesses can be heard and affected interest groups make their case. But not, I think, otherwise. On the other hand, the major standing committees with their greater expertise are much more likely to accomplish serious scrutiny of the administration of government, a task which is not made easy by the greatly reduced number of items in the estimates brought about by program budgeting.

The central need is to provide the House of Commons with the machinery to do its job. And its primary job is not simply to grind out legislation, The House is the only place left for a serious inquest on the political party which—as a price for governing the country—must account for its actions.

THE STRIKING THING about the matters I have been talking about is that they have happened almost without public discussion. There has been much furious debate about the constitution, about the nature of Canadian federalism, and about the meaning of Canadian independence. But little serious argument has been devoted to what has happened to the institutions of government in the last fifteen years. The reorganization of the executive has taken place as a result of largely invisible debate within the government, although some of the issues can be discerned in the work of the Glassco Commission and in a few papers and speeches by senior civil servants who can hardly be expected to depart from their occupational discretion. There was some public discussion of the workings of cabinet government under Mr Pearson and Mr Trudeau, but this has been mostly by journalists. Even the reform of parliamentary procedure, which in part was the work of an all-party parliamentary committee, took place with little public debate and aroused only small interest among political scientists largely preoccupied with electoral behaviour and party anatomy. Perhaps it is time to take a harder look at our machinery of government before it runs down.

**4**

## *Editors' Introduction*

Eugene Forsey was both a public official and an experienced commentator on Canadian political life. His Ph.D. dissertation, published as *The Royal Power of Dissolution in Parliament*, remains an unparalleled explanation of the reserve powers of the Crown. Attuned to Canadians' feeble understanding of their constitution, he regularly wrote letters to the editor to rectify others' mistakes and errors. This also motivated him to craft a guide to *How Canadians Govern Themselves*, which is available online at the Parliament of Canada's official website and remains a staple for anyone looking for a simple introductory overview on the matter. However, the selection here is from an obscure study he authored at the behest of the government to explain the foundational principle of the Canadian constitution: responsible government. It is amazing how so basic a principle is so poorly understood, especially by those who it is meant to govern, that is, politicians and even the government's own civil servants. This piece, although not well-known, is a succinct explanation by the country's foremost scholar of Canada's constitutional principles.

Source: Eugene Forsey and G.C. Eglinton, *The Question of Confidence in Responsible Government* (Ottawa: Special Committee on the Reform of the House of Commons, 1985), 1–20, 119.

Eugene Forsey and G.C. Eglinton

# The Question of Confidence in Responsible Government

## CONFIDENCE

A seat in this House is equal to any dignity derived from posts or titles, and the approbation of this House is preferable to all that power, or even Majesty itself, can bestow: therefore when I speak here as a minister, I speak as possessing my powers from His Majesty, but as being answerable to this House for the exercise of those powers.

Sir Robert Walpole in the House of Commons, February 1, 1739.

I have lived long enough in the world, Sir, to know that the safety of a minister lies in his having the approbation of this House. Former ministers, Sir, neglected this and therefore they fell. I have always made it my first study to obtain it, and therefore I hope to stand.

Sir Robert Walpole in the House of Commons, November 12, 1739.

## PART I: INTRODUCTION

The confidence of the House of Commons lies at the heart of responsible government. Responsible government is the very foundation of our modern polity, a constitutional and parliamentary monarchy. That polity, sharing its essential features with other members of the Commonwealth, is distinctive and, in our view, distinctly superior to that existing in the United States of America which serves as the stated, or more often unstated, model on which much criticism of our system of governance is based. We make no bones about stating this view at the outset. We also wish to make plain our opinion that it is extremely difficult to borrow particular features of the United States constitutional and political system without all the others, and without importing grave difficulties for ourselves. Our constitutional order is one organic whole and we graft alien features on to it at considerable peril to ourselves and our freedoms. The Members of the House of Commons have particular reason to know this because of the reduction in their significance, status and power brought about by the adoption of the Convention method of electing the Leaders of our political parties.

Even admirers of the American system of governance must, if honest, admit that the American system is different from ours and that it is not possible to borrow from it certain of its distinguishing features unless we are prepared to adopt the others. The two systems of governance are incompatible precisely because we have responsible government and they do not; because the Government of Canada must enjoy the confidence of the House of Commons, while the President of the United States need not and often does not find his policies supported by one or both Houses of the Congress. From this essential incompatibility all other differences flow. It is impossible to take over further American constitutional practices without attacking the central difference. Change along American lines must mean constitutional revolution. The American practices we have already adopted have contributed to the weakening and severe straining of our system of responsible government and have, at the least, tended to pervert it in the direction of a plebiscitary autocracy.

One other matter needs to be stated plainly before we begin. The constitutional law and custom of Canada are based on and derived from those of England, of Great Britain and of the United Kingdom. This may not appeal to some, but it is fact. Consequently, we have no apologies to make for referring to precedents and practices in the United Kingdom, its predecessor kingdoms or in other parts of the Commonwealth which have chosen to take advantage of the genius of the English people for sound, common sense approaches to governance and of their horror of abstract, general principles.

If asked: "How are we governed?", the average Canadian would probably answer along the following lines. There are three main parties, each of which chooses its leader at a popular national convention. Every election time the voters decide which of these Leaders and his party shall be the Government. While many people are loyal to parties for decades or even throughout life, a lot of others deliberately pick on a particular Leader as their choice for Prime Minister and then vote for his party by voting for the candidate of that party in the 282 local constituencies. The Leader of the party which wins the most seats in Parliament becomes the Prime Minister and he governs, assisted by other members of his party who have got themselves elected to the House of Commons (or,

occasionally, who are Senators) and by personal aides of his own choosing. The Government, thus constituted, makes the laws, runs the country and generally does what it likes until the next election, unless it runs into stiff opposition from one of the Premiers of the powerful provinces, or from a group of provincial Premiers, or falls foul of the Supreme Court. If a Prime Minister or his Ministers or aides annoy enough voters, then at the next election another Leader and his party will get the most seats and take over the government.

This layman's view of our system of government is sufficiently at variance with classical statements of the functions of the formal parts of our policy to make one take a deep breath before writing at length on one particular part of the central theory of our constitution. It causes one to reflect on the profound differences that can exist between reality, or perhaps the real world as almost universally misunderstood by journalists and voters, and theory. While the way the average citizen sees things may serve well enough when the political world runs smoothly, it is important to understand how things are supposed to operate in theory so that one can tell what can and cannot be done when the smooth running of the political machine breaks down. It may also be useful to know what can happen in constitutional theory in case we wish to alter or to improve the way we are governed now.

As the part of the constitution we are to examine involves ordinary Members of the House of Commons, it is important to see how politicians view the present system of government. The Special Committee itself will be the best judge of this. It is our conclusion that the popular view corresponds fairly closely to that of most politicians, the Members of Parliament (themselves chosen by local conventions) who constitute their Leaders' infantry and the visible members of the political parties which compete for the voters' favour and for government. Their appeals are cast in the form: "elect our Leader and our Party to government, and we shall do this and that as promised by the Leader." There are no party manifestos or settled platforms, merely loose, and loosely acknowledged, tendencies characteristic of each party. Once elected, Members of the House of Commons regard themselves not primarily as controllers of the Executive, or even as legislators, but as followers of the Leaders who are either in or out of power, as representatives of the parties and as constituency liaison or grievance officers for those needing redress, support or money from the manifold tentacles of modern government. Given that the Members cannot even control the legislative policies of their parties in their caucuses (the distinguishing feature of New Zealand and to a lesser extent Australian political life), the distinction between executive and legislative powers has entirely disappeared, a reality reinforced in Canada by the vast delegated law-making powers of the Executive, powers untramelled by any general power of disallowance in either House of Parliament. Both the legislative and executive functions are exercised by the Leader of the majority party, the Prime Minister, and his closest layer of supporters, his Ministers and his personal advisers and aides. Legislation agreed to by this inner group almost invariably is passed by Parliament, unless enormous outside pressure is brought to bear or powerful provincial Premiers are actively opposed. The Government party members in the House of Commons may be on the receiving end of this pressure, and may pass it on, but they are in no sense responsible to a wider political party in the country. The Government party members cannot in their caucus, as of right, reject or attend proposed legislation. Nor do they feel themselves able or entitled to exercise their own deliberative judgment very often. They will, however, ultimately be held responsible by the electorate at large for the sins or virtues of the Leader and his inner group of supporters.

This system does not leave a great role for Parliament.[1] It has been reduced to the status of a medium through which the governing Leader and his inner cadre legitimize their legislative acts and the opposing Leaders and their supporters seek to expose the blunders, follies and iniquities of the reigning Leader's executive or administrative acts and those of his Ministers.

The salient characteristics of this system are that it provides a strong government with few limits on its capacity to act on behalf of society; it is simple

and easily understood in that it centralizes power and authority in one dominant body, and it provides for direct responsibility of government to the governed.[2]

The Leader and his inner group of followers rule untrammelled through his and their control of the House of Commons, saving only the safeguards of a Charter of Rights, a written constitution, the theoretical but remote possibility of rejection of Bills in the Upper House, and powerful provincial governments. These safeguards, operating principally through delay, may be enormous, and compared with safeguards against tyrannical government in, say, the United Kingdom, they are powerful indeed. Yet, they are likely, and sensibly, to be dismissed by the average voter as merely constituting the rules of the game. They do leave a large field for the naked exercise of power, a field it might be thought ordinary, non-Ministerial Members of the Commons would be keen to enter. Why have they not been keen? Why have they not from time to time been tempted in large numbers to seize the opportunity afforded by the legitimizing process of the passage of bills and passing or resolutions in the Commons and its Committees to demonstrate their own powers, which are in theory enormous? These are the central questions facing any who purpose upon reform of the House of Commons.

It should hardly need stating that the theory of the constitution is quite different from the view of modern government just put. The *divergence* between the popularly perceived model and the theoretical one may for very long periods of time be of little or no significance. As long as one party or another retains a majority in the Commons, party revolts or schisms are avoided, and large scale resignations from the Ministry on matters of principle do not occur, it matters little that only greybeards or fussy purists seek to see the constitutional processes at work beneath the calm surface. Any *convergence* between the popularly perceived model and generally accepted ideas as to how the constitutional order *should* operate raises immediately the question as to whether it is worth worrying about the fate of the House of Commons and its Members, far less about enhancing their role in the polity. To the

---

1    Evans, H.: "Party government versus Constitutional Government," *The Australian Quarterly*, Vol. 56, No. 3 page 265 at page 266. We are indebted to Mr. Evans, Clerk-Assistant of the Senate of the Commonwealth of Australia for suggesting our initial method of approach to this work.

---

2    Ibid.

extent that the popularly perceived model is seen to be "legitimate" or "valid" or the way of the future, there is neither incentive nor reason to attempt to rescue the ordinary Member from his fate as a trained seal. If we see no need for change in how the House of Commons and its Members play their part in the political system, then there is no point in studying the theory of "confidence." It is only if we believe that the orthodox constitutional model is worthwhile and proper, and that it has suffered abuse, neglect and misconstruction bordering upon perversion—that it is a model resiled from by successive governments, and not in Canada alone—in other words, it is only if we accept the need for change in the way the political system works now, that there is any point in studying what the relationships between Government and the House of Commons are in constitutional theory, how those relationships should operate, and the extent to which they can and should operate differently from the way the Executive controls the House of Commons now. It is only if we believe that the House should ultimately control the Government—and not vice versa—that there is any point in proceeding further.

## PART II: WHAT IS "RESPONSIBLE GOVERNMENT"?

### a) General Principles

The power in this realm of Canada is divided in two different ways. It is divided first in accordance with the division of the legislative and consequent executive powers between the Dominion and the provinces in accordance with the provisions of the Constitution. Power is also divided in the traditional English way between the Queen, the Senate, the House of Commons and the Courts. To the Crown belongs the supreme authority over all save the courts, checked by the doctrine of the legislative sovereignty of Parliament, the doctrine of ministerial responsibility and the power of the House of Commons to refuse supplies. To the House of Commons belongs the control over the purse and, therefore, control over the Crown's Ministers, checked by the royal prerogative of dissolution.[3] To the Senate belongs

a full share in all legislation except the initiation of Appropriation and taxing Bills as provided in section 53 of the Constitution Act 1867. To the Courts belongs the maintenance of the rule of law, the holding of the Crown's servants liable for any wrongdoing and the preservation of the rights and liberties of the people. The network of constitutional relationships thus established is governed by conventions. Conventions are observed rules of constitutional and political behaviour. They are not rules of law and are unenforceable in the Courts, which may, however, on occasion take notice of them. The conventions governing ministerial responsibility or responsible government are arguably the most important because they define the essential characteristics of the way we are in fact governed.

Responsible government concerns the relationship between the Executive and the Parliament, and the House of Commons most directly. In our modern world of adult suffrage it is not possible to state theories without acknowledging the overwhelming power of the electorate which must be reckoned as having a place in the chain of responsibility in our Constitution. The membership of the House of Commons is, by periodic elections, brought into accord with the popular will from time to time, and by this means the continuance of a Ministry comes to depend on the periodic judgment of the electors, which to a great degree settles the questions of confidence.

The relationships between the Executive and House of Commons are sometimes summed up in a generalized and, therefore, incomplete way in the rule that the Government must enjoy the confidence of the House of Commons. What does this mean, and what does it entail?

"Responsible government" is an expression with which great care must be taken because it does not mean the same thing in all contexts and because the nature of "responsibility" is not always clear. "We must not be misled by abstract terms ... There is no cut-and-dried institution called responsible government, identical in all countries where it exists."[4]

Perhaps the best statement of the concept of confidence, and of responsible government, is still that

---

3    Lord Loreburn, L.C.H. of L., 22 November 1909, c.754.

4    Holroyd, J., quoted by Sir Kenneth Bailey in *Cambridge History of the British Empire*, Cambridge University Press, 1933, Vol. 7, page 395.

contained in a mere two sentences in the Durham Report.

[If] the Crown … has to carry on the government in unison with a representative body, it must consent to carry it on by means of those in whom that representative body has confidence … Every purpose of popular control might be combined with every advantage of vesting the immediate choice of advisers in the Crown, were the Colonial Governor to be instructed to secure the co-operation of the Assembly in his policy, by entrusting its administration to such men as could command a majority …[5]

Responsible government is but an application of the English system of parliamentary control over the Crown's finances and of the principle of redress of grievance before supply. Responsible government did not come about by Act of Parliament; nor by any alteration of or in institutions. There was simply an adjustment by the Executive, over a considerable period in the United Kingdom, over a much shorter period in the Canadian colonies, and almost at a point in time in the Australasian colonies, in the terms on which the chief servants of the Crown were to hold their places. They would be removed if political considerations made that desirable or necessary in order to secure passage of the Crown's business. The terms of the Crown's adjustment and the conditions of the retention and loss of office by the Sovereign's Ministers are settled by constitutional conventions. Responsible government requires that the Executive be responsible for its actions to an elected Legislature and it necessarily implies that there will be a policy-making body of Ministers bound to provide unanimous advice to the Sovereign and that the several departments of the public service will be under the control of political heads responsible to the Legislature. Responsible government also implies that both Executive and Legislature bear responsibility to the people. The Legislature is obviously so responsible, the Executive perhaps less so. Yet the periodic elections, and especially the necessary right of the Crown to dissolve the Legislature, all bear witness to that responsibility of the Executive

to the people and its right in proper circumstances to appeal to the people against an unworkable Legislature, an appeal which in the modern world alone affords to our system of government its acceptance by the governed, an acceptance without which it cannot survive.

In a sense, the English Crown from mediaeval times onwards was always forced to carry on government in such a way as to enjoy the confidence of the Commons. Without the confidence or support of the Commons, taxes and aids could not be raised to supplement the prerogative and casual revenues of the Crown, revenues which were wholly inadequate in themselves to sustain government. The continuing poverty of our Kings ensured the growth of the popular element in the constitution. Without the compliance of the Commons, no major domestic policy changes could be carried through whether in land law or matters affecting the relations between Church and State. The support or compliance of the Commons could often be garnered by political skill, by fear, by appeal to loyalty, by the prospect of office or other reward—all features incidentally of a modern day Prime Minister's armory in dealing with his backbenchers or the members of another party whose support is desired. The failure of Charles I's eleven years of Christian rule and the catastrophe of his relations with the Long Parliament demonstrated that government by sheer governmental will against the majority of the Commons could not work. Thenceforth, Crown and Commons have been forced to work together, and especially they have had to come together in money matters and matters of significant policy, though these were few until the passage of the first Reform Bill.

This situation, however, is merely the avoidance of tyranny. It does not describe our peculiar form of government known as responsible government. It is equally consonant with that other form of democratic government practised in the United States of America. Both may be classified as representative but ours necessarily achieves *harmony* between Executive and Legislature and operates in a remarkably different way from that employed in the United States of America.

Since the United States model is put so often before Canadians by the media it is as well to state simply how accord between President and Congress is achieved, if indeed it is, for there is no necessity that Executive and Legislature agree. Compromise is frequent, as is

---

5    House of Commons Paper No. 3 of 1839 quoted, Sir William Dale, *The Modern Commonwealth*, Butterworths, London, 1983, page 5.

the abandonment of Presidential policies requiring legislation the Congress will not make. The Congress itself may take policy and financial initiatives but these may be and often are vetoed by the President. In the day to day operation of the Government of the United States of America the President and his administration are free to act, unanswerable to Congress. Congress may, however, pass legislation interfering with this Presidential freedom, legislation which the President may feel constrained not to veto as part of a compromise designed to secure Congressional approval for some other legislative scheme he desires. It is the *independence* of the Legislature and the Executive from each other which is the hallmark of the American way; the *harmony* between Executive and Legislature the mark of ours. The Presidency, the United States Senate, the House of Representatives and the Supreme Court—each has a different power base and source of legitimacy, and a distinct set of constitutional powers that may enable each to check and balance the others. The independence of each is both demonstrated and enhanced by the different terms for which each, or the members of each, are elected or appointed.

The result of the United States Constitution is a system which works against any one election being decisive. It is nearly impossible for a candidate or a party to take control of the political system by winning on a wave of public enthusiasm. The different methods of election or appointment and the different terms from two years to life mean that no party can come to full power in the United States as it can and often does in a parliamentary democracy. Congress and the President, whatever their party-political colourings, seem pitted in a perpetual struggle for power and institutional dominance. This struggle disappeared in Britain and in the British North American colonies when the Crown ceased trying to govern independently of the lower House. A President of the United States is required to govern independently for the Constitution forbids the mingling or sharing of powers. The President is locked into a position akin to that of the Stuarts by an eighteenth century sedan-chair constitution.

There have been efforts at various times to bend the United States Constitution in the direction of responsible government. All have failed. President Lincoln, taking advantage of the Civil War, asserted a doctrine of "inherent power." His successor, Andrew Johnson, could not carry such a claim to overwhelming power as against the Congress. Impeached in the House, he escaped by one vote in the Senate. At the core of the struggle between President and Congress was an attempt by the Legislative Branch to dictate the appointment of Cabinet officers.[6] It failed.

An apparent attempt for increased presidential power in the 1960's and 1970's failed; an overweening President was driven from office and his experiment in "impounding" appropriations he disapproved of and seeking to retain them for his own desired expenditures failed. The "line veto" on appropriations is now sought by Mr. Reagan by constitutional amendment. In an interesting development thirty states have now agreed to call for a constitutional convention. If a few more join the call, the United States will have its first constitutional convention since 1786 and the want of harmony between Executive and Legislature may be directly addressed.

Responsible Government is the term we use to describe that harmony between the Executive and the Legislature we have already achieved. It is the essential and distinctive feature of British parliamentary democracy, practised now not only in countries like Canada, Britain, Australia and New Zealand, but also in other democratic states from Denmark to Japan. The essence is simple: the Executive is accountable to and owes its continued existence to the Legislature. The Executive is accountable and answerable, not only for its budget, its money measures and legislative proposals, but also for the whole range of its activities. The servants of the Sovereign can continue in office only so long as they retain the confidence of the Legislature; which means only so long as they can secure the grant of Supply—the making of the appropriations from the Consolidated Revenue Fund necessary to carry on the programmes they desire; only so long as they can secure passage of the major elements of their basic legislative programme; and only so long as they can turn back any censure of their policies, and retain the general support of the Commons for their competence and handling of any and all of the myriad of administrative acts which make up modern government.

6     Nicholas von Hoffman, "The Test of King Ronald," *Time and Tide*, Winter, 1984, p. 14.

"Responsible Government" does not mean that such a government will necessarily behave more prudently or act more responsively to the wishes of the public or the opinions of Members of the Legislature than will administrations under other democratic forms of government.[7] On the contrary, it is often a ground of complaint about responsible government, as it has come to be badly practised in the party systems of the British Commonwealth in the late twentieth century, that it has come to be an irresponsible form of government with the Executive treating Parliament as a rubber stamp.[8] The members belonging to the majority party for the time being are dragooned into supporting whatever measure the party caucus approves (Australia and New Zealand) or the Party Leader and Cabinet direct (Canada and the United Kingdom), and into sustaining the Government however incompetent, corrupt or misguided. However badly it may be practised, or even perverted, responsible government does achieve a harmony between Executive and Legislature by the erection of a chain of responsibility[9] in which the people elect the House of Commons, the Ministry is chosen from amongst the group capable of securing passage of the Crown's business through the Commons, the civil service carries out the will of that Ministry and the Sovereign of her representative, through the reserve powers of the Crown, ensures that the chain of responsibility is observed. The civil service is responsible to the Ministers for the execution of their lawful commands, the Ministers to the House of Commons, individually and collectively, and to the Sovereign, and the Members of the House of Commons to the people.

A significant feature of the Canadian Constitution is that the basic rules as to how this harmony is achieved are nowhere set out. The Executive Government is not even described in terms most people would recognize. The Cabinet is not there, neither is the Prime Minister except as the person required by Sections 37 and 49 of the Constitution Act, 1982 to convene two constitutional conferences and as a participant in and convenor of the further constitutional conferences required by Sections 35.1 and 37.1 of that Act as

amended by Proclamation in 1984. There are no provisions relating to appointment of the Prime Minister and other Ministers from the group commanding a majority in the House of Commons or requiring those Ministers to resign or advise a dissolution if they lose the confidence of the House. The responsibility of Ministers, whether collective or individual, to the House is not mentioned. All these matters are governed by convention, which is to say by precedent and common sense.

The relevant precedents are often misunderstood and confused and the common sense with which all constitutional matters should be approached is often lacking. Professor J.L.J. Edwards was even moved to write:

> The modern realities of administering a Government and being the Minister in charge of a major Department, have led to some serious questioning as to the current constitutional meaning of ministerial responsibility. It is not necessary to look further than the series of debates and question periods in the Canadian House of Commons in recent times to perceive the degree of confusion as to the nature and limits of this doctrine that exists among parliamentarians.
>
> Inevitably, the gulf in its interpretation between the Government and the Opposition parties has been transmitted into the public domain. Simplistic attitudes become hardened in the process and doubts are cultivated as to the effectiveness of the entire parliamentary system. Especially is this so when the yardstick of effectiveness is viewed exclusively in terms of extracting ministerial resignations following upon allegations and proof of ministerial ineptitude.[10]

A straightforward statement of responsible government is easy to make but the simple statement masks a complexity of operation which has led to the confusion Professor Edwards has noticed. The Constitution Act 1867 recognizes that the executive power of Canada is

7  J. McMillan, G. Evans and H. Storey, *Australia's Constitution: Time for Change?* George Allen & Unwin, Sydney 1983, p. 209.
8  Ibid.
9  Ibid., p. 210.

10  J.L.J. Edwards, "Ministerial Responsibility for National Security," Study prepared for Commission of Inquiry concerning certain Activities of the Royal Canadian Mounted Police, Ottawa, 1980, p. 7.

vested in the Queen (section 9). The unwritten constitution grafts on to that section the principle that both the prerogative powers (save the reserve powers) and the powers delegated by Parliament are exercised by the Sovereign or her representative, the Governor General, according to the advice of Ministers having the confidence of the House of the Legislature which represents the people, which is to say, who enjoy the support of the majority of that House. Perhaps this should be put more accurately by saying the Ministers must not find themselves opposed by a majority of that House who wish them out of their offices which constitute a monopoly on tendering advice to the Sovereign or the Governor General in her Cabinet or closet. The practical result, as Bagehot noted,[11] is that the executive power is placed in the hands of a Committee made up of members of both Houses of Parliament, called the Cabinet, and that the real head of the Executive in terms of having his will carried out is not the Queen or the Governor General but the Chairman of that Committee, known as the Prime Minister. This finds expression in the deferential language of section 11 of the Act of 1867.

> There shall be a Council to aid and advise in the Government of Canada, to be styled the Queen's Privy council for Canada and the Persons who are to be Members of that Council shall be from Time to Time chosen and summoned by the Governor General and sworn in as Privy Councillors …

This is the sole legal basis for the Cabinet.

There is thus a very real sense in which the popular view of the Government both making the laws and administering the country is true. According to Bagehot, the "separation" of the legislative and executive powers under responsible government is better described as a "fusion of powers."

> The efficient secret of the English constitution may be described as the close union, the nearly complete fusion, of the executive and legislative powers.[12]

This fusion takes place in the Cabinet which as Bagehot put it:

> … is a combining committee—a *hyphen* which joins, a *buckle* which fastens, the legislative part of the State to the executive part of the State. In its origin it belongs to the one, in its functions it belongs to the other.[13]

It is worth noting why the word "responsible" is used. As Sir Samuel Griffith observed[14] it does have a meaning and was not plucked out of the void for use in constitutional jargon. The person who does an act or at whose will an act is done is the proper person to be held responsible for it. So long as acts of government are done by or at the volition of the head of a state alone, he alone is responsible for them. If he can be called to account or controlled by no-one, the only remedy for intolerable or deeply unpopular acts is revolution, a fate which befell Charles I. Responsible government stems from the maxim that the King can do no wrong which is given sense, and harmony with the idea of accountability, by requiring that the Sovereign does not do a governmental act (except for the exercise of reserve powers) of his own volition or motion, but follows the advice of Ministers, on whom the responsibility for acts done in order to give effect to their will falls. Some Minister is always legally responsible for every act of the Crown. If Ministers do wrong, or commit distinctly unpopular acts they can be punished by recourse to the law or forced from office without effecting any change in the Sovereign (the Head of State). Revolution is no longer necessary; the executive is controlled by both the law and by convention. The person of the Sovereign is removed from political debate and warfare, and from the consequences of a failure of Ministers to carry on government by securing supply or to carry with them the will of the electorate. Consequently, when the popular House, the House of Commons, disapproves of the actions or policies of the Ministers, refuses to grant to their administration the moneys necessary to carry on the country's affairs, or expresses its censure of or want

---

11  W. Bagehot, *The English Constitution*, Collins' Fontana Library, London, 1963, p. 66.
12  Ibid., p. 65.

13  Ibid., p. 68.
14  Quoted J. Quick and R.R. Garran, *The Annotated Constitution of the Commonwealth of Australia*, Angus and Robertson, Sydney, 1905, p. 703–704.

of confidence in the Ministers, the Sovereign or the Governor General dismisses them from Her service or accepts their resignation and appoints new Ministers or, alternatively, grants those Ministers an opportunity, by appealing to the country, to secure the return of a House of Commons which will support the Ministers, their policies and actions and will grant to them the necessary supplies of money. The effect is that the actual government is conducted by men and women who to an approximate degree enjoy the confidence of the electorate, which now a days means the adult population.

The ultimate sanctions in this system are two: first, the power of the Commons to withhold money from Ministers in whom it has no confidence and, secondly, the power of the Sovereign or Her representative to dismiss Ministers who, wanting the confidence of the House and being in consequence unable to govern, either immediately or proximately, and who, having neglected to ask for a dissolution or having been refused one, refuse to resign.

As a practical matter the Ministers combine together as a body, partly because they are appointed on the recommendation of the chief amongst them, and partly because the confidence of the House cannot be tested or determined if there is not one Ministry, and one policy. Thus, even an expression of want of confidence in one Minister's administration of his own individual departmental affairs may be treated by the Ministers as a censure of all, but need not be.

A further and necessary corollary of responsible government is that in the formation of a Ministry or Cabinet the essential first step is the appointment of its principal member, the Prime Minister. In the choice of a Prime Minister, however, the discretion of the Sovereign is fettered. She or her representative is constrained to select only that one man or woman who can, or expects to be able to, command the confidence of a majority of the House of Commons. The other members of the Ministry are selected by the Prime Minister and appointed by the Sovereign or Governor General on his recommendation, subject to the Sovereign's or Governor General's right to warn and advise on the suitability or limitations of particular persons suggested for office. It is in the methods by which popular Houses and modern political parties produce that one person who commands a majority in the House that the greatest diversity of constitutional practice has developed in the modern Commonwealth.

If we take our stand with Erskine May in 1862, who gave what may already have been an anachronistic summary, we may begin to grasp the perspective and the complexity of an easily oversimplified concept.

> [Ministers'] resolutions upon every important measure of foreign and domestic policy are submitted for [the King's] approval; and when that approval is withheld, his Ministers must either abandon their policy, or resign their offices. They are responsible to the King on the one hand, and to Parliament on the other; and while they retain the confidence of the King, by administering affairs to his satisfaction, they must act upon principles, and propose measures, which they can justify to Parliament … As [the King] governs by responsible Ministers, he must recognize their responsibilities. They are not only his Ministers, but also the public servants of a free country.[15]

There is no single doctrine of ministerial responsibility. Rather there is a trinity: three responsibilities in one doctrine. First, there is the responsibility of a Minister to the Queen or Governor General, so often overlooked, but basic to our constitutional order in which governments are *not elected* but are *appointed* and Ministers serve, not for a term, but until they die, resign or are dismissed. Ministers are just what the word means, *servants*, the Queen's confidential, political servants upon whom devolves the good government of Her subjects.

When responsibility or accountability to Parliament became an ingredient of our constitution, flowing from the original cry of redress of grievances before granting of Supply, each Minister came to be responsible *individually* for the policies of his Department and to some extent at least for individual acts and decisions taken within that Department. The second responsibility is, therefore, an individual accountability to Parliament by each of the Crown's servants having the administration of some part of the public

---

15  *The Constitutional History of England, 1760–1860*, Crosby and Nichols, Boston, 1862, p. 25.

service. The Minister may be subjected to criticism in the Commons, especially at Question Period, or he may have to meet a motion of censure. Again, he may be subject to such criticism outside Parliament that either he feels constrained to resign or the Prime Minister asks for or insists on his resignation.

The third responsibility is that most commonly thought of under the rubric of responsible government, the collective responsibility of the Ministry to the Parliament, and to the popular House in particular.

Each of these three responsibilities will now be dealt with in turn.

### b) Responsibility to the Sovereign

The cornerstone of our constitution is the Sovereign whose government is carried on in Her several realms. Centuries of constitutional evolution have not blurred this one central point: government is a trust which the Sovereign discharges; it is a trust that cannot be thrown up or ignored in some nihilistic whim. The Queen's business must be carried on and She must have a Government that has "the right and power to govern" and can carry on "the Queen's Service."[16] Ministers, therefore, owe their first responsibility to the Sovereign whom they serve, to carry out the terms of Her trust and to enable Her to honour Her Coronation Oath. This primary duty can only be honoured if the Ministers can carry with them the co-operation of the Commons House, for the carrying on of government requires money, and our constitution has developed in such a way that the Crown has no revenues save those voted by Parliament. Ministers, who rejoice in the title of "Minister of the Crown," sometimes, so it seems,

need to be reminded whence flow their appointments and whom they serve.

It is only if Ministers serve the Queen that we can ensure that they serve the people, and not themselves. It was not for naught that Mr. Churchill, at the height of his glory, was regularly photographed in deep obeisance before King George VI or that in February 1952 he paid public homage to his new Sovereign on his knees.

The responsibility of Ministers to the sovereign involves more than acknowledgment of allegiance and the successful prosecution of Government business in the Parliament. It entails frankness and openness with the Sovereign or Her personal representative and a proper respect for the royal or vice-regal right to warn and to advise. The Sovereign or Her representative must be kept fully informed of all Government initiatives and must never be placed in a position in which a careful consideration of her views and advice is pre-empted by premature announcements of policy.

Responsibility to the Sovereign also requires that Ministers who have been refused a dissolution or have been dismissed accept the exercise of the reserve power of the Crown like men.

### c) Responsibility of a Minister to the House

The question of a Minister's individual responsibility resolves itself into the question: When should a Minister in the eye of a storm offer his resignation or when should it be accepted or asked for? This question was studied by Professor Edwards for the Commission of Inquiry Concerning Certain Activities of the Royal Canadian Mounted Police. His opinion canvassed many of the relevant precedents and stands as the latest, most complete statement.

---

16   Sir Ivor Jennings, *The Queen's Government*, Pelican 1957, 41–2.

5

---

## Author's Introduction

Introductory comments on a paper about Senate reform have an advantage, when compared, for instance, with discussions about constitutional amendment or rule changes in the House of Commons, in that, unlike them, reform of the Senate never—or almost never—happens. Except for the introduction in 1965 of a retirement age of seventy-five, in place of the original provision for life-appointment, and in 1982 of a suspensive veto for the upper chamber on constitutional reform, all things are as they were in 1867. Why is this such an ever-green topic—so much talk and so little action? Part of the answer is that the public, despite its professed negative opinion of the Senate, puts reform of the institution low on its order of priorities. Another part is that the provincial governments distrust reform initiated by the federal government, and this is true whether the province in question is large or small. Thus, public apathy and provincial suspicion are disincentives to any successful reform initiative.

These considerations provide background to the following essay, "The Canadian Senate: What Is to Be Done?" Essentially, it argues that there are two principal questions to address when the subject is Senate reform. They are, what is the role of the upper chamber in the Canadian Parliament and how should that body be constructed in order to realize that object? Moreover, the chapter maintains that the questions should be answered in that order. It is not enough to say that appointed legislative bodies are out of date in the twenty-first century and that, therefore, the Senate must be elected. For if that were to happen, how would the work of two elected bodies in one bicameral Parliament be harmonized? The strength of the Senate today lies more in its investigative work than as a representative body. To the extent that the Senate's structure and composition were altered by the successful introduction of a reform (for example, eight, ten or twelve year terms), how would that change affect the existing hierarchy of duties performed by the upper house, and—never to be forgotten—what implication would that change have for the operation of the House of Commons?

Source: David E. Smith, "The Canadian Senate: What Is to Be Done?" in *The Canadian Senate in Bicameral Perspective* (Toronto: University of Toronto Press, 2003), 149–175.

---

David E. Smith

# The Canadian Senate: What Is to Be Done?

NOT ALL UPPER houses are the same: the United States Senate is the most powerful, the House of Lords the most exotic (Gilbert and Sullivan devoted one of their operas, Iolanthe, to it), the Australian Senate the most unexpected since it constitutes a strong, elected upper house in a parliamentary system, and the Canadian Senate the most controversial and criticized. For instance, in none of the first three is abolition of the chamber suggested as an option since in none does the upper house lack acceptance. That does not mean that the action of senators elsewhere is uncontroversial: the role of Australia's Senate in the drama leading to the dismissal of the Whitlam Government in 1975 or the repeated test of wills that takes place between a United States Senate and the House of Representatives or between the Senate and the White House stand as proof of that claim. By way of contrast, in the United Kingdom, the House of Lords may throw a government off its stride but poses no permanent obstacle to a government determined to realize its objective. This is true regardless of the political make-up of the government.[1]

Thus among second chambers, the Canadian Senate is the exception, and on several grounds. First, it is an appointed body, once with life terms and now to age seventy-five; second, it is an all-powerful body (with the customary limitations on financial initiatives understood); and third, it is a model of restraint in the exercise of its powers. The story of the GST aside, the rare occasions when the government does not see its will prevail underlines the Senate's generally cooperative nature. Like the Lords, the Canadian Senate is regularly celebrated by its members and a few academics for the breadth and quality of its investigative and scrutiny functions in committee, but just as regularly ignored by the media for this activity. At the same time, while less theatrical in appearance than the Lords (there have been no Canadian "enrobed bishops"), the Senate too is the subject of "media sensationalism and public fascination with the idiosyncrasies and quirkiness of the … Chamber."[2]

The House of Lords "problem" from the last quarter of the nineteenth century onward was what its role should be once the House of Commons had come to represent the popular will through the domination of electoral politics by mass parties.[3] In time, this problem was corrected by the introduction of the suspensive veto (1911) and, much later, by the passage of the Life Peerages Act, 1958. The Wakeham Commission has characterized the arrival of life peers as a modernizing development because it diluted the influence of hereditary peers. Critics described the act as deeply reactionary, since "it served to prolong the enfeeblement of the Second Chamber by deflecting rising criticism of the continuing appointment of hereditary peers and to strengthen the premier's powers of political patronage."[4] Life peers did not contradict the first principle of the Lords' composition, that it was a hereditary body, or the ensuing fact that most peers were Tory by birth and persuasion. This bias in partisan loyalty disguised another feature of the Lords that is often ignored—the contribution its members make to incorporating the provinces and principalities that comprise the United Kingdom. The Wakeham Commission recommends that a portion of the new Lords be elected in the regions and nations of the United Kingdom. Popular election will be new but not the incorporative function of the new peers. Indeed, the history of the British Parliament of the last two centuries has to be seen against the incorporative motif: in the late nineteenth century the Irish Nationalists and in the late twentieth century the Ulster Loyalists posed a threat to the unity the House of Commons symbolized—a threat the presence of non-English peers at Westminster helped moderate. And yet, the principle of territorial incorporation has never been articulated forthrightly in discussions about the Westminster Parliament. At best, it has been treated as an afterthought.

The reason for belabouring this point is that territorial incorporation was a central theme at the creation of Canada's upper house in the mid-1860s. Representation in the Senate was Confederation's answer to the concern the Maritime provinces and Quebec experienced at retaining "adequate representation" in Parliament, either because the Maritimes saw a large measure of self-government surrendered at Confederation, or the French-Catholics of Quebec sensed their vulnerability as a large but nonetheless minority population. As a federal negotiator of Newfoundland's Union with Canada said six decades later, accession would "tend to strengthen the centrifugal forces within the Dominion."[5]

In varying combinations, language, religion and schools—for instance, New Brunswick and Manitoba, Ontario and most recently Newfoundland—have destablized the bargain on which Confederation is based. Part of the potential for these issues to disrupt lay in the failure of the Fathers of Confederation to provide a basis for adjustment. Some federal theorists see constitutional amendment as a test of the resilience of federalism.[6] If so, Canada fails the test: it had no general domestic amending formula until 1982, and since that date "there have been more unsuccessful than successful attempts to amend the Constitution of Canada."[7] Constitutional amendment is never easy in federal systems; in the United States there have been only twenty-six in 214 years, in Australia forty-nine attempts but only eight successes in the century since the Commonwealth's creation. Still, Canada's constitution, with its multiple amending formulas and even sometimes needed unanimity, is extraordinary. Rather than enabling change, the formulas appear to prevent it.

To be clear on this matter, it is useful to summarize the amendment terms. Part V of the Constitution Act, 1982, sets out a general amending procedure (section 38) that requires resolutions of the two houses of Parliament and seven provincial legislatures with 50 per cent of the population; another formula for specified matters (section 41) requires unanimity on the part of Parliament and all ten legislatures; and a third procedure (section 44) permits amendments in relation to the executive government, Senate and House of Commons by ordinary act of Parliament. In addition, An Act Respecting Constitutional Amendments (SC 1996, c.1), although an ordinary statute, prohibits the government from proposing certain amendments to the Constitution unless the amendment has first been consented to by a certain configuration of provinces. The result is to lend the political veto to Ontario, Quebec, British Columbia, the Atlantic provinces and the Prairie provinces.[8] Finally, it needs to be recalled that under section 47(1) "an amendment to the Constitution of Canada … may be made without a resolution of the Senate … if … within one hundred and eighty days after the adoption by the House of Commons of a resolution … the Senate has not adopted such a resolution and if … the House of Commons again adopts a resolution."

This suspensive veto is logical because the determination of the fate of the amendment passes to the provincial legislatures. Amendments and bicameralism both involve delay and maybe even defeat. It would be illogical, therefore, to require constitutional change to clear both hurdles. Thus the Senate may delay but not prevent constitutional change. Technically this is true, but it does not go far enough in explaining the Senate's role, for during the amendment process the upper house offers a forum for both public participation and public understanding. The House of Commons may do the same thing, although past evidence demonstrates that Senate committees are more accessible and less subject to government-imposed deadlines.

The Senate was the great mollifier of 1867. The terms of the bargain awarded jurisdictional and financial dominance to the central government but also placed the protection of sectional interests in the Senate and—at a time when the Lords' absolute veto was beginning to be contested—conferred an absolute veto on the Senate as well. As a protector of sectional interests the Senate was not alone—there were the courts and the cabinet—nor was it the most effective defender. Controversy over sectional and minority rights often arose as a result of third-party actions, such as by provincial governments, over whom the upper chamber had minimal influence.

It is a refrain of critics of Canada's upper chamber that the Great Compromise (on the composition of the two houses of Congress), achieved at Philadelphia, recognized the equal claims of population and territory; here, they say, was a precedent the Canadian founding fathers chose to ignore. It is true that equality of representation of the new provinces in the Senate was never an option for serious discussion. And for a practical reason: the Senate was intended "to fill out" the representation deficit in Quebec and the Maritimes. (Arguably, the Senate "corrective" might be resorted to once more at the beginning of the twenty-first century in order to redress the weight of two new sections— the Prairie provinces and British Columbia—which by any comparative test of federal upper chamber representation would be found wanting in their current Senate numbers.) One of the arguments advanced in favour of the higher age and property qualifications for senatorial appointments than for members of the House of Commons was that these criteria would guarantee a higher quality of representation from the regions in terms of the professional and life experience of the senators selected. Continuous tenure in the Senate versus high turnover in the Commons reinforced the quality of representation. More than that, the Fathers recognized the claims of population in the lower house but allowed for weighted territorial representation in the upper, so that both provinces and regions might be recognized. The result was that each of the three regions, of which two were provinces in themselves, had almost as many senators at the outset as all the original states of the American Union together had senators in 1787.

In this difference there is no intended claim to superior achievement on the part of Canadians, only a plea to acknowledge the difference between the two upper houses and to recognize the role the Canadian Senate was given to accomplish this representational end. A number of reasons may be suggested for explaining why the Senate did not perform as the Fathers of Confederation expected it would. Most significant were the long periods of one-party rule that followed Confederation and the expansion of the national party system into the provinces of Canada. The emergence of disciplined parties and a political executive that controlled the House of Commons made impossible any sense of balanced power, as there was in the United States with its separated institutions, or in Great Britain with its monarchy, hereditary aristocracy ensconced in the Lords, and the Commons. The independence of the Senate "alike of the people and the Crown" was, because of its creation through patronage appointment, viewed by critics as a counterfeit independence.[9]

The concept of balanced powers may be inapplicable to Canada's constitutional structure, but it may be inappropriate to other systems as well. Balance conveys a mechanical (Newtonian) analogy of planes and surfaces. When applied "to the British Constitution" of responsible government, the mechanical metaphor, in the following case the image of a clock, must be abandoned. That at least was Issac Issacs's view when the delegates in the Australian conventions of the 1890s were weighing the comparative advantages of the British and American constitutions:

> The view formerly entertained with regard to the British Constitution, that deadlocks were an element of safety, and rather to be courted than guarded against, has now been abandoned, and ... we have ceased to regard as a proper form of government a constitution in which the hour and the minute hands and the striking part should all be governed by different mechanisms, with no provision for the various indicators marking the correct and the same time.[10]

Chemistry rather than physics would offer more illustrative metaphors in a study of parliamentary bicameralism, for chemistry suggests an interaction between bodies. At the same time, to the unscientific mind it implies mutability rather than a fixed state. And change, contrary to popular opinion, is a feature of the Canadian Senate. "It is a fact, that the Senate—almost alone among our political institutions—has evolved to meet new needs and challenges." That is Senator Lowell Murray's opinion, and as supporting evidence he uses the familiar Senate committee studies but also the Senate's autonomy, compared to the Commons, to provide "some check on the power of the cabinet and its Commons majority without challenging or offending today's democratic culture."[11]

Senator Murray's proposition that the Senate is a resilient institution would go some way to help explain one feature of Senate reform proposals: that

they forever remain proposals, reformers being long on talk but short on action. This is more than a debating point; there is something fundamentally at issue in the perenniality of the debate. Of course, there are practical reasons why reform is difficult. One is the different roles the Senate is expected to perform—oversight, protection, innovation, representation, and more. Reforms can have contradicting effects depending on which role is being evaluated. Another is the current amending formula which requires a majority of the population and a majority of the provinces to amend the Senate's powers and the method of selection of its members. A third reason, of much older vintage, is the restrictive influence of the House of Lords. While it is true that that limitation disappeared when the Asquith government forced radical change on the Lords in the form of the Parliament Act of 1911, for decades before then the colonial and Westminster upper chambers were bound in a self-limiting relationship. Consider, for instance, the assertion by English Liberal George Grote (MP for London, 1832–41) on the eve of the 1837 Rebellions that

> He would not degrade the House of Lords by a comparison with the Legislative Council of Canada to the House of Lords.... The hon. Member [George Richard Robinson, Conservative (Worcester)] ... had ... alluded to the division of the population of Canada into two distinct races, and had contended that the Legislative Council was necessary for the protection of the minority. He could not admit any such necessity. The House of Assembly represented not only the majority, but the whole of the population of Canada, and though the decisions of that body were necessarily determined by a majority, the interests of the minority were not the less duly represented. If, indeed, a separate legislature was to be established for every separate class or minority, every principle of a representative government would be totally disregarded. Those hon. Gentlemen who maintained such a doctrine with regard to Canada were bound, in consistency, to apply the same principle to Ireland, and to support a proposition for the repeal of the Union.[12]

The implication of change in Canada's upper house for the precedent it might pose for House of Lords' reform was another disinclination for those in Canada who wanted reform of the Senate.

As important as these reasons might be, there is a more fundamental explanation for why Senate reform languishes. If metaphors such as the one about equilibrium are misapplied and misleading, then what constitutional image does fit the Canadian case? The answer is none. Or several. The Canadian constitution is about fiscal federalism and linguistic federalism; it is about two nations (perhaps) and First Nations; it is about executive federalism and representational federalism; it is about the common law, the civil code and an entrenched charter of rights. Canada is made up of a number of little constitutional images in only a minority of which the Senate (and thus its reform) bulk large. This proposition can be pressed still further: it is not the Senate that fails to figure in the constitutional scheme but bicameralism because, except for the upper chamber in Ottawa, Canadians have before them only unicameral legislatures.

This is why Senate reform proposals never succeed, why "interest dies down, the reform promised … forgotten."[13] In truth, the Triple E proposal may not be forgotten but interest in it is at best episodic. Despite the amount that has been written about the proposal, it too remains a little constitutional image. Too much is left out; for example, Triple E has nothing to say to Quebec or First Nations. As with the German Bundesrat before it, Triple E is all about foreground; there is no depth to the proposal because there is no depth to the analysis. How will the new Senate work with the House of Commons? What provision will there be for breaking deadlocks—will it be joint sittings, referendums, or double dissolution? How will campaigning for election to one chamber affect campaigning (and party organization) for the other. Will political careers in the two chambers overlap and, if so, to what effect? How well will the symmetrical Senate the Triple E system proposes serve Canada's asymmetrical federalism? Here, as with all Senate reform proposals, it is necessary to look behind the rhetoric in order to move from theory to practice. Especially is it necessary to acknowledge what is never discussed, that the Senate is one part of a bicameral legislature whose houses share a common workload but play different roles. Until that is admitted, reform proposals will encounter objections from the lower chamber and

the government who is its master, on the grounds that any rehabilitation above will come at the expense of those below. Arguably, an elected (partisan) Senate might add to the prime minister's already large powers. But the prime minister is not the House of Commons and, in this case, both chambers would be weaker.[14]

An elected Senate poses more than an institutional problem; there is a theoretical challenge as well. It is no coincidence that Australian defenders of Senate power are also advocates of popular sovereignty. Do Canadian proponents of an elected second chamber share the same theoretical predisposition? And, more importantly, are they prepared to accept the consequences that flow from that argument? Angus Hawkins maintains that the theory of parliamentary sovereignty demands the exclusion of the sovereign and the people. Would not a theory of popular sovereignty demand the inclusion of the people in practice as well as in words? In short, would it not demand a reconceptualization of Canada's British-inherited constitution? One piece of evidence invariably cited to sustain the claim of popular sovereignty in Australia is the referendum-centred amending formula. Could Canada move to a constitution based on the people rather than the Crown-in-Parliament and maintain its current legislatively based amendment formula? Popular sovereignty is not a selective phenomenon in Australia. On the contrary, Australians are inordinately committed to the principle of equality in the counting of votes and the drawing of constituency boundaries. This is a shared national characteristic that long predates the creation of the Commonwealth and is, perhaps, the country's political hallmark. Certainly, in Australia claims are neither acknowledged nor, even more surprising, made to "effective," or "traditional," or "historic" representation.

Putting to one side the problem that Canada's amending formula presents any move toward Senate elections, there is a more fundamental question: whether an elected upper house is desirable. The answer to that question demands an answer to a prior question: what role should the Senate play in Canada's constitution? Despite criticism the Senate is credited on all sides with doing good work. But is this the work a second chamber should be doing, and is it work an elected house would do better than an appointed one? Once there is consensus on the role of the Senate, then it is possible to move on to discuss the characteristics an upper house with this role will have, including, for instance, whether it should possess an absolute veto. As the matter currently stands, there is no logical argument either for retaining the absolute veto or replacing it with some variant of a suspensive veto. John Turner, the only political leader to study the Senate (it was the subject of his honours thesis), observed that "the Senate has never overstepped its bounds … and scarcely deserves the tirades hurled against it on this score. Therefore, a limitation on the 'veto' power would merely be a further emasculation of the chamber without any compensatory cure of an abuse."[15]

Thus, the central problem for the Canadian Senate and for Canadian bicameralism is a conceptual one. Until there is agreement on what the Senate is supposed to do, there will be no agreement on its modification. More than that, until there is inevitable recognition that change to the composition of the upper chamber will necessitate change to the lower one also, and that the pair of alterations must be seen as valid if they are to gain acceptance—until this occurs, the prospect of reform is slight. In its place, agreements such as the Charlottetown Accord, which proposed equal Senate representation for every province but reduced power for the chamber and more seats in the Commons for the populous provinces, will not command the support they require for approval. Unless there is a logic to compensatory adjustments, as there was in the distribution of seats by senatorial region in 1867 coupled to representation in the lower chamber, then institutional redesign will not happen.

Yet there is a practical need to do something in order to enhance the upper house and thereby make it a constructive element of Parliament within current constitutional arrangements. Thus, the discussion that follows concerns improving the Senate by non-constitutional means. To date, reformers have addressed the Senate as a one-dimensional institution with the result that a discrepancy prevails between the content of the reform they propose and the context in which it is to take place. The great expectations associated with large-scale institutional change are as inappropriate as they are unrealizable. Better a gradual, cautious strategy to make the most of the current Senate.

Before turning to this question, the meaning of the phrase "non-constitutional" should be clarified,

since, while convenient, it is imprecise. Some of the improvements cited below are constitutional in that they technically include unilateral amendments to the Constitution that can be made by Parliament (section 44 of the Constitution Act 1982). These changes, whether by an act of Parliament or modification of the Rules of the Senate, require only the development of a clear vision among parliamentarians in order to bring about results. (Of course, what cannot be done by this means, for instance, is to add new senatorial regions and more senators to correct perceived imbalance in the present upper chamber.)

## ROLE AND FUNCTIONS OF THE SENATE OF CANADA

Much can be done without constitutional amendment to make the Senate a more constructive and credible institution. The first step is to determine what the Senate is supposed to do, or what proponents of change want it to do, and then recommend how it might be altered to secure that result. Adopting this procedure for institutional design imitates Louis Sullivan's dictum for early twentieth-century architects: "Form ever follows function." It also reverses the process followed by most reformers: usually, for example, those who say the Senate should have a suspensive veto only to delay rather than an absolute veto to kill legislation, or those who campaign for an elected Senate, or start at the other end. Grounding their arguments on "democratic" or "representational" propositions, reformers give no thought to the effect the changes they advocate will have on the operation of the chamber nor on the operation of the lower house. By contrast, Viscount Cranborne, the first Conservative opposition leader in the House of Lords after the Labour Party came into power in 1997, acknowledged the importance of bicameralism to second chamber reform: "Any examination of Parliament should start with the House of Commons…. Once we have addressed the House of Commons—and only then—would it make sense to think of the House of Lords."[16]

If, as will be argued below, the Senate is found to have a role to protect regional and sectional interests, a role the Fathers of Confederation expected the upper chamber to play, then loss of the power to veto legislation the Senate deems a threat to those interests, and which it also determines was fundamental to achieving the Canadian federation, would render the role useless. Similarly, to recast the composition of the Senate so that each province had an equal number of senators would also have direct implication for its role as protector of minorities. In this discussion the statement by the Supreme Court of Canada in the Senate Reference must be recalled once more: "The smaller provinces only consented to Confederation on the understanding that there would be a regional Upper House."[17]

The primary function of the Senate is to complement the House of Commons. Because the Senate is not a confidence chamber, it does not compete with the House of Commons in its most important elective function—that is, to make and unmake governments. Rather than compete, the upper house completes the work of the lower house. It is from this activity that the deliberative role of the Canadian Senate or the House of Lords in the United Kingdom arises. Redundancy is as central an element of bicameralism as it is of federalism, and Canadian senators, who are free from the pressures of constituency and electoral duties, have the time to consider and become educated on issues in a manner different from that of members in the House of Commons. However, duality does not mean repetition; nor does it imply superfluousness. It is one of the paradoxes of modern politics in parliamentary systems that the upper houses are in a stronger position today to carry out the deliberative work of Parliament, which Walter Bagehot described as its expressive, teaching and informing functions, than is the House of Commons to which Bagehot originally assigned the tasks.[18]

In the study of bills, the Senate has an advantage over the House of Commons because of its small numbers, because with shorter and fewer speeches, procedure is informal and flexible, and because senators have more time, freedom, and expert knowledge as well as greater independence than do members of Parliament. That independence is a product not only of subdued partisanship (every commentator on the Senate remarks invidiously upon the adversarial tone of the Commons and its general absence in the upper house) but of distinctive procedures. The manipulation of House committee chairmen and members has no

equivalent in the Senate. Where volatility characterizes the former, stability and continuity mark the latter.[19] The Senate's purpose is to deliberate, to build up its legislative case through debate, the taking of testimony from witnesses, and the collection of a broad range of opinion from Canadians in all walks of life and all parts of the country. In the political marketplace, the Senate's capital, so to speak, lies not in its skill at brokering interests (that clearly belongs to the Commons) but in distilling arguments. While the Senate is not an academic body, the influence it exerts is intellectual in content. This is why the senators spend more time in committee than in the full house: the Senate sat on sixty-two calendar days in 1997–8, and its committees held meetings on ninety-five days.

Another technique is to use Senate committees for investigative purposes, as in such highly regarded studies as the Croll report on poverty, the Lamontagne report on science policy, the Davey report on the media and communications policy.[20] There have also been proposals to use special Senate committees in lieu of far more costly royal commissions and inquiries. This option merits serious consideration, particularly as the composition of special committees, unlike standing committees, could be constructed to ensure the most appropriate membership in terms of expertise and representativeness.

Like royal commissions, investigative studies by the Senate can be a source of public policy. On the other hand, like royal commissions, their recommendations and findings may languish unregarded by government. The government is free to reject a committee report, and the outcome then would be no different from the case of the unamended Clarity Bill. Yet the argument used to assess the work of the Senate on that bill applies with equal force to all committee activity: the deliberative role of the Senate is important because of the diminished capacity of the lower chamber and of citizens generally to frame public debate. The Senate provides a forum for broadened participation. Its structure and procedures are more receptive to encouraging focused debate and less susceptible to domination. In short, the Senate provides ballast to a system that seems increasingly weightless. This is an opinion widely shared: "The work of Commons' committees in Canada is now almost as irrelevant as debate in Parliament"; "[M]inisters …

say that Cabinet is no longer where important decisions are made...." "Rather, it is a kind of focus group for the prime minister"; "Canadians continue to feel that they do not have much say over what government does and that their elected representatives are not in touch with the people."[21]

If the primary function of the Senate is to complement the House of Commons, then in its deliberative role it helps to complete the legislative process. Improvements to the manner in which that deliberation takes place—the organization, size, and membership of committees, the frequency with which they meet, the possibility of a timetable of fixed sittings, whether or not the pre-study of bills should be reintroduced as a regular feature of Senate procedure, and whether the government should be pressed to introduce more government bills into the upper chamber—these and similar matters can all be accomplished by non-constitutional means. The internal arrangement of Parliament's business is Parliament's business. In other words, if it is agreed that the work of the Senate described above is its principal activity, then improving its performance lies solely with members of the two houses of Parliament, including the government of the day.

What is problematic about this depiction of the Senate at work is the proposal to transform the chamber into an elected body. While plausible, an elected Senate is not probable, for reasons already given. Still it helps focus attention on the Senate's current operation to consider the adjustments election would bring. To begin with, there would be greater, sustained partisanship in a manner comparable to the Commons. Of course, there is partisanship now, as critics never tire of pointing out, usually by referring to the period between 1984 and 1993.[22] There is nothing wrong with partisanship in an upper chamber; in fact, bicameralism would be in jeopardy if the government could not look to supporters there to shepherd its bills through that legislative process. (It is one of the new concerns of some Senate critics that were a Canadian Alliance government, minority or majority, to be formed at some point in the future, there would have been no Canadian Alliance senators appointed to the upper house.) All that may be admitted, but as every commentator on the operation of the Senate states, partisanism there is muted and, sometimes, inverted. It

is not uncommon to see senators speaking and even voting in opposition to a bill that originated in the Commons with their party.

Elected senators, like elected members of Parliament, would have constituents to serve and a voting base to protect and mobilize. Independent MPs do not get elected in Canada, nor would independent senators. Party support at the time of nomination and party resources during campaigns would assume an importance now absent in an unelected chamber. At the same time, the changed relationship to the House of Commons cannot be ignored. That relationship would deepen: if parties are inevitable, equally certain is it that the same parties would be active in the two chambers.[23] In this scenario, the future of Canada's minor or third parties would substantially change, since either they would be pressed out of the lower house or they would make their appearance in the upper house. The type of electoral system used would be all-important. The question to be asked is whether an elected Senate would perform its deliberative role more fully and more faithfully than the Senate as presently constituted. If the answer is no, then improvers of the Senate should focus on what the Senate does and concentrate on non-constitutional means to bring about those changes deemed desirable. If the answer is yes, then proponents of reform must show how election would strengthen deliberation; and once this is done, they are then confronted with the impenetrability of constitutional reform.

The Senate does more than deliberate; it also represents. It is well known that the Fathers of Confederation spent longer at Quebec City in 1864 discussing the composition of the Senate than any other institution of government. The reason is with Canadians still: the provinces now are manifestly unequal in population. They are unequal in other respects, but it is population that is the issue here. One of the attractions of bicameralism in the 1860s—perhaps the main attraction—was that it offered a counterweight to "rep-by-pop" enthusiasts such as George Brown. Unlike other federations, which also experienced population disparities among their states or provinces but which used the states and provinces as units for equal representation in the upper chamber, Canada opted for senatorial regions of equal representation. These reasons lay partly in the lessons Canadians drew from the causes of the Civil

War in the United States and partly in the value they placed on government being responsible to an elected chamber. (It should be remembered that Confederation came only thirty years after the Rebellions of 1837.) Those reasons notwithstanding, the agreement on the Senate illustrates an important feature of British North American political culture—a tolerance of difference or, phrased more bluntly, a recognition that equality would undermine the federation altogether.

It needs to be remembered that treating the provinces unequally in the matter of Senate representation in 1867 was not a cause for sorrow. For their part, the Fathers of Confederation did not envision the Senate acting as a House of the Provinces. Originally appointed by the governor-in-council for life, Canadian senators were in a position to be independent of provincial governments, of the people of the provinces, and of public opinion in the country.[24] The federative principle in Canada concerned jurisdiction, not representation. Equality of power in the matter of jurisdiction for the provinces, normally unconstrained by the exercise of superordinate federal power in the form of disallowance or declaratory legislation—that was the view of how Canadian federalism should work. Neither equality of representation nor popular representation of provincial electors was possible. Nor was the Senate's composition a source of grievance with the founding provinces, since the sectional and regional interests the Senate was expected to protect were not viewed as territorially confined to provinces. A variation on this theme is the concept of interest-based constituencies. In the words of the study on The Senate Veto:

> Individual senators over the years have become advocates for children, the poor, the aged, visible minorities, prisoners, veterans and illiterates. Their ability to knit together national constituencies of people who might otherwise have an inadequate voice in Parliament can be attributed at least in part to not having to run for election in a geographically defined constituency.[25]

That quotation is drawn from a section of the report that describes the Senate as a "house of equalization." If in its deliberative role the Senate acts as a house of legislative completion, then in its representative role it acts as a house of compensation. From its personnel it can replenish the depleted ranks of a government, witness Mr Trudeau's selection of the three western senators as ministers in 1980. Again, it may inject sectional interests into a debate from which they are being excluded. An example of this occurred following the 1993 election: Liberal MPs supporting the Chrétien government "occupied all but one of the thirty-two seats from the Atlantic region. For the next four years, Conservative senators from that region provided almost the only parliamentary debate and serious questioning of government policies affecting Atlantic Canadians."[26]

A house of equalization perhaps, but the Senate has never functioned as a House of the Provinces, although it is fair to say, as Jack Stilborn does, that today "regional representation ... [is] virtually the universal preoccupation of reformers."[27] The preoccupation of these reformers focuses on neither sectional nor regional but rather provincial interests defined by territory and articulated by provincially appointed or, better still, periodically elected senators. The federal principle as embraced by the Fathers of Confederation and institutionally embodied in the Senate disappears. So, too, does the constitution's internal architecture which harmonized the Senate's deliberative and representative roles. Deliberation, as applied to national policies, cannot be reconciled with the promotion or defence of provincial interests.

Foreign practice in this matter is informative. Australia's Senate has been exceptional among upper houses in parliamentary systems, for since its inception it has been elected. Indeed, three electoral systems have been employed—plurality, preferential and, since 1949, proportional. Each change was introduced to respond to unexpected problems that arose with the previous method. From the perspective of Canadian reformers committed to an elected upper house of Parliament, the instructive lesson to draw from Australian experience is that it has never acted as a House of the States. Either parties dominated its activities or it provided a forum for minority representation. There is no question, as one Australian political scientist has said, that "state identity continues to be a potent force in Australian politics, but it has been joined by cross-cutting sources of sectional or minority identity."[28]

Since the introduction of the Charter of Rights and Freedoms two decades ago, Canadians have grown familiar with this latter form of interest aggregation. Up to the present, these interests have been more prominent in the judicial than in the electoral arena, although a pattern appears to be emerging of the Senate responding to minority interests and debating issues that eventually reach the courts. Nor does Canada have a system of proportional representation from which minority interests might profit. Nonetheless, Australian experience with upper chamber reform serves as a reminder that the interests of states (or provinces) in a federation are less easily transferred to national politics than reformers may suppose.

The history of the Australian Senate affords one other cautionary note in the discussion of the role and function of upper chambers. There, as here, the constitution requires that appropriation measures be introduced in the lower house only. There, as here, the upper chamber refuses to acknowledge any limitation on its potential action even with regard to financial bills. But there, unlike here, the Senate has used its powers to block the passage of budgetary measures proposed by a government that controls the lower house. The outcome of that impasse in 1975 has already been discussed. The incident is notable only to underline the extension of partisan politics into the second chamber of the Australian Parliament to a degree unknown in Canada. Whatever its putative failings, the Senate of Canada has never been the cause of a constitutional crisis.

There is a third role the Senate plays, one less commented upon than the previous two but which illustrates the special duty it was given to protect. In a comparison made to highlight the unique circumstances and expectations surrounding the creation of Australia's Senate, Australian political scientist John Uhr explained why the framers of the Commonwealth were attracted to the example of American federalism but lukewarm about the Canadian variant:

> Stripped of exclusive constitutional functions, the Australian Senate had no need for those other structural devices designed to differentiate the Senate from the House and so enhance the review capacity: such as the different age qualification ... and commitment to as small an upper house as feasible.

The Canadian model should have been of great interest, since the whole rhetoric of "responsible government" derived from the Canadian struggle for self-government; but the Canadian federal model in the 1867 British North America Act attracted very little support during the Conventions.[29]

Unlike Australia, Canada initially had no domestic amending formula for its constitution. Only in 1982 was the constitution patriated with a set of amending formulae. Originally, therefore, protection of the rights of sectional minorities rested, on the one hand with the executive (for example section 93 of the Constitution Act, 1867, assigns to cabinet the responsibility to hear appeals on the actions of provincial authorities that affect the educational rights of denominational minorities where they exist, and, if necessary, to initiate remedial legislation to restore those rights) and, on the other hand, with the Senate, as indicated in Uhr's description above. In Australia an amendment is an amendment is an amendment: initiated by the federal government, passed by both houses of Parliament, and supported by a majority of voters in a majority of states. There is no partitioning of the Constitution, of which Canadians are so fond. Questions about the degree of consent, the determination of who gives the consent, the classification of subject matter according to requirements for different levels of consent—none of these issues afflict Australian politics.

## POWERS

The roles and functions of the Senate are finite, but except for the requirement that money bills be introduced in the House of Commons, the formal powers of the Senate are infinite. What the Senate does with these powers, and whether they are appropriate to the functions it performs, are central issues in any discussion of improving the Senate. There is no question that the ability to reject legislation rather than simply delay or amend it is exceptional among upper chambers. Certainly, there is no unelected chamber that possesses similar power. And even elected bodies with this power, such as the Senate of Australia, are vulnerable to criticism from government and the public when they contemplate exercising it. Parliamentary democracies based on the Westminster model are strongly imbued with the belief that "governments should be allowed to govern." Opposition, whether elected or appointed, is unpopular.[30]

In his study of *The Senate Veto*, the law clerk and parliamentary counsel to the Senate presents an appendix entitled "Senate Use of the Veto to Defeat Bills." That list shows that the veto was used forty-four times in the twentieth century. For those critics who oppose the Senate as currently constructed, that figure may appear excessive. From any other vantage, it indicates voluntary restraint on the part of senators. That judgment emphasizes a point sometimes overlooked by reformers who want to see an elected upper house; there is no reason to believe and some cause to doubt that an elected body would approach the use of power in the same way as an appointed body does.

This was the issue on which the referendum on an Australian republic foundered in 1999: how to give the majority of citizens the popularly elected president they wanted but, at the same, to guarantee that the president would honour the conventions of the constitution whereby the prerogative powers of the Crown are exercised (except in the most extraordinary situation) only on ministerial advice.

More than in most political systems, the constitutions of Canada and Australia depend upon understandings for their operation; the written portions of those documents are worse than useless, since they falsify the modern arrangement of political power. This is particularly the case with the executive, defined as the Crown and in whom all executive power is vested, but it is also true of other institutions, none more so than the Senate of Canada.

The Senate possesses broad powers which it uses sparingly. This is not to say that it would make no difference if the Senate were to exchange its absolute veto for a suspensive one. The Wakeham Commission is precise in recommending that the reformed second chamber should have no more than a suspensive veto in the future. The House of Commons is the confidence chamber and the commission believes that any stronger power on the part of the upper house would set up a rival to the Commons. While the new upper chamber in the United Kingdom will incorporate representation from the country's regions and nations, the vast majority of the members will be centrally appointed. All of Canada's senators are regional in that they all are appointed for some province. It is that regional and sectional complexion that sets Canada's Senate apart from the House of Lords and which defenders of the Senate veto cite in defence of their position.

Proponents of a Triple E Senate seek institutional change in order to achieve greater regional (that is, western) influence over national policies. They believe that those policies reflect central Canadian interests because the government dominates the House and the House is dominated by members from Ontario and Quebec. While reformers talk about little other than an upper chamber that is equal, effective, and elected, they should still favour retention of the Senate veto. Otherwise, a reformed Senate, if that could ever be achieved by constitutional amendment, would have less power than the present body. Thus, from the perspective of reformers, and of improvers who maintain constitutional amendment is not a practical alternative at present, the status quo as regards the veto is acceptable.

## COMPOSITION

The composition of the Senate is subordinate to agreement about the role it should fulfil as a second chamber. That purpose is to complement the House of Commons, first, as a deliberative body that amplifies, clarifies, and scrutinizes legislation and, second, as a representative institution that articulates and protects regional and sectional interests. The primacy awarded here to function over form is not universally shared. Indeed, the *National Post* echoes many critics who reverse these priorities and who say that "the Senate's central flaw is that it is filled through patronage appointments [made on the prime minister's recommendation] that last until age 75."[31] From this "flaw," they say, follows others: senators are either accountable to no one or they are in the pocket of the prime minister; senators are privileged, partisan, and in the service of special interests; and senators are old, out of touch with society, and a standing rebuke to Canada's democratic pretensions.

Critics in Canada no more like the patronage system of selection than did critics in the United Kingdom like the hereditary base of the House of

Lords. The difference between the two situations is that, paradoxically, it was easier to sever the peerage from the Lords (by simple statute) than it will be to agree on an alternative senatorial selection process in Canada. The Wakeham Commission proposed a statutory appointments commission to appoint the independent members of the reformed Lords. While nominations may come from several sources, including the political parties, the final say rests with the commission. It would work under a set of guidelines that is supposed to keep the chamber broadly representative of the larger society, balanced between the parties in light of the last general election vote, and moderately independent. The majority of members of the new Lords would be nominated by the political parties, but in proportions intended to reflect the shares of the national vote and with the actual number of seats determined by the commission. The age of swamping has finally passed. The prospect of a second chamber at Westminster acting wilfully independent, if only temporarily because of the suspensive veto, has disappeared. Because any move to elect senators in Canada will require constitutional amendment, whose passage is improbable because of the conflicting interests at stake in the bicameral Parliament, discussion of the Senate's composition must look to non-constitutional means to improve selection process.

And it needs improvement on several fronts. One of these is the current retirement age of seventy-five. In the Constitution Act, 1965, Parliament unilaterally set an age limit to Senate membership, since prior to 1965 senators were appointed for life. This establishes a precedent for further unilateral (defined here as non-constitutional) action.[32] However, rather than an age limit, tenure could be defined as a term, one long enough to ensure a Senate that possesses both independence and experience. The average tenure of a senator is about fifteen years or approximately three Parliaments. A fixed term would have the advantage of equalizing appointments, since it would translate what is now an average into fixed tenure. At the same time, it would respect the deliberative function of the second chamber. More practically, it would also conform to the Supreme Court's 1980 opinion that changes to the Senate should not "affect the fundamental features, or essential characteristics, given to the Senate

as a means of ensuring regional and provincial representation in the federal legislature process."

The unilateral or non-constitutional formula could also be used to change the minimum age requirement and property qualification for senators, although the latter provision as it applies to senatorial divisions in Quebec may require that province's consent to abolition.

The heart of the criticism of the selection process remains the prime minister's monopoly to name senators. Over the past two decades similar arguments have been heard about the Crown's prerogative in the making of all appointments, for example judicial and diplomatic, on the sole advice of the first minister. There have been suggestions that this task should be shared with Parliament, just as the President and the Senate are required to cooperate under the United States Constitution. Arguably, appointments per se are not the issue but, rather, who makes the appointments. Is there some way, within the scope of section 44 of the amendment procedure, to limit the prerogative of the prime minister? Is it possible to frame a set of objectives to guide prime ministerial appointments? In other words, can Canada approximate the procedure the Wakeham Commission proposes the United Kingdom follow.[33] It should be recalled that, for some years now, the prime minister and the minister of justice have been assisted by advisory committees (composed, among others, of members of the provincial bar) in selecting judges for appointment by the governor general. And this has been done without constitutional amendment.

Of course, the guidelines would be dictated by different considerations and concerns. Compared with his British counterpart, a Canadian prime minister appoints few members to the upper house. In his first three years in office, Mr. Blair made nearly two hundred appointments.[34] In a comparable period, Mr. Chrétien appointed one-fifth that number, although the regular selection of at least some aged appointees (three over seventy), with few years to acquire the deliberative skills senators must have increases these opportunities. The explanation lies in the fact that historically the Lords had no upper limit on its number. The swamping power was absolute, and its thrust immense—as witness the events that preceded passage of the Parliament Act, 1911, which deprived the Lords of their absolute veto.

Perhaps because the number of senators a prime minister appoints is comparatively few, the impact appointments have is all that much greater.

There seems little doubt that if the Fathers of Confederation were devising an upper chamber for the Parliament of Canada today, they would shun an appointed chamber. But even if this were the case, the Fathers would still be confronted with the conundrum of how to harmonize two elected bodies. Their original answer to the clash that would inevitably occur between elected chambers was to make the Senate appointed. This assured that a government enjoying the confidence of the House of Commons would normally be able to have its legislation adopted by Parliament, but gave the Senate the ability to act as a check in those rare instances when it was absolutely necessary. Australian experience is one indication of how Canadian history might have unfolded. Canada, however, must live with the institutions it has and the constitutional amendment formula its elected politicians have given it. In that circumstance, it seems less than constructive to criticize every Senate appointment simply because he or she is an appointee.

## ACCOUNTABILITY

Advocates of an elected Senate want senators to represent their provinces. They explicitly say that senators do not do this now because they are appointed on the recommendation of the prime minister. Yet it is neither the role nor the function of senators to advance the cause of specific interests, territorially defined or otherwise. First and foremost, they are expected to bring their considered judgment to bear on questions of national importance, including the maintenance of the federation. A necessary condition to that end is the independence of the Senate and senators. The age and property qualifications, the term of appointment, the absolute veto, the cap on membership, along with the restrictive provision for the appointment of senators these and other characteristics of the operation of the chamber are explicable as guarantees of institutional and personal independence.

Those who want to anchor senatorial selection in provincial electorates champion improved accountability as well as representation. In their eyes, senators

appointed by the Crown on prime ministerial advice are unaccountable. This is one variant of the argument that permeates criticism of existing governmental institutions and reveals itself in calls for initiative, recall and referendum and for legislative confirmation of federal (but, seldom, provincial) appointments. As with representation, the concept of accountability is narrowly defined.

The critics of the Senate are correct: the chamber is not responsible to the people or to interests outside of Parliament. On the contrary, it is responsible to Parliament. If the Senate possesses a veto on the legislative process, so does the House of Commons. Laws are made when the two parts of Parliament act as one. When comity fails, then some means of reparation must be found. All legislative bodies are self-governing institutions who police themselves and, occasionally, others. Again, this is understandable only when the primacy historically accorded the independence of Parliament is appreciated.[35] Rather than focus on that dimension of parliamentary life, critics increasingly call for improvements in the internal administration of the Senate.

Here, perhaps more than anywhere else, the Senate is open to improvement by non-constitutional means. Here, too, the benefits to be gained from improvement are greatest. Too often reform and media critics depict the Senate as a private club whose members act without regard to interests beyond their immediate personal concern. This is quite the reverse of the way private clubs function, and it is a misinterpretation of the Senate's mode of operation.[36]

The parallel between the two lies in the Senate's small size and the long tenure of its members. The result is that the Senate has operated largely on unwritten rules agreed to by members of the Liberal and Progressive Conservative parties. This is not altogether true; from Confederation onward the Senate has listed members in attendance in the daily *Journals*, and since 1990 those names along with committee attendance have been available to the public. Nonetheless, controversy surrounding non-attendance of individual senators and the fact that existing Senate rules provided no penalty for the most infrequent attendees depreciates Senate governance in the eyes of the public. To this should be added public displeasure at the Senate's response to criminal charges brought against its members. The Senate must design and implement codes or frameworks of conduct to guide itself in dealing with controversy. Thus procedural change would accompany clarification in the public mind of Senate practice and policy in matters involving dereliction (or charges of dereliction) of duty.

That being said, a caveat or warning is in order. The Senate is a small chamber where codified rules can be kept to a minimum. Indeed, they should be kept that way if the flexibility and informality of the chamber are to be retained. The fear of some senators, such as Michael Pitfield, is that if the Senate does not remain that way, it will become but a "pale image of the other place." The threat lies in not valuing the second chamber for its distinctiveness—particularly its comparative independence—but subjecting it to performance criteria drawn from the much more partisan House of Commons.[37] At the same time as Senator Pitfield voiced his fears, an echo of concern was heard at Westminster. A former long-time member of the British House of Commons, Sir Robert Rhodes James, addressed "the plague of reform" and its wake, an explosion of career politicians "anxious for preferment." In this situation, "the obsequious got on ... the critics ... did not." If the partisan lower house is to become the standard for conduct in the upper house, then only the executive stands to gain.[38]

Under the general heading of accountability fall policies on retirement and disability. Until 2001 the absence of policies permitting early retirement with improved pension programs, as exist for judges, has meant that senators who would favourably consider early retirement continued in office.[39] If the objective of improvement is to rejuvenate the Senate, to make it more responsive to public opinion, then early retirement is one alternative that rests with Parliament to implement. Senators should not be placed in the position that they must incur financial hardship if they vacate their seats early. On a related matter of finance, it has been official policy of the Reform and Canadian Alliance parties to favour an elected upper house and also to oppose election expense legislation that sought to control the cost of House of Commons elections. By any measure, the Senate is an economical institution: "During 1995–96, Senate operating expenses were 21% of those of the House of Commons. The Senate cost approximately $1.50 per Canadian annually, compared

with $7.13 for the House of Commons. The per capita costs for provincial legislatures ranged from $6.97 in British Columbia to $17.79 in Prince Edward Island."[40]

## CONCLUSION

Improvement of the Senate by non-constitutional means is both necessary and possible. In its role as a deliberative and representative institution, in its powers which include the veto, in its composition as an appointed body and in its accountability procedures, the Senate is a more substantial and responsible legislative chamber than its critics allow. That does not mean that there is no room for improvement, but this can be done by turning the existing Senate to good account rather than transforming it by introducing the elective or some other principle. There is no sovereign reform for the Senate of Canada. It needs emphasizing once again that the Senate is not an embalmed institution that the Fathers of Confederation would immediately recognize. In fact, Canada's upper chamber has been transformed out of all recognition from its nineteenth and earlier twentieth-century character. Largely, and in spite of the criticism reformers direct against the Senate, this has happened because of the use of the appointment power. It is because of the transformation in appointments that the Senate has a more diversified membership in terms of gender, language, and race than any comparable second chamber in the Anglo-American world or than the House of Commons.

With this composition the Senate is a national institution; and ... it is an institution with experience, memory and a long view of policy and events. Although the Canadian people no longer believe it is credible in its present form, yet it is these features that are the chamber's fundamental characteristics. Any improvements must reinforce these features at the same time as they complement the work of the House of Commons. It may not be impossible, but it is futile, to consider changes to the upper house that do not take account of its relationship to the lower house. In short, in the matter of improvements to the Senate by non-constitutional means, context is everything.

The Senate already does excellent committee work. Improvements would see greater use of special committees as well as of the Committee of the Whole. If the latter committee's meetings were televised, the Canadian people would have the rare opportunity of seeing a national institution at work. Through electronic communication, as now happens in non-televised committee work, such as study of the amendment to Newfoundland's Term 17, the Senate moves "closer to the people."[41] Its debates and hearings on questions like minority rights present rare occasions for citizens to be heard and listened to. There are a number of organizational and procedural matters with regard to committee meetings that need study—[such as] their timetabling, size, work allocation. These are matters that fall within the mandate of the Senate to determine. In other words, they are non-constitutional matters which, nonetheless, have the potential to energize and reconfigure public perception of the Senate as an operating institution.

A standing criticism of the Senate is its partisan complexion. However, the problem is not partisanism in and of itself but the monopoly of the selection process in the hands of the prime minister and the imbalance in party standings which results. A major improvement of the Senate would result if agreement were reached on its desired composition and if that agreement were accepted as a guide by the prime minister in the use of the prerogative of appointment. Two examples make the point. First, prime ministers should agree not to let the ranks of the opposition in the Senate fall below a certain floor, say one-third of the total. Mr Trudeau's actions two decades ago foreshadowed support for this norm, but they constituted no convention of the constitution.[42] Second, while exercise of the prerogative is discretionary, agreement on a limit on the amount of time taken to fill Senate vacancies would help counter the perception that appointments occur solely according to the prime minister's personal judgment. Finally, it is vital that senators have enough time to gain experience of the chamber and of its symbiotic relationship to the House of Commons. For that to happen, senators should have the experience of one full Parliament. It therefore seems desirable that the maximum age of senators at their appointment should be no more than seventy and, ideally, less than that.

A final general area where improvements are needed is in the standards and enforcement of senatorial behaviour. Matters such as conflict of interest,

non-attendance, travel expenses and complaints from the public or from within the chamber about improper behaviour, require a forum in which to be heard. One of the great difficulties the Senate faces is that, to many observers, it appears sequestered and deaf to criticism. Prime ministerial appointment and the Senate's style of self-government convey (perhaps erroneously) both a lack of attention and a disregard for public opinion. The House of Commons may be in as much need of improvement as the Senate, but at least the public thinks their members of Parliament represent a channel through which criticism can be made.

Events subsequent to the terrorist attacks on the United States in September 2001 may give cause to reconsider that view: John Reid, information commissioner and thus as officer of Parliament, looked to the Senate for protection (in the form of amendments) to the sweeping powers of Canada's anti-terrorist legislation (Bill C-36) passed through the Commons under closure. Otherwise, he said, "the independence of an officer of Parliament would be at risk if a government could ... terminate its investigations at will."[43] Nor was he alone. The Special Senate Committee that studied Bill C-36 broadened its concern to include the privacy commissioner and the potential interference in the conduct of his office posed by the legislation. However, two of the committee's recommended amendments, as set out in its final report—creation of a new "Officer of Parliament to monitor the exercise of powers under [the] Bill" and "the application of a true sunset clause to virtually all parts of the Bill"—were ignored by the House of Commons.[44] The government and Parliament's handling of this extraordinary matter requires the perspective of time before it can be judged. Still, from the perspective of this study, the assessment of one close observer deserves attention. In an essay entitled "Terrorism's Challenge to the Constitutional Order," Lorraine Weinrib reminds readers that "bicameral, multi-party examination of government policy ... can prevent and remedy abuses before they would come to the attention of the judiciary."[45]

The Senate may not be a representative body like its lower house partner in Parliament. Nor need it be, since parliamentary democracy does not require that a useful and legitimate second house of Parliament be elected. Nonetheless, it is a public body, and the public has lost confidence in its ability and commitment to rehabilitate itself in the absence of non-constitutional change of the order discussed in this chapter.

## NOTES

1  "[I]n 1991 … the Conservative Party which has traditionally championed the role of the House of Lords—chose simply to overrule the Second Chamber's carefully considered rejection of the War Crimes Act and proceed to enact the legislation without peers' consent under the terms of the Parliament Acts." Robert Blackburn, "The House of Lords," in Robert Blackburn and Raymond Plant, eds., *Constitutional Reform: The Labour Government's Constitutional and Reform Agenda* (London: Longman 1999), 22.

2  Ibid., p. 19.

3  See Angus Hawkins, "'Parliamentary Government' and Victorian Political Parties, c. 1830–c. 1880," *English Historical Review*, CIV (no. 412, July 1989), 638–69.

4  Blackburn, "The House of Lords," 24. See too Lord Ponsonby of Shulbrede, "The House of Lords: An Effective Restraint on the Executive?," *The Parliamentarian*, 69 (no. 2, April 1988), 83–5.

5  N.A. Robertson, "Memorandum from the Under-Secretary of State for External Affairs to Prime Minister," 25 September 1945, topic: "'Policy Towards Newfoundland' in Documents on Relations between Canada and Newfoundland" (2 Vols, compiled by Paul Bridle, Department of External Affairs, Ottawa: Supply and Services Canada, 1984), II, 170.

6  See Donald S. Lutz, "The Theory of Consent in the Early State Constitution," *Publius*, IX (1979) 11–42.

7  James Ross Hurley, *Amending Canada's Constitution: History, Processes, Problems and Prospects* (Ottawa: Supply and Services Canada, 1996), 99, and especially chapter 6.

8  Mark Audcent, *The Senate Veto: Opinion of the Law Clerk and Parliamentary Counsel* (Ottawa: Senate of Canada, 1999), 72.

9  This opinion was not shared by all senators: "We are a nominated body, and we are not subject to the conditions that render such legislation [The Independence of Parliament Act] necessary in the other House … These considerations do not apply to us." Senate Debates, 20 August 1891, 477. (A.C. Miller.)

10  Convention Debates (Sydney), 16 September 1897, 660.

11  Senator Lowell Murray, "Which Criticisms Are Founded?" in Serge Joyal, ed., *Protecting Canadian Democracy: The Senate You Never Knew* (Montreal: McGill-Queen's University Press, 2005), 137.

12  Great Britain, Parliamentary Debates, Commons, 14 April 1837. The Canada Debate, cols. 1261–2. A Benthamite, champion of the Great Reform Bill, and frequent author of pamphlets on electoral reform, Grote sat as MP from 1832–41. Author of a renowned history of Greece, Grote displayed a sharp sensitivity to the question of representing small, distinctive communities. Sir Leslie Stephen and Sir Sidney Lee, eds., *The Dictionary of National Biography* (Oxford University Press, London: Geoffrey Cumberlege, 1921–22), VIII, 727–36. Three-quarters of a century later, in 1918, the shoe was on the other foot: "[The Canadian Senate] rejected any analogy between [itself] and the British House of Lords which, after a constitutional crisis which included a threat of swamping, had its financial power eliminated in 1911." Henry Albinski, "The Canadian Senate: Politics and the Constitution," *American Political Science Review*, 57 (no. 2 June 1963), 382.

13  W.P. M. Kennedy, *Some Aspects of the Theories and Workings of Constitutional Law* (New York, 1932), 107, quoted in Albinski, "The Canadian Senate," 391.

14  For a sample of the argument, see Senate Debates, 26 March 1998, 1306 (Senator D. Nino).

15  John N. Turner, "The Senate of Canada. Political Conundrum," in Robert M. Clark, ed., *Canadian Issues: Essays in Honour of Henry F. Angus* (Vancouver: University of Toronto Press for University of British Columbia, 1961), 74.

16  "Parliament, Government and the Constitutional Balance" (Lecture delivered to Politeia, London, 1 April 1998), 9 and 12 (in typescript).

17  Reference re. Legislative Authority of Parliament in relation to the Upper House [1980] 1 SCR 54 at 10.

18  Marsh, "Opening up the Policy Process," in Marian Sawer and Sarah Miskin, eds., *Representation and Institutional Change: 50 Years of Proportional Representation* (Papers of Parliament, No. 34, Canberra: Department of the Senate, 1999), 195. Bagehot's discussion is in *The English Constitution* (Garden City: Dolphin Books, 1961), chapter 5.

19  Paul G. Thomas, "Comparing the Lawmaking Roles of the Senate and the House of Commons," in Joyal, ed., *Protecting Canadian Democracy: The Senate You Never Knew*, 218–9.

20  See *A Review of Senate Committee Studies* (Ottawa: Parliamentary Research Branch, Library of Parliament, December 1999).

21  *Ottawa Citizen*, 1 May 2000, A4; Donald J. Savoie, *Governing from the Centre: The Concentration of Power in Canadian Politics* (Toronto: University of Toronto Press, 1999), 260; Paul Howe and David Northrup, "Strengthening Canadian Democracy: The Views of Canadians," *Policy Matters* (Institute for Research on Public Policy), 1, no. 5 (July 2000), 52.

22  For a description of this period, see C.E.S. Franks, "Not Dead Yet, But Should It Be Resurrected? The Canadian Senate," in Samuel C. Patterson and Anthony Mughan, eds., *Senates: Bicameralism in the Contemporary World* (Columbus: Ohio State University Press, 1999), 120–61, and "The Canadian Senate in Modern Times," in Joyal, ed., *Protecting Canadian Democracy: The Senate You Never Knew*, 155ff.

23  In this context, two remarkable features about elections in the United States should be noted: the United States is (and has always been) a twoparty system when it comes to election returns; and for the last century and a half, it is the same two parties that compete for election nationally and in every state (the Non-Partisan League in North Dakota and the Farmer Labor Party in Minnesota were surrogates for mainstream parties). The explanation for this phenomenon lies in the electoral college requirement that, in order to keep the choice of president out of the hands of Congress, a candidate must receive more than 50 percent of the electoral college vote. That is possible only if there are two parties. The electoral college was not intended to work this way. At the time the framers of the constitution agreed upon indirect election of the president and vice president by state coteries of notables there were no political parties. Here is an example of the law of unintended consequences working with a vengeance. For details, see William H. Riker, 'The Senate and American Federalism,' 452–69.

24  Canadian experience with an elected upper chamber, the Legislative Council of the United Provinces of Upper and Lower Canada from 1854 to 1867, did not recommend its continuation in the new federation: "A Comparison of the votes polled in general elections and in the elections for councillors indicates that less interest was taken in the contests for council than for the assembly…. [The Council] still occupied a position of definite subordination to the popular assembly." See Duncan McArthur, "A Canadian Experiment

with an Elective Upper Chamber," *Transactions of the Royal Society of Canada* 24 (1930), Section II, 86–7.

25  Audcent, *The Senate Veto*, 11.

26  Senator Lowell Murray, "Which Criticisms are Founded?" in Joyal, ed., *Protecting Canadian Democracy: The Senate You Never Knew*, 144.

27  Jack Stilborn, *Comments on Twenty-Four Recent Senate Reform Proposals Provided for Analysis* (Parliamentary Research Branch, Library of Parliament July 1999), 6.

28  Marsh, "Opening the Policy Process," in *Representation and Institutional Change*, 194.

29  John Uhr, "Why We Chose Proportional Representation," in Marian Sawer and Sarah Miskin, eds., Paper for presentation to Representation and Institutional Change: A Conference to Mark 50 Years of Proportional Representation in the Senate, Papers of Parliament No. 34 (Canberra: Department of the Senate, 1999), 24.

30  See Harry Evans, Clerk of the Senate, "Accountability Versus Government Control: The Effect of Proportional Representation," in Brian Costar, ed., *Deadlock or Democracy?: The Future of the Senate* (Sydney: University of New South Wales Press, 2000), 48–57. "Upper houses," says Evans, "have only one hold over governments, their ability to withhold assent from government legislation" (p. 55). In reply, Senate critics say that the House of Representatives is the more "democratically legitimate House," because its constituencies are designed to reflect "one vote, one value." Senator Helen Coonan, "Safeguard or Handbrake on Democracy?" in ibid., 12–28.

31  *National Post*, 10 August 2000, A15.

32  Henry S. Albinski, "The Canadian Senate: Politics and the Constitution," *American Political Science Review*, 57 (no. 2, June 1963), 378–91.

33  This is not a new suggestion; see Senate Debates, 19 March 1998, 1235–8 and 26 March 1998, 1308 for commission schemes.

34  Constitution Unit, Weedon, "Wakeham in the Long Grass," 26.

35  For a study of the House of Commons policing itself and others within its precincts see Norman Ward, "Called to the Bar of the House of Commons," *Canadian Bar Review* (May 1957), 529–46. See, also, Ward, *The Canadian House of Commons: Representation* (Toronto: University of Toronto Press, 1950), especially chapter 5. Recent judicial confirmation is found in Ontario (Speaker of the Legislative Assembly) v. Ontario, 8 June 2001, C35182, Court of Appeal for Ontario.

36  According to one close observer of Parliament, "While such institutional loyalty runs high in the Senate, it does not appear to run as high in the House of Commons." Gary O'Brien, 'Legislative Folkways: The Example of the Canadian Parliament,' paper presented to the 105th Inter-Parliamentary Conference and meeting of the Association of Secretaries General, Havana, April 2001, 11.

37  Senate Debates, 9 June 1998, 1705.

38  See Robert Rhodes James, "Some Thoughts on Parliamentary Reform," in Jack Beatson, Christopher Forsyth and Ivan Hare, eds., *Constitutional Reform in the United Kingdom: Practice and Principles* (The University of Cambridge Centre for Public Law, Oxford: Hart Publishing, 1998), 112. See too Rt. Hon. Robert MacLennan, "The Taylor Reforms to Commons Business and Reform of the House of Lords," in ibid., 119–24.

39  As part of a new salary package for MPs and Senators, passed by Parliament in June 2001, members of the upper chamber will be able to go on long-term disability after age sixty-five, according to the *Globe and Mail*, "Senators who take advantage of the change would be replaced and could not return," 7 June 2001, A1/A4.

40  Senate of Canada, *The Senate Today* (Ottawa, 1997), 12.

41  The phrase is taken from Elaine K. Swift, *The Making of an American Senate: Reconstitutive Change in Congress, 1787-1841* (Ann Arbor: The University of Michigan Press, 1996), 117. It is Swift's thesis that "between 1809 and 1829 … the [US] Senate cultivated strong bonds with the people and distanced itself from state legislatures" (p. 140). Once aristocratic and British-like, it became a popular American institution.

42  The Wakeham Commission recommended that appointments to the new House of Lords should reflect party balance "as expressed in votes cast at the most recent general election." Report, 113. Writing in *Saturday Night* half a century ago, Senator A.W. Roebuck said much the same thing: "I would like to see representation of the political parties more evenly divided. No change in Constitution or Reform of the Senate is required in this connection. Appointments to the Senate are made by the government of the day … and the Administration is free to consider this as well as other factors involved." "Tinkering with Senate of Doubtful Value," *Saturday Night*, 27 February 1954, 8.

43  "Ramming terror bill into law could backfire," *Globe and Mail*, 29 November 2001, A14.

44  The Special Senate Committee deliberations constituted "pre-study" of the omnibus bill. As the chairman noted in an early meeting of the Committee, pre-study "has not … been a regular practice for a considerable period of time." Proceedings of the Special Senate Committee on Subject Matter of Bill C36, 17 October 2001, 1:12. The serious subject matter (but not the bill proper) and the urgency of quick action prompted the break from recent practice. The committee's First Report (1 November 2001) and its Second Report (10 December 2001) are available at http://www.parl.gc.ca/37/17parlbus/commbus/senate/com-e/sm36-e.

45  Lorraine Weinrib, "Terrorism's Challenge to the Constitutional Order," in Ronald J. Daniels, Patrick Macklem, and Kent Roach, eds., *The Security of Freedom: Essays on Canada's Anti-Terrorism Bill* (Toronto: University of Toronto Press, 2001), 105.

# 6

## Author's Introduction

The sharp and overwhelming reaction in Quebec to the demise of the Meech Lake Accord in 1990 and the resulting unprecedented extent of public support in Quebec for sovereignty led immediately to renewed demands for a major constitutional restructuring. At the same time there was considerable pressure from many other quarters in Canada for other sorts of constitutional change, such as Senate reform and Aboriginal self-government. Recognizing that Canada was facing a renewed and potentially disastrous constitutional crisis, a group of leading academic commentators from the fields of political science, economics, philosophy, and law produced early in 1991 a collection of papers exploring a range of possible solutions and the opportunities and risks associated with them under the title *Options for a New Canada*.

Among the papers included in that volume was "The Federative Superstructure" in Canada. The organization of effective federal systems involves not only the constitutional distribution of jurisdiction (legislative, executive, and financial) but, equally important, the organization and character of the shared superstructure that manages the common areas of jurisdiction. This article focuses on the latter and takes account of two basic considerations. The first concerns the form of common institutions required to manage the shared powers and responsibilities effectively. The second concerns the character of the common institutions required to ensure that the interests of the citizens in the different constituent units are effectively represented, protected, and harmonized in central policy-making. In considering these two objectives, the pros and cons of federal versus confederal and parliamentary versus non-parliamentary institutions are reviewed and possible reforms to the House of Commons, the Senate, regulatory agencies, intergovernmental instruments, and the Supreme Court are examined. Subsequently, in 1992, during the negotiations that led to the Charlottetown Agreement, extensive attention to these issues was included.

Source: Ronald L. Watts, "The Federative Superstructure," in *Options for a New Canada* (Kingston: Institute of Intergovernmental Relations, 1991), 309–36.

Ronald L. Watts

# The Federative Superstructure

## INTRODUCTION: THE ISSUES

### Federative Superstructures and the Current Canadian Impasse

The term "federative superstructure" is used in this paper to encompass the central institutions that are responsible for the areas of common jurisdiction and also the institutions that affect relations between the central government and the governments of the constituent units.

In considering Canada's constitutional options, the shape of the federative institutional structures is a particularly important issue for two reasons. First, the character of the federative superstructure needs to be related to the functions and powers assigned to

it. The current constitutional debate has focused upon the desires for a major revision in the jurisdiction to be assigned to the provinces and to the central superstructure. These issues will be significant regardless of whether the final form is one of a revised federalism, a looser confederation or sovereignty-association. Such proposals raise the further issue, however, of the form the common institutional superstructure should take if it is to manage its powers most effectively.

Second, if there is to be mutual agreement upon a resolution to the current constitutional impasse, account will have to be taken of the concerns not only of Quebec but of the provinces elsewhere. These other sources of dissatisfaction with the status quo, arise largely because of the perception in the western and Atlantic provinces that they have lacked influence in the operations of central government. Indeed, for the past decade and a half the major thrust of western sentiment has been for constitutional reforms that would provide for greater participation in and recognition by the national government. This has expressed itself in various proposals since 1976 for improved "intrastate federalism" (a term used by Canadian political scientists to refer to the provisions for regional representation in central institutions). The most recent example has been the advocacy of a Triple-E Senate in which the members would be elected, provinces would be represented equally, and the Senate would possess effective powers. Indeed the tentative but ill-fated agreement reached in support of the Meech Lake Accord in Ottawa on 9 June 1990 included as a major element a commitment to a process of significant Senate reform.

The solution is not a simple one, however. There is a problem in attempting to meet the concerns of the western and Atlantic provinces about their perceived insufficient input into policy-making within the central institutions. That is, that any increase in their representation, for instance by treating all provinces equally, means a commensurate reduction in the representation not only of Ontario but also of Quebec. In the latter province, the federal union tends to be regarded as primarily binational, uniting one province with its French-speaking majority with nine English-speaking provinces. Representation of Quebec as just one of ten equal provinces is feared as leading to a permanent under-representation of a major and historic Canadian minority that constitutes a quarter of the federal population. Indeed, some advocates of sovereignty-association or of a confederal system have argued for equality of status for Quebec and "English Canada" within a binational federative superstructure. Here there is a clash between equality of provinces and adequate representation of major minority communities as principles of representation in central institutions. Thus, the issue of the representation of the constituent units within the federative superstructure has to be resolved as part of any resolution to the current constitutional difficulties.

### The Role of Federative Superstructures

In the organization of all federal or confederal unions there are two fundamental sets of issues. The first set relates to the form and scope of the distribution of jurisdiction (legislative and executive powers and financial resources) between the governments of the constituent units and of the federative superstructure. The economic and political implications of possible revisions to the distribution of jurisdiction in Canada have been analyzed in the preceding chapters by Robin Boadway, Peter Meekison and David Milne.

A second and equally important set of issues arising in the design of any federal or confederal system relates to the organization and character of the shared superstructure that manages the common areas of jurisdiction. That is the aspect upon which this paper focuses. There are two basic considerations here. The first concerns the form of institutions that will enable them to manage those shared powers and responsibilities most effectively. The second concerns the arrangements required to ensure that the interests of the constituent units—of either the governments or the residents of these units—are channelled through and protected by the structures and operations of the common institutions. Significantly, in the original negotiations for the founding of the Canadian and also the American and Australian federations, it was not the constitutional distribution of powers that proved to be the most intractable issue in each of these federations, but rather conflicts among the constituent units about the composition, powers and structure of the central institutions, particularly the Senate. Because control of the common institutions and particularly the legislature is a major element in central power, the organization of those common institutions has proved a contentious issue during the creation of every federal or confederal union.

### FEDERAL VERSUS CONFEDERAL SUPERSTRUCTURES

#### The Relationship of Federative Institutions to the Form of Polity

Among the nine basic structural options ... were five federal variants, three confederal variants (of which sovereignty-association was one), and complete separation. The appropriate form for the common institutions will vary according to the choice made from among these basic options.

To begin with, the basic distinction between federal and confederal systems has implications for the type of federative institutions that are appropriate. The basic distinction between federal and confederal systems is that the former are communities of both individuals and constituent polities, while the latter are primarily communities of the constituent political units. In *federal* systems sovereignty is divided between two orders of government—strong constituent governments and a strong general government—each assigned specific sovereign powers by the constitution and each empowered to deal directly with the citizenry in the exercise of their powers. Consequently, the common government in parallel with the constituent governments is elected by and acts directly on the people. In *confederal* systems, which are primarily communities of political units, it is those units themselves that provide the basis for the representation in the federative institutions. Consequently confederal institutions are usually composed of delegates from the constituent governments and relate to the citizenry only indirectly through these constituent governments.

In federations the federative institutions have as a rule been structured to express their compound character as a community of both individuals and of constituent governments. Thus common to virtually all federal systems has been the adoption of a bicameral central legislature. These have usually involved representation according to population in one house, and the weighted or equal representation of constituent units in the other house. Members of the second house are either directly elected by the citizens, indirectly elected by the state legislatures, or appointed by the state governments. Most federations have paid particular attention, therefore, to facilitating the representation and accommodation of distinctive regional interests, both of smaller constituent territories and of significant linguistic or religious minorities, not only within the central legislature but also in the executive and other institutions.

In confederal systems, representation within the confederal superstructure has typically taken the form of indirectly elected representatives, selected by the legislatures or governments of the constituent units, with each of the constituent units equally represented. Sometimes, although not invariably, the representatives of each constituent unit are granted a veto in the most important matters. For example, under the American Articles of Confederation (written in 1777 and fully ratified in 1781), delegates to Congress were appointed annually, each state had one vote in Congress and each state could veto any constitutional amendment to the Articles. A majority of 9 out of 13 states was required for most decisions. Only minor matters were dealt with by majority rule. In the Swiss Confederation of 1815–47 each canton had one vote in the Diet, but the requirement of unanimity on important questions which had existed in previous Swiss confederations was replaced by the requirement of a three-quarters majority. Thus, in a confederal system, the operation of the central institutions is normally controlled to a large extent by the views of the constituent governments. This means that there is usually a heavy reliance as well upon a multitude of other collaborative institutions involving representatives of the constituent governments. Where each constituent government plays such an important role in the development of common policies, agreement has often been difficult to reach, particularly where any redistribution of resources has been involved.

There are also examples of hybrid political unions that involve elements of both federal and confederal unions. The European Community until recently has represented to a large extent an example of confederal central institutions, although the development of a directly elected European Parliament and the introduction of majority voting in some areas in the Council of Ministers represents a movement towards more typically federal institutions.

While one may identify in broad terms these basic alternative forms of union and the character of the federative superstructures appropriate to them, many variations are possible within each type of political union. These variations will themselves have implications for the appropriate design of the federative superstructure. For instance, in federations where there is asymmetry in the powers assigned to the constituent governments there will be implications for the number of representatives or the voting powers in the central institutions of representatives from those constituent units having greater jurisdictional autonomy. (This is discussed further in the section on the reform of the parliamentary federal institutions.) Federations composed of only two constituent units, for example,

Pakistan and Czechoslovakia, have invariably been marked by contention over the appropriate representation of the two units where there is a significant difference in their populations. Representation according to population would result in the larger unit dominating permanently. But parity of representation has in practice usually produced permanent deadlocks, an experience not unknown in Canadian history, as exemplified by the problems of the Province of Canada under the Act of Union, 1840–67. Even where there are more than two units the number and size of the constituent units can be a complicating factor in balancing the representation of citizens and of constituent units in the common institutions. Disparity of population and wealth raises problems of the appropriate weight that should be given to the representation of provinces as provinces within the federal institutions and raises questions as to whether some provinces should be grouped together or others divided. Canada provides one of the more extreme examples of the problem with provinces ranging from Ontario with 36.5 percent of the population and 41.4 percent of the Gross Domestic Product (GDP) to Prince Edward Island with 0.5 percent of the population and 0.3 percent of the GDP.[1] Furthermore, the 3 to 1 population imbalance in any proposal for a binational two-unit structure composed of Quebec and the rest-of-Canada would clearly create problems for the design of the federative superstructure.

There are variations among confederal systems as well. The complexity and range of common collaborative institutions has varied with the extensiveness of the common functions. These range from the complex array of the almost-federal common institutions and the judicial arm in the European Community to one rudimentary governing Council with no formal dispute settling mechanisms in the European Free Trade Area.

## The Effectiveness of Confederal and Federal Superstructures
Up to the eighteenth century, most political unions that were not unitary were confederal. Among examples were the Holy Roman Empire, the medieval city

leagues of Germany, Belgium and Italy, and the United Provinces of the Netherlands, all of which either disintegrated or were subsequently reconstituted as consolidated nation-states. In both the United States in 1789 and Switzerland in 1848 previously ineffective and troubled confederal institutions were replaced by federal institutions that since their establishment have proved more effective and stable. The German Confederation established in the nineteenth century eventually evolved by way of the quasi-federal Empire, the Weimar Republic and the Third Reich into the current Federal Republic of Germany. Thus, the historical record seems to suggest that confederal, by comparison with federal, superstructures have been less effective and ultimately prone to instability, either dissolving or evolving into federal or even unitary systems.

In the late twentieth century, there have been indications that the European Community with its functional arrangements presages a revival of confederal unions.[2] Unlike earlier confederations that focused particularly upon common action relating to foreign affairs and defence, the European Community has proceeded through creating common institutions for specific economic functions rather than through a general act of confederation. Thus the construction of common institutions has proceeded stage by stage in a way that has minimized the threat to the existing states who wish to retain independence in the areas not assigned to the common institutions. How far these confederal arrangements of the European Community represent permanent ones or merely way stations along the way to more fully federal ones, is difficult to assert conclusively. Pressures to change voting patterns in the Council, to make the Commission more accountable, and to reduce the "democratic deficit" in common policy-making by increasing the powers of the European Parliament all indicate efforts to modify the federative superstructure of the European Community in a direction that would be closer to those normally found in federations.

On the basis of historical and comparative experience, one would have to conclude that the prospects for effective and cohesive common policies

1  *1990 Corpus Almanac and Canadian Source Book* (Toronto: Corpus Information Services, 1990), pp. 17–237, 17–305.

2  Daniel Elazar, *Exploring Federalism* (Tuscaloosa: The University of Alabama Press, 1987), pp. 50–4.

are likely to be greater in a federal rather than a confederal form of federative superstructure. But even within the category of federal superstructures there is room for considerable variation, and it is to a consideration of such variations that the balance of this paper turns.

## PARLIAMENTARY AND NONPARLIAMENTARY FEDERAL SUPERSTRUCTURES

### The Current Canadian Form
The Canadian political structure created in 1867 was a hybrid combining the institutions of parliamentary responsible government following the British model with those of federalism derived from the American model. Canadians have attempted to combine a British inheritance with an American model, each based on fundamentally different premises and apparently contradictory to each other. The tradition of British parliamentary institutions is based on the notion that power should be tamed by concentrating it under the control of a majority of the electorate's representatives in a parliament where executive and legislative power is fused. The United States Constitution was based on a very different premise: that power is to be tamed by dispersing it among multiple separated decision-making centres, no one of which should dominate. The federal division of power between national and state governments and the separation within each government of executive, legislative and judicial power were seen as different expressions of the same fundamental principle of dispersed power and therefore inherently interrelated.

Until the past decade, the efficacy of the combination of parliamentary and federal institutions in Canada went largely unchallenged. In recent years, however, it has come increasingly into question. There have been three sets of concerns. The first has been the dominance of the cabinet and of party discipline constraining the expression of regional concerns within Parliament. The second has been the difficulty of creating an effective Senate as a house for the expression of regional views in a parliamentary system where the cabinet is responsible to the House of Commons. The third has been the inevitable corollary of "executive federalism" as the predominant

mode of intergovernmental relations when the executive dominates within each level of government. These three concerns have led to the expression of increasing dissatisfaction with the operation of the present form of Canadian parliamentary institutions.

### Three Alternative Models for the Form of Executive
Broadly speaking, executives in federations have followed one of three forms: the presidential, collegial and the parliamentary.

The classical example of the presidential system in a federation is that of the United States. There, in both the national and state governments the chief executive (i.e., the president or the governor) is directly elected for a fixed term and selects his or her own ministers without restriction.[3] Within the federal government authoritative decision-making power is dispersed among the President, the House of Representatives, the Senate and the Supreme Court. In this presidential-congressional system, the various institutions have been assigned powers that check and balance each other, and central decision-making requires compromises that take into account the variety of regional, local, and minority views.

Switzerland has incorporated into its federal system a collegial form of executive. It is based on the same fundamental principle of dispersed but interacting multiple centres of power as in the United States. Its adoption involved a conscious departure from the American example, however, in making the federal executive a collective one composed of a group of seven members rather than a single individual. The members of the Federal Council, while elected by the two houses in joint session from their membership, are then excluded from membership in either chamber and hold office for a fixed term of four years. The chairmanship rotates annually. The Swiss collegial executive with its fixed term and nonmembership in the legislative houses contrasts with the parliamentary form found in Canada. The collegial executive is not responsible to the legislature for its continuance in office and, as in the United States, the principle of the

---

3   Strictly speaking, the president is indirectly elected by an electoral college, but to all intents and purposes the system is now in practice one of direct election.

separation of powers between the various branches of government operates generally. This creates plural centres of political power interacting to balance and check each other in order to facilitate the resolution of conflicts through the emergence of widely accepted compromises.

Canada was the first, but a number of federations, notably Australia, Germany and a host of successful and unsuccessful new federations established in former British colonies since World War II, have attempted to incorporate parliamentary executives. By contrast with the United States and Switzerland the executives in the parliamentary systems are responsible to the legislature and stay in office only as long as they have the support of the legislature. This means that unless there is a stable majority in the legislature, an unstable executive is likely to result, a problem that does not arise in the American or Swiss arrangements. The requirement in a parliamentary system of a stable majority and the power of dissolution placed in the hands of the prime minister has invariably induced a pattern of strong party discipline and cabinet dominance not found in the American and Swiss legislatures.

## Implications for Federal Cohesion

The form of the common institutions has an important bearing upon the ability to encourage cohesion among the diverse groups within a federation. On the whole, the presidential system of the United States has in the past been relatively successful in resolving conflicts within the central institutions. The one significant exception was during the period leading up to the Civil War in the nineteenth century. Generally, however, the need to capture a single presidential post has induced political parties to seek compromises in order to win maximum electoral support through aggregating a wide range of political demands. Furthermore, the separation of powers and the multiple checks and balances have usually provided a strong inducement for compromises among the various elements involved in central policy-making. But this beneficial influence has been achieved at a price. The various checks and balances have often meant that a solution has taken a long time to emerge or that sometimes there have been serious deadlocks, especially when the President and Congress have been controlled by different political parties. The result is that some fundamental problems have remained unresolved, and this lack of resolution has in certain periods contributed to considerable stress.

The Swiss federal system, created in 1848 after the previous confederacy had disintegrated into civil war, has been renowned for the manner in which since then it has reconciled unity with religious and linguistic diversity. The Swiss collegial form of executive combines the stability of the fixed-term executive and the checks and balances found within the American system with the further benefits of explicit representation of different regional and minority groups in the federal executive.[4] There has also been a pattern of broad multiparty governing coalitions encompassing not just a bare majority but the support of virtually all the major parties and interest groups. The incentive for these broad governing coalitions has been the existence of the arrangement whereby any federal legislation challenged by a specified number of citizens must be put to a referendum. To forestall such challenges, the tendency has been to ensure widespread support by all major parties of any major legislation before it is enacted. This system would appear to have maximized the inducements for reconciling political conflicts and cleavages and to have minimized adversarial politics. But it too has its price. As in the United States, decision-making is protracted and there are sometimes difficulties in achieving urgent action, or even any action at all, in areas where diverse groups are disagreed. Nevertheless, the Swiss system has ensured the avoidance of action that would sharpen political cleavages.

The parliamentary federations, by contrast to those employing the other two forms of federal executive, have been able, by concentrating political power in cabinets possessing majority legislative support, to undertake more rapid and coherent decision-making and action. But this arrangement has exacted its own price. Within the central institutions, it has in effect placed complete political control over those functions assigned to the federal government in the party and government enjoying majority support in the lower

---

4  For example, the Federal Council is constitutionally limited to no more than one representative from any canton and the Roman Catholic and French minorities have always been represented in it.

house. This is exemplified by the resulting typical relative weakness of the second chambers in most parliamentary systems, contrasting with the relative strength of the American and Swiss federal second chambers. It is also exemplified by the dominance in parliamentary federations of cabinet initiative in legislation and of party discipline within both federal houses. The lack of institutional checks upon the majority in parliamentary federations has usually put the responsibility for reconciling regional and minority interests directly upon the internal organization and processes of the federal political parties themselves. Where the political parties have failed in this task, and particularly where a fragmented multiparty system or a primarily regional differentiation of federal parties has developed, parliamentary federations have been prone to instability. The clearest examples of this are Pakistan before 1958, Nigeria before 1966, and the current situation in India.

## Implications for Intergovernmental Relations

The form of executive established within a federal system has also had a fundamental impact upon the character of intergovernmental relations. The American and Swiss forms of presidential or collegial executive, incorporating within both levels of government the separation of powers and multiple centres of decision-making, have meant that not just the executive but all the various branches of both levels of government have been heavily involved in intergovernmental relations. By contrast, in parliamentary federations the central role of the cabinet within each level of government has made the cabinets the dominant focus for intergovernmental relations. This has resulted in what has come to be known as "executive federalism," a pattern of intergovernmental relations that is not unique to Canada but rather is typical of all parliamentary federations.[5] In these federations the major instrument for intergovernmental relations has been consultation and negotiation between the executives (and their officials) of the different governments. As a result, intergovernmental relations in parliamentary federations have often taken on a

character similar to international diplomacy, serving as a place for public confrontation as much as a place for resolving differences, and as a place where agreements are more likely to be possible only behind closed doors.

## Conclusion: The Choice among Alternatives

Given the current conditions and pressures for radical change what should be the preferred form of federal superstructure for Canada?

To most Canadians, the American presidential-congressional system is the best known alternative form for structuring federal institutions. But while that example has some advantages, it is for a number of reasons a dubious solution for Canada. As noted above it has some serious disadvantages with respect to effective decision-making. It lacks the advantages possessed by the Swiss federal institutions for providing regional and minority representation within the collegial executive and for reducing adversarial relations between parties. Furthermore, since parliamentary institutions are one of the major features distinguishing Canada from the United States, the removal of this distinctiveness would probably contribute significantly to a reduction in the sense that Canadians have of their own distinct identity in relation to the republic to the south. Finally, while there is increasing grumbling among Canadians about cabinet dominance, overly rigid party discipline and "executive federalism," there is no clear evidence that a majority of Canadians are at present clamouring for an American-style presidential-congressional system.

What then about conversion to a collegial form of fixed-term executive? The conversion itself would not be difficult to achieve. All that would be required is to institute in the constitution a fixed term for parliament and the cabinet. Since the life of the House of Commons would no longer depend upon the discretion of the prime minister or the continued cohesion of party support for the cabinet, party discipline and confrontation in Parliament would be substantially weakened. Furthermore, were the Canadian party system to evolve, as it may, into a multiparty system with no party having a majority, a fixed-term collegial executive would ensure governmental stability. It is noteworthy that in Australia after

---

5   Ronald L. Watts, *Executive Federalism: A Comparative Analysis*, Research Paper no.26 (Kingston: Institute of Intergovernmental Relations, Queen's University, 1989).

the constitutional crisis of 1975 there was for a time considerable pressure to move towards a fixed-term federal Parliament, although in the end that has not come to pass.[6] But so far, there has been little discussion in Canada about the advantages or disadvantages. In many respects a fixed-term Parliament and executive might best meet longer-run Canadian needs. Should public debate and education eventually make a fixed-term Parliament publicly acceptable, it could be adopted at that point simply by introducing a constitutional amendment specifying a fixed term between elections.

Nevertheless, at the present time Canadians do not appear to be prepared for a radical alteration of federal institutions towards a fixed-term federal legislature and collegial executive. Therefore, the more promising direction may be to consider modifications to the existing parliamentary institutions that would enable them to overcome some of their present difficulties and to work more effectively. It is worth noting that among the many proposals for constitutional reform that have been advanced in the past decade none have advocated abandoning parliamentary institutions. The proposals of the Quebec Liberal Party for a renewed Canadian federalism in the 1980 Beige Paper, for example, expressly called for preserving the parliamentary system and responsible government although some modifications were suggested.[7] The recent report of the Constitutional Committee of the Quebec Liberal Party (Allaire), of 28 January 1991, also envisages the continuation of Parliament, although it advocates abolition of the Senate. Nor have the proposals for reform of federal institutions emanating from western Canada envisaged abandoning parliamentary responsible government as such. They have focused instead upon reforms, particularly relating to the Senate. Since modification to the existing parliamentary institutions appears to be the preferable path, the next section will deal with such reforms.

## REFORM OF THE PARLIAMENTARY FEDERAL INSTITUTIONS

### The Working Executive

In the past two decades or so there have been two contradictory forces at work in the structure and operations of the Canadian federal executive.

First, there has been the movement towards organizational rationalization expressed in a variety of forms such as the "Program Planning and Budgeting System," "Management by Objectives," long-term budgetary projections, the vastly extended role of cabinet committees, the increased size and power of the Prime Minister's Office and of other central agencies, ministries of state, and the increased reliance on research.

Second, there has been a continued effort to ensure regional representativeness. At the time of Confederation it was recognized that, given the importance of the cabinet, the representation of regional interests in the cabinet would be more important than representation in the Senate. Every cabinet has been formed with a careful eye to the representation of regions as well as of other interests. Nevertheless from the point of view of less populous provinces, the cabinet as a device for accommodating regional concerns and demands is perceived to suffer from the same basic limitations as the House of Commons since both reflect majoritarian tendencies and decisions in caucus or the cabinet are made behind closed doors. Furthermore, it is often argued that the organizational rationalization of the cabinet that has occurred in recent decades has further limited the ability of the cabinet to accommodate and reconcile regional claims and demands. Nevertheless, some studies indicate that regional ministers have continued to play a significant role in the making of policy.[8] This has been a natural response to the regional pressures exerted upon the federal government in any federation.

The tension between the two impulses—the technocratic and the regional—will continue, and any effective federal executive will have to achieve a balance between the two. If that balance is to be attained,

---

6   George Winterton, *Parliament, the Executive and the Governor-General* (Melbourne: Melbourne University Press, 1983), pp. 158–60.

7   Constitutional Committee of the Quebec Liberal Party, *A New Canadian Federation* (Montreal, 1980), recommendations 5 and 7, pp. 39–40, 45–7.

8   Herman Bakvis, "Regional Politics and Policy in the Mulroney Cabinet 1984–88: Towards a Theory of the Regional Minister System in Canada," *Canadian Public Policy*, vol. 15, no. 2, June 1989, pp. 121–34.

conscious efforts will need to be made to overcome the actual and perceived unresponsiveness of federal officialdom to the provinces and regions, and to ensure a more effective input of regional concerns into central executive and administrative decision-making. A number of steps might be considered for countering the general disposition of the structure and operation of the federal government to down-play values and interests that are spatially delimited. These include the structuring of central agencies so as to provide more regional information upon which the cabinet and the prime minister can base policy decisions, the decentralization of federal departments and agencies incorporating a regional dimension into departmental planning and policy development, and arrangements for ensuring that those reaching senior executive positions in the public service have served both in the field and in the national capital region.[9] Most such reforms would not require formal constitutional amendments to be achieved.

## The Symbolic Executive

Canada from its inception as a federation has been a constitutional monarchy, a feature that distinguishes it from the republic to the south. The question of the monarchy's continued utility as a unifying symbol at a time when Canadians of British stock have become a minority needs to be considered. The meaningfulness of the symbolic executive would seem to be limited not only for those in Quebec but for the many Canadians elsewhere whose roots lie in continental Europe, Asia or Africa. Is the monarchy as a symbol of unity now more divisive than unifying?

Raising the issue of abolishing the monarchy, however, is itself likely to stir considerable controversy, especially among the minority who find in it significant symbolic value. Such opposition might well be counter-productive to the effort to find grounds for more common agreement. Since the issue of the monarchy is not at the moment one of explicit contention, it may be more fruitful to concentrate upon those features of the federal institutions where there is overt contention rather than to create yet another.

Calls for reform of the House of Commons to improve its representativeness have generally proceeded from two main perspectives. The first asserts that the influence of the political parties is too strong and that members of Parliament (MPs) unduly subordinate the interests of the regions, provinces and localities from which they come to party interests. Consequently, there have been numerous suggestions that party cohesion should be weakened. The second perspective argues that there is a need to ensure that representation of the parties in the House of Commons reflects more accurately the degree of support for them in each province. In certain periods major parties have been shut out of major regions of the country, even though they draw a significant proportion of the popular vote in those regions. The deficiency can be remedied, it is claimed, by changes to the electoral system. The following sections deal with these two issues.

*Pervasiveness of party.* Many Canadian exponents of the enhanced independence of MPs are explicitly or implicitly thinking in terms of the independence from party enjoyed by American legislators. Such independence of legislators is possible within the American and Swiss systems of the separation of powers in which the tenure of the executive does not depend on the continuing support of legislative majorities. However, these models have little relevance so long as we maintain the parliamentary system. All parliamentary systems with responsible cabinets have been marked by strong party discipline and cohesion.

Nevertheless, the degree of party cohesion in the contemporary Canadian House of Commons is high even by comparison with other parliamentary systems such as Britain. Studies have suggested that this is attributable more to self-imposed norms than to the sanctions at the disposal of the party leaders and also to the active role that party caucuses have assumed since the late 1960s. While it was hoped that the major overhaul of the committee system in 1968–69 would give MPs increased opportunity to act independently of their respective parties, in practice partisanship has permeated the committees just as it has the other dimensions of parliamentary life. As long as the cabinet is responsible to the House of Commons, the Commons will continue to act in a relatively cohesive way, despite the wishes of many outside the House

---

9   See, for instance, Royal Commission on the Economic Union and Development Prospects for Canada, Report, vol. 3 (Ottawa: Minister of Supply and Services, Canada, 1985), pp. 92–5, 464–5.

that backbench MPs should act otherwise. Moreover, it should not be overlooked that the requirement of party cohesion is one of the processes for reconciling differences and finding implementing solutions where there is a diversity of opinion represented within the party. One of the problems, however, is that in parliamentary systems these compromises are worked out in party caucuses behind closed doors. In the age of heightened television and media attention a key problem with caucus secrecy and party discipline is that opportunity is not provided for federal parliamentarians to be seen to be representing regional or other diverse interests. Nevertheless, the degree of overt party voting might be moderated if it were more generally recognized by the House of Commons and by the public that only defeats on a specific vote of confidence would require the government to resign or the prime minister to request a dissolution. The posturing and media attention that accompanies every case where a private MP of the governing party fails to vote with the government might then be reduced.

*Changes in the electoral system.* The second major set of possible reforms involving the House of Commons relates to the electoral system. Compared to many other countries Canadians have been remarkably conservative about their federal electoral system. During the 1970s and 1980s, elections to the House of Commons which over-represented regional majority votes and returned virtually no Liberals from the west and almost no Progressive Conservatives from Quebec led many students of Canadian politics to see the electoral system itself as a cause of disunity. As a result in recent years a number of specific proposals for electoral reform have been advanced. Their major impulse has been to bring the distribution of seats won by each party in the various provinces more in line with the proportion of the popular vote cast for each. Many of them would involve some form or element of proportional representation.

Electoral reformers have tended to overestimate the extent to which the electoral system explains the behaviour of federal parties towards the provinces and regions. Nevertheless, there is good reason to attempt to reduce the distorting effect of the current electoral system and its impact upon party behaviour. The major objectives of electoral reform should be to

make the House of Commons more effectively representative and give political parties more incentives than they now have to build support in areas where they are weak. Such reforms might be expected also to enhance representation of women and other groups now relatively under-represented in the Commons. Some variant of proportional representation such as the use of the single transferable vote in multimember urban ridings and the alternative vote procedure in other areas may be worth considering.[10] While electoral reform is no panacea, it may contribute towards a more representative House of Commons and hence improve its legitimacy as a focal point for federal policy-making. Under existing constitutional provisions electoral reform could be achieved by ordinary legislation and would not require a formal constitutional amendment.

## The Senate

The federal institution that has received the most attention during the past two decades as a candidate for reform has been the Senate.[11] This is hardly surprising since among federations Canada does less than any other to use the second chamber as a body for ensuring effective participation for distinctive regional and minority interests in the formation of federal policies and decisions. Nearly all other federations have found a bicameral central legislature (i.e., with two houses) essential. The few rare exceptions have been cases where the constituent units have been given equal representation in a unicameral legislature. While from time to time, and most recently in the Allaire report of the Quebec Liberal Party, abolition of the Senate without any replacement has been advocated in Canada, and that would seem to fly in the face of federal experience elsewhere.

*Federal second chambers elsewhere.* These have taken a variety of forms. In terms of method of appointment members may be: (1) directly elected, as is now the case in the United States, Switzerland and Australia;

10  For an elaboration of such a proposal see Donald Smiley and Ronald L. Watts, *Intrastate Federalism in Canada* (Toronto: University of Toronto Press, 1985), pp. 113–5.

11  For a summary of many of the proposals, see, Attorney General of Ontario, *Rethinking the Senate: A Discussion Paper* (Toronto, 1990), pp. 51–101.

(2) indirectly elected (i.e., chosen by state legislatures), as was originally the case in the United States and Switzerland and is now the case for most second chamber members in India and Malaysia (a small proportion in the former and a substantial number in the latter are appointed by the central government to represent particular minorities or interests); or (3) appointed as delegates of the state governments as in the German Bundesrat. In Switzerland the method of selection is left to each canton to decide.

In terms of composition, constituent units may be: (1) equally represented, as in the United States, Australia and Malaysia; (2) represented by categories, as in Switzerland (where 20 cantons classed as full cantons have two seats each and six cantons classed as half cantons have one seat each); or (3) based on some formula related to population, but giving additional weighting to smaller states, as in Germany and India.

In terms of formal powers relative to the first chambers, those in the United States and Switzerland have formally equal powers, but those in all the parliamentary federations, where the cabinet is responsible to the first house, have more limited formal powers. Nevertheless, the powers of the Australian Senate and the German Bundesrat are not inconsiderable. The Australian Senate can in some circumstances force a government to face the electorate through a "double dissolution" (i.e., calling an election for both the Senate and the lower house, the House of Representatives). The German Bundesrat possesses an absolute veto over all federal legislation in the extensive areas of concurrent jurisdiction.

*Canadian proposals for a "house of the provinces."* In Canada the late 1970s saw many proposals for establishing a body composed of persons appointed by and taking their instructions from the provincial governments on the lines of the German Bundesrat.[12] Canadian critics of these proposals have feared that such a "house of the provinces" might operate as

a "house of obstruction" preventing effective and cohesive federal action. Such critics have overlooked the integrative dynamics that in practice have been induced by the Bundesrat. This occurs in intergovernmental relations because Bundesrat decisions do not require unanimity, thus reducing the leverage of hold-out states. The Bundesrat also has an integrative influence on federal-state party relations because state election results affect the ability of a governing federal party to achieve its legislative objectives in the Bundesrat. This has made the governing parties more sensitive to state interests. A more valid criticism is to point out that the significant role of the Bundesrat derives from the particular form which the distribution of jurisdiction between the federal and state governments takes in Germany. The constitution requires administration by the states for a large area of federal legislation. This makes the consent of a majority of the states (through the Bundesrat) for such legislation a necessary vehicle for coordination. In Canada where most executive powers are assigned to the same government as that having legislative jurisdiction the context is different.

*Canadian proposals for an elected Senate.* More recently, during the past decade, attention has shifted to proposals for a Senate whose members would be directly elected by the Canadian people.[13] The overwhelming popular preference for this alternative derives from its clearly democratic appearance. A major focus of interest in western Canada, arising out of a continued sense of lack of influence in Ottawa, has been the advocacy of a Triple-E Senate, elected directly, equal in representation from every province, and effective in power. While some have questioned the appropriateness of such a Senate for Canada because of its parliamentary institutions, the Australian Senate which is in every respect a Triple-E Senate shows that such a

---

12  Among such proposals were those of British Columbia (1978), the Ontario Advisory Committee on Confederation (1978), the Progressive Conservative Party of Canada (1978), the Canada West Foundation (1978), the Canadian Bar Association (1978), the Task Force on Canadian Unity (Pepin-Robarts) (1979), the Quebec Liberal Party (Beige Paper) (1980), and the Government of Alberta (1982).

13  Among such proposals have been those of the Canada West Foundation (1981), the Minister of Justice of the Government of Canada (1983), the Special Joint Committee of the Senate and the House of Commons on Senate Reform (1984), the Royal Commission on the Economic Union and Development Prospects for Canada (Macdonald) (1985), the Alberta Special Select Committee on Upper House Reform (1985), the Government of Newfoundland and Labrador (1989), Gordon Robertson in *A House Divided* (1989), and the First Ministers' Meeting on the Constitution, Final Communique, 9 June 1990.

body is not incompatible with a system of parliamentary responsible government. The tentative June 1990 constitutional agreement arrived at by the first ministers in Ottawa when they were attempting to save the Meech Lake Accord set out a process involving a commission of federal, provincial and territorial representatives to prepare specific proposals for Senate reform. The commission was to give effect to the following objectives:

- The Senate should be elected.
- The Senate should provide for more equitable representation of the less populous provinces and territories.
- The Senate should have effective powers to ensure the interests of residents of the less populous provinces and territories figure more prominently in national decision-making, reflect Canadian duality and strengthen the Government of Canada's capacity to govern on behalf of all citizens, while preserving the principle of responsibility of the Government to the House of Commons.

That agreement died with the demise of the Meech Lake Accord, but it indicates the direction in which agreement upon Senate reform might be possible to achieve.

The general principle of a Senate directly elected by the people appears to be popular among the general public. It has two particular attractions. First, it suggests a way of specifically representing the interests of the provincial electorates within the federal institutions while bypassing the provincial governments. Second, a directly elected Senate employing a method of proportional representation (as occurs in Australia) would provide another way of correcting electoral distortions in Ottawa.

Equal representation of all provinces has been a major element in western Canadian proposals for Senate reform. This is understandable given the present representation by under-representation of the four western provinces. Not only do each of them have fewer senators than the less populous provinces of Nova Scotia and New Brunswick, but the two largest provinces (Ontario and Quebec) are actually somewhat more favourably represented in relation to their population than British Columbia and Alberta. This is clearly a ridiculous anomaly with no justification. But the proposal for equal representation of provinces, often advocated as the solution, in turn raises particular difficulties in the Canadian context. The function of federal second chambers as a check on majoritarian interests is not simply to favour the representation of smaller provinces but also of non-majoritarian minority interests in general. In the Canadian case this presents a particular problem: equal representation for all provincial units would require reducing the representation of the one province whose majority is French-speaking from its current 23 percent to 10 percent. This clearly violates the principle of reinforcing the representation of significant federal minorities.

To balance these two pressures the distribution of seats in the Senate will have to be a pragmatic one, weighted to favour the less populous provinces and territories, but also taking account of the special needs for both adequate francophone and aboriginal representation while at the same time correcting the present anomalies. This requirement was recognized in the communique of the First Ministers' Meeting on 9 June 1990 identifying the objectives of a "more equitable" representation of the less populous provinces and territories and of the need to "reflect Canadian duality." A number of proposals have attempted to make major corrections in regional representation along these lines [...] An alternative or supplementary approach would be to adopt rules of procedure requiring special majorities or the concurrence of Quebec representatives or of francophone representatives on legislation identified as being in areas of their special interest.

A number of other federations, notably India and Malaysia, have reserved a number of places in the federal second chamber for members nominated to represent special minority interests. Such an approach might be incorporated in a reformed Canadian Senate to guarantee a minimum number of seats to representatives of the aboriginal peoples. A system of election rather than nomination for these reserved seats would be preferable, however.

A persuasive case can be made that a popularly elected Senate should have effective powers to influence and even to obstruct governments backed by House of Commons majorities. Some of the hesitation about establishing a strong elected Senate appears to have arisen from a fear that such a Senate would undermine the principle of responsible cabinet government and from Canadian interpretations of the Australian constitutional crisis of 1975. Closer analysis of Australian experience suggests, however, that while an effective Senate at the federal level will inevitably operate in tension with cabinet government, the existence of a powerful and autonomous upper house in the federal institutions helps in practice to ensure that the values implicit in federalism are pervasive in the system.[14]

Senate reform would be an important element in improving the effectiveness of our federal institutions. At the same time Canadians should be wary of expecting too much from Senate reform by itself. It will be no panacea. It is only one element in a total solution. As long as a Senate operates within a system of parliamentary responsible government, there will be limits to its impact. The Australian example shows that an effective elected Senate can operate within a system of parliamentary institutions. But that experience also indicates that it will not diminish the tendency to "executive federalism" as the primary mode of intergovernmental relations within parliamentary federations, nor diminish the predominance of party coherence. To press for a Senate isolated from party ties is to confine the Senate to virtual irrelevance in a parliamentary system where parties are a fundamental part of the political process. The primary contribution of an effective elected Senate would be to sensitize the federal parties to the need to accommodate provincial and minority concerns. As Campbell Sharman has put it: effective bicameralism "is the ally of federalism; both imply preference for incremental rather than radical change, for negotiated rather than coerced solutions, and for responsiveness to a range of political preferences rather than the artificial simplicity of dichotomous choice."[15]

## Federal Institutions in an Asymmetrical Federation

There remains the issue of the arrangements and procedures within the federal institutions that might be required in a federation with a significant asymmetry in the distribution of powers—i.e., one providing substantially greater legislative and executive autonomy for one or more provinces. Since an element of asymmetry is one of the possible options for a revised Canadian federation, the implications for the operation of the federal institutions must be considered. The basic issue raised in the earlier chapters by Alan Cairns and David Milne is whether representatives from provinces with more autonomy should vote in federal institutions on those subjects where their province has autonomy.

In other federations where asymmetry in the distribution of powers has not been substantial or has resulted from incremental delegations of authority over time, no such adjustments have been made. Indeed, while the *Constitution Act, 1867,* included some asymmetrical features, no corresponding adjustment of provincial representation in federal institutions was envisaged. Nor did the asymmetry relating to the separation of the Canada and Quebec Pension Plans in the 1960s lead to any change in the role of Quebec MPs. The issue appears to come to the fore only where the degree of asymmetry is substantial.

*Reduction of representation in federal institutions.* Other federations such as India, Pakistan, and Germany (in the arrangements for German reunification) have involved a considerable measure of jurisdictional asymmetry without limiting the participation of the representatives of the more autonomous units deliberations within the federal institutions. However, the Federation of Malaysia after the accession of the Borneo states and Singapore in 1963, and the Federation of Rhodesia and Nyasaland 1953–63, provide significant examinations of federations where some states with more autonomy were given reduced representation in the central legislature.[16] In the case of Singapore, to balance greater autonomy,

---

14  Campbell Sharman, "Second Chambers," in H. Bakvis and W.H. Chandler (eds.), *Federalism and the Role of the State* (Toronto: University of Toronto Press, 1987), p. 96.

15  Ibid., p. 96.

16  Ronald L. Watts, Multicultural Societies and Federalism, Study no. 8 for the Royal Commission on Bilingualism and Biculturalism (Ottawa: Information Canada, 1970), pp. 47–50.

the proportion of its representation in the central legislation was reduced (to 9 percent although its population was 17 percent of the federal total) and the federal franchise of Singapore citizens outside Singapore was restricted. The consequent resentment in Singapore, and the annoyance of the federal governing party at the failure of the different governing party in Singapore to confine its activities to its own state, resulted in mounting tension that culminated in the complete separation of Singapore only two years after it joined the federation. By contrast, when the two Borneo states, Sarawak and Sabah, joined the Malaysian Federation at the same time as Singapore, and were also granted substantially greater autonomy than the other states in the federation, they did not have the same disabilities in terms of representation applied them. They have continued to the present as member states of the Malaysian federation. The experience of Singapore and also of the Federation of Rhodesia and Nyasaland which lasted for only a decade suggests that the reduction in the number of representatives in the federal legislature for a more autonomous province does not work well as a solution. It is likely to foster an increased sense that the citizens of that province are second-class citizens in the federation and lead to federal instability and perhaps disintegration in the long run.

*Special voting rules and procedures.* An alternative adjustment to reducing the presentation of the more autonomous provinces in the federal legislature, is to adopt voting rules and procedures whereby these representatives would abstain in votes on matters over which their province has autonomous jurisdiction. This might involve some complexity and difficulties in deciding when these representatives should not vote, but procedural rules should not be possible to devise. The German Bundesrat has an absolute veto over matters that are under concurrent jurisdiction and only a suspensive veto over matters that are under exclusive federal jurisdiction. The line between the two has not always been easy to draw, but it has been workable. Given that experience, it would be no more difficult to define procedures for when representatives of a more autonomous province should abstain in voting within the federal legislate. Such an arrangement would certainly be a more logical solution than

reducing the proportionate representation of the more autonomous provinces within the federal institutions, thereby also reducing their weight in federal policy-making in those areas that do affect them.

## OTHER FEDERATIVE INSTITUTIONS

### Regulatory Agencies

While it is appropriate to avoid as far as possible unnecessary and costly duplication in the jurisdiction of federal and provincial governments, in practice no federal system has been able to avoid overlaps. One area where this situation has a particular significance is in the operation of major regulatory agencies. Concern is often expressed that such bodies established by the federal government are insensitive to the needs and concerns of the constituent governments and the different groups and regions of Canada. Consequently, it has been argued that "the constitution should state the principle that federal bodies charged with the responsibilities in key sectors of Canadian affairs and those of a political nature must reflect the duality and regional character of Canada."[17] One approach to realizing this objective is to provide provincial governments with a role in appointments to major regulatory agencies including the Bank of Canada. Indeed, the Constitutional Committee of the Quebec Liberal Party (Allaire) has argued for reform of the Bank of Canada to ensure regional representation, citing the Federal Reserve of the United States as an example.[18]

The Macdonald Commission recommended that regional representation should receive consideration in nominations to the boards of crown corporations and regulatory agencies in order to enhance their political legitimacy and improve their sensitivity to regional concerns. It went on to suggest that a reformed elected Senate with strengthened regional representation would be the appropriate body to scrutinize through a committee all appointments of the heads of crown corporations and all the members of major regulatory agencies.[19] Such a public process of

---

17  *A New Canadian Federation*, recommendation 8.2, p. 50.
18  Constitutional Committee of the Quebec Liberal Party, *A Quebec Free to Choose: Report of the Constitutional Committee* (Montreal: Quebec Liberal Party, 1991), pp. 42 and 62.
19  *Report*, vol. 3, pp. 464–5.

appointment would both promote greater public confidence in the representative character of such bodies and encourage these bodies to be more sensitive to regional considerations in conducting their operations and coming to decisions

## Collaborative Institutions

In confederal systems, the common institutions of the federative superstructure used to be primarily collaborative in form, being composed of delegates of the constituent governments and dealing primarily with areas for collaborative action, but even in federations, where common federal institutions directly representing and acting upon the citizens are established, there is a need for institutions facilitating collaboration between the federal and provincial and among provincial governments. The notion of a strictly dual federal polity of two levels of government operating independently of each other has in all federations proved both impossible and undesirable in practice. While it is appropriate to avoid as far as possible unnecessary and costly duplication in the responsibility of governments within a federation, overlaps can never be completely avoided. All federations have found it necessary, therefore, to establish institutions and processes to facilitate consultation, cooperation, coordination and harmonization, and to moderate intergovernmental conflict in those areas where activities of their governments interpenetrate.

While greater intergovernmental harmonization is desirable, the diversity of action inherent in a federal system also makes a positive contribution to society, balance must be found, therefore, between encouraging institutional diversity competition and establishing institutions and procedures producing federal provincial coordination. Furthermore, in parliamentary federations, where "executive federalism" is a logical dynamic resulting from the marriage of federal and parliamentary institutions and is, therefore, unavoidable, there is a need to harness "executive federalism" in order to make it more effective and accountable.

*Informal and formal collaborative institutions.* Most often in federations the intergovernmental collaborative bodies and procedures have not been specified in the constitutions, but have been established simply by agreement as the need arose. This has the

advantage of enabling flexible and pragmatic arrangements, nevertheless, in some federations intergovernmental institutions have actually been specified in the constitutions. In some of these cases there are special voting rules that do not necessarily require unanimity, and in some these bodies have powers to make decisions binding upon the participating governments, long such examples are the Australian Loans Council, the German Bundesrat which shapes the character of intergovernmental relations in that federation, in a variety of councils and commissions established in the newer parliamentary federations in the Commonwealth.

*Canadian proposals.* In Canada, by contrast with the examples referred to above, there has been some resistance to constitutionalizing such arrangements in fear that they might encroach upon the sovereignty of Parliament and of the provincial legislatures. Nevertheless, there is a need to improve the operation of our intergovernmental collaborative institutions. The Quebec Liberal Party's Beige Paper of 1980 advanced an interesting proposal in this respect for an "intergovernmental institution which will frame the interdependence of the two orders of government."[20] The proposed Federal Council would have involved weighted representation of different provincial governments and territories and a voting procedure not requiring unanimity. The Federal Council would have had advisory powers in certain areas, and powers of ratification in others. There would have been a "Dualist Committee" with advisory or ratification powers in some other specified areas relating to the maintenance of cultural duality. While envisaged as a body supplementing a unicameral federal parliament, a revised adaptation of this proposal could serve as a supplement to a bicameral federal parliament even with a reformed Senate.

A less radical approach directed at making "executive federalism" more effective was that of the Macdonald Commission in 1985.[21] While emphasizing the value of intergovernmental diversity and competition, it proposed (1) that the First Ministers' Conference be formally established in the constitution

20  *A New Canadian Federation*, recommendation 9, pp. 51–6.
21  *Report*, vol. 3, pp. 473–5.

with the requirement that it meet at least once a year; (2) that the First Ministers' Conference appoint a network of Councils of Ministers to serve in major functional policy areas and particularly in the fields of finance, economic development and social policy, and (3) that to ensure that governments are held accountable for their conduct of intergovernmental affairs, Parliament and the provincial legislatures should establish permanent standing committees responsible for intergovernmental relations. These proposals could all be implemented without having to resort to formal constitutional amendments.

The Allaire report of the Quebec Liberal Party, after defining a restricted list in which Parliament would share authority with Quebec and other provinces, suggests that "as far as the coordinating functions are concerned, the decisions of Parliament will have to be ratified by the Quebec National Assembly and the assemblies of all the other legislatures (provincial or regional) that have adopted the same approach as Quebec."[22] It goes on to suggest that specific targets would be set to limit severely the power of central institutions to contract debts. These proposals are only sketched out and, therefore, the full implications are not clear. They do seem to imply that any coordination in areas of shared jurisdiction would require the formal consent of the legislatures of the provinces involved rather than mere intergovernmental agreement implying a primarily confederal rather than a federal arrangement. The reference to limits on the contracting of debts might require a body like the Australian Loans Council. That body coordinates public borrowing but makes decisions binding on both federal and state governments.

## Adjudicative Bodies: The Supreme Court

Adjudicative institutions for resolving jurisdictional disputes between governments in federations have most often taken the form of a Supreme Court, examples elsewhere are the United States, Australia, India, and Malaysia. An alternative is the establishment of a specialized constitutional court dealing solely with constitutional matters, as in Germany. In Switzerland, cantonal legislation is subject to judicial review by the Federal Tribunal, but adjudication of the validity of federal legislation involves the process of the legislative referendum.

In the past there have been few proposals for Canada to abandon employing Supreme Court as the ultimate constitutional adjudicative body. But if the Supreme Court is to be the ultimate umpire in disputes between governments, s anomalous that its status is not entrenched in the constitution and that appointments to it are solely in the hands of only one of the governments: the federal government.

*Arrangements in other federations.* In most federations the status of the Supreme Court, Constitutional Court or Federal Tribunal is entrenched in the institution. Furthermore, appointments are not made simply by the federal executive but involve the states (or their representatives) through one of the following: (a) the requirement of Senate ratification, as in the United States; appointment of half the members by the state governments, as in effect in Germany through the Bundesrat; or (c) the requirement of prior consultation either with state governments or chief justices of the state high courts as occurs in Australia, Malaysia, and India.

*Canadian proposals.* Various proposals relating to the procedure for appointments to the Supreme Court have been advanced in Canada such as the institutional requirement of mandatory consultation with the provinces ratification by a reformed Senate, ratification of federal appointments by proves, nomination by federal-provincial nominating commissions, or selection an Appointing Council composed of both federal and provincial appointees, a Meech Lake Accord proposed a system of federal government appointments from lists of provincial nominations. If the Supreme Court is to continue the ultimate constitutional adjudicator, there still remains, as a result of the promise of the Meech Lake Accord, the need to entrench in the constitution the status of the Supreme Court as the ultimate adjudicative body. This should prelude a procedure for appointments that does not leave them solely at the discretion of one level of government. Of the various appointment procedures that have been advocated, two would seem to recommend themselves most for consideration. One would be

---

22 Constitutional Committee of the Quebec Liberal Party, *A Quebec Free to Choose,* p. 41.

mandatory consultation of the provinces by the federal government prior to it making nominations that would have to be ratified by a reformed Senate. The other would be appointments by an independent Appointing Council, half of whose members would be appointed by the federal government and half by the provincial governments.[23]

The Allaire report of the Quebec Liberal Party proposes a special "common tribunal to ensure compliance with the Constitution and enforcement of laws under the new central state."[24] It would not act as a court of appeal for Quebec courts and decisions of Quebec superior courts would no longer be subject to appeal to the Supreme Court of Canada. Under this proposal the Supreme Court of Canada would no longer be the ultimate constitutional adjudicative body, that function being performed by the new common tribunal. The details are not spelled out and so it is not clear whether this tribunal would be limited to ruling on the constitutionality of central and not provincial actions, or whether it would be a specialized constitutional court ruling on all constitutional matters along the lines of that in Germany. In any case the elimination of appeals from the Quebec courts would contrast with the stronger judicial authority of the European Court. The proposal will clearly need clarification.

## CONCLUSIONS

The effectiveness and stability of any future federal or confederal union in Canada will depend not only upon the way in which jurisdiction is distributed between the common and constituent governments but also upon the federative superstructure that is established. Historically the predominantly collaborative form of federative superstructure that typifies confederal systems has been less effective than those normally associated with federal systems. But even among federations there is considerable variety in the form that the central institutions may take. While a fixed-term collegial executive and legislature has much to recommend it, there appears to be continued general support in Canada for parliamentary institutions. Consequently, the appropriate path would seem to be to retain those parliamentary institutions, but to reform them substantially to improve their effectiveness in managing the responsibilities assigned to the federal government and to provide greater confidence in their representativeness in terms of provincial interests, of Canadian duality and of significant minorities including the aboriginal peoples.

A number of reforms that do not require formal constitutional amendment could be made to achieve a better balance between the technocratic and regional impulses within the executive and administration. In the case of the House of Commons there is a need to reduce the pervasiveness of party cohesion. This could be done through a more general recognition by the House of Commons and the public that only defeats on a specific vote of confidence would require the government to resign or the prime minister to request a dissolution. To improve the representativeness of the House of Commons electoral reform involving some variant of proportional representation may be worth considering.

While it should not be considered a panacea, Senate reform would be an important element in improving both the effectiveness and representativeness of our federal institutions. An elected and effective Senate can be compatible with parliamentary institutions. The need for more equitable representation of the less populous provinces and territories will need to be balanced against the need to reflect adequately Canadian duality and the need to provide reserved representation for representatives of the aboriginal peoples.

Should constitutional revision involve a substantial measure of asymmetry in the allocation of jurisdiction to the provinces, voting rules and procedures will need to be developed for both Houses of Parliament limiting the votes of the representatives of a province on those matters where their province has autonomous jurisdiction.

Steps should also be taken to improve the legitimacy and effectiveness of federal and regulatory agencies, the intergovernmental collaborative institutions,

---

23  For the latter proposal see C.F. Beckton and A.W. MacKay, *Recurring Issues in Canadian Federalism*, Research Studies of the Royal Commission on the Economic Union and Development Prospects for Canada, vol. 57 (Toronto: University of Toronto Press, 1986), pp. 60–1.

24  Constitutional Committee of the Quebec Liberal Party, *A Quebec Free to Choose*, pp. 42 and 62.

and the ultimate constitutional adjudicative body. Regional representation on the major federal regulatory agencies would enhance their political legitimacy and improve their sensitivity to regional concerns. Executive federalism is an inevitable feature of any parliamentary federation, but it could be better harnessed by the establishment of standing legislative committees for intergovernmental relations to ensure greater accountability of governments for their conduct of intergovernmental affairs. The operation of the First Ministers' Conference might also be made more systematic. The status of the ultimate constitutional adjudicative body, the Supreme Court or possibly a separate specialized Constitutional Court, and the procedure for appointments to that body involving a role for both the federal and provincial governments, should be constitutionalized.

Such reforms to Canadian federal institutions could assist in restoring confidence in their representativeness and effectiveness. This in turn would make a major contribution to restoring a sense of legitimacy and loyalty to the Canadian federation.

# *Part Two*
# Federalism

ALONG WITH THE United States, Switzerland, Australia, and perhaps Germany, Canada counts among the world's classic federations. Canada's founding fathers took their cue from the United States. At the same time, they were fully aware of the apparent flaws of American federalism that were thought to have given rise to the civil war that was raging south of the 49th parallel while they crafted what would become the BNA Act, 1867. Most Canadians know that Canada is a federation. Few can tell you what a federal system is. Fewer yet know why Canada got a federal system in the first place, let alone why it evolved in such an ironic way. Is it not curious that Canada began as a highly centralized federation only to end up as one of the world's most decentralized federations without much constitutional change along the way?

This second part of the reader begins with a short excerpt by George Stanley that details the circumstances that led up to the eventual institutionalization of a federal solution. Lord Durham notwithstanding, the only way to make the Union Parliament work meant making it function akin to a federal compact. Ergo, the federal compromise should not be interpreted as the magnanimous coming-together of kindred spirits. As George Rawlyk explains in the following excerpt, Confederation was highly controversial in the Maritimes, whose concerns were not without cause: many of them bore out. With respect to Quebec,

A.I. Silver analogizes in his essay that Confederation is better understood as a divorce rather than a marriage; it governs how to live apart, not how to live together.

Confederation is often portrayed as a quintessentially pragmatic historical moment, imprinted by John A. Macdonald's highly centralized vision. Donald Creighton bears the burden of having rehabilitated Macdonald's centralist vision as gospel. The myth has taken on almost biblical proportions: Macdonald single-handedly brings salvation to the nation. Had Macdonald's vision prevailed, Canada as we know it surely would have not. Creighton's bias notwithstanding, he usefully outlines some of the motivations driving Confederation and the rationale behind the way powers ended up being divided between the Dominion government and the provinces. However, had it not been for George-Étienne Cartier and a federal compromise that accounted for provincialism, there would not have been a deal.

Closing this section is Samuel LaSelva's contribution that deconstructs the centralist-pragmatist myth which most Canadians have come to associate with Confederation. LaSelva's careful re-examination of the intellectual origins of Confederation demonstrates that, contrary to popular belief, the federalist vision that prevailed was far more theoretically informed (by a classic conception of federalism) than many people realize.

# 7

## Introduction by D.M.M. Stanley

(Professor Emerita, Mount Saint Vincent University, and George Stanley's daughter)

More than a century has passed since provincial rights advocates such as L. Houlton, D. Mills, and Honoré Mercier espoused the "Compact Theory" interpretation of the *British North America Act*. Over that time, the "Act or Pact?" debate has marked practically all discussions of the Canadian constitution. The debate between those who believe it was a British law passed on the advice of the colonial politicians and intended to ensure the existence of a strong central government and those who argue that it was a cultural compact, even a regional compact, with the status of a treaty, negotiated by the Fathers of Confederation on behalf of the British government and designed to highlight provincial rights, continues unabated. One need only note that in February 2006, at the Supreme Court nominee hearing for Justice Marshall Rothstein, his views of this debate were solicited. George Stanley was an advocate of the "Compact Theory" school as he clearly states in his introduction to *The Short History of the Canadian Constitution*. Stanley is widely recognized for his contributions to the historiography of western Canadian history, Canadian military history, and Acadian history. Unfortunately, his important contribution to the writing about Canada's constitutional history has often been overlooked, perhaps because of the unpopularity of his views in English Canada. Not that his views were revolutionary. In fact, as he noted himself, the "Racial Compact Theory" largely dominated political thinking and vocabulary in the decades prior to World War I and the Great Depression. It is only at this point that the "Centralist Theory" emerged as "the accepted constitutional dogma" in English Canada.

Stanley's concise, textbook-style account of the evolution of Canada's constitution from the start of the French colonial period up to the *Dunton-Laurendeau Report* and the constitutional conferences of the late 1960s, directly challenged the "Centralist Theory." This challenge to many of his peers, such as Norman McL. Rogers, J.S. Ewart, F. Scott, A.R.M. Lower, and D.G. Creighton, was first raised publically in Stanley's presidential address to the Canadian Historical Association in 1956, which was entitled "Act or Pact?" Coincidentally, this speech was delivered the same year Thomas Tremblay released his report on constitutional issues in Quebec, in which he too advocated the "Compact Theory." This interpretation formed the framework for Stanley's courses in Canadian constitutional history taught over the years at UBC, RMC, Mount Allison University, and the University of Victoria. Not since W.M.P. Kennedy's *Constitution of Canada* (1922) had there been a general, chronological historical tracing of the constitution. Stanley was motivated to fill that gap while also arguing his interpretation of the constitution, one which was widely accepted in French Canadian circles. For example, Quebec writers such as L. Groulx, C. Ryan, J.C. Bonefant , and L-A. Pigeon argued in favour of the "Compact Theory." Among English Canadian historians there were a few like R. Cook, F. Underhill and M. Wade who shared Stanley's understanding of French Canada's vision of the constitution, and there were those such as W.R. Lederman, J.A. Corry and J.E. Hodgetts who were willing to acknowledge that to some extent a "moral compact" had existed in 1867, although not a legally binding treaty/compact. Initially, because of its interpretative approach, Stanley's book was denounced by a host of centralist constitutional experts, led by E. Forsey, and was often ignored in English Canada. However, as the constitutional debate heated up in subsequent decades, ignited by the rise of such things as le Parti Québécois and the FLQ and events like the patriation of the constitution and the Meech Lake Accord, this text was "rediscovered" by students seeking to understand the implications and relevance of the cultural/regional compact approach. Many discovered that its straightforward chronological layout offered a valuable and easily accessible source of information about the evolution of the constitution, even though it stopped with events in 1969.

The following text looks not at the debates that determined the content of the BNA *Act*, but at the political realities of the legislative union, the United Canada, created by London in 1840 on the recommendation of Lord Durham. Stanley argues that this period provides the historical evidence that the intended legislative union never materialized and in its place there emerged a form of quasi-federalism based on a mutual acceptance of the cultural duality of Canada East and Canada West. This, he maintains, was a well-established situation by the time the Confederation discussions began in Charlottetown in 1864, a reality that formed the basis for the federal system and the nature of the division of powers laid out for the British Parliament's approval by the Fathers of Confederation. As Stanley notes, in the 1840s and 1850s, "the parts remained" ensuring that regional and racial duality were reflected in the nominal identities, the administrative structures, the legal systems, bilingualism, and the principles of double majority. Although, admittedly, New Brunswick and Nova Scotia were not shaped by this same reality, looking instead for economic advantages in a new union, Stanley suggests that union in 1867 was only possible once Canada East and Canada West reached an agreement that was modelled on the Union's previous two decades. In the end, he says, the BNA *Act* "was simply the reduction into proper legislative form and language of the resolutions agreed upon by the various provincial delegates."

George Stanley's understanding and appreciation for Quebec's vision of the BNA *Act*, for provincial rights and for linguistic and cultural duality in a changing modern Canadian society led him to conclude in 1969 that "the constitutional problem remains the most pressing one facing our country…." He warned that, while there were different interpretative positions, the time had come when that debate was no longer relevant or productive, and that what was essential was an understanding of the differing positions and the will to enter into a political negotiation that would ensure national unity and survival. *The Short History of the Canadian Constitution* was Stanley's contribution to that understanding, one that offered an explanation of a perspective that saw in the BNA *Act* not only a compact between two colonial linguistic groups but also between provinces, particularly in central Canada.

Source: George Stanley, *A Short History of the Constitution* (Toronto: Ryerson Press, 1969), 71–80.

George Stanley

# A Short History of the Constitution

## DUALISM AND QUASI-FEDERALISM UNDER THE UNION

The *Act of Union*, in spite of a preamble which recited the expediency of uniting the two Canadas, Upper and Lower, failed to bring about the extinction of its two component parts. Instead it recognized and confirmed the continued existence of the very provinces which Durham had hoped to make one single political and cultural unit.

Section XII of the *Act of Union* read as follows:

And be it enacted that in the Legislative Assembly of the Province of Canada … the parts of the said Province which now constitute the Provinces of Upper and Lower Canada respectively, shall … be represented by an equal number of representatives to be elected for the places and in the manner hereinafter mentioned.

This section changed the whole course of Canadian history as originally mapped by Lord Durham. It was a denial of the doctrine of representation according to population and an assertion of the doctrine of equality of the two Canadas regardless of the numbers of electors in each. In 1841 the census figures gave Canada West (Upper Canada) a population of 455,688 and Canada East (Lower Canada) an estimated population of 650,000. By 1844 these totals had increased to 560,000 (estimated) and 697,084 respectively. The rate of growth was faster in Canada West than in Canada East, and by 1850 the two provinces were roughly equal in size. Eleven years later the respective populations of Canada West and Canada East were 1,396,091 and 1,111,566. Of these totals, 33,287 were French Canadians in Canada West, and 847,615 French Canadians in Canada East. The numerical strengths of the two racial groups in the United Province were 1,626,755 English Canadians and 880,902 French Canadians. On the basis of these figures, it will be seen that, in 1841, there was one elected member of the Legislative Assembly for every 10,850 people in Canada West, and one for every 15,476 in Canada East. The lower province was thus placed at a political disadvantage. However, by 1861 there was one member for each 21,478 electors in Canada West, and one for each 17,101 in Canada East. Regardless of these changes in the provincial populations, the principle of equality remained unchanged until the advent of federation in 1867.

Not only did the *Act of Union* recognize the political equality of the two provinces, it also ensured, by sections XLVI and XLVII, that each should retain its own laws and courts as previously established. Section XLVI stated:

> And be it enacted that all laws, statutes and ordinances which at the time of the union of the Provinces of Upper and Lower Canada shall be in force within the said Provinces or either of them or any part of the said Provinces respectively, shall remain and continue to be of the same force, authority, and effect in those parts of the Province of Canada which now constitute the said Provinces respectively as if this Act had not been made, and as if the said two Provinces had not been united …

Steps had previously been taken in both provinces to revise and consolidate the various provincial statutes and these revisions were proceeded with and published, in 1843 in the case of Canada West and 1845 in the case of Canada East. Subsequently the *Consolidated Statutes of Canada* were published in 1859. But this consolidation did not include the statutes of the two original provinces which still remained in force. Thus, during the Union, there were three bodies of statute law, those applying to Canada as a whole, and those applying to the two original provinces.

The regional and racial duality apparent in the Parliament and in the law was also reflected in the organization of the Administration. The first Ministry which assumed office under Lord Sydenham was, for practical reasons if for no other, obliged to appoint duplicate Ministers to look after the peculiar needs of each province, such as William Draper as Attorney-General West, Charles Ogden, Attorney-General East, Robert Baldwin, Solicitor-General West and Charles Day, Solicitor-General East, Samuel Harrison, Provincial Secretary West, and Dominick Daly, Provincial Secretary East. Assimilation may have been what the Imperial Government in London hoped for from the *Act of Union,* but the practical political realities of the Canadian situation forced Sydenham into the acceptance of the very duality he was expected to erase.

Once the French Canadians had been accepted into the Administration by Sir Charles Bagot, duality was emphasized by the addition of the racial representation which had been absent under Sydenham. The alliance of LaFontaine and Baldwin in a joint Administration set a precedent which was followed for the remainder of the Union period, with the exception of the short-lived Government of Henry Sherwood. The dual, bi-racial Administrations included those of LaFontaine-Baldwin (16 September, 1842–11 December, 1843); Draper-Viger (12 December, 1843–17 June, 1846); Draper-D.B. Papineau (18 June, 1846–28 May, 1847); Sherwood-D.B. Papineau (29 May, 1847–7 December, 1847; Sherwood (8 December, 1847–10 March, 1848); LaFontaine-Baldwin (11 March, 1848–27 October, 1851); Hincks-Morin (28 October, 1851–10 September, 1854); Morin-MacNab (11 September, 1854–26 January, 1855); MacNab-Taché (27 January, 1855–23 May, 1856); Taché-MacNab (24 May, 1856–25 November, 1857); Macdonald-Cartier (26 November 1857–1 August, 1858); Brown-Dorion (2–5 August, 1858); Cartier-Macdonald (6 August, 1858–23 May, 1862); J.S. Macdonald-Sicotte (24 May, 1862–15 May,

1863); J.S Macdonald-Dorion (16 May, 1863–29 March, 1864; Taché-Macdonald-Brown (30 March, 1864–6 August, 1865); Belleau-Macdonald (7 August, 1865–1 July, 1867). It may be noted that, although the Ministries were all bi-racial ministries, the parties supporting them were not always representative of the two races. There was, for instance, little or no French support for the Draper-Viger, the Draper-D.B. Papineau or the Sherwood-D.B. Papineau Ministries. And the entry of George Brown into the Taché-Macdonald coalition was not followed by the adhesion of the *Rouges* to the policy advocated by the Great Coalition. Nevertheless, bi-racial leadership became a fact which could not be ignored and every Government endeavoured to the best of its ability to find support from both national groups in Canada. During the Union, Canada was, in fact, a quasi-federal state, governed by the co-operation of the two national groups which made up its population.

Not only was there duality in the leadership of the Governments of the Union period. Each hyphenated Ministry had its parallel Ministries for each province, including the Attorney-General's office and the Solicitor-General's office. There were two Provincial Secretaries between 1841 and 1844, after which the appointment alternated between Canada East and Canada West. The Receiver-Generalship also alternated between the two provinces, as did the speakership. Even more extensive than at the Ministerial level was the dualism in the Civil Service. The Department of Public Works included a Commissioner and an Assistant Commissioner, the two offices alternating between French- and English-Canadian appointees. The Provincial Secretariat, even after it was reduced to a single Minister, was organized at the lower level in two separate establishments for each province. Duality was the rule in the Surveyor-General's Branch, in the Crown Lands Department, and in the Education offices.

Despite the fact that the *Act of Union* had implied a unilingual state for the United Province, bilingualism was a political fact from the opening session of the first meeting of Parliament in Kingston. The first speaker was a French Canadian (Augustin Cuvillier, a former colleague of Papineau) and the *Standing Rules and Regulations of the Legislative Assembly* included provisions for the translation of papers and the reading of motions in both languages. Lord Elgin was aware of the strength of the national feeling of the French Canadians and in his communications with the Colonial Secretary urged the Imperial authorities to remove the restriction imposed by the *Act of Union* upon French as a language of record. Writing to Grey on 4 May, 1848, he said "I, for one, am deeply convinced of the impolicy of all such attempts to denationalize the French. Generally speaking, they produce the opposite effect from that intended, causing the flame of national prejudice and animosity to burn more fiercely." At Elgin's request, the Imperial Parliament changed the language section of the *Act of Union*. When the Canadian Legislature met in January, 1849, the Governor-General announced that French had been placed on the same basis as English as an official language, and for the first time read the speech from the throne in both languages.

Dualism also marked the procedures of the Canadian Legislature. The idea that the people in each province should not have to submit to measures peculiarly applicable to it, unless these measures had received a majority vote from the representatives of the province concerned (the principle of the double-majority) seems first to have been spoken of by William Draper in the last days of the Metcalfe regime, when he was endeavouring to enlist the support of Louis LaFontaine. It was an idea which appealed to the French Canadians (and to the French-language press in Canada East) who felt frustrated at their exclusion from office. LaFontaine liked the idea, too, but he resisted Draper's blandishments, preferring to maintain his alliance with Robert Baldwin. Baldwin did not think highly of the double-majority principle. It would, he said "perpetuate distinctions, initiate animosities, sever the bonds of political sympathy, and sap the foundations of public morality." But he was compelled to accept it in order to maintain effective collaboration with his French-language colleagues. The principle, although not applied in every instance, never lost its popularity in the United Province, and continued to be an important factor throughout the days of the Union. John A. Macdonald even proposed that formal recognition should be given the principle as an essential convention of the Canadian constitution; and his namesake, John Sandfield Macdonald, tried hard to adhere to it during his months in office. It is ironic that it was during Sandfield Macdonald's regime that the *Separate Schools Bill* in Canada West was forced through the House of Assembly by means of a majority of votes in Canada East. Perhaps it would be accurate to say that the double-majority, in Canadian history, was a matter of practical expediency rather than a constant requirement or a political convention.

John A. Macdonald described the working of the double-majority principle in this fashion during his speech on the *Quebec Resolutions* in February, 1865:

> We, in Canada, already know something of the advantages and disadvantages of a Federal Union. Although we have nominally a Legislative Union in Canada—although we sit in one Parliament, supposed constitutionally to represent the people without regard to sections or localities, yet we know, as a matter of fact, that since the union in 1841, we have had a Federal Union; that in matters affecting Upper Canada solely, members from that section claimed and generally exercised the right of exclusive legislation, while members from Lower Canada legislated in matters affecting only their own section. We have had a Federal Union in fact, though a Legislative Union in name; and in the hot contests of late years, if on any occasion a measure affecting any one section were interfered with by members from the other—if, for instance, a measure locally affecting Upper Canada were carried or defeated against the wishes of its majority, by one from Lower Canada—my honorable friend the President of the Council, and his friends denounced with all their energy and ability such legislation as an infringement of the rights of the Upper Province. Just in the same way, if any act concerning Lower Canada were pressed into law against the wishes of the majority of her representatives, by those from Upper Canada, the Lower Canadians would rise as one man and protest against such a violation of their peculiar rights.

## THE TRANSITION FROM QUASI-FEDERALISM TO FEDERALISM, 1864–1867

The federal union which was finally achieved in 1867, may be said to have arisen from various factors, some external and some internal. One of the most significant was the fear of the British North American provinces of the unfriendliness and aggressiveness of the United States. In Canada the memories of the invasions of 1775, 1812 and 1838 were too deep to forget, and the calculated delay on the part of the American authorities in dealing with the Fenian invaders of 1866 too recent to overlook. Strength might be found in union. Other factors included the demands of an expanding nation for an extension of the railway system and a linking of the interior provinces with the ice-free ports of the Maritimes; the desire to emulate the western expansion of the United States by acquiring and exploiting the rich resources of the lands, at this time, still under the control of the Hudson's Bay Company; and finally the hopes of countering the uncertainties of an American market, about to be restricted by the unilateral denunciation of the Reciprocity Treaty by the United States, with increased intercolonial trade.

The idea of uniting the central colonies and those of the Atlantic seaboard began with Chief Justice William Smith in Quebec in 1790. Later, union was advocated by Chief Justice Sewell and supported by the Duke of Kent in 1814. It was talked about by Lord Grey in London in 1847, and by Sir Edmund Head in Canada in 1854. In 1858 everybody seemed to have something to say about it, including J.W. Johnston in Nova Scotia, Alexander Morris in Canada West and Alexander Gait and J.C. Taché in Canada East, It was tentatively discussed on an official basis at an Interprovincial Conference on communications at Quebec in 1862. Federal union was not, however, an idea which appealed generally to French Canadians. Not without reason they felt that the economic advantages which might accrue to them from such a union would be outweighed by the political disadvantages it would bring in its train. Nor were the Maritimers very enthusiastic about it. To them the one great advantage would be the extension of their railway system to the St. Lawrence valley and a linking with the Grand Trunk railway system of Canada West. The chief partisans of the federation scheme were, therefore, the Anglo-Canadians of Canada West and the English minority of Canada East.

But, even if there were economic advantages to be derived from federation which seemed more compelling to the people of Canada West than to those of Canada East, there were also political advantages which influenced the people of both provinces. Perhaps federation was the answer to the problem of political instability which had plagued Canada ever since 1763. There were, of course, other possibilities, such as George Brown's suggestion that Canada should abandon the principle of equality in the provincial administration and adopt representation according to population, or "Rep. by Pop." John Sandfield Macdonald, another Grit, believed that the solution for Canada's problems rested in a more rigid adherence to the principle of the double-majority. George E. Cartier's *Bleus* from Canada East, owing perhaps to their leader's interest in the Grand Trunk Railway, were prepared to go along with the idea of interprovincial federation, provided it included the Maritime Provinces as a counterbalance to Upper Canada; but Antoine Dorion's *Rouge* party wanted no change at all; if anything, they preferred to return to the situation as it had existed prior to the Act of 1840. Macdonald's Conservatives were federalists and willingly followed their leader's pragmatic approach to the problem, once he had been convinced by Gait that federal union was both a necessary and practical measure of politics. With such a variety of opinions and attitudes the cause of federation might well have languished had not George Brown and his Upper Canada Clear Grits, finally crossed the floor of the House to join forces with John A. Macdonald and George E. Cartier and the Liberal-Conservative party in the Taché-Macdonald coalition of 1864. Thus federation seemed to offer the one means of obtaining "Rep. by Pop.," while at the same time granting a large measure of autonomy to the French Canadians. Without Brown's support it would have been impracticable for the Government of Canada to have entered into negotiations with the Maritime provinces.

The initial meetings between the Canadians and the Maritimers took place at Charlottetown, Prince Edward Island, in September, 1864. Here, in secret sessions, the delegates of all the provinces agreed upon the desirability of forming a federal union of the British North American provinces. The next month, in October, they met again at Quebec, as a Constituent Assembly, in order to hammer out the details. The

outcome was a draft federal constitution called the *Quebec Resolutions*. The decision to adopt a federal form of government rather than a legislative union was not the result of any philosophical theories of government, but of practical necessities. No other form of union was possible, regardless of the voiced preference for a unitary system on the part of some of the Canadian delegates. The French-Canadian province and the Maritimes possessed too strong a sense of their own identity willingly to surrender it for the sake of being ruled by an alien or a central Canadian majority. This determination to retain the maximum power over their own local affairs while yielding broad general powers to a central government was the basic fact of the negotiations, both at Charlottetown and at Quebec. The union was a compromise, and unless there had been some positive assurances that the critics, like the New Brunswicker who contended that the provinces were left no powers beyond making regulations "to prevent cows from running on the Commons, providing that sheep should wear bells and to issue tavern licences," or the Nova Scotian who contended that the union would make "a second Downing Street at Ottawa," were in error, there could have been no intercolonial union. Even so, the suspicious New Brunswickers succeeded in defeating their Confederate opponents in the election of 1865; while in Prince Edward Island the legislature rejected Confederation, and in Nova Scotia and Newfoundland the *Quebec Resolutions* were never put to a vote either of the members of the legislature or of the electors of the province.

In Canada the *Quebec Resolutions* were thoroughly discussed in the Parliament of the United Province. Among the most fervent supporters of Confederation in the House of Assembly were John A. Macdonald (Kingston), Alexander Galt (Sherbrooke) and George Brown (South Oxford); George E. Cartier (Montreal East), Hector Langevin (Dorchester) and Joseph Cauchon (Montmorency) the editor of the influential *Journal de Quebec*. Opposed were Antoine Dorion (Hochelaga), Joseph Perrault (Richelieu) and Henri Taschereau (Beauce) a former *Bleu* and follower of Cartier. In the Legislative Council the principal proponents of the federal scheme were Sir Narcisse Belleau (Quebec), Alexander Campbell (Cataraqui) Macdonald's law partner in Kingston, and Colonel

Sir E.P. Taché (Montmagny). The opponents included Letellier de St. Just (Grandville), David Reesor (King's) and J.C. Aikins (Home).

The great debate lasted from 3 February until 13 March, 1865. Several votes were taken. In the Assembly the most important vote was that taken on 10 March, when the Government proposals supporting the *Quebec Resolutions* were carried by 91 votes to 33. The members for Canada West gave strong support to the Government with 54 votes favouring Confederation and only 8 against. In Canada East the margin was much less decisive. Thirty-seven members voted for federation and 25 opposed it. As far as the French Canadians were concerned, the Government resolutions secured a majority of no more than four votes. Narrow as this majority was, it was sufficient to argue that there had been no departure from the principle of the double-majority and that the Confederation proposals had obtained a majority in both sections of the United Province. In the Upper House, an attempt to postpone further discussion on the proposed federation until the *Quebec Resolutions* had been endorsed by the people was rejected 36 votes to 19. The final expression of approval was 45 votes to 15. Among those who would not vote for Confederation were 7 members from Canada West and 8 from Canada East. Of the elected members of the Legislative Council, 32 supported Confederation and 12 opposed it. Thirteen appointed members supported it and 3 opposed it. From the standpoint of the double-majority principle, 28 members from Canada West and 17 members from Canada East voted for the federal scheme with contrary votes of six and nine respectively. The racial vote was 32 Anglo-Canadians for and 9 against; and 13 French Canadians for and 6 against.

Still, Confederation did not come for two more years. Not until after the Confederates of Samuel Tilley regained power in New Brunswick in another general election in 1866, and Charles Tupper forced a resolution through the Nova Scotia legislature asking for a resumption of negotiations with the other colonies for union, was it possible for Canada West, Canada East, New Brunswick and Nova Scotia to send delegates to London to take a third look at the problem of intercolonial union. The *Quebec Resolutions* were reviewed, a few minor changes were made and a Bill, drafted with the assistance of the British Colonial Office, was introduced into the Imperial Parliament in the spring of 1867. This Bill, known as the *British North America Bill* was simply the reduction into proper legislative form and language of the resolutions agreed upon by the various provincial delegates; and the lack of interest taken in the Bill in the Imperial Parliament was, no doubt, a reflection of the fact that Parliament was being asked to rubber-stamp the provisions of an agreement already mutually arrived at by Canada West, Canada East, New Brunswick and Nova Scotia. After a rather desultory debate, the Bill passed both Houses and received the royal assent. Four months later, on 1 July, 1867, the new federal union, under the name *Canada* was proclaimed in the capitals of the four original contracting provinces. New Brunswick and Nova Scotia retained their old names, but Canada East and Canada West were renamed respectively, Quebec and Ontario.

**8**

## Editors' Introduction

Nowadays, George Rawlyk is best known for his ground-breaking work on Canadian religious history, espe-cially as it pertains to certain Protestant denominations in Atlantic Canada. He spent his early years, however, researching Atlantic history more generally. In the process, he wrote on the issues the Atlantic provinces were facing at the time of Confederation and how it affected their position vis-à-vis the prospect of federating. Of course, many of those concerns were borne out in the end, especially insofar as the economic, demographic, and political shift toward Ontario and Quebec is concerned. In a sense, Atlantic Canada is also the cradle of Canadian democracy, Nova Scotia under Joseph Howe having been the first entity in the entire British Empire to introduce responsible government.

Source: George A. Rawlyk, "The Historical Framework of the Maritimes and the Problems of Confederation," in *The Atlantic Provinces and the Problems of Confederation* (St. John's: Breakwater, 1979), 8–18.

George Rawlyk

# The Historical Framework of the Maritimes and the Problems of Confederation

## THE CONFEDERATION CRISIS

It may seem paradoxical that just as the Maritime Provinces were reaching social and political maturity, the underpinnings of their economy began to crum-ble, and Confederation threatened their painfully won collective identities. With the advent of steam and steel technology, the days of the wooden sailing ves-sels were numbered; similarly, hitherto isolated parts of a vast continent could be sewn together by a ribbon of steel as railway development gripped the entre-preneurial imagination of the age. The long-term trends towards a continental economy, with all of its diso-rienting consequences for the Maritimes, were evi-dent to only the most far-sighted, for the effects of the changes in transportation and industrial technology came only slowly to the region, and the staple, seaward economy of the provinces did not collapse until at least the 1870s. Moreover, the security offered by so-called conservatism shielded most residents of the region from the harsh realities of the contagion of "change."

In all three Maritime Provinces there were, by the late 1850s, leaders whose interests began to be rooted in the new technologies and, eventually, in the conti-nental economy. These men usually started as railway promoters, seeking the advantages that railway links would bring to the commerce and industry of the dispersed communities of their provinces. Many of them ended as supporters of Confederation, foresee-ing the same advantages through a transcontinental British North American union made possible by the railway age. But it would be too simplistic to conclude that Confederation was just a political scheme to give legitimacy to railway empires and power and influ-ence to their entrepreneurs. Some railway promoters, like Joseph Howe for instance, did not share the "glo-rious image" of Confederation that fellow Maritimers Charles Tupper of Nova Scotia or Peter Mitchell of New Brunswick attempted to project. Yet, it seems clear that railways prepared the way for the Maritime Provinces to enter Confederation, and that without the guarantee of such railways, Confederation was an "impossible dream."

The Confederation scheme, as might be expected, ran head-on into the deep residual confidence and prosperity of a long-established and traditional society. Beneath most of the anti-Confederation sentiment of the period lay a fundamental belief in an established system—the cultural, economic, social and political aspects of the "Golden Age"—which the new faith only slowly eroded. During the ensuing often bitter political conflict, Maritimers were torn between the competing ideologies of a yet-to-be-realized transcontinental nation and an existing way of life which seemed to many to suit admirably their needs and aspirations.

The formation of pro-Confederation and anti-Confederation camps in the Maritime provinces exhibited, among other things, the diverging perspectives, attitudes and values of the elite. In New Brunswick, where the Canadian Confederation scheme found strong support in the government of Samuel L. Tilley, there had been hopes for an intercolonial railway for some time.[1] However, an equally strong group among the Saint John mercantile elite had for years been promoting the "Western Extension" railway from that port to Maine, where it was to link with American lines. These Saint John interests contributed to the defeat of the Tilley government in 1865 in an election that was called to seek approval of the province's entry into Confederation on the basis of the "Quebec Resolutions" of 1864.[2] There were, of course, other reasons for the Tilley defeat. Many New Brunswickers distrusted the Central Canadian politicians, particularly after the latter had been perceived as reneging on the Intercolonial railway project agreed to earlier; moreover, New Brunswickers feared it would mean higher taxes to support the "spend thrift" Canadians who were eager to build canals and other public projects in Central Canada. More important than this, however, was a profound opposition to any change in the *status quo* for the alleged purpose of ensuring material "progress." It has been pointed out that New Brunswickers resisted Confederation not because of a parochial or conservative disdain for change, but rather because of a shrewd pragmatic assessment that the scheme "seemed to offer very little that they lacked, while requiring them to sacrifice their prized political autonomy to the mistrusted Canadians."[3] Given a clear choice over the issue in 1865, the province voted overwhelmingly against Confederation, striking an unexpected blow to the union cause.

In Nova Scotia there had emerged by the 1860s a "new and vital dichotomy" among the elite of the province. The old group was based on the mercantile economy of "Iron Men and Wooden Ships"; the new group stressed the importance of a new industrialism based upon the railways and the large coal resources of the northern part of the province, where an iron and

steel industry was in its infant stages.[4] Led by Charles Tupper, premier of Nova Scotia since May, 1864, the pro-Confederation party pitted its "new industrial ideology" against the older, more established and, for the moment, stronger elite, based in Halifax but also influential throughout most of the province. While it was slow to get organized, the Anti-Confederation League became a formidable political force; and following Tilley's defeat in New Brunswick, Tupper was determined to avoid an election on the Confederation issue which he knew he could not win. The Tupper government succeeded in bringing Nova Scotia into Confederation without an election, but following the official birth of the new Canada, his party suffered ignominious defeat in both the provincial and federal elections held in the fall of 1867. In the former, 36 out of 38 anti-Confederationists were elected, and in the latter, 18 out of 19. It had been argued that "It was a question of the traditional leaders of society successfully standing off a challenge from an emerging and politically immature group...."[5]

As in New Brunswick, prevailing distrust of the Canadians—Howe referred to Canada spitefully as "a nation with a helot race in its bosom"—and fear of taxation were important issues in the Confederation debate in Nova Scotia. Even more significant a factor than in New Brunswick was the attachment of many Nova Scotians to a provincial identity, an identity which they instinctively felt would be submerged in the Canadian-dominated Dominion government.[6] In its appeal to the past and present glories of Nova Scotian autonomy, the Anti-Confederates enjoyed the nominal leadership of Joseph Howe, the political spokesman of the old order. Howe's rhetoric in the campaign stressed the "traitorous" deeds of his antagonist, Tupper, in stripping Nova Scotia of its rights without consulting the people; he struck a responsive chord with his demands that the province seek redress in the form of secession from the new union and the restoration of its full stature as a self-governing nation within the British Empire.

While the Confederation issue prompted a widespread debate in the two mainland Maritime provinces, Prince Edward Island was virtually unanimous in its rejection of the union. "The issue," it has recently been argued, "created a deep and extraordinary sense of peril within the community."[7] After the Charlottetown Conference of 1864, some Island politicians cautiously approved of Confederation in principle, but at the Quebec Conference it became clear that Prince Edward Island stood to lose more of its autonomy than the Island delegates had previously envisaged. The province soon became virtually unanimous in its rejection of further co-operation with the Confederates. Conscious of and defensive concerning their unique identity, Islanders rejected the union scheme as they had rejected annexation threats in the past. In the words of one eloquent anti-Confederate spokesman:

> And considering that we would be such a small portion of the Confederacy, our voice would not be heard in it. We would be the next thing to nothing. Are we thus going to surrender our rights and liberties? It is just a question of "self or no self."[8]

In the face of such opposition it took the concerted and combined effort of local pro-Confederationists, Canadian politicians, and the British Colonial Office to defeat their opponents in the Maritimes. In each province, the effects of British pressure to conform with the "Queen's" wish that they be united played upon the essentially colonial mentality of the region and its powerful attachment to "loyalty." A creeping fatalism, moreover, undermined the determination of the opposition as the union's inevitability became apparent to all but the most recalcitrant anti-Confederationists.

In New Brunswick, opposition to Confederation peaked with the election of the Smith government in 1865. Weakened by disunity and an initial financial crisis, the government exhibited what has been called a "psychological defensiveness" towards the Confederation issue.[9] The competing railway interests—the north shore supporters of the Intercolonial and the Saint John supporters of the Western Extension—as well as financial problems meant that the provincial government was unable to deal effectively with the important problem of railway construction.[10] This failure persuaded a growing number of New Brunswickers that the Smith government could not implement any development strategies which could ensure provincial economic progress and prosperity. Furthermore, strong pro-Confederation statements from the Mother Country strengthened the Confederation forces and placed the anti-Confederationists on the defensive. As early as 1864, most

New Brunswick political observers had pointed out that the province would eventually follow the dictates of "duty" to the Empire, even when that duty conflicted with its best commercial "interest."[11] This theme of "loyalty" to Britain's wishes was exploited by Tilley and his allies, with the full collaboration of the Colonial Office. The "political, financial and moral resources" of the pro-Confederationists was "overwhelming; and the unionist press was able to demonstrate very successfully that support for the Smith government was a diminishing minority in the province."[12]

It would be misleading to suggest, however, that New Brunswickers were simply bowing to imperial pressure and Canadian money. Other considerations led a majority in 1866 to believe that Confederation was desirable. The inability of the Smith government to proceed with the Western Extension railway, the failure of reciprocity trade negotiations with the United States in 1866, and defence considerations because of Fenian raids, all pointed to the benefits of a colonial union cemented by the promised Intercolonial railway. When the real doubts of the Smith government concerning the value of prolonged opposition to Confederation are also taken into account, the province's sudden shift away from the anti-Confederation camp is understandable. In April 1866, barely a year after its election to office, the Smith government caved in, and in the subsequent election Samuel Tilley led the Confederates to a convincing victory, securing for his cause the "keystone" of the Confederation arch.[13]

The defeat of the anti-Confederationists in New Brunswick demonstrated the province's new dependent status. It was unable independently to negotiate either reciprocity with the United States or the railway development that continuance of the old economic order required. Politicians like W.H. Needham could proclaim bravely in the legislature that:—

> When I forget my country so far as to sell it for Confederation, may my right hand forget its cunning, and if I do not prefer New Brunswick as she is, to Canada with all her glory, then let my tongue cleave to the roof of my mouth.[14]

But Confederation seemed inevitable to most who rushed, in 1866, to enjoy the spoils of victory and share in Tilley's success. Only the die-hards like Needham were left to commiserate on their defeat.

While effective opposition to Confederation in New Brunswick petered out rather quickly, in Nova Scotia, Howe and his anti-Confederationists were faced with the task of fulfilling the mandate of their 1867 election: to secure the secession of the province from the evil union. From the beginning, Howe was faced with a cruel personal dilemma which in many ways reflected the problems of the anti-Confederation movement as a whole. At the crux of Howe's political philosophy was a deeply abiding faith in the British Empire and British justice.[15] His "reluctance to support Canadian Confederation and his concomitant apathy towards the idea of autonomous local legislatures" were both rooted in his hopes of an imperial federation. His dream of a British North America as part of a unitary imperial state was shattered with Britain's whole-hearted support of Confederation; and as Howe left for London early in 1868, ostensibly to secure Nova Scotia's secession, he must have known in advance that "repeal" was impossible.[16] His "British Nova Scotianess became bankrupt in the fact of imperial intransigence with respect to the demands of the province."[17]

When faced with Britain's refusal to grant repeal, what could Howe do? Annexation to the United States was certainly out of the question, as was a declaration of Nova Scotia independence. In the final analysis, there was only one choice for Howe: the choice provided by the Colonial Office—Confederation. There is no evidence to suggest that Howe, before he entered John A. Macdonald's Cabinet on January 30, 1869, made a serious attempt to force the restructuring of Confederation to meet Nova Scotia's special needs.[18] The "Better Terms" arrangement which he alone negotiated for the province were, it should be stated, "deliberately and narrowly financial in nature,"[19] consisting of revised debt allowances and annual revenue subsidies to compensate for the trading province's lost revenues.[20]

With Howe's entry into Macdonald's Cabinet, the Repeal movement in Nova Scotia received a fatal blow. Conceived in frustration and economic discontent, it had a relatively short life in Nova Scotia, and when signs of an economic upturn appeared in 1869, the movement lost most of its momentum and much of its popular support. Nevertheless, the bitterness towards Confederation in the province remained near the surface of the collective mentality of its people.[21]

Unable to find "any alternative policy to replace the decrepit and oft-repeated repeal policy," the provincial wing of the anti-Confederation party had virtually disappeared by 1870.[22] As for the Nova Scotian Members of Parliament, they had "tacitly recognized the new regime" by sitting in the new Dominion House of Commons in the first place; and they had, moreover, left themselves open to ideological compromise and to the inducements of patronage.[23] It was relatively easy for them to swallow their principles—to accept the hard political facts of life—and to take advantage of the system. They, like Joseph Howe, saw the *cul-de-sac* that Repeal was forcing them into, and they abandoned their attachment to a Nova Scotia nationalism, and their Atlantic past, and appropriated John A. Macdonald's vision of a new Canada, and a continental future.

As far as Prince Edward Island was concerned, the familiar patterns of British pressure, Canadian manipulation and local fatalism combined to undermine the opposition to Confederation in the tiny province as well. However, unlike New Brunswick and Nova Scotia, the Island was not an essential link in the Confederation chain. Both the Canadian and the Imperial governments were willing to wait for time and circumstance to alter Island intransigence. Unhampered, too, by internal division, the province sought an alternative to Confederation, of which neither of its neighbours seemed capable. An American Congressional mission headed by Massachusetts Congressman Benjamin ("the Beast") Butler, arrived in Charlottetown in 1868, where, through shrewd manipulation of the Islanders' sentiments, they preached the benefits of reciprocal trade for their own political benefit back in the United States.[24] In a flood of enthusiasm, most Islanders thought that they could regain the peak of prosperity reached during the Civil War years while at the same time continuing to reject the threat posed by Confederation. But to their dismay, the British authorities completely squashed the Islanders' hopes that they could negotiate a separate treaty with the United States.[25]

While the Imperial rejection of the Butler initiative marked a "moment of supreme frustration for P.E.I.," it did however shake the Macdonald government out of its lethargy. Late in 1869 the Dominion government once again submitted a union proposal to the Island, featuring a more generous debt allowance and annual subsidies, communication and transportation guarantees, and a promise to deal with the absentee-landlord problem. The provincial government once again rejected the overture and cited inadequate provision for the settlement of the land question as its main reason. As has been pointed out, however, "The refusal of the terms was, as the Canadians surmised, only an excuse, for the real factor in the situation was the absence of some compelling emergency which could cause the islanders to sink their doubts in favour of union."[26]

That Prince Edward Island agreed in 1873 to enter Confederation on terms which were only slightly more generous than those offered in 1869 indicates not, perhaps, that they were only shrewdly waiting for a better deal, but that the islanders took longer to accept the apparent inevitability of the union, and that they required final proof of the province's absolute inability to "go it alone" before they took the dreaded step. Denied reciprocity, the helpless Island government was grasping at any scheme which promised to recapture the prosperity that had been slipping from its grasp since 1866. In the 1870 provincial election, J.C. Pope was returned at the head of a coalition government which "made railway their politics." Thus, in this typical "mainland fashion," the Islanders *set out* to build themselves a railway, "and the tracks led straight to Ottawa."[27] In the eyes of the vociferous opponents to the development at the time, the railway was a plot to bring the island into Confederation; and as many predicted, the Union Bank of P.E.I. triggered a "phony crisis" when it found it had little chance of selling railway securities on the London markets in 1872. The government quickly succumbed. A poor harvest, an economic recession, and the unrelenting pressure of the British Government had finally weakened the provincial resistance. Early in 1873, island politicians journeyed to Ottawa where "onerous terms were mutually agreed upon."[28] Most Islanders met the end of their independent history with bitter resignation and, as was the case in the other two Maritime Provinces, the legacy of resentment against those responsible remained. One popular Island poet expressed what he knew to be the point of view of many Islanders when he declared:—

With dishes fine their tables shine,
They live in princely style,
They are the knaves who made us slaves,
And sold Prince Edward Isle.

An idealized island past had been transformed by Confederation into the grim modern Canadian hell of the present:

In days of yore, from Scotland's shores
Our Fathers crossed the main;
Tho dark and drear, they settled here
To quit the "Tyrant's" chain,
With hearts so stout, they put to rout
The forest beasts so wild;
Rough logs they cut, to build their huts
Upon Prince Edward Isle.

With ax well ground, they levelled down
The forest far and wide;
With spade and hoe the seed they sowed,
The plow was left untried;
With sickle hooks they cut their stooks,
No "Buckeyes" ever in style;
They spent their days—their aches lay
Upon Prince Edward Isle.

The place was new, the roads were few,
The people lived content,
The landlords came, their fields to claim;
Each settler must pay rent.
So now you see, the turning tide
That drove us to exile,
Begin again to cross the main,
And leave Prince Edward Isle.

But changes great have come of late,
And brought some curious things;
Dominion men have brought us in,
The Isle with railways ring;
There's maps and charts, and towns apart,
And tramps of every style,
There's doctors mute and lawyers cute,
Upon Prince Edward Isle.[29]

In the response of the three Maritime Provinces to Confederation are to be found certain common features. There was a widespread and stubborn resistance to political and economic change that was perceived to be contrary to the interests of an apparently prosperous and settled society. And in the political manifestations of the anti-Confederation movement, the strength of the provincial identities was clearly revealed.

However, in all three provinces the opposition was eroded by the psychological and political skill of pro-Confederation politicians and the British officials. In each province the combined power of pro-union forces undermined the viability of options upon which the anti-Confederationists depended. The failure to re-negotiate reciprocity, in particular, had the important effect of burning the bridge to the past on which the anti-Confederates had placed so much of their hopes. By dwelling upon the *status quo*, or rather upon attempts to restore an order that was being lost forever, the opponents to Confederation failed to take a creative role in the nation-building process. In neither Nova Scotia nor Prince Edward Island's "better terms" is there evidence of a serious attempt to re-shape Confederation to meet the special economic needs of the Maritime region. Tilley, Tupper, and their supporters, who shared the Macdonald-Cartier vision of Canada, appropriated the future; those distrustful of the ultimate effects of Confederation took no significant part in ensuring that their worst fears would not be realized. They reluctantly and almost fatalistically accepted the inevitable, and found solace and escape in praising a "Golden Age" that could never be reconstructed.

The success of the pro-Confederation forces in gaining the initiative under the Macdonald government in 1867 would have a great effect on the subsequent political development of the Maritime Provinces. The "close connection forged between Macdonald and his supporters in Canada and Tilley and his supporters in New Brunswick … did much to solidify a political party" where "solid" parties had been virtually non-existent before.[30] Successors of Tilley's 1866 government held power in the province until 1884; and their opponents, who gradually came to consider themselves as Liberals, supported the government and party of Alexander Mackenzie at the federal level.

Confederation held the same results for Nova Scotia and Prince Edward Island. In the former province, the integration of provincial parties into national counterparts was complete by 1874, when, as the anti-Confederation movement finally died, the parties submerged "the one issue that permitted meaningful cleavage of the electorate along party lines."[31] On Prince Edward Island the absorption of local parties into federal ones took longer, although for all intents and purposes, opposing Island candidates in federal elections were readily identified as "government" or "opposition" by 1878.[32]

Throughout the region the disintegration of any political movement which did not correspond to the sole Canadian cleavage of Liberal and Conservative signified the complete political integration of the Maritimes into Canada. In spite of lingering dissatisfaction with the policies of the national government, there would be no significant attempts to channel regional protest outside the traditional two-party system.

The economic, cultural, and social integration of the Maritimes into the new nation came only slowly when compared with the political integration. It was largely in non-political spheres that the regional identities continued to assert themselves, reflecting the painful adjustment of the region to the new situation. The legacy of opposition to Confederation remained strong in some quarters, and with the economic depression of the 1870s and 1880s, many Maritimers, especially those who had taken an "anti" stand at an earlier period, began to re-articulate their old prophecies of doom. Resentment towards Confederation often took on an "anti-Upper Canadian" flavour, as the press and politicians exploited popular opposition to outsiders. An editorial in the Halifax *Morning Chronicle* in 1886 superbly captured this feeling:—

The people of Nova Scotia know the Ontario or Quebec man but we know him principally in the shape of the commercial traveller. He comes here to sell, but he buys nothing but his hotel fare and in this respect he makes a rather ostentatious display. He is usually a genial enough sort of fellow, has a diamond ring, smokes fair cigars, "sets them up with the boys" in an off-hand way, and generally conveys the impression that in his own estimation he is a very superior being, whose condescending patronage it is a great privilege to enjoy. He spreads himself periodically throughout the province, in number he equals the locust and his visit has about the same effect. He saps our resources, sucks our money and leaves a lot of shoddy behind him. He has been able—at least the people whose agent he is—to have laws passed that compel us to buy his wares or submit to a tremendous fine, if we purchase from John Bull or brother Jonathan.... Our interests—the very genius of our people, all our instincts, everything that is calculated to foster and encourage national spirit, are so utterly foreign and dissimilar that fusion is absolutely impossible.[33]

Both the strengths and the weaknesses of this traditional regional protest were clearly demonstrated by the Nova Scotian "Repeal Movement" of 1886–87. By 1886 the Liberal government in Nova Scotia, led by the taciturn W.S. Fielding, like its Conservative predecessor, found itself in a financial strait-jacket during a period of economic stagnation. As early as 1878 the provincial government had asked the Ottawa authorities for a continuation of the temporary arrangements provided by Howe's "Better Terms," in order to compensate the province for the still serious loss of revenue being endured because of the British North America Act. For their troubles, the Nova Scotian governments received from the Macdonald government a series of "stinging rebukes."[34] Unable or unwilling to realize the seriousness of Nova Scotia's financial problems, neither national party responded favorably to Nova Scotian Members of Parliament's urgent requests for *still* "Better Terms." In February, 1885, a Liberal member of the provincial Legislature, J.A. Fraser, proposed a resolution championing his favourite solution for the province's ills: secession from Confederation. While Fielding suppressed this motion at the time, he gradually became convinced of the political effectiveness of threatened repeal. In a series of resolves passed in May, 1886, the Fielding Government proposed that:—

> the financial and commercial interests of the people of Nova Scotia, New Brunswick and Prince Edward Island would be advanced by these provinces withdrawing from the Canadian federation and uniting under one government.

If Maritime union was found to be impossible, the province should then ask:

> permission from the imperial parliament to withdraw from the union with Canada and return to the state of a province of Great Britain, with full control over all fiscal laws and tariff regulations ... as prevailed previous to Confederation.[35]

It is doubtful if any but a few of the members of the Nova Scotia Legislature were actually willing to go as far as to take the province out of Confederation. In Premier Fielding's speech to the Assembly following his tabling of the motion, he had to admit that

> ... Even if we fail, (to obtain repeal) we shall have done justice to ourselves by placing on record these views; and I submit that, as the repeal agitation of 1867–69 failed to accomplish the object proposed, yet nonetheless it accomplished great good....[36]

As has been observed, the repeal agitation was "part of the political ritual," part of the rhetoric of regional protest which had little basis in actual intention.[37] Whatever the motives of the politicians, the rhetoric struck a responsive chord throughout the province, awakening the latent anti-Confederation sentiment of a previous generation. As an editorial in the Halifax *Morning Chronicle* stated, the resolutions "will inspire the hearts of our people in a long smothered hope," and it proceeded to ask the rhetorical question: "How long are proud spirited people of Nova Scotia going to submit to a condition of vassalage...?"[38]

Having called an election shortly after the repeal resolutions passed in the House, Fielding's government was swept back to office. It would be a serious mistake, however, to argue that repeal was the only issue in the election. The so-called progressive administration of the Fielding government and railway policy were issues as important as that of repeal.[39] It has been argued that:

> The secession threat was little more than political blackmail. In the past, John A. Macdonald had often been willing to purchase support or quell discontent when the cries of protest became too shrill for his sensitive ears and it was a well-known fact that

all provinces had their grievances, and it was also realized that they also had their price.[40]

Following the provincial election of 1886, Fielding found himself in something of a quandary. Even less probable than in 1867–68 was the possibility of securing from the British government an agreement to Nova Scotia's secession from Confederation. The Conservative Party and press had, both during and after the election campaign, condemned Fielding for "dragging out 'the putrid carcass of repeal'";[41] and as the months passed it became clearer and clearer that most Nova Scotians had grown suspicious of the measure and of its possible implications. Rhetoric was one thing, action—especially anti-British action—was another. By the time of the 1887 federal election, the "repeal issue became the Liberal party's albatross,"[42] and Fielding's support of the Liberals in the election revealed, as has been recently suggested, some of the contradictions inherent in his repeal policy. "Fielding was asking Nova Scotians, on the basis of their provincial nationalism, to vote for a federal party that, by definition of its position in the structure of Canadian politics, was antagonistic to repeal."[43] The Conservatives underscored this contradiction and won a majority of the Nova Scotian seats, burying the repeal movement in the process—but not the anti-Confederation and anti-Upper Canadian feeling.

The 1880s repeal agitation in Nova Scotia illustrated at least two important features of the Maritime's adjustment to Confederation. First of all there existed among the provincial population a deep and widespread, though not perhaps overwhelming, sense of grievance with their place in the new nation. This latent or perhaps residual nationalism was strong enough to be manipulated by the political leaders in an attempt to pry concessions from the Dominion government.

Secondly, the episode demonstrated the inability of the federal party organizations to "accommodate themselves to the language of local discontent."[44] In the only arena where regional grievances could be effectively redressed, the House of Commons in Ottawa, Nova Scotians, as well as other Maritime Members of Parliament willingly sacrificed their regional interests on the altar of party loyalty. Maritimers came, by the end of the 1880s, to identify and to locate their political goals and ideologies within the framework provided by their Central Canadian "overlords." As elsewhere in the Dominion, the debate over Macdonald's National Policy became the central political issue of the day; and Maritimers took part in the debate echoing the arguments of Upper Canadians with a growing sense of commitment. Their grievances and their local identities would thus be submerged in the New Dominion and its future.

## NOTES

1 A.G. Bailey, "Railways and the Confederation Issue in New Brunswick," in *Culture and Nationality* (Toronto, 1972), pp. 78–83.
2 *Ibid.*, p. 91.
3 D.G. Bell, "The Confederation Issue in Charlotte County, New Brunswick" (Unpublished M.A. thesis, Queen's University, 1976), p. 95.
4 See D.A. Muise, "The Federal Election of 1867 in Nova Scotia: An Economic Interpretation," *Collections of the Nova Scotia Historical Society*, Vol. 36 (1968), pp. 327–351.
5 *Ibid.*, p. 348.
6 See K.G. Pryke, "Nova Scotia and Confederation, 1864–1870" (Unpublished Ph.D. thesis, Duke University, 1962).
7 D. Weale and H. Baglole, *The Island and Confederation: The End of an Era* ([Charlottetown] 1973), pp. 103–104.
8 Quoted in *ibid.*, p. 116.
9 Bell, pp. 101–102.
10 Bailey, "The Basis and Persistence of Opposition to Confederation in New Brunswick," in *Culture and Nationality*, pp. 104–106.
11 Bailey, "Railways," pp. 86–87.
12 See Bell, "The Federal Election," pp. 109; Bailey, "The Basis," pp. 106–111.
13 See Bailey, "New Brunswick, Keystone of the Arch," *Culture and Nationality*, pp. 118–127.
14 New Brunswick, Debates of the House of Assembly for 1866, p. 89.
15 For an excellent summary of this philosophy see J.M. Beck, "Joseph Howe: Opportunist or Empire Builder," *Canadian Historical Review*, XLI (Sept., 1960), pp. 185–202.
16 Pryke, "Nova Scotia and Confederation," p. 152; Colin D. Howell, "Nova Scotia's Protest Tradition and the Search For a Meaningful Federalism," in D.J. Bercuson (ed.), *Canada and the Burden of Unity* (Toronto, 1977), p. 173.
17 G.C. Burrill, "Maritime Nationalism and the Decline of Maritime Political Culture: An Alternative View" (Unpublished M.A. thesis, Queen's University, 1978), p. 76.
18 Howell, "Nova Scotia's Protest Tradition," p. 172.
19 G.A. Rawlyk, "The Maritimes and the Canadian Community," in M. Wade (ed.), *Regionalism in the Canadian Community* (Toronto, 1969), p. 104.
20 Pryke, "Nova Scotia and Confederation," p. 198.
21 *Ibid.*, p. 152.
22 *Ibid.*, p. 290.
23 J.M. Beck, *The Government of Nova Scotia* (Toronto, 1957), p. 151.
24 See G.A. Rawlyk, "The Island and the States: Prince Edward Island Views the United States, 1763 to 1968" (Unpublished paper, 1977), pp. 105–107.
25 Weale and Baglole, *The Island and Confederation*, pp. 135–137; F.W.P. Bolger, *Prince Edward Island and Confederation 1863–1867* (Charlottetown, 1964), pp. 175–192.
26 F. MacKinnon, *The Government of Prince Edward Island* (Toronto, 1951), pp. 129–130.
27 Weale and Baglole, *The Island and Confederation*, p. 141.

28  See Bolger, *Prince Edward Island*, pp. 235–242; R.T. Naylor, *The History of Canadian Business 1867–1914*, Vol. 1 (Toronto, 1975), pp. 34–35.

29  Quoted in E.D. Ives, *Lawrence Doyle, The Farmer Poet of Prince Edward Island: A Study in Local Song Making* (Orono, 1971), pp. 68–70.

30  H.G. Thorburn, *Politics in New Brunswick* (Toronto, 1961), p. 13.

31  J.M. Beck, "The Party System in Nova Scotia: Tradition and Conservatism," in Martin Robin (ed.), *Canadian Provincial Politics* (Scarborough, 1972), p. 181; see also Beck, *Government of Nova Scotia*, pp. 154–156.

32  MacKinnon, *Government of Prince Edward Island*, pp. 245–247.

33  Quoted in Rawlyk, "The Maritimes," p. 101.

34  Howell, "Nova Scotia's Protest Tradition," pp. 175–177.

35  Nova Scotia Assembly, Journal, 1886, pp. 147–149.

36  Quoted in P.R. Blakeley, "Party Government in Nova Scotia 1878–1897" (Unpublished M.A. thesis, Dalhousie University, 1945) p. 94.

37  Rawlyk, "The Maritimes," p. 111–113.

38  Halifax *Morning Chronicle*, May 10, 1886.

39  Rawlyk, "The Maritimes," p. 111.

40  *Ibid.*

41  Howell, "Nova Scotia's Protest Tradition," p. 178.

42  *Ibid.*, p. 180.

43  Burrill, "Maritime Nationalism," p. 89.

44  Howell, "Nova Scotia's Protest Tradition," p. 181.

# 9

## *Editors' Introduction*

This selection was written at a time when Confederation was commonly interpreted as a great national unification. The provinces of British North America had naturally come together to form one nation, one people, under a strong and dominant central government. French Canadians had been persuaded by a far-sighted George-Étienne Cartier that they should be part of this nation—that they should come together with other Canadians to form a single people. Older versions of the story held that what was needed for French Canadians to be persuaded was to grant them modest cultural rights in Quebec. The version that had become popular in the 1970s held that pan-Canadian bilingualism had been part of the deal, making it possible for French Canadians to be at home all over the Confederation and thus fully part of the single Canadian people. Historian W.L. Morton described John A. Macdonald as one of the four great unifiers of the nineteenth century, along with Cavour, Bismarck, and Lincoln.

In French Canada, however, the objective of Confederation had been portrayed not as centralizing but as decentralizing, not as unification but as separation. Somehow, English-Canadian nationalist scholars, from F.R. Scott on the left to Donald Creighton on the right, had overlooked the fact that before Confederation, Quebec and Ontario had been more unified than after, that they had not even existed as distinct entities but had together formed one single province. Disaggregating that province was the main selling point of those promoting Confederation in French Canada. Far from merging with others to form a single Canadian nation, the French-Canadian nation would become more distinct and more autonomous under Confederation, having a province of its own—Quebec—with laws and institutions chosen by its French-Canadian majority. Associated with other provinces in a federal partnership to promote economic and security interests, Quebec would always be distinct and autonomous, representing and embodying a distinct French-Canadian nation.

Source: A.I. Silver, "Confederation and Quebec," in *The French-Canadian Idea of Confederation: 1864–1900*, 2nd ed. (Toronto: University of Toronto Press, 1997), 33–50.

A.I. Silver

# Confederation and Quebec

WHEN FRENCH LOWER Canadians were called on to judge the proposed confederation of British North American provinces, the first thing they wanted to know was what effect it would have on their own nationality. Before deciding whether or not they approved, they wanted to hear "what guarantees will be offered for the future of the French-Canadian nationality, to which we are attached above all else."[1] From Richelieu's Rouge

---

1    *La Gazette de Sorel*, 23 June 1864.

MPP to Quebec's Catholic-Conservative *Courtier du Canada,* everyone promised to judge the work of the Great Coalition according to the same criterion.[2] Even Montreal's *La Minerve,* known to be George-Étienne Cartier's own organ, promised to make its judgement from a national point of view:

> If the plan seems to us to safeguard Lower Canada's special interests, its religion and its nationality, we'll give it our support; if not, we'll fight it with all our strength.[3]

But this quotation reminds us that concern for the French-Canadian nationality had geographical implications, that Canadians in the 1860s generally considered French Canada and Lower Canada to be equivalent. When French Canadians spoke of their *patrie,* their homeland, they were invariably referring to Quebec. Even the word *Canada,* as they used it, usually referred to the lower province, or, even more specifically, to the valley of the St Lawrence, that ancient home of French civilization in America, whose special status went back to the seventeenth century. Thus, when Cartier sang "O Canada! mon pays! mes amours!" he was referring to the "majestic course of the Saint-Laurent";[4] and Cartier's protégé, Benjamin Suite, versifying like his patron, also found French Canada's "Patrie ... on the banks of the Saint-Laurent."[5]

Throughout the discussion of Confederation, between 1864 and 1867, there ran the assumption that French Canada was a geographical as well as an ethnic entity, forming, as the *Revue Canadienne* pointed out optimistically, "the most considerable, the most homogeneous, and the most regularly constituted population group" in the whole Confederation.[6] *La Minerve,* which, as has been seen, characterized Lower Canada by a religion and a nationality, referred also to a "Franco-Canadian nationality, which really exists today on the banks of the St Lawrence, and which has affirmed itself more than once."[7] Nor was the equation of Lower Canada with French Canada only a pro-Confederationist notion. The editors of the *Union Nationale* also maintained that the way to defend the French-Canadian nationality was to defend the rights of Lower Canada.[8]

It followed from this equation that provincial autonomy was to be sought in the proposed constitution as a key safeguard of the interests of French Canada. "We must never forget," asserted the *Gazette de Sorel,* "that French Canadians need more reassurance than the other provinces for their civil and religious immunities...." But since French Canada was a province, its immunities were to be protected by provincial autonomy; hence, "this point is important above all for Lower Canada...."[9]

On this key issue, French Canadians felt themselves to have different interests from those of other British North Americans. Thus, Carder's organ:

> The English ... have nothing to fear from the central government, and their first concern is to ensure its proper functioning. This is what they base their hopes upon, and the need for strong local governments only takes second place in their minds.
>
> The French press, on the contrary, feels that guarantees for the particular autonomy of our nationality must come before all else in the federal constitution. It sees the whole system as based on these very guarantees.[10]

2   Perrault quoted in the *Gazette de Sorrel,* 3 Sept. 1864; Le Courrier du Canada, 24 June 1864.
3   *La Minerve,* 9 Sept. 1864. After the Quebec Resolutions were known, journalists, politicians, and clergy still claimed to judge them by the same criterion. See, eg., *Le Journal de Quebec,* 24 Dec. 1864. Joseph Cauchon, *L'Union desprovinces de l'Amerique britannique du Nord* (Quebec: Cote 1865), pp. 19, 41; *Nouvelle constitution du Canada,* p. 59.
4   Most relevantly quoted in Auguste Achintre and J.B. Labelle, *Canute: La Confederation* (n.p., n.d.), p. 4. Cartier, indeed, saw French Canada as geographically defined. J.-C. Bonenfant claims that while he fought for the French Canadians, "seuls a ses yeux comptent ceux qui habitent le Bas-Canada." See Bonenfant's article, "Le Canada et les hommes politique de 1867," in the *RHAF,* xxi, 3a (1967), pp. 579-80. At the 1855 funeral of Ludger Duvernay, the founder of the Saint-Jean-Baptiste Society, Cartier had warned that every nationality, including French Canada, must possess an "élément territorial" in order to survive. See Joseph Taise, ed., *Discours de Sir Georges Cartier* (Montreal: Senecal et Fils 1893), p. 95. Cartier also used the very expression 'French Canada' in a geographical sense, meaning Lower Canada. See, eg., Tasse, p. 83.
5   *La Revue Canadienne,* 1 (1864), p. 696.

6   Ibid., iv (1867), p. 477.
7   *La Minerve,* 25 Sept. 1865.
8   *L'Union Nationale,* 3 Sept. 1864. All of these quotations, of course, are merely variations of Louis-François Laflèche's statement (in *Qaelques considérations,* p. 43), "Les Canadiens-français sont réellement une nation; la vallée du St-Laurent est leur patrie."
9   *La Gazette de Sorel,* 14 Jan. 1865. Also, *La Minerve,* 10 and 14 Sept. 1864.
10  *La Minerve,* 14 Sept. 1864.

*Le Courrier de St-Hyacinthe* agreed that "we do not have the same ideas as our compatriots of British origin concerning the powers which are to be given to the central government.... We cannot consent to the loss of our national autonomy...."[11] The Rouges also saw opposition between French and English-Canadian interests. It was because of this opposition, they commented pessimistically, that George Brown had been able to reveal details of the Quebec Resolutions in Toronto, to the evident satisfaction of Upper Canadians, while in Lower Canada the ministers refused to make any information public.[12]

New Brunswick's governor, A.H. Gordon, in whose house Cartier had been a guest after the Charlottetown Conference, also saw an opposition between English and French-Canadian aspirations. He reported to the Colonial Secretary that while the former seemed to expect a very centralized union, "'federal union' in the mouth of a Lower Canadian means the independence of his Province from all English or Protestant influences...."[13]

This was, indeed, what it seemed to mean to the French-Canadian press. Thus:

We want a confederation in which the federal principle will be applied in its fullest sense—one which will give the central power control only over general questions in no way affecting the interests of each separate section, while leaving to the local legislatures everything which concerns our particular interests.[14]

A confederation would be a fine thing, but only "if it limited as much as possible the rights of the federal government, to general matters, and left complete independence to the local governments."[15] As early as 1858, French-Canadian advocates of a British North American confederation had argued that "it would certainly be necessary to give the separate [provincial] legislatures the greatest possible share of power," and even that the federal government should only

have its powers "by virtue of a perpetual but limited concession from the different provinces."[16]

While most papers did not go so far as to support the provincial sovereignty which that last implied,[17] they did opt for co-ordinate sovereignty:

The federal power will be sovereign, no doubt, but it will have power only over certain general questions clearly defined by the constitution.

This is the only plan of confederation which Lower Canada can accept.... The two levels of government must both be sovereign, each within its jurisdiction as clearly defined by the constitution.[18]

What, after all, could be simpler than that each power, federal or provincial, should have complete control of its own field?

Isn't that perfectly possible without having the local legislatures derive their powers from the central legislature or vice versa? Isn't it possible for each of these bodies to have perfect independence within the scope of its own jurisdiction, neither one being able to invade the jurisdiction of the other?[19]

To be sure, the fathers of Confederation were aware that French Canadians would reject complete centralization. John A. Macdonald told the Assembly that though he would have preferred a legislative union, he realized it would be unacceptable to French Canadians. Nevertheless, he felt the Quebec Resolutions did not provide for a real federalism, but would "give to the General Government the strength of a legislative and administrative union." They represented "the happy medium" between a legislative and a federal union, which, while providing guarantees for those who feared the former, would also give "us the strength of a Legislative union."[20] In short, he appeared to

11 Le Courrier de St-Hyacinthe, 23 Sept. 1864. Also, *Le Journal de Québec*, 4 July 1867.
12 *Le Pays*, 8 Nov. 1864.
13 In G.P. Browne, ed., *Documents on the Confederation of British North America* (Toronto: McClelland and Stewart, 1969), pp. 42–3. Also, pp. 47, 49, 168 for Gordon's other assertions on the matter.
14 *Le Courrier de St-Hyacinthe*, 2 Sept. 1864.
15 *La Gazette de Sorel*, 30 July 1864.
16 J.-C. Taché, *Des Provinces*, pp. 147, 148.
17 Some did support provincial sovereignty, however—at least at times. See, eg., *La Gazette de Sorel*, 27 Aug. 1864.
18 *Le Courrier de St-Hyacinthe*, 2 Sept. 1864. Also, 28 Oct. 1864.
19 *Le Journal de Québec*, 1 Sept. 1864. Also, 6 Sept. 1864; *Le Courrier du Canada*, 30 Sept. 1864, and 10 Oct. 1864.
20 In P.B. Waite, ed., *The Confederation Debates in the Province of Canada, 1865* (Toronto: McClelland and Stewart 1963), pp. 40, 41, 43. Macdonald's belief that he had obtained something more centralized than a federation is dramatically expressed in his well-

understand the Quebec scheme to provide for the closest thing possible to a legislative union, saving certain guarantees for the French Canadians' "language, nationality and religion."

This interpretation was hotly rejected by French Canadians of both parties, including those who spoke for Macdonald's partner, Cartier:

> Whatever guarantees may be offered here, Lower Canada will never consent to allowing its particular interests to be regulated by the inhabitants of the other provinces.... We want a solid constitution ... but we demand above all perfect freedom and authority for the provinces to run their own internal affairs.[21]

Let there be no mistake about it: anything close to a legislative union "cannot and will not be accepted by the French-Canadian population." A centralized union would be fatal to the French-Canadian nationality.[22] The *Courrier de St-Hyacinthe*, in fact, summed up the whole French-Canadian position when it said:

> But whatever guarantees they decide to offer us, we cannot accept any union other than a federal union based on the well-understood principles of confederations.[23]

In taking this view, French Canadians were led to reject another position adopted by John A. Macdonald: that the United States example proved the necessity of a strong central government. He argued that the Civil War had occurred there because the individual states had too much power under the American constitution—power which had given the federation too much centrifugal thrust. To avoid this, British North America must have a dominant central authority.[24]

In French Canada, even *La Minerve* considered Macdonald's reasoning to be nonsensical. "We believe that this is a specious argument. The United States have a strongly centralized government, which is even capable of acting despotically, as we can see every day." If you gave a central government too much power over too many localities, it would inevitably antagonize some of them.

This is precisely what happened in the United States, where the war was caused not by the excessive power of the local governments, but by the central government, whose tyrannical actions came into direct opposition to the particular interests of a considerable part of the confederation.[25]

*Le Journal de Québec* agreed whole-heartedly. The causes of the American Civil War were to be sought, not in the powers of the states, but in "the awful tyranny which the central government of the United States imposes on the state authorities, by taking them over and stealing their most inalienable powers...."[26]

There was agreement between Bleus and Rouges that the autonomy of a French-Canadian Lower Canada was the chief thing to be sought in any new constitution. Accordingly, the Confederation discussion revolved around whether or not the Quebec plan achieved that aim. As far as the opposition was concerned, it did not. The Rouges maintained that this was an "anglicizing bill,"[27] the latest in a line of attempts to bring about the "annihilation of the French race in Canada," and thus realize Lord Durham's wicked plans.[28] And it would achieve this goal because it was not really a confederation at all, but a legislative

known letter of 19 Dec. 1864 to M.C. Cameron (PAC, Macdonald papers), in which he predicts that within a lifetime, "both local Parliaments and Governments [will be] absorbed in the General power."

21  La Minerve, 15 Oct. 1864. See also Le Courrier de St-Hyacinthe, 2 Sept. 1864.

22  Le Courrier du Canada, 16 Sept. 1864.

23  Le Courrier de St-Hyacinthe, 18 Oct. 1864. See also Le Pays, 13 Oct. 1864; L'Ordre, 14 Oct. 1864; Contre-poison: la Confédération c'est le salut du Bas-Canada (Montreal: Senécal 1867), p. 9.

24  The argument is stated clearly and briefly in a letter to M.C. Cameron. See also Donald Creighton, John A. Macdonald (2 vols.;

Toronto: Macmillan 1966), 1, 369, 375–6, 378–80; P.B. Waite, "The Quebec Resolutions and the Courrier du Canada, 1864-1865," in the CHR, XL, 4 (Dec., 1959), p. 294; etc., etc.

25  La Minerve, 15 Oct. 1864.

26  Le Journal de Québec, 27 Aug. 1864. See also Joseph Cauchon, L'Union des provinces, p. 39. Le Courrier du Canada, far from seeing the U.S. constitution as embodying the error of excessive decentralization, found it an apt model for the Quebec Conference to follow. See J.-C. Bonenfant, "L'Idée que les Canadiens-français de 1864 pouvaient avoir du federalisme," in Culture, xxv (1964), p. 316. Some Rouges, notably Médéric Lanctôt in L'Union Nationale, went so far as to maintain that it would be more desirable for Lower Canada to join the U.S. than the British North American Union, precisely because it would have more autonomy as an American state.

27  Le Pays, 27 Mar. 1867.

28  Ibid., 2 Apr. 1867. Also, 23 July 1864; and La Confédération couronnement, p. 5.

union in disguise, a mere extension of the Union of 1840.[29] "It is in vain," cried C.-S. Cherrier at a Rouge-sponsored rally, "that they try to disguise it under the name of confederation.... This *quasi* legislative union is just a step toward a complete and absolute legislative union."[30]

The evidence of Confederation's wickedness could be seen by its opponents on every hand. Did it not involve representation by population—the dreaded "Rep by Pop" which French Canadians had resisted so vigorously till now?[31] And were not English Canadians proclaiming that centralization was to be the chief characteristic of the new regime? The Canadian legislature had even ordered the translation and publication of Alpheus Todd's essay on the provincial governments—an essay which included the remark that these would be "subject to the legal power of the federal parliament."[32] Indeed, argued the Rouges, it was hardly worthwhile for Quebec to have such an elaborate, two-chamber parliament as was proposed, since, as Todd made clear, the federal legislature "will be able to quash and annul all its decisions."[33]

The Quebec Resolutions themselves indicated that Todd was right, that the provincial powers would be scarcely more than a mirage:

Mind you, according to everything we hear from Quebec, the prevailing idea in the conference is to give the central government the widest powers and to leave the local governments only a sort of municipal jurisdiction....[34]

*Le Pays* had been afraid of this from the time the Great Coalition had announced its programme. "Without finances, without power to undertake major public works, the local legislature will hardly be any-thing other than a big municipal council where only petty matters will be discussed."[35] When the Quebec Conference had ended, opposition papers still had the same impression: "In short, the general parliament will have supreme control over the local legislatures."[36] Even provincial control of education was an illusion, since the governor-general at Ottawa could veto any provincial legislation in the field.[37]

Finally, English-Canadian talk of creating a new nationality only strengthened Rouge fears that Confederation meant centralization and assimilation. When the legislature refused to pass A.-A. Dorion's resolution of January, 1865, that Canadians neither desired nor sought to create a new nationality, his brother's newspaper became convinced that it was all over for Lower Canada and its French-Canadian nationality.[38]

In answering all these opposition arguments, the Bleus certainly did not attempt to defend the notion of a strong or dominant central government. But, they maintained, that was not at all what British North America was going to get. Lower Canada, liberated from the forced Union of 1840, would become a distinct and autonomous province in a loose and decentralized Confederation—that was the real truth of the matter.

The defenders of Confederation refuted the opposition's arguments one after another. Did the Rouges speak of Rep by Pop? Why, any schoolboy ought to see the difference between Rep by Pop, which the Bleus had opposed as long as the legislative union remained, and a "confederation which would give us, first of all, local legislatures for the protection of our sectional interests, and then a federal legislature in which the most populous province would have a majority *only in the lower house*."[39] As long as there was only a single legislature for the two Canadas, Rep by Pop would have put "our civil law and religious institutions at the

29  *La Confederation couronnement*, pp. 5, 8; *Le Pays*, 12 Nov. 1864, 9 Feb. 1865, 2 Apr. 1867.
30  C.-S. Cherrier et al., *Discours sur la Confederation* (Montreal: Lanctot, Bouthillier et Thompson 1865), p. 13.
31  *Le Pays*, 23 and 28 June, 14 July, 8 Nov. 1864; *L'Ordre*, 27 June 1864; *L'Union Nationale*, 8 Nov. 1864; *Confédération couronnement*, p. 13.
32  Alpheus Todd, *Quelques considérations sur la formation des Gouvernements beaux du Haut et du Bas-Canada ...* (Ottawa: Hunter, Rose et Lemieux 1866), p. 5.
33  *Le Pays*, 28 July 1866. Also, 27 Sept. 1864, and 19 July 1866.
34  *Le Pays*, 25 Oct. 1864.
35  Ibid., 23 July 1864. Also, *L'Ordre*, 22 July 1864.
36  *L'Union Nationale*, 11 Nov. 1864. Also, 3 Sept. 1864; *Le Pays*, 14 and 23 July 1864.
37  *L'Ordre*, 14 Nov. 1864.
38  *Le Défricheur*, 25 Jan. 1865. All these fears which inspired the opposition also provoked doubts in the minds of some people who were otherwise supporters of the government. "Nous avons toujours dit," remarked *Le Canadien*, on 3 Aug. 1866, "que dans le plan de confédération actuel, on n'avait pas laissé assez de pouvoir aux gouvernements locaux et trop au gouvernement général." See also, eg., 3 Feb. 1865.
39  *Le Journal de Québec*, 5 July 1864.

mercy of the fanatics." But Confederation would eliminate that danger by creating a separate province of
Quebec with its own distinct government:

> We have a system of government which puts under
> the exclusive control of Lower Canada those ques-
> tions which we did not want the fanatical partisans
> of Mr Brown to deal with....
>
> Since we have this guarantee, what difference
> does it make to us whether or not Upper Canada
> has more representatives than we in the Commons?
> Since the Commons will be concerned only with
> general questions of interest to all provinces and not
> at all with the particular affairs of Lower Canada, it's
> all the same to us, as a nationality, whether or not
> Upper Canada has more representation.[40]

This was central to the Bleu picture of Confederation:
all questions affecting the French-Canadian nationality as such would be dealt with at Quebec City, and
Ottawa would be "powerless, if it should want to invade
the territory reserved for the administration of the
local governments."[41] As for the questions to be dealt
with at Ottawa, they might divide men as Liberals
and Conservatives, but not as French and English
Canadians. "In the [federal] Parliament," said Hector
Langevin, "there will be no questions of race, nationality, religion or locality, as this Legislature will only be
charged with the settlement of the great general questions which will interest alike the whole Confederacy
and not one locality only."[42] Cartier made the same
point when he said that "in the questions which will
be submitted to the Federal parliament, there will be
no more danger to the rights and privileges of the
French Canadians than to those of the Scotch, English
or Irish."[43] Or, as his organ, La Minerve, put it, Ottawa
would have jurisdiction only over those matters "in
which the interests of everyone, French Canadians,
English, or Scotch, are identical."[44] For the rest—for
everything which concerned the French Canadians

*as* French Canadians—for the protection and promotion of their national interests and institutions, they
would have their own province with their own parliament and their own government.

And what a parliament! and what a government!
Why, the very fact that Quebec was to have a bicameral legislature was proof of the importance they were
to have. "In giving ourselves a complete government,"
argued the Bleus, "we affirm the fact of our existence as
a separate nationality, as a complete society, endowed
with a perfect system of organization."[45] Indeed, the
very fact that Ontario's legislature was to have only one
house while Quebec's had two served to underline the
distinctiveness, the separateness, and the autonomy of
the French-Canadian province:

> It is very much in our interest for our local leg-
> islature to have enough importance and dignity
> to gain respect for its decisions.... For us, French
> Canadians, who are only entering Confederation
> on the condition of having our own legislature as a
> guarantee of our autonomy, it is vital for that legis-
> lature not to be just a simple council whose delib-
> erations won't carry any weight....
>
> The deeper we can make the demarcation line
> between ourselves and the other provinces, the more
> guarantee we'll have for the conservation of our spe-
> cial character as a people.[46]

Here was the very heart and essence of the pro-
Confederation argument in French Lower Canada: the
Union of the Canadas was to be broken up, and the
French Canadians were to take possession of a province
of their own—a province with an enormous degree of
autonomy. In fact, *separation* (from Upper Canada)
and *independence* (of Quebec within its jurisdictions)
were the main themes of Bleu propaganda. "As a distinct and separate nationality," said *La Minerve*, "we
form a state within the state. We enjoy the full exercise of our rights and the formal recognition of our
national independence."[47]

40  *Réponses aux censeurs de la Confédération* (St-Hyacinthe: *Le Courrier* 1867), pp. 47–9.
41  *La Minerve*, 20 Sept. 1864. Also, *Le Courrier du Canada*, 11 July 1864.
42  *Parliamentary Debates on the Subject of the Confederation of the British North American Provinces* (Ottawa 1865), p. 368.
43  Ibid., pp. 54–5.
44  *La Minerve*, 15 Oct. 1864.
45  Ibid., 17 July 1866.
46  *Le Journal des Trois-Rivières*, 24 July 1866. Also, *Le Courrier de St-Hyacinthe*, 10 July 1866.
47  *La Minerve*, 1 July 1867. Also, 2 July 1867: "[Comme] nation dans la nation, nous devons veiller à notre autonomie propre...."

The provinces, in this view, were to be the political manifestations of distinct nationalities. This was the line taken in 1858 by J.-C. Taché, when he wrote that in the provincial institutions, "the national and religious elements will be able to develop their societies freely, and the separate populations realize ... their aspirations and their dispositions." And it was widely understood that Taché had played a vital role in influencing the course of the Quebec Conference.[48] Cartier himself had told that conference that a federal rather than a unitary system was necessary, "because these provinces are peopled by different nations and by peoples of different religions."[49] It was in this light that *La Minerve* saw the Quebec programme as establishing "distinctly that all questions having to do with our religion or our nationality will be under the jurisdiction of our local legislature."[50] All the pro-Confederation propagandists were agreed that "the future of our race, the preservation of everything which makes up our national character, will depend directly on the local legislature."[51] It was the Lower Canadian ministers who had insisted, at the Quebec Conference, that education, civil and religious institutions should be under provincial jurisdiction, in order that Quebec should have the power to take charge of the French-Canadian national future.[52] Indeed, that power extended well beyond civil and religious institutions. It included "the ownership and control of all their lands, mines, and minerals; the control of all their municipal affairs"[53]— everything "which is dearest and most precious to us"[54]—all power, in fact, necessary to promote the national life of French Canada.

All these powers were to be entrusted to the government of a province in which French Canadians would form "almost the whole" of the population, and in which everyone would have to speak French to take part in public life.[55] Yes, Confederation, by breaking up the union of the two Canadas, would make the French Canadians a majority in their own land,"[56] so that "our beautiful French language will be the only one spoken in the Parliament of the Province of Quebec...."[57]

What was more, the control which French Canadians would exercise over their wide fields of jurisdiction would be an absolute control, and "all right of interference in these matters is formally denied to the federal government."[58] The Bleus, in fact, claimed to have succeeded in obtaining a system of co-ordinate sovereignty. "Each of these governments," they explained, "will be given absolute powers for the questions within its jurisdiction, and each will be equally sovereign in its own sphere of action."[59] Some over-enthusiastic advocates of the new régime even claimed that the provinces alone would be sovereign, "the powers of the federal gove[r]nment being considered only as a concession of specifically designated rights."[60] But even the moderate majority was firm in maintaining that the provinces would be in no way inferior or subordinate to the federal gove[r]nment, that they would be at least its equal, and that each government would be sovereign and untouchable in its own sphere of action:

In the plan of the Quebec conference there is no delegation of power either from above or from below,

48 Taché, *Des Provinces*, p. 151: "Les éléments nationaux et religieux pourront à laise opérer leurs mouvements de civilisation, et les populations séparées donner cours ... a leurs aspirations et à leurs tendances." During the Confederation Debates, Joseph Blanchet claimed that the Quebec Resolutions were, essentially, the very scheme which Taché had presented in his 1858 pamphlet (p. 457 of the Ottawa edition of the debates). Joseph Tassé asserted in 1885 that Taché had acted as special adviser to the Canadian ministers at the Quebec Conference. (See J.-C. Bonenfant, "L'Idée que les Canadiens-français de 1864," p. 314.) And Taché's son told an interviewer in 1935 that his father (whose uncle, Sir E.-P. Taché, had repeatedly recommended the nephew's scheme to the conference) had several times been called into the sessions, "vraisemblablement pour donner des explications sur son projet." See Louis Taché, "Sir Etienne-Pascal Taché et la Confédération canadienne," in the *Revue de l'Université d'Ottawa*, v (1935), p. 24.
49 In Browne, *Documents*, p. 128.
50 *La Minerve*, 30 Dec. 1864. See also *Le Journal de Québec*, 24 Dec. 1864.
51 *Le Courrier de St-Hyacinthe*, 28 Oct. 1864. Also, 23 Sept. and 22 Nov. 1864.
52 *Le Courrier de St-Hyacinthe*, 28 Oct. 1864. Also, 23 Sept. and 22 Nov. 1864.
53 *Le Courrier du Canada*, 13 Mar. 1867. Also, 28 June 1867.
54 *La Minerve*, 1 July 1867. Also, 2 July 1867; and the speech of Sir Narcisse Belleau in the *Confederation Debates* (Waite edition), p. 29.
55 *Le Courrier de St-Hyacinthe*, 10 July 1866.
56 Cauchon, *L'Union*, p. 45.
57 *Contre-poison*, p. 20. See also *Réponses aux censeurs*, p. 48.
58 *Contre-poison*, p. 20. Also, *Le Journal de Québec*, 15 Nov. 1864, and 24 Dec. 1864; Cauchon, *L'Union*, pp. 45–6; *L'Union des Cantons de l'Est* (Arthabaskaville), 4 July 1867; Governor Gordon in Brown, *Documents*, p. 75; Bishop Larocque in *Nouvelle constitution*, p. 75.
59 *Le Courrier de St-Hyacinthe*, 28 Oct. 1864.
60 E.-P. Taché, quoted in Bonenfant, "L'Idée que les Canadiens," p. 315.

because the provinces, not being independent states, receive their powers, as does the federal authority, from the imperial parliament.[61]

Politicians and journalists expressed this same view, in the legislature as well as in print. Thus, Joseph Blanchet told the Assembly: "I consider that under the present plan of confederation the local legislatures are sovereign with regard to the powers accorded to them, that is to say in local affairs."[62]

It may be that French-Canadian Confederationists went farther than they ought to have done in interpreting the Quebec Resolutions the way they did. Part of the reason for this may have been ignorance. A Bleu back-bencher like C.B. de Niverville of Trois-Rivières could admit in the legislative debates that he had not read the resolutions, and what's more, that his ignorance of the English language had prevented him from following much of the debate. In this very situation he saw—or thought he saw— an argument for Confederation. For as he understood it, the new arrangement would remove French-Canadian affairs from an arena where men such as he were at a disadvantage, and place them before a group of French-speaking legislators:

Indeed, what sort of liberty do we have, we who do not understand the English language? We have the liberty to keep quiet, to listen, and to try to understand! (Hear! hear! and prolonged laughter.) Under Confederation, the Upper Canadians will speak their language and the Lower Canadians will speak theirs, just as today; only, when a man finds that his compatriots form the great majority in the assembly in which he sits, he'll have more hope of hearing his language spoken, and as they do today, members will speak the language of the majority.[63]

Such an argument seems virtually to have ignored the very existence of the federal parliament, or at least of the authority it would have over French Canadians.

The case of de Niverville may have been extreme, but it was certainly not the only case of Bleus interpreting the Confederation plan in such a way as to maximize the powers of the provinces and minimize those of Ottawa far beyond anything we have been accustomed to. The federal power to raise taxes "by any mode or system of taxation" was interpreted so as to exclude the right of direct taxation.[64] The federal veto power was represented not as a right to interfere with provincial legislation, but only as an obligation upon Ottawa to act as "guardian of the constitution" by keeping clear the distinction between federal and provincial jurisdictions.[65]

But more important than any of these *specific* arguments was the wide-ranging exuberance of pro-Confederation propaganda. Here was a source of rhetoric that seemed to be promising that Confederation would give French Canadians virtual independence. Quebec was "completely separated from Upper Canada and has a complete governmental organization to administer *all its local affairs* on its own."[66] In the legislative council, E.-P. Taché interrupted his English-language speech on Confederation to tell his French-Canadian followers in French: "If a Federal Union were obtained, it would be tantamount to a separation of the provinces, and Lower Canada would thereby preserve its autonomy together with all the institutions it held so dear."[67] This could not be too often repeated: "The first, and one of the principal clauses of the constitution is the one that brings about the repeal of the Union, so long requested by the Rouges, and separates Lower Canada from Upper Canada."[68] What patriotic French

61    Joseph Cauchon, *Discours ... sur la question de la Confédération* (n.p., n.d.), p. 8: "les provinces, n'étant pas des états independants, reçoivent, avec l'autorité supérieure, leurs organisations politiques du Parlement de l'Empire. Il n'y a que des attributs distincts pour l'une et pour les autres." See also Cauchon's *L'Union*, pp. 40, 52; *Le Courrier du Canada*, 7 Nov. 1864, and in Waite's "The Quebec Resolutions and," pp. 299–300.

62    Joseph Blanchet in *Débats parlementaires sur la question de la Confédération des provinces de l'Amérique Britannique du Nord* (Ottawa: Hunter, Rose et Lemieux 1865), p. 551.

63    Ibid., p. 949.

64    *L'Union des Cantons de l'Est*, 12 Sept. 1867. This argument about direct taxation will not be as unfamiliar to historians as to other payers of federal income tax.

65    *La Minerve*, 3 Dec. 1864. Also, 11 Nov. 1864; *Le Courrier de St-Hyacinthe*, 22 Nov. 1864; *Le Courrier du Canada*, 7 Nov. 1864.

66    *Contre-poison*, p. 13.

67    *Confederation Debates* (Waite edition), p. 22.

68    *Contre-poison*, p. 11. Episcopal statements recommended Confederation on the same basis. Bishop Baillargeon of Tloa, who administered the diocese of Quebec, noted in his pastoral letter that, although there would be a central government, Confederation would, nevertheless, comprise four distinct provinces. "C'est ainsi que le Bas-Canada, désormais séparé du Haut, formera sous le nouveau régime une province séparée qui sera nommé 'la Province de Québec'" (in *Nouvelle constitution*, p. 53).

Canadian could fail to be moved by what the fathers of Confederation had achieved?

> We've been separated from Upper Canada, we're called the Province of Quebec, we have a French-Canadian governor … we're going to have our own government and our own legislature, where everything will be done by and for French Canadians, and in French. You'd have to be a renegade … not to be moved to tears, not to feel your heart pound with an indescribable joy and a deserved pride at the thought of these glorious results of the patriotism and unquenchable energy of our statesmen, of our political leaders, who … have turned us over into our own hands, who have restored to us our complete autonomy and entrusted the sacred heritage of our national traditions to a government chosen from among us and composed of our own people.[69]

This sort of exaggerated rhetoric invited an obvious response from the opposition. If you really are serious about separation from Upper Canada, they asked, if you really do want to obtain autonomy for French Lower Canada, then why not go the whole way? Why not break up the old union altogether, instead of joining this confederation? "Everyone is agreed that only the repeal of the union would give us the independence of action needed for the future of Lower Canadians."[70] If necessary, some sort of commercial association would be sufficient to satisfy Upper Canada in return for political separation.[71] The Confederationists answered this, not by saying that Quebec's independence was an undesirable goal, not by saying that French Canadians wanted to join together with English Canadians to form a Canadian nation, but by claiming that complete independence was simply not practicable:

> The idea of making Lower Canada an independent State … has appealed to all of us as schoolboys;

but we don't believe that any serious adult has taken it up so far…. We simply cannot do everything on our own….[72]

This was, perhaps, a temporary condition, and it was to be hoped that one day Quebec *would* be in a position to make good her independence. Yes, French Canada "can and must one day aspire to become a nation";[73] for the moment, however, "we are too young for absolute independence."[74] Of course, whoever says "we are too young" implies that one day we shall be old enough—and Confederation, in the meanwhile, would preserve and prepare French Quebec for that day of destiny.[75]

One obvious reason why complete independence was not a realistic goal for the present was that Lower Canada was still part of the British Empire, and imperial approval, without which no constitutional change was possible, could not be obtained in the face of intense English-Canadian opposition.[76] But beyond that, it should be clear that an independent Quebec would inevitably be gobbled up by the United States. "We would be on our own, and our obvious weakness would put us at the mercy of a stronger neighbour."[77] French Canadians must understand, therefore, that, "unless we hurry up and head with all sails set toward Confederation, the current will carry us rapidly toward annexation."[78]

The weakness of an independent Quebec would be both military and economic. The first of these weaknesses could hardly be more apparent to Quebeckers than it was in the mid-1860s, for just as the Anglo-American frictions created by the Civil War were impressing upon them the dangers arising from American hostility, the desire of British politicians to disengage themselves from colonial defence

69  *Contre-poison*, p. 3.
70  *L'Union Nationale*, 3 Sept. 1864. Also, *Confédération couronnement*, p. 5.
71  *L'Union Nationale*, 7 Nov. 1864. Even the pro-Conservative *Gazette de Sorel* admitted, on 23 June 1864, that it had always preferred a straightforward breakup of the union as the best solution for French Canada. Also, 30 July 1864.
72  *La Minerve*, 5 Jan. 1865.
73  *Le Journal de Québec*, 17 Dec. 1864.
74  *Le Pionnier de Sherbrooke*, 9 Mar. 1867.
75  See Cauchon, *L'Union*, p. 29.
76  *La Minerve*, 28 Sept. 1864.
77  *Le Courrier de St-Hyacinthe*, 25 Nov. 1864. Also, *Le Courrier du Canada*, 10 Oct. 1864.
78  Cauchon, *L'Union*, p. 25. Cartier put the same alternative to the legislative assembly, when he said: "The matter resolved itself into this, either we must obtain British American Confederation or be absorbed in an American Confederation." (*Confederation Debates*, Waite edition, p. 50.) See also *La Minerve*, 13 Jan. 1865; and *Nouvelle constitution*, pp. 60, 66–7, 78ff.; *La Revue Canadienne*, 11 (1865), p. 116, on Confederation as an alternative to "le gouffre et le néant de la république voisine."

responsibilities was causing Canadians to think as never before of their own defences. Intercolonial co-operation seemed a natural response to the situation:

> No-one could deny that the annexation of the British colonies, either by their consent or by force, is intended and desired by the northern states; it is a no less evident truth that, as things stand today, we could resist their armies with help from Europe; but that on their own, without a political union, without a strong common organization, the colonies could, in the foreseeable future, sustain such a combat—that is something which no-one would dare to maintain....[79]

It was in these circumstances that the Confederation project presented itself. Only weeks after the end of the Quebec Conference, the St Alban's raid brought the fear of imminent war with the United States. Yet at the same time, recent British military reports on colonial defence made Quebeckers wonder how much help they could expect if war broke out. "We must not place unlimited hopes on the support of the mother-country in case of war with our neighbours. Circumstances more powerful than the will of men could render such confidence illusory."[80] Yet the prospect for the separate British North American colonies without British support was bleak: "separate from each other, we'd be sure to be invaded and crushed one after the other."[81] Not only would Confederation give Quebec the advantage of a joint defence organization with the other colonies, but also, by this very fact, it would make Britain willing to give more help in case of war than she would have been willing to give to the isolated and inefficient defence effort of a separate Quebec.[82]

Quebec's economic weakness could be seen already in the flood of emigration directed toward the United States. Clearly, French Lower Canada's economy was not able, on its own, to support all its population. To keep her people at home, the province must co-operate with others to create opportunities. As French Canadians went to seek manufacturing jobs in New England, manufacturing must be established in Lower Canada;[83] by 1867, Quebec papers were appealing to outside capital to set up mills in the province.[84] Long before, Hector Langevin, in a prize-winning essay, had looked to the development of the St Lawrence transportation system to check emigration by providing jobs in commercial enterprises.[85] But the St Lawrence was an interprovincial organization—even more in the era of railroads than in that of the canal.[86]

Thus, the need for economic viability dictated some form of central authority and prevented Quebec's independence from being complete:

> The more provinces there are gathered together, the greater will be the revenues, the more major works and improvements will be undertaken and consequently, the more prosperity there will be. What Lower Canada was unable to do on its own, we have done together with Upper Canada; and what the two Canadas have been unable to do together will be done by the confederation, because it will have markets and sea ports which we have not had.[87]

The British North American provinces had been endowed with resources enough. If they worked together to develop them, they could enjoy abundance, material progress, and even economic power.[88] But if they failed to co-operate, if they remained separate and isolated, then their economies would be weak, and inevitably they would become dependent on the United States, the prosperous neighbour to the south. "But we know that where there is economic dependence there will also be political dependence...."[89]

79  *La Revue Canadienne*, 11 (1865), p. 159.

80  *La Minerve*, 7 Dec. 1864. The danger of war with the U.S. was announced not only by *La Minerve* in December 1864, but also by *Le Courrier du Canada*, 16 Nov. 1866, and *La Gazette de Sorel*, 19 Nov. 1864, while the need to prepare for British disengagement was urged by the *Journal de Québec*, 17 Dec. 1864, and *Le Courrier du Canada*, 5 Oct. 1864.

81  Cauchon, *L'Union*, p. 32. See also Jules Fournier, *Le Canada: Son présent et son avenir* (Montreal: *La Minerve* 1865), p. 4.

82  *Contre-poison*, p. 8.

83  *L'Union Nationale*, 19 July 1866.

84  *L'Union des Cantons de l'Est*, 3 Jan. 1867.

85  Hector Langevin, *Le Canada, ses institutions, ressources, produits, manufactures, etc., etc., etc.* (Quebec: Lovell et Lamoureux 1855), p. 96.

86  *L'Union des Cantons de l'Est*, 8 Aug. 1867.

87  *Contre-poison*, pp. 48–9.

88  Taché, *Des provinces*, pp. 10–11; *Le Courrier de St-Hyacinthe*, 23 July 1867; *Réponses aux censeurs*, pp. 3–4; Achintre and Labelle, *Cantate*, pp. 2–3, 8; Cauchon, *L'Union*, p. 3; Henry Lacroix, *Opuscule sur le présent et l'avenir du Canada* (Montreal: Senecal 1867).

89  *La Revue Canadienne*, 11 (1865), p. 103. See also Fournier, pp. 2–3, who argued that as long as Canada was economically dependent

THERE WERE STRONG reasons, then, why Quebec's independence could not be complete, why the nationalist longing for separateness had to compromise with the practical need for viability. But if some form of association with the rest of British North America was necessary, the degree of unification must be the minimum required to make Quebec viable. In the spring of 1867, on his way home from London, where he had helped write the BNA Act, Cartier told a welcoming crowd at a station-stop in the Eastern Townships that his main preoccupation had always been to protect the French-Canadian nationality, language, and institutions. "That is why I was careful to make sure that the federal government would receive only that amount of power which was strictly necessary to serve the general interests of the Confederation."[90] This meant, as E.-P. Taché had explained in 1864, that Ottawa would have enough power "to do away with some of the internal hindrances to trade, and to unite the Provinces for mutual defence," but that the provinces would remain the agencies to which the "majority of the people" would look for the protection of their "rights and privileges" and "liberties."[91]

Perhaps this arrangement was not *ideal*; perhaps, even, Confederation was only "the least bad thing in a very bad world."[92] The French-Canadian leaders, after all, had not been alone at the constitutional conferences, and French Canada's own needs and aspirations had had to be reconciled with "our condition of colonial dependence and the heterogeneous elements which make up our population."[93]

Nevertheless, it had to be admitted that, despite Rouge protestations to the contrary, the old union could not have continued longer,[94] that the only alternative to Confederation would have been Rep by Pop,[95] and that, whatever degree of central authority there might be in the confederation, the patriotism of French-Canadian leaders could be relied on to promote the interests of their nationality, just as their patriotism had already won so much for French Canada in the making of the confederation.[96]

And what, then, in the final analysis, had they won? According to Bleu propaganda, Confederation was to be seen as an "alliance" or "association" of nations, each in its own autonomous province, and co-operating for the common welfare.[97] And this "alliance with your neighbours,"[98] this *"federal alliance among several peoples,"*[99] was to be regulated by the terms of a treaty or pact drawn up freely among them. Even the imperial authorities, according to Cartier, in preparing and passing the British North America Act, had accepted that they were only giving the official stamp of approval to an interprovincial compact. "They understood … that the Quebec plan was an agreement among the colonies, which had to be respected, and they respected it."[100]

on overseas trade, she would be politically at the mercy of the U.S., unless she had her own all-British rail link with an ice-free port in New Brunswick or Nova Scotia. See also Cauchon, *L'Union*, pp. 34–5.

90 *L'Union des Cantons de l'Est*, 23 May 1867.

91 Taché was speaking at the Quebec Conference. In Browne, pp. 127–8.

92 Quoted in Waite, 'The Quebec Resolutions and', p. 297. See *Le Courrier du Canada*, 11 Nov. 1864.

93 *Le Courrier de St-Hyacinthe*, 22 Nov. 1864. The opposition tried to stress the weakness and isolation of the French-Canadian delegates to the constitutional conferences as a reproach to them. Eg., *Le Pays*, 13 Oct. 1864. But Confederationists thought it only reasonable to take realities into account. Eg., *La Minerve*, 25 Feb. 1865; *La Gazette de Sorel*, 1 Sept. 1866.

94 *La Gazette de Sorel*, 23 June and 23 July 1864, 14 Jan. 1865; *Le Courrier du Canada*, 24 June 1864; *Le Courrier de St-Hyacinthe*, 8 Nov. 1864; *L'Union des Cantons de l'Est*, 4 Apr. 1864; *La Minverve*, 9 Sept. and 30 Dec. 1864; *Le Journal de Quebec*, 15 Dec. 1864;

Cauchon, *L'Union*, p. 19; *Contre-poison*, p. 7; the pastoral letters of Bishops Cooke and Larocque, in *Nouvelle constitution*, pp. 58–9, 68.

95 *La Minerve*, 28 Dec. 1864; *La Gazette de Sorel*, 30 July 1864; Louis-Francois Lafleche and Bishop Baillargeon, quoted in Walter Ullmann, 'The Quebec Bishops and Confederation', in the CHR, xliv, 3 (Sept., 1963), reprinted in G.R. Cook, ed., *Confederation* (Toronto: University of Toronto Press 1967), pp. 53, 56, 66.

96 *Le Courrier du Canada*, 22 June 1864; Bishops Baillargeon and Cooke in *Nouvelle constitution*, pp. 54–5, 60; E.C. Parent to J.I. Tarte, Ottawa, 4 Sept. 1866, in PAC, Tarte papers (MG 27, N, D16). Just as they had promoted French-Canadian interests at the constitutional conferences, Quebec's sixty-five MPs would watch over French Quebec's interests at Ottawa. For they would be sent to Ottawa as representatives of Quebec, the French-Canadian province, and their responsibility would be toward that province and its autonomy. See Bonenfant, "L'Idée que les Canadiens français," p. 317; *Le Courrier de St-Hyacinthe*, 22 July 1864.

97 *La Gazette de Sorel*, 25 Feb. 1865; *La Minerve*, 1 July 1867. It was perfectly clear, of course, what Quebec's nationality was considered to be. It was French-Canadian. But what nationalities were to be attributed to the other provinces was never certain. French Canadians were aware of distinctions among the English, Scottish, and Irish nationalities … and they may have seen the other provinces as having unique national characters determined by their respective blends of these various elements. But they were always vague on this point. Cartier, however, did suggest a similar distribution of religious characteristics when he said (in the legislative debate on the Quebec resolutions) that Ontario would be Protestant, Quebec Catholic, and the Maritimes pretty evenly divided between the two denominations (eg., in Tassé, p. 422).

98 *L'Union des Cantons de l'Est*, 4 July 1867.

99 *Contre-poison*, p. 8. Also, p. 10.

100 *L'Union des Cantons de l'Est*, 23 May 1867.

Confederation had, thus, been achieved because four separate colonies had formed "a pact" among themselves.[101]

And in the federal alliance thus formed, Quebec was to be the French-Canadian country, working together with the others on common projects, but always autonomous in the promotion and embodiment of the French-Canadian nationality. "Our ambitions," wrote a Bleu editor, "will not centre on the federal government, but will have their natural focus in our local legislature; this we regard as fundamental for ourselves."[102] This was, no doubt, an exaggerated position, like the statement of de Niverville in the Canadian legislature, but what it exaggerated was the general tendency of the Confederationist propaganda. It underlined the Quebec-centredness of French Canada's approach to Confederation, and the degree to which French Quebec's separateness and autonomy were central to French-Canadian acceptance of the new régime.

101 *Le Journal de Québec*, 4 July 1867. See also the Bishop of St-Hyacinthe, in *Nouvelle constitution*, p. 65. J.-C Taché had assumed, in 1858, that a confederation would necessarily be brought about by an intercolonial pact. See his *Des provinces*, p. 139.

102 *Le Courrier de St-Hyacinthe*, 10 July 1866. We shall find this point of view adopted not infrequently by French-Quebec journalism in the first decades after Confederation.

## 10

### Editors' Introduction

Donald Creighton was a realist, a proponent of national history rather than "social history." Arguably no historian has had greater influence over the vernacular interpretation of Confederation and the national myth of elevating John A. Macdonald to founding father of the nation. In his two-volume biography of Macdonald, Creighton exerted quite intentional an effort to rehabilitate Macdonald's Golden Age and vision for Canada at the expense of the long slide owing to missed opportunities, thwarted ambitions, and dashed hopes under what Creighton perceived as Liberal continentalism. Creighton was enamoured of the BNA *Act, 1867*, especially the division of powers and the status of the French language. He opposed the federal policy of official bilingualism promulgated in the 1960s. Favouring a strong central government, he was staunchly opposed to the growth in provincial powers especially to Quebec's demands for more powers, which he felt would only further separatist aspirations. So Creighton's depiction of the distribution of federal and provincial powers is as authoritative an account by one of Canada's foremost national historians as it is a normative centralist vision of Canada. The excerpt stems from the Royal Commission on Dominion–Provincial Relations (commonly known as the *Rowell-Sirois Report*), which was established unilaterally by the federal government in 1937 to re-examine "the economic and financial basis of Confederation and the distribution of legislative powers in the light of the economic and social developments of the last 70 years."

Source: Donald G. Creighton, "The Division of Economic Powers at Confederation," in *British North America at Confederation*. A Study Prepared for the Royal Commission on Dominion–Provincial Relations (Ottawa, 1939), section IX, pp. 49–58.

Donald Creighton

# The Division of Economic Powers at Confederation

### I

In conformity with the method employed throughout this study, the division of economic powers at Confederation will be subjected to a purely historical examination. Such an inquiry differs essentially, in both purpose and method, from a legal investigation. It is concerned, not only with the British North America Act, but also with the forces and purposes which lay back of it; and it relies for its authority upon contemporary historical evidence and not upon subsequent judicial decisions and opinions. For the purposes of such historical study, there exists a considerable and varied body of evidence, of unimpeachable authenticity. Confederation was not, as sometimes seems to be imagined, the result of some mysterious crisis in the remote dark ages; it was the product of a period which until very recent times was regarded by historians as "contemporary history"; and it has left materials much more voluminous than those which support generally accepted interpretations of events far more remote in the past. This evidence comprises among other things, the resolutions and proceedings of the Quebec and London Conferences, the debates in the imperial parliament and the provincial legislatures, the official and private correspondence of the time, and the printed matter, official and otherwise, which was current at the period. The results of an investigation into such materials may be regarded as speculative and debatable; some of the conclusions must admittedly remain in the realm of inference. It should be emphasized, of course, that a considerable measure of agreement exists among historians concerning some of these inferences; but differences of opinion do still exist. And there is no final historical court of appeal whose decisions are absolute and binding.

There can be little doubt that one important general principle was used to determine and to explain the division of legislative powers in the projected Canadian federation. From their speeches at the time of the Charlottetown and Quebec Conferences, and from their explanations in the debates in the different provincial legislatures, it is apparent that the Fathers of Confederation intended that all matters of a general or national importance should be entrusted to the general legislature, and that all matters of merely local significance should be confided to the local legislatures.[1] The second of the Quebec Resolutions—which, we are told in the official minutes, was carried unanimously in the Conference[2]—declared that: "In the

Federation of the British North American Provinces the system of government best adapted under existing circumstances to protect the diversified interests of the several provinces, and secure efficiency, harmony, and permanency in the working of the Union— would be a General Government charged with matters of common interest to the whole country, and Local Governments ... charged with the control of local matters in their respective sections...." This clear distinction between a general government or legislature on the one hand and local governments or legislatures on the other—between matters of general or common interest on the one hand and local matters on the other—was maintained throughout the Quebec and London Resolutions and throughout all the explanations of the Quebec Resolutions which were presented by their principal authors. In his opening speech on the Quebec Resolutions in the Canadian Assembly, John A. Macdonald repeatedly and emphatically stressed this essential contrast, "In the proposed constitution," he declared, "all matters of general interest are to be dealt with by the General Legislature; while the local legislatures will deal with matters of local interest, which do not affect the Confederation as a whole, but are of the greatest importance to their particular sections.... We have strengthened the General Government. We have given the General Legislature all the great subjects of legislation ... any honourable member on examining the list of different subjects which are to be assigned to the General and Local Legislatures respectively, will see that all the great questions which affect the general interests of the Confederacy as a whole, are confided to the Federal Parliament, while the local interests and local laws of each section are preserved intact, and entrusted to the care of the local bodies.... Besides all the powers that are specifically given, the 37th and last item of this portion of the Constitution, confers on the General Legislature the general mass of sovereign legislation.... We thereby strengthen the Central Parliament, and make the Confederation one people and one government, instead of five peoples and five governments...."[3]

This clear distinction between a general government charged with all matters of general interest and local governments entrusted with matters of purely

1  W. P. M. Kennedy, *Essays in Constitutional Law* (London, 1934), pp. 85–94; F.R. Scott, "The Development of Canadian Federalism" (*Proceedings of the Canadian Political Science Association*, vol. 3. 1931, pp. 231–47); V.C. MacDonald, "Judicial Interpretation of the Canadian Constitution" (*University of Toronto Law Journal*, vol. 1, No. 2, 1936, pp. 260–85).

2  Pope, *Confederation Documents*, p. 8.

3  *Canadian Confederation Debates*, pp. 30, 33, 40, 41.

local concern was affirmed by Galt in his Sherbrooke speech and in his address to the Canadian assembly.[4] It was stated by Cartier and D'Arcy McGee in their speeches in the Canadian legislature.[5] "The real object which we have in view," said Lord Carnarvon, the colonial secretary, in introducing the British North America Act to the House of Lords, "is to give to the central government those high junctions and almost sovereign powers by which general principles and uniformity of legislation may be secured in those questions that are of common import to all the Provinces; and, at the same time, to retain for each Province so ample a measure of municipal liberty and self-government as will allow and indeed compel them to exercise those local powers which they can exercise with great advantage to the community.… Just as the authority of the Central Parliament will prevail whenever it may come into conflict with the local legislatures, so the residue of legislation, if any, unprovided for in the specific legislation … will belong to the central body."[6]

It is reasonable to assume that, in dividing between the Dominion and the provinces the legislative authority to control the economic affairs of the country, the Fathers of Confederation attempted to observe this broad distinction between general and local matters. They may have failed to appreciate the limitations of their guiding principle, as applied to economic activities; they may appear to have made distinctions which were artificial and ambiguous. But the existing conflicts of jurisdiction are not necessarily their responsibility; and, from the historical point of view, the intelligibility of their decisions is to be tested solely by reference to the conditions of British North America at that time and to the historical forces which had created those conditions. To the Dominion the Fathers assigned a relatively large number of economic powers, including the important authority to regulate trade and commerce. To the provinces they confided the control and beneficial interest in the public domain, together with the power to legislate in relation to property rights and civil rights. Any theory designed to account for the division of these

powers into the two categories of general and local matters, must admittedly be tentative in character; but it is suggested here that the Fathers of Confederation attempted to separate the affairs and interests associated with commerce from certain rights and customs dependent upon land. The former, which covered the great bulk of the economic activities of British North America as they knew it, they gave to the control of the Dominion; the latter, which included matters of minor economic, or of largely cultural, importance, they entrusted to the provinces.

… [L]and and commerce were the two great economic interests of British North America. From the very beginning, the basic inducements to settlement in the new world had been free land and trade; and trade and land had constituted the economic foundations of successive stages of European civilization. The political and legal structure supported by land had come to be termed feudalism, that based on commerce had been known as mercantilism. The ancient rights of the sovereign in the land and the basic property rights and civil rights of the subject were derived historically from feudal times. The laws, regulations and practices designed to encourage trade and commerce were the special contribution of the mercantilist era. These rights and authorities, transferred across the Atlantic to the new world, had, if anything, gained rather than lost in significance. British North America, which had developed for nearly a century under the protection of the British mercantile system, was a commercial civilization and so regarded itself; but, at the same time, it had good cause to appreciate the importance of the legacies of feudalism. The presence of the vast natural resources of the new world enhanced the value of the rights of the crown in the public domain. The preservation of the distinctive laws and customs of semi-feudal Quebec had contributed to the difficulties and disputes which arose between the two races. The control of these subjects had been, and remained, a matter of importance; but how were they to be divided between the two categories of general and local affairs?

In the light of the conditions existing at that time in British North America, the solution of these problems would not appear to have been excessively difficult. The affairs of commerce were mobile and ubiquitous in character; the range of trade was

4   Galt, *Speech on the Proposed Union*, p. 7; *Canadian Confederation Debates*, p. 70.
5   *Canadian Confederation Debates*, pp. 60, 145.
6   Quoted in V.C. MacDonald *"Judicial Interpretation of the Canadian Constitution,"* p. 263.

transcontinental and transoceanic in scope; and the laws by which it was regulated had an international origin in the Law Merchant of Europe. Moreover, the chief economic objective of the Dominion was the commercial integration of the country on a continental scale; and, as the authority which was obviously designed to assume the role of leadership in material development, the federal government was naturally accepted as the regulator of the business affairs of the new, commercial federation. While this decision could be regarded as relatively natural and easy, the allocation of the two other powers might appear, at first sight, to have been a matter of some difficulty. On the one hand, natural resources were certainly fixed and localized in space; but, on the other, the greatness of their extent and the magnitude of their value could be taken to justify their inclusion in the class of general, national interests. Property rights and civil rights might be presumed to be a matter in which no genuine local or provincial interest could exist; but, at the same time, the laws by which these rights were secured differed fundamentally as between Canada East and the rest of British North America. Thus, on the application of the Fathers' guiding principle of division, there followed certain apparently contradictory results; but these contradictions appear less formidable under a closer scrutiny of the facts.

At that time, it was only in certain areas of the projected Dominion that the magnitude of the domain still awaiting development appeared to constitute a genuine national interest. In the west, where settlement and exploitation had barely commenced, the lands were significantly appropriated by the federal government "for the purposes of the Dominion"; but in the four original provinces of Confederation, where large-scale settlement and exploitation appeared to be approaching its limits under the conditions of the time, the natural resources could be logically transferred to the provinces. The Fathers of Confederation could not possibly foresee the enormous general importance which the public domain would acquire in the industrial Canada of the 20th century; and to them, therefore, the natural resources of the eastern and central provinces appeared to have passed from the category of general to that of local affairs. As for the laws relating to property and civil rights, they might

seem to represent two broad, cultural interests rather than a number of genuine local or provincial interests. But the use of the distinctive body of law and custom derived from France had been historically limited to the territory which was to be included in the province of Quebec; and, in so far at least as the cultural autonomy of Quebec was concerned, the laws relating to property and civil rights might be regarded as a provincial interest.

## II

That the Fathers of Confederation should consider commercial matters to be of general interest, as well as of great importance, is to be expected in view of the nature and development of the communities in which they lived. Colonial societies are forced, by the number and complexity of the problems of physical adjustment which confront them, to be largely, if not chiefly, preoccupied with material concerns. The British North American provinces had been, and remained, intensely commercial in spirit. Their enterprises may appear now to have been small in size, but they were not parochial in character. The very structure of the physical environment of British North America invited and, indeed, compelled its citizens to develop commercial systems which were international as well as interprovincial in scope. The St. Lawrence was a great imperial trade route penetrating far into the heart of the international American West; the Atlantic coastline was the centre of a commercial network which stretched to Newfoundland, the West Indies, South America, Great Britain, Europe and the Mediterranean. The Maritimes had competed with New England for the carrying-trade of the Atlantic; the Canadas had struggled with New York for the commerce of the American West. In view of the economic history of British North America, it would have been virtually impossible for its citizens to look upon commerce as a local affair; they thought of it, and were habituated to think of it, in terms truly oceanic and transcontinental. Galt assumed, as a question beyond dispute, that commercial matters were matters of general interest. "There is one advantage which I feel that I enjoy on this occasion," he said in addressing the Canadian Assembly on the Quebec Resolutions, "and it is that this House is not called upon, in dealing with the commercial and financial interests involved in the proposed changes, to consider the form or mode of government by which such interests are to be promoted. It makes little difference to the consideration of this branch of the subject whether the Constitution of the new Government be that of a Legislative or Federal Union—the points with which I am about to deal, are those which concern the public at large, and bear no reference to what may be the creed, nationality or language of portions of the people."[7] It followed that, since commercial affairs were unquestionably matters of general interest, they should be entrusted to the control of the general legislature. "It would have the regulation of all the trade and commerce of the country," said Galt, "for besides that these were subjects in reference to which no local interest could exist, it was desirable that they should be dealt with throughout the Confederation on the same principles."[8]

The necessity of entrusting the commercial welfare of the country to the control of the general legislature was the more fully appreciated in Canada in the light of the experience of the past. For fifty years, during which time the provinces of Upper and Lower Canada maintained their separate existence, the control of the St. Lawrence and its commerce had been divided between two distinct and independent governments. This division had not only encouraged conflicts between the two provinces; it had also exaggerated the rivalries between the commercial and agrarian parties in each.[9] Upper Canada had disagreed with Lower Canada, and the Montreal merchants had quarrelled with the leaders of the *Patriote* party, over many economic matters of common interest to the whole St. Lawrence valley. The deadlock which followed had hampered commercial Canada in a critical phase of its struggle with New York for the prize of the western trade; and the resulting embitterment of the merchants was a factor of no small importance in the rebellions of 1837. In 1864, these events were not remote and forgotten; they were part of the living memory of many of the statesmen who made Confederation. Moreover, the moral of these events for commercial men was

plain: the control of a commercial system which was interprovincial and international in character must not again be surrendered to local political bodies.

In the discussions and debates of the Confederation period, these commercial difficulties of the past were recalled with the evident purpose of demonstrating the impossibility of their recurrence under the provisions of the new constitution. It was recognized that the British merchants of Canada East had vital material interests which they wished to safeguard, just as the French Canadians had cherished customs and institutions which they desired to preserve; and it was repeatedly asserted that, under the new constitution, the control of each of these classes of subjects had been entrusted to the very legislative authority which in each ease the interested parties would themselves have selected. In this connection, the remarks of Galt, Cartier and John Rose are of considerable interest. Galt and Cartier were members of the existing Canadian government and Rose was soon to become Minister of Finance. Cartier and Rose represented ridings in the city of Montreal and Galt was member for Sherbrooke. All three men were closely connected with the business of the country; and all three laboured to remove those apprehensions concerning the future of commercial interests which had naturally arisen in the minds of many of the British in Lower Canada. "We could easily understand," said Cartier, in a passage of great historical interest, "how a feeling against the Federation project was raised in the minds of a few of the British residents of Lower Canada by fears of such difficulties as those which occurred in the days of Mr. Papineau, relative to the passing of laws relating to commercial matters. These difficulties had been of a very inconvenient nature, Mr. Papineau not being a commercial man, and not understanding the importance of these measures. He considered Mr. Papineau was right in the struggle he maintained against the oligarchy at that time in power; but he had never approved of the course he took with reference to commercial matters, and in opposition to measures for the improvement of the country. But this precedent could not be urged as an objection to Federation, inasmuch as it would be for the General Government to deal with our commercial matters."[10]

7   *Canadian Confederation Debates*, p. 62.
8   Galt, *Speech on the Proposed Union*, p. 10.
9   These conflicts are examined in detail in D.G. Creighton, *The Commercial Empire of the St. Lawrence 1760–1850.*
10   *Canadian Confederation Debates*, p. 61.

It was in very much the same fashion that Galt dealt with this problem in his address at Sherbrooke. "And to speak more particularly," he said, "with regard to the British population of Lower Canada, he would remark that, in the General Government they could have nothing to fear.... Their interests would be safe there. The interests of trade and commerce, those in which they felt more particularly concerned, which concerned the merchants of Montreal and Quebec, would be in the hands of a body where they could have no fear that any adverse race or creed could affect them. All those subjects would be taken out of the category of local questions, would be taken away from the control of those who might be under the influence of sectional feelings animated either by race or religion...."[11] Similarly, John Rose, who spoke frankly from the point of view of the British and commercial minority of Lower Canada, endeavoured to quiet the fears of his fellow countrymen. "What," he inquired, "are you afraid of? Where is the interest affecting you that is imperilled? You have, in conjunction with a majority of your own race, power in the General Legislature ... to make laws respecting the post office, trade, commerce, navigation; and you have all the great and important interests that centre in the community I represent—all matters that affect the minority in Lower Canada—within your control in the Federal Legislature."[12] It may be said that commercial Canada, whose leadership lay in the city of Montreal, abandoned its favourite plan of legislative union on the clearly understood condition that all the economic matters with which it was most deeply concerned should be entrusted to the general legislature of the proposed federation.

## III

In entrusting commercial matters, as well as all other general matters to the control of the general legislature, the Fathers of Confederation made use of terms of great historical import. The phrases "peace, welfare and good government" were phrases of all-embracing significance in the legislative history of the British Empire.[13] They were, in fact, the phrases habitually used by the colonial office and the Imperial government in conveying to colonial legislatures the entire range of their legitimate legislative authority. In the statutes passed by the British Parliament in respect of the different colonies, in the commissions and instructions issued from time to time to the different colonial governors, it was not customary to enumerate specific legislative powers; it was customary merely to grant, in one or other of these accepted phrases, the entire measure of jurisdiction which was deemed compatible with imperial control. In the Quebec and London Resolutions, the Fathers of Confederation used the phrase "peace, welfare and good government" because it was most familiar to them. It had appeared in the Royal Proclamation of 1763, in the Quebec Act of 1774, in the Constitutional Act of 1791, and in the Union Act of 1840.[14] But though "peace, welfare and good government" was the phrase employed in all the chief Imperial statutes relating to the Canadian Constitution, it had not become stereotyped as the only phrase by which colonial legislative authority might be conveyed. In the instructions given to James Murray in 1763, the governor is required "to make such Rules and Regulations, by the Advice of Our said Council, as shall appear to be necessary for the Peace, Order and good Government of Our said Province...";[15] and it is to be observed that the phrase "peace, order and good government" was here used to describe the same legislative authority which, by the Royal Proclamation of the previous October, had been conveyed in terms of "Public Peace, Welfare and good Government." In the Act for the government of New South Wales and Van Diemen's Land of 1842, as well as in the New Zealand Government Act of 1846, authority was granted to make laws for the "peace, welfare and good government" of these colonies; but, in the New Zealand Constitution Act of 1852, the phrase "peace, order and good government" was used in the same connection to grant similar powers.[16] Thus in both the

---

11  Galt, *Speech on the Proposed Union*, p. 20.

12  *Canadian Confederation Debates*, p. 409.

13  C.H. Cahan, *The British North America Act, 1867* (an address delivered before the Canadian Club of Toronto, Sept. 15, 1937).

14  W.P.M. Kennedy, *Statutes, Treaties and Documents of the Canadian Constitution, 1713–1929* (Toronto, 1930), pp. 36, 139, 194, 433.

15  Ibid., p. 44.

16  K.N. Bell and W.P. Morrell (eds.), *Select Documents on British Colonial Policy, 1830–1860* (Oxford, 1928), pp. 56, 90, 152.

18th and 19th centuries, and in both the American and Australasian Colonies, the terms "peace, welfare and good government" and "peace, order and good government" had been employed frequently and, apparently, indifferently, to convey the entire body of legislative authority which Great Britain was willing to surrender to its colonies. In effect, these historic phrases are the title deeds of the legislative powers now enjoyed by the self-governing Dominions of the British Empire.

In the enumeration of specific powers, by which the Fathers of Confederation sought to illustrate and exemplify the authority conveyed to the Dominion under the comprehensive phrase of "peace, order and good government," there are a considerable number of clauses which relate directly to the economic activities of the new confederation. The meaning of these clauses, as it was understood by the men who drafted the Quebec resolutions, can best be realized in the light of the economic and political history of the provinces, and of the British empire as a whole. In the development of the empire, the phrase "the regulation of trade and commerce" had come to acquire the greatest importance and the widest amplitude. Even at the height of the American Revolution, when Great Britain at length renounced its claim to tax the colonies, it reserved the right to impose such duties as might seem expedient for the "regulation of commerce"[17] and two generations later, Lord Durham excepted, from the powers which he was willing to assign to the local colonial legislatures "the regulation of foreign relations, and of trade with the mother country, the other British colonies, and foreign nations...."[18] From the beginning, the commerce of the colonies had constituted, for Englishmen, the main value and the chief justification of an overseas empire; and up to the time of the American revolution, all questions relating to the colonies were referred originally to the imperial Board of Trade. The duty of the Board was to advise the various departments of government in their task of maintaining that great body of laws—called generally the mercantile system—by which the trade of the whole empire was regulated.

This system of regulation was both comprehensive and detailed.[19] Back of it lay the design of a united and self-sufficient empire, in which the interests of the colonies were to be clearly subordinated to those of the mother country; and this purpose inevitably necessitated a strict supervision and control over the economic activities of the whole empire, so far as this was possible in the conditions of the time. The course of colonial trade was directed by means of tariffs, bounties and total prohibitions. Certain enumerated products of the American possessions could be shipped only to England or to other colonies; and all the produce of Europe could be transported to the colonies only via the mother country. The exports and imports of the new world could be carried only in ships which were built and owned in the empire, and manned by predominantly British crews; and since it was intended that Great Britain should be the financial and industrial centre of the empire, the imperial government watched the currency, banks and manufactures of the colonies with a jealous and scrutinising eye. Great Britain checked inflationary tendencies, regulated the colonial banking system, and subjected the woollen and iron manufactures of the new world to legislative control. The maintenance of this system was entrusted, in the colonies, to the colonial governors, and to imperial customs officials and imperial courts of Vice-Admiralty; and the customs officials, by means of "writs of assistance," were permitted to make forcible entry into residences and warehouses and to seize property. The mercantile system, however imperfectly executed, was ambitious in design. It involved the control and regulation of tariffs, shipping, banks, currency and manufactures. The phrase, "the regulation of trade and commerce" acquired its comprehensive significance during the mercantilist age. It was in the light of this historical experience, that the term was used by the inhabitants of British North America.

In the seventy-five years which followed the American Revolution, Great Britain gradually abandoned its mercantile system and its imperial controls. Little by little the colonies assumed the direction of their economic life; but the controls which they regarded as

17  Kennedy, *Statues, Treaties and Documents*, p. 168.
18  C.P. Lucas (ed.), *Lord Durham's Report on the Affairs of British North America* (Oxford, 1912), vol. 2, p. 282.
19  C.M. Andrews, *The Colonial Period of American History*, vol. 4, *England's Commercial and Colonial Policies* (New Haven, 1938).

necessary and advisable could still be summed up under the traditional mercantilist formula, "the regulation of trade." As has been seen, the economic activities of the American possessions were changing and developing; but manufacturing, though it had made considerable progress in the years preceding Confederation, was still definitely ancillary to the main extractive industries and staple trades of British America. Contemporaries of Confederation conceived of their economy and its future in commercial terms. For them, trade and commerce still signified the general business of the country. In all the colonies at that time, the export of staple commodities and the import of manufactured goods were the dominant forms of economic activity. In Halifax and Saint John, as well as in Toronto and Montreal, the most important concerns were the great importing and exporting houses; and everywhere the words "merchant" and "trader" were the accepted equivalents of the modern term "business man."

The comprehensive significance of "trade and commerce" was apparent in the legal, as well as in the popular, usages of the time. The contents of the consolidated statutes of Canada, published in 1859 were divided into eleven titles or chapters, two of which were directly related to the economic activities of the country.[20] Title IV, which was called simply "Trade and Commerce," included the laws relating to navigation and shipping and the inspection of lumber, wheat, flour and provisions, together with the legislation concerning weights and measures, banks, interest, promissory notes, limited partnerships and other matters. Title V, which was called "Trading Companies and Corporations," comprised the laws relating to the incorporation of public utilities, railway, telegraph, mining and insurance companies, as well as companies engaged in various manufactures. These two titles, which are among the most important in the book and which include the great bulk of the legislation referring to economic matters, suggest the wide meaning which contemporaries ascribed to "trade and commerce" and their adjectival derivatives. When, therefore, the Fathers of Confederation entrusted the regulation of trade and commerce to the general legislature, without restricting the grant, as was done in the American constitution, to foreign and interprovincial trade, it

was only natural that contemporaries should have been impressed by the comprehensiveness of the clause.

In the subsections relating to shipping, banks, bills of exchange, interest and bankruptcy, certain aspects of the regulation of trade and commerce were particularized. It is possible but not certain that these details were added for much the same reason that the enumerated powers were included in section 91 in the first place. In both cases, it was "for greater certainty, but not so as to restrict the generality of the foregoing terms." There was a certain amount of overlapping in the enumerated powers; but since they were all intended to serve as examples or illustrations of the general authority to legislate for the peace, order and good government of Canada, a certain amount of overlapping was unexceptionable and might even serve a useful purpose. In the past, there had been a good deal of dispute in Lower Canada over bankruptcy legislation; and, as was observed during the Confederation debate in the Canadian legislature, the French Canadians had held strong views on the subject of usury and were opposed to complete "free trade" in money.[21] The enumeration of these definite powers did not exhaust the trade and commerce clause any more than the trade and commerce clause exhausted the economic powers implied in the general authority to make laws for the peace, order and good government of Canada. But the inclusion of these particular, and sometimes controversial, matters, did presumably make more clear to the average intelligent Canadian the kind of authority which was being given up. In view of the history of British North America and of the empire as a whole, it must have seemed clear that the general government was assured of the right to regulate the business life of the country.

Parliament was given not only the right to regulate commerce but also the power to control the major avenues of trade. By the clauses relating to navigation and shipping, to railways, canals, steamships and ferries, and to postal service and telegraphs, the Dominion was charged with the control of all forms of interprovincial transport and communications which existed at that time. The federal government was empowered, moreover, to declare that any public work, though situated wholly in one province, was for the general

20 *The Consolidated Statutes of Canada* (Toronto, 1859).

21 *Canadian Confederation Debates*, 192.

advantage of Canada; and such a declaration automatically brought the work in question under the legislative authority of the Dominion. Finally, the federal administration was given the right to disallow any provincial statute; and just as the imperial government had used the power of disallowance to defend the provisions of the mercantile system, so the federal government was likely to employ it to protect the economic policies designed for the general interest of Canada. In the first report on the use of the power of disallowance, which was dated June 8, 1868, Macdonald assumed, as a matter of course, that provincial acts would be scrutinized to determine whether they "affected the interests of the Dominion generally";[22] and since that time the power has been used to protect, among other things, the railway and financial policies of the federal government.

## IV

While the federal parliament was charged with the regulation of matters coming under the head of trade and commerce, the provincial legislatures were empowered to legislate concerning those rights and authorities which had their historical origin in the feudal communities of western Europe. On the one hand, were the fundamental rights of the subject, such as those which had been embodied in the new Civil Code of Canada East; on the other hand, were the rights of the sovereign, as feudal lord, in the land and its resources. The control and beneficial interest of natural resources, like the control of taxation, fiscal policy, commercial policy, communications and defence, had devolved upon the provincial administrations of British North America with the coming of responsible government. The natural resources which remained, after the wholesale alienations made by the imperial authorities, could be regarded as national or local in interest on the basis simply of their extent and value; and the Fathers of Confederation proceeded to distribute the domain by applying their general principle in this very realistic fashion. The vast unpeopled and undeveloped lands of the west were regarded by everybody at that time as a national interest which could only be exploited by national policies; and accordingly, in strict and

significant conformity with the general principle of division, the western natural resources were appropriated by the federal government "for the purposes of the Dominion." In the eastern and central provinces, the state of the public domain at that time appeared to be very different. In 1867, the great bulk of the good lands in all the original provinces of Confederation had already been alienated. Nobody could then foresee the mining, newsprint and hydro-electric developments of the future; and the vast areas of Quebec and Ontario which lay north of the timberline could only be regarded as a liability rather than an asset. It seemed, therefore, that in these provinces the domain had ceased to form a part of the materials essential for nation-building; and it was therefore entrusted to the control of the provincial governments.

In addition, the provincial legislatures were assigned the authority to make laws in relation to "property and civil rights in the province." The reasons which prompted the grant of this power, and the contemporary understanding of the significance of the authority so conveyed, are highly debatable subjects; but even a cursory examination of Canadian history reveals what would appear to be a probable explanation of these problems. If there had been, up to that time, a paramount theme in the cultural history of British North America, it was the persistent defence by French Canada of the distinctive laws and customs which formed the basis of its provincial culture; and it is beyond a doubt that any federal constitution for British North America would, of necessity, have included some provision for the preservation of this legal heritage. If differences at all comparable in importance had existed between the English-Canadian provinces, the right to make laws in relation to property and civil rights could have been regarded as a genuinely local or provincial interest throughout the Dominion; but in fact, of course, Ontario, Nova Scotia and New Brunswick, being common law provinces, were distinguished by relatively minor differences in respect of these laws. The arrangements embodied in the British North America Act appear to have been devised in strict conformity with these facts; and accordingly it was only in so far as the province of Quebec was concerned that the power to legislate in relation to property and civil rights was accepted as an unquestionable and permanent local interest. By

22 *Provincial Legislation*, vol. 1, pp. 61–2.

section 94 of the British North America Act, it was expressly provided that authority to make laws relating to property and civil rights for the whole Dominion except Quebec would be transferred to the federal legislature, so soon as the Dominion parliament had made provision, with the consent of the provinces concerned, for the uniformity of these laws in the three common law provinces of Ontario, Nova Scotia and New Brunswick. There were apparently no vital provincial rights involved which would require the permanent retention of these powers by the provinces; but obviously there were practical difficulties of assimilation which would for a while delay their transference to the Dominion. The provinces were willing to provide that the transfer should be effected, once the uniformity of laws had been achieved; and the work of assimilation was regarded by Macdonald as a practical task which it would be one of the first duties of the federation to perform. It would appear, therefore, that the fundamental purpose of the property and civil rights clause was to protect the cultural autonomy of Quebec by safeguarding the laws and customs which were most characteristic of it and most essential to it; and it is arguable that this power would never have been given to the provinces if it had not been for the peculiarities of the basic civil law of French Canada.

If it was the intention of the Fathers of Confederation to permit Quebec to preserve the peculiarities of its distinctive legal system, then the powers conveyed by the property and civil rights clause would presumably extend only so far as was necessary to attain this purpose. Since imperial and Canadian officials had been preoccupied ever since the conquest, with the problem of French-Canadian law and custom, there could be no serious misunderstanding of its essential and distinctive elements; and opinion was still further clarified at the time of Confederation by the opportune publication of the Civil Code of Canada East, which was given legislative authority in the very session which witnessed the debate on the Quebec resolutions. Historically, the new Civil Code was derived from the Custom of Paris and from a variety of commercial laws and usages;[23] and the Custom of Paris

was, from the point of view of English-speaking British America, the most distinctive and peculiar element in the French system. Commercial law was international in origin, just as commerce was international in character; and both English commercial law and the French *Code Marchand* were derived ultimately from the Law Merchant of western Europe. The Custom of Paris, however, belonged to a different category. It was the creation of a local feudal community of northern Europe; it became the cherished possession of a local seigniorial community in North America; and it was the chief source of those laws and customs which most intimately affected the lives of the French Canadians and to which they had been most devotedly attached. These were the fundamental laws and customs which concerned the relations of citizen with citizen, which regulated the ownership, transfer and inheritance of property, and which determined the rights arising from personal status and family relationships. Such laws were evidently most essential to the preservation of the traditional social order in Quebec; and, accordingly, these were the very laws which the imperial authorities after the conquest showed the least disposition to disturb with the rough hand of the conqueror. Their attitude to the problem may be illustrated by the instructions issued to Governor Carleton in 1775. Read in conjunction with the Quebec Act, to which they were obviously intended to act as an explanatory guide, the instructions serve to reveal the nature of the laws and customs whose continuance was believed to be most essential to the contentment of the French Canadians. "... On the one hand" read the instructions, "it is Our Gracious purpose conformable to the Spirit and Intention of the said Act of Parliament, that Our Canadian Subjects should have the benefit and use of their own Laws, Usages and Customs in all Controversies respecting Titles of Land, and the Tenure, Descent, Alienation, Incumbrances and Settlement of Real Estates, and the distribution of the personal property of Persons dying intestate; so on the other hand, it will be the duty of the Legislative Council to consider well in framing such Ordinances, as may be necessary for the Establishment of Courts of Justice, and for the better Administration of Justice, whether the Laws of England may not be, if not altogether, at least in part the Rule for the decision in all Cases of personal Actions, grounded upon

23  A.L. Burt, *The Old Province of Quebec* (Toronto, 1933); H.M. Neatby, *The Administration of Justice under the Quebec Act* (Minneapolis, 1937).

Debts, Promises, Contracts and Agreements, whether of a Mercantile or other Nature; and also of Wrongs proper to be compensated in damages...."[24]

The evidence already presented in this section suggests that the Fathers of Confederation attempted to settle the problem of legislative power along somewhat the same lines as had been contemplated in the instructions of 1775 for the solution of the legal difficulty. Like the imperial authorities, they made a distinction between what was, and what was not regarded as essential for the preservation of the cultural autonomy of Quebec. To the Dominion they specifically confided the power to amend a substantial portion of the commercial law, together with what seemed to them the comprehensive authority to regulate trade and commerce. To the province of Quebec they assigned the right to amend and supplement a body of fundamental law and custom which at once expressed and supported the distinctive culture of an agrarian society. As Rose, Galt and Cartier argued, the business affairs characteristic of a commercial city like Montreal were to be entrusted to the federal parliament, while the laws which time out of mind had regulated the traditional transactions of village society and family life were to be confided to the safe keeping of the provincial legislature. In the light of all the disputes and controversies of the past, this application of the guiding principle which separated general from local matters, must have appeared to be a natural, and even an inescapable, solution; it would seem to have been enjoined by history as the settlement which alone could satisfy the historic requirements of both races. To a people which had lived with the problem for generations, the meaning and purport of the compromise would surely have been beyond question; and this general understanding may well explain what was not said, as well as what was said, in the documents and speeches of the time. If the contemporaries of Confederation had placed upon the property and civil rights clause a construction even remotely comparable to that which the courts have now established, it is reasonable to assume that they would have given some time to a discussion of conflicts of jurisdiction over economic matters; but in fact, of course, the assurances given by Galt and Rose

to the commercial minority of Lower Canada that its chief interests would be entrusted to the general legislature, were not qualified by any references whatsoever to subsection 13 of section 92; and even Christopher Duncan, the voluminous critic of Confederation who devoted considerable space to possible conflicts of jurisdiction, never attempted to set the property and civil rights clause against the Dominion power to regulate trade and commerce. If, again, the representatives of the provinces had believed that the subsection on property and civil rights protected important and vital local interests which were equally valuable for all the provinces, they would scarcely have made legislative provision for the transfer of these powers to the Dominion; yet this was precisely what they did do in section 94 of the British North America Act. In his famous speech at Sherbrooke, Alexander Galt presented one of the few explanations of the property and civil rights clause which were ever given by the Fathers of Confederation; and he significantly assumed that the fundamental purpose of the subsection was to confide to the province of Quebec the body of distinctive private law which was essential to the preservation of its cultural autonomy. "From the peculiar position of Lower Canada," he said, "it was felt impossible to confide the matter of civil law to the General Legislature. The principles upon which the civil law of Lower Canada were founded differed entirely from those of the English law. Under it property was secured, and civil rights of every kind maintained, and the people had no particular wish to see it changed, especially at this moment, when the work of codifying and simplifying it was about completed and when they knew that within the next three or four months they would have it put into their hands in one volume.... He thought they should rejoice that at the moment when they were obliged to confide to the local Legislatures the administration of this law there should have been put before them, at the start, a volume which would contain in a succinct, beautiful and simple manner the whole civil law of Lower Canada...."[25]

In this section, an attempt has been made to explain certain particular decisions of the Fathers of Confederation in relation to the general design which

24  Kennedy, *Statutes, Treaties and Documents*, p. 156.

25  Galt, *Speech on the Proposed Union*, p. 15.

appears to have governed their work. It is suggested that this is at least a reasonable method of procedure. Explanations of particular decisions will derive part of their authority in so far as they can be reconciled with the established historical facts concerning the general design; and, at the same time, interpretations of the general design must find a large measure of their justification in the available historical evidence concerning a number of particular decisions and arrangements. The study of the purposes of Confederation as parts of a general Confederation plan has not as yet formed the subject of any great number of detailed historical treatises; and, as was suggested at the beginning the argument of this section represents only one approach to the problem. Objections, both in principal and in detail, may be lodged against it, and it should be admitted at once that it depends in part upon interpretations of particular clauses of the British North America Act which have not been accepted by certain authorities on the subject.[26]

The explanation of the phrase "property and civil rights" must of necessity be an important part of the interpretation of the purposes of the Fathers of Confederation: and it is here perhaps that authorities have differed most markedly in their views. It has been urged, for example that the expression "property and civil rights" has always had a very wide meaning in Canadian constitutional history. This argument has its

basis in an action of Louis XIV, who in 1663 created a sovereign council in Quebec and entrusted to it the power "de connaître de toutes causes civiles et crimmelle, pour juger souverainement et en dernier ressort selon les lois et ordonnances de notre royaume." It is contended that this royal edict established in Quebec the entire French law and not merely portions of it; and that, at the conquest, these laws were all in force, whether or not they had been applied. It is therefore, according to this view, irrelevant to attempt to determine the nature and scope of the laws which were actually in use at the time of the conquest; and the foments made by British officials and the instructions given to British governors regarding this problem should not be used as evidence to limit the laws which were actually in force. The Quebec Act, in determining that the laws and customs of Canada should provide the rule of decision in controversies relative to property and civil rights, thus restored without limitation the entire French civil law to the colony. A wide meaning is thus attributed to the expression "property and civil rights" as it was used in the Quebec Act; and it is contended that the phrase retains its significance in later statutes, except where some express limitation is introduced. No express limitation was inserted in the British North America Act; and there is therefore no reason to restrict the amplitude of meaning which the phrase originally possessed. This argument is only one of a number which any survey of the literature of the subject would reveal; and it has been used to illustrate important opinions which are at variance with those expressed in the body of this section.

---

26 P.B. Mignault, "Nos Problèmes Constitutionnele" (15, *Revue du Droit*, p. 577); V.E. Gray, "The 'O'Connor Report' on the British North America Act" (17, *Canadian Bar Review*, p. 309).

# 11

## Author's Introduction

Canada is a federation and the foundation of the Canadian federation is the Confederation Settlement of 1867. The adoption of the Charter of Rights in 1982 has of course added significant new dimensions to the Canadian constitutional landscape. It has further restricted the legislative sovereignty of the provincial and national legislatures, enhanced the status and powers of the Supreme Court, and promoted the creation of a multicultural society and a more politically active citizenry. No less significant are the failed constitutional initiatives that followed the adoption of the Charter, namely, the Meech Lake Accord of 1987 and the Charlottetown Accord of 1992. Moreover, in 1995 there was a nearly successful sovereignty referendum in Quebec and in 1998 the Supreme Court issued its much discussed opinion on Quebec's asserted right to secede unilaterally from the Canadian federation. Canadian Aboriginals have also asked fundamental questions about Canada. Although Canada is often described as one of the oldest and most successful federations in the world, Canadians disagree intensely about the identity and future of their country, and no subject is more contested than Canadian federalism.

The following essay attempts to contribute to the continuing debate about Canadian nationhood by re-examining the Confederation settlement of 1867. Confederation is often portrayed as a purely pragmatic historical event, as devoid of fundamental principles, and even as part of a now lost constitutional world. Moreover, it is frequently identified with Sir John A. Macdonald's highly centralized constitutional vision, with his admiration of British political institutions, and with his deep distrust of federalism and provincialism. However, an examination of the Confederation debates of 1865 reveals that Macdonald's constitutional vision did not go unchallenged and, ultimately, it did not prevail. Macdonald was compelled to concede far more to federalism, provincialism, and the diversity of Canada than he wished and, in the clash of competing constitutional visions, it was George-Étienne Cartier who came closest to articulating the spirit of Confederation and capturing the middle ground without which it would have remained a political dream. Cartier was an unequivocal federalist and a proponent of minority rights. He rejected assimilation, celebrated the existence of pluralism and multiple identities, and identified Confederation with the creation of a new kind of nationality, which he called political nationality. He articulated a distinctively Canadian federalist theory that differs in important respects from the American variant and forms an enduring pillar of Canadian nationhood. In the era of the Charter of Rights, there is still much to learn about Canadian nationhood from the competing constitutional visions that figured so prominently in Canada's founding debates.

Source: Samuel V. LaSelva, *The Moral Foundations of Canadian Federalism: Paradoxes, Achievements, and Tragedies of Nationhood* (Montreal: MQUP, 1996) 31–48.

Samuel LaSelva

# Confederation and the Beginnings of Canadian Federalist Theory

DISAGREEMENTS ABOUT FEDERALISM are not new in Canada. Canadians have almost always disagreed about it, and their disagreements were, if anything, even more intense in the years that immediately preceded Confederation. In 1867 Confederation had supporters as well as opponents, but few Canadians were unequivocal federalists. "The Fathers of Confederation," Donald Creighton wrote more than a century later, "recognized the inevitability of federalism, [but] they could not help regarding it as a suspect and sinister form of government."[1] It was suspect partly because federation was commonly believed to be an unstable form of government. In 1865 John A. Macdonald believed that the unitary features of the Constitution would save Canada from the common afflictions of federations; yet even he later admitted that the difficulties raised by federation could not be settled so simply. The divisive question of "States Rights," Macdonald complained in 1869, "has already made its appearance in Canada!"[2]

But states rights was an old question, and it did not emerge only after Confederation. In fact, the issue was raised repeatedly in the Confederation debates of 1865 and was frequently coupled with the even more explosive issue of nationality. Opponents of Confederation warned that Canada would suffer the common and unhappy fate of federations, of which the American Civil War was the immediate reminder. Even Switzerland, Henri Joly insisted, was no exception; it too had had a civil war.[3] Others believed that "the old aggression of race against race ... has not disappeared" and was destined to disrupt Confederation.[4] Those who supported Confederation did not evade such objections. In speeches delivered at the Quebec Conference and published in the Confederation debates of 1865, they insisted that Canada could succeed, even if other federations had failed. Moreover, the debates contain at least two distinctive justifications for such a belief. One of them is contained in Macdonald's now-famous speech in support of Confederation; the other was given classic expression by George-Étienne Cartier.

The debates of 1865 provide an image of Confederation that is obscured by the orthodox accounts. Canadian Confederation is often fitted into a practical mould, devoid of philosophical interest; yet the Confederation debates raise vital questions of political and constitutional theory. Once the Fathers agreed that Canada was to be a federation, difficult issues of political and constitutional theory could no longer be avoided. Opponents of Confederation raised those issues in their discussions of federalism, and the Fathers responded to them. The Fathers had to justify their adoption of a federal form of government to those who believed that the aggressions of race had not disappeared and who regarded the American Civil War as symptomatic of federations. As a result,

the debates of 1865 record an important Canadian discussion about federalism and the beginnings of a distinctively Canadian federalist theory. This chapter seeks to recover the original significance of Canadian federalist theory by focusing in large measure on the debates of 1865. Those debates not only record the ideological context from which Canadian federalist theory emerged, but they also provide evidence of the crucial role assumed by Cartier in its formulation, a role that is not adequately recognized. Like James Madison before him, Cartier provided middle ground between opposing positions, neither of which could prevail in the social and political conditions from which Canadian Confederation emerged. Madison had focused on American problems and had created an American federalist theory; Cartier addressed Canadian problems and provided the beginning of a Canadian federalist theory.

## THE IDEOLOGICAL CONTEXT OF CONFEDERATION

In its accomplishment, Confederation was a practical achievement as well as the achievement of practical men. Macdonald has been described as a natural empiricist and Cartier as a man who avoided abstract ideas. As a consequence, Canadians are said to lack the kind of ideological debate that surrounded the adoption of the United States Constitution.[5] But such a view is unsatisfactory, partly because it neglects the ideological origins of the *idea of Confederation*. Proposals for the union of British North America, as a recent study has shown, not only preceded the accomplishment of Confederation by a century or so, but also took sides in the eighteenth-century debate between commercial wealth and classical republican virtue.[6] That debate continued into the nineteenth century, became a key component in the debate over Confederation, and gave Canadian Confederation commercial, as well as ideological, dimensions. The eighteenth-century debate between wealth and virtue also divided federalists and anti-federalists in the ideological debate over the United States Constitution. Not only did Canadian Confederation have ideological dimensions, but the earliest proposals for Confederation produced debates similar to those in the United States. In the case of

Canada, however, the eighteenth-century debate between wealth and virtue was eventually linked to the nineteenth-century one about nation and nationality, with the result that Canadian Confederation also acquired ideological dimensions that were absent from the American debate.

There is, however, a traditional understanding of Canadian Confederation and of the American influence that owes much to Macdonald himself. In the debates of 1865, he described the United States Constitution as "one of the most skillful works which human intelligence ever created"; but he quickly added that it was "not the work of Omniscience." The United States Constitution "commenced … at the wrong end" because it declared that "each state was a sovereignty in itself."[7] By contrast, the Canadian constitution, Macdonald said, would confer all the great powers of legislation, as well as the residuary power, on the general legislature, thereby avoiding the fatal defect in the United States Constitution that had resulted in civil war. "Canadian Confederation," Peter Waite has written, "was a native creation. There was no intention of imitating the United States."[8] Behind Waite's assessment is Macdonald's belief that the United States Constitution was not to be emulated so much as improved upon.

This belief—that Confederation corrected American errors—did not go unchallenged in the debates of 1865. Christopher Dunkin not only accused Macdonald of failing to respect the distinction between legislative and federal union, but also predicted the early demise of Confederation.[9] Others warned that that the proposed Confederation would cause rebellion among French Canadians, who wanted "a real confederation, giving the largest powers to the local governments, and merely delegated authority to the General Government."[10] Such a union was similar to the kind of union that the United States Constitution was believed to have established, but which Macdonald rejected. According to Robert Vipond, it was the Reformers who, unlike Macdonald, "defended a constitutional position in 1865 that was in many ways similar to the Federalists' defense of the American Constitution some eighty years before." Moreover, the ideas of the Reformers, Vipond adds, acquired new importance in the years after Confederation by providing "a foundation" on which advocates of provincial rights could build a constitutional theory that treated "Macdonald's centralizing mechanisms as if they were impurities that had to be removed from the constitutional system."[11] What Reformers and other opponents of Canadian Confederation did not probe, however, were the political theories behind the United States Constitution. For the Reformers, as for Macdonald, it was the American Civil War, together with its implications for federalism, that required attention.

The Framers of the United States Constitution had not concerned themselves with the problem of civil war. Their attention was fixed on a different issue. For the American Framers, the crucial problem had been raised by Montesquieu, who believed that large countries turn into despotisms and destroy republican liberty.[12] So long as his problem remained unsolved, most Americans could see no alternative to the ineffectual Articles of Confederation, other than Alexander Hamilton's unacceptable proposals for consolidated government. A solution to Montesquieu's problem was eventually provided by James Madison in his classic discussion of republicanism. Smallness, said Madison, was fatal to republicanism because faction would be worse in small states; but consolidated government was equally unacceptable because it destroyed republican liberty. His famous middle ground was the idea of a compound or extended republic, whose constitution was both national and (con)federal in character.[13] A stable republican state required the compounding of various economic interests of a large territory with a federal system of semi-sovereign political units, and the adoption of a scheme of indirect elections that would refine the voice of the people at the national level.[14] The compound republic, so Madison believed, provided the commercial and military advantages of energetic union without sacrificing either republican government or the states.

The theory of the compound republic was not unchallenged. In the debates over the ratification of the Constitution, anti-federalists reasserted their belief in the small-republic theory and the virtues presupposed by it. They defended their belief in homogeneity, their contempt for extremes of wealth, their sympathy for Christian piety, and their conviction that republican government depended on the citizen's active participation in public affairs and his devotion to the public good. They argued that standing armies and commerce would undermine classical republican virtues and lead to a decline of morals.[15] Although anti-federalists were unsuccessful in their campaign, their protests were instrumental in securing the adoption of the original Bill of Rights and have become a recurring theme of American political thought. But there was at least one crucial assumption that anti-federalists did not dispute in 1789. Everyone agreed, including the anti-federalists, that the United States was one nation; their disagreement, as Herbert Storing said, was about the kind of government it should have.[16]

Such an assumption was precisely what Canadians could not take for granted in 1867. In his famous report of 1839, Lord Durham found in Canada "a struggle not of principle, but of races": "two nations warring in the bosom of a single state."[17] The debates of 1865 constantly returned to Durham's theme. Henri Joly, for example, spoke of the "great difference of nationality, which is certainly fated to play an important part in the destinies of the future Confederation."[18] Joseph Perrault admitted that times have changed, but denied that racial hatred had disappeared. French and English had come to the New World, he said, but had brought their old national hatreds with them.[19] And Christopher Dunkin surmised that "the two differences of language and faith ... [were] the real reasons" for the supposed federal union, whose purpose it was to meet a "probable clashing of races and creeds."[20] Students of American federalism have frequently noted the great difference that exists between their federalism and that of Canada. "Canadians ...," wrote Carl Friedrich, "had a very special problem to deal with which found no parallel in the American experience: that was how to arrange a federal system that would satisfy their French-speaking citizens."[21]

Because Canadians had special problems, Canadian Confederation had a distinctive ideological context. But Canadians also had problems and objectives similar to those that shaped the United States Constitution. "The American Union and the Canadian Federation," wrote W.B. Munro, "were the outcome of essentially similar conditions. Both arose in part from a desire to promote the common defense, and in part from the hope that commercial prosperity would be attained through union."[22] In Canada, commercial prosperity was frequently connected to Tory ideas of union. In 1854 a Halifax newspaper called for the union of the

British North American colonies and insisted that "the union should be perfect, unqualified and absolute."[23] In pre-Confederation Canada, it was the Tories who most favoured union, and their proposals for union were highly centralized and supported executive power. They tended to associate the provinces with local prejudices, regarded democracy as a faction-ridden system of government based on the will of uneducated and uncultivated people, and looked to commercial empire in order to provide opportunities for ambitious men. Tories, it has been said, wanted the kind of imperial or consolidated government that Alexander Hamilton had failed to obtain.[24]

The leading proponent of the Tory vision of Canada was Macdonald himself. His preference, as he revealed in the debates of 1865, was for a legislative union because such a union was "the best, the cheapest, the most vigorous, and the strongest system of government we could adopt." Moreover, Macdonald urged the provinces of British North America not only to establish a commercial union, but also to become "a great nationality, commanding the respect of the world, able to hold our own against all opponents."[25] "The Nation," Donald Creighton wrote in his account of Macdonald's idea of Union, "transcends the group, the class, or section."[26] Macdonald admitted, however, that the Tory idea of Legislative Union was "impracticable", not only because Lower Canada refused to accept it, but also because the Maritime provinces rejected it. A federal union was the only "practicable" solution. Yet Macdonald seemed to imply that the Canadian union would still be a Tory union because only minimal concessions were made to the federal principle.[27]

The concessions were limited, but powerful social and political forces had made them necessary in the first place. Behind the concessions was Lower Canada and the issue of French Canadian nationality. Moreover, the idea of a distinct local identity and a distinct provincial destiny also had wide support in the Maritimes. Such local identities and provincial destinies had received recognition from the British colonial practice, beginning in 1791, of granting popular representation in local legislatures. "The democratic element in Canadian politics," wrote W.L. Morton, "was always stronger than any other, including allegiance to the Crown."[28] Tory ideas of imperial government were also challenged by Reformers in Upper and Lower Canada in the decades before Confederation. Mackenzie and Papineau had defended local democracy and civic virtue against élite control and centralized government, and Canadians witnessed the articulation of political ideas not unlike those of anti-federalists in 1789.[29] Opposition to Tory union came from of a variety of ideological sources and represented powerful social and political forces.

Federation was offered as the compromise solution, even though federalism was widely regarded as a sinister doctrine. Not surprisingly, Macdonald provided a pragmatic account of Confederation and assured Canadians that they would avoid the maladies of American federalism. Confederation, he said, improved on the American union. But the story of Confederation is more complicated than Macdonald made it appear. Confederation was a practical achievement, but the idea had ideological origins, as well as a complex ideological context, from which it finally emerged. As a proponent of Tory union, Macdonald wanted a legislative union; he settled for a federal union. The difficult problems of Canadian federalism did not emerge only after Confederation; many of them already existed before 1867 and were canvassed in the debates of 1865. In the years after 1867, Canadian federalism avoided the malady of civil war that had disrupted the United States, but it continued to confront the Canadian problems that had compelled the adoption of federation in the first place. Macdonald had little enthusiasm for such a prospect. "It is generally believed," wrote Alfred DeCelles, that while the British North American Act was before the British parliament, "Macdonald desired ... to have it modified so that a legislative union should be substituted for the proposed federation."[30] Apparently, Cartier's intervention rescued the federation idea.

## THE BEGINNINGS OF CANADIAN FEDERALIST THEORY

So long as federalism was understood as the American error, Macdonald occupied pride of place. But it was also intended as a solution to Canadian problems. In the debates of 1865, it was Cartier who most directly addressed the kinds of problems that distinguished

Canada from the United States. Macdonald regarded federalism as a suspect idea; Cartier was an unequivocal federalist. "If Macdonald is entitled to be called the 'Father of the Canadian Constitution,'" wrote W.B. Munro, "... Alexander Hamilton has some claim to be designated as its grandfather."[31] But neither Alexander Hamilton nor John A. Macdonald obtained the kind of constitution he preferred; both were compelled to concede more than they wished to federalism. In the case of Canada, it was Cartier who was instrumental in obtaining crucial concessions. His demands could not be ignored if Confederation was to include French Canada. Cartier, it has been said, was the Jefferson of Confederation.[32] But he did not share Jefferson's democratic sympathies, and in any case, his role was more like Madison's. He broke the deadlock that had developed between those who favoured the Tory idea of legislative union and those who either could see no alternative to the status quo or looked to a weak confederacy. In so doing, Cartier also provided the beginnings of Canadian federalist theory.[33]

In the United States, federalist theory frequently returns to its early beginnings in the debate between classical republicanism and the compound republic. That debate creates a tension in American federalist theory and gives richness to it. But the tension, it has been said, is comparable to "differences within the family."[34] The differences are far from negligible, but they are normally differences about the best means for the realization of republican liberty. Canadian federalist theory also contains a tension. The Canadian tension relates not to liberty but to identity and to the relation (or clash) between local identities and national identity.[35] Moreover, the Canadian debate about identity often takes place between those who dispute "family" membership. Put differently, American federalist theory has focused on the kind of government the nation should have; Canadian federalist theory has concerned itself with whether there is a nation at all.

Questions of identity and nationhood were prominent in discussions of Confederation. In 1867, the Toronto *Globe* hailed the "birthday of a new nationality. A united British North America ... takes its place among the nations of the world."[36] But the issue of nationality was far more controversial than the *Globe* made it appear. Not only was nationality the single most divisive issue of Confederation, but almost all the important questions of Confederation were somehow connected to it. The debates of 1865 record its significance and its contentiousness. Some speakers, such as Macdonald, urged that the happy opportunity of founding a great nation should not be allowed to pass. Others, including Joseph Perrault, complained that the real object of Confederation was not merely the creation of a new nationality and a vast empire, but the obliteration of the French-Canadian nationality. Christopher Dunkin, on the other hand, believed that there was no common nationality to which Confederation could appeal. "Have we any class of people," he asked, "… whose feelings are going to be directed to … Ottawa, the centre of the new nationality that is to be created?"[37]

In the years after Confederation, Dunkin's question retained its importance. In fact, the apparent failure of the Macdonaldian constitution, as demonstrated by the genesis of provincial rights, has been traced to the lack of attachment to Ottawa that he foresaw. The weakness of Macdonald's constitutional programme, Norman McL. Rogers wrote, "lay in the fact that it presupposed a general sentiment in the country which would support the dominion government in a dispute with a province." This assumption, Rogers added, "was not correct," partly because Ottawa was "a new and untried entity," whereas the provinces "were old and familiar friends."[38] In the debates of 1865, however, the task of meeting Dunkin's objection fell as much to Cartier as to Macdonald. Macdonald's general response was that the proposed Confederation had disposed of the problem of provincial rights because it created a centralized federation and radically diminished the authority of the provinces. Cartier's response was the idea that Confederation would bring into existence a new kind of nationality, which he called a political nationality.[39]

Connected to Cartier's idea of a Canadian political nationality was his philosophy of federalism. This philosophy distinguished him not only from Macdonald, who favoured Tory union, but also from early American federalists who assumed the existence of a single nation. As a federalist, Cartier's focus was multiple identities and their implications for Canadian nationhood. In the debates of 1865, he noted that opponents of Canadian federation either lamented the existence of racial and local diversities, and thus called

for their elimination through a legislative union, or appealed to such diversities and particularities in their attempt to discredit any scheme of union, other than a weak confederacy, a defence league, or a free trade area. The implicit issue was homogeneity, and the belief that a nation either presupposed homogeneity or was compelled to create it. Not only had Lord Durham arrived at such a conclusion, but his assumption reappeared in the debates of 1865 and became an obstacle to Canadian Confederation. Cartier's response was to dismiss projects such as Durham's as "utopian." "The idea of unity of races," he said, "was … impossible."[40]

At the core of his dismissal of Durham was his philosophical affirmation of diversity and his distinctive conception of Canadian nationhood. Against Durham, Cartier insisted that diversity of race would always exist because "dissimilarity … appeared to be the order of the physical world and of the moral world, as well as in the political world."[41] The project of racial unity was not only utopian but impossible. Cartier also objected to those who used Durham to argue that the Confederation project of creating a great nation was misconceived because Upper Canada was British and Protestant, whereas Lower Canada was French and Catholic. Such an objection seemed to suppose not only that racial hatreds existed, but that they were irreducible. Cartier responded by insisting, in part, that racial diversity should be regarded as "a benefit rather than otherwise." The British Empire, he said, had diversity of race, and each race contributed to the greatness of the Empire. "We were of different races," he observed, "not for the purpose of warring against each other, but in order to emulate for the general welfare."[42]

At one level, Cartier provided an exhortation on racial harmony. But he coupled his exhortation with a defence of federalism. He had come to the conclusion "that federation was desirable and necessary" because it was the most practical means of bringing the colonies together, "so that particular rights and interests should be properly guarded."[43] Those who supposed that federation would not work, on account of the differences of race and religion, "were in error." On the contrary, it was on account of the variety of races and local interests that "the Federation system ought to be resorted to, and would be found to work well."[44] As Cartier understood it, federalism was an exercise in the art of separation. The general interest was to be separated from local interests, and questions of race and religion were assigned to their proper place. As an exercise in the art of separation, Canadian federalism, in his understanding of it, did not presuppose the nation so much as create it.

Canadian federalism did not create the Canadian nation out of nothing. Cartier supposed that the provinces of British North America had common "sympathies and interests" and "desired to live under the British Crown."[45] Canadian federalism separated common interests and sympathies from the local interests and racial particularities that were distinctive to the provinces. In so doing, it brought into existence a Canadian nation that was an "agglomeration of communities" having "kindred interests and sympathies," as well as a common political nationality.[46] Moreover, the Canadian political nationality was a new nationality, in the sense that it did not displace the French-Canadian nationality or existing allegiances to the provinces. In a classic discussion of federalism, A.V. Dicey expressed a similar idea. For him, federalism presupposed a peculiar kind of sentiment because it required citizens to possess both a desire for national unity and the determination to maintain a separate political existence.[47] In the debates of 1865, Cartier appealed to such a sentiment not only to justify Canadian federalism, but also to legitimate the creation of the Canadian nation.

Canada was to be a nation in which multiple loyalties and multiple identities flourished. But Canada, in Cartier's understanding of it, also presupposed strong institutions at the national level, as well as the continued existence of English and French minorities within the provinces. Both beliefs were criticized in the debates of 1865. French Canadians, it was said, would be outnumbered in the federal parliament and their interests ignored. Others complained that the rights of the English minority would be trampled on in Quebec. In the case of the federal parliament, Cartier admitted that he once opposed representation by population as being adverse to the interests of French Canadians, who were the weaker party. However, he was now willing to allow such representation in the House of Commons because he realized that it "would not involve the same objection if other partners were drawn in by a federation." "If three parties

were concerned," he added, "the stronger would not have the same advantage."[48] In the case of minorities, Cartier appealed to considerations of fairness as well as to legal and constitutional remedies. "Any attempt to deprive the minority of their rights," he said, "would be at once thwarted." If unfairness occurred, he added, "it would be censured everywhere."[49] In Cartier's understanding of it, the Canadian nation presupposed the existence of multiple identities and allegiances, the solution of complex institutional problems, and a sense of fairness throughout the country.

In the debates of 1865, Cartier also addressed the issue of the American Civil War. The American union, he said, had fallen into civil war because it was a democracy, and "purely democratic institutions could not be conducive to the peace and prosperity of nations." But the Canadian union would form "a Federation with a view of perpetuating the monarchical element."[50] Cartier associated pure democracy with mob rule and political instability, and monarchy with national dignity and respect for principle. French Canadians, he said, supported constitutional monarchy because "their adherence to the British Crown" had secured for them "their institutions, their languages, and their religions intact to-day."[51] They also knew that their own nationality would enjoy no such guarantees in the American democracy. "There was the instinctive feeling … in French Canada," W.L. Morton wrote, "that monarchical allegiance allowed a diversity of customs and rights under law in a way that the rational scheme and abstract principles of republican democracy did not."[52] The Crown, in Cartier's understanding of it, typified a type of federal union that differed not only from the American union but also from Tory union. Its symbols were permanence, order and unity; its practice was the difficult art of separation, which was crucial for the creation of the Canadian nation.

## AFTER CONFEDERATION

Cartier died in 1873. Macdonald lived until 1891 and presided in large measure over the consolidation of the Canadian Confederation. But the Macdonaldian constitution was already faltering by the 1870s, and by the 1890s the Canadian constitution had moved decisively away from Macdonald's centralism and towards provincial rights. What eventually emerged was described in 1947 as "two streams of constitutional thought in violent opposition, represented by the supporters of federal authority ... and the advocates of the 'compact theory.'"[53] By the 1970s, Canada's constitutional crisis had acquired new dimensions. The governments of Canadian federalism, it was suggested in an influential study, were bent on increasing their own jurisdictions without regard to the self-defeating competition engendered by such policies. The new crisis was described as a crisis of big governments, which had turned the Canadian constitution into "a lame-duck constitution," and called into question even the limited goal of keeping Quebec in Confederation.[54] Behind the new crisis, however, was Macdonald's failure to settle the issue of provincial rights. Moreover, his vision of Canada—a vision that privileged imperial government and regarded federalism with suspicion—was as likely to fuel doctrines of provincial rights as to eliminate them.

In the years after Confederation, advocates of provincial rights challenged Macdonald's centralism by developing alternative constitutional visions. In some cases, the alternative vision presupposed Canadian nationhood and offered a new understanding of it. Oliver Mowat was the leader of the provincial rights movement in Ontario, but he also professed devotion to the success of Confederation. Unlike Macdonald, Mowat believed that the success of Confederation was to be obtained through the autonomy of the provinces and not through central power.[55] Confederation was itself described as a compact of provinces. In other cases, the affirmation of Canadian nationhood was less manifest, if not altogether absent. Some French Canadians focused on culture and race, and believed that Confederation rested on a compact between two races, in which each affirmed the right of the other to live according to its own culture. Confederation was understood as a racial *modus vivendi*, and Canada was taken to be a country that allowed two cultures or two nations to exist side by side.[56] In both cases, central authority was eroded and the idea of a common Canadian nationality diminished.

There were also provincialists, such as David Mills of Ontario, who associated the protection of provincial rights and the vitality of provincial communities with liberal principles that included respect for the rule of law, as well as a strong commitment to individual rights. "The provincialists," Robert Vipond has suggested, "strongly defended the autonomy and integrity of community, but they were also the carriers of a genuinely liberal strain in Canadian political culture that those like Charles Taylor would say threatens community."[57] For them, the Macdonaldian constitution represented not only centralism and paternalism, but also arbitrary power and corrupt government. Ultimately, provincialists such as Mills "could find no logically necessary and empirically rigorous connection between provincialism and liberalism."[58] But in their own minds at least, there was a deep association between provincial rights and liberal values, and their critique of centralized power in some respects laid a foundation for the eventual adoption of a charter of rights.

For Macdonald, however, provincial rights and the compact theory represented the refusal of the provinces to accept the subordinate status that Confederation conferred on them. "It is difficult to make the local Legislatures understand," he complained, "that their powers are not so great as they were before the Union."[59] The enhancement of provincial power also reminded Macdonald of the American Civil War, which he attributed to the weakness of central power and to the strength of states rights. But the expansion of provincial power did not simply diminish central authority; it also eroded minority rights. A survey of the growth of provincial jurisdiction in the decades after Confederation, undertaken by Frank Scott, dismissed as a "popular myth" belief in the protection of minority rights by the Judicial Committee of the Privy Council. The decisions of the Privy Council had reduced the jurisdiction of the central government, expanded the powers of the provinces, and upheld provincial jurisdiction at the expense of minority rights. Given the apparent hostility of provincial governments to minority rights, wrote Scott, "it is little comfort for the French-Canadian minorities [throughout Canada] ... to realize that the provincial governments on which they depend for their educational privileges and civil rights have had their powers enlarged."[60] Macdonald was more concerned about the reduction of central power, but the erosion of minority rights also raised questions about Confederation.

One of the most controversial cases of minority rights arose in 1871, as a result of the New Brunswick School Act. This act established a system of tax-supported, non-sectarian free schools, thereby abolishing the state-supported denominational schools that had existed before Confederation. Roman Catholics appealed to Macdonald to disallow the act under the powers given to the central government by the British North America Act; but he refused on the ground that the Roman Catholics had lost no legal rights, since their denominational schools had only the sanction of practice. Macdonald's opinion was eventually upheld by the Judicial Committee of the Privy Council; it was supported at the time by Cartier, among others. Strict law aside, the School Act not only disturbed New Brunswick politics, but also raised questions about the spirit of Confederation. Some of those opposed to the act believed that the spirit of Confederation was to maintain all minority rights enjoyed at the time of union, whether embodied in law or not.[61]

The New Brunswick School Act also raised questions about Canadian federalist theory because it opened old issues about the war of races, nationalities, and religions that Confederation was to have settled. In the debates of 1865, Étienne Taché had addressed the war of races and dismissed it. "Much had been said on the war of races," he noted, "but that war was extinguished on the day the British Government granted Canada Responsible Government."[62] The Fathers of Confederation settled on a more complex response that included both federalism and minority rights. Moreover, minority rights were to enjoy the protection, in Cartier's understanding of them, not only of the law courts and the power of disallowance, but also of the sense of fairness that pervaded the country. Taché also spoke of fairness in 1865. French Canadians, he said, had taken pains "to give our fellow subjects of English origin the whole of their rights and fair play in every respect."[63] In the Confederation debates, fairness for minorities was a critical issue, so much so that Cartier made it part of Canadian federalist theory.

In the United States, questions of fairness acquired critical importance in the decades before the war and produced new understandings of American federalism. Behind the Civil War was the issue of slavery, as well as difficult questions of economic policy and territorial expansion. Those questions also provided the background to John Calhoun's *Disquisition on Government*. As he understood the issue, the northern states, which formed a majority and opposed slavery, had used the central government to enact policies detrimental to the interests of the southern states, which formed a minority and favoured the continuation of slavery. Calhoun offered a complex solution to the problem, which included his famous idea of a concurrent majority. The will of the people, he said, could not be correctly ascertained merely by consulting the numerical majority. In a country such as the United States, which was composed of different interests and sections, it was also essential to obtain special consent for central government action by way of a concurrent majority of interests and sections.[64] The requirement of special consent also implied that interests and sections possessed a veto on central government action. Calhoun's proposal for a plural executive was a practical device for the achievement of a concurrent majority. The Framers of the United States Constitution had created a single chief magistrate; Calhoun regarded their creation as "a great mistake" and believed that a plural presidency would create harmony in the country since one section could not oppress the other.[65]

Calhoun's ideas did not attract the attention of the Fathers of Confederation. There is, however, an indirect connection between him and Canadian Confederation that comes through Lord Acton. In twentieth-century discussions of Canadian federalism, Acton's essay on "Nationality" occupies a distinguished place. Pierre Trudeau, for example, frequently cited Acton in his own studies on Canadian federalism. Citation of Acton began at least as early as 1921, with W.P.M. Kennedy's critique of nationalist doctrines.[66] Since then Acton has been cited by scholars and statesmen to justify the kind of state that the Fathers of Confederation are thought to have created. "Not Mill and Durham," it has been said, "but Lord Acton was the thinker who provided the intellectual foundation which British North America ... was already destined to take."[67] It was Acton who said that "the coexistence of several nations under the same State is the test ... of its freedom [as well as] one of the chief instruments of civilization."[68] He said more about federalism in his 1861 essay on the United States Constitution, where Calhoun's ideas are described as "profound" and as "applicable to the politics of the present day."[69]

What Acton found attractive about Calhoun's theory was its rejection of absolutist politics. In the United States, such politics operated through Jeffersonian democracy, which Acton likened to "the spurious democracy of the French Revolution."[70] As he understood it, the French Revolution began by proclaiming a democratic republic and ended by creating a new theory of nationality, in which the nation was regarded as an indivisible whole and the diverse interests of the people were absorbed in a fictitious and tyrannous unity. The alternative was the spirit of English liberty, which substituted diversity for uniformity and harmony for unity. In the case of the United States, the spirit of English liberty produced the original constitution as a compromise based on "mutual concessions ... between opposite principles, neither of which could prevail."[71] Such mutual concessions, Acton said, were also the basis of Calhoun's concurrent majority. In other situations, the spirit of English liberty enabled several nations or races to coexist under the same state, thereby reviving exhausted nations and giving to every people "an interest in its neighbour." So understood, English liberty was antithetical to the nationalist state, under which "all other nationalities that may be within the boundary ... are exterminated or reduced to servitude."[72] For Acton, the spirit of English liberty produced an understanding of federalism that rejected extremist politics, whether based on principle or nationality.

Canadian Confederation also relied on English liberty and the spirit of compromise. Despite such similarities, Actonian federalism has limited relevance for the critical issues of Confederation. In the case of Canada, it produces a critique of the nationalist state and a justification of the multinational state. Confederation shared such objectives, but it also attempted to create a single nation. Put differently, federalism, in the sense presupposed by Canadian Confederation, "is a device designed to cope with the problem of how distinct communities can live a common life together without ceasing to be distinct communities."[73] The Fathers of Confederation did not merely believe that nationalities could coexist under the same state; they also sought to create a great and single nation, united by a strong central government and a common nationality. Moreover, the Fathers had to confront the problem of minorities within the provinces, a problem that Actonian federalism does not address. Acton's federalism is premised on the rejection of absolutist and extremist politics. The Fathers of Confederation also rejected extremist politics, but coupled this rejection with a conception of nationhood that was not confined to the boundaries set by Lord Acton.

In their effort to create a great nation, the Fathers of Confederation accepted federalism. The Framers of the United States Constitution also sought to create a great nation, but unlike the Canadian Fathers, they could take the nation for granted, provided they solved the problem of republican liberty. Madison's solution was the idea of a compound republic. Years later, Calhoun attempted to improve on his checks and balances by adding the idea of a concurrent majority. But American theories of federalism contained assumptions that the Fathers of Confederation implicitly rejected. "The last thing the Canadian delegates wanted," Jennifer Smith has written, "was the petty and paralyzing intrusion of local concerns in their proposed new national forum."[74] Under the proposed Confederation, the federal principle would help to ensure that local and particular concerns were left at the local level. Madison and Calhoun made no such assumption. The Fathers of Confederation took pains to distinguish their federalism from the American form. For some of the Fathers, federalism, even in its Canadian version, represented an uneasy compromise. For others, such as George-Étienne Cartier, Confederation promised to create a nation that solved Canadian problems.

## CONCLUSION

Canadian Confederation, it is often noted, was not a popular movement, but "the work of a few master-builders."[75] In the debates of 1865, Christopher Dunkin made a similar observation. The United States Constitution, he said, was adopted after a "successful war of independence", in which the men who framed it had gone "shoulder to shoulder" through a great trial, and "their entire communities ... had been united as one man." Moreover, Americans had tried "the system of mere confederation" and were ready "to build up a great nationality that should endure in the future." But Canadian Confederation, Dunkin observed, was "very different indeed" because it was preceded, not by a common struggle, but by a struggle that "pitted our public men one against another, and ... even our faiths and races against each other."[76] Such difficulties, coupled with the belief that federalism had contributed to the American Civil War, undermined the popularity of Canadian Confederation. Confederation, it has been said, "was imposed on British North America by ingenuity, luck, courage and sheer force."[77] But neither its opponents nor its supporters took its accomplishment for granted. At the Quebec Conference of 1864 and after, Canadians engaged in a full and famous debate. That debate contains a plurality of constitutional visions, in which ideas about imperial government were opposed to beliefs about popular sovereignty, and the war of races and nationalities was opposed to ethnic harmony and to the Canadian political nationality.

Macdonald initially favoured a unitary state; his opponents favoured either "state sovereignty" as embodied in a "real confederation" or defended the status quo. Cartier provided middle ground. Moreover, his middle ground differed in important respects from that provided by Madison some eighty years before. Madison had addressed the problem of republican liberty; Cartier confronted the issue of multiple identities, the war of races, and minority rights. In the debates of 1865, he not only addressed those problems, but he also believed that solutions were at hand. The years after Confederation demonstrated that Cartier's middle ground was politically and philosophically less secure than he seemed to suppose in 1865. Canadians continued to address issues that Confederation was to have settled, and they witnessed the articulation of new constitutional visions. Even if Cartier did not solve the problems of Canadian nationhood, he did provide a new beginning for federalist theory.

## NOTES

1 Donald Creighton, *Canada's First Century* (Toronto: Macmillan, 1970), 10. See also Creighton, *The Road to Confederation* (Toronto: Macmillan, 1964), 141–6.
2 Cited in Norman McL. Rogers, "The Genesis of Provincial Rights," *Canadian Historical Review* 14 (1933): 18.
3 *Parliamentary Debates on the Subject of the Confederation of the British North American Provinces* (Quebec: Hunter, Rose, 1865), 347. Subsequently cited as *Confederation Debates*.
4 *Confederation Debates*, 589, 350.
5 L.F.S. Upton, "The Idea of Confederation: 1754–1858," in *The Shield of Achilles*, ed. W.L. Morton (Toronto: McClelland and Stewart, 1968), 184.
6 Peter J. Smith, "The Ideological Origins of Canadian Confederation," *Canadian Journal of Political Science* 20 (1987): 3.
7 *Confederation Debates*, 32–3.
8 Peter Waite, *The Life and Times of Confederation* (Toronto: University of Toronto Press, 1962), 115.
9 *Confederation Debates*, 501, 493.
10 Such was Henri Joly's protest. See *Confederation Debates*, 250.
11 Robert Vipond, *Liberty and Community: Canadian Federalism and the Failure of the Constitution* (Albany: State University of New York Press, 1991), 27–8, 35–6.
12 See, for example, Douglass Adair, *Fame and the Founding Fathers* (New York: Norton, 1974), 93–106.
13 For a discussion of the difficulties raised by the word "federalism," see Martin Diamond, "What the Framers Meant by Federalism," in *A Nation of States*, ed. Robert Goldwin (Chicago: Rand McNally, 1974), 25–42.
14 Alexander Hamilton, James Madison, and John Jay, *The Federalist*, ed. B.F. Wright (Cambridge: Harvard University Press, 1961), 129–36. See also David Epstein, *The Political Theory of the Federalist* (Chicago: University of Chicago Press, 1984), 147.
15 Isaac Kramnick, "The 'Great National Discussion': The Discourse of Politics in 1787," *William and Mary Quarterly* 45 (1988): 4. See also J.G.A. Pocock, *The Machiavellian Moment* (Princeton: Princeton University Press, 1975), 506–9, 521–35.
16 Herbert J. Storing, *The Complete Anti-Federalist*, vol. 1 (Chicago: University of Chicago Press, 1981), 24. See also Alpheus Mason, *The States Rights Debate* (Englewood Cliffs: Prentice-Hall, 1964), 15.
17 G. Craig, ed. *Lord Durham's Report* (Toronto: McClelland and Stewart, 1963), 23.
18 *Confederation Debates*, 350.
19 *Confederation Debates*, 599, 607.
20 *Confederation Debates*, 509.
21 Carl J. Friedrich, *The Impact of American Constitutionalism Abroad* (Boston: Boston University Press, 1967), 60–1.
22 William B. Munro, *American Influences on Canadian Government* (Toronto: Macmillan, 1929), 11.
23 Peter Waite, *Confederation, 1854–1867* (Toronto: Holt, Rinehart, and Winston, 1972), 28.
24 Smith, "The Ideological Origins of Canadian Confederation," 28.
25 *Confederation Debates*, 27.
26 Donald Creighton, *Towards the Discovery of Canada* (Toronto: Macmillan, 1972), 217.
27 "A federation," wrote W.L. Morton, "so like a legislative union Macdonald could accept, for he could hope that the same forces, the needs of defence and development, which had produced a confederation would continue to strengthen the central power." W.L. Morton, "Confederation, 1870–1896," in *Contexts of Canada's Past*, ed. A.B. McKillop (Toronto: Macmillan, 1980), 208. Macdonald's views are of course complex as is federalism. His strongest objections were to intergovernmental relations; he was more accepting of binationality. Still, Macdonald desired such a high degree of centralization that his position is widely and perhaps correctly regarded as inimical both to intergovernmental relations and to binationality.
28 Morton, "Confederation, 1870–1896," 224–5.
29 Smith, "The Ideological Origins of Canadian Confederation," 12–9.
30 Alfred DeCelles, "Sir Georges-Étienne Cartier," in Stephen Leacock et al., *Mackenzie, Baldwin, Lafontaine, Hincks, Papineau, Cartier* (New York: Oxford University Press, 1926), 102.

31  Munro, *American Influences on Canadian Government*, 20.
32  F.R. Scott, "French-Canada and Canadian Federalism," in *Evolving Canadian Federalism*, ed. A.R.M. Lower (Durham: Duke University Press, 1958), 61.
33  Recent biographical studies of Cartier include Alastair Sweeny, *George-Étienne Cartier* (Toronto: McClelland and Stewart, 1976) and Brian Young, *George-Étienne Cartier* (Montreal: McGill-Queen's University Press, 1981).
34  Storing, *The Complete Anti-Federalist*, 1:5. See also Thomas Pangle, *The Spirit of Modern Republicanism* (Chicago: University of Chicago Press, 1988), 124–7.
35  See, for example, J.M.S. Careless, "'Limited Identities' in Canada," *Canadian Historical Review* 50 (1969): 1.
36  Cited in Waite, *Life and Times of Confederation*, 322.
37  *Confederation Debates*, 511.
38  Rogers, "The Genesis of Provincial Rights," 20–1. See also Vipond, *Liberty and Community*, 89.
39  See Donald V. Smiley, *The Canadian Political Nationality* (Toronto: Methuen, 1967), 8–9, 128–35.
40  *Confederation Debates*, 60.
41  *Confederation Debates*, 60.
42  *Confederation Debates*, 60.
43  *Confederation Debates*, 57. See also Joseph Tasse, ed., *Discours de Sir Georges Cartier* (Montreal: Eusebe Senecal, 1893), 399–447.
44  *Confederation Debates*, 57. Cartier's understanding of federalism is also discussed in Ramsay Cook, *Canada and the French-Canadian Question* (Toronto: Macmillan, 1966), 44–7; and Ramsay Cook, *The Maple Leaf Forever* (Toronto: Macmillan, 1971), 72–5.
45  *Confederation Debates*, 55, 60.
46  *Confederation Debates*, 60. See also John Cooper, "The Political Ideas of George Etienne Cartier," *Canadian Historical Review* 23 (1942): 291.
47  A.V. Dicey, *An Introduction to the Study of the Law of the Constitution*, 10th ed. (London: Macmillan, 1959), 142–3.
48  *Confederation Debates*, 54.
49  *Confederation Debates*, 60.
50  *Confederation Debates*, 59.
51  *Confederation Debates*, 59.
52  W.L. Morton, *The Canadian Identity* (Toronto: University of Toronto Press, 1972), 105.
53  F.R. Scott, *Essays on the Constitution* (Toronto: University of Toronto Press, 1977), 176–7.
54  Alan C. Cairns, *Constitution, Government and Society in Canada* (Toronto: McClelland and Stewart, 1988), 183, 190.
55  Ramsay Cook, *Provincial Autonomy, Minority Rights, and the Compact Theory, 1867–1921* (Ottawa: Information Canada, 1969), 2. See also Vipond, *Liberty and Community*, 47–82.
56  Cook, *Provincial Autonomy, Minority Rights, and the Compact Theory*, 51, 57.
57  Vipond, *Liberty and Community*, 152.
58  Vipond, *Liberty and Community*, 190.
59  Cited in Rogers, "The Genesis of Provincial Rights," 17.
60  F.R. Scott, "The Privy Council and Minority Rights," *Queen's Quarterly* 37 (1930): 677.
61  Morton, "Confederation, 1870–1896," 213–5.
62  *Confederation Debates*, 10.
63  *Confederation Debates*, 238.
64  John C. Calhoun, *A Disquisition on Government*, ed. C. Gordon Post (Indianapolis: Bobbs-Merrill, 1953), 22, 29.
65  Calhoun, *A Disquisition on Government*, 102.
66  W.P.M. Kennedy, "Nationalism and Self-Determination," *Canadian Historical Review* 2 (1921): 11.
67  David Cameron, "Lord Durham Then and Now," *Journal of Canadian Studies* 25 (1990): 11. See also David Cameron, *Nationalism, Self-Determination and the Quebec Question* (Toronto: Macmillan, 1974), 76–80.
68  Lord Acton, *Essays on Freedom and Power*, ed. Gertrude Himmelfarb (Cleveland: Meridian, 1962), 160.
69  Acton, *Essays on Freedom and Power*, 199.
70  Acton, *Essays on Freedom and Power*, 224.
71  Acton, *Essays on Freedom and Power*, 174.
72  Acton, *Essays on Freedom and Power*, 168.
73  Cameron, *Nationalism, Self-Determination and the Quebec Question*, 107. See also K.C. Wheare, "Federalism and the Making of Nations," in *Federalism Mature and Emergent*, ed. Arthur Macmahon (New York: Russell & Russell, 1962), 35.
74  Jennifer Smith, "Intrastate Federalism and Confederation," in *Political Thought in Canada*, ed. Stephen Brooks (Toronto: Irwin, 1984), 271. See also Jennifer Smith, "Canadian Confederation and the Influence of American Federalism," *Canadian Journal of Political Science* 21 (1988): 443.
75  Rogers, "The Genesis of Provincial Rights," 14.
76  *Confederation Debates*, 514.
77  Waite, *Life and Times of Confederation*, 323. See also Ged Martin, ed., *The Causes of Canadian Confederation* (Fredericton: Acadiensis Press, 1990), 19.

*Part Three*

# Intergovernmental Relations

FINDING A FEDERAL compromise was one thing, making it work quite another. Disputes over the distribution of powers have been shaping the federation since its inception. Donald Smiley analyzes these competing interpretations of the division of powers in light of their historical merit. Richard Simeon follows by examining the way environmental, institutional, and constitutional patterns shape the patterns of intergovernmental relations in Canada.

With Smiley and Simeon setting the scene, the chapter taken from Peter H. Russell's well-known *Constitutional Odyssey* provides an unparalleled synopsis of the key events that defined the debate over the meaning of sovereignty and the intellectual origins of Confederation over the first three decades, and how conceptions of classical federalism and co-ordinated sovereignty eventually won out over post-Confederation centralism. Today, Quebec and perhaps Alberta are at the forefront of Canadians' minds in terms of the quest for provincial rights. The original impetus for provincial autonomy, however, came from Ontario. To clarify this matter on Ontario's legacy in intergovernmental relations, a short excerpt by Christopher Armstrong from Donald Swainson's edited collection on *Oliver Mowat's Ontario* follows. This excerpt is meant to raise awareness about how the actions of Oliver Mowat, the province's longest-reigning premier, affected the turn of events in federal-provincial relations between 1872 and 1896. This section closes with another article by Peter H. Russell in which he argues that the provincial and federal governments' political use of the courts was not just a phenomenon during the early years of Confederation but continues right through to this day.

# 12

## Editors' Introduction

Donald Smiley ranks among the most distinguished experts on Canadian federalism as well as its constitutional dimensions. A selection from Smiley's abridgement of the *Rowell-Sirois Report* seemed like a fitting way to pay homage to his legacy. The Report is significant on a number of fronts, not the least of which being that it set the course of Canada's institutional, policy, and political developments coming out of the Second World War. In 1937, the Liberal government under Mackenzie King established the Royal Commission on Dominion–Provincial Relations to conduct an inquiry into whether the balance of legislative responsibilities and fiscal resources between the central and provincial governments needed adjustments to deal with the challenges facing Canada as a modern industrial society. Smiley's abridged version of Book 1 of the Report details some of the economic drivers of Confederation and the accompanying division of legislative powers but, more importantly, the problems associated with its interpretation. The piece is notable for suggesting that sound historical grounds to support an expansive interpretation of either provincial or federal powers notwithstanding, both interpretations are problematic.

Source: Donald V. Smiley, ed. *The Rowell-Sirois Report: An abridgement of Book 1 of the Royal Commission Report on Dominion-Provincial Relations,* Carleton Library No. 5 (Toronto: McClelland and Stewart, 1940), 30–43, 70–81.

Donald Smiley

# The Rowell-Sirois Report: An abridgement of Book 1 of the Royal Commission Report on Dominion-Provincial Relations

FEDERAL UNION WAS a plan whereby, through mutual concession, cultural and local loyalties could be preserved and reconciled with the political strength and solidarity of the whole. These separate loyalties were strong and their existence was keenly realized. They existed not only in Canada but also in the Maritimes where they had helped to frustrate projects for Maritime legislative union. Mutual concession required the English-speaking elements of Lower Canada to relinquish their integral union with the English-speaking people of Upper Canada while the French-speaking Canadians abandoned their objections to a superior political authority in whose councils they would be in a minority. In compensation, the broad questions of trade and commerce which so intimately concerned the English-speaking people of Lower Canada were to be given to the federal authority, thus securing the benefits of single control in these matters of general interest while French-speaking Canada was to

be secured in sole control of the cherished values it so tenaciously held. Equally, this solution offered security for the historic traditions firmly rooted in the Maritimes.

Economically, the first objectives of Confederation were to establish a free-trade area comprising the five old provinces and to develop interprovincial transportation facilities. The resources and industries of the several provinces, it was thought, would prove complementary to each other, and would increase prosperity and self-sufficiency. To make this a reality, the Intercolonial Railway was to link the Maritime Provinces with the St. Lawrence Valley and to give Canada winter access to the sea.

Another great economic objective of Confederation, to be realized as soon as circumstances permitted, was the opening up of the Northwest and the inclusion of the Pacific province. For the Province of Canada, in particular, this westward expansion was to provide an escape from a *cul-de-sac* and the threatened economic stagnation. New frontiers and new resources would provide opportunities for settlement and development. It was recognized as an immense undertaking for which no specific detailed plan could be made under the urgencies and limitations of the moment.

This project had to await the acquisition of the lands of the Hudson's Bay Company. It required the building of a transcontinental railway. This, in turn, depended upon attracting new capital and capital, at that time, had become shy of Canadian ventures. Collective effort and resources on a scale which only government could secure were necessary and, at the same time, conditional on the restoration of the public credit.

Although these plans were necessarily vague in 1867, they were nevertheless resolutely held. The new political framework was designed to give the Federal Government ample powers for the prodigious task of opening up the West. The Federal Government was intended to give a vigorous lead in the development of the new national transcontinental economy and in matters relating to that development there was to be no doubt, such as had recently arisen in the United States, about its authority.

There were some among the Fathers of Confederation who favoured a unitary state as an instrument for realizing these plans. As is well known, John A. Macdonald had a strong preference for a unitary state and Galt accepted the federal scheme with reluctance and hoped it might later coalesce into a legislative union.[1] But legislative union was not acceptable to the French-speaking Canadians or to the Maritime Provinces. Furthermore, municipal institutions had not yet been established in the Maritimes, and they were still in the early stages of development in Lower Canada. The centralization of all governmental powers under one government was, therefore, impracticable from an administrative point of view. The distractions of local administration might well have diverted some of the energies of the central government from its larger creative tasks. Thus, for various reasons, the builders of the new nation planned a federation comprised of a central government with authority over matters of general and common interest and provincial governments with authority over matters of local concern.

## THE DIVISION OF LEGISLATIVE POWERS

The British North America Act was the final embodiment of their scheme. The acknowledged necessity of a federal type of union was recognized by the preamble to the Act which recited the desire of the Provinces of Canada, Nova Scotia and New Brunswick "to be federally united into One Dominion." The vital core of a federal constitution is the division of legislative powers between the central authority and the component states or provinces. This division represents the compromise between the forces which make union possible and those which inhibit the formation of a closer union. It marks the limits of what can be done by common agreement and the extent to which the separate states must be permitted to differ and work out their own destinies. In sections 91 to 95 of the British North America Act, the main lines of this division were set forth.

In section 92, certain classes of subjects were enumerated and the provinces were given exclusive power to make laws in relation to matters coming within these classes of subjects. These classes included such things as the administration of justice, municipal institutions, the establishment and maintenance of prisons, hospitals, asylums, and charitable institutions, and control over the public lands of the province. The provinces were also given control over local works and undertakings. But an exception reserved international and interprovincial lines of transport and communication to the Dominion and authorized the Dominion to take legislative power over any local work at any time by declaring it to be for the general advantage of Canada or for the advantage of two or more provinces. A power of direct taxation to raise revenue for provincial purposes was given, although it was thought that expanding revenues from the public lands would make it generally unnecessary for the provinces to exercise this power.[2]

The classes of subjects in section 92 included two of vague and general reference, viz., "Property and Civil Rights in the Province" and "Generally all Matters of a merely local or private Nature in the Province." Section 93 gave the provinces control over education, subject to certain clauses designed to protect the rights of Roman Catholic and Protestant religious minorities. By section 95, the Dominion and the provinces were given concurrent powers over agriculture and immigration, federal legislation to prevail in case of conflict.

The opening paragraph of section 91 gave the Dominion power "to make Laws for the Peace, Order and good Government of Canada, in relation to all Matters not coming within the Classes of Subjects by this Act assigned exclusively to the Legislatures of the Provinces." That is to say, the residue of powers not expressly given to the provinces was reserved to the Dominion. The section then proceeded with a specific enumeration of twenty-nine classes of subjects, illustrating but not restricting the scope of the general words used earlier in the section.

This enumeration included such classes of subjects as defence, criminal law, naturalization and aliens, and the postal system. It also included regulation of trade and commerce, fisheries, banking, currency and coinage, commercial paper, weights and measures, bankruptcy and insolvency, and certain other topics of primarily economic reference. It also gave the Dominion unlimited powers of taxation. The concluding paragraph of section 91 provided against these enumerated topics being "deemed to come within the Class of Matters of a local or private Nature comprised in the Enumeration of the Classes of Subjects" assigned to the provinces by section 92. An exception to section 92 gave the Dominion control over all interprovincial and international transportation and communications.

## THE PROBLEM OF INTERPRETING THE DIVISION OF LEGISLATIVE POWERS

No amount of care in phrasing the division of powers in a federal scheme will prevent difficulty when the division comes to be applied to the variety and complexity of social relationships. The different aspects of life in a society are not insulated from one another in such a way as to make possible a mechanical application of the division of powers. There is nothing in human affairs which corresponds to the neat logical divisions found in the constitution. Therefore, attempts to exercise the powers allotted by the constitution frequently raise questions as to its meaning in relation to particular circumstances.

The British North America Act has not escaped this difficulty. Manifestly, it would be difficult for the Dominion to make any law for the "Peace, Order and good Government of Canada" without affecting, in some way, one or other of the specific subjects in relation to which the provinces were given exclusive powers. On the other hand, laws made by the provinces under the heads of jurisdiction given by section 92 would frequently have direct implications for the "Peace, Order and good Government of Canada" or would bear in some unexpected way upon the enumerated classes of subjects in section 91 over which the Dominion was given exclusive power. The implications and sometimes the express provisions of legislation would seem to cross the line which, in theory, divided the spheres of legislation assigned to the provinces and the Dominion. In a variety of circumstances, the problem of what amounted to an invasion of the field of one by the other would raise difficult questions of interpretation.

The task of interpretation was complicated by the existence, in sections 91 and 92, of several general descriptions of the ambit of legislative power given to the Dominion and the provinces which lacked a clear, legal meaning. "Peace, Order and good Government," "Regulation of Trade and Commerce," "Property and Civil Rights in the Province" do not convey precise signification. Since 1867, the Privy Council has had the last word on the meaning of the British North America Act and has laid down rules of construction for determining when section 91 was to have primacy over section 92. By a process of textual criticism, it has given some concreteness to the general phrases just mentioned. In this way, it has elucidated the legal meaning of the constitution and imparted greater certainty to the division of powers than could have existed when the Act first came into operation. This legal meaning is binding on all other courts and on the Dominion and provincial legislatures.

The British North America Act was a statute of the British Parliament and the Privy Council brought to its task of elucidation an elaborate set of rules binding on the courts in their interpretation of all statutes. These rules required the Privy Council to consider the literal meaning of the words used without any conjectures as to the intentions of those who framed the Quebec and London Resolutions. The Privy Council as a court was not free to consider historical evidence about intentions but was bound to restrict itself to a consideration of what may be called, by contrast, legal evidence—the intention actually expressed by the words used in the Act.[3] Much controversy, past and present, has centred on the question whether the intention which the Privy Council has found to be expressed in the Act accords with the actual intention of the Fathers; in short, whether we now have the constitution which they intended to give us.

Some are satisfied that the Privy Council has merely made explicit what the Fathers intended. Others dismiss the controversy on the ground that we cannot now know what they intended. Others, again, hold that the constitution today is vastly different from what its framers meant it to be and seek to support their contentions from certain historical evidence. The interpretation given by the Privy Council will be considered in later chapters. In an account of the forces behind Confederation and of the nature of the constitution established in 1867, it is important to note the historical arguments which form the basis of many current criticisms of the Privy Council.[4] For purposes of record, we summarize these arguments here but, as we shall indicate later, we do not accept them as conclusive upon certain points, some of them of considerable importance. The critics of the Privy Council do not appear to have fully substantiated their case but, at the same time, they do marshal an impressive mass of historical evidence in support of their general conclusions and their arguments cannot be dismissed as mere hypotheses. Confederation being relatively close to us in time, and the records of its achievement being relatively ample, it is argued we have no reason to assume that it is inherently impossible to determine now the intentions of the Fathers, although it may well be admitted that it is difficult to establish with conclusive finality the meaning of some of the phrases which they employed. The historical case presented by the critics of the Privy Council has not been accepted by all authorities but it merits the attention and consideration of serious students of the problem.

## HISTORICAL INTERPRETATION OF THE INTENTIONS OF THE FATHERS —ARGUMENTS SUPPORTING A BROAD VIEW OF DOMINION POWERS

Some historians urge that the Fathers intended to give wide, sweeping powers to the Dominion and to restrict the provinces to a narrow range of functions, in the exercise of which they were to be subject to the control and supervision of the Dominion.[5] They claim that the general phrases in section 91, "Peace, Order and good Government" and "Regulation of Trade and Commerce," to which the Privy Council has given a restricted meaning were intended to have a broad interpretation and that the general phrase, "Property and Civil Rights in the Province," in section 92, to which the Privy Council has given an extended meaning, was intended by the framers to have a much more limited interpretation.

Some of the leading figures among the framers of the federal scheme evidently intended the general government, as it was called, to have broad and far-reaching powers. John A. Macdonald explained that "all the great questions which affect the general interests of the Confederacy as a whole, are confided to the Federal Parliament."[6] Galt declared that among the subjects given to the general government would be found "all that could in any way be considered of a public and general character."[7] Lord Carnarvon, the Colonial Secretary, introducing the scheme to the House of Lords said it proposed to give to the central authority "those high functions and almost sovereign powers by which general principles and uniformity of legislation may be secured in those questions that are of common import to all the provinces."[8]

Some of the opponents of the scheme criticized it on much the same grounds. A.A. Dorion claimed that it "gives all the powers to the Central Government, and reserves for the local governments the smallest possible amount of freedom of action,"[9] and J.B.E. Dorion opposed the scheme "because we are offered local parliaments which will be simply nonentities, with a mere semblance of power on questions of minor importance."[10]

Supporters of this historical interpretation urge that this view of the relative importance of the Dominion and provincial governments in the new scheme is borne out by various sections of the constitution. They point to the power of the Dominion to appoint the Lieutenant-Governors of the provinces and emphasize the fact that while the provinces were given power to amend the provincial constitutions, they were forbidden to alter in any way the office of Lieutenant-Governor. They contend that the intention to give the

Dominion a dominating position is confirmed by the power to reserve and disallow provincial legislation which was given to the Dominion.

In support of this general position, they place great importance on the opening paragraph of section 91 which gave the Dominion power to make laws for the "Peace, Order and good Government of Canada" in relation to all matters not exclusively assigned to the provincial legislatures. This phrase had acquired a wide, though not very precise, significance in the legislative history of the British Empire before 1867.[11] "Peace, order and good government," and the variation, "peace, welfare and good government" were the phrases habitually used by the British colonial authorities in vesting colonial legislatures with the full range of their legislative powers.

In conferring these powers on colonial legislatures, it was not customary to enumerate specific powers; it was customary merely to grant, in one or other of these well-worn phrases, the entire measure of jurisdiction deemed compatible with imperial control. As imperial control in the internal affairs of the colonies was mainly exercised through the power of disallowance, these phrases carried complete internal legislative competence. In fact, they are the title-deeds of the legislatures of the self-governing Dominions, not again added to by imperial legislation until the Statute of Westminster. The exponents of this historical interpretation, emphasizing the breadth of Dominion powers, infer from the insertion of this phrase in section 91 that the framers must have intended its full historic meaning to prevail, saving only the powers expressly given to the provinces in section 92.

It is similarly urged that the Fathers meant an extended signification to be given to the phrase "Regulation of Trade and Commerce," in section 91. At the time of Confederation, Canada was just beginning to emerge from the commercial into the industrial age. The distinguishing feature of the commercial age was its preoccupation with exchange, the trading of raw or crudely processed products on a world-wide scale. This required an extended organization, interprovincial and international in its scope. It was a delicate system, for its life-lines were everywhere exposed. Prosperity depended on its maintenance and its maintenance and development, in turn, depended on the sympathetic consideration, if not the positive assistance,

of governments. Nothing showed this more clearly than the British imperial trading organization of the 18th and early 19th centuries. British North American statesmen had lived with this system and had seen what control over extended trading relationships by a single government could achieve. Trade and commerce, because of their nature and scope, were inevitably public matters of great import and it is argued that the phrase "the regulation of trade and commerce" had a very wide significance both historically and in the current usage of the Confederation period.

In addition, it is contended, they must have been acutely aware of the confusion which arises when control over such matters is parcelled out among several governments. During the fifty years in which the Provinces of Upper and Lower Canada maintained their separate existence, the control of the St. Lawrence and its commerce had been divided between two distinct and independent governments. This division led to conflicts between Upper and Lower Canada and to bitter struggles between the commercial and agrarian parties in each.[12] Upper Canada had disagreed with Lower Canada and the commercial interests in Montreal had quarrelled with the leaders of the Patriot party over many economic matters of common concern to the whole St. Lawrence Valley.

The impossibility of arriving quickly at a vigorous common policy in these matters had hampered Canada in its bid for the trade of the mid-continent. The frustrations engendered by divided authority formed part of the living memory of public men at the time of Confederation and this appeal to history for a broad interpretation of Dominion powers argues that the Fathers, who wanted to create a robust national economy, must have intended the control of such matters to be placed in the hands of a single government.

In support of this thesis, they draw attention to the reluctance among the commercial element in Montreal to give up the Union of 1841 which had established a common government to deal with these economic matters. The confederation plan asked them to abandon this union and one of the tasks of the advocates of a wider union was to convince them that the establishment again of two provinces in the St. Lawrence Valley would not mean a return to the old confusions. John Rose assured them that they had nothing to fear because the general legislature would have control over the post office, trade, commerce, navigation:— "all the great and important interests ... that affect the minority in Lower Canada...."[13] Galt reiterated that "the interests of trade and commerce ... would be taken out of the category of local questions...."[14] Cartier, stating that he could understand the concern of the commercial minority of Lower Canada lest there should be a return of the old difficulties, said these fears were groundless because "it would be for the General Government to deal with our commercial matters."[15] On the basis of these statements, supporters of this historical interpretation argue that the words "Regulation of Trade and Commerce," were intended to transfer a wide range of economic matters to the control of the central authority.[16]

A historical interpretation which would magnify the scope of Dominion powers by attaching a limited special meaning to the phrase, "Property and Civil Rights in the Province" has also been urged. This phrase has had a long history in British North America, rising out of the relationships of French and English in the valley of the St. Lawrence. British statesmanship sought a solution of this racial problem which would preserve to French Canada the institutions which were vital to its way of life. The Quebec Act of 1774 secured "His Majesty's Canadian subjects within the Province of Quebec" in the enjoyment of their property and civil rights and provided that "in all matters of controversy relative to property and civil rights, resort shall be had to the laws of Canada as the rule for the decision of the same."

In the constitutional and legislative enactments of both Upper and Lower Canada, there were a number of references to the law "relating to property and civil rights." In these references, the phrase was used to signify either the common law of England or the French customary law. That is to say, it denoted the set of laws and customs which were at once the expression and support of the distinctive ways of life of the French-speaking and English-speaking Canadians. The phrase found its way into sections 92 and 94 of the British North America Act.

Supporters of a broad view of federal power argue that the sole purpose of introducing the phrase "Property and Civil Rights in the Province" into section 92 was to protect the unique institutions and ways of life of the Province of Quebec. They lay strong emphasis on section 94 which contemplates certain conditions under which the federal authority may secure unrestricted power to make uniform laws "relative to the Property and Civil Rights in Ontario, Nova Scotia and New Brunswick." To them, this section suggests that the phrase had reference only to matters on which these three provinces were in fundamental agreement and that regional differences of interest were not involved. Ontario, Nova Scotia, and New Brunswick, with their acceptance of the English common law, were in agreement on precisely those matters in which each differed so completely from Quebec. Thus, it is argued that the inclusion of this phrase in section 92 was not designed to express genuinely local as against national interests nor to fix the spheres of the different levels of government but rather to protect regional interests only in so far as they were specifically cultural in character.

This historical interpretation, therefore, maintains that the phrase, "Property and Civil Rights in the Province," as used in section 92, was intended to cover only what was necessary for this limited but important purpose of safeguarding the cultural autonomy of Quebec. It appeals to statements of British officials prior to the passing of the Quebec Act of 1774 and to the instructions of the British Government to the Governors of Quebec after 1774 as showing what were long understood to be the essential laws for safeguarding the fundamental institutions and ways of life of Quebec. These instructions to the Governors repeatedly commanded that the Canadians were to enjoy the "benefit and use of their own Laws, Usages and Customs in all Controversies respecting Titles of Land, and the Tenure, Descent ... of Real Estates, and the distribution of the personal property of Persons dying intestate...."[17] Accordingly, the phrase in question would include matters of civil law concerning the relations of citizen and citizen, such as ownership, transfer and various dealings in property, inheritance and succession by will, rights arising from personal status, such as minority and capacity to make contracts, and from the intimate domestic relations of the family. It would include a variety of other matters of private law but it would not include a number of matters inextricably bound up with the public law such as nation-wide regulation of industry and trade. Still less could it include social insurance which had formed no part of either French or English law and the idea of which was unknown to those who framed the British North America Act. In this way, it is sought to infer from historical evidence the intention to give the phrase "Property and Civil Rights in the Province" a much more restricted meaning than that given to it by the Privy Council.

## HISTORICAL INTERPRETATION OF THE INTENTIONS OF THE FATHERS —ARGUMENTS SUPPORTING A BROAD VIEW OF PROVINCIAL POWERS

These historical arguments as to the intentions of the Fathers of Confederation and the meaning assigned by them to general phrases such as "Peace, Order and good Government," "Regulation of Trade and Commerce" and "Property and Civil Rights in the Province" have not gone without challenge on historical grounds.[18] For example, it is urged that the expression "property and civil rights" has always had a very wide meaning in our constitutional history.

By Royal Edict in 1663, Louis XIV of France created a sovereign Council at Quebec giving it the power "de connaître de toutes causes civiles et criminelles, pour juger souverainement et en dernier ressort selon les lois et ordonnances de notre royaume,"[19] thus, it is claimed, establishing in Quebec the entire French law which ruled New France at the time of the conquest.

The Royal Proclamation of George III of England in October, 1763, which proposed to introduce the English common law into the conquered territory in North America was naturally resented as a grave injustice by the people of Quebec. The Quebec Act of 1774 which was passed to meet this grievance, repealed the proclamation of October, 1763. Section 8 of the Act declared that "His Majesty's Canadian Subjects, within the province of Quebec … may also hold and enjoy their Property and Possessions, together with all Customs and Usages relative thereto, and all other their Civil Rights, in as large, ample, and beneficial Manner, as if the said Proclamation … had not been made" and then continued to provide, as quoted above, that the laws of Canada should provide the rule of decision in controversies "relative to Property and Civil Rights." This section of the Quebec Act has never been repealed.

The French law in its entirety was in force in New France at the time of the conquest and the people of Quebec desired to retain it. This was the ground of their objection to the Proclamation of 1763 and the Quebec Act was passed to meet this grievance. On the basis of these facts, it is argued that the Quebec Act was intended to meet the grievance fully and that the expression, "Property and Civil Rights," as used in the Act, was intended to comprise the entire French civil law and not merely certain selected portions of it. The only thing which is important for understanding the scope of the Act is the purpose for which it was passed. The statements of British officials and the instructions of the British Government to colonial governors merely reveal their opinions. They do not give clues to the meaning of phrases used in the Quebec Act.

This argument attributes a very wide meaning to the expression "Property and Civil Rights" as used in the Quebec Act, and holds that when used in later statutes, the expression bears the same extended meaning unless an express limitation is introduced. No express limitation on the meaning of the phrase occurs in the British North America Act and therefore it is concluded that the broad meaning given to it by the Privy Council is in accordance with its original historical meaning.[20]

## THE LIMITATIONS OF THE HISTORICAL ARGUMENTS

All the historical interpretations go far afield for their arguments. There is no final certainty as to what the framers meant by the use of these phrases. The records of the time have not preserved all their opinions on all points. Clear statements of the views of some on particular points have come down to us; of the views of others, nothing is known.[21]

All that is certainly known is that the framers had large plans for the new Dominion and they proposed a strong central government with ample financial powers to carry the program through. The financial settlement which gave the Dominion the unrestricted taxing power, and the exclusive use of the most important revenue sources of the time (nearly four-fifths of the former provincial revenues were given to the new Dominion Government) is the most significant evidence of the leading role cast for the new Federal Government and of the responsibilities which it was expected to assume. In the provisions for reservation and disallowance of provincial legislation, the Fathers gave the Dominion legal power to supervise and control the legislatures of the provinces. At the same time, it was agreed that the state should be federal with exclusive spheres of power reserved to both the provinces and the Dominion. But the exact meanings intended to be given to the general words used in outlining these exclusive spheres of legislative power remain a matter for speculation.

There is no doubt that some of the framers had wanted a legislative union. Those who expected to be members of the new Federal Government naturally wanted a large stage on which to exhibit their capacity as statesmen.[22] But whatever their intentions, they could not overcome the limitations imposed by physical conditions. They could not ignore the social forces rooted in the history of the colonies any more than they could presume to bind the future indefinitely to the past.

There is a further limitation inherent in all historical interpretation of political constitutions which are to govern the distant future. The framers of the constitution could not foresee the revolutionary economic and social changes that have since taken place and therefore could have no intention at all concerning them. Whatever powers Confederation was intended to confer on the Dominion, these intentions cannot provide answers for many of the questions which agitate us now for the simple reason that the conditions out of which present difficulties arise were not even remotely considered as possibilities. The intentions of the founders cannot, except by chance, provide solutions for problems of which they never dreamed.

• • •

REGIONAL AND PROVINCIAL DISCONTENT —THE CHALLENGE TO THE DOMINANCE OF THE DOMINION

A bald statement of the length of the depression gives little hint of its effect upon the lives of the people. Federal policies had burdened them with debt and failed to bring prosperity. The only large-scale remedy which the Dominion had been able to offer was the National Policy of 1879. In these circumstances, communities had to do what they could to help themselves, looking to the provinces for the help which the Dominion failed to give. The provincial governments attempted to promote expansion on their own frontiers by railway building and immigration policies. But most of them quickly discovered the strait jacket in which the financial settlement of Confederation had placed them. The agitation for better terms gathered strength and led to differences with the Dominion. The failure of the Dominion's economic policies, which formed such important elements in the new national interest, discouraged the growth of a strong, national sentiment; and local loyalties and interests began to reassert themselves.

Indeed, there had never been any large transfer of loyalty from the older communities to the new Dominion created for urgent common purposes. The achievement of Confederation and the spectacular activity of the Federal Government in the early years had merely overshadowed or, at most, temporarily subordinated the separate interests of the distinct regions and communities. From the very date of the union, there had been a widespread and burning conviction in Nova Scotia that it had been manoeuvred into a bargain prejudicial to its vital interests. In the provincial election—held late in 1867—thirty-six out of thirty-eight members elected to the legislature were anti-Confederates. The new Government tried desperately to extricate the Province from the bonds of the union. Although these efforts were unavailing, the sentiment against Confederation remained strong in Nova Scotia and was significant in New Brunswick.

Confederation had not succeeded in eliminating the clash of racial and religious differences which had agitated the Province of Canada in the past. It had been hoped that the creation of two provinces, allowing free play to these cultural differences in separate spheres, would remove these antagonisms from deliberations on matters of common interest in the federal councils. When the western insurrections of 1870 and 1885 raised a racial and religious conflict in the valleys of the Red River and the Saskatchewan which disturbed the peace in the new federal territories, the opinions of the dominant groups in Ontario and Quebec clashed over the action taken by the Federal Government. Quebec's deepest feelings were outraged by the execution of Louis Riel and a wave of resentment against the Federal Government swept the Province. It became clear at once that there were federal issues in which conflicts of opinion might follow in the main provincial lines. In such circumstances, any solution was bound to create Dominion-provincial friction.

Such Dominion-provincial friction was not limited to cases of the resurgence of loyalties antedating Confederation. The problems of the Pacific railway embittered the relations of British Columbia and the Federal Government during the seventies; and in the eighties the requirements of federal railway policy brought Manitoba and the Dominion into sharp conflict. The appropriation of western lands "for the purposes of the Dominion" deprived Manitoba of its natural resources and the monopoly clause in the charter of the Canadian Pacific Railway Company prevented the Province from promoting a competitive transport system. Repeatedly the Provincial Legislature chartered railway companies to build lines to the international boundary and repeatedly the Dominion Government disallowed them on the ground that the projected lines would divert traffic to the United States and thus conflict with the settled transport policy of the Dominion. Dominion policy was hard to reconcile with the interests of the settlers in Manitoba and the Provincial Government became the spearhead of local demands.

British Columbia was irritated by federal tariff policy and its long controversy with the Dominion over Oriental immigration began in this period. Large sections of opinion in the Maritimes were antagonized by the introduction of the National Policy in 1879. In 1886, a series of resolutions was introduced in the Legislature of Nova Scotia advocating secession on the ground that the commercial and financial interests of the Province had been vitally injured by Dominion policies. By 1887, agricultural and lumbering interests in Ontario were straining against federal tariff policy and urging commercial union with the United States. Ontario clashed with the Dominion over the location of the Ontario-Manitoba boundary and the ownership of its northern natural resources. Mowat, as Premier of Ontario, fortified the principle of "provincial rights" when he claimed and won the right of the provinces

to regulate the sale of liquor within their boundaries and for years he conducted an unwearying attack on the federal power of disallowance.

These various grievances culminated in the provincial conference held at Quebec in 1887. The five provincial premiers who attended included all the leaders of provincial protest. The procedure of the provincial premiers seems to indicate that they claimed the right to examine and correct the operation of the federal system. Although their interests differed widely, they were able to agree that a considerable curtailment of federal power would be desirable. They proposed to increase the subsidies to the provinces, to abolish the federal power of disallowance, and to make the right of the Dominion to declare public works to be for the general advantage of Canada conditional on the approval of the province concerned. Lieutenant-Governors were to be acknowledged to be representatives of the Sovereign rather than of the Dominion, and each province was to nominate half of the Senators from the province in the Senate.

The conference challenged the view that Confederation was designed to set up a highly centralized and pervasively dominating government at Ottawa. In its swing to the other extreme, emphasizing the primacy of the provinces, it was no doubt employing a theory of federalism similar to the doctrine of "states rights" in the United States. But the strength of diversity of provincial interests shown by the conference indicated that, under the conditions of the late nineteenth century, the working constitution of the Dominion must provide for a large sphere of provincial freedom.

The policies of the Federal Government were in discredit and the Government itself was embarrassed by its difficulties in the late eighties. Except for a short interval between 1874 and 1878, the Federal Government throughout this period had been identified with Sir John A. Macdonald and his associates. Sir John's views of the nature of Confederation, so clearly stated both before and after the union, are well known. It is not known how many of the other framers of the British North America Act shared his views. But it is important that, for nearly thirty years, Macdonald and those who thought like him were the Federal Government of the new Dominion. The views which they took of the functions of the Lieutenant-Governor and the use to be made of the powers of reservation and disallowance have already been discussed. Their practice in revising the financial arrangements with the provinces and securing constitutional amendments has been noted. Their actions reveal clearly their conception of the primacy of the Dominion and the subordinate position of the provinces.

It is highly significant that the realities of the later years of the period forced a modification of this conception on the very men who held it most strongly. Their interpretation of the general interest failed to command widespread assent in the different provinces. The ineradicable, particularist interests, always associated with different regions and ways of life, demanded free expression. In face of the formidable provincial protest, the Government was forced to retreat. In 1884, the Ontario Rivers and Streams Act, already thrice disallowed by the Dominion, was re-enacted by the Provincial Legislature and the Dominion acquiesced. Later, the Dominion abandoned its policy of protecting the Canadian Pacific Railway Company from competition through the power of disallowance and finally repealed the monopoly clause itself. During the early nineties, it began the downward revision of the tariff.

## PROVINCIAL RIGHTS AND THE CONSTITUTION—THE INTERPRETATIONS OF THE PRIVY COUNCIL WIDEN THE POWERS OF THE PROVINCES

It is a matter for speculation what would have been the ultimate issue between the Dominion and the provinces if the conditions of the eighties had continued. The equilibrium was becoming very unstable. On the one hand, there was the conception of federal dominance which the Dominion Government tried to enforce and which was strongly supported by powers of reservation and disallowance. There were the sweeping words of the opening paragraph of section 91 which, it might be argued, gave to the Dominion those "high functions and almost sovereign powers" which at least some of the framers intended it to have. The power to tap all the really productive sources of revenue was in the hands of the Federal Government.

On the other hand, there was the patent failure of the great general projects of the Dominion to meet

what the provinces deemed to be their particular interests. There was the provincial revolt, focused by the provincial conference of 1887, which significantly demanded a drastic reduction of federal powers. There were straitened provincial governments representing large bodies of opinion and demanding greater revenues.

The preamble of the British North America Act announced the formation of a federal union, but it was not clear how far this was consistent with the wide general powers conferred on the Dominion by the opening words of section 91. Dominion-provincial friction was not lessened by these seeming obscurities in the constitution. It was becoming vital to know what the constitution meant and whether it could be harmonized with the realities which had appeared. In this crucial decade, the Privy Council began to give its first important decisions on the British North America Act. By the end of the period under review, the main lines of the working constitution had emerged through these decisions. It is therefore necessary to turn to them to see how the constitution was moulded by their influence.

It would be difficult to say how far these decisions influenced the concessions made by the Federal Government. At any rate, some of the earliest of these cases bore on the nature of the provincial governments and their relation to the Dominion and to the Crown. In particular, decisions in 1883 and 1892 denied some of the main tenets of the Macdonald school. In *Hodge v. The Queen*, in 1883, their Lordships, by implication, denied that the provincial legislatures were inferior bodies. They held that, within the limits of subjects and areas as prescribed by section 92, "the local legislature is supreme and has the same authority as the Imperial Parliament or the Parliament of the Dominion, would have had under like circumstances"[23] to confide powers to bodies of its own creation.

In *Liquidators of the Maritime Bank* v. *Receiver-General of New Brunswick* in 1892, it was necessary to decide how far the provincial Executive was entitled to exercise the ancient prerogatives of the Crown. In answer to the argument that the British North America Act had severed all connection between the Crown and the provinces and reduced the latter to the rank of Liverpool or Manchester, the Privy Council replied that the provinces were not subordinated to the Federal

Government or depreciated to the level of municipal institutions. The supremacy of the province in its field of jurisdiction was reiterated. Their Lordships were pressed to say that, as the Lieutenant-Governor was appointed by the Dominion, he was purely a creature of the Dominion. Lord Watson denied this conclusion saying that the Governor General, in appointing, was acting for the Queen and that a "Lieutenant-Governor, when appointed, is as much the representative of Her Majesty for all purposes of provincial government as the Governor-General himself is for all purposes of Dominion government."[24]

These decisions magnified the provinces and struck at the theory that they were merely a superior kind of municipal institution. They also raised acutely the question of how far the enactments of a legislature endowed with the same kind of supremacy as the Imperial Parliament should be subject to an unrestricted power of disallowance. These decisions, at least, made it harder for the Federal Government to maintain its positions and foreshadowed the steep decline in the use of the powers of reservation and disallowance which came in succeeding years.

A detailed review of the Privy Council decisions of this period would be out of place here. But there were several cases of historic importance in determining the lines of constitutional development which must be considered. In 1882, the Privy Council had to decide whether the Canada Temperance Act was within the powers of the Dominion. This Act forbade the sale of intoxicating liquor under penalty of fine and imprisonment in those municipalities which exercised the "local option" of applying its provisions.

Naturally, it was argued that this prohibition would interfere with property and civil rights in the local areas where it was adopted. However, the Act recited the desirability of uniform legislation promoting temperance throughout the Dominion and the Privy Council concluded that the traffic in liquor was being dealt with as a matter of public order and safety and not in relation to the aspects of property and civil rights which were admittedly involved. They decided that general liquor legislation so conceived was exclusively within the general power of the Federal Parliament "to make laws for the peace, order and good government of Canada." General legislation, genuinely "deemed to be necessary or expedient for national safety or for political reasons" or "designed for the promotion of public order, safety or morals," was held to fall within the general power of section 91. Of course, in almost every case, such legislation would "in some incidental way, affect property and civil rights." Thus, "the true nature and character of the legislation in the particular instance under discussion must always be determined in order to ascertain the class of subjects to which it really belongs."[25]

This decision asserted the clear primacy of the "peace, order and good government" clause over section 92 and argued the validity of all federal laws dealing with general and national aspects of any subject matter even though that subject matter, in its local aspects, might be within the enumerations of section 92.[26] However, it left the criterion of what might be "necessary or expedient for national safety or for political reasons" and of what might be "designed for the promotion of public order, safety and morals," vague and unsettled. Such questions as these could only be determined by reference to the political, economic and social conditions of the time and to certain broad considerations bearing on the problem as to what it is proper for governments to try to do.

The decision did not explain how "the true nature and character of the legislation in the particular instance" was to be determined. There were only two alternatives. Either the existence of that urgent general or national aspect which was to justify untrammelled federal legislation under the "peace, order and good government" clause should be decided by the court before which the validity of the legislation was raised, or it would have to depend on the simple assertion of national urgency by the Federal Parliament.

In the first event, the court would be required to say whether the federal legislation in question had such a general or national aspect—in short, whether, in view of all the circumstances, the legislation might conceivably be desirable in the national interest. But this is a question which the courts always dislike to answer on the sound ground that it is not a question of law at all. The answer, if given, would inevitably depend upon the temperament of the judge and his personal views on public policy. Judges, like other people, differ profoundly in their views on public policy and their decisions would become essentially unpredictable. The hope of drawing a clear line between the legislative sphere of the Dominion on the one hand, and that of the provinces, on the other, would disappear. Moreover, because the principal test of the validity of the provincial and Dominion legislation would be the judgment of the court on large issues of expediency and public policy, the final court of appeal would become the arbiter of public policy rather than the guardian of the constitution and, therefore, the storm-centre of Dominion-provincial disputes.

The court might escape from this invidious task by limiting itself to the question of whether the Federal Parliament had decided, in good faith, that general and national aspects were involved. Careful reading of *Russell* v. *The Queen* gives some reason for thinking that the personnel of the Privy Council in that case conceived its duty to be discharged by this limited scrutiny. In the nature of things, it would be a rare case where bad faith on the part of the Federal Parliament could be established and therefore the first alternative might, in practice, come to little more than the second, which is now to be considered.

The second alternative would be that the bare assertion by the Federal Parliament of a general or national aspect in the subject matter of the legislation would, of itself, justify the legislation under the "peace, order and good government" clause. That clause would then confer tremendous power on the Federal Parliament, giving it, as Macdonald had proposed, "the general mass of sovereign legislation."[27] The exclusive sphere ensured to the provinces by section 92 might, if the Dominion so desired, become very small indeed. The power of the Dominion Parliament under the "peace, order and good government" clause would become so overwhelming that the federal character of the constitution would be open to grave doubt. Indeed, under these conditions, the constitution in its working, would approach the legislative union which some of the Fathers desired but which, as they recognized, they could not secure by agreement.

These implications of *Russell* v. *The Queen* must be kept in mind and related to the growing revolt of the provinces against the paternalism of the Dominion when considering the case now to be discussed. "The Local Prohibition Case,"[28] as it has come to be called, which was decided in 1896, is the most important case in the period, and one of the most significant of all interpretations of the British North America Act by

the Privy Council. In it, the Privy Council upheld the validity of the Ontario Temperance Act which provided for Ontario a structure of regulation of the liquor traffic similar to that which the Canada Temperance Act provided for the Dominion as a whole.

The technique of interpretation used to reach this result need not be discussed here. It is sufficient to say that while Lord Watson held that the Dominion, relying on the enumerated heads of section 91, could validly enact legislation which affected subjects enumerated in section 92, he also declared that the Dominion, when legislating under the general "peace, order and good government" clause, "has no authority to encroach upon any class of subjects which is exclusively assigned to the provincial legislatures by s. 92." He stated that the exercise of legislative power under the general clause of section 91 must be "strictly confined to such matters as are of unquestionably Canadian interest and importance," admitting that "some matters, in their origin local and provincial, might attain such dimensions as to affect the body politic of the Dominion and to justify the Canadian Parliament in passing laws for their regulation or abolition in the interest of the Dominion."[29] Under the authority of this decision, the general clause of section 91 has come to be regarded as justifying little more than emergency legislation in the stress of great national crises.

While not challenging the correctness of *Russell* v. *The Queen*, this decision struck directly at the reasoning on which it was based. It denied the primacy of the "peace, order and good government" clause of section 91 over the enumerations of section 92 and as a result Dominion jurisdiction became, for most purposes, restricted to the specific heads enumerated in section 91. In the main, interpretation of the legislative powers of the Dominion and the provinces settled down to a competition between the specific enumerated heads of sections 91 and 92. In this competition, the provinces enjoyed an advantage because section 92 contained two heads capable of a general and inclusive signification, *viz.*, "Property and Civil Rights in the Province" and "generally all Matters of a merely local or private Nature in the Province" while section 91 contained only one such head, "the Regulation of Trade and Commerce" and, as will be pointed out below, it received a restricted interpretation. Thus the

stage was set for the subsequent course of interpretation which has provoked the comment, in recent
times, that the residuary powers under the constitution are now to be found in section 92.

There are some who believe that the Local
Prohibition Case involved a textual violation of section
91 of the British North America Act.[30] Logical exposition, limited to sections 91 and 92, might lead to that
conclusion. But it must be remembered that, according to the preamble of that Act, what was desired by
the provinces was a federal union. It has been pointed
out that the decision in *Russell* v. *The Queen*, which, in
practical effect, was over-ruled by the Local Prohibition
Case, would have imperilled the federal character of
the union if it had become the ruling decision. There
seems to be no doubt that this consideration weighed
heavily with Lord Watson. In an earlier case, he had
pointed out that "the object of the Act was neither to
weld the provinces into one, nor to subordinate provincial governments to a central authority, but to create a federal government ... each province retaining its
independence and autonomy."[31] In justifying his construction of sections 91 and 92 in the Local Prohibition
Case, he made the following significant statement: —

> To attach any other construction to the general
> power which, in supplement of its enumerated pow-
> ers, is conferred upon the Parliament of Canada
> by s. 91, would, in their Lordships' opinion, not
> only be contrary to the intendment of the Act, but
> would practically destroy the autonomy of the prov-
> inces. If it were once conceded that the Parliament
> of Canada has authority to make laws applicable to
> the whole Dominion, in relation to matters which
> in each province are substantially of local or private
> interest, upon the assumption that these matters
> also concern the peace, order, and good govern-
> ment of the Dominion, there is hardly a subject
> enumerated in s. 92 upon which it might not legis-
> late, to the exclusion of the provincial legislatures.[32]

It may be that the insight which guided his decision
was solely derived from a theoretical analysis of the
requisites of a federal state. It may be that he was also
aware of the growing provincialism, then assailing the
pretensions of the Federal Government. At any rate,
he perceived and stated the lines of what he regarded

as a tolerable compromise between Dominion power
and provincial claims in the Canada of his day. And
compromise is always the essence of the federal state.

It is necessary to notice briefly a foreshadowing in
this period of the limited interpretation later given
to the Dominion power under head 2 of section 91,
"the Regulation of Trade and Commerce." In a case
before the Privy Council in 1881, the question of the
meaning to be attached to this phrase was considered.
Their Lordships pointed out that the words "regulation of trade and commerce, in their unlimited sense
are sufficiently wide, if uncontrolled by the context
and other parts of the Act, to include every regulation
of trade ... down to minute rules for regulating particular trades."[33] By a process of textual criticism for
which the enumerated heads of section 91, taken as a
whole, give some warrant, they reached the conclusion that the words were not used in their unlimited
sense,[34] and suggested limitations which were later
adopted and pushed still further by the courts. The
case also made a significant contribution to the interpretation of head 13 of section 92, holding that, in the
phrase "Property and Civil Rights in the Province," the
expression "civil rights" includes rights arising from
contract as well as rights directly maintained by the
law itself such as the status of persons.

One other case, relating to the taxing power of
the provinces, requires to be considered. Section 92
gave the provinces a power of "Direct Taxation within
the Province in order to the raising of a Revenue for
Provincial Purposes." In 1882, the Quebec Legislature
passed a statute imposing on certain commercial corporations, a tax the amount of which varied with the
paid-up capital and the number of places of business.
A number of corporations resisted collection of the tax
and an appeal was finally taken to the Privy Council.[35]
Their Lordships were obliged to decide whether or
not it was a direct tax.

"Direct taxation" is a phrase which lacks precise
signification. From an economic point of view, it is
impossible to say that any particular tax is direct in
its final incidence because of the opportunities which
may exist for shifting its burden. Economists would
agree that a corporation tax generally is an indirect tax
because of the ease of shifting it. However, the Privy
Council felt bound to find a criterion for the validity
of provincial taxation which would not involve the

impossible task of trying to find out, in each case, whether the burden had, in fact, been shifted.

Adopting from John Stuart Mill a statement that "a direct tax is one which is demanded from the very persons who it is intended or desired should pay it," they inferred from the legislation itself that the legislature must have intended it to be finally borne by the very corporations from whom it was demanded and held it to be "direct taxation" within the meaning of section 92. The decision was one of great significance. From the point of view of the provincial governments it made available an important and increasing source of revenue since corporate enterprise was expanding rapidly. From the point of view of the economy as a whole it was the legal basis of the growth of much of the duplication, confusion, and uneconomic types of taxation which today weigh oppressively on the national income.

## NOTES

1  *Speech on the Proposed Union of the British North American Provinces*, delivered at Sherbrooke on Nov. 23, 1864, p. 22.
2  Speech by Galt, *Confederation Debates*, p. 68.
3  In interpreting the British North America Act, "the question is not what may be supposed to have been intended but what has been said." Lord Sankey in *Edwards v. Attorney General of Canada* (1930) A.C. 124 at p. 137.
4  E.g., C.H. Cahan, *The British North America Act, 1867*, an address delivered before the Canadian Club of Toronto, September 15, 1937; cf. *Report pursuant to Resolution of the Senate to the Honourable Speaker, by the Parliamentary Counsel relating to the Enactment of the British North America Act*, Ottawa, 1939.
5  For historical interpretations in general supporting this view, see … D.G. Creighton, *British North America at Confederation*; R.G. Trotter, *Canadian Federation* (Toronto, 1934); "The Coming of Confederation," *Cambridge History of the British Empire*, Vol. VI, pp. 438–62; Chester Martin, "British Policy in Canadian Federation," *Canadian Historical Review*, Vol. XIII, pp. 3–19; W.M. Whitelaw, *The Maritimes and Canada before Confederation* (Toronto, 1934); W.P.M. Kennedy, *Essays in Constitutional Law*, p. 85ff; V.C. MacDonald, "Judicial Interpretation of the Canadian Constitution," *University of Toronto Law Journal*, Vol. I, No. 2, p. 26off. For careful description of the Quebec Conference see W.M. Whitelaw, "Reconstructing the Quebec Conference," *Canadian Historical Review*, Vol. XIX, pp. 123–37.
6  *Confederation Debates*, p. 40. See also pp. 30, 33, 41.
7  *Speech on the Proposed Union*, p. 10.
8  Quoted by V.C. MacDonald, "Judicial Interpretations of the Canadian Constitution" (1936), *University of Toronto Law Journal*, p. 263.
9  *Confederation Debates*, p. 250.
10  *Ibid.*, p. 859.
11  C.H. Cahan, *op. cit.*
12  These conflicts are examined in detail in D.G. Creighton, *The Commercial Empire of the St. Lawrence, 1760–1850*.

13  *Confederation Debates*, p. 409.
14  *Speech on the Proposed Union*, p. 20.
15  *Confederation Debates*, p. 61.
16  See D.G. Creighton, *British North America at Confederation*, pp. 50–52.
17  W.P.M. Kennedy, *Statutes, Treaties and Documents*, p. 156.
18  P.B. Mignault (formerly Mr. Justice Mignault of the Supreme Court of Canada), "Nos Problemes Constitutionnels" (1928), *16 Revue du Droit*, p. 577; V. Evan Gray, "The O'Connor Report on the British North America Act" (1939), *17 Canadian Bar Review*, 309.
19  "to deal with all civil and criminal cases, to judge finally and in the last resort according to the laws and ordinances of our kingdom."
20  For this argument, see P.B. Mignault, *op. cit.*
21  The agreement reached by delegates to the Quebec Conference is acknowledged to have been a compromise and it is unlikely that the delegates, in the subsequent discussions, always distinguished clearly between the compromise and their own conception of what Confederation should have been. For a clear statement of the difficulties attending historical interpretation, see V. Evan Gray, "The O'Connor Report on the British North America Act," (1939), *17 Canadian Bar Review*, 309 at pp. 315–8.
22  John A. Macdonald probably had the possibility of a great future in mind when he said, "We are all mere petty provincial politicians at present; perhaps by and by some of us will rise to the level of national statesmen." Quoted by A.R.M. Lower in "Sir John A. Macdonald," (1939), *19 Dalhousie Review*, p. 86.
23  (1883) 9 A.C. 117, at p. 132.
24  (1892) A.C. 437, at p. 443.
25  *Russell v. The Queen* (1882) 7 A.C. 829, at pp. 838–40.
26  Although *Russell v. The Queen* is frequently cited in the courts, the general principle which it lays down has not been followed and it must be regarded as virtually over-ruled by later decisions.
27  *Confederation Debates*, p. 41.
28  *Attorney-General of Ontario v. Attorney-General of the Dominion* (1896) A. C. 348.
29  *Ibid.*, pp. 360–61.
30  The most cogent and complete statement of this view is to be found in the *Report pursuant to Resolution of the Senate to the Honourable the Speaker, by the Parliamentary Counsel relating to the Enactment of the British North America Act*, Ottawa, 1939. For criticism see V. Evan Gray, *Canadian Bar Review*, 17, p. 309.
31  *Liquidators of the Maritime Bank v. Receiver-General of New Brunswick* (1892) A.C. 437 at pp. 441–2.
32  *Attorney-General of Ontario v. Attorney-General of the Dominion* (1896) A.C. 348 at p. 361.
     Lord Watson assumes, it is to be noted, that, if *Russell v. The Queen* remained the ruling decision, the Privy Council would shrink from deciding whether particular Dominion legislation might be "necessary or expedient for the national safety or for political reasons" and would, in practice, leave that question to the discretion of the Dominion Parliament—in other words, the second alternative discussed above would rule. In these circumstances, it is not surprising that the Privy Council exerted itself to make the specific and more concrete enumerated heads of section 91 the main test of the validity of Dominion legislation.
33  *Citizens' Insurance Co. v. Parsons* (1881) 7 A.C. 96, at pp. 112–13.
34  Their reasons for thinking so are given in *Bank of Toronto v. Lambe* (1887) 12 A.C. 575 at p. 586, where it is said that in Parsons Case, "it was found absolutely necessary that the literal meaning of the words ('regulation of trade and commerce') should be restricted in order to afford scope for powers which are given exclusively to the provincial legislatures."
35  *Bank of Toronto v. Lambe* (1887) 12 A.C. 575.

**13**

## Editors' Introduction

It is rare for scholarship dealing specifically with Canada to have a major impact outside of the country. In 2005, *Federal-Provincial Diplomacy* became the first Canadian monograph to receive the Martha Derthick Award from the American Political Science Association "for its lasting significance for federalism and intergovernmental relations." Early on in his career, Richard Simeon came to the realization that Canada's experience had comparative and practical value far beyond Canadian parochialism. The book has the rare distinction of having gone into reprint thirty-five years after it was originally published. Rather than examining federalism using conventional historical institutionalism, Simeon's pioneering rational-choice variant is concerned with institutions as coordination mechanisms that generate or sustain equilibrium. Contrary to much of the scholarship on federalism, Simeon is not concerned with the way institutions change and the way institutions emerge from and are embedded in concrete temporal processes. Rather, as illustrated in this excerpt, Simeon is preoccupied with institutional stability in the form of measurable independent social and institutional effects and the way they shape the patterns of federal-provincial relations. In fact, toward the end of the book, he vindicates his approach when he points out how surprisingly little effect the profound social, political, and economic changes since the 1960s—the continental north–south economic integration, the "decline of deference," the rise in the status and political claims of cities—have had on the centrality and conduct of federal-provincial relations in Canada.

Source: Richard Simeon, "The Social and Institutional Context," in *Federal-Provincial Diplomacy: The Making of Recent Policy in Canada* (1972; reprint, Toronto: University of Toronto Press, 2006), 20–42.

Richard Simeon

# The Social and Institutional Context of Federal–Provincial Diplomacy

## THE SOCIAL ENVIRONMENT

The basic elements of the "federal" basis of Canadian society have been described many times. We need only summarize them.

The most salient characteristic of Canadian society is its regional diversity—geographic, economic, cultural, and historical.[1] Geographic differences stemming from long distances and a scattered population persist even after the barrier of distance itself has been reduced by modern technology. This simple geographic distance appears to be one factor accounting for the great sense of remoteness and isolation from Ottawa found in British Columbian respondents. "Victoria is

only some 2,700 miles from Ottawa," said one BC official, "but Ottawa is 27,000 miles away from Victoria."

But added to geography are much more important regional influences. Great economic differences among the regions persist—in wealth, income, and the nature of regional economies.[2] These differences have led to great variations in outlook, with, for example, the central provinces more interested in tariff protection of secondary manufacturing and the west stressing free trade. Regional economic interests have been an important source of conflict in Canadian history, from battles between protectionists and free traders over the tariff to the rise of third party movements

---

1   See essays in Mason Wade, ed., *Regionalism in the Canadian Community, 1867–1967* (Toronto, 1969).

2   See, for example, H.A. Innis and W.T. Easterbrook, "Fundamental and Historical Elements," in John Deutsch, Burton Keirstead, Kari Levitt, and Robert Will, eds., *The Canadian Economy: Selected Readings* (rev. ed., Toronto, 1965), pp. 440–8.

on the prairies, which based much of their appeal on resisting the exploitation of the bankers and manufacturers of the east.[3] These regional differences remain a prime source of conflict.

Coupled with economic influences are differences in historical tradition between the various regions. Ontario, Quebec, the Maritimes, and British Columbia all had an independent existence as British colonies long before Confederation. Many of the distinctive characteristics engendered by the pre-Confederation experience have persisted, especially in Quebec and the Maritimes. As a result it appears reasonable to conceive of Canada as a collection of regional cultures rather than one "national" culture.

The most salient and historically most important basis of social diversity in Canada, of course, is the existence of what is commonly referred to as the "two cultures" of French and English Canada.[4] The French-Canadian minority, about 30 per cent of the population, is highly distinctive in its language, history, religion, and culture. It is heavily concentrated in Quebec, where 81 per cent of the population is of French-speaking origin. New Brunswick, where 35 per cent of the population is of French origin, is the only other province with a large proportion of French Canadians.[5] In all other provinces the proportion is less than 10 per cent.

Quebec is the home of a distinct subculture. It has an autonomous educational system, code of civil law, and a distinctive pattern of institutional and associational life. In addition it has its own political voice, the provincial government. Moreover, French Canadians have been imperfectly integrated into national life. The province's economy has been dominated by English-Canadian-owned industry. Nationally, French Canadians are underrepresented in professional and financial occupations. Only 6.7 per cent of the Canadian "economic élite" are French Canadian; only 13 per cent of higher federal bureaucrats are French Canadian; and there has been less, but still significant, underrepresentation in a "political élite" defined to include federal cabinet ministers, provincial premiers, and senior members of the judiciary.[6] Official policies to increase French-Canadian participation both in government and in national life generally are recent developments. Thus, not only are French Canadians a highly distinctive minority but also they are a disadvantaged one.

As a result French-English relations have been a central problem facing the Canadian system since before Confederation. Indeed, a major reason for federation itself was the political deadlock which developed when what are now Ontario and Quebec were combined in the united province of Canada. Since 1867 there have been recurrent conflicts between French and English Canadians, over language and religious rights, education, conscription during both world wars, and other matters. The "crisis" of the 1960's, while different in many ways from previous conflicts, is only the most recent. Relations with Quebec have been a central preoccupation of national leaders since 1867.

The effect of these widespread regional differences in Canada has been to make regional and ethnic cleavages the most important source of conflicts within the system. The "great issues" of Canadian politics have revolved around questions of national unity and survival rather than around class and economic problems.

These factors have also had a profound effect on Canadian political behaviour. Thus, electoral cleavages are largely regional, religious, and ethnic. "Class voting," Robert Alford has found, is lower in Canada than in any of the other Anglo-Saxon democracies, and there is no evidence that it is increasing,[7] or that

3   See C.B. Macpherson, *Democracy in Alberta: Social Credit and the Party System* (2nd ed., Toronto, 1962); S.M. Lipset, *Agrarian Socialism: The Cooperative Commonwealth Federation in Saskatchewan* (Anchor ed., Garden City, NY, 1968).

4   There are many analyses of French-Canadian society. A good general introduction is found in Edward M. Corbett, *Quebec Confronts Canada* (Baltimore, 1967). See also Ramsay Cook, *Canada and the French-Canadian Question* (Toronto, 1967); Philippe Garigue, *L'option politique du Canada français : une interprétation de la survivance nationale* (Montreal, 1963); D. Kwavnick, "The Roots of French-Canadian Discontent," *Canadian Journal of Economics and Political Science* 31 (1965), pp. 509–23; Marcel Rioux and Yves Martin, *French-Canadian Society* (Toronto, 1964); Mason Wade, ed., *Canadian Dualism / La dualité canadienne* (Toronto, 1960); Royal Commission on Bilingualism and Biculturalism, *A Preliminary Report* (Ottawa, 1965); André Siegfried, *The Race Question in Canada* (New York, 1908).

5   *Census of Canada*, 1961, catalogue number 92-549, vol. I, part 2: "Population: Official Language and Mother Tongue."

6   John Porter, *The Vertical Mosaic: An Analysis of Social Class and Power in Canada* (Toronto, 1965), pp. 87, 286, 441, 389.

7   *Party and Society* (Chicago, 1963), passim, and his "The Social Bases of Political Cleavage in 1962," in John Meisel, ed., *Papers on the 1962 Election* (Toronto, 1964), pp. 203–34. For a more detailed examination of the relation of class, religion, and ethnic factors to

regionalism in electoral behaviour is on the decline.[8] Another consequence (when combined with some more institutional factors, as we shall see later) has been the recurrence of regionally based parties, like Honoré Mercier's Parti National in nineteenth century Quebec, the Cooperative Commonwealth Federation and Social Credit in the west, and the Union Nationale in Quebec. Regionalism has also affected the structure and behaviour of national parties, forcing them to become loose coalitions of diverse elements. Even so, the national parties have traditionally drawn disproportionate strength from different regions. The Liberals, for example, are the most nearly "national party" with support in all sections. But their strength has come primarily from Quebec and, to a lesser extent, Ontario.

Thus the social basis for Canadian federalism is strong. Even without Quebec regional diversities would persist. But how does this affect the relationship of provinces and central government? At a minimum the great diversity, organized largely along regional or territorial lines, means that Canadian political institutions will give great weight to regional interests. More particularly, the degree of regionalism, both in mass publics and various élite groups, will be a central factor in determining the relative weights of central and provincial governments. But at the same time the nature of the federal society is not sufficient to explain the particular patterns of adjustment between central and regional interests. Given the Canadian social structure one would expect that regional interests in national policy-making will be strong, but one could still imagine a variety of institutional and operational forms within which the adjustment process could take place. The United States also has much regional diversity, but its federal system operates very differently from Canada's.

Another basic characteristic of Canadian society, which operates in the same direction as regionalism,

is a weak sense of national identity.[9] This is, of course, related to regional diversity. In particular, the Quebec government provides a very important focus of loyalty for Quebec citizens. In that province it is still unclear whether the crises of legitimacy and integration, to use LaPalombara's and Weiner's terms,[10] will be resolved in favour of the Quebec or national polities. But this lack of a strong sense of national identity has other causes as well. Canada lacks a central national myth around which a strong sense of national identity could form. Until recently the country has had few of the common symbols of nationhood. Lipset and others suggest that this is related to the lack of a revolutionary tradition.[11] Formal independence in 1867 was followed by a gradual and relatively conflict-free weaning from imperial ties, of which vestigial elements remain. Many Canadians maintain emotional ties to Britain. The economic and cultural influence of the United States adds to the diffusion of loyalties and identity and to the lack of a single distinctive Canadian social or political culture. This situation may be changing. D.V. Smiley, for example, suggests that English Canadians are forming a distinct national identity oriented around the federal government.[12] But this sense of community is clearly not shared by many French Canadians. The effect of the weak sense of identity, of strong and persisting regional identities,[13] and of the divergent French and English identities, is to deny the federal government a

voting, see John Wilson, "Politics and Social Class in Canada: The Case of Waterloo South," *Canadian Journal of Political Science* 1 (1968), pp. 289–309. Wilson suggests class may be becoming more important, and that while religion and ethnicity continue to be important, working class voters are becoming more homogeneous. We may expect these patterns to vary considerably from constituency to constituency. National patterns of cleavage can obscure great variations in the patterns from area to area.

8   The most careful analysis of electoral regionalism is by Donald E. Blake. "The Measure and Impact of Regionalism in Canadian Voting Behaviour," paper presented to the Canadian Political Science Association, 1971.

9   See Mildred Schwartz, *Public Opinion and Canadian Identity* (Berkeley and Los Angeles, 1967), esp. chaps. 1 and 2.

10  Joseph LaPalombara and Myron Weiner, eds., *Political Parties and Political Development* (Princeton, 1966), pp. 15–17.

11  S.M. Lipset, *The First New Nation: The United States in Historical and Comparative Perspective* (London, 1964), p. 87. Lipset finds many other traits of Canadian political culture traceable to the lack of revolutionary tradition; see *Revolution and Counter-Revolution: Change and Persistence in Social Structures* (New York, 1968), pp. 47–52.

12  "The Two Themes of Canadian Federalism," *Canadian Journal of Economics and Political Science* 31 (1965), pp. 88–93.

13  Many writers have suggested there are inevitable "nationalizing" forces in modern society, which would tend to weaken more parochial regional identities. Such forces as a "national" economy with "national" interest groups, urbanization, development of the mass media, and so on are expected to promote national feeling. However, this does not seem to be happening—regional identities do not appear to be weakening significantly, and, indeed, it has been argued that such factors as urbanization have actually enhanced regional orientations. See J.M.S. Careless, "'Limited Identities' in Canada," *Canadian Historical Review* 50 (1969), pp. 1–10.

large measure of authority and legitimacy. It is reasonable to assume that if a stronger sense of national community developed Canadians would be more hostile to local and particularistic interests, so that the long-run influence of provincial governments would decline.

This brief discussion suggests that some basic characteristics of Canadian federal society underlie the relationship between federal and provincial governments and help to determine the relative balance between the two. The effects of these broad factors can be detected, as we shall see, even in the day-to-day discussions of federal and provincial officials. They are reflected in the goals of the actors, the degree of conflict between them, their political resources, and even their tactics.

## THE INSTITUTIONAL FRAMEWORK

Canadian political institutions help to account for the distinctive pattern of direct negotiations between the executives of federal and provincial governments in several ways. This framework—including the nature of the national and provincial legislatures, the party system, and the courts—provides some of the fundamental parameters to which the decision-makers must accommodate themselves as they work out their differences. It helps to channel and direct political activity, and in large measure has made the Canadian pattern of federal-provincial relations both necessary and possible.

Where will the interaction of federal and regional or unit interests take place? Two alternatives suggest themselves: these interests may be adjusted *within* the central government, or they may be adjusted in relations *between* the levels. In most federations both forms are likely to exist, but broad differences are apparent. Thus in the United States the party system, the role of the states in national political recruitment, and the decentralized nature of the Congress and bureaucracy facilitate a high level of federal-state accommodation within national political institutions. In Canada the second pattern dominates: accommodation takes place not within but between governments.

### National political institutions as arenas for adjustment

Canada's Parliament represents an interesting grafting of British parliamentary forms onto the highly diverse federal society already described. The Canadian Parliament was a direct transplant rather than an indigenous creation of Canadian political requirements.[14] The result, S.M. Lipset suggests, is a basic incompatibility between the logic of the British model and the requirements of federalism. "Contemporary Canadian politics should be seen as the product of the failure of British Parliamentary institutions to work in a complex North American federal union."[15] Lipset and others see the existence of many regionally based third parties as one consequence of this incompatibility. But another consequence is that the Canadian Parliament, unlike the American Congress, has failed to provide an important arena within which local and provincial interests are worked out.

The reason for this failure is that a fundamental requirement of British parliamentary or cabinet government is party unity and discipline. Crossing party lines is extremely rare in Canada. Legislative party unity, says Hugh McD. Clokie, is expected by both politicians and public as "the very condition of party government of the cabinet variety."[16] In such circumstances it is almost impossible for members of Parliament to push for policies favourable to their regions if they clash with government policy. Similarly, members from different parties are unlikely to form powerful regional blocs or caucuses.[17] Even within the general party caucus there is little evidence that regional groups play an important role in overall policy formation,[18] though there are some intra-party regional caucuses. A Manitoba MP summed up his relationship to the provincial government: "[Being a provincial spokesman] is a pretty minor role for MPs.

---

14  See Leon Epstein, "A Comparative Study of Canadian Parties," *American Political Science Review* 58 (1964), p. 48.

15  "Review of *Democracy in Alberta*," *Canadian Forum* 34 (1954–5), p. 196.

16  "The Machinery of Government," in George W. Brown, ed., *Canada* (Berkeley and Los Angeles, 1950), p. 307. See also Epstein, "A Comparative Study of Canadian Parties," p. 52.

17  For the New Brunswick example, see H.G. Thorburn, *Politics in New Brunswick* (Toronto, 1961), pp. 172, 178.

18  See Allan Kornberg, "Caucus and Cohesion in Canadian Parties," *American Political Science Review* 60 (1966), pp. 84–7.

You hardly ever hear from the provincial government. Lines are all party down here."

There are, of course, exceptions. Thus members of the Ralliement des créditistes, based entirely in Quebec, have been vocal spokesmen for their interpretation of Quebec's interests, but it seems highly unlikely that they have ever been a channel for communication between the federal and Quebec governments. For most MPs, especially those in the government party, the political environment within which they operate and the structure of incentives that surrounds them stress loyalty to the party leadership. They have few debts to provincial governments. Thus, while they may act as provincial spokesmen on minor matters of local interest, on overall policy questions, such as I am considering, contact with the province is negligible. In these circumstances it is impossible for the legislature to act as an important forum for federal-provincial adjustment. "Because of the discipline imposed by cabinet government in Canada and Australia, regional interests cannot express themselves as freely in the national Parliaments as they do in the United States."[19]

But what of the cabinet? As the central policy-making body, does it serve to accommodate provincial interests? To some extent it does. The cabinet, says R. MacGregor Dawson, is federalized. Strong norms dictate that all provinces will be represented, as will major religious and ethnic groups: "The cabinet has, in fact, taken over the allotted role of the Senate as the protector of the rights of the provinces and it has done an incomparably better job."[20] R. Gordon Robertson, secretary to the cabinet, suggests that: "It is behind the closed doors of the cabinet, and in the frankness of its confidence, that we achieve much of the vital process of accommodation and compromise that are essential to make this country work."[21]

Thus the cabinet is an important element in the adjustment process. But it has some important weaknesses. First, like Parliament, it is governed by norms of unity and solidarity, which may make it hard for members to act as regional spokesmen. Second, provinces represented by weak or very junior ministers may find "their" members are not effective. Or a federal minister may be a political opponent of the provincial premier.[22] Quebec, which traditionally has several members in the cabinet, has suffered from a "hidden underrepresentation" because Quebec ministers have received lesser cabinet posts and have had less political experience.[23] Vincent Lemieux suggests that Quebec ministers have much less power and status than the senior federal ministers on the one hand and provincial cabinet ministers on the other.[24] With a French-Canadian prime minister and a strong Quebec delegation in the cabinet this underrepresentation does not appear to exist today, though it is impossible to tell whether the change is permanent.

But some other fundamental factors appear to weaken the ability of the cabinet to act as a forum for adjustment. Federal ministers operate in the federal environment. They are oriented to winning national office, to formulating national policies in areas of federal jurisdiction, and to survival in the House of Commons. Provincial governments are only a part of that environment. It would therefore be unrealistic to view the minister's chief role as that of regional spokesman. This is not to say they never play this role. In fact, the example of Forestry Minister Sauvé in the pension negotiations and Manpower and Immigration Minister Marchand in the manpower negotiations provide two examples of Quebec ministers playing crucial roles as intermediaries between the governments. It is also clear that much tacit negotiation takes place within the cabinet. Policies, such as the education and equalization proposals of 1966, will often be drawn up to meet provincial objections in advance. Trudeau, Marchand, Sauvé, and other

19  J.A. Corry, "Constitutional Trends and Federalism," in A.R.M. Lower, ed., *Evolving Canadian Federalism* (Durham, NC, 1958), pp. 120–1. See also Leon Epstein, *Political Parties in Western Democracies* (New York, 1967), p. 62.

20  *The Government of Canada*, revised by Norman Ward (5th ed., Toronto, 1970), p. 179. See also Paul Fox, "The Representative Nature of the Canadian Cabinet," in Fox, ed., *Politics: Canada* (Toronto, 1962), pp. 140–3.

21  R.G. Robertson, "The Canadian Parliament and Cabinet in the Face of Modern Demands," paper presented to the Institute of Public Administration of Canada, 1967, p. 18.

22  See Paddy Sherman, *Bennett* (Toronto, 1966), esp. pp. 135–8.

23  Richard Van Loon, "The Structure and Membership of the Canadian Cabinet," report prepared for the Royal Commission on Bilingualism and Biculturalism, 1966, pp. 56–7. This point was frequently made by Quebec respondents.

24  "Les partis et le pouvoir politique," *Recherches sociographiques* 7 (1966), p. 51. See also Jean-Charles Bonenfant, "L'évolution du statut de l'homme politique canadien-français," *ibid.*, p. 117.

French-Canadian ministers played a very important part in shaping the 1966 federal proposals to accommodate Quebec's position on shared-cost programmes and on federal involvement in educational matters. In this sense, then, the cabinet is an arena for adjustment, but that is only one of its functions.

Its success in this task will also depend greatly on the number and seniority of ministers from any region, their perceptions of their role, and the kinds of problems competing for their attention. But, in sum, the cabinet's activity in adjustment, according to R.B. Bryce, former deputy minister of finance, is unprofessional, sporadic, overlain by personal and partisan differences; it "consequently has not been by any means an effective channel."[25]

Finally, and perhaps most important, if cabinet ministers do represent regions and have important regional bases of support, that is not at all the same thing as saying they represent *governments*. The distinction is vital. Thus federal ministers from Quebec and Quebec government ministers have very different views about the nature of the federation and Quebec's place in it, but both groups can argue they equally represent Quebec, seen as a region. Provincial governments have few claims on ministers from the province. Indeed, during the pension negotiations the partisan complexion of seven of the ten provinces differed from Ottawa's. Two federal ministers from Ontario—Judy LaMarsh and Walter Gordon—were the chief opponents of the Ontario government. Federal-provincial disagreements are differences between governments as much as if not more than between the regions the governments represent. Therefore cabinet success in adjusting regional interests does little to resolve intergovernmental conflicts. "In no way are the cabinet ministers spokesmen for provincial governments," said one respondent.

The cabinet, then, is one forum for the adjustment process. But it is far more concerned with federal policy-making and execution than with expression and accommodation of provincial interests. Similarly the bureaucracy is organized primarily on functional or interest-group lines rather than regional ones.

A third element in the national Parliament is the Senate, which does provide for fixed representation from each province. However, any role it might have played was vitiated because senators are named by the federal government. A bicameral legislature with one House effectively representing the states is virtually impossible to reconcile with responsible cabinet government on the British model.[26] As a result the Senate has been primarily a retirement home for party warhorses, with little policy-making significance and even less function in federal-provincial relations.[27] The Constitutional conference discussed in vain proposals to make the Senate truly representative of regional and provincial interests.

A fourth potential site for the working out of federal-provincial conflicts is the Supreme Court, whose equivalents have played an important role in other federations. Until 1949 final judicial review of Canadian legislation rested with the Judicial Committee of the British Privy Council, one of the last appendages of Canadian colonial status. Its decisions had a fundamental effect on the meaning of the British North America Act, the written part of the constitution.[28] "The just-short-of-unitary state that [Sir John A.] Macdonald thought he had achieved," says A.R.M. Lower, "was cut down to something just short of a Confederacy."[29] The Judicial Committee drastically reduced federal powers through its interpretation of sections 91 and 92 which described federal and provincial powers.[30] Although its position moderated somewhat after 1935, one product of the committee's line of constitutional interpretation appears to have been a reluctance by the Canadian governments to submit conflicts to the courts for judicial review. Thus, after the war Ottawa took massive initiatives in fields of social policy, basing its activity on the federal spending power and using shared-cost programmes. Their constitutionality has seldom been tested in the courts,

25  Bryce, "Discussion," Canadian Institute of Public Administration, *Proceedings*, 1957.

26  Carl J. Friedrich, *Trends of Federalism in Theory and Practice* (New York, 1968), p. 100.

27  See Dawson, *The Government of Canada*, pp. 279–303.

28  For a thorough description of the workings of the process of judicial review, both in the JCPC and later, see W.R. Lederman, ed., *The Courts and the Canadian Constitution* (Toronto, 1964).

29  "Theories of Canadian Federalism: Yesterday and Today," in his *Evolving Canadian Federalism*, p. 40.

30  See, among many others, A.H. Birch, *Federalism, Finance and Social Legislation* (Oxford, 1955), pp. 158–62.

at least partly because no government has been willing to risk the programmes' being shot down. The Canadian Supreme Court has been Canada's final court only since 1949, and has so far not established itself as an important factor in federal-provincial relations. It is not—unlike the American court—enshrined in Canadian political life and tradition, and, in fact, it has frequently been criticized in French Canada as an English-dominated institution which should not play the role of constitutional court.[31] It appears unlikely the court will play a much larger part in the future. When Ottawa referred a federal-provincial dispute about who controls mineral resources located off Canada's shores, it was widely interpreted as a violation of the rules of the game since the matter was a political conflict which should be settled politically.[32] Thus the Supreme Court is not an important arena for federal-provincial discussion. Quebec has suggested a constitutional court with fairly wide powers and membership appointed by both federal and provincial governments, but the idea has little support from other governments which share a suspicion of a political judiciary and the danger of limiting parliamentary sovereignty.

This discussion suggests that the traditional institutions of the central government have been relatively ineffective as sites for federal-provincial negotiation. This is not to say these institutions never act as arenas for accommodation, but they do so only rarely. The result has been that the adjustment process has grown up in an *ad hoc* fashion outside traditional institutional forms, notably in the federal-provincial conferences. The inadequacy of the institutions at the national level is one reason why intergovernmental negotiations have taken the form of direct confrontations between governments. Were regional interests accommodated better within Parliament, as they are

within the United States Congress, there would be less need for governments to negotiate directly with each other, or for new institutional arrangements to be built.

*Political parties: separate political systems*

The Canadian party system also fails to provide an adequate mechanism for federal-provincial coordination in policy-making. On the face of it, one might expect parties to be a frequent channel of provincial demands. The major parties have small and weak national organizations, nominations are made at the constituency level, and, parties are in large measure federations of provincial associations. "The Canadian party structure," writes Leon Epstein, "resembles that of Republicans and Democrats in its federative character."[33]

But this local dominance is not translated into provincial influence at the national level. There are several reasons. First, partly because they are diverse the major Canadian parties are non-doctrinal and play little policy-making role in any case. Indeed, John Meisel suggests that the growth in importance of federal-provincial intergovernmental negotiation has weakened still further the parties' policy-making concerns.[34] The locus of party *policy-making* is in the disciplined parliamentary party, which, as I have suggested, is not dominated by provincial interests.

Another reason is that the logic of federal-provincial negotiations means provincial governments must be able to deal with governments of a different political stripe in Ottawa, and vice versa. Conservative Ontario must negotiate with Liberal Ottawa. There is little point in trying to influence the federal government through the Conservative opposition in Ottawa, because the parliamentary system gives little policy-making importance to the opposition. Hence, just as it may be dangerous for interest groups to become too closely identified with one party, so it is unwise for provincial governments to stress party differences in the negotiations.

A broader reason seems to be in what appears to be a high degree of separation between federal and provincial branches of the same parties. "[I]n provincial politics one cannot understand the Canadian

31  For example, the famous Tremblay Commission investigating Quebec's constitutional problems declared that in creation, jurisdiction, and personnel the Supreme Court is a creature of the federal government, which made it "fundamentally repugnant to the federative principle." See Royal Commission of Enquiry on Constitutional Problems, *Report*, vol. III (Quebec, 1956), pp. 289–96. Prime Minister Johnson of Quebec has repeated this contention in his *Egalité ou indépendance* (Montreal, 1965), p. 77. See also Quebec's "Propositions" to the Constitutional Conference.

32  Edwin R. Black, "Oil Offshore Troubles the Waters," *Queen's Quarterly* 72 (1966), p. 592.

33  "A Comparative Study of Canadian Parties," p. 50.

34  John Meisel, "Les transformations des partis politiques canadiens," *Cahiers de la Société canadienne de science politique*, no 2, 1965, pp. 11–12.

political system *except* as a series of discrete compartments contained by political boundaries."[35] Again, this is because the parties operate in different environments with different perspectives: "The national party structure is designed to help provide leaders and decisions in Ottawa; the provincial party structures help to perform these functions in the various provincial governments."[36]

There are many indications of this apparent separation of federal and provincial party systems. In few provinces is the national party pattern reproduced; in British Columbia, the most extreme example, the two major provincial parties are both minor parties at the national level. Provincial electorates frequently return members of different parties to provincial and federal legislatures. One study of an Ontario constituency suggests 38 per cent of the voters voted for different parties at the federal and provincial levels in recent elections.[37] Stephen Muller suggests that Canada has a "two-layer" party system of provincial and national levels.[38] He goes on to postulate a cyclical pattern by which voters elect a national party and then, because it does not adequately reflect provincial viewpoints, the voters gradually become disaffected and elect governments of opposing parties in the provinces. The federal government eventually finds itself faced with hostile governments in most provinces, and finally it is replaced by the opposition and the cycle begins over. There is little evidence for this view, which seems to imply an exceedingly calculating electorate, but it does seem clear that election of minor parties at the provincial level, especially in Quebec and the west, is in a sense a safety valve for the expression of regional disaffections from the major parties.[39] Another possible explanation for provincial electorates' returning different parties at different levels is simply that,

since federal and provincial elections are held at different times, many voters approach each separately, reacting to a different set of issues, candidates, parties, and concerns.

The relative separation of federal and provincial parties takes other forms. Federal parties do not attempt to control nominations in provincial parties; seldom do national parties play an active role in provincial elections[40] or try to influence the policies of provincial parties.[41] Much more than in the past, provincial parties have their own sources of funds.[42] In some provinces federal and provincial party organizations are quite distinct,[43] though there appears to be wide variations between provinces and informal relations may still provide important links. In July 1964 the federal and provincial wings of the Quebec Liberals formally separated. Premier Lesage said at the time: "It has become evident that the Canadian reality demands more and more that the political parties which work on the federal level be distinct from provincial parties and vice versa… In effect … the interests are too divergent between federal and provincial governments at the high political level, so that the members of the [party] executive and those on the committees are constantly in a dilemma which I describe as almost insoluble for them."[44]

It is clear, therefore, that the party system does not often serve as a channel for intergovernmental adjustment. Partisan factors are little help in understanding or explaining either federal-provincial conflict generally or the particular conflicts examined here. Like the

35  David E. Smith, "The Membership of the Saskatchewan Legislative Assembly: 1905–1966," in Norman Ward and Duff Spafford, eds., *Politics in Saskatchewan* (Don Mills, Ont., 1968), p. 178.

36  F.C. Engelmann and M.A. Schwartz, *Political Parties and the Canadian Social Structure* (Scarborough, 1967), p. 143.

37  Patti Peppin, "Split-Ticket Voting," unpublished undergraduate honours essay, Queen's University, Kingston, 1969.

38  "Federalism and the Party System in Canada," in Wildavsky, *American Federalism in Perspective*, pp. 144–62. Similar points were made earlier by Dawson in *The Government of Canada*, p. 486.

39  See Lipset, "Review of *Democracy in Alberta*," passim. The Union Nationale in Quebec, he suggests, is the functional equivalent of a United States primary.

40  The Quebec election of October 1939 is the most famous exception. Premier Duplessis threatened to make it a referendum on Canadian participation in the Second World War and was defeated after a massive invasion of the province by federal ministers who warned that to so cut off Quebec from the rest of Canada could be disastrous.

41  Engelmann and Schwartz, *Political Parties and the Canadian Social Structure*, pp. 198–9. More often provincial governments run "against Ottawa." That is standard election fare in Quebec, British Columbia, and other provinces. For a good description of a campaign in Nova Scotia by the Conservative government of Premier Robert Stanfield against alleged unfair treatment at the hands of federal Liberals, in a federal election, see J. Murray Beck, "The Electoral Behaviour of Nova Scotia in 1965," *Dalhousie Review* 46 (1966), pp. 29–39.

42  Khayyam Z. Paltiel, "Federalism and Party Finance: A Preliminary Sounding," in Committee on Election Expenses, *Studies in Canadian Party Finance* (Ottawa, 1966), pp. 5–6.

43  Engelmann and Schwartz, *Political Parties and the Canadian Social Structure*, p. 143.

44  Speech to la Fédération libérale du Québec, 5 July 1964.

operation of the traditional institutions, the Canadian party system does not greatly integrate politics at the provincial and national levels. The party subsystems are largely separate and distinct, and again this fosters the pattern of government-to-government negotiation, more analogous to that between nation-states than that between units in the same political system. The governments are interdependent, but truly autonomous.

This may be broadened to a more general hypothesis about federal and provincial political systems, although there is only fragmentary and impressionistic evidence. Federal and provincial political systems are to a high degree separate and distinct, with few connecting links. Not only parties but also electoral behaviour, political leadership, and dominant political traditions, culture, and issues distinguish politics in the provinces from national politics and from each other. In the matter of political leadership, for example, there is very little mobility between federal and provincial governments. Between 1919 and 1971 only three of the eleven national leaders of the two major parties have been provincial premiers. All were Conservatives; none has become prime minister. In the United States, however, nine of twenty-two first-time presidential candidates since 1896 were at one time state governors.[45] Another indication is that among English-Canadian cabinet ministers appointed between 1948 and 1965 only 4 per cent were premiers, 7.5 per cent provincial cabinet members, and 19 per cent members of provincial legislatures. No French-Canadian ministers had been provincial premiers or cabinet ministers, and only 8 per cent had been MLAs.[46] Of twenty-six Liberal cabinet members in January 1966, none had been in a provincial cabinet and just two had been MLAs, but ten had once worked in the federal civil service.[47] By contrast 22 per cent of United States senators were state governors immediately before election to the Senate.[48] About 13 per cent of Canadian MPs have prior experience in provincial

government and legislatures; in the United States the comparable figure is 38 per cent, in Australia 27.4 per cent. Immediately prior to election to the lower house of the national legislature, 27 per cent of American, 17.5 per cent of Australians, and only 8 per cent of Canadians served in state or provincial positions.[49] Similarly, since Confederation, only nine federal cabinet ministers have returned to provincial politics.[50] Some data on the individual perspectives of members of the Ontario and Michigan legislatures, collected by E.J. Heubel, also indicate the separation of provincial and national politics. Asked which level of government best met its responsibilities, 76 per cent of the Ontario legislators said the province; only 4 per cent felt the federal government did. But 42 per cent of the Michigan legislators opted for the federal government, and only 19 per cent for the state government.[51] Three times as many Michigan representatives often mentioned national issues in speeches (27 per cent to 9 per cent); twice as many planned to run for national office (19 per cent and 9 per cent); and, while two-thirds of the Michigan respondents would run for national office if asked, only a fifth of the Ontario ones would. Michigan legislators, Heubel concludes, are "clearly supportive of a nation-centred polity," but in Ontario "national sentiment, though expressed, is heavily discounted by provincial regard and interests."[52] If, as seems likely, these orientations can be generalized to other provinces, they should have important implications for federal-provincial relations. They reinforce the impression of relative separation of provincial and federal political systems. They also suggest that in dealings with Ottawa provincial representatives are unlikely to identify with the interests and concerns

45  Paul David, "The Role of Governors at the National Party Convention," in Daniel J. Elazar *et al.*, eds., *Cooperation and Conflict: Readings in American Federalism* (Itasca, Ill., 1969), p. 373.

46  Van Loon, "The Structure and Membership of the Canadian Cabinet," p. 111.

47  Calculated from biographical material in the *Canadian Parliamentary Guide*.

48  Donald R. Matthews, *U.S. Senators and Their World* (New York, 1960), p. 55.

49  Joseph A. Schlesinger, "Political Careers and Party Leadership," in Lewis Edinger, ed., *Political Leadership in Industrialized Societies* (New York, 1967), pp. 266–93; calculated from tables on pp. 277 and 279. The data is based on the 1957 Canadian election, 1956 American elections, and 1964 Australian elections. Only 4 per cent of a sample interviewed by David Hoffman and Norman Ward reported provincial experience. *Bilingualism and Biculturalism in the House of Commons*, Documents of the Royal Commission on Bilingualism and Biculturalism, 3 (Ottawa, 1970), p. 63.

50  Van Loon, "The Structure and Membership of the Canadian Cabinet," p. 123.

51  E.J. Heubel, "Michigan and Ontario Legislators: Perspectives on the Federal System," *Canadian Journal of Economics and Political Science* 32 (1966), p. 450.

52  *Ibid.*, p. 454.

of federal negotiators, are unlikely to perceive them as potential colleagues or to see themselves as future incumbents of federal roles, and are more likely to see disputes in the form of "your government versus my government." Thus, at many different levels, what evidence there is suggests that the two levels of government are clearly differentiated from each other. Party, Parliament, and other institutions provide few channels between them, and few ways of meshing activity at one level with that of another. As a result, the adjustment process takes the form of separate, distinct, and autonomous organizations dealing directly with each other, rather than a diffuse pattern of relations through parties, the Congress, and the bureaucracy as in the United States, or rather than a pattern in which centralized programmatic parties serve to greatly integrate politics at the two levels as in Germany. [53]

## Internal organization: centralization
So far I have suggested a pattern of separation *between* governments. Equally important as a determinant of the shape of federal-provincial relations is internal organization within governments. Here the pattern is one of relative centralization, and the principal explanation, again, seems to lie in the transplantation of British governmental forms, together with a tradition of strong executive authority. All provincial governments, like the federal, are organized after this model. In Ontario, for example, "There can be no denying the fact of cabinet domination over the whole of government operations."[54] Provincial legislatures have little impact on policymaking, and, with the exception of Quebec, appear to spend very little time discussing federal-provincial relations. One consequence of this cabinet dominance, and the absence of separation of powers, is that premiers and prime ministers can firmly commit their own governments, since there is very little chance of their being repudiated by a recalcitrant legislature.

In the United States, says William Anderson, the "splitting up of the political authority of the states and the national government has the effect that no one in the national government can promise the states what the national government will do for them; and no one in the state government can commit the state in advance to any agreement with the national government."[55] In contrast, the Australian and Canadian premiers "have been able to speak with the full authority of their states and to drive hard bargains with the prime minister and cabinet of the central government."[56] This greatly simplifies the bargaining process by making it possible for agreements to be worked out in face-to-face meetings of relatively few persons. It is also one reason why federal-provincial conferences have been able to become such important sites for negotiation.

The centralization of governments also means that development of horizontal relations between ministers or officials with similar interests at both levels will be inhibited. Edward Weidner finds such relationships to be a central characteristic of intergovernmental relations in the United States.[57] Similar "collaboration" is common in Canada as well, particularly among officials sharing common professional values in particular programme areas. The extensive federal reliance on shared-cost programmes in the postwar period fostered its development.[58] Federal and provincial officials often made common cause to promote and protect their programmes against the interference of federal and provincial central agencies like finance departments, treasury boards, and prime ministers' offices; they knew that if they failed to resolve conflicts among themselves, then it would be done by outsiders who did not share their programme concerns.[59]

By the 1960s, however, the significance of such horizontal relationships, especially in matters of broad policy like those discussed here, began to weaken. In part, this is because provincial premiers and other central officials began to make greater use of the

53  See Arnold J. Heidenheimer, "Federalism and the Party System: The Case of West Germany," *American Political Science Review* 52 (1958), pp. 809–28.
54  Fred Schindeler, "The Organization and Functions of the Executive Branch in Ontario," *Canadian Public Administration* 9 (1966), p. 431. For a more extended discussion, see his *Responsible Government in Ontario* (Toronto, 1969), pp. 28–55.
55  *Intergovernmental Relations in Review* (Minneapolis, 1960), p. 15.
56  *Ibid.*, p. 139.
57  "Decision-making in a Federal System," in A.W. Macmahon, ed., *Federalism Mature and Emergent* (New York, 1955).
58  See D.V. Smiley, *Conditional Grants and Canadian Federalism* (Toronto, 1963), esp. pp. 37–42.
59  D.V. Smiley, "Public Administration and Canadian Federalism," *Canadian Public Administration* 7 (1964), p. 378.

hierarchical controls at their disposal to exert greater dominance over programme departments. Several provincial governments became much more committed to their own long-term planning and to developing their own priorities, and recruited officials with general concerns less tied to particular programmes.[60] Thus Quebec centralized all federal-provincial relations within a new Department of Federal-Provincial Affairs; Ontario gradually strengthened its Treasury Board, increased the role of the cabinet secretariat, and established the Office of the Chief Economist with major responsibilities in federal-provincial relations;[61] Manitoba strengthened the Treasury Board and developed a personal staff for the premier centred in the cabinet secretariat;[62] New Brunswick greatly strengthened its Treasury Department. In addition, the strong personal control exerted by such premiers as Bennett in British Columbia contributed to increased centralization within provincial governments. Wrote a senior Ontario official: "These agencies will all tend to diminish the independence of specialist relationships between operating departments, by attempting to develop common policies for all federal-provincial relationships."[63] Ottawa also moved in the direction of centralization, especially after the 1968 election. A cabinet committee on federal-provincial relations expanded its role, and a strong Federal-Provincial Relations Division was set up in the Privy Council Office. A greatly decreased emphasis on shared-cost programmes also promised to weaken cross-governmental officials' relationships.

These developments, while not eliminating horizontal relationships, do reduce their significance for federal-provincial relations. The most important consequence of centralization within governments is to channel conflicts through to the cabinets and senior central officials of the governments. Instead of being diffused throughout the bureaucracy, and settled in adjustments at lower levels, many issues will emerge at the political level. If it is assumed that political leaders of the governments have fewer areas of common interest than officials concerned with particular programmes, then such channelling of disagreements to the political level should increase the level of conflict. The values of the central officials predominate over those of programme officials and the values of the two groups often differ.[64] More important, this channelling gives a certain shape to the conflict. The participants are not scattered through the system in the form of federal cabinet members, members of Parliament, bureaucrats, and party leaders; rather they are concentrated and limited largely to provincial premiers, senior cabinet members, and senior officials on the one hand, and their federal counterparts on the other. Being thus expressed as *intergovernmental* conflicts, it seems more likely that considerations of institutional status and prestige become inextricably intermingled with more substantive programme differences. The concentration also makes it less likely that alliances in policy-making will cut across governmental lines. Thus the institutional arrangements of the constituent governments are a fundamental factor shaping intergovernmental relations in Canada. Combined with the inadequacy of national political institutions as arenas for adjustment, and the apparent isolation of federal and provincial political systems, they provide an essential reason for the overall pattern of direct negotiations between senior executives as the dominant form of adjustment.

A final, very simple, institutional factor also facilitates this pattern: the relatively small number of units in the federation. This may have two effects. First, it might help to explain the degree of provincial influence, since the smaller the number of units, presumably, the greater the influence of each. However, the German case, for one example, shows that this is by no means a sufficient condition. Second, the small number of units facilitates the pattern of direct relations between governments by keeping the number of participants at a manageable level. It is hard to imagine decision-making in a body like the federal-provincial conference with five times as many units. Coordination among eleven governments, we shall see, is hard enough; to coordinate fifty would be much

60  *Ibid.*, pp. 380–1.
61  Schindeler, "The Organization and Functions of the Executive Branch in Ontario," pp. 410–28. See also H. Ian Macdonald, "The 'New Economics' and the Province of Ontario," *Ontario Economic Review* 4, no 4 (1966), pp. 4–9.
62  M.S. Donnelly, *The Government of Manitoba* (Toronto, 1963), p. 99.
63  Don Stevenson, "Federalism and the Provision of Public Services: A Canadian Viewpoint," paper presented to seminar on federalism, Indiana University, June 1967, p. 8.
64  See J.A. Corry, *Difficulties of Divided Jurisdiction* (Ottawa, 1939), p. 16.

more difficult. At the least, one would expect more tacit or indirect bargaining, and many more relationships between the central government and groups of a few states. It would be a much more complex and diffuse process, and this very diffuseness should be expected to change not only its outward form but also its results.

Thus the coexistence of British models of governmental organization at both federal and provincial levels with the diverse social and economic environment of Canadian federalism is a crucial determinant of the nature of federal-provincial relations. Both sets of factors help to create a characteristic form of decision-making, one narrowly focused in direct relations between distinct governments, which have relatively few links with each other except through direct contacts between their political leaders. The institutional arrangements do not, of course, completely explain the pattern of negotiation: underlying them are the great regional differences, differences in perspectives of different governments, the nature of the problems facing the system, and the activism of provincial governments. But it does seem clear that these institutional arrangements have had a significant independent effect: the contrast of the Canadian pattern with that in the United States, which does not differ greatly in social characteristics but does have a very different set of institutions, is adequate illustration of the point.

## THE CONSTITUTION

Just as the institutional environment sets some basic parameters for the decision process, so too does the constitutional framework. The Canadian constitution lies partly in the written British North America Act, which established the Dominion in 1867, and its later amendments and judicial interpretation, and partly in unwritten custom and tradition, like the British model.[65] As already mentioned the BNA Act originally envisioned a highly centralized union, but its judicial interpretation has made it highly decentralized. What are some of its effects on federal-provincial relations?

First, the interplay between constitutional provisions and problems raised in the system helps to shape the kinds of issues the governments negotiate. Thus, if the constitution allocated both functions and the resources to perform them unambiguously, then presumably there would be less interdependence. But to the extent that problems cut across constitutional provisions, or the allocation of revenue sources and the allocation of legislative responsibilities do not match, or functions are shared among governments, then the need for interaction increases. All three conditions obtain in Canada. The BNA Act is vague or silent on many of the important issues of modern times, requiring the development of new forms and procedures to handle them. Similarly, a chronic imbalance between revenues and responsibilities has dogged federal-provincial relations since 1867, especially since the constitution gives Ottawa very broad taxing powers while at the same time consigning such areas as health, education, and welfare, which have assumed crucial importance in the twentieth century, to the provinces. Moreover, many important matters are shared between governments. For example, both levels have the right to impose personal income taxes.[66] As a result of a 1951 amendment to the BNA Act, which gave Ottawa authority to establish the Old Age Security programme, pensions became a matter of shared jurisdiction. Therefore when the issue arose in 1963 it was immediately a federal-provincial one. Finally, rigidities in the constitution, or its failure to permit resolution of important questions, may lead to attempts to circumvent its provisions and develop new mechanisms. Thus, in response to widespread demands, including some from the provinces, Ottawa became deeply involved in many provincial responsibilities, partly through constitutional amendment, as in the pension case, but even more through extensive use of the spending power.[67]

One factor preventing a major reallocation of functions to Ottawa in the postwar period of relative centralization was the extreme difficulty of amending the British North America Act. Amending procedures

---

65 For a good brief summary of the principal features of Canadian constitutionalism, see R.I. Cheffins, *The Constitutional Process in Canada* (Toronto, 1969).

66 For an exhaustive analysis of constitutional provisions concerning taxation, see Gerard V. La Forest, *The Allocation of Taxing Power under the Canadian Constitution* (Toronto, 1967).

67 See D.V. Smiley, *The Canadian Political Nationality* (Toronto, 1967), pp. 39–43.

were not spelled out in the act and have themselves been the subject of extensive and continuing federal-provincial negotiations.[68] This difficulty has partially prevented the removing of some issues from the federal-provincial arena, and has so fostered a continuing high level of interaction.[69] Thus, one basic effect of the constitutional provisions is to shape the kind and degree of federal-provincial relations as well as to affect what sorts of issues arise. It does so not by itself but rather as it interacts with the goals and objectives of governments, the demands of other élites, and basic problems facing the system.

The constitution has other effects on the process. It is a crucial element in the allocation of political resources and hence also in strategies and tactics. Constitutional factors will help to shape outcomes. The form of federal aid to higher education proposed in 1966 is an example. It was designed partly to reconcile widespread demands for federal involvement in an area with provincial constitutional jurisdiction. The pension outcome would almost certainly have been different had the provinces not had precedence in the pension field. More broadly, Birch suggests "the complications of federalism,"[70] in particular the inappropriateness of the constitution to contemporary problems and the inflexibility of amendment, slowed progress in the development of social legislation in Canada, despite widespread demands, by giving veto power to reluctant provincial governments and by giving provinces jurisdiction in such fields without giving them sufficient financial resources. Without assessing the goodness or badness of such "complications," it is clear, however, that while the constitutional provisions did make agreement on such welfare programmes more protracted and difficult to attain, it did not, as the pension case shows, prevent the establishment of a welfare state in Canada.[71]

None of this is to suggest that the constitution is fixed or immutable. Its omissions and ambiguities are often as important as its more definite provisions. Federal-provincial relations are often attempts to get around constitutional strictures, and in doing so they may result in de facto constitutional changes. The whole structure of federal-provincial conferences, to mention one example, is now an essential part of Canada's governmental structure, though unmentioned in the British North America Act. Piecemeal adjustments such as the development of shared-cost programmes, the contracting-out legislation of 1965 which implied a special status for Quebec, and the more recent federal attempt to draw a fairly strict line between federal and provincial responsibilities and revenues all have implications for the operating constitution. The frequency of constitutional discussions is a good indicator of the importance of constitutional matters in shaping relations among governments.

THIS DISCUSSION HAS shown that institutional and constitutional arrangements play their part in directing not only the overall pattern of federal-provincial negotiations but also the operation of the process in specific cases. They provide some of the basic parameters within which the decision-makers operate. They provide both constraints on behaviour and opportunities which can be exploited.

Together, the social and institutional foundations of the system help to determine the broad outlines of the relationship between federal and provincial governments, and the patterns of decision-making they have evolved. Alone, neither provides sufficient explanation. Thus, Australia has many institutional characteristics, especially parliamentary government and party discipline, which are much like the Canadian ones. As in Canada, conferences of premiers and prime ministers are an important mechanism for adjustment.[72]

---

68   See W.S. Livingston, *Federalism and Constitutional Change* (Oxford, 1956); and Department of Justice, *The Amendment of the Constitution of Canada* (Ottawa, 1965); see also Alexander Brady, "Constitutional Amendment and the Federation," *Canadian Journal of Economics and Political Science* 29 (1963), pp. 486–94, and articles in the section on "Constitutional Amendment" in Fox, *Politics: Canada*, pp. 81–98. For a description of one noted attempt to develop a formula for amendment, see Agar Adamson, "The Fulton-Favreau Formula: A Study of Its Development, 1960–1964," paper presented to the Canadian Political Science Association, Ottawa, 7 June 1967.

69   Smiley, "Public Administration and Canadian Federalism," p. 372.

70   *Federalism, Finance and Social Legislation*, p. 204.

71   For a strong argument that the BNA Act provides a flexible form for change in the federal system, see Barry Strayer, "The Flexibility of the BNA Act," in Trevor Lloyd and Jack McLeod, eds., *Agenda 1970: Proposals for a Creative Politics* (Toronto, 1968), pp. 197–216. See also Cheffins, *The Constitutional Process in Canada*.

72   J.D.B. Miller, *Australian Government and Politics* (London, 1954), pp. 137–8.

However, the overall degree of centralization appears to be much greater in Australia, and the reason seems to lie in differences in social structure. Australia is a much less "federal society."[73] Together, the social and institutional patterns in Canada facilitate a pattern of federal-provincial relations which not only gives great weight to regional interests in national policy-making but also takes the form of direct negotiations between the executives of different governments.

73  Alexander Brady, *Democracy in the Dominions: A Comparative Study in Institutions* (3rd ed., Toronto, 1958), p. 178.

# 14

## Author's Introduction

Despite the intentions of John A. Macdonald and other Canadian anglophone Fathers of Confederation, the Canadian federation did not come to operate as a highly centralized federation. This was largely because of political forces favouring provincial rights that came into play soon after Confederation and before the Judicial Committee of the Privy Council began to interpret the constitution. Too often commentators on the Canadian constitution fail to give sufficient emphasis to the way political forces shape how a constitutional structure plays out in the living experience of a country. Some decry this politically-driven departure from the legal text of the constitution. The politics of the provincial rights movement in Canada teaches us, whether we like it or not, how politics trumps pure law in the constitutional evolution of a country.

Source: Peter H. Russell, "Provincial Rights," in *Constitutional Odyssey*, 3rd ed. (Toronto: University of Toronto Press, 2004), 34–52.

Peter H. Russell

# Provincial Rights

THE GREAT CONCEIT of constitution-makers is to believe that the words they put in the constitution can with certainty and precision control a country's future. The great conceit of those who apply a written constitution is to believe that their interpretation captures perfectly the founders' intentions. Those who write constitutions are rarely single-minded in their long-term aspirations. They harbour conflicting hopes and fears about the constitution's evolution. The language of the constitution is inescapably general and latent with ambiguous possibilities. Written constitutions can establish the broad grooves in which a nation-state develops. But what happens within those grooves—the constitutional tilt favoured by history—is determined not by the constitutional text but by the political forces and events that shape the country's subsequent history.

Canada's constitutional development in the decades immediately following Confederation is a monument to the truth of these propositions. Although a majority of the Fathers of Confederation favoured a highly centralized federation, it soon became apparent that their aspirations would not be fulfilled. Instead, the most effective constitutional force in the new federation was the provincial rights movement. Far from moving towards a unitary state, Canada, by the end of the nineteenth century, had become a thoroughly federal country.

One might have expected the stiffest challenge to Macdonald's centralism to have come from Nova Scotia or Quebec. Nova Scotians, as we have seen, voted against Confederation in the provincial and federal elections of 1867. Immediately following Confederation a significant secessionist movement was developing in the province.[1] In 1868 Joseph Howe led a delegation to London seeking a repeal of the union. Nova Scotian opposition to Confederation, however, was not based on a desire for stronger provincial powers. In the end, Nova Scotian separatism was quelled by persuading Howe to join the federal cabinet and by offering Nova Scotia better terms, not through a constitutional amendment but by bringing its debt allowance into line with New Brunswick's.

From the very beginning, the Province of Quebec, in the words of A.I. Silver, "was seen as the geographical and political expression of the French-Canadian nationality, as a French-Catholic province and the French-Canadian homeland."[2] It was not just the *rouge* opponents of Confederation who championed the cause of provincial autonomy and resisted federal interference in provincial affairs. The *Bleus* had promoted Confederation in Quebec largely on the grounds that it would give the French majority in Quebec exclusive control over matters basic to their culture. A *bleu* paper in 1872, for example, claimed that "as Conservatives we must be in favour of provincial rights and against centralization."[3]

It was not Quebec but Ontario that spearheaded the provincial rights movement. Ontario would seem the least likely province to play this role. After all, support for Confederation had been stronger in Ontario than in any other province. With the largest and fastest-growing population, Ontario was expected to be able to dominate national politics. Why at this formative stage in the federation's history should its provincial government be in the vanguard of the provincial rights movement?

The answer is to be found in the pattern of partisan politics that developed soon after Confederation and has endured ever since. Even before Confederation, the Great Coalition of Conservatives and Reformers had broken up. The first federal government after Confederation was headed by the Conservative leader John A. Macdonald. As Ontario Reformers and Quebec Liberals began to organize a competing national party, they naturally took up the provincial cause. In the words of Christopher Armstrong, "If Macdonald's Conservatives were the party of centralism, then its opponents would become the party of localism and provincialism, recruiting the anti-Confederates of the Maritimes to the Reform cause."[4]

The Conservatives dominated the first thirty years of federal politics, holding office in Ottawa for all but four of those years. During that same period the Liberals were having their greatest success at the provincial level. Nowhere was this more true than in Ontario, where Oliver Mowat's Liberals won six successive elections between 1875 and 1896. While Mowat found Liberal allies in other provincial capitals, notably Quebec's Honoré Mercier, he was in office the longest and built the strongest record of provincial rights advocacy. Mowat's championing of this cause is remarkable in that he began his professional career as a junior in John A. Macdonald's law office, was a Father of Confederation, and had moved the Quebec Resolutions setting forth the division of powers between the two levels of government.[5]

The pattern of politics in which one party dominates at the federal level while its main opposition gathers strength in the provincial capitals has been repeated several times in Canadian history. For a long stretch of the twentieth century the Liberals dominated the federal scene while the Conservatives and other opposition parties won in the provinces. The reverse has been developing since the Mulroney Conservatives came to power in Ottawa in 1984. The fact that the largest national parties have gone through long periods in which their experience in government has been concentrated at the provincial level has done much to make provincial rights a cause that transcends partisan politics.

Although this phenomenon is one that stems from the fluctuating fortunes of partisan politics, it is closely tied to the Canadian system of parliamentary government. Responsible government ... tends to concentrate power in the hands of the prime minister and the cabinet. After Confederation it soon became apparent that this concentration of power would occur in the provincial capitals as well as in Ottawa. In Canada, provincial premiers emerged as the strongest political opponents to the federal prime minister. State governors in the United States, hemmed in by an elaborate system of checks and balances, are political pygmies compared with provincial premiers who perform as political giants on the national stage. Canadians, without any conscious design, found their liberal check and balance not within the national or provincial capitals but in the rivalry and tensions between those capitals.

The success of the provincial rights movement cannot be attributed to weak governments at the national level in Canada's formative years. Quite to the contrary, federal administrations presided over by John A. Macdonald, who was prime minister of Canada for nineteen of the country's first twenty-four years, were strong nation-building governments not at all shy about asserting federal power. Under Macdonald's leadership, Canada's "manifest destiny" of becoming a continental nation-state was quickly fulfilled. In 1869 the Hudson's Bay Company's territories covering the prairies and the far north were purchased and added to Canada. A year later, following military suppression of the Métis led by Louis Riel, the Province of Manitoba was carved out of the North-West Territories. In 1871 Canada was extended to the Pacific, when British Columbia became a province on terms agreeable to its colonial government. Prince Edward Island became the seventh province, agreeing to join Confederation in 1873. To this expanding national territory Macdonald's Conservatives applied a National Policy, completing the transcontinental rail link, erecting tariff walls to protect manufacturing, and stimulating immigration to populate the west and provide a market for the protected industries.[6]

Important as the achievements of Macdonald's governments were in building the material conditions of nationhood, they contributed little to a Canadian sense of political community. Nor did they translate into constitutional gains for the federal government. The Conservatives' economic nationalism, as Reg Whitaker has observed, relied "on elites and on their exclusively economic motives."[7] It did not have much emotional appeal at the mass level. Government in faraway Ottawa had difficulty competing with provincial governments for the allegiance of citizens in the new provinces. During these years it was the provinces, not Ottawa, that seized and held the initiative in constitutional politics.

The first objective of the provincial rights movement was to resist and overcome a hierarchical version of Canadian federalism in which the provinces were to be treated as a subordinate or junior level of government. An early focal point of resistance was the office of provincial lieutenant-governor. From a Macdonald centralist perspective, the lieutenant-governors were essentially agents of the federal government in provincial capitals. In the 1870s, however, Ontario, under Mowat's leadership, began to insist that lieutenant-governors had full Crown powers in matters of provincial jurisdiction and that they exercised these powers on the advice of provincial ministers. Not surprisingly, the issue first arose over a question of patronage—the power to make lawyers queen's counsels.[8] Implicit in the provincial claim was an assertion of the provinces' constitutional equality with the federal government.

No element of the Constitution was potentially more threatening to provincial autonomy than the federal powers of reservation and disallowance. These powers derived from an imperial rather than a federal structure. Under the reservation power, the lieutenant-governor of a province could refuse to sign a bill that had passed through the provincial legislature and could reserve it for consideration by the federal cabinet. If, within a year, the lieutenant-governor was not instructed to give royal assent, the bill would die. Disallowance was simply a veto power under which the federal government could render null and void any provincial law within a year of its passage by the provincial legislature. These federal powers mirrored powers of reservation and disallowance over federal legislation that the imperial government retained and that were also written into the BNA Act.[9] The only difference was that the British government had two years rather than one to decide whether to block Canadian legislation.

The powers of reservation and disallowance are classic examples of how a shift in political sentiment and principle can render formal legal powers unusable. Well before Confederation, the British government had greatly reduced the use of its imperial powers of control over the British North American legislatures. Soon after Confederation these powers fell into desuetude. In the first decade a few Canadian bills were reserved, but royal assent was always granted and there were no reservations after 1878. Only one Canadian act was disallowed, in 1873, and the act in question was clearly unconstitutional.[10] At imperial conferences in the late 1920s declarations were made that these imperial powers would never be used and that steps would be taken to remove them from Canada's Constitution. Although the latter step was never taken, no one really cares that the powers remain formally in the Constitution because there is a clear political understanding—a constitutional convention—on both the British and Canadian sides that the powers are completely inoperative.[11] This convention of desuetude was established because use of the imperial powers was incompatible with the principle of Canadian self-government, a principle which, at least in matters of domestic policy, was so firmly in place by the 1870s that breach of it would have had the gravest political consequences.

A similar process occurred with respect to the federal government's powers of reservation and disallowance. Over time, the principle of provincial autonomy—self-government in those areas constitutionally assigned to the provincial legislatures—became so strongly held in the Canadian political system that the federal powers of reservation and disallowance, though remaining in the Constitution, became politically unusable. This did not happen all at once. It occurred only because the idea that the provinces are not subordinate to but coordinate with the federal government became the politically dominant conception of Canadian federalism.

At first federal governments—not only Macdonald's but the Liberals too when they were in power in the 1870s—made extensive use of the powers of reservation and disallowance.[12] Macdonald's first administration withheld assent on sixteen of twenty-four provincial bills reserved by lieutenant-governors. Between 1867 and 1896, sixty-five provincial acts were disallowed by the federal government. Although the powers continued to be used, they came under increasing attack from the provinces, and from no province more than Ontario. Even when, as was most often the case, the rationale for using these powers was the federal government's view that the legislation was outside the province's jurisdiction, provincial rights advocates were inclined to argue that questions concerning the division of powers should be settled in the courts, not by the federal cabinet. When the Macdonald government in 1881 disallowed Ontario's Rivers and Streams Act primarily to protect the interests of a prominent Conservative, Mowat decided to fight back. He promptly had the legislation re-enacted. After being disallowed and re-enacted three more times, the legislation was allowed to stand. The courts had the final say when the Judicial Committee of the Privy Council upheld the provincial law in 1884.[13]

Abolition of the federal disallowance power topped the list of constitutional proposals emanating from the Interprovincial Conference of 1887. The conference was called by Honoré Mercier, premier of Quebec, who had come to power largely on the strength of Quebec's resentment of the use of federal power in the hanging of Louis Riel. Macdonald and the Conservative premiers of British Columbia and Prince Edward Island declined Mercier's invitation. Delegates from the Liberal governments of the four original provinces and from Manitoba's Conservative administration, "angered by repeated disallowances of their railway legislation,"[14] met for a week under Mowat's chairmanship behind closed doors. The twenty-two resolutions that they unanimously endorsed amounted to a frontal attack on the centralist conception of Confederation. Besides calling for the abolition of federal disallowance and an increase in federal subsidies, the conference proposed that half of the federal Senate be chosen by the provinces. Once these proposals had been approved by the provincial legislatures, they were to be submitted to London for enactment as constitutional amendments by the imperial Parliament.

In the end, nothing concrete came of these proposals. Only the lower houses of New Brunswick and Nova Scotia sent them on to London. The imperial authorities refused to act without having heard from the federal government or the other provinces.[15] Nonetheless, the 1887 conference is a significant landmark in Canada's constitutional politics, for it clearly demonstrated that the constitutional initiative had passed to the provinces. Strong centralist voices could still be heard, not least John A. Macdonald's, but the centralist view was losing its ascendancy in both French and English Canada.

During the first thirty years of Confederation, the provinces made their most tangible constitutional gains not through the process of formal constitutional amendment but through litigation in the courts. Their judicial victories were achieved in London before the Judicial Committee of the Privy Council. The Supreme Court of Canada had been created by the federal Parliament in 1875, but it was supreme in name only. Although the Liberal government which had sponsored the Supreme Court Act aimed at making the court Canada's highest tribunal, the Conservative opposition and the Colonial Office were able to thwart this objective.[16] The right of appeal to the highest court in the British Empire, the Judicial Committee of the Privy Council, was retained in Canada until 1949.

Retaining the Judicial Committee as Canada's highest court had significant consequences for the development of the Canadian Constitution. In the 1870s when the practice of bringing constitutional challenges against legislation in the courts was just beginning, the newly created Supreme Court of Canada decided a few cases very much in the federal government's favour. In *Severn* v. *The Queen*, decided in 1878, the Supreme Court found an Ontario law licensing brewers unconstitutional or ultra vires, outside the powers of the provincial legislature.[17] The Supreme Court judges gave the widest possible interpretation of the federal Parliament's exclusive power to make laws in relation to "the Regulation of Trade and Commerce," and supported this judgment by arguing that the Constitution's framers wished to avoid the "evils" of states rights that had plagued the American federation. A year later in *Lenoir* v. *Ritchie*, the Supreme Court firmly rejected provincial pretensions to Crown prerogative by denying provincial governments the power to appoint queen's counsel.[18]

It did not take long for the English law lords who manned the Judicial Committee of the Privy Council to reverse the Supreme Court's approach to the Constitution. By the 1880s a steady stream of constitutional cases was being taken on appeal to London. The fact that so many constitutional questions were coming before the courts gives the lie to the pretension of the Fathers of Confederation to have settled all questions of jurisdiction.

One of the Judicial Committee's earliest decisions, *Citizens Insurance Co.* v. *Parsons*,[19] is a good example of the kind of issue that arose and the kind of outcome that obtained in the Judicial Committee. Section 91(2) of the BNA Act gave the federal Parliament exclusive jurisdiction over "the Regulation of Trade and Commerce." Section 92(13) gave the provincial legislatures exclusive jurisdiction over "Property and Civil Rights in the Province." At issue in the Parsons case was whether an Ontario statute regulating fire insurance contracts was within provincial powers. Such a law would seem clearly to be a regulation of trade and commerce and a regulation affecting property and civil rights in Ontario. Under which power did the

Ontario legislation fall? The Judicial Committee reasoned that unless some limits were attached to trade and commerce and to property and civil rights, such broadly phrased powers would contradict each other. In this case they chose to put limits on the federal trade and commerce power, ruling that it applied to interprovincial and international commerce and to trade "affecting the whole Dominion," but not to the regulation of an industry within a province. Thus the Ontario act was upheld as a law relating to property and civil rights.

Between 1880 and 1896 the Judicial Committee decided eighteen cases involving twenty issues relating to the division of powers. Fifteen of these issues (75 per cent) it decided in favour of the provinces. What is even more important, as Murray Greenwood has observed, is that in these decisions the committee reversed "every major centralist doctrine of the [Supreme] Court."[20] No area of policy making was as hotly contested as the consumption of alcohol. At first, the Judicial Committee appeared to favour federal power by upholding the Canada Temperance Act, a federal law providing a nationwide system whereby towns and cities could opt for local prohibition.[21] However, in subsequent decisions it ruled that only the provinces could provide for the licensing of taverns and retail liquor outlets in areas that did not opt for prohibition.[22] Finally, in 1896, the Judicial Committee upheld an Ontario local prohibition scheme. It was in this case that the imperial court called for a restrained interpretation of the federal Parliament's general or residual power to make laws for the "Peace, Order, and good Government of Canada." That power should be confined "to such matters as are unquestionably of Canadian interest and importance," and must not encroach on any of the subjects assigned exclusively to the provinces. "To attach any other construction of the general power which, in supplement of its enumerated powers, is conferred upon the Parliament of Canada, would," wrote Lord Watson, "not only be contrary to the intendment of the Act, but would practically destroy the autonomy of the provinces."[23]

The Judicial Committee went beyond the details of the division of powers to articulate a conception of federalism which would have been anathema to John A. Macdonald. The key judgment came in 1892 in the Maritime Bank case and involved that touchiest of constitutional questions—sovereign Crown powers.[24] At issue was New Brunswick's use of the Crown's prerogative to claim priority over other creditors seeking to recover funds from the liquidators of an insolvent bank. In upholding the province's right to use this power, Lord Watson set down the following thesis about the purpose of the BNA Act:

> The object of the Act was neither to weld the provinces into one, nor to subordinate provincial governments to a central authority, but to create a federal government in which they should all be represented, entrusted with the exclusive administration of affairs in which they had a common interest, each province retaining its independence and autonomy.

So much for John A. Macdonald's view that "the true principle of a Confederation lay in giving to the General Government all the principles and powers of sovereignty."[25] For the tribunal which had the final say in interpreting the Canadian Constitution, the provinces were not a subordinate level of government. The federal and provincial governments were coordinate levels of government, each autonomous within the spheres allotted to them by the Constitution.

The theory espoused by the Judicial Committee of the Privy Council is often called the theory of "classical federalism."[26] There can be no doubt that Macdonald and many of Canada's constitutional founders did not think of the country they were building as a classic federation. Some of the Fathers of Confederation, however, especially Quebec leaders like Cartier and Taché, were apprehensive of the centralist view and hoped that the provinces would be autonomous in the areas of law making reserved for them. The Quebec supporters of Confederation realized they could not retain their political support if they portrayed Confederation publicly in centralist terms. The political coalition that put Confederation together never came to a clear and explicit accord on federal theory.[27] What the Judicial Committee did was to give official legal sanction to a theory of federalism congenial to those who, at the time of Confederation and afterwards, could not accept centralism.

The impact of the Judicial Committee's constitutional decisions demonstrates a fundamental feature of constitutional development which is still, at most, only dimly understood by the Canadian public. In countries with written constitutions stipulating the powers of government and the rights of citizens, and in which the constitution is taken seriously, judges will play an important role in enforcing the constitution. The process through which judges play that role is called "judicial review." In performing the function of judicial review, judges review the acts of the executive and legislature and rule null and void those that do not conform with the constitution. Through these determinations, especially those of the highest court, the meaning of the constitution's general terms is fleshed out. This process of judicial review has been so important in the United States that it is said that "the constitution is what the judges say it is."[28]

The Fathers of Confederation did not discuss judicial review. Although some of them were aware of the important role the Supreme Court was playing in the United States, they did not see that there would be an immediate need for a Canadian Supreme Court.[29] Their constitutionalism was much more British than American, and hence more attuned to an unwritten constitution. They were accustomed to having the Judicial Committee of the Privy Council, as the highest imperial court, review colonial laws for their conformity with imperial law. Since the Canadian Constitution took the form of an act of the imperial Parliament, it was logical that this mechanism of imperial judicial control would apply to the BNA Act. For enforcing the rules of federalism internally, within Canada, it is evident that the Fathers of Confederation looked more to the federal executive using its powers of reservation and disallowance than to the judiciary. Also, it was to the federal executive, not the judiciary, that the BNA Act directed minorities to appeal if they believed a province had infringed their constitutional right to denominational schools.[30]

Federal government enforcement of the Constitution made sense, of course, so long as Canadian federalism was viewed primarily as a hierarchical, quasi-imperial structure in which the provinces were a junior level of government. From this perspective, the objective of constitutional enforcement was to keep the provinces from exceeding their powers. John A. Macdonald never contemplated that Canadian courts would find federal laws unconstitutional.[31]

Once, however, the hierarchical view of federalism began to be eclipsed by the theory of classical federalism and dual sovereignty, it was much more logical for a judicial tribunal independent of both levels of government to exercise the primary responsibility for applying the Constitution.

Judicial review in Canada could not be justified in the same way as it was in the United States. There it was possible to justify judicial review on the grounds that in vetoing laws passed by popular majorities, the judiciary was giving effect to the enduring will of the American people as expressed in the Constitution.[32] Given the imperial and undemocratic foundations of the Canadian Constitution, this justification could hardly be advanced in Canada. Nonetheless, the Judicial Committee's constitutional interpretation could not have made the impact it did had it not coincided with powerful political forces in Canada. By the late nineteenth century, Canada had moved too far away from colonialism towards self-government to have complied with the rulings of an imperial tribunal that were out of line with political opinion in the country. The federal election of 1896 demonstrated that in Canada's national politics, the tide was running in favour of provincial rights and a balanced view of Canadian federalism.

The 1896 election was won by the Liberals led by Wilfrid Laurier. The Liberals and Laurier were to remain in power for the next fifteen years. Laurier's political success stemmed in part from his championing of provincial rights. This support occurred in a most ironic setting—the Manitoba Schools crisis.[33] In the 1896 election, Laurier, a French Catholic from Quebec, opposed the Conservative government's threat to force Manitoba to restore the denominational schools of that province's Roman Catholic minority.

In 1890, Manitoba, which by that time had developed into a largely English Protestant province, passed legislation reducing the rights of the French Catholic minority.[34] One law made English Manitoba's official language, ignoring the clause in Manitoba's terms of union guaranteeing the use of English and French in the province's courts and legislature.[35] Nearly a century would pass before this statute would be effectively challenged in the courts.[36] The other statute replaced a dual system of Roman Catholic and Protestant schools in existence since 1871 with a system of secular public schools to be supported by all taxpayers, including parents of children attending the Roman Catholic schools. This legislation was immediately challenged on the grounds that it violated another clause in Manitoba's terms of union guaranteeing denominational school rights held "by law or practice" at the time of union.[37] Although the challenge was initially successful in the Supreme Court of Canada, it failed in the Judicial Committee of the Privy Council.[38] Nevertheless, in a subsequent decision, the Judicial Committee ruled that Manitoba's Catholics could, under another section of the constitutional guarantee, appeal to the federal cabinet to introduce remedial legislation forcing Manitoba to restore their school rights.[39] A few months before the 1896 election, the Conservatives, now led by Charles Tupper, agreed to submit a remedial bill to Parliament. This was the bill that Laurier successfully opposed in the ensuing election campaign.

It was not the substance of that bill which Laurier and the Liberals opposed. They were strongly committed to the restoration of Catholic school rights in Manitoba. In national politics the Laurier Liberals provided the main resistance to a growing movement within English Canada led by D'Alton McCarthy, president of the Ontario Conservative Association, calling for a Canada free of papism and rejecting "the nationaliste thesis that the French were a permanent and equal element in Canada."[40] Still, Laurier, who drew his strongest political support from Quebec, remained as committed to provincial rights as to minority cultural rights. Instead of federal coercion of a province, Laurier proposed the "sunnier ways" of negotiating an accommodation with the provincial government. In the end, it was Laurier's "sunnier ways" and his respect for provincial rights that prevailed politically.[41]

The success of the provincial rights movement did not mean that in terms either of governmental power or of citizens' allegiance the provincial political realm had come to surpass the federal. Laurier, after all, was a national leader whose government would pursue important initiatives in domestic and international politics. Indeed, Laurier and other Quebec leaders, by supporting the rights of French Catholics outside Quebec, were encouraging Quebecers, in the words of A.I. Silver, to look beyond "the still-special home of Quebec" and see that "all Canada should yet be a country for French-Canadians."[42] Since the 1890s there have been shifts back and forth in the balance of power between the two levels of government, but there has always been a balance; neither level has been able to dominate the other. Canada's citizens have been thoroughly schizophrenic in their loyalties, maintaining strong associations with their provincial governments as well as the federal government. In this sense Canada, despite the ambiguities and contradictions in its Constitution, became, as Donald Smiley put it, "in the most elemental way a federal country."[43]

One measure of how ingrained the balanced view of federalism has become is the fate of those imperial powers of reservation and disallowance which the federal government held over the provinces. They are still in the Constitution, but they are simply not used any more. Disallowance has not been used since 1943. The last time a lieutenant-governor reserved a provincial bill was 1961, and then his action was totally repudiated by the federal prime minister, John Diefenbaker, as violating the basic principles of Canadian federalism.[44] When the Parti Québécois came to power in Quebec in the 1970s and enacted Bill 101, the Charter of the French Language, the Trudeau government in Ottawa, which bitterly opposed this legislation, did not ever indicate that it would disallow it. And again in 1988, when Quebec adopted Bill 178 to overcome a Supreme Court ruling and restore a unilingual French sign policy, although Prime Minister Mulroney and opinion leaders throughout English Canada denounced the legislation, neither government nor opposition leaders called for disallowance of the legislation. By the 1980s political parties and leaders of all persuasions, like Laurier and the Liberals a century earlier, would not protect minority rights at the cost of violating provincial rights.

The sovereignty at issue in the struggle for provincial rights was not the sovereignty of the people but the sovereignty of governments and legislatures. The sovereignty claimed and won for provincial legislatures and governments within their allotted sphere of jurisdiction was primarily a top-down kind of sovereignty.[45] Canadian constitutional politics continued to be highly elitist, with federal and provincial leaders contending against each other in intergovernmental meetings and the courts. Still, traces of a more democratic constitutionalism were beginning to appear in the rhetoric, if not the reality, of the constitutional process.

Robert Vipond has shown how exponents of provincial rights defended the sovereignty of provincial "parliaments" against federal intrusions by emphasizing the right to self-government of local electorates. Provincial leaders attacking federal intervention in provincial affairs appealed to the same principles of self-government as earlier colonial politicians had invoked in objecting to imperial intervention in internal colonial affairs. The exercise of the federal powers of disallowance and reservation was portrayed as "autocratic and tyrannical" whereas, according to Liberal leader Edward Blake, to support provincial autonomy was to sustain "the educating and glorious attributes which belong to self-government, to a government of the people, by the people, for the people."[46] Although the provincial leaders were still too British, too wedded to the notion of parliamentary sovereignty, to talk about the people as sovereign in the constituent American sense, they were edging closer to this conception of popular sovereignty when they referred to the rights of provincial legislatures as powers entrusted to them by the people.[47]

Out of this rhetoric and the political success of its authors was born the myth of Confederation as a compact entered into by sovereign provincial communities. According to the compact theory, the provinces as the founding, constituent units of the federation retained the right to alter the terms of their original union.[48] This was the theory promulgated by Honoré Mercier and the other provincial premiers who attended the 1887 Interprovincial Conference: "the conference represented all of the original parties to the compact of 1864, and the partners should now assess the state of their joint enterprise."[49] Not surprisingly, the theory found its most articulate spokesmen in Quebec, where the notion of the province as a founding community could be infused with a sense of ethnic nationalism.

What is meant in referring to the compact theory as a "myth" is that its validity depends not on its historical accuracy but on its capacity to serve as a set of "beliefs and notions that men hold, that they live by or live for."[50] Confederation, as we have seen, did involve a two-stage agreement, first between English- and French-Canadian politicians and then between Canadian and Maritime politicians. Leading participants in the agreement, including John A. Macdonald and George-Étienne Cartier, as well as some of the imperial authorities, frequently referred to the Quebec Resolutions as a treaty or pact. But it is not clear that when they used this terminology they had the same thing in mind. It is most unlikely that when John A. Macdonald talked of a treaty he meant that the parties to the agreement exercised and retained sovereign political authority.

From a strictly legal point of view, the founding colonies in 1867, as colonies, did not have sovereign powers to retain. They did not formally sign or give legal authority to the Constitution. Further, given the elitist quality of the process and the failure, indeed the disinclination, to seek a clear popular mandate for the Confederation deal, it is a total fabrication to maintain that the peoples of the founding provinces had covenanted together to produce the Canadian federal union. This fabrication flies in the face of the top-down process whereby new provinces were added—especially the two provinces carved out of the North-West Territories in 1905. As Arthur Lower observed, "there was not the slightest vestige of a 'compact' in the Acts of Parliament that created the provinces of Alberta and Saskatchewan in 1905."[51]

Nor was the compact theory strictly followed in constitutional practice. If the Canadian Constitution was a compact or treaty among the provinces, then no changes should have been made to it without the consent of all the provinces. Formally constitutional changes, as amendments to the BNA Act, were enacted by the British Parliament, but that body would act only on a request from Canada. During the period that the compact theory was gathering force, however, several amendments were made to the BNA Act at the request of the federal government and Parliament without consulting the provinces or seeking their consent. While none of these amendments directly affected the powers of the provinces, two of them related to the structure of the federation: one empowered the federal Parliament to create new provinces and the other provided for the representation of territories in the federal Parliament.[52] Prior to the 1907 amendment,[53] which revised the subsidies paid to the provinces, Laurier did hold a federal-provincial conference and eight of the nine provinces (British Columbia held out for better terms) agreed to the federal proposal. But the provinces were not consulted on the 1915 amendment that redefined the divisions of the Senate, forming a new section out of the four western provinces.[54]

Even though the compact theory was not consistently observed in the constitutional amendment process, it had become a powerful constitutional ideal by the turn of the century. Provincial rights and the compact theory had, as Ramsay Cook put it, "attained a position close to motherhood in the scale of Canadian political values. It would be difficult to find a prominent politician who was not willing to pay lip-service to the principle of provincial rights and its theoretical underpinning, the compact theory."[55] As a constitutional doctrine, the compact theory may have contained ambiguities and lacked precision, but its strength as a political value in Canada meant that the Canadian political community that was forming would be complex and deeply pluralist. Canada would take its place in the world as an interventionist state and its nationwide activities would take on increasing significance in the lives of its citizens, but the provinces would nonetheless endure as strong constituent elements of the Canadian community.

The ambiguities of the compact theory were intensified by the coexistence of two competing versions of the compact: a compact of founding provinces and a compact of founding peoples.[56] The latter contended that Canada was founded on the basis of a covenant between English Canadians and French Canadiens. In the final analysis, the making of Canada in 1867 was "the free association of two peoples, enjoying equal rights in all matters."[57] These were the words of Henri Bourassa, the theory's most eloquent spokesman and founder of the great Montreal newspaper Le Devoir in 1910. Again, the significance of this theory in Canada's constitutional politics rests not on its historical accuracy but on its potency as a political myth. It is easy to show that neither in law nor in politics was the BNA Act a formal agreement between the French and English people of British North America. Nonetheless, that constitutional settlement depended, as we have seen, on English- and French-Canadian leaders agreeing to a federal structure with a province in which the French Canadians would remain a majority. For many English Canadians, assent to this agreement was only grudgingly given; for French Canadians it represented liberation from Lord Durham's scheme to assimilate them into a unicultural English political community, the triumph of their cultural survival—and, indeed for many, of national survival. The expectations on the French side flowing from that agreement gave rise to the theory that Confederation was based on a compact between two founding peoples.[58]

As originally espoused by Bourassa and other French Canadians, the two founding peoples theory was applied to all of Canada. Indeed, it was advanced as the theoretical underpinning for a pan-Canadian nationalism that viewed all Canada in dualist terms. Its exponents defended the rights of the French minorities outside Quebec and of the English minority in Quebec. In this sense, it may have provided "moral support for minimizing the consequences of the compact of provinces" and of provincial rights.[59] At the same time, this dualist view of Canada always retained a special place for the province of Quebec. As the homeland of one of the founding peoples, it had the right to be secure against intrusions into its culture by the general government answerable to an English-speaking majority.

Lurking within these rival compact theories were deep-seated differences on the nature of Canada as a political community. The idea that Quebec has a special place in Confederation as the only province in which one of the founding peoples forms the majority would collide with the doctrine of provincial equality. More fundamentally, the idea of a Canada based on the English and the French as its two founding peoples would be challenged at the end of the twentieth century by Canadians who were neither British nor French in their cultural background and by the aboriginal peoples.

So long as Canadians were not interested in taking custody of their Constitution into their own hands, this conflict over the nature of Canada as a political community was of no great political importance. It was bound, however, to become salient once that condition changed. The time arrived in 1926, when the Balfour Declaration declared Canada and the other self-governing dominions to be "autonomous Communities" within the British Commonwealth.[60] Canada's political leaders then faced the challenge of arranging for Canada to become constitutionally self-governing.

## NOTES

1  For an account see W.P.M. Kennedy, *The Constitution of Canada, 1534-1937: An Introduction to Its Development, Law and Custom*, 2nd ed. (London: Oxford University Press, 1938), 318–320.
2  A.I. Silver, *The French-Canadian Idea of Confederation, 1864–1900*. (Toronto: University of Toronto Press, 1982), 111.
3  *Ibid.*, 121.
4  Christopher Armstrong, *The Politics of Federalism: Ontario's Relations with the Federal Government, 1867–1942* (Toronto: University of Toronto Press, 1981), 14.
5  A. Margaret Evans, *Sir Oliver Mowat* (Toronto: University of Toronto Press for The Ontario Historical Studies Series, 1992).
6  For a succinct account of the National Policy see Craig Brown, "The Nationalism of the National Policy," in Peter H. Russell, ed., *Nationalism in Canada* (Toronto: McGraw-Hill 1966), 155–63.
7  Reginald Whitaker, "Democracy and the Canadian Constitution," in Keith Banting and Richard Simeon, eds., *And No One Cheered: Federalism, Democracy and the Constitution Act* (Toronto: Methuen, 1983), 250.
8  For a full account see Paul Romney, *Mr. Attorney: The Attorney General for Ontario in Court, Cabinet and Legislature, 1791–1899* (Toronto: University of Toronto Press, 1986), chap. 6.
9  Sections 55–7.
10  R. MacGregor Dawson, *The Government of Canada*, 4th ed. revised by Norman Ward (Toronto: University of Toronto Press, 1966), 142.
11  For a contemporary statement on this point see Peter W. Hogg, *Constitutional Law of Canada*, 2nd ed. (Toronto: Carswell, 1985), 38.
12  For a full account of the use of these powers see Gerard V. LaForest, *Disallowance and Reservation of Provincial Legislation* (Ottawa: Department of Justice, 1965).
13  For a detailed account see Romney, *Mr. Attorney*, 255–6.
14  Armstrong, *Politics of Federalism*, 29.
15  See Paul Gerin-Lajoie, *Constitutional Amendment in Canada* (University of Toronto Press, 1950), 142–3.
16  For a full account see Frank MacKinnon, "The Establishment of the Supreme Court of Canada," *Canadian Historical Review*. 27 (1946): 258–74.
17  [1878] 2 S.C.R. 70. For a compendium of Supreme Court and Judicial Committee decisions on the constitution see Peter H. Russell, Rainer Knopff, and Ted Morton, *Federalism and the Charter: Leading Constitutional Decisions* (Ottawa: Carleton University Press, 1989).
18  [1979] 3 S.C.R. 575.
19  [1881] 7 App. Gas. 96.
20  F. Murray Greenwood, "Lord Watson, Institutional Self-interest and the Decentralization of Canadian Federalism in the 1890's," *University of British Columbia Law Review*. 9 (1974): 267.
21  *Russell v. The Queen* (1882), 7 App. Gas. 829.
22  *Hodge v. The Queen* (1883), 9 App. Gas. 177 (upholding provincial power), and the McCarthy Act Reference (not reported). For a discussion see Russell et al., *Federalism and the Charter*, 53.
23  *Attorney General for Ontario v. Attorney General for Canada*, [1896] A.C. 348.
24  *Liquidators of the Maritime Bank of Canada v. Receiver General of New Brunswick* [1992] A.C. 437.
25  P.B. Waite, ed., *The Confederation Debates in the Province of Canada, 1865* (Toronto: McClelland and Stewart, 1963), 156.
26  For a classical statement of the theory see K.C. Wheare, *Federal Government*, 4th ed. (London: Oxford University Press, 1963). On the basis of the centralizing elements in the constitutional text,

Wheare concluded that Canada was not a true federation but a "quasi-federation."

27 On the absence of a theoretical understanding or agreement on federalism at the time of Confederation see P.B. Waite, *The Life and Times of Confederation, 1864–1867: Politics, Newspapers, and the Union of British North America*, 2nd ed. (Toronto: University of Toronto Press, 1962), 44.

28 The saying is attributed to Charles Evans Hughes, later chief justice of the United States. See A.T. Mason and W.M. Beaney, *American Constitutional Law* (Englewood Cliffs, NJ: Prentice-Hall, 1959), 3.

29 For a discussion of the views of the Fathers of Confederation on this subject see Jennifer Smith, "The Origins of Judicial Review in Canada," *Canadian Journal of Political Science.* 16 (1983): 115–34.

30 Section 93(4).

31 For the evidence see Peter H. Russell, *The Supreme Court of Canada as a Bilingual and Bicultural Institution* (Ottawa: Queen's Printer, 1969), chap. 1.

32 See Alexander Hamilton, "The Federalist No. 78," *The Federalist Papers* (New York: Modern Library, 1937).

33 For an account see W.L. Morton, *The Kingdom of Canada: A General History from Earliest Times*, 2nd ed. (Toronto: McClelland and Stewart, 1969), chap. 19.

34 On the demographic changes see Janice Staples, "Consociationalism at Provincial Level: The Erosion of Dualism in Manitoba, 1870–1890," in Kenneth McRae, ed. *Consociational Democracy: Political Accommodation in Segmented Societies* (Toronto: McClelland and Stewart, 1974), 288–99.

35 Section 23 of the Manitoba Act, 1870.

36 *Attorney General for Manitoba v. Forest* [1979] 2 S.C.R. 1032. Earlier challenges that were successful in the local courts were simply ignored.

37 Section 22 of the Manitoba Act, 1870.

38 *City of Winnipeg v. Barrett* [1892] A.C. 445.

39 *Brophy v. Attorney General for Manitoba* [1895] A.C. 445.

40 Morton, *Kingdom of Canada*, 379.

41 After the election, Laurier worked out a compromise with Manitoba premier Greenway that allowed periods of minority language and religious instruction where numbers warranted.

42 Silver, *French-Canadian Idea of Confederation*, 243.

43 D.V. Smiley, *Canada in Question: Federalism in the Eighties*, 3rd ed. (Toronto: McGraw-Hill Ryerson, 1980), 1.

44 See Edwin Black, *Divided Loyalties: Canadian Concepts of Federalism* (Montreal and London: McGill-Queen's University Press, 1975), 132–5.

45 For a fuller elaboration see Whitaker, "Democracy and the Canadian Constitution."

46 Quoted in Robert Vipond, *Liberty and Community: Canadian Federalism and the Failure of the Constitution* (Albany: State University of New York Press, 1991), 79.

47 *Ibid.*, especially chap. 3.

48 For a full account of the theory see Ramsay Cook, *Provincial Autonomy, Minority Rights and the Compact Theory, 1867–1921* (Ottawa: Queen's Printer, 1969).

49 Black, *Divided Loyalties*, 154.

50 This is the definition of myth given by R.M. MacIver in *The Web of Government* (New York: Macmillan, 1947), 4. For the application of this sense of myth to the compact theory see Donald V. Smiley, *The Canadian Political Nationality* (Toronto: Methuen, 1967), 30.

51 Arthur R.M. Lower, *Colony to Nation: A History of Canada*, 4th ed. (Toronto: Longmans, 1964), 432.

52 The British North America Act of 1871 and the British North America Act of 1886. The third, the Parliament of Canada Act, 1875, concerned the privileges and immunities of the House of Commons. For a brief account of all constitutional amendments up until 1964 and how they were obtained see the Honourable Guy Favreau, *The Amendment of the Constitution of Canada* (Ottawa: Queen's Printer, 1965).

53 The British North America Act of 1907.

54 The British North America Act of 1915.

55 Cook, *Provincial Autonomy*, 44.

56 For an analysis of the relationship between the two compact theories see Filippo Sabetti, "The Historical Context of Constitutional Change in Canada," *Law and Contemporary Problems.* 45 (1982): 11–32.

57 Quoted *ibid.*, 21.

58 For an analysis of this tendency for French-speaking Canadians to view the Constitution as a compact between two peoples while the English-speaking population view the Constitution as an organic development see Daniel J. Elazar, "Constitution-making: The Preeminently Political Act," in Keith G. Banting and Richard Simeon, eds., *Redesigning the State: The Politics of Constitutional Change* (Toronto: University of Toronto Press, 1985), 245–6.

59 Sabetti, "Historical Context of Constitutional Changes in Canada," 20.

60 Dawson, *Government of Canada*, 63.

**15**

## Editors' Introduction

Oliver Mowat was Ontario's third, longest-reigning, and most influential premier (1872–96). He was re-elected an unprecedented six times. Although in 1836 he had articled in one of John A. Macdonald's Kingston law practices, little love ended up being lost between the two of them once both men went into politics. In 1837 he had joined the crowd at Montgomery's Tavern on Yonge St., just north of Eglinton (it no longer exists but is commemorated by a plaque in front of the flag pole of Postal Station "K" which now stands in its place) that would become the Upper Canada Rebellion. Before Confederation, Mowat sat in the Union Parliament for George Brown's Reformers, which fostered his mistrust of Macdonald and George-Étienne Cartier. Significantly, he was part of the Great Coalition of 1864 and took part in the Quebec Conference that settled the Articles of Confederation, notably the division between federal and provincial powers. As exemplified by Christopher Armstrong's piece, over the years to come his disagreements with Macdonald as to what had been agreed to would irrevocably shape federal politics and the role of the provinces in Confederation. Yet Mowat was no radical, working consistently to bridge rifts between Protestants and Catholics, and rural and urban dwellers. Mowat is also notable for having been a judge before going into provincial politics. Can you imagine a judge running for public office in Canada today? Mowat went into federal politics where he was Minister of Justice under Wilfrid Laurier, appointed to the Senate, and eventually became Lieutenant-Governor of Ontario. There may not be a politician in Canada whose career spanned as long and wide a range.

Source: Christopher Armstrong, "The Mowat Heritage in Federal–Provincial Relations," in *Oliver Mowat's Ontario*, ed. Donald Swainson (Toronto: Macmillan, 1972), 93–118.

## Christopher Armstrong

# The Mowat Heritage in Federal–Provincial Relations

SIR OLIVER MOWAT deserves the title, "father of the provincial rights movement in Canada." It was he who challenged Sir John Macdonald upon the use of the power of disallowance, over the granting of "better terms" to some provinces without the others being consulted, and over the functions of the lieutenant-governor. He took a hand in the calling of the first Interprovincial Conference, which dutifully passed a number of resolutions he had drafted demanding for the provinces sovereign control of their affairs within their sphere of jurisdiction. He appeared personally before the Judicial Committee of the Privy Council with conspicuous success and persuaded them to accept his contentions in a number of important constitutional cases. All in all, he made it certain that the provinces would be far more than the glorified municipalities which some Fathers of Confederation, not least himself, had envisaged.[1]

Some might say that Canadians have little reason to be grateful to Mowat for his efforts. It must be admitted that the conduct of federal-provincial relations seems to bring out the worst in our political leaders. In the intervals between delivering long-winded speeches, most of which are no more than platitudinous humbug, premiers and prime ministers alike have engaged in back-biting and name-calling on a grand scale. Witness, for example, Mackenzie King's description of Howard Ferguson as a "skunk," or Sir James Whitney declaring that the federal minister of

---

1    All students must be indebted to J.C. Morrison's study, "Oliver Mowat and the Development of Provincial Rights in Ontario: A Study in the Dominion-Provincial Relations, 1867–1896," in *Three History Theses* (published under the auspices of the Ontario Department of Public Records and Archives, 1961), passim.

Justice, "'Baby' Aylesworth, … is without exception the most infantile specimen of politician or statesman that ever came to my notice," or that master of invective, Mitchell Hepburn, reviling King in 1941 as an "assassin of Confederation," fiddling with the Canadian constitution while London burned.[2] None of this has raised the tone of our political life, and such bitterness might be said to have retarded the growth of Canadian national feeling.

Mowat, of course, can hardly be blamed for the whole unedifying spectacle. What should be remembered is that during almost twenty-five years as premier of Ontario he defined the objectives of the province's external policy, of its relations with the federal government and with the other provinces. These his successors continued to pursue long after his retirement. He recognized that Ontario occupied a unique place in the Canadian federation owing to its size, its wealth, and its population. The poorer provinces might look upon federalism as a means of overcoming regional disparities, but Ontarians, loyal to the Clear Grit tradition, valued separation more than equalization. The province wished to be left on its own to develop its bountiful resources without outside interference. Mowat sensed that "Empire Ontario" must have its emperor, and during his premiership did his best to enhance the province's power and influence along with his own.[3]

Mowat's first objective then was to secure the fullest control over the province's economic development. Federal policies which threatened to restrict this must be strenuously resisted. Indeed, there developed a sort of dialectic in federal-provincial relations: any "interference" by Ottawa was opposed by provincial politicians, almost as a conditioned reflex. Whenever federal policies failed to meet Ontario's needs, or threatened to work against her best interests, the province tried to substitute its authority for that of the federal government. More often than not, it should be noted,

the dynamic force which provoked such clashes was a private interest group, attempting to use whichever level of government best met its needs and desires. The province would take up the cudgels on behalf of its clients, whose opponents were usually pressing just as hard for Ottawa's aid.

Because of its vast domain Ontario was rich enough to resist the efforts of the federal government to bully it or bribe it into line. While the other provinces clamoured for "better terms," Ontario held aloof. Since almost half of federal tax revenues were supplied by Ontarians, any increase in federal transfer payments to the other provinces held a limited appeal for them. When the other premiers went cap in hand to Ottawa, Mowat could afford to stay at home and denounce any changes made in the financial relations between the Dominion and the provinces without consulting him. Occasionally, however, Ontario might wish the support of the other provinces for some demand it was making upon the federal authorities. Then the premier could unbend a little and ensure the necessary backing by approving the demands of the poor relations for increased subsidies.

Sir Oliver was quick to realize that both of these objectives could better be attained if Ontario were to secure a veto over constitutional change. He could not only torpedo those amendments of which he disapproved but demand favours in return for his assent. Since the British North America Act contained no formula for its own amendment, there was no statutory basis for such a demand, but the "Compact theory" of Confederation, which explained the constitution as a treaty between the provinces, offered a historical and conventional justification for this claim. Mowat early became an ardent exponent of the theory, and while his efforts bore little fruit during Macdonald's lifetime, his successors reaped the benefits.

Only a few illustrations can be offered here of the way in which Mowat and his successors pursued these aims, but they are sufficient to show that the premiers of Ontario, regardless of party, have been surprisingly faithful to them. As a result the Mowat heritage in federal-provincial relations long remained a vital part of our national life.

The most serious threat to the Ontario domain during Mowat's premiership arose from Macdonald's

2   King Diary, June 17, 1930, quoted in H.B. Neatby, *William Lyon Mackenzie King*, vol. 2, *1924–1932, The Lonely Heights* (Toronto, 1963), p. 337; Public Archives of Ontario, Whitney Papers, Whitney to R.L. Borden, September 11, 1907; *ibid.*, Mitchell F. Hepburn Papers, draft of speech to Dominion-Provincial Conference, January 1941, p. 12.

3   H.V. Nelles "Empire Ontario: The Problems of Resource Development," in Donald Swainson, *Oliver Mowat's Ontario* (Toronto: Macmillan, 1972), pp. 189–210.

determination to cut the province down to size by handing over a huge area west of the Lakehead to the new province of Manitoba. To the *Globe* the issue was a simple one:

> Shall Ontario be deprived of the railway terminus on Lake Superior, with the city which is certain to spring up there?
> Shall Ontario be robbed of 60,000 acres of fertile land?
> Shall Ontario lose the revenue of $125,000,000, the sum which the pine timber alone, to say nothing of other valuable timber on the disputed territory, is computed to be worth?
> Shall Ontario be defrauded of a mineral region the wealth of which may exceed anything else in the known world?

Mowat threw himself vigorously into the fight; in 1882 he went so far as to threaten secession, boldly stating that

> if they could only maintain Confederation by giving up half their province, then Confederation must go … and if they could not demand the large amount of property to which they were entitled without foregoing the advantages of Confederation then it was not worth maintaining.[4]

Eventually the matter was fought out before the Judicial Committee. With Mowat personally arguing the province's case, Ontario won its point. He returned home to a hero's welcome, and while touring the province the premier told the crowd at a reception in Niagara Falls,

> I rejoice to know that the one great cause, the principal cause of your enthusiasm, is that you love Ontario as I love it. The display that you have made this night shows that you are for Ontario, and that you are for those who maintain Ontario's cause.[5]

When Macdonald continued to claim the timber and minerals in the disputed area, Mowat entered another suit to establish full possession. In 1888 the Privy Council again upheld him, and a settlement with the Dominion was finally arrived at in 1889.

The way in which private interest groups could create tension between the Dominion and the province was also dramatically demonstrated in Mowat's time by the row over the Rivers and Streams Act. The significant fact was that one of the lumbermen involved in the dispute was a Grit, the other a Tory. The Grit naturally turned to the provincial government for help, while the Tory hitched his fortunes to the government in Ottawa. Four times the legislature passed the act and three times it was disallowed by Macdonald. The two levels of government were drawn into serious conflict through a private quarrel. Neither premier nor prime minister emerged from this fracas with an enhanced reputation, but a pattern had been fixed which would frequently be repeated in future.[6]

Macdonald was convinced that Canada's economic development could best be achieved through the National Policy. So long as it seemed to promote the fullest development of Ontario resources and the creation of an industrial base there, the province's politicians were content to accept its benefits. But as soon as Ontario's interests seemed threatened, the province stood ready to challenge federal policies, to substitute an "Ontario policy" of its own. The need did not arise during Mowat's premiership, but in 1897 the Dingley Tariff imposed a duty of $2 per thousand board feet on Canadian pine lumber, while the unprocessed raw material, pine sawlogs, was admitted free to the United States. Ontario lumbermen were naturally upset at the closing of the huge and profitable American market. They pressed the federal government to impose an export duty on sawlogs to force the McKinley administration to negotiate. But Sir Wilfrid Laurier was reluctant to act, not only because the Dingley Tariff included certain retaliatory provisions, but because he had fixed his hopes for freer trade on the pending negotiations aimed at settling all Canadian-American differences.

4  *Globe*, May 20, 1882, quoted in Morrison, "Mowat and Provincial Rights," pp. 147–48, 296.
5  *Globe*, September 16, 1884, quoted in K.A. Mackirdy, "Regionalism: Canada and Australia" (unpublished Ph.D. thesis, University of Toronto, 1959), p. 186.
6  For an analysis of the conflict over the Rivers and Streams Act, see Morrison, "Mowat and Provincial Rights," pp. 206–15.

Unable to get relief in Ottawa, some Ontario lumbermen turned to the provincial government and demanded that it require the sawing of all Ontario pine in Canada. They succeeded in convincing the public and both political parties that Ontarians would become mere "hewers of wood and drawers of water" for their richer, industrialized American neighbours if they failed to act. Facing a provincial election in 1898, Mowat's successor and longtime subordinate, Arthur S. Hardy, bowed to this skilfully promoted public clamour and inserted a manufacturing condition in all timber licences so that the exportation of pine sawlogs cut on crown land was forbidden.[7]

American lumbermen who owned limits in Ontario protested both to Washington and to Ottawa. Secretary of State Day suggested that the federal government might disallow the export embargo legislation. Premier Hardy began to fear that the federal government might do so in order to persuade the McKinley administration to accept a reciprocity agreement. Laurier refused, however, to interfere with the provincial policy, for Hardy had warned that this would seriously damage the Liberal party's prospects in Ontario. Efforts were then made by the American lumber interests to have prohibitive duties imposed on lumber and other Canadian imports. Meanwhile, the Colonial Office urged Laurier to persuade Hardy to suspend the embargo until the courts decided whether it was a regulation of trade and commerce and, hence, a federal responsibility. The premier stood firm in the face of pressure from Washington, London, and Ottawa. He refused to suspend the act or to join in a reference to the courts, and eventually the embargo was declared valid by the Judicial Committee in a private suit.

… [T]he government of Ontario wished to force companies exploiting the province's natural resources for sale in the United States to do their processing in Canada. This was intended to create jobs as well as capital investment in plant. The success of the sawlog export embargo in forcing the relocation of a number of American sawmills in the province led the government to extend the manufacturing condition to pulpwood, nickel ore, and hydroelectricity too, though with varying degrees of success. Ontario sought, then, to impose her own development policy, which sometimes clashed with the consistent federal policy of seeking to secure free access to the American market for Canadian raw materials.

The mediating influence of party loyalty, both Hardy and Laurier being Liberals, had helped to prevent any open federal-provincial conflict over the sawlog embargo. With the election of the Conservative Whitney administration in 1905 this influence disappeared. Over the next half-dozen years bitter rows between the two levels of government over development policy were frequent. Technological innovations in the fields of transportation, hydroelectricity, and pulp and paper held out the lure of such large profits that one observer was moved to declare, "If Solomon were on hand today, he would say, 'With all your getting, get a water power and a lighting and electric railway franchise.'"[8] Astute entrepreneurs were quick to take note of these opportunities; owing to the vagueness of the B.N.A. Act about the division of authority to incorporate companies,[9] men like James Conmee became convinced that they could play a kind of game and evade provincial control by obtaining federal charters. Attempts at regulation by the Ontario government could then be denounced as attacks upon vested interests and the sacred right of private property.

Conmee himself was specially favourably situated as a Liberal Member of Parliament, able to call upon the government to back his schemes. But others were quick to follow his lead in seeking to obtain at Ottawa what they were denied at Toronto. So complaisant did the Laurier administration prove in meeting the demands of company promoters, that Whitney was forced to retain the services of a watchdog in Ottawa to alert him to trouble ahead.[10] A good deal of time

---

7    Nelles op cit.

8    P.A.C., Willison Papers, Alex Smith to J.S. Willison, October 2, 1905, 27826–7; Smith was the secretary of the Ontario Reform (Liberal) Association.

9    The provinces could charter companies "with provincial objects," but it was not clear whether this phrase was to be construed territorially, so that only concerns operating within one province were covered, or jurisdictionally, so that any company with objects covered by Section 92 was included. The federal government could incorporate companies whose objects were covered by Section 91, such as banking and shipping concerns, and also claimed the right to charter any company whose works were declared to be "for the general advantage of Canada." The province contested the latter claim and pressed for the jurisdictional interpretation of provincial objects.

10   The provincial agent was an Ottawa lawyer, R.G. Code; see the Code-Whitney correspondence, 1905–10, in the Whitney Papers.

and energy was spent by both provincial and federal Conservatives in denouncing charter-mongering by the Liberals, though their protests usually fell upon deaf ears. A reservoir of ill-will built up which did much to embitter the relations of the province and the Dominion as long as Laurier remained in power.

Ontario's single most valuable resource was hydro-electricity, the province's only domestic power source. For over thirty years Mowat's successors resisted federal attempts to take control of the electrical industry. Here, too, the conflict was rooted in a constitutional ambiguity. While the province owned its lands and natural resources, the B.N.A. Act gave the Dominion control of navigation. The greatest hydro potential lay on navigable rivers like the St. Lawrence and the Ottawa. If the existing canals were improved, creating new waterpowers, the federal government might claim them as "incidental" to navigation. Or else it might block the construction of provincially owned generating stations indefinitely as impediments to shipping. Once the province had taken the decision to develop all its power through an arm of the provincial government, the Hydro-Electric Power Commission, conflict between Ontario and the Dominion seemed unavoidable.

The First World War produced an enormous upsurge in the demand for electricity, and by the mid-1920s the H.E.P.C. was casting longing eyes at a share of the two million horsepower potential of the International Section of the St. Lawrence. This development obviously required the cooperation of the United States government which was ready to support the construction of the St. Lawrence Seaway as a joint power-navigation project. However, Prime Minister Mackenzie King was determined that if there was to be a Seaway it should be paid for through the sale of power and not from federal revenues. Should the federal government establish control over this development, it would have sufficient leverage to establish a national electricity policy.

Premier Howard Ferguson of Ontario was equally determined to prevent this. The very idea of a national electricity policy was repugnant to his government, and he rejected the notion that the H.E.P.C's customers should finance the Seaway through higher electricity rates. To bolster its position the province fell back upon the Compact theory of Confederation:

Canada was created by the act of the separate provinces. They established a federal union, yielding to the union the rights and functions appropriate to the national endeavour. Navigation went to the federal authority in the interests of national trade and commerce.... On the other hand, it was only natural that the more local aspects, the more particular property rights, the power, the domestic and sanitary uses [of waterways], which physically are applicable only to local industry and endeavour and should be retained within the sphere of the Provinces.

Ottawa's claim that power was "incidental" to navigation was

a concealed assault upon the provincial position under our federal system. In effect, if admitted, it would mean that federal action could completely oust the province from all benefits whenever a stream could be made navigable.

Such tactics "could slowly convert Canada from a federal union into a legislative union under supreme control of the Parliament at Ottawa."[11]

Efforts to clarify the constitutional position through a reference to the Supreme Court in 1928 proved abortive, for the learned judges confined their replies almost entirely to vague hypotheticals. Efforts to negotiate a settlement during the next two years were equally fruitless. During the federal election campaign of 1930 Ferguson and King traded insults over who was to blame for the delay. The new prime minister, R.B. Bennett, was more enthusiastic about the Seaway than his predecessor; and a fellow-Conservative, George Henry of Ontario, proved more cooperative once it was clear that Bennett was prepared to concede the province's demands. By the Canada-Ontario agreement, which preceded the St. Lawrence Deep Waterway Treaty of 1932 with the United States, the federal government agreed to pay the entire cost of works required for navigation alone plus 30 per cent of the cost of joint navigation and power works. The remaining 70

11   Unsigned memorandum entitled, "Federal and Provincial Rights in Waterways, Georgian Bay Canal Charter and Dominion Lease of Carillon Rapids to National Hydro Electric Company," February 24, 1927, p. 8, in P.A.C., Howard Ferguson Papers.

per cent, about $37.7 million, along with the $66.5 million to equip the powerhouses, was to be met by the province. The H.E.P.C. would own all the power.

The treaty failed to get approval in the United States Senate, but Ferguson's struggle had not been in vain. When the Roosevelt administration persuaded Mackenzie King to take up the Seaway project again in the late 1930s, it was simply assumed that Ontario would control Canada's share of the power. Under the St. Lawrence Basin Agreement of 1941 the province's share of the cost of joint works was also reduced from 70 per cent to 62.5 per cent. Just as Mowat had done in the case of the Manitoba boundary, his successors successfully defended the province's control of a vital resource on which its industrial base and future prosperity were heavily dependent.

The second part of Mowat's legacy was opposition to increases in federal transfer payments to the provinces. As early as 1869 Edward Blake led the Ontario Reform party in denouncing the grant of better terms to Nova Scotia as a violation of the Confederation compact. Ontario's first premier, Sandfield Macdonald, accumulated such a large surplus that the provincial government weathered the depression of the 1870s with relatively little difficulty. However, when the Mowat administration found itself faced with large deficits in the early eighties, his ministers turned their fire upon Macdonald's habit of soothing discontented provinces with financial titbits taken from the pockets of Ontarians. Christopher Fraser, the Commissioner of Public Works, told the legislature in 1885:

[W]e who have charge of Ontario affairs would be recreant to our trust, if in the face of what we see going on, and what is absolutely certain to occur again, we made no sign, and did not indicate that Ontario would not continue submitting to these raids by the other Provinces.... We do not care to get these indirect and unwarranted grants, and that Ontario shall be the milk cow for the whole concern.[12]

When Honoré Mercier suggested an Interprovincial Conference in 1887, Mowat at once agreed that federal encroachment on provincial autonomy must be resisted, but added pointedly that Ontario "was satisfied with the provisions of the British North America Act, and would still prefer them to any changes if the principle on which they are based were faithfully carried out by the Dominion Parliament with the approval of all the provinces."[13] Yet he realized that subsidy increases were the chief concern of Mercier and the other premiers. In what would become a classic ploy for Ontario leaders, he agreed to throw his weight behind their demands, despite his reservations, in return for the backing of the other provinces in his demand for greater provincial autonomy. The conference called for hefty increases in the scale of grants to civil government (in Ontario's case involving a rise from $80,000 to $240,000 per year), and proposed that the annual per capita subsidy of 80 cents be tied to the current census figures rather than the 1861 ones. Such a "basis for a final and unalterable settlement" meant, of course, that the Mowat administration would get the tidy sum of $600,000 a year to dispose of.[14]

Macdonald simply ignored the resolutions passed at the conference. The subsidy question was not raised again until 1900 when the Liberal premiers of Quebec and the Maritime provinces secured better terms. Premier George W. Ross of Ontario immediately protested to Laurier "about the reopening of questions of public policy which were considered settled years ago."[15] The other provinces were insistent on an all-round subsidy increase, however, and an Interprovincial Conference met in December 1902. Ross, who was occupied with a crucial series of by-elections, did not even bother to attend or to send an Ontario representative. In a memorandum read to the delegates, he simply reaffirmed support for all the resolutions passed in 1887, although he did suggest more

---

12  *Globe*, February 23, 1885, quoted in Morrison, "Mowat and Provincial Rights," pp. 260–61.

13  *Globe*, March 31, 1887, quoted in Morrison, "Mowat and Provincial Rights," p. 263.

14  The deliberations of this conference, and the subsequent ones, may be studied in Dominion Provincial and Interprovincial Conferences from 1887 to 1926, and Dominion-Provincial Conferences, November 3–10, 1927, December 9–13, 1935, January 14–15, 1941 (Ottawa, 1951). See also J.A. Maxwell, *Federal Subsidies to Provincial Governments in Canada* (Cambridge, Mass., 1937), passim.

15  P.A.C., Laurier Papers, Ross to Laurier, May 14, 1901, Private, 56180–1.

generous grants for the support of civil government. Premier S.N. Parent of Quebec, by contrast, wanted the per capita subsidy fixed at $1. In the end the delegates merely repassed the earlier resolutions.

Laurier showed no more inclination to act upon these demands than had Macdonald, but as the federal surplus mounted the provinces became increasingly restive. By 1904 even Ontario faced a deficit of $800,000 on ordinary account, although the proceeds from the sale of timber limits covered this. Ross was still convinced that piecemeal grants of better terms were a poor way to cope with financial difficulties. Nevertheless, the financial pinch made him less high-minded; he pleaded with Laurier for a subsidy of $6,400 per mile for the provincially owned Temiskaming and Northern Ontario Railway. Laurier refused, however, to treat the province like "an ordinary railway company," opening the way for a flood of similar demands from the other provinces.[16]

The election of Whitney's Conservative government in 1905, ending almost thirty-five years of Liberal rule, saw no reversal of the province's policy on transfer payments. When Premier Lomer Gouin of Quebec sought the new premier's support for another Interprovincial Conference, Whitney agreed coolly that "fixity of arrangement between the Federal Government and the Provinces ... would, for more than one reason, be very desirable...."[17] It was left to the Liberal premiers to persuade Laurier to call a meeting in October of 1906. Whitney recognized that the original subsidies had become quite inadequate. The 1887 proposal to tie the per capita subsidy to the growth of population had several attractions. It had been twice approved by Interprovincial Conferences. The subsidy would automatically increase through time, so that periodic revisions would be unnecessary. Such an arrangement would be both elastic and yet permanent. Last but not least, the largest province would get the biggest increase. Whitney therefore decided to propose that the conference simply endorse the 1887 subsidy resolution once more.

The other premiers were prepared to agree to this, but insisted that each province should have the right to demand additional special allowances.

Whitney fought a stubborn rearguard action against this, but was eventually overborne. He then proposed that British Columbia, the most importunate in its demands, should receive a special grant of $100,000 annually for ten years. An attempt by the other western provinces to obtain similar grants was turned down largely at Whitney's insistence. Laurier agreed, to accept these terms as a "final and unalterable" settlement of the subsidy question, and the B.N.A. Act was amended the following year.

The steadily increasing demand for provincial services like highways and education soon absorbed these increases completely. The years immediately before the First World War found even a rich province like Ontario sufficiently hard-pressed that its opposition to greater federal transfer payments was again relaxed somewhat. The election of Robert Borden in 1911 was the signal for the repayment of a number of political debts owed to Conservative premiers like Whitney, Rodmond Roblin and Richard McBride. The boundaries of both Ontario and Manitoba were extended, and conditional grants to agricultural education and highway construction proposed. Still provincial spending mounted inexorably. In 1913 another Interprovincial Conference was held to consider the subsidies. Whitney and the other premiers approved a resolution demanding that 10 per cent of federal tariff revenue be channelled into subsidies. Grants to civil governments were to be increased 50 per cent to $2,610,000, while the remaining $10,710,000 (for 1913) would be distributed according to population. The beauty of this scheme, from Whitney's point of view, was that it would return to Ontarians a fairer share of the money which the federal government would collect from them in any case, so that any increase in transfer payments financed by the province would be comparatively small. Despite strongly worded pleas from Whitney, Borden refused to consider this ingenious suggestion, which would have made every tariff revision the occasion for a federal-provincial donnybrook.

In 1927 there came another occasion when the Mowat ploy proved effective. A Dominion-Provincial Conference was called by Mackenzie King in the midst of his dispute with Howard Ferguson over the control of waterpower on navigable rivers. Since the prime minister was content to drag his feet, to refuse to negotiate seriously, Ontario faced a severe power shortage

---

16   Ibid., Laurier to Ross, February 29, 1904, 83607–12.
17   Whitney Papers, Whitney to Gouin, September 18, 1905.

with no prospect of early development of either the St. Lawrence or the Ottawa rivers. Ferguson and Premier L.A. Taschereau of Quebec were confident that the courts would uphold the claims of the provinces, but a reference case required the consent of the federal cabinet. The conference provided a heaven-sent opportunity for forcing King's hand.

Both the Maritimes and the western provinces wanted better terms. When the question of subsidies was raised, Ferguson seized his chance. He reminded the delegates that Ontario paid the largest amount into the federal treasury, yet he supported the demands of the poorer provinces. "He did not," he said,

> intend … to cavil about small things. He regarded it as supremely important to bring about a situation which would be satisfactory to all the provinces.
>
> The basis of financing laid down by the British North America Act could not be regarded as permanent and must be subject to readjustment…. The big problem was to promote satisfaction and prosperity by giving fresh inspiration to those who needed help…. The expenditure of a few hundred thousand dollars was nothing if optimism, harmony, and industry could be inspired.[18]

Lest the other premiers forget their duty, he suggested that the power question should be eliminated from the agenda and referred to the courts. Despite an invitation from the prime minister to discuss this matter the other premiers remained quiet as mice. Doubtless they were too busy savouring the "fresh inspiration" of "a few hundred thousand dollars." Outmanoeuvred, King gave way and allowed the matter to go to the Supreme Court, though not without taking care to frame the questions so as to render most of the answers irrelevant.

The Compact theory of Confederation, the third element in the Mowat heritage, provided an underpinning for the other objectives. It could be called into play to defend Ontario's interest in controlling its development or in the financing of the federal system. To insist upon consultation concerning constitutional

change proved the surest defence of provincial rights against federal encroachment. The grant of better terms to Nova Scotia had been attacked by Edward Blake in 1869, on the grounds that the assent of all the provinces was required to change the financial terms of the B.N.A. Act. As Blake's successor, Mowat quickly adopted the Compact theory as a weapon in his disputes with Macdonald.

The Interprovincial Conference of 1887 was represented as the reconvening of the Quebec Conference of 1864, at which the original compact had been agreed to. Under Mowat's influence, the 1887 meeting resolved that the provincial legislatures "should at the earliest moment take steps with a view of securing the enactment by the Imperial Parliament of amendments to the British North America Act…." In return for his agreement to support an all-round subsidy increase, the premiers gave their support to Mowat's proposals to widen the powers of the provinces and make them even more immune to federal interference.

Mowat's successors were equally loyal to the Compact theory. George Ross declared that it was

> quite evident that in every stage of its progress it [the B.N.A. Act] was regarded by its framers as a treaty under which the Provinces agreed to transfer a certain portion of their sovereignty to a central Government, which would undertake to discharge the duties common to all, while at the same time leaving the residuum of their sovereignty intact and unimpaired….
>
> Now is it not clear that a trusteeship so formed cannot be dissolved, or its powers abridged or increased without the consent of the parties by whom it was made?[19]

By the turn of the century, indeed, politicians of both parties paid lip service to some version of the Compact theory. The influence of Blake and Mowat remained strong within the Liberal party, and Robert Borden admitted that,

> In very many matters touching the everyday life of the people, the policy and aims of any provincial

---

18  "Precis of Discussions, Dominion-Provincial Conference, November 3 to 10, 1927," p. 25, in *Dominion-Provincial Conferences, 1927, 1935, 1941.*

19  Sir George Ross, *The Senate of Canada, Its Constitution, Powers and Duties Historically Considered* (Toronto, 1914), pp. 31–32.

administration are of the greatest possible interest and importance. The Liberal-Conservative party for many years past has been inclined to regard Provincial issues as of somewhat minor consequence.

This he now promised to change.[20]

Nevertheless, the provinces did not succeed in establishing a firm conventional right to be consulted about constitutional change. The 1907 subsidy revision was agreed upon at the Interprovincial Conference, and its recommendations accepted by Laurier, but later amendments were not the product of consultation. However, at the 1927 Dominion-Provincial Conference Ernest Lapointe laid before the delegates an amending formula for the B.N.A. Act, declaring that

> The Government has taken the ground that the B.N.A. Act is an agreement between different parties and that no substantial change should be made without consulting the contracting parties. The B.N.A. Act is the charter of the provinces in which powers have been fixed and determined between the Dominion and the provinces. Consequently, the provinces have the right to be consulted about establishing a new procedure to amend it.[21]

Lapointe's plan would have allowed amendments concerning exclusively federal matters to be made without reference to the provinces. Changes concerning education, the use of French, the administration of justice, property rights and the like, would have required unanimous provincial consent, and other changes could be made with the consent of any six of the nine provinces.

The dangers inherent in this proposition cannot have escaped Ferguson. Federal powers could now be altered without any reference to the provinces. More important, on all but a few matters, any six provinces could join with the federal government to approve an amendment even if both Ontario and Quebec opposed it. Better to allow the existing confusion to continue, meanwhile loudly claiming the right to be consulted about every alteration, than to tie oneself up in such an

unsatisfactory arrangement. Ferguson felt the change might "affect the fundamental structure of our constitution" and declared that he could "see no substantial reason in favour of it." Strong support for this stand came from Premier Taschereau, and Lapointe had to abandon his efforts.

In 1930 the problem recurred. Newly elected, R.B. Bennett prepared to depart for London and an Imperial Conference to approve a draft of the Statute of Westminster, which would have repealed the Colonial Laws Validity Act of 1865 insofar as the Dominions were concerned. Thereafter, British legislation would apply to Canada only if the Dominion expressly requested that it should do so. But the B.N.A. Act was a British statute. Could the division of powers between Dominion and province be altered at the request of the federal Parliament alone once the Statute of Westminster took effect leaving the provinces with no recourse?

Premier Ferguson was much upset, and suggested to Taschereau

> that the provinces should enter a vigorous protest against what is being done without the original parties to the Confederation agreement being consulted.... [W]e should at least be consulted about it before representations are made to the Imperial Parliament. I have made strong protest to Mr. Bennett in one or two discussions I have had with him, and at his suggestion I am putting my views in writing and have asked him to give voice to them at the Conference.[22]

The premier put his position in an open letter to Bennett.[23] Confederation had been "brought about by the action of the Provinces," and the constitution was "the crystallization into law ... of an agreement made by the provinces...." Accordingly, Ferguson claimed the right to veto any changes: "The Province of Ontario holds strongly to the view that this agreement should not be altered without the consent of the parties to it." He protested vigorously against the proposed statute

---

20  P.A.C., Borden Papers, Borden to W.B.A. Ritchie, June 15, 1909, 6646–7.

21  P.A.C., Bennett Papers, Precis of Discussion, Dominion-Provincial Conference, 1927, 16298–312.

22  Ferguson Papers, Ferguson to Taschereau, September 10, 1930.

23  This letter and the accompanying memorandum were published as a pamphlet entitled *Amendment of the Canadian Constitution, Statement and Protest by the Prime Minister of the Province of Ontario* (Toronto, 1930).

and demanded that nothing be done until "the parties to the original compact" had been consulted and were satisfied. Any other course, he warned, would "not only greatly disturb the present harmonious operation of our Constitution, but I fear may seriously disrupt the whole structure of our Confederation."

In an accompanying memorandum the Compact theory of Confederation was further explained. First came a number of bald assertions: "the Quebec resolutions … were in the nature of a treaty between the provinces…."; "the Dominion was … created at the instance of the provinces…." Then came the "proof": Macdonald, Cartier, and Brown had all referred to the agreement as a "treaty" at various times. Moreover, the federal Parliament had not been given the power to amend the constitution; if it had had such power "the long and hitherto successful controversy [*sic*] as to the constitutional rights of the provinces would have had a very different outcome, because at any stage of the struggle the Dominion Parliament would have had the power to enact legislation setting aside the pretensions of the provinces." Skating lightly around the difficult question of who was now party to the compact, the memorandum merely insisted that all the provinces, even those created since 1867, had the same rights. The fact that the provinces had only been formally consulted about a constitutional change on one occasion was dismissed; it simply showed the perfidy of the federal authorities. After all, Ontario had been demanding to be consulted since 1869. A new era had begun in 1927, when Lapointe had at last admitted that the provinces had a right to be consulted. There could be no turning back now, and Ontario would bring all its influence to bear to prevent the power to amend the constitution unilaterally being handed over to Ottawa by the British parliament.

Coming from the Conservative premier of the largest province, this protest proved effective. The Imperial Conference was adjourned "until an opportunity has been given to the provinces to determine whether their rights would be adversely affected…."[24] In April 1931,

a Dominion-Provincial Conference met and Bennett somewhat reluctantly agreed that the statute should be amended so that it conferred no new powers upon either the Dominion or the provinces to amend the B.N.A. Act or to alter their legislative jurisdiction. The broader question of an amending formula was ignored. The outcome satisfied Premier Henry of Ontario, since provincial powers had not been reduced.

Pressure for constitutional amendment was naturally increased by the Depression. The fashion of the day in many quarters was to insist that the federal government should assume full responsibility for unemployment and for relief. Not surprisingly, however, neither the Henry government nor the Liberal administration of Mitchell Hepburn was enthusiastic about such a constitutional change. Both premiers suspected that proposed amendments would simply be designed to place all effective power in federal hands. Arthur Roebuck, Hepburn's attorney general, was alarmed by Bennett's aggressive attitude towards the provinces: "Wherein lies the need for immediate revision?" he asked J.W. Dafoe. "The tory-minded would like to centralize power. The Divine Righters always did, and every battle for freedom has been directed to decentralization." In any event, Roebuck added, nothing should be done until the provinces all agreed upon an amending formula. He was confident that tactical skill in these negotiations could "head off a Dominion grab."[25]

In 1935 Mackenzie King accepted the recommendation of a Select Committee of the Commons that an amending formula should be discussed at a Dominion-provincial conference. Roebuck insisted that any method must be "satisfactory to all provinces."[26] Some progress was made; he and W.J. Major of Manitoba proposed that all the constitutional statutes should be consolidated and divided into four categories, each with a different amending procedure. Matters exclusively federal, like disallowance or the creation of new provinces, could be handled by Parliament alone. Changes concerning the Dominion and some, but not all, the provinces could be made if the provinces

24  Bennett Papers, Bennett to George S. Henry, Feb. 23, 1931; Ferguson had been succeeded by Henry upon the former's appointment as Canadian High Commissioner in London by Bennett. J.W. Dafoe greeted the news this way: "What a gift for Ontario but imagine him at Canada House! Part of the harvest of the regime of bunk, blather, bluster, blasting, braggadocio, Bennett—a swarm of B's."

P.A.C., Dafoe Papers, Dafoe to Harry Sifton, November 29, 1930.
25  *Ibid.*, Roebuck to Dafoe, January 7, 1935.
26  "Dominion-Provincial Conference, 1935, Record of Proceedings, Ottawa, December 9–13, 1935," p. 50, in *Dominion-Provincial Conferences, 1927, 1935, 1941.*

concerned concurred in amendments approved by Parliament. All ten legislative bodies would have to approve changes in minority rights. The remainder of the constitution, in particular the distribution of powers under Sections 91 and 92 of the B.N.A. Act, could be altered with the consent of Parliament and two-thirds of the provinces if they represented 55 per cent of the population.

A number of meetings of a committee of attorneys general were held to discuss this plan during 1936. It was approved in principle, although fears expressed by Maritimers that the other six provinces might gang up on them were met by treating "property and civil rights" and "all matters of a merely local or private nature" in the same way as minority rights. Moreover, a province was to be permitted to opt out of any amendments and to retain its exclusive jurisdiction. Ontario certainly supported this formula; with one-third of Canada's population, its veto would operate unless all the other provinces united against it. The attraction of the formula, as the province's deputy attorney general pointed out, was that, "This method definitely recognized the compact or contract theory. Changes cannot be made without the consent of the provinces affected, and this settles for all time the question as to whether the provinces should be consulted or not."[27] The long struggle begun under Mowat and carried on by his successors had apparently been won.

Unfortunately, it proved impossible to secure the unqualified assent of all the provincial governments to the formula. Mackenzie King's announcement in the spring of 1937 that a Royal Commission would be appointed to study Dominion-provincial relations led to the suspension of negotiations pending its report. Premier Hepburn considered the Rowell-Sirois Commission a waste of time and money. Loyal to the Compact theory he bluntly told the Commissioners: "I have always regarded Confederation as the outcome of a conference…. If there is to be a change in Confederation, it can be brought about only by renewed conference of the representatives of the people and with unanimity of approval."[28] The *Report*,

therefore, realized his worst fears. Already at odds with Mackenzie King over his handling of the war effort, the Premier drafted a blistering speech for delivery to the Dominion-Provincial Conference in January 1941. He described the Commission's recommendations as "a scrapping of Confederation, that robs the provinces of their fiscal independence and of their full autonomy." When the conference opened he immediately declared that he would not be a party to "national vandalism," to the handing over of the constitution to the tender mercies of any "mushroom government that may in future take office at Ottawa…." When Premier John Bracken of Manitoba suggested that the Ontario leader should show the same breadth of vision that George Brown had displayed in joining the Great Coalition of 1864, Hepburn was defended by his Highways Minister, T.B. McQuesten: "[I]n taking the attitude he has, Hon. Mr. Hepburn has been living up to the tradition of Brown and has defended and upheld all that Brown stood for, and is safeguarding the rights and responsibilities vested in the separate provinces by Confederation."[29] In the face of such opposition the conference hastily adjourned. Hepburn's performance, if not his manners, had been firmly in the Mowat tradition, and the aim of securing provincial consultation concerning constitutional change had at last been achieved.

Although the illustrations given here cover only the period up to the Second World War, there is evidence that Mowat's legacy retains its vitality. Premier William Davis has declared that if federal action is not forthcoming to offset the effects of the 10 per cent surcharge on imports, imposed by President Richard Nixon in August 1971, upon Ontario businesses, then the provincial government will take independent action. Arthur Wishart, attorney general in the Robarts administration, expressed his belief in the Compact theory of Confederation on a number of occasions. And in April 1971, former Premier Robarts attacked the increase in the federal equalization payments drawn from Ontario taxpayers, which he claimed had

27  I.A. Humphries, Observations on a Proposed Method of Amending the British North America Act (n.p., n.d.), pp. 17–18.
28  Royal Commission on Dominion-Provincial Relations, *Statement by the Government of Ontario* (n.p., 1938), Book I, Statement by Premier M.F. Hepburn, pp. 3–4.
29  Mitchell F. Hepburn Papers, draft of speech to Dominion-Provincial Conference, January 1941, p. 14; "Dominion-Provincial Conference, Tuesday, January 14, 1941, and Wednesday, January 15, 1941," pp. 15, 76, in *Dominion-Provincial Conferences*, 1927, 1935, 1941.

risen from $1.4 billion in 1970 to $2 billion in 1971, or over 40 per cent in one year.[30]

Since the Mowat heritage has been so consistent and long-lasting, it seems proper to ask whether it has been a constructive force in Canadian development. Mowat's own achievements have not been kindly dealt with. He has been criticized for misleading the Privy Council, and they for heeding his arguments in favour of provincial rights. It has been pointed out, quite rightly, that Mowat was inspired as much by partisanship as by principle. More important, his heedless use of the provincial rights movement is said to have hindered the development of national feeling in Canada. As early as 1889 D'Alton McCarthy argued that

> The worship of local autonomy, which some gentlemen have become addicted to, is fraught … with great evils to this Dominion. Our allegiance is due to the Dominion of Canada. Our separation into provinces, the rights of local self-government which we possess, is [sic] not to make us less anxious for the promotion of the welfare of the Dominion.

Canada's uncertain response to the economic crisis of the 1930s seemed to many to confirm that Mowat's legal and political guile had subverted the intentions of the Fathers of Confederation. The nation had been reduced to a collection of enfeebled but semi-independent principalities, no longer capable of providing Canada with a minimum level of social and economic services, and resistant to the development of a strong and cohesive national identity.[31]

Mowat and his successors were certainly partisans. They identified their possession of power with the public good. But the very relentlessness with which they pursued their objectives in federal-provincial relations suggests that they sensed a strong, deep-laid Ontario particularism, on which they could draw. The Clear Grits had expressed this feeling

before Confederation, and it did not disappear in 1867. Reinforced by Mowat's political skills and legal successes, it became a resource upon which the politically astute, the Whitneys, the Fergusons, and the Hepburns, could depend. Ontarians resent being the "milk cow" of Confederation, just as much in 1971 as in 1941 or 1885. The Compact theory of Confederation, however shoddy historically or legally, is important as an expression of the province's self-consciousness.

Perhaps, however, sectional loyalties like this do pose a bar to the development of strong national feeling. Certainly, it has usually been assumed that they do so, but David Potter has recently pointed out "the general similarity between nationalism and other forms of group loyalty." The attachment of the citizen to his nation can be a by-product of loyalty to non-national groups and goals, for in Morton Grodzins' words, "… one is loyal not to nation but to family, business, religion, friends. One fights for the joys of his [sic] pinochle club, when he is said to fight for his country." Nationalism and sectionalism are not necessarily antithetical, though they may sometimes conflict. The editor of the *Globe* grasped as much when he wrote in 1883: "Only upon condition that Provincial rights are respected is there any hope of building up a Canadian nationality." National loyalty flourishes not by overpowering other loyalties but by subsuming them and keeping them in a mutually supportive relationship. Loyal Canadians can also be loyal Ontarians.[32]

Professor Maurice Careless has suggested that we should explore "limited identities" in Canada.[33] Big, rich, and successful, Ontario has not hesitated to express its feelings, its distinctive identity. Indeed, its government has been the foremost crusader for

30  For Robarts' speech, see *Globe and Mail*, April 20, 1971.

31  Sir Charles Tupper quoted McCarthy in Canada, House of Commons, *Debates*, March 17, 1896, p. 3700; D.G. Creighton has severely criticized the trend towards decentralization in his essay, "Federal Relations in Canada Since 1914," in Chester Martin, ed., *Canada in Peace and War: Eight Studies in National Trends Since 1914* (Toronto, 1941), p. 48; similar criticisms may be found in F.R. Scott, "The Development of Canadian Federalism," *Proceedings of the Canadian Political Science Association* (1931), pp. 231–58.

32  David M. Potter, "The Historian's Use of Nationalism and Vice Versa," *American Historical Review*, vol. 67 (1962), p. 931; Morton Grodzins, *The Loyal and the Disloyal; Social Boundaries of Patriotism and Treason* (Chicago, 1956), p. 29; *Globe*, February 5, 1883, quoted in Morrison, "Mowat and Provincial Rights," p. 299; John Robarts remarked in the spring of 1971, that Ontario now had the "capability to devise and offer alternatives to major federal policies and programmes. While the alternatives are developed in Ontario, they cannot be based only on an Ontario standpoint. Rather, if they are to serve Ontario's interest, they must represent national alternatives, and by national I do not mean simply federal. They must be based on a recognition of the fact that what is good for Canada is good for Ontario...." *Globe and Mail*, April 20, 1971.

33  J.M.S. Careless, "'Limited Identities' in Canada," *Canadian Historical Review*, L (1969), pp. 1–10.

provincial rights. The cultural and ethnic distinctiveness of Quebec has made it particularist, too, yet
French-Canadian politicians have never been able to
ignore the existence of the minority outside Quebec.
The Manitoba school question showed vividly how
minority rights and provincial rights could collide.
How, then, could French Canadians commit themselves fully to provincial rights for Quebec if this
meant the sacrifice of the diaspora? Federal power,
as they saw, could be called upon to serve ethnic ends,
for the Official Languages Act has a lengthy pedigree.
But Ontario's leaders have been hampered by no such
ambivalence. They have committed themselves fully
to the cause of provincial rights and so given expression to Ontario's particularism or, as some might say,
its imperial ambitions. In this they have reflected the
desire of Ontarians to fasten their version of Canadian
nationalism upon the rest of the country, making little
copies of what they see as the "real" Canada.

Where Mowat led his successors have followed.
He taught them all the moves: how to rally the other
provinces against Ottawa; when to form accords and
when to go it alone; above all, he revealed the value of
persistence and tenacity. He was not an enemy of the

national spirit, but one who understood how it would
develop in a new country, by grafting itself onto older,
deeper, loyalties. His vision of Canada's development
was different from Macdonald's, but time has proved
him more far-sighted. When the Ontario legislature
met in 1897, that stubby, determined, myopic figure
was absent from the premier's chair for the first time
in a quarter of a century. Andrew Pattullo recalled his
past triumphs for the cause of provincial rights. "In
this long series of constitutional victories," Pattullo
told the Assembly,

lies perhaps Oliver Mowat's highest claim to enduring fame and everlasting gratitude of his countrymen. For it was essential to the stability and very
existence of Confederation that the rights and privileges of the Provincial and Federal Governments
should be clearly and justly defined. Without such
just consideration and protection of the rights of
the Provinces by the Privy Council, it is quite certain that the Provinces would not have remained
in the same union.[34]

34  *Globe*, February 12, 1897.

## 16

### Author's Introduction

It is one thing for a government to win a court case. It is quite another thing for a government to cash in on its victory and use the power that appears to flow from the victory. This is certainly true of some of the division of powers cases that the federal government has won as well as some that add to the legal resources of the provinces. Governments certainly like to win these cases because they welcome additions to the resources in their legal arsenal. But the decision to make use of such resources and push the government's presence further into areas where the other level of government has important interests is a political one. Often, as this article shows, political leaders will be cautious about exploiting the full potential of a court victory because they fear a political backlash and will prefer to use the case they have won as leverage in intergovernmental negotiations.

Source: Peter H. Russell, "The Supreme Court and Federal-Provincial Relations: The Political Use of Legal Resources," *Canadian Public Policy* 11(2) (1985): 161–70.

Peter H. Russell

# The Supreme Court and Federal–Provincial Relations: The Political Use of Legal Resources

FROM A PURELY quantitative point of view judicial decisions appear to be a significant factor in federal-provincial relations in Canada. Looking only at the Supreme Court of Canada and decisions reported in the *Supreme Court Reports*, I find that from 1950 (when the Supreme Court took over from the Privy Council as Canada's highest court) to the end of 1982, 158 cases concerned issues arising under Canada's original Constitution and its amendments. Nearly all of these concerned the division of powers between the two levels of government. The main exceptions were three cases dealing with entrenched language rights. The volume of constitutional litigation has increased in recent years: over half (80 out of 158) of all the Supreme Court's constitutional decisions since it became Canada's final court of appeal have been reported in the last eight years, 1975–82.

Not only has the Supreme Court rendered many decisions concerning federal issues but a number of them have involved issues of great political importance. Challenges to the Trudeau Government's anti-inflation program and to provincial energy policies, and questions relating to the conventions governing constitutional amendments readily come to mind. And this is only at the Supreme Court level. There were other cases relating to federal provincial relations decided in the lower courts and not appealed to the Supreme Court. I doubt if the judiciary of any other federation is more active than Canada's in umpiring the federal system.[1]

A great many decisions is one thing. But what overall effect have they had on federal provincial relations? Such a question is prompted by Canada's experience under the Judicial Committee of the Privy Council. The Judicial Committee as Canada's highest court clearly had a decentralizing effect on the federation. Canadians differ as to whether this was a good or bad thing. Scholars differ as to whether it was a correct interpretation of the Constitution. Conventional wisdom in English Canada is that the Judicial Committee reversed the intentions of the Fathers of Confederation, while French Canadians and a few maverick English Canadians, including the author, believe that the Confederation coalition harboured a very complex and somewhat contradictory amalgam of hopes and fears. Historians will never be able to agree on the weight to be attached to the Judicial Committee's decisions as compared with other political, economic and cultural factors in causing Canada to be one of the most decentralized federations. But surely everyone agrees that the overall impact of the Judicial Committee's decisions was decentralizing—and significantly decentralizing at that.

When we turn to an appraisal of the Supreme Court of Canada's influence on the federation it is important to distinguish two kinds of consequences that flow from its decisions. The most immediate results of court decisions are their effect on the legal powers of government. These legal results shape the constitutional capacity of government. But they do not determine how that capacity is used. Here we encounter the political as opposed to the legal consequences of judicial decisions. Government responses to judicial decisions contacting or expanding their powers—the changes they make in policy, the strategies they adopt for constitutional change—are not controlled by law. These political consequences are determined by the intentions and resources of politicians. Constitutional capacity is one of those resources and an important resource, particularly in a society that reveres the rule of law. But it is not the only resource. In a democratic federation it will often be less important than popularity or the general level of allegiance that a level of government enjoys. Thus the political significance of judicial decisions for federal-provincial relations may not be the same as the purely legal results.

## LEGAL RESULTS

First let us briefly consider the main tenor of Supreme Court decisions in terms of their effect on Canada's constitutional law, A few years ago it could be said that the Supreme Court tended to favour the federal government.[2] Such a verdict was based primarily on decisions concerning peace, order and good government, property and civil rights and trade and commerce up to the early 1970s. Since then two scholars, Gilbert L'Ecuyer and Peter Hogg, writing in the later 1970s, have concluded that a review of the Supreme Court's decisions does not show a marked bias towards either level of government but an overall balance (L'Ecuyer, 1978; Hogg, 1979).

I think this verdict of balance is correct so far as constitutional jurisprudence is concerned. Indeed, writing now a few years after L'Ecuyer and Hogg, I would add that the Supreme Court's overall record

shows an uncanny balance. In so many areas the net outcome of its decision making is to strike a balance between federal and provincial powers.

Quantitatively, there has been very little change in the federal victory ratio (federal laws upheld + provincial laws found unconstitutional as a % of all constitutional cases). The federal victory ratio in constitutional decisions of the Supreme Court rose only slightly from 50.5 per cent before 1949 to 54.7 per cent for the two decades following 1949 (Russell, 1975). For 1970 to 1982 the ratio fell a little to 53.9 per cent. But these figures mean very little. One victory in a big case on a major point of constitutional interpretation may be worth many losses in relatively minor cases. It is when we look at the treatment of major points of doctrine that we can see how balanced the Court has been.

With regard to the most important federal powers—peace, order and good government, trade and commerce, taxation and criminal law—the Court has balanced what it has conceded to the central government with one hand by denying federal power or granting power to the provinces with the other. In the *Anti-Inflation* case, peace, order and good government for the first time served as the constitutional basis for a major, peace time federal economic policy.[3] But the Court's majority rejected the expansive national dimensions interpretation of this power which the Court had appeared to endorse in the 1950s and 1960s. The Court, as *Caloil*[4] and the 1978 *Agricultural Marketing Act Reference*[5] indicate, has been more willing than the Judicial Committee to use the trade and commerce power as a basis for federal regulation of economic activity which is essentially although not entirely international or interprovincial. But in *Vapor Canada*[6] and *Labatt*,[7] the Court in vetoing federal economic regulations that were not tied to distinctively interprovincial or international commerce, indicated that it would be very cautious about opening up what sounds like the branch of trade and commerce with the greatest potential—"general regulation of trade affecting the whole Dominion." In *C.I.G.O.L.*[8] it restricted provincial power to tax natural resources, but then in the *Exported National Gas Tax*[9] case it ruled that resources could be immunized from federal taxation if they are owned by the provincial government when they are exported from the province. While the Court in the *Canadian Indemnity Co.*[10] case upheld British

Columbia's 'nationalization' of the automobile insurance despite the interprovincial nature of the industry, in *Central Canada Potash*[11] it would not permit provincial management of a province's natural resources to embrace direct control of international trade in a resource. Overall, the Court's decisions affecting constitutional capacity for economic management have not tilted the balance of power decisively in one direction or the other.

In the criminal justice field the timing has been different but the result the same. The Court's 1978 decisions in *McNeil*,[12] *Dupond*[13] and *Di lorio*[14] capped a long developing tendency to dilute the exclusive federal jurisdiction over criminal law and procedure. These decisions eliminated the division of powers as a significant constitutional protection against provincial encroachments on civil liberties and, in that way, helped pave the way to the Charter. But in another series of cases beginning with *Hauser*,[15] *Corofes*[16] and *Keable*[17] in 1979 and running through *Putnam*[18] to *Canadian Natural Transportation*[19] and *Wetmore*[20] decided in the fall of 1983, the Court has restricted provincial power in the area of prosecuting and policing. As a result, with regard to the enforcement of the criminal law, the Supreme Court appears to have given the central government precisely what it has denied that level with regard to the making of criminal law—namely exclusive constitutional power.

We can see the same kind of balance in the Supreme Court's treatment of the distribution of constitutional powers with respect to the judiciary. Some might regard this as a perverse balance for it is an even-handedness in the distribution of frustration. The Court has attempted to clarify earlier jurisprudence by formulating a test for determining whether provincial administrative tribunals or expansions of provincially appointed judges' functions run afoul of the guarantee of federally appointed provincial judges' jurisdiction based on section 96.[21] While this jurisprudence has enabled a number of provincial innovations in public administration to survive constitutional challenge, still it has not saved them all. Major provincial policies concerned with housing,[22] the unification of family courts,[23] and the regulation of professions[24] have recently foundered on the Supreme Court's enforcement of section 96. However the Court has balanced the books by restricting the federal power to establish

courts under section 101. Its decisions in *McNamara Construction*[25] and *Quebec North Shore*[26] have reduced the jurisdiction of the Federal Court and in *Fuller*[27] destroyed the possibility of overcoming the inconveniences to litigants resulting from its interpretation of section 101. These decisions must reduce federal policy-makers' incentive to make further use of that constitutional power.

In the cultural field we find the same balance. The Court's decision in *Capital Cities*[28] confirmed hegemony in regulating the physical means of broadcasting and in *Dionne*[29] denied Quebec the power to develop local culture through the licensing of Cable TV outlets. But then in *Kellogg's*[30] the Court upheld provincial power to police advertising in the mass media. This decision together with the Court's rejection of federally-enforced product standards in *Labatt*[31] and *Dominion Stores*,[32] leave the provinces with considerably more constitutional clout than Ottawa in the general field of consumer protection.

Most dramatically, the balance can be seen in the Supreme Court's decision on constitutional amendment. In 1979, the Court denied the federal Parliament the power to change the Senate[33] and in 1982 it denied that Quebec had, as a matter of convention, a veto over amendments affecting its powers.[34] In between, in the 1981 *Patriation Reference*,[35] the outcome was the epitome of balance—half a loaf to each side. The Prime Minister could legally proceed to patriate the Constitution with an amending formula and Charter of Rights, but, if he did so without a substantial measure of provincial support, he would violate a convention of the constitution.

When we turn to explaining these decisions it is not easy to find evidence that the balance is the result of the conscious intentions of the justices. As Noel Lyon has pointed out, constitutional theory has not been the Court's long suit.[36] It is only a few judges who have occasionally put forward as a deep underlying premise the importance of maintaining a well-balanced federal system in Canada. There is a bit of this in Justice Beetz's reasons, in the *Anti-Inflation Reference*, for rejecting the national dimensions interpretation of peace, order and good government. The most carefully worked out and eloquent defence of balance that I am aware of is our new Chief Justice's opinion in the *Hauser* case. Ironically this was a dissent, and the historic balance Mr. Justice Dickson appealed to—a primary role for the federal Parliament in making criminal law balanced by a primary role for local authorities in the administration of criminal law—is the very opposite of the balance the Court has been moving towards in criminal justice.

One is tempted to adopt a more Hegelian style of explanation—an explanation in terms of the cunning of institutional history.[37] That is why I have referred to the balance as uncanny. While this will no doubt offend strict empiricists, is it really so mysterious? How often we have observed in other contexts—especially the sports arena—the pressure on umpires or referees to "even things up." Justices of Canada's Supreme Court must feel some of that pressure. After all, they are human too! They are umpiring a contest which the main protagonists—federal and provincial politicians—take very seriously. As umpires they know they have a credibility problem because one side, the federal government, appoints them and constitutionally controls their institution. It may, indeed, turn out that, if the Constitution is ever amended so that this federal control over appointments is modified and the Court becomes a creature of the Constitution, the Court will be under less pressure to retain its credibility.

Whatever the explanation of the balance achieved by the Court, one of its likely effects is to encourage constitutional litigation. Whatever side you are on in a constitutional dispute over the division of powers, the record of balance makes it reasonable to believe you might win. Most constitutional cases in recent years have been initiated by corporations resisting regulation or defence counsel in criminal cases. The frequency with which division of powers arguments have succeeded is an incentive to lawyers to raise constitutional issues at least as an auxiliary line of attack. Once private litigants have commenced constitutional litigation, governments tend to jump in as intervenants to make sure that their constitutional resources are adequately defended and that no opportunity is lost to whittle down the other side's. Governments themselves through the reference case procedure have initiated 16.5 per cent of constitutional litigation since 1950.[38] While governments seldom turn to the Courts as the first arena of combat, a government is quite apt to do so when it is frustrated with political negotiations.

## POLITICAL EFFECTS

Thus, one effect of judicial decision-making on Canada's federal system is simply that it has sustained litigation as a significant phase of federal-provincial relations. But beyond this what effects has it had on federal-provincial relations? One might be tempted to say that because its decisions have not tilted sharply in one direction it has had no significant effect on intergovernmental relations. But this would be a mistaken conclusion. Even though the decisions overall may not have altered the balance of power, many have had an important bearing on policy issues and on the bargaining resources of government.

Two kinds of policy or political effects of constitutional decisions can be distinguished. First, a decision on the division of powers usually means that a particular law stays on the books or is removed. This may have important implications for government policy. Of course, this is not always the case. Sometimes when a law is found *ultra vires*, government is able to achieve pretty much the same policy objective through a better drafted law or using some other constitutional power. Saskatchewan's recovery of oil revenues through an oil well income tax after having other taxes and royalties ruled unconstitutional in *C.I.G.O.L.* is a case in point. Some years ago Barry Strayer pointed out that "our constitution can sustain strong government at either level."[39] As recent initiatives of the federal government in the fields of medical insurance and higher education indicate, the level of a government's activity in a given field of policy depends less on its constitutional resources than on its will to use the resources it has.

But it would be a mistake to stretch this point too far. Court decisions on specific pieces of legislation may not exclude a level of government from a policy field but they will certainly influence the choice of instruments available to government in any given field. A classic example is the way in which the Privy Council's decisions forced the federal government to put its anti-combines legislation in the form of criminal law.[40] This has had important policy ramifications: the criminal justice approach to competition policy has, to say the least, not been very effective. Here it is interesting to note that in the *Canadian National Transportation* case Justice Dickson, in a concurring opinion supported by two other judges, found that the *Combines Investigation Act* could be supported as a general regulation of trade and commerce. Even if this position were to be adopted by a majority of the Court, the power of the big business lobby would seriously constrain the federal government's willingness to use its expanded constitutional resources as the basis for a more effective competition policy.

Besides their direct effect on the policy options of governments, constitutional decisions on the division of powers can have a second kind of effect which may be of more interest to the student of federal provincial relations. This is the effect decisions have on the bargaining strength and position of governments in negotiating policy arrangements or constitutional change. From this perspective constitutional power should be viewed as a political resource just as popularity or a good international economic climate are resources for democratic politicians. Through constitutional litigation governments may gain or lose constitutional capacity in any given field. How governments use their constitutional gains or seek to overcome their losses depends on their political will and skill, and their other resources.

Recent Supreme Court cases provide some fascinating illustrations of court decisions as political resources. The *Patriation Reference* is a textbook example. The federal government was not willing to use the resource it gained in this case—namely the legal power to proceed unilaterally with its constitutional package—because it was apprehensive of the resource its provincial opponents had acquired in the same case—namely the Supreme Court's endorsation of the proposition that unilateralism violates a convention of the Canadian constitution. The provinces, on the other hand, realized that if they remained inflexible in opposition to Mr. Trudeau's package, legally he could and probably would "go it alone." As a consequence both sides went back to the bargaining table with reasonably equal constitutional resources and a compromise resulted.

More often in recent years, it is the federal government that appears to have taken advantage of bargaining resources it has gained from judicial decisions. This is in a political context where the provinces have been on the offensive so far as changing the constitutional division of powers is concerned. For example,

the Supreme Court's decision in the *C.I.G.O.L.* case provided the Trudeau Government with a very handy bargaining resource. The case did not have a significant effect on federal or provincial energy policies. However it gave Trudeau an exclusive power (the power to impose indirect taxes on non-renewable natural resources regardless of their destination) which he could offer to share with the provinces through a constitutional amendment "strengthening" provincial power over resources. Such an amendment was then used to meet the price Mr. Broadbent set for obtaining the federal NDPs support for Trudeau's constitutional package.[41] The other major resource case the federal government won during this period, *Central Canada Potash*, was not nearly so useful, because here the federal government was not willing to modify its exclusive control over foreign trade. Section 92A limits provincial power over non-renewable natural resources exported from the province to interprovincial trade.

The federal victories in the cable television cases, *Capital Cities* and *Dionne*, may be useful, in much the same way, in dealing with Quebec. If a federalist party comes to power in Quebec and demands some constitutional changes in the division of powers, the federal government may be forced to take the renewal of this aspect of federalism half seriously. In such a situation, federal politicians may find that a constitutional amendment partially reversing these cases and giving the provinces, especially Quebec, a share of the regulatory power over cable TV is something they can give up without threatening major policy objectives. It is interesting that immediately following these decisions, the then federal Minister of Communications, Jeanne Sauvé, offered to consider moving in that direction. In federal-provincial relations it is nice to have goodies on the shelf that you can afford to give away if it becomes politically necessary to make concessions.

The Supreme Court's two decisions on off-shore mineral rights (BC in 1967[42] and Newfoundland in 1984[43]) illustrate both what politicians can and cannot do with a court decision favouring their level of government. The political strength of provincialism in Canada is such that federal politicians have not gone ahead and exercised the total and exclusive control over offshore mineral resources to which, by virtue of Court decisions, they are entitled. They have continued to try and negotiate a deal with the provinces over revenue sharing and regulatory control. The decisions, however, greatly increase the federal politicians' bargaining strength in these negotiations. While the federal Liberals are, no doubt, pleased with these judicial outcomes, federal Conservative leaders are in a somewhat different position. Some of them, especially Mr. Mulroney's recently defeated rivals for the Conservative Party leadership, Clarke and Crosbie, appear committed to giving back to Newfoundland by means of a constitutional amendment what the Supreme Court has denied that Province. Such undertakings may put an additional constraint on the extent to which a conservative Government could take advantage of the court victory. For Mulroney that victory may almost be an embarrassment.

Indeed, it is possible that a government may win too much in a constitutional case. The Supreme Court's recent decisions in *Canadian National Transportation* and *Wetmore* may be cases in point. Chief Justice Laskin's majority opinions in these cases are not entirely clear but they seem to give the federal government exclusive power to prosecute federal offences. If that is so, then the provinces may argue that the federal government should fiscally compensate them for their very substantial contribution to what is entirely a central government responsibility. Or, alternatively, the provinces might press for a constitutional amendment which will give them expressly what they believed to be implicitly theirs under their responsibility for the Administration of Justice in the province. Even though, at the level of popular opinion, there may have been some shift of allegiance to the central government in the 1980s, I doubt if an assertion by the federal government of exclusive power over the direction of criminal prosecutions would be politically acceptable in Canada today. Provincial demands resulting from these federal constitutional victories will be difficult to resist. From a political and fiscal point of view, the federal government may have been better off winning less—for example, paramountcy in a concurrent field.

Normally, I should think governments are happy to win as much as they can in constitutional cases, even though they may not be interested in making immediate use of what they have won. The Court's decisions in the *Chicken and Egg Reference*[44] and *Burns Food*[45] restricting the provinces' power to regulate commodities, a portion of which comes in from other provinces, is of assistance to a federal government that wishes to foster competition within the Canadian economic union. However, in agricultural marketing, inter-provincial competition has not been an objective of federal policy. In fact, Ottawa, using the delegation device (a Court created resource for getting around judicial decisions on the division of powers), gave provincial marketing boards the opportunity of setting provincial quotas.[46] Still, the Court decision enabled the federal Minister to orchestrate this structuring of the market—an opportunity which no doubt contributed to his political career.

Although for political reasons a government may not wish to make immediate use of a court victory, the very existence of a judicial decision containing a favourable doctrinal development might be a background factor in intergovernmental relations. Ottawa-Alberta negotiations over energy policy provide an example. No doubt, the federal government would like to have come out of the *Anti-Inflation* case with a more expansive interpretation of peace, order and good government than the Court's majority gave it. Still, the deference the majority showed to federal use of emergency powers was significant. The Trudeau government for political reasons was not interested in using this power to combat continuing high inflation in the late 1970s and early 1980s. It even acted as if it could not on its own introduce a comprehensive system of controls. But in the fight with Alberta over energy pricing, when Premier Lougheed threatened to curtail drastically Alberta's petroleum supplies, the Supreme Court's willingness to attribute virtually unlimited power to Ottawa to deal with an emergency and its unwillingness to question the government's assessment of emergency conditions must have been a comfort to federal strategists. On the other hand, the Court's decision in the *Exported Natural Gas Tax* appeal seems to have set an outer limit on the extent to which Ottawa can control tax revenues from exports. However to use this constitutional resource against the federal government, a province would have to re-arrange the legal ownership of developed resources in a manner that may be politically and ideologically unattractive. For the provinces, this diminishes the political value of the Court's holding in this case.

In certain contexts it is possible for governments to derive some value from losing constitutional cases. This is most likely to be the case for governments involved in agitating for constitutional change. A classic example is René Levesque's attack on the Supreme Court decision in the Quebec veto case as "the end of all illusions" about the possibility of Quebec achieving its proper status within the Canadian federation.[47] More subtle is the way in which provincial losses in section 96 cases have strengthened the provinces' case for an amendment to that section designed to remove the restrictions judicial interpretation have placed on the provinces' freedom to establish administrative tribunals. The Supreme Court's decision in *McEvoy*[48] indicates just how subtle are the political advantages which may result from losing section 96 cases. Here the Court indicated that the judicature sections of the Constitution prevent the federal Parliament as well as the provinces from unifying criminal jurisdiction in an "inferior" provincial court. This gives the federal government a constitutional excuse for not co-operating with provincial proposals to unify criminal or family jurisdiction under provincially-appointed judges.

So win, lose or draw, judicial decisions continue to affect the resources of the chief protagonists in the never-ending struggle for power that goes on within Canadian federalism. Viewed from this perspective we should not expect judicial decisions to tilt the balance of power decisively one way or the other. Instead the practical impact of decisions should be studied in terms of how they combine with the other resources of federal and provincial politicians within a particular political or policy context. In recent years, it is my assessment that despite a reasonable balance in terms of doctrine, as well as quantitatively, Supreme Court decisions on the division of powers have been more useful to federal than to provincial politicians in the struggle over constitutional change. This perhaps has had more to do with the skill and coherence of federal players in the constitutional game than with the inherent value of the resources the Supreme Court has given them.

## THE FUTURE OF CONSTITUTIONAL LITIGATION

In 1958, J.A. Corry suggested that there was some ground for thinking that the Supreme Court of Canada was being retired from "its post as supervisor of the federal balance in Canada ... by forces outside itself."[49] Corry thought that the effectiveness of federal-provincial conferences in resolving disputes and the open-ended nature of the federal government's fiscal powers were such that there should in the future be much less resort to the judicial forum to settle disputes about constitutional powers. However our federal history has not worked out this way. Corry was basking in the warm glow of a co-operative federalism that did not endure. The provinces became more constitutionally aggressive than he anticipated. As inflation increased federal policy-makers could not satisfy all of their ambitions through the spending power.

But if asked to explain why Corry's prediction turned out to be wrong, I would be inclined to give more weight to a factor that is extraneous to federal-provincial relations per se: a general increase in litigiousness. A few of the constitutional decisions handed down by the Supreme Court can be traced to a failure of politicians to resolve an issue through informal bargaining. The *Patriation Reference* and the offshore mineral cases are clear examples. But most cases, as has been pointed out, originated in the private sector when a lawyer representing a corporation, a trade union or an individual raised a constitutional objection to a law or regulation that adversely affected his or her client. In the 25 years since Corry wrote a major expansion of the legal profession and the advent of legal aid have made legal advice much more accessible to Canadians.[50] Government legal departments have expanded, and may have become more independent of political control over litigation decisions. The Supreme Court of Canada's balanced response to federal and provincial claims has, as I have noted, not discouraged constitutional litigation. Indeed, the very sophistication of some of its jurisprudence—for instance its test for determining whether a provincial administrative body is performing a function appropriate for a section 96 superior court judge—sometimes creates new opportunities for resourceful, well-educated lawyers. In addition, the Supreme Court has made constitutional litigation more accessible by being far more generous in granting "standing" to individuals to raise constitutional issues in the courts.[51]

The addition of a constitutional charter of rights adds a whole new dimension to constitutional litigation. There can be no doubt that the Charter of Rights will generate many more cases than the division of powers. But it would be a serious mistake to think that division of powers cases will disappear. In 1983, for example, while the Supreme Court heard 25 requests for leave to appeal in cases involving the Charter of Rights it also heard 13 requests for leave to appeal in cases involving sections 91, 92 and 96 of the "old constitution."[52] Where legislation is challenged on both division of powers and Charter of Rights grounds, the Supreme Court will likely be inclined to treat the former as the threshold issue. If the legislation is found *ultra vires* in a division of powers sense, the court will not have to deal with the Charter issue.[53]

Those, like Paul Weiler who believe that the Canadian federal system might work better if there were no external judicial arbiter and the main political actors had to rely entirely on their capacity for negotiation and compromise to manage conflict, may be dismayed at the continuing significance of the Supreme Court as umpire of the Canadian federal system (Weiler, 1974). But so long as both political and legal power in the Canadian federation are so finely balanced between the two levels of government, disputes over jurisdiction are inescapable. Adjudication and informal negotiation in this context as in others should not be seen as mutually exclusive dispute settlement mechanisms.[54] In federal disputes as in family affairs negotiations in which the two parties work out mutually acceptable solutions is the preferable way of settling conflicts. But the negotiation process may be enhanced rather than impeded when it takes place in the shadow of a creditable and balanced adjudicator. The availability of such an adjudicator may in itself moderate extravagant claims of the protagonists. And when informal negotiations fail, as they often do between passionate and powerful adversaries, it is comforting to be able to turn to a body which can provide an authoritative determination of the legal points at issue. If the Supreme Court of Canada's record as

constitutional umpire does nothing else, it at least establishes the Court's claim to legitimacy in this role.

## NOTES

1 The United States Supreme Court and West Germany's Constitutional Court settle more constitutional cases concerning fundamental rights but not more cases concerning federalism. For a survey of the role of courts as constitutional arbiters in Australia, Canada, Ireland, Japan, the USA and West Germany, see Murphy and Tanenhaus (1977).

2 Peter H. Russell "The Supreme Court's Interpretation of the Constitution from 1949 to 1960," and "The Supreme Court Since 1968" in Fox (1977: 523).

3 *Reference Re Anti-Inflation Act* [1976] 2 S.C.R. 373.

4 *Caloil Inc. v. A.-G. Canada* [1971] S.C.R. 543.

5 *Reference: Re Agriculture Products Marketing* [1978] 2 S.C.R. 1198.

6 *MacDonald v. Vapor Canada Ltd.* [1977] 2 S.C.R. 134.

7 *Labatt v. A.-G. Canada* [1980] 1 S.C.R. 914.

8 *Canadian Industrial Gas & Oil Ltd. v. Government of Saskatchewan* [1978] 2 S.C.R. 545.

9 *Re Exported Natural Gas Tax* [1982] 1 S.C.R. 1004.

10 *Canadian Indemnity Co. v. A.-G. B.C.* [1977] 2 S.C.R. 504.

11 *Central Canada Potash Co. Ltd. and A.-G. Canada v. Gov't of Saskatchewan* [1979] 1 S.C.R. 42.

12 *Nova Scotia Board of Censors v. McNeil* [1978] 2 S.C.R. 662.

13 *A.-G. Canada and Dupond v. Montreal* [1978] 2 S.C.R. 770.

14 *Di Iorio v. Wardens of the Montreal Jail* [1978] 1 S.C.R. 152.

15 *The Queen v. Hauser* [1979] 1 S.C.R. 984.

16 *Cordes v. The Queen* [1978] 1 S.C.R. 1062.

17 *A.-G. Quebec and Keable v. A.-G. Canada* [1979] 1 S.C.R. 218.

18 *A.-G. Alberta v. Putnam* [1981] 2 S.C.R. 267.

19 *A.-G. Canada v. Canadian National Transportation Ltd.* Released Oct. 13, 1983.

20 *The Queen v. Judge Wetmore, Kripps Pharmacy et al.* Released Oct. 13, 1983.

21 See Dickson J.'s formulation of this test in *Re Residential Tenancies Act* [1981] 1 S.C.R. 714.

22 *Ibid.*

23 *Re B.C. Family Relations Act* [1982] 1 S.C.R. 129.

24 *Crevier v. A.-G. Quebec* [1981] 2 S.C.R. 220.

25 *McNamara Construction v. The Queen* [1977] 2 S.C.R. 655.

26 *Quebec North Shore Paper Co. v. C.P.R.* [1977] 2 S.C.R. 1054.

27 *The Queen v. Thomas Fuller Construction* [1980] 1 S.C.R. 695.

28 *Capital Cities Communications v. C.R.T.C.* [1978] 2 S.C.R. 141.

29 *Public Service Board v. Dionne* [1978] 2 S.C.R. 191.

30 *A.-G. Quebec v. Kellogg's Co.* [1978] 2 S.C.R. 211.

31 [1980] 1 S.C.R. 914.

32 *Dominion Stores Ltd. v. The Queen* [1980] 1 S.C.R. 139.

33 *Reference Re Legislative Authority of Parliament to Alter or Replace the Senate* [1980] 1 S.C.R. 54.

34 *Re Objection to a Resolution to Amend the Constitution* [1982] 2 S.C.R. 793.

35 [1981] 1 S.C.R. 753.

36 Noel Lyon, "Constitutional Theory and the Martland-Ritchie Dissent," in Russell, Decary et al. (1982).

37 A somewhat similar explanation of the Judicial Committee's decisions on the Canadian Constitution is offered in Greenwood (1978).

38 Reference cases were most frequent at the beginning and end of the period: of the 26 references between 1950 and 1982, 12 were in the 1950s and 7 in the 1980s. For a review of the use of Reference cases see Strayer (1983).

39 Barry L. Strayer, "The Flexibility of the BNA Act," in Lloyd and McLeod (1968: 216).

40 In re Board of Commerce [1922] 1 A.C. 191 and Proprietary Articles Trade Association v. A.-G. Canada [1931] A.C. 310.

41 Section 92A(4) added by the Constitution Act 1982 to the list of provincial legislative powers.

42 Reference Re The Offshore Mineral Rights of British Columbia [1967] S.C.R. 792.

43 Reference Re Property in and Legislative Jurisdiction Over the Seabed and Subsoil of the Continental Shelf Offshore Newfoundland. Released March 8, 1984. The Supreme Court of Canada's third decision on offshore resources released on May 18, 1984, making a provincial lake out of the sea between Vancouver Island and mainland B.C. appears to be yet another chapter in the Supreme Court's balancing act.

44 A.-G. Manitoba v. Manitoba Egg and Poultry Association et al. [1971] S.C.R. 689.

45 Burns Food Ltd. v. A.-G. Manitoba [1978] 1 S.C.R. 494.

46 With one minor qualification this was upheld by the Supreme Court in Reference Re Agricultural Products Marketing [1978] 2 S.C.R. 1198.

47 Toronto Globe and Mail, Dec. 7, 1982.

48 McEvoy v. A.-G. N.B. [1983] 1 S.C.R. 705.

49 J.A. Corry, "Constitutional Trends and Federalism," in Lower, Scott, et al. (1958).

50 In Ontario, for instance, the ratio of lawyers to population has changed from 1:1142 in 1960 to 1:574 in 1981. See Law Society of Upper Canada (1983).

51 See Strayer (1983) ch. 6.

52 Bulletin of Proceedings taken in the Supreme Court of Canada, February 3, 1984.

53 In Westendorp v. The Queen [1983] 1 S.C.R. 43, Counsel of the appellant abandoned his Charter of Rights challenge to Calgary's by-law prohibiting street-soliciting by prostitutes and won the case on division of powers grounds. The Supreme Court ruled that the by-law encroached upon exclusive federal jurisdiction over criminal law.

54 For an analysis of the relationship between adjudication and informal methods of dispute settlement see Auerbach (1983).

# REFERENCES

Auerbach, Jerold S. (1983) Justice Without Law? Resolving Disputes Without Lawyers (New York: Oxford University Press).

Fox, Paul ed. (1977) Politics: Canada, 4th ed. (Toronto: McGraw Hill-Ryerson).

Greenwood, Murray (1978) "Lord Watson, Institutional Self Interest, and the Decentralization of Canadian Federalism in the 1980s," UBC Law Review, IV: 244.

Hogg, P.W. (1979) "Is the Supreme Court of Canada Biased in Constitutional Cases?" Canadian Bar Review, LVII: 721.

Law Society of Upper Canada (1983) "Report of the Special Committee on the Number of Lawyers," Gazette, XVII:2: 227.

L'Ecuyer, Gilbert (1978) La cour suprème du Canada et le partage des compétences 1949–1978 (Quebec: Gouvernement du Québec, Ministère des Affaires intergouvernementales).

Lloyd, Trevor and Jack McLeod (1968) Agenda 1970: Proposals for a Creative Politics (Toronto: University of Toronto Press).

Lower, A.R.M., F.R. Scott et al. (1958) Evolving Canadian Federalism (Durham, N.C.: Duke University Press).

Murphy, Walter F. and Joseph Tanenhaus (1977) Comparative Constitutional Law (New York: St. Martin's).

Russell, Peter H. (1975) "The Political Role of the Supreme Court of Canada in its First Century," Canadian Bar Review, LIII: 589–90.

——, Robert Decary et al. (1982) The Court and the Constitution (Kingston: Institute of Intergovernmental Relations, Queen's University).

Strayer, Barry L. (1983) The Canadian Constitution and the Courts (Toronto: Butterworths).

Weiler, Paul (1974) In the Last Resort: A Critical Study of the Supreme Court of Canada (Toronto: Carswell).

*Part Four*

# The Judiciary

THE PURPOSE OF this section is to provide insights into the role of the judiciary in constitutional politics and to introduce some of the controversies that have arisen over the years and that continue to shape debate. Judicial review—the power of the courts to nullify actions of the executive and legislative branches of government that are found to conflict with the Constitution—is fundamental to the rule of law in common-law systems. Jennifer Smith opens this section by explaining the emancipation of the process of judicial review in Canada. Just how long a road it was for the courts to establish their independence is the subject of William Lederman's article on the subject. Legislation made by Parliament had been subject to some external review through the Judicial Committee of the Privy Council. Yet, as Alan Cairns explains in his piece that follows Smith's, the JCPC's decisions were often quite controversial, in part because the JCPC was not always forthcoming about the principles it applied in its interpretations. In this article,

among the most quoted to appear in the *Canadian Journal of Political Science*, Cairns defends the JCPC decisions on sociological grounds.

In the following essay, John Saywell delves into the long-standing debate about the logic behind some of the key JCPC decisions that would come to alter irreversibly the course of Canadian federalism. One of Canada's earliest and most influential legal scholars, Frank R. Scott, then reflects on the impact of the JCPC in a witty poem. On its heels follows another classic article by Alan Cairns on the way a document that has seen surprisingly little change to its text can nonetheless prove sufficiently flexible to continue to serve as the country's guiding political framework almost 150 years after it was first written. With the courts playing such a significant role in shaping Canadian constitutional politics, perceptions of potential bias by a court whose members are federally appointed are not far-fetched. The extent to which these premonitions pan out is the subject of Peter Hogg's essay, which closes this section.

## 17

### Author's Introduction

The origins of judicial review in this country have been the subject of debate among legal scholars. This selection examines the conflicting accounts provided by W.R. Lederman and B.L. Strayer and attempts to assess them in the light of the Confederation debate, 1864–67, and the debate surrounding passage of the *Supreme Court Act* in 1875. It arrives at these considerations: that the intentions of the founders are of greater significance than has hitherto been suggested; that both the founders themselves and the legislators in 1875 held conflicting expectations on the role of the Supreme Court in constitutional matters; and that this conflict has left its mark on the court. This article concludes that reflection on the origins of judicial review ought to temper the enthusiasm with which many Canadians have greeted the advent of the Charter of Rights and Freedoms.

Source: Jennifer Smith, "The Origins of Judicial Review in Canada," in *Law, Politics, and the Judicial Process in Canada*, ed. Ted Morton (Calgary: University of Calgary Press, 1987), 433–41.

Jennifer Smith

# The Origins of Judicial Review in Canada

FOR MANY YEARS, students have been taught that the practice of judicial review in Canada is less important than it is in the United States. This is because it has had less scope, and it has had less scope because until recently Canada's written constitution, unlike the American Constitution, included no bill of rights. Whereas in both countries the courts, acting as "umpires" of their respective federal forms of government, have had the power to declare laws beyond the competence of the jurisdiction enacting them, the American courts have had the additional and, to many, fascinating power to enforce against governments the guarantees of the rights of citizens contained in the Bill of Rights. Obviously this line of comparison is outmoded now. After a prolonged and at times bitter debate, the federal government and nine of the ten provincial governments reached agreement last year on a set of amendments to the *British North America Act*, among them a Charter of Rights and Freedoms. As a result, the breadth of the courts' power of judicial review more closely approximates that possessed by their American counterparts. Is this development consistent with the nature of Canada's constitutional arrangements? Does the Charter provide the basis of the completion of an initially limited power? ...

... One of the most thorough studies available is B.L. Strayer's *Judicial Review of Legislation in Canada*.

Strayer argues that the BNA Act, 1867 and related acts did not vest explicitly in the courts the power of judicial review. Nor can our common law inheritance be held responsible for it. Instead, judicial review is a product of the British colonial system, "implicit in the royal instructions, charters, or Imperial statutes creating the colonial legislatures." Since these legislatures were bodies of limited power, the colonial charters establishing them typically included clauses prohibiting them from passing laws repugnant to Imperial statutes....

... As early as the fifteenth century, it was customary for the King's Privy Council rather than English domestic courts to hear appeals arising out of colonial matters. This practice was regulated by the Privy Council Acts of 1833 and 1844, which established the Judicial Committee of the Privy Council, specified its membership, and authorized it to hear appeals from colonial courts. Thus the Judicial Committee acted as the highest appellate court for the colonies. As Strayer points out, it showed no inclination to question its authority to review the validity of colonial legislation, undoubtedly because the colonies themselves possessed only limited or subordinate legislative powers. He attributes considerable importance to the precedent it set throughout the Empire for the exercise of a similar power by colonial courts. According to Strayer, we must look to the British colonial system, and especially its doctrine of judicial review of colonial legislation, for the origin of judicial review in Canada: "The constitutional law of the Empire in 1867 apparently embraced the convention that where legislative powers were granted subject to limitations the courts would enforce those limitations. The BNA Act was drafted and enacted in this context." ...

... Thus he [Strayer] is faced with the fact that following Confederation, the Canadian courts took up the power of judicial review, and concludes that this was the result of both pre-Confederation practice and the federal character of the new constitution: "There was a continuity of judicial practice because the Imperial structure had not changed basically.... Colonial legislatures, whether Dominion or provincial, were limited legislatures, and courts could enforce the limitations." The inner logic of federalism with its distribution of legislative powers pointed to the need for something like the kind of judicial enforcement that pre-Confederation practice had established.

Strayer's search for an explanation of judicial review arises out of his insistence that it is not "absolute," that is, not fully guaranteed in the BNA Act. In his opinion, the relevant clauses of the Act gave Parliament and the local legislatures too much regulatory power over the courts to support such a view, power more in keeping with the principle of parliamentary as opposed to judicial supremacy. Indeed, according to W.R. Lederman, Strayer implies that an "element of judicial usurpation" figures in its establishment, an implication Lederman cannot accept. By contrast, Lederman reads into sections 96 to 100 of the Act an "intention to reproduce superior courts in the image of the English central royal courts." If he can demonstrate that these English courts had acquired a "basic independence" enabling them to withstand even the undoubted supremacy of the British Parliament, then courts deliberately modelled after them in Canada would assume a similar status. In "The Independence of the Judiciary," Lederman undertakes such a demonstration....

... Strayer takes note of this argument and dismisses it by observing that the jurisdiction of Lederman's royal courts was subject to the British Parliament's control and that in any event it never included the power to review the validity of Parliament's acts "in spite of the pretensions of Coke and others." Canadian

superior courts can hardly claim by inheritance an inviolable right of judicial review their English forebears never possessed. Lederman's rejoinder is that Canadian courts, both before and after 1867, have never faced legislatures equipped with the full supremacy of the British Parliament. Indeed, until 1931 they dealt with subordinate colonial legislatures, and while the Statute of Westminster substituted equality in the place of subordination, the constitution itself remained a British statute. Thus the power to review acts of subordinate bodies undertaken by Canadian courts before 1931 was well established by "history, custom, precedent, and the needs of federalism" and after 1931 merely continued as a matter of course.... Yet a closer examination of the framers' views may throw some light on this debate.

According to the records of the Quebec Conference edited by Joseph Pope, Macdonald alluded to the need for some form of judicial review in his initial argument on the desirability of federal union. Having put the case for a strong central government, he warned the delegates not so much of the importance of provincial governments per se but of the need of the people in each "section" to feel protected, that is, secure from the reach of an overweening central authority. One way of encouraging this feeling was to provide a guarantee of the test of legality against which centralist incursions on sectional matters might be measured. Since the new constitution would take the form of a British statute, he continued, British courts could supply an answer to the question, "Is it legal or not?" The availability of some form of judicial arbitration might satisfy local partisans fearful of abandoning local autonomy to the mercies of a strong central power.

The issue was raised once more towards the end of the Quebec Conference, again in connection with the extent of jurisdiction appropriate to local governments. R.B. Dickey of Nova Scotia, expressing some sympathy for the opinion of E.B. Chandler of New Brunswick that the delegates were in danger of establishing a legislative rather than a federal union by insisting on reserving all unspecified subject matters to the central government, proposed a "Supreme Court of Appeal to decide any conflict between general and state rights." He was supported by George Brown, leader of the "Grits" in Upper Canada, who suggested that provincial courts determine jurisdictional disputes, with provision for appeal to a superior court. Both men appeared to contemplate a Canadian court of last resort on constitutional questions. Jonathan McCully of Nova Scotia, however, disputed this proposal. Throughout the Conference, he had made no bones about his preference for a legislative over a federal union, although he was prepared to accept a highly centralized form of federalism. From this perspective, he succinctly stated the difficulty posed by a constitutional court: "Mr. Brown will land us in [the] position of [the] United States by referring [the] matter of conflict of jurisdiction to [the] courts. You thus set them over the General Legislature." ...

... In the Maritime provinces, even less attention was paid to the issue despite the fact that a number of anti-Confederates were sorely exercised by what they deemed the insufficiently federal character of the proposed scheme.... Their major concern was the lack of any provision for the scheme's amendment, but in an aside they observed that the "wise framers" of the American Constitution had given the Supreme Court the "power to decide all questions of jurisdiction and authority, between the general Government and those of the several States." The Quebec scheme, by contrast, did not require the establishment of any such court. Indeed, in their view, it contained no safeguards at all for the provinces in the event of conflict between their legislatures and the central Parliament. Guided by the American example, they recommended establishment of a tribunal authorized to decide disputes arising out of the division of powers. In New Brunswick A.J. Smith, recently defeated by Tilley's pro-union party in a second election over the Confederation issue, similarly advocated "a court for the determination of questions and disputes that may arise between the Federal and Local governments as to the meaning of the Act of Union."

Such clearly worded statements indicated a view of federalism rather more in line with the American example than that set out in the Quebec scheme. Taken together with the views expressed at the Quebec Conference and in the debate in the Parliament of Canada, they also suggest that no one had any illusions about the significance of judicial review, particularly as it related to the distribution of legislative powers between Parliament and the local legislatures. The point at issue was whether the type of federalism

set out in the Quebec Resolutions required it. Under the Resolutions, the central government possessed the power to disallow local laws just as the British government retained the power to disallow Parliament's enactments, a parallel feature not unnoticed by critics of the scheme like Christopher Dunkin. Disallowance not only undermined the need for judicial arbitration, whether by the Judicial Committee or a national court, it also suited partisans of parliamentary supremacy like Jonathan McCully, who clearly understood the threat to this supremacy posed by a tribunal patterned after the American Supreme Court.

The question of whether to establish a final appellate court was settled eight years after Confederation when Parliament finally used the power it possessed under section 101 of the BNA Act. The debate at the time is illuminating, since in picking up the threads of the earlier arguments it does so in the light of some years' experience of union. It also reveals an attitude towards the new court and its power of judicial review somewhat at variance with that held today....

... While the constitutionality of the bill was generally accepted, there remained the question of members' understanding of the Court's position in relation to the central government. Here opinions varied. In introducing the bill, Fournier stressed the need for a court to settle disputes arising out of conflicting jurisdictional claims, particularly when the extent of provincial powers was in question. In this sense he portrayed the proposed court as the completion of the "young construction" established at Confederation, citing earlier remarks by Cartier and Macdonald in support of this view. Along side the notion of the court as an impartial arbiter, however, there is present in his speech the rather different view of it as a substitute for the failing remedy of disallowance. As he explained, the government was required daily to "interfere" with provincial legislation considered *ultra vires* the provinces' jurisdiction, and it was falling behind in the task. The result was that the statute books were filled with an "enormous mass of legislation" of dubious constitutionality, leaving citizens uncertain about what was and was not law. In light of this definition of the problem, namely, the excesses of provincial legislatures, the suggestion that the new court could resolve it more speedily than the central government's power of disallowance must have struck his listeners as doubtful.

Indeed, it quickly became clear he was seeking legitimacy, not speed. The Governor-General, he pointed out, could disallow provincial laws only on the advice of the federal cabinet, in turn advised by law officers of the Department of Justice, and this state of affairs, predictably, was "not satisfactory." What was needed was a tribunal whose decisions—especially those adverse to the provinces—were acceptable to all parties. Apparently Fournier viewed his "independent, neutral and impartial court" as an instrument of the central government. He contended that Ottawa needed "an institution of its own" in order to ensure proper execution of its laws because, however contrary to the spirit of Confederation, the time might come when "it would not be very safe for the Federal Government to be at the mercy of the tribunals of the provinces."

Some members feared that the powers conferred on the court would conflict with the principle of parliamentary supremacy. An Ontario member, Moss, excused the length of his speech by emphasizing the gravity of establishing a tribunal whose power to determine jurisdictional disputes finally rendered it "paramount" to Parliament itself. Rejecting this view, Macdonald interpreted the Court's role under the "Special Jurisdiction" clauses as one of informing the "conscience" of the government. It would function simply as an adviser to the government in much the same way as the Judicial Committee did when asked for advice by the British Crown. Macdonald's view was consistent with Fournier's exposition of these clauses for, as noted earlier, the Minister of Justice had stated that the Court's decisions in such instances were to have the same effect as its decisions in reference questions, namely, a kind of "moral weight." Since moral weight undoubtedly influences but does not command, it would appear that for both men the supremacy of Parliament remained unimpaired. Their position seemed well grounded for neither the reference case provision nor the special jurisdiction clauses gave the new court's opinions the status of legal judgments. Yet many of their colleagues assumed that it did, especially Robert Haythorne, a Liberal senator from Prince Edward Island, who warned members that "their power of interpretation [on constitutional matters] ceased when the bill passed."

Concern over the precise nature of the Court's advisory function on constitutional questions surfaced again in discussion of the reference case clause. Moss thought it "extreme" that the Governor-General in Council might ask the court for an opinion on any matter, since this would result in the Governor-General relying on others for the advice "he ought under our system of Government to obtain from his responsible advisers." However, he was persuaded that the practice was not incompatible with responsible government on the ground that the British, the greatest authorities on responsible government, used the Judicial Committee in the same manner. Others were not so easily persuaded. Senator Haythorne argued that a ministry under pressure to exercise its power of disallowance might be tempted to refer a provincial act to the court for an opinion on its constitutionality, thus relieving itself of the burden of taking a decision and defending it before Parliament. He also thought it unwisely mixed law and politics because it substituted judicial review for disallowance, that is, a judicial ruling in the place of a political decision. From this flowed his third objection, namely, that judicial review was a greater threat to the small provinces' legislative programme than the power of disallowance since any ministry advising the Crown to exercise the latter power was required to defend publicly its advice in the Commons and, more important, the Senate, the very institution in which the provinces could expect support. The Court's opinion faced no such political test....

... Yet while both the constitution and practical necessity apparently pointed in the same direction, members of Parliament clearly entertained two different views of the role of the proposed court in the very area that was thought to stand most in need of its services, namely, jurisdictional conflicts. As is evident from the above, some saw in the court an instrument of the federal government that would enable it to deal more satisfactorily with provincial pretensions. How else to interpret Senator Scott's contention?: "The fact that so many of the Acts in the different Provinces were *ultra vires* showed that a bill of this kind was necessary." The raft of suspect provincial statutes, for Scott, posed a problem for which the central government was inadequately equipped. But why was it ill equipped when it possessed the power of disallowance? As noted earlier, for Fournier the central government's problem was its inescapable partisanship. Only a court and its long-standing reputation of nonpartisanship could tame the aggression of the provinces without provoking bitter controversy. Left unstated was the assumption that the central government, by contrast, was unlikely to experience the embarrassment of an adverse ruling in its exercise of legislative power. Thus the view of the court as a tribunal whose very impartiality would serve the federal cause ignored the obvious tension between that impartiality and the central government's partisanship. The opinion of men like Macdonald that the proposed bill must not and, indeed, did not affect the principle of parliamentary supremacy simply overlooked it in favour of the central government. Had he not said that the special jurisdiction clauses were "principally for the purpose of informing the conscience of the Government"? Despite his interest in setting up the court, he was obviously unwilling to relinquish ultimate determination of the constitution to it.

At the same time, as we have seen, many supposed that the new court did signal a shift from the central government's control over the distribution of legislative powers to judicial determination of disputes arising out of it. It might be objected that this view was as incorrect as Macdonald's on the grounds that the executive's control in this respect was only partial to begin with, limited to supervision of provincial enactments through its power of disallowance, and that Parliament's own enactments in turn were subject to disallowance by the British government. Moreover, the Judicial Committee, representing the judicial mode of constitutional arbitration, had retained its position as the highest court of appeal for the new colony at the outset of Confederation. Nevertheless, it is clear that for many participants in the debate, the Court's institution spelled a retreat from the executive fiat of disallowance in favour of the judicial remedy. And they assumed, contrary to Macdonald's supposition, that its jurisdiction would extend to impugned federal as well as provincial enactments. Indeed, opponents of the court, such as Senator Kaulbach of Nova Scotia, criticized it precisely because it would "take from this Parliament the right to decide constitutional questions." ...

... In the event it appears that those who subscribed to the second view were closer to the mark. Certainly the new Supreme Court agreed with them. As Strayer points out, in its first reported constitutional decision, *Severn v. the Queen* (1878), the court, "without showing any hesitation concerning its right to do so," found an Ontario licensing statute invalid on the ground that it interfered with Parliament's jurisdiction over trade and commerce. The following year, in *Valin v. Langlois*, it reviewed and upheld the Dominion Controverted Elections Act, 1874 as a valid exercise of Parliament's legislative power. In the latter case, Chief Justice Ritchie set out the Court's power of judicial review with unmistakable clarity:

> In view of the great diversity of judicial opinion that has characterized the decisions of the provincial tribunals in some provinces, and the judges in all, while it would seem to justify the wisdom of the Dominion Parliament, in providing for the establishment of a Court of Appeal such as this, where such diversity shall be considered and an authoritative declaration of the law be enunciated, so it enhances the responsibility of those called on in the midst of such conflict of opinion to declare authoritatively the principles by which both federal and local legislation are governed.

Commenting on Ritchie's declaration, Strayer states: "And so the Canadian courts were launched on a course from which they have never swerved. The ease with which they could take up judicial review of legislation after Confederation must have been the result of the situation existing prior to 1867." He nowhere suggests that the Chief Justice might have based his understanding of the Court's role on the terms of the Supreme Court Act or the expectations of many of those who participated in its passage four years earlier. But then, as indicated earlier, Strayer pays little attention to the debate surrounding its passage. Thus he is open to Lederman's charge, namely, that his argument implies an assumption of judicial review on the part of the court, an assumption possibly unwarranted. Yet Lederman too ignores the very debate in the light of which Ritchie's view is surely intelligible. The Chief Justice clearly favoured the side of those who, like Moss, thought that the proposed court would be able "to determine the [constitutional] controversy finally, virtually therefore, the Supreme Court could overrule the decisions of this legislature."

Although the Chief Justice's generous conception of the court's role in constitutional matters reaffirmed both the hopes and fears of those who supposed its decisions would be as authoritative as he claimed they were, the notion of the court as an instrument of the central government was not wholly eliminated. There remained the reference case provision of the Supreme Court Act, which obliged the court to advise the executive on any question referred to it. To the extent that this obligation is understood as an executive advisory function as opposed to a judicial one, it recalls Macdonald's view of the court as an aid to the government, or the "conscience" of the government. If so, it is hardly surprising that the provinces were uncomfortable with the comprehensiveness of the reference case provision, especially since it enabled the government to refer provincial laws to the court for a ruling on their validity. In the event, Parliament's competence to enact it was tested before the Judicial Committee in *Attorney-General for Ontario* v. *Attorney-General for Canada* (1912). The provinces choosing to intervene argued that it imposed an executive function on the court and thereby violated section 101 of the BNA Act, which permitted Parliament to establish a tribunal possessed of judicial powers only. In his judgment delivered on behalf of the Judicial Committee, Earl Loreburn, L.C., appeared to accept their contention that the Court's task in the reference case was in essence merely advisory and therefore nonjudicial, but he did not consider this fatal to its judicial character as a whole....

... The competing views of the court apparent at its inception have left their mark on it. For example, those who approve its role as umpire of the federal system are critical of the fact that its establishment was permitted rather than required under the terms of the BNA Act, that its members are appointed formally by one level of government rather than both, and that the reference case procedure remains. On the other hand, partisans of parliamentary supremacy, understandably less enamoured of the American Supreme Court whose example inspires the criticisms just mentioned, prize these very features as symbols of the Court's ultimate dependence on the will of Parliament. This tension between the Court's judicial independence and the claims of the executive figures in the debate between Lederman and Strayer. Lederman, seeking to strengthen and reaffirm its independence, prefers to locate the origins of its power of judicial review in both the tradition of the old English royal courts and the logic of federalism, that is, beyond the reach of Parliament. Thus the intentions of the legislators who founded the Court are of little interest to him. By ignoring them, he avoids confronting not only the view of those who supposed they were withholding the full power of judicial review but, more important, the opinion of those who assumed that Parliament could confer it. As a result, he overlooks the possibility that judicial review was deliberately, if tentatively, advanced as a remedy for the failing power of disallowance. In short, since Lederman wishes to secure judicial review, he cannot derive it from anything so precarious as legislators' intentions. This leaves him open to the criticism implied in Strayer's thesis. Strayer, much more sensitive to the claims of the executive, highlights the limitations on the Court's power to review legislative enactments. Yet he is left with the new Court's easy assumption of the power, and since he too disregards the debate surrounding its establishment he looks beyond Parliament to past colonial practice. Thus he does not see the tension between judicial review and executive claims which he ably expands as a reflection of clashing legislative intentions.

Viewed in the light of the older controversy about the Court, the debate culminating in the recent set of amendments contained in the Constitution Act, 1982 took a familiar turn. In the earlier contest, both opponents and partisans of judicial review focused attention on its implications for the distribution of legislative powers so critical to the shape of the country's federalism. While some saw in it a solution to conflicts arising out of competing jurisdictional claims, others interpreted it as a direct challenge to their presumption in favour of Parliament's control of the constitution. Over a century later, the issue of judicial versus parliamentary supremacy surfaced again in connection with the proposed Charter of Rights and Freedoms. Prime Minister Pierre Trudeau, a determined champion of the notion of a charter, often defended his cause without even referring to the task it necessarily imposes on the courts. Instead, he claimed that it would "confer power on the people of Canada, power to protect themselves from abuses by public authorities." A charter would liberate people by preventing governments from denying specified freedoms. On the other hand, opponents of the idea like the then Premier of Saskatchewan, Allan Blakeney, attempted to counter the undeniable appeal of this claim by drawing attention to the role of the courts that it implied. According to Blakeney, including rights in a written constitution means transferring responsibility for them from duly elected legislatures, the democratic seat of governments, to nonelected tribunals. It amounts to requiring the courts to make "social judgments" in the course of interpreting a charter's clauses, judgments which, in his view, properly belong to "the voters and their representatives." In the event, a Charter of Rights and Freedoms now forms part of Canada's newly amended constitution. Are we entitled to conclude, then, that acceptance of the Charter, and the increased scope for judicial review that it entails, signals a resolution of the issue of parliamentary versus judicial supremacy in favour of the latter? The answer is not quite.

It is true, as Peter Russell points out, that section 52 of the Constitution Act, 1982, by declaring the Constitution of Canada to be the "supreme law" and any law inconsistent with its provisions to be of "no force or effect," gives the courts' power to invalidate unconstitutional laws an explicit constitutional footing for the first time. Further, under the provisions of the new amending formula, the composition of the Supreme Court is protected from easy change by the stringent requirement of unanimity on the part of the Senate, the House of Commons and provincial legislative assemblies. The Court is also listed under section 42(1) as an item that can be amended only in accordance with the general formula set out in section

38(1). Thus the court is constitutionally entrenched. However, neither the federal government's power to appoint Supreme Court justices nor the nonjudicial advisory task required by the reference mechanism is affected. More important still is the fact that the Charter itself, to the disappointment of its partisans, contains a provision enabling the legislative bodies of both levels of government to override some of its guarantees, namely, those dealing with fundamental freedoms, legal rights, and equality rights. The provision is qualified to the extent that legislatures choosing to avail themselves of it are required to declare expressly their intention and reconsider the matter every five years, and there has been speculation about the likely effect of these qualifications on politicians' willingness to resort to the "override." Nevertheless, its very appearance in the context of the Charter strikes an incongruous note and is testimony to the strength of the lingering tradition of parliamentary supremacy. Finally, there is the first clause of the Charter which subjects its guarantees to "such reasonable limits prescribed by law as can be demonstrably justified in a free and democratic society." Ultimately it is up to the Supreme Court to stake out the "reasonable limits." In the meantime, we do know that they are held to exist, that there is thought to be something higher than, or beyond the Charter's guarantees to which appeal can be made in order to justify their denial or restriction. And the initiative in this regard is secured to governments. While the courts' power of judicial review has undoubtedly surmounted the rather narrow, partisan function envisaged for the new Supreme Court in 1875 by Macdonald, the principle of parliamentary supremacy persists.

# 18

## *Author's Introduction*

This article was my contribution to the debate over the performance of the Judicial Committee of the Privy Council in interpreting the *British North America Act.*

In the depression of the 1930s, legal scholarship in English Canada launched a barrage of criticisms in extremely harsh language of the JCPC's performance. The critics were deeply troubled by the incapacity of the federal government to grapple with the evils of the Depression, an incapacity they blamed on the JCPC.

There were two streams of criticisms. One argued that Canada had begun its constitutional life with the 1867 *BNA Act*, which these critics viewed as the framework for a centralized federalism with the central government playing the leading role which, they argued, was what Canada needed in that deeply troubled Depression decade. The blame for leading Canada away from the wisdom of the fathers of the 1867 Constitution was affixed on the JCPC, especially several provincializing decisions in the 1880s and 1890s, as well as in the Depression itself. The solution was to correct the judicial errors that had turned the constitution on its head. These critics I called the fundamentalists who, in effect, said let us stick to the clear understanding of the Fathers of Confederation that Canada was to be a centralized polity. A profoundly different criticism was made by what the article called the constitutionalists. They argued that the failure of the JCPC was its inability to understand that its responsibility was to bring the *BNA Act* up-to-date by interpretations that would be sensitive to the evolving contemporary requirements of governance.

The supporters of these two views, labelled fundamentalists and constitutionalists, obviously held contradictory views of the judicial role, although several commentators managed to hold both views simultaneously. In sum, the article concludes that the incoherence of, or internal contradictions in criticisms of, the JCPC reflected an immature Canadian jurisprudence.

Source: Alan C. Cairns, "The Judicial Committee and Its Critics," in *Constitution, Government and Society in Canada: Selected Essays by Alan C. Cairns,* ed. Douglas E. Williams (Toronto: McClelland and Stewart, 1988) pp. 45–85, notes 261–81.

Alan C. Cairns

# The Judicial Committee and Its Critics

THE INTERPRETATION OF the British North America Act by the Judicial Committee of the Privy Council is one of the most contentious aspects of the constitutional evolution of Canada. As an imperial body the Privy Council was unavoidably embroiled in the struggles between imperialism and nationalism which accompanied the transformation of Empire into Commonwealth. As the final judicial authority for constitutional interpretation its decisions became material for debate in the recurrent Canadian controversy over the future of federalism. The failure of Canadians to agree on a specific formula for constitutional amendment led many critics to place a special responsibility for adjusting the BNA Act on the Privy Council, and then to castigate it for not presiding wisely over the adaptation of Canadian federalism to conditions unforeseen in 1867.

Given the context in which it operated it is not surprising that much of the literature of judicial review, especially since the depression of the thirties, transformed the Privy Council into a scapegoat for a variety of ills which afflicted the Canadian polity. In language ranging from measured criticism to vehement denunciation, from mild disagreement to bitter sarcasm, a host of critics indicated their fundamental disagreement with the Privy Council's handling of its task.

Lords Watson and Haldane have been caricatured as bungling intruders who, either through malevolence, stupidity, or inefficiency channelled Canadian development away from the centralized federal system wisely intended by the Fathers.[1]

This article will survey the controversy over the performance of the Privy Council. Several purposes will be served. One purpose, the provision of a more favourable evaluation of the Privy Council's conduct, will emerge in the following discussion. This, however, is a by-product of the main purpose of this article: an assessment of the quality of Canadian jurisprudence through an examination of the most significant, continuing constitutional controversy in Canadian history. The performance of the Privy Council raised critical questions concerning the locus, style, and role of a final appeal court. An analysis of the way in which these and related questions were discussed provides important insights into Canadian jurisprudence.[2]

## VARIETIES OF CRITICISM

Criticisms of the Privy Council can be roughly separated into two opposed prescriptions for the judicial role.[3] One camp, called the constitutionalists in this essay, contained those critics who advocated a flexible, pragmatic approach so that judges could help to keep the BNA Act up to date. Another camp, called the fundamentalists, contained those who criticized the courts for not providing a technically correct, logical interpretation of a clearly worded document.

According to the fundamentalists the basic shortcoming of the Privy Council was its elementary misunderstanding of the Act. The devotees of this criticism, who combined a stress on the literal meaning of the Act with a widespread resort to historical materials surrounding Confederation, had four main stages in their argument.[4] Naturally, not all critics employed the full battery of arguments possible.

1. The initial requirement was the provision of documented proof that the Fathers of Confederation intended to create a highly centralized federal system. This was done by ransacking the statements of the Fathers, particularly John A. Macdonald, and of British officials, for proof of centralist intent. Given the known desire of some Fathers for a "legislative union," or the closest approximation possible in 1867, a plethora of proof was readily assembled.

2. The next logical step was to prove that the centralization intended was clearly embodied in the Act.[5] This was done by combing the Act for every indication of the exalted role assigned to Ottawa and the paltry municipal role assigned to the provinces. This task required little skill. Even the least adept could assert, with convincing examples, that the division of powers heavily favoured Ottawa. If additional proof seemed necessary the dominance of the central government could also be illustrated by referring to the provisions of the Act dealing with the disallowance and reservation of provincial legislation, and with the special position of the lieutenant governor as a federal officer.

Once concordance was proved between what the Fathers intended and what they achieved in the Act the critics could then delve into a vast grab bag of pre-Confederation sources for their arguments. This greatly increased the amount of material at their disposal, and strengthened their claim that a prime reason for Privy Council failure was its unwillingness to use similar materials.

3. The third feature of this fundamentalist approach was a definition of the judicial role which required of judges no more and no less than the technically correct interpretation of the Act to bring out the meaning deliberately and clearly embodied in it by the Fathers. Where necessary the judges were to employ the methods of historical research in performing this task. This point was explicitly made by H.A. Smith in his criticism of the English rule against extrinsic evidence in the interpretation of statutes. This, he asserted, was to forbid the courts "to adopt historical methods in solving a historical problem." The consequences were grave:

> … an arbitrary and unreasonable rule of interpretation has produced the very serious result of giving Canada a constitution substantially different from that which her founders intended that she should have. A study of the available historical evidence gives us a clear and definite idea of what the fathers

of Canadian confederation sought to achieve. By excluding this historical evidence and considering the British North America Act without any regard to its historical setting the courts have recently imposed upon us a constitution which is different, not only in detail but also in principle, from that designed at Charlottetown and Quebec.[6]

In brief, the judge, like Ranke's ideal historian, was to find out "the way it really was," and then apply his historical findings to the cases which came before him.

4. Proof that the Fathers had intended and had created a centralized federal system in the terms of the BNA Act, coupled with the transformation of the judge into a historian, provided conclusive evidence of the failure of the Judicial Committee. This was done by contrasting the centralization intended and statutorily enacted with the actual evolution of the Canadian polity towards a more classical decentralized federalism, an evolution to which the courts contributed. Since the judges were explicitly directed to apply the Act literally it was obvious that they had bungled their task. As W.P.M. Kennedy phrased it, their "interpretations cannot be supported on any reasonable grounds. They are simply due to inexplicable misreadings of the *terms* of the Act."[7] The same point was made in more polemical fashion by J.T. Thorson in a parliamentary debate on the Privy Council's treatment of the Bennett New Deal legislation:

> … they have mutilated the constitution. They have changed it from a centralized federalism, with the residue of legislative power in the dominion parliament, to a decentralized federalism with the residue of legislative power in the provinces—contrary to the Quebec resolutions, contrary to the ideas that were in the minds of the fathers of confederation, contrary to the spirit of confederation itself, and contrary to the earlier decisions of the courts. We have Lord Haldane largely to blame for the damage that has been done to our constitution.[8]

In summary, the fundamentalists simply asserted that the Privy Council had done a bad job in failing to follow the clearly laid out understandings of the Fathers embodied in the BNA Act. O'Connor, the author of the most influential criticism of the Privy Council, viewed their decisions as indefensible interpretations of a lucidly worded constitutional document. He felt that the act was a marvellous instrument of government, the literal interpretation of which would have been perfectly consonant with the needs of a changing society.[9] The same literal criticism was brandished by a critic of the decision in *Toronto Electric Commissioners* v *Snider* who "arose in his place in the House of Commons and protested against 'a condition which allows the Judicial Committee … to shoot holes in our constitution.'"[10] For such critics the failure was technical, a simple case of misinterpretation. All critics who appealed to the intentions of the Fathers or to the clearly expressed meaning of the Act when criticizing the "deviations" of the Judicial Committee fell into this category. Since this gambit was almost universal, this fundamentalist criticism was widespread.[11]

In documenting the emasculation of federal authority critics concentrated on the opening "peace, order, and good government" clause of section 91, and on 91 (2), dealing with "the regulation of trade and commerce." The former, "the foundation of Macdonald's whole federal system,"[12] was the "favourite whipping-boy of most of the articles and comments on Canadian constitutional law.…"[13] According to critics, the peace, order and good government clause was clearly designed to be the primary grant of federal authority with the enumerated clauses being illustrative, or "for greater certainty but not so as to restrict the generality" as section 91 declared. The destruction of the utility of the residuary clause, and its subsequent partial revival as a source of emergency power, evoked a series of violent critiques from a host of embittered commentators.[14]

The Privy Council's handling of the trade and commerce power evoked only slightly less indignation. W.P.M. Kennedy, the most influential constitutional analyst of the period from the early twenties to the middle forties, spoke for the bulk of the critics when he protested that it "is reduced to the almost absurd position of being a power which the Canadian Parliament can only call in aid of a power granted elsewhere.…" It had been "relegated to a position utterly impossible to defend on the clearest terms of the Act, and one which makes any reliance on it barren and useless."[15]

The decline of peace, order, and good government and the virtual nullification of trade and commerce on the federal side were counterbalanced by the remarkable significance which came to be attached to "property and civil rights" in section 92.[16] It was this provincial head that H. Carl Goldenberg described as "wide enough to cover nearly all legislation outside of criminal law," including the whole field of social legislation.[17]

In brief, the critics argued, the Privy Council seriously misinterpreted the division of powers in sections 91 and 92, to the extent that the provinces were left with responsibilities they were neither intended, nor competent, to handle. Several key decisions raised the status of the provinces,[18] while other decisions enhanced the significance of provincial jurisdiction in section 92, especially property and civil rights. Conversely, the federal government, originally endowed with potent problem-solving and nation-building capacities, had its powers cribbed and confined to such a degree that the Fathers would not recognize their creation. As a consequence, an explicitly centralized federal system was transformed into its reverse, a decentralized system approximating a league of states.[19]

The previous approach defined the judicial role in terms of the literal, almost technical, task of correctly interpreting a historic document in terms of the intention of its framers. From this perspective the trouble with the Privy Council was that it had got its history wrong, or had misinterpreted the clear phraseology of the BNA Act.

The second stream of criticism rested on contrary assumptions. These critics, the constitutionalists, took their stand with John Marshall's assertion that judges must not forget that they were expounding a constitution.

Critics of this school were hostile to the Privy Council for treating the BNA Act as a statute to be analysed by "the ordinary rules of statutory construction." They asserted that the Judicial Committee should have been an agent for constitutional flexibility, concerned with the policy consequences of their decisions. They flatly rejected the Judicial Committee's own interpretation of its task, to treat "the provisions of the Act in question by the same methods of construction and exposition which they apply to other statutes."[20]

Contrary to the narrow statutory approach officially adopted by the Privy Council the critics favoured a more generous, flexible, liberal approach which clearly recognized the constitutional significance of judicial review, with its corollary of a policy role for judges. In positive terms these critics spoke variously and vaguely of the need to keep the BNA Act up to date, particularly in its federal aspects. In a variety of ways they believed that a Canadian version of the United States Supreme Court was required. They spoke especially favourably of Lord Sankey, the closest approximation to a hero they could find on the Privy Council, and they delighted in the analogy of the "living tree" which he had applied to the BNA Act.[21]

The general tenor of the desired approach is readily apparent from the felicitous phrases used. MacDonald spoke of the need for interpreting the act "progressively so as to keep it as apt an instrument of government in new conditions as it was in the conditions current at its enactment."[22] Elsewhere he wrote of the necessity for "constant effort to bring and keep the Constitution up-to-date as the source of power adequate to present needs,"[23] and the desirability of "the flexible interpretation that changing circumstances require."[24] Laskin wrote favourably of "those sentiments in existing constitutional doctrine which express principles of growth." He contrasted "the higher level of constitutional interpretation" with the "lower level of statutory interpretation."[25] F.R. Scott, one of the most prolific critics of the Privy Council, praised the "clear recognition" by courts in the United States "that a constitution is primarily intended, not to rivet on posterity the narrow concepts of an earlier age, but to provide a living tree capable of growth and adaptation to new national needs."[26] To A.R.M. Lower the act should have been interpreted "as the vehicle for a nation's growth. If the Act is the vehicle of a nation, then the broadest construction must be put on it in order that under it all parts of the nation may have adequate life."[27]

Essentially, these critics were strong on general exhortation and weak on specifics. What they disliked was very clear. Positively, they were concerned with consequences. They recognized the policy role of the judiciary, and the dangers of being tied down to the constitutional assumptions of a previous era. The difficulties of formal amendment encouraged them to look to the courts for the injection of flexibility into an ancient document. They also frequently noted the necessity of incorporating a broader range of facts into the judicial decision-making process. From this perspective their orientation was salutary, for the brunt of their message was to make judges more self-conscious than hitherto.

Inevitably the advocates of a living tree, liberal, flexible approach to constitutional interpretation were hostile to *stare decisis*. MacDonald spoke of the "shackles of previous decisions,"[28] Laskin of "the inertia of *stare decisis*," and the "encrustation of *stare decisis*,"[29] and W.P.M. Kennedy of "that uncanny stranglehold with which *stare decisis* seems doomed to rob the law of creative vitality.[30] They were far more concerned with the suitability of the developing constitution to new circumstances than with a narrow fidelity to previous constitutional case law.

Underlying the specific criticisms of the Privy Council there was the overriding assumption that a powerful central government endowed with broad-ranging legislative authority and generous financial resources was an essential requirement of modern conditions. "The complications of modern industry and of modern business," asserted W.P.M. Kennedy in 1932, "will sooner or later demand national treatment and national action in the national legislature."[31] In the mid-thirties Vincent MacDonald favourably noted "prevailing political theories which indicate the propriety or necessity of a greater degree of national control over, and governmental intervention in, matters of social welfare and business activity."[32] The general centralist basis of the critics is most clearly found in the writings of the socialist law professor, F.R. Scott, the "unofficial constitutional advisor" of the CCF.[33] On numerous occasions Scott criticized the Privy Council for departing from the centralist federalism established in 1867 and for leaving Canada with a constitution which gravely hampered attempts to solve important public problems. In 1931 he stated:

Canadian federalism has developed continuously away from the original design. Constitutionally we have grown disunited, in spite of the fact that in other respects, as a result of the increased facility of communication, the rise of our international status, and the general spread of what may be called our national consciousness, we have grown more united. The Dominion Parliament does not play today the full part which the Fathers of Confederation planned for her.... Just at the time when the exigencies of the economic situation call for drastic action, for increased international co-operation and for a planned internal social order, we find ourselves with cumbrous legislative machinery and outworn constitutional doctrines.[34]

The same point was made by Laskin in an article shortly after the Second World War. After noting the provincial bias of the Privy Council, he continued: "But has provincial autonomy been secured? In terms of positive ability to meet economic and social problems of interprovincial scope, the answer is no. A destructive negative autonomy exists, however, which has as a corollary that the citizens of a province are citizens of the Dominion for certain limited purposes only."[35]

In the thirties when the impotence of the provinces was highlighted by the Great Depression this kind of opinion was greatly strengthened.[36] The interdependence of a modern economy, the growth of national corporations, national unions, and a national public opinion inevitably focused attention on the need for a strong national government. The recently formed CCF with its centralist orientation was inevitably hostile to the decentralizing tenor of Privy Council decisions. The intellectual spokesmen of the left in the League for Social Reconstruction viewed the provinces as reactionary supports of the business community.[37] The Conservatives, who had seen their New Deal program harshly treated by the Privy Council, reacted by raising the issue of abolishing appeals.

In the international arena a different set of factors existed to require strong central governments capable of decisive action by means of treaties which could be negotiated, ratified, and implemented without the inhibitions of a federalist division of powers. In these circumstances Lord Atkins's decision in the Labour Conventions case was viewed as an unmitigated disaster. "While it is true," his judgment stated, "... that it was not contemplated in 1867 that the Dominion would possess treaty-making powers, it is impossible to strain the section [132] so as to cover the uncontemplated event."[38]

This particular decision elicited a veritable flood of intemperate, polemical abuse of the Judicial Committee, both at the time and subsequently. The critics found it insulting to Canadian dignity and incompatible with Canadian autonomy that the evolution of Canadian independence from Great Britain should leave the federal government so seriously hampered in its relations with foreign states. F.R. Scott dramatized the choice as between local sovereignty and world peace.[39] W.P.M. Kennedy asserted in 1943 that the treaty situation was fraught with grave consequences for Canadian performance of postwar peace treaties.[40] Vincent MacDonald satirically noted:

The Dominion's power of treaty implementation is absolute as to types of treaty now obsolete. It is, however, almost non-existent as to many types of treaty called for by modern conditions; for these latter tend in point of subject matter to fall, entirely or largely, within Provincial heads of jurisdiction, as greatly expanded by judicial interpretation. This is a fact of the utmost importance in a day requiring co-operative action of many nations to control international forces of an economic, social or political character.[41]

Thus the critics, particularly the constitutionalists, were convinced that both domestic and foreign policy requirements necessitated the dominance of the central government in the federal system. Their opposition to the Privy Council on grounds of policy was backed by a growing Canadian nationalism. Even some of the early supporters of the Privy Council had recognized that in the fullness of time the elimination of appeals was inevitable. Nationalist arguments had been used by Edward Blake when the Supreme Court was established in 1875.[42] They were later to form a staple part of John S. Ewart's long campaign for Canadian independence in the first three decades of this century. To Ewart the appeal was "one of the few remaining badges of colonialism, of subordination, of lack of self-government."[43] A later generation of critics reiterated Ewart's thesis. In 1947 F.R. Scott stated that the continuation of appeals "perpetuates in Canada that refusal to shoulder responsibility, that willingness to let some one else make our important decisions, which is a mark of immaturity and colonialism."[44] The

nationalist argument was incorporated in the official justifications of the Liberal government when appeals were finally abolished in 1949.[45]

The fact that the elimination of appeals occurred simultaneously with the admission of Newfoundland to Canada and a renewed attempt to find a domestic amending procedure was not accidental. On the one hand the meaning and value of the Commonwealth was not what it had been prior to the Second World War. A weakened Britain and an attenuated Commonwealth combined with a stronger and more self-confident Canada to diminish the significance of ties with the mother country, a phrase which had begun to sound quaint and archaic.[46]

The nationalist attack on the Privy Council was fed by the special pride with which many Canadian writers asserted the superiority of Canadian over American federalism. The centralized variant of federalism established north of the "unguarded frontier," in reaction to the destructive effects of a decentralized federalism which the American Civil War allegedly displayed, was for many critics part of the political distinctiveness of Canada which they prized. In these circumstances for a British court to reverse the intentions of the farsighted Fathers was doubly galling. This helps to explain the bitterness with which Canadian writers frequently contrasted the divergent evolutions of the American and Canadian federal systems away from their respective points of origin.

## EXPLANATIONS OF THE JUDICIAL COMMITTEE

Critics of the Privy Council attempted to explain, as well as condemn, the results they deplored. In addition to explanations in terms of incompetence critics offered specific interpretations of the Privy Council's conduct. One explanation was legal, the assertion that it was natural for judges to attempt to reduce the discretion involved in interpreting vague phrases such as peace, order and good government. Frank Scott held that the decline of the federal residual power was due to the displeasure of a court of law at the task of having to distinguish between local and general matters. "Rather than commit themselves they have on the whole preferred to support legislation under some specific power, and thus the general residuary power has died of non-use."[47] A legal explanation of the Privy Council's conduct has been given recent support by Professor Browne's attempted justification of the claim that the act was in fact properly interpreted in the light of its evident meaning.[48]

Occasionally critics suggested that Privy Council decisions were influenced by political considerations inappropriate to a court. While the nature of these considerations was seldom made clear, the most frequent accusation was that imperial interests were best served by a weak central government.[49] This explanation was consistent with the political bias most frequently attributed to the court, the protection and enhancement of the position of the provinces in Canadian federalism.[50] Proof of this was found in cases favouring the provinces, or restricting federal legislation, and in the provincialist statements which these cases frequently contained. Critics also pointed to the several occasions on which the Privy Council referred to the BNA Act as a compact or a treaty.[51] Further proof could be found in the speeches by Lord Haldane explicitly noting a protective attitude to the provinces, especially by his predecessor Lord Watson.[52] Haldane's candid admissions are of special significance because of the propensity of Canadian critics to single out these two judges for particularly hostile treatment.[53] Haldane stated of Watson:

> ... as the result of a long series of decisions, Lord Watson put clothing upon the bones of the Constitution, and so covered them over with living flesh that the Constitution of Canada took a new form. The provinces were recognized as of equal authority co-ordinate with the Dominion, and a long series of decisions were given by him which solved many problems and produced a new contentment in Canada with the Constitution they had got in 1867. It is difficult to say what the extent of the debt was that Canada owes to Lord Watson....[54]

Haldane was also explicit that a judge on the Privy Council had "to be a statesman as well as a jurist to fill in the gaps which Parliament has deliberately left in the skeleton constitutions and laws that it has provided for the British colonies."[55] In view of these overt indications of a policy role favouring the provinces

there can be no doubt that Watson and Haldane consciously fostered the provinces in Canadian federalism, and by so doing helped to transform the highly centralist structure originally created in 1867.

An alternative policy explanation deserves more extensive commentary. This was to identify the court with more or less subtlety as defenders of free enterprise against government encroachments. Spokesmen for the Canadian left, such as Woodsworth and Coldwell, were convinced that "reactionary interests have sought to shelter and to hide" behind the BNA Act.[56] F.R. Scott asserted that the "large economic interests" opposed to regulation sided with the provinces, which would be less capable of their effective regulation than would the federal government.[57] The courts, as both Scott and Professor Mallory noted, responded favourably to the protection from control which business sought.[58]

Mallory's description is apt: "The force that starts our interpretative machinery in motion is the reaction of a free economy against regulation.... In short the plea of *ultra vires* has been the defence impartially applied to both legislatures by a system of free enterprise concerned with preventing the government from regulating it in the public interest."[59] Business was opposed by labour which has fought consistently for "greater Dominion jurisdiction, based on the facts of everyday life as they must be met today by the Canadian working class population, looking to broader Dominion powers in questions touching the welfare of the wage earners."[60] The tactics of business and labour were pragmatic reflections of self-interest. A necessary consequence of a federal system is that each organized interest will seek to transform the most sympathetic level of government into the main decision-maker in matters which concern it. The evaluation to be put on these tactics, and the responses of the courts to them, however, is another matter. Regardless of the groups which align themselves with different levels of government at different times, it is far from clear that support for provincial authority is necessarily reactionary and support for federal authority necessarily progressive.

There is considerable evidence that influential groups in Canada, including prominent lawyers, opposed the growing regulatory role of the modern state. Sir James Aikins, founder and first president of the Canadian Bar Association, frequently spoke in satirical and hostile terms of modern legislation and the politicians who inspired it. Unlike former times when harsh and antiquated law was softened by judicial fictions, "changes are dangerously empirical by reason of the easiness with which legislation can be secured, and the lack of comprehension in the legislator of the general principles of the law."[61] He deprecated the fact that experiments in social control had been transferred from courts to legislatures which produce "an impromptu statute and try ... [it] ... out on a resigned public, amending or repealing according to the pained outcry." Legislatures, he felt, had an ephemeral membership unlike courts or "organized law bodies." Their members were not experts in the law, "only amateurs, and their acts, too often crude and inartistic, run the gauntlet of interpretation and construction by courts and lawyers before they are put right, usually at the expense of some unfortunate litigant."[62] Aikins's antipathy to collectivism was shared by many. The report of the Committee on Noteworthy Changes in Statute Law in 1939 to the Canadian Bar Association expressed strong hostility to the growing role of government in the closing years of the depression. It reported ominously on the extent of socialism in Canada, and stated the belief that "private property is the pillar on which our whole civilization rests."[63] Critics of collectivism were disturbed by the "new despotism" of government by order-in-council, and the developing authority of proliferating tribunals which handled business felt to be the prerogative of the courts.[64]

In brief, collectivism, in Canada as elsewhere, had to be fought out in a variety of arenas, before mass electorates,[65] in parliaments, and in courts.[66] In each arena there were supporters and opponents of the emerging transformation in the role of public authority. The real question is not whether courts were embroiled in the controversy, or whether some judges sided with "reactionary" forces. It would be astonishing if such were not the case.

The important questions are more difficult and/or more precise. Were the courts more or less receptive than other elite groups to collectivism? Where did they stand in the general trend to the welfare, regulatory state?[67] What were the links between judges and courts and the various influential groups that appeared

before them? How did the Privy Council compare with other final appeal courts, or with lower Canadian courts, in its response to collectivism? Research on these questions would be extremely informative in pinning down the role of courts in the transition from the night watchman state to the era of big government.

## SUPPORTERS OF THE JUDICIAL COMMITTEE

Depression criticism, followed in the next decade by the elimination of appeals, had the effect that the period in which the Privy Council was under strongest attack has probably had the greatest effect on contemporary attitudes to it. Some of the most influential academic literature dealing with judicial review comes from that period and its passions.[68] As a consequence the Privy Council has typically received a very bad press in numerous influential writings by historians, political scientists, and lawyers in the past forty years.

In these circumstances, it is salutary to remember that if its critics reviled it, and turned Watson and Haldane into almost stock figures of fun, the Privy Council nevertheless did have a very broad body of support. Many highly qualified and well-informed analysts gave it almost unstinting praise. Indeed, if its critics reviled it too bitterly, its supporters praised it too generously. Often they wrote in fulsome terms, replete with awe and reverence for this most distinguished court.[69]

It was described as "this splendid body of experts,"[70] as "one of the most unique tribunals in the world,"[71] as a body of judges which "possesses a weight and efficiency as a supreme Judicial tribunal unequalled in the history of judicial institutions ... a tribunal supremely equipped for the task—equipped for it in unexampled degree."[72] In 1914 Sir Charles Fitzpatrick, the chief justice of Canada, claimed that "amongst lawyers and Judges competent to speak on the subject, there is but one voice, that where constitutional questions are concerned, an appeal to the Judicial Committee must be retained."[73] In 1921 the Hon. A.C. Gait, justice of the Court of King's Bench, Manitoba, replied to the objection that the Privy Council derogated from the dignity of Canadians with the assertion that it was always sensible to employ experts. "Now it so happens that the Privy Council possesses all the advantages, as experts, to deal with legal ailments which the Mayo Brothers possess in dealing with physical ones."[74] Howard Ferguson, premier of Ontario, ended a eulogy of the Privy Council in 1930 with special praise for Haldane, who protected "the Constitution of this country ... giving it sane and sound interpretation.... In this country of ours we will ever revere the memory of that great man."[75] Another writer observed that it was neither necessary nor "in good taste" for counsel to cite authorities before the Privy Council, "as owing to the great learning and vast experience of the members of the Board, they are usually familiar with such as have a bearing on the matters in question."[76] Supporters referred in an almost bemused way to the diversity of jurisdiction, extent of territory, and range of cases which it handled. "Imagination without actual experience," stated Justice Duff, "is hardly adequate to realize the infinite variety of it all...."[77]

The defenders and supporters of the Judicial Committee typically intermingled judicial and imperial arguments. The alleged contribution of the board to uniformity of law between Britain and her colonies and dominions straddled both arguments,[78] while the general assertion that the court was a link of empire was explicitly imperial.[79] It was also from this vantage point—that of a British citizen across the seas—that appeals were viewed and defended as a birthright, and much sentiment was employed over the right to carry one's appeals to the foot of the throne.[80]

A reading of the eulogies of the Privy Council prior to 1930 makes it clear that its most important source of Canadian support was imperial, and only secondarily judicial. The bulk of its supporters regarded it as an instrument of empire. Rather than viewing its dominant position in the judicial structure as a symbol of Canadian inferiority, they derived pride and dignity from the empire of which it was a part. They were British subjects first, and Canadians second, although from their perspective there was no conflict between these two definitions. The sentiments which inspired them are well presented in a statement of Justice Riddell in 1910 in which he spoke of

... the idea of fundamental union in all British communities—made manifest in concrete form in one great Court of Appeal for all the lands beyond the

seas ... to me there is no more inspiring spectacle than that body of gentlemen in the dingy old room on Downing street, Westminster, sitting to decide cases from every quarter of the globe, administering justice to all under the red-cross flag and symbolizing the mighty unity of an Imperial people.... One name we bear, one flag covers us, to one throne we are loyal; and that Court is a token of our unity.[81]

The immediately preceding set of arguments was essentially imperial. One important set of arguments, however, was jurisprudential. This was the frequently reiterated thesis that the great virtue of the Privy Council was its impartiality, a product of its distance from the scene of the controversies it adjudicated, and, unlike the Supreme Court, its absence of any direct link with either level of the governments whose interests clashed in the court room. In the quaint phraseology of the time, the committee was without those local prepossessions, so the argument went, which inevitably influence the decisions of local courts, and thus prejudice the impartiality necessary in the judicial role.[82]

In his presidential address to the Canadian Bar Association in 1927 Sir James Aikins spoke critically of the role of the American Supreme Court in augmenting national power, a court "appointed and paid by that central government, resident in the same place and within the influence and atmosphere of Congress and the Executive, consequently removed from any contact with the capitals or governments of the several states." He went on to mention that largely similar conditions prevailed in Canada, and similar results might be expected should the Supreme Court become the final appeal court. He concluded with the rhetorical question: "will it not be in the best interests of all to have constitutional interpretation made by an Empire Court which is not appointed or paid by or in the immediate environment of one of the parties interested?"[83]

To the critics of the Privy Council, impartiality, or absence of local prepossessions, simply meant ignorance. Nevertheless, the argument is of some importance if only because of its durability. It is prominent in the contemporary debate over the Supreme Court. In recent years English Canadians have defended the Supreme Court on grounds of its impartiality, while

French Canadians have criticized it on grounds of its insensitivity to their distinctive culture and special position in Canadian federalism. Further, this particular image of a good court is a reflection of one of the enduring visions of the judicial role—the blind eye of justice. It is also very close to the ideals behind the principle of judicial independence, and it is integrally related to the positivist conception of the judicial role, to the concept of the impartial third party as chairman, and to the concept of neutrality. This image, in brief, includes one of the ubiquitous central values which inevitably and properly intrudes into discussions of the role of public officials in general and judges in particular.

## SOCIOLOGICAL JUSTIFICATION OF
## THE JUDICIAL COMMITTEE

The defence of the Privy Council on grounds of its impartiality and neutrality is, however, difficult to sustain in view of the general provincial bias which ran through their decisions from the 1880s. This was the most consistent basis of criticism which the Judicial Committee encountered. A defence, therefore, must find some support for the general provincialist trend of its decisions.

It is impossible to believe that a few elderly men in London deciding two or three constitutional cases a year precipitated, sustained, and caused the development of Canada in a federalist direction the country would otherwise not have taken. It is evident that on occasion the provinces found an ally in the Privy Council, and that on balance they were aided in their struggles with the federal government. To attribute more than this to the Privy Council strains credulity. Courts are not self-starting institutions. They are called into play by groups and individuals seeking objectives which can be furthered by judicial support. A comprehensive explanation of judicial decisions, therefore, must include the actors who employed the courts for their own purposes.[84]

The most elementary justification of the Privy Council rests on the broad sociological ground that the provincial bias which pervaded so many of its decisions was in fundamental harmony with the regional pluralism of Canada. The successful assertion of this

argument requires a rebuttal of the claim of many writers that the Privy Council caused the evolution of Canadian federalism away from the centralization of 1867.[85]

From the vantage point of a century of constitutional evolution the centralist emphasis of the Confederation settlement appears increasingly unrealistic. In 1867 it seemed desirable and necessary to many of the leading Fathers. "The colonial life had been petty and bitter and frictional, and, outside, the civil war seemed to point to the need of binding up, as closely as it was at all possible, the political aspirations of the colonies."[86] Further, it can be argued that what appeared as overcentralization in the light of regional pluralism was necessary to establish the new polity and to allow the central government to undertake those nation-building tasks which constituted the prime reasons for union.

It is, however, far too easily overlooked, because of the idolatry with which the Fathers and their creation are often treated, that in the long run centralization was inappropriate for the regional diversities of a land of vast extent and a large, geographically concentrated, minority culture. The political leaders of Quebec, employing varying strategies, have consistently fought for provincial autonomy. The existence of Quebec alone has been sufficient to prevent Canada from following the centralist route of some other federal systems. In retrospect, it is evident that only a peculiar conjuncture of circumstances, many of them to prove ephemeral, allowed the degree of central government dominance temporarily attained in 1867.[87]

In the old provinces of Canada and the Maritimes provincial loyalties preceded the creation of the new political system. Nova Scotia and New Brunswick were reluctant entrants into Confederation, while Lower Canada sought to obtain as much decentralization as possible. A striking series of successes for the new Dominion might have generated the national loyalty necessary to support the central government in struggles with the provinces. Instead, the economic hopes on which so much had been placed in the movement to Confederation proved illusory and contributed to the undermining of federal prestige. Intermittent depression for most of the first thirty years of the new polity seriously eroded the flimsy supports for centralization on which Macdonald and some of his colleagues depended. The military dangers which had been an important original justification for a strong central government rapidly passed away. The thrusting ambitions of provincial politicians, bent on increasing the power and resources of their jurisdictions, wrested numerous concessions from the federal government by a variety of methods, of which resort to the courts was only one. Their conduct was sustained by the almost inevitable rivalry between politicians of the two levels of government, especially when belonging to opposed political parties.[88]

The provinces, which had initially been endowed with functions of lesser significance, found that their control of natural resources gave them important sources of wealth and power, and extensive managerial responsibilities. By the decade of the twenties, highways, hydro-electric power, a host of welfare functions, and mushrooming educational responsibilities gave them tasks and burdens far beyond those anticipated in 1867. By this time the centralizing effect of the building of the railways and the settlement of the west was ended by the virtual completion of these great national purposes.

As the newer provinces west of the great lakes entered the union, or were created by federal legislation, they quickly developed their own identities and distinct public purposes. Their populations grew. Their economies expanded; their separate histories lengthened; their governmental functions proliferated; and their administrative and political competence developed. They quickly acquired feelings of individuality and a sense of power which contributed to the attenuation of federal dominance in the political system.

Only in special, unique, and temporary circumstances—typically of an emergency nature—has the federal system been oriented in a centralist direction.[89] The focus of so many Canadian academic nationalists on the central government reflected their primary concern with winning autonomy from the United Kingdom. An additional and less visible process was also taking place. Canadian political evolution has been characterized not only by nation-building, but by province-building.[90] Further, it is too readily overlooked that with the passing of time Canada became more federal. In 1867 there were only four provinces in a geographically much more compact area than the nine provinces which had emerged by 1905, and the ten

by 1949. If a province is regarded as an institutionalized particularism the historical development of Canada has been characterized by expansion which has made the country more heterogeneous than hitherto.

In response to this increasingly federal society the various centralizing features of the BNA Act fell into disuse, not because their meaning was distorted by the courts, but because they were incompatible with developments in the country as a whole. In numerous areas, decentralizing developments occurred entirely on Canadian initiative, with no intervention by the Judicial Committee. The powers of reservation and disallowance were not eroded by the stupidity or malevolence of British judges but by concrete Canadian political facts. The failure to employ section 94 of the BNA Act to render uniform the laws relating to property and civil rights in the common law provinces was not due to the prejudice of Lords Watson and Haldane, but to the Utopian nature of the assumptions which inspired it, and the consequent failure of Canadians to exploit its centralizing possibilities.

The preceding analysis of Canadian federalism makes it evident that the provincial bias of the Privy Council was generally harmonious with Canadian developments. A more detailed investigation provides added support for this thesis.

At the time when Privy Council decisions commenced to undermine the centralism of Macdonald there was a strong growth of regional feeling. During the long premiership of Oliver Mowat, 1872–96, Ontario was involved in almost constant struggle with Ottawa. The status of the lieutenant governor, the boundary dispute with Manitoba and the central government, and bitter controversies over the federal use of the power of disallowance constituted recurrent points of friction between Ottawa and Ontario. Friction was intensified by the fact that with the exception of the brief Liberal interlude from 1873 to 1878 the governing parties at the two levels were of opposed partisan complexion, and by the fact that Mowat and Macdonald were personally hostile to each other.[91] The interprovincial conference of 1887, at which Mowat played a prominent part, indicated the general reassertion of provincialism. The "strength and diversity of provincial interests shown by the conference," in the words of the *Rowell-Sirois Report*, "indicated that, under the conditions of the late nineteenth century, the working constitution of the Dominion must provide for a large sphere of provincial freedom."[92] Nationalism had become a strong political force in Quebec in reaction to the hanging of Riel and the failure of the newly opened west to develop along bicultural and bilingual lines. Nova Scotia was agitated by a secession movement. The Maritime provinces generally were hostile to the tariff aspects of the National Policy. Manitoba was struggling against federal railway policies. British Columbia was only slowly being drawn into the national party system after the belated completion of the CPR in 1885. It was entering a long period of struggle with the Dominion over Oriental immigration. In addition, the late eighties and early nineties constituted one of the lowest points of national self-confidence in Canadian history.[93] It was a period in which the very survival of Canada was questioned. By the late 1890s, when economic conditions had markedly improved, a new Liberal government, with provincial sympathies, was in office. The year of the much criticized Local Prohibition decision was the same year in which Laurier assumed power and commenced to wield federal authority with much looser reins than had his Conservative predecessors. "The only means of maintaining Confederation," he had declared in 1889, "is to recognize that, within its sphere assigned to it by the constitution, each province is as independent of control by the federal Parliament as the latter is from control by the provincial legislatures."[94]

The Privy Council clearly responded to these trends in a series of landmark decisions in the eighties and nineties.[95] Unfortunately it is not possible to provide detailed information on whether or not their decisions were supported or opposed by a majority or minority of the Canadian people. What can be asserted is that provincial political elites vigorously used the courts to attain their objectives of a more decentralized federal system. Further, they apparently received widespread popular support for their judicial struggles with Ottawa.[96] Premier Mowat of Ontario, who used to go personally to London for the appeals,[97] was received as a hero on his return from his engagements with the federal government.[98] It can thus be safely asserted that the Privy Council was not acting in isolation of deeply rooted, popularly supported trends in Canada. For critics of the Judicial Committee to appeal to the

centralist wishes of the Fathers is an act of perversity which denies these provincialist trends their proper weight and influence.

It would be tedious and unnecessary to provide detailed documentation of the relative appropriateness of the decisions of the Judicial Committee to subsequent centrifugal and centripetal trends in Canadian society. It can be generally said that their decisions were harmonious with those trends. Their great contribution, the injection of a decentralizing impulse into a constitutional structure too centralist for the diversity it had to contain, and the placating of Quebec which was a consequence, was a positive influence in the evolution of Canadian federalism.[99] Had the Privy Council not leaned in that direction, argued P.E. Trudeau, "Quebec separatism might not be a threat today: it might be an accomplished fact."[100] The courts not only responded to provincialism. The discovery and amplification of an emergency power in section 91 may have done an injustice to the intentions of Macdonald for the residuary power, but it did allow Canada to conduct herself virtually as a unitary state in the two world wars in which centralized government authority was both required and supported.

The general congruence of Privy Council decisions with the cyclical trends in Canadian federalism not only provides a qualified sociological defence of the committee but also makes it clear that the accusation of literalism so frequently levelled at its decisions is absurd. Watson and Haldane in particular overtly and deliberately enhanced provincial powers in partial defiance of the BNA Act itself.[101] The Privy Council's solicitous regard for the provinces constituted a defensible response to trends in Canadian society.

Prior to the great outburst of criticism against the Privy Council in the depression of the thirties, strong approval for its decisions and their consequences was voiced by a variety of commentators. In 1909 J.M. Clark pointed out "what is too well known to require argument, namely, that the earlier decisions of our Supreme Court would have rendered our Constitution quite unworkable," a fate prevented by the existence of appeals to the Privy Council.[102] A few years later another writer praised the Privy Council for the political astuteness it combined with its legal abilities: "Better for the Canadian Constitution that the highest tribunal is composed of judges who are

also politicians, rather than of lawyers who are merely judges. The British North America Act is nearly forty-nine years old and works more easily every year; the American Constitution, admittedly a more artistic but less elastic document, is daily falling behind."[103]

In 1921 another supporter strongly criticized the opponents of the Privy Council "whose interpretations have evolved for us all that is great, splendid and enduring in the Constitution under which the Dominion has flourished."[104] An unsigned, eulogistic editorial in the *Canadian Law Times* (1920) sums up the approbation with which many viewed the work of the Judicial Committee:

I have read many of the decisions of the Privy Council relating especially to the Constitutional questions of Canada which have come before it; and I say that if it never did anything else for the purification of our legal conceptions, it has by its interpretations of the BNA Act rendered services to this country which should assure to it an abiding and grateful memory. With steady, persistent, and continuous adherence to the true lines of demarcation it has kept the Province and Dominion apart; and it has built up the Provincial fabric into a semi-sovereignty independent alike of the Dominion and of the United Kingdom. Its declarations on the Provincial Legislative powers alone are worthy of our gratitude and endless admiration. They are reverberant of that splendid independency which the several entities of Canada enjoy. These powers which the Dominion at one time thought subject to its control and doubtless would have striven to make them so, the Privy Council has declared are not delegated at all or subordinate to any authority except the Crown, but on the contrary that they are powers granted and surrendered by the Imperial Parliament directly in favor of the Legislature of each Province of Canada, and not even through the medium of the confederate Dominion.

How splendid an inheritance! This is not the letter of the B.N.A. Act but its spirit interpreted or declared for us by the Sovereign through his Privy Council in the light of aspirant freedom and of future nationhood.

Well may the upholder of our Constitution who stands aghast at the invectives of the would-be demolisher of the Privy Council say: *Si quaeris monumentum circumspice.*[105]

Any plausible defence of the Privy Council must come to grips with the *cause celebre* which more than any other indicated to its critics its incompetence and insensitivity as a final appeal court. In 1937, in a series of decisions, the Privy Council largely invalidated the New Deal legislation of the Bennett government. By so doing it indicated, to the fury of its critics, that even the emergency of a worldwide depression provided insufficient justification for central government authority to grapple with a devastating economic collapse. In these broad terms the case of the critics seems irrefutable. The New Deal decisions, more than any other, are responsible for the general hostility to the Privy Council in the literature of recent decades. The critics, however, have ignored a number of factors which place the action of the Privy Council in a much more favourable light.

The constitutionality of most of the New Deal legislation was in doubt from the moment of its inception.[106] Further, the final decisions by the courts were entirely predictable to a number of critics. Ivor Jennings' British law class "correctly forecast five of the decisions; and we were wrong on the sixth only because we took a different view of 'pith and substance.'"[107] W.P.M. Kennedy anticipated every New Deal decision but one before they went to the Supreme Court or the Privy Council.[108] The decisions therefore were not wayward, random, or haphazard. The judges did what men trained in the law expected them to do.

Any impression of an aloof court slapping down a determined Canadian leadership backed by widespread support is wrong.[109] R.B. Bennett, the initiator of the legislation, was decisively beaten in the federal election of 1935. The victor, Mackenzie King, had questioned the constitutionality of the legislation from the outset, never displayed any enthusiasm for its retention on the statute books, forwarded it willingly, almost eagerly, to the courts for their opinion, and uttered no anguished cries of rage when the decisions were announced.

In brief, the decisions were legally predictable and politically acceptable. In addition, there were extremely powerful centrifugal forces operating in the depression. Hepburn in Ontario, Duplessis in Quebec, and Aberhart in Alberta symbolized the developing regionalism unleashed by massive economic breakdown. French-Canadian separatists loudly resisted the claim that the depression could only be fought by centralization.[110] In these circumstances it is at least arguable that the political situation of the time was scarcely the most apposite for the enhancement of federal authority. The centralist bias of the critics ignored this fact. They unquestioningly assumed that the scale and nature of the problems facing the Canadian people could only be handled by the central government, and that no other considerations mattered. The critics were supported by the contribution of the Statute of Westminster in 1931 to Canadian autonomy. They were also encouraged by the dramatic development of "an astonishing number of voluntary, non-political, national associations" dealing with social, cultural, and intellectual affairs.[111] Given these factors the critics' position is understandable and defensible. Equally so, however, is the conduct of the Privy Council. The real controversy is not over the performance of the Judicial Committee, but over the proper criteria for the evaluation of judicial decisions.

## THE WEAKNESS OF THE JUDICIAL COMMITTEE

The Judicial Committee laboured under two fundamental weaknesses, the legal doctrine which ostensibly guided its deliberations, and its isolation from the setting to which those deliberations referred.

The basic overt doctrine of the court was to eschew considerations of policy and to analyse the BNA Act by the standard canons for the technical construction of ordinary statutes. The objection to this approach is manifold. Numerous legal writers have pointed out that the rules of statutory construction are little more than a grab bag of contradictions. It is also questionable whether a constitution should be treated as an ordinary statute, for clearly it is not. In the British political system, with which judges on the Privy Council were most acquainted, it is at least plausible to argue that the doctrine of parliamentary supremacy, and the consequent flexibility of the legislative process, provides some justification for the courts limiting their

policy role and assigning to parliament the task of keeping the legislation of the state appropriate to constantly changing circumstances. The BNA Act, however, as a written constitutional document, was not subject to easy formal change by the amending process. Consequently, the premise that the transformation of the act could be left to law-making bodies in Canada, as in the United Kingdom, was invalid. A candid policy role for a final appeal court seems to be imperatively required in such conditions.

Even in the absence of this consideration it is self-evident that no technical analysis of an increasingly ancient constitutional document can find answers to questions undreamt of by the Fathers. The Privy Council's basic legal doctrine was not only undesirable, therefore, it was also impossible. In reality, as already indicated, the Privy Council obliquely pursued a policy of protecting the provinces. The clear divergence between the act as written and the act as interpreted makes it impossible to believe that in practice the Privy Council viewed its role in the narrow, technical perspective of ordinary statutory construction. The problem of the court was that it was caught in an inappropriate legal tradition for its task of constitutional adjudication. It partially escaped from this dilemma by occasionally giving overt recognition to the need for a more flexible, pragmatic approach, and by covertly masking its actual policy choices behind the obfuscating language and precedents of statutory interpretations.

The covert pursuit of policy meant that the reasoning process in their decisions was often inadequate to sustain the decision reached. This also helps to explain the hypocritical and forced distinguishing of previous cases which was criticized by several authors.[112] Further, the impossibility of overt policy discussion in decisions implied the impossibility of open policy arguments in proceedings before the court. Inevitably, the court experienced severe handicaps in its role as policy-maker.

Caught in an unworkable tradition the Judicial Committee was unable to answer the basic question of constitutional jurisprudence, how it should apply the discretion it unavoidably possessed. The application of a constitution to novel conditions provides a court with the opportunity for creative statesmanship. To this challenge the Judicial Committee evolved no profound theories of its own role. Its most basic answer was silence, supplemented by isolated statements of principle dealing with the federal system, and occasional liberal statements concerning its role in contributing to the growth and evolution of the constitution. The confusion in Privy Council philosophy was cogently described by MacDonald:

> Uncertainty and inconsistency in … matters which lie at the very threshold of the problem of interpretation have played a large part in making the ascertainment of the meaning of the Canadian constitution the precarious task that it is today; for the chief element of predictability of legal decision inheres in a known and uniform technique of approach. It is a prime criticism of the Privy Council that it has had no uniform technique of approach to the act; for it has sought now the intention of the framers of the act, now the meaning of its terms; sometimes excluding, sometimes being influenced by, extraneous matters, and sometimes interpreting the terms of the act as speaking eternally in the tongue of 1867, and sometimes in the language of contemporary thought and need.[113]

The second main weakness of the Privy Council was its isolation from the scene to which its judgments applied. Its supporters argued otherwise by equating its distance from Canada with impartiality. Judges on the spot, it was implied, would be governed or influenced by the passions and emotions surrounding the controversy before them. British judges, by contrast, aloof and distant, would not be subject to the bias flowing from intimate acquaintance.

The logic of this frequently espoused position was curious. The same logic, as J.S. Ewart satirically observed, implied the desirability of sending British cases to the Supreme Court at Ottawa, but no such proposals were forthcoming. "Local information and local methods," he continued, "are very frequently essential to the understanding of a dispute. They are not disqualifications for judicial action."[114]

The critics were surely right in their assertions that absence of local prepossessions simply meant relative ignorance, insensitivity, and misunderstanding of the Canadian scene, deficiencies which would be absent in Canadian judges. "The British North America Act,"

Edward Blake had asserted in 1880, "is a skeleton. The true form and proportions, the true spirit of our Constitution, can be made manifest only to the men of the soil. I deny that it can be well expounded by men whose lives have been passed, not merely in another, but in an opposite sphere of practice…."[115] The same argument was reiterated by succeeding generations of critics until the final elimination of appeals.[116]

The weakness flowing from isolation was exacerbated by the shifting composition of the committee which deprived its members of those benefits of experience derived from constant application to the same task. "The personnel of that Court," stated a critic in 1894, "is as shifting as the Goodwin Sands. At one sitting it may be composed of the ablest judges in the land, and at the next sitting its chief characteristic may be senility and general weakness."[117] This instability of membership contributed to discontinuities in interpretation as membership changed. It also allowed those who sat for long periods of time, as did Watson and Haldane, to acquire disproportionate influence on Privy Council decisions.

The professed legal philosophy of the Judicial Committee helped explain away the disadvantages allegedly flowing from isolation, by stressing the mechanical, technical, legal character of the judicial task. This minimized the advantages of local understanding for judges. Conversely, the position of the critics was strengthened when they stressed the policy component in judicial interpretation. While a plausible case might be made that technical, legal matters could be handled as well, or even better, by a distant court the same argument could scarcely be made of policy matters, where local understanding was obviously of first-rate importance. It necessarily followed that the Supreme Court of Canada, composed of men thoroughly conversant with Canadian social and political conditions, had a greater capacity to be a more sophisticated and sensitive court of appeal.

The understanding of Canadian politics held by British judges was well summarized by a sympathetic observer, Jennings:

> The Atlantic separates them from the political disputes of Canada. Their information about the controversies of the Dominion is obtained from the summary cables of the London press, which is far

more interested in problems nearer home. If Mr. Dooley came to London he could not say that the Judicial Committee followed the Canadian election returns. Unless their functions make them particularly interested in Canadian news, they are probably as uncertain of the politics of the governments in power as is the average Englishman. The controversies which appear to them to be merely legal disputes as to the meaning of Sections 91 and 92 of the Act often have a background of party strife and nice political compromises. The judges may know enough to realize that politics are involved, but not enough to appreciate exactly why and how.[118]

These considerations add a special cogency to Vincent MacDonald's plea for abolition of appeals on the ground that "even in matters of dry law decision is affected by the national character and personal background of the judiciary." One could not ignore, he continued, "the temperament, the experience, the social background and training of the final court," especially when interpretation dealt with policy matters.[119] Tuck's argument was equally to the point:

> Resort to the Privy Council is unnecessary where the two tribunals agree; and where they disagree, since constitutional interpretation turns largely on matters of policy, its development would be best directed by a Canadian court with first-hand experience of Canadian conditions and needs. The Privy Council, with its constantly shifting personnel, working always at a distance from the scene of operations, is hardly the appropriate body for this kind of work.... It is unlikely, therefore, that the board will ever be thoroughly familiar with the spirit of the Canadian constitution, or the environment necessary to its successful working.[120]

Given the difficulties which inevitably flowed from its London location, and given the sterilities of the legal tradition it espoused, the decisions of the Privy Council were remarkably appropriate for the Canadian environment. The Privy Council, in its wisdom, was partially able to overcome some of the dangers caused by its own ignorance. That it did so imperfectly was only to be expected. Watson and Haldane have been criticized by McWhinney on the ground that if they were

consciously influenced "by a bias in favour of provincial powers, their approach seems nevertheless to have been a vague, impressionistic one, without the benefit of a detailed analysis and weighing of the policy alternatives involved in each case."[121] Essentially the same criticism is made by MacGuigan who criticizes the abstract natural law approach adopted by the Privy Council in coming to its policy decisions. They were policy-makers without the necessary tools of understanding.[122] These criticisms, while valid, reflect failings that were inevitable for a body of men who adjudicated disputes emanating from the legal systems of a large part of the world, and who could not be expected to become specialists in the shifting socio-economic contexts in which each legal system was embedded.[123] This particular weakness could not be overcome by a body of British judges. If local knowledge was a necessary attribute of a good court the Privy Council could only be a second best interim arrangement.

The context in which the Privy Council existed deprived it of the continual feedback of relevant information on which wise and sensitive judging depends. Superficially this could be described as a deficiency of local knowledge. This deficiency, however, is sufficiently complex and important to require elaboration.

An effective court does not exist in a vacuum. It is part of a complicated institutional framework for the amelioration of the human condition through the device of law in individual nation states. Law is unavoidably national. It cannot be otherwise as long as the basic political unit is the nation state. Laws are not designed for men in general, but for Canadians, Americans, Germans, etc.

Within these national frameworks a variety of procedures has been developed to make law sensitive to the needs of particular communities. This is readily recognized and admitted for legislatures and executives. For courts, however, the attributes of objectivity and impartiality, combined with the status of judicial independence, tend to distract attention from the task similarity between judges and legislators. Both, however, are concerned with the applicability of particular laws to particular communities. There is consequently an important overlap in their mutual requirements. Both must be provided with the institutional arrangements which facilitate an adequate flow of the relevant information for their specific tasks.

A strong and effective court requires a variety of supporters. It must be part of a larger system which includes first class law schools, quality legal journals, and an able and sensitive legal fraternity—both teaching and practising. These are the minimum necessary conditions for a sophisticated jurisprudence without which a distinguished judicial performance is impossible. Unless judges can be made aware of the complexities of their role as judicial policy-makers, and sensitively cognizant of the societal effects of their decisions, a first-rate judicial performance will only occur intermittently and fortuitously. In brief, unless judges exist in a context which informs their understanding in the above manner they are deprived of the guidance necessary for effective decision-making. Most of the conditions required as supports for a first class court were only imperfectly realized in Canada prior to the abolition of appeals to the Privy Council. A shifting body of British judges, domiciled in London, whose jurisdiction covered a large part of the habitable globe, existed in limbo. This isolation of the court not only reduced its sensitivity to Canadian conditions, but rendered it relatively free from professional and academic criticism.[124] A related part of the problem was noted by Ewart in his observation that the Privy Council either had the assistance of English barristers devoid of an intimate understanding of Canadian circumstances, or "Canadian barristers, who speak from one standpoint and are listened to from another."[125]

The position of the Judicial Committee at the apex of a structure of judicial review of global extent virtually necessitated the conceptualizing approach found offensive to so many of its critics. The court was not, and could not be, adequately integrated into a network of communication and criticism capable of transmitting the nuances and subtleties which a first class appeal court required.

The single opinion of the court, while it possibly helped to sustain its authority and weaken the position of its critics,[126] had serious negative effects. Jennings pointed out that "the absence of a minority opinion sometimes makes the opinion of the Board look more logical and more obvious than it really is. The case is stated so as to come to the conclusion already reached by the majority in private consultation. It is often only by starting again and deliberately striving to reach the opposite conclusion that we realize that ... there were two ways of looking at it."[127] The absence of dissents hindered the development of a dialogue over the quality of its judgments. Dissents provide a lever for the critic by their indication of a lack of judicial unanimity, and by their provision of specific alternatives to the decisions reached. Unanimity of its published opinion thus made its own contribution to the isolation of the court. In addition, as a final appeal court, it had "no dread of a higher judicial criticism."[128] Finally, much of the debate which swirled around its existence and performance was so inextricably intertwined with the larger controversy between nationalism and imperialism that the question of the judicial quality of its task was not faced head on. These extraneous considerations partly account for the extremes in the evaluations made of the court, ranging between "undiscriminating praise and ... over-criticism."[129]

## THE CONFUSION OF THE CRITICS

For the better part of a century the performance of the Judicial Committee has been a continuing subject of academic and political controversy in Canada. Even the elementary question of whether its work was basically good or fundamentally bad has elicited contrary opinions. The distribution of favourable and critical attitudes has shifted over time. From the turn of the century until the onset of the depression of the thirties informed opinion was generally favourable. Subsequently, English-Canadian appraisals became overwhelmingly critical. It is a reasonable speculation, sustained by Browne's recent volume,[130] by the contemporary strength of regional forces in Canadian society, and by the fact that Canadian judicial autonomy is now in its third decade, that more favourable evaluations of the Judicial Committee will begin to appear. For example, the Labour Conventions case (1937), which so aroused the ire of the critics who feared the emasculation of Canadian treaty-making, now seems to present a defensible proposition in contemporary Canadian federalism.

In the period up to and subsequent to the final abolition of appeals in 1949 there was a consistent tendency for opposed evaluations of the Judicial Committee to follow the French-English cleavage in Canada.[131] This divergence of opinion was manifest in French-Canadian support for the Judicial Committee,[132] with opposition on grounds of nationalism and its provincial bias largely found in English Canada. Many English-Canadian writers hoped that the Supreme Court, as a final appeal court, would adopt a liberal, flexible interpretation, eroding at least in part the debilitating influence of *stare decisis*. In practical terms, their pleas for a living tree approach presupposed a larger role for the central government than had developed under the interpretations of the Judicial Committee. In essence, one of the key attitudes of the predominantly English-Canadian abolitionists was to view a newly independent Supreme Court as an agent of centralization.[133] The very reasons and justifications which tumble forth in English-Canadian writings caused insecurity and apprehension in French Canada which feared, simply, that if English-Canadian desires were translated into judicial fact the status and influence of the provinces which had been fostered by British judges would be eroded.[134] The American-style supreme court sought by the constitutionalist critics of the Privy Council was justifiably viewed with apprehension by French-Canadian observers. They assumed, not unfairly, that if such a court heeded the bias of its proponents it would degenerate into an instrument for the enhancement of national authority. These contrary English and French hopes and fears are closely related to the present crisis of legitimacy of the Supreme Court.

An additional significant cleavage in Canadian opinion was between those fundamentalist critics who opposed the Judicial Committee for its failure to provide a technically correct interpretation of a clearly worded document, and the constitutionalists who castigated it for its failure to take a broad, flexible approach to its task.

The fundamentalist approach, already discussed, imposed on the courts the task of faithfully interpreting a document in terms of the meanings deliberately embodied in it by the Fathers of Confederation. This approach was replete with insuperable difficulties:

1. If the task of the courts was to provide a literally correct interpretation of the agreement of 1867 it is possible to differ on the degree of their success or failure. The standard interpretation adhered to by MacDonald, O'Connor, and numerous others is that the performance of the Judicial Committee, from this perspective, was an abject failure. Recently, however, a new analysis by Professor G.P. Browne has lauded the Privy Council for the consistency of its interpretation, and has categorically asserted that refined textual analysis of sections 91 and 92 indicates that they were given a proper judicial interpretation. According to Browne, British judges were not acting out a bias in favour of the provinces, but were simply applying the logic of the BNA Act to the legal controversies which came before them for adjudication.[135] Browne's revisionist thesis has been both praised and harshly criticized.[136] Its truth, if such a word can be applied to such a subject as constitutional interpretation, is not germane to our purposes.[137] What is germane is the fact that a century after Confederation the question of the technically correct interpretation of the act can still produce violently opposed positions among serious, competent scholars. One is tempted to ask if the pursuit of the real meaning of the act is not a meaningless game, incapable of a decisive outcome.[138]

2. There is controversy over the relationship between the intentions of the Fathers and the BNA Act they created. The centralist argument is that the Fathers both intended and produced a centralized federal system. It has, however, been asserted by Professor Philippe Ferland that there is a discrepancy between the intentions and the result. This approach claims that the pre-Confederation statements of the Fathers favoured a legislative decentralization, but they drafted a text which devoured the provinces. The judges then, according to Ferland, concentrated on the text, ignored the external evidence, and thus damaged the interests of the provinces.[139] It is impossible to overlook the fact that here, as elsewhere, legal scholars have displayed an ingenious ability to locate evidence for the kind of intentions they sought.

3. LaBrie noted that even if it could be assumed that the Fathers of Confederation did have views on the newer areas of government "there remains the question whether, in the light of our own greater experience in the problems of federal government, these intentions ought to rule us at the present day."[140] By implication the fundamentalists attempted to tie succeeding

generations of Canadians down to the constitutional assumptions of a small body of men in the 1860s. For a completely static society, in which the original settlement was perfectly suited to existing social values and needs, such an approach has some plausibility. But as society changes it seems evident that the faint glimmers of insights of the Fathers should be overruled by the more comprehensive understandings of their successors. Literalism, consequently, is an inadequate guide for judges. This was tacitly admitted by those fundamentalist critics who applied their literalism to the division of powers, but often proudly noted the flexibility of other portions of the Act. They were, for example, happy to accept the evolving conventions which transformed the roles of the governor general and the lieutenant governor. They tended to be literalist only when it suited their purposes.

Further, literalism, either as a description of what judges can or should do, is so clearly preposterous that its frequent employment as a tactic of criticism is, to say the least, surprising. M.R. Cohen's comment dealing with judicial review in the United States is no less applicable to Canada: "The pretence that every decision of the Supreme Court follows logically from the Constitution must ... be characterized as a superstition. No rational argument can prove that when the people adopted the Constitution they actually intended all the fine distinctions which the courts have introduced into its interpretation. Nor can we well deny the fact that judges have actually differed in their interpretations...."[141]

4. Most obvious, and noted by various writers, was the fact that the new and developing areas of government activity, where uncertainty was greatest, could not be fitted into the intentions of a previous generation ignorant of the problems involved.[142] The courts themselves have had to recognize the novelty of the issues they frequently encounter. When the Privy Council faced the question of whether a Canadian legislature could regulate appeals, the judgment stated that "it is ... irrelevant that the question is one that might have seemed unreal at the date of the British North America Act."[143]

5. It can be argued that the relevant intentions of the Fathers include not only their specific intentions for the Canadian political system as they visualized it in 1867, but also their attitudes to the possibility that future generations might wish to transform the nature of their creation. Lord Haldane, for example, argued that the Fathers intended the courts to work out the constitution.[144]

6. The question of the intentions of the Fathers is part of the larger controversy over the desirability of going beyond the wording of the act to a variety of pre-Confederation material that conceivably could throw light on its meaning.[145] Many critics recommended the use of the historical material surrounding Confederation as an aid to interpretation. Others asserted that not only was it the custom of the courts to exclude such materials, but that they were correct in doing so.[146] They agreed with Lord Sankey in the Edwards case that in interpreting the BNA Act "the question is not what may be supposed to have been intended, but what has been said."[147] Evan Gray, a critic of O'Connor, asserted that all pre-Confederation material "is illusory and inconclusive. It is not merely because a rigid rule of legal procedure binds our courts that we reject such material, but because as a matter of common sense we know that any other method of enquiry is unreliable, being speculative rather than logical and adding to uncertainty instead of resolving it."[148] The use of such materials was also undesirable, according to Vincent MacDonald, because the tying down of interpretation to the intentions of the Fathers "allows the horizon of that year [1867] to restrict the measures of the future." It was wiser, he argued, to interpret the words of the statute which allowed flexibility, and the incorporation of new meanings.[149]

The use of pre-Confederation material to document the intentions of the Fathers as an aid to interpretation would not have improved the Privy Council's performance. In addition to the much greater ambiguity of pre-Confederation speeches and resolutions compared to the BNA Act itself, their use is subject to all the criticisms of those who resist the binding of future generations by the restricted foresight of their predecessors. A living constitution incorporates only so much of the past as appears viable in the light of new conditions. A further weakness of the use of pre-Confederation material is that its contribution to understanding the BNA Act was greatest at the general level of the nature of the act as a whole, and weakest in the more specific areas covered by constitutional cases. It is significant that critics of the Privy Council tended to focus on pre-Confederation statements about the nature of the political system as a whole. Judges inevitably interpreted particular powers rather than the entire BNA Act, "because there was no machinery for the interpretation of the constitution as such."[150]

In summary, the intellectual rigour of the fundamentalist critics of the Privy Council leaves much to be desired. Their case is destroyed by its essential shallowness.

The constitutionalist critics of the Privy Council based themselves on a much more promising normative and analytical stand. They welcomed and recognized a policy role for the courts in judicial review. They appreciated both the impossibility and undesirability of complete fidelity to a statute conceived in former times by men who lacked the gift of foresight. To this extent, they were judicial realists. They could easily document, when so inclined, the inevitable policy content of judicial decisions, and by so doing could puncture the slot machine theory of law. This was their achievement. Their recognition of a policy-making role helped to initiate normative discussions on what a final appeal court should do with the discretion inherent in its task.[151] However, their own prescriptive statements were frequently shallow and seldom placed in a carefully articulated philosophy of the judicial role. An important contributing reason for the inadequacy of their normative contribution was that they were not clearly distinguished in policy objectives from the fundamentalists. Unlike the United States where the advocates of strict constitutional construction were usually state rightists,[152] Canadian centralists could and did find in the 1867 agreement constitutional support for their position. Thus the distinctions between the constitutionalists and the fundamentalists were blurred by the fact that both were centralists.[153] Constitutionalists, accordingly, could always fall back on literalist justifications for their centralist policy position. They were not therefore under an obligation to prescribe a carefully defined policy justification, either for their centralization, or for the role of the court in helping to attain it. They thus lapsed into uncritical support

for centralization on the general ground that it was required by the needs of the time.[154] This, however, as B.N. Cardozo pointed out, is not even the beginning of a judicial philosophy:

> I have no quarrel, therefore, with the doctrine that judges ought to be in sympathy with the spirit of their times. Alas! assent to such a generality does not carry us far upon the road to truth. In every court there are likely to be as many estimates of the "Zeitgeist" as there are judges on its bench.... The spirit of the age, as it is revealed to each of us, is too often only the spirit of the group in which the accidents of birth or education or occupation or fellowship have given us a place. No effort or revolution of the mind will overthrow utterly and at all times the empire of these subconscious loyalties.[155]

The critics did not develop a consistent and meaningful definition of the judicial role in constitutional review. The much maligned Judicial Committee was criticized on two mutually exclusive grounds.[156] The fundamentalists, fluctuating back and forth between the Act itself and pre-Confederation material, charged it with departing from the clear meaning of the act and the obvious intent of its framers. The constitutionalists, concerned with policy, charged it with a failure to interpret the act in the flexible manner appropriate to a constitutional document. Their policy approach tended to be based on whether or not a given decision, or series of decisions, agreed with their values, which usually meant whether or not it facilitated government action regarded as desirable, or inhibited government action regarded as undesirable. The fundamentalist castigated the Privy Council for reaching decisions which every historian knew to be untrue, the very kind of decision which the logic of the constitutionalists invited the Bench to make. The fundamentalist demanded a technically correct performance of a mechanical act, the interpretation of a clearly worded document. The constitutionalist appealed less to the act than to the contemporary conditions to which it was to be applied. While they did not write off the BNA Act as irrelevant, the constitutionalists tended to be hostile when the act, or its judicial interpretation, stood in the way of their objectives. Their prime purpose was to allow the federal government to grapple with problems they deemed to be beyond provincial competence, or which they expected provincial governments to handle in some undesirable way. The simultaneous or sequential employment of these divergent fundamentalist and constitutionalist rationales was effective as a debating device. It was productive of great confusion over the basic question of the proper role for the court.

The critics of the Judicial Committee were moved more by the passions of nationalism and desires for centralization than by federalism. By the mid-thirties the two main perspectives on the judicial role agreed that the act, as interpreted, was increasingly irrelevant to the environment to which it applied. Both groups of critics "took it as axiomatic that the application of the appropriate techniques of interpretation of the BNA Act, whether in the form of a larger dose of knowledgeable judicial statesmanship or greater fidelity to the true meaning of the constitutional text, could only be achieved by transferring the highest judicial power from English to Canadian judges."[157] Both groups of critics were centralists, although they found different constitutional justifications for their position. Neither group wrote favourably of the provinces, or expected much of them. They pinned their hopes on Ottawa. They shared Underbill's evaluation of the provinces: "The only province," he wrote in 1931, "which has not been subject to the regular alternation between short periods of comparatively good government and long periods of decay is Quebec. In Quebec they enjoy bad government all the time."[158] The critics assumed that industrial, technological, urban, or some other set of conditions required centralization. They stressed the difficulties of divided jurisdiction as barriers to the effective regulation of an interdependent economy. They placed great emphasis on the national structure of an economy no longer capable of meaningful delimitation by provincial boundaries. They assumed economic forces to be uncompromisingly centralist, and never regionalist in impact. They shared Laski's thesis that federalism was obsolete, paid little attention to the varying kinds of pluralism rooted in non-economic factors, and were hostile to the institutional arrangements which preserved and protected federalism. They were prone to stress the national-local distinction as crucial to the proper understanding of the BNA Act, and thus to employ a national dimension or general interest justification for federal legislation. This was an approach to which French Canadians took strong exception because of its obvious threat to provincial autonomy.[159]

The really dramatic cleavage between the supporters and opponents, especially the constitutionalists, of the Privy Council, was, as hinted above, in their opposition over the kinds of non-legal facts which should be of significance in constitutional adjudication. The supporters stressed either the governmental pluralism of the federal system, or the underlying, regionally grouped diversities on which it was deemed to be based. Judicial decisions which protected and fostered this pluralism were praised. Judicial interpretation hostile to pluralism was opposed. The constitutionalists, by contrast, downplayed the significance of pluralism, which they frequently saw as a cover for vested interests seeking to avoid regulation. To them the paramount extra-legal factors were the ties of economic and technical interdependence and the corporate power behind them. These, by implication, had either undermined the sociological supports for pluralism or, by generating problems of national importance or scope which imperatively required central government authority for their resolution, had reduced pluralism to secondary significance.

There is no easy way by which these contrary definitions of relevant extra-legal facts can be categorized as more or less true. Both provided plausible justifications for the kind of federal system their advocates sought and the kind of judicial review required to achieve or sustain it.

Several speculations are in order. It is evident that with the passage of time since 1867 ties of interdependence have been generated which have helped to knit the Canadian economy together. It seems clear, however, that an economic interpretation of Canadian history which presupposes that this economic interdependence has undermined pluralist values is largely wrong. Canadians have remained pluralist in spite of economic change.

Economic interdependence is an omnibus concept which conceals as much as it reveals. To the extent that it does exist it is not always seen as beneficial by all the parties caught in it. The National Policy incorporated the prairies into the Canadian economy in a manner which has generated disaffection ever since Manitoba began to fight the railway monopoly of the CPR shortly after being constituted as a province. French-Canadian provincial politicians have not been notably pleased with a system of interdependence in which capital and management were English and the workers were French.

The concept of interdependence is thus too general to be helpful in describing the nature of the Canadian economy or the kinds of political authority necessary to manage it. The concept also contributes to a disregard for the distinctive nature of the regional economies which have grown since Confederation. The importance of provincial control of natural resources, and the foreign markets to which these resources are sent, sustain distinct regional or provincial interests frequently hostile to a national approach. The nature of the Canadian economy has never been such as to offer unequivocal support for central government authority.

It is also probable that the alleged disastrous effects of Privy Council support for the provinces have been exaggerated. In recent years, at least, the provinces, particularly the larger and wealthier ones, have not been the impotent units of government which critics of the Privy Council assumed. They are neither synonyms for reaction nor backwaters of ineptitude. In the long view judicial support for the provinces has contributed to the formation of competent governments. It is also clear that the paralysing effect of judicial decisions on the federal government has been overstressed. For a decade and a half after the Second World War Canada was run in a highly centralist fashion despite nearly a century of judicial interpretation which was claimed to have reduced Ottawa to a powerless non-entity. Judicial review scarcely seems to have been as important a determinant of constitutional evolution as has often been imagined. Professor Corry has indeed speculated that judicial interpretation adverse to Ottawa precipitated the "spectacular refinement of the techniques of economic and fiscal powers after the war" on which postwar centralization was based. "Perhaps the Privy Council interpretations have, in the sequel, pushed effective centralization further and faster than it would otherwise have gone."[160]

Professor McWhinney is critical of the quality of the controversy over the Privy Council because it too frequently proceeded "in the form of a dispute over alternative rules of statutory construction, rather than in terms of the actual consequences to Canadian

national life flowing from the individual decisions."[161] This is neither entirely true nor entirely fair. At bottom, the critics, of whatever school, were motivated by a concern for the consequences of constitutional interpretation. Especially in the depression of the thirties, it was the perceived consequences of the New Deal decisions that aroused their ire.

Hostility to the Judicial Committee was fed by the inability of Canadians to develop an amending procedure which would facilitate transfers of power from the provinces to the central government. In this situation the courts were viewed as the last resort. When they failed to respond to the challenge in the thirties, their critics retaliated with passionate hostility as the federal system appeared impotent when confronted with economic breakdown and social dislocation. In general, criticisms resulted from an antipathy to the negative effects of Privy Council decisions on the capacity of Canadians to pursue certain objectives. The Privy Council left Canadians, in the phrase of one critic, with a "hardly workable polity."[162] In area after area, argued the critics, the situation was intolerable in terms of administrative efficiency, the scope of the problem, or the power of the interests requiring regulation.[163]

The constitutionalists, in particular, were much concerned with the consequences of judicial decisions. They inevitably sought legal justification for the decisions they favoured, but they can scarcely be faulted for that. They were simply playing the game in the accustomed manner. As indicated above, they exaggerated both the harmful consequences of the decisions and the role of the Judicial Committee in the evolution of Canadian federalism. They cannot, however, be criticized for a lack of concern with policy. Their chief weakness lies elsewhere, in their failure to produce a consistent, comprehensive definition of what can legitimately be expected from a particular institution, a definition necessarily related to the specific task of that institution in the complex of institutions which make up the political system as a whole. In a discussion of the Privy Council's handling of the New Deal, A.B. Keith asserted that from a "juristic point of view" he was able to accord "cordial appreciation" to the decisions. It was, he continued, a "completely different question" whether the constitution was an apt instrument for the solution of new problems; but this, he concluded, was "a work for the statesmen and people of the Dominion, and not for any court."[164] The particular distinction made by Keith may or may not be valid. What is relevant is that he made a distinction. It is not necessary to fall into the textbook simplification between those who make the laws, those who administer them, and those who interpret them to suggest that different institutions are entrusted with different tasks. The failure to make any kind of differentiation denies the validity of the institutional division of political labour which has been painfully evolved over centuries of western history. To blame the milkman for not delivering bread, or the doctor for the mistakes of the laundryman is a recipe for chaos. The basic, prior, and determining question is simply what can properly be expected of judicial review. In a constitutional system the function of judicial review must be more than simply allowing desirable policies to be implemented by whatever level of government so wishes. A worthwhile court of final appeal is bound on occasion to prevent one level of government from doing what a group of temporary incumbents or its supporters would like to do. Criticism of a court based on the fact that it has prevented a desirable objective from being attained is not good enough. Like the American legal realists, with whom the constitutionalists had some affinity, Canadian critics were effective at the task of demolition, and weak at telling the judge what he should do.[165]

In sum, Canadian jurisprudence was deeply divided on the question of the relevant criteria for the guidance of judges in the difficult process of constitutional interpretation. Neither critics nor supporters of the Judicial Committee were able to develop consistent and defensible criteria for judicial review. Admittedly, Canadians were not alone in their confusion. Professor Corry asserted in 1939 that "one would have to search far to find a more confused portion of the English law" than "the rules to be followed in interpreting statutes and constitutions." He continued:

> The text writers and judges all insist that the basic rule is to find the "expressed intention" of the makers of the constitution and that, in the case of constitutions, this intention is to be liberally rather than narrowly construed. The trouble is that constitutions often do not have "expressed intentions"

about many of the situations to which they must be applied. The Fathers of Confederation could not express any intention about aviation and radio. At best then, in such circumstances, the court can only argue by analogy, making inferences as to what the framers would have said if they had thought about the problem. Even then, there are numerous situations where no compelling inferences can be found by logical processes. Nor does it help to propose that the constitution should be liberally construed, for one must still ask for what purpose and to what end. Liberal construction of Dominion power is, at the same time, strict construction of provincial power and *vice versa*.[166]

In brief, if the performance of the Privy Council was, as its critics suggested, replete with inconsistencies and insensitivity, the confused outpourings of the critics displayed an incoherence completely inadequate to guide judges in decision-making. To contrast the performance of the Judicial Committee with the performance of its opponents is to ignore the dissimilarity of function between artist and critic. It is however clear that the Judicial Committee was much more sensitive to the federal nature of Canadian society than were the critics. From this perspective at least the policy output of British judges was far more harmonious with the underlying pluralism of Canada than were the confused prescriptive statements of her opponents.[167] For those critics, particularly on the left, who wished to transform society, this qualified defence of the Judicial Committee will lack conviction. However, such critics have an obligation not only to justify their objectives but also the role they advocated for a non-elected court in helping to attain them.

Whether the decline in the problem-solving capacity of governments in the federal system was real or serious enough to support the criticism which the Privy Council encountered involves a range of value judgments and empirical observations of a very complex nature. The purpose of this paper has been only to provide documentation for the minimum statement that a strong case can be made for the Judicial Committee, and to act as a reminder that the basic question was jurisprudential, a realm of discussion in which neither the Privy Council, its critics, nor its supporters proved particularly illuminating.

## THE ABOLITION OF APPEALS AND AN INADEQUATE JURISPRUDENCE

It is valid, if somewhat perverse, to argue that the weakness and confusion of Canadian jurisprudence constituted one of the main justifications for ending appeals to the Privy Council. The attainment of judicial autonomy was a prerequisite for a first class Canadian jurisprudence.[168] Throughout most of the period of judicial subordination the weaknesses in Canadian legal education produced a lack of self-confidence and a reluctance to abolish appeals.[169] As long as the final court of appeal was an alien body the jurisprudence which did exist was entangled with the emotional contest of nationalism and imperialism, a mixture which deflected legal criticism into side issues. In these circumstances the victory of nationalism was a necessary preliminary to the development of an indigenous jurisprudence which has gathered momentum in the past two decades.

It is also likely that the quality of judicial performance by Canadian courts was hampered by subordination to the Privy Council. The existence of the Privy Council undermined the credibility of the Supreme Court and inhibited the development of its status and prestige. The Supreme Court could be overruled by a superior, external court. In many cases it was bypassed as litigants appealed directly from a provincial court to the Privy Council. Finally, the doctrine of *stare decisis* bound the Supreme Court to the decisions of its superior, the Privy Council. The subject status of the Supreme Court and other Canadian courts was further exacerbated by the absence of dissents which reduced the potential for flexibility of lower courts in subsequent cases. In spite of the quality of its performance the dominant position of the Privy Council in the Canadian judicial hierarchy was an anomaly, incompatible with the evolving independence of Canada in other spheres, and fraught with too many damaging consequences for its elimination to be regretted.

The inadequate jurisprudence, the legacy of nearly a century of judicial subordination, which accompanied the attainment of judicial autonomy in 1949, has harmfully affected the Supreme Court in the last two decades. The Supreme Court, the law schools, the legal profession, and the political elites have been unable to devise an acceptable role for the court in Canadian

federalism. Shortly after the court attained autonomy the institutional fabric of the Canadian polity, the court included, began to experience serious questioning and challenges to its existence. The Diefenbaker Bill of Rights was succeeded by the Quiet Revolution with its confrontation between rival conceptions of federalism and coexistence. Additional uncertainty has been generated by the proposed Trudeau Charter which, if implemented, will drastically change the significance of the judiciary in our constitutional system. In the unlikely event that a significantly different BNA Act emerges from the present constitutional discussions the court will face the task of imparting meaning to a new constitutional document delineating a division of powers different from the existing division. To these factors, as indications of the shifting world of judicial review, can be added the possibility that the court may be reconstituted with a new appointment procedure, with a specific entrenched status, and perhaps even as a special court confined to constitutional questions.

It would be folly to suggest that the above problems would not exist if Canadian jurisprudence had been more highly developed. Their source largely lies beyond the confines of the legal system. On the other hand, the confused state of Canadian jurisprudence documented in this article adds an additional element of difficulty to their solution.

## NOTES

In writing this article I have received assistance from numerous friends and colleagues, including Leo Barry, Ed Black, Alexander Brady, Ronald Cheffins, Peter Finkle, Martin Levin, Susan McCorquodale, Donald Smiley, Paul Tennant, and Walter Young.

1  "Within the last twenty years in particular," wrote G.F.G. Stanley in 1956, "it has been the common sport of constitutional lawyers in Canada to criticize, cavil and poke fun at the *dicta* of the judges of the Privy Council and their decisions in Canadian cases. Canadian historians and political scientists have followed the legal party line with condemnations of 'the judicial revolution' said to have been accomplished by Lord Watson and Lord Haldane, and the alleged willful nullification of the true intentions of the Fathers of Confederation." "Act or Pact? Another Look at Confederation," in Ramsay Cook, ed., *Confederation* (Toronto, 1967), p. 112.

2  I have not confined my sources to the writings of the legally trained. Historians and political scientists are also considered.

Their approach, although less influenced by technical considerations, did not differ significantly in orientation from that of the lawyers.

Canadian criticism of the Privy Council was part of the more general dissatisfaction present in many of the jurisdictions for which it was a final appeal court. See Hector Hughes, *National Sovereignty and Judicial Autonomy in the British Commonwealth of Nations* (London, 1931), for an analysis.

3 Peter H. Russell, *The Supreme Court of Canada as a Bilingual and Bicultural Institution* (Ottawa, 1969), pp. 34–5, identifies the same two streams of criticism singled out in this article. André Lapointe, "La jurisprudence constitutionnelle et le temps," *Thémis, 7* (1956), pp. 26–7, adds a third main criticism, the failure to use adequate legal arguments, but this is clearly subsidiary and is not in fact discussed in his article.

4 V.C. MacDonald, "Judicial Interpretation of the Canadian Constitution," *University of Toronto Law Journal* (hereafter *UTLJ*), 1 (1935–36), provides a general centralist interpretation of the intentions of the Fathers and the BNA Act they created, which he contrasts with the judicial interpretation of the act. See also H.A. Smith, "The Residue of Power in Canada," *Canadian Bar Review* (hereafter *CBR*), 4 (1926), 438–9.

5 MacDonald, "Judicial Interpretation," p. 267, after noting that a centralized federation was intended, observed "how closely the language of the act reproduces that intent...." W.F. O'Connor stated: "there are not any material differences between the scheme of distribution of legislative powers between Dominion and provinces as apparently intended at the time of Confederation and the like legislative powers as expressed by the text of Part VI of the British North America Act, 1867." *Report Pursuant to Resolution of the Senate to the Honourable the Speaker by the Parliamentary Counsel Relating to the Enactment of the British North America Act, 1867, any lack of consonance between its terms and judicial construction of them and cognate matters* (hereafter the *O'Connor Report*) (Ottawa, 1939), p. 11.

In his most recent publication, Donald Creighton states that the Fathers regarded federalism as a "suspect and sinister form of government ... British American union, they admitted, would have to be federal in character; but at the same time it must also be the most strongly centralized union that was possible under federal forms....This basic principle guided all the planning whose end result was the British North America Act of 1867." *Canada's First Century: 1867–1967* (Toronto, 1970), p. 10 (see also pp. 44–46).

The extent of Macdonald's centralist bias is evident in his prediction in a letter to M.C. Cameron, dated December 19, 1864: "If the Confederation goes on you, if spared the ordinary age of man, will see both local governments and all governments absorbed in the General Power." Cited in A. Brady, "Our Constitutional Tradition," mimeo, paper presented to the Progressive Conservative Party Policy Conference, Niagara Falls, Autumn, 1969, p. 16n.

For additional support for the thesis that a centralized federal system was both intended and embodied in the BNA Act, see R.I. Cheffins, *The Constitutional Process in Canada* (Toronto, 1969), p. 37; D.G. Creighton, *British North America at Confederation* (Ottawa, 1939); R.M. Dawson, *The Government of Canada*, rev. by Norman Ward (4th ed., Toronto, 1963), chapters 2 and 5; W.P.M. Kennedy, *The Constitution of Canada, 1534–1937: An Introduction to Its Development, Law and Custom* (2nd ed., London, 1938), chapter 19; Kennedy, *Some Aspects of the Theories and Workings of Constitutional Law* (New York, 1932), pp. 86–87; A.R.M. Lower, *Colony to Nation* (Toronto, 1946), pp. 329–31; E. McInnis, *Canada:*

*A Political and Social History* (rev. ed., New York, 1960), chapter 13; *Report of the Royal Commission on Dominion-Provincial Relations* (hereafter the *Rowell-Sirois Report*) (Ottawa, 1954), I, pp. 32–35; F.R. Scott, "The Development of Canadian Federalism," *Papers and Proceedings of the Canadian Political Science Association* (hereafter *PPCPSA*), 3 (1931); Scott, "The Special Nature of Canadian Federalism," *Canadian Journal of Economics and Political Science* (hereafter *CJEPS*), 13 (1947); Scott, "Centralization and Decentralization in Canadian Federalism," *CBR*, 29 (1951); Scott, *Canada Today* (London, 1938), pp. 75–78; R. Tuck, "Canada and the Judicial Committee of the Privy Council," *UTLJ*, 4 (1941–42), pp. 41–43.

6 H.A. Smith, "The Residue of Power in Canada," p. 433. For additional assertions that the failure of the Judicial Committee to use pre-Confederation evidence was partially responsible for their misinterpretation of the BNA Act, see Tuck, "Canada and the Judicial Committee," pp. 40–41. V.C. MacDonald, "Constitutional Interpretation and Extrinsic Evidence," *CBR*, 17 (1939), is a helpful discussion of the actual practice of the Privy Council.

7 W.P.M. Kennedy, "The Terms of the British North America Act," in R. Flenley, ed., *Essays in Canadian History* (Toronto, 1939), p. 129.

8 *Can. H. of C. Debates*, April 5, 1937, pp. 2584–85.

9 *O'Connor Report*, pp. 11–14, and Annex 1.

10 R.W.S., "Criminal Appeals," *CBR*, 4 (1926), p. 410.

11 J.R. Mallory, *Social Credit and the Federal Power in Canada* (Toronto, 1954), p. 29, notes that generally historians, political scientists, and lawyers have argued that the courts misinterpreted the BNA Act. See, for example, Lower, *Colony to Nation*, pp. 376–77; D.G. Creighton, *Dominion of the North* (Boston, 1944), pp. 380–81; C.H. Cahan, *Can. H. of C. Debates*, April 5, 1937, p. 2575; W.P.M. Kennedy, "The Interpretation of the British North America Act," *Cambridge Law Journal*, 8 (1943), pp. 156–57, 160; V.C. MacDonald, "The Constitution in a Changing World," *CBR*, 26 (1948), pp. 29–30, 41; MacDonald, "The Privy Council and the Canadian Constitution," *CBR*, 29 (1951), p. 1035; Smith, "The Residue of Power in Canada," p. 434.

12 Creighton, *Canada's First Century*, p. 49.

13 B. Laskin, "'Peace, Order and Good Government' Re-examined," *CBR*, 25 (1947), p. 1054.

14 The vehemence that ran through many of these criticisms is evident in Laskin's assertion: "My examination of the cases dealing with the Dominion's general power does not indicate any inevitability in the making of particular decisions; if anything, it indicates conscious and deliberate choice of a policy which required, for its advancement, manipulations which can only with difficulty be represented as ordinary judicial techniques." *Ibid.*, p. 1086. Kennedy, "Interpretation of the British North America Act," pp. 153–56, and Tuck, "Canada and the Judicial Committee," pp. 56–64, describe the development of the misinterpretation of this clause. See also Creighton, *Dominion of the North*, pp. 380, 466–67; Dawson, *Government of Canada*, pp. 94–102; MacDonald, "The Constitution in a Changing World," pp. 33–34, 41; *O'Connor Report*, Annex 1, pp. 52–78; E.R. Richard, "Peace, Order and Good Government," *CBR*, 18 (1940); D.A. Schmeiser, *Civil Liberties in Canada* (London, 1964), pp. 8–9.

15 Kennedy, "Interpretation of the British North America Act," p. 156 and 156, n42. The situation was so anomalous that Anglin C.J. asserted that he found it difficult to accede to the proposition that "it should be denied all efficacy as an independent enumerative head of Dominion legislative jurisdiction." *King v Eastern Terminal Elevator Co.*, [1925] S.C.R. 434, at 441. Lionel H. Schipper, "The Influence of Duff C.J.C. on the Trade and Commerce Power,"

*University of Toronto Faculty of Law Review*, 14 (1956), discusses the influence of the provincial bias of Duff on the evolution of this clause. For critiques of the Privy Council interpretation, see B. Claxton, "Social Reform and the Constitution," *CJEPS*, 1 (1935), pp. 419–22; A.B. Keith, "The Privy Council and the Canadian Constitution," *Journal of Comparative Legislation*, 7 (1925), pp. 67–68; MacDonald, "The Constitution in a Changing World," pp. 36–42; M. MacGuigan, "The Privy Council and the Supreme Court: A Jurisprudential Analysis," *Alberta Law Review*, 4 (1966), p. 421; F.R. Scott, "Constitutional Adaptations to Changing Functions of Government," *CJEPS*, 11 (1945), pp. 332–33; A. Smith, *The Commerce Power in Canada and the United States* (Toronto, 1963); Tuck, "Canada and the Judicial Committee," pp. 64–69.

16 Smith, "The Residue of Power in Canada," p. 433; H.A. Smith, "Interpretation in English and Continental Law," *Journal of Comparative Legislation*, 9 (1927), pp. 162–63; Creighton, *Dominion of the North*, p. 381; Dawson, *Government of Canada*, pp. 96–98; Thorson, *Can. H. of C. Debates*, April 5, 1937, p. 2584.

The critics asserted that the original and intended meaning of property and civil rights was much more restrictive than it came to be under judicial fostering. See W.F. O'Connor, "Property and Civil Rights in the Province," *CBR*, 18 (1940).

17 H. Carl Goldenberg, "Social and Economic Problems in Canadian Federalism," *CBR*, 12 (1934), p. 423.

18 *Hodge* v *The Queen* (1883), 9 App. Cas. 117; *Liquidators of the Maritime Bank of Canada* v *Receiver-General of New Brunswick*, [1892] A.C. 437; *A.G. Ont.* v *Mercer* (1883), 8 App. Cas. 767. See Cheffins, *Constitutional Process in Canada*, pp. 38–39, 107–08. Ramsay Cook, *Provincial Autonomy, Minority Rights and the Compact Theory, 1867–1921* (Ottawa, 1969), pp. 21–22, discusses the successful attempt of Premier Mowat of Ontario "to make the lieutenant-governor as much the representative of the Queen in the province as the governor general was the representative of the Queen in federal affairs." See also G.F.G. Stanley, *A Short History of the Canadian Constitution* (Toronto, 1969), pp. 99–102, and J.C. Morrison, "Oliver Mowat and the Development of Provincial Rights in Ontario: A Study in Dominion-Provincial Relations, 1867–1896," in Ontario Department of Public Records and Archives, *Three History Theses* (Toronto, 1961), chapter 2.

19 This is the gist of comments by Mallory, *Social Credit and the Federal Power*, p. 29; Creighton, *Dominion of the North*, p. 381; J.M.S. Careless, *Canada: A Story of Challenge* (Toronto, 1963), pp. 364–65; MacDonald, "The Constitution in a Changing World," p. 44.

20 *Bank of Toronto* v *Lambe* (1887), 12 App. Cas. 575, at 579. Critics of the Privy Council for its adoption of a narrow legal approach were legion. See, for example, Creighton, *Canada's First Century*, p. 49; Lower, *Colony to Nation*, p. 334; MacDonald, "The Privy Council and the Canadian Constitution," pp. 1029–31; MacDonald, "Judicial Interpretation of the Canadian Constitution," pp. 267–70; Kennedy, "Interpretation of the British North America Act," pp. 151–52; Kennedy, *Some Aspects of the Theories and Working of Constitutional Law*, pp. 70–72; MacDonald, "The Constitution in a Changing World," p. 23; Thorson, *Can. H. of C. Debates*, April 5, 1937, p. 2582; F.R. Scott, "Section 94 of the British North America Act," *CBR*, 20 (1942), p. 530; E. McWhinney, *Judicial Review* (4th ed., Toronto, 1969), pp. 16–17, 29–30; Tuck, "Canada and the Judicial Committee," pp. 36–41.

Even supporters of the Privy Council agree that this was its approach. In the midst of the furore over the New Deal decisions, Ivor Jennings wrote: "It is not reasonable to expect that the members of the Judicial Committee of the Privy Council would interpret the Act in any way different from that adopted in the interpretation of other statutes. The Act is an ordinary statute, passed by Parliament at the request of certain rather troublesome and very remote colonists on the other side of the world. The judges did not think of themselves as determining the constitutional development of a great nation. Here was a statute in essence not different from many other pieces of legislation; and the judges naturally interpreted it in the usual way, by seeing what the statute said. They were concerned not with the desires of the Fathers, but with the progeny they had in fact produced." "Constitutional Interpretation. The Experience of Canada," *Harvard Law Review*, 51 (1937), p. 3 (see also p. 35).

21 Lord Sankey's bias was "clearly against pettifogging lawyers' arguments that interfered with the effective control of social life and the freedom of Dominion action, and this led him to infuse a new spirit into the process of interpretation." Jennings, "Constitutional Interpretation," p. 36. He also suggested (p. 36) that had he been on the court at the time, the New Deal decisions might have been sustained. He discusses Sankey's "liberal" approach on pp. 28–30. A "liberal" interpretation "implies a certain impatience with purely formal and technical arguments" (p. 31). "Liberal" decisions most frequently favourably cited by critics of the Privy Council were *Edwards* v *A.G. Can.*, [1930] A.C. 124; *In re Regulation and Control of Aeronautics in Canada*, [1932] A.C. 54; *In re Regulation and Control of Radio Communication in Canada*, [1932] A.C. 304; *British Coal Corporation* v *The King*, [1935] A.C. 500; *A.G. Ont.* v *A.G. Can. and A.G. Que.*, [1947] A.C. 127.

22 MacDonald, "The Privy Council and the Canadian Constitution," p. 1034.

23 MacDonald, "The Constitution in a Changing World," p. 24.

24 *Ibid.*, p. 41.

25 Laskin, "'Peace, Order and Good Government' Re-examined," p. 1087.

26 A. Brady and F.R. Scott, eds., *Canada after the War* (Toronto, 1943), p. 77.

27 Lower, *Colony to Nation*, p. 334.

28 MacDonald, "The Constitution in a Changing World," p. 45.

29 Laskin, "'Peace, Order and Good Government' Re-examined," pp. 1086–87.

30 Kennedy, "The British North America Act: Past and Future," *CBR*, 15 (1937), p. 399.

31 Kennedy, *Some Aspects of the Theories and Workings of Constitutional Law*, pp. 92–93.

32 MacDonald, "Judicial Interpretation of the Canadian Constitution," p. 282. See also MacDonald, "The Constitution in a Changing World," pp. 26, 44.

33 Michiel S.D. Horn, "The League for Social Reconstruction: Socialism and Nationalism in Canada, 1939–1945," (Ph.D. thesis, University of Toronto, 1969), p. 158.

34 Scott, "Development of Canadian Federalism," p. 247; see also Scott, *Canada Today*, pp. 32–33, 80–82.

35 Laskin, "'Peace, Order and Good Government' Re-examined," p. 1085.

36 In 1936 Vincent MacDonald wrote of the "inability of the Canadian constitution to meet the social, economic, and political needs of today and of the necessity for its revision … great problems affecting the social and economic life of the country demand legislative capacity and solution. The second great fact at the moment is that effective solution of these contemporary problems is, in part, handicapped, and, in part, rendered impossible by (a) the terms of the act of 1867, and (b) previous decisions thereon, which, together, withhold jurisdiction where it is necessary that jurisdiction should be, divide jurisdiction where unity of jurisdiction is essential, and in other cases, paralyse action because

of doubt as to jurisdiction where certainty of jurisdiction is vital." "Judicial Interpretation of the Canadian Constitution," p. 282. According to A.R.M. Lower, "Objection to Privy Council appeals did not become considerable until about 1930, but it rapidly increased during the Depression when certain decisions visibly hampered the country's ability to cope with the situation." "Theories of Canadian Federalism—Yesterday and Today," in Lower *et al.*, *Evolving Canadian Federalism* (Durham, N.C., 1958), p. 30. J.A. Corry, *Law and Policy* (Toronto, 1959), p. 26, notes how "the Great Depression of the thirties came perilously close to a breakdown in public order." See also Jean Beetz, "Les attitudes changeantes du Québec à l'endroit de la constitution de 1867," in P.A. Crépeau and C.B. Macpherson, eds., *The Future of Canadian Federalism/L'avenir du fédéralisme canadien* (Toronto, 1965), pp. 134–35.

37 Horn, "League for Social Reconstruction," p. 468.

38 *A.G. Can.* v *A.G. Ont.*, [1937] A.C. 326, at 350.

39 Scott, "Centralization and Decentralization in Canadian Federalism," p. 1113.

40 Kennedy, "Interpretation of the British North America Act," p. 159.

41 MacDonald, "The Constitution in a Changing World," p. 42.

42 See Russell, *Supreme Court*, pp. 11–17, for the controversy attending the establishment of the court and the failure to eliminate appeals at that time.

43 J.S. Ewart, *The Kingdom of Canada* (Toronto, 1908), p. 227; see also p. 22, and Ewart, *The Kingdom Papers* (Ottawa, 1912), I, p. 88. For a study of Ewart, see Douglas L. Cole, "John S. Ewart and Canadian Nationalism," Canadian Historical Association, *Historical Papers*, 1969. "Canadian history as Ewart viewed it had but one chief theme —Canada's fight for freedom from imperial control" (p. 65). Nationalist criticisms of the Privy Council waxed and waned up until the thirties. There was a brief flurry immediately prior to the First World War. See W.E. Raney, "Justice, Precedent and Ultimate Conjecture," *Canadian Law Times* (hereafter *CLT*), 29 (1909), p. 459; W.S. Deacon, "Canadians and the Privy Council," *CLT*, 31 (1911), p. 9, and "Canadians and the Privy Council," *CLT*, 31 (1911), pp. 126–27; J.S. Ewart, "The Judicial Committee," *CLT*, 33 (1913), pp. 676–77; also "Address by W.E. Raney," *Proceedings of the Canadian Bar Association* (hereafter *PCBA*), 5 (1920), pp. 221–24. McWhinney points out that the very low repute of Privy Council judges in the Depression represented not only dissatisfaction with "economically conservative judicial decisions ... [but] ... also, in part, an outpouring of local nationalism in that the court ... was an alien (in the sense of English) tribunal...." *Comparative Federalism* (Toronto, 1962), pp. 21–22.

44 Scott, "Abolition of Appeals to the Privy Council: A Symposium," *CBR*, 25 (1947), p. 571; see also Scott, "The Consequences of the Privy Council Decisions," *CBR*, 15 (1937), pp. 493–94.

45 Hon. Stuart S. Garson (minister of justice), *Can. H. of C. Debates*, Sept. 20, 1949, pp. 69, 74–75.

46 Michel Brunet, "Canadians and Canadiens," in R. Cook, ed., *French-Canadian Nationalism: An Anthology* (Toronto, 1969), p. 289, discusses the war and post-war nationalist drive to centralism, of which the abolition of appeals was a part.

47 Scott, "The Development of Canadian Federalism," p. 245. See also J.A. Corry, review of G.P. Browne, *The Judicial Committee and the British North America Act* (Toronto, 1967), in *Canadian Journal of Political Science*, 1 (1968), pp. 217–18; *Rowell-Sirois Report*, I, pp. 57–59, and Browne, *The Judicial Committee*, pp. 40, 84, 158–59.

48 *Ibid.*, Browne.

49 As John Dafoe believed. See R. Cook, *The Politics of John Dafoe and the Free Press* (Toronto, 1963), p. 217. Modified versions of this view were also presented by A.R.M. Lower, "Theories of

Canadian Federalism," p. 38; Jacques Brossard, *La Cour Suprême et la constitution* (Montreal, 1968), p. 172; and Giuseppe Turi, "Le déséquilibre constitutionnel fiscal au Canada," *Thémis*, 10 (1959–60), p. 38. Hughes, *National Sovereignty and Judicial Autonomy*, pp. 98, 104–05, discusses the possibility of Judicial Committee bias "where the issue is one between a Dominion and the British Government or between a Dominion person or firm and a British person or firm ... This is based on its composition which is predominantly English and partly political...." Unspecified allegations of political expediency are contained in Thorson, *Can. H. of C. Debates*, April 5, 1937, p. 2582, and MacDonald, "Judicial Interpretation of the Canadian Constitution," p. 285.

50 For discussions of the provincial bias of the Judicial Committee, see F.E. LaBrie, "Canadian Constitutional Interpretation and Legislative Review," *UTLJ*, 8 (1949–50), pp. 318–23; McWhinney, *Judicial Review*, pp. 51 n7, 67, 69; MacDonald, "The Privy Council and the Canadian Constitution," pp. 1030–32, 1035; MacDonald, "The Constitution in a Changing World," p. 23; MacGuigan, "The Privy Council and the Supreme Court," pp. 426–27. R.F. McWilliams, "The Privy Council and the Constitution," *CBR*, 17 (1939), p. 582, attempts to prove that the Privy Council was not a defender of the provinces or responsible "for whittling down the powers of the Dominion." See also Browne, *The Judicial Committee*, p. 77.

51 Privy Council treaty references are summarized in R. Arès, *Dossier sur le pacte fédératif de 1867* (Montreal, 1967), pp. 66–68, and criticized in MacDonald, "Privy Council and the Canadian Constitution," pp. 1030–31.

52 Cheffins, *Constitutional Process in Canada*, p. 130, provides a summary of the speculation on the reasons for the provincial bias of Watson and Haldane. Some interesting reflections on Haldane are contained in the "Address by the Right Honourable Sir David Maxwell Fyfe," *PCBA*, 37 (1954), pp. 149–51. Jonathon Robinson, "Lord Haldane and the British North America Act," *UTLJ*, 20 (1970), and Scott, *Canada Today*, p. 77, refer to the relevant writings of Haldane. Robinson attempts to explain Haldane's provincial bias as an outgrowth of his Hegelian philosophy. See also the obituary of Watson given by Haldane, *CLT*, 23 (1903), pp. 223–25.

53 See, for example, Creighton, *Dominion of the North* , p. 466; Thorson, *Can. H. of C. Debates*, April 5, 1937, p. 2585; Laskin, "'Peace, Order and Good Government' Re-examined," p. 1077; MacGuigan, "The Privy Council and the Supreme Court," p. 425; Scott, *Canada Today*, pp. 77–78.

Jennings asserted that "Lord Watson held to the fixed idea that Canada was a true federation and that it was the function of the Board to maintain something called 'provincial autonomy' which was not in the Act." Jennings is an exception, however, in claiming that Haldane favoured the provinces reluctantly because of the "weight of the previous decisions." "Constitutional Interpretation," pp. 35–36, 21.

54 Lord Haldane, "The Work for the Empire of the Judicial Committee of the Privy Council," *Cambridge Law Journal*, 1 (1923), p. 150.

55 Cited in Ewart, *Kingdom of Canada*, p. 20.

56 *Can. H. of C. Debates*, Feb. 1, 1937, pp. 426, 444.

57 *Special Committee on British North America Act: Proceedings and Evidence and Report* (Ottawa, 1935), p. 82. R.M. Dawson, ed., *Constitutional Issues in Canada, 1900–1931* (London, 1933), pp. 343–44, reprints a 1912 editorial from the *Ottawa Journal* strongly critical of several decisions in which the Privy Council supported "vested right against the public weal," while the decisions of the Canadian courts had been "in favour of the public." These cases are briefly noted by C.G. Pierson, *Canada and the Privy Council* (London, 1960), p. 47. For Depression fears that business would

seek to shelter behind the provinces, see R.A. MacKay, "The Nature of Canadian Federalism," in W.W. McLaren *et al.*, eds., *Proceedings, Conference on Canadian-American Affairs* (Montreal, 1936), p. 202. F.H. Underhill wrote that the use of provincial rights to obstruct social reform was "largely camouflage put up by our industrial and financial magnates. None of these worthy gentlemen wants a national government with sufficient constitutional power to be able to interfere effectively with their own pursuit of profits." "Revolt in Canadian Politics," *Nation*, 139 (December 12, 1934), p. 673, cited in Horn, "League for Social Reconstruction," p. 439.

58  Scott, "Centralization and Decentralization in Canadian Federalism," p. 1116; Scott, "The Consequences of the Privy Council Decisions," p. 492; J.R. Mallory, "The Courts and the Sovereignty of the Canadian Parliament," *CJEPS*, 10 (1944), pp. 166–73. Since the Revolution Settlement, asserted Mallory, British judges "have been activated by an acute suspicion of the motives of both the executive and the legislature and have conceived it their duty to confine the application of statute law to cases where its meaning could not be mistaken" (p. 167). "Upon occasion the very novelty of government expedients has seriously strained the impartiality of the type of judicial mind which is shocked by the unorthodox" (p. 173). See also Mallory, "The Five Faces of Federalism," Crépeau and Macpherson, *The Future of Canadian Federalism*, pp. 6–7, and *Social Credit and the Federal Power*, pp. 53–56 and chapter 3.

When Australia sought to restrict appeals to the Privy Council, the British Colonial Secretary, Chamberlain, stated: "The question of the right of appeal must also be looked at from the point of view of the very large class of persons interested in Australian securities or Australian undertakings, who are domiciled in the United Kingdom. Nothing could be more prejudicial to Australia than to diminish the security felt by capitalists who desire to invest their money there. One element in the security which at present exists is that there is the possibility of an ultimate appeal to the Queen in Council…." Cited in Ewart, *Kingdom of Canada*, p. 232. In 1909 J.M. Clark stated that the right of appeal "is also regarded as an important security and safeguard by British foreign investors." "The Judicial Committee of the Privy Council," *CLT*, 29 (1909), pp. 352–53.

The high cost of appeals, which played into the hands of the wealthy and thus buttressed the position of the economically strong, was a frequent criticism of the Privy Council. See Editorial, "Procedure before the Judicial Committee," *CLT*, 25 (1905), pp. 29–30; W.S. Deacon, "Gordon v Horne: Canadians and the Privy Council," *CLT*, 30 (1910), p. 877; Deacon, "Canadians and the Privy Council," *CLT*, 31 (1911), p. 128, and "Canadians and the Privy Council," *CLT*, 31 (1911), p. 10; C.E. Kaulbach, *Can. H. of C. Debates*, February 26, 1880, p. 241; "Labor's Views on Dominion-Provincial Relations," *Canadian Congress Journal*, 17 (February, 1938), p. 15; Pierson, *Canada and the Privy Council*, pp. 41–42, 70.

Sir Allen Aylesworth, a former Liberal minister of justice (1906–11), admitted in 1914 that the wealthy had an advantage in appeals due to their high cost, but that was "after all, but one of the advantages which the possession of wealth carries with it in every walk of life." "Address of Sir Allen Aylesworth, 7th Annual Meeting of the Ontario Bar Association," *CLT*, 34 (1914), p. 144.

59  Mallory, "The Courts and the Sovereignty of the Canadian Parliament," p. 169.

60  "Labor's Views on Dominion-Provincial Relations," p. 10.

61  Presidential address, *PCBA*, 6 (1921), p. 110.

62  Presidential address, *ibid.*, 12 (1927), pp. 112–113.

63  *Ibid.*, 24 (1939), pp. 204–05 . In their report the previous year the committee referred to the disallowance of Alberta legislation

as a "reversion to sound thought. Disallowance in some cases is just as important as enactment." The report continued to warn, however, that "quite apart from certain notorious Acts, much of this year's product reveals an inspiration which is wholly alien to our usual habits of thought…. The Committee believes that it is the general view of the profession that unless we can govern ourselves according to settled and generally recognized principles of right and wrong, we are headed either for anarchy or despotism … it can find no place in any civilized system of law for several Acts passed at the last Session of the Legislature of Alberta … these are only high water marks which stand above the general level and are more conspicuous on that account." The committee went on to castigate open-ended legislation in British Columbia and Saskatchewan that gave significant, vaguely defined authority to the Lieutenant-Governor-in-Council to make regulations for the carrying out of legislation. *Ibid.*, 23 (1938), pp. 191–93.

64  W.S. Johnson, "The Reign of Law Under an Expanding Bureaucracy," *CBR*, 22 (1944). Cheffins, *Constitutional Process in Canada*, chapter 3, contains a brief discussion of the factors behind this evolution in the procedures of government operation.

Cecil A. Wright stated in 1938: "we have to a great extent underestimated the importance of administrative tribunals and the place of modern legislation as regulating forces in modern society. Legislation has always been viewed with disfavour by the common law lawyer because of the traditional view of the common law broadening down from 'precedent to precedent,' and undoubtedly the general attitude of the profession today is not different from that of Lord Halsbury who is reputed to have said that 'the best Act you can have is a repealing Act.' One consequence of this is that our whole technique and approach to legislation is weak, and as a result antagonism between the legal profession and legislative and administrative bodies becomes more marked.

"We have, indeed, paid so much attention to past judicial policy, that courts and lawyers are frequently in danger of limiting present legislative policy by restrictive interpretations. The notion that a statute shall be deemed to have departed as little as possible from common law principles runs throughout many judicial decisions, yet, as a member of the House of Lords recently said, 'it is an unsafe guide in days of modern legislation, often or perhaps generally based on objects and policies alien to the common law.'" "Law and Law Schools," *PCBA*, 23 (1938), p. 115.

65  See G.L. Caplan, "The Failure of Canadian Socialism: The Ontario Experience," *Canadian Historical Review*, 44 (1963), for the extreme anti-socialist campaign waged by business in the closing years of the Second World War.

66  For American experience, see Benjamin R. Twiss, *Lawyers and the Constitution: How Laissez-Faire Came to the Supreme Court* (New York, 1962).

67  W.H. Hamilton, "The Path of Due Process of Law," *Ethics*, 48 (1938), p. 296, asserted that American courts were more resistant to laissez faire than other parts of the body politic. "It seems strange that so many jurists stood steadfast against the seductions of laissez-faire; history, political science, and economics can boast no such record … does the whole story, in irony, paradox, and compromise, derive from the innate conservatism of the law—a rock of ages which even the untamed strength of laissez-faire could move but could not blast."

68  Stanley, "Act or Pact?" pp. 112–13.

69  Given the strong criticism it subsequently received it is worthwhile to document the extent of its support in earlier years. See, for example, John T. Small, "Supreme Court and Privy Council Appeals," *CLT*, 29 (1909), pp. 51–52; Clark, "The Judicial Committee of the Privy Council"; "Address of Sir Allen Aylesworth," p. 139; "By the Way," *CLT*,

36 (1916), pp. 354–55, 662–63; W.E. Wilkinson, "Our London Letter," *CLT*, 41 (1921), p. 61, reporting Lord Cave; B[ram] T[hompson], "Editor's Note," *CLT*, 41 (1921), pp. 62–63; "Editorial," *CLT*, 41 (1921), pp. 83–86; Bram Thompson, "Editorial," *CLT*, 41 (1921), pp. 161–65; Edward Anderson, "Address to Manitoba Bar Association," *CLT*, 41 (1921), pp. 252–53; "Appeal to the Privy Council," *CLT*, 41 (1921), pp. 525–26; Pierson, *Canada and the Privy Council*, p. 39.

70 A.C. Galt, "Appeals to the Privy Council," *CLT*, 41 (1921), p. 172.

71 W. Nesbitt, "The Judicial Committee of the Privy Council," *CLT*, 29 (1909), p. 252.

72 Sir L.P. Duff, "The Privy Council," *CBR*, 3 (1925), pp. 278–79.

73 Sir Charles Fitzpatrick, "The Constitution of Canada," *CLT*, 34 (1914), p. 1031.

74 Galt, "Appeals to the Privy Council," pp. 168–69.

75 *PCBA*, 15 (1930), p. 37. Another writer stated that Viscount Haldane was "recognized as the greatest living authority on the interpretation of the British North America Act." W.E. Raney, "Another Question of Dominion Jurisdiction Emerges," *CBR*, 3 (1925), p. 617.

76 Nesbitt, "The Judicial Committee," p. 244.

77 Duff, "The Privy Council," p. 278. See also Nesbitt, "The Judicial Committee," pp. 243, 245–46; W.R. Riddell, "The Judicial Committee of the Privy Council," *CLT*, 30 (1910), pp. 305–06; W.H. Newlands, "Appeal to the Privy Council," *CBR*, 1 (1923), pp. 814–15.

78 Nesbitt, "The Judicial Committee," pp. 250–51; Riddell, "The Judicial Committee," p. 304. Ewart, *Kingdom of Canada*, p. 228, argued that if the Privy Council did try to produce uniformity of laws in the Empire appeals should be abolished, for each community required its own laws. In fact, however, he asserted that the Privy Council endeavoured to keep the various systems of laws distinct.

79 Nesbitt, "The Judicial Committee," pp. 250–51; Clark, "The Judicial Committee," pp. 349, 352–53; "By the Way," *CLT*, 37 (1917), pp. 624–25; "Address of Sir Allen Aylesworth," p. 140; Bram Thompson, "Editorial," *CLT*, 41 (1921), pp. 162–63; Howard Ferguson, *PCBA*, 15 (1930), p. 37. The desire of the Macdonald Conservatives to retain appeals to the Privy Council when the Supreme Court Act of 1875 was under discussion was based "primarily on their concern for preserving Canada's links with the Empire." Russell, *Supreme Court*, p. 16.

80 Clark, "The Judicial Committee," p. 352; Galt, "Appeals to the Privy Council," p. 172.

81 Riddell, "The Judicial Committee," p. 304.

82 This argument was used by British officials in 1876 when the Liberal government attempted to cut off appeals to the Privy Council. See L.A. Cannon, "Some Data Relating to the Appeal to the Privy Council," *CBR*, 3 (1925), pp. 460–62. In discussions on the Australian constitution in 1900 Chamberlain stated that "questions … which may sometimes involve a good deal of local feeling are the last that should be withdrawn from a tribunal of appeal with regard to which there could not be even a suspicion of prepossession." Cited in Ewart, *Kingdom of Canada*, p. 232. The British constitutional expert, A.B. Keith, asserted that the "true value of the appeal … lies in the power of the Judicial Committee to deal in perfect freedom from local or racial prejudice with issues deeply affecting the relations of the two nationalities in Canada, or of the provinces and the Federation, or of the provinces *inter se*." Cited in W.E. Raney, "Appeal to the Privy Council," *CBR*, 5 (1927), p. 608. For the widespread Canadian support for this line of reasoning, see "Editorial Review," *CLT*, 27 (1907), pp. 403–04; Small, "Supreme Court and Privy Council Appeals," p. 51; Nesbitt, "The Judicial Committee," p. 249; Riddell, "The Judicial Committee," p. 304;

Fitzpatrick, "The Constitution of Canada," p. 1031; "Appeal to the Privy Council," *CLT*, 41 (1921), p. 525, reporting Premier Taschereau of Quebec; James Aikins, "President's Address to Conference of Commissioners on Uniformity of Legislation," *PCBA*, 6 (1921), p. 286; Brossard, *La Cour Suprême*, p. 171.

83 "Presidential Address," *CBR*, 5 (1927), pp. 562–63.

84 Evan Gray made this point with vigour. "It is time the chief 'indoor sport' of constitutional lawyers in 'lambasting' the Privy Council and cavilling at decisions of that body was discontinued. The 'sport' never had any merit or excuse and it violates 'good form'—an essential element of all 'sport.' All this talk about distortion of the framework of Confederation and defeat of our national purposes by judicial authority is silly and puerile. If there is distortion, we Canadians all must take the responsibility for the distortion. If there is defeat of national purposes, let us do something worthy of our autonomy rather than continue to accept and complain of the defeat. Our constitution is what our forefathers made it and as we have applied it—not what British judges gave us. If we do not like the constitution as it is, we have always had leave to change it; let us change it—now—in an open, forthright and well-considered manner." "'The O'Connor Report' on the British North America Act, 1867," *CBR*, 17 (1939), pp. 333–34.

85 The issue was posed but not answered by R. Cheffins: "It could be argued that the type of strong federal government envisaged by the political founders of the Canadian nation was impractical and not realizable in a country as large geographically and as culturally diverse as Canada. It could also be argued that the Judicial Committee was recognizing the realities of the social and political life of the nation in upholding the validity of provincial statutes. On the other hand it could be maintained that if the Privy Council had not ruled the way it did, then the provincial governments would never have assumed the importance which they did, and thus their position would not have to be continually sustained by judicial decisions." "The Supreme Court of Canada: The Quiet Court in an Unquiet Country," *Osgoode Hall Law Journal*, 4 (1966), p. 267.

Both Morton and Careless lay great stress on the contributions of the Judicial Committee to the strong position of the provinces in the 1920s. W.L. Morton, *The Kingdom of Canada* (Toronto, 1969), p. 444; Careless, *Canada*, p. 364. D.G. Creighton also emphasizes the causal role of the Judicial Committee in breaking down Macdonald's centralized federalism. "The Decline and Fall of the Empire of the St. Lawrence," Canadian Historical Association, *Historical Papers, 1969*, p. 24. See also Scott, "The Development of Canadian Federalism," pp. 238–47; Goldenberg, "Social and Economic Problems in Canadian Federalism."

86 Kennedy, *Some Aspects of the Theories and Workings of Constitutional Law*, p. 100.

87 See N. McL. Rogers, "The Genesis of Provincial Rights," *Canadian Historical Review*, 14 (1933), for an incisive analysis of the weakness of the centralist basis of Confederation from the moment of its inception.

88 "The failure of the Dominion's economic policies, which formed such important elements in the new national interest, discouraged the growth of a strong, national sentiment; and local loyalties and interests began to reassert themselves." *Rowell-Sirois Report*, I, p. 54. See also E.R. Black and A.C. Cairns, "A Different Perspective on Canadian Federalism," *Canadian Public Administration*, 9 (1966), p. 29, and Cook, *Provincial Autonomy, Minority Rights and the Compact Theory*, chapter 3, especially p. 19.

89 Black and Cairns, "A Different Perspective," p. 29.

90 *Ibid.*, pp. 38–43.

91 Morrison, "Oliver Mowat," *passim*.

92  *Rowell-Sirois Report*, I, p. 55.

93  F.H. Underhill, *The Image of Confederation* (Toronto, 1964), p. 27.

94  Cited in A. Brady, "Quebec and Canadian Federalism," *CJEPS*, 25 (1959), pp. 260–61.

95  See the *Rowell-Sirois Report*, I, pp. 55–59, for a discussion. André Lapointe, "La jurisprudence constitutionnelle et le temps," is a suggestive impressionistic study to the effect that Privy Council decisions, 1880–84, constituted appropriate responses to the forces of regionalism developing at that time.

96  Gray, "'The O'Connor Report,'" pp. 334–35.

97  "The Late Lord Watson," *CLT*, 23 (1903), p. 224.

98  For Mowat's position on the role of the provinces, his success with the Privy Council, and his favourable reception by the people of Ontario, see Lower, *Colony to Nation*, pp. 376–79. Creighton, *Canada's First Century*, p. 47, provides a critical assessment of Mowat's philosophy and conduct. G.W. Ross, *Getting into Parliament and After* (Toronto, 1913), pp. 187–88, states that "Sir Oliver Mowat's success in the courts of Canada, and particularly before the Privy Council, raised him greatly in the estimation of the whole people of Ontario. Were it not for these conflicts with the Dominion Government I doubt if Sir Oliver would have survived the general election of 1883." Morrison, "Oliver Mowat," provides the most detailed analysis of Mowat's strategy.

99  There is considerable academic support for the proposition that the federal system established in 1867 was too centralist for the underlying regional pluralism of Canadian society, and the related proposition that it was an act of creative judicial statesmanship for the Privy Council to adapt the constitution to pluralist realities. O.D. Skelton stated that the "provincial trend of court decisions paralleled or rather followed, with some time lag, the changes in Canada itself." *Special Committee on the British North America Act: 1935*, p. 27. "In all justice to the Judicial Committee," asserted Professor Brady, "they probably did no more than what the majority of Canadians in the earlier period desired. They gave judicial expression to the upsurge of provincialism, evident from the early eighties to the decade after the First World War...." *Democracy in the Dominions* (2nd ed., Toronto, 1952), pp. 45–46. See also Brady, "Our Constitutional Tradition," p. 16. Michael Oliver states of the centralist intentions of the Fathers: "It must be concluded that they either seriously overestimated the range of shared assumptions between the two cultures, or badly underestimated the degree of unity on fundamentals which was necessary to run the centralized state they had tried to create." "Quebec and Canadian Democracy," *CJEPS*, 23 (1957), p. 504. Cheffins states that the "ineffectiveness" of the centralist features of the BNA Act "serves as a classic example of the futility of written positive law in the face of a social environment which refuses to accept the original statutory intention." *Constitutional Process in Canada*, pp. 37–38 (see also p. 132). G.P. Glazebrook states: "the Judicial Committee was a make-weight in scales that were otherwise uncertainly balanced. The committee did not create the provincial school of thought; and it is worthy of note that it was long after it had ceased to have jurisdiction that provincialism took on its most extreme form. Nevertheless the strong slant in the legal decisions ... may be regarded as influential in the years in which the constitutional debate began." *A History of Canadian Political Thought* (Toronto, 1966), pp. 186–87. J.R. Mallory praised the political acumen of the Local Prohibition Case in 1896, but added that "No other judge since Lord Watson's time has attempted the judicial realignment needed by the times and comparable to that achieved by the Supreme Court of the United States after 1937." "The Courts and the Sovereignty of the Canadian Parliament," p. 177.

Even the leading Canadian constitutional expert, W.P.M. Kennedy, later to be so critical of the Privy Council, had strongly praised it in earlier writings. In 1930 he wrote: "I often wonder ... with the inevitable divergencies in our national life due to race, religion, geography and such like, whether after all the way of the Privy Council up to 1929 has not been the better way. We might, apart from the Privy Council, have followed paths of greater juristic cohesion. We might have created a stronger legal nation; but it is problematical, had we done so, whether our legal cohesion would not have been compelled, if federation was to have survived, to give ground ultimately to those more compelling forces ... and whether we should not have been forced ultimately, in the interest of continuing the union, to retrace our legal steps." Book review of E. Cameron, *The Canadian Constitution as Interpreted by the Judicial Committee, 1916–1929*, in *CBR*, 8 (1930), p. 708. Kennedy made the same point on several other occasions: see *Essays in Constitutional Law* (London, 1934), pp. 59–60, 101–02; *Some Aspects of the Theories and Workings of Constitutional Law*, pp. 93, 101–02.

See also J.A. Maxwell, "Aspects of Canadian Federalism," *Dalhousie Review*, 16 (1936–37), p. 277n; E. McWhinney, "Federalism, Constitutionalism. and Legal Change: Legal Implications of the 'Revolution' in Quebec," in Crépeau and Macpherson, *The Future of Canadian Federalism*, pp. 159–60; McWhinney, *Judicial Review*, pp. 25–26, 70–71; E. Forsey, "Concepts of Federalism: Some Canadian Aspects," in J.P. Meekison, ed., *Canadian Federalism: Myth or Reality* (Toronto, 1968), p. 349; Stanley, *A Short History of the Canadian Constitution*, p. 142.

100  P.E. Trudeau, *Federalism and the French Canadians* (Toronto, 1968), p. 198.

101  Cheffins, *Constitutional Process in Canada*, pp. 130–31, and W.R. Lederman, "Thoughts on Reform of the Supreme Court of Canada," *Alberta Law Review*, 8 (1970), p. 3, both point out the inappropriateness of a literal criticism of Privy Council decisions.

102  Clark, "The Judicial Committee," p. 348.

103  E.W., "Random Remarks Regarding the Judicial Committee," *CLT*, 36 (1916), pp. 370–71.

104  Bram Thompson, "Editorial," *CLT*, 41 (1921), p. 165.

105  "Editorial," *CLT*, 40 (1920), p. 261.

106  MacDonald, "Judicial Interpretation of the Canadian Constitution," pp. 282–83.

107  Jennings, "Constitutional Interpretation," p. 38.

108  Kennedy, *The Constitution of Canada*, p. 550. See also F.C. Cronkite, "The Social Legislation References," *CBR*, 15 (1937), p. 478.

109  Left-wing critics of the time disagree with this interpretation. See *The Canadian Forum* (March, 1937), p. 4, and Dorothy Steeves in CBC, *The Canadian Constitution* (Toronto, 1938), pp. 97–98.

110  R. Cook, *Canada and the French Canadian Question* (Toronto, 1966), p. 53.

111  Creighton, *Canada's First Century*, pp. 213–14.

112  MacDonald, "The Privy Council and the Canadian Constitution," p. 1036.

113  MacDonald, "Judicial Interpretation of the Canadian Constitution," p. 281. MacDonald, "The Privy Council and the Canadian Constitution," pp. 1034–35, reiterates his earlier statement, and adds that we do not even have certainty (p. 1036). Laskin, "'Peace, Order and Good Government' Re-examined," p. 1056, accused the Privy Council of laying down too many unnecessary dicta and generalities. McWhinney, *Judicial Review*, p. 54, suggests that the need for compromise in the committee may have produced obscurities in their decisions. Some earlier technical criticisms may be found in "Editorial Review," *CLT*, 6 (1886), p. 375, and A.H. Marsh, "The Privy Council as a Colonial Court of Appeal,"

*CLT*, 14 (1894), p. 92. See, by contrast, E.W., "Random Remarks Regarding the Judicial Committee," pp. 371–72, who praises the committee for its statesmanlike willingness to be inconsistent and to override legal quibbles. The caveat of H.A. Innis is also worthy of consideration: "But though interpretations of decisions of the Privy Council have been subjected to intensive study and complaints have been made about their inconsistency, inconsistencies have implied flexibility and have offset the dangers of rigidity characteristic of written constitutions." "Great Britain, the United States and Canada," in M.Q. Innis, ed., *Essays In Canadian Economic History* (Toronto, 1956), p. 404.

114 Ewart, *Kingdom of Canada*, pp. 226–28. Ewart repeated his opposition to this defence of the Privy Council on numerous occasions: *ibid.*, p. 20; *Kingdom Papers*, I, p. 88; "The Judicial Committee," *CLT*, 34 (1914), pp. 221, 230–31; "The Judicial Committee," *CLT*, 33 (1913), pp. 676–78; "Some Further Comments on Dominion-Provincial Relations," *PPCPSA* , 3 (1931) , pp. 253–58.

115 *Can. H. of C. Debates*, February 26, 1880, pp. 253–55, and see Blake, cited in MacDonald, "The Privy Council and the Canadian Constitution," p. 1026. For Blake's later partial change of mind, see Russell, *Supreme Court*, p. 251, n173.

116 Raney, "Justice, Precedent and Ultimate Conjecture," p. 460; Thorson, *Can. H. of C. Debates*, April 5, 1937, pp. 2581–82; Scott, *Canada Today*, p. 77; Tuck, "Canada and the Judicial Committee," pp. 71–73; Mallory, "The Five Faces of Federalism," p. 6.

117 A.H. Marsh, "The Privy Council as a Colonial Court of Appeal," *CLT*, 14 (1894), p. 94. See also Deacon, "Canadians and the Privy Council," pp. 126–27. This criticism was popular among the opponents of the New Deal decisions. Cahan, *Can. H. of C. Debates*, April 5, 1937, p. 2574, and Scott, "The Consequences of the Privy Council Decisions," pp. 493–94.

Jennings, "Constitutional Interpretation," is the best attempt to discuss the influence of Privy Council personnel on its judgements.

118 Jennings, "Constitutional Interpretation," pp. 1–2.

119 MacDonald, "The Canadian Constitution Seventy Years After," *CBR*, 15 (1937), pp. 426–27.

120 Tuck, "Canada and the Judicial Committee," p. 73 (see also pp. 55–56, 71–72). Versions of this point were made by various commentators. LaBrie, "Canadian Constitutional Interpretation and Legislative Review," p. 346; W.R. Lederman, "The Balanced Interpretation of the Federal Distribution of Legislative Powers in Canada," in Crépeau and Macpherson, *The Future of Canadian Federalism*, p. 111; Lederman, "Thoughts on the Reform of the Supreme Court of Canada," pp. 3–4.

121 McWhinney, *Judicial Review*, p. 72.

122 MacGuigan, "The Privy Council and the Supreme Court," pp. 425–26.

123 D.G. Creighton, speaking of the diversity of jurisdiction of the Privy Council, stated: "An expert knowledge of one of these legal systems might be regarded as a respectable accomplishment for an ordinary man. But the titans of the Judicial Committee, from long practice and profound study, have grown accustomed to the multifarious and exacting requirements of their office; and they apparently leap, with the agility of quick-change performers, from one legal metamorphosis to another.... To an outsider it might seem that there was at least the faint possibility of some bewilderment and confusion in these endlessly varied deliberations. The outsider might even be so far misled as to conceive of a noble judge who continued obstinately to peruse the Koran when he ought to have been consulting the *British North America Act*." "Federal Relations in Canada since 1914," in Chester Martin, ed., *Canada in Peace and War* (Toronto, 1941), pp. 32–33.

124 Ewart, "The Judicial Committee," p. 676. He also asserted that the Judicial Committee "suffers from a conviction of its own superiority—a conviction due (*a*) to the ruling character of the race to which its members belong, and (*b*) to the fact that, by sending our cases to it, we appear to acknowledge our incapacity."

125 *Ibid.*, p. 676.

126 "What gives its imposing respectability, its ponderous finality to a decision of the Privy Council is its unity. There may be considerable diversity of opinion, doubts, hesitations and dissents behind the curtain. But when the curtain goes up one judge delivers the opinion of the Court and it is law. It does not sprinkle like a garden hose; it hits like the hammer of Thor." A.T. Hunter, "A Proposal for Statutory Relief from the Privy Council Controversy," *CBR*, 4 (1926), p. 102. See McWhinney, *Judicial Review*, pp. 52–53, for a discussion of the practice and suggested explanations for its survival.

127 He continued: "Though the reports summarize the arguments of counsel, the emphasis given to the written opinion minimizes the case that the majority did not accept. Finally, the opinion of the whole Board is given by one member. The substance is, no doubt, agreed to by the rest of the majority; but it is never certain that all the expressions would have been accepted by the majority if they had fully considered them. The type of opinion differs according to the judge who renders it. He comes to the conclusion desired by the majority and states the reasons acceptable to the majority; but anyone who has drafted a document knows that there are many ways of saying the same thing and that a draft often says more than is intended." Jennings, "Constitutional Interpretation," pp. 2–3.

128 Ewart, "The Judicial Committee," p. 676.

129 E.W., "Random Remarks Regarding the Judicial Committee," p. 370.

130 Browne, *The Judicial Committee and the British North America Act*.

131 The reference is to a tendency, not to ethnic unanimity. Frank Scott was correct in pointing out in 1947 that Quebec had "no single view" on the question of the retention of the Judicial Committee, and in noting that a minister of justice from Quebec, Télésphore Fournier, who introduced the bill to establish the Supreme Court in 1875, stated that he "wished to see the practice put an end to altogether," and that Ernest Lapointe held similar views. "Abolition of Appeals to the Privy Council: A Symposium," p. 571. Scott had earlier argued that minority rights had received better protection from the Supreme Court than from the Privy Council. "The Privy Council and Minority Rights," *Queen's Quarterly*, 37 (1930). It is also worthy of note that the elimination of appeals occurred under a French-Canadian Prime Minister. Pierson, *Canada and the Privy Council*, pp. 69–70, provides some evidence of French-Canadian opposition to appeals. The 1927 Labrador decision of the Privy Council turned some French Canadians against the system of appeals. See Brossard, *La Cour Suprême*, p. 189, and Dale C. Thomson, *Louis St. Laurent: Canadian* (Toronto, 1967), pp. 91, 208. Further, it is clear that there have been many English-Canadian supporters of the Privy Council right up to its final abolition. These observations do not, however, invalidate the statement about a tendency for opposed evaluations of the Judicial Committee to follow the French-English cleavage.

132 For French-Canadian support of the Privy Council's interpretation of the BNA Act and/or support for its continuation as a final appeal court, see L.P. Pigeon, "The Meaning of Provincial Autonomy," *CBR*, 29 (1951); Pigeon, "French Canada's attitude to the Canadian Constitution," in E. McWhinney, ed., *Canadian Jurisprudence* (Toronto, 1958); Jean Beetz, "Les attitudes changeantes du Québec à l'endroit de la constitution de 1867," pp. 117–18; *CLT*, 40 (1920), p. 315, reporting a speech by Mr. Horace J. Gagne of the Montreal

Bar; "Appeal to the Privy Council," *CLT*, 41 (1921), p. 525, reporting a speech of Premier Taschereau of Quebec. Russell notes that in the nineteenth century French-Canadian support for the Judicial Committee, and opposition to the Supreme Court were primarily based on the belief that the composition, training, and background of the former was much to be preferred to that of the latter for interpretations of Quebec civil law. *Supreme Court*, chapter 1, *passim*. See also Brossard, *La Cour Suprême*, p. 125.

133 On this attitude of the abolitionists, see Jonas L. Juskaitis, "On Understanding the Supreme Court of Canada," *School of Law Review*, University of Toronto, 9 (1951), pp. 7–8; and Leonard H. Leigh, "The Supreme Court and the Constitution," *Ottawa Law Review*, 2 (1967–68), p. 323. Jacques Brossard, "The Supreme Court and the Constitution," in Ontario Advisory Committee on Confederation, *Quebec in the Canada of Tomorrow* (Toronto, n.d.), translated from *Le Devoir*, special supplement, June 30, 1967, stated: "It was, moreover, in opposing the centralizing aims of the federal government that the Judicial Committee signed its own death warrant; it was accused, not without reason, of having violated the centralizing spirit of the BNA Act of 1867."

134 Beetz, "Les attitudes changeantes," pp. 119–21. The divergent evaluations of the Judicial Committee and of a proposed independent Supreme Court are discussed by Peter Russell, "The Supreme Court's Interpretation of the Constitution since 1949," in Paul Fox, ed., *Politics: Canada* (2nd ed., Toronto, 1966), pp. 117–18. See also Russell, *Supreme Court*, pp. 31–32, 36–37. In addition to the ethnic-based opposition from French Canada there was also considerable provincial opposition to the unilateral nature of the federal action in abolishing appeals. P. Gérin-Lajoie, *Constitutional Amendment in Canada* (Toronto, 1950), pp. xvii–xviii. By 1949 French Canadians had become critical of the Privy Council's treatment of French civil law, but this "was counter-balanced by approval of its interpretation of the BNA Act." Russell, *Supreme Court*, p. 31.

135 Browne, *The Judicial Committee and the British North America Act*.

136 J.A. Corry, while doubtful of the final validity of Browne's thesis, gives the book a very favourable review in *Canadian Journal of Political Science*, 1 (1968), pp. 217–19. Critical reviews are provided by B. Laskin, *Canadian Public Administration*, 10 (1967), pp. 514–18, and E.R. Alexander, *UTLJ*, 17 (1967), pp. 371–77.

137 See the eminently sensible criticism by Corry, *ibid.*, pp. 218–19. Jennings's observation is also relevant. "The idea that judges spend days on end in reading all the decisions on any particular topic is one which is sometimes assumed by academic writers; it can, however, be designated as clearly false by anyone who has watched a court give judgement immediately at the end of an argument." "Constitutional Interpretation," p. 27.

138 W.R. Lederman, after noting the antithetical literal interpretations of the BNA Act by Browne and O'Connor, states that in his view "Browne and O'Connor simply cancel one another out. The truth is that the BNA Act was simply ambiguous or incomplete in many respects as originally drafted and the answers just were not in the Act as to how these ambiguities were to be resolved and the gaps filled." "Thoughts on the Reform of the Supreme Court of Canada," p. 2.
    Note also the chronic "historical" controversy over the validity of the compact theory and between centralist and provincialist interpretations of the BNA Act and/or the intentions of the Fathers. Glazebrook's comment is apt: "one has only to sample the speeches and writings of politicians, academics, and jurists to appreciate the wealth of interpretation of the intent and terms of the original union. It needs a conscious effort to realize that they are describing the same episode in Canadian history. Confederation, in fact, was

what you thought it was—or often what it should have been. Which seems to suggest that particular interpretations and points of view were rationalized by tailored versions of the Constitution." *A History of Canadian Political Thought*, p. 264 (see also pp. 153, 258).

139 Philippe Ferland, "La Confédération à refaire," *Thémis*, 5 (1954), p. 105. Stanley, "Act or Pact?" p. 114, asserts that the pre-parliamentary history of the BNA Act appears to confirm the interpretation of the Judicial Committee rather than that of the critics.
    The 1887 Interprovincial Conference, which advocated a much more decentralized federal system than prevailed under Macdonald's prime ministership, claimed that two decades of experience with the BNA Act have "disclosed grave omissions in the provisions of the Act, and has shown (when the language of the Act came to be judicially interpreted) that in many respects what was the common understanding and intention had not been expressed, and that important provisions in the Act are obscure as to their true intent and meaning." *Dominion, Provincial and Interprovincial Conferences from 1887 to 1926* (Ottawa, 1951), p. 20.

140 LaBrie, "Canadian Constitutional Interpretation," p. 310. K.N. Llewellyn's statement is also apt: "there is no quarrel to be had with judges *merely* because they disregard or twist Documentary language, or 'interpret' it to the despair of original intent, in the service of what those judges conceive to be the inherent nature of our institutions. To my mind, such action is their duty. To my mind, the judge who builds his decision to conform with his conception of what our institutions must be if we are to continue, roots in the deepest wisdom." "The Constitution as an Institution," *Columbia Law Review*, 23 (1934), p. 33.

141 M.R. Cohen, *Reason and Law* (New York, 1961), p. 84.

142 G.H. Ross, "Interpreting the BNA Act," *CBR*, 7 (1929), p. 704. LaBrie, "Canadian Constitutional Interpretation," pp. 310, 318; *Rowell-Sirois Report*, I, p. 36.

143 *A.G. Ont.* v *A.G. Can.*, [1947], A.C. 127, at 154.

144 Robinson, "Lord Haldane and the British North America Act," p. 58. See also A.M. Bickel, "The Original Understanding and the Segregation Decision," *Harvard Law Review*, 69 (1955).

145 Various American writers have noted that the appeal to history in American constitutional interpretation has led to an abuse of history and does not in fact act as a control on the court. See, in particular, A.H. Kelly, "Clio and the Court: An Illicit Love Affair," in P.B. Kurland, ed., *The Supreme Court Review* (Chicago, 1965); J. TenBroek, "Admissibility and Use by the United States Supreme Court of Extrinsic Aids in Constitutional Construction," *California Law Review*, 26 (1937–38), pp. 448, 451; C.S. Hyneman, *The Supreme Court on Trial* (New York, 1964), pp. 207–08. Felix Frankfurter, "Reflections on Reading Statutes," in A.F. Westin, ed., *The Supreme Court: Views from Inside* (New York, 1961), pp. 75, 84–85, 88–92, argues the advantages in appealing to historical materials, although he also notes the difficult problems this entails. The difficulty in using historical material is also noted by W.O. Douglas, "Judges as Legislators," in Westin, *ibid.*, pp. 68–69. A.A. North, *The Supreme Court, Judicial Process and Judicial Politics* (New York, 1966), pp. 18–29, provides a neutral discussion. E. Bodenheimer, *Jurisprudence* (Cambridge, Mass., 1962), pp. 348–53, is a good discussion of whether courts should take the original meaning at the time of statutory creation, or the contemporaneous ones understood at the time of decision.

146 See MacDonald, "Constitutional Interpretation and Extrinsic Evidence," for a discussion.

147 *Edwards* v *A.G. Can.*, [1930], A.C. 124, at 137.

148 He added: "it seems to us fallacious, as well as reckless, for the author to suggest that seventy years after Confederation he can

assist us by such contemporary records to say that those who framed the Confederation Act intended to do other than what they embodied in the words of the statute.

"Indeed the matter goes deeper than that; what they are seeking to discover who speak of the pre-confederation intention of the framers of confederation or of the constituent provinces has no real existence. The search is pursuit of a 'will-O-wisp'; when once you leave the natural light afforded by the text of the BNA Act, you are in a realm of unreality....

"Neither should we continue the pretension of the author that by a miracle of understanding and foresight, the Canadian Fathers of Confederation provided in 1867 a constitution suitable to any future." Gray, "'The O'Connor Report' on the British North America Act 1867," pp. 316–18, 334.

See also Stanley, "Act or Pact?" p. 112, for the morass of contradictions involved in attempting to determine the "intentions" of the Fathers. "The one sure guide as to what the Fathers really agreed to agree upon, was the language of their resolutions, or better still, the language of the British North America Act itself. And in construing this Act in the way they have, the judges probably arrived at a more accurate interpretation than have the multitude of critics who have so emphatically disagreed with them."

149 MacDonald, "Judicial Interpretation of the Canadian Constitution," pp. 280–81. His approach agreed with K.N. Llewellyn's assertion that with an ancient statute "the sound quest does not run primarily in terms of historical intent. It runs in terms of what the words can be made to bear, in making sense in the new light of what was originally unforeseen." *The Common Law Tradition* (Boston, 1960), p. 374. See also W. Friedman, *Law and Social Change in Contemporary Britain* (London, 1951), pp. 252, 254–55.

150 Mallory, "The Courts and the Sovereignty of the Canadian Parliament," p. 173.

151 W. E. Rumble attributes the same achievement to the American legal realists. *American Legal Realism* (Ithaca, 1968), pp. 232–33.

152 H.V. Jaffa, "The Case for a Stronger National Government," in R.A. Goldwin, ed., *A Nation of States* (Chicago, 1968), p. 121.

153 Browne suggests that the "constituent statute argument equates 'liberal' with 'federal' (and so 'literal' with 'provincial')." *The Judicial Committee and the British North America Act*, p. 31. This is not entirely true. As indicated in this essay there was also a critique of the Privy Council that was both "literal" and "federal."

154 The weak reasoning is similar to that noted by Smiley in "national interest" justifications for conditional grants. D.V. Smiley, *Conditional Grants and Canadian Federalism* (Toronto, 1963), pp. 48–52.

155 B.N. Cardozo, *The Nature of the Judicial Process* (New Haven, 1960), pp. 174–75.

156 Lapointe also notes the incompatibility of the two, and argues that the Privy Council conducted itself in accordance with the constitutional rather than the fundamentalist approach. "La jurisprudence constitutionnelle et le temps," pp. 27–28.

"The manner of framing the question," writes Llewellyn, "is psychologically of huge importance. 'Is this within the powers granted by the Document?' throws the baseline of inquiry back a century and a half, constricts the vision to the static word, turns discussion into the channels of logomachy. It invites, and too often produces, artificial limitation of attention to the non-essential, the accidental: to wit, what language happens to stand in the Document, or in some hoary—or beardless—text of its 'interpretation'....

"Contrast the effect of framing the question thus: 'Is this within the leeway of change which our going governmental scheme affords? And even if not, does the nature of the case require the leeway to be widened to include it?' The baseline then becomes so much of the past only *as is still alive*, and the immediate future comes to bear as well. The tone and tendency of the very question is dynamic. The 'nature of the case' invites attention to explicit policy. While that continuity with the past which, if not a duty, is wisdom quite as well as a necessity, is carefully preserved—only that the past concerned is that embodied not in an ancient Text, but in a living Government." "The Constitution as an Institution," pp. 32–33.

157 Russell, *Supreme Court*, p. 35.

158 F.H. Underhill, "O Canada," *The Canadian Forum*, 11 (June, 1931), p. 332, cited in Horn, "League for Social Reconstruction," p. 433.

159 Ferland, "La Confédération à refaire," pp. 106–07; Beetz, "Les attitudes changeantes du Québec à l'endroit de la constitution de 1867," p. 120.

160 Corry, "Commentaries," in Crépeau and Macpherson, *The Future of Canadian Federalism*, p. 38.

161 McWhinney, *Judicial Review*, p. 69.

162 Tuck, "Canada and the Judicial Committee," p. 75.

163 J.R. Mallory recently contrasted the capacity of the Supreme Court of the United States to "'follow the election returns'" with the Privy Council, which "was so deficient in both sense and sensibility that the allocation of power in the constitution, by the end of the 1930's, had achieved a remarkable incongruity between the resources, capacities, and responsibilities of the federal and provincial governments." "The Five Faces of Federalism," p. 7. See also MacDonald, "The Privy Council and the Canadian Constitution," pp. 1032–33, 1035, 1027; MacDonald, "The Constitution in a Changing World," pp. 43–44; MacDonald, "Judicial Interpretation of the Canadian Constitution," p. 278; Tuck, "Canada and the Judicial Committee," p. 34; B. Laskin, "Reflections on the Canadian Constitution after the First Century," in Meekison, *Canadian Federalism*, p. 139.

164 A.B. Keith, "Privy Council Decisions: A Comment from Great Britain," *CBR*, 15 (1937), p. 435.

165 Rumble, *American Legal Realism*, pp. 220–21, 227, 232.

166 J.A. Corry, "Decisions of the Judicial Committee, 1930–9," *CJEPS*, 5 (1939), pp. 511–12. See also Rumble, *American Legal Realism*, p. 231, on the difficulty of defining relevant criteria for judicial decisions. Herbert Wechsler, "Toward Neutral Principles of Constitutional Law," *Harvard Law Review*, 73 (1959), is an important attempt to define a judicial process that is "genuinely principled, resting with respect to every step ... in reaching judgement on analysis and reasons quite transcending the immediate result ... on grounds of adequate neutrality and generality." He is hostile to criteria concerned with immediate results that turn the court into a "naked power organ" rather than a court of law. He describes the resultant *ad hoc* evaluation as the "deepest problem of our [American] constitutionalism" (pp. 15, 12).

167 A related question is whether or not Canadian federalism would have had a less turbulent history if the task of judicial interpretation had been undertaken by the Supreme Court. McWhinney, *Judicial Review*, pp. 73–74, provides evidence on both sides of the question, although personally doubtful that the Supreme Court would have acted differently. Glazebrook, *A History of Canadian Political Thought*, p. 258, finds no proof that the Supreme Court would have done otherwise than the Judicial Committee. MacGuigan argues that, from the evidence, it is impossible to decide whether or not the Supreme Court approved of the decisions of the Judicial Committee. "The Privy Council and the Supreme Court:

A Jurisprudential Analysis," p. 421. R.F. McWilliams, "The Privy Council and the Constitution," p. 579, also doubts that the Supreme Court would have differed in its interpretation from the Privy Council. Russell, *Supreme Court*, pp. 255–56, n5, notes the difficulty in arguing that the Supreme Court was more pro-dominion than the Privy Council. On the other hand, supporters of the Supreme Court, who note that it and the Judicial Committee usually agreed, have been cautioned not to ignore the fact that the Supreme Court had to take the previous decisions of the committee as the major premise in its thinking. MacDonald, "The Canadian Constitution Seventy Years After," p. 426. Scott argues that an independent Supreme Court would have produced decisions much more favourable to the federal government. *Canada Today*, p. 77; "Development of Canadian Federalism," p. 246.

168 A point strongly made by W.E. Raney sixty years ago. "Justice, Precedent and Ultimate Conjecture," p. 461.

169 Innis, "Great Britain, the United States and Canada," p. 404. Sir Allen Aylesworth told the Ontario Bar Association that "It is …

no disparagement to Canadian lawyers or to Canadian judges to say that the men, or some of the men at any rate, who constitute the Judicial Bench in England, and some of the men who sit at the Council Board as members of the Judicial Committee are better read lawyers, are stronger lawyers than any men we have, either at the Bar or upon the Bench, in Canada, and in these circumstances it is a matter of actual daily practical advantage to the people of this country that they should have still the right to take to that Court their complicated cases as between citizen and citizen for final adjudication." "Address of Sir Allen Aylesworth," p. 143.

Bram Thompson stated: "The reader of the Law Reports is constantly confronted with cases which the Privy Council decisions prove to have been decided in our local Courts upon the grossest misconception of even elementary principles. Indeed, some of our Courts seem to delight in rendering judgements which are, to say the least of them, utterly perverse." "Editorial," *CLT*, 41 (1921), p. 164. Russell notes that the early weakness of the Supreme Court inhibited moves to abolish appeals. *Supreme Court*, p. 24.

# 19

## Editor's Introduction

The way the Judicial Committee of the Privy Council adjudicated some of the key decisions pertaining to Canadian federalism has long been the subject of debate. Donald Creighton and Robert MacGregor Dawson were the dominant proponents of vilifying the JCPC and its decisions. This is not surprising given Creighton's pro-Macdonald centralist credentials. G. Peter Browne reacted by rallying to the JCPC's defence, demonstrating that the law lords simply applied traditions and rules of legal interpretation as they were understood at the time. Some of the most critical decisions in this respect were reached under the auspices of Lord Watson. His decisions changed the trajectory of Canadian federalism from a highly centralized federation to what would become one of the most decentralized federations in the world, with little formal constitutional change along the way. While legal scholars puzzle over the reasons and principles that informed Watson's logic, John Saywell's structural-functionalist approach that accounts for Watson's socialization provides a convincing explanation for the apparent puzzle. Saywell's piece and approach undermine the pedestal to which judges are often elevated. Notwithstanding their aspirations to objectivity, they cannot divorce themselves from their humanity.

Source: John Saywell. "The Watson Era, 1889–1912, " in *The Lawmakers: Judicial Power and the Shaping of Canadian Federalism* (Toronto: University of Toronto Press for the Osgoode Society for Canadian Legal Studies, 2002), 114–49.

John Saywell

# The Watson Era, 1889–1912 *

The mind of a master and the hand of a great craftsman …
—Lord Denning, 1963

AFTER TWO DECADES of judicial review in the Canadian courts and the Judicial Committee, the structure of sections 91 and 92 and their inter-relationship remained substantially as was intended and legislated. Differences of judicial opinion were less on the structure than on the determination of the "matter" of challenged legislation and on the

---

\* The substance of this chapter was first presented at the founding conference of the Organization for the Study of the National History of Canada in Ottawa on 5 November 1995.

appropriate content or scope of the enumerations. Although the principle of coordinate federalism was generally accepted (with [Macdonald-appointed Judge John Wellington] Gwynne a vocal exception), the theoretical and practical status of the lieutenant governor remained legally and politically controversial. But, by the end of the century, the Judicial Committee had imposed a radically different template on sections 91 and 92, and authoritatively asserted the independent status of the lieutenant governor as the representative of the crown for all purposes of provincial government. However mysterious the inner workings of the committee, the author of the decisions embodying the new doctrines was William Watson.

When Watson became a lord of appeal in 1880, wrote Richard Haldane, "he found himself face to face with what threatened to be a critical period in the history of Canada." The country was torn by conflicts between the advocates of federal paramountcy and provincial autonomy. The Supreme Court of Canada endorsed the principle of federal paramountcy, Haldane asserted, but in the appeals to the Judicial Committee, Lord Watson "made the business of laying down the new law that was necessary his own. He completely altered the tendencies of the Supreme Court … In a series of masterly judgments, he expounded and established the real constitution of Canada."[1] Haldane's claim obviously lingered in the mind of the Judicial Committee. It fell to Watson "to shape the destinies of Canada," wrote Lord Denning in 1963. "The British North America Act was a skeleton. The mind of a master and the hand of a great craftsman were needed to endow it with a lasting and expanding virtue, and at the right moment the mastermind appeared in the person of Lord Watson, a truly dominant figure. Like the prophet of old, He had the daring to ask himself: Can these dry bones 'live'? and proceeded to vivify their framework with the impulse of a progressive interpretation."[2]

Lord Watson was acclaimed on his death as one of the great jurists of his day, and among his distinguished contemporaries, the *Times* noted, "probably none of them have so largely influenced the jurisprudence of the British Empire."[3] Haldane found Watson to be the ideal imperial judge, whose function, "sitting in the supreme tribunal of the Empire, is to do more than decide what abstract and familiar legal conceptions should be applied to particular cases. His function is to be a statesman as well as a jurist, to fill in the gaps which Parliament has deliberately left in the skeleton constitutions and laws that it has provided for the British Colonies."[4] Watson was admirably fitted to be the statesman-jurist. Despite his declared commitment to the conventional principles of statutory interpretation and judicial restraint, he was cavalier in embedding his speculations and assumptions in the constitutional law of Canada as seemed to be appropriate for a jurist shouldering his imperial responsibility.

Among scholars of the law and of federalism jurisprudence, Watson remains a central and controversial figure. In a highly literalist, positivist, almost tautological verbal analysis of his decisions and doctrines, G.P. Browne maintained that they were not only consistent with, but the only possible reading of, the language and structure of the BNA Act.[5] W.F. O'Connor and Bora Laskin concluded from their historical and textual analysis that Watson's rendering of the act was either a confused or wilful distortion.[6] Paul Romney, besides insisting that the traditional centralist interpretation of Confederation is a "vast fabric of myth,"[7] claims that in setting out the "guidelines by which to construe the distribution of powers as a whole" Watson was right, apparently because his decisions "were about as close" to Oliver Mowat's "analysis as one could get without using the same words."[8]

Other scholars have been more nuanced. William Lederman, who considered Watson "the greatest of the Privy Council judges concerned with the Canadian Constitution," commended the Judicial Committee for reducing uncertainty and making "the distribution of powers system meaningful," obviously because Watson and his colleagues had captured what Lederman believed to be the ideal balance between unity and diversity.[9] Alan Cairns accepts the "vast fabric of myth" argument but believes that it was the constitution, not Lord Watson, that was at fault. Bad law meant good statecraft, for the decisions that "deliberately enhanced provincial powers in partial defiance" of the constitution and revealed a "solicitous regard for the provinces" were a necessary and thus defensible, if not conscious, response to the "fundamental pluralism" of Canada.[10] While Cairns suggests that "a few elderly men in London" could not have pushed the country in a direction it would not have otherwise taken,[11]

Robert Vipond, in his admirably nuanced study of the provincial-rights movement in Ontario, rightly counters that Watson and the Judicial Committee gave judicial sanction to the advocates of decentralization and helped shape the political and constitutional debate over federalism.[12]

WATSON'S EARLY CAREER was as unremarkable as it was unrewarding; only the death or elevation of his seniors explained the growth of his practice and his appointment to office. Born in 1827, "he was never an ardent politician," wrote a contemporary, "but by nature, taste, and conviction he was a Conservative."[13] With Conservatives a rarity among Scots lawyers, Watson was appointed solicitor general when Disraeli returned to office in 1874. Two years later, when Lord Gordon was made the first Scots lord of appeal under the 1876 act, Watson succeeded him as lord advocate with a seat in the House of Commons as the representative of the universities of Aberdeen and Glasgow. Disraeli had regarded the Lord of appeal as a "plumb job" and "an appointment to make a Scotsman's mouth water." However, after Gordon died in 1879, Lord Chancellor Cairns spent five fruitless months trying to persuade leading Scottish judges to accept the appointment. In 1880, he turned to Watson, who accepted and was given a life peerage as Baron Watson of Thankerton.[14]

Watson first sat with the Judicial Committee in the appeal from Quebec in *Dobie* in 1881 and wrote the decision.[15] He did not sit on another Canadian appeal until 1888 but often heard petitions for leave to appeal. He was also a member of the board in civil law appeals from Quebec, probably because of his civilian training in Scots law.[16] From 1888 until his death in 1899, Watson was the pre-eminent Canadian specialist on the Judicial Committee. He was a member of the board in the sixteen cases concerning the constitution and delivered the decision in ten. With one exception, these decisions advanced, or invented, interpretive doctrines.[17]

By 1888, the committee was composed largely of the law lords. Lord Herschell, lord chancellor from 1892 to 1895, sat on five cases and delivered the judgment in four, and Lord Halsbury (lord chancellor in 1885, from 1886 to 1892, and from 1895 to 1905) sat on six and wrote the decision in one. Lord Macnaghten,

an Irish lord of appeal appointed in 1887, sat on fourteen appeals and, after expressing strong personal views during the argument, wrote the controversial decision upholding Manitoba's right to abolish denominational schools.[18] Lord Hobhouse sat on ten appeals and Lord Morris on nine, but neither wrote decisions.[19] Before joining the board in 1894, Horace Davey, as counsel, fought five appeals included here, all but one for the provinces. In the seven appeals for which there are transcripts of the oral arguments, Watson, Herschell, and Halsbury dominated the proceedings, with Watson usually the most persistently vocal.

Although there was considerable continuity on the board, with Watson present at all appeals and presiding in those when neither Herschell nor Halsbury was present, it is impossible to find a coherent or consistent approach to judicial review. Watson and the board professed to endorse Hobhouse's principle in *Lambe,* that cases arising under the BNA Act would be determined "by the same methods of construction and exposition"[20] applied to any other case, pleading strict rules of statutory construction and refusing to examine extrinsic aids or Canadian context. Although Watson was emphatic that the "'intention of the Legislature' is a common but slippery phrase," in practice he did not hesitate to provide his own version of what must have been the intention of the legislature. Similarly, Sir Montague Smith's admonition that the court should decide each case "without entering more largely upon an interpretation of the statute"[21] than was necessary was sometimes cited in principle but usually ignored in practice. Watson in particular, in argument and decision, indulged himself in wide-ranging conclusions and speculations about language, history, intentions, and policy.

Lord Watson's first major judgment originated as a territorial dispute between Ontario and Ottawa over the Ontario-Manitoba border but became a landmark definition of the nature of aboriginal land rights.[22] The Indians had surrendered the disputed territory in the Treaty of 1873. Arbitrators had accepted Ontario's claim in 1878, but Macdonald refused to accept the decision. With an appeal to the Judicial Committee likely, Macdonald injected a new element into the controversy when he boasted during the 1882 election that its decision would be of little consequence.

Although the land had belonged to the Hudson's Bay Company, he argued, "it was subject to the Indian title. They and their ancestors had owned the land for centuries until the Dominion Government purchased them.… By seven treaties the Indians of the Northwest conveyed the lands to Canada; and every acre belongs to the people of Canada, and not to the people of Ontario."[23]

When Macdonald refused to accept the decision of the Judicial Committee in 1884 awarding the territory to Ontario, Mowat launched a suit against the St. Catherine's Milling Company which had been given a federal licence to cut timber in the disputed territory. D'Alton McCarthy, who was to act for the company (and Ottawa), had not been keen about forcing the issue, but in the end he agreed that "if the question is to be raised it had better be as a matter of law than as a matter of politics."[24]

The matter of law as it emerged in court depended in part on title to the surrendered land: if title was in the crown, it would pass to the province under section 109, the property provision of the 1867 BNA Act; if it was in the Indians, the federal government could claim ownership through purchase. There was also the unsettled jurisdictional question about the meaning of section 91(24), which gave the federal government jurisdiction over "Indians, and Lands reserved for the Indians." When Mowat won in Chancery, Sir Alexander Campbell urged Macdonald not to wage another legal battle with Mowat. Rather "put to one side the fact that the money came from the Dominion—and ask ourselves for whom is the crown now trustee, and that the answer to that is for those who have ultimately come to be the owners of the country, and who are represented by the Government of Ontario—I think that we shall have to come to this and that we should come to it."[25]

But Macdonald refused and, after losing in the Ontario Court of Appeal, went to the Supreme Court. For the majority, Ritchie held that the Indians had a legal right of occupancy but the crown held legal title to the land which passed to Ontario in 1867. Strong (with Gwynne concurring) dissented on the grounds that the Indians did have some legal rights and that, while unsurrendered lands were the property of the crown, they were lands reserved for Indians which passed to the Dominion in 1867.[26] Macdonald

stubbornly appealed in the name of the company to the Judicial Committee.[27]

The argument at the Judicial Committee continued for seven days before Selborne, Watson, Hobhouse, Peacock, Smith, and Couch. Mowat and Blake appeared for Ontario, aided by Davey and Haldane. Mowat led off with what Blake described as a "lamentable failure … no judgment, no capacity for answering questions, no facility for meeting difficulties and a persistent presentation of minor unimportant and untenable points against the mind of the court." The outcome, wrote Blake (openly worried about his £6,000 fee if they lost), "is distinctly worse still than it was before he spoke, and is still in danger."[28] Blake then had the polite attention of the board for two days. He conceded that the Indians had the right of occupancy but argued ownership was vested in the crown and had passed to Ontario.[29] "Our chances of success are distinctly improved," he wrote triumphantly to his wife, "and poor Mowat who thought our case absolutely lost has recovered spirits and we both think we shall win … my argument has made a sensation … my *opponents* said it was the most brilliant piece of eloquence they had ever heard … nevertheless the case hangs by a thread."[30]

In a mixture of law and policy, the Judicial Committee rejected the argument of Sir Richard Webster and McCarthy that the Indians had owned the land, and confirmed the decisions in the Canadian courts. Aboriginal title to the land, wrote Watson, was only a "personal and usufructuary right" but ownership was vested in the crown.[31] As a result, the beneficial interest in the lands surrendered in the Treaty of 1873 was transmitted to the province under section 109 of the BNA Act.

Long held as a classic statement of the nature of aboriginal tenure, as recognized by the Royal Proclamation of 1763, Watson's opinion has been largely discredited in the Supreme Court. "The subsequent jurisprudence has attempted to grapple with this definition," noted Chief Justice Antonio Lamer, "and has in the process demonstrated that the Privy Council's choice of terminology is not particularly helpful to explain the various dimensions of Indian title."[32] Although the issues remain complex, Canadian courts now recognize that aboriginal title arises from occupation of the land prior to the conquest, the assertion of British sovereignty, and the Royal Proclamation.

In decision, Watson accepted the Ontario position that section 91(24) gave the federal government only legislative power, not proprietary rights, over "Indians, and Lands reserved for the Indians." However, he rejected the argument that "lands reserved for the Indians" were simply Indian reserves created after the surrender. Again falling back on the language used, as well as grounds of public policy, he concluded that "the words actually used are, according to their natural meaning, sufficient to include all lands reserved, upon any terms or conditions, for Indian occupation. It appears to be the plain policy of the Act that, in order to ensure uniformity of administration, all such lands, and Indian affairs generally, shall be under the legislative control of one central authority."[33]

In the end, Canada could legislate for aboriginals in the unsurrendered lands it did not own, and the province could not legislate for or secure a surrender of lands it would own. Perhaps that was less a complication than having a huge federal enclave in northwestern Ontario and later in western Canada. It was the prospect of that outcome that Webster believed influenced the decision: "For a long time the result seemed to be in great doubt. I think, and thought at the time, that the decision was largely governed by questions of policy, which were undoubtedly very much in favour of the view taken by Canadian Courts, as it would have been most inconvenient that there should be established a province within a province as would have been the case if the reserves had been held to be the property of the Dominion."[34]

To complicate the outcome further, Watson gratuitously added that since the benefits of the surrendered land accrued to the province, it "must, of course, relieve the crown, and the Dominion, of all obligations involving the payment of money which were undertaken by Her Majesty, and which are said to have been in part fulfilled by the Dominion Government."[35] It was inevitable that Ottawa would someday attempt to recover its outlay. When it did, Lord Loreburn agreed with the majority in the Supreme Court that Ottawa had not acted as an agent of the provincial government but "with a view to great national interests." As a matter of "fair play" the province might be liable but "in point of law" it was not. Loreburn admitted that,

while Watson's statement "does give strong support to the view of those who rely on it," it was "quite possible that Lord Watson did not intend to pronounce upon a legal right. If he did so intend, the passage in question must be regarded as *obiter dictum*."[36]

Blake's eloquence had been less apparent in his argument over substance than in his oratorical portrayal of the provinces as an endangered species needing the protection of the court if they were to survive. The court's preliminary task was to understand the "general scheme" of the constitution:

> In truth the Act is in many points little more than a skeleton, which is to be clothed with flesh and muscle, nerve and sinew, into which the breath of life is to be breathed by interpretation ... the word federal is the key which unlocks the clauses, and reveals their contents. It is the glass which enables us to discern what is written. By its light the Act must be construed....
>
> It was not the intention of Parliament to mutilate, confound and destroy the provinces mentioned in the preamble, and having done so, from their mangled remains, stewed in some legislative cauldron, to evoke by some legislative incantation absolutely new provinces into an absolutely new existence ... it was the design, I say ... by gentle and considerate treatment to preserve the vital breath and continue the political existence of the old provinces. However this may be, they were being made, as has been well said, not fractions of a unit, but units of a multiple. The Dominion is a multiple, and each province is a unit of that multiple.[37]

Blake's invitation to give the constitution a "very large, liberal and comprehensive interpretation" in the provincial interest and to escape the narrow confines of rigid statutory interpretation may not have influenced Watson. But the history and theory of federalism he later advanced was not dissimilar, and in his decisions could be heard echoes of the need to protect that endangered species. And Blake's anatomical analogy appears to have had a lasting and agreeable effect on Richard Haldane, his junior in the case.

WATSON'S NEXT JUDGMENT has aroused less attention but is equally problematic. The reasoning is not convincing historically and the argument has recently been criticized by the Canadian courts, although they did not directly question the decision. What is known as the *Precious Metals* case involved the ownership of the gold and silver in the forty-mile belt of railway land transferred from British Columbia to Canada by the 11th article in the terms of union in compensation for the construction of the Canadian Pacific Railway.[38] The terms were initially negotiated by Sir George-Étienne Cartier, a lawyer, and three laymen from British Columbia. There was no suggestion in the negotiations, in the terms themselves, in the statute authorizing the transfer, or in the 1883 revisions that precious metals were excluded or included. The legal contention that they were not included was based on a sixteenth-century English decision in which, after lengthy deliberations, the justices and barons decided that "all mines and gold and silver" belonged to the queen, even those on the Earl of Northumberland's land.[39] The rule derived from the decision was that a grant of land to private persons would not include the prerogative ownership or 'royalties' of precious metals unless the intention of the crown was expressed, as Horace Davey said in argument at the Judicial Committee, by "apt and precise words."

A majority of the Supreme Court found that the rule governing private grants was inapplicable and that all mineral rights were transferred to Canada. Chief Justice Ritchie stated that the terms of union should not be regarded as a transaction between the crown and a private individual or between private parties but as a statutory arrangement "in settlement of a constitutional question between the two governments, or rather, giving effect to, and carrying out, the constitutional compact under which British Columbia became part and parcel of the Dominion of Canada, and as a part of that arrangement the government of British Columbia relinquished to the Dominion of Canada … all right to certain public lands belonging to the crown."[40]

Ritchie also found persuasive—both for what it said and what it did not say—an 1883 provincial minute of council stating that one of the conditions of the transfer was that Ottawa "shall establish a land system equally liberal as to mining and agricultural industries, as that in force in the province at the present time."[41] Gwynne (Taschereau concurring) agreed that

the ancient precedent was inapplicable: "The case must be regarded not at all in the light of a grant of land by the crown to a subject, but in the light of a treaty between two independent contracting parties upon the faith of which alone the Province of British Columbia was received into and became part of the Dominion of Canada."[42]

Without elaborate reasons, Watson reversed the decision of the Supreme Court. If the agreement could be regarded as either "a separate and independent compact" or "an independent treaty," the conclusion reached by the Supreme Court "would have been inevitable." But their Lordships found that the 11th article of the terms of union simply "embodies the terms of a commercial transaction, by which one Government undertook to make a railway, and the other to give a subsidy, by assigning part of its territorial revenues." Section 109 of the BNA Act, which provided that "all lands, mines, minerals, and royalties" belonging to the province would be retained, should be read to include British Columbia. The 11th article was an exception, but it did not profess to deal with the "jura regia" and the province retained ownership of the precious metals in the railway belt.[43]

Three Canadian courts have recently criticized Watson's language, and implicitly his reasons. Chief Justice William Esson of the British Columbia Supreme Court observed in 1989 that while the decision "must no doubt be taken as stating the law on the specific issue raised in the case," Watson's "crabbed view" of the 11th article "as merely settling the turns of a commercial transaction" was unacceptable. "That view simply ignores the enormous scope of the project to which the Dominion committed itself, and the essential part it played in creating a dominion from sea to sea. To Lord Watson, this was no more significant than, say, an agreement to extend a Glasgow tramway into an adjoining suburb. Ritchie C.J. and Gwynne J. were surely closer to the mark."[44] The British Columbia Court of Appeal also agreed with Ritchie's characterization of the terms of union and, with reference to Watson's reasons cited above, stated that "if we consider ourselves bound by that pronouncement we would, of course, be bound to follow it, leaving it to the Supreme Court of Canada to correct what is obviously a serious misapprehension of Canadian constitutional history."[45]

In the Supreme Court of Canada, Justice Frank Iacobucci found Watson's language "troubling":

If Lord Watson meant to suggest that Term 11 is simply a commercial and not a constitutional provision, then the judgment of the Privy Council must be regarded as having been rendered per *incuriam* [politely, through inadvertence; less respectfully, through ignorance] for reasons I have already noted. If, then, Lord Watson erred in this fashion, the Court of Appeal below was correct to assert that the Privy Council "seriously misapprehen[ded]" Canadian history and the learned trial judge was correct to refer to its "crabbed" view of Term 11 (assuming without deciding that, as a matter of *stare decisis,* either court had sufficient justification to ignore the perceived authority of the Privy Council).[46]

However, Iacobucci preferred "a more generous view of Watson's reasons," which involved reinterpreting what Watson must have meant and elaborating the argument Watson might have made. He concluded lamely that at least in his decision Watson's "exceptional treatment" of royalties was consistent with other judgments of the Judicial Committee.[47]

WATSON'S OPINIONS IN *St. Catherine's Milling* and *Precious Metals* were based in part on his interpretation of the rights of the crown in the province. And, in 1892, Watson had the opportunity to settle finally the troublesome but critical issue of the constitutional status of the lieutenant governor. The Supreme Court decisions in *Lenoir* and *Mercer*, neither of which had been argued or settled precisely on the point, suggested that the lieutenant governor did not represent the crown directly and possessed only the prerogatives expressly stated in the constitution. However, Ritchie's dissent in *Lenoir* (with Strong's apparent concurrence) that the lieutenant governor continued to represent the crown, "though doubtless in a modified manner," was endorsed in the provincial courts.[48] In the Ontario Court of Appeal, George Burton "respectfully" but pointedly stated that, if "it had not been for the expression found in some judicial utterances placing within very narrow limits the powers of the executives of the provinces, I should have thought it too

clear for argument, that the powers formerly exercised by the Lieutenant-Governors of the other Provinces, and by the Governor-General of Canada in reference to provincial matters ... were now vested exclusively in the Lieutenant-Governors."[49]

That had always been Mowat's position. The lieutenant governor, he insisted, was "entitled *virtute officii* and without express statutory enactment, to exercise all prerogatives incident to the Executive authority in matters over which the Provincial Legislatures have jurisdiction." This was a matter not only of law but of history, for it was the "undoubted and unquestioned understanding on which the subject of Confederation was considered, on which the resolutions which formed the basis of the BNA Act were framed and accepted, and was the understanding which, without any express provision to this effect in the Act, has been acted upon as of course by the Dominion and Provincial authorities ever since."[50] As the courts circled the issue and the federal minister of justice refused Mowat's request for a reference to the Judicial Committee, the Ontario premier seized the initiative.[51]

In 1888 he passed an Act respecting the Executive Administration of the Laws of this Province which in declaratory language stated that the meaning of section 65 of the BNA Act confirmed that the lieutenant governor had executive authority over all matters within provincial jurisdiction as his predecessors had before 1867, including the power of commuting and remitting sentences for offences against the laws of the province.[52] John Thompson, the federal minister of justice, found the act objectionable but, to avoid "any unnecessary conflict," did not recommend disallowance.[53] In the end, he and Mowat agreed to a stated reference case in the Ontario courts in the first instance rather than to the Supreme Court or the Judicial Committee where no reasons would be given.

The case was first heard in Chancery in June 1890; Edward Blake acted for Ontario. In a unanimous decision on 6 December, the court found the act *intra vires.* While the intention of section 92(1) was "manifestly intended to keep intact the headship of the Provincial Government, forming, as it does, the link of federal power," declared Chancellor Boyd, that did not prevent a statutory increase in the constitutional position or functions of the lieutenant governor. More broadly, he continued, although "no direct or immediately representative coordination of queen and people may exist in the provincial Assembly, yet sovereign power must substantially operate and be manifested in Ontario legislation in order to the efficient exercise of territorial government under the sanctions of the Imperial Act."[54] The decision was confirmed by the Court of Appeal in January 1892.[55] As the appeal was proceeding to the Supreme Court, Lord Watson made it largely unnecessary with his decision in *Liquidators of the Maritime Bank of Canada* v. *Receiver-General of New Brunswick,* delivered in July 1892.[56]

The case originated with the collapse of the Maritime Bank, which was indebted to the provincial government.[57] Arguing before the Supreme Court of New Brunswick, A.G. Blair, premier and attorney general, contended that the *Bank of Nova Scotia* case, "which determined the crown, in the exercise of its prerogative rights in the country can claim a preference over creditors of the same class, narrows the first question down to this, whether the crown, as represented by the local government, has been bereft of its prerogative right." Citing sections 64, 65, and 72 of the BNA Act and observing that the provinces possessed a Great Seal, Blair concluded that there was not "a syllable in the Act excluding the crown from the exercise of its rights in respect of matters retained by the Local Executive." Divest the crown in the province "of its executive rights as represented by the lieutenant governor, and the whole machinery of Government would stop." The lieutenant governor was appointed by the governor general in the name of the queen and thus "the whole Scheme of Union is made consistent and harmonious. The Sovereign is not only the chief, but the sole magistrate of the nation, and all others act through her. The executive authority, as represented by the Federal and Provincial Governments, reaches out in both directions and covers the whole ground."[58]

The court easily found for the provincial government. "It is true that the prerogative rights of the crown were by the Statute apportioned between the Provinces and the Dominion," Chief Justice John Allen stated, "but this apportionment in no sense implies the extinguishment of any of them, and they there continue to subsist in their integrity, however their locality might be altered by the division of powers contained in the new constitutional law." Justice John Fraser agreed

that the prerogatives possessed by the lieutenant governor were co-extensive with the division of powers.[59]

The decision was immediately and unsuccessfully appealed to the Supreme Court. In the most confirming judgment, Christopher Patterson, who had joined the court in October 1888, found the decision consistent with "the spirit and tenor of the British North America Act" and "in accordance with the views which prevail in the bulk of the decisions under the statute although all the opinions expressed, particularly in the earlier cases, may not have been in harmony." Patterson cited Lord Watson's decisions in the *St. Catherine's Milling* and the *Precious Metals* cases, "not that these bear directly on the point at hand: they are merely instances of late utterances where the Provincial Governments are spoken of in the same terms as the Dominion Government as representing the queen."[60]

Gwynne dissented vigorously and predicted that the judgment "will no doubt give to the dispensers of the Prerogative in London … another opportunity to indulge their favorite game … to exalt the provinces of the Dominion of Canada at the expense of the Dominion and to neutralize or repeal the BNA Act." Indeed, so successful had they played the game, he wrote to his old friend Judge J.R. Gowan, that "old as I am I fully expect that both you and I shall be present as mourners at the funeral of Confederation cruelly murdered in the house of its friends."[61]

The appeal was heard at the Judicial Committee in May 1892 when Watson presided at the two-day argument. Sir Richard Webster was retained by the liquidators and Sir Horace Davey appeared with Blair for the province. It was an uneven battle in talent and in precedent.

Foolishly adopting Gwynne's extreme centralist reasoning, which had never been accepted in the Judicial Committee (or the Supreme Court), Webster argued that the governor general alone represented the queen and that the lieutenant governor of a province, "with functions different from the old government and legislatures, and with powers limited and defined by statute and municipal in their general character," neither represented the crown nor possessed any prerogatives not expressly granted. Davey observed that sections 64 and 65 continued the executive authority of the provincial governments unless "cut down by express enactment and there is nothing in the Act of 1867 or in any subsequent Act which abolishes or alters them." More broadly and in line with decision, "according to the true effect of that Act the provincial governments and legislatures are within their respective spheres sovereign.... The intention was that the Dominion and the provinces should have coordinate authority within their respective spheres, all subject to the control of the Imperial Parliament."[62]

In his judgment, Watson summarily dismissed what he described as the "sum and substance" of Webster's argument that Confederation had severed the connection between the crown and the provinces and had reduced the provinces "to the rank of independent municipal institutions" as propositions for which "their Lordships have been unable to find either principle or authority."[63] The appointment by the governor general was under the Great Seal, or the "Executive Government of the Dominion," which, by section 9, was declared "to continue and be vested in the Queen," and was thus "the act of the Crown; and a Lieutenant-Governor, when appointed, is as much the representative of Her Majesty for all purposes of provincial government as the Governor General himself is for all purposes of Dominion Government."[64] Citing *Mercer, St. Catherine's Milling,* and *Precious Metals* as authority, Watson concluded: "Seeing that successive decisions of this board, in the case of territorial revenues, are based upon the general recognition of Her Majesty's continued sovereignty under the Act of 1867, it appears to their Lordships that, so far as regards vesting in the crown, the same consequences must follow in the case of provincial revenues which are not territorial."[65]

The legal position of the crown in the right of the province and thus of the office of the lieutenant governor had been settled. As Edward Blake commented later in the Supreme Court, during the argument in the case involving the provincial authority to appoint queen's counsel, there was nothing new in Watson's decision but "it appears to me that in that case the Judicial Committee had concluded to make a definite statement of their view of the position of the province, and to place their decision upon a broad and clear view of the result of previous decisions affecting the rights of the different provinces of the Dominion."[66]

Watson was not content just to declare the law, but in one long *obiter* he placed the Judicial Committee's imprimatur on his view of the history and philosophy of Canadian federalism:

The object of the Act was neither to weld the provinces into one, nor to subordinate provincial governments to a central authority, but to create a federal government in which they should all be represented, entrusted with the exclusive administration of affairs in which they had a common interest, each province *retaining* its independence and autonomy. That object was accomplished by distributing, between the Dominion and the provinces, *all powers executive and legislative,* and all public property and revenues which had previously belonged to the provinces; so that the Dominion Government should be vested with such of these *powers,* property and revenues as were necessary for the due performance of its constitutional functions, and that the *remainder should be retained by the provinces* for the purposes of provincial government. But, in so far as regards those matters which, by sect. 92, are specially reserved for provincial legislation, the legislation of each province continued to be free from the control of the Dominion, and as supreme as it was before the passing of the Act.[67]

Watson had, in fact, redefined, perhaps even realigned, the nature of Canadian federalism. His long *obiter dictum,* unnecessary for the determination of the issue before the court, not only confirmed the legal foundations for provincial sovereignty but also, in placing all residual powers—apparently including legislative—within the province, was an endorsement of the compact theory of the delegated capacity of the federal government and of provincial pre-eminence.[68]

Over the next few years, Watson and his colleagues had to confront more explicitly the task of mastering the structure of sections 91 and 92 and the scope of their enumerations. The first occasion was *Tennant v. Union Bank of Canada,* a challenge to the provisions of the federal Bank Act which had validated warehouse receipts as negotiable instruments, unlike Ontario's *Mercantile Amendment Act* which did not. D'Alton McCarthy, counsel for Tennant, argued that the federal government's jurisdiction over banking "must be so exercised as not to interfere with property and civil rights." Horace Davey, for the bank, argued the exclusivity of federal power over banking and, on the precedent of *Cushing,* that even if the subject could be brought within section 92, the power of the Dominion was "paramount."[69]

The decision, wrote Watson, turned upon the construction of sections 91 and 92. Section 91 gave the federal government power to make laws in relation to all matters not assigned exclusively to the provinces, "and also" exclusive legislative authority in relation to certain enumerated subjects, one of which was banking. As the statutory regulations at issue "unquestionably relate to property and civil rights," opposition to the provisions of the act would be "unanswerable if it could be shewn that, by the Act of 1867, the Parliament of Canada is absolutely debarred from trenching to any extent upon matters assigned to the provincial legislatures by sect. 92. But sect. 91 expressly declares that, 'notwithstanding anything in this Act,' the exclusive legislative authority of the Parliament of Canada *shall extend* to all matters coming within the enumerated classes; which plainly indicates that the legislation of that Parliament so long as it strictly relates to these matters, is to be of paramount authority."[70]

In the decision, however, Watson stated that the federal power over banking was "wide enough to embrace every transaction coming within the legitimate business of a banker" and confirmed the validity of the Bank Act.[71]

Watson's bifurcation of section 91 with the words "and also" could be attributed to sloppy language rather than deliberate intention had it not been followed by a more explicit separation of the residual clause and the enumerations in *Local Prohibition* two years later. W.F. O'Connor and G.P. Browne, the former to denounce and the latter to praise, agreed that "and also" represents what Browne described as the "first incontestable precursor" of the separation of section 91 into two compartments.[72] They also agreed that the substitution of the enacting tense "shall extend" for the declaratory "extends" reinforced the division.[73] And while the decision confirmed the paramountcy of the section 91 enumerations, the words "strictly relates" added a narrow interpretive dimension to the words "in relation to."

A few days after he delivered the decision in *Tennant,* Watson was on the board for the appeal on *Voluntary Assignments,* a challenge to Ontario legislation providing relief to insolvent debtors and enabling them to make a voluntary assignment of assets among creditors.[74] The act had been challenged as relating to "Bankruptcy and Insolvency" (section 91[27]) although the 1875 federal insolvency had been repealed in 1880 there was no federal legislation on either bankruptcy or insolvency. After inconclusive judgments in the Ontario courts, E.L. Newcombe, the deputy minister of justice, agreed to facilitate an appeal to the Judicial Committee in 1893. Mowat believed that the committee would appreciate the importance of the appeal "if informed by counsel that the Ontario Act in question is the only substitute for a bankruptcy or insolvency law which this province has; and that in consequence of the differing opinion in various sections of the Dominion, the Government has hitherto been unable to frame a law which the Canadian Parliament is prepared to accept."[75]

The Judicial Committee was undoubtedly influenced by the absence of federal legislation. Both during the argument and in his decision, Herschell pointed to the absence of compulsion or the creation of the legal status of a bankrupt or insolvent as provisions which were common to schemes of bankruptcy and insolvency, and thus found the act a valid exercise of jurisdiction under property and civil rights. However, he added, such provisions could be contained in a federal act and the province would thus be "precluded from interfering.… But it does not follow that such subjects, as might properly be treated as ancillary to such a law and therefore within the powers of the Dominion Parliament, are excluded from the legislative authority of the provincial legislature when there is no bankruptcy or insolvency legislation of the Dominion Parliament in existence."[76] Herschell's suggestion of the "unoccupied field" would soon be clarified.

The discussion during the pleadings provide important additional insights into Watson's view of the distribution of legislative jurisdiction and his theory of Canadian federalism. When the case was first heard in the Court of Appeal, E.F.B. Johnston, the deputy attorney general, advanced a proposition novel even far the Mowat government:

The Province, apart from the British North America Act, would have the power inherently to deal with property as it dealt with by the Act in question. The British North America Act does not destroy such right, but suspends it only. The restriction as against the province is merely the result of a political arrangement whereby the provinces are united in a Federal Government without their rights being abrogated.

If the Dominion Government therefore does not exercise its rights as regards bankruptcy, the power to deal with that law may be exercised by the Local Legislatures. The reason is, that if the Dominion practically waives its right to legislate on that branch of property and civil rights, which was excepted in its favor, the local Government would have the power under the wide term, and because that power only remained in suspense during the exercise of Dominion rights....[77]

Opening his argument before the Judicial Committee, Blake did not go so far as to suggest that the provincial power over property and civil rights was merely suspended by the existence of federal legislation; instead, he contended that, "even though the Dominion Parliament might be legislation passed under one or the other heads in section 91, appropriate some particular Provincial field otherwise occupied by section 92 so as to exclude the Province from its further occupation, yet it by no means follows that, in the absence of such Dominion legislation, the Provincial field is to be taken as limited by the possible range of unexercised power by the Dominion Parliament." Watson's interjection, although somewhat impenetrable, suggests that he saw the section 91 enumerations as exceptions from section 92: if the power were exercised, provincial laws as to property and civil rights could be modified, but if not exercised they remained untouched. "That," replied Blake, "is the line of argument I intend to pursue."[78]

Watson repeatedly interjected to the same effect during Sir Richard Webster's argument that, occupied or not, federal jurisdiction *was* exclusive: "If they passed legislation which did trench quite properly an area in which the Province might exercise legislation then if it rescinded that legislation you are thrown back upon the old and prime question what is the area allowed to them and is it trenched on?"[79] Later,

when Webster argued that you were to "read out" of section 92 anything in section 91, Watson observed:

That is rather suggesting this—the area of the Legislative Power is defined and capable of definition, and is absolutely exclusive in all cases. That is not the view which has been suggested by the decisions of this board. The decisions of this board rather point to this—and at present I am rather inclined to agree with them—that there is a certain extent of that Legislation which might be reserved to the Province, but there are many ancillary regulations which might be made in carrying out their primary object and the power given to them which they can over-ride the Provincial Authorities. But the provincial Authority is there.[80]

Or again: "It is not exclusive as soon as they [the federal government] retreat from it and do not occupy it by legislative means."[81]

Watson's sentiments and his view of the appropriate constructions of sections 91 and 92 were clearly in harmony with Blake's final pleas that "the deeper the wound Parliament can make in 'Property and Civil Rights,' the larger the area in which it can infringe ... the more indefinite and elastic the range of its potential action, the more important it is to decide that at any rate until Parliament chooses to act the other Legislature shall not be disabled from acting."[82]

Watson obviously believed that as a matter of law the province could legislate within its enumerations, not only on property and civil rights, unless and until the field was occupied by federal legislation under its enumerated powers. As he restated his proposition during the oral argument in *Fielding* v. *Thomas:* "I think you may take this as a general proposition, that the provincial legislature cannot be debarred from exercising any of the power specified by reason of the ability of the Canadian Parliament to deal with the same matter. There is no bar in the way of the provincial parliament until there is legislation by the Dominion Parliament."[83] A few months later, during the argument in *Brewers and Malsters*, he was even more decisive:

I do not see that the powers in 91 have any effect whatever in limiting the powers of the provincial Legislature under 92 except in those circumstance where in virtue of those powers given by 91 there has been actual legislation by the Dominion Parliament.... As long as there is legislation in the Dominion Parliament on the same subject the provincial Legislature has full power to exercise the specific rights given it by section 92. You have no power to include in 91 powers given by 92.[84]

In his judgment in the *Fisheries Reference* in 1898, however, Herschell had to correct or clarify the unoccupied-field doctrine drawn from *Voluntary Assignments*.[85] The declaratory clause unmistakably asserted the exclusivity of federal legislative authority under the enumerations, he observed, and provincial legislation in relation to any enumeration was "incompetent." It had been suggested during the argument, "and this view has been adopted by some of the judges of the Supreme Court, that although any Dominion legislation dealing within the subject would override provincial legislation, the latter is nevertheless valid, unless and until the Dominion Parliament so legislates. Their Lordships think that such a view does not give due effect to the terms of s. 91, and in particular to the word 'exclusively.'"[86]

The decision was given in May 1898 and, in view of the "collegial" practices of the committee, presumably had been read by Watson. Yet, during the argument in *Bonsecours* in March 1899, Watson could lecture Blake that the "power of exclusive legislation given to the Dominion Parliament by section 91 can never take effect till the legislation exists, and until it exists and occupies the field, which is the expression that has been used aptly enough, the law of the province must subsist."[87]

However, a few months later, in his last decision, Watson seemed to qualify his position.[88] The British Columbia Supreme Court had upheld a provincial statute prohibiting the employment of Chinese in coal mines as coming within property and civil rights, and it was on that ground that Haldane argued its validity. Blake contended that the federal government had exclusive jurisdiction over aliens by section 91(25), and as "the Dominion Parliament had dealt with the subject as completely as it saw fit ... it was not competent to the provincial legislature to further impose restrictions and disabilities upon the Chinese alien immigrants into British Columbia."[89]

Watson agreed that the "whole pith and substance" of the regulations established prohibitions "which affects aliens or naturalized subjects, and therefore trench upon the exclusive authority of the Parliament of Canada." He rejected the argument, which had found favour in the lower court, that the federal naturalization act had established only partial control over the rights of aliens: "The abstinence of the Dominion Parliament from legislating to the *full limit of its powers*, could not have the effect of transferring to the provincial legislature the legislative power which had been assigned to the Dominion by s.91 of the Act of 1867."[90] Watson's decision was to be "distinguished" (to use the legal term for "altered") almost beyond recognition but his belated and partial denial of the unoccupied-field doctrine, even if the federal government had not legislated "to the full limit of its powers," was not.[91]

THE JUDICIAL COMMITTEE was also given the opportunity to write another chapter in the long political and legal battle over liquor regulation. Despite the apparent trade-off in *Russell, Hodge,* and the *McCarthy Act Reference,* Mowat could not escape the political pressure from the temperance forces for total prohibition. After repeatedly tightening the regulations, he passed an act in 1890 giving the municipalities their pre-Confederation local-option powers. The act was found *intra vires* in the Ontario Court of Appeal, largely under section 92(8). Chief Justice John Hagarty stated that "it may safely be said that there is no apparent intention in the Confederation Act to curtail or interfere with the existing general powers of municipal councils unless the Act plainly transfers any of existing such powers to the Dominion jurisdiction."[92] However, the court upheld the prohibition of retail sales only, although Burton stated that without the binding precedents of *Fredericton* and *Russell* he would have upheld total prohibition.[93]

Although Mowat professed to support total prohibition, he said in the legislature that he "wondered whether there was any lawyer in the house who was prepared to say we had jurisdiction."[94] Requesting Sir John Thompson to agree to a Supreme Court reference, he wrote that rather than claiming jurisdiction for the province, "I have expressed great doubts as to whether the Courts would hold that jurisdiction was in the Provinces, though it is of course my duty to uphold that view before the courts until the point is decided."[95] Thompson finally agreed.

Before the reference reached it, the Supreme Court had heard what was in effect an appeal on the local-option act but had delayed announcing the decision until the reference was heard. Strong, Fournier, and Taschereau had held that the province could prohibit retail sales under 92(8); while Gwynne and Robert Sedgewick, the former deputy minister of justice, had held the pre-Confederation municipal practice was irrelevant, given the redistribution of power in 1867, and that provincial prohibition was an unconstitutional interference with trade and commerce.[96] When the reference itself was heard in May 1894, the federal government readily conceded the provincial power to prohibit retail sales but contended that only Ottawa could prohibit the manufacture or importation of liquor and also determine what was retail or wholesale.[97] Taschereau did not sit on the reference, and George King, who had recently joined the court, supported Gwynne and Sedgewick in finding the act unconstitutional.[98] In the result, two different decisions were announced on 15 January 1895: by a majority of 3–2 the court had found the Ontario legislation both *ultra* and *intra vires*. As Lord Watson sarcastically commented early in the argument before the Judicial Committee, "they must have been right once."[99]

The substantive question before the Judicial Committee was the right of the province to prohibit the sale of liquor, but there were other questions concerning manufacture, importation, and "what ifs," or, as Lord Chancellor Halsbury put it, "all the things which may happen in the course of this world's history, which may or may not render temperance legislation or any other legislation proper."[100] The sarcasm was understandable, for it was the fourth time the committee had been asked to determine who could stand between Canadians and their beer. Four members of the board had heard it all before; only Watson and Lord Morris had not.[101] On the other side of the table, John Maclaren, counsel for Ontario, had acted in *Fredericton, Russell,* and *Local Prohibition* in the Court of Appeal and the Supreme Court, and Haldane had acted in *McCarthy*. Much to Mowat's dismay, Edward Blake had been retained by the distillers, as had Wallace Nesbitt, who had fought the legislation before the Supreme Court. E.I. Newcombe, the deputy minister of justice, was senior counsel for the federal government, but most of the burden fell on Blake.[102]

Maclaren relied almost exclusively on the section 92(8) argument which had always won favour in the Canadian courts and had been accepted by the Judicial Committee in *Hodge*. But it was evident at once that Herschell, Halsbury, and Watson believed that pre-Confederation law or practice was legally irrelevant because the province could not endow municipal institutions with powers it did not itself possess. Herschell did muse, however, that since local governments had been given the power for the "good order and sobriety of the community ... I think there is a good deal to be said for that being one of the subjects of a local nature."[103] Maclaren was constantly pressed, by Herschell in particular, to go to 92(16), but he was hesitant not only because of *Russell* but also because he feared the application of the deeming clause. Herschell agreed that "if it is within the specific subjects mentioned in section 91, then clearly all matters although merely local if they are within any of those specific subjects are under section 91."[104]

Any legislature, Blake stated, had the power to prohibit any trade for social, moral, economic, fiscal, or political reasons, and "I am going to contend that both under the general and under the enumerated powers of the Dominion the jurisdiction to prohibit on any of these grounds rests in, and rests solely in, the Dominion."[105] Blake's structural analysis of section 91 and the purpose of the residual, declaratory, and deeming clauses was exemplary, as were his attempts to revisit *Parsons* and re-examine the trade and commerce power. But whether it was general weariness by the third day of argument or hostility to a counsel who was by now an Irish nationalist member of parliament, the court engaged in constant interruptions and interjections as well as long irrelevant musings. Never overly deferential before the committee, Blake was often exasperated: "Surely, when you come to the enumerated powers. Which I hope to reach some time"—or "I ventured to assume that your Lordships would understand the language that your Lordships used."[106] Watson was by far the worst offender and his performance is ample witness to the comments of a contemporary: "Recently, too, he became oblivious of the interruptions of the other judges, unceremoniously breaking in even upon interruptions, and when his brethren turned round and looked aghast, no doubt expecting the customary apology, the noble lord audibly pursued the thread of his own thoughts without deferring to his right hand or his left."[107]

Nine months after the argument, Lord Watson delivered the decision. Agreeing to give only a qualified answer to some of the questions, describing them as "academic rather than judicial," the committee upheld the Ontario legislation and confirmed the provincial power to prohibit the sale of liquor. All that was necessary in decision was to determine that in "pith and substance," a phrase Watson was to create in Union Colliery, local prohibition was a local and private matter which had always been entrusted to local authorities and was not a matter in relation to trade and commerce despite its incidental effects. But, with a careful selection and revisiting of some precedents, a rejection of others, and some jurisprudential inventions, Watson seized another opportunity to reconstruct Canadian federalism to his own satisfaction, a reconstruction that could not have secured unanimity or probably even a majority.[108]

The law could not be upheld under section 92(8), wrote Watson. Despite the many decisions in the Canadian courts, the committee had properly concluded that while the province possessed the power to create municipal institutions, it could delegate only those powers it possessed. Therefore, jurisdiction had to lie in either section 92(16) or 92(13) and, since it could not be in both, Watson's preferred choice was the former. However, his difficulty was that, by its wording, reinforced by precedent and frequent and undisputed judicial comment in argument, the deeming clause withdrew from 92(16) any matter infringing on the enumerations in section 91. Moreover, there was the precedent in Russell, not overruled in Hodge, that the power to prohibit lay within the federal government's residual power and could also be said to fall within trade and commerce. With an imaginative reconstruction of sections 91 and 92, aided by equally imaginative assumptions about the intentions of the framers, Watson warmed to his task of overcoming these obstacles in what was in many ways a fifteen-page obiter dictum.

Watson first redefined the purpose of the deeming clause. In Parsons, Sir Montague Smith had observed that the declaratory and deeming clauses were both designed to give "pre-eminence to the dominion parliament in cases of a conflict of powers" but pointed out that the latter "applies in its grammatical Construction only to No. 16 of sect. 92."[109] Although Gwynne and the others in Supreme Court had felt that it applied to, and limited, all of section 92, the Judicial Committee never wavered from Smith's observation. Smith repeated his conviction during the argument, in Russell and both Horace Davey and Collier reaffirmed it during the argument in Hodge, as did Davey in the McCarthy Act Reference argument.[110]

During the argument, Maclaren and Herschell had agreed that the clause applied to 92(16), and, as Herschell stated, "if the thing is one of the things specifically mentioned in 91 section then you are thrown."[111] Watson seemed to agree during a brief discussion when Blake cited Smith's observation in Parsons and Herschell interjected: "But more than that surely. The effect of that provision at the end of section 91 is to exclude from sub-section 16 certain things that otherwise would have come distinctly within it." To which Blake replied, "I do not know my Lord, that it was necessary at all," because the declaratory clause protected the federal enumerations from all of section 92. Davey interjected, "And for greater certainty still," and Watson added, "They put it for greater certainty twice over."[112] And later no one disagreed when Blake stated that "it is conceded that if the subject we are now dealing with is embraced within this enumeration it is withdrawn from 'merely local and private' by the express terms at the close of the section."[113]

When Blake, Davey, and Herschell were commenting on the "sting" in both the "head and tail" of section 91, a perplexed Watson observed, "I am afraid there may be a difficulty which we will have to get out of in that respect." In his decision, without apology or evidence, Watson disagreed with his own court and removed the difficulty.[114] Smith's observation "was not material to the question arising in that case, and does not appear to their Lordships to be strictly accurate." On the contrary, it was "apparently contemplated by the framers … that the due exercise of the enumerated powers conferred upon the Parliament of Canada by s. 91 might, occasionally and incidentally, involve legislation upon matters which are prima facie committed exclusively to the provincial legislatures by s. 92." In order to provide for that contingency, the deeming clause was added. Not only did the clause apply to all of section 92, but its purpose was not to subtract from section 92(16) the power to legislate in relation to anything coming within the section 91 enumerations. On the contrary, it was to permit the federal government "to deal with matters local or private in those cases where such legislation is necessarily incidental to the exercise of powers conferred upon it by the enumerative heads of clause 91."[115] In short, its object in effect was to diminish federal jurisdiction as protected by the declaratory and deeming clauses.

The residual clause was next to be explained. Watson's comments during the argument amply confirmed Lord Macnaghten's friendly observation that he did not have "the precision of thought and language which distinguished Lord Westbury ... or that singular facility of lucid exposition which in the hands of Lord Cairns made argument superfluous."[116] An anonymous contemporary was less kind: "Watson's mind, like his body and his gait, was singularly massive, and its movements deliberate. In his early days he was therefore considered slow."[117] In fact, Watson certainly appeared to have difficulty determining the purpose of the residual clause. At one point during the argument he observed that the

> effect of the original first words—they have not been a great deal considered, and may some day require considerable attention—appears to me to be to override to a certain extent nearly all the clauses giving jurisdiction. If that is thought good for one, each Province may enact for itself, because it thinks it for the benefit of the Province. The Dominion Parliament apparently have power if they are really justified, and I assume they are acting fairly and honestly in the matter, to enact it as a general regulation.[118]

Whatever may have been his expository problems, his grasp of the clause was at best uncertain. "Every power that is not entrusted, I take it, to the Parliament of Canada, which does not belong to it, is with the province," he commented. "No; it is the other way," Herschell quickly interjected. "Everything which is not expressly enumerated to the Province is with the Canadian Parliament." To which Watson replied: "It belongs either to the Dominion by virtue of one of

the sub-sections 1 to 29, or by virtue of it not coming under section 92, in which case the last sentence of section 91 gives it."[119]

Watson made it all much clearer, if only to himself, in his decision. The declaratory clause simply indicated that there may "be matters not included in the enumerations upon which the Parliament of Canada has power to legislate because they concern the peace, order and good government of the Dominion." But since the deeming clause did not apply to such matters, any federal legislation "ought to be strictly confined to such matters as are unquestionably of Canadian interest and importance, and ought not to trench upon provincial legislation with respect to any of the classes of subjects enumerated in s. 92." This was a matter not only of law but of politics: "To attach any other construction to the general power which, *in supplement* of its enumerated powers, is conferred upon the Parliament of Canada by s. 91, would, in their Lordships' opinion, not only be contrary to the intendment of the Act, but would practically destroy the autonomy of the provinces."[120]

However, the residual clause did have a purpose. During an irrelevant discussion about the possible manufacture of cordite, Watson commented, "It rather occurs to me that if any question arose as is now suggested, the legislature of Canada would have full power to legislate under the general words with which section 91 commences and which are not limited by the words which follow. Any subjects may be dealt with which is necessary, which, in the opinion of the Government is required for the peace, order or good government of Canada." Later, during a rambling discussion of what was "local," Watson observed that what may once have been a "local evil ... may attain such dimensions as to become a threatened danger to the whole Dominion and in that case I should be sorry to doubt that there in power, given to the Dominion Parliament to intervene."[121] The observation passed without comment. Nevertheless, Watson decided to add his "national concern" and "national dimension" doctrines to the constitution:

> Their Lordships do not doubt that some matters, in their origin local and provincial, might attain such dimensions as to affect the body politic of the Dominion, and to justify the Canadian Parliament

in passing laws for their regulation or abolition in the interest of the Dominion. But great caution must be observed in distinguishing between that which is local and provincial, and therefore within the jurisdiction of the provincial legislature, and that which has ceased to be merely local or provincial, and has become a matter of national concern, in such sense as to bring it within the jurisdiction of the Parliament of Canada.

As an illustration, he suggested that restricting the sale of arms to young people would be a provincial matter, but traffic in arms for seditious purposes might become a matter of national concern.[122]

In his decision, Watson next turned to "the regulation of trade and commerce," the scope of which had been extensively discussed in argument. Arguing for federal jurisdiction over prohibition, Blake had insisted that by decision it lay within the residual clause and trade and commerce. Reminded that *Parsons* had rejected the view that the federal government had authority over "every particular dealing," Blake first emphasized that Smith had explicitly not defined the scope of trade and commerce. He then began to argue the greater relevance of Canadian language and practice than Smith's extrinsic aids, when Lord Davey cut him off with, "Is that admissible?" Clearly it was not. "I have no right to ask your Lordships to depart" from *Parsons*, Blake continued. "And if your Lordships think that the attempt at a definition or suggestion, made *obiter* perhaps, and stated in *Lambe's* case to be thrown out rather than otherwise, is not important to be discussed, I will not trouble your Lordships." Obviously they felt it was not important.[123]

During the argument, Watson had admitted that he had no idea of the scope of trade and commerce. "I do not think any of the cases afford a definition or anything like a precise definition of what precisely is meant by the expression 'regulation of trade' in sub-section 2," he had lectured Newcombe. "There are explanations of it, but the explanations, as far as I can find, require as much explanation as the section itself."[124] As Newcombe argued that prohibition could fall within trade and commerce, Watson anticipated his ultimate decision. "If it had been 'Trade and Commerce' I could quite well have understood that these words might have implied abolition as well

as regulation," he countered, "but when the power given expressly is confined to the regulation of the liquor trade could they abolish it. I could quite understand their doing it in virtue of the general power at the commencement of the section."[125] Thus, just as Blake was anxious to reopen *Parsons* to find in trade and commerce a home for prohibition, Watson was determined to close that door and keep it within the residual clause in order to leave the 92(16) door open.

No sooner had Blake begun his trade and commerce argument than Watson asked him whether the Canada Temperance Act in reality had been upheld under trade and commerce or the residual clause. "You see the importance of the distinction between these two … The distinction may be important when you come to consider the enactments of the last clause of section 92."[126] Blake persisted in arguing the authority to prohibit under 91(2), and, faced with Watson's strenuous opposition, was heartened by the lord chancellor's intervention. "I made an observation the other day which, I think, I ought to retract upon consideration," Halsbury informed Blake. "What occurred to me was, and it is relevant to our present discussion, that these words 'Regulation of Trade' could not be satisfied by prohibition. I think I was too hasty. Trade generally may be regulated by prohibiting a particular trade." That admission, Blake said later, seemed to make further argument on the point unnecessary.[127] In the last moments of the argument, Watson seemed to concede the possibility that the words could include prohibition, although, as usual, it was difficult to decipher his code: "You cannot put a general meaning on them, you must refer to the context of the statute to discover what the Legislature meant in employing them. I do not doubt that the Regulation of Trade and Commerce may very fairly include prohibition. If the context gave an indication I should not be surprised at its being either way in one statute, but then being construed one way in one statute would not lead to its being similarly construed in another."[128]

In his decision, Watson reluctantly accepted *Russell* as precedent that the Canada Temperance Act was valid under the residual clause (but ignored Smith's pointed statement that the committee did not dissent from the Supreme Court's finding that it was also valid under trade and commerce). That being so, the only remaining obstacle was the possibility that prohibition could fill within trade and commerce. "If it were so," wrote Watson, "the Parliament of Canada would, under the exception from 92 which has already been noticed [the deeming clause], be at liberty to exercise its legislative authority, although in so doing it should interfere with the jurisdiction of the provinces." No such danger need be apprehended, however, for despite Halsbury's intervention, Watson had no difficulty in asserting that a "power to regulate, naturally, if not necessarily, assumes, unless it is enlarged by the context, the conservation of the thing which is to be made the subject of regulation."[129] As authority, Watson reached for Davey's recent decision in *City of Toronto* v. *Virgo,* a case in which he had participated, which struck down a city by-law prohibiting hawkers from plying their trade in certain sections of the city, with the argument that a "power to regulate and govern seems to imply the continued existence of that which is to be regulated or governed."[130]

Mowat's liquor legislation, with some qualifications, could stand.

In so deciding, Lord Watson had reconstructed sections 91 and 92 of the constitution. The path of reconstruction was tortuous indeed. Watson strayed far from precedent and ignored previous judicial comment: he reversed the application of the deeming clause, excluded any meaningful purpose for the declaratory clause, explained (almost away) the content and possible application of peace, order, and good government, and advanced the novel proposition that federal regulation excluded prohibition. The pretense that the committee's single decision was collegial was revealed as the myth it was. Given the views expressed by his colleagues during the argument, Watson's judgment in all its particulars could not have been delivered without strong dissent—if anyone cared nine months after the argument when the judgment was delivered.[131] But his reasons, doctrines, and *obiter dicta* became embedded in the law of the constitution.

With something less than the precision of a scholar, Watson had written the text for symmetrical federalism. In *Liquidators,* Watson's provinces had fathered Confederation, delegated a limited capacity to the national government, and retained a direct connection with the crown. In *Local Prohibition,* he expanded their legislative jurisdiction by the process of redefining and

limiting federal jurisdiction. It is no wonder that, on his death in 1899, Richard Haldane could prophesy that "nowhere is his memory likely to be more gratefully preserved than in those distant Canadian provinces whose rights of self-government he placed on a basis that was both intelligible and firm."[132]

APART FROM THOSE few who maintain that Watson's jurisprudence was a reasonable and faithful rendering of the 1867 constitution, the intellectually curious have attempted to determine his motive. Unfortunately, Watson is of little assistance. Unlike his disciple, Lord Haldane, he bequeathed neither correspondence nor memoirs. Conclusions about motive must be reached on the basis of his published opinions on behalf of the committee and his participation in the arguments, although some scholars assume that his opinions were obviously derived from currents of nineteenth-century political and legal thought.

Watson's solicitude for the autonomy of the provinces has led Murray Greenwood to conclude that the motive was "institutional self-interest." In its support of provincial jurisdiction, Greenwood argues that the committee avoided being labelled superfluous and created a supportive political constituency in Canada. The motive was not the perfection of Canadian federalism but the preservation of appeals and the continuation of judicial imperialism. However provocative, it is impossible to find in the constitutional decisions, at least, quantitative support for this speculation.[133] Suzanne Birks also finds imperialism lurking in the committee's law. Analysing the apparent logic of the decisions, she suggests that the provincial crown served not only, or even primarily, as a vehicle to establish provincial executive autonomy or sovereignty, but was essential to establish or re-establish a direct link between the provinces and the empire. The interesting but intuitive argument is most fairly stated in her words:

At the banning of the activist period in the 1890s, the issue of Canada's incomplete sovereignty operated as a fundamental, sustaining presumption for Lord Watson in the enunciation of the *Maritime Bank* doctrine. Lord Watson made it clear in the decision that the Canadian federal system had to be bolted to the constitutional framework of the Empire. The independence of the provinces from

Ottawa's control was by no means independence from Great Britain and the sovereign, any more than Ottawa's powers could exclude the authority of London. This interweaving of the Canadian and imperial structures established a point of departure in the interpretation of the Canadian constitution which was necessarily detrimental to the federal cause.... Faced with the energetic drive of the provinces, who participated with considerable vigour in the constitutional disputes before the Judicial Committee, and given the inclination of the board to preserve the integrity of the imperial structure, the Privy Council's redirection of Confederation is entirely comprehensible.[134]

David Schneiderman looks for the roots of Watson's solicitousness in late-nineteenth-century legal thought. In his determined exclusion of prohibition from regulation, he suggests, "Watson was faithful not necessarily to the text of the constitution but to the ideological presuppositions of the constitutional lawyer of the late nineteenth century." Those presuppositions included a judicial penchant for limited or weak government, and the belief that personal liberty and property were best protected in "the repositories of counter power" in federal state. Schneiderman implies that these presuppositions explain much more than the limits of regulation: "It is this understanding of federalism—as a means of limiting legislative authority and promoting provincial autonomy—that fits the conception of federalism as facilitative of liberty. It also makes more coherent the Privy Council's application of the common law rules of interpretation to the *British North America Act*."[135]

Similarly, although Richard Risk finds both the reasoning and the result of *Local Prohibition* difficult to explain, he agrees in large part with Schneiderman. Although Watson's restrictions on the residual clause "may simply have been a product of misunderstanding of the structure of sections 91 and 92," more generally, both in the analysis of the residual clause and throughout the judgment, Risk finds confirmation of the presence, if not the dominance, of the "rule of law thought." This principle, "with its general model of autonomous powers divided by sharp lines policed by courts, was a foundation of Dicey's analysis of federalism, and any reading of 'peace, order, and good

government' as an indefinite power or a threat to the (autonomous) powers of the province was fundamentally inconsistent." Risk finds further confirmation of the "rule of law thought" in what he sees as the court's unwillingness to consider context and values, preferring to rely instead on the supposedly plain meaning of the words in the constitution.[136]

Neither Watson's opinions nor his comments during argument provide direct confirming evidence for these and other plausible arguments. But, however much Watson may have professed to rely on the "plain meaning of the words in the constitution," in both argument and decision he enthusiastically engaged in substantive, if idiosyncratic, lawmaking, which might have had roots more personal and experiential. For his comments in argument and *dicta* in decision do reveal that he had an instinctive predisposition both to decentralization and to judicial lawmaking, which might be expected from a partially assimilated Scots lawyer trained in the civil law.

Lord Watson, wrote a contemporary, was a striking example of early training in civil law which, with its liberal views of the law and sense of historical development, "furnished him when he came to sit on the Judicial Committee, with the key to the legal puzzles which make up the legal mosaic of our Empire."[137] His training and experience were not the same as those of his southern colleagues. Scots law was not fundamentally a case-law system. Precedent and *stare decisis* were relatively recent English imports, which were still not firmly entrenched and certainly far less rigid in Scots law and practice.

For that reason, Watson felt less restraint in disregarding precedent or lower-court reasoning, as he indulged in speculation about the nature of Canadian federalism and solved the legal puzzles to his satisfaction. As he once said in the House of Lords, before Halsbury's 1898 statement on the binding nature of precedent, "so long as such revising discretion remains in the highest tribunal in the land there is wisdom in the practice that cobblers in less exalted places should stick to their lasts and leave to the supreme tribunal the task of making such modifications as the times may require to previously established rulings."[138]

Unlike other Scots lawyers who migrated south, Watson remained what a colleague described as a "typical and ardent Scot" whose education and experience were exclusively Scottish until he was middle- aged, when he was drawn south by promotion not envy.[139] Watson was familiar with the unique federal system that united England and Scotland in the new state called Great Britain. Original Scottish proposals for this union had called for a version of a federal system in which their legal system, religion, and other matters of concern to a permanent minority could be guaranteed. Although the British insisted on a unitary state and, like "whiskey polluted with soda, previous separate elements had been superseded by a new species altogether," the union "took effect as a skeletal, but nonetheless fundamental, written constitution for the new Kingdom of Great Britain" when it came into being. "It does not seem to be widely realised that the basic constitution of this new kingdom was the prototype of written constitutions which expressly limit the powers of organs of government in relation to each other," explained a leading Scottish authority, "in particular which, by restricting the powers of the legislature which makes laws for the whole country, protect the interests of a permanent minority from being overridden by a permanent majority."[140]

During his four years in the Commons and later in the Lords, Watson showed no interest in politics but was assiduous in protecting and promoting Scottish interests—Scot law, religion, local government, the universities. And, just as he was solicitous for Scottish interests while in parliament, so too was he solicitous for minority interests in Canada. Although he felt that the Judicial Committee might be tied by the statutory language of the Manitoba Act, Watson was almost alone in expressing sympathy for the minority in Barrett.[141] Trained in the civil law, he became familiar with the Civil Code of Quebec and, in a judgment overruling a decision of the Supreme Court, referred to the "general importance to the province of Quebec of the question arising upon the construction of its Civil Code," noting in justification that his judgment confirmed that of all seven judges who heard the case in Quebec.[142] With the civil law of the other provinces embedded in property and civil rights, it was natural that he would show, as he constantly did, a similar concern for their jurisdiction and for the significance of the stillborn section 94.

It is dangerous to draw definitive conclusions from Watson's comments during the oral arguments, for, even more than his considered opinions, they confirm the judgment of a contemporary that "he was no grammarian or philologist. No one accustomed to listen to him could ever predict how any sentence was to end; and we are quite sure that many of his propositions ended in an entirely different manner from what their author intended or the listener expected."[143] A modern student of his jurisprudence is much less kind: "One of the difficulties in writing about contributions such as those of Lord Watson, is that they are—with respect—too confused to classify."[144] However, his language in Liquidators, even more than the result, supports the compact theory of Confederation. As he commented during the argument in Brophy, Confederation was "by consent and there were no means of compelling it. Of course the Imperial Parliament might have it in their power, but it certainly never was the intention of the imperial legislature to compel it, and certainly the adjustment of the terms were left to the contracting parties."[145] A similar understanding of federalism would appear to explain his proposition that provincial jurisdiction was the rule and federal legislative authority the exception.

Although he did not say so in as many words, Watson seemed to anticipate Haldane's belief that the provinces were "like independent kingdoms"[146] under the British sovereign. It followed that, in the resolution of federal-provincial disputes, the committee was involved in "some really international questions between Canadian governments."[147] All that was necessary was to restructure the BNA Act to fit the theory, a task made easier by Watson's view that "bills are drawn in order that they may pass, as razors are manufactured in order that they may sell—in other words the legislator instead of clothing his purpose in plain and unambiguous language, resorts to all kinds of verbal disguises in order to make it appear colourless and innocent in the eyes of those from whom opposition is expected."[148] On many occasions Watson admitted or revealed that sections of the BNA Act were difficult to understand and that someday the apparent ambiguities or uncertainties would have to be resolved. In Local Prohibition he stripped the act of its "verbal disguises" to make it coherent and consistent with his conception of Canadian federalism.

THE FIRST DECADE of the twentieth century was a quiet interlude between the doctrinal turbulence of the Watson and Haldane courts. There were fourteen federalism appeals. Eleven decisions of the Canadian courts were confirmed, including all from the Supreme Court, and nine upheld federal jurisdiction. Several of the appeals fell within Watson's precedents.[149] The Judicial Committee held on five appeals that federal railways and Bell Telephone were immune from provincial or municipal regulations. Federal ownership of the foreshore in Vancouver and the right of the Canadian Pacific Railway to obstruct passage to the water were confirmed and the provincial attempt to control water rights in the railway belt was rejected.[150]

Dismissing an appeal of a Supreme Court decision finding the attempt of the Grand Trunk Railway to contract out of liability for personal injury to their employees, on the ground that a federal statute prohibiting it fell within property and civil rights, Lord Dunedin wrote that the decisions in *Voluntary Assignments* and *Tennant* established two propositions: "First, that there can be a domain in which provincial and Dominion legislation may overlap, in which case neither legislation will be *ultra vires*, if the field is clear; and secondly, that if the field is not clear, and in such a domain the two legislations meet, then the Dominion legislation must prevail." To the doctrine of paramountcy, Dunedin added that of ancillarity. The "true question" was not whether the law "deals with a civil right—which may be conceded—but whether this law is truly ancillary to railway legislation." In his opinion it was, and because such railways were "mere creatures of the Dominion legislature … it cannot be considered out of the way that the Parliament which calls them into existence should prescribe the terms which were to regulate the relations of the employees to the corporation," although the legislation did "touch what may be described as the civil rights of those employees."[151]

In a surprising decision, the committee found Ontario's Sunday observance legislation, which prohibited working, "tippling," swearing, fishing, sports, and excursions, *ultra vires*. It was openly unsympathetic to arguments based on 92(13) or 92(16). After three days of argument, Halsbury, the lord chancellor, was exasperated: "We are drowning everything in words. The Act of Parliament says you shall not work

on Sunday, putting it in its broadest form, if you do you shall be indicted and punished. Is that not a criminal offence made so by Statute?"[152] Immediately after the argument, Halsbury delivered a decision, in which he stated that the "reservation of the criminal law for the Dominion of Canada is given in clear and intelligible words which must be construed according to their natural and ordinary signification" and it was "impossible to doubt" that an infraction of the Ontario act was "an offence against the criminal law."[153]

The Laurier government was as unhappy with the decision as was the Lord's Day Alliance. After prolonged negotiations with the provinces and appeals to the Supreme Court and the Judicial Committee,[154] the government passed An Act respecting the Lord's Day, which prohibited a wide variety of activities under the criminal law. But the act allowed the provinces to opt out of many provisions and left prosecution to the provincial attorney general. The act remained in force until 1985 when, in *Big M. Drug Mart,* it was deemed to be in violation of the *Charter* guarantee of freedom of religion.

However, the Judicial Committee was given the opportunity to revisit and confirm Lord Watson's doctrines in 1911 with a Quebec challenge to the federal Railway Act, which subjected provincial railways to its provisions relating to through traffic. Intervening for Ottawa, E.L. Newcombe chose to base his argument on the residual clause, national dimensions, and the regulation of trade and commerce, thus inevitably inviting the court to return to *Local Prohibition*.[155] In his decision, Lord Atkinson chose not only to reject the arguments but, seldom altering Watson's language, to extract and codify the doctrines found in Watson's decision:

1. The deeming clause did not derogate from provincial legislative authority under *92(16)* except to enable the federal government to deal with "matter, local or private, in those cases where such legislation is necessarily incidental" to the exercise of power under the section 91 enumerations.
2. The deeming clause had no application to anything but the enumerations, and, in legislating on matters not enumerated, the Dominion parliament had "no authority to encroach" upon the classes of subjects in section 92.

3.  Sections 91 and 92 indicated that, under the residual clause, federal legislation "ought to be strictly confined to such matters as are unquestionably of Canadian interest and importance, and ought not to trench upon provincial legislation."

4.  To "attach any other construction of the general powers which, in supplement of its enumerated powers, are conferred upon the Parliament of Canada by s. 91 would not only be contrary to the intendment of the Act, but would practically destroy the autonomy of the provinces."

5.  If the federal government had power to legislate for the whole country on matters which were in each province "substantially of local or private interest, upon the assumption that these matters also concern the peace, order and good government of the Dominion, there is hardly a subject upon which it might not legislate to the exclusion of provincial legislation."

The same considerations, Atkinson continued, applied to the regulation of trade and commerce. "Taken in their widest sense these words would authorize legislation by the Parliament of Canada in respect of several of the matters specifically enumerated in s. 92 and would seriously encroach upon the local autonomy of the province."[156]

The act could not be justified on the grounds that it concerned the peace, order, and good government of Canada, or that it dealt with the regulation of trade and commerce, or that it was necessarily incidental to the control of federal railways. It was *ultra vires* as "an unauthorized invasion of the rights of the Legislature of the province of Quebec."[157] Although Atkinson admitted that Watson's decision had "little if any application," he had embedded the latter's construction of the BNA Act even more deeply into federalism jurisprudence.[158]

The doctrinal stage was set for Viscount Haldane, eagerly waiting in the wings.

## NOTES

1  "Lord Watson" (1899) 11 *Juridical Review*, 272 at 279. See also R.B. Haldane, "The Appellate Courts of the Empire" (1900) 12 *Juridical Review*, 4.

2  Lord Denning, *Borrowing from Scotland* (Glasgow: Jackson, Son 1963), 34.

3  *The Times*, 15 September 1899.

4  "Lord Watson" (1899) 11 *Juridical Review*, 278 at 279.

5  G.P. Browne, *The Judicial Committee and the British North America Act: An Analysis of the Interpretative Scheme for the Distribution of Legislative Powers* (Toronto: University of Toronto Press 1967).

6  [W.F. O'Connor] Canada, Senate, *Report pursuant to Resolution of the Senate to the Honourable Speaker by the Parliamentary Counsel relating to the Enactment of the British North American Act, 1867, Any Lack of Consonance between Its Terms and Judicial Construction of Them and Cognate Matters* (Ottawa: King's Printer 1939); Bora Laskin, "'Peace, Order and Good Government' Re-Examined" (1947) 25 *Canadian Bar Review*, 1054.

7  Paul Romney, "The Nature and Scope of Provincial Autonomy: Oliver Mowat, the Quebec Resolutions and the Construction of the *British North America Act*" (1992) 25 *Canadian Journal of Political Science*, 3 at 28.

8  "Why Lord Watson was Right," in Janet Ajzenstat, ed., *Canadian Constitutionalism, 1791–1991* (Ottawa: Canadian Study of Parliament Group 1991), 177 at 191.

9  "Unity and Diversity in Canadian Federalism" (1975) 53 *Canadian Bar Review*, 597 at 608, 607.

10  "The Judicial Committee and Its Critics" (1971) *Canadian Journal of Political Science*, 301 at 324–5.

11  Ibid., 319.

12  Robert Vipond, *Liberty and Community: Canadian Federalism and the Failure of the Constitution* (Albany: State University of New York Press 1991), 158–9. On the historiography of the controversy, see also Richard Risk, "The Scholars and the Constitution: P.O.G.G. and the Privy Council" (1966) 23 *Manitoba Law Journal*, 496; and "Constitutional Scholarship in the Late Nineteenth Century: Making Federalism Wor'" (1996) 46 *University of Toronto Law Journal*, 427.

13  "Lord Watson" (1899) 15 *Scottish Law Review*, 235. This obituary is the fullest account of Watson's life. See also the entry in the *Dictionary of National Biography*, vol. 22 (London: Oxford University Press 1901), 1380; and "EM.," "Lord Watson," *London Law Times*, reprinted in *Canadian Law Times* (June 1903), 551.

14  Alan Paterson, "Scottish Lords of Appeal, 1876–1988" (1988) *Juridical Review*, 238.

15  *Dobie v. The Temporalities Board* (1881–2) 7 A.C. 136, appropriately since it involved the Presbyterian Church and the Church of Scotland.

16  See George J. Wheeler, *Confederation Law of Canada: Privy Council Cases on the British North America Act 1867* (London: Eyre and Spottiswoode 1896). T.B. Smith notes that, when preparing the English-language version of the Quebec Civil Code in 1866, "Scottish legal terminology was used to ensure a civilian construction." (*British Justice: The Scottish Contribution* [London: Stevens and Sons 1961], 42.)

17  The sixteen are conveniently printed in Richard A. Olmsted, *Decisions of the Judicial Committee of the Privy Council relating to the British North America Act, 1867 and the Canadian Constitution, 1867–1954* (Ottawa: Queen's Printer 1954). The exception was *A.G. Ontario v. A.G. Canada*, [1894] A.C. 189, known as the *Voluntary Assignments* case, which led to the controversial unoccupied-field doctrine. Among the sixteen are two on the Manitoba schools question on which he sat but did not deliver the judgments.

18  *City of Winnipeg v. Barrett*, [1892] A.C. 445. The oral argument is printed in Canada, *Sessional Papers*, no. 33B, 1893.

19  Morris, a prominent Irish Catholic, was appointed in 1889. Described as a Tory of independent temperament, distrustful of democracy and hostile to Home Rule, in the Judicial Committee

"he not infrequently dissented from the majority." Judging from the oral argument in *Barrett*, he must have dissented in that case. (*Dictionary of National Biography* [supplement, vol. 1, London: Oxford University Press 1912], 653.)

20 *Bank of Montreal v. Lambe* (1887), 12 A.C. 575 at 579.

21 *Citizens Insurance Company v. Parsons* (1881), [1881–2] 7 A.C. 96 at 109.

22 *St. Catherine's Milling and Lumber Company v. The Queen* (1888), 14 A.C. 46. Sidney Harring, in an excellent legal account, described the case as "one of the most significant cases on native rights in the common law world." Sidney L. Harring, *White Man's Law: Native People on Nineteenth-Century Jurisprudence* (Toronto: University of Toronto Press 1998), 125. The decision is still before the courts. See the judgment of Justice Archie Campbell in *The Chippewa Band of Sarnia v. A.G. Canada, A.G. Ontario et al.* [released April 1999], Ontario, Superior Court of Justice, court file no. 95-CU-92484. On the dispute generally, see Christopher Armstrong, *The Politics of Federalism: Ontario's Relations with the Federal Government, 1867–1942* (Toronto: University of Toronto Press 1981), 14–22.

23 Cited in Anthony J. Hall, "*The St. Catherine's Milling and Lumber Company v. The Queen*: Indian Land Rights as a Factor in Federal-Provincial Relations in Nineteenth Century Canada," in Kerry Abel and Jean Friesen, eds., *Aboriginal Land Use in Canada: Historical and Legal Aspects* (Manitoba: University of Manitoba Press 1991), 267 at 271.

24 National Archives of Canada (NAC), Macdonald Papers, McCarthy to Macdonald, 5 January 1885.

25 NAC, Macdonald Papers, 83015, Campbell to Macdonald, 23 October 1885. Campbell had retired as minister of justice a month earlier.

26 Strong's dissenting opinion held that to interpret the BNA Act as "by implication abolishing all right and property of the Indians in unsurrendered lands … would attribute to the Imperial Parliament the intention of taking away proprietary rights, without express words and without any adequate reason." Such an interpretation would constitute a departure from "the long cherished and most successful policy originally inaugurated by the British Government for the treatment of the Indian tribes … and must be rejected." (*St. Catherine's Milling and Lumber Co. v. R.* (1887), 13 S.C.R. 577 at 616.) Strong's dissent has become more appealing given the direction of modern decisions on aboriginal rights. See, for example, Hamar Foster, "Forgotten Arguments: Aboriginal Title and Sovereignty in *Canada Jurisdiction Act* Cases" (1992) 21 *Manitoba Law Journal*, 343.

27 During the hearing on the petition to appeal, opposed by Haldane acting for Ontario, the board requested that the federal government be a formal party to the litigation given the size of the territory at stake. John Thompson reluctantly agreed and retained Sir Richard Webster, who appeared with McCarthy. The transcript of the hearing on appeal and subsequent correspondence is in Archives of Ontario (AO), Irving Papers, MU1480, file 41/08/5 and 41/06/2. Webster, better known as Lord Alverstone, also acted in *Precious Metals*, *Voluntary Assignments*, and *Barrett*, losing all three. The transcript of the oral argument in *Barrett* confirms John Ewart's bitter comment that he "didn't look at the brief, knew nothing of the case, and blundered from start to finish." (NAC, Thompson Papers, N.C. Wallace to R. White, 6 August 1892, enclosed in White to Thompson, 8 August 1892.) The contributor to the *Dictionary of National Biography* (vol. 24, 1912–31, 562) wrote that "he was not a clever man, nor a learned lawyer, nor a good speaker—either in the courts or in parliament, his equipment as an advocate consisted mainly in splendid physique, a forcible personality, and immense

industry." In fact, as attorney general Webster boasted of his large, private practice. (Viscount Alverstone, *Recollections of Bar and Bench* [London: Edward Arnold 1915], 227.)

28 Blake to Margaret Blake, 21 July 1888, cited in Joseph Schull, *Edward Blake: Leader and Exile* (Toronto: Macmillan 1976), 108.

29 Blake printed his argument: *In the Privy Council: The St. Catherine's Milling and Lumber Company v. The Queen: Arguments of Mr. Blake, Counsel for Ontario* (Toronto: 1888).

30 Blake to Margaret Blake, 25 July 1888, cited in Schull, *Blake*, 110.

31 *St. Catharine's Milling and Lumber Co. v. The Queen* (1889), 14 A.C. 46 at 54.

32 *Delgamuukw v. British Columbia*, [1997] 3 S.C.R. 1010 at 1081 (Lamer). See also the judgment of Justice Archie Campbell n.22 above. Of Watson's decision, Harring concludes that while it remains important in modern title cases, "almost no part of its analysis, taken element by element, is good law." (Harring, *White Man's Law*, 146–7.)

33 *St. Catherine's Milling* at 59. In *Delgamuukw* (at 1117) the Supreme Court, following Watson's opinion, determined that the provision extended to all "lands held pursuant to aboriginal title" and that only the federal government could extinguish aboriginal title.

34 Alverstone, *Recollections*, 224–5.

35 *St. Catherine's Milling* at 60.

36 *Dominion of Canada v. Province of Ontario*, [1910] A.C. 637 at 647.

37 Blake, *The St. Catherine's Milling and Lumber Company*, 5–7.

38 *A.G. British Columbia v. A.G. Canada* (1889), 14 A.C. 295.

39 In *Re Earl of Northumberland's Mines*, I Plowd. 310, 75 *English Reports* (1907) 471.

40 *A.G. British Columbia v. A.G. Canada* (1887), 14 S.C.R. 345 at 357–8.

41 Ibid. at 361.

42 Ibid. at 372–3. Fournier believed that the Earl of Northumberland's case applied, and Henry concluded that title to the land was not vested in the crown.

43 *A.G. British Columbia v. A.G. Canada* (1887), 14 A.C. 295 at 303–4.

44 *B.C. (A.G.) v. Can. (A.G.)* (1989), 45 B.C.L.R. (2d) 339 at 358.

45 *British Columbia (Attorney General) v. Canada (Attorney General)* (1991), 59 B.C.L.R. (2d) 280 at 302.

46 *AG. Canada v. A.G. British Columbia*, [1994] 2 S.C.R. 41 at 97. Indexed as *British Columbia (Attorney General) v. Canada (Attorney General): An Act Respecting the Vancouver Island Railway (Re)*. In a lengthy judgment for the court, Iacobucci reviewed the judgments in the lower courts on the railway in question but included the comments on the quality of Watson's reasons. At issue was the federal government's responsibility not only to build but to continue to operate the railway.

47 Ibid.

48 For example, *Molson v. Chapleau* (1883), 6 *Legal News* 222 at 224, where Justice Auguste Papineau asserted that if the queen was not part of the provincial government, the province could not be part of the empire.

49 *St. Catherine's Milling and Lumber Company v. The Queen* (1886), 13 O.A.R 158 at 165.

50 Lieutenant governor to the secretary of state, 22 January 1886, Ontario, *Sessional Papers*, 1888, no. 37, 20.

51 NAC, Lansdowne Papers, reel 627, Lansdowne to Thompson, 17 July 1886; Thompson to Lansdowne, 28 July 1886. The governor general pressed Thompson to agree to the reference. Thompson refused and replied officially to Mowat that "so long as the judgement in *Lenoir v. Ritchie* is not revised, it is the duty of Governments and individuals in Canada to respect and conform to that judgement." (Secretary of State to the Lieutenant Governor, 27 September 1886, Ontario, *Sessional Papers*, 1888, no. 37, 27–9.)

52  51 Vict. c. 5. See Paul Romney, *Mr Attorney: The Attorney-General of Ontario in Court, Cabinet, and Legislature, 1791–1899* (Toronto: Osgoode Society/University of Toronto Press 1986), 258.

53  Thompson to Mowat, 4 February 1889, in W.E. Hodgins, comp., *Correspondence, Reports of the Ministers of Justice, and Orders in Council upon the Subject of Dominion and Provincial Legislation, 1867–1895* (Ottawa: Government Printing Bureau 1896), 206.

54  *A.G. Canada v. A.G. Ontario* (1890), [1891] 20 O.R. 222 at 247, 249. The arguments and decisions in the courts are fully examined in Suzanne Marthe Birks, "The Survival of the Crown in the Canadian State: The Political Components of Monarchy" (LLM thesis, Osgoode Hall, 1980), 51–60.

55  Blake's argument was published privately: *The Executive Power Case: Argument* (Toronto: 1892).

56  [1892] A.C. 437. Though the Supreme Court did hear the appeal, Taschereau stated that the appeal should have been abandoned because of Watson's decision or gone directly to the Judicial Committee: "Constitutional questions cannot be finally determined in this court. They never have been, and can never be under the present system." *A.G. Canada v. A.G. Ontario* (1893), 23 S.C.R. 458 at 472. At the Judicial Committee, where the issue was the validity of acts of Ontario in 1873 to appoint queen's counsel, the case was decided without reference to *Liquidators*. "Assuming it to have been within the competency of the provincial legislature to vest the power in some authority other than the Sovereign," wrote Watson, "the Lieutenant-Governor appears to have been very properly selected as its depositary," citing the provisions of section 65. And under heads 4 and 14 of section 92, it lay within provincial authority to determine who should represent the crown in its courts. (*A.G. Canada v. A.G. Ontario* (1897), [1898] A.C. 247 at 253.)

57  The bank also owed money to the federal government but, for purposes of the stated case, it was agreed that the federal government would be regarded as a simple creditor of the bank. This may have been to avoid the question raised in *The Queen v. The Bank of Nova Scotia* (1885), 11 S.C.R. 1, where it was argued that, since the federal government was attempting to recover money owed by the bank, only the crown in the right of the province had the prerogative right of preference over other creditors. The argument was rejected by the court and the right of the federal government upheld.

58  *The Provincial Government of New Brunswick v. The Liquidators of the Maritime Bank* (1888), 17 N.B.R. 379 at 382, 384.

59  Ibid, at 396.

60  *Liquidators of the Maritime Bank v. The Receiver General of New Brunswick* (1889), [1892], 20 S.C.R. 695 at 707.

61  NAC, Gowan Papers, Gwynne to Gowan, 24 December 1889.

62  *Liquidators of the Maritime Bank of Canada v. Receiver-General of New Brunswick*, [1892] A.C. 437 at 438–9.

63  Ibid, at 441.

64  Ibid, at 443. Watson neglected to point out that the appointment was made on advice and at no point received royal approval, as did that of the governor general. It also seemed irrelevant to question whether the lieutenant governor's capacity to reserve provincial legislation on the advice of the federal executive compromised his position as a regal representative.

65  Ibid. at 444–5.

66  *A.G. Canada v. A.G. Ontario* (1893), 23 S.C.R 458 at 463.

67  Ibid, at 441–2. Italics added. That the provinces were still subject to federal powers of disallowance and reservation, transferred from the imperial authority, obviously did not influence Watson's opinion although his judgment weakened the powers themselves.

Watson continued with a long quotation from the decision Hodge, cited in chapter 3, n.74, but he conveniently omitted the last clauses—"would have under like circumstances...." This suggested the equality of the imperial, Dominion, and provincial governments, something that Fitzgerald may not have intended.

68  See David Smith, *The Invisible Crown* (Toronto: University of Toronto Press 1995). Smith notes that in *Liquidators* "the courts redefined the nature of Canadian federalism by recourse to the Crown's prerogative" (139).

69  (1893), [1894] A.C. 31 at 35–6. The constitutional question had arisen in the Ontario Court of Appeal but was not discussed because it was at variance with the decision in *Merchants' Bank of Canada v. Smith* (1883), 8 S.C.R. 512, which was binding on the provincial court. When it arose at the Judicial Committee in July 1892, further argument on that question was delayed until July 1893 because the Judicial Committee had undertaken to hear the Labrador case. In the interim, the bank had replaced Christopher Robinson with Davey as lead counsel. Since the government of Ontario, whose retainer Davey held, was not party to the litigation, he could plead in support of federal jurisdiction for the only time in his career.

70  Ibid., at 45. Italics added.

71  *Tennant v. Union Bank of Canada* at 46.

72  Canada, *Report pursuant to Resolution of the Senate to the Honourable Speaker*, 36; Browne, *The Judicial Committee and the British North America Act*, 43. André Tremblay has also noted that "à ce moment-là, on n'avait pas encore distingués les pouvoirs énuméres des pouvoirs généraux du Parlement Canadienne." (*Droit Constitutionnel: Principes* [Montreal: Les Éditions Thémis 1993], 230.)

73  "The substitution is most important," O'Connor emphasized, "for the word extends indicates that the existing necessary exclusiveness of the enacted residuary power extends to the 29 declared exemplary enumerations of classes of subjects which all 'come within' the enacted general legislative powers of the Dominion, whilst the words 'shall extend' imply a new creation and distribution of exclusive powers." O'Connor, *Report*, 37.

74  *A.G. Ontario v. A.G. Canada*, [1894] A.C. 189. Legislation similar to An Act Respecting Assignments and Preferences by Insolvent Persons (R.S.o.1887, c. 124) had existed in Ontario since Confederation.

75  Thompson had refused to agree to a reference to the Supreme Court (AO, RG 4-32, file 1891, no. 576, Mowat to Thompson, 16 October 1891). Mowat believed that Thompson would agree "all the more readily because I believe that you approve of the provincial Legislature's dealing with the subject so far as practicable while there is no Dominion legislation respecting Bankruptcy or Insolvency." (Ibid., file 1892, no. 1052, Mowat to Newcombe 20 May 1893.)

76  *A.G. Ontario v. A.G. Canada*, [1894] A.C. 189 at 200–1.

77  *Edgar v. Central Bank* (1888), 15 O.A.R. 193 at 197–8.

78  The MSS oral argument is in AO, Irving Papers, MU 1489, file 1027: *The Ontario Insolvency Case in the Privy Council ... Argument of Mr. Blake for the Appellant* (Toronto: Bryant Press 1894). See also Blake, *Ontario Insolvency Case*, 6.

79  Oral argument, 12 December 1893, 75.

80  *Ibid.*, 100.

81  Oral argument, 13 December 1893, 60.

82  Blake, *Insolvency Case*, 21. Nor apparently did other members of the board. Forwarding the transcript of the oral argument, the London solicitors noted that "you will gather from a perusal of this

that there is every reason to believe the judgement will be in favour of your Province." (AO, RG 4-32, file 1052, Freshfields and Williams to J.R. Cartwright, 15 December 1893.)

83 [1896] A.C. 66, cited in A.H.F. Lefroy, *The Law of Legislative Power in Canada* (Toronto: Toronto Law Book 1897–98), 537n.1.

84 SCC Library, oral argument, 97. *Brewers and Malsters' Association of Ontario* v. *A.G. Ontario* [1897] A.C. 231.

85 *A.G. Canada* v. *A.G. Ontario, Quebec, Nova Scotia*, [1898] A.C. 700 (*Fisheries Reference*) Supreme Court of Canada, Library, oral argument, 135.

86 *Fisheries Reference*, 715.

87 *Canadian Pacific Railway* v. *Corporation of the Parish of Notre Dame de Bonsecours*, [1899] A.C. 367, Supreme Court of Canada Library, oral argument, 30–1.

88 *Union Colliery Company of British Columbia* v. *Bryden*, [1899] A.C. 580.

89 Ibid., at 582.

90 Ibid., at 585, 588. Italics added.

91 See, for example, Peter Hogg, *Constitutional Law of Canada* (Toronto: Carswell 1992), 404; W.R. Lederman, "The Concurrent Operation of Federal and Provincial Laws in Canada (1962–3)" 9 *McGill Law Journal*, 185 at 188. The British Columbia Supreme Court had reluctantly felt Watson's precedent binding and found *ultra vires* the B.C. elections act denying Japanese, naturalized or not, the right to vote. As Chief Justice McColl stated, "apart from the decision binding upon me I would have considered that the authority of the Dominion Parliament becomes exhausted with the naturalization." (In *Re The Provincial Elections Act and in Re Tomey Homma, a Japanese* [1900], 7 B.C.R. 368 at 372.) On appeal, Lord Halsbury found that the exclusivity of federal jurisdiction over naturalization and aliens was trumped by the power of the provinces, "notwithstanding anything in this Act," to "exclusively make Laws" in relation to the provincial constitution. (*Cunningham* v. *Tomey Homma* (1902), [1903] A.C. 151.) Moreover, in argument, members of the committee insisted that naturalization did not extend to the consequences of naturalization, thus distinguishing *Union Colliery*. (SCC Library, oral argument, *Cunningham* v. *Tomey Homma*.) Watson's decision was distinguished to the point of rejection by the Judicial Committee in *Brooks-Bidlake and Whitall* v. *A.G. British Columbia*, [1923] A.C. 450.

92 In re *Local Option Reference* (1891), 18 O.A.R. 572 at 580.

93 Ibid., at 591.

94 *Globe*, 3 May 1893.

95 MAC, MG 26 D, vol. 187, Thompson Papers, Mowat to Thompson, 10 October 1893.

96 *Huson* v. *South Norwich* (1895), 24 S.C.R. 145.

97 NAC, RG 125, vol. 15, file 147, Supreme Court of Canada, "Subject Provincial Jurisdiction, Prohibitory Liquor Law. Factum of the Solicitor General of Canada," 2 April 1894.

98 *A.G. Ontario* v. *A.G. Canada* (1895), 24 S.C.R. 170.

99 *Liquor Prohibition Appeal: An Appeal from the Supreme Court of Canada to Her Majesty the Queen in Council* (London: 1895), oral argument at 31.

100 Ibid., at 153.

101 Couch had sat on the three earlier cases; Halsbury on the *McCarthy Reference*; Davey, now on the committee, had been counsel in *Hodge* and *McCarthy*; and Herschell had opposed Davey in *McCarthy*.

102 Maclaren and Blake between them were responsible for more than 250 of the 325 pages of argument.

103 *Liquor Prohibition Appeal* at 114.

104 Ibid., at 77.

105 Ibid., at 224.

106 Ibid., at 242, 239.

107 "Lord Watson" (1899) 15 *Scottish Law Review*, 241. Blake might have taken some comfort in the reply Watson once made to an eminent counsel who complained about his interruptions: "Eh! man, you should never complain about that for I never interrupt a fool." *The Times*, 19 September 1899, letter to the editor.

108 *A.G. Ontario* v. *A.G. Canada*, [1896] A.C. 348.

109 *Citizens Insurance Company of Canada* v. *Parsons* (1881), [1881–2] 7 A.C. 96 at 108.

110 *Russell* at 100, 91; *Hodge* at 88; *McCarthy* at 168.

111 *Liquor Prohibition Appeal*, oral argument, 94. See also 163, 185, 194.

112 Ibid., 244.

113 Ibid., 292.

114 Ibid., 256.

115 *A.G. Canada* v. *A.G. Ontario*, [1896] A.C. 348 at 360. During the oral argument in *Fielding* v. *Thomas* in July 1896, Watson elaborated his understanding of the clause. "I think that clause plainly shows the consciousness of those who framed that Act, that the things given to the one parliament by section 92 and the supreme parliament by section 91, did run into each other or override each other, and they got rid of the difficulty by the declaration that nothing done by the supreme legislature under the express and exclusive power given them by section 91 should be deemed to come within the exclusive power given to the province by section 92. In other words, if the Dominion exercise that power, the matter is no longer within the exclusive power committed to the province. It is a very wise provision and shows a good deal of foresight." (Cited in A.H.R Lefroy, *The Law of Legislative Power in Canada* [Toronto: 1897–8], 649n.2.) Clearly, Watson confused the purpose of the declaratory and deeming clauses and virtually ignored the former.

116 "Lord Watson" (1899) 11 *Juridical Review*, 270–1.

117 "Lord Watson" (1899) 15 *Scottish Law Review*, 229 at 237.

118 *Liquor Prohibition Appeal* at 141.

119 Ibid., at 45.

120 *A.G. Canada* v. *A.G. Ontario*, [1896] A.C. 348 at 360–1. Emphasis added. In *Tennant*, Watson had divided section 91 into two distinct grants of legislative jurisdiction: the residual clause "and also exclusive legislative authority in relation to certain enumerated subjects." (*Tennant* v. *Union Bank of Canada*, [1894] A.C. 31 at 45.) Here he went further and stated that "these sources of jurisdiction are in themselves distinct, and are to be found in different enactments" (at 359). It is impossible to reconcile this with the wording of section 91.

121 *Liquor Prohibition Appeal* at 130, 236.

122 *A.G. Canada* v. *A.G. Ontario*, [1896] A.C. 348 at 361. In fact, he borrowed the example from Herschell who had commented that the right to carry arms might be purely local, but during a war the federal government might prohibit the carrying of arms. (Oral argument, 118.) The head-note to the case, cited more often than the decision, was misleading: "The general power conferred upon the Dominion Parliament … in supplement of its therein enumerated powers must be strictly confined to such matters as are unquestionably of national interest and importance; and must not trench on any of the subjects enumerated in s.92 … *unless* they have attained such dimensions as to affect the body politic of the Dominion' (at 348). Watson did not go as far as 'unless.'"

123 *Liquor Prohibition Appeal* at 303, 296. If Blake had read the oral argument in *Russell*, he would have had a stronger case,

citing Smith's own words, although it would have been termed inadmissible. See Chapter 5, n.23.

124 Ibid., at 210. He said precisely the same about the word "commerce." Ibid., at 103.

125 Ibid., at 179.

126 Ibid., at 218. In *City of Fredericton* v. *The Queen* (1880), 3 S.C.R. 505. The Supreme Court had no doubt that the power to prohibit lay within "The Regulation of Trade and Commerce." Ritchie did "not entertain the slightest doubt that the power to prohibit is within the power to regulate" (537) and Taschereau stated emphatically that "A prohibition is a regulation" (559).

127 Ibid., at 225, 306.

128 Ibid., at 353.

129 *A.G. Canada* v. *A.G. Ontario*, [1896] A.C. 348 at 362–3. Watson's opinion later caused some difficulty in the Supreme Court in *Gold Seal Limited* v. *A.G. Alberta* (1921), 52 S.C.R. 424, but Duff found a way around it (457–8). Years later, Chief Justice Rinfret rejected Watson's proposition: "In my opinion such a contention cannot be supported … It stands to reason that, if you regulate, you may prohibit things that are not in accordance with those regulations." (Re *Validity of Section 5 [a] of the Dairy Industry Act*, [1949] S.C.R. 1 at 25.)

130 (1895), [1896] A.C. 88 at 93. The regulation/prohibition issue is thoroughly discussed in two articles by David Schneiderman, who sees it as much more than a refinement necessary to suit the immediate purpose. The decision on that point, he argues, "reflects the cast of mind of the common lawyer that Dicey so ably captured in The Law of the Constitution … Federal government was meant to mean weak government, and laws were to be tested against the same standards as those of a delegated authority under British constitutionalism [such as a by-law made by a railway company]." ("A.V. Dicey, Lord Watson and the Law of the Canadian Constitution" [1998] 16 *Law and History Review*, 495 at 510.) In an earlier article, using "a conception of productivity" traceable to John Locke, Schneiderman argued that this aspect of "*Local Prohibition* can best be understood as a manifestation of judicial anxiety about the potential implications of energetic federalism for property and productivity, anxieties which were prevalent in late-nineteenth century legal thought." ("Constitutional Interpretation in an Age of Anxiety: A Reconsideration of the Local Prohibition Case" [1996] 41 *McGill Law Journal*, 411 at 415.)

131 The comment of Lord Denning to Alan Paterson that within six weeks of the argument he ceased to take an interest in the details of the judgment seems apt. Watson's decision was delivered nine months after the argument. See Chapter 4, no.51. (*The Law Lords* [London: Macmillan 1982], 99). However, someone on the board or in the registrar's office cared enough to change the answer to the question, had a province "jurisdiction to prohibit the importation of liquors into the province?" The answer, in Watson's judgment, which was printed in the *Appeal Cases*, was: "Their Lordships answer this question in the negative. It appears to them that the exercise by the provincial legislature of such jurisdiction in the wide and general terms in which it is expressed, would probably trench upon the executive authority of the Dominion Parliament." However, the certificate of judgment issued by the clerk of the Privy Council read: "No useful answer can be given to this question in the absence of a precise statement of the facts to which it is intended to apply. There may be some circumstances in which a Provincial Legislature will and others in which it will not have such jurisdiction." (The certificate is printed in E.R. Cameron, "The House of Lords and the Judicial Committee" [1923] 1 *Canadian Bar Review* 223 at 231.)

132 "Lord Watson" (1899) 11 *Juridical Review*, 278 at 281.

133 Murray Greenwood, "Lord Watson, Institutional Self-Interest, and the Decentralization of Canadian Federalism in the 1890s" (1974) 9 *University of British Columbia Law Review*, 244 at 261.

134 Birks, "The Survival of the Crown," 158–9.

135 Schneiderman, "A.V. Dicey, Lord Watson, and the Law of the Canadian Constitution," 510, 524.

136 Richard Risk, "Canadian Courts under the Influence" (1990) 40 *University of Toronto Law Journal*, 687 at 731–2, 733.

137 "Lord Watson" (1902) 4 *Journal of the Society of Comparative Legislation* (new series), 9 at 9. Watson was a member of the Comparative and Historical Jurisprudence Committee of the Society, on which he sat with A.V. Dicey, Sir F. Pollock, and F.W. Maitland.

138 *Nordenfelt* v. *Maxim-Nordenfelt Co.* [1894] A.C. 535 at 553. See T.B. Smith, *The Doctrine of Judicial Precedent in Scots Law* (Edinburgh: Green and Son 1952). It is significant that the catalyst for change in the rigid adherence to precedent in the House of Lords in 1966 came from the Scottish Law Commission, which wanted a statement that the doctrine of precedent in the Lords did not apply in Scottish appeals. The movement resulted in the 1966 practice statement loosening the doctrine of precedent. (See Alan Paterson, *The Law Lords* [London: Macmillan 1982] 149–53).

139 Moir T. Stormont-Darling, "Lord Watson" (1899) 11 *Juridical Review* 272, 277.

140 T.B. Smith, *British Justice: The Scottish Contribution* (London: Stevens and Son 1961), 205, 202.

141 *Winnipeg* v. *Barrett*, [1892] A.C. 445. The oral argument is printed in *Sessional Papers*, no. 33, 1893.

142 *Robinson* v. *Canadian Pacific Railway*, [1892] A.C. 481 at 485, 490.

143 "Lord Watson" (1899) 15 *Scottish Law Review*, 237.

144 George L. Gretton, "Trust and Patrimony," in H.L. MacQueen, ed., *Scots Law into the 21st Century* (Edinburgh: Green Sweet 1996), 187.

145 *Brophy* v. *A.G. Manitoba*, [1895] A.C. 202; *Sessional Papers*, no. 20, 1895, 246.

146 Canada, Department of Labour, *Judicial Proceedings respecting Constitutional Validity of the Industrial Disputes Investigation Act, 1907 and Amendment of 1910, 1918 and 1920: Toronto Electric Commissioners* v. *Snider et al.* (Ottawa: King's Printer 1925), 116.

147 *A.G. Canada* v. *A.G. Ontario* (Indian annuities) (1896), [1897] A.C. 199 at 213.

148 Lord Watson, "Recent Legal Reform" (1901) 13 *Juridical Review*, I at 17, a speech given in 1883 and printed after his death.

149 *Ontario Mining Company* v. *Seybold* (1902), [1903] A.C. 53, following *St. Catherine's*; *A.G. Manitoba* v. *Manitoba License Holders Association* (1901), [1902] A.C. 73, following *Liquor Prohibition*; and *Canada* v. *Ontario* [1910] A.C. 637, following *St. Catherine's*.

150 *A.G. British Columbia* v. *Canadian Pacific Railway*, [1906] A.C. 204; *Burrard Power Company* v. *The King* (1910), [1911] A.C. 87.

151 *Grand Trunk Railway* v. *A.G. Canada*, [1907] A.C. 66 at 68. The two doctrines occasioned a good deal of scholarly comment. See Hogg, *Constitutional Law* (1992), 405, 418; W.R. Lederman, "The Concurrent Operation of Federal and Provincial Laws in Canada" (1962–3) 9 *McGill Law Journal*, 185; Bora Laskin, "Tests for the Validity of Legislation: What's the 'Matter'?" (1944) 11 *University of Toronto Law Journal*, 114.

152 Supreme Court of Canada Library, *Hamilton Street Railway Company*, oral argument, third day, 13.

153 *A.G. Ontario* v. *Hamilton Street Railway Co.* (1902), 1 *Ontario Weekly Reports* 312.

154 When one draft bill was appealed to the Privy Council, Lord Davey caustically commented that they had expressed themselves on this "Sunday question before" and unceremoniously declined the opportunity, as Newcombe requested, to "set the matter finally at rest." (AO, RG 4–32, file 1905, no. 458 (2), "In the Privy Council on Appeal from the Supreme Court of Canada, July 1905," transcript of hearing.) The federal-provincial correspondence may be found in RG 4–32, various files in 1903–5.

155 *City of Montreal* v. *Montreal Street Railway*, [1912] A.C. 333. In the Supreme Court, Davies and Anglin dissenting, the majority

rejected the "necessarily incidental" and ancillary powers arguments. (1910), 43 S.C.R. 197.

156 *City of Montreal* v. *Montreal Street Railway* at 343–4.

157 Ibid., at 346.

158 Ibid., at 344. See, for example, Lord Tomlin's abbreviated statement of the accepted propositions in the *B.C. Fish Canneries* case (*A.G. Canada* v. *A.G. British Columbia* (1929), [1930] A.C. 111 at 118.)

## 20

### *Introduction by Roderick A. Macdonald*

F.R. Scott Professor of Constitutional and Public Law, McGill University

Francis Reginald Scott (1899–1985) was Canada's pre-eminent constitutional lawyer, scholar, and activist of the twentieth century. A graduate of McGill's law faculty, he was professor of constitutional law from 1927 to 1967 and dean from 1960 to 1964. In the 1930s he was a founding member of the League for Social Reconstruction, and served as national chair of Canada's socialist political party, the CCF, during the 1940s. Perhaps best known for his role in Supreme Court litigation involving Jehovah's Witnesses in Quebec, beginning with *Saumur* v. *Quebec*, through *Chaput* v. *Romain*, *Switzman* v. *Elbing*, and culminating in *Roncarelli* v. *Duplessis* in 1959, he was also a tireless champion for a constitutional Bill of Rights and an expansive view of federal legislative jurisdiction. Both Prime Minister Pierre Trudeau and Chief Justice Laskin would draw inspiration from Scott's constitutional vision.

Throughout the period of his academic and political activities he pursued—in the manner of another jurist, Wallace Stevens—a parallel career as a poet. In 1978 he received the Governor-General's Award for non-fiction for his collection *Essays on the Constitution*, and in 1982 he received the Governor-General's Award for poetry for his *Collected Poems*. The poem that follows is a repetition of Scott's general take on the division of powers jurisprudence of the Privy Council. Scott was annoyed, especially in light of the economic crisis of the 1930s, that the Privy Council failed to give an appropriately expansive reading to federal jurisdiction. For Scott, the sacrifice of federal power on the altar of section 92(13) "Property and Civil Rights," the erection of barriers to federal trade and commerce jurisdiction in the name of "water-tight compartments," and the requirement that invocation of the mantra of "Peace, Order and Good Government" be limited to "emergencies" were the enduring legacies of the Privy Council, and the rationale for the poem.

Source: Frank R. Scott, "Some Privy Counsel," *Canadian Bar Review* 28 (1950): 780.

Frank R. Scott

# Some Privy Counsel

"Emergency, emergency," I cried, "give us emergency,
This shall be the doctrine of our salvation.
Are we not surrounded by emergencies?
The rent of a house, the cost of food, pensions and
        health, the unemployed,
These are lasting emergencies, tragic for me."
Yet ever the answer was property and civil rights,

And my peace-time troubles were counted as nothing.
"At least you have an unoccupied field," I urged,
"Or something ancillary for a man with four children?
Surely my insecurity and want affect the body politic?"
But back came the echo of property and civil rights.
I was told to wrap my sorrows in water-tight
    compartments.
"Please, please," I entreated, "look at my problem.
I and my brothers, regardless of race, are afflicted.
Our welfare hangs on remote policies, distant
    decisions,
Planning of trade, guaranteed prices, high
    employment—
Can provincial fractions deal with this complex whole?
Surely such questions are now supra-national!"
But the judges fidgeted over their digests
And blew me away with the canons of construction.
"This is intolerable," I shouted, "this is one country;
Two flourishing cultures, but joined in one nation.
I demand peace, order, and good government.
This you must admit is the aim of Confederation!"
But firmly and sternly I was pushed to a corner
And covered with the wet blanket of provincial
    autonomy.
Stifling under the burden I raised my hands to Heaven
And called out with my last and expiring breath
"At least you cannot deny I have a new aspect?
I cite in my aid the fresh approach of Lord Simon!"
But all I could hear was the old sing-song,
This time in Latin, muttering *stare decisis*.

## 21

### Author's Introduction

Like so much of the scholarly commentary on the Canadian constitution in the last half century, "The Living Canadian Constitution" was intended as a contribution to the ongoing debate about the desirability of major constitutional reform—to bring the constitution up-to-date, as the issue was often defined.

I argued that much of the discussion was superficial, based on a misunderstanding of what a constitution is. In particular, the article suggested, much of the criticism was based on the premise that, by definition, a constitution more than a century old was unavoidably irrelevant. What could John A. Macdonald know about the demands confronting the governments of the 1960s?

"The Living Canadian Constitution" claimed, as its title suggested, that the constitution, correctly seen as more than the BNA Act, was a constantly evolving set of constitutional principles and practices by which Canadians confronted the never-ending challenges of the new worlds to which we had to fashion a response. From this perspective, the age of the constitution was a tribute to its resilience. Viewed this way, the Canadian constitution was a remarkable achievement, such that its age was a tribute to its adaptability, not an indicator of its imminent demise. In other words, Canadians had in 1970, when this article was published, a "living constitution," which should not be attacked on the spurious ground that it was obsolete because the BNA Act, one of its founding documents, had just entered its second century.

Source: Alan C. Cairns, "The Living Canadian Constitution," *Queen's Quarterly* 77 (4) (1970): 1–16.

Alan C. Cairns

# The Living Canadian Constitution

THE DUSTBIN OF recent history is littered with discarded constitutions cast aside after brief and withering exposure to reality. Constitutions capable of responding and adapting to the perils of change have sufficient scarcity value to be treated with the deference appropriate to rare achievements. All the more curious, therefore, has been the detached, unappreciative Canadian attitude to one of the most durable and successful constitutions in the world.

A partial explanation is found in the nature of the British North America Act. It is a document of monumental dullness which enshrines no eternal principles and is devoid of inspirational content. It was not born in a revolutionary, populist context, and it acquired little symbolic aura in its Subsequent history. The movement to Confederation was not a rejection of Europe, but was rather a pragmatic response to a series of economic, political, military, and technological considerations. There was no need for the kind of political

theorizing that accompanied the American experience of creating a new political entity and exercised a spell on subsequent generations. With the important exception of the federal system, Canada was endowed "with a Constitution similar in Principle to that of the United Kingdom." Constitutional monarchy and responsible government in a parliamentary setting were already part of the Canadian heritage, which was approvingly translated to the larger sphere of action the new Dominion created. No resounding assertions of human rights accompanied the creation of the new polity. The British tradition precluded any approach to their protection premised on comprehensive declarations of principle.

The absence of an overt ideological content in its terms, and the circumstances surrounding its creation, have prevented the BNA Act from being perceived as a repository of values by which Canadianism was to be measured. Further, the first thirty years of its existence were troubled by depression, threats of secession, and constant bickering over its terms. These scarcely constituted the circumstances for the Act to become the symbolic focus for the nascent political system. Consequently, a conscious ideological adherence and loyalty to the BNA Act and the constitution of which it was a part never became overt integral components of the Canadian civic identity.

An additional factor in the Canadian lack of appreciation for the constitution is a confused understanding of the meaning of age and time for institutions. With the passage of time, the intentions of the Fathers of Confederation unavoidably became an increasingly artificial concept with an ever attenuated contact with reality. Their visions were responses to the problems they faced in the light of prevalent conceptions of the role of government. Many of the conditions to which they addressed themselves faded away, to be replaced by conditions they could not predict. In such circumstances deference to their intentions became impossible, for they had none. Nevertheless, the BNA Act, which represents a consolidation of some of their intentions, remains an important constitutional document. This raises the question of how relevant for a contemporary evaluation of the Canadian constitution is the fact that the BNA Act is a century old.

At the most abstract level of institutional analysis, age has a double significance. Positively, a functioning institution of ancient origin acquires the special credibility that derives from its continuing utility for the attainment of one or more specified human goals. In the Darwinian process of institutional competition for survival it has emerged triumphant. Negatively, it is placed on the defensive by the fact that the contemporary circumstances to which it now applies are significantly different from the circumstances to which it was originally a response. Hence, it appears to be tinged with mortality. The graveyard, sooner or later, is its inevitable destination.

To continue the discussion on this level, however, is to grant to the question of age an undeserved importance and a spurious relevance. Institutions do not have a natural life span. They are, when wisely constructed and carefully tended, evolving human arrangements for avoiding the ravages of time by flexibly responding to the demands confronting them. Therefore to discuss the relevance of an institution in terms of its age, defined by the lapse of time since its first beginnings, is to misconceive what an institution is.

Canadian understanding of the constitution would have been much improved had it been consistently viewed in the significant American phrase as a "living constitution."[1] The wise admonition of Holmes reveals a perspective sadly lacking in Canada:

> The provisions of the Constitution are not mathematical formulas having their essence in their form; they are organic living institutions transplanted from English soil. Their significance is vital, not formal; it is to be gathered not simply by taking the words and a dictionary, but by considering their origin and the line of their growth....When we are dealing with words that are also a constituent act, like the Constitution of the United States, we must realize that they have called into life a being the development of which could not have been foreseen completely by the most gifted of its begetters. It was enough for them to realize or to hope that they had created an organism; it has taken a century and has cost their successors much sweat and blood to prove that they created a nation. The case before us must be considered in the light of our whole experience and not merely in that of what was said a hundred years ago.[2]

The virtual absence of this understanding of a living constitution has produced the mistaken belief that the constitution is a century old, that it has already outlived its allotted life span, and that *younger* means *better* and *older* means *worse*. Given this belief it is possible to advocate a new constitution simply because the BNA Act was drafted a century ago. The rather trite conclusion automatically follows that a constitution, or a constitutional document, so heavy with years must be out of date.

In the 1960s there has been a recurrence of the criticism of the constitution as obsolete that was so widespread in the Depression of the thirties. In that troubled decade, the constitution as judicially interpreted was roundly condemned by centralists for the barriers it placed in the way of decisive action by the federal government. The contemporary attack has different roots. One source is the spurt of nation-building and constitution-making that followed the demise of Western imperialism. In much of the Third World, constitution-making became a normal political activity interrupted by secession movements, coups, assassinations, and civil war as the new states struggled to overcome appalling problems and to find a framework for modernization. Whatever the justification for their endemic efforts to resolve their constitutional difficulties, and there are many, only a masochist would find their experience worthy of emulation.

An additional source is the French-Canadian view of recent years that the existing constitution restricts the process of nation-building in Quebec. Hence Marcel Faribault, the late Premier Daniel Johnson, Father Ares, Professor A. Dubuc, and numerous others have issued clarion calls for a new constitution to usher in the new age of emancipation which is part of the rhetoric of the Quebec nationalist intelligentsia. Their search for a new constitution is sustained by English-Canadian writers such as Peter O'Hearn, who finds the "battered hulk of the British North America Act and its train of amendments" unacceptable.[3] Other English-Canadian support is found in politicians who capitalize on any groundswell of opinion, or who naively assume that to be progressive requires a repudiation of the past, at least at the level of oratory. They sympathize with T.C. Douglas, whose own party is more trapped by the shibboleths of the nineteenth century than any other Canadian party, when he states: "The time has come for Canadians to free themselves from the dead hand of the past and forge a constitution that will enable Canada to keep its rendezvous with destiny.... I do not think that the dead hand of the past should be allowed to stay the onward march of progress. Human rights are sacred but constitutions are not."[4]

In an age when rapid obsolescence is viewed as the natural and inevitable end for every man-made product, such a thesis quickly finds attentive, receptive hearers. Superficially, it has compelling force, for clearly the conditions of 1867 have passed away. It logically follows that decisions made in the light of those conditions must become increasingly irrelevant with the passage of time.

Crucial to this widespread position is the belief that the constitution is by and large what the Fathers bequeathed to us a century ago. From this perspective the constitution emerged in 1867 in the form of the British North America Act and its accompanying understandings, the product of a small political elite, the Fathers of Confederation, and barring formal amendments, is now what it was then. The confusion is subtle. To view the constitution in terms of what the Fathers intended and immediately achieved fails to see that the constitution is a continuous creation. It accords too much deference to the constitution as it existed in 1867, and too little attention to the contribution of subsequent generations to its evolution.

The Canadian constitution is the body of understandings defining the basic institutions of government and the relationships between them, plus the relationships between governments in the federal system, and between the citizens and those governments. At any given point of time the content of the constitution is a series of living practices worked out by successive generations. It is a product of continuous selection, rejection, and addition. It is always, in a practical sense, contemporary. It is a living instrument of government, wider in scope than the BNA Act, and not restricted to the 1867 intentions of the Fathers. It is an evolving institution that has responded to pressures and flexibly accommodated itself to a variety of needs and changing demands.

The distinction between the constitution as an institution and the key statute that went into its formation is cogently described by Llewellyn in his discussion of the American constitution:

> The discrepancy between theory and fact found in private law is exaggerated in the constitutional field, because under a code of rigid words no easy and gradual rewording of outmoded rules in such manner as to hide the changes made in their content, is possible. The consequence is that with growing age all force in the actual words of a code withers and dies. What is left, and living, is not a code, but an institution. Many of the institution's roots trace back through time into the code. *Many do not.* But the living institution is neither the dead code nor its "interpretation." It is not even by any parthenogenesis descended from its great-grandmother code alone. It is new, it is different, it is growing; and in its blood run so many other streams that resemblance to the code is seldom strong and always confined to single traits.[5]

Evidence on the living nature of the constitution is ubiquitous. The settlement of 1867 was only a beginning. It has been under constant transformation since that time. The major evidence is as follows:

1. The instruments of federal control—disallowance, reservation, and refusal of assent by the Lieutenant-Governor—have fallen into virtual desuetude. If not entirely dead, there is no likelihood that they will ever again be used in the coercive fashion of the early post-Confederation years.

2. The transformation of Empire into Commonwealth—from "Colony to Nation"—has reduced the ties to Great Britain until all that remains is an increasingly attenuated emotional link, a similarity in the institutions of parliamentary and monarchical government, and an embarrassing leftover in the continuing (entirely formal) role of the British Parliament in the amending procedure.

3. As is well known, the division of powers in the BNA Act was importantly affected by the Judicial Committee of the Privy Council. While its decisions aroused much resentment and may or may not have been appropriate to Canadian needs, it cannot be denied that they made a fundamental contribution to the constitutional evolution Canadians actually experienced.

4. The division of powers was also transformed by the massive engine of the federal spending power and the conditional grants mechanism. Once again the evaluation may be favourable or unfavourable, but it is clear that the result was a marked change in the practical significance of Sections 91 and 92 of the BNA Act. Perhaps the spending power was used indiscriminately. Perhaps its use should have been (or should be) more tightly controlled, but that is not the issue here.

5. The proliferation of federal-provincial meetings of administrators and politicians, culminating in conferences of premiers and prime ministers, has added, as many have pointed out, an important new mechanism of co-ordination for the federal system.

6. Since the onset of World War II the fiscal system has not been the chaos of clashing taxing jurisdictions it was in the Depression. Further, as part of a succession of fiscal agreements, huge equalization grants have been paid to the less well-endowed provinces. The original compulsory federal subsidies have been rendered financially trivial by comparison.

7. The parliamentary system has been transformed by the development of the party system, the institution of party discipline, the emergence of third parties and their recognition, the institution of research staffs for the opposition parties, etc. Recently we have been told that before our very eyes the parliamentary system is being transformed into a presidential system without the requisite checks and balances. The truth of this latter statement is irrelevant for our purposes. What is relevant is that the parliamentary half of the Canadian wedding of parliamentary government and federalism has not stood still.

8. Even prior to the passage of the Diefenbaker Bill of Rights, the Supreme Court, and particularly Mr. Justice Rand, began to develop a court-supported jurisprudence for the protection of civil liberties. Basing their decisions largely on the flimsy constitutional basis of the preamble to the BNA Act, which stated that Canada was to have "a Constitution similar in Principle to that of the United Kingdom," the court enunciated an important series of civil liberties decisions.

9. Finally, the formal amendments to the Act contributed to its evolution.

Even in the cryptic fashion expressed above, these changes have been of momentous significance in the evolution of the Canadian constitution.

The agents of these changes were largely the politicians and civil servants of both levels of government responding to the demands and opportunities that the possession of office imposed on them. To examine the above list is to have it confirmed that the constitution never has been, and is not now, only what the courts say it is. The evolution of the constitution has been largely guided by successive generations of political leaders and their influential bureaucratic advisers. Admittedly, they did not have a clean slate to work with. Admittedly, the result has been evolution rather than revolution. Admittedly, certain key parts of the constitutional framework remain, in form at least, as they were originally established in 1867. It is also true that a different beginning would have produced a different outcome, but that is true of all human experiments. The point is not that what happened in 1867 did not matter, but that the decisions then made did not constitute a cake of custom that has held subsequent generations of Canadians in unwilling thralldom in a world they never made. The point is that the constitution has worked and grown in response to the shifting conditions thrown up by the passage of time. A constitution which had accommodated for a century the often competing demands of two ethnic groups, which had survived through depression and war, the transformation of a rural society into an urban society, the settlement of the West, and the technological revolution of recent years might have been appreciated in more prosaic times for its real practical virtues, rather than, as was so often the case, being scorned for its absence of symbolic appeal and criticized for a non-existent inflexibility. In the words of Eugene Forsey, "There is no point in change for its own sake, or just for the sake of having the very latest thing in constitutions. (What matters in a constitution is not how new *it is* but how good it is, how well it works.) The bigger the change, the heavier the onus upon those who propose it to prove that it is necessary, or even useful."[6]

It may be taken for granted that the Canadian constitution, like any other, prejudices some and fosters other public policy outputs. Any constitution, particularly a federal one, will regularly prevent some group of officeholders from attaining some of their policy objectives. To criticize a constitution because it entails this consequence, however, is similar to criticizing the law of gravity. The more precise and relevant question is comparative, whether or not the existing constitution erects more barriers to desired governmental output than would its successor. The answer depends on the nature of the particular new constitution that is advocated. Until that information is available, it is entirely proper to note the flexibility of the existing constitution.

All of the changes noted above are obvious and well known. Why then has so little heed been paid to the message they contain about the flexibility of a living constitution? What explains the constant confusion implicit in the attacks on the constitution because of its age? First, there is sometimes failure to distinguish

between the BNA Act and the constitution. Then the relative paucity of formal amendments, especially dealing with the division of powers, has produced a misleading impression of stability belied by our actual experience even in that area. Much of the change that has occurred has not been formally designated as constitutional, and it has not been accompanied by fanfare. It has simply represented the handiwork of busy men attempting to work an ongoing system of government.

A good part of the explanation simply lies in a compartmentalization of the minds of the critics and analysts. While all the changes have been recognized and noted, they have frequently co-existed with the assumption that the constitution is a century old. The absence of the concept of a living constitution has aided in this compartmentalization. The confusion has been deliberately sewn by propagandists who hate undertaken partisan attacks on the constitution because it stood in the way of their pet panacea. No century-old document (or constitution), they contend, should be allowed to stand in the way of the people. At the opposite pole, blindness on the part of some constitution-worshippers, who have been reluctant to believe that their god could be affected by anything so mundane as the passage of time, has had some influence.

Finally, the scholarship of historians and lawyers, and to a lesser extent of political scientists, has been obsessed with discovering the true meaning of 1867. Centralists and provincialists, compact theorists and their opponents, have all fought over the BNA Act in an attempt to discover its true meaning, and often to further their partisan objectives. By so doing they have exaggerated the importance of the original agreement of 1867 and have downgraded the changes it underwent in its subsequent expression.

In view of the preceding, two frequent tendencies in the discussion and evaluation of the Canadian constitution have been based on dangerous misunderstandings. It is simply mistaken to attack the existing constitution because of the age of the BNA Act, one of the key documents that went into its making a century ago. Llewellyn describes a working constitution "as being in essence not a document, but a living institution built (historically, genetically) in first instance around a particular document."[7] "With every passing decade," stated Carl Brent Swisher, "a constitution written long ago provides less and less guidance for its own interpretation amid patterns of social change and with sheer change in the dictionary meanings of familiar terminology."[8] It is equally fallacious to transform the constitutional settlement of 1867 into a measuring rod against which subsequent deviations can be assessed and their perpetrators chastised. Two American authors describe the "intentions of the framers" as a "filio-pietistic notion that can have little place in the adjudicative process of the latter half of the twentieth century.... A nation wholly different from that existing in 1787, facing problems obviously not within the contemplation of the Founding Fathers, can scarcely be governed—except in broadest generality—by the concepts and solutions of yesteryear."[9] The same point was lucidly expressed by Chief Justice Hughes of the United States Supreme Court:

It is no answer to say that this public need was not apprehended a century ago, or to insist that what the provision of the Constitution meant to the vision of that day it must mean to the vision of our time. If by the statement that what the Constitution meant at the time of its adoption it means today, it is intended to say that the great clauses of the Constitution must be confined to the interpretation which the framers, with the conditions and outlook of their time, would have placed upon them, the statement carries its own refutation.[10]

To attack the constitution on grounds of age is to fail to see its living nature. The same failure produces the description of post-1867 changes as deviations.

This latter approach was very widespread in discussions of judicial review, particularly in criticisms of the Privy Council. Since lawyers constitute the professional group which has arrogated specialized expertise to itself in this matter, they have an important responsibility for the misconceptions which heavily influence our constitutional discussion. I do not forget that one category of legal criticism of the Judicial Committee was based on the alleged failure of British judges to treat the BNA Act as a living instrument of government. It is true that to this group Lord Sankey,

with his "living tree" analogy, was the closest thing to a judicial hero that is found in the law periodicals. However, the other major group of criticisms was specifically based on the unacceptable conduct of the Judicial Committee in departing either from the intentions of the Fathers or the clear meaning of the BNA Act in which those intentions were presumably embodied. Further, the "living tree" school of Canadian criticism typically also reproached the Privy Council for leading Canada down the provincial path away from the limited, centralized federalism so wisely chosen in the sixties of the nineteenth century. This was partly because those critics willing to overtly discuss the constitution in terms of current need were usually centralists. Consequently, they could not resist appealing to the Fathers and their original creation as the touchstone of constitutional wisdom.

In general, the basic language of both constitutional case law and its Canadian critics stressed fidelity to an ancient document. O'Connor, the author of the classic fundamentalist statement that judges should apply the Act in terms of the meanings deliberately embodied in it by its creators, strongly attacked the Judicial Committee for "most serious and persistent deviation ... from the actual text of the Act." He was highly critical of Lord Watson's "assumption of the guardianship of the autonomy of the provinces. His proper function was merely that of an interpreter of the meaning of the words of a statute."[11] This position reflected the British tradition, which instructs judges to apply statutes literally. Thus, jurisprudence in Canada, both in the language of courts and in that of their critics, has not devised adequate criteria to guide judges in the employment of the discretion they unavoidably possess. This has been unfortunate, for it has meant that much constitutional advocacy has been, literally, meaningless. It has also contributed to the misunderstanding of what a constitution is.

The critics of the Privy Council frequently asserted that its failure rested on an unwillingness to use the variety of historical evidence available to throw light on the intentions of the Fathers, and thus clarify obscurities in the BNA Act. This approach was always fraught with difficulties, but with the passage of time its desirability became increasingly questionable. This was recognized by Professor Strayer in a recent publication. He noted the "very limited" evidence available on the formation of the Act, and, more importantly, questioned its utility in principle. "Conditions have so drastically changed since 1867," he pointed out, "that the particular context in which the Act was passed may have little bearing on the context in which it is now expected to operate."

This position represents a marked change from the obsessive concern with the intentions of the Fathers in the decades prior to the abolition of appeals to the Privy Council. Yet Strayer is still caught in an historical quagmire of his own making. The obligation to appeal to the past is irresistible. His argument continues: "The more crucial question now is: What would the framers have intended had conditions been in 1867 as they are today? Even if the courts could now be induced to make use of external evidence as to the conditions of that time such evidence would be of limited value in answering this hypothetical question."[12]

Unfortunately, we are not told what evidence would be helpful. Given the impossibility of deciding how to undertake this pseudo-historical quest, one wonders why it should be undertaken at all. The assertion of Learned Hand is as valid for Canada as for the United States: "It is impossible to fabricate how the 'Framers' would have answered the problems that arise in a modern society had they been reared in the civilization that has produced those problems. We should indeed have to be sorcerers to conjure up how they would have responded."[13]

In the evolution of a constitution, it is evident that the passage of time does and should reduce the weight to be given to the views and desires of the Fathers or of influential moulders of the constitution at other points of time. As time transforms the conditions to which the constitution must be responsive, the search is not for what was originally intended but for what can be creatively extracted from a constitutional heritage, of which the BNA Act is only a part. The search for the contemporary meaning of the constitution does not consist in minute examination of what was said or intended or achieved a century ago. Such an approach would deny to constitutional unfolding the benefits a century of experience has given us. This generation, its predecessors, and successors partially have and certainly should view the constitution for

what it is, a developing responsive tradition neither to be lightly departed from nor to be casually obeyed.

The arrangements of 1867 were never a sacrosanct body of holy writ. Approaches that so regarded them constituted a disservice to the Canadian polity and rested on a misunderstanding of the nature of a constitution. They inhibited change and thus reduced the flexibility essential for survival. Equally important, they blinded their possessors to the changes that did occur. Realistically, all working constitutions are living constitutions springing from, but not bound and gagged by, history. Inadequate recognition of this truth is a significant cause of the constitutional morass in which we now find ourselves. Cryptically, we might say that the constitution has not failed us, so much as we, by our inadequate understanding of its living nature, have failed it. In a living constitution all generations are simultaneously Fathers and Sons, by necessity even if not by choice. King, Bennett, Diefenbaker, and their provincial counterparts were in their own way Fathers as were Macdonald and Cartier. Like Macdonald and Cartier, they were also Sons in that they built on the achievements of their predecessors. There can be no quarrel with the fact that each succeeding generation of Canadians has decided what parts of the constitution they received were viable and worthy of continued life, and which were not. However, we can quarrel with those who, blinded by a deification of the past, resist new departures because the Fathers intended otherwise, or those who propose a new constitution on the mistaken grounds that the existing one, because of its time of origin, is necessarily an inflexible, incompetent instrument for new conditions. The first approach makes us prisoners of the past. The second deprives us of the benefits a rich tradition provides.

To view a constitution as a living constitution has important consequences. It is to recognize that the processes of constitutional change are manifold and unpredictable. The processes of formal amendment and judicial review are neither the only nor the most important vehicles for change. The constitution is constantly interpreted and modified by the men who work it. No new division of powers can prevent the intermingling of the activities of both levels of government in modern conditions. Predictable, clear-cut procedures for change can be obtained in the area of formal amendment, but nowhere else. The Supreme Court can be revamped in various ways, but "the history of judge-made law invites no other view than this: that the parties to the original federal 'bargain' can never be certain that the words in which they have clothed their intentions can ever be more than a rough guide to political activity, or that the range of permissible activity at any time after will bear any exact relation to their intentions."[14]

The terribly difficult problem, frequently overlooked because of obsession with the written text and the more blatant methods of change by amendment and judicial review, is how to devise conventions and understandings by which the other, less obvious methods of change can be brought within a framework of constitutionalism. The main weakness, for example, of the compact theory as a set of criteria for constitutional change did not lie in its hotly contested validity, but in the restricted scope of its intended operation. Even if wholehearted agreement to its terms had existed, this would have represented no more than a control of the amending procedure, one of the least important methods of constitutional change in Canadian history.

This problem is, of course, recognized by influential Quebec spokesmen. The late Premier Daniel Johnson, for example, stated in 1967:

Canada today is faced with a whole series of problems which the Fathers of Confederation ... could not conceivably have foreseen.... Therefore, when a new problem arises in Canada, we are more and more likely to base each government's responsibilities for it, not on constitutional principles, but on considerations of the moment which, in turn, derive from a variety of factors such as relative capacity to act, financial resources or merely the political power wielded by a given area of government. Hence even though there is a written document called the British North America Act from which we may expect some light to be cast on such traditional fields as education and municipal institutions, the allocation of new tasks among governments has not been guided by this document but by decisions mainly based on exigencies of the day.... Our present Constitution, perhaps admirable during the

age of steam trains, no longer suits Canada's needs in this era of interplanetary rockets.[15]

At the 1966 federal-provincial conference on taxation, Johnson stated:

Having reached what it considers a turning point in its history, Quebec expects some specific things from the present constitutional system. First, it wants proof that the division of powers written in the constitution is not mere window-dressing and that, accordingly, it can count on the fiscal and financial resources it requires in order to discharge its obligations properly.... Quebec also wants assurance that it can exercise, fully and without interference from any quarter, all its powers under the present constitution. It wants the Government of Canada to withdraw from fields which are not federal or in which the provinces have priority.[16]

Essentially the same point was made by Professor Dubuc, who asserted that a century of change had rendered the BNA Act "too far removed from the basic structure and values of ... [contemporary] ... society to remain the touchstone for the division of powers," with the consequence that the "most important conflicts are settled on the political level and become confrontations of power; these are the conditions of political chaos."[17]

The general cogency of these critiques can be accepted. The question, however, is what can be done about them. To Johnson and Dubuc the obvious answer is a new constitution whose division of powers reflects the worked-out results of a contemporary agreement, responding to today's conditions, as to what the responsibilities of each level of government should be. Assuming for the moment that agreement could in fact be reached on a new constitution, the contribution this would make to the solution of the problem that troubles Dubuc and Johnson is debatable. Obviously, if Quebec were to be granted greatly enhanced jurisdictional authority, the seriousness of the problem from Quebec's viewpoint would be greatly diminished. The problem would still exist, but its scope would be less extensive. If, however, as seems more likely, a new division of powers did not deviate markedly from the existing division, we would be little better off. It is not entirely clear that an ancient division of powers is more likely to produce "decisions mainly based on exigencies of the day" than is a division freshly minted at a constitutional conference. To some extent the problem arises from the impossibility of devising a comprehensive catalogue of powers into which all proposed legislation can be easily fitted. The operations of modern governments are too complex, the future is too unpredictable, and words are too full of imprecision and ambiguity for such an achievement. Further, the very political processes Johnson and Dubuc decry for the uncertainties they generate can be seen as the instruments to produce the concordance between the division of powers and contemporary requirements they seek. If such processes did not exist, we would really be in a bad way. The difficult problem, as suggested earlier, is to find ways by which they can be brought within a framework of constitutionalism.

The assault on the existing constitution has led to a process of constitutional review out of which a new, or at least a drastically modified, constitution is supposed to emerge. Unfortunately, the justification for this review does not reside in any self-evident likelihood that a new and better constitution can be created. The existing constitution was caught in a barrage of criticism based on its age, which is largely a fraudulent consideration, and a confused battery of French-Canadian demands to break with the past and stake out for themselves a status in Canadian federalism superior to what was apparently possible under the constitution as they perceived it.

From the evidence available, there is little possibility that a new constitution will emerge. Most of the political leaders engaged in constitutional review are dutifully going through the motions with little hope or desire that any major changes will transpire. If their pessimism is correct, Canadians will be left with the existing constitution whose limited sanctity has been further eroded by the criticism to which it has been subjected in the process of review. Its claim to our continued allegiance may come to rest on the flimsy basis that it is the only constitution Canadians have.

The perspective on the constitution adopted in this essay is a reminder that a constitution is not merely a piece of paper. It is a set of relationships between governments and between governments and peoples which has become embedded in the evolving habits and values of successive generations of Canadians. Tinkering with constitutional documents in an era of laissez faire might have left the mass of the citizenry unaffected. However, when governments increasingly involve themselves in the nooks and crannies of our lives, dramatic constitutional change presents a less attractive and less plausible face. It is only necessary to observe the difficulties of successfully introducing major policies, such as medicare or tax reform, to question the feasibility of attempting to change a large part of the constitutional framework from which governments derive their authority and by means of which citizens deal with the government.

A new constitution can be no more than a point of departure. The day after it is proclaimed its evolution away from the agreement just reached will commence. The new settlement will inevitably be subject to the informal processes of change and growth that helped "undermine" the BNA Act. The security and control of the future that can be obtained from a written document are only relative. Further, if a new constitution is created, the short-run result of its implementation inevitably will be an increase in uncertainty and insecurity until the text is fleshed out by the actions of men struggling to make it work. This, of course, is in addition to the uncertainties automatically generated by the simple fact of change from the old constitution to the new. Given these corollaries of a new constitution, we might consider whether constitutions are not like wine—much better when well aged. Perhaps, however, 1867 was not a good year for constitutions.

## NOTES

1  For an excellent American discussion of the living constitution, see K.N. Llewellyn, "The Constitution as an Institution," *Columbia Law Review*, 34 (1934).

2  Cited in Archibald Macleish and E.F. Pritchard, Jr., eds., *Law and Politics: Occasional Papers of Felix Frankfurter* (New York, 1962), p. 71. The eloquence of Holmes can be supplemented by Marshall's famous description of "a constitution intended to endure for ages to come, and consequently, to be adapted to the various crises of human affairs."

3  Peter Joseph Thomas O'Hearn, *Peace, Order and Good Government* (Toronto, 1964), p. 6.

4  *Globe and Mail*, April 13, 1966, p. 7.

5  Llewellyn, "The Constitution as an Institution," p. 6.

6  "Constitutional Monarchy and the Provinces," *Ontario Advisory Committee on Confederation: Background Papers and Reports* (Toronto, 1967), p. 180. Ronald I. Cheffins, *The Constitutional Process in Canada* (Toronto, 1969), provides a well-argued defence of the existing constitution. See especially chapter I and pp. 150–151, 167.

7  Llewellyn, "The Constitution as an Institution," p. 3.

8  *The Supreme Court in Modern Role*, rev. ed. (New York, 1965), p. 192.

9  Arthur S. Miller and Ronald F. Howell, "The Myth of Neutrality in Constitutional Adjudication," *University of Chicago Law Review*, 27 (1960), p. 683.

10  Cited in Paul Abraham Freund, *The Supreme Court of the United States* (New York, 1965), p. 20.

11  *Report Pursuant to Resolution of the Senate to the Honourable the Speaker by the Parliamentary Counsel Relating to the Enactment of* the British North America Act, 1867, any lack of consonance between its terms and judicial construction of them and cognate matters (Ottawa, 1939), 11, Annex 1, p. 47.

12  Barry L. Strayer, *Judicial Review of Legislation in Canada* (Toronto, 1968), p. 156.

13  Learned Hand, *The Bill of Rights* (Cambridge, Mass., 1958), pp. 34–35.

14  Rufus Davis, "The 'Federal Principle' Reconsidered," in Aaron B. Wildavsky, ed., *American Federalism in Perspective* (Boston, 1967), p. 14.

15  *The Confederation of Tomorrow Conference: Proceedings* (Toronto, 1968), Appendix B, p. 8.

16  *The Federal-Provincial Conference, Quebec—Federal-Provincial Tax Structure Committee* (Ottawa, 1966), pp. 56–57.

17  Alfred Dubuc, "The Decline of Confederation and the New Nationalism," in Peter Russell, ed., *Nationalism in Canada* (Toronto, 1966), p. 131.

# 22

## Editor's Introduction

Today, we take an independent judiciary for granted as part and parcel of Canadian democracy. This is not the way it always was. As William Lederman explains, the "judicial system" used to work quite differently with most of the power lying with appointed colonial administrators. Even a careful reading of the American constitution shows that the role the judiciary plays in the United States today is not really what the founders had in mind. The judicial branch had to work at establishing its independence in reviewing legislative decisions. This selection details the evolution of the judiciary's independence; more importantly, however, it works through the implications, that is, the means by which that hard-won independence is to be preserved. A key means to this end is the appointment of qualified individuals to the bench and a sound legal education. As the first dean of the school of law at Queen's University, Lederman left a lasting impression on the country's legal profession by practising what he preached. There is yet a broader implication to Lederman's piece, one he does not actually spell out: democracy should not be taken for granted; rather, democracy needs to be defended, a role in which post-secondary education has an important hand.

Source: William R. Lederman, "The Independence of the Judiciary," in *Law, Politics and the Judicial Process*, ed. F.L. Morton (Calgary: University of Calgary Press, 2002), 183–88.

## William Lederman

# The Independence of the Judiciary

### INTRODUCTION

An independent judiciary has long been an established feature of our Constitution in Canada, coming to us as a primary part of our great inheritance of English public law and governmental institutions. My purpose here is an ambitious one—to explain the essential *positive* functions of an independent judiciary as an integral part of our total constitutional system. This involves examining the relations between the judiciary on the one hand, and parliaments and cabinets on the other, as they play their respective parts in making and applying laws for our country, at both the provincial and the federal levels. Also, of course, this task requires some examination of the institutional arrangements that are the basis of judicial independence, and some assessment of the relevance of such independence to the needs of our time for good government under law. Obviously, in this relatively brief paper, I can speak only of certain high lights concerning the matters mentioned. The other topics in this book are more specialized and will no doubt be treated with suitable detail in due course. I construe my assignment to be to provide the general picture of judicial independence in the context of our total constitution. I attempt to paint the general picture for its own sake, and as background for the more particular topics that are to follow. What I have to say falls under three main headings:

1.  Our English Constitutional Inheritance,
2.  Essential Operational Elements of Judicial Independence, and
3.  Judicial Independence, Democracy, and The Rule of Law.

## 1. OUR ENGLISH CONSTITUTIONAL INHERITANCE

Sir Arthur Goodhart has told us, in his distinguished lectures on "English Law and the Moral Law," that the English are not as much without a constitution as they frequently profess to be. He gives four principles which he maintains are equally basic as first or original principles of the English constitution.[1] They are briefly as follows: (1) "That no man is above the law" (among other things, this means that all official persons, the Queen, the judges and members of Parliament included, must look to the law for the definition of their respective positions and powers). (2) "That those who govern Great Britain do so in a representative capacity and are subject to change…. The free election of the members of the House of Commons is a basic principle of English constitutional law." (3) That there shall be freedom of speech, of thought and of assembly. (4) That there shall be an independent judiciary. "The fourth and final principle which is a basic part of the English constitution is the independence of the judiciary. It would be inconceivable that Parliament should today regard itself as free to abolish the principle which has been accepted as a cornerstone of freedom ever since the Act of Settlement in 1701. It has been recognized as axiomatic that if the judiciary were placed under the authority of either the legislative or the executive branches of the Government then the administration of the law might no longer have that impartiality which is essential if justice is to prevail." Sir William Holdsworth expressed a very similar view on the status of the judiciary. He said:

The judges hold an office to which is annexed the function of guarding the supremacy of the law. It is because they are the holders of an office to which the guardianship of this fundamental constitutional principle is entrusted, that the judiciary forms one of the three great divisions into which the power of the State is divided. The Judiciary has separate and autonomous powers just as truly as the King or Parliament; and, in the exercise of those powers, its members are no more in the position of servants than the King or Parliament in the exercise of their powers … it is quite beside the mark to say that modern legislation often bestows undivided executive, legislative and judicial powers on the same person or body of persons. The separation of powers in the British Constitution has never been complete. But some of the powers in the constitution were, and still are, so separated that their holders have autonomous powers, that is, powers which they can exercise independently, subject only to the law enacted or unenacted. The judges have powers of this nature because, being entrusted with the maintenance of the supremacy of the law, they are and always have been regarded as a separate and independent part of the constitution. It is true that this view of the law was contested by the Stuart kings; but the result of the Great Rebellion and the Revolution was to affirm it.[2]

For England then, secure tenure and autonomy in office for the superior court judges came as one of the primary results of the Great Rebellion and Revolution at the end of the 17th Century. It took some time before the same guarantees of judicial independence were extended to the governmental systems of the United States and British North America, but extended they were in due course. Suffice it to say that one of the main complaints of the American colonists before 1776 concerned the subservience of colonial judges because they held office at the pleasure of the Crown or the Royal Governor. When the American colonists won the revolutionary war, they promptly established both the State and the Federal Court Systems of the new United States on the model afforded by the English Act of Settlement of 1701. It is true that the position was later modified in most state court systems, starting in 1846, by provision that judges were to be elected for relatively short and fixed terms. But no change has occurred in the Federal Court system of the United States respecting these essentials to this day.

In British North America after the American Revolution, the independence of the Superior court judiciary on the same model—the Act of Settlement model—was accomplished by local colonial statutes in the 1830's and the 1840's, as a matter of peaceful evolution toward greater constitutional maturity. It is surely striking that this sort of separation of powers in favour of the independence of the judiciary emerged as part of the settlement of great constitutional issues in England at the end of the 17th Century, in the United States at the end of the 18th Century, and in British North America in the early part of the 19th Century, well before the grant of responsible government and the achievement of Confederation, Accordingly, historical evidence suggests that such a separation of the judiciary from both the legislature and the executive is a distinct governmental virtue of great importance, worthy of cultivation in its own right.

To return to Canada, we find that the constitutional requirement for an independent judiciary was carried forward into the Confederation period, both expressly and by necessary implication, in the judicature provisions of the B.N.A. Act of 1867. Moreover, these provisions establish that Canada shall have for the most part a unitary judicial system, though we are a federal country. The English-type separation of powers in favour of the judiciary makes this not only feasible but desirable. Accordingly, we find that Provincial Parliaments and Governments share with the Federal Parliament and Government responsibility and power to provide the various elements of this single system. Certain courts of limited and specialized original jurisdiction are constituted by the respective Provinces, their judges are appointed by the Provincial Cabinets and are paid from the Provincial treasuries. Examples are the Provincial Criminal Courts and the Provincial Family Courts, which I need not emphasize are very important courts indeed, both in terms of subject-matter and volume of cases. In the case of the Superior, District, or County Courts, they are constituted Province by Province by Provincial legislation, but the judges must be appointed by the Governor General in Council, that is by the Federal Cabinet. Also, they must be drawn from the legal profession and paid out of the Federal treasury, under statutory authority from the Parliament of Canada. The characteristic mark of the Superior Courts is their very broad, if not unlimited, original or appellate jurisdiction or both. This includes, for example, the Provincial Courts of Appeal. Finally, there is the Supreme Court of Canada which is entirely constituted by legislation of the Parliament of Canada and whose judges are appointed by the Governor General in Council, that is by the Federal Cabinet. It has plenary appellate jurisdiction for all of Canada on all subjects, and is thus the final court at the apex of our judicial system. To complete the picture, we should note that the Federal Parliament is also empowered to establish courts devoted to the trial of issues arising under laws which, as to their subject-matter, are within the legislative powers of the Parliament of Canada only. Parliament has in fact established the Federal Court of Canada, with Trial and Appeal Divisions, as a superior court with some specialized jurisdiction concerning a few federal subjects.

For present purposes, two things are noteworthy about the Canadian judicial system. First, while it is true that the guarantee of removal from office only by joint address of the Parliament of Canada is explicitly specified by the B.N.A. Act just for the Superior courts of the Provinces, this most emphatically does not mean that there is no constitutional protection for the security of tenure in office of other judges in the total judicial system just described. The same point applies concerning the explicit guarantee of salaries in the B.N.A. Act, which mentions only the Superior, District, and County courts of the Provinces. The position in my view is that the Superior Courts, by virtue of the explicit provisions for them in the B.N.A. Act afford the prototype—the model—which should be followed for all other Canadian courts.

In other words, I am saying that security of tenure and salary for judges in Canada, as a matter of basic constitutional law and tradition, is not limited to the strictly literal reach of sections 99 and 100 of the B.N.A. Act. I remind you of the words of Goodhart and Holdsworth. They make it clear that essential provision for the independence of the judiciary generally has long been deeply rooted as an original principle in the basic customary law of the constitution. In Britain herself, the explicit provisions about judicial security are in the ordinary statutes—but these ordinary statutes, including the Act of Settlement itself, manifest the more fundamental unwritten constitutional principle I have described, as Goodhart and Holdsworth insist. The same point can and should be made about the status of Canadian judges. In Canadian Federal statutes we have provisions ensuring the independence of the County and District Court judges, the judges of the Federal Court of Canada, and the judges of the Supreme Court of Canada itself. In various Provincial statutes, security is likewise provided for provincially-appointed judges, for example the Provincial Criminal Court judges in Ontario. My point is that though these are ordinary statutory provisions, they are "ordinary" in form only because they are declaratory of basic constitutional principles and traditions.

Now of course, for the judges who depend on ordinary statute in this respect, there is room for variations in just how their basic constitutional independence is to be implemented. But, provided they are guaranteed security of tenure in office until a reasonable retirement age, subject only to earlier removal for grave misconduct or infirmity, after full due process by way of enquiry, then the basic constitutional mandate for their independence is satisfied. I am not arguing that all judges are, or have to be, under the parliamentary joint address procedure in order to be secure and independent. Adequate due process leading to removal for cause may take several forms. In this respect, we should note the recent advent of the Canadian Judicial Council, under which the federally-appointed judges as a group themselves apply due process and self-discipline concerning any of their own members against whom complaints may have been entered. This is a progressive step in safeguarding the independence of the judiciary that is quite in harmony with the concept of independence.

The second major point I wish to make about the Canadian judicial system is to emphasize the implications of its unitary character. All through the system, with the exception of the Federal Court of Canada, the respective judges and courts have power to try issues that arise under both provincial laws and federal laws, singly or in combination. Hence, for the most part our citizens need look only to the one system of courts for complete disposition of matters that concern them, though we live in a federal country. There is a case for some carefully limited exceptions respecting the Federal Court of Canada, but in my view, the jurisdiction of that court should remain quite limited and exceptional, so as not to prejudice the great benefit for Canadians of the essentially unitary judicial system we presently have and were intended to have. In this way we avoid the very wasteful and frustrating forum-shopping that goes on between the separate State and Federal Court systems in the United States.

Nevertheless, to maintain an essentially unitary judicial system in a federal country like ours requires a great deal of intergovernmental consultation and collaborative action, between the Federal Government and Parliament and the respective Provincial Governments and Parliaments. Also involved is some consultation with the judges collectively, for they should have some input concerning the decisions these governments and parliaments make concerning such matters as the structure of the court system, the jurisdiction of various courts, the management of the flow of cases, and so on.

This brings me to my second main heading, a more careful look at the operating elements of judicial independence.

## 2. ESSENTIAL OPERATIONAL ELEMENTS OF JUDICIAL INDEPENDENCE

What I have said so far implies that the elements of judicial independence fall into two groups, individual elements and collective ones.

The individual elements may be stated in these terms. A judge is not a civil servant, rather he is a primary autonomous officer of state in the judicial realm, just as cabinet ministers and members of parliament are the primary official persons in the executive and legislative realms respectively. No minister of the Crown, federal or provincial, and no parliament, federal or provincial, has any power to instruct a judge how to decide any one of the cases that comes before him. If a parliamentary body does not like the judicial interpretation of one of its statutes in a particular case, then it can amend the statute, use different words, and hope that this will cause a different judicial interpretation when next the statute is before a court. But that is all a parliamentary body can do or should attempt to do under the constitution. As for ministers of the Crown, when the government is an interested party in litigation or prosecution before the courts, then the minister can instruct counsel to appear and argue in court for the result the executive government would prefer, but that is all a minister can do or should attempt to do under the constitution. The judge remains autonomous, both as to his determinations of fact and his interpretations of the applicable law. As Chief Justice Laskin said recently, the judge must supply his own answers from his own resources, and thus there is something of the loneliness of the long distance runner in every judge. Long term security of tenure in office with the corresponding guarantee of salary ensures that the judge can maintain this position, especially as he is not allowed to hold any other office concurrently with his judicial office.

The reason for this individual independence of judges is best explained in the words of the late Robert MacGregor Dawson, as follows:

> The judge must be made independent of most of the restraints, checks and punishments which are usually called into play against other public officials … He is thus protected against some of the most potent weapons which a democracy has at its command: he receives almost complete protection against criticism; he is given civil and criminal immunity for acts committed in the discharge of his duties; he cannot be removed from office for any ordinary offence, but only for misbehaviour of a flagrant kind; and he can never be removed simply because his decisions happen to be disliked by the Cabinet, the Parliament, or the people. Such independence is unquestionably dangerous, and if this freedom and power were indiscriminately granted the results would certainly prove to be disastrous. The desired protection is found by picking with especial care the men who are to be entrusted with these responsibilities, and then paradoxically heaping more privileges upon them to stimulate their sense of moral responsibility, which is called in as a substitute for the political responsibility which has been removed. The judge

is placed in a position where he has nothing to lose by doing what is right and little to gain by doing what is wrong; and there is therefore every reason to hope that his best efforts will be devoted to the conscientious performance of his duty.[3]

As Dr. Dawson makes clear, it is of great importance to the success of the system that only highly qualified persons should be appointed to judicial office. How one may ensure the making of such appointments is indeed a matter of great importance, but I do not pursue it further here because appointment is scheduled as the next topic on the programme of this conference.

But, assuming the appointment of able people to judicial office, this is not in itself enough to ensure that the judicial system functions well as a whole and in all its parts. There are problems of the whole system of courts that have an important bearing on the independence of the judiciary.

If there are too few judges for the work to be done, then, able and independent though they are as individuals, they will be too much overworked and hurried to take the time they should to think through the problems that come before them. Moreover, the public will be frustrated and exasperated over long delays. We are in some trouble of this sort now because we do not have enough judges in Canada. Also, if the divisions of jurisdiction for the courts are unsatisfactory, or if civil or criminal procedure is unnecessarily wasteful of time and energy, again justice will be down-graded in spite of the ability and independence of individual judges. The same kind of points about the efficacy of the judicial system collectively can be made concerning the adequate staffing of the courts with necessary support personnel for the judges, concerning the provision of suitable court houses, and concerning systems for the assignment of judges to case lists and the management of the flow of cases generally.

■ ■ ■

First, my outline of the many parts that make up the unitary Canadian judicial system shows that responsibility for necessary appointments and legislation is shared between the federal and provincial levels of government. Accordingly, for the solution of these system problems, there must be a great deal of federal-provincial consultation and collaboration at the cabinet and parliamentary levels. This applies also to the provision of adequate financial support for the judicial system. Generally speaking, the administration of justice in Canada has been seriously underfinanced, and both levels of government are to blame for this.

In the second place, in certain vital respects, collective responsibility for the effective operation of the judicial system should be invested in the judges themselves. Here the role of the Chief Justices and the Chief Judges is very important, as spokesmen for themselves and their brother judges. This refers particularly to the assignment of judges to case lists, and to determination of priorities for the grouping and hearing of cases. In my view, to safeguard the basic independence of the judiciary, the Chief Justices and the Chief Judges should be in operational control of these matters for their respective courts, with adequate administrative staff responding to their directions.

I have now spoken of the individual and the collective elements that go to make up an independent judiciary. But there is a final question that remains to be answered. *What*, in the end, *is the main purpose of maintaining an independent judiciary?* Sir William Holdsworth said, "The judges hold an office to which is annexed the function of guarding the supremacy of the law." My third and final topic is an attempt to explain why he said this.

## 3. JUDICIAL INDEPENDENCE, DEMOCRACY, AND THE RULE OF LAW

At this point I return with particular emphasis to the special importance of our superior courts of general jurisdiction. We say that we have the rule of laws rather than of men, but that this has a special dependence on the men who are the superior court judges. Constitutionally they have the last word on what the laws mean, so, does this not really mean the personal supremacy of superior court judges? I deny this, for the following reasons. It is basic to the rule of law that doctrines, ideas, and principles are supreme, not persons. The great case of *Roncarelli* v. *Duplessis*[4] confirmed this as the position in Canada. In aid of this supremacy, we find that the superior courts possess under the

constitution a final supervisory review function over lesser courts, and over officials, boards and tribunals of all kinds, to ensure that they stay within the limits of the powers respectively given them by the constitution, or by statute, or by common law. The superior courts have power to nullify decisions of other officials and tribunals for excess of jurisdiction or breach of natural justice in procedure. But here we encounter that basic constitutional dilemma—Who watches the watchman? Who checks the superior courts themselves for excess of jurisdiction or breach of natural justice in procedure? The answer is that, at this primary level of constitutional responsibility, the superior court judges must be trusted to obey the laws defining their own functions, and to check themselves. Believing in the supremacy of law, they must themselves scrupulously obey it. They must be all the more careful about this precisely because there is no one to review their powers, as they review the powers of others. Judicial restraint on these terms at the superior court level is the ultimate safeguard of the supremacy of the law, enacted and unenacted, to use Holdsworth's terms. Remember too that at the intermediate and final levels of judicial appeal you have a plural bench, so that a majority of several judges is necessary to reach a decision. Several heads are better than one, and in the process purely personal peculiarities are likely to be cancelled out. It seems to me that this is as close as we can get to the rule of laws rather than of men.

There are further reasons for confidence in the independent judiciary, and I am speaking now of all judges, both provincially-appointed and federally-appointed. The conditions on which they hold office mean that they have no personal career interest to be served by the way they go in deciding cases that come before them. The laws to be interpreted and applied must be expressed in words, and words are not perfect vehicles of meaning. Hence there is frequently room for partisan interpretation, and that is precisely what you would get if one of the interested parties was in a position to make his interpretation prevail. At least the judges have no such personal interest in biased interpretation one way or the other, hence, in the words of Sir Arthur Goodhart, they are able to bring to the administration of the law that impartiality which is essential if justice is to prevail.

Finally, I assert that the power of the independent appointed judiciary is neither undemocratic nor anti-democratic. The statutes of our popularly elected legislatures do have priority, and will be made to prevail by the courts, if the parliamentarians speak plainly enough. But often their statutes speak only in general terms that must be further particularized by someone else, or they speak in ambiguities that must be resolved by someone else. These tasks fall to interpretative tribunals, especially the courts at all levels of the judicial system. Judicial procedure respects the individual by giving him a fair hearing and allowing him and his counsel to argue that the reason of the law is in their favour. This is as much a feature of democracy as it is to give the same citizen a vote, as a

means of influencing his own fate. As for judicial law making, the judicial tasks just referred to do involve discretions that are at times legislative in character.

**NOTES**

1. A.L. Goodhart, *English Law and the Moral Law* (Stevens & Sons Limited, London, 1953), pp. 55–60.
2. Sir W.S. Holdsworth, "His Majesty's Judges," (1932), 173 *Law Times* 336, at pp. 336–7.
3. R. MacGregor Dawson, *The Government of Canada* (Toronto, The University of Toronto Press, 2nd edition, 1954), p. 486.
4. [1959] S.C.R. 121.
5. Generally, on this whole topic, see also W.R. Lederman, "The Independence of the Judiciary" (1956), 34 *Can. Bar Rev.*, 770–809, and 1139–1179.

# 23

## *Editor's Introduction*

There is a long-standing debate in Canada as to whether the Supreme Court is biased. The selection of judges for the Supreme Court of Canada is an executive prerogative in Canada, subject only to the convention that those judges be regionally representative and that three of those judges be from Quebec (so as to be able to hear civil-law cases). So the presumption that the government may be prone to picking judges with a federal/centralist bias is not far-fetched. First, then, there is the issue as to whether the government is prone to selection bias. Second, even if this were the case, is there any evidence that such selection bias is manifest in the Court's judgments? A subsequent piece by Choudhry and Howse wrestles with the competing pressures judges have to reconcile in their earnest attempt to ensure their judgments are seen to be legitimate. Peter Hogg was instrumental in putting the debate about perceived bias to the test in an article that continues to stand the test of time for both its method and its findings. On this matter, there is no better source than Hogg: he is the author of the best-selling *Constitutional Law in Canada*, the most-cited book on decisions by the Supreme Court.

Source: Peter Hogg, "Is the Supreme Court of Canada Biased in Constitutional Cases?" *Canadian Bar Review 57* (1979): 721–39.

## Peter Hogg

# Is the Supreme Court of Canada Biased in Constitutional Cases?

### I. THE ISSUE

In recent public discussions of the Supreme Court of Canada the allegation has occasionally surfaced that the court has been biased in favour of the federal interest in constitutional cases.[1] The allegation has

been especially stimulated by the decisions in the two broadcasting cases,[2] which denied provincial power

1    Charges of bias in the press prompted a defence of the court by

the Chief Justice: Laskin, "Judicial Integrity and Supreme Court of Canada," [1978] Law Soc. Gaz. 116.
2    *Capital Cities Communications* v. *Canadian Radio-Television Commission*, [1978] 2 S.C.R. 141; *Public Service Board* v. *Dionne*, [1978] 2 S.C.R. 191; but compare *A.-G Que.* v. *Kellogg's Co. of Canada*, [1978] 2 S.C.R. 211.

over cable television, and by the CIGOL[3] and *Potash*[4] cases, which limited provincial power to tax and regulate the production of natural resources located in the province. It is true that over the last few years there has been an increase in both the number and the importance of the constitutional cases before the Supreme Court of Canada, and the federal interest has fared much better than the provincial interest.[5]

When a province loses a case which engages vital provincial policies it is only to be expected that the province's politicians will be upset with the result, and that their criticism will depart from the conventions of polite legal discourse. But in my view the allegation of bias has to be taken seriously by lawyers and political scientists. It casts doubt upon the efficacy of judicial review as a means of resolving federal-provincial controversies. It underlies the proposals to entrench the court in the constitution and to provide a role for the provinces in selecting the judges. The purpose of this article is to examine the allegation of bias on its merits.[6]

We must start with the trite proposition that the law rarely supplies a clear answer to the questions which come before the Supreme Court of Canada. A litigant is not likely to spend good money taking an appeal to the Supreme Court of Canada unless he is convinced that there is a fair chance that the Supreme Court will reverse the decision which was arrived at by the provincial (or federal) court of appeal. The Supreme Court is not likely to give leave to appeal if a simple point of law is involved. The fact is that the Supreme Court often does reverse the court of appeal, and is often divided itself. All of the constitutional controversies which come before the court are cases where the language of the constitution does not speak clearly with respect to the question at hand, and the precedents either do not quite cover the question at hand

or are conflicting. Obviously, differences of opinion as to the "correct" result in such cases do not imply bias on the part of anyone.

There is a longstanding controversy among legal scholars as to how judges do decide these difficult cases where a judge has to choose between competing interpretations of the existing legal materials. The extreme "positivist" point of view that a judge simply applies the pre-existing rules to the case at hand is entirely unhelpful, because it is the ambiguous or vague condition of the pre-existing rules which has caused the litigation, and the judge's decision will itself define for the first time the rule which is applicable to the case at hand (and like cases). In this situation a new rule has been created (or developed or elaborated). In formulating that new rule the judge exercises a choice which cannot be wholly explained by the pre-existing rules. How is that choice made? The extreme "realist" point of view would be that judges are inevitably free to indulge their own personal policy preferences in choosing between competing interpretations of the pre-existing rules. But it seems clear that judges do not feel that they have this kind of freedom, and the shared assumption of appellate advocacy is that the judge is not free to develop the law along lines which would be congenial to his own preferences. The moderate position, which seems to me to be accurate, is that the judicial choice is primarily governed by the body of legal policies and principles which underlie the more specific rules and which emerge from the statutes, cases, and other conventional sources of law; the judge formulates the legal rule which seems to him to flow most plausibly from those conventional sources of law, even if the result does not accord with his own policy preferences.[7] But it is undeniable that the decision of a difficult case may, as Oliver Wendell Holmes said long ago, "depend on a judgment or intuition more subtle than any articulate major premise";[8] and precisely because that crucial judgment or intuition

---

3   *Canadian Industrial Gas and Oil* v. *Govt. of Sask.*, [1978] 2 S.C.R. 545, hereinafter referred to as CIGOL.

4   *Central Canada Potash Co.* v. *Govt. of Sask.*, [1979] 1 S.C.R. 42.

5   See K. Lysyk, "Reshaping Canadian Federalism" (1979), 13 U.B.C.L. Rev. 1, at pp. 16–21, who does not, however, allege bias.

6   There is an important study in existence, commissioned by the government of Quebec, Gilbert L'Ecuyer, *La Cour suprême du Canada et le partage des compétences 1949–1978* (Gouvernement du Québec, Ministère des Affaires intergouvernementales, 1978), which rejects the allegation of bias. The present article, while agreeing with L'Ecuyer's conclusion, investigates the issue by different methods.

7   Out of the vast literature on judicial decision-making, I cite as particularly useful on this point, Paul C. Weiler, "Two Models of Judicial Decision-Making" (1968), 46 Can. Bar Rev. 406; Paul C. Weiler, "Legal Values and Judicial Decision-Making" (1970), 48 Can. Bar Rev. 1.

8   *Lochner* v. *New York* (1905), 198 U.S. 45, at p. 76, per Holmes J. dissenting; see also "The Path of the Law" (1897), 10 Harv. L. Rev. 457, at p. 466.

is inarticulate, it can be influenced—unconsciously no doubt—by the judge's predispositions.[9]

I conclude that it is at least possible for a judge to be biased in federal-provincial controversies. Of course, the Supreme Court of Canada consists of nine judges at any one point of time, and a total of fifty-seven judges have sat on the court. In investigating the charge of bias in federal-provincial controversies it is necessary to ask whether the numerous judges of the court are likely to share a predisposition to favour the federal or centralist side of the case.

## II. FEDERAL APPOINTMENT OF JUDGES

The simplest form of the argument for bias is that the judges are appointed and paid by the federal government, and will feel beholden to the federal government. Sometimes this argument is reinforced by the argument that the institution itself—the Supreme Court of Canada—was created by a federal statute, and could be abolished the same way. These facts, it would be said, may serve to inculcate gratitude or fear (or a mixture of the two) in the minds of the Supreme Court judges, predisposing them to render decisions pleasing to the federal government. It is obviously not necessary to embark on a detailed rebuttal of this argument. The fact is that once a judge has been appointed—admittedly by the federal government—he has nothing to hope for or fear from the federal government. Constitutional guarantees and powerful political traditions of judicial independence render the judge invulnerable to any kind of governmental action.[10]

The objective fact of judicial independence would not preclude the existence of a sycophantic psychology on the part of the judges. The fact here, however, is that the judges are all longstanding members of the legal profession; in most cases they have been engaged in the private practice of law; they have all been nurtured in a professional tradition which is highly unsympathetic to governmental authority especially when exercised from Ottawa; and they are unlikely to have developed attitudes which are unduly deferential to the federal government. The strong likelihood is that they value the assessment of their work by the legal profession infinitely more highly than they value the opinions of the members of the federal cabinet and civil service. The reputation of a judge in the legal profession is established partly through scholarly writing but mainly through informal discussion among lawyers, and it develops primarily as a result of professional assessment of craftsmanship and fairness. The judge who could always be counted on to vote for the federal government would be regarded with contempt by the profession.

A more subtle form of the bias argument holds that the federal government exercises its appointing power in favour of people with known centralist predispositions. It is only to be expected, so the argument runs, that a government intent on strengthening its power would make such appointments. In fact, however, it seems unlikely that the government does engage in this kind of court-packing. It is not easy to find eminent lawyers and judges who are in favour of increased centralization of power in Ottawa. If obvious candidates for appointment were being passed over in favour of committed centralists, or if enquiries were being made about the constitutional opinions of potential candidates, I think it is obvious that these facts would become known and would be the subject of a considerable protest.[11]

To be sure, there are well-qualified candidates who have publicly recorded their views on some aspects of federal-provincial relationships. It is well known that Chief Justice Laskin, as a law professor, was a vigorous critic of the Privy Council decisions which strengthened provincial power at the expense of the federal government.[12] It is less well known that Mr. Justice Pigeon and Mr. Justice Beetz before their

---

9   In *Lochner* v. *New York, ibid.*, it will be recalled that the Supreme Court of the United States struck down a state law prescribing maximum hours of labour in bakeries as "an unreasonable, unnecessary and arbitrary interference" with freedom of contract.

10  The federal Parliament retains power over judicial salaries, and the Prime Minister decides who will be promoted to Chief Justice when that office is vacant. But the tradition of judicial independence ensures that these powers will not be used to punish or reward judges who render decisions adverse to or favourable to the federal government.

11  For an account of the procedure which is followed in making judicial appointments, see E. Ratushny, "Judicial Appointments: The Lang Legacy," in A.M. Linden (ed.), *The Canadian Judiciary* (1976), ch. 2.

12  B. Laskin, "Peace, Order and Good Government Re-examined" (1947), 25 Can. Bar Rev. 1054.

appointments had published articles which vigorously defended the decisions of the Privy Council.[13] So far as I am aware, none of the other judges had before appointment recorded his opinions on constitutional law.[14] On the basis of the precedents of Laskin C.J., Pigeon and Beetz JJ., it is impossible to substantiate any charge of court-packing. In any case it is impossible to predict with confidence how a person will vote when he assumes judicial office. For example, Laskin C.J. has written the court's opinion, or a separate concurring opinion, in every case in which a federal statute has been held unconstitutional;[15] Pigeon and Beetz JJ. have often written or agreed to opinions holding a provincial statute to be unconstitutional.[16]

It must be remembered too that constitutional cases form only a very small part of the work of the Supreme Court of Canada. The great majority of cases are appeals in civil or criminal cases which involve no constitutional issues at all. One of the factors which is taken into account by the federal government in making appointments is the securing of an appropriate mix of legal experience and expertise among the judges. It would be impossible for the federal government to give due weight to this consideration, as well as conforming to the conventional regional balance of the judges,[17] at the same time as it was pursuing judges

who could be relied upon to vote the "right" way in constitutional cases.

The truth is, I suspect, that the federal government does not see the winning of constitutional law cases as a major policy objective, does not see the role of the Supreme Court in constitutional cases as being of major importance in determining the balance of power between the centre and the provinces,[18] and does see that any evidence of packing the court would provoke a storm of protest. If these viewpoints correspond with reality, as I believe they do, then one must conclude that it is good politics to make good appointments.

## III. FREQUENT INVALIDATION OF PROVINCIAL STATUTES

The only remaining argument for bias is based on the outcomes of constitutional cases[19] decided in

---

13  L.-P. Pigeon, "The Meaning of Provincial Autonomy" (1951), 29 Can. Bar Rev. 1126; J. Beetz, "Les attitudes changeantes du Québec à l'endroit de la Constitution de 1867," in P.-A. Crépeau and C.B. Macpherson, *The Future of Canadian Federalism* (1965), p. 113.

14  Judges, appointed to the Supreme Court of Canada from the bench of another court would normally have decided the occasional constitutional case.

15  *MacDonald v. Vapor Canada*, [1977] 2 S.C.R. 134; *McNamara Construction v. The Queen*, [1977] 2 S.C.R. 655; *Quebec North Shore Paper Co. v. Canadian Pacific*, [1977] 2 S.C.R. 1054; *Reference re Agricultural Products Marketing Act*, [1978] 2 S.C.R. 1198.

16  E.g., *Amax Potash v. Govt. of Sask.*, [1977] 2 S.C.R. 576; *Canadian Industrial Gas and Oil v. Govt. of Sask.*, supra, footnote 3; *A.-G. Que. v. Farrah*, [1978] 2 S.C.R. 638.

17  The Supreme Court Act, R.S.C., 1970, c. S-19, s. 6, stipulates that three of the nine judges must come from Quebec. Until December 1978 the practice was to appoint three judges from Ontario, two from the four Western provinces, and one from the Atlantic provinces. In December 1978, on the retirement of Spence J. who had been appointed from Ontario, McIntyre J. was appointed from British Columbia. The present composition of the court therefore includes (as well as the three judges from Quebec and the one from the Atlantic provinces) two judges from Ontario, two judges from the prairie provinces and one judge from British Columbia. It remains to be seen whether this is now to be the permanent regional distribution of appointments.

18  The federal-provincial financial arrangements, which are made by agreement between the eleven governments, and which encompass the sharing of tax "room," equalization grants, and shared-cost programs, are incomparably more significant. When a judicial decision does have a serious impact on the federal-provincial sharing of power, an accommodation is usually reached by agreement among the various governments. On three occasions that agreement has led to a constitutional amendment to reverse the effect of a judicial decision: s. 91(2A) of the British North America Act (added by British North America Act, 1940, 3–4 Geo. VI, c. 36 [U.K.]) and s. 94A (added by British North America Act, 1951, 14–15 Geo. VI, c. 32 [U.K.] and revised by British North America Act, 1964, 12–13 Eliz. II, c. 73 [U.K]), hereinafter referred to as B.N.A. Act, were designed to abrogate *A.-G. Can v. A.-G. Ont* (Unemployment Insurance), [1937] A.C. 355. More commonly, the effect of the decision can be overcome or modified by revenue-sharing arrangements (e.g., modifying effect of *Reference re Offshore Mineral Rights*, [1967] S.C.R. 792) or by federal inter-delegations of various kinds (e.g., those upheld in *Lord's Day Alliance v. A.-G. B.C.*, [1959] S.C.R. 497; *P.E.I. Potato Marketing Board v. Willis*, [1952] 2 S.C.R. 392; *Coughlin v. Ont. Highway Transport Board*, [1968] S.C.R. 569; *Reference re Agricultural Products Marketing Act*, supra, footnote 15, each of which was a response to a judicial decision). I predict that current controversies over the control and taxation of natural resources and over cable television will also be settled reasonably agreeably to the contending governments. Indeed, one scholar has argued that judicial review could be abolished in view of the existence of consensual methods of resolving federal-provincial controversies: Paul C. Weiler, "The Supreme Court of Canada and Canadian Federalism" (1973), 11 Osgoode Hall L.J. 225; Paul C. Weiler, *In the Last Resort* (1974), ch. 6.

19  I included only cases which raised a constitutional issue of federalism. Constitutional cases on points not bearing on the distribution of powers were excluded, for example, cases on the Canadian Bill of Rights, R.S.C., 1970, Appendix III. I excluded cases

the Supreme Court of Canada from the abolition of appeals to the Privy Council on December 23rd, 1949, to the present.[20] I have looked at all those cases, and I find that sixty-five provincial statutes were attacked in the Supreme Court of Canada and twenty-five of them were held to be unconstitutional in whole or in part,[21] or to be inoperative through paramountcy. In the same period thirty-seven federal statutes were attacked in the Supreme Court of Canada and four of them were held to be unconstitutional in whole or in part.

This kind of raw data must be treated with the utmost caution. Consider some of the complicating factors.

First of all, there are ten legislative bodies busy enacting provincial laws and only one legislative body enacting federal laws. Even allowing for the fact that many provincial statutes duplicate those of other provinces, the volume and variety of provincial laws are so much greater that there are bound to be, and there are, more challenges to the constitutionality of provincial laws. In the period of my study, January 1950 to May 1979 inclusive, as I have just indicated above, there were sixty-five decisions on the validity of provincial laws, and thirty-seven decisions on the validity of federal laws. Of course, this point goes to explain

the number of challenges to provincial laws, not the ratio of success to failure.

Secondly, in such a large and diverse country as Canada, the provinces really are the "social laboratories" that they are supposed to be. Innovative and even radical political ideas tend to find political expression at the provincial level. Federal governments, by contrast, cannot get elected except on middle-of-the-road policies which appeal to a broad cross-section of the country. Since the Second World War cautious or weak federal governments have undertaken few initiatives which would invite a plausible constitutional challenge. The Trudeau government was quite exceptional in its willingness to intervene in the economy. The provinces, however, especially in the west and in Quebec, frequently elect governments with strong mandates to intervene in the economy. These interventions naturally provoke constitutional challenges.

Thirdly, technological developments have tended to diminish provincial powers of economic regulation and increase federal powers.[22] Even in 1867 shipping and rail could move products from their producers to distant markets; but those means of transportation have now been joined by the highways and the airlines. Similarly, the printing press has now been joined by the motion picture, the telephone, radio, and television. The improvements in transportation and communication, and other technological developments, have led to larger and larger business units which can take advantage of the techniques of mass production, mass distribution, and mass advertising. This has led to the gradual disappearance of locally-produced consumer goods. The general tendency of technological change is to convert activities which were once local and private, and which could be governed by the private law of contract, tort, and property, into activities which extend across the entire nation, make use

in which the majority opinion was not based on a constitutional issue, even though the point may have been strenuously argued, or even formed the basis of a dissenting opinion (as in *Breckinridge Speedway* v. *The Queen*, [1970] S.C.R. 1975). I also excluded cases in which a constitutional point was referred to in the majority opinion, but was in my view either an obiter dictum or a subsidiary ground of decision; these exclusions are more controversial, but it must be appreciated that the constitution is argued in many cases and often receives passing reference in the decisions, for example, in administrative law cases.

20  The cases comprise all the decisions of which I was aware, from the beginning of 1950 up to June 1st, 1979. This included all the cases reported in the Supreme Court Reports up to Part 2 of [1979] 1 S.C.R. together with four cases decided, but unreported in S.C.R. at that time, namely, *Construction Montcalm* v. *Commission du salaire minimum*, December 21st, 1978; *Tropwood A.G.* v. *Sivaco Wire and Nail Co.*, March 6th, 1979; *Mississauga* v. *Peel*, March 6th, 1979; *The Queen* v. *Hauser*, May 1st, 1979. I excluded *Winner* v. *S.M.T. Eastern*, [1951] S.C.R. 887 because, although it was decided after 1949, it still went on appeal up to the Privy Council.

21  In six cases a statute was not held invalid, but "read down" or interpreted narrowly so that it was held inapplicable to the facts on the ground that a literal application of the statute would have been unconstitutional. On reading down, see Hogg, *Constitutional Law of Canada* (1977), pp. 90–92. I counted these cases as holdings of partial invalidity.

22  Paralleling technological developments has been the rise of egalitarian values reflected in social policies to provide income support and security from illness, disability, and old age. Many of these policies are within provincial legislative jurisdiction, but there is also a heavy federal presence reflected in federal programs of unemployment insurance, family allowances, Canada pension plan, old age security, guaranteed income supplement, and in shared-cost programs of income support, hospital insurance, and medical care. Unlike economic regulation, programs of income distribution and social security rely primarily upon extensive spending powers and are rarely vulnerable to constitutional challenge.

of public facilities, and require regulation in order to protect the public from predatory or monopolistic practices. These developments do not necessarily answer the question of which level of government should be the regulator. But in many instances the need for a single national policy is so clear that the federal claim is very plausible.

Fourthly, in a federal system—any federal system—provincial laws are vulnerable to constitutional challenge on the basis of their extraterritorial impact. Various doctrines are either expressed in the constitution or are inferred by the courts to limit the power of a provincial legislature, which is elected by and answerable to the people of only that province, to enact policies which will have an impact on the people of other provinces. This is the underlying policy behind many of the limits on the powers of the provinces, even though the limits may be expressed in terms of encroaching on interprovincial trade and commerce, imposing indirect taxation, as well as the more straightforward prohibition on extraterritorial laws. The federal Parliament, by contrast, is elected from all over the country. No doctrine has developed and none is needed to prevent it from overreaching in a territorial sense.[23]

Fifthly, in Canada, and apparently in all modern federations,[24] provincial laws are vulnerable to constitutional challenge on the basis of their inconsistency with federal law. This is a judge-made doctrine in Canada, to be sure, but one for which the Privy Council, and not the Supreme Court of Canada, bears the responsibility. In any event, I think there would be little quarrel with the general proposition that where national and provincial laws come into conflict it is the national law—the law with the broadest political support—which should prevail.[25] The doctrine of federal paramountcy provides a ground for challeng-ing provincial laws which is not available in respect of federal laws.[26]

What all this means is that we must expect many more successful constitutional challenges to provincial laws than federal laws. This situation stems from the nature of the Canadian federal system, not from any bias on the part of the judges. Even during the Privy Council period this was true. I only have figures from 1919 to the end of appeals, but that was the period when the Privy Council established doctrines highly favourable to the provinces. In that period there were thirty-five challenges to provincial statutes of which nineteen were held invalid in whole or in part, and twenty-two challenges to federal statutes of which eight were held invalid in whole or in part.[27] The Privy Council was less restrained in judicial review than the Supreme Court of Canada. Therefore the rate of invalidation is higher for both classes of statutes. But a similar discrepancy in the numbers of challenges and in the proportions of successful challenges is obvious.

## IV. DOCTRINES ESTABLISHED BY THE COURT

### 1. Legacy of the Privy Council

Let us now move away from the raw data and ask whether the doctrines established by the judges indicate a pro-centralist bias.

The legacy left by the Privy Council was a very broad provincial power over property and civil rights in the province, and correspondingly narrow federal powers over the peace, order, and good government of Canada and over the regulation of trade and commerce. As new kinds of legislation emerged, even when the initiative had come from the federal Parliament, the Privy Council had often allotted the new law to provincial jurisdiction, usually, property and civil rights in the province. The regulation of insurance, and therefore of other industries and occupations, most labour relations, trades, and professions, wages and prices, combinations, health, and

---

23  It may be objected that the federal Parliament is subject to a comparable limitation in the sense that it is precluded from legislating in relation to matters which are local. Perhaps the answer is that this fourth point is really only a corollary to the third point, which is that fewer and fewer matters are genuinely local.

24  K.C. Wheare, *Federal Government* (4th ed., 1963), p. 74.

25  The practice of other federal systems, see Wheare, *op. cit., ibid.,* supports this proposition. This is not to deny that in a revised Canadian constitution there may well be some areas of concurrent legislative power where the general rule should be reversed so that provincial laws would be paramount.

26  In the period under study, 1950–1979, *supra,* footnote 20, only two provincial statutes were actually held inoperative by reason of federal paramountcy. The paramountcy cases are discussed later in this article.

27  Paul C. Weiler, *In the Last-Resort* (1974), p. 309, note 3.

welfare, and the marketing of natural products were all topics which the Privy Council ruled were outside the competence of the federal Parliament, except in time of war. During the depression of the 1930s the federal Parliament did not have the power to undertake measures designed to alleviate the distress and prevent its recurrence. Federal laws providing for unemployment insurance, minimum wage and maximum hours laws, as well as marketing regulation, were all held to be unconstitutional.[28]

The decisions of the Privy Council were widely if not universally deplored by English-Canadian constitutional lawyers, although not by French-Canadian constitutional lawyers.[29] From a doctrinal point of view, however, there was surely force in the criticism that the decisions had virtually emptied the major federal powers of content. It was not a particularly plausible interpretation of the peace, order, and good government power that it applied only in wartime. It was not a particularly plausible interpretation of the trade and commerce power that it would not permit the regulation of any intraprovincial trade and commerce. Indeed, the Privy Council itself had left a number of decisions and dicta which reflected quite different opinions than those which became dominant during the Haldane period.

## 2. Peace, Order, and Good Government
When we look at the extensions of the peace, order, and good government power which have occurred since 1949, we have to remember how severely that power had been attenuated by the Privy Council and how inevitable it was that there would be a movement away from the Privy Council's more extreme views. In fact, the decisions of the Supreme Court of Canada have been quite cautious in departing from Privy Council precedents. The "national concern" branch of peace, order, and good government has been used to uphold federal power over aviation,[30] the national capital commission,[31] the minerals off the shore of

British Columbia,[32] and the control of narcotics.[33] None of these outcomes would surprise a visitor from another federation. But in the *Anti-Inflation Reference* (1976),[34] a case which shows up in the raw data as a federal victory, the Supreme Court of Canada refused to extend the national concern test to wage and price controls. These could only be enacted as a temporary emergency measure in wartime or in a peacetime crisis. To be sure, the court found that the requisite crisis existed, and upheld the Anti-Inflation Act; but the court emphasized that permanent controls were outside federal competence. I suggest that a visitor from another federation would be surprised that permanent wage and price controls cannot be enacted by the federal Parliament. This means, of course, that they cannot be enacted at all, because provincial controls could not be effective while there is free movement across provincial boundaries of personnel, capital, goods, and services. The opinions in the *Anti-Inflation Reference*, and especially that of Beetz J., abundantly demonstrate the continuing life of the Privy Council extensions of property and civil rights in the province.

## 3. Trade and Commerce
The history of the trade and commerce power is similar. Few people would quarrel with the Supreme Court of Canada's acceptance of federal marketing legislation for wheat[35] and oil,[36] products which flow across provincial boundaries.[37] But when the federal government sought to use the trade and commerce power to uphold a law which afforded a civil remedy for loss caused by an act or business practice which was "contrary to honest industrial or commercial practice in Canada'" the Supreme Court of Canada in *MacDonald*

28  See generally, Peter W. Hogg, *op. cit.*, footnote 21, chs 14, 15, 17.
29  Compare the articles cited, *supra*, footnotes 12 and 13; and see Alan C. Cairns, "The Judicial Committee and its Critics" (1971), 4 Can. J. Pol. Sci. 301.
30  *Johannesson* v. *West St. Paul*, [1952] 1 S.C.R. 292.
31  *Munro* v. *National Capital Commission*, [1966] S.C.R. 663.
32  *Reference re Offshore Mineral Rights, supra*, footnote 18.
33  *The Queen* v. *Hauser, supra*, footnote 20. This is a surprising decision, because it appears to resuscitate *Russell* v. *The Queen* (1882), 7 App. Cas. 829, a decision widely regarded as wrong, and because narcotics law had hitherto been generally regarded as criminal. But the allocation of narcotics law to federal power is not at all surprising.
34  [1976] 2 S.C.R. 373.
35  *Murphy* v. *Canadian Pacific Railway*, [1958] S.C.R. 626.
36  *Caloil* v. *A.-G. Can.*, [1971] S.C.R. 543.
37  See also *Reference re Agricultural Products Marketing Act, supra*, footnote 15, where an egg marketing scheme was upheld. The scheme was the fruit of a federal-provincial agreement and supported by both federal and provincial statutes; the federal statute was carefully expressed in most of its provisions to be limited to interprovincial and export trade.

v. *Vapor Canada* (1976),[38] unanimously condemned the law. Once again, the viability of the old cases on property and civil rights in the province was reaffirmed. In the *Anti-Inflation Reference* (1976),[39] counsel for the federal government did not even argue that the trade and commerce power could sustain the wage and price controls, and the tenor of the opinions makes clear that at least five of the nine judges would have emphatically rejected such an argument.

The Supreme Court of Canada has used an expanded view of the trade and commerce power to strike down several provincial marketing schemes, including Manitoba's egg marketing scheme[40] and Saskatchewan's scheme to control the production and price of potash.[41] The essential basis of these decisions is that the provincial law had too severe an impact on interprovincial trade and commerce. In my opinion, these decisions are hard to reconcile with earlier decisions and therefore do represent a shift in doctrine by the Supreme Court of Canada;[42] it is a shift which is unfavourable to provincial power. But, as I noted earlier, every federal system has to define limits on the power of its provincial (or state) governments to affect people in other parts of the country. The litigation which this same issue has spawned in the United States[43] and Australia[44] demonstrates that this is a real problem upon which people of equal intelligence and equal good faith are simply not going to agree. Moreover, while the provinces have lost some of the cases where the effects of provincial laws have rippled outside the province, they have won others, most notably, *Carnation Co.* v. *Quebec Agricultural Marketing Board* (1968),[45] in which a provincial marketing scheme was held applicable to a processor of milk who shipped the bulk of the processed product out of the province,[46] and *Canadian Indemnity Co.* v.

*A.-G. B.C.* (1976),[47] in which the creation of a provincial monopoly of automobile insurance was upheld despite the interprovincial character of the business of writing automobile insurance. The latter case reaffirmed the Privy Council precedents upholding provincial jurisdiction over the insurance industry. In the United States, by contrast, initial holdings of state jurisdiction over insurance were reversed in 1944 on the basis that the nation-wide character of the industry brought it within the commerce clause and thus within federal jurisdiction.[48]

One must conclude that while the federal trade and commerce power has expanded at the hands of the Supreme Court of Canada, it has not expanded very much. As a support to federal jurisdiction the expansion has been very cautious, confined to marketing schemes over wheat and oil and (with co-operative provincial supplementation) eggs. An observer from the United States would be astonished to learn that the trade and commerce power cannot be employed to regulate the insurance industry, or to impose nation-wide wage and price controls, and that the constitutional validity of federal regulation of foreign ownership, anti-trust and securities regulation are still matters of argument among constitutional lawyers. As a barrier to provincial jurisdiction, the trade and commerce power has been applied more boldly—to the chagrin of some of the provinces. Even here, however, the results have not been uniformly unfavourable to provincial power to regulate activity which spills outside provincial borders; and the difficulty of drawing the line between that which is predominantly local, and that which is predominantly interprovincial, is one which simply cannot be denied.

## 4. Cable Television
The recent decisions affirming federal regulatory authority over cable television[49] and denying provincial authority over cable television[50] came as a blow

---

38  *Supra*, footnote 38.

39  *Supra*, footnote 34.

40  *A.-G. Man.* v. *Man. Egg and Poultry Assn.*, [1971] S.C.R. 689; see also *Burns Foods* v. *A.-G. Man.* [1975] 1 S.C.R. 494.

41  *Central Canada Potash Co.* v. *Govt. of Sask.*, *supra*, footnote 4; see also *Canadian Industrial Gas and Oil* v. *Govt. of Sask.*, *supra*, footnote 3.

42  Peter W. Hogg, *op. cit.*, footnote 21, p. 311.

43  Laurence H. Tribe, *American Constitutional Law* (1978), ch. 6.

44  P.H. Lane, *The Australian Federal System* (1972), pp. 597–675.

45  [1968] S.C.R. 238.

46  See also *Reference re Agricultural Products Marketing Act*, *supra*, footnote 15, where provincial controls on the production of eggs

were upheld, although the controls applied regardless of the ultimate destination of the eggs.

47  [1977] 2 S.C.R. 504.

48  *United States* v. *South-Eastern Underwriters Assn.* (1944), 322 U.S. 533.

49  *Capital Cities Communications* v. *Canadian Radio-Television Commission*, *supra*, footnote 2.

50  *Public Service Board* v. *Dionne*, *supra*, footnote 2; but compare *A.-G. Que.* v. *Kellogg's Co. of Canada*, *supra*, footnote 2.

to Quebec where the issues were perceived in terms of the protection of French-Canadian language and culture. However, federal jurisdiction over broadcast (non-cable) radio and television had been established by the Privy Council in the *Radio Reference* (1930),[51] and the argument over cable television boiled down to the question whether it was feasible to regard the cable system as a local undertaking separate from the undeniably federal broadcasting system. The Supreme Court's decision that the cable system should not be regarded as separate was in accord with a virtually unanimous accumulation of prior decisions and published articles.[52] The point was still open, as is evidenced by the dissents of the three French-Canadian judges, but it should be noted that the Federal Court of Appeal in the *Capital Cities* case and (more significantly, perhaps) the Quebec Court of Appeal in the *Dionne* case was each unanimously of the same opinion as the majority in the Supreme Court of Canada.

My opinion, for what it is worth, is that the competing federal and provincial claims to regulate cable television are each founded on real interests. A judicial decision which allocates jurisdiction to one level of the government or the other cannot be entirely satisfactory, whichever level of government emerges as the winner. It is most unlikely that the judicial resolution will turn out to be final. What is required is an agreement for the sharing of jurisdiction, either spelled out in a revised constitution, or embodied in sub-constitutional arrangements.

## 5. Taxation

In *Canadian Industrial Gas and Oil* v. *Government of Saskatchewan* (1977),[53] the Supreme Court of Canada struck down a provincial tax on oil produced in the province. The tax was designed to appropriate to the province the dramatic increase in the price of oil which had started in 1973. Because of the huge sums involved the decision was a serious blow to the province of Saskatchewan, and it attracted severe criticism from the government of that province. The legal issue before the court was whether the tax was direct or indirect, because the provinces are confined to direct taxes by section 92(2) of the B.N.A. Act. Previous decisions established that a tax which tended to enter into the price of a commodity was an indirect tax and was incompetent to the provinces. The Saskatchewan Court of Appeal held that this tax was direct because the price of oil determined the tax rather than the other way around. This was also the view of Dickson J. (with de Grandpré J.) dissenting in the Supreme Court of Canada. But Martland J. for the seven-judge majority of the Supreme Court of Canada viewed the facts differently, emphasizing the power which the statute conferred on the provincial minister to fix the price at which oil was to be sold when the minister was of opinion that oil had been sold at less than fair value.

*CIGOL* must be accounted an important loss to the provinces in federal-provincial litigation. I find the majority opinion of Martland J. much less persuasive than the minority opinion of Dickson J. I do not see the answer to Dickson J.'s point that "purchasers would be paying the same price whether the tax existed or not."[54] The ministerial power to fix the price, which was relied upon by Martland J., seems to me to be satisfactorily explained by Dickson J. as a subsidiary provision to block evasion of the tax by "such practices as sale of oil between related companies at artificially low prices."[55] However, the legal issue turned on one's perception of exactly how the tax and associated regulations would impinge on the price of Saskatchewan oil. Differences of opinion on complex issues of this kind should not lay the judges open to a charge of bias.

The Supreme Court of Canada recently made another decision upon the provincial taxing power. In the *Ontario Egg Reference* (1977),[56] the court held that marketing levies were not indirect taxes; the levies were regulatory charges which could be imposed by the provinces as an incident of a valid provincial marketing scheme. This holding involved an unprecedented overruling of the decision of the Privy Council in the *Crystal Dairy* case,[57] which had decided that marketing

51  [1932] A.C. 304.
52  The case-law and commentary before *Capital Cities* and *Dionne* are discussed in Peter W. Hogg, *op. cit.*, footnote 21, pp. 336–342.
53  *Supra*, footnote 3. See also *Amax Potash* v. *Govt. of Sask. supra*, footnote 16.
54  *Ibid.*, at p. 593.
55  *Ibid.*, at p. 592.
56  *Reference re Agricultural Products Marketing Act, supra*, footnote 15.
57  *Lower Mainland Dairy Products Sales Adjustment Committee* v. *Crystal Dairy*, [1933] A.C. 168.

levies were indirect taxes which were incompetent to the provinces. It was also necessary to overrule (on this point) a previous decision of the Supreme Court of Canada, the *Farm Products Marketing Act Reference* (1957).[58] The court applied the new doctrine by striking down a federal statute authorizing the imposition of marketing levies by provincial marketing boards, notwithstanding the fact that the federal statute had been enacted in 1957 in reliance on the fact that the *Crystal Dairy* doctrine had been reaffirmed by the Supreme Court of Canada in the *Farm Products Marketing Act Reference* in 1957. This unanimous holding is a remarkable example of judicial activism, and of course its effect was to augment provincial power.

## 6. Administration of Justice

Federal power over the administration of justice by federal courts, which is granted by section 101 of the B.N.A. Act, has been severely limited by the decisions of the Supreme Court of Canada in *Quebec North Shore* (1976)[59] and *McNamara Construction* (1977),[60] which hold that the federal Parliament can confer jurisdiction on federal courts only over issues governed by federal statute law. This has gravely undermined or rendered uncertain much of the jurisdiction of the Federal Court of Canada, introduced terrible complexities to multi-party litigation, especially where the federal Crown (which can only be sued in the Federal Court) is involved, and spawned a flood of litigation which is now working its way up through the system.[61] I have criticized these decisions elsewhere.[62] For present purposes it suffices to note that the new doctrine is highly unfavourable to federal power.

Provincial power over the administration of justice in the province has been contentious in recent years. In *Di Iorio* v. *Montreal Jail Warden* (1976),[63] the Supreme Court of Canada decided by a majority that the province of Quebec had the jurisdiction to establish an inquiry into organized crime, despite the close relationship with the federal subject of criminal law. However, in the *Keable* case[64] the court decided unanimously that the province of Quebec did not have the jurisdiction to establish a broad-ranging inquiry into the policies, procedures, and methods of the Royal Canadian Mounted Police, although the inquiry could be continued in respect of particular criminal acts allegedly committed in Quebec by the force. In *The Queen* v. *Hauser* (1979),[65] the court decided by a majority that the federal Parliament had the jurisdiction to provide for the federal prosecution of offences under the Narcotic Control Act. This decision, *like Keable*, was unfavourable to the provincial point of view, but, also like *Keable*, it was based on rather narrow grounds. The court in *Hauser* did not affirm federal power to provide for the prosecution of criminal law (as many observers expected); a majority of the court managed to avoid this vexed issue by holding that the Narcotic Control Act was not really a criminal law after all,[66] which enabled the court to decide the case on the basis that the federal Parliament had the power to provide for the enforcement of its non-criminal laws.

Frequent attacks on provincial administrative agencies (or inferior courts), based on the allegation that the agencies (or courts) were exercising judicial powers analogous to those of a superior court in contravention of section 96 and the other judicature provisions of the B.N.A. Act, have met with success in three cases,[67] but have usually failed. The court has emphasized that "it is not the detached jurisdiction or power alone that is to be considered but rather its setting in the institutional arrangements in which it appears and is exercisable under the provincial legislation."[68] This pragmatic

---

58  [1957] S.C.R. 198.

59  *Quebec North Shore Paper Co.* v. *Canadian Pacific, supra,* footnote 15.

60  *McNamara Construction* v. *The Queen, supra,* footnote 15.

61  At the time of writing only one case had reached the Supreme Court of Canada, namely, *Tropwood A.G.* v. *Sivaco Wire and Nail Co., supra,* footnote 20, upholding federal jurisdiction in admiralty.

62  Comment (1977), 55 Can. Bar Rev. 550.

63  [1978] 1 S.C.R. 152.

64  *A.-G. Que. and Keable* v. *A.-G. Can.,* [1979] 1 S.C.R. 218.

65  *Supra,* footnote 20.

66  *Supra,* footnote 33.

67  *Toronto* v. *Olympia Edward Recreation Club,* [1955] S.C.R. 454; *Seminary of Chicoutimi* v. *A.-G. Que.,* [1973] S.C.R. 681; *A.-G. Que.* v. *Farrah, supra,* footnote 16.

68  *Tomko* v. *Labour Relations Bd. (N.S.),* [1977] 1 S.C.R. 112, at p. 120; see also *Reference re Quebec Magistrate's Court,* [1965] S.C.R. 772; *Dupont* v. *Inglis,* [1958] S.C.R. 535; *Brooks* v. *Pavlick,* [1964] S.C.R. 108; *Tremblay* v. *Commission des relations de travail du Québec,* [1967] S.C.R. 697; *Jones* v. *Edmonton School Trustees,* [1977] 2 S.C.R. 873; *Mississauga* v. *Peel, supra,* footnote 20. This pattern of judicial restraint in support of provincial power had been established by the Privy Council in *Labour Relations Bd. (Sask.)* v. *John East Iron Works,* [1949] A.C. 134.

contextual approach is of course favourable to the provincial power to set up administrative agencies.

## 7. Civil Liberties

In the 1950s the Supreme Court of Canada rendered decisions which tended to limit if not deny provincial power to legislate in relation to speech and religion. The *Saumur* case (1953)[69] held that the City of Quebec could not prevent the distribution of religious tracts in the streets. *Switzman* v. *Elbling* (1957)[70] held that a provincial law prohibiting the use of a house to propagate communism was invalid. These cases were unfavourable to provincial power, to be sure, but they had their roots in well-respected dicta by Duff C.J. and Cannon J. in the *Alberta Press* case (1938),[71] and they were widely applauded for their support of civil libertarian values. Recently, however, the court has upheld provincial restraints on civil liberties. In *Nova Scotia Board of Censors* v. *McNeil* (1978),[72] provincial censorship of movies was upheld as being merely the regulation of a business (the movie business) and of property (films) in the province; and this despite the absence of any explicit criteria laid down by the statute or regulation or by the censorship board itself to limit the kinds of movies which could be forbidden. In *A.-G. Can. and Dupond* v. *Montreal* (1978),[73] a Montreal by-law prohibiting all demonstrations in the streets and parks of the city for a specified period of time was upheld as a regulation of the use of the municipal public domain.

It is difficult to believe that *McNeil* and *Dupond* would have been decided the same way by the Supreme Court of the 1950s. For present purposes, the point is, of course, that the value of provincial autonomy over local matters has been held to encompass even speech and assembly despite the nation-wide implications of speech and assembly for the democratic process. Whatever else one may say about the recent decisions, they are certainly favourable to provincial power.

## 8. Paramountcy

The B.N.A. Act says nothing explicit about conflict between federal and provincial laws. The Privy Council early developed the rule of federal paramountcy: in the event of conflict the federal law was to prevail. Surprisingly, however, there were only a few occasions for the application of this rule by the Privy Council, and their lordships never developed any jurisprudence as to the degree of inconsistency which would amount to a conflict which would attract the rule. Here then was an opportunity for the court to give effect to any centralizing predispositions. Given the overriding force of federal law, a wide definition of inconsistency would result in the defeat of provincial laws in the same "field" as a federal law. In the United States and Australia there are many precedents for this covering-the-field test of conflict. On the other hand, a narrow definition of inconsistency would allow provincial laws to survive so long as they did not expressly contradict the federal law.[74]

The Supreme Court of Canada has not followed the covering-the-field precedents of the United States and Australia. It has not taken the course of judicial activism in favour of central power. On the contrary, it has insisted upon a direct contradiction between the federal and provincial law to trigger the paramountcy doctrine. There are many cases in which the court has refused to render a provincial law inoperative for paramountcy,[75] and only two where the conflict was deemed sufficient to render the provincial law inoperative.[76] The cases have been described elsewhere,[77] but it is perhaps worth briefly describing one case. In *Ross* v. *Registrar of Motor Vehicles* (1973),[78] the court was concerned with the effect of a federal Criminal Code provision dealing with penalties for drunk driving and conferring a discretion on the sentencing court

---

69   *Saumur* v. *City of Quebec*, [1953] 2 S.C.R. 299.

70   [1957] S.C.R. 285.

71   *Reference re Alberta Statutes*, [1938] S.C.R. 100.

72   [1978] 2 S.C.R. 662.

73   [1978] 2 S.C.R. 770.

74   For general discussion, see Peter W. Hogg, *op. cit.*, footnote 21, ch. 6.

75   The leading cases are *Reference re s. 92(4) of the Vehicles Act 1957* (Sask.), [1958] S.C.R. 608; *Smith* v. *The Queen*, [1960] S.C.R. 776; *O'Grady* v. *Sparling*, [1960] S.C.R. 804; *Stephens* v. *The Queen*, [1960] S.C.R. 823; *Mann* v. *The Queen*, [1966] S.C.R. 238; *Ross* v. *Registrar of Motor Vehicles*, [1975] 1 S.C.R. 5; *Bell* v. *A.-G. P.E.I.*, [1975] 1 S.C.R. 25; *Robinson* v. *Countrywide Factors*, [1978] 1 S.C.R. 753; *Construction Montcalm* v. *Commission du salaire minimum*, *supra*, footnote 20.

76   *A.-G. B.C.* v. *Smith*, [1967] S.C.R. 702; *A.-G. Ont.* v. *Policy-holders of Wentworth Insurance Co.*, [1969] S.C.R. 779.

77   *Op. cit.*, footnote 21, ch. 6.

78   *Supra*, footnote 75.

to prohibit driving on an intermittent basis—"at such times and places as may be specified in the order." In the *Ross* case this power had been exercised by prohibiting the defendant "from driving for a period of six months, except Monday to Friday, 8:00 a.m. to 5:45 p.m., in the course of employment and going to and from work." The question was whether the Criminal Code discretion, as exemplified by the *Ross* order, conflicted with a provincial law which automatically suspended the driving licence of anyone convicted of drunk driving. The provincial law had the effect of nullifying the spirit if not the letter of the carefully tailored order made under the Criminal Code because the order obviously contemplated that the defendant be free to drive in the periods which were exempt from the prohibition. Yet the Supreme Court of Canada held that the provincial law was not rendered inoperative by paramountcy. Ross's licence was suspended.

While the *Ross* case is the most extreme example, many others could be cited to show the length to which the court has been willing to go in support of provincial laws.[79] In this area the Supreme Court of Canada has developed doctrine highly favourable to provincial power.

## 9. Conclusion

My conclusion is that the Supreme Court of Canada has generally adhered to the doctrine laid down by the Privy Council precedents; and that where the court has departed from those precedents, or has been without close precedents, the choices between competing lines of reasoning have favoured the provincial interest at least as often as they have favoured the federal interest. There is no basis for the claim that the court has been biased in favour of the federal interest in constitutional litigation.

---

79  *Supra*, footnote 74, but see especially the decisions in *Reference re s. 92(4) of the Vehicles Act* 1957 (Sask), *Smith* v. *The Queen,* and *Mann* v. *The Queen, supra,* footnote 75.

## Part Five

# Bilingualism and Binationalism

ONE MIGHT SAY that the creative tension between French and English is the well-spring of Canadian constitutional politics. These two communities have been called Canada's two solitudes. The description is apt, given how poorly they appear to understand each other, best efforts and intentions notwithstanding. Although the fire had continued to smolder since Confederation, the first real test, as A.I. Silver explains, came with the Manitoba School Crisis. It proved to be an event of historic proportion that would come to shape the role of the federal government vis-à-vis language politics, would offer an implicit recognition of the special role reserved for Quebec in the federation, and mark the beginning of the end of Ottawa's use of the reserve powers to assert its hegemony over the provinces. A second yet short piece on the tactical dimensions of the Crisis by J.W. Dafoe shows just what a political minefield language politics can be and the way crafty political operatives with inclination for what is at stake can exploit it for political gain.

Two insightful pieces on "what Quebec wants" follow. Judge L.-P. Pigeon's article stands out as one of the earliest, most articulate, and clearest accounts of the particular relevance of provincial autonomy for Quebec. Pigeon's article is complemented by Alexander

Brady's assessment of the *Tremblay Report*, which appeared only a few years later. The *Tremblay Report* was a seminal statement of traditional culture. It discussed the implications for Quebec of preserving this traditional culture in a federation where the federal government was increasingly seen as encroaching on constitutional jurisdiction that Quebec feels it must control if it is to fulfill its ultimate raison d'être: preserving the particularity of the French fact in North America.

The final part of this section illustrates two of the definitive positions held with respect to the controversy over the role of the federal and Quebec governments with respect to the protection and promotion of the French language. Pierre Elliott Trudeau embodies the visceral reaction of one of the country's best-known francophone Quebeckers to the nationalist positions taken by Pigeon and the *Tremblay Report*. The essay included here is perhaps his most famous exposition that rationalizes the precedence-taking role of the federal government. Trudeau's position contrasts starkly with that defended by Guy Laforest, whose essay offers a lucid historical explanation of francophone Quebeckers' concerns and the implications that could follow.

# 24

## Editor's Introduction

The first major test of the resilience of Confederation and its ability to reconcile and protect two different languages came from the most unlikely of places: not Quebec, not Ontario, but … Manitoba. The Manitoba School Crisis is illustrative of the perils of language politics for francophones, politicians and political parties. At the same time, it is indicative of the controversy surrounding the use of reservation and disallowance as reserve powers of the Crown. Just when they would ostensibly have needed the interventionist protection of the federal government, none other than Canada's first francophone prime minister, Wilfrid Laurier, ends up giving the impression of leaving Manitoba's francophones to their own devices. Why would he do that? This selection explains why. As it turns out, there was a postscript to the crisis some hundred years later when a savvy Manitoba motorist challenged his English-only speeding ticket all the way up to the Supreme Court of Canada—and won! It pays to know your constitutional rights.

Source: A.I. Silver, "Manitoba Schools and the Rise of Bilingualism," in *The French-Canadian Idea of Confederation, 1864–1900*, 2nd ed. (Toronto: University of Toronto Press, 1997), 180–217.

A.I. Silver

# Manitoba Schools and the Rise of Bilingualism

THE RIEL AGITATION did not end with the 1886 provincial elections. During the 1887 federal campaign all Liberals and Nationals again stressed the Riel affair, looking forward to "the hour of national revenge,"[1] and reminding voters that Macdonald had authorized "the plundering of our compatriots and co-religionists of the North-West"[2] and sacrificed Riel "to the Orange lodges."[3] Conservatives, for their part, put some considerable effort into arguing that Riel had not been worthy of Quebec's sympathy, that he had pushed the Métis into unjustified rebellion for his own selfish purposes,[4] had been responsible for the murders of priests and the deaths of 150 soldiers, and even as far back as 1870 had shown his wickedness by causing "the brutal and senseless shooting of Scott, who was laid still breathing into his grave."[5] Whatever effect

this arguing may have had on the election results,[6] it was still not the last of Riel. By the end of the decade polemicists were still contending whether he had been an impostor or the noble victim of "a judicial murder,"[7] and Wilfrid Laurier could say, during the 1890 debate on the language question, that the agitation begun in 1885 still had not ended.[8]

Nevertheless, the most important continuing impact of the Riel execution was indirect. It came from the fact that the affair had increased English-Canadian sensitivity to the dangers of French-Canadian nationalism while at the same time calling forth new assertions of that nationalism.

Mercier, as we have seen, came to power by stressing the traditional concern for the autonomy of the

---

1   *L'Electeur*, 16 Nov. 1886.

2   Ibid., 10 Jan. 1887. Also 10 Feb.

3   *Le Mot de la fin* (n.p., n.d.), pp. 7, 22. Also, *L'Etendard*, 4 Feb. 1887, and *La Vérité's* interpretation of the election results, 26 Feb. 1887.

4   *Rébellion du Nord-Ouest: faits pour le peuple* (n.p., n.d.).

5   *Electeurs, attention, ne vous laissez pas tromper* (n.p., n.d.), p. 6. Also, *Elections de 1887: la vraie question* (n.p., n.d.); *Le Journal des Trois-Rivières*, 10, 14, 21, and 24 Feb., 1887; *Le Courrier de St-Hyacinthe*, 26 Feb. 1887.

6   The Bleus just barely managed to hold Quebec in 1887, but the gains which the Liberals made may well be attributable to other factors than Riel. See H.B. Neatby, *Laurier and a Liberal Quebec* (Toronto: McClelland and Stewart 1973), pp. 33–4.

7   *Le Courrier de St-Hyacinthe*, 20 Apr. 1889; *Le Journal des Trois-Rivières*, 23 Dec.; *L'Etendard*, 14, 17, and 23 Aug. 1889; Adolphe Ouimet, *La Vérité sur la question métisse au Nord-Ouest* (Montreal 1889), esp. pp. 188, 288–9, 397.

8   *Wilfrid Laurier à la tribune*, pp. 588–9. See also *Le Nouveau Monde*, 17 Feb. 1890.

French-Catholic province. His followers still spoke of Quebec as the homeland of the French Canadians,[9] and he responded by telling them: "This province of Quebec is Catholic and French, and it shall remain Catholic and French."[10] The autonomy of this homeland must not be weakened, for it was the key to French Canada's national future.[11] Provincial autonomy, claimed an 1890 Parti National brochure, was the "first article of the national programme." No sooner had Mercier come to power than he "took up the fight for the province's rights."[12]

Conservatives could not help being annoyed at the way in which Mercierites spoke of provincial autonomy. Autonomy was a splendid thing, they observed during the 1886 campaign. "But this is precisely the doctrine championed by the present Conservative administration...."[13] The Liberals had attacked provincial autonomy in the past—witness the Letellier *coup d'état*—and even now, for the sake of gaining power, they seemed willing to endanger it by obscuring the boundary between federal and provincial powers in the Riel affair.[14] No, it was the Conservatives who had always been "the true friends of the 1867 federal pact," the true friends of provincial autonomy.[15]

But if Mercier's conception of an autonomous French-Catholic Quebec was not original, he thrust it more jarringly than the Bleus had ever done upon the attentions of English Canadians—and this at a time when the Riel affair had already caused them to become nervous about the implications of French-Canadian nationalism.[16] Mercier's manner of campaigning, his appointment of a priest as deputy-minister of colonization, his grand trips abroad and acceptance of high honours from the French government and the papacy[17]—these alone might well have worried English Canadians. But he took other initiatives as well.

Shortly after coming to office, Mercier began to organize an interprovincial conference at Quebec in an attempt to enhance the autonomy of the provinces. Praising the idea, Jules-Paul Tardivel warned that unless it succeeded in its aim, Confederation could not endure much longer.[18] As the delegates gathered at Quebec, *L'Electeur* referred to them as "the foreign ministers," and published banner headlines of welcome and pictures of the Ontario delegation.[19] During and after the conference Mercierite publications emphasized its importance for provincial autonomy in general and Quebec in particular.[20]

Naturally, the Bleus would not admit that this "Mowat-Mercier picnic" might serve any useful purpose.[21] How could one expect anything from a group of Liberals gathered together to complain (for example) about the federal veto power, when they themselves had been guilty of an "immoderate use" of the veto between 1873 and 1878? The Liberals would do well to "tune their fiddles before they begin the dance."[22]

But while the Bleus may have been right in saying Mercier's conference achieved no concrete gains for the province, it was probably also true that the meeting helped build up an image of Mercier as a challenger of Confederation, and a man who aimed to loosen its bonds. What else could have been the effect of this comment from a pro-Mercier newspaper:

---

9   Eg., *La Vérité*, 10 Sept. 1887, 15 Jan. 1888; *L'Electeur*, 9 Mar. 1892.

10  Mercier's speech at Quebec, 24 June 1889, quoted in Rumilly, *Honoré Mercier et son temps*, 11, 94.

11  *L'Etendard*, 29 Jan. 1887; *La Vérité*, 15 Jan. 1888.

12  *Elections provinciales, 1890: le gouvernement Mercier* (Quebec: Belleau et Cie 1890), p. 259.

13  *Le Journal des Trois-Rivières*, 8 July 1886.

14  *Le Courrier de St-Hyacinthe*, 11 Sept. 1886. Also, 25 Oct. 1887; *Le Nouveau Monde*, 13 Oct. 1886; *Le Journal des Trois-Rivières*, 11 Jan., 8 Feb., 29 Mar., 5 Apr., and 6 Sept. 1886.

15  *Le Courrier de St-Hyacinthe*, 24 Aug. 1889. Also 10 Dec. 1887.

16  Accepting the trial as legitimate, convinced of Riel's sanity not only by the testimony but also by the lucidity and rationality of his own final address to the court, English Canadians apparently tended to consider the execution a normal consequence of a valid conviction. If Riel had been English, Scotch, or even Turkish, they felt, the execution would have taken place without any protest. The French Canadians seemed to be demanding that Riel should be saved—that he be made an exception—simply because he was French and Catholic. They seemed to be saying, in fact, that there should be

two different laws in Canada: one for French Canadians and one for everyone else. Such a pretension surely implied a rejection not only of equality but also of any real cohesion in the Canadian confederation.

17  We have seen in our own time how nervous English Canadians can become when the French government makes a Quebec premier commander of the Légion d'Honneur, as it did Mercier.

18  *Quoted in Rumilly*, Histoire de la province de Québec, *v*, 265–6.

19  *L'Electeur*, 12 and 15 Oct. 1887, and following issues. Also, *La Patrie*, 19 Oct.; *L'Union des Cantons de l'Est*, 22 Oct. 1887.

20  Eg., *La Vérité*, 5 and 26 Nov.; *L'Etendard*, 21 and 28 Oct. 1887; *Elections provinciales, 1890*, pp. 260–3.

21  *Le Nouveau Monde*, 26 Oct. 1887.

22  *La Minerve*, 31 Oct. 1887. Also, *La Presse*, 21 Oct.; *Le Pionnier de Sherbrooke*, 27 Oct.; *Le Journal des Trois-Rivières*, 24 Oct.; *Le Courrier de St-Hyacinthe*, 10 Dec. 1887.

"Some people are afraid of seeing a weakening of the federal bonds. It's precisely because we want to see a weakening of those bonds, which are much too strong, that we approve most of the resolutions passed by the conference."[23] But this sort of image could be a source of great danger if it provoked English Canadians into some sort of militant backlash. Bleu leaders, in fact, had feared such a backlash since the beginning of the Riel agitation.[24] It seemed certain to them "that the coalition of French Canadians would provoke a union of English MPS against us. And as we are the minority, the province of Quebec would be crushed by the other provinces.[25] French Canadians must stand up for their rights, of course; but their appeal should be to justice and right, not to race and nationality:

> Is it wise, in an affair like that of the North-West, and in a Parliament like the one at Ottawa, where the other races outnumber us three to one, to raise so heatedly the question of nationality? Clearly not. How can we win at this game if the other races decide to do the same thing?[26]

By the beginning of 1887 it seemed these fears were already being realized. "The agitation, which, thank heaven, has not been universal among us, has nevertheless provoked an opposite agitation in Ontario and Manitoba—an anti-French and anti-Catholic agitation."[27]

The situation became worse after the passing of the Jesuits' Estates Act, for this act, more than anything Mercier had done before, helped convince English Canadians that French-Catholic assertiveness threatened both Canadian unity and the rule of law.[28] The angry agitation against the act could not fail to impress Quebeckers, whatever their party. Conservatives blamed Mercier for having provoked

it by his own aggressiveness: "Mr Mercier stuffed the preamble to the law with Latin and Italian in order to arouse the fanaticism of his Protestant confederates against the Conservative government in Ottawa."[29] Rejecting this blame, Liberals still had to admit that the act had provoked a fearsome reaction against French Catholicism. Ontario's Anglo-Protestant press seemed to have "declared an out-and-out war against Canadian Catholicism over the settlement of the Jesuits question."[30] Everywhere, the "Orange fanatics have been unleashed against the Pope, against the Church, against the religious orders, and against the French Canadians of the province of Quebec."[31]

French Canadians had every reason to be frightened by the "insults against the Catholics and the French Canadians" that were said to fill Ontario newspapers[32]—every reason to be frightened by "this regrettable agitation which seems to threaten the peace and tranquility of the country."[33] Things had gone too far, and everyone could see the need to abandon appeals to race and religion. "Appeals to prejudice and to religious and national fanaticism are always dangerous, because they tend to disrupt the harmony among the different races which inhabit this country…."[34] Confederation's very existence depended on this harmony. "It is only by maintaining peace in the country, by maintaining harmony between the two races, that we can come to full development."[35] All public-spirited men must desire "peace and harmony between the races of this country."[36] Mercierites as well as Bleus could see the need for racial harmony, the need for the present "mistrust between the races,

23  *La Vérité*, 26 Nov. 1887.
24  See Laurier LaPierre, "Politics, Race and Religion in French Canada: Joseph Israel Tarte" (unpublished Ph.D. thesis, Department of History, University of Toronto, 1962), p. 158.
25  *Le Nouveau Monde*, 26 Mar. 1886.
26  *Le Journal des Trois-Rivières*, 20 Dec. 1886.
27  *Electeurs, attention, ne vous laissez pas tromper*, p. 2.
28  See J.R. Miller's book, *Equal Rights: The Jesuits' Estates Act Controversy* (Montreal: McGill-Queen's University Press 1979). Also his article, "D'Alton McCarthy, Equal Rights, and the Origins of the Manitoba School Question," in the *CHR*, LIV, 4 (Dec., 1973).

29  *Le Nouveau Monde*, 5 Aug. 1889. Also, 26 Mar.; *Le Courrier de St-Hyacinthe*, 24 Aug. 1889; *La Presse*, 12 Oct. 1888.
30  *L'Union des Cantons de l'Est*, 23 Feb. 1889.
31  Ibid., 21 Sept. 1889. Also, 26 Jan.; *L'Electeur*, 18 Oct. and 7 Dec. 1889; *Elections provincials*, 1890, p. 306; *Laurier à la tribune*, pp. 499–503, 567; *La Vérité*, 26 Feb. 1887; *Elections provincials de 1892* (Quebec: Belleau et Cie 1892), p. 121.
32  *Le Nouveau Monde*, 26 Mar. 1889. Also, 5 Oct. 1888, and 9 Feb. 1889.
33  *Le Journal des Trois-Rivières*, 13 Jan. 1890. Also, *Le Courrier de St-Hyacinthe*, 18 July and 24 Aug. 1899; *La Presse*, 25 and 26 Oct. 1888, 30 Mar., 1, 20, and 26 Apr., 15 and 17 June 1889; *L'Electeur*, 18 Oct. 1889.
34  *Le Nouveau Monde*, 25 Oct. 1888. Also, 30 May 1887, 9 Feb. and 30 Mar. 1889; *Le Courrier de St-Hyacinthe*, 8 and 24 Aug. 1889.
35  *Le Journal des Trois-Rivières* (quoting Sir John A. Macdonald), 21 Oct. 1889. Also, 20 Dec. 1886; *La Presse*, 29 Mar. 1889.
36  *Le Courrier de St-Hyacinthe*, 5 Sept. 1889. Also, 26 Feb. 1887, and 24 Aug. 1889.

mistrust between the religions" to be replaced by "good will and mutual respect."[37]

In the long run, then, the Riel affair led to fears of racial conflict which French Canada would necessarily lose, and consequently, to a new insistence in French-Canadian rhetoric on the need for the two races, English- and French-Canadian, to live together in peace and harmony, to share Canada between them on friendly and equitable terms.

It did not take long to see just where the English-Canadian backlash was directed. Convinced that Canada could only survive if it had "national unity" and a single Canadianism, that only these could check the disruptive influence of Mercierism, many English Canadians began to press for measures of unification. And since the maintenance of the French language and of Catholic separate school systems seemed to encourage French-Canadian separateness and prevent the growth of a community of feeling among Canadians, these institutions became, more than ever, the objects of criticism. In Ontario, attacks were directed against the use of French in schools and against the Catholic school system.[38] Similar attacks had begun in Manitoba by the summer of 1889.[39] That fall both Manitoba and the North-West Territories moved to drop the French language from their official gazettes.[40] And before the end of the year an appeal reached Quebec from Alberta's Bishop V.-J. Grandin, who complained that Catholic schools were being persecuted in the Territories.[41]

To the Bleus, at least, it was clear why all this was happening. In these attacks on the French language and Catholic schools, "the English majority continues

to give its answer to the useless and senseless provocations of the national movement and the so-called Catholic party!"[42] Having sown the wind of nationalism, French Catholics must now reap a whirlwind of "fanaticism, intolerance, and prejudice."[43] It all showed once again the need to establish peace and harmony between the two races. "The two nationalities should live in perfect harmony, but in order to reach that goal they must not treat each other unjustly."[44] They must realize that both races in Canada "are equal before the constitution and before the law."[45]

The war against French and Catholic institutions was accelerated at the beginning of 1890. In the House of Commons, D'Alton McCarthy presented his bill to end the official use of French in the North-West Territories, since it was "expedient in the interest of the national unity of the Dominion that there should be community of language among the people of Canada."[46] Meanwhile, at Winnipeg, the Manitoba government was preparing legislation of its own to end both the dual school system and official bilingualism.

Quebec's reaction to the McCarthy bill set the tone of debate for the 1890s. It was called "a declaration of war … against the French race."[47] To pass it would be "an infamy" and a "defiance of the French-Canadian nationality"[48]—an acceptance of "domination and intolerance toward the French minority."[49] It would bring about "the complete anglicization of

37  L'Union des Cantons de l'Est, 12 Oct. 1889.

38  Laurier à la tribune, p. 503; L'Union des Cantons de l'Est, 23 Mar. 1889; La Presse, 26 Mar. and 31 Aug.; La Patrie, 28 Aug.; Le Nouveau Monde, 26 July; L'Electeur, 13 Nov.; Le Courrier de St-Hyacinthe, 31 Aug. 1889.

39  Le Courrier de St-Hyacinthe, 8, 13, 15, 20, and 22 Aug., 12 Sept., 24 and 31 Oct. 1889; L'Electeur, 13 Nov.; Le Journal des Trois-Rivières, 5 and 10 Sept. 1889.

40  L'Etendard, 21 Sept. 1889; L'Electeur, 2 Nov.; Le Courrier de St-Hyacinthe, 22 and 24 Oct., 7 and 16 Nov. 1889.

41  Le Journal des Trois-Rivières, 19 Dec. 1889; L'Union des Cantons de l'Est, 28 Dec. Grandin's letter to the bishops of Quebec, dated 20 Nov. 1889, was published in 1891 under the title Un Suprême appel: l'Evêque du Nord-Ouest supplie tous les amis de la justice de l'aider à protéger ses ouailles contre les tyrans d'Ottawa.

42  La Presse, 14 Sept 1889. Also, 14 and 20 Aug., 16 and 19 Sept.; Le Courrier de St-Hyacinthe, 8 Aug. 1889.

43  La Minerve, 5 Mar. 1890.

44  La Presse, 13 Feb. 1890. Also, La Patrie, 14 Feb.

45  L'Electeur, 18 Feb. 1890. These calls for harmony and equitable sharing between the races continued from the late 1880s through the 1890s. See, eg., L'Electeur, 8 and 27 Nov., 7 Dec. 1889; L'Union des Cantons de l'Est, 3 July 1890, 26 Mar. 1891; La Presse, 21 Feb. 1894; Laurier à la tribune, pp. 534, 544, 596, 604; Elections provinciales de 1892, pp. 120–1; Honoré Mercier, L'Avenir du Canada (Montreal: Gebhardt-Berthiaume 1893), p. 88; Honoré Mercier, Reponse de l'hon. Honoré Mercier au pamphlet de l'Association des "Equal Rights" contre la majorité des habitants de la Province de Québec (Quebec 1890).

46  Quoted in numerous common books, eg., O.D. Skelton, Life and Letters of Sir Wilfrid Laurier (2 vols.; Toronto: McClelland and Stewart 1965), I, 129. For reports on the presentation of the bill and progress of the debate, see, eg., Le Courrier de St-Hyacinthe, 25 Jan., 1, 20, and 22 Feb. 1890; Le Journal des Trois-Rivières, 27 Jan., 17, 20, and 27 Feb., 3 Mar.; L'Electeur, 13 and 15 Feb.; La Minerve, 22 Feb.; Le Nouveau Monde, 18 Feb.; La Presse, 14, 15, and 19 Feb. 1890.

47  Laurier à la tribune, p. 580.

48  La Presse, 13 Feb. 1890, and La Patrie, 14 Feb.

49  L'Electeur, 18 Feb. 1890. Also, 20 and 21 Feb.

the North-West … the complete exclusion from it of French-Canadian and Catholic influence."[50] And that was only the beginning. "The abolition of French in the territories … is only the prelude to the general abolition throughout the dominion, not only of the official use of French, but also of the separate school system."[51]

Such designs must not come to fruition. It was not by eliminating one of the races in Canada that you could bring about unity between them,[52] especially when this was done in opposition to "the sense of equity of the 1877 Parliament,"[53] when it meant that Parliament would be vilely taking back what it had given already (imagine it doing that with homesteads!)[54] and when it meant taking away "a right which is solemnly established by law."[55] French was secured in the territories both by federal law and by the terms upon which the North-West agreed to enter Confederation in the first place—in other words, by "the fundamental law of that vast country."[56] To abolish it, therefore, would be "to admit that the most solemn guarantees, the most sacred rights of the minority are at the mercy of the first political intriguer who takes it into his head to remake the constitution according to his own whim…." It would be to treat French Canadians as a people without rights. "Is there a caste of conquerors here and a caste of conquered slaves? Are we not all British subjects in the same right?"[57]

Certain characteristics of the above comments are to be noted. First, there seems to be, among French Quebeckers, greater concern for and closer identification with the people of the North-West than we have seen in the past. Second, there is a much greater readiness than in the past to see French Catholic rights as constitutionally guaranteed and irrevocable.

In the past, embattled minorities had been Acadians or Métis—not exactly French Canadians—but this time there could be no doubt that the targets of the attacks were "our French-Canadian compatriots,"[58] the "French Canadians of Manitoba,"[59] and even "our own people"[60] or "us."[61] At stake in the West were "our institutions, our schools, our language."[62] Not surprisingly, therefore, the western language and schools questions were debated more heatedly and more persistently than any previous minority question.

Moreover, while French Quebeckers had not even imagined there could be constitutional rights when the West was annexed, and had accepted readily enough that the constitution did not protect Catholic schools in the Maritimes,[63] they did not hesitate at all in 1890 to assert that actions taken against the French language and Catholic schools in the West were illegal or unconstitutional. Language and school rights were "conferred by the constitution."[64] To take them away was to "violate the law and the constitution,"[65] and to maintain them was to defend the "integrity of the constitution."[66] Accordingly, there was a spontaneous desire and expectation that Ottawa should "disallow the iniquitous

50  *L'Etendard*, 11 Feb. 1890. Also, 20 Feb.
51  *L'Electeur*, 17 Feb. 1890. Also, *La Patrie*, 27 Jan.; *Laurier à la tribune*, pp. 585–6; *L'Etendard*, 26 Feb. 1890.
52  *Laurier à la tribune*, p. 589. It is interesting to note that this debate saw not only the rejection of a single Canadianism but also the refutation of one of the most common arguments against bilingualism: its expense. When McCarthy argued that it was too costly to translate documents into French, Sir Hector Langevin offered to pay the whole cost of translation for the North-West Territories out of his own pocket. See *La Minerve*, 19 Feb. 1890, and Hector Langevin, *Speech on the French Language in the North-West*, in the House of Commons, 13 Feb. 1890 (n.p., n.d.).
53  *L'Etendard*, 11 Feb. 1890.
54  *Le Journal des Trois-Rivières*, 10 Feb. 1890.
55  *La Minerve*, 16 Feb. 1890.
56  Ibid., 16 Feb. 1890.
57  *La Patrie*, 27 Jan. 1890. The need for harmony between two races of loyal British subjects was a natural theme for politicians who had to try to appeal to both. See, e.g., Laurier's speech in *Laurier à la tribune*, Langevin's *Speech on the French Language in the North-West* and J.A. Chapleau's *Speech on the French Language in the North-West* (Ottawa: Brown, Chamberlain 1890).

58  *L'Electeur*, 13 June 1890. Also, 20 Feb.; *La Patrie*, 8 Apr.; *L'Union des Cantons de l'Est*, 17 July 1890, 15 Sept. 1892, 16 Feb. 1893, 15 Oct. 1896; *Le Courrier de St-Hyacinthe*, 29 Aug. 1889, and 17 July 1890; *La Presse*, 22 June 1896.
59  *Le Courrier de St-Hyacinthe*, 12 Sept. 1889. Also, *La Presse*, 27 Aug.
60  *L'Etendard*, 19 Aug. 1889. Also, 23 Aug. 1892, *Le Courrier de St-Hyacinthe*, 19 Oct. 1895.
61  *La Minerve*, 28 Jan. 1890; *Le Courrier de St-Hyacinthe*, 12 Nov. 1896.
62  *La Minerve*, 5 Apr. 1890 (emphasis added).
63  See *Le Courrier de St-Hyacinthe* as late as 20 Feb. 1896.
64  *La Presse*, 27 Aug. 1889. Also, 23 Aug.
65  *L'Electeur*, 4 Aug. 1892. Also, 3 Aug. 1892, 6 Mar. 1893.
66  *La Presse*, 19 Sept. 1889. Also, 17 Aug.; *Le Courrier du Canada*, 4 Sept.; *Le Courrier de St-Hyacinthe*, 12 Sept. and 24 Oct. 1889, 17 and 22 July 1890; *Le Journal des Trois-Rivières*, 5 and 10 Sept. 1889, and 2 Oct. 1890; *La Minerve*, 28 Jan. and 20 Feb. 1890; *L'Etendard*, 2 Apr. 1890, and 30 Aug. 1892; *Le Nouveau Monde*, 9 Oct. 1888, 10 and 23 Aug. 1889, and 29 Oct. 1891; *La Patrie*, 11 Sept. 1889, 27 Jan. and 21 Feb. 1890; *L'Union des Cantons de l'Est*, 9 Apr. 1891; A.-A. Taché, *Ecoles séparées: partie des négociations à Ottawa en 1870* (n.p., 1890), pp. 7–8.

laws which deprive Manitoba's French Canadians and Catholics of their constitutional rights."[67] Disallowance was, for the federal government, "a responsibility which the constitution imposes upon it."[68]

The readiness of Quebeckers in the 1890s to believe that the constitution guaranteed French language and Catholic school rights in Manitoba and the North-West Territories can be explained partly by the twenty years of history we have followed to this point. The increasing anxiety since 1869 to protect the Métis in their difficulties had ... convinced French Quebeckers that they had something important at stake in the West—had committed them firmly to French Catholicism there. And this emotional commitment was the more easily translated into a belief in constitutional rights because of the concern for peace and harmony between the races—yes, and even for Canadian unity—which had developed within the past few years. It might be desirable for Canada to form a single great nation, allowed L'Electeur in a generous moment, "but that does not mean that this nation must not speak any other language than English." On the contrary, unity could only be based on duality, on a recognition that both races "are equal before the constitution and before the law."[69]

But certainty about the immutability of western language and school rights was also based on the specific circumstances in which Manitoba and the North-West Territories had been established. The constitution of Manitoba, for example, was contained in a federal act, the Manitoba Act of 1870, which had been confirmed by the imperial British North America Act of 1871. Manitoba, therefore, was incompetent to amend it. "It is not in the power of the Manitoba legislature to abolish the use of the French language and separate schools. The law which governs these matters is under the jurisdiction of the parliament at Ottawa."[70]

But behind the Manitoba Act had been a more fundamental commitment: the agreement between the Canadian government and the Red River authorities, which had been the basis of the West's agreement to join Canada in the first place. This was an argument put forward repeatedly by Archbishop Taché. He maintained that Catholic school rights in Manitoba "are not only the result of an act passed in Parliament, but are also part of an arrangement or treaty concluded between the Dominion of Canada and the inhabitants of Red River before the admission of our province into the confederation."[71] In a number of articles and pamphlets, the archbishop described again and again the negotiations between the Red River delegates and the federal ministers, the insistence of imperial authorities that the Red River demands be met, and the inclusion of school and language rights among the conditions which Red River required to be satisfied before it would agree to Confederation.[72] These arguments did not fail to impress Quebeckers. Manitoba's Catholic schools and French language, they maintained, had been absolutely protected in the new province's constitution. "It was on these conditions that the province of Manitoba was admitted into the Canadian confederation."[73]

Belief in the constitutional protection of French and Catholic rights in the West could only be

67  L'Union des Cantons de l'Est, 17 July 1890. Also 9 Apr. 1891.

68  Ibid., 16 Feb. 1893. Also, L'Etendard, 8 Apr. 1890, and 30 Aug. 1892; Le Courrier de St-Hyacinthe, 26 Feb. 1891; L'Electeur, 3 Feb. 1891, and 4 Aug. 1892; Le Journal des Trois-Rivières, 2 Aug. 1890, and 16 Feb. 1891.

69  L'Electeur, 18 Feb. 1890. Also, Le Journal des Trois-Rivières, 23 Dec. 1892.

70  Le Courrier de St-Hyacinthe, 13 Aug. 1889. Also, L'Etendard, 13 Aug. 1889 and 7 Jan. 1890; La Minerve, 16 Feb. 1890; La Patrie, 14 Feb. 1890.

71  In L'Etendard, 7 Jan. 1890.

72  Ibid. Also, Ecoles séparées, pp. 1–4, 7; Mémoire de Monseigneur Taché sur la question des écoles en réponse au rapport du comité de l'honorable Conseil Privé du Canada (Montreal: Beauchemin et Fils 1894), pp. 25, 32, 33; Une Page de l'histoire des écoles de Manitoba (Montreal: Beauchemin et Fils 1894), 6–7, 27–35.

73  La Revue Canadienne, XXVII (1892), p. 465. Also, Le Courrier de St-Hyacinthe, 31 Jan. 1895, and 20 June 1896; L'Electeur, 6 Mar. 1893; L'Etendard, 2 Apr. 1890; Le Journal des Trois-Rivières, 23 Dec. 1892; La Minerve, 16 Feb. 1890; Le Nouveau Monde, 7 Mar. 1890. The emphasis on the 1870 negotiations as the guarantee of French and Catholic rights sometimes led to a certain reinterpretation of the events of 1869–70, in which the resistance was no longer seen as the defence of the old buffalo-based way of life against a foreign invasion of settlement, but as a French-Catholic defence against an Anglo-Protestant threat. Eg., Taché, Une Page de l'histoire, pp. 18–19. It should be noted, as well, that all the arguments mentioned above with regard to the Manitoba schools question were also applied through the 1890s to the language and schools question in the territories. Eg., La Presse, 21 Feb. 1894; L'Electeur, 12 Jan. and 20 Mar.; La Minerve, 8 Feb. 1894; La Revue Canadienne, XXX (1894), pp. 118, 163; L'Union des Cantons de l'Est, 16 Feb. 1893, and 22 Mar. 1894; Taché, Memoire, pp. 25–35, 41.

strengthened by the court cases fought over them. In 1890–1 Archbishop Taché had reluctantly agreed not to press for disallowance of the Manitoba school law, having been persuaded by Quebec leaders that the courts would declare it unconstitutional, or that, if they did not, Ottawa would act to remedy the situation.[74] This last promise, made by a leading federal minister, J.A. Chapleau, implied Ottawa's acknowledgement that the Manitoba Catholics had indeed been deprived of something to which they were legally entitled. Consequently, when the Judicial Committee of the imperial Privy Council ruled in 1892 that the Manitoba school law was constitutionally valid, French Canadians were not so much weakened in their conviction as angered by the judgement:

> We consider it an injustice toward Roman Catholics, for it is obvious that the aim of the legislators who passed the Manitoba Act (which was afterwards sanctioned by an imperial statute) was to grant separate schools to the Catholics. This is a basic principle of Canadian legislation: it's what we have in Ontario and Quebec, and the federal parliament up till now has also declared itself favourable to the maintenance of separate schools in the North-West.[75]

It was hard to see, therefore, how the Privy Council could deliver so wrong-headed a judgement[76]—a judgement which set at naught all "those so-called guarantees which the fathers of Confederation thought to have assured to the minorities,"[77] and which would provoke a new round of "the most terrible sort of strife, based on nationality, language, and religion."[78] Nevertheless, rights were rights, and if the courts would not restore them, Ottawa must do so.[79] This contention was the subject of a second Privy Council judgement in early 1895. This time the Council found that Manitoba Catholics did have a legitimate complaint and that the federal government did have the

power to remedy it—though it did not say what action, if any, Ottawa had to take.[80]

Despite their lordships' warning that the "particular course to be pursued must be determined by the authorities to whom it has been committed by the statute"[81]—that is, by the federal government—French-Canadian commentators took the judgement as a definite confirmation that the constitution guaranteed Catholic separate schools in Manitoba. "The imperial privy council declares that the rights of the Catholics have been ignored and trampled upon, and that they must be restored."[82] Ottawa must act "to carry out Her Majesty's judgement, rendered by the Sovereign's Judicial Council." This did not involve any political decision by the federal government. "It is only the High-Sheriff of the Queen, charged with a writ of execution of which it does not have the right to change the terms."[83] It was the constitution that compelled action, as interpreted by "the highest court in the empire."[84] In 1896, when the Quebec bishops issued a pastoral letter to guide voters on the school question, they claimed that what they wanted was to give "the Catholic minority of Manitoba the school rights which have been recognized by the Honourable Privy Council of Great Britain."[85] And when the federal government produced first an order-in-council and then remedial legislation on this subject, its aim, according to its supporters, was, in compliance with the Privy Council's instructions, to "impose upon [Manitoba] the respect of the constitution and of the minority's rights."[86]

74  On this see Paul Crunican, *Priests and Politicians: Manitoba Schools and the Election of 1896* (Toronto and Buffalo: University of Toronto Press 1974), pp. 18–33.
75  *L'Union des Cantons de l'Est*, 4 Aug. 1892.
76  *Le Journal des Trois-Rivières*, 20 Dec. 1892. Also, 13 Dec.
77  *L'Electeur*, 4 Aug. 1892.
78  *L'Etendard*, 23 Aug. 1892.
79  *La Presse*, 3 Aug. 1892; *L'Electeur*, 3 Aug.
80  *Le Nouveau Monde*, 30 Jan. 1895; *L'Electeur*, 30 Jan.
81  The decision is most easily accessible in Lovell Clark, ed., *The Manitoba School Question: Majority Rule or Minority Rights* (Toronto: Copp Clark 1968), pp. 116–7. "It is not for this tribunal," said the judgement, "to intimate the precise steps to be taken." And Lord Watson added in a separate comment that the federal authorities "may legislate or not as they think fit." (Quoted in Crunican, *Priests and Politicians*, p. 43.)
82  *La Minerve*, 21 June 1895.
83  *La Presse*, 4 Mar. 1895. Also, *La Minerve*, 7 Jan.
84  *Le Courrier de St-Hyacinthe*, 23 Mar. 1895. Also, 20 Feb. 1896.
85  Published in *Le Courrier de St-Hyacinthe*, 19 May 1896; *L'Electeur*, 18 May; *Le Nouveau Monde*, 18 May; *La Patrie*, 18 May; *L'Union des Cantons d l'Est*, 21 May; etc.
86  *Le Nouveau Monde*, 22 Mar. 1895. Also, *Le Courrier de St-Hyacinthe*, 31 Jan. and 2 Feb. 1895, 5 Mar. and 7 May 1896; *La Minerve*, 8 Jan. 1896; P. Bernard, *Un Manifeste libéral* (Quebec: Brousseau 1896), pp. 28–9, 33.

By 1896, then, French Quebeckers had acquired, first, an emotional concern about the treatment of the minorities; second, a desire for harmony and mutual respect between English and French; and third, a belief in "constitutional" guarantees for minority language and school rights, at least in the West. It was easy to go from these to generalizations about the nature of Confederation.[87] Confederation, it now began to be asserted, had been meant to establish "perfect equality of the two races before the law."[88] The very "stability of the constitution" depended on "the peace and harmony which must exist between the two great races which form the Canadian confederation."[89] But this required the preservation of the very rights which were in dispute during the 1890s:

> The education of youth, in which religion and language occupy so large a place, was deliberately put out of reach of any attack, and never would Confederation have been accepted, nor will it ever be consolidated in a durable way, if this spirit of mutual esteem and tolerance ceases to prevail in all levels and all parts of the edifice.[90]

In short, bilingualism—or biculturalism—was the very basis, the *sine qua non,* of Confederation. It was not just a question of the Manitoba Act, but of "a pact made in 1867 to guarantee equal rights to all in matters of education."[91] Without such a guarantee, "it is certain that Confederation would never have been adopted."[92] Aside from separate schools, it had been "the intention of the original federal pact to admit the official use of the two languages in each and every province of the confederation."[93]

The novelty of this conception is evident. In 1867 French Quebeckers had seen their province alone as the home of the French-Canadian nationality, and looked to Confederation to separate it as much as possible from the others. But many were now coming to accept some notion of a Canadian nation based on equality between two races, each having guaranteed rights in *all* provinces. This view emerged from events in the intervening decades. It was only *after* French Quebeckers had discovered and become concerned about the French-Catholic minorities, only *after* they had tried to help the Métis, only *after* the Riel affair, the racial agitation of the late 1880s, and the controversies of the 1890s—only *after* all this that the bilingual theory of Confederation could emerge. Only then could an Henri Bourassa appear on the scene.

More than anyone before him, Bourassa expressed the new ideas clearly, coherently, and systematically. To the English-Canadian nationalism of the time, his theory replied that it was possible for English and French Canadians to work together, but not on the basis of cultural unity. Confederation must be seen as an agreement between two nations—English and French Canada—to live together on terms of equality. The British North America Act, claimed Bourassa, was only the official sanctioning of this agreement. Its aim was to build a Canada

> that would be French and English in each of its parts as well as in its whole—not French and English in the sense of some bastard fusion of the two races, in which they would lose their distinctive qualities and characteristics, but a fruitful alliance of the two races, each one remaining distinctly itself, but finding within the Canadian confederation enough room and liberty to live together side by side.[94]

Perhaps the BNA Act did not spell this out in so many words; but after all, only scribes and pharisees split hairs about the wording of texts. What counted was

---

87  It will be apparent that expressions like "guaranteed by the constitution" or "constitutional guarantees" were used in vague and varied ways in these discussions of the 1890s. It was precisely this vagueness about what "the constitution" was and what it contained that permitted people to claim it guaranteed minority rights or perfect equality between English and French Canadians, and thus permitted the emergence of the bilingual theory of Confederation.

88  *La Patrie,* 27 Jan. 1890.

89  *Le Courrier de St-Hyacinthe,* 5 Mar. 1896.

90  *La Presse,* 21 Feb. 1894. Also, 3 Aug. 1892; *L'Electeur,* 13 June 1890 and 7 Mar. 1893; *L'Etendard,* 30 Aug. 1892; *Le Nouveau Monde,* 24 Feb. 1896; *La Revue Canadienne,* XXVIII (1892), p. 471; *L'Union des Cantons de l'Est,* 4 Aug. 1892, 25 July and 22 Aug. 1895; Taché, *Mémoire,* p. 35; Mercier, *Avenir du Canada,* p. 26.

91  *Le Nouveau Monde,* 7 Mar. 1893.

92  *La Revue Canadienne,* XXVIII (1892), pp. 464–5.

93  *La Patrie,* 21 Feb. 1890. It was unusual for so strong a statement to be made at such an early date. Such an assertion would have been more usual later in the decade. See also *L'Electeur,* 7 Mar. 1893; *Le Nouveau Monde,* 22 Feb. and 16 Apr. 1896.

94  Henri Bourassa, *Pour la justice* (Montreal 1912), p. 12.

the "spirit of Confederation," and it was clear that according to that spirit, French Canadians had a right to their language, schools, and religion "throughout the entire confederation."[95]

These ideas became increasingly current among Bourassa's contemporaries. The newspaper, *Le Nationaliste*, with which he was associated, proclaimed that the "entire edifice of the Canadian confederation rests on the equality of the races,"[96] on the "duality of origins, language, and religion of the Canadian people."[97] Even school textbooks were influenced by this idea. Thus, a 1911 geography text:

> By its political constitution, as Mr Henri Bourassa recently said, by its ethnic composition, and by natural law, Canada is an Anglo-French confederation, the product of the fruitful union of two great and noble races. It must remain, under the protection of the British Crown, the heritage of a bilingual people.[98]

In the light of such conceptions, Laurier's failure in 1905 to secure adequate protection for French language and Catholic schools in the new provinces of Saskatchewan and Alberta could only seem the violation of a contract "which was supposed to ensure the permanence of their separate school system for our compatriots in Ontario, New Brunswick, and the North-West Territories."[99] Similarly, the Ontario Department of Education's Regulation 17, which, in 1912, virtually ended the use of French in Ontario schools, also seemed to betray a constitution which had guaranteed that French Canadians should be "at home in Ontario as everywhere else in Canada."[100]

The appearance of the bilingual theory of Confederation did not, however, mean the abandonment of older conceptions. Neither Bourassa nor any other French Quebecker was prepared to forget about provincial autonomy, or to deny that, whatever rights might be claimed elsewhere, Quebec would always be the homeland in a most particular sense. Only in Quebec, after all—that province which Bourassa described as the "particular inheritance of French Canada"[101]—were French Canadians a majority. Only there could they control the government; only there were they in a position to build a society reflecting their own distinctive national characteristics and aspirations.

Quebec, therefore, always continued to be referred to as the French Canadians' special country. Even the editors of *Le Nationaliste* referred to it as "the French Province of the Dominion."[102] Poets still described the banks of "the Great River" as "our country,"[103] and pamphleteers still advised their compatriots to "remain in our dear province, which is fertile enough to support all its children."[104] Those who left Quebec, even for a province as near as Ontario, might wish for cultural privileges. "But as they have committed themselves to Ontario, the best thing for them to do is to face their situation bravely and work vigorously and persistently for the improvement of their lot."[105] It was still population—the majority in each province—that must ultimately determine cultural rights. That was why Wilfrid Laurier rejected a proposal in the Commons in 1905 to make French official in the new provinces of Saskatchewan and Alberta:

> By virtue of what principle or what law would you give the French population of the North-West Territories the privilege of permanently establishing its language in the constitution? ...
>
> My answer to this question is that I do not recognize any right of parliament to impose the French language on the new provinces.[106]

95  Ibid., pp. 31, 33. Also, Henri Bourassa, *Le Patriotisme canadien-français: ce qu'il est, ce qu'il doit être* (Montreal: Revue Canadienne 1902), p. 8.
96  *Le Nationaliste* (Montreal), 12 Mar. 1905.
97  Ibid., 3 Apr. 1904.
98  Abbé Adélard Desrosiers and Abbé Fournet, *La Race française en Amérique* (Montreal: Beauchemin 1911), p. x.
99  *La Revue Canadienne*, LVII (1909), p. 133. Also, *Le Nationaliste*, 12 Mar. and 23 Apr. 1905.
100  Jules Tremblay, *Le Français en Ontario* (Montreal: Nault 1913), p. 33. Also, p. 23-4, 25-8; *La Revue Canadienne*, LXIII (1912), pp. 442-4; Charles Langelier, *Etude historique: la Confédération, sa genèse, son établissement* (Quebec: Le Soleil 1916), p. 43.
101  Bourassa, *Le Patriotisme canadien-française*, p. 3.
102  *Le Nationaliste*, 16 Oct. 1904.
103  Albert Ferland in *La Revue Canadienne*, LVII (1909), p. 477.
104  Denys Lanctot, *Avenir des Canadiens-Français* (Montreal 1902), p. 11.
105  *La Minerve*, 24 Oct. 1887.
106  *La Langue française dans l'Alberta et la Saskatchewan* (n.p., n.d.), p. 13. Just as Laurier argued that the majority in the new provinces was entitled to decide on language matters, so French

Even *Le Nationaliste* seemed at least partly to accept this, for its first criticism of the 1905 autonomy bills was not concerned with language or school rights but with the boundaries of the new provinces. Given the distributions of the French and English populations, an east-west boundary would have created "one English province and one largely French province."[107] The actual north-south line divided the French-Catholic group and left it weak in both the new provinces. This "unnatural and anti-French-Canadian geographic division … destroys forever the French influence in Saskatchewan."[108]

Control of provinces was essential because provinces were still seen as the basis of the Canadian edifice. One had only to recollect the way in which the régime had been founded:

Representatives of *four* provinces—Upper Canada, Lower Canada, Nova Scotia, and New Brunswick—met in a convention at Quebec to discuss a plan for federation. *Each one* had certain rights and privileges which had been granted to it by the metropolis, and, within the limits of its jurisdiction, and as long as these rights are not withdrawn, each one was and still remains sovereign.[109]

The provinces were thus "the constituent power" of the confederation,[110] and their autonomy remained the basis of the whole system. This was as necessary for Quebec now as in 1864—and for the same reasons. Thus, a strong central government could still be seen as "the common enemy."[111]

Indeed, the feeling for Quebec's autonomy appeared even to strengthen toward the end of the century, for some writers now began to refer to separatism no longer just as a vague dream but as something French Canadians ought actively to prepare themselves for. "The province of Quebec belongs to us French Canadians; this is what we must love, develop, strengthen, and prepare for independence."[112] Yes, it was an "imperious duty to prepare for the complete and definitive independence of French Canada, for therein, and only therein, is our salvation."[113] This was not only French Canada's duty; it had always been her inevitable destiny and her heart's innermost desire.[114]

We can see, therefore, a persistence of traditional attitudes toward Confederation and provincial autonomy at the end of the nineteenth and beginning of the twentieth century. Provincial affairs still usually predominated in the press—even (for example) during the debate on the 1890 McCarthy bill and at a time when the Manitoba school and language laws were being passed. Federal MPS were still referred to not as representatives of their constituencies but as delegates of their provinces or of the cultural or national groups which the provinces embodied. Thus, there were men who "represent the French and the Catholics in the cabinet"—this referring to the Quebec ministers at Ottawa.[115] This was a notion which the Liberals naturally exploited after Laurier became their federal leader: "for our province and our race, he has a particular quality" because of "the honour he reflects upon them…."[116]

This provincial approach to things could even be seen in the discussion of minority affairs. Thus, loss of rights by French-Catholic minorities was still particularly hard to bear because Quebec was obliged to be so liberal with its Anglo-Protestants. Quebeckers, commented one paper with bitter irony, "continually pamper the English minority of Quebec with

Quebeckers too appealed to their demographic position to justify their contention that Quebec was a French-Canadian country. Eg., *Laurier à la tribune*, pp. 614–16; *L'Union des Cantons de l'Est*, 30 Mar. 1889, and 4 Aug. 1892; Honoré Mercier, *Réponse au pamphlet de l'Association des "Equal Rights,"* pp. 59–60, 84; L.-O. David, *Le Clergé canadien: sa mission, son œuvre* (Montreal 1896), p. 40; *Canada: la province de Québec, pays de langue française* (Quebec 1918), pp. 5, 10, 11, 13; *La Vérité*, 10 Sept. 1887, 15 Jan. 1888.
107 *Le Nationaliste*, 5 Feb. 1905.
108 Ibid., 26 Feb. 1905.
109 *L'Etendard*, 22 Oct. 1887. Also, 29 Sept. 1887; *La Presse*, 21 Feb. 1894; *La Vérité*, 16 Apr. 1892; *Canada: la province de Québec*, pp. 15–16.
110 *L'Electeur*, 2 Feb. 1895.
111 *La Revue Canadienne*, XXIV (1888), p. 271. Ottawa was not only the common enemy of Quebec's own political parties; it was the common enemy of the provinces, as shown by Manitoba's defence of provincial rights in the matter of railroads. See pp. 198, 270.
112 *La Presse*, 20 Mar. 1894.
113 *La Revue Canadienne*, LVII (1909), pp. 137–8.
114 Jules-Paul Tardivel, *Pour la patrie* (Montreal: Cadieux et Derome 1895), pp. 7–8, 9–10, 150; Denys Lanctot, *Avenir des Canadiens-Français*, pp. 9–10, 13. The increasing prominence of separatism was reflected in the pains which someone like Laurier took to repudiate it. (Eg., *Laurier à la tribune*, pp. 546–7.)
115 *L'Electeur*, 26 Mar. 1895.
116 Ibid., 6 Feb 1891. Also, *L'Union des Cantons de l'Est*, 26 Mar. 1891.

righteous generosity and delicate attentions."[117] After all, what Manitoba Catholics wanted was what "the Protestants have here even though they're only a minority in the province of Quebec."[118] Were the English, then, to "keep for themselves alone the guarantees they have obtained?"[119] It was certain that if Quebec were to abolish its minority's language and schools as Manitoba had done, Ottawa would disallow the act in an instant.[120]

The capacity of the western language and school questions to provoke concern about Quebec's own identity can also be seen in the reappearance of the "domino theory".… This is particularly apparent in the case of McCarthy's 1890 language bill. The preamble, with its contention that unilingualism was necessary for the sake of national unity, was "a declaration of war against the French language not only in the North-West but in the whole dominion."[121] This was undoubtedly why Bleu and Rouge leaders alike could accept Sir John Thompson's amendment, which dropped the threatening preamble but authorized the territorial council, after holding elections, to end the use of French in its own proceedings and records.[122] But fear of the domino effect was provoked throughout the decade. Manitoba's abolition of Catholic schools would soon be copied by other provinces, it was feared, after which "they'll descend upon Quebec to force a legislative union on us, and then the name of Mr McCarthy will go on to posterity while that of the French race goes down to oblivion."[123] The rise of the Protestant Protective Association in Ontario showed that the wave of intolerance was moving eastward

from Manitoba. "Isn't it obvious that the current is rushing straight toward the province of Quebec?"[124]

Like the western minority problem, western railroads and development were also still seen in a provincial light: they were advantageous for the commerce they brought to Quebec ports—"a continual tribute which will increase with the whole commerce of the North-West."[125] As for settlement, it was still, as it always had been, the westerners themselves who took the initiatives;[126] and their appeals became increasingly desperate as Quebec continued not to respond. We do not wish to depopulate Quebec, wrote Bishop Grandin in his *Ultimate Appeal,* by taking away those who are not already planning to emigrate to the United States; "but without weakening your province, at least give us the crumbs from your table."[127] Some Quebeckers were willing at least to go this far; but all the concern about western school rights did not change old priorities when it came to migration:

> The best thing for a French Canadian is to stay in his own country, where there is still so much good land covered with rich forest and only awaiting men of stout heart and good will to exploit it. As for those who are forced by hard circumstances to leave the province of Quebec, it is to Manitoba that they ought to turn.[128]

117 *Le Nouveau Monde,* 22 Aug. 1889.
118 *La Presse,* 3 Aug. 1894. See also 21 Feb. 1894; *La Revue Canadienne,* XXX (1894), p. 174; Tremblay, *Français en Ontario,* p. 30.
119 *L'Union des Cantons de l'Est,* 16 Mar. 1893. Also, 23 Mar. 1889, 22 Mar. 1894; *L'Electeur,* 27 Nov. 1889; *La Minerve,* 25 Feb. 1890; *Laurier à la tribune,* p. 567.
120 *L'Electeur,* 7 Mar. 1893. Also, 7 Dec. 1889; *Le Courrier de St-Hyacinthe,* 28 Sept. 1889; *La Minerve,* 5 Apr. 1890; Taché, *Mémoire,* p. 39; Mercier, *Réponse au pamphlet,* especially pp. 59–60.
121 *La Minerve,* 20 Feb. 1890. Also, *L'Electeur,* 17, 18, and 20 Feb.; *Le Journal des Trois-Rivières,* 27 Jan.; *La Patrie,* 27 Jan. and 21 Feb. 1890; *Laurier à la tribune,* p. 614.
122 *Laurier à la tribune,* pp. 614–16; *La Minerve,* 20 Feb. 1890; *L'Electeur,* 25 Feb.; *Le Nouveau Monde,* 24 Feb.; *La Presse,* 21 and 22 Feb.; *Le Courrier de St-Hyacinthe,* 4 Mar. 1890.
123 *L'Electeaur,* 3 Aug. 1892.

124 Ibid., 23 Jan. 1894. Also, 13 Nov. 1889, 6 Mar. 1893, and 15 Jan. 1894; *La Presse,* 13 and 14 Sept. 1889; *Le Nouveau Monde,* 24 Feb. 1896; *La Revue Canadienne,* LVII (1909), p. 135.
125 Honoré Beaugrand, *De Montréal à Victoria par le transcontinental canadien* (Montreal 1887), pp. 5–6. Also, *Le Canadien,* 8 Feb. 1889; *L'Electeur,* 10 Jan. 1887; *La Presse,* 9 Mar. 1888; *Elections de 1887: la vraie question,* p. 21.
126 Eg., note how the matter was raised in *Le Courrier de St-Hyacinthe,* 4 July 1889; *Le Journal des Trois-Rivières,* 19 Dec. 1889; *L'Union des Cantons de l'Est,* 8 Mar. 1890. Public meetings continued to be organized by men sent from St Boniface for the purpose (eg., Abbé Beaudry, referred to in the *Union des Cantons de l'Est,* 16 Mar. 1889, or in *Le Courrier de St-Hyacinthe,* 11 June 1889). Again, in this post-Riel period, brochures encouraging western settlement continued to be the work of westerners: eg., M.J. Blais, *Le Manitoba* (Ottawa: Imprimerie de l'Etat 1898), T.A. Bernier, *Le Manitoba: champ d'immigration;* Georges Dugas, *Manitoba et ses avantages pour l'agriculture* (n.p., n.d.); Albert Lacombe, *Un Nouveau champ de colonisation: la vallée de la Saskatchewan;* Morin, *Le Nord-Ouest canadien et ses ressources agricoles;* Morin, *La Terre promise aux Canadiens-Français: le Nord-Ouest canadien.*
127 Grandin, *Suprême appel,* p. 4; *Le Journal des Trois-Rivières,* 19 Dec. 1889.
128 Bishop Laflèche, in the *Union des Cantons de l'Est,* 16 Mar. 1889. For the same set of priorities see *Le Courrier de St-Hyacinthe,* 11

Many, however, were not even willing to go this far. To them, the arrival in Manitoba of French Canadians with enough capital to establish themselves meant "just so much capital and population lost to our province."[129] It was more satisfying to see English Quebeckers make the move—or Ontarians, who might depopulate their own province to Quebec's advantage.[130]

On the other hand, there does seem to be in this period—indeed, during all the 1880s and 1890s—an increasing acceptance of settlement in the United States and confidence in the possibility of French-Canadian national survival there. Though some articles (often inspired by Manitoba colonizers) still complained of unemployment, poverty, and assimilation in the States,[131] many more spoke of prosperity,[132] the successes of French Canadians in American public life,[133] and the manifestations of national vitality among the Franco-Americans. They had their own schools,[134] continued to speak French,[135] and worked energetically to organize conventions and societies to promote their national interests.[136] Living under a

free and tolerant constitution,[137] and reinforced continually by emigration from Canada, they appeared destined to take over and gallicize considerable portions of the United States. Already New England was being transformed into a New France. "The Yankees are all headed toward the West; French Canadians are replacing them."[138]

This growing predominance of French Canadians in the northeastern United States represented, in effect, an expansion of Quebec itself. Unlike those who went to Manitoba, separating themselves by a thousand miles from their native province, emigrants to New England remained next door, as it were, in geographical contact with Quebec. Their movement was "simply the normal extension of a people which is little by little pushing its advance guard toward the south."[139] Like the movement of French Quebeckers into those parts of Ontario and New Brunswick which bordered on Quebec, this expansion into contiguous parts of the U.S. enabled French Canadians to remain "united on a consolidated territory" rather than being "dispersed among heterogeneous groups and assimilated to the other races."[140] In a sense, Quebec was being enlarged to include the surrounding areas; "the East of America" was becoming a larger French-Canadian homeland.[141] This would soon be true even in a political sense, "for within twenty years [the Franco-Americans] will have become our compatriots once more...." Annexation might be a preliminary step, but not the last. For "once the United States have engulfed the whole of North America, then their dismemberment will begin, and from that ephemeral confederation will be born a number of independent republics, of which not the least will be a New France."[142] French Canadians would

June 1889, 6 May 1890, 24 Jan. 1891, and 28 Feb. 1895; *Le Canadien*, 14 Mar. 1889; *La Minerve*, 6 Oct. 1886; *La Revue Canadienne*, xxiv (1888), p. 406; C.-E. Rouleau, *L'Emigration: ses principales causes* (Quebec: Brousseau 1896), p. 146.

129 *L'Union des Cantons de l'Est*, 30 Mar. 1889. See also Louis Beaubien, *Discours: agriculture et colonisation* (Montreal: Senécal et Fils 1894), p. 18.

130 *Le Canadien*, 23 Feb. 1889. One does, however, begin to see some expressions of regret that more had not been done in the past to settle French Canadians in the West, since a more numerous community might not have had to endure a Riel affair or loss of language and school rights. Eg., *Le Nouveau Monde*, 22 Aug. 1889; *La Minerve*, 5 Apr. 1890; *Le Courrier de St-Hyacinthe*, 22 Oct. 1889; A.-B. Routhier, *De Québec à Victoria* (Quebec: L.-J. Demers et Frère 1893), p. 105.

131 Eg., *Le Courrier de St-Hyacinthe*, 24 Jan. and 22 July 1890.

132 *L'Electeur*, 29 Nov. 1890; Joseph Tassé, *Les Canadiens de l'Ouest* (Montreal: Imprimerie Canadienne 1878); N.E. Dionne, *Etats-Unis, Manitoba et Nord-Ouest*, pp. 21–2; Honoré Beaugrand, *Jeanne la fileuse*.

133 *Le Courrier de St-Hyacinthe*, 20 Sept. 1884, and 17 Jan. 1885; *Le Nouveau Monde*, 26 Oct. 1888; *La Presse*, 24 Oct. 1888, and 27 Mar. 1890; *L'Union des Cantons d l'Est*, 15 Sept. 1892; *L'Electeur*, 11 Nov. 1889, and 1 Apr. 1890.

134 *Le Courrier de St-Hyacinthe*, 7 July 1881; *La Presse*, 24 Apr. 1889.

135 *L'Electeur*, 2 Feb. 1891; *La Presse*, 9 Nov. 1888; Tassé, *Les Canadiens de l'Ouest*, p. XXIX; E. Hamon, *Les Canadiens-Français de la Nouvelle-Angleterre* (Quebec: N.S. Hardy 1891), pp. 33–4, 75.

136 *Le Pionnier de Sherbrooke*, 12 Aug. and 2 Sept. 1881; *L'Union des Cantons de l'Est*, 23 and 30 July 1881, and 2 June 1885; *La Revue Canadienne*, XVIII (1882), pp. 377–80; *La Minerve*, 3 Aug. 1885; *Le Courrier de St-Hyacinthe*, 4 July 1889; *L'Electeur*, 23 Oct., 6, 11,

and 14 Nov. 1889; *La Presse*, 15, 18, and 25 June 1888; *Le Nouveau Monde*, 26 Oct. 1888; Desrosiers and Fournet, *La Race française en Amérique*; Hamon, *Les Canadiens-Français de la Nouvelle-Angleterre*, pp. 22–8, 50ff., 113–7.

137 *L'Electeur*, 13 Nov. and 7 Dec. 1889.

138 Ibid., 12 Nov. 1889. Also, *La Revue Canadienne*, XXVII (1891), pp. 42ff., 513–21; Joseph Tassé, *Aux Canadiens français émigrés* (Ottawa 1883), p. 13; J.-B. Proulx, *Le Curé Labelle et la colonisation* (Paris 1885), pp. 11–12.

139 Hamon, *Canadiens-Français*, p. 127. Also, *La Vérité*, 12 June 1886.

140 Edmond de Nevers, *L'Avenir du peuple canadien-français* (Paris: Henri Jouve 1896), pp. 424–5.

141 Edmond de Nevers, "Les Anglais et nous," in *La Revue Canadienne*, XLII (1902), p. 12. See also, *La Revue Canadienne*, XL (1901), p. 478; XXXIX (1901), p. 493; LVII (1909), pp. 106–16 and 296–301.

142 Lanctot, *L'Avenir*, p. 13. Also, *La Vérité*, 8 Oct. 1887.

ultimately control "an independent state formed by a part of the present dominion together with a fragment of the American bloc...."[143]

Meanwhile, they were having to fight for cultural rights in the United States just as in Manitoba and the North-West. There was a "school question in the United States," brought on, like Manitoba's by the desire to replace free Christian schools by compulsory non-sectarians ones.[144] Franco-Americans too had to fight for the rights of their language, in schools, in public life, and even within the Church.[145] Melting-pot pressures for Americanization, the hostility of Americans toward autonomous cultures, obliged Franco-Americans to struggle to keep alive their nationality.[146] And this they did with an attitude not unlike that of the Franco-Manitobans. "They were conscious of not being intruders on American soil: 'We've been here longer than the Irish; it's they who are the foreigners.'"[147] Their rights were based on natural law, Church law, and the spirit of the American constitution itself—"the principles of liberty which are so dear to the Americans."[148] Indeed, Franco-Americans, in demanding French and Catholic rights, "have the constitution for them, and the liberty which protects them under the shelter of the stars and stripes."[149]

In their struggles, Franco-Americans could count on support from Quebec, for Quebec was their motherland, to which they showed their attachment by their determination to maintain their nationality.[150] Thus it was Quebec that sent most of the priests and teachers to the New England francophone parishes.[151] And it was Quebec's premier, Mercier, who told the provincial legislature: "For the French Canadians of the United States, we are the mother country. We have the rights and duties of the mother country."[152] He backed up these words by granting Quebec government subsidies to Franco-American organizations, participating in Franco-American conventions, and using an 1891 audience with the Pope to ask for the appointment of a French-Canadian bishop in New England.

These attitudes toward the Franco-Americans and their rights must affect our conclusions about the Canadian question. For they do seem to indicate that the French-Canadian expectation of linguistic and scholastic rights was not based solely on the conditions or institutions of the Canadian confederation. Even where there was no argument to be made about racial equality, the BNA Act, or a binational compact, there was still an expectation of a French-Canadian national life and of French-Canadian rights. Comments about justice, natural law, or the American spirit of liberty suggest a general principle of respect for ethnic life and aspirations, a spirit of tolerance and equity.

As a matter of fact, arguments for minority rights even in Canada did not always depend on interpretations of the BNA Act or the meaning of Confederation. As in the U.S., so in Canada French Canadians were not newcomers, and they were not unwilling to assert the right of first exploration or settlement to justify minority demands. Thus, French had rights in the North-West as the "language first used to evangelize the savages of the country"[153] and in Ontario as "the first civilized language to echo by the Great Lakes and

143 G. Bourassa, *Conférences et discours* (Montreal: Beauchemin 1899), p. 171. Also, N.H.E. Faucher de St-Maurice, *La Question du jour; resterons-nous français* (Quebec: Belleau 1890), pp. 135–6; Hamon, *Canadiens-Français*, pp. 125–50; *La Revue Canadienne*, XXVII (1891), p. 521, and XL (1901), p. 493. This idea of a Greater Quebec reflected the continued belief that national survival depended less on laws or constitutional rights than on demographic strength. The same belief shows up in the argument that French Canadians must colonize northern Ontario before Manitoba, so as to form a continuous belt of settlement from Quebec westward. See, eg., Routhier, *De Québec à Victoria*, p. 107; Association catholique de la Jeunesse canadienne-française, *Le Problème de la colonisation* (Montreal: ACJC 1920), p. 90.
144 *La Revue Canadienne*, XXVIII (1892), pp. 324ff., 513ff.; *Le Courrier de St-Hyacinthe*, 21 Mar. 1889; *Le Nouveau Monde*, 9 Feb. 1889.
145 Robert Rumilly, *Histoire des Franco-Américains* (Montreal 1958), pp. 129–30; *La Vérité*, 8 Oct. 1887; *La Presse*, 2 Apr. 1890; *L'Electeur*, 29 Mar. 1890, and 2 Feb. 1891.
146 Hamon, *Canadiens-Français*, pp. 39–40, 65–86; *L'Electeur*, 31 Oct. 1889; *La Revue Canadienne*, XL (1901), p. 478.
147 Rumilly, *Histoire des Franco-Américains*, p. 150.
148 Hamon, *Canadiens-Français*, p. 117. Note also Henri Beaudé, *Le Français dans le New Hampshire* (n.p., 1919), p. 17.
149 *L'Electeur*, 10 Mar. 1890.
150 Ibid.
151 G.F. Theriault, "The Franco-Americans of New England," in Wade and Falardeau, *Canadian Dualism*, p. 400; Hamon, *Canadiens-Français*, p. 62; Rumilly, *Franco-Américains*, p. 44.
152 In Rumilly, *Franco-Américains*, p. 121.
153 *Elections provinciales de 1892*, p. 154. Also, *L'Electeur*, 15 Jan. and 3 Feb. 1890; *La Minerve*, 30 Jan. 1890; *Le Courrier de St-Hyacinthe*, 7 Nov. 1889, and 17 July 1890; *L'Electeur*, 20 Feb. 1890, 6 Mar. 1893; *L'Union des Cantons de l'Est*, 3 Dec. 1896; *Le Nationaliste*, 12 Mar. 1905; Georges Dugas, *L'Ouest canadien* (Montreal: Cadieux et Derome 1896), pp. 5–6; Lewis Drummond, *The French Element in the Canadian North-West* (Winnipeg: The North-West Review 1887), p. 14.

in the forests of this sister province."[154] Such rights were also referred to the terms of the 1760 capitulation, early post-Conquest precedents and custom, and the law of nations.[155] Church law was said to guarantee language rights,[156] and of course, so was natural law. Thus, Manitoba Catholics held their right to separate schools "from nature,"[157] and French belonged in Ontario schools by "natural law, historic right, political right, and true national interest."[158] So, in Canada as in the States, we find the demand for French-Catholic rights based on a broad principle of equity, tolerance, and right.

This is certainly not to suggest that the demand for rights in Canada was based on such a principle alone. We have seen clearly enough the emergence of a constitutional theory which made bilingualism or biculturalism an essential basis of Confederation itself. But that theory did not represent the whole of what French Canadians thought about the place of their nationality in Canada or in America. It shared a place in their minds with a more traditional Quebec nationalism as well as with a general concern about rights in the continent as a whole. In other words, we must recognize a certain ambivalence or ambiguity in the attitudes we are seeking to identify.

This ambivalence shows up in the matter of Quebec support for the minorities. Quebeckers certainly liked to think that minorities benefited from their aid and could depend on it.[159] The minorities themselves, however, were apt to take a different point of view, and to complain that Quebeckers did not really care about them and were all too ready to let them down in a pinch.[160] The fact was that Quebeckers still

did expect the others to take the initiatives on their own behalf, and they awaited those initiatives before doing anything themselves. Thus, as the North-West schools question began to be raised, Jules-Paul Tardivel warned western Catholics that their failure to stand up for themselves by supporting the Riel agitation had "weakened as much as possible" the support that Quebec could give them now.[161]

However, once minority initiatives had made them aware of the problems, most Quebeckers were ready to proclaim themselves their supporters. Thus, a plea from *Le Manitoba* that Quebeckers should be on guard against proposed anti-French and anti-Catholic measures in the West brought this response: "Our colleague can be certain that he'll find in our province courageous combatants for the defence of the dearest rights of our brothers out there."[162] Quebeckers, after all, were "those who, by the constitution and by circumstances, ought to be protecting them...."[163] Quebec's MPS at Ottawa were particularly bound by this duty.[164] But, to provide a really solid support for the minorities, Quebec must be strong:

> Those who are protected by the strong are not oppressed, and if the province of Quebec were rich and strong, nobody in the confederation would dare to touch the schools of the North-West or speak of

---

154 Langelier, *Etude historique*, p. 37. Also, Tremblay, *Français en Ontario*, pp. 9–16.

155 *L'Etendard*, 29 Aug. 1889; Tremblay, *Français en Ontario*, pp. 9–16.

156 [J. Sasseville], *Dialogue entre un Acadien et un Canadien-Français* (Quebec: L.-J. Demers et Frère 1889), pp. 18–19.

157 *Le Journal des Trois-Rivières*, 7 Dec. 1892.

158 *La Revue Canadienne*, LXXI (1916), p. 555. Also, LXIII (1912), p. 443; Desrosiers and Fournet, *La Race française*, p. x.

159 *Dialogue entre un Acadien et un Canadien-Français*, p. 9: *Le Courrier de St-Hyacinthe*, 19 Apr. 1890; *La Revue Canadienne*, LVII (1909), pp. 106, 116.

160 *Dialogue entre un Acadien et*, p. 9. Acadian disappointment and resentment at the Quebec attitude is a major theme in Martin Spigelman's "The Acadian Renaissance and the Development of Acadien-Canadien Relations, 1864–1912" (unpublished Ph.D. thesis, Dept of History, Dalhousie University, 1975), eg., pp. 147, 256–8, 368–75, 383, 436ff. Western feelings of betrayal by

Quebec are explored in Robert Painchaud, "French-Canadian Historiography and Franco-Catholic Settlement in Western Canada, 1870–1915," in the *CHR*, LIX, 4 (Dec., 1978), while Gilbert-L. Comeault indicates that Quebec action was often independent of the appeals or even the real needs of the Franco-Manitobans, which Quebeckers often failed to understand, in his paper, "Les Franco-Manitobains face à la question des écoles," given to the 1978 annual meeting of the Institut d'Histoire de l'Amérique Française.

161 *La Vérité*, 5 Nov. 1887. The tendency of Quebeckers to wait for these affairs to be brought to them, as it were, is probably reflected in the very skimpy coverage newspapers gave to the Manitoba schools question in 1890 and 1891. After the Privy Council decisions, however—especially the second one—the question came to dominate the Quebec press.

162 *Le Courrier du Canada*, 3 Sept. 1889. Also, *La Minerve*, 24 Feb. 1890.

163 *La Revue Canadienne*, XXVIII (1892), p. 478. Also, *La Minerve*, 5 Apr. 1890.

164 *L'Electeur*, 7 Mar. 1893. Also, 15 Jan. 1894; *Le Courrier de St-Hyacinthe*, 17 July 1890; *L'Etendard*, 19 Aug. 1889; *L'Union des Cantons de l'Est*, 15 Sept. 1892; Bernard, *Manifeste libéral*, pp. 42–3, 220.

expelling French Canadians from the places they occupy.[165]

So, then, it came back to Quebec, its strength, influence, and autonomy. Between the old Quebec patriotism and the new Canadian biculturalism there was a tension, a balance, but ultimately an interdependence. Some might still fear that to protect minority rights effectively might endanger provincial autonomy;[166] others might find it necessary to explain that restrictions of provincial autonomy on behalf of minorities need not always be dangerous for Quebec;[167] nevertheless, when it came down to it, it was no longer a question of choosing between provincial autonomy and minority rights at all, for in fact, they went together. Each implied the other. In forming the confederation, after all, the provinces had insisted on autonomy in order to protect their respective nationalities. It followed that they must respect each other's nationalities:

> The confederated nations did not unite for the purpose of fusion; on the contrary, each one of them was careful to preserve its autonomy; each one of them insisted on having its nationals or co-religionists respected. In a word, the basis of a confederation is the respect of minorities.[168]

Of course, Quebec's case was the clearest. We have seen it in the fear that elimination of French rights in the West was only the first stage in a campaign whose ultimate goal was legislative union. Obviously, this was where the PPA's reasoning led:

> If a Catholic is unworthy of making a good policeman, then *a fortiori* a Catholic people is incapable of governing itself. So down with our legislature, all our provincial institutions, our civil laws, our schools, our traditions, our language![169]

But if French Quebeckers had insisted on governing themselves, on having their own autonomous province, it was for the sake of promoting the French-Canadian nationality. For the sake of that nationality, declared Bourassa, Cartier had insisted on and obtained a federal structure, "in opposition to the principle of 'fusion,' of legislative union, advocated by Sir John Macdonald."[170] But if the basis of Confederation was provincial autonomy, and if the *raison d'être* of provincial autonomy was the protection of Quebec's nationality, then it surely followed that the sharers of Quebec's nationality should have "a right to equality throughout the whole of this confederation."[171] To attack the minorities was to work against the very aim of Confederation, just as much as to attack provincial autonomy:

> If their elements of national individuality were certainly the heritage which the contracting parties [provinces] intended to protect above all against outside enemies, then at the very least they have the right to see that heritage respected first of all by the co-signatories of the pact.[172]

Thus, as the idea of bilingualism, or cultural duality, emerged toward the end of the nineteenth century, it was not seen by its advocates as an alternative to the traditional conception of Confederation as an alliance of autonomous provinces with distinct identities, but as a corollary of it. This is what gives the air of ambivalence or ambiguity to the attitudes we have been examining.

The emergence of these new attitudes was not unconnected with the political process by which the Liberals came to replace the Bleus as the dominant political party in Quebec. An important first step in both these changes was the appropriation by the Liberals of the principle of provincial autonomy. Having protested at first that provincial autonomy had always been *their*

165 *La Presse*, 20 Mar. 1894. Also, *La Revue Canadienne*, LVII (1909), p. 137.
166 *L'Electeur*, 25 Feb. 1890, 4 Aug. 1892; *La Patrie*, 23 Mar. 1895; *Laurier à la tribune*, pp. 614–16.
167 Taché, *Mémoire*, p. 32; *Le Nationaliste*, 12 Mar. 1905.
168 *La Revue Canadienne*, XXVIII (1892), p. 469. Cf. *Le Nationaliste's* reference to Canada (3 Apr. 1904) as a "federation of distinct races and autonomous provinces." See also *L'Union des Cantons de l'Est*, 1 Mar. 1890.
169 *L'Electeur*, 15 Jan. 1894.
170 Bourassa, *Pour la justice*, p. 12.
171 Ibid., p. 32.
172 Lionel Groulx, "Ce Cinquantenaire," first published in *L'Action Française*, July, 1917, reprinted in the *RHAF*, XXI, 3a (1967), p. 669. See also *L'Etendard*, 29 Jan. 1887; *La Minerve*, 28 Jan. 1890; *Le Nationaliste*, 3 Apr. 1904.

policy,[173] the Bleus ultimately reacted to Mercier by rallying to the federal government and institutions. Since Quebec was now Liberal, Bleus must turn to Ottawa, where their party still ruled. And since Mercier rocked the federal boat by demanding more autonomy for Quebec, Bleus responded by defending the present constitutional arrangements. This constitution, they claimed, contained precious advantages for Quebec, and Quebeckers ought to oppose any change in it.[174] Nor should Quebec seek conflict with Ottawa, as Mercier did:

> Mr Mercier has become a political radical in the full sense of the word, since he is undermining our written constitution and seems to desire, between the federal and provincial governments, a continuous state of war and dispute, from which our province only stands to lose. For we must not forget that the *status quo* contains all the guarantees we could want for the happiness, liberty, and independence of the French-Canadian population.[175]

French Canadians, the Bleus began to assert, were part of a "heterogeneous people" whose different groups should be "working together in common agreement for the general prosperity."[176] They must, therefore, place emphasis on the common government, and participate fully in *common* political movements, of which the federal Conservative Party was the archetype.[177] The Bleus claimed, in fact, that the Ottawa Conservatives—the government of Sir John A. Macdonald—were French Canada's best friends. As proof of this, they stressed Macdonald's decision not to disallow the Jesuits' Estates Act,[178] and pointed out that English-Canadian "fanatics" criticized him for being under the influence of the French Catholics.[179] Moreover, Bleu newspapers began to quote Macdonald's statements and manifestos at great

length.[180] In short, they countered Mercier's Quebec nationalism by rallying to Confederation, which they identified with the central government.

The effect of this strategy (in so far as it had a positive effect) was to encourage people to look to the *federal* government to act in the interest of French Canada. This would certainly affect the discussion of the Manitoba school question. While we saw that in the 1870s French Quebeckers had been reluctant for Ottawa to intervene on behalf of New Brunswick's Catholics, we find them in the 1890s demanding and expecting such intervention in the West.

The belief that Manitoba's 1890 legislation had exceeded the limits of the province's jurisdiction reinforced the tendency to look to Ottawa because it implied the need for disallowance. "The Martin law was manifestly unconstitutional; the federal government should have disallowed it…."[181] The failure to disallow caused "the federal government to bear the odium of this unjust legislation."[182]

Once the time had passed within which disallowance was possible, and once the Privy Council had declared the school law to be valid, Ottawa was looked to for remedial action. The federal government must produce "special legislation to ensure Manitoba's Catholic minority the separate schools which were promised them, as was perfectly well understood, when that province entered the union."[183]

The notion of federal responsibility for minority rights was emphasized in the motion which Joseph Israel Tarte presented to the House of Commons in 1893, to censure the government for its handling of the Manitoba schools issue. In supporting it, Tarte expressed many of the ideas we have seen emerging in the 1890s: the need for mutual tolerance and respect between the races, the idea that Confederation had sought to ensure that tolerance by a pact which guaranteed minority rights, and the idea that the West's entry into Canada had been dependent on specific

---

173 Above, pp. 181–2.

174 *Le Courrier de St-Hyacinthe*, 16 Feb. 1887; *Le Nouveau Monde*, 1 Apr. 1889.

175 *La Presse*, 12 Oct. 1888.

176 *Le Courrier de St-Hyacinthe*, 2 July 1889. Also 11 Sept. 1886, and 25 Oct. 1887.

177 *Le Journal des Trois-Rivières*, 20 Dec. 1886.

178 *La Presse*, 21, 26, and 28 Jan.; 1 and 4 Apr., 23 Aug. 1889.

179 *Le Courrier de St-Hyacinthe*, 24 Aug. 1889; *Le Nouveau Monde*, 5 Aug. 1889.

180 Eg., *Le Nouveau Monde*, 9 Feb. 1891; *Le Courrier de St-Hyacinthe*, 15 Oct. 1889, 12 Feb. 1891. Note also *Le Nouveau Monde*, 13 Oct. 1888. This emphasis on the federal government and federal party fits perfectly, of course, with the Bleu insistence, at the same time, on the need for harmony and co-operation between the two races.

181 *L'Etendard*, 30 Aug. 1892.

182 *L'Union des Cantons de l'Est*, 9 Apr. 1891. Also, 17 July 1890.

183 *L'Electeur*, 3 Aug. 1892. Also, *La Presse*, 3 Aug.; *L'Union des Cantons de l'Est*, 11 Aug. 1892.

guarantees of French-Catholic rights. Because equality between the races and religions was the very "basis" of the constitution, "the Manitoba legislature had no right to abolish the French language and Catholic schools," and once it had done so, Ottawa had the duty to intervene.[184] Thus, concluded Tarte's journalistic commentators, it was the federal ministers who were "the cause of the present agitation. If they had acted as statesmen, if they had faced up to the constitution and forced Manitoba to respect the law, then we would not be having our present troubles."[185]

The second Privy Council decision made federal action inescapable—at least as it was interpreted in Quebec. It was in the interest of both parties, in fact, to interpret the judgement in this way: it enabled the Bleus to reassure their French and Catholic voters while encouraging their Tory colleagues to act; and it enabled the Liberals to embarrass their opponents. In any case, by interpreting the judgement as a clear statement that Catholic schools were constitutionally guaranteed, both sides focused attention on Ottawa as the enforcer of these guarantees. Thus: "The question of the rights and powers of the federal parliament is now settled; it only remains for it to do its duty."[186] The responsibility was not avoided by the federal order-in-council of 1895, which called on Manitoba to restore the lost school rights. For if Manitoba failed to comply, there could be "only one possible result: the intervention of Parliament."[187] When Manitoba's refusal was announced, therefore, the reaction was predictable:

There is great excitement here and all eyes are turned toward Ottawa. Catholics are convinced that the federal government will intervene, and they even prefer that the redress of their grievances should be the work of the central power rather than of the local legislature, which could have subjected them to constant vexations.[188]

The federal remedial bill was the logical outcome of these expectations. Through that bill Bleus claimed to be carrying out the federal duty "to do justice, and to protect the minorities against majorities, be they Catholic or Protestant."[189]

The Liberals were able to exploit this expectation of federal action as long as the Conservatives were in power at Ottawa. The Bleus could be made to look bad, first of all, by their failure to obtain disallowance. They had "allowed the law and the constitution to be violated without saying a word."[190] After the second Privy Council decision they had issued an order-in-council which was merely an attempt to "decoy" the minority by "dilatory means" in the face of clear instructions from "the highest court in the empire" about what the constitution required.[191] As for remedial legislation, Liberals proclaimed the need for it. They would even support the Conservative ministry "if it would only make up its mind to give justice to the Catholic minority of Manitoba" by effective action.[192] But the "so-called remedial bill"[193] which the Tories presented to Parliament in 1896 was nothing but a "legislative hoax"[194] which left itself open to every sort of sabotage by unco-operative Manitobans.[195] It represented a failure of Ottawa to carry out its duty as defender of the minority.

The effect of all this was to help bring about the changes we have seen in French-Canadian views of Confederation. First, the more the Liberals succeeded in making the Conservatives look guilty for their failure to restore Catholic schools in Manitoba, the more they reinforced the belief that the constitution contained guarantees for those schools. The Liberal approach, after all, was that the Conservatives were failing to act according to the constitution. Conversely, the more people became persuaded that the constitution guaranteed minority rights and that the federal government ought to be enforcing it, the more

184 L'Electeur, 6 and 7 Mar. 1893.
185 Le Nouveau Monde, 7 Mar. 1893. Also, L'Union des Cantons de l'Est, 16 Feb. and 16 Mar. 1893, 17 May and 21 June 1894; L'Electeur, 7 Mar. 1891.
186 La Minerve, 7 Jan. 1895.
187 Ibid., 14 June 1895.
188 Le Courrier de St-Hyacinthe, 14 June 1895.
189 Ibid., 5 Mar. 1896. Also, 15 Feb., 21 and 31 Mar., 16, 21, and 30 Apr.; La Presse, 4 and 23 Mar. 1896; Bernard, Manifeste libéral, pp.68ff; La Minerve, 14 Apr. 1896.
190 L'Electeur, 4 Aug. 1892.
191 Ibid., 23 Mar. 1895. Also, La Patrie, 23 Mar.
192 L'Electeur, 15 Apr. 1895. Also, 20 Apr.
193 La Patrie, 9 Apr. 1896.
194 L'Union des Cantons de l'Est, 2 Apr. 1896. Also, L'Electeur, 17 Apr.; La Patrie, 16 Apr. 1896.
195 L'Union des Cantons de l'Est, 20 Feb. 1896.

the Conservatives, who controlled that government, must appear reprehensible. But also, the effect of all the factors which encouraged the expectation of federal action—from Bleus' rallying to Ottawa in the time of Mercier to Liberals' criticizing the federal Conservatives for not acting—was to make cultural rights seem no longer dependent on the provinces alone (as in the view of the 1860s) but on the confederation itself. This made possible the emergence of the theory that French-Catholic institutions were guaranteed not only in Quebec but throughout the dominion.

The Conservatives, however, were not to profit from the remedial action which they did eventually take. Their long delays and evasions, which had enabled the Liberals to criticize them so often, had hurt their credibility among Catholic voters. They had missed chance after chance to do something, from 1890, when Sir John A. Macdonald had instructed Manitoba's lieutenant-governor not to refuse to sign the infamous bills into law,[196] till 1896, when they introduced remedial legislation so late and so ineffectively as to indicate clearly that they did not really intend it to pass.[197] Especially after the 1895 Privy Council decision, the Liberals were able to mock their opponents for their delays, and to conclude from them that they did not intend to remedy the situation. After five years of stalling, they complained, and in spite of the clear instructions of the Privy Council, things were still at the same point as in 1890.[198] The vulnerability of the remedial bill itself to Liberal criticism also hurt the Conservatives. Since it failed to ensure that Catholic schools would receive their share of provincial grants, or some equivalent, Liberals could oppose the bill as "vague, incomplete, unjust, and in reality [giving] nothing at all to the Manitoba Catholics."[199]

The Bleus also suffered from the English-Canadian company they kept. Already in the 1880s Mercierites had begun claiming that Sir John A. Macdonald was an Orangeman—a member of the "Black Degree"[200]—and

sworn "to work for the annihilation of the Catholic religion in Canada and consequently of the French-Canadian race, which professes it."[201] Other English-Canadian Conservatives were much more embarrassing to the Bleus: D'Alton McCarthy, and William Meredith, the Ontario Conservative leader who had been attacking French and Catholic schools in that province since the late 1880s.[202] McCarthy, a president of the Ontario Conservative Association and prominent Tory MP, had been a leader of the anti-Jesuit agitation, had led the attack against the French language in the North-West, and was accused of having stirred up the hornets' nest of anti-separate school legislation in Manitoba in 1889, when "Sir John sent [him] to Manitoba to arouse the fanaticism of the Protestants."[203] It was this intolerant Ontario wing, which even a leading Bleu had described as "a collection of factions led by Meredith and McCarthy,"[204] that seemed to rule the Conservative Party, while the servile Bleus bowed to their Orange allies and let slip chance after chance to aid the Manitoba minority.[205] Could one really trust such a party to follow through with effective remedial action, when even during the 1896 election campaign its Anglo-Protestant leader told a Winnipeg audience "that it was a lie to claim that the Conservatives favoured the re-establishment of separate schools"?[206]

The Liberals, on the other hand, had been looking more and more like defenders of French and Catholic rights, ever since Mercier won ultramontane support for the formation of his government and went on to appoint the Curé Labelle deputy minister, correspond with and receive great honours from the Pope, make a flamboyant appearance at the great 1889 Baltimore

196 *La Patrie*, 14 Mar. and 8 Apr. 1890.

197 *L'Electeur*, 17 Feb. 1896; *La Patrie*, 9 Apr.

198 *L'Union des Cantons de l'Est*, 7 Feb. 1895.

199 David, *Le Clergé canadien*, p. 64. Also, *L'Electeur*, 7 Mar. 1896; *L'Union des Cantons de l'Est*, 13 Feb., 19 Mar., and 30 Apr. 1896.

200 *L'Etendard*, 22 Feb. 1889. See also 15 Feb. 1890, where Macdonald's Orange sympathies are said to be manifest in his support for the incorporation of the order.

201 *L'Electeur*, 13 Oct. 1885. Also, 16 Nov.

202 Ibid., 20 Feb. 1890; *L'Union des Cantons d l'Est*, 23 Mar. 1889.

203 *L'Union des Cantons de l'Est*, 24 Aug. 1889. Also, *L'Electeur*, 18 Oct. and 30 Nov. 1889, 25 Mar., 11 Apr., and 6 May 1891; 23 Jan. and 21 Nov. 1894. While there were Liberals involved in the anti-Jesuit agitation, and while the Manitoba government itself was Liberal during this period, the role of Conservatives seemed most prominent, and it was that party's image that suffered from identification with the anti-French and anti-Catholic agitation. See J.R. Miller, "'This Saving Remnant': Macdonald and the Catholic Vote in the 1891 Election," in the Canadian Catholic Historical Association, *Study Sessions*, 1974, pp. 36-7.

204 *L'Union des Cantons de l'Est*, 21 May 1896.

205 *L'Electeur*, 26 Mar. 1895; *L'Union des Cantons de l'Est*, 14 Mar.

206 *L'Electeur*, 16 May 1896. Also, 27 Jan., 17 Feb. and 7 Mar.

convention of American Catholicism, and settle the Jesuits' estates question.[207] It certainly helped at the federal level also to have in Laurier a French-Catholic leader, who upheld the Catholic theory of education,[208] could be reported to have attended mass all over the country, and was praised by a Catholic bishop as "the first among the Canadians."[209]

Liberal publicists had been trying hard to free the party from its old anticlerical image:

> There was a time when the idea was firmly set in the minds of certain community leaders that the Liberal Party was hostile to the Church.
>
> But Mr Mercier came to power, and he did more in four years to consolidate our Catholic institutions in the province than all his predecessors since Confederation.
>
> It's been said that the clergy later forgot his services; but that is a mistake and a grave injustice to the clergy.
>
> Before the coming of Mr Mercier, influenced by prejudices stirred up in the interest of the Bleus, there were not ten priests in the province who were sympathetic to the Liberal Party.
>
> Today there are more than five hundred out of a thousand.[210]

Liberals need not fear, therefore, that the clergy would intervene in politics against them. If some clerics still occasionally did so, it was only because the Bleus had hoodwinked them into mistaking their true friends.[211] "It's not the clergy who go running after the politicians; it's rather the latter who are continually chasing them…."[212] But good Liberals would not try, like the Bleus, to manipulate the clergy. They were "submissive in every way to the teachings of our holy mother Church, devoted to the interests of religion more than

to those of politics,"[213] and they knew that their duty was to follow clerical guidance while encouraging the electorate to do the same.[214]

In claiming to be the pro-Catholic party, Quebec Liberals were aided by their English-Canadian allies. Ever since the days when Edward Blake had attacked Macdonald's government for allowing the execution of Louis Riel, English-Canadian Liberals had been losing their old stench of Grit francophobia and taking on a sweeter aroma.[215] When McCarthy the Tory attacked the French language in the North-West, Blake the Liberal declared himself "the champion of the French language in Canada" and defended it.[216] It was the Ontario Liberal premier, Oliver Mowat, who had chaired the 1887 interprovincial conference at Quebec and worked with Mercier to defend provincial autonomy. It was that same Liberal Mowat whose government maintained French and Catholic schools in Ontario while the Tories attacked him for it.[217]

All these circumstances were cleverly exploited by Liberal publicists. Their psychological astuteness is well illustrated by an 1894 report in *L'Electeur* about a provincial by-election in London, Ontario. The Conservative candidate, who had lost to his Liberal opponent, had been the leader of the infamous Protestant Protective Association. "Catholics and Protestant Liberals had united," commented the paper, "to crush the bigots." At the head of the article was a sketch of the red ensign, and over it were printed the words "Catholic and Liberal."[218] This was

207 *L'Etendard*, 22 Feb. 1889, 15 Jan. 1890; *L'Electeur*, 14 Nov. 1889; *Elections provinciales de 1892*, pp. 109, 117–18.

208 *La Presse*, 6 Mar. 1895.

209 *L'Electeur*, 19 Sept. 1894.

210 Ibid., 17 Apr. 1895. Also, 29 June 1896.

211 Ibid., 28 Jan. 1896.

212 *La Patrie*, 4 May 1896. That it was Conservative politicans who dragged a reluctant clergy into the remedial bill question and the 1896 elections is borne out by Professor Crunican in *Priests and Politicians*.

213 *L'Electeur*, 14 Feb. 1896. Also, 16 Apr. 1895.

214 *L'Union des Cantons de l'Est*, 4 June 1896. Not content with proclaiming their piety and obedience, Liberal editors opened their columns to Ultramontane articles by priests (eg., *L'Electeur*, 10 Apr. 1895), and *L'Electeur* even referred to Jules-Paul Tardivel as a guide to political events (17 Feb. 1896)! No wonder *L'Union des Cantons de l'Est*, could claim (21 Mar. 1895) that the old notion that Liberals were hostile to the clergy while Bleus were the champions of Catholicism was, in fact, the very opposite to the truth.

215 Even the Ultramontane *L'Etendard* (4 Feb. 1887) reprinted passages from Blake's speech on the censure motion to win Quebec support for the Liberals.

216 *L'Electeur*, 17 Feb. 1890. Also 8 Nov. 1889. J.R. Miller points out that Blake had also helped the Liberals win Catholic sympathy by opposing the incorporation of the Orange order and by choosing Laurier to succeed him as party leader ("This Saving Remnant," p. 34). Even the Conservative *La Presse* had to praise Blake's good will and benevolence toward French Catholics (15 Feb. 1890).

217 *Laurier à la tribune*, p. 503; *L'Etendard*, 1 Apr. 1890; *La Patrie*, 28 Aug. 1889; *L'Electeur*, 1 Apr. 1890.

218 *L'Electeur*, 21 Nov. 1894.

the image which a decade of Liberal propaganda finally succeeded in establishing.

When, in the midst of the 1896 election campaign, the Quebec episcopacy issued its collective pastoral letter on Manitoba schools and the duty of Catholic voters, it reflected the new constitutional and political attitudes. What they wanted, said the prelates—what all Catholics must want—was "the triumph of rights which have been guaranteed by the Constitution." To restore Catholic schools in Manitoba would be to show "the respect due to the Constitution and to the British Crown." In saying this, the prelates were expressing the new Quebec views about the constitution and minority rights, and in telling Catholic voters that they should vote only for candidates who would support remedial action in Parliament, they expressed the new view of the role of Ottawa in enforcing those rights.[219]

The pastoral letter also expressed the new political outlook by declining to give any explicit support to the Conservatives, who had already presented remedial legislation in Parliament. Bleus might claim that the letter "approved the government's conduct,"[220] but in reality they were disappointed by it. Liberals reported gleefully that after the reading of the letter from the pulpit, Bleus had come out of church complaining that it "favours the Liberals—we're done for."[221] Indeed, the letter's very neutrality did favour the Liberals, for the declining credibility of the Bleus and the increasingly Catholic aura which had come to surround the Liberals in recent years made it possible for the latter to gain a better hearing when they gave the undertaking required by the bishops. Well, then, might Liberals praise the letter for putting an end to the Bleus' "odious exploitation of a holy authority." French-Canadian Catholics would now have an even "greater respect, livelier affection, and higher consideration for the hierarchy which commands us all, Conservatives and Liberals alike, in the spiritual domain."[222]

In fact, the Rouges claimed they would get more than the Bleus for the Manitoba Catholics. Years of stalling and evasion had proved the duplicity of the Conservatives, who simply would not "respect the constitution" by remedial action. The Liberals, on the other hand, "would have done it five years ago."[223] The Orangemen had realized this all along, and had attacked Laurier because "his policy would have been favourable to the Catholic minority of Manitoba."[224] Liberal papers proclaimed this in Laurier's own words:

> What I want and what I ask is that the minority in Manitoba should obtain the privilege of teaching their children their duties toward God and society in the manner in which they have been instructed by their religious authorities....
>
> The Liberal Party's policy has always had as its aim to protect the minorities. I want the Liberal Party to follow that policy under my leadership, and I believe that, in the name of all the members of the Liberal Party, I can make a solemn commitment that the Liberal Party will undertake to settle the present problem on a basis which will be found just, equitable, and satisfactory by the minority, on that liberal basis of equal rights and justice for all which is the spirit of our constitution.[225]

In other words, while the Tories' remedial bill only *pretended* to help the Manitoba Catholics, the Liberal Party was "committed to the re-establishment of separate schools just as they existed before 1890."[226] Thus the Liberals outbid the Conservatives in their claim to satisfy the demands of Quebec's Catholic voters in 1896—to satisfy, that is, the demands which arose from the new conception of the constitution and of the nature of Confederation.

219 The pastoral letter was published in most or all newspapers between the 18th and the 21st of May, 1896.
220 *Le Courrier de St-Hyacinthe*, 20 June 1896. Also, *Le Nouveau Monde*, 22 May; *La Presse*, 22 June; Bernard, *Manifeste libéral*, p. 36.
221 *La Patrie*, 18 May 1896.
222 *L'Electeur*, 18 May 1896. The Liberals did so well with the pastoral letter that their opponents later accused them of having shamelessly and dishonestly exploited it. Eg., Bernard, *Manifeste libéral*, p. 52; *La Minerve*, 25 June 1896.

223 *L'Electeur*, 28 Jan. 1896. Also, *L'Union des Cantons de l'Est*, 7 Feb. 1895. On the duplicity and unreliability of the Conservatives, see *L'Electeur*, 25 Mar. and 10 Apr. 1895; *L'Union des Cantons de l'Est*, 4 and 11 Apr. 1895.
224 *L'Union des Cantons de l'Est*, 23 Mar. 1893.
225 This was printed in every issue of the *Union des Cantons de l'Est* from 25 July to 22 Aug. 1895. It was all in bold-face capital letters, with the words SOLEMN COMMITMENT standing out in extra-large type.
226 *L'Electeur*, 13 Mar. 1896. Also, 17 and 29 Sept. 1894; *La Patrie*, 16 Apr. 1896; *L'Union des Cantons de l'Est*, 21 May 1896; David, *Le Clergé canadien*, p. 68.

What made the Liberals particularly unbeatable, however, was that in satisfying new demands they were able to respect old values. Here Laurier's race and religion were precious assets. To vote for the party he led was to get rid of "the Orange machine and put at the head of the country [a] compatriot and co-religionist."[227] English Canadians understood what that meant. "COMPATRIOTS!!" screamed a giant headline in *L'Electeur*. "LEND AN EAR." Here was what Tupper, the Tory leader, had said two days before in a speech at Port Arthur: "Can you vote to overthrow the present government and put into power a French and Roman Catholic prime minister?"[228] In Quebec, of course, this sort of thing could only lend credibility to Liberal promises to do more than the Bleus for the Manitoba minority. That it did so, however, was a reflection of the continued belief that MPs were the representatives in Parliament of their nationality and religion. And as, in the traditional view, race and religion were connected with province, so that MPs were also seen as the representatives of their provinces, it was particularly important that Laurier was a Quebecker. "We of the province of Quebec should be particularly proud of the statesman who is now the leader of our party; he is of our race and our little homeland."[229] His coming to power would enable "his province to gain the ascendancy in Confederation."[230] But it was also a traditional view (still current, as we have seen) that Quebec was the protector of the minorities. Was it not clear, then, that a federal leader who was also the representative of French Quebec would be the man most likely to bring justice to the Manitoba Catholics? In February, Laurier had told the House of Commons that he would not take his stand as a Catholic and a French Canadian on the remedial issue. But in the Quebec campaign, that was exactly what the Liberals promised that Laurier would do.

This was borne out by the post-election commentaries. To the rueful Bleus it seemed Quebeckers had been taken advantage of, "and that in voting for Mr Laurier they imagined that they were really giving their support to a French Canadian, who would defend the rights of our Manitoba brothers."[231] Liberals, far from rueful, noted that Manitoba had voted Tory, and concluded that Manitobans, like Quebeckers, had understood which party was really for Catholic schools.[232]

The same ideas show up in the comments on the settlement which was negotiated in the fall of 1896. While the talks were going on, Bleus found it prudent to remind Laurier "that you are a Catholic and that your MPs got themselves elected by promising, in compliance with the pastoral letter of the bishops, to vote for a remedial law."[233] When the agreement was announced, Bleus found it particularly disappointing because it was the work of a French Quebecker. The Liberals had only been elected because Quebeckers were "convinced that Laurier, a Catholic of French race, would do more and better for our oppressed brothers than an English Protestant like Sir Charles Tupper."[234] Instead of keeping his promise, though, "Mr Laurier has signed the abdication of his race and the subservience of his brothers in Catholicism."[235] Interestingly, Liberal commentators agreed with the Bleus' assessment both of Laurier's election promise and of his duty. That was why, in *praise* of the settlement, they maintained that he had acted as "a patriot, a devoted friend of all his brothers by race and by religion."[236]

But in the election campaign Laurier offered more than the promise to act as leader of French Quebec and defender of the minorities. While, in 1872, Cartier had claimed that the New Brunswick Catholics could not be defended without some threat to Quebec's autonomy, Laurier undertook in 1896 to restore the schools of the Manitoba Catholics without endangering provincial autonomy.

Since Conservatives had looked increasingly to the central government over the past decade for action,

227 *L'Electeur*, 28 Jan. 1896.
228 Ibid., 15 May 1896. Also, 16 May; *La Patrie*, 8 May; *L'Union des Cantons de l'Est*, 21 May 1896.
229 *La Patrie*, 24 Apr. 1896.
230 *L'Electeur*, 24 Nov. 1894.

231 *Le Courrier de St-Hyacinthe*, 27 June 1896. That the Liberals had won credibility for their promises by stressing Laurier's nationality was the contention of *La Minerve*, 25 June 1896; *Le Nouveau Monde*, 24 June; *La Presse*, 24 June; *La Revue Canadienne*, XXXII (1896), p. 444; Bernard, *Manifeste libéral*, pp. 56–8.
232 *L'Electeur*, 29 June 1896. Also, David, *Clergé canadien*, pp. 98–9.
233 *Le Courrier de St-Hyacinthe*, 12 Nov. 1896. Also, 17 and 21 Nov.
234 *Le Nouveau Monde*, 21 Nov. 1896.
235 *Le Courrier de St-Hyacinthe*, 26 Nov. 1896. Also, Bernard, *Manifeste*, pp. 215, 220.
236 *L'Electeur*, 21 Nov. 1896. Also, 20 and 23 Nov.; *L'Union des Cantons de l'Est*, 15 Oct., 26 Nov., and 3 Dec. 1896.

responsibility, and identification, it was not surprising that they ended up with a remedial bill that seemed to *coerce* Manitoba into restoring Catholic school rights. The logic of the situation seemed to require it. Was it not federal action, after all, that Liberals had been demanding all this time? And what other choice was there once Manitoba had refused to comply with the order-in-council?

> The more it goes, the more we're convinced that negotiating with fanatics of this sort ... is a waste of time. There only remains one thing to do: to act on the privy council decision and *force* them to do their duty.[237]

But was coercion really the only recourse? Was it really desirable, or was it only the natural tendency of a Conservative Party which had been accused for years of excessively centralizing tendencies? Had not Mercier already had to face "a conspiracy of Sir John Macdonald against the independence of the provinces"?[238] Macdonald had always preferred legislative union to federalism, and his party remained a party of centralization.[239] All in all, therefore, it was easy to see the Conservatives in 1896 as offering a solution to the schools problem which, while not effectively restoring Catholic rights, nevertheless endangered provincial autonomy.

Was it not safer all round to turn to Laurier, who offered to get more for the minority by "sunny ways,"

by negotiation? Laurier was a French Quebecker and therefore understood the value both of minority rights and of provincial autonomy. And he proposed to make Oliver Mowat a special commissioner to resolve the school problem to everyone's satisfaction—Mowat, who, as an English-Canadian Liberal, could deal with the Manitobans, who had fought for provincial rights as premier of Ontario and chairman of the interprovincial conference, and "who for so long has fought against the Tory leader Meredith to preserve the separate schools of the Ontario Catholic minority."[240]

This was an unbeatable programme. It responded to the ambivalence of Quebec attitudes, to the need for *both* provincial autonomy and minority rights. Here we see how the notion of a bilingual or bicultural Canada came to coexist with the vision of an autonomous Quebec in alliance with other autonomous provinces. Although Laurier would inevitably disappoint some of the expectations his own campaign had encouraged (for it was impossible to be at once both a *federal* leader and the special representative of French Quebec), these ideas were carried into the new century. Henri Bourassa, who had followed Laurier in 1896 precisely because he believed in the implications of the campaign,[241] expounded them in opposition to Laurier, developing them into his bilingual theory. By the generation of Lionel Groulx, these ideas had become commonplace. They would remain so until the rise of modern separatism in the 1960s.

---

237 *Le Courrier de St-Hyacinthe*, 19 Oct. 1895 (emphasis added). Also, 21, 28, and 30 Jan., and 3 Mar. 1896.
238 *L'Electeur*, 12 Oct. 1889. Also, 5 and 9 Mar. 1892; *Elections provinciales de 1892*, pp. 153, 155.
239 *L'Electeur*, 2 Feb. 1895.
240 *L'Union des Cantons de l'Est*, 21 May 1896. Also 21 Mar. 1895. For an extra hedging of bets, Laurier added that if this method didn't work, he would resort to remedial legislation—and more effective legislation than what the Tories proposed. See the report of his St-Roch speech in *L'Electeur*, 8 May 1896.
241 Bourassa, *Pour la justice*, p. 28.

**25**

## Editor's Introduction

This pithy piece offers an alternative take on the Manitoba School Crisis, painting it with the brush of political expediency. Rather than sanitizing the events of the day, it shows the fickleness of the politics of language and how one sharp political operative who is sensitive to the electoral idiosyncrasies can turn the tables. It is a riveting account of the trade-offs national politicians make and the political tactics they use to get around thorny constitutional issues as they continue to shape the country's political vernacular.

Source: J.W. Dafoe, "The Tactics of Victory," from *Laurier: A Study in Canadian Politics* (Toronto: McClelland and Stewart, 1968), 34–39.

J.W. Dafoe

# Laurier: A Study in Canadian Politics

THE STORY OF the Manitoba school question and the political struggle which centred around it, as told by Professor Skelton,[1] is bald and colourless; it gives little sense of the atmosphere of one of the most electrical periods in our history. The sequelae of the Riel agitation, with its stirring up of race feeling, included the Jesuit Estates controversy in parliament, the Equal Rights movement in Ontario, the attack upon the use of the French language in the legislature of the Northwest Territories and the establishment of a system of National schools in Manitoba through the repeal of the existing school law, which had been modelled upon the Quebec law and was intended to perpetuate the double-barrelled system in vogue in that province. The issue created by the Manitoba legislation projected itself at once into the federal field to the evident consternation of the Dominion government. It parried the demand for disallowance of the provincial statute by an engagement to defray the cost of litigation challenging the validity of the law. When the Privy Council, reversing the judgment of the Supreme Court, found that the law was valid because it did not prejudicially affect rights held prior to or at the time of union, the government was faced with a demand that it intervene by virtue of the provisions in the British North America Act, which gave the Dominion parliament the power to enact remedial educational legislation overriding provincial enactments in certain

circumstances. Again it took refuge in the courts. The Supreme Court of Canada held that under the circumstances the power to intervene did not exist; and the government breathed easier. Again the Privy Council reversed the judgment of the Supreme Court and held that because the Manitoba law prejudicially affected educational privileges enjoyed by the minority after union there was a right of intervention. The last defence of the Dominion government against being forced to make a decision was broken down; in the language of to-day, it was up against it. And the man who might have saved the party by inducing the bishops of the Catholic church to moderate their demands was gone, for Sir John Thompson died in Windsor Castle in December, 1894, one month before the Privy Council handed down its fateful decision. Sir John was a faithful son of the church, with an immense influence with the clerical authorities; he was succeeded in the premiership by Sir Mackenzie Bowell, ex-grand master of the Orange Order. The bishops moved on Ottawa and demanded action.

There ensued a duel in tactics between the two parties, intensely interesting in character and in its results surprising, at least for some people. The parties to the struggle which now proceeded to convulse Canada were the government of Manitoba, the author of the law in question, the Roman Catholic hierarchy in their capacity of guardians and champions of the Manitoba minority, and the two Dominion political parties. The bishops were deadly earnest in attack; so was the Manitoba government in defence; but with

---

1   O.D. Skelton, *The Life and Letters of Sir Wilfrid Laurier* (Toronto: Gundy, 1921).

the others the interest was purely tactical. How best to set the sails to catch the veering winds and blustering gusts to win the race, the prize for which was the government of Canada? The Conservatives had the right of initiative—did it give them the advantage? They thought so; and so did most of the Liberal generals who were mostly in a blue funk during the year 1895 in anticipation of the hole into which the government was going to place them. But there was at least one Liberal tactician who knew better.

The Conservatives decided upon a line of action which seemed to them to have the maximum of advantage. They would go in for remedial legislation. In the English provinces they would say that they did this reluctantly as good, loyal, law-abiding citizens obeying the order of the Queen delivered through the Privy Council. From their experiences with the electors they had good reason to believe that this buncombe would go down. But in Quebec they would pose as the defenders of the oppressed, loyal co-operators with the bishops in rebuking, subduing and chaining the Manitoba tyrants. Obviously they would carry the province; if Laurier opposed their legislation they would sweep the province and he would be left without a shred of the particular support which was supposed to be his special contribution to a Liberal victory. The calculation looked good to the Conservatives; also to most of the Liberals. As one Liberal veteran put it in 1895: "If we vote against remedial legislation we shall be lost, hook, line and sinker." But there was one Liberal who thought differently.

His name was J. Israel Tarte. Tarte was in office an impossibility; power went to his head like strong wine and destroyed him. But he was the man whose mind conceived, and whose will executed, the Napoleonic stroke of tactics which crumpled up the Conservative army in 1896 and put it in the hole which had been dug for the Liberals. On the day in March, 1895, when the Dominion government issued its truculent and imperious remedial order, Tarte said to the present writer: "The government is in the den of lions; if only Greenway will now shut the door." At that early day he saw with a clearness of vision that was never afterwards clouded, the tactics that meant victory: "Make the party policy suit the campaign in the other provinces; leave Quebec to Laurier and me." He foresaw that the issue in Quebec would not be made by the

government nor by the bishops; it would be whether the French-Canadians, whose imagination and affections had already been captured by Laurier, would or would not vote to put their great man in the chair of the prime minister of Canada. All through the winter and spring of 1895 Tarte was sinking test wells in Quebec public opinion with one uniform result. The issue was Laurier. So the policy was formulated of marking time until the government was irretrievably committed to remedial legislation; then the Liberals as a solid body were to throw themselves against it. So Laurier and the Liberal party retired within the lines of Torres Vedras and bided their time.

But Tarte had no end of trouble in keeping the party to the path marked out. The fainthearts of the other provinces could not keep from their minds the haunting fear that the road they were marching along led to a morass. They wanted a go-as-you please policy by which each section of the party could make its own appeal to local feeling. Laurier was never more indecisive than in the war councils in which these questions of party policy were fought over. And with good reason. His sympathy and his judgment were with Tarte but he feared to declare himself too pronouncedly. The foundation stone of Tarte's policy was a belief in the overwhelming potency of Laurier's name in Quebec; Laurier was naturally somewhat reluctant to put his own stock so high. He had not yet come to believe implicitly in his star. Within forty-eight hours of the time when Laurier made his speech moving the six months' hoist to the Remedial bill, a group of Liberal sub-chiefs from the English provinces made a resolute attempt to vary the policy determined upon. Their bright idea was that Clarke Wallace, the seceding cabinet minister and Orange leader, should move the six months' hoist; this would enable the Liberals to divide, some voting for it and some against it. But the bold idea won. With Laurier's speech of March 3, 1896, the death-blow was given to the Conservative administration and the door to office and power opened to the Liberals.

The campaign absolutely vindicated the tactical foresight of Tarte. A good deal might be said about that campaign if space were available. But one or two features of it may be noted. In the English provinces great play was made with Father Lacombe's minatory letter to Laurier, sent while the issue was trembling in the balance in parliament: "If the government … is beaten … I inform you with regret that the episcopacy, like one man, united with the clergy, will rise to support those who may have fallen in defending us." In his Reminiscences, Sir John Willison speculates as to how this letter, so detrimental to the government in Ontario, got itself published. Professor Skelton[2] says boldly that it was "made public through ecclesiastical channels." It would be interesting to know his authority for this statement. The writer of this article says it was published as the result of a calculated indiscretion by the Liberal board of strategy. As it was through his agency that publication of the letter was sought and secured, it will be agreed that he speaks with knowledge. It does not, of course, follow that Laurier was a party to its publication.

The campaign of 1896 was on both sides lively, violent, and unscrupulous. The Conservatives had two sets of arguments; and so had the Liberals. Those of us who watched the campaign in Quebec at close range know that not much was said there by the Liberals about the high crime of coercing a province. Instead, stress was laid upon the futility and inadequacy of the proposed remedial legislation; upon the high probability that more could be got for the minority by negotiation; upon the suggestion that, negotiation failing, remedial legislation that would really accomplish something could still be invoked. This argument, plus the magic of Laurier's personality and Tarte's organizing genius, did the business. Futile the sniping of the curés; vain the broadsides of the bishops; empty the thunders of the church! Quebec went to the polls and voted for Laurier. Elsewhere the government just about held its own despite the burden of its remedial policy; but it was buried under the Quebec avalanche. The Liberals took office sustained by the 33 majority from the province which had once been the citadel of political Conservatism.

"Now is the winter of our discontent
Made glorious summer by this sun of York;
And all the clouds that lour'd upon our house
In the deep bosom of the ocean buried.
Now are our brows bound with victorious wreaths;
Our bruised arms hung up for monuments;
Our stern alarums changed to merry meetings;
Our dreadful marches to delightful measures."

---

2    *Ibid.*

## 26

### *Editor's Introduction*

Largely unknown in English Canada, Maître Louis-Philippe Pigeon was among the most important judges to be called to the bench in Quebec and, eventually, to the Supreme Court of Canada. Much of his scholarship is available only in French. However, included here is a piece in English that provides a lasting explanation of just how high the stakes are in disputes about the balance between self-rule and shared-rule in the Canadian federation. The selection is significant, for the understanding of provincial autonomy it advances, for its unique insights into continuity as a hallmark of Quebec's perspective on provincial powers that long predates the advent of the Quiet Revolution; and for a perspective brought to bear by someone who is a judge first—and a Quebec francophone judge at that. A greater appreciation of this perspective goes a long way toward understanding the constitutional position Quebec governments defend with respect to Canadian federalism.

Source: Louis-Philippe Pigeon, "The Meaning of Provincial Autonomy," *Canadian Bar Review* 29 (1951): 1126–35.

Louis-Philippe Pigeon

# The Meaning of Provincial Autonomy

A PROPER STUDY of the problem of provincial autonomy requires consideration of some fundamental principles. Laws are the framework of society. Without them, relations between men would be governed by individual brute force. Any order of things means laws in one form or in another. Laws in turn imply an authority empowered to make and to enforce them. Under any form of government the power of this authority over individuals is of necessity very great, and very great also is its influence on their living conditions.

For any given group of humans the constitution of the civil authority by which they are governed is therefore of prime importance. Obviously this will cause any human group possessing special characteristics to desire an authority of its own. A group forming what is sociologically termed a "nation" normally aspires to independence. Small states are apt however to encounter very serious difficulties owing to their inherent military and economic weakness. Instead of precarious military alliances or trade agreements, a federation offers stability and permanency. The federal state is an attempt to reconcile the need of military, political and economic strength, which large units only can offer, with the desire for self-government that is inherent in any human group having distinct collective feelings.

Of course federation necessarily implies that some powers become vested in a central authority. The real problem is the definition of these powers or, its corollary, of the powers remaining in the federated states or provinces.

In the eyes of some men, a federal state is an instrument of unification, in other words, a means of bringing about the gradual disappearance of the segmental differences opposed to complete political unity. In the eyes of others, federation of itself implies this complete political unity, the component states or provinces being looked upon as mere administrative entities whose functions should be restricted to the application of general policies defined by the central authority. In the eyes of autonomists, federation implies a division of political authority so that the component states or provinces are free to define their general policy in their own sphere of activity, without being obliged to conform with any pattern set down by the central authority.

In the construction of the British North America Act the courts, and especially the Judicial Committee of the Privy Council, have fairly consistently adopted the autonomist conception of federation:

> They [the Federal Government] maintained that the
> effect of the statute has been to sever all connections

between the Crown and the provinces; to make the government of the Dominion the only government of Her Majesty in North America; and to reduce the provinces to the rank of independent municipal institutions. For these propositions, which contain the sum and substance of the arguments addressed to them in support of this appeal, their Lordships have been unable, to find either principle or authority … and a Lieutenant-Governor, when appointed, is as much the representative of Her Majesty for all purposes of provincial government as the Governor-General himself is for all purposes of Dominion government.[1]

The scheme of the Act passed in 1867 was thus, not to weld the Provinces into one, nor to subordinate Provincial Governments to a central authority, but to establish a central government in which these Provinces should be represented, entrusted with exclusive authority only in affairs in which they had a common interest. Subject to this each Province was to retain its independence and autonomy and to be directly under the Crown as its head.[2]

Their Lordships do not conceive it to be the duty of this Board—it is certainly not their desire—to cut down the provisions of the Act by a narrow and technical construction, but rather to give it a large and liberal interpretation so that the Dominion to a great extent, but within certain fixed limits, may be mistress in her own house, as the Provinces to a great extent, but within certain fixed limits, are mistresses in theirs.[3]

All the arguments advanced against these decisions by numerous writers are based either on the "Peace, Order and good Government" clause or on the so-called "historical construction" of the Act.

In support of the first argument it is contended that the courts have failed to give full effect to the opening words of section 91[4] and that the authority thus con-ferred on the federal Parliament should be broadly construed.[5] But it is significant that seldom do those who advance this contention quote the complete sentence. They speak of the importance of the grant of legislative authority for the "Peace, Order and good Government of Canada." They point out that such expressions were traditionally used to grant general legislative authority; but they pay slight attention to the fact that these pregnant words are immediately followed by the all-important restriction: "in relation to all Matters not coming within the classes of Subjects by this Act assigned exclusively to the Legislatures of the Provinces." If due attention is paid to these words, it becomes impossible to construe the grant of residuary power otherwise than as saving provincial authority instead of overriding it.

The "historical construction" is a pretended inquiry into the intentions of the framers of the Canadian constitution, otherwise than by a consideration of the meaning of the words used in the final document. The fallacy of this method lies not only in the fact that it runs counter to a fundamental rule of legal interpretation[6] but also in the fact that it is most unreliable. The B.N.A. Act is not the expression of the intention of one man, whose ideas might perhaps be gathered from extrinsic evidence with a reasonable degree of certainty; it is the expression of a compromise between

1   *Liquidators of the Maritime Bank of Canada v. Receiver-General of N.B.,* [1892] A.C. 437, at pp. 441–443.

2   In *re The Initiative and Referendum Act,* [1919] A.C. 935, at p. 942.

3   "*Persons*" case, [1930] A.C. 124, at p. 136.

4   "It shall be lawful for the Queen, by and with the Advice and Consent of the Senate and House of Commons, to make Laws for the Peace, Order, and good Government of Canada, in relation to all Matters not coming within the Classes of Subjects by this Act assigned exclusively to the Legislatures of the Provinces…."

5   See, for example, Bora Laskin, "'Peace, Order and Good Government' Re-examined" (1947), 25 Can. Bar Rev. 1054, at p. 1085: "Some sixty years ago the Judicial Committee said in *Riel v. The Queen* that the words 'peace, order and good government' were words 'apt to authorize the utmost discretion of enactment for the attainment of the objects pointed to.' The remark was not made in relation to sections 91 and 92 of the British North America Act and in the context of the Act it is undoubtedly too wide. But in its reference to legislative objects it indicates the type of problem which a court must face in interpreting sections 91 and 92. It is beside the point that the words of the introductory clause are too large and loose for comfortable adjudication. The Judicial Committee has not been reticent about its ability to give content to the large and loose provincial legislative power in relation to property and civil rights in the province, although it may be noted that it has done so largely in terms of thwarting exercises of federal legislative power, whether for the peace, order and good government of Canada or in relation to the regulation of trade and commerce."

6   "The question is, not what may be supposed to have been intended, but what has been said": *Brophy v. A.-G. of Manitoba,* [1895] A.C. 202, at p. 216. See also *Ladore v. Bennett,* [1939] A.C. 468. This is not a rule of interpretation of statutes but a general rule applicable to all legal documents, such as wills: *Auger v. Beaudry,* [1920], A.C. 1010, at p. 1014.

many men holding different and opposed viewpoints. When agreement was reached on a text, are we justified in assuming that agreement was also reached on intentions?

We know that the Fathers of Confederation were far from unanimous in their conception of the proposed federation. Some, like Sir Charles Tupper, held complete unification as their ideal, while others, like E.B. Chandler,[7] favoured a large measure of provincial autonomy. A compromise formula was finally devised to which both groups assented. Does this mean that their conflicting points of view had been reconciled?[8]

Experience in the practice of law shows that it is extremely difficult to visualize all the implications of a complex statute. Taxation statutes, for example, are prepared by specialists and scrutinized by experienced parliamentary counsel. Even then amendments introduced for the express purpose of avoiding unintended and undesired results are far from uncommon. Obviously, the long-term consequences of constitutional enactments are much more difficult of exact appreciation than the immediate consequences of taxation statutes.

Another important and often overlooked factor contributing to the difficulty of interpreting the B.N.A. Act is the fact that words actually lose much precision of meaning when used to define broad and fundamental political conceptions. The meaning of words is conventional. In final analysis it rests on generally accepted usage. It is really precise only to the extent that the category of acts or things described by any given word is susceptible of exact and objective definition.

This is the kind of precision which is almost totally lacking in the definitions of legal categories and concepts. They are precise only when applied to a given existing system of laws. Within this existing framework, such words as civil, criminal, municipal, have a clear and unmistakable meaning. But when the same words are used to define fields of legislative activity, any great degree of precision disappears. This is because, to a certain extent, the distinction between classes of laws is not based on an objective classification of the activities which are their subject-matter, but on the technique used in regulating them.[9] In fact, the same activities are the subject-matter of different classes of laws from different aspects. As an illustration of the many judicial pronouncements in which this is recognized, I should like to quote these words of the late Chief Justice Duff:[10]

> The fallacy lies in failing to distinguish between legislation affecting civil rights and legislation "in relation to" civil rights. Most legislation of a repressive character does incidentally or consequentially affect civil rights. But if in its true character it is not legislation "in relation to" the subject matter of "property and civil rights" within the provinces, within the meaning of section 92 of the British North America Act, then that is no objection although it be passed in exercise of the residuary authority conferred by the introductory clause.

On what basis is the "true character" to be ascertained, once it is decided, as it should be, that "civil law" and "criminal law" are not to be confined to the content they had in 1867?[11]

When the question is critically examined it becomes apparent that human activities as a whole are the subject matter of legislation and that these activities are, in our modern society, so inter-related that, if every possible degree of connexity is explored, there is no limit to the permissible extension of any given field of legislation. For instance, in Australia, federal power over "national defence" has, in wartime, been construed as extending to any measure deemed necessary. In Canada, unlimited federal authority for emergency legislation was held to be *implied* in the Constitution:

---

7   See Pope's Confederation Documents, p. 84.
8   There are definite indications that Sir John A. Macdonald had yielded to the desire of the delegates of Lower Canada, who insisted on a definite measure of autonomy. He is reported to have said at the Quebec Conference (Pope's Confederation Documents, p. 86): "New Zealand constitution was a Legislative Union, ours Federal. Emigrants went out under different guarantees. Local charters jarred. In order to guard these, they gave the powers stated to Local Legislatures, but the General Government had power to sweep these away. That is just what we do not want. Lower Canada and the Lower Provinces would not have such a thing."

9   If a repressive technique is resorted to, the law is classified as "criminal" or "penal"; if a remedy by private lawsuit is created, the law is classified as "civil."
10  *Gold Seal Ltd.* v. *A.-G. Alberta* (1921), 62 S.C.R. 424, at p. 460.
11  *Proprietary Articles Trade Ass.* v. *A.-G. for Canada*, [1931] A.C. 310.

It is proprietary and civil rights in new relations, which they do not present in normal times, that have to be dealt with…. In a *sufficiently great* emergency such as that arising out of war, there is implied the power to deal adequately with that emergency for the safety of the Dominion as a whole.[12]

It is thus seen that a most important distinction rests on the appreciation of a "degree" of necessity. If any degree were held sufficient, federal authority would be practically unlimited. As illustrations of this principle let me consider briefly the jurisprudence of the Supreme Court of the United States on the "Commerce clause" as contrasted with the decisions of the Privy Council and of the Supreme Court of Canada on the federal power to regulate "Trade and Commerce."

In the United States, pre-New-Deal decisions had established the principle that local activities could be regulated by Congress under the commerce clause only if they were "directly" related to "interstate commerce." More recent decisions of the Supreme Court of the United States have brushed aside this distinction,[13] however, with the result that the commerce clause has acquired practically unlimited meaning: "The federal commerce power is as broad as the economic needs of the nation."[14]

In Canada, on the other hand, federal authority over trade and commerce, although unlimited in its terms, was held to be strictly limited to the regulation of interprovincial operations, because to hold otherwise would have deprived provincial legislatures of powers they were clearly intended to possess:

The scope which might be ascribed to head 2, s. 91 (if the natural meaning of the words, divorced from their context, were alone to be considered), has

necessarily been limited, in order to preserve from serious curtailment, if not from virtual extinction, the *degree* of autonomy which, as appears from the scheme of the Act as a whole, the provinces were intended to possess.[15]

I have italicized the word "degree" in this last quotation because I wish to stress the point that here again, as in the definition of the federal emergency power, it is a question of "degree," not a specific distinction. In my view it is wrong to read the generally accepted definition of legislative autonomy ("that the Dominion to a great extent, but within certain fixed limits, may be mistress in her own house, as the Provinces to a great extent, but within certain fixed limits, are mistresses in theirs"[16]) as implying limits defined with mathematical accuracy. To do so is to conceive political science as an exact science ascertainable in the same manner as the natural sciences.

The government of men is essentially a moral problem. Moral problems are not solved by mathematical formulas but by the exercise of prudent judgment based on fundamental principles of morality. These principles rest on belief in God, and in this sense "Christianity is part and parcel of the law." Moral principles, by their very nature, imply concepts which, in their application to contingencies, cannot be divorced from a certain degree of subjective appreciation, a fact illustrated by the "prudent man" referred to in negligence cases. The proper standard of conduct is not to be ascertained by statistical methods but by a consideration of the "proper" duty to be discharged. What is "proper" is a question to be decided according to conscience, not otherwise.

If any one doubts the correctness of the statement that words used to describe "degrees" in moral (including legal) questions are of necessity imprecise and open to subjective appreciation, let him consider, on the one hand, the meaning ascribed to the word "gross" in the construction of statutes restricting the right of action to "gross negligence" in gratuitous passenger or sidewalk accident cases and, on the other, the meaning ascribed to the same adjective in the

---

12  *Fort Frances Pulp & Power Co. v. Manitoba Free Press*, [1923] A.C. 695 at pp. 704–705 (italics added).

13  "But even if … [an] activity be local and though it may not be regarded as commerce, it may still, whatever its nature, be reached by Congress if it exerts a substantial economic effect on interstate commerce, and this irrespective of whether such effect is what might at some earlier time have been defined as 'direct' or 'indirect.'" Per Mr. Justice Jackson in *Wickard v. Filburn* (1942), 317 U.S. 111, at p. 125.

14  Per Mr. Justice Murphy in *American Power and Light Co. v. SEC* (1946), 67 S. Ct. 133.

15  Per Duff J. (as he then was) in *Lawson v. Interior Tree Fruit Committee*, [1931] S.C.R. 357, at p. 366 (italics added).

16  *"Persons"* case, [1930] A.C. 124, at p. 136.

application of the wartime wages orders restricting wage adjustments to cases of "gross injustice." In the former, anything short of murder or wilful maiming is held excluded; in the latter the slightest inequality is held included.[17]

As a further illustration of the difficulty of precisely defining fundamental legal terms, let us consider the meaning of the word "free." It was discussed by the Privy Council in the construction of the "free trade" provision of the constitution of Australia and the following observations were then made:

> "Free" in itself is vague and indeterminate. It must take its colour from the context. Compare, for instance, its use in free speech, free love, free dinner and free trade. Free speech does not mean free speech; it means speech hedged in by all the laws against defamation, blasphemy, sedition and so forth; it means freedom governed by law, as was pointed out in McArthur's case. Free love, on the contrary, means licence or libertinage, though, even so, there are limitations based on public decency and so forth. Free dinner generally means free of expense, and sometimes a meal open to any one who comes, subject, however, to his condition or behaviour not being objectionable. Free trade means, in ordinary parlance, freedom from tariffs.[18]

The fundamental idea, the basic truth, expressed in those observations is that freedom is not something absolute. This is strikingly revealed by the practical consequence of the political regime that promises absolute freedom: communism. It yields freedom, but for one man: the dictator. It cannot be otherwise: total emancipation of any one man means total domination over all others. True freedom means freedom under the law. Autonomy is nothing else than freedom under the constitution.

The true concept of autonomy is thus like the true concept of freedom. It implies limitations, but it also implies free movement within the area bounded by the limitations: one no longer enjoys freedom when free to move in one direction only. It should therefore

be realized that autonomy means the right of being different, of acting differently. This is what freedom means for the individual; it is also what it must mean for provincial legislatures and governments. There is no longer any real autonomy for them to the extent that they are actually compelled, economically or otherwise, to act according to a specified pattern. Just as freedom means for the individual the right of choosing his own objective so long as it is not illegal, autonomy means for a province the privilege of defining its own policies.

It must be conceded that autonomy thus understood allows the provinces on occasion to work at cross purposes. But it would be a grave mistake to assume that this is wrong in itself, or that it is necessarily against the national interest. Unfortunately this assumption is all too frequently made and it is also all too frequently the only argument invoked against autonomy (if it can be termed an argument). Here is a typical specimen:

> The most serious specific threat to any orderly kind of future for Canada lies in the nature of our Constitution. The "property and civil rights" clause of section 92 of the British North America Act will make short work of our war-time measures and will very quickly reduce us to the bedlam of provincialism again. Can any sane person believe that the competing authorities, mostly parochial, will give us anything but anarchy leading perhaps to revolution?[19]

It will be noted that autonomy is deprecated here as a mark of insanity, but no other argument is advanced. Obviously the underlying assumption is that diversity in legislation concerning property and civil rights is against national interest. Implicit in this assumption is the belief that uniform legislation enacted by the federal Parliament would be better. Of course uniformity has its advantages, but it also has its disadvantages.

The framing of legislation, as already pointed out, is a political task.[20] Hence it is not an exact science

---

17  This observation is not meant as a criticism of the decisions; on the contrary it cannot be doubted that they carry out the intent of the enactments.

18  *James v. Commonwealth of Australia*, [1936] A.C. 578, at p. 627.

19  From the introduction by A.R.M. Lower to "War and Reconstruction," a pamphlet published in 1943 by the Canadian Institute on Public Affairs.

20  In the Aristotelian sense, not necessarily in the familiar sense of partisan politics.

but a matter of prudent judgment, on which even popularly elected men may sometimes go wrong. Why should competition be assumed to be undesirable in this sphere of action, when it proves to be such a valuable force in the economic field? It should not be assumed that, in such matters, there is necessarily one right solution, all others being wrong. Human affairs are more complex than that and, very often, several possible courses of action are open among which one may choose. Such is the situation in individual life and such it is in collective action.

This is especially so when the characteristics of individuals or of collectivities are different. Educators have long ago recognized that human beings are not robots and that varying methods and different institutions are necessary to suit varying types of intelligence and differences in character. The same difficulty is met in devising legislation: it is wrong to assume that the same laws are suitable for all peoples. On the contrary, laws have a cultural aspect; hence due consideration should be given in framing them to the character, condition, and beliefs of those for whom they are made. Autonomy is designed for the very purpose of meeting this requirement. The French-speaking population of the province of Quebec is obviously the group of Canadian citizens specially interested in it. For them autonomy is linked up with the preservation of their way of life.

Of course, it cannot be denied that the general welfare of a country requires that collective action be made uniform in some important fields, such as defence, tariff, currency. More than that, it must be conceded that the area of uniformity cannot be defined without allowing for extension in emergencies. But the increased need for uniformity in emergencies cannot be relied on as an argument against autonomy in normal times. It is already provided for.

All this means that tests of constitutional validity cannot be rigidly devised. Almost invariably they involve judgment on questions of "degree." The courts have therefore been compelled to rest their decisions touching constitutional issues on broad principles and on a general conception of what the B.N.A. Act intended to secure to the provinces and to the federal authority, respectively, rather than on an impossible technical construction:

Inasmuch as the Act embodies a compromise under which the original Provinces agreed to federate, it is important to keep in mind that the preservation of the rights of minorities was a condition on which such minorities entered into the federation, and the foundation upon which the whole structure was subsequently erected. The process of interpretation as the years go on ought not to be allowed to dim or to whittle down the provisions of the original contract upon which the federation was founded, nor is it legitimate that any judicial construction of the provisions of ss. *91* and *92* should impose a *new* and different contract upon the federating bodies.[21]

On this basis the courts have consistently refused to allow any particular clause of the B.N.A. Act to be construed in a way that would enable the federal Parliament to invade the provincial sphere of action outside of emergencies. "Such a result would appear to undermine the constitutional safeguards of Provincial constitutional autonomy"[22] was the main reason given by Lord Atkin for his refusal to construe section 132 as enabling the federal Parliament to encroach on provincial matters in order to implement labour conventions adhered to by Canada.

The same principle was applied in dealing with provincial legislation. For instance, the Supreme Court of Canada has invalidated an Alberta law interfering with the freedom of the press, because it would have jeopardized the working of federal parliamentary institutions:

Some degree of regulation of newspapers everybody would concede to the provinces. Indeed, there is a very wide field in which the provinces undoubtedly are invested with legislative authority over newspapers; but the limit, in our opinion, is reached when the legislation effects such a curtailment of the exercise of the right of public discussion as substantially to interfere with the working of the parliamentary institutions of Canada as contemplated by

---

21 In re *The Regulation and Control of Aeronautics*, [1932] A.C. 54, at p. 70.

22 *A.-G. for Canada v. A.-G. for Ontario (Labour Conventions)*, [1937] A.C. 326, at p. 352.

the provisions of *The British North America Act* and the statutes of the Dominion of Canada.[23]

Let it be noted that, here again, it is a question of "degree." Undoubtedly the task of construing our constitution would be made lighter for our courts if provincial autonomy could be defined in more specific words, but that hardly appears possible. The great value of the numerous decisions rendered since 1867 lies in the illustrations they afford of the "degree" of autonomy secured to the provinces.

A great volume of criticism has been heaped upon the Privy Council and the Supreme Court on the ground that their decisions rest on a narrow and technical construction of the B.N.A. Act. This contention is ill-founded. The decisions on the whole proceed from a much higher view. As appears from passages I have quoted, they recognize the implicit fluidity of any constitution by allowing for emergencies and by resting distinctions on questions of degree. At the same time they firmly uphold the fundamental principle of provincial autonomy: they staunchly refuse to let our federal constitution be changed gradually, by one device or another, to a legislative union. In doing so they are preserving the essential condition of the Canadian confederation.

23 *Reference re Alberta Statutes*, [1938] S.C.R. 100, at p. 134.

# 27

## Editors' Introduction

Alexander Brady was among the foremost anglophone scholars of Canadian federalism of his day. In this essay, he provides an original analysis of the *Tremblay Report*, generally considered a classic depiction of the traditional culture of Quebec and the powers needed to secure Quebec's francophone future in the sea of English North America. In 1955, the Government of Quebec under Maurice Duplessis set up the Royal Commission on Constitutional Problems, headed by Judge Thomas Tremblay. The Commission was to conduct an inquiry into problems arising from what were seen as centralizing encroachments on the power and resources granted to the provinces at the time of Confederation: tax sharing among the federal, provincial, and municipal governments and school boards; federal intervention in the field of direct taxation, particularly taxes on revenue, corporations, and inheritances; the consequences of these interventions for Quebec's legislative and administrative system and for its people; and, more generally, to examine constitutional problems of a legislative and fiscal nature. Starting with the premise that the role of the political system established in 1867 was to create an infrastructure within which the English- and French-speaking communities could benefit from federalism, the Commission concluded that the federal government is a creation of the provinces. It inferred an expansion of provincial autonomy, especially in areas of social policy, and new fiscal arrangements to accompany these policy fields. Ergo, the *Tremblay Report* is a pivotal document in Canadian constitutional politics as it articulates the agenda that would inform Quebec's position with respect to reforming Canadian federal arrangements over the coming decades.

Source: Alexander Brady, "Quebec and Canadian Federalism," *Canadian Journal of Economics and Political Science* 25(3) (1959): 259–70.

Alexander Brady

# Quebec and Canadian Federalism

CANADA'S FEDERATION IS distinct from the other two major federations in the English-speaking world in resting upon an alliance of two peoples and two cultures. Other differences exist, but this is fundamental. Since 1867 the dualism of culture has been slowly woven into the political fabric of the nation, although outside Quebec its implications are still not always appreciated or wholly accepted. With the appearance in 1956 of the *Report of the Royal Commission of Inquiry on Constitutional Problems*,[1] English-speaking Canadians have little excuse for misunderstanding the position of their French-speaking compatriots. The Commission was appointed by provincial statute in January, 1953, under the chairmanship of Judge Thomas Tremblay. Its bulky report is never likely to be widely read. It is prolix and sometimes repetitious to the point of tedium; its analysis would have been more telling had it been tidier and more compressed.

Yet, despite such flaws, it is a landmark in the literature of federalism: it describes and explains more fully than any other public document the position and anxieties of Quebec in the federal state, and defends the concept of a strict federalism as the essential basis for the success of Canada's national experiment. For the Tremblay Commissioners the issue of Quebec in the federation and the issue of the French in the nation are one and the same. In harmony with their theme they submit numerous recommendations. We cannot, however, assess these or do justice to their premises, without first reviewing briefly the historical position of Quebec in Canadian federalism.

I

At Confederation the political thinking of leaders in British North America swung between two positions, both empirical. Some of the Fathers had originally

---

1    Four vols. (Quebec, 1956). Hereafter called the *Tremblay Report*.

feared that the federal principle, especially as exemplified in the neighbouring republic, implied a dispersal of power that would drain the strength, increase the cost and jeopardize the survival of a new state in North America. Sir John A. Macdonald's first preference, like that of Sir Charles Tupper, was a legislative rather than a federal union. Yet he and his associates quickly yielded to the logic of the fact that the existing colonies enjoyed local autonomy and were unwilling to surrender it.[2] The two Canadas, moreover, possessed a single legislature, but had been compelled by the differences in their cultures to conduct their affairs almost as in a federation This was the main circumstance which changed Macdonald's mind on the nature of the new State: the French as a minority feared that in legislative union "their institutions and their laws might be assailed, and their ancestral associations, on which they prided themselves, attacked and prejudiced."[3] The French were emphatic in contending for genuine federalism, and those among them who opposed the projected confederation did so because it appeared to offer a provincial autonomy that was shadowy and insufficient. The presence of dual cultures and diverse social values among the people of the St. Lawrence Valley was thus basic in shaping the decision of the Fathers for a federal state.

Since 1867 Quebec has remained consistently attached to a strict federalism as a protector of its own culture and the cultural dualism of Canada. It has been the chief citadel of resistance to centralizing conceptions and homogenizing tendencies. Its position has sometimes been backed by Ontario, which usually however acts independently for reasons of its own. In the first three decades after Confederation Ontario might seem to have been even more emphatic in assailing the centralizing pretensions of Ottawa. Under Oliver Mowat (1872–96) it checkmated the manoeuvres of Sir John A. Macdonald, who never wholly subdued his original bias for a legislative union and persistently endeavoured to restrict the role of the provincial legislatures and to exalt that of the national Parliament. But, in Mowat's successive legal contests and triumphs before the Privy Council, Quebec was Ontario's vigilant and reliable ally. Its jurists and

politicians were equally keen to elaborate the powers of the provinces under section 92. In Judge T.J.J. Loranger among others it had a constitutional expert who in the eighties presented with distinguished clarity the provincial case. "If the federal pretensions prevail," wrote Loranger in 1883, "and if the principle of the provinces' inferiority and dependence of their legislatures with regard to the federal authority is recognized, in less than half a century their absorption will be accomplished and the federal system will give way to the legislative union so rightly feared in our province."[4]

In politics, two Quebec figures in the first half-century of federation especially advanced the provincial cause: Honoré Mercier and Wilfrid Laurier. Both reflected the inflamed feelings of French Canadian nationalism in the eighties provoked by the sorry events of the Riel Rebellion and its aftermath. Both, and especially Laurier, also responded to the more stable emotions about provincial rights which in greater or lesser degree have inspired all French leaders since 1867. Mercier's principal achievement was his convening an interprovincial conference in 1887 to examine the relations of the provinces with the federal government. Under the chairmanship of Oliver Mowat five provincial premiers there adopted resolutions that challenged and rejected the centralist policies of Macdonald. Although their requests, including a surrender by the federal government of its power to disallow provincial acts, were not acceptable to Ottawa, the case for provincial autonomy received an important impetus from its formal affirmation.

Laurier's leadership of the national Liberals (1887–1919) secured, by quiet persuasion at the highest levels in Ottawa, a sympathy for Quebec's position and for provincial autonomy in general. "The only means of maintaining Confederation," he declared in 1889, "is to recognize that, within its sphere assigned to it by the constitution, each province is as independent of control by the federal Parliament as the latter is from control by the provincial legislatures." This dictum is important, not for its novelty, but for the fact that it influenced Laurier's tactics and policies throughout his career. It was evident in his stand on the Manitoba school question before his electoral triumph in 1896,

2   See, e.g. *Confederation Debates*, 29.
3   *Ibid.*
4   Quoted in *Tremblay Report*, I, 67.

and in office he never lost a French Canadian's anxiety for the autonomy of the provinces. Admittedly he was aided by the stream of events. In successive decisions from that of *Hodge* v. *the Queen* in 1883, the Privy Council consolidated and fortified the power of the provincial legislatures, while the growth in population and industry of Quebec and Ontario enhanced the prestige of their governments and goaded them to seek in the courts that larger legislative competence essential for developing their natural resources. In employing the power of disallowance Laurier and his colleagues sought to pursue a fresh course. They did not consider the power obsolete (although privately Laurier told Blake that it was alien to the federal idea), but generally avoided its use as a corrective of the alleged errors and injustices committed by provincial legislatures, and confined it to cases where the legislation affected Federal or imperial interests. No other view, they were convinced, could secure provincial autonomy and local democracy. Laurier's governments between 1896–1911 admittedly disallowed thirty provincial statutes, but of these twenty issued solely from the legislature of British Columbia and affected both Canadian and imperial interests by dealing adversely with the employment and status of Asiatics. Since 1896 only one Quebec act has been disallowed compared with five in the preceding twenty-nine years and only two Ontario acts compared with eight in the earlier period.[5]

Soon after the passing of the Laurier régime, there appeared fresh threats to provincial autonomy, which were mainly related, as they still are, to the issues of finance. On a small scale before the First World War and on a larger scale after it, national governments began to make grants to the provinces on conditions which implied a federal control over their use. This new procedure came from a quickened and wider sense of national interest in the policy-makers at Ottawa, coupled with a desire to circumvent the restrictions imposed on them by the constitution. They were persuaded that, without loss of provincial autonomy, the provinces and the national government might create an *ad hoc* partnership for certain desirable ends with funds jointly contributed. Grants,

such as those provided in 1919 to encourage technical education, trespassed on the legislative field of the provinces, but the provincial governments could not resist the temptation to accept virtual supplements to provincial revenue.

From the outset leaders in Quebec viewed this form of federal largesse with disquiet or positive disfavor. Ernest Lapointe, a prominent French Canadian spokesman in the Liberal Opposition at the close of the First World War, attacked conditional grants. In his view they intruded on provincial jurisdiction and were unfair to non-concurring provinces, whose citizens were taxed to benefit those in other provinces.[6] Indirectly but forcibly, a federal government thus exerted coercion in fields where its action was either constitutionally ambiguous or invalid. It practised generosity at the price of provincial autonomy, and employed its own relative affluence to entice and bribe impecunious provinces, whittle away their independence, and generally impair their freedom to manoeuvre. In Quebec this argument has ever since rendered doughty service in the polemic of federal-provincial relations.

The inter-war ministries of Mackenzie King, wherein Ernest Lapointe as an influential member, were on the whole unsympathetic to conditional grants, although the social and political compulsions of the time involved them in this policy to some degree. In July, 1924, a special committee of the Commons advocated that the federal and provincial governments should share the costs of old age pensions for needy persons over seventy. The Liberals were reluctant to reject a proposal that might win popularity. King himself was deeply interested in policies of social welfare and alert to their importance in political strategy. Hence in 1927 his Government sponsored a scheme whereby it would pay half the cost to every province which agreed to provide old age pensions. The provinces, beginning with British Columbia, made such agreements, and finally in 1936 New Brunswick and Quebec participated, although the Quebec government still viewed old age pensions as an undesirable federal intrusion into the provincial field. It could not, however, continue to ignore the unpalatable fact that if it remained outside the scheme

---

5   See G.V. La Forest, *Disallowance and Reservation of Provincial Legislation* (Ottawa, 1955), Appendix A.

6   *House of Commons Debates*, 1919, p. 3794.

its people would be helping to pay for pensions they were not free to enjoy.

Despite the precedent of old age pensions, the inter-war administrations of Mackenzie King, influenced by their French Canadian supporters, never displayed enthusiasm for conditional grants. Quebec resented them as the vehicle of a vigorous federal policy. Its leaders had no wish to see the national government in a position to exert pressure on the provinces. Such grants placed it in this position because they implied centralized authority in making decisions by lawmakers and officials in Ottawa, the majority of whom were English Canadians.[7]

Since 1939 profound changes in Canadian society and ways of thought have involved a heavier subsidization of the provinces. National enactments have multiplied conditional grants until today there are half a hundred different kinds. Some, such as those relating to the reclamation of land and to fisheries, mainly concern specific provinces and regions. Others, such as those in public health and old age assistance appeal to all the provinces, and enlist the active support of all, including Quebec. This accentuated trend in federal action is traceable to social forces linked with industrialism and nationalism, accelerated by war and the preparation for war. The appetite of a growing industrial people for public services within provincial jurisdiction has sharpened, especially for highways, welfare and health services, and education. Federal governments, of course, might have left the provinces alone to cope with these services as best they could, but they have been persistently pressed by public opinion to feed them with federal funds. In some cases the pressure has been strongest from people in the relatively poor and less favoured areas, but it commonly comes from certain organized interests in all the provinces and especially from the more industrialized regions. The more rapid the pace of urbanization, the more varied and insistent are the demands on the national treasury. On their part federal politicians are loath to miss an opportunity of winning votes by spending money, and now find it easy to justify expenditure on the grounds of a compelling national interest. Since their primary concern is to placate the electors, they

must listen to the numerous pressure groups which often are indifferent to the political and legal facts of federalism and rationalize their own interests in terms of a national interest. Thus the Liberal party, ascendant in Ottawa for the first dozen years after the Second World War, became fired by a stronger nationalism, and rapidly retreated from its former scruples about encroaching on provincial jurisdiction. In successive enactments after 1940 it sponsored abundant grants, conditional and unconditional.

The Tremblay Commission, in surveying this panorama of post-war change, admit with evident sorrow that "a vast network has been spread which binds the provinces to the central government and which, to a certain extent, provides them with the financial means of discharging their legislative functions but always at the discretion and on the terms of the wealthy and powerful donor."[8] In all this the French Canadians as the chief defenders of traditional federalism face a difficult dilemma. Either they must patiently resign themselves to a course of events that threatens to erode the older federalism, or pursue more resolutely than hitherto the policy of survival by withdrawal. Some fear that they have no choice, and that the decision is made for them by the speed and inexorable strides of an industrialism which transforms their society, exposes them to a stream of influences from outside, and assimilates them in character to English-speaking Canadians. Since 1939 Quebec with rich mineral resources, abundant water power, and a high birth rate, has shared substantially in the country's material expansion. Its industrial production has multiplied fivefold, and light industries such as textiles have yielded ground to heavy industries such as mining and metallurgy. Industrialism in the province was born long before, but the Second World War accelerated its growth. The drift from farm to factory was quickened. The old rural framework of life, in which for generations the relatively isolated culture of the French Canadians was sustained, is crumbling now that only a fifth of the people live in strictly rural areas. As urban dwellers and industrial workers they undergo much the same experience as labour elsewhere in Canada, respond to the prevalent appetite for social security, and are likely to be no less eager for

---

7   For Mackenzie King's concern for the position of the provinces in this matter see *ibid.*, 1931, pp. 1959 ff.

8   *Tremblay Report*, II, 214.

the services that the federal treasury can ensure. With the progress of industrialism a variety of interests in French Canadian society, notably organized labour, establish a rapport with like interests in Ontario and other provinces, and become less diffident in dealing with a government in Ottawa. Quebec may still resemble a cultural island within the nation, but an island now with numerous bridges that diminish its isolation.

The Union Nationale party led by Maurice Duplessis has held office in Quebec since 1944, and in the face of these forces has vehemently defended the province's autonomy. It has freely exploited the sentiments of French Canadian nationalism aroused by the depression of the thirties and the subsequent tensions of the Second World War. Yet it is difficult to determine precisely how much the longevity of M. Duplessis' régime is due to his display of autonomist convictions. Other obvious factors contribute: his smoothly working political machine, his rare art in winning support by dexterous use of patronage, and his gains from an electoral distribution of seats that bears little relation to the rapid urbanizing of the population. Despite his strong position, he has found it expedient to accept many conditional grants from Ottawa; others he has brusquely rejected. His criterion for acceptance or rejection is the extent of the threat to the traditional autonomy of the province. Thus he entered into agreements to obtain substantial grants from the federal treasury for health services, including hospital construction, general public health, and the control of tuberculosis and cancer. Although he also accepted the conditions prescribed in 1952 for joint provincial and federal old age assistance for the needy, he rejected the federal subsidies to aid in building the Trans-Canada Highway through Quebec. Even more emphatically he rejected the subsidizing of Quebec universities from federal funds because it touched, not merely traditional provincial jurisdiction, but the sensitive nerves of culture. For him this was an appropriate battle ground. "What counted in Judas' betrayal of Christ," he declared, "was not the sum of thirty pieces of silver but the fact that Judas had betrayed his Master." Acquiescence in such federal action would merely stimulate Ottawa to indulge further in an interference all the more unwarranted in being needless, since the provincial government itself could adequately sustain the colleges of the province,

especially if the federal authority left it appropriate fields for direct taxation. This point raises the controversial and basic question of the taxing power, which has occasioned the most prolonged and wordy debates between Ottawa and Quebec.

The modern issue of taxation originated as a by-product of the First World War, when the national government in 1916 resorted to direct taxes on war profits and in the next year on general income. After the war the income tax survived as an important instrument in federal policy, and provoked in Quebec strong protests. "Ottawa," asserted Premier Taschereau in 1920, "has unceremoniously arrogated to itself Our Own sources of revenue." But the federal income tax was there to stay, and the facts of the depression in the thirties helped to secure its permanence. The depression, however, had contrasting and conflicting effects within the federation. In English-speaking Canada, especially in the west, the current of opinion now ran more strongly than before towards a heavy reliance on Ottawa. The taxing power of the federal government was accepted as an inevitable adjunct to its responsibility. In Quebec, by contrast, the current of opinion ran turbulently in the opposite direction. The harsh tensions of the depression merely exacerbated French Canadian nationalism, raised more urgently the persistent theme of cultural survival, and made the régime of M. Duplessis after 1936 more uncompromising than any previous government in clinging to every element of provincial autonomy. In the economic and social facts of the time Quebec sensed a new and greater menace to the position that it was obligated by long tradition to defend. The Sirois Commission (appointed in August, 1937) was naturally viewed by M. Duplessis as objectionable because it was appointed without prior consultation with the provinces and unilaterally investigated matters that were crucially important to them. His government made explicit to the Commission its opposition to any abridgment of provincial rights, or any significant change in the federal pact unless accepted by all the provinces.

At that time, however, Quebec's position was not isolated. Four other provincial governments also argued before the Sirois Commission against any drastic change, fiscal or otherwise, in the existing distribution of federal power. Only the four then most needy provinces, Manitoba, Saskatchewan, Nova Scotia, and

Prince Edward Island, were ready to barter their right to tax for provincial aid. All four proclaimed fidelity to federalism, but, in their precarious financial plight, a secure revenue had more appeal than fiscal liberty. The conference of January, 1941, convened by Ottawa to get agreement for implementing the principal recommendations of the *Sirois Report*, adjourned in failure on the second day because Ontario, British Columbia, and Alberta rejected a revision of the federal system on the terms recommended, and the national Government would consider no others. From September, 1939, to August, 1944, Quebec was ruled by the Liberals under Adélard Godbout, who cautiously did not commit himself. "We are here," he remarked, "to study; we will listen and we are ready to co-operate."

After the Second World War the issue of federal taxation appeared to Quebec in a more ominous light. To meet the urgent necessities of war the federal Government had secured (in 1912) the agreement of all the provinces to vacate in its favour the right to levy personal income and corporation taxes and to accept compensation in annual grants. Here was a means that with provincial consent and without a constitutional amendment might at any time augment the fiscal initiative of Ottawa, and for many reasons Ottawa was anxious that it should endure into the peace. Public sentiments at the time incessantly pressed the federal Government to do and prepare for countless things. Fears of a post-war depression and haunting memories of unemployment in the thirties were in the air. Conceptions of an economy managed through fiscal controls seeped into the thinking of federal ministers and public servants. The ideas of Maynard Keynes took root in the Department of Finance, and to lend them scope it seemed essential to have federal control over the major and most remunerative taxes. Hence at the Dominion-Provincial Conference on Reconstruction (1945–6) Ottawa submitted to the provinces far-ranging proposals, buttressed by a series of supplementary studies, which among other things would have left to it an exclusive access to personal income and corporation taxes and succession duties, while in return Ottawa provided per capita provincial grants.

Quebec, like some other provinces, viewed these plans of Ottawa as a serious menace to federalism. If they were fully implemented, the major initiative in social policy would irretrievably shift to the national

capital, and provincial independence in finance and manoeuvrability in policy would drastically diminish. In the words of the Quebec brief the proposals would "exclude the provinces from the most important fields of direct taxation and to that extent deprive them of the exercise of the powers assigned to them by the constitution." Ontario's plea was similar. It denied, moreover, that centralization could provide protection against depression, although it would certainly violate federal principles. Yet neither Quebec nor Ontario outdid in vigorous and eloquent protest the Premier of Nova Scotia, who declared that if the proposals ware accepted, "provincial autonomy will be gone. Provincial independence will vanish. Provincial dignity will disappear. The provincial governments will become mere annuitants of Ottawa."

The Conference of 1945–6 dissolved in acrimony and without accomplishment. The wartime agreements, however, ran their course to 1947. In the interval certain fundamental facts in the situation worked inexorably in favour of Ottawa, especially the inequality of the provinces in economic and financial strength and hence their divergence in interpreting the nature of the federal bond. The financially weak or less favoured naturally saw advantages in retaining payments from Ottawa. On principle they were not really averse to rental agreements provided that they got good terms, although for purposes of bargaining they might appear appropriately coy. Their outlook on the federation fundamentally differed from that of Quebec, because they were not preoccupied with the feeling of having to defend through federalism a distinct culture. Consequently they were disposed to take a short-run view of federal matters. The necessities of the day dominated, for under pressure from their electorates they thought primarily of services to which they were committed and must become committed, and of how to secure the revenue necessary to finance them. Even the strong and affluent among the English-speaking provinces do not act very differently, but their strength commonly permits them to take longer views.

This circumstance in the situation makes plain why Ottawa, after failing to obtain agreement for a general scheme, could successfully resort to the tactic of individual agreements on the basis of new formulae. By the beginning of 1948 seven provinces and in 1949 Newfoundland had signed such agreements. Quebec and Ontario then alone remained outside, but in 1952 Ottawa, armed with different formulae, was able to win Ontario and isolate Quebec. The history of these years illustrates how expediency dominates in Canadian federalism. With the rapidly changing society an elaborate process of individual and constant bargaining between the federal and provincial governments is the accepted norm, and the provinces rarely present a united front. On such a basis the federation will continue to operate, for it serves best the short-run interests of Ottawa and all the provinces except Quebec.

## II

The Tremblay Commission, aided by the numerous briefs of organized interests in the province, assess Quebec's place in the federation in the light of history and philosophy. Much of their detailed report, with its wealth of facts, surveys the past and analyses the present in order to underline the special identity of the French community in Canada's evolution, its relation to the federal structure after 1867, and the threats to its survival and the survival of federalism that result from the forces of the twentieth century, especially industrialism, depression, and war.

The historical section of the report is invaluable, and, despite a bias on some matters, is likely to be acceptable to scholars outside Quebec. Agreement on facts, however, does not imply agreement on their interpretation. The historical struggle of the French Canadian for cultural survival gives him a special point of view, which the Tremblay Commission express in terms of an appropriate philosophy. This philosophy is a form of Catholic pluralism, emphasizing the necessary freedom for cultural groups to operate and survive, combined with the assumptions of a liberal nationalism. Federal policy, it is argued, should be determined, less by the material conditions and appetites of the society, than by the wholesome impulses towards the freedom of cultural groups and the freedom of the individual to develop his personality in a group. The goals of the Canadian nation should be association not assimilation, diversity not uniformity, the vitality of all the distinct groups in the state and

not their standardization. These concepts of liberal Catholic philosophers, such as Jacques Maritain, are readily translated into the traditional French Canadian attachment to a strict federalism, stressing the full autonomy of the province with its aggregate of usages and traditions. This pluralist philosophy might have found an uncongenial environment in the Quebec of the nineteenth century under its dominant ultramontanism. But in the 1950's it seems to fit comfortably into the French Canadian heritage.

What kind of offspring in practical recommendations does this marriage of history and philosophy produce? The Tremblay Commission are explicit about what it should produce. They formulate many recommendations, some of which differ greatly in content and purpose from those of the Sirois Commission twenty years ago. They primarily seek to stop the erosion of federalism, threatened by the centralizing pressures of Ottawa especially in finance. They launch what they hope are destructive assault against the "new federalism" and its apologists, English and French, and single out for criticism the views of a French Canadian advocate, Maurice Lamontagne, author of Le Féderalisme canadien.[9] "To believe and to try to have it believed," they wrote, "that there is respect, in Canada, for the autonomy of the provinces, because they are allowed to exist as mere administrative units to which the central authority will distribute living allowances, is mere self-deception and an attempt to deceive others. It confronts true federalism with mere administrative decentralization which is to be found in any state but which does not truly allow autonomy of the regional and local communities."[10]

The Tremblay Commission think of a genuine federal state as one wherein financial and political powers are so apportioned between the federal and unit governments that their self-operating and self-governing functions are unfettered by interferences from one another. "There can be no federalism," they write, "without autonomy of the state's constituent parts, and no sovereignty of the various governments without fiscal and financial autonomy."[11] Such a federal structure must ensure the identity of the whole and the identity

9   Quebec, 1954.
10  Tremblay Report, II, 276.
11  Ibid., III, 294.

of the parts. It implies, not isolation, but close co-operation among the several governments. This general concept of federalism is one to which many modern political theorists would readily subscribe. The inevitable question, however, is, what division of power has most logic in a given situation? Even among genuine liberal pluralists it is far from easy to secure agreement on this thorny issue in view of the speed of economic and social change. The modem industrial economy never stands still, and every major innovation affects profoundly the federal jurisdiction.

The Tremblay Commission naturally enough use a criterion calculated to ensure for a province an authority sufficiently broad to protect its culture. They are confident that the constitution drafted by the Fathers provided this authority, and that in the past the Judicial Committee and the Supreme Court of Canada jealously upheld it. The real threat to the federation in the present generation comes from the centralizing actions of an Ottawa forgetful that federalism implies two orders of government and not one. The national authority has employed various expedients, such as conditional grants, to encroach on provincial jurisdiction. It has freely invoked ancillary powers in the B.N.A. Act and has used the financial incapacity of the provinces as an excuse for doing countless things, while its own inroads in the field of direct taxation accentuate their incapacity. The Commission are particularly critical of the national government for exercising powers, as in some forms of education, allegedly ancillary to those in Section 91. Ottawa may properly legislate for the Indians, the penitentiaries, the armed forces, agriculture, immigration, and radio, but assumes that each of these subjects has an educational aspect that justifies its intervention in the field of education associated with the subject. Judge Tremblay and his colleagues comment caustically on the manner in which the Massey Commission, by what they deem a series of specious arguments, establish a right of the federal government to intervene in certain fields of education and then transfer this right into a duty in the name of the public welfare and spiritual values. They think that the extravagant use of ancillary powers seriously threatens the survival of the federation, and quote with approval Justice Duff's view that the "division of legislative authority is the principle of the British North America Act, and if the doctrine

of necessarily incidental powers is to be extended to all cases in which inconvenience arises from such a division, that is the end of the federal character of the Union."[12]

On this premise the Tremblay Commission consider that for the future federal power should be employed, not to displace the province but to establish the conditions, including a sufficient and independent revenue, that would allow them to play the special role assigned to them under the constitution. The provinces need fiscal powers commensurate with their legislative powers, and can secure them only by a logical division of the field of direct taxation between them and the national government. Yet, even with a careful division of the taxing power, some provinces would likely remain unable to obtain revenue sufficient to finance services comparable with those of their wealthier or mere industrialized neighbours, and for this situation the Commissioners think that the appropriate remedy is a "financial equalization organism."[13] Instead of leaving solely to Ottawa the major task of combatting economic depressions, the provinces should for this purpose be brought into a close co-operative relation with Ottawa and be organized to participate in the anti-cyclic policy according to their capacity and the requirements of their institutional role.[14] In a period of depression they, like the federal government, should be able to sell bonds to the Bank of Canada. The Commission emphasize the value of a permanent committee of the federal-provincial conferences to secure continuity of co-operation in the interval between conferences, and in addition a permanent council of the provinces, confined exclusively to them, somewhat on the lines of the Council of State Governments in the United States. One body that they have in mind now already exists in the Federal-Provincial Continuing Committee on Fiscal and Economic Matters.

Such briefly is the main case of the Tremblay Commission for a revitalized federalism. It is both radical and controversial. Its chief argument and proposals are derived from briefs submitted to the Commission, and unquestionably represent important bodies of

---

12  *Ibid.*, II, 236.
13  *Ibid.*, III, 297.
14  *Ibid.*, III, 299.

opinion in the province of Quebec, although not all that province's opinion is necessarily well represented. A convinced federalist elsewhere in Canada could accept the main thesis of the Tremblay Commission that decentralization is desirable to invigorate local autonomy in all the provinces. But the patent fact is that in English-speaking Canada, in the post-war years especially, the current of nationalism has run powerfully in the opposite direction and has been stimulated by the evident insecurities of the national state in the contemporary world. The dangers to Canada's survival as a political entity have among English-speaking Canadians weakened the federal spirit. Moreover there is a growing sense that many problems of social life can best be settled nationally and that social progress demands national standards. Hence the pressure of special interests for action from Ottawa has increased rather than diminished. With its larger and more flexible source of income Ottawa can most effectively achieve what these special interests want. Federal politicians, moreover, with the indispensable help of the national treasury, never cease to angle for votes by promising many things and doing many things. The very nature of democracy is contributory to this end. Here are nationalizing forces, which at present are not easy to control in order to guarantee the complete integrity of the federal system.

Yet federalism in Canada has not suffered a final eclipse. It is not on the road to dissolution. Many of the provinces constitute immense territories with abundant resources, and already have grown into populous and prosperous communities which are destined to become more populous and more self-confident. They will increasingly require all the legislative and administrative powers that they now possess to achieve effective regional planning and development. Consequently their political leaders will be anxious to erect defences against the continued seepage of power and initiative to Ottawa. Much of the distinctiveness in Canada's nationality in the future must derive from the recognition of its cultural dualism, and the more this fact is appreciated the more sensitive will be the concern for federalism. In the meantime Quebec's devotion to the federal idea has served a national purpose; it has helped to lessen the danger of excessive centralization in Ottawa and the equal danger of a rigid framework advantageous to Ottawa. Rigid arrangements acceptable today may be intolerable tomorrow. Flexibility is a prime condition for a healthy federalism, and paradoxically Quebec by its unbending position has been its guarantor.

## 28

### Editors' Introduction

This well-known chapter from *Federalism and the French Canadians*, published on the eve of Pierre Elliott Trudeau becoming leader of the Liberal Party and prime minister in 1968, lays out his motivation for going into politics as well as his constitutional and political vision for Canada's federal future. In an infamous televised clash between the then federal minister of justice and Quebec premier Daniel Johnson, Trudeau, a bilingual francophone Quebecker, vehemently opposed Johnson's demands for special status for Trudeau's home province. The logic informing Trudeau's position is set out in this famous chapter. Both the chapter and its logic continue to epitomize that position in Canadian constitutional politics, which holds that the federal government ultimately has the responsibility for defending French across Canada. His thinking was influenced by Eli Kedourie who, having become a refugee during World War II, warned about the excesses of ethnic nationalism and militated for civic nationalism as the antidote.

The book, and especially this particular chapter, garnered considerable attention and attracted just as much criticism. The most stinging rebuke came in 1985 from Trudeau's intellectual nemesis, Charles Taylor in his *Philosophical Papers*, where he objects to Trudeau's liberal atomism which holds that "men are self-sufficient outside of society." Taylor sparred with Trudeau on the campaign trail as well, unsuccessfully contesting his home riding in four separate elections as a candidate for the NDP. The controversy of Trudeau's constitutional politics notwithstanding, has Canada gone from Trudeaumania to Trudeauphobia to Trudeau-nostalgia? Does Trudeau's constitutional legacy as manifest in today's Canada not approximate that which he had set forth to accomplish and that is outlined in large part in the excerpt below?

Source: Pierre Elliott Trudeau, "Quebec and the Constitutional Problem," in *Federalism and the French Canadians* (Toronto: Macmillan, 1968), 3–51.

Pierre Elliott Trudeau

# Quebec and the Constitutional Problem

Translated from the French by Joanne L'Heureux

### INTRODUCTION

The mandate given to the "Constitution Committee" of the Quebec Legislative Assembly on May 22, 1963, by a unanimous vote of the Assembly, reads as follows: "To determine the objectives that should be pursued by French Canada in the revision of the Canadian constitution, and the best means of attaining them."

I understand the great importance of Canada's ethnic problem, and I can also see that the Legislature of a province that is the home of 83 per cent of all Canadians whose mother tongue is French (according to the 1961 census) should take this fact into account when considering constitutional questions.

Having said this, however, I should like to make a few comments on the mandate of the Constitution Committee.

(a) From a constitutional point of view, the Quebec Legislature has no authority to speak on behalf of "French Canada." French Canada includes 850,000 Canadians whose mother tongue is French, who live outside Quebec, and over whom the Legislature has no jurisdiction. On the other hand, Quebec includes a million people whose mother tongue is not French and from whom the Legislature cannot constitutionally disassociate itself. I do understand, however, that because of historical circumstances Quebec has had to, and must still, assume responsibility for the French language and culture; and that in any case it will always have to protect and give particular consideration to the values held by the majority of its citizens.

(b) From a philosophical point of view, the aim of a political society is not the glorification of a "national fact" (in its ethnic sense). A state that defined its function essentially in terms of ethnic attributes would inevitably become chauvinistic and intolerant. The state, whether provincial, federal, or perhaps later supra-national, must seek the general welfare of all its citizens regardless of sex, colour, race, religious beliefs, or ethnic origin.

(c) From a practical point of view, most labour organizations in Quebec, despite their very large majorities of French Canadians, do nevertheless contain important ethnic minorities. These organizations are obliged by their own constitutions as well as by law to represent all their members without distinction of sex, belief, colour, or national origin. If the mandate of the Constitution Committee is to be taken literally, how could these organizations possibly appear before it?

These remarks are necessary to indicate the perspective of this review, in which, first and foremost, I have attempted to formulate a line of thought acceptable to workers and farmers as members of the political society in Quebec, rather than as members of a specific ethnic group. I leave the pursuit of properly nationalistic ideologies to so-called "national" or patriotic organizations. Such a role would be unsuited to labour or agricultural associations whose primary function is promoting the social or economic interests of workers. Should these organizations—or the state itself for that matter—direct the whole of their action towards obtaining the specific good of one ethnic group, thus becoming the vehicles of ethnocentric ideologies, they would inevitably be moving in the wrong direction.

This is not to say that the state must disregard cultural or linguistic values. Among the many values that a political society must protect and develop, these have high priority. It is therefore entirely desirable that a state ensure, through its constitution and legislation, the protection of such values. Moreover, it is inevitable that its policies will serve the interests of ethnic groups, and especially of the majority group in proportion to its numbers; but this will happen as a natural consequence of the equality of all citizens, not as a special privilege of the largest group.

Similarly, private organizations must consider the rights of the French-speaking group to which the majority of its members belong. Because the main object of the present review is to discuss the social and economic repercussions of our country's political structures upon the working classes, the reader should not conclude that I am indifferent to the other problems arising from the fact that two great linguistic communities have coexisted in Canada for the past two centuries. Not only am I far from indifferent about this matter, but I greatly fear that if, through stubbornness, indifference, or fanaticism, no adequate solution to these problems is found in the near future, Confederation will face serious difficulties. Canada must become a truly bilingual country in which the linguistic majority stops behaving as if it held special and exclusive rights, and accepts the country's federal nature with all its implications.

It seems quite evident to me that the English-speaking majority has behaved, historically, as though French Canadians were merely one of the country's ethnic minorities, with a few special privileges. The most striking example of this attitude occurs in the federal civil service, where English is, to all intents and purposes, the only working language. In the past, the Department of External Affairs has built up an image of Canada as a unilingual, English country. I could almost say the same of other departments and Crown corporations. The federal capital is an English capital. The Canadian army is an English army in which French Canadians have to overcome serious handicaps, especially from a linguistic point of view.

With regard to language and education, French Canadians in other provinces do not enjoy rights comparable to those of Quebec's English Canadians. This is true even of New Brunswick, where Acadians constitute two-fifths of the population.

The C.B.C., despite all its efforts in the past few years, has not yet managed to extend its French radio and television network from coast to coast.

Many companies established in Quebec have not respected the language and culture of their employees, nor those of the population. French Canadians have been and often still are in an inferior position as far as hiring or promotion are concerned.

On the other hand, sometimes by agreement and sometimes not, the federal government has often encroached on areas of provincial jurisdiction. It took advantage of wars and crises to seize the lion's share of tax revenues; and it also took advantage of the negligence or weakness of the provincial government in Quebec, which did not always defend its jurisdiction (the best way would have been simply to occupy it), and which did not secure a large enough share of revenues to be able to fulfil its constitutional obligations.

Where should a solution to all these problems be sought? In my opinion, it would be an illusion to look for it in sweeping constitutional changes. A constitution by itself cannot provide adequate protection against the enormous influence exerted by the great mass of Anglo-Saxons that occupies most of North America and penetrates deeply even into Quebec. This influence is not merely the result of our powerful modern means of communication; it comes from the fact that we have at our doorstep a country that is the richest in the world, the most advanced industrially, and strategically one of the poles in our planet's military equilibrium.

In such a situation, legal guarantees by themselves are far too fragile to ensure the survival of French language and culture. People who think such guarantees are enough may be the most dangerous enemies of the traditions we wish to safeguard and perpetuate.

I do not consider a state's political structures or constitutional forms to have absolute and eternal value. But it would be wrong to think that I am merely reluctant to touch the constitution. History teaches us that diversity rather than uniformity is the general rule in this land. With the exception of a certain number of basic principles that must be safeguarded, such as liberty and democracy, the rest ought to be adapted to the circumstances of history, to traditions, to geography, to cultures, and to civilizations.

Thus I am neither shocked nor astonished that individuals and groups are advocating constitutional changes in Canada. There are dozens of ways of thinking politically about the country, from Quebec separatism to the idea of a unitary Canadian state. If we were confronted with a population that had just immigrated to a new territory, several hypotheses would be possible and they could be the subject of heated debate. But this is not the case. Even though our country is young, it has a history, and has lived through some profound experiences which have left their mark upon it, and which it would be vain and childish to ignore.

May I make a comparison with trade unionism? The unions know that they have a relatively large freedom to manoeuvre when the first collective agreement is negotiated; but this no longer holds for subsequent renewals. They cannot, for the mere pleasure of it, play around with those sections of their contract that have not given rise to difficulties. Nor does the opposition come solely from the employer's side: the workers themselves are not prepared to engage in battles simply to obtain a contract that would be theoretically more satisfactory.

I want to make these points at the very beginning of this article, to emphasize that I am far from disagreeing with many of the complaints brought before the Constitution Committee by individuals or organizations. What I do dispute is the validity of the solutions proposed, especially those simplified, unrealistic formulas designed only to inflame existing passions.

In any case these briefs have not, generally speaking, paid much attention to the fate of the working classes and the consequences for them of the proposed constitutional transformations. The main characteristics of these proposals are the emphasis constantly placed upon so-called "national" questions and the almost total lack of discussion of their effect upon the working classes as such. I am afraid that excessive preoccupation with the future of the language has made certain people forget the future of the man speaking it. A working man may care about his language and cultural values; he also cares very strongly about having a decent life without the risk of losing the little he has through some misguided political adventure. This is why, in the present article, I shall often insist on economic realities; these realities constitute one of the main preoccupations of the working class.

Apart from their professional and sometimes even ideological differences, the various working classes occupy more or less the same position in their political society; the position of people whose material security is quite precarious, and whom the slightest illness or economic recession can plunge into misery.

(a) The prosperity of the agricultural class, since it includes producers, is related in the long term to that of urban workers. All these people contribute in complementary ways to the same general economic activity. The farmers of Quebec, for example, spent $41,250,509 in 1963 for agricultural equipment alone. This economic interdependence becomes even more evident in times of crisis. The mobility of labour, which has long been expressed in Quebec as an exodus from rural areas, means that in effect the two classes are lumped together on the employment market; one group's unemployment impoverishes all the others; and though they may be stricken at different times, they are all left perilously close to actual destitution.

(b) It is in the interests of all labouring classes, as consumers, to have a sound economy capable of supporting a high standard of living. They are aware of the dangers of closed commercial policies which may give a temporary advantage to one class or to a certain percentage of workers, but which in the long term carry the risk of impoverishing the entire population.

In short, labouring classes, whether urban or rural, will be the more or less immediate victims of any political or economic mistakes that might be made by the governing classes. It is characteristic of these victims, however, that their social and economic situation renders them incapable of protecting themselves adequately against the consequences of such mistakes. They are therefore the first to be concerned in constitutional discussions that claim to define new instruments of power within society. It is time people realized that in a democratic country the constitution is the shield protecting the weak from the arbitrary intervention of power.

These preliminary points having been made, I would now like to examine the problem that the Constitution Committee has been set up to resolve: the kind of constitution that would best promote the full development of those values considered important by the political society of Quebec.

## THE BASIC FACTS OF THE PROBLEM

The first law of politics is to start from given facts. The second is to take stock of the real relationship between forces that may divide or unite the existing political factors. Thus, it will soon become evident, even to the least acute of Quebec observers, that no constitutional reform—indeed not even a declaration

of independence—could make French a major language of business and industry in North America, or make Quebec a state capable of dictating its terms to the rest of the continent.

The basic facts of the constitutional problem faced by Quebec are, in brief, as follows:

(a) Economic facts. The economy of Quebec is closely linked with that of Canada and both are largely dominated by the economy of the United States. This means that Quebec workers cannot discuss their prospects without taking into account the fact that they are integrated into a continental economy. For better or worse, Quebec is linked to the most powerful economic giant the world has ever known: a giant with whom its territories are contiguous. Capital, employment, and technology tend to cross the border as a result of legislation favourable to them.

(b) Linguistic facts. In North America, French is the mother tongue of five or six million people, while English is the mother tongue of one hundred and eighty-two million. The only considerable territory in the Western hemisphere in which French-speaking people are grouped in sufficient numbers and are sufficiently attached to French for this language to be a political society's first idiom is Quebec, a province with a population of 5,260,000 in a country of 18,240,000 and on a continent of 233 million. Even if New Brunswick were eventually to be added to it, the two provinces would still have fewer than six million people. In Quebec, the number of persons *speaking only French* tends to increase in absolute numbers (2,016,000 in 1941 and 3,255,000 in 1961) and even, it seems, as a percentage of the total population (60.5 per cent were in this category in 1941 and 61.9 per cent in 1961). In New Brunswick, the absolute number increased from 82,000 to 112,000 during the same period, and the percentage from 18 per cent to 18.7 per cent. In the rest of Canada, the percentage of persons *speaking only French* is insignificant, reaching a maximum of 1.5 per cent in Ontario. Everywhere in North America, except in Quebec (and perhaps New Brunswick, Prince Edward Island, and the Yukon), the phenomenon of cultural assimilation tends therefore to reduce the importance of French as a language used by the population.

These economic and linguistic realities result in a certain balance of power that no amount of exhortation—even incorporated into a constitutional document—can change. The world might be a better place if Quebec were economically self-sufficient, or if a hundred million French-speaking people lived in North America. But politics cannot take into account what might have been; and any constitutional reform based on such suppositions would lead only to disillusion and disaster. On the other hand, an objective appraisal of the basic facts allows one to make the best possible use of these facts and, over a long period, to bring forces of change to bear upon them so that new policies become not only desirable, but possible.

These forces of change are many and various, acting sometimes on men and sometimes on things. For example, it was a search for religious freedom that touched off the immigration of the Puritans to New England, and of the Doukhobors to Canada. Another example is that the demand for independence in Indonesia caused a flow of European capital away from that country. And a final example: in an attempt to escape from misery, Irishmen have fled to England, Englishmen to Canada, and French Canadians, by the tens of thousands, to the United States—proof that faithfulness to one's language and native soil cannot long withstand urgent economic pressures.

It is important to look more closely at how these variations occur. Let us for this purpose consider three areas in which forces of change may affect the basic facts of reality.

## Men

The search for a better life, which has been at the root of nearly all migrations in the world since the beginning of time, is one of the forces also motivating the people of Quebec. But it must be borne in mind that the idea of a better life can be interpreted according to many different standards. If the only pressure is an economic one, workers will tend to go wherever they can obtain the highest wage or salary, and this is also where their contribution to society will be greatest. This may express itself in a change of linguistic allegiance, as when many French Canadians in the West forget their mother tongue; or by a physical displacement of population, as when the awakening of Quebec attracted civil servants from Ottawa but was unable to prevent some forty unemployed workers at Thetford from emigrating to the United States (as happened in 1964). On the other hand, economic pressures may be counterbalanced by moral, patriotic, or sentimental forces. These sometimes affect the mobility of workers, making them accept situations that are economically less rewarding, but more satisfactory on another scale of values: compensation for accepting lower salaries will be found, for example, in the genuine pleasure of speaking French or of living among their own people.

The forces influencing human decisions are, therefore, many and varied. And this is precisely where political factors become important.

The state may resist certain pressures, but not others; it may work to transform the basic situation so that migrations go in one direction and not in another. But the state must take great care not to infringe on the conscience of the individual. I believe that, in the last analysis, a human being in the privacy of his own mind has the exclusive authority to choose his own scale of values and to decide which forces will take precedence over others. A good constitution is one that does not prejudge any of these questions, but leaves citizens free to orient their human destinies as they see fit.

## Capital

The richer a country, the more it can save, and consequently invest; the more it can invest, the greater the profits it can make, and consequently the richer it becomes. This explains, roughly, why the economic lead that the United States has over other countries tends to increase rather than decrease. From another point of view, a very wealthy country, with an overabundance of capital available, is always looking for profitable investments. Left to its own devices, capital will tend to go wherever it can obtain the highest return. Thus it happens that American investment (limited in its own country by anti-trust laws) is naturally attracted to such countries as Canada and the nations of Western Europe, which have social stability and an industrial economy sufficiently advanced to support a high level of consumption. The result is a sort of economic dependence which is sometimes described in such emotional terms as "colonialism" and "colonization." This may give rise to simplified solutions: as Cuba has demonstrated, it is easy enough to get rid of American capital. But one must be prepared to accept the consequences. And there are no indications that a friendly country would be ready to supply Quebec with $300 million a year as Russia did for Cuba.

The answer here is not to chase away foreign capital, since the standard of living must then be lowered so that foreign capital can be replaced by indigenous capital. The answer, in the first place, is to use foreign capital within the framework of rational economic development; and secondly, to create indigenous capital and direct it toward the key sectors of the future: computers, services, and industry in the age of nuclear energy. Movements of capital, like movements of people, are sensitive to political decisions. I must therefore repeat what I said earlier: in a commendable attempt to change economic facts, the state must never use legal or moral violence against its citizens. A sound economic policy must never be based on the assumption, for example, that workers would be ready to accept a drastic lowering of standards of living for the mere pleasure of seeing a national middle class replacing a foreign one at the helm of various enterprises. Governments must remember that sentimental campaigns to promote the purchase of home-produced goods, or appeals to racial feeling, are often subterfuges hiding the desire of owners of business and industry to protect their profits against foreign competition.

On these matters as well, a constitution of free men must be free from bias.

## Technology

In an age when industrial development is dependent on science and technical inventions, economic facts are subject to pressures from technology as well as from capital. Because of this, France was recently unable to prevent the takeover of Bull Equipment by General Electric; at that point, it was not lack of capital that prevented France from retaining control over these crucially important industries; it was lack of scientific knowledge. This deficiency resulted from the fact that France was, and still is, unable to finance research on the scale required by our current industrial revolution. Twenty billion dollars a year are now being spent to finance research in the United States, and this is nearly twenty times as much as in France, and 3.3 times as much as in the eighteen countries of the Organization for Economic Co-operation and

Development (O.E.C.D.) put together.[1] The consequences of this are striking: "In the case of France alone, there is one patent sold for every five we buy from the States, whereas three years ago we sold one for every three."[2] And Mr. Louis Armand, one of the greatest experts on technology in France, states:

> Before the last war, if you had raw materials, manpower, capital and energy, you could be an industrial country, whatever your human or financial potential. This is no longer the case. The only material that counts now is grey matter. That is to say, the number and quality of research workers ceaselessly contributing to the progress ... of science and technology. What these researchers need is not blackboards, but equipment that costs billions of dollars, and quickly becomes obsolete. To meet the needs of a new economy based on science, it is no longer enough merely to be wealthy: you must be colossally rich. Actual needs destroy the idea of nations; they imply—and impose—great industrial complexes, and a sharing of manpower, markets and capital.... There are no longer any solutions on a national scale.[3]

These last sentences lead us to think that the role of politics is even more delicate regarding technology than it is regarding population or capital. For if laws and constitutions create a situation that is not favourable to the entry and development of technology and technicians, the country will be hopelessly outclassed economically, and its industries soon outdated and inefficient. On the other hand, if technology is free to enter, the country must irrevocably step into the era of great communities, of continental economies. It will have to pay the price in terms of its national sovereignty. And its constitutional law will have to take this factor into account.

We have now seen what basic facts are at the root of our constitutional problem in Quebec; we have seen that forces of change can affect these facts; and lastly we have seen that political power itself can influence these forces of change. In other words the state—which

---

1   *Le progrès scientifique*, 1/9/64, published by the Committee on Scientific Research.
2   Michel Drancourt, in *Communauté européenne*, November 1964.
3   *Réalités*, January 1965.

embodies political power—can play a crucial role in guiding the destiny of Quebec.

One might be tempted to conclude that a weak state would be unable to put up much resistance to demographic, economic, and technological pressures, whereas a strong state would be able to counterbalance them with forces of another order. For such a proposition to be tenable, however, two things must be considered:

(a) The expression "strong state" can only be applied to the United States and to the Soviet Union, other states being out of the race altogether. The latter may certainly pass laws to intervene in the movement of men, capital, and techniques; but far from applying political pressure to these factors, the states themselves are often forced to yield to economic and, especially, to technological laws. For example, France could have passed legislation to prohibit the introduction of processes based on English and American patents into the country, but then it could not have built the Caravelle. As soon as France had decided to build the Caravelle, with its English jet engines and American electronics system, however, the French state was no longer free to sell the plane as it wished: "The Caravelle cannot be exported to China due to an American licence on the pressurization system."[4]

(b) The notion of sovereignty is not the most important one to help us appreciate, in these circumstances, the relative strength or weakness of various states. For example, Guatemala, which enjoys complete legal sovereignty, is at an even greater disadvantage when faced with foreign economic pressures than is Quebec, despite the fact that Quebec shares its sovereignty with the federal state.

Another way of expressing this would be to say that states are free to intervene in the action of demographic, economic, and technical forces, but they must pay the price of their intervention.

However, the price to be paid is not the same for all categories of the population. In the case of France, Michel Drancourt, in the article quoted above, expressed it as follows:

[For most people] the fact of becoming a Ford employee may seem bearable even though one would have preferred to remain the employee of a French company. It is at the administrative or governing level that the change is felt most painfully, but then how can one take into account administrators or directors who have failed to retain any real power?

Nevertheless, there is a plausible (and, personally, I think it an extremely probable) alternative: a national reaction along socialist lines.

To combat "American imperialism," a few countries, and France in particular, would engage in a kind of enlightened "Castroism." This would not help the material prosperity of Frenchmen, since it would imply a return to a certain autarchy and considerable sacrifice on the level of consumption; but they might be "sold" such policies by persuasion, or indeed by force.

In the case of Quebec, state intervention in demographic, financial, and technological variables, and its results, can take the form of either of two extreme alternatives:

(a) We can demand that Quebec be given complete sovereign powers, thereby saving Quebec particularism by subordinating all other needs to it. So much the worse if the economy is slowed down and the standard of living lowered as a result. That is the price we must pay to end the cultural alienation of a conquered and demoralized nation. When this nation has gained new confidence in itself, it will at last be able to take vigorous and economically valid action.

This alternative is most attractive to those people who are discontented with their situation, but possess some kind of economic security. Since they are not on the verge of misery, they—as well as young people not yet concerned with such matters—may more easily risk a lowered standard of living. In addition, they have more to gain from a separate Quebec, for, in fact, this group will provide the new ruling class.

(b) We can minimize the importance of the state's sovereignty, obtain the maximum advantage from our integration into the American continent, and make Quebec an ideal province for industrial development. So much the worse if the particular qualities of Quebec (including language) must suffer: this is the price that

4  B. Goulet, "Brevets industriels et indépendance nationale," *Economie et Humanisme*, December 1964, p. 40.

must be paid if the people of Quebec are to attain a higher standard of living and of technical development. Their improved material position will later enable them to affirm more strongly what remains of the French fact in North America.

Those who live in slums and are already on the brink of destitution or unemployment, as well as those who have no reason to fear international competition—for example, true scientists or true financiers—tend very often to favour this second alternative. From their point of view, it is better first to free man through technical progress: to liberate him from physical misery so that he may then concern himself with culture.

Between these two extreme options there is, of course, a whole range of intermediary positions. But it seems clear that each person's constitutional or political options depend upon his particular scale of values and the priorities he attributes to the various objectives he wishes to attain. In the next section, I shall examine a few options that have traditionally been adopted in Quebec. After this, in section IV, I shall outline the objectives that I think present themselves today to the working classes of Quebec. Lastly, in section V, I shall state what constitutional alternatives, in my opinion, result from these objectives.

By way of conclusion to the present section, however, I want to affirm the following. Basic facts as well as the variables that may affect them seem to require the people of Quebec to commit themselves to realistic policies. Whatever constitutional direction we may decide to take, the destiny of our province will be shaped by a balance of forces in which, acting alone, we would have very little weight. Quite apart from our constitutional arrangements, the government of Quebec has but limited power to intervene in capital or technical markets; consequently, it must use these powers wisely and economically, and always in sectors advantageous to the entire population.

## TRADITIONAL CONSTITUTIONAL OPTIONS

If there was any constant factor in Quebec policies from Honoré Mercier to Maurice Duplessis, it was the state's passive attitude toward capital investment. From mines to forests, from hydroelectric resources to urban property, there was scarcely a resource that

could not be exploited by private investment without political difficulty. This was also true in the fields of manufacturing and services. True, the state could be bothersome at times, and partisan politics were not above imposing taxes on money-lenders. But on the whole, the main characteristic in Quebec's economic history over the past hundred years has been the absence of any coherent policy on private investment; and the same could almost be said of public investment as well.

With regard to technology, the state of Quebec maintained more or less the same policy of non-intervention. Contractors were free to introduce whatever techniques they liked, in whatever way they liked. With very few exceptions (such as working on Sunday), it never occurred to the government to direct technological movements in any way. It would be an understatement to say that the state did not think of being generous in its support of scientific research: it did not even plan for technical schools (which were supported by Ottawa). As for promoting the formation of French-speaking industrial management, there was no question of it, since no effort was made even to protect the language itself against the invasion of foreign technical vocabulary.

Nor can Quebec governments be said to have done much more to direct the movement of manpower. In matters of immigration, Quebec's attitude was consistently the negative one of refusing to exercise its constitutional powers. In matters of emigration, the state was at first indifferent about the exodus to the United States. When it finally decided to act, it did so as a result of emotional rather than purely rational considerations. To take possession of the soil was presented as an eminently patriotic and moral duty: a great deal of energy and a fair amount of money were spent gaining access to territories that could be colonized, and establishing settlers upon them. It is obvious that had these efforts been directed instead toward consolidating viable agricultural enterprises, establishing industries, and training contractors and skilled workers, we would now be much closer to having first-hand control over our own affairs.

It should be pointed out that, by contrast, the central government as well as certain other provincial governments were much more interested and skilful than ours in directing economic, technical, and demographic forces. A glance at Macdonald's "National Policy," C.D. Howe's Crown corporations, provincial policies concerning education, health, immigration, nationalization, and social security, makes it obvious that English-speaking Canadians had a much greater awareness of the state's interventionist role.

The recent history of Quebec serves to illustrate the following paradox: despite the fact that our ideology recognized the primacy of spiritual over material matters and that our constitutional powers enabled us to uphold this primacy, economic forces were allowed free reign to influence the destiny of our society. We believed ourselves to be guided by a providential mission bolstered by patriotic motives; but by reducing the powers of the state to a minimum or by badly directing its action, we cleared the way for the most relentless kind of economic liberalism: capital was allowed to enter, manpower to leave, and the technology we obtained was of the sort attracted by docile, ignorant, and cheap labour. Worse still, the language and culture to which we attached such importance became debased, since they were identified with a people placed in a condition of inferiority.

It would, however, be a childish error to condemn our entire past as an unmitigated disaster. For one thing, we must remember that our political strength was at best quite modest. Then too, it may be a consolation to think that one result of the play of economic forces is that our province has attained a relatively high level of industrial development and now possesses relatively important technical equipment.

These last two considerations may serve as a warning against the opposite extreme: absolute subordination of economic forces to political forces.

In recent years a segment of opinion in Quebec has been rushing in the direction of this extreme, thus rejoining a form of protest that often crops up among us. The state was nothing in Quebec: now it must be everything.

So that the state can indeed be everything, one line of thought rejects federalism, and goes so far as to advocate complete independence for Quebec. People speak of the principle of nationalities, affirm the right of these nationalities to govern their own destiny, and conclude that, for reasons of dignity and pride, French Canadians (Quebeckers) must have their own national state endowed with more or less complete sovereignty.

I recognize the right of nations to self-determination. But to claim this right without taking into account the price that will have to be paid, and without clearly demonstrating that it is to the advantage of the whole nation, is nothing short of a reckless gamble. Men do not exist for states: states are created to make it easier for men to attain some of their common objectives.

Therefore, people who wish to undermine or to destroy the Canadian federal system must define clearly the risks involved and demonstrate that the new judicial and political situation they want to establish would be in the general interests of our people.

Far from doing that, this school of thought is content to affirm that independence would not *necessarily* involve a drastic drop in our standard of living—although it recognizes that we do not have enough facts at the moment to be entirely sure. Such people admit that a "free" Quebec might be dominated by a backward and authoritarian *bourgeoisie*; yet they are prepared to take the risk. They fully expect that a sovereign state will put an end to the real or imagined sense of cultural alienation that afflicts some Quebeckers; but they admit that to achieve this Quebec may have to suffer through a period of stagnation. They do not condescend to show how all this constitutes a necessary step to helping people who live in slums or vegetate on farms. And by way of consolation they assure us that after independence, the mistakes we make will at least have the advantage of being our own!

It seems to me that, faced with such attitudes, the working classes must feel the need of entering the debate. For in the end it is always they who have to pay; it is they who would suffer most from a lowering of the standard of living, who would be hardest hit by a period of political and social stagnation, and who would be the first to suffer from unemployment and destitution. In short, the consequences of whatever mistakes "our" ruling classes might make would be borne mainly by the working Confederation.

This is not to say that representatives of labour should systematically oppose constitutional reform. They are certainly not people to be frightened of change; but they must be convinced that any particular change is for the better, not the worse. They also want the most urgent matters attended to first. Under our present constitution, the government of Quebec is free to undertake economic and social reforms that seem more important and certainly more urgent than revision of the very foundations of Confederation.

The working man knows very well what benefits he might derive from a better organization of justice, a system of health insurance, better labour or agricultural legislation, or policies promoting low-cost housing. That is why he attaches priority to these reforms, knowing that they will create conditions more favourable to cultural development. And before diverting considerable amounts of time and energy into Quebec separatism—or into annexation to the United States for that matter—he wants to know, *in a concrete way*, what is involved. In theory, of course, everything is possible.

In theory, an economist can demonstrate perfectly well that separation would be entirely to Quebec's advantage. All he needs to postulate, for example, is that if Quebec were independent, foreign contractors and technologists would bring in capital and inventions at an increased rate. (On the other hand, what an odd way to "repossess" our economy!) Or again, that our markets—including English Canada—would buy even more agricultural or industrial products from an independent Quebec than they do now. Or that our governments and all our institutions would overnight become miraculously progressive and well adapted to the technological revolution. Or, finally, that our middle class, after independence, would suddenly discover that its talents lay in high finance instead of ambassadorial service.

If in practice it turned out that these postulates were groundless, however, the whole adventure would end in disaster. Another economist might justifiably postulate that Quebec's independence would result in loss of both capital and markets, in technological stagnation, and in administrative inefficiency. Nor is it entirely impossible that our rising middle class would discover that it still had less taste for finance than for diplomacy.

Clearly, an economist alone cannot tell us what the future would hold for an independent Quebec. To his knowledge must be added sociology, political science, history, and, if at all possible, a gift for prophecy. Faced with such contradictory and uncertain possibilities, a man by himself may decide to take the plunge. From dignity and pride—or even in the hope of raising his own social rank—he may declare himself ready to try national independence, especially if he has intellectual or financial reserves to fall back on should the adventure miscarry.

But this does not hold for those people who have, at best, a precarious economic security. Organizations concerned with the working classes in Quebec would plainly be irresponsible to scuttle Confederation with an attitude of "Come what may!" These associations must give the benefit of the doubt to established political institutions that have helped Canadians attain the second or third highest standard of living in the world. Let the burden of proof fall upon people who would lead an entire nation into an unknown speculation.

In my opinion, nothing said before the Constitution Committee or published in the province has been sufficient to undermine confidence in the federal system. It is true that in practice the system has not been free from inequalities and injustices; for example, all Canadians do not have a reasonable share of our highly praised standard of living. On this point, however, Quebec's position is not the worst, and if it were a question of economic colonialism, the Maritimes would have far greater right to complain than we.

It is clear, then, that the position I am outlining here is not at all based on smug satisfaction. In the past, popular movements have worked for economic, social, political, or even, when there was need, for constitutional changes; and they will continue to work for them. But, for reasons I have just explained, and for other reasons which will become apparent in subsequent chapters, the fact remains that an open federal system is the aim assumed in this review.

## OBJECTIVES

The function of a state is to ensure the establishment and maintenance of a legal order that will safeguard the development of its citizens. This order, as I conceive it, must be based on a certain number of objectives which, for convenience, I shall class as economic, social, and cultural.

### Economic objectives

What counts for an economist is not the size of a country, but the size of each inhabitant's income. Thus, the United States' particular virtue is not that it possesses extensive territory or a large population—in these China is far richer—but that it has the highest per-capita income in the world. At the other extreme, Switzerland, which is a small country on the basis of both territory and population, nevertheless has a standard of living that classes it among the four most prosperous countries on earth. It seems, therefore, that a country's wealth is not necessarily related to the size of its home markets, but may just as well result from its capacity to produce goods and services that are competitive everywhere in the world. For example, the most interesting aspect of the European Common Market is not the Market as such, but the gradual abolition of protective tariffs between member countries, which will force each one of them to develop greater efficiency if its standards are to be maintained.

As is well known, neither Sweden nor Switzerland depends on the Common Market for its high standard of living; they have achieved it partly by keeping out of European wars and partly by adapting to their own needs the very latest developments of technology and finance over the past fifty years. (In 1963, for example, the balance of payments on manufactured goods between France and Switzerland was eight to one in favour of Switzerland.)

Looked at solely from the point of view of economic objectives, the important question is not whether Quebec will become a sovereign state, remain integrated with Canada, or be annexed to the United States, although these options are not unrelated to the kind of political means used to attain economic goals. In the last resort, what really matters is that the per-capita income be increased as quickly as possible. To achieve this, the economy of Quebec must become extremely efficient, technologically advanced, quite specialized, and capable of offering the best products at the best prices in all the markets of the world.

In practice this means that the economy of Quebec must not be isolated, but open to the whole world, for then it will find new markets as well as the competition it has to expect.

Whatever may be said to the contrary, it seems clear that a large part of the constitutional upheaval so fashionable in our province at the moment would in fact tend to isolate Quebec. It is proposed, for example, that Quebec be given exclusive jurisdiction over banks,

immigration, manpower placement, foreign trade, customs duties and tariffs, and many other things as well. The stated aim—to regain control over our economic destiny—seems very laudable. But all the evidence indicates that the motive for using these legal instruments is to protect our capital, businessmen, and the top ranks of management from foreign competition. And this is precisely the way to render them inefficient, and to make certain that our products are rejected in foreign markets. Quebec would then have to oblige its consumers to "buy French Canadian"; and farmers and workers would have to pay more—either in prices or in subsidies—for these products. This argument applies to steel as well as to blueberries, and it would be a mistake to think that the working classes would derive any long-term benefit from being turned into a captive market.

The objection is sometimes made that this is not at all what is intended; far from wishing to isolate Quebec once it has gained the constitutional powers mentioned above, the government will seek to integrate it within some kind of common market. A most peculiar line of thought! For in general, such a common market would require Quebec to abandon its autonomy on the migration of capital, techniques, and manpower, as well as on such matters as the value of currency, external trade, customs, and tariffs. In other words, from an economic standpoint a "new" Quebec would have more or less the same sovereign powers, the same measure of independence, and probably the same competitive protection if it joined a common market as it does at the moment within the Canadian Confederation.

As producers and consumers, therefore, the working classes in Quebec must strive for an economy based on world-wide markets and as competitive as possible. That is the only way for Quebec to become richer in the long run; and that is why we must reject constitutional reforms that not only give no indication of increasing economic efficiency, but seem to imply protectionist and isolationist policies the benefit of which will be measured in terms of increased prestige and dividends for propertied classes.

On the whole, our present constitution allows the provinces—and therefore Quebec—extensive jurisdiction over the means of achieving the objectives mentioned above. Provinces are responsible for education, and it is mainly through education that labour and administrators will acquire the financial and scientific knowledge they need in order to act efficiently at a time when industry is so dependent upon research, and production techniques upon computers. Furthermore, provinces have jurisdiction over land and resources, which allows them to develop the land, complete the network of industrial support (roads, bridges, electricity, services, and the rest), and develop resources, each according to its own pace and set of priorities.

On the other hand, the fact that the provinces do not have jurisdiction over tariffs and international commerce could only be inconvenient for Quebec in these two particular cases:

(a) If Canada's policies were more protectionist than Quebec wished them to be, there would be a danger of fostering a "hot-house" culture, unable to face outside competition. I can only say that this is highly unlikely. As far as we can judge from the attitudes and slogans adopted by Quebec opponents of Confederation, it seems certain that free trade would find greater (if still inadequate) support from the federalists. In any case we must not forget that, protection being equal, Canada would still have an advantage over a separated Quebec, first because its markets are three times as large, which means economizing through larger-scale production, and second because its competition is three times as strong, which stimulates efficient production.

(b) If Canada's tariff system were detrimental to Quebec products as compared to other Canadian products, it is clear that Quebec would be justified in demanding control over its tariffs and external commerce. This hypothesis is just as improbable as the first. In the past, Canadian tariff regulations have on the whole worked against the West and the Maritimes. And it is difficult to see how in the future an alert, and, more important, a knowledgeable Quebec could be victimized by adverse tariff regulations from Ottawa. There are too many vested interests—and not only French Canadian—involved in the matter.

It would certainly be an advantage if the federal government consulted the provinces about matters that affect them, even if these matters are entirely within federal jurisdiction. I do not see why we could not establish permanent consulting bodies to ensure that our trade, tariff, customs, or monetary policies

really reflect the opinions of people throughout the country, and that no province feels undermined by the exercise of central power.

Before turning to the next section, I should like to add one more comment: these objections to economic chauvinism are valid for English Canadians as well as French Canadians. It is always costly and inefficient to choose men or to favour institutions on the basis of their ethnic origin rather than their particular aptitude or competence. Great industries cannot promote maximum efficiency by ethnocentric policies, any more than by nepotism. Now, speaking only of Quebec, no matter how backward the province may have been in its technical and administrative education, neither this backwardness nor pure chance is sufficient to account for the fact that in all levels of industry, from the very top down to the foreman, French Canadians have been poorly represented in proportion to their number. It even happens that a Quebec worker being hired for industry is required to speak English as well as French—a form of discrimination that should be rigorously forbidden by Quebec law.

Quebec does not need to extend its jurisdiction to questions of tariffs in order to condemn the form of protection most harmful to the province: that which operates against French Canadians in high finance and large industries. There is no doubt that the whole of Quebec suffers as a result of these practices. The number of English-Canadian financiers and industrialists able to compete in our North American big league is pathetically small; and it is almost certain that the inefficiency of the Montreal group is at least partly due to their chauvinism.

The conclusion that must be drawn is this: from the point of view of its economic objectives, Quebec will find Canadian Confederation not only an acceptable system, but indeed the one most conducive to its full development.

## Social objectives
Economic forces operating in the way I have outlined—that is to say, according to certain laws but unhampered by administrative red tape or territorial barriers—will tend to enrich the community as a whole. For this wealth to be fairly distributed within the community, however, a certain number of social objectives must necessarily be pursued.

In a very general way, these consist in so organizing a political community that all its members have the essential before a few are allowed to enjoy the superfluous. Of course, the concepts of the "essential" and the "superfluous" will be defined variously in different countries and at different times; and even in one country at any given time they will be defined according to each person's social philosophy. As for labour organizations, they also have their own definition of these concepts and have frequently elaborated them in the briefs they regularly submit to their governments. This side of the question therefore need not be re-examined in detail by the Constitution Committee.

It must be pointed out, however, that social objectives sometimes conflict with economic objectives; and whereas the latter can only command limited state intervention, the former can command a great deal. For example, automation is good for the progress of industry but bad for the labourer who becomes redundant as a result; and a state that allows automation must also be responsible for workers affected by it.

The conflict is not always easy to resolve. It would be a great oversimplification to adopt the attitude: social needs first, then economic. For, as I mentioned in section II, it is a rare state that can disregard economic or technological laws with impunity. A government trying to do so, even though for excellent social motives, would so impoverish its economy that its social goals became unattainable. In fact, unless the economy is fundamentally sound, a strong, progressive social policy can be neither conceived nor applied. All social security measures, from family allowances to old age pensions, from free education to health insurance, must remain theoretical if the economic structure is incapable of bearing the cost. Even the right to work remains no more than a pious hope if economic cycles or the stagnation of business creates unemployment for industrial labourers, or prevents farmers from selling their products profitably.

In the matter of social objectives, then, we must begin by applying the same constitutional considerations that I outlined for economic objectives in subsection A. This means in effect that we must oppose the dismemberment of our country, because the result would be to weaken the economy of Quebec and therefore to some extent prevent the province from pursuing social objectives or being able to assume the cost.

From another point of view, our Canadian constitution gives provinces the widest possible jurisdiction in matters of social security. This permits the government of each province to apply whatever social philosophy is best suited to its own population. The resulting diversity can create a healthy rivalry between provinces on matters relating to taxation and to the benefits to be derived for the various taxpayers. In the Canadian federal system, therefore, a citizen has a multiple choice, and this increases his democratic freedom: within the Canadian economy as a whole, manpower and capital will tend to move toward whatever balance of fiscal charges and social services suit them best. Obviously, because of language considerations, a French Canadian will be relatively less mobile; this is merely another reason why the government of Quebec must choose its fiscal and social policies with great care and in the most democratic way possible.

To the foregoing considerations must be added these three observations:

(a) First, the rivalry mentioned in the preceding paragraph carries some risks: for example, a province might be tempted to attract capital and industry by adopting anti-cooperative and anti-union laws, as well as by reducing its expenditures for social purposes to a minimum. This can constitute a real danger for labour and agricultural workers who, lacking other means of protection, will wish to transfer some constitutional jurisdiction over these matters to the central government. I would consider this kind of centralization to be a last resort, however, and would prefer to retain, as far as possible, the freedom and diversity arising from federative decentralization. This is why I consider it so urgent to negotiate interprovincial agreements establishing certain minimum standards of social legislation, at least in the larger industrial provinces.

Within this context, I can only consider premature and inappropriate the preoccupation in certain circles with constitutional reforms designed to give provinces the right to conclude treaties with foreign powers without consulting the federal government. As long as Quebec has not negotiated agreements with other provinces regarding trade union legislation, can it be very urgent, or indeed economically wise, for the province to sign treaties that would bind it to standards established in other countries?

Similarly, the province has recently concluded certain agreements with France, without overstepping the bounds of constitutional legality. I am not one of those who greeted this initiative with great enthusiasm; to be quite frank, I am not all that preoccupied with the "image" that Quebec as a province projects on the international scene. As for the future, I am of the opinion that Quebec has better things to do than, for example, to be seen at every meeting of UNESCO, especially considering that it has not even begun serious negotiations with a neighbouring province about the education of that province's French minority.

(b) My second remark concerns provinces that are too poor to achieve minimum standards of social security by themselves. Under our present constitution, the central government can remedy this lack by equalization grants, and this is a system that must continue. From this point of view, I find it regrettable that Ottawa and Quebec should have quarrelled about the division of federal tax revenues.

A concept of tax sharing that does not take into account the beneficiary's needs, and which seems to claim that any given group of taxpayers must receive as benefits at least the equivalent of what it pays in taxes, makes a mockery of the equalizing function of taxation and identifies itself as completely reactionary.— And speaking of taxes, it is perhaps not inappropriate to denounce another idea widespread in Quebec: that the province should recover from Ottawa the funds drawn from it in the last World War. I shall content myself with saying that this was a political, never a constitutional matter; and that on a political level, Mr. Duplessis and after him Mr. Lesage established ways of allowing Quebec to receive a far greater proportion of personal and corporate income taxes, and succession duties, than was ever yielded during the war.

(c) My third remark concerns planning and anti-cyclical policies, both of which presuppose some form of state intervention in economic mechanisms for social purposes such as full employment or rational development. It would not be appropriate to go very deeply into such technical concepts in this review. I shall merely say that in the Canadian constitutional system, these two kinds of policies presuppose a measure of co-operation between the federal and provincial levels. The federal government is of course mainly responsible for the economy of the whole country, but its action cannot be efficient unless it has the support of the provinces.

Both planning and anti-cyclical policies have very great priority for the agricultural and working classes. If a federal régime made these goals harder to attain, these classes might be obliged to advocate reforms leading to greater centralization. It is precisely to prevent the necessity of such a move that I am suggesting, instead of constitutional modifications, a more systematic recourse to consultation and to federal-provincial agreements.

In conclusion, it appears that from the point of view of social objectives federalism is the form of government that can best serve the interests of the Quebec community.

## Cultural objectives

We have seen that the state must occasionally intervene in the play of economic forces to better ensure the pursuit of social objectives. But it must not stop there; if it does, we could find ourselves promoting the development of a community that was rich, technologically advanced, equitably structured, but completely depersonalized. We would be struck with the disease that threatens every society in an advanced stage of industrialization. Technology, which brings abundance and material happiness, presupposes an undifferentiated mass of consumers; it also tends to minimize the values that let a human being acquire and retain his own identity, values that I am grouping here under the vague term "cultural." The political order created by the state must struggle against this kind of depersonalization by pursuing cultural objectives.

The state must use its legal powers to compel the economic community to favour certain values that would otherwise be destroyed by the pressure of economic forces. In other words, just as the state intervenes in economic matters to protect the weak through social legislation, so it must intervene to ensure the survival of cultural values in danger of being swamped by a flood of dollars.

This principle does not create problems when it is a question of intervening in favour of painting, music, films, the "Canadian content" of radio or television, and other similar matters. But it may be useful to recall that even this kind of cultural investment is only achieved at some cost, not only economic, but also cultural. For it supposes that the state knows better than the citizen what is "good" for him culturally, and such a hypothesis must always be applied with utmost prudence and consideration. More than any other, this kind of value is international and common to all men; in the long term, then, the state should ideally promote an open culture. There is also a danger that cultural protection, like its economic counterpart, would tend eventually to produce a weak, "hothouse" culture.

Having made this point, I must now turn to the much more difficult question of cultural values directly related to ethnic background; or, to be more precise, the values for which the French language is the vehicle in Canada and in Quebec.

Let us start by recalling the facts: 28 per cent of all Canadians speak French as their mother tongue, and 58.4 per cent speak English. (The next largest percentage is German, with 3.0 per cent.) And of those whose mother tongue is French, 83 per cent live in the province of Quebec.

Because of this last fact, many people are tempted to consider Quebec the "national state of French Canadians." But, as I mentioned in the Introduction to this review, I believe that a definition of the state that is based essentially on ethnic attributes is philosophically erroneous and would inevitably lead to intolerance. Moreover, this definition seems to me strategically unacceptable. If Quebec defines itself constitutionally as the "national state of French Canadians" on the grounds that it contains the majority of French-speaking Canadians, the same logic—the logic of numbers—would lead all the other provinces, and indeed the federal state itself, to define themselves (at least pragmatically) as the national states of English-speaking Canadians. French Canadians would then have gained nothing and have lost a great deal: they would be neither more numerous nor more cultured, and it is most improbable that even in Quebec they could succeed in noticeably reducing the use and influence of the language that dominates North American life so completely. On the other hand, French-Canadians in all other provinces—and in Ottawa as well—would have to abandon forever the hope of being anything but a minority among—or after—many others. No longer would there be any question of English and French Canadians possessing equal linguistic rights within Confederation.

The idea of a national state is thus unacceptable both in theory and in practice to any person who does not wish to see French Canadians withdraw from the Canadian scene and limit themselves exclusively to Quebec.

I have shown that the option of withdrawing from Canada, with its attendant constitutional reforms, is inadmissible from an economic or social point of view. I now wish to demonstrate that the same is true from a cultural point of view.

Let me make it very clear from the beginning that the issue at stake is not the mere survival of the French language and of the cultural values relating to it. Their survival is already assured. French is spoken in Quebec by an ever increasing number of persons. If one discounts the possibility of genocide or of some major cataclysm, it seems certain that in this part of America French will continue to be spoken regardless of what happens to the constitution.

The problem is therefore to stimulate our language and culture so that they are alive and vital, not just fossils from the past. We must realize that French will only have value to the extent that it is spoken by a progressive people. What makes for vitality and excellence in a language is the collective quality of the people speaking it. In short, the defence of the French language cannot be successful without accomplishments that make the defence worthwhile.

Given these facts, should French-speaking people concentrate their efforts on Quebec, or take the whole of Canada as their base? In my opinion, they should do both; and for the purpose they could find no better instrument than federalism.

If French Canadians are able to claim equal partnership with English Canadians, and if their culture is established on a coast-to-coast basis, it is mainly because of the balance of linguistic forces within the country. Historical origins are less important than people generally think, the proof being that neither Eskimo nor Indian dialects have any kind of privileged position. On the other hand, if there were six million people living in Canada whose mother tongue was Ukrainian, it is likely that this language would establish itself as forcefully as French. In terms of *realpolitik,* French and English are equal in Canada because each of these linguistic groups has the power to break the country. And this power cannot yet be claimed by the Iroquois, the Eskimos, or the Ukrainians.

This reality is sometimes expressed in Canada by the "two nation" concept. In my opinion, this concept is dangerous in theory and groundless in fact. It would be disastrous if—at the very moment when French Canadians are at last awakening to the modern world and making their presence count in the country—their politicians were to be won over to anti-federalist policies. The consequence would be that French Canadians in Ottawa, Washington, and all capitals of the world would represent a country of five million inhabitants, and could expect to exert an influence in proportion to this population. On the other hand, if Quebec were part of a Canadian federation grouping two *linguistic* communities as I am advocating, French Canadians would be supported by a country of more than eighteen million inhabitants, with the second or third highest standard of living in the world, and with a degree of industrial maturity that promises to give it the most brilliant of futures.

This is what *could* happen. But on two conditions:

(a) First, French Canadians must really want it; that is to say, they must abandon their role of oppressed nation and decide to participate boldly and intelligently in the Canadian experience. It is wrong to say that Confederation has been a total failure for French Canadians; the truth is rather that they have never really tried to make a success of it. In Quebec, we tended to fall back upon a sterile, negative provincial autonomy; in Ottawa our frequent abstentions encouraged paternalistic centralization. If we lack the courage and the strength to launch out in Canadian politics, where at worst the odds are only two to one, how can we claim that we should be confronting the world, where the odds would at best be a hundred to one?

(b) The second condition is that the dice are not loaded against French Canadians in the "Confederation game." This means that if French Canadians abandon their concept of a national state, English Canadians, must do the same. We must not find Toronto or Fredericton or, above all, Ottawa exalting the *English*-Canadian nation. On the contrary, when either the federal or provincial governments intervene in the economy to protect cultural values, they must apply the same rules of equity toward the French as Quebec has always applied toward the English segment of its population.

Just as the central state invests tax funds in such various enterprises as railways, radio and television, and the flag, in order to develop that non-commercial value, a specifically Canadian identity; and just as provincial governments are ready to patronize the arts in the hope of enriching the lives of their citizens; so these governments have the duty to intervene in favour of certain linguistic values whose preservation constitutes a *sine qua non* for the existence of Canada.

The Canadian community must invest, for the defence and better appreciation of the French language, as much time, energy, and money as are required to prevent the country from breaking up. Just as the federal government can use equalization grants to impose a just sharing among the provinces in economic matters, so the constitution must without delay extend these concepts of just sharing to the cultural field.

In practice, this can be achieved by a constitutional amendment granting French minorities in other provinces, as well as in Ottawa, the same rights and privileges as the English minority in Quebec. I shall have more to say on this point in the recommendations presented at the end of this article.

In the last analysis, those who clamour for French Canadians to be heard in the concert of nations should be glad that our community, despite its limited number of voices, has, in Canada, an enormous sound-box, and, in Ottawa, an excellent amplifier.

Precisely because they are such a tiny minority in North America, French Canadians must refuse to be enclosed within Quebec. I am opposed to what is called "special status" for these two reasons, among others: first, I would not insult Quebeckers by maintaining that their province needs preferential treatment in order to prosper within Confederation; and second, I believe that in the long run this status can only tend to weaken values protected in this way against competition. Even more than technology, a culture makes progress through the exchange of ideas and through challenge. In our Canadian federal system, French-Canadian cultural values have a good balance of competition and protection from a fairly strong state.

But the fact remains that French-Canadian strength is concentrated in Quebec. And as I wrote in section II:

"The only considerable territory in the Western hemisphere in which French-speaking people are grouped in sufficient numbers and are sufficiently attached to French for this language to be a political society's first idiom is Quebec."

It is clear that the way in which a nation is governed is part of its culture, in the widest sense of the word. The anatomy and physiology of political institutions constitute one of the most important characteristics of a nation, and serve to distinguish it from its neighbours.

On this basis as well, Canadian federalism is ideal. The federal system obliges Quebec's political culture to stand the test of competition at the federal level, while allowing Quebec to choose the form of government best suited to its needs at the provincial level. Under our present constitution, Quebec may modify its own constitution (except in those sections relating to the function of the Lieutenant-Governor) and create the political institutions its people desire. It is true that in the past the people did not really desire very much: witness the survival of the Legislative Council! But this was due to the people themselves, not to any lack of freedom.

Consequently, there is no need to evoke the notion of a national state to turn Quebec into a province "different from the others." In a great number of vital areas, and notably those that concern the development of particular cultural values, Quebec has full and complete sovereignty under the Canadian constitution.

I believe in provincial autonomy. I think it was important for French Canadians to have had a place of their own in which to learn the art of democratic and responsible government. But I hope that our people and their leaders will soon have developed sufficient political maturity to no longer feel the need of engaging in purely symbolic battles. Doubtless it is still important to resist the central government's paternalistic tendencies, or to block massive use of joint planning. But we can be mature and responsible without rejecting out of hand every form of administrative co-operation with Ottawa. After all, our human resources are not so unlimited that we can afford to systematically refuse help in carrying those burdens we share with the rest of the country. Nor are we short of work to do in Quebec.

First and foremost, on a strictly material level Quebec must assert itself as a society undergoing rapid economic development. Otherwise some of our workers will emigrate and lose their maternal language, while others will stay but will be ashamed of a language identified with an economically weak people. As we have seen, however, federalism is a system that can be extremely advantageous to Quebec on the purely material level.

On a spiritual level Quebec must assert itself as a province that fosters moral, intellectual, artistic, scientific, and technical values. When Quebec has produced or attracted a sufficient number of real philosophers, real scientists, real film directors, real economists, real experts in computer technology, and a large enough number of true statesmen, the "French fact" will prosper in North America, and will have no need of the separatist crutch. These values on the whole are developed through education and through interaction with other cultures; from this point of view as well, our present constitutional institutions are satisfactory for the province since they give it complete jurisdiction over education. Consequently, it is up to Quebec to put its population in the forefront of progress in such matters. And as the majority of French Canadians live in this province, it is up to us to assure the triumph of French cultural values. (As for French minorities in other provinces, they can only have a future if Quebec establishes itself as a strong, progressive force *within* Confederation; if Quebec withdraws into itself or secedes, these French minorities will have approximately the same rights and the same influence as cultural groups of German origin in Canada.)

To sum up, the political culture of French Canadians will be what they decide to make it. As a group, they are free to direct provincial policies as they wish; and those who complain of a colonial mentality need to see to their own political re-education. Naturally, this education will still have to occur in a hostile world; but the world is not likely to be any less hostile simply because Quebec has revised its constitution. In the field of political culture, no less than in other fields, our institutions do not deserve to survive at all unless they can successfully survive external competition. And Canadian federalism is a closed field in which the French-Canadian province can seek to rival other provinces in political maturity and administrative efficiency, on a more or less equal footing. It is not at all certain that were Quebec

to find itself isolated on the North American continent, it would find the game any easier, or its rules
any more favourable.

## THE ELEMENTS OF A SOLUTION

In attempting to specify the goals to be sought by
political communities, we have seen that for some
purposes it is desirable that the state be limited in
size, while for others a larger territory is definitely
preferable. For example, in social or cultural matters,
where needs often vary from region to region and
where a citizen must feel that he can communicate
directly with the source of power, there is an advantage in limiting the territorial jurisdiction of the state.
In other areas, such as economic matters, it is much
more efficient for the geographical unit to be considerably extended. In still other areas, such as peace or
trade agreements, the trend will be toward international political groupings.

The ideal state would therefore seem to be one with
different sizes for different purposes. And the ideal
constitution for it would be one that gave the various
parts, whatever their size, the powers they needed to
attain their own particular objectives.

In practice, the federal state comes closest to this
ideal. Its advantage is to be able to create a state that
fits the dimensions of the problem; there are two levels of government, and the measure of sovereignty
each one has is dictated by necessity.

For these reasons, the present writer opts for federalism. And, in particular, our own form of federalism seems to me the system best suited to French
Canadians, for it allows them to take full advantage
of the province, country, and continent in which they
are destined to live. Under our present constitution,
the federal government has jurisdiction over foreign
affairs, defence, criminal law, navigation, railways,
and postal and telegraph services, as well as over most
areas required to establish a large and stable basis for
sound economic development: international trade,
customs, financial institutions, currency, and statistics. It is important to notice, however, that with the
possible exceptions of marriage and broadcasting,
federal jurisdiction covers only those areas having

minimal cultural content. In these matters it is safe
to assume that, except in times of crisis, linguistic factors will not be involved, and public opinion will be
governed by criteria in which ethnic considerations
play very little part.

Provincial governments, on the other hand, have
jurisdiction over all matters of a purely local or private nature; over education, natural resources, property and civil rights, municipalities, roads, social and
labour legislation, and the administration of justice;
and more generally over all matters relating to cultural
development or development of the land.

With regard to agriculture and immigration, the
federal and provincial governments have concurrent
jurisdiction. For all practical purposes, the powers of
any government in matters concerning the levying and
spending of taxes are limited only by the fact that politicians are ultimately answerable to their taxpayers.

This division of powers no doubt results in a constitution that is less than perfect, and in this respect
the fundamental law of Canada is just like any other
human institution. Industrialists or businessmen
might prefer to see greater power vested in the central government; jurists or men of letters might wish
that the provinces had more extensive jurisdiction. But
any discussion between these two sides would soon
make it clear that each was basing its argument solely
on its own particular point of view. The former attach
very little importance to purely social or cultural values; the latter often neglect to take account of the most
elementary laws of technology or political economy.

If we look at all aspects of the problem, therefore, I
think we shall find the general spirit of Canadian federalism quite acceptable. I should be very surprised if
real statesmen, given the facts of the problem, arrived
at the conclusion that our constitution needs drastic
revision. At the one extreme, I have said enough in
sections III and IV to indicate why I believe Quebec
must resist the temptation to isolate itself. Granted
the province would then be safe from competition
or other dangers, but it would also be quite safe from
any form of progress!

At the other extreme, I would be opposed to either
merging our province with Canada if the country
were to become a unitary state, or allowing it to be
absorbed by the United States. I cannot believe that

a pan-Canadian or pan-American form of nationalism would be any less prone to chauvinism than the French-Canadian form.

In terms of personal or political maturity, a citizen of Quebec—especially if he is French-speaking—does not stand to gain anything from total assimilation within a continental or semi-continental macrocosm. On the contrary, faced as we are by the gigantic complexes forced upon us by our third industrial revolution—that of thermo-nuclear energy and computers—it is absolutely vital that we maintain psychological equilibrium as well as democratic responsibility by strengthening local ties and keeping regional governments on a human scale as much as possible.

To my mind, neither Canada's present constitution nor the country itself represents an eternal, unchangeable reality. For the last hundred years, however, this country and this constitution have allowed men to live in a state of freedom and prosperity which, though perhaps imperfect, has nevertheless rarely been matched in this world. And so I cannot help condemning as irresponsible those people who wish our nation to invest undetermined amounts of money, time, and energy in a constitutional adventure that they have been unable to define precisely but which would consist in more or less completely destroying Confederation to replace it with some vague form of sovereignty resulting in something like an independent Quebec, or associate states, or a "special status," or a Canadian common market, or a confederation of ten states, or some entirely different scheme that could be dreamt up on the spur of the moment, when chaos at all levels had already become inevitable.

That the Canadian federal system must evolve is obvious. But it is evolving—radically—and has been for a hundred years without requiring any fundamental constitutional reform. In our history, periods of great decentralization have alternated with periods of intense centralization, according to economic and social circumstances, external pressures, and the strength or cunning of various politicians. A recent factor in politics, which is also a verifiable law in most industrial countries, is that the state must nowadays devote an ever increasing proportion of an ever increasing budget to purposes that in Canada are the constitutional responsibility of provincial governments. In other words, Canadian federalism is

presently evolving in the direction of much greater decentralization.

Since the end of the Second World War, Canada has undergone profound transformation. The rapid growth of our school-age population has created hitherto unknown needs at all levels from elementary schools to universities and technical colleges. At the same time, the proliferation of services, combined with an unprecedented industrial growth, has resulted in an urban concentration that is increasing at perhaps the fastest rate in the world and thereby creating many new needs at the municipal level: the need for expansion of welfare services; public health programs for slum areas; control of air and water pollution; development of low-cost housing; extension of urban transport; provision of better facilities for police and fire departments, hydro, water supplies, electricity, and telephone; development of new recreational facilities such as parks, libraries, green belts; and many others.

At the same time as these new needs were being created by the evolution of external circumstances (and this includes the substantial rise in incomes throughout the country), another transformation was taking place in the minds of men ("the revolution of rising expectations"). In our province, this transformation expressed itself in terms of increased public action: the various social movements, especially labour unions and agricultural organizations, brought increasing pressure on the state to intervene in such fields as education, medical and hospital services, welfare, the development of natural resources, and social, agricultural, and industrial legislation.

Our present constitution places all these needs and services without exception under provincial jurisdiction. Already the situation has produced the following statistics (for the years 1953 to 1963): during this decade, provincial expenditure for goods and services rose from 3 per cent of the gross national product to 4 per cent; similar expenditures at the municipal level (which also falls within provincial jurisdiction) increased from 5 per cent to 8 per cent; while federal expenditure fell from 10 per cent to 7 per cent. This realignment of state expenditures has naturally brought about changes in the division of tax revenues between the central and provincial governments. So much so that from 1961 to 1963, for example, provincial income and corporate taxes rose from $655 million to $1,144 million, while federal taxes increased only by $114 million.[5] This trend towards decentralization is even more striking if one compares the gross general revenue for 1954 and 1962: at the federal level, it rose from $4.44 to $6.6 billion; at the provincial level, from $1.58 to $4.24 billion; at the municipal level, from $1.02 to $2.11 billion. In brief, then, the total revenue increased in those eight years by 48.6 per cent for the federal, as opposed to 144.2 per cent for the provinces (including municipalities).[6]

The phenomenon becomes even more obvious when one considers the total sum of government expenditure, excluding intergovernmental transfers. "Final" expenditure at the federal level rose from $4.198 billion in 1954 to $6.550 billion in 1964, which represents an increase of 56 per cent. During the same period, provincial and municipal expenditure went from $2.652 to $8.065 billion, which is an increase of 204 per cent.[7]

Clearly, an enormous amount of power is being transferred to provincial governments by the natural operation of demographic, social, and economic forces, without the necessity of amending a single comma of the constitution. In the circumstances, it seems rather surprising that some Quebeckers should choose this very moment to clamour for a new constitution. Twenty years behind the times as usual, they are at last coming to terms with the reality described in the *Rowell-Sirois Report* of 1940, and preparing to charge the centralizing dragon just when it has stopped breathing fire.

The error, especially in terms of strategy, is glaring. For anyone who really wishes a return to greater centralization will be only too glad—despite some feigned reluctance—to reopen constitutional negotiations. No doubt a few legal gestures would be made in the direction of Quebec's particular characteristics, but in all probability, Quebec would receive less than it is gradually obtaining through the force of circumstances. Meanwhile, the modifications we had thus introduced into our constitution might well alter our entire economy: it is a well-known fact that the slightest change in the letter of constitutional law would be sufficient

to annul a hundred years of constitutional precedent and judicial decisions—most of which tended on the whole to favour the provinces. And therefore I must repeat: is this the time for such action, since both the letter and interpretation of the law are presently so favourable to provincial autonomy?

I must confess that, seen from this angle, the Fulton-Favreau formula for repatriation and constitutional revision does not fill me with wild excitement. I can certainly appreciate its many merits: it is no mean achievement to have finally found a compromise allowing our constitution to become a completely Canadian document, as well as a way of placing checks upon the arbitrary use of power permitted under the 1949 clause of Section 91(1) of the B.N.A. Act.

In my opinion, however, these merits are not so great, nor the reforms proposed so urgent, that they can entirely override the following considerations:

I consider it illogical that the Legislative Assembly should commit Quebec to an irrevocable constitutional move before it has even had time to hear the report of its Constitution Committee. It is not true, as some have claimed, that the Fulton-Favreau formula (where it relates to constitutional revision) merely expresses in precise terms an existing body of custom and accepted practices. Quite the contrary, the formula represents a radical innovation, and one that would be practically irreversible.

In the first place, the formula provides that the jurisdiction of Parliament may be extended in certain matters if this is supported by two-thirds of the provinces, representing 50 per cent of the population. Furthermore, the federal government and four provinces may proceed to delegate legislative powers relating to several fundamental matters between the two levels of government.

It is my fear that in the present situation, the two-thirds formula and the technique of delegating powers will serve on the whole to weaken the theory and application of federalism in Canada; my reasons follow.

We have seen that, within the framework of our present constitution, natural forces are now tending to strengthen provincial autonomy. If we wish this situation to continue, there is no need for the new amendment formula. Indeed, its effect, if any, would merely be to allow a certain number of provinces

5    The Bank of Nova Scotia, *Monthly Review,* September 1964.

6    *House of Commons Debates,* February 22, 1965, p. 11, 565.

7    *National Accounts, Income and Expenditure,* Table 37. Data revised in July 1965.

to increase the legislative jurisdiction of the central Parliament. The two-thirds amendment would permit Ottawa to invade certain legislative fields; and, although provinces would theoretically retain their right to act (according to the Honourable Mr. Favreau, *Le Devoir*, March 5, 1965), very few would in practice wish to duplicate federal action. In addition, the technique of delegation would mean that some groups of provinces abandoned their autonomy in certain matters while other groups abandoned it in other matters. This process would, of course, be reversible; but we must not delude ourselves that provinces would be particularly keen to re-establish abandoned ministries or government services.

Thus, the two new elements of the Fulton-Favreau formula would tend systematically to weaken the reality of federalism in most provinces, to break the opposition of the provinces as a whole to centralization, and to create divisions between them along lines that are not yet clear, but that would probably depend on the relative wealth or poverty of the provinces, their leaning toward right-wing or left-wing politics, or their ethnic composition.

It must be obvious that this kind of blurring of the boundary lines between the two levels of government could only be disastrous. Parliament's jurisdiction over Canadian citizens would vary depending on the area in which they lived; during federal elections, voters in provinces that had chosen to remain autonomous would be called on to judge the way in which the government had administered the public good in other provinces; Members of Parliament would have to take a stand and vote on laws not applicable to their own constituents; and taxpayers would have to finance the application of laws from which they themselves could derive no benefit.

Moreover, considering our present political climate, there is reason to fear that above all this kind of confusion would tend to isolate Quebec. Our province would in fact achieve a "special status" constitutionally, but only at the cost of deriving least benefit from the situation. After other provinces had used the two-thirds and delegation formulas in order to modify the constitution for their own benefit and to suit their own needs, Quebec would be left with what remained of the B.N.A. Act. And then where would we be with our right to veto?

In brief, it seems almost certain that if the Fulton-Favreau formula were put into effect, Quebec would tend to evolve, at least in practice, toward the formation of a national state that would have every reason to disparage whatever remained of federalism. As I have already made clear, I prefer the federal system for economic, social, and psycho-cultural reasons. In my opinion, politicians or commentators on public affairs who encourage other provinces to establish interprovincial or federal-provincial relationships that differ from those used for Quebec, thereby fostering the isolation of this province, do a very great disservice to the country they claim to serve.

Our existing constitution, skilfully exploited, modified if need be (but in such a way that the division of power between the two government levels is the same in all provinces), creates a country in which Quebec may call upon the support of nine allies to protect provincial autonomy, and yet still feel that it struggles against even—not overwhelming—odds in its attempt to develop French culture in North America.

At the same time, this constitution prevents Quebec from becoming a closed society, which could only spell extinction for French Canadians living outside Quebec, and the development of a ghetto mentality for those living within it.

And this is the constitution our innovators want to change! Let them first come up with a system in which the rules of the game are really more favourable than the present one, and then we shall perhaps listen to them with greater interest.

## CONCLUSION AND CONCRETE PROPOSALS

Essentially, a constitution is designed to last a long time. Legal authority derives entirely from it; and if it is binding only for a short period it is not binding at all. A citizen—to say nothing of a power group—will not feel obliged to respect laws or governments he considers unfavourable to him if he thinks that they can easily be replaced: if the rules of the constitutional game are to be changed in any case, why not right now? A country where this mentality is prevalent oscillates between revolution and dictatorship. France, once it had started down the slippery path, gave itself eighteen constitutions in 180 years.

I do not believe that Quebec is powerful enough to afford such waste. Our province must have a long period of constitutional stability if it is to establish a sound basis for the great economic, social, and cultural development it wishes to achieve. Furthermore, the rest of the country would refuse to negotiate seriously with us if it had reason to suspect that any constitutional concession granted to Quebec would merely lead to new and greater demands. This means that the "revision of the Canadian constitution" mentioned in the mandate of the Legislative Assembly's Constitution Committee must be interpreted as taking place over several generations.

All the evidence seems to indicate that at the moment Quebec is not ready to say precisely what constitutional system of government it would like to have during the next half-century. When it comes to constitutional matters, political thinking in Quebec tends on the whole to be vague and self-contradictory. For example, our public opinion has long maintained that provincial unanimity should be required for any constitutional amendment; now that the idea of unanimity is embodied in the Fulton-Favreau formula, however, it is rejected as an obstacle to Quebec's "special status"! One need only glance at the briefs presented to the Constitution Committee to realize just how various and fluctuating our public opinion can be. It is now fashionable to be for change—but for *what* change, exactly? That, alas, is where there is a complete lack of consensus.

To my mind, this only goes to prove that we must not meddle with the constitution just yet. The real danger is that all these constitutional debates will provide an escape valve for our energies, and useful diversionary tactics for those who fear the profound social reforms advocated by the progressive element in our province. Worse still, if we did succeed at this stage in imposing a new constitutional framework, we would merely fetter this progressive element instead of giving it greater freedom of action.

If it is indeed true that Quebec is on the march, let us first find out just where it wishes to go, and where it in fact *can* go. There will still be ample time for lawyers to incorporate both what is desirable and what is feasible into the law.

All these reasons, taken together, lead me to exercise great restraint in suggesting constitutional reforms; and they account for the fact that in recent years I have appeared as a supporter of the constitutional *status quo*. As I have demonstrated in previous sections, the constitution has very little to do with the state of economic, technical, and demographic inferiority in which the French Canadians of Quebec find themselves today. I am not in a frantic hurry to change the constitution, simply because I *am* in a frantic hurry to change reality. And I refuse to give the ruling classes the chance of postponing the solving of *real* problems until after the constitution has been revised. We have seen only too often how, in the past, discussions centring on ideas such as the form of the state, nationhood, provincial autonomy, and independence have served to conceal the impotence of the ruling classes when faced with the profound transformation of our society by the industrial revolution. All I ask of our present ruling classes is that they stop being so preoccupied with the hypothetical powers an independent Quebec might have, and start using powers the real Quebec does have a bit more wisely.

In the economic field, it is infinitely less important to dream up new constitutional phrasing that would allow Quebec to recoup a larger percentage of federal taxes (this is already happening under our present constitution) than it is to move our province to the forefront of industrial progress (the result of which would be to increase substantially the very basis of provincial taxation).

Similarly, in the social and cultural fields, it is infinitely less important for Quebec to modify the constitution so as to acquire an international judicial identity, than to invest immense energy in agrarian reform and better urban planning, and concentrate all the strength it can muster upon educational reforms.

It should not be concluded from what I am saying that I am less aware than others of imperfections in the B.N.A. Act and the rules of federalism embodied in it. There is nothing easier than proposing constitutional reforms, and I could very easily outline several points that would some day have to be taken into account by a new constitution. For example:

(a) A Bill of Rights could be incorporated into the constitution, to limit the powers that legal authorities have over human rights in Canada. In addition to protecting traditional political and social rights, such a bill would specifically put the French and English languages on an equal basis before the law.

(b) The protection of basic rights having thus been ensured, there would be no danger in reducing the central government's predominance in certain areas (for example, by abolishing the right of reservation and disallowance); at the same time, this would have the advantage of getting rid of some of the constitution's imperial phraseology.

(c) The organic law relating to the central government could be revised in order to give it a more authentically federal character. In particular, conflicts in jurisdiction between federal and provincial levels could be judged by an independent body deriving its authority directly from the constitution. The Senate could also be reformed so that it represented the provinces more directly. Far from diminishing the authority of Parliament, such a measure would increase provincial confidence in the legislation that emanates from Ottawa (for example, in matters of tariffs or macro-economic policy).

These points are certainly important, and no doubt Canadians will have to face them some day—perhaps following the repatriation of the constitution. But I refuse to propose them formally at the moment, for the reasons I have already given, which I would like to summarize briefly once again:

Natural forces are presently favouring provincial autonomy. It is the centralizers who should be pressing for constitutional changes. If Quebec negotiators were cannier, they would affect supreme indifference, saying blandly: "Oh, the constitution isn't all that bad after all…. We are so busy trying to change the social and economic *status quo* that we simply haven't time for constitutional reforms just at the moment…. But if you are really keen about it, of course we are prepared to discuss revisions with you—say in a few months' time, or perhaps next year?"

Meanwhile, decentralization would have continued apace, the strong provinces would have established competent administrations which would be difficult to dislodge, and Quebec would have found several allies in its struggle for an improved federal system. Better still, our progress in the province would have raised the prestige of Canada's entire French-speaking population.

And so when constitutional negotiations finally began—at the instigation of other provinces!—Quebec could concentrate all its bargaining power

on the most crucial point, which I have called in section v "a very small constitutional modification." In conclusion I should like to make a few comments on this modification.

It is obvious that most of Canada's constitutional crises, like the present one, arise from ethnic problems, and more precisely from the question of the rights pertaining to the French language. As I have said earlier (in section III), the French language will be able to express progressive values only if North Americans who speak it are themselves in the forefront of progress, that is to say if they compete on an equal basis with English-speaking Canadians.

But the competition *must* be on an equal basis. Otherwise, the French population is in danger of becoming paralysed by an excess of defensive mechanisms. We shall develop the mentality of a beleaguered people, withdrawing into Quebec the better to sustain the siege. In other words, French Canadians may be forced by *English-Canadian* nationalism to push Quebec nearer to a national state and sooner or later to independence.

On this matter as on many others, the Fathers of Confederation showed great wisdom. Although they may have suspected that French Canadians would *in fact* always remain a linguistic minority, it seems that they wished to avoid making them feel a minority as far as *rights* were concerned. To put it in another way, while recognizing that French Canadians might always feel more at home in Quebec, they attempted to prevent the law from fostering in them a sense of inferiority or from giving them any excuse to feel like aliens in other parts of Canada.

According to Section 92 of the constitution, education became the responsibility of the provinces, as French Canadians had wished. The first paragraph, however, made it unconstitutional for provinces to interfere with confessional schools; and it is mainly through these, as is well known, that French Canadians develop and transmit their particular cultural values. Moreover, the last two paragraphs gave the central government power to rectify infringements upon "any right or privilege," including linguistic rights, of the (religious) group that includes almost all French Canadians.

Section 133 gave the French language official status for the exercise of the following political rights:

(a) At the federal level, the two languages were placed on an absolutely equal basis for all legislative as well as judicial functions. There was no mention of executive functions, but very likely this was due partly to the fact that in 1867 there was a much smaller number of people involved in the military and civil services, and partly to the fact that the cabinet was not defined by the constitution, but by custom; and in practice custom has gradually ensured that the number of French Canadians in the cabinet is more or less proportionate to their population. In so far as federal political institutions are concerned, then, the intention seems to have been to place English and French on an equal basis throughout Canada, and consequently to give the central government a genuinely bilingual character.

(b) In so far as provincial political institutions are concerned, the French language obtained equal rights only in those provinces where there was a considerable number of French Canadians. In practice, this meant Quebec; but the future was left open—for, according to Section 92, paragraph 1, each province could give the French language a position corresponding to the size of the French-Canadian population in that province. The spirit in which this was intended is evident if one considers that three years later, when the central government created Manitoba, whose population contained a large percentage of French-speaking people, French was placed on a par with English in this province.[8]

In substance, then, the Canadian constitution created a country where French Canadians could compete on an equal basis with English Canadians; both groups were invited to consider the whole of Canada their country and field of endeavour.

Unfortunately, for reasons that I cannot go into here, but that on the whole reflect less credit on English than on French Canadians, the rules of the "constitutional game" were not always upheld. In the matter of education, as well as political rights, the safeguards so dear to French Canadians were nearly always disregarded throughout the country, so that they came to believe themselves secure only in Quebec.

Worse still, in those areas not specifically covered by the constitution, the English-speaking majority used its size and wealth to impose a set of social rules humiliating to French Canadians. In the federal civil service, for example, and even more so in the Canadian armed forces, a French Canadian started off with an enormous handicap—if indeed he managed to start at all. This was true also in finance, business, and at all levels of industry. And that is how English became the working language, even in Quebec, and at all levels from foreman to bank president.

These social "rules of the game" do not lie within the mandate of the Constitution Committee. But a complete transformation of these rules is most urgently needed. And I have already described, especially in section IV, the conditions that are necessary if French Canadians are to revise these rules so that they operate in their favour.

The Constitution Committee, however, must propose amendments to the constitutional rules. The constitution must be so worded that any French-speaking community, anywhere in Canada, can fully enjoy its linguistic rights. In practice, this means that for the purpose of education, wherever there is a sufficient number of French-speaking people to form a school (or a university), these people must have the same rights as English Canadians in the matter of taxes, subsidies, and legislation on education. Of course, the concepts of "sufficient number" and "equal rights" will often have to be defined judicially or administratively; but both judges and administrators have as a guide the fact that these concepts have been applied for the past hundred years in remote areas of Quebec wherever there lived a "sufficient number" of English-speaking Canadians.

(a) At the federal level, the two languages must have absolute equality. With regard to legislative and judicial functions, this is already theoretically the case, according to Section 133 of the constitution; but the theory must be completely incorporated into actual practice so that, for example, any law or ruling is invalid if the English and French texts are not published side by side. Like the United States, we must move beyond "separate but equal" to "complete integration."

With regard to the executive functions, innovation is clearly required. Of course, it would be difficult to

---

8    *The Manitoba Act*, Section 23. See also Section 22, relating to education.

test the bilingualism of ministers of the Crown, and no doubt the whole thing will rest upon which men the voters decide to elect. (But it might also be decided by the fact that unilingual ministers would become frustrated when decisions were sometimes taken in French, and sometimes in English within the cabinet.) Everywhere else, and notably in the civil service and the armed forces, the two languages must be on a basis of absolute equality. This concept of equality must also be put into effect by management and by the courts. A simple, fair way of doing this might be to institute reciprocal rules: for example, if an infantry corporal or a minor Post Office official is exempted from knowing French because his functions bring him into contact with only a small percentage of French-speaking people, the same rule should apply to English when English-speaking people constitute the same small percentage. Or, to take another example, if a knowledge of English is required in the higher echelons of the civil service, then the same should be true of French. It is obvious that if such rules were applied overnight, they would result in a great many injustices and might indeed bring the state machinery grinding to a halt. But the introduction of such reforms must nevertheless be carried out according to a fixed schedule set by law (we could take the example of the Supreme Court of the United States which, in matters of racial integration, bases its decisions on the spirit, the general tendency, and to some extent upon the chronological intentions of the legislation brought before it).

(b) At the provincial level, similar reciprocal rules must be applied. In principle, the language of the majority will be the only official one. However, when a province contains a French or English minority larger than, say, 15 per cent, or half a million inhabitants, legislative and judicial functions must be exercised in such a way that the two languages are given absolute equality. It is very doubtful whether the same rule could be applied to the executive function; regardless of the size of its minorities, a province will therefore be able to remain unilingual on this point, provided of course that any citizen has the right to an English-French interpreter in his dealings with officials. (In practice, this could lead to the establishment of a bilingual civil service in those provinces where there was a sufficiently large and concentrated French or English minority.)

Such reforms must certainly be incorporated into constitutional law. It would not be very realistic to rely upon good will or purely political action. For example, in a province containing a greater number of Canadians of Ukrainian origin than of French origin, it would be rash to think that an elected provincial legislature would risk giving French schools privileges that Ukrainian schools did not have. Nor is it wise to rely entirely upon federal intervention: the ill-fated "remedial legislation" of 1896, relating to Manitoba schools, taught us to be cautious on this score.

The reforms I am proposing must therefore be written into the constitution itself, and must be irrevocably binding upon both the federal and provincial governments. As I suggested earlier, the guarantees contained in Sections 93 and 133 of the constitution must be extended and incorporated into a clear, imperative text which could be worded more or less along these lines: "Any law passed by the Parliament of Canada and relating to its executive, legislative, and judicial functions, as well as any law on matters of education passed by a provincial Legislature, or any constitutional text, will be invalid if it does not place the English and French languages on a basis of absolute judicial equality." And also: "In any province where there is a French or English minority exceeding 15 per cent or one-half million inhabitants, no law relating to legislative or judicial functions will be valid if it does not place the English and French languages on a basis of absolute judicial equality; however, a number will not be considered to exceed 15 per cent or one-half million inhabitants, unless it has been so established at two successive decennial censuses." And lastly: "It will be the right of every citizen to have an English-French interpreter in his dealings with any level of authority either in the central or the provincial governments."

Those are more or less the comments I wished to make about the constitution. The reforms I am proposing may seem quite modest in comparison with the vast upheaval favoured by so many Quebeckers these days; but this is because I want to keep to what I consider to be the absolute essential. This essential, however modest, implies an immense transformation of attitudes and of what I have called the social rules of the game. If this is achieved, sterile chauvinism will disappear from our Canadian way of life, and other useful constitutional reforms will follow suit without too much difficulty. If, on the other hand, the essential is not achieved, there is really no point in carrying the discussion any further; for this will mean that Canada will continue to be swept periodically by the storms of ethnic dispute, and will gradually become a spiritually sterile land, from which both peace and greatness have been banished.

# 29

## Editor's Introduction

Guy Laforest is among the sharpest of Quebec's nationalists. He has an uncanny ability to explain the nationalist cause, its causes, and its objective to audiences in the rest of Canada in a way few others can. Yet it is all too easy to equate nationalism with separatism. Francophone Quebeckers are, by and large, nationalists but not necessarily separtists. The controversy centres on the best means of protecting the French, and Quebec as a primarily francophone province, against the constant peril of being gobbled up in the anglophone sea that is North America. Laforest is sometimes accused of being inconsistent for not offering unqualified backing for Quebec separatism. From a nationalist perspective, though, his position is actually quite principled: if the objective is to preserve the French fact in North America and if its fortune is coterminous with Quebec's, then the means best suited to that end are a matter of time and the right conditions. In this fairly recent piece, Laforest offers a second take on one of Canada's most infamous historical documents, *Lord Durham's Report*. Most students will have some familiarity with the anglophone interpretation of the Report; however, understanding the vernacular francophone Quebec reading of that same Report and why it is interpreted differently than in English Canada is indispensable to grasping Quebec nationalism and Quebec's take on the federation. In addition to this fresh reading of the Durham Report that will be virgin territory to most anglophone students, the Durham Report is notable for making two key contributions to Canadian politics. The first is one that most Canadians will have some familiarity with: the assimilationist inference Lord Durham drew from his conclusion about "two nations warring in the bosom of a single state" (which, if understood in historical context, is not all that surprising given his time, his own socialization, and the constraints under which he carried out his report). The second is easily overlooked. From the vantage point of the twenty-first century, it is easy to pounce on "radical Jack's" nineteenth-century biases while neglecting his enduring contribution to constitutional government in Canada: responsible government.

Source: "Lord Durham, French Canada and Québec: Remembering the Past, Debating the Future," in *Lord Durham's Report: A Re-Edition*, ed. J. Azjenstat (Montreal: McGill-Queen's University Press, 2007), 177–203.

### Guy Laforest

# Lord Durham, French Canada, and Québec: Remembering the Past, Debating the Future

LORD DURHAM'S REPORT is still important reading, both for social scientists and for those with a general or scholarly interest in politics, philosophy, and history. It is helpful to a larger public that is dealing, in a variety of vexing circumstances, with finding the appropriate way to remember a troubled past and to delineate the moral and political consequences of specific ways of interpreting historical facts and events.

Deciding these questions requires entering a perennial philosophical debate, that of how to make sense of the relationship between history, memory, and politics. To show why the Durham Report is as indispensable as ever for political theorists of all stripes, I will slightly reformulate a question that is a recurrent theme in Janet Ajzenstat's introduction to [the 2007 edition of *Lord Durham's Report*]: Can the universalistic pull of liberal modernity be reconciled with the preservation of particular identities and cultures? In the past twenty years, this question has been a central issue in the republic of letters. It is no mere coincidence that Canadians have played leading roles in such a debate[1] and … the pedagogical value of the Durham Report is nowhere more important than in Canada and Quebec.

In 1963, when the last edited version of the Report was published in English, Quebec was going through the political phase of its own process of late and brutal modernization, known as the "Quiet Revolution."[2] Canada as a whole, on the eve of the 1967 Centennial of Confederation, was moving equally rapidly towards establishing its own national identity at a greater distance from Britain. In 1963 the Canadian federal government led by Lester Pearson put together the Royal Commission on Bilingualism and Biculturalism, co-chaired by Davidson Dunton and André Laurendeau, whose mandate was based on the idea of an equal partnership between the French- and English-speaking founding peoples of Canada.[3] It is, of course, beyond the scope of this [chapter] to address at length the political evolution of Quebec and Canada from 1963 to the present day, although I will not completely ignore it.[4] It is sufficient at this stage to mention that this new edition of the Report, in its own right a commemoration of Durham's legacy, is being published at about the same time as two major historical celebrations: we are about to mark the 400th anniversary of the founding of the City of Quebec and of Canada by Champlain in 1608 as well as the 25th anniversary of the 1982 constitution, the last step in Canada's adventure of quiet decolonization from Britain and the dawn of the era of the Canadian Charter of Rights and Freedoms. In our days as well as in 1963 and in the epoch of Durham, the historical paths of Canada and Quebec remain intertwined in their joint struggle for greater political freedom and the development of secure, distinct identities in North America.

My argument here is thus premised on the idea that the Durham Report has both universal and particular meanings. Given how debatable and contradictory these meanings may prove to be, I do not pretend to be able to end the debate. But it is my hope that fifty years from now, when the Report undergoes yet another edition, readers will still find in this [chapter] useful notes and arguments to help them make up their own minds on these matters.

I will start logically, dealing in the first section with the fate of the Report in French Canada and Quebec and attempting to assess how it has been viewed by previous generations and how it is being discussed in current historiographical debates. Variations abound, but the basic idea remains the same: Lord Durham and his Report are causally connected to the emergence and the development of a specific form of national self-consciousness. I will then discuss Janet Ajzenstat's views … starting with the key figure of Étienne Parent. Much of what my colleague says throughout her introduction about the meaning of the Durham Report for Canadian history and the evolution of federalism is very enlightening; I will supplement her general view with my particular perspective. Following some notes on Durham as a human being and as a thinker, I will focus on two other themes: the place of the Durham Report in one of Quebec's most important ideological and intellectual aspects, "melancholy nationalism" (an expression developed by political philosopher Jocelyn Maclure) and the role of the fundamental tension between universalistic and particularistic aspects in the tribulations of modernity—a key feature of the Report—and how this tension is being played out in Canada and Quebec.[5]

## COMING TO TERMS WITH LORD DURHAM'S REPORT IN FRENCH CANADA AND QUEBEC

Canada is a member of an elite G-8 group of industrialized states in the global age of the internet. Quebec is a majority French-speaking province in a federal, highly developed country that prides itself on official bilingualism. Canada and Quebec thus share two autonomous but equally interconnected public spheres, two communicational and scientific networks operating in the great languages of Western modernity,

English and French. The development of this social environment from 1963 to 2006 has produced greater academic and scholarly sophistication in all fields. History, the art of understanding the past, has not been left behind in this evolution. The task of revisiting the Durham Report is made even more challenging by the complexity and vigour of historiographical debates throughout Canada, particularly in Quebec.[6] There has also been, since the last English edition of the Report, a quantum leap in the level of interest in the international academic community about Canadian affairs. To highlight the perennial importance of Lord Durham and of the constitutional blueprint that arose at least partly based on his Report, I shall start with one such foreign voice, that of Dresden Professor Ingo Kolboom: "For French Canadians, it was the genesis of a historical trauma. The repression of the Patriotes and the sanctions on French Canadians, institutionalized by the Union Act in 1840, were their true historical defeat, inasmuch as they saw these events as a traumatizing deception on the part of the British, who revealed themselves to be the Conquerors of 1763. French Canadians re-lived the defeat of 1760 through the sanctions of 1840."[7]

I believe that Kolboom's interpretation in this passage reflects the hegemonic view of Lord Durham and his influence that has affected both the history and intellectual life of French Canada and Quebec. Durham's legacy has become even more present in academia in the last decade due to a rejuvenated interest in political history and a corresponding decline in interest in more positivistic and technically oriented economic and social history.[8] With Durham, as with other matters, Quebec and other Canadian historians now engage in more frequent and energetic debates, searching for insightful ways to debunk the historical myths at work in their respective communities.[9] I want to briefly consider two questions stemming from these recent exchanges. The first arises from attempts to establish the primary cause of the 1837–38 Rebellions. Was the crisis fundamentally linked to political reasons or was it rather, as Lord Durham forcefully argued, the apotheosis of a long-standing and insurmountable ethnic conflict? University of Toronto historian Allan Greer, an expert on the Rebellions in Lower Canada, has this to say about the archival evidence on this matter:

An influential school of thought in Canadian historiography that dates back to Lord Durham and others says that all fine phrases about political rights and freedom spouted by the patriots were a cover for an essentially xenophobic movement and that what is fundamental in Lower Canada is the conflict of English and French. Everything else is secondary. I would argue that the argument is almost exactly the reverse of reality.... The conflict that came to an acute stage in 1837 and 1838 had everything to do with the breakdown of politics as usual and a crisis of the state, which called forth a mobilization of the majority of the population.... The really acute strife and conflict between English and French came after that; it followed from that fundamentally political conflict.... What seems to have resulted is something that happens in a lot of revolutionary crises in other parts of the world and other eras of history. Ethnic and linguistic minorities became quite uncomfortable, as a reaction to the revolutionary process itself.[10]

The myth that Allan Greer helps to dismantle with regard to the source of the conflict is not the only one to have survived until quite recently, bringing me to the second issue. Obsessed by Durham's scathing language throughout his Report and by the cold severity of his prescription concerning assimilation, French Canadians and Quebec thinkers have tended to portray him as a formidable figure. Fernand Dumont summarizes this trend when he characterizes Lord Durham's implacable logic and "remarquable hauteur d'esprit" as "immense."[11] Durham as a spiritual semi-God? John Ralston Saul begs to differ with this judgment:

In a way our attitudes can be summarized through our relationship to Lord Durham. We have turned his four-month visit during 1838 into the touchstone of the Canadian condition.... The words aimed at francophones have been particularly retained by part of their elite as a sore to be scratched open on a regular basis. But consider the real Durham, beyond mythology. He was neither a great figure nor a great aristocrat. He inherited money and through political activity was paid off with a title. He was of marginal junior-minister importance....

His one original idea—the union of the two provinces would provoke the assimilation of the francophones—was completely wrong…. This is the context in which Durham's gratuitous insults must be seen. It was just the sort of language you'd have expected from an immature graduate of Eton in the nineteenth century…. The combination of personal privilege, marginal success, an unstable personality and class prejudice are enough to perpetuate this sort of juvenile wilfulness in a man who cannot engage with reality.[12]

Saul certainly has a point, although I believe that there is a room for greater nuance in the assessment of Lord Durham as a human being and as a thinker. Such a careful re-examination requires a journey through current historiographical developments. McGill Professor Yvan Lamonde is Quebec's pre-eminent historian of ideas and has provided a path toward a more balanced evaluation of Lord Durham's Report through his scholarly work, particularly a masterful synthesis on the nineteenth century.[13] Aside from his impeccable bibliographical work, Lamonde's essential contributions are a precise chronicling of the mounting dissatisfaction of Lower Canadian colonial elites vis-à-vis metropolitan authorities in the 1830s, a much needed determination of the intellectual climate at the time of the Rebellions through a detailed examination of the printed sources at the disposal of Lower Canadians in order to establish their knowledge of contemporary developments and struggles in the Americas and Europe, a profound analytical and contextual analysis of the political thought of Étienne Parent and Louis-Joseph Papineau (their personal intellectual evolutions, the transition from their close collaboration to their estrangement in the camps of moderation and revolution, their opinions on Lord Durham's mission during his sojourn in the Canadas, and their reactions to his Report), and finally a lucid understanding of the complex reasons that explain the failure of the Rebellions.[14] Indispensable reading in general, Lamonde makes one key point about Lord Durham that can easily be neglected by twenty-first century readers. Durham did not belong to a neutral, fact-finding commission of the International Court in The Hague trying to assess the causes of a conflict, determine responsibilities, and draw the contours of a durable and just

institutional peace that would respect the premises of human rights conventions. Rather, Lord Durham was a British imperialist first and foremost, culturally and politically biased about the matters he had to enquire into and report about. This is particularly obvious, according to Lamonde, in his lack of criticism of the Legislative Council, the one colonial institution that Lower Canadians had constantly identified, starting with Pierre Bédard in 1814, as an essentially English ethnic structure that contradicted the spirit of British constitutionalism.[15]

French Canada (rather than Lower Canada—a fundamental distinction) as a self-conscious national community begins with Lord Durham's Report and its political consequences. Starting with the nostalgic, quasi-Romantic figure of François-Xavier Garneau, a contemporary of Durham, and going from the conservative urbanity of Thomas Chapais, the ultramontane and anti-modern nationalism of Lionel Groulx, the post-1945 Montréal School (Maurice Séguin, Guy Frégault and Michel Brunet, a generation obsessed by the negative consequences of the Conquest that set the stage politically for Quebec's post-1960 independence movement) and its Laval counterpart (Fernand Ouellet, Jean Hamelin, pioneers in a more positive evaluation of the British regime and of Canadian Confederation), to arrive finally at Lamonde's generation of scholars, historians have dated the birth of an ideology or doctrine of national survival in French Canada to the early 1840s. The ideology developed at this time focused on the conservation of the cultural, linguistic, religious, and other traditional institutions of the community, a program of survival that seems to confirm Lord Durham's verdict by delineating a national life that remains largely distant from the struggles of liberal politics and the challenges of market economic practices in America. Lord Durham and his Report have played a role in all phases of this historiographic saga. For those who are curious about the centrality of Lord Durham's legacy for contemporary Quebec society, it is useful to consider the work of the late Fernand Dumont and of Gérard Bouchard, two major thinkers who, as public intellectuals, have enjoyed wide respect beyond the walls of academia.

Both Dumont and Bouchard support the project of political sovereignty for Quebec. For both thinkers, independence is the political telos of political modernity. Nations are truly normal and healthy when they are completely sovereign. Trained in anthropological philosophy, psychology, and sociology, Dumont in his master narrative, *Genèse de la société québécoise*, emphasized the role of Lord Durham in producing the key individual and collective historical consciousness pathologies in French Canada. In doing this, Dumont integrates all the elements that led Durham to prescribe forced assimilation: the spirit of contempt and disrespect for most things French Canadian and the disparaging comparisons and prophecies of inevitable doom in America. He thus makes Durham one of the most important examples of the British—later transmuted into Canadian—Other for French Canada and French Canadians. This negative discourse of necessary assimilation based on inescapable inferiority has been slowly, subtly, and systematically internalized by French Canadians in their attempts to formulate their own discourse of national self-consciousness.[16] The Durham Report led to their permanent political subordination and to the development of a profound minority complex. In the next section I will discuss some problems associated with Dumont's narrative. My point here is simply to reiterate that Dumont holds that Lord Durham is directly linked to the existence of a deep problem of false consciousness in the historical trajectory of French Canada and of Quebec, the kind of problem that can only be cured by sovereignty. Whatever one may think of the validity of its thesis, Dumont's book remains useful for its comprehensive discussion of historical materials, particularly with regard to the generation of François-Xavier Garneau, which lived in the immediate aftermath of Lord Durham's Report and had to interpret—in truth had to invent narratively—French Canada in his shadow.

Gérard Bouchard, trained in sociology and in history, provides a nice complement to Dumont's approach. Whereas the latter is fascinated by the unfolding dramas of subjective consciousness, Bouchard is more interested in the apparently more objective comparative analysis of the structural patterns at work in the evolution of modern societies. In his magnum opus, *Genèse des nations et cultures du nouveau monde: Essai d'histoire comparée*, Bouchard studies the historical trajectories of Canada and Quebec by contrasting them with movements and trends in the experiences of Australia, Latin America, the United States, and New Zealand. His excellence in the art of synthesizing intellectual doctrines is illustrated in his very useful analytical summary of the doctrine of "la survivance" for French Canada, the paradigm of survival for a national culture and a collective memory.[17] According to Bouchard, Quebec is essentially the sole exception to a pattern that saw the full political emancipation, most often through processes of radical rupture, of all New World collectivities subordinated to European empires. On this narrative, Lord Durham and his Report stand at a critical historical juncture, one that saw a definitive break in the march of Lower Canada towards full societal and political maturity.[18] There is a teleological philosophy of history at work in Bouchard's thinking that sees Quebec's sovereignty as a normal end-point—the fulfilment of the promises of its roots and destiny on the American continent.[19]

How does Lord Durham fare, ultimately, in the work of these two widely admired figures of Quebec's sovereigntist intelligentsia? In Fernand Dumont's elegant prose, Durham is respected, critically dissected without being demonized. In Gérard Bouchard's more coldly scientific but equally compelling narratives, Durham is almost completely ignored but the consequences of his thoughts and actions are omnipresent. In both cases, his name is associated with the dark side of the past.

## JANET AJZENSTAT'S [ARGUMENT]: DEBATING LORD DURHAM'S INFLUENCE ON CANADA AND ASSESSING HIM AS A HUMAN BEING AND AS A THINKER

Janet Ajzenstat is quite right to emphasize the importance of Étienne Parent, editor of the newspaper *Le Canadien* in the 1830s and arguably Quebec's first real intellectual.[20] Throughout that decade, Parent attempted to articulate the reasonable middle ground, marching in the footsteps of Bédard and thus embracing British constitutionalism while at the same time attempting to balance his support for Enlightenment liberalism with the defence of Canadian nationality ("la nationalité canadienne," as it was referred to in pre-Durham years). In April 1837, when it became clear following the Russell Resolutions that authorities in Britain would remain deaf to the grievances of Lower Canada, Parent advocated renewed prudence and warned his compatriots to take care lest they suffer a fate similar to that of Poland in 1831 at the hands of Russia. In some circumstances, writes Parent, "there is both an honourable submission and a dishonourable domination."[21] In the aftermath of Lord Durham's Report, as Ajzenstat notes, Parent had his great moment of despair, contemplating the inevitable disappearance of "la nationalité canadienne" and the assimilation of his compatriots. As Ajzenstat lucidly argues, the history of Canada would not have unfolded as it has if Parent had not found ways to reconsider this bleak judgment. She fails, however, to mention that Parent lived through his darkest hour while he was in jail. He remained in custody from late December 1838 onwards, for a period about as long as Durham's own stay in the Canadas. His imprisonment occurred during a tough colonial winter and he became deaf. Parent was jailed—not on Durham's orders, for he had gone back to Britain two months before—on the basis of an article he had written in *Le Canadien* where he argued in quasi-Lockean terms that the real conspirators, those who were primarily responsible for the disturbance of order, were those in authority who had multiplied provocations, pushing the people from excesses to new excesses by harshness and renewed harshness.[22] Parent despaired after such repressive means were used to crush and subjugate him. Durham and his era are more than a theoretical chapter in the history of liberal doctrine. These were dark times and Parent, as Allan Greer remarks, was not the only one to suffer from the politics of terror:

> There was another version of terror, the counter-revolutionary terror, that occurred after the patriots were defeated and that took very harmful forms. Houses were burned down by the dozens, possibly by the hundreds, in the wake of the fighting in 1837–38. People were killed, people by the hundreds were thrown into jail. Many were taken into custody, probably thousands, for shorter periods, although it was not well recorded. So the population in the District of Montreal, in the rural areas,

was well and thoroughly frightened into submission by these tactics.[23]

… Ajzenstat seems to suggest that Lord Durham felt that the safeguards of the parliamentary system would overcome the potential intolerance of the French majority and the flaws of Lower Canada's colonial regime. Following this logic, she writes, "Unconstrained rule by the French majority would soon become as intolerant as unconstrained rule by Governors and their cronies."[24] However—and this question seems to me as poignantly relevant in 2006 as it was to those who first had to live with the Report in 1839—how could Durham have been so utterly certain about that, given his studied and complete ignorance, throughout his Commission, of those such as Étienne Parent and Louis-Hyppolite LaFontaine who represented the camp of moderate Canadian patriotism and support for British constitutionalism?[25] Lord Durham, preceded by his reputation as a Liberal reformer, was greeted with sympathetic anticipation when he disembarked in Quebec City in late May 1838. The turning point in the gradual disenchantment with him and his mission was his hiring of Adam Thom, also known in Lower Canada under his pen name of "Camillus" and the author of a series of "Anti-Gallic Letters" in the *Montreal Herald*.[26] Janet Ajzenstat argues persuasively that Durham was a coherent and far-reaching liberal thinker. If his attitude toward Lower Canadians of French background—to coin a new category—gives us an accurate measure of the man, fair-mindedness (otherwise put, a respect for the key humanistic concept of *audi alteram partem*) was not one of his cherished principles.

In addition to the doctrine of responsible government, has Lord Durham left other structural legacies to the architecture of the Canadian state and the spirit of Canadian federalism? On this matter, I would like to add a couple of notes to Ajzenstat's remarkably instructive remarks. With regard to responsible government, she is trying to re-assess whether or not Lord Durham wanted to maintain "the crucial powers of control and compliance" in Great Britain at the same time that he envisaged greater political autonomy for the Canadian colonies.[27] With regard to the division of powers in Canadian federalism, she is attempting to portray him as the forefather of a coherent, over-arching principle for allocation of such responsibilities: the central government would take care of general matters with representatives in the federal Parliament debating, in the language of liberal universalism, the issues of concern to all citizens without consideration of their origins, whereas provincial governments would take care of local matters, with legislative representatives embracing the language of human particularities in their debates and paying primary attention to the interests of their citizens as these pertained to their cultural or national origins.[28] On the first matter, I suspect that in 1867 the Dominion of Canada was indeed the middle of a three-tiered hierarchical structure: some crucial powers of control remained with Westminster—legislative supremacy, organization of courts and ultimate jurisdiction over judicial arbitration, determination of foreign and defence policies, and overall coordination of the political association—while the Dominion enjoyed greater autonomy than previously and thus retained substantial control of those same areas in its relationships with its provincial counterparts.[29] Provinces, while remaining subordinate in key areas, also claimed greater autonomy. If this meta-interpretation is correct, then I would certainly agree with Ajzenstat when she writes that we in Canada have forgotten both this organization and Lord Durham's role in its conception. I want to point out, however, that the idea of this principled distribution is used yet again in two recent, seminal essays, written by André Burelle and Eugénie Brouillet, that attempt to make sense of the project of federal harmony for French Canada and Quebec around 1867.[30] Thus, at least in Quebec, this particular scheme has not been forgotten, but Ajzenstat is correct that Lord Durham's role in its formulation has been completely disregarded.

What should we make in the end of Lord Durham as a human being and as a thinker? Perhaps paradoxically, I think that in the above-mentioned passages John Ralston Saul has been too harsh on him. The man who arrived here with the promise of spring in 1838, and even more the one who departed with the bitterly cold rains of November, was tired, sick, overwhelmed with sadness in his personal life, and considerably weakened as a political animal—thoroughly diminished and thus incapable of moving beyond the

prejudices associated with his own complex identity as a doctrinaire liberal politician, an English aristocrat, and a self-conscious British imperialist. On a more theoretical plane the most thought-provoking evaluation of Lord Durham and his times comes, in my judgment, from Stéphane Dion. According to him, it served Durham's purposes to assert that it was French Canada that espoused the principles and practices of anti-liberalism. This apparently objective sociological assessment made it possible for him to reconcile his liberal ideas with his geo-political preoccupations. As Dion rhetorically asks himself, "Would Durham have recommended the autonomy of Lower Canada if he had considered the patriots to be sincere in their professed liberalism? We will never know, because Durham and Alexis de Tocqueville (the two preeminent figures of liberal colonialism in the nineteenth century) formulated their arguments in ways that allowed them to avoid choosing between empire and liberty."[31]

I have so far been preoccupied with what could be called a critical hermeneutics that privileges an understanding of the past for the sake of the past. In the next section I will put much more emphasis on considerations of the present and the future—for Lord Durham and his Report continue to be significant not only for Canada and Quebec but for humankind in general.

## A CRITICAL HERMENEUTICS FOR THE PRESENT AND THE FUTURE

In a key philosophical essay on the theories and histories of identity in Quebec, Jocelyn Maclure shows that people, particularly the intelligentsia, in Quebec, a province where the majority of the population is French-speaking, are still obsessed by the spirit of Lord Durham and have failed to liberate themselves from his shadow. According to Maclure, discussions of collective identity are narrative projects. These narratives are important to the emergence and consolidation of national communities. The fundamental criteria for judging the importance of such narratives is their continued presence in the writings and minds of interpreters.[32] Beyond the contributions that Lord Durham and his Report have made to the nature of the Canadian state and Canadian federalism, described in Ajzenstat's introduction, Maclure shows that both man and report strongly influenced the dominant ideological doctrine in interpretations of the past in Quebec. Maclure characterizes this all-encompassing feature of intellectual life in Quebec as "melancholy nationalism," a meeting point of history, memory, and politics. Discussing the ramifications of melancholy nationalism allows me to begin addressing the broader significance of Lord Durham's Report, moving outside French Canada and Quebec toward the idea of an inescapable tension between particularistic and universalistic dimensions of reality. To delineate the phenomenon of melancholy nationalism as precisely as possible, I will start with two quotations: one from Maclure's essay and one from Jocelyn Létourneau's critical work on the narrative construction of memory and identity in Quebec.

There exists in Quebec a whole discourse about the fragility, the precariousness, the tragic existence, the fatigue, the modesty, the philistinism, the mediocrity, the immaturity, and the indecision of the Québécois people. Those who intone this sombre national chant are drinking from a stream with many confluents. By searching a little and by adopting a certain relationship to the past, one can indeed find in the genesis of Quebec society, as well as in its recent history, the fuel for a major depression— or more precisely, a case of collective melancholia. In Freud's terms, melancholia is experienced as a kind of mourning whose sources elude us, which we cannot ascribe to a specific, identifiable loss. That is, melancholia is an elusive, diffuse, latent feeling of grief. From generation to generation, Quebec intellectuals and writers have attempted to follow the thread of this melancholia, in the belief that they can work back to the origins of Quebec's modern-day ills.[33]

This sad view of the past was created by the great French Canadian and Québécois intellectuals, from Garneau to Dumont, loyally and in good faith—albeit with varying degrees of modulation, subtlety, and complexity.... For these pioneers of historical consciousness, the inherent fragility of the community required that they carry the country as one holds a child. Thus, for them memory had to be at the beginning of method, misery had

to structure the purpose, melancholy had to set the tone, and the text had to nurture memory.[34]

According to the narrative of melancholy nationalism, the vast majority of people remain completely unconscious of their alienation because they have "internalized in their identity the belittling, traumatizing, even insulting gaze of the other."[35] Their imagination is perpetually haunted by this gaze. The highest literary expression of the perspective of melancholy nationalism can be found in the essays and novels of Hubert Aquin, who coined the famous expression "the cultural fatigue of French Canada" to describe the psychological traits that emerged, at the level of both individual and collective consciousness, as a result of Lord Durham's verdict that the French should remain permanent minors: "self-punishment, masochism, a sense of unworthiness, 'depression,' the lack of enthusiasm and vigour."[36] The highest theoretical, philosophical, and historiographical expression in the tradition of melancholy nationalism is the narrative articulated by Fernand Dumont in *Genèse de la société québécoise*. Dumont shows that internalization and appropriation of the Other's degrading contempt has led to a state of permanent mental colonization in French Canada that has both individual and collective dimensions, even in contemporary Quebec.[37] While doing research and thinking about this [chapter], I could not help but be aware that Lord Durham was, and remains to this day, the first significant Other under whose gaze the narrative of melancholy nationalism perpetually unfolds. Consider the following passages near the end of the Report, when Lord Durham vividly recapitulates the gist of his analysis:

I know of no national distinctions marking and continuing a more hopeless inferiority.... There can hardly be conceived a nationality more destitute of all that can invigorate and elevate a people, than that which is exhibited by the descendants of the French in Lower Canada, owing to their retaining their peculiar language and manners. They are a people with no history, and no literature.[38]

The fate of such a destitute nationality could only be that of permanent political subordination under the rule of law, or, in Durham's own words, obliteration through assimilation into the numerical majority of a loyal English population reinforced by a systematic policy of encouraging like-minded immigrants.[39] With these passages in mind, Lord Durham seems a good candidate for the true "Other" of melancholy nationalism. Aside from the works of Aquin and Dumont, there are two persuasive illustrations of this connection in essays written by André D'Allemange and Jean Bouthillette in the 1960s, the period in Quebec history that witnessed the apex of French Canada's collective alienation in the context of global decolonization.[40] The fate of Lord Durham as the historical embodiment of the British or English Other is not restricted to the narratives of melancholy nationalism: "anti-Durhamism" plays a fundamental role in a number of ideological statements in support of Quebec's aspirations towards full political sovereignty. Université de Montréal political scientist Denis Monière argues that sovereignty is necessary, first and foremost, because since 1867 Canada has fulfilled Lord Durham's vision, subjecting French Canadians in Quebec to all the social and psychological consequences that result from their status as a debilitated and paralysed political minority.[41] In an attempt to rekindle support for Quebec sovereignty, Gérard Bouchard makes very explicit the link between Lord Durham's heritage, the vocabulary of melancholy nationalism, and the ideal of political independence. Bouchard advocates returning to the founding ideals of the sovereignty movement: the vision that Quebec, as a Francophone and American nation, should be master of its own destiny; the goal of granting greater status to Francophone Québécois by revaluing, nationally and internationally, all areas of collective life; and, finally, the re-making of the identity of French Canadians, to repudiate the heritage of colonialism and restore the confidence and self-respect of Québécois.[42] According to Jacques Beachemin, the goal of sovereignty for Quebec is inseparable from a desire to redress the march of history.[43] From this perspective, achieving sovereignty would be to bury, at long last, Lord Durham and his Report.

I would now like to discuss overcoming Lord Durham's heritage, and all other similar heritages, by looking at the insights of French philosopher Paul Ricoeur on the necessity of finding an equilibrium between remembrance and forgetfulness in the search for a moral way to deal with History.

For individuals as well as for groups, the fall of historical memory into the abyss of melancholy is catastrophic. It seems to me that this is the arresting conclusion reached by Paul Ricoeur near the end of his long and remarkably productive life.[44] Whenever a community closes itself to its own sufferings, thus becoming "blind and deaf to the sufferings of other communities," history must intervene to criticize and correct the memory of the first community. According to Ricoeur, memory, with the help of a critical historical hermeneutics, is able to achieve a certain sense of justice for, as he rhetorically puts it, "How could there be a happy memory that was not, as well, a just memory?"[45] Following the triumph of melancholy, the problem for identity is a Self that suffers from its own devaluation, from its own condemnation, from the consequences of its own downgrading, resulting in depression and anxiety.

Can French Canada and Quebec, influenced by their nationalist and sovereigntist historians, be put in the category of these communities that, following Ricoeur's logic, have traced the unhappy path towards the abyss of melancholy? This is the argument propounded by Maclure and Létourneau and the view of John Ralston Saul when he portrays Lord Durham's insults as resulting in a "sore to be scratched open on a regular basis." There is undeniably an element of truth in this critical assessment. As Jean-Philippe Warren contends, it may be that in its desire to focus on a psychoanalytical approach to the understanding of history, Dumont's generation has nourished and possibly even generated an overdeveloped sense of anxiety.[46] Université Laval sociologist Simon Langlois, closely associated with Dumont's school of thought, recognizes that the author of Genèse de la société québécoise clearly privileged the memory of a certain French Canadian past in the history of Quebec, neglecting aspects of diversity in the past and the present of this society, and neglecting as well the duty of every nation to re-imagine the future in a new light.[47] It would be an over-simplification, however, to conclude that the dominant intellectual characteristic of modern-day Quebec is the perpetuation of a fall into the abyss of melancholy, a fall inaugurated by Lord Durham's narrative in his Report.

In the social sciences, literature, and philosophy, the last two decades have been marked by a series of debates on the pluralistic nature of Quebec's collective identity and on the need to allow much greater space to these different memories in the reconstruction of Quebec's national history.[48] It is only fair to recognize the leading role played in this enterprise by Gérard Bouchard, who has probably become Quebec's pre-eminent historian and intellectual figure since the death of Fernand Dumont in 1997.[49] As well, echoing Ricoeur's admonitions about the importance of a happy and just historical memory, Jacques Beauchemin and Daniel Jacques have argued that in Quebec the politics of conquest and re-conquest must be replaced by a politics of concord, a politics marked by processes of dialogue and reciprocal recognitions, where people steeped in their plural identities argue their way towards reasonable compromises.[50] In the politics of concord, no one vision of the collective future can claim the language of historical inevitability. Newcomers to such a society have to accept that they have climbed aboard a train or joined a movie that has started without them.[51] They should not, moreover, be over-burdened by the memory of any particular group. In Quebec as elsewhere in the world, as Daniel Jacques concludes, the wounds of the past, the duty to remember, should not be the sole guiding principle in matters of political conduct.[52]

Jocelyn Maclure, following Freud, has described melancholia as a sort of mourning "whose sources elude us." I shall now venture to identify one such possible source for this kind of mourning, rejoining Ajzenstat … when she finds at the heart of Lord Durham's Report a fundamental tension between universalistic and particularistic dimensions in the unfolding of modernity. What would have happened, in the 1840s, if Lord Durham had recommended, and British imperial authorities had implemented, a regime of Dominion-like status or responsible self-government for Lower Canada? Would the French majority have acted despotically, ruling Lower Canada in an unconstrained, intolerant, and absolutist fashion? Or would this regime have inaugurated an era of tolerance, fairness, and pluralism in the history of the modern state, establishing an edifying precedent in a world attempting to deal with the conflicting challenges of liberalism and nationalism—of

universalism and particularism—in the middle of the nineteenth century? There are no guarantees either way, but in the humanities and social sciences we have known since Max Weber that it is instructive to think through such counterfactual possibilities.[53] Lower Canada stood at the crossroads of these possibilities when Lord Durham, with his Report, directed it away from the optimistic alternative. I believe that this is a major source of the mourning that can be found in the narrative of melancholy nationalism. Remember Ajzenstat's key question: is universalism implacably hostile to expressions of particularity? Political philosophers ponder such difficult questions, whereas political communities act upon them. In his seminal work, *Critique de l'Américanité: Mémoire et démocratie au Quebec*, University of Ottawa sociologist Joseph-Yvon Thériault argues that this central question that fascinates Ajzenstat has been, since the advent of Lower Canada through the Constitution of 1791, the question that dominated public debates in the colony and later in French Canada and Quebec. Thériault calls it the question of the people and then suggests that the intellectual and political configurations stemming from this question can best be understood as the "Durham moment."[54] This question has always had a double nature, with a universalistic axis—envisaging the nation as a contractual community of individuals with liberal rights—and a particularistic one—emphasizing the broad cultural heritage of the national community. Lord Durham saw the French majority in Lower Canada as too anchored in a destitute and parochial heritage to be able to reach by itself the good of universality. The general spirit of his Report follows a rather Manichean logic: either tradition or modernity; either a nation of individual citizens or a community of heritage. Durham fails to integrate into his narrative the fact that, since the first session of its Parliament in 1792, Lower Canada had been struggling, however imperfectly, to find its own balance between the good of universality and the good of particularity.[55] In the end, there is nothing mysterious about such a tension in philosophy or politics. As Ajzenstat herself remarks, the idea of the ineluctability of this tension is generally accepted by the contemporary political theory.[56]

Lord Durham's Report still makes remarkable sense in contemporary Canada and Quebec not only because it affected both the nature of the emerging Canadian federal state in 1867 and the whole intellectual history of French Canada and Quebec, whether we prefer to look at it from Maclure's perspective of melancholy nationalism or from Thériault's approach insisting on a "Durham moment," but because his reductive and doctrinaire view of the conflict between universality and particularity had a great influence on the philosophical make-up of Pierre Elliott Trudeau, Canada's most important statesman in the twentieth century and the father of our 1982 constitutional revision and of our Charter of Rights and Freedoms. Having written about this extensively elsewhere, I do not want to belabour the point.[57] I shall only add that with regard to Trudeau's own understanding of the struggle between liberal universalism and national particularism in French Canada, major thinkers such as Thériault and Lamonde make an explicit connection between Lord Durham's interpretation and the one propounded by Canada's former prime minister.[58] Moreover André Burelle, a friend of Trudeau who worked for him as a speech-writer and a close collaborator in the crucial stages of his career, has just documented the triumph of doctrinaire liberalism in Trudeau's intellectual evolution that led to the ultimate exclusion of any meaningful recognition of Quebec's difference, of its particularity, in the constitution that Canada and Quebec have inherited from him.[59] If we are to believe Ajzenstat, there are ways to cope with the tension between universalism and particularism: "Politics is a matter of compromise; even fundamental principles must be bent sometimes—a little—on occasion."[60] If we are to believe André Burelle, Trudeau thought otherwise with regard to French Canada and Quebec. If the connection between Lord Durham and Trudeau holds true, then the spirit of the famous Report belongs not only to our past but is also intimately related to the present and to the future of Canada and Quebec.

## CONCLUSION

Historians should not forget that the task of making history in our liberal and democratic world belongs to citizens. Paul Ricoeur adds that although thinkers only narrate history, they remain responsible for what they say, particularly when their work applies to wounded memories.[61] Delineating the existence of a link between a sense of "wounded dignity" and manifestations of national patriotism in French Canada and Quebec is certainly not the exclusive province of the authors normally associated with melancholy nationalism. But how should we deal with these aspects of our collective memory? I am no expert on this issue. My best answer, using Lord Durham's Report as an edifying example for us and for people elsewhere, is this Afterword. More to the point, I believe, with Ricoeur, that the memory of those who actually suffered in the past must be honoured. Thus Quebec is right to honour the memory of the Patriotes, particularly the memory of the twelve who died on the scaffolds erected by colonial despotism. Once this is done, however, I believe it is appropriate to place one's historical wounds in comparative perspective, paying due respect to the wounds of the other groups and communities with whom one has shared parts of the past and with whom one hopes to share parts of the future. I am careful when discussing the future, because I believe it is open-ended. Constructing an appropriate historical memory for any community should be done without prejudging the "normal" unfolding of history, particularly since I believe that the idea of normality is a blatant illusion. It should be recognized, as John Ralston Saul has argued, that Quebec historians of all stripes have paid greater attention to the various conflicts between francophones and anglophones than to periods of greater harmony and collaboration. A happy and just memory requires a better balance between these two poles than has been achieved so far. A happy and just memory requires that, in a complex modern society made of groups and individuals with plural identities, we should pay equal attention to what we have done together and to one another in the past, and to what we dream of accomplishing in the future.

Where does that leave us with Lord Durham and his Report? According to Ajzenstat, Lord Durham's lasting question is the problem of the relationship between universalism and particularism. In his reflections on the same question, Joseph-Yvon Thériault called it both the question of the people in French Canada and the question of Quebec. I believe that Lord Durham's question IS the question of Quebec. And dealing with this question requires not only answering it for Quebec but finding a vitally important answer for the world in the twenty-first century.

## NOTES

1 Beiner, Ronald and Wayne Norman, eds., *Canadian Political Philosophy* (Toronto: Oxford University Press, 2001).

2 Gagnon, Alain-G., *Quebec, State and Society* (Peterborough: Broadview Press, third edition, 2003); Simard, Jean-Jacques, "Ce siècle où le Québec est venu au monde," in Côté, Roch, ed. *Québec 2000: rétrospective du XXe siècle* (Montreal: Fides, 1999), 17–78; Cook, Ramsay, *Watching Quebec: Selected Essays* (Montreal and Kingston: McGill-Queen's University Press, 2005).

3 McRoberts, Kenneth, *Misconceiving Canada: The Struggle for National Unity* (Toronto: Oxford University Press, 1997), 38–41.

4 Up-to-date political science textbooks are the right place to start addressing this question. See MacIvor, Heather, ed., *Parameters of Power: Canada's Political Institutions* (Toronto: Nelson Canada, fourth edition, 2006); and Pelletier, Réjean, and Manon Tremblay, eds., *Le parlementarisme canadien* (Quebec: Presses de l'Université Laval, third edition, 2005). For my own views, see Laforest, Guy, *Pour la liberté d'une société distincte* (Quebec: Presses de l'Université Laval, 2004), 325–55.

5 Maclure, Jocelyn, *Quebec Identity: The Challenge of Pluralism* (Montreal and Kingston: McGill-Queen's University Press, 2003), 19–59. As Maclure acknowledges, it must be said in fairness that Jocelyn Létourneau had previously, and critically, established a link between misery and melancholy in Quebec's historiography. See the essays collected in Létourneau, Jocelyn, *A History for the Future: Rewriting Memory and Identity in Quebec* (Montreal and Kingston: McGill-Queen's University Press, 2004), 101.

6 To grasp the basic trends in the historiography of Quebec, see Rudin, Ronald, *Making History in Twentieth-Century Quebec* (Toronto: University of Toronto Press, 1997); Gagnon, Serge, *Quebec and Its Historians: 1840 to 1920* (Montreal: Harvest House, 1982); Gagnon, Serge, *Quebec and Its Historians: The Twentieth Century* (Montreal: Harvest House, 1985).

7 Kolboom, Ingo, *Pièces d'identité: signets d'une décennie allemande* (Montreal: Presses de l'Université de Montréal, 2001), 192. I find a clear and coherent expression of this dominant view in Dufour, Christian, *A Canadian Challenge, Le défi québécois* (Vancouver: Oolichan Books, 1990), chapter 3. Even those who disagree with this paradigm agree on its centrality. See Létourneau, Jocelyn, *Le Québec, Les Québécois: un parcours historique* (Quebec: Musée de la civilisation and Editions Fides, 2004), 30.

8 This recent development is discussed by the editor in the introduction to his book in Kelly, Stéphane, ed., *Les idées mènent le Québec* (Quebec: Presses de l'Université Laval, 2003), 1–11; see also Kelly, Stéphane, and Guy Laforest, "Aux sources d'une tradition politique," in Ajzenstat, Janet, Paul Romney, Ian Gentles, and William D. Gairdner, eds., *Débats sur la fondation du Canada, Québec* (Presses de l'Université Laval, 2004), 527–46. The return of political history is illustrated and discussed in a series of new journals that have emerged in Quebec in the last decade: *Argument, Bulletin d'histoire politique, Mens: revue d'histoire intellectuelle de l'Amérique française, Cahiers d'histoire du Québec au vingtième siècle, Les Cahiers du 27 Juin, Globe: Revue internationale d'études québécoises*. For developments throughout Canada, see Owram, Doug, "Narrow Circles: The Historiography of Recent Canadian Historiography," *National History: A Canadian Journal of Enquiry and Opinion* 1, no.1 (1997): 5–21.

9 Institute for Research on Public Policy with the collaboration of Meisel, John, Guy Rocher, and Arthur Silver, *As I Recall Si Je Me Souviens Bien: Historical Perspectives* (Montreal: IRPP, 1999).

10 These excerpts are taken from an interview with Allan Greer in Bothwell, Robert, ed., *Canada and Quebec: One Country Two Histories* (Vancouver: UBC Press, 1995), 32–3. Lengthier discussion in Greer, Allan, *The Patriots and the People* (Toronto: University of Toronto Press, 1992).

11 Dumont, Fernand, *Genèse de la société québécoise* (Montreal: Boréal, 1993), 128.

12 Ralston Saul, John, *Reflections of a Siamese Twin: Canada at the End of the Twentieth Century* (Toronto: Viking, 1997), 363–5.

13 Lamonde, Yvan, *Histoire sociale des idées au Québec: 1760–1896* (Montreal: Fides, 2000). For an annotated introductory bibliography on Quebec, the reader should start with Gagnon, Alain-G., *Quebec* (Oxford: Clio Press, 1998). For a summary of Lamonde's own bibliographical progress through the history of ideas in Quebec, see Lamonde, Yvan, *Histoire sociale des idées au Québec, 1896–1929* (Montreal: Fides, 2003), 11. Étienne Parent—the learned journalist and moderate constitutionalist—and Louis-Joseph Papineau—the great Parliamentarian turned rebel and exiled radical Republican—are the most important of Durham's contemporaries in Lower Canada. Lamonde has made it much easier to arrive at a comprehensive understanding of their intellectual evolution. See Parent, Étienne, *Discours*, edition prepared by Yvan Lamonde and Claude Couture (Montreal: Presses de l'Université de Montréal, 2000); see also Lamonde, Yvan, and Claude Larin, *Louis-Joseph Papineau, un demi-siècle de combats: interventions publique* (Montreal: Fides, 1998).

14 Lamonde, *Histoire sociale des idées au Québec: 1760–1896*, 183–282. Two enlightening recent essays attempting to further the work of Lamonde in his areas of originality are Harvey, Louis-Georges, *Le printemps de l'Amérique française: Américanité, anticolonialisme et républicanisme dans le discours politique québécois, 1805–1837* (Montreal: Boréal, 2005); and Bellavance, Marcel, *Le Québec au siècle des nationalités: essai d'histoire comparée* (Montreal: VLB éditeur, 2004).

15 Lamonde, *Histoire sociale des idées au Québec: 1760–1896*, 261.

16 Dumont, *Genèse de la société québécoise*, 123–38. For a critical yet sympathetic introduction to Dumont's project, see Beauchemin, Jacques, "Dumont: historien de l'ambiguïté," *Recherches sociographiques* 42, no.2 (2001): 219–38. See also Warren, Jean-Philippe, "L'hiver de la mémoire," in Warren, Jean-Philippe, *Un supplément d'âme: Les intentions primordiales de Fernand Dumont (1947–1970)* (Quebec: Presses de l'Université Laval, 1998), 159–93.

17 Bouchard, Gérard, *Genèse des nations et cultures du nouveau monde: Essai d'histoire comparée* (Montreal: Boréal, 2000), 107–10.

18 Ibid., 98–9.

19 This interpretation is shared by sympathetic and more critical readers of Bouchard as shown in, respectively, Beauchemin, Jacques, *L'histoire en trop: La mauvaise conscience des souverainistes québécois* (Montreal: Boréal, 2002), 142–3 and Létourneau, Jocelyn, *A History for the Future: Rewriting Memory and Identity in Quebec* (Montreal: McGill-Queen's University Press, 2004), 55–64. To gain a sense of Bouchard's position among Quebec historians, see Bédard, Eric, "Genèse des nations et cultures du Nouveau Monde: le magnum opus de l'historiographie moderniste," *Bulletin d'histoire politique* 9, no.2 (2001): 160–73.

20 Bergeron, Gérard, *Lire Étienne Parent: notre premier intellectuel (1802–1874)* (Quebec: Presses de l'Université du Québec, 1994).

21  Parent, Étienne, "Une soumission honorable," in Lamonde, Yvan, and Claude Corbo, eds., *Le rouge et le bleu: une anthologie de la pensée politique au Québec de la Conquête à la Révolution tranquille* (Montreal: Presses de l'Université de Montréal, 1999), 100.

22  I am trying here to render as concisely as possible a key passage; a longer excerpt can be found in Lamonde, Yvan, *Histoire sociale des idées au Québec: 1760–1896*, 267.

23  This quotation comes from Bothwell, *Canada and Quebec*, 33.

24  Ajzenstat, Janet, Introduction to *Lord Durham's Report. A Re-Edition* (Montreal and Kingston: McGill-Queen's University Press, 2007), xxvi.

25  Lamenting Lord Durham's failure to hear the voices of the representatives of the Lower Canadian French majority is a perennial theme. See Desrosiers, Léo-Paul, *L'accalmie: Lord Durham au Canada* (Montreal: Le Devoir, 1937), 123; see also Viau, Roger, *Lord Durham* (Montreal: Editions HMH, 1962), 163.

26  Bindon, Kathryn M., "Adam Thom," *Dictionary of Canadian Biography/Dictionnaire biographique du Canada, 1881–1890*, vol. 11 (Toronto and Quebec City: University of Toronto Press and Presses de l'Université Laval, 1982), 874–6.

27  Ajzenstat, Janet, Introduction, XXV.

28  Ibid., xxviii–xxviv.

29  Caron, Jean-François, Catherine Vallières-Roland, and Guy Laforest, "Le déficit fédératif au Canada," in Gagnon, Alain-G., ed., *Le fédéralisme canadien contemporain: Fondements, traditions, institutions* (Montreal: Presses de l'Université de Montréal, 2006), 158–61.

30  Burelle, André, *Pierre Elliott Trudeau: L'intellectuel et le politique* (Montreal: Fides, 2005), 433–69; Brouillet, Eugénie, *La négation de la nation: L'identité culturelle québécoise et le fédéralisme canadien* (Quebec: Septentrion, 2005), 192–8.

31  Dion, Stéphane, "Durham et Tocqueville sur le colonialisme libéral," *Journal of Canadian Studies/Revue d'études canadiennes* 25, no.1 (1990): 75. My translation.

32  Maclure, *Quebec Identity*, 8–15.

33  Ibid., 20.

34  Létourneau, *A History for the Future*, 101–2. In the second chapter of his essay, Maclure engages critically with Létourneau's work and with my own. As he remarks, Létourneau began to focus on the centrality of this melancholical dimension in two important articles: Létourneau, Jocelyn, "'Impenser' le pays et toujours l'aimer," *Cahiers internationaux de sociologie* 105 (1998): 363; "Pour une révolution de la mémoire collective: Histoire et conscience historique chez les Québécois," *Argument* 1 (1998): 41–57.

35  Létourneau, *A History for the Future*, 101.

36  Aquin, Hubert, "La fatigue culturelle du Canada français," in Aquin, Hubert, *Blocs erratiques* (Montreal: Quinze, 1977), 88. In English, see Aquin, Hubert, *Writing Quebec* (Edmonton: University of Alberta Press, 1988), 35. I am following here the analysis in Maclure, *Quebec Identity*, 25–8.

37  Ibid., 41–4.

38  *Lord Durham's Report. A Re-Edition* (Montreal and Kingston: McGill-Queen's University Press, 2007), 147 and 153.

39  Ibid., 153.

40  D'Allemagne, André, *Le colonialisme au Québec* (Montreal: Agone, 2000), 20; Bouthillette, Jean, *Le Canadien Français et son double* (Montreal: L'Hexagone, 1972), 50–1. D'Allemagne makes a connection between the failure of the Rebellions, their demoralizing consequences, and the emergence of a deep inferiority complex; Bouthillette describes how French Canadians have become strangers to themselves, how the defeat of the Patriotes remains their definitive loss, and how the fall into nostalgia has been accompanied by regret and disconsolate pain.

Readers should be warned: if you believe that Marx, Hegel, Jean-Paul Sartre, and Franz Fanon are too abstract and imprecise about alienation, just read Bouthillette.

41  Monière, Denis, *Pour comprendre le nationalisme au Québec et ailleurs* (Montreal: Presses de l'Université de Montréal, 2001), 138–40.

42  Bouchard, Gérard, "Le projet de souveraineté du Québec: Sortir de l'impasse en revenant aux idées fondatrices," *Le Devoir*, 17 June 2006, B-5.

43  Beauchemin, *L'histoire en trop*, 181.

44  Ricoeur, Paul, *La Mémoire, L'Histoire, L'Oubli* (Paris: Seuil, 2000), 81.

45  Ibid., 650

46  Warren, Jean-Philippe, *Un supplément d'âme: Les intentions primordiales de Fernand Dumont (1947–1970)*, 161.

47  Langlois, Simon, "Refondation de la nation au Québec," in Côté, Roch, and Michel Venne, eds., *L'annuaire du Québec 2003: Toute l'année politique, sociale, économique et culturelle* (Montreal: Fides, 2002), 11.

48  Elbaz, Mikhaël, Andrée Fortin, and Guy Laforest, eds., *Les frontières de l'identité: Modernité et postmodernisme au Québec* (Quebec and Paris: Presses de l'Université Laval and Editions de l'Harmattan, 1996); see also Venne, Michel, ed., *Penser la nation québécoise* (Montreal: Quebec Amérique, 2000); Maclure, Jocelyn, and Alain-G. Gagnon, *Repères en mutation: Identité et citoyenneté dans le Québec contemporain* (Montreal: Québec Amérique 2001); Seymour, Michel, *La nation en question* (Montreal: L'Hexagone, 1999); Laforest, Guy, *De l'urgence* (Montreal: Boréal, 1995).

49  Bouchard, Gérard, *La nation québécoise au futur et au passé* (Montreal: VLB éditeur, 1999).

50  Jacques, Daniel, "Des 'conditions gagnantes' aux 'conditions signifiantes,'" in Venne, Michel, *Penser la nation québécoise*, 71–6; Beauchemin, *L'Histoire en trop*, 182–3. These authors agree with Maclure when he defines dialogue as a process of "reciprocal elucidation"; see Maclure, *Quebec Identity*, 15.

51  Taylor, Charles, "Nation culturelle, nation politique," in Venne, *Penser la nation québécoise*, 42.

52  Jacques, "Des 'conditions gagnantes' aux 'conditions signifiantes,'" in Venne, *Penser la nation québécoise*, 83.

53  Weber, Max, *Essais sur la théorie de la science* (Paris: Plon, 1965), 290–300.

54  Thériault, Joseph-Yvon, *Critique de l'américanité: Mémoire et démocratie au Québec* (Montreal: Québec Amérique, 2002), 296–300.

55  Ibid., 294–5.

56  Ajzenstat, Janet, Introduction, xxvii. See for instance Taylor, Charles, "Les sources de l'identité moderne," in Elbaz, Mikhaël, Andrée Fortin, and Guy Laforest, eds., *Les frontières de l'identité: Modernité et postmodernisme au Québec*, 357–60; and Kymlicka, Will, "Misunderstanding Nationalism," in Kymlicka, Will, *Politics in the Vernacular: Nationalism, Multiculturalism and Citizenship* (Toronto: Oxford University Press, 2001), 242–53.

57  Laforest, Guy, *Trudeau and the End of a Canadian Dream* (Montreal and Kingston: McGill-Queen's University Press, 1995), 171–84.

58  Thériault, *Critique de l'américanité*, 311; see also Lamonde, Yvan, *Trajectoires de l'histoire du Québec* (Quebec and Montreal: Musée de la civilisation et Editions Fides, 2001), 14–15.

59  Burelle, André, *Pierre Elliott Trudeau: L'Intellectuel et le politique*, 68–74 and 462–44.

60  Ajzenstat, Janet, Introduction, xxvii.

61  Ricoeur, Paul, "Mémoire, histoire, oubli," *Esprit*, March–April 2006, 323.

*Part Six*

# The Charter

THE CHARTER OF Rights and Freedoms has received much scholarly attention over the past two decades. This section contains only four pieces drawn from some of the earliest scholarship that subsequently defined some of the constitutional debates that followed. The short excerpt from Alan C. Cairns exposes the Charter as an instrument with distinctly political ulterior motives. Following on its heels are two essays that capture the widely cited debate about one of the most unique elements of the Charter, the notwithstanding clause. While John Whyte finds it highly problematic, Peter H. Russell mounts a spirited defence of its benefits. The advent of the Charter also raised the ire of commentators on both sides of the political spectrum who were concerned that it would tilt judicial outcomes ideologically. From the perspective of the social sciences, the debate is an interesting one because of its potential for empirical falsification. Richard Sigurdson's article is significant insofar as it is among the first to apply empirical social-science methodology to testing propositions about the Charter.

**30**

## Author's Introduction

This short extract is from a longer article, "Reflections on the Political Purposes of the Charter: The First Decade." The article was delivered as a talk at a conference dominated by lawyers, which had, as one of its objectives, to make the point that political scientists and the law trained did not see the same Charter. In particular, the legal professoriate tended not to see the political purposes of the Charter (the focus of the following excerpt), which provided the impetus for Trudeau's passionate Charter advocacy.

The Charter was much more than a legal instrument primarily of concern to lawyers and judges. It was an instrument of nation-building designed to enhance the role of the citizenry in the constitutional order, to vest sovereignty in the people, and to strengthen a pan-Canadian consciousness and weaken provincial identities.

These were clearly political objectives that Ottawa sought and that most provincial premiers feared. The following excerpt discusses the four main political purposes of the Charter.

Source: Alan C. Cairns, "Reflections on the Political Purposes of the Charter: The First Decade," in *Reconfigurations: Canadian Citizenship & Constitutional Change*, Alan C. Cairns (Toronto: McClelland and Stewart, 1995), 197–99.

Alan C. Cairns

# Reflections on the Political Purposes of the Charter

FOUR POLITICAL PURPOSES[1] provided the dynamic for Prime Minister Trudeau's unyielding Charter advocacy.

(1) The Charter's constitutional language policy, especially the section 23 minority-language educational rights, was the servant of a country-wide view of French Canada, in opposition to the Quebec-centred view of Quebec nationalists, who redefined French Canadians in Quebec as Québécois, a national people, whose real government wielded the lever of *l'état du Québec*. If the former view could be kept alive by constitutional succouring, and if simultaneously the Anglophone minority could be sustained in Quebec to invalidate the dangerous (to Trudeau) equation of a French-speaking nation with the totality of the Quebec people, then the Quebec nationalist drive toward an assertive provincialism or an independent Quebec would be muted.

Clearly, as our present constitutional disarray testifies, the erosion of Quebec nationalism has not occurred. On the other hand, the Charter has definitely stimulated official minority-language rights holders to see themselves in Canadian terms and to see the constitution as their defender. However, the Charter's language regime provides constitutional support to a particular view of the appropriate relationship between the two official-language communities and thus impedes the development of an alternative territorial language policy that some scholars deem preferable.[2] The application of the Charter's language regime to Quebec is the focal point of Quebec nationalist criticism.

(2) More generally, the citizenry's possession of Charter rights was designed to transform the base of the constitutional order. A citizenry seized of the constitutional recognition accorded by the Charter would be drawn out of provincialism into a pan-Canadian sense of self. Viewed this way, the Charter would support a positive answer by Canadians to Renan's thesis that a nation is a plebiscite of every day. Put differently, the Charter was a nationalizing, Canadianizing constitutional instrument intended to shape the psyches and identities of Canadians. The Charter, accordingly, was a constitutional weapon analogous to disallowance, with its objective of constraining the diversities that federalism both reflects and sustains. At the time of its implementation, it was a rival to the constitutional definition of Canada as a community of

communities espoused by Conservative leader Joe Clark, Brian Peckford of Newfoundland, and others.

The Charter was to be ubiquitous, monitoring Canadian presence within every province. That presence was not intended to be detached and impersonal, an esoteric subject in law faculties and pulled off the shelves in courtrooms, but a perpetual, embedded presence socialized into the psyches and identities of the citizenry. The latter, as bearers of Charter rights, were to evaluate provincial performance through the lens of a constitutional rights-defined Canadianism.

From the Diefenbaker Bill of Rights to the 1982 Charter, the federal government had led the drive for entrenched rights binding on both orders of government, with opposition or reluctance coming from most of the provincial governments. That the 1982 notwithstanding clause was a response to provincial demands and has been employed only by provincial governments, that successive federal governments either opposed its introduction, sought to make its application tougher, or advocated its elimination—these all reflect the self-interested, federalism-driven political logic of the competing government actors in the constitutional order. The strongest government support for the notwithstanding clause, therefore, logically should and does come from the Quebec government. Political understanding of the Charter, accordingly, begins with the recognition that it was not introduced as a neutral instrument, but as a weapon in the never-ending struggle of the competing governments of Canadian federalism for influence and survival. Federal government support via the Charter for intraprovincial minorities, for example, psychologically erodes the latter's attachment to the provincial community by inducing them to look outward to find their protection. In the conflict between rights and parliamentary supremacy, the tendency of the federal government to support the former and the provinces the latter is not fortuitous.

At a very general level, with important exceptions noted below, this political purpose has been achieved. The Charter has generated a powerful, vocal clientele of supporters who see themselves in Canadian terms and who tend to defend a strong federal government role, sometimes, as in Meech Lake, to the embarrassment of the federal government. The Charter, therefore, impedes constitutional changes that would

markedly strengthen provincial jurisdiction. It also, along with the equality of the provinces norm, provides ammunition for opponents of special status for any province that might lead to province-specific differences in citizenship entitlements.

(3) Linked to the previous point, the Charter was an instrument to relocate sovereignty in the people rather than in the governments of Canadian federalism. The fact that the original federal proposals of 1980 combined the Charter and an amending formula with a referendum component underlines the coherence of the constitutional theory of the then federal government. To give rights against governments to citizens in normal politics and to deprive those same citizens of a role in the formal amending process by which those rights could be eliminated, enhanced, or reduced was simply illogical. However, that very illogic was embedded in the 1982 Constitution Act that brought together an amending formula designed by provincial governments according to federalism criteria and a Charter whose basic pan-Canadianizing and democratizing thrust presupposed that the constitution belonged to the Canadian people. This contradictory legacy of the 1982 Constitution Act, little noticed at the time, was played out in the Meech Lake conflict between executive federalism and the participant constitutional culture stimulated by the Charter.

The post-Meech difficulty of finding a *modus vivendi* between the elitist assumptions of executive federalism and the participant dynamic unleashed by the Charter, and by Aboriginal constitutional ambitions, runs like a connecting thread through the hearings and reports of the Spicer Commission, the Beaudoin-Edwards Committee, and the Beaudoin-Dobbie Committee.[3] The six public constitutional conferences in the winter of 1992 provided tentative short-term answers to pressures for participation. More fundamental institutional answers are suggested by the ubiquitous proposals for referenda and constituent assemblies in the post-Meech era.[4]

(4) Finally, the prominence accorded to a Charter in federal proposals throughout the Trudeau period was a tactic to delay constitutional discussion of the division of powers until Ottawa's objectives had been achieved in terms of rights and the reform of central institutions. In the interim, the federal government could employ, as the Kirby memorandum of 1980

underlined, a rhetoric of a people's package versus a government package dealing with powers and institutions.[5] This allowed the federal government to contrast its high-minded support for the people's package of rights and patriation with the grubby, self-interested provincial concern for more powers. The deeper federal strategy was to view constitutional reform in stages so that by the time the division of powers appeared on the agenda, the federal government's legitimacy would be so enhanced by the Charter's support for a Canadian versus provincial view of Canada that public support for provincial jurisdictional aggrandizement would be greatly reduced. The reform of central institutions, not yet achieved, of course, had the same objectives; if the federal government could successfully respond to provincial diversity by change internal to itself, the competing claim that accommodation of a frustrated provincialism required more powers for provincial governments, and hence a weaker Ottawa, could be countered.[6]

While this federal tactic worked in the minimum sense that it delayed grappling with division of powers issues, the Charter's arrival has not reduced provincial government appetites for more jurisdiction. Centrifugal pressures for enhanced provincial jurisdiction were evident in the contents of the Meech Lake package, and are likely to be even more so in any post-Meech settlement. Nevertheless, the pressures for decentralization are countered by the Charter Canadians who support a strong central government.

## NOTES

1 For a nuanced discussion of many of the points in this section, and indeed of much of the rest of this chapter, see R. Knopff and F.L. Morton, *Charter Politics* (Scarborough, Ont., 1992).
2 See K. McRoberts, "Making Canada Bilingual: Illusions and Delusions of Federal Language Policy," in D.P. Shugarman and R. Whitaker, eds., *Federalism and Political Community: Essays in Honour of Donald Smiley* (Peterborough, Ont., 1989), for strong advocacy of the territorial principle.
3 *Citizens' Forum on Canada's Future: Report to the People and Government of Canada* (Ottawa, 1991); *Report of the Special Joint Committee on a Renewed Canada* (Ottawa, 1991); *The Process for Amending the Constitution of Canada: The Report of the Special Joint Committee of the Senate and the House of Commons* (Ottawa, 1991).
4 See P. Monahan *et al., Constituent Assemblies: The Canadian Debate in Comparative and Historical Context: Background Studies of the York University Constitutional Reform Project, Study no. 4* (North York, Ont., 1992), for an assessment of the Canadian debate on constituent assemblies. A national referendum is advocated by Patrick J. Monahan, "Closing a Constitutional Deal in 1992: A Scenario," in D.M. Brown *et al.,* eds., *Constitutional Commentaries: An Assessment of the 1991 Federal Proposals* (Kingston, 19921), p.105–06.
5 "Report to Cabinet on Constitutional Discussions, Summer 1980, and the Outlook for the First Ministers Conference and Beyond," Ministers' Eyes Only, August 30, 1980.
6 See D.V. Smiley and R.L. Watts, *Intrastate Federalism in Canada* (Toronto, 1985), for a helpful discussion.

# 31

## *Author's Introduction*

Many commentators have attempted to locate a justification for the legislative override in section 33 of the Charter on the basis of Canadian constitutional theory. This selection argues that the abolition of the not-withstanding clause would conform comfortably with the premises that underlie the Canadian constitutional regime. The first among these is the principle of legalism, the process by which we have chosen to adjudicate the resolution of public issues. Second, the principle of democracy, it is contended, provides some support for judicial control over political choices on the basis that, at the very least, certain Charter rights enhance the democratic process. The final principle examined, that of federalism, provides a historical perspective within which the disruption caused by judicial nullification can be assessed. Constitutionalism already exacts a high price on the autonomy of electoral politics and that the capacity of governments to regulate for the public good has not been seriously hampered as a result. Lastly, the selection examines the rationale for the Charter, as a tool to circumvent oppressive legislative measures, and why the judiciary can be relied upon to protect the radically dispossessed when they have no alternative route for the vindication of Charter values.

Source: John Whyte, "On Not Standing for Notwithstanding," *Alberta Law Review* 28 (1990): 347–57.

John Whyte [*]

# On Not Standing for Notwithstanding [**]

## I. INTRODUCTION

In our political culture we tend to believe that resolution of conflict comes about either by way of choosing policies or by way of following principle. Under this dichotomy, claims that are supported by appeals to principle are seen to enjoy a moral advantage. In constitutional discourse, our sense is that both adjudication and the process of constitutional reform should be driven by appeals to principle. There is good reason for this; a constitution is an ethical document revealing what a nation recognizes as a good social arrangement. In my view, however, it is mistaken to conflate the ethical nature of constitutional discourse with the claim that such discourse should invariably be principled. For instance, critics of the *Canadian Charter of Rights and Freedoms* have shown that in *Charter* adjudication, simple appeals to the text of the *Charter*, or to the political principles that are embodied in that text, are not dispositive of conflict. They have argued that it is the preferences of judges that determine results. (They also argue that it is a defeat for democracy that policies adopted by judges should prevail over policies chosen by legislators.) The critics'

description of the weakness of principle is supported by Michael Ignatieff:[1]

> It is a recurring temptation in political argument to suppose that these conflicts can be resolved in principle.... Yet who really knows whether we need freedom more than equality? Modern secular humanism is empty if it supposes that the human good is without internal contradiction. These contradictions cannot be resolved in principle, only in practice.

Yet, the critics miss the point of constitutional principles. They do not lead to crisp conclusions but, rather, to a focussed arbitration of conflicting claims. As David Dyzenhaus has observed:[2]

---

[*]   Faculty of Law, Queen's University, Kingston, Ontario.

[**]  This article is adapted from a paper delivered to the Constitutional Law Section of the 1989 Annual Meeting of the Canadian Bar Association, Vancouver, British Columbia, August 21st, 1989. I am grateful for the research assistance of Christopher Kendall and for the helpful comments of Andrew Petter, David Schneiderman and Bryan Schwartz.

1   M. Ignatieff, *The Needs of Strangers* (New York: Viking Penguin, 1984) at 137.

2   D. Dyzenhaus, "The New Positivists" (1989) 39 U.T.L.J. 361 at 378.

… [A] charter that promises not only freedom and justice for all but also equality provides a forum in which consciousness can be raised. Lawyers can aim to raise consciousness and provoke participation by focusing public attention on the ways in which society fails to live up to its formally enacted promise.

This unclear relationship between the role of policy preferences and the role of principles of public ordering in constitutional adjudication is matched in those political processes that are directed at reforming the constitution. Deciding whether Canada should have in its constitution a clause that permits a legislative override of otherwise entrenched rights is not the same sort of question as the distributional issues that arise under the *Charter* and it might seem that this question is more susceptible to principled resolution. However, in constitutional reform the question of which institutional arrangements—which long term political commitments—match best the ethical conceptions of the state are in the end also resolved by the choice of policies for the state. Although the resolution of difference on these issues is based on notions of the good state, these notions are, ultimately, chosen. I take the position that, with respect to the future of the override clause, the role of policy choice is dominant and the answer cannot be found by resort to principle. There are no principles that determine how we ought to vote on keeping or abandoning the legislative trump over rights contained in the *Charter of Rights*. Furthermore, our usual expectation that questions of the appropriate institutional arrangement can be answered by inference from the commitments reflected in our basic constitutional order cannot be met in this particular debate.

Nevertheless, with respect to the debate on whether to continue the override clause, the usual starting point has been to advance arguments rooted in Canadian constitutional principle. For instance, a claim made by Professors Peter Russell and Paul Weiler in their opinion piece on the issue is that the legislative override is a uniquely Canadian feature of our constitution.[3] What must be being expressed by this observation is that there are other elements of our constitution—other

constitutional arrangements that reveal fundamental commitments—that fit well with permitting legislative override of *Charter* protections. Professors Russell and Weiler, in arguing against repeal of the override power, provide a rudimentary explanation of what those commitments are:[4]

… nothing in our constitution is so distinctively Canadian as this manner of reconciling the British tradition of responsible democratic government with the American tradition of judicially enforced constitutional rights.

Another version of principled justification of the override clause is to label it as the perfect device for accommodating a regime for vindicating civil rights with the constitutional principle of parliamentary supremacy. Professor Peter Hogg, for example, has explained the clause as "a concession to Canada's long tradition of parliamentary sovereignty."[5]

In my view these attempts to locate a justification for the override procedure in Canadian constitutional theory are wrong for two reasons. First, the principles at work in the design of the Canadian state support not allowing any legislative exemptions from court-enforced rights at least as powerfully as they support including such a power in the constitution. Second, arguments rooted in constitutional principle distract us from enquiry into the actual social goods and bads that are likely to be produced by the practice of exercising the legislative power to override *Charter* rights. In short, this sort of debate keeps us from choosing a policy that is good because it reflects the actual aspirations of political community.

## II. LOOKING FOR THE LESSON FROM CONSTITUTIONAL THEORY

The position that is advanced in this paper is that the debate over keeping the override power should be conducted in terms of what will produce the soundest government and fairest society and that we should

---

3    Note, for example, the title of P. Russell's and P. Weiler's, opinion article: "Don't scrap override clause—it's a very Canadian solution," *The Toronto Star* (4 June 1989) B3.

4    *Ibid.* Later in the same article Professors Russell and Weiler call the constitution's override procedure "quintessentially Canadian."

5    P. Hogg, *Constitutional Law of Canada* (2nd edn.) (Toronto: Carswell, 1985) at 692.

approach this question by trying to anticipate how effective courts and legislatures actually will be in making various sorts of social and political accommodation.[6] For this reason it is not essential to demonstrate that Canadian constitutional theory requires repeal of an override power for legislatures. What I do want to demonstrate is that the values inherent in our constitutional arrangements do not require (or even tend towards) including in the constitution a trumping authority for legislatures over courts in the complex business of mediating between claims of right and the general social interest.

The basic constitutional principles that I perceive to be at work in the formal structure of the Canadian state are legalism, democracy, and federalism. I do not include as a fundamental constitutional principle, at least for the purposes of this debate, individual and collective rights. It is clear that, ever since the Second World War, human rights have become politically constituted in the Canadian state. And of course, the Constitution Act, 1982, gave human rights immense constitutional status. (Our experiences over the last seven years have confirmed how ripe Canadian society was to absorb the constitutionalization of human rights.) Nevertheless, to argue against continued inclusion of the override clause on the basis that the legislative override power undermines the concept of rights would be a bootstrap argument.

An argument might be made that, from a purely semantic point of view, the override power is inconsistent with a rights regime (at least, a rights regime as we understand such a thing in a legalist society). The problem with basing an argument against the override provision on the prior constitutional commitment to rights is that it begs the question of the nature and extent of the actual constitutional commitment. It is not morally defective for Canada not to have granted to courts hearing claims arising under the *Charter* ultimate authority over other political processes and choices. However, not having done so means that arguments from constitutional principle, based on the claim that Canada has adopted the

principle of entrenched human rights, proceed on an inaccurate premise.

Let us look at the constitutional principles that are less equivocally present in our constitutional arrangement—legalism, democracy, and federalism.

## A. Legalism

Public authority in Canada derives at least a part of its legitimacy from its legal base. What a government does must accord with what, from a legal perspective, it is entitled to do. This idea that the legitimacy of state power can be measured through legal adjudication is, in our culture, well over half a millennium old. We understand authoritative social relationships to be formed and governed by enforceable promises and the keystone of the system is that enforceability is produced through legal evaluation. In order to produce a system for legal evaluation that has some degree of formality, specialized legal agencies grew up. Furthermore, we attached to those agencies political attributes that were designed to conduce to legal or formal evaluation (as opposed, say, to self-interested evaluation). These attributes were expertise and independence. Of course, we are right to be highly sceptical about the role of expertise and formality when the legal order that requires expertise and formal elaboration is as indeterminate as it is. We are also right to be sceptical about the actual degree of independence from social forces that can be achieved simply through protecting pay and tenure, the devices that are provided by the 1867 *Constitution*. However, it is not important to this argument that we subscribe to the purity of formalism or complete independence. All that is necessary is to see that they are long-standing constitutional values; it is through the identification of certain ideals and values that we can determine what arguments from principle can be made.

If it is accepted that these values have been recognized in Canadian constitutional ordering then other conclusions might be drawn. The chief one is that our state structure seems to be based on the idea that formal commitments represent binding promises that restrain future power. This idea is perhaps derived from the development of the law of contract. In any event, the commitment to legal enforceability of promises extends to binding governments as well as individuals. Legalism is what makes possible constitutionalism, the

6  An example of pure functional analysis of the override clause issue is found in A. Petter, "Canada's shield against despotic courts," *The Toronto Star* (25 July 1989) A17.

process by which political expressions from one age can bind future ages unless equally formal political processes are mustered to remove the constitutional constraint. In short, Canadian constitutionalism is not in thrall to the idea that populations are free to determine their own best interests from moment to moment. Judicial control over governmental authority and legislative choices is no alien concept for Canada. We are a nation in which past solemn commitments are allowed to work to the disadvantage of current preferences. For instance, perfectly clear legislative preferences about the administration of laws are frequently frustrated by the prior constitutional commitment to the separation of powers. The separation of powers is seen as a relevant doctrine to the maintenance of a commitment to legalism and the implications of that commitment are tolerated by the people of this democratic state.

My claim is simply this. As a matter of principle we have adopted the notion that there are adjudicable public issues. Furthermore, we have come to terms with these issues being *ultimately* adjudicable—not subject to legislative review and revision. If Canada wants to say about human rights claims that not only are they adjudicable at the first stage of resolution, but they are adjudicable as a matter of ultimate resolution, this would be entirely consistent with our commitment to legalism in public ordering.

However, in the context of the *Canadian Charter of Rights and Freedoms,* section 33 means, first, that what were once political problems have been transformed into legal problems but, second, that when political interests are sufficiently compelling these issues can revert to being resolved through political choice. This arrangement gives rise to a further principled argument. The idea that some problems may be adjudicated—may be made subject to legal determination—requires there to be substantive constitutional value to be interpreted and applied. It is necessary to the conception of legalism that adjudication of disputes be based on previously expressed normative standards. When there is a sense that there are no constraints, or no interpretative processes (for instance, when there is no textual basis for decision-making), no genuine adjudication is possible.[7] Canada, in enacting the *Charter*

*of Rights,* accepted that some political problems were capable of adjudication and at the same time, created a normative order (a text, in other words) to ensure that those issues could be resolved through adjudication. The nation expressed its commitment to, first, the rightness of social resolution being produced by the interpretation of rights and, second, the capacity of the terms of the *Charter* to be interpretable—to be the subject matter of adjudication. This assessment of what was possible and appropriate for adjudication does not fit well with the idea that the ultimate method of resolution of conflicting claims is through a purely political process. In other words, once the advantages of constitutional interpretation were accepted, as a general matter, it is not easy to see why the framers of the 1982 Constitution then saw political judgment to be a preferred form of political accommodation in each and every instance in which political interests wished to suspend the operation of legalism.

## B. Democracy[8]

Judicial enforcement of human rights standards poses a serious challenge to majoritarianism. The advantage of pure majoritarianism is that there is no situation which cannot be responded to and no strategy of social regulation that cannot be tried once a majority of the people wish to act.

The problem with truly entrenched rights is that it undermines the majoritarian principle. Legislative calculations of social need are subject to being substituted by courts which are not representative and are not amenable to majoritarian control. The will of the electors is not sovereign. The question is whether the shift away from majoritarianism through removal of the override power reflects a conception of democracy that is as fundamental as the popular conception of democracy—that state policies ought always to reflect the preferences of a majority of electors.

Democratic theory rests not so much on the mechanisms of expressing political preferences (or who should represent the voters in making political choices) and on who should govern, as it does

7    See, S. Levinson, "Law as Literature" (1982) 60 Texas L. Rev. 373 at 400–401.

8    A longer version of the ideas expressed here is found in J. Whyte, "Legality and Legitimacy: The Problem of Judicial Review of Legislation" (1987) 12 Queen's L. J. 1 at 5–12. A better version of these ideas is found in W. Bishin, "Judicial Review in Democratic Theory" (1977) 50 Southern California L. Rev. 1099 at 1112–1117.

on deeper conditions such as political participation, equality, autonomy, and personal liberty. From the now fully developed constitutional idea that people have the right to participate in public choices it is possible to tease out a series of non-derogable conditions. For example, we know that duly elected and popularly supported governments can, and do, believe that the appropriate conditions for democratic politics include such things as censored political speech, restrictions on political participation,[9] political campaigns that are funded by government, and perhaps most currently, in at least two Canadian jurisdictions, gerrymandering.[10] In considering this list, it is not difficult to see the connection between the use of judicially enforced fundamental rights of speech, equality and due process, and the vindication of principles that are designed to protect democratic processes.

Of course it would be wrong to suggest that the whole array of interests identified in the *Charter of Rights* are justifiable on the basis that they enhance the democratic process. Some rights, (for example, an expanded notion of personal security being protected from substantive injustice under section 7 of the *Charter*) must be explained by reference to other political commitments. However, the point that needs to be made is that the democratic principle provides a powerful pedigree for judicial control over political choices that erode some fundamental human rights.

## C. Federalism

There are two points to make about Canada's adoption of federalism in organizing state power. The first is that the chief justification for the federal arrangement (and this is particularly true in the Canadian experience) is that it provides protection to minorities from the political choices of national majorities.[11] Federalism is a political arrangement that is designed to blunt the force of majoritarianism because groups within the nation are recognized as having special interests that deserve entrenched protection. It is true that this mode of protection does not entail courts engaging in the same kind of social accommodation as they do under the *Charter*. Nevertheless courts do intervene to protect specific constitutionally recognized interests. Federalism is quite simply a substantial check on the exercise of national popular will. As such it is a further instance of seeing our constitutional order as consisting of commitments that have been embraced so that, as we live out our life as a community, certain ideals or images will prevail over power.

The second point is that by looking at the history of court adjudication over federalism we might get a better perspective on the significance of the debate over the override clause. Courts have been involved in disallowing back to work legislation and Sunday closing legislation, in adjudicating refugee claims and rules for qualifying as a profession, and in setting out the modes of proof of criminal liability and the allowable strategies for criminal investigations, each of which produces some disruption of public administration.[12] These outcomes require the abandonment of administrative processes and, sometimes, governmental policies. Indeed, some of these policies have become

9  Professors Russell and Weiler, *supra*, note 3, seem to believe restrictions on political participation is an appropriate policy to adopt in the context of elections and argue that the override power should be used to counteract any court decision that protected political participation on the basis of freedom of speech or equal protection of the laws. They write: "Having just experienced in the last federal election the wave of private election advertising, American-style, we would strongly endorse the use of Canada's override procedure if our Supreme Court were to … interpret 'freedom of expression' in the Charter [to preclude legislative restriction on the amount spent on an election campaign]."

It is not, of course, likely that freedom of expression protects limitless political campaigns (although it may protect limitless spending by an individual in his or her own campaign). Furthermore, it is not evident that the wave of privately funded advertising on the issues of the November 1988 federal general election did not serve a positive role in educating Canadians on important issues. Do Professors Russell and Weiler really prefer that our information on free trade or tax reform, as well as critical analysis of what they mean for Canada, be limited to what we are provided by the political parties?

10  In British Columbia, see *Dixon* v. A.G.B.C. (1989), 35 B.C.L.R. (2d) 273 (B.C.S.C.); the other jurisdiction in question is Saskatchewan. See "New ridings to be passed," *The Leader-Post* [Regina] (22 August 1989) A-8; Professor Howard McConnell of the University of Saskatchewan is reported as saying "If Saskatchewan's [electoral] boundaries were challenged in court it's likely the result would be the same as in B.C.," *The Leader-Post* [Regina] (20 April 1989) A-11.

11  See, for example, R. Whittaker, *Federalism and Democratic Theory* (Kingston: Institute of Intergovernmental Relations, 1983); and F. Neumann, "Federalism and Freedom, A Critique," in A. Macmahon (ed.), *Federalism: Mature and Emerging* (New York: Doubleday, 1955) at 44–57.

12  I do not, of course, wish to minimize the political impact of decisions under the Charter. Judicial nullification of legislation has been fairly extensive. See, F. Morton, G. Solomon, I. McNish and D. Poulton, *Judicial Nullification of Statutes Under the Charter of Rights and Freedoms, 1982–1988* (1990) XXVIII Alta. L. Rev. 396.

established within the country as the standard way of accommodating social conflict. *Charter* decisions that cause an abandonment of established accommodations will produce periods of dislocation and adjustment and could effect long term changes in the distribution of social benefits. However, the capacity of governments to regulate society for the public good has not, yet, been fundamentally hampered by *Charter* decisions. The major determinants that shape well-being in society are not frequently at stake in *Charter* decisions. For instance, compare the significance of any of the *Charter* cases alluded to above to the significance of a court decision that prevents a province from controlling trans-boundary environmental damage produced by pollution that is licensed by an adjoining province.[13] Compare any *Charter* decision with the significance to a province's economic development of deciding that it is unconstitutional to ration production of a resource with a view to sustaining a viable market for the resource.[14] Or compare the impact of any *Charter* decision with the consequence for a province of limiting its capacity to control the distribution of benefits from its most valuable natural attribute.[15] This is not a country in which governments have never been seriously frustrated in implementing policies that make a difference to the health, wealth, and well-being of every person in their jurisdiction. It is not credible to argue that removal of the override clause will produce a shift in the balance of power between political decision-makers and courts that will change the nature of our society. Constitutionalism already exacts a high price on the autonomy of electoral politics. Most Canadians see this as legitimate and fair in order to maintain the integrity of our national commitment to federalism. Undoubtedly the *Charter of Rights* has produced additional restraints on democratic politics. However, it has not made irrelevant the role of politics in shaping the nature of our society.[16] Our experience

under federalism has clearly shown us that politics lives (that political initiatives are vital and that political mobilization makes an important contribution to the well-being of society) even when courts have the authority to protect constitutional values.

As I have stated, it is not my ambition to demonstrate that the override provision cannot coherently be included in our constitutional arrangements. My goal has been simply to show that it doesn't earn its place in the Constitution because of its logical fit with the general constitutional pattern. The most basic features of our constitutional arrangements do not, as it happens, create a logical or principled argument for the legislative override of the *Charter of Rights*.

## III. FINDING A LESSON IN POLITICAL PRACTICE

There is a hope about the override clause. It is that it will be used to preserve social arrangements that have been carefully worked out by legislators through a process in which competing interests have been fully explored and understood and compromises have been thoughtfully constructed. Sometimes this hope takes stronger forms. One is that uses of section 33 are reviewable by courts to determine whether the exercise has been reasonable.[17] Another is that use of section 33 is limited to situations in which a court has already struck down the legislative provision that is being granted legislative immunity from *Charter* review.[18]

political accommodations are made, nor does it subordinate the role of politics in the conflict between the state and the individual." Professor Andrew Petter in his review of *Canada ... Notwithstanding* ("'Duck Soup'—Canada Style" [1985] 7 Supreme Court L. Rev. 553) commented on this sentence: "Clearly this is incorrect" (at 556). Clearly he is correct; the Charter does have an impact on the role of politics. (I suppose the sentence could be justified by giving the most abstract reading to the concepts of the "way" of political accommodation and the "role" of politics. In any event I have expressed the minimalist position differently, and more cautiously, in this paper.)

13  *Interprovincial Co-operatives Ltd.* v. *The Queen*, [1976] 1 S.C.R. 477.

14  *Central Canada Potash* v. *Saskatchewan*, [1979] 1 S.C.R. 42.

15  *Churchill Falls (Labrador) Corp.* v. *Attorney General of Newfoundland; Reference re. Upper Churchill Water Rights Reversion Act*, [1984] 1 S.C.R. 297.

16  Minimizing the impact of the Charter of Rights on the respective roles of courts and legislature is something that I (with others) have done before. See, R. Romanow, J. Whyte, and H. Leeson, *Canada ... Notwithstanding* (Toronto: Carswell/Methuen, 1984) at 219: "The Charter does not change the way that important

17  B. Slattery, Legislative Note, "Canadian Charter of Rights and Freedoms—Override Clause Under Section 33—Whether Subject to Judicial Review Under Section 1" (1983) 61 Can. Bar Rev. 391.

18  Discussed in D. Greschner and K. Norman, "The Courts and Section 33" (1987) 12 Queen's L. J. 155 at 188–9. This position is supported by the judgment of Jacques, J.A. in *Alliance des Professeurs de Montreal* v. *Attorney General of Quebec* (1985), 21 D.L.R. (4th) 354 at 364.

An instance of this sort of use may be the enactment by Saskatchewan of the *S.G.E.U. Dispute Settlement Act.*[19] However, even the rather narrow use of section 33 to confirm the provinces' right to stop rotating strikes in the public sector was challenged as anything but a thoughtful accommodation of competing public and group interests. It was viewed by some as opportunistic and gratuitous, two characteristics that get to the heart of what it means to act repressively.

The constitutional patterns that we create are, happily, hardly ever pure.[20] There are many visions of a good society and we act wisely when we find ways not to deny the legitimacy and place of perfectly plausible visions. Hence, one of the virtues of the override power is that it has allowed Canada to create a regime for protecting human rights and it has left room for determined legislators to maintain social arrangements that they consider particularly important.

The unfortunate aspect of this benign description of the override clause as a restrained tool, instrument of thoughtful response, and balancer of constitutional ideologies is its use is simply not likely to be restricted to instances that match this description. The primary reason for wishing to do away with the override clause is that the anxiety that produced the political demand for entrenched rights cannot rationally be calmed in the face of the legislative power granted by section 33. That anxiety is simply this: political authority will, at some point, be exercised oppressively; that is, it will be exercised to impose very serious burdens on groups of people when there is no rational justification for doing so.

Furthermore, the more that we succeed in marginalizing section 33 by pointing to its rare use and speaking of its deployment in extraordinary circumstances only, the more that legislative override will become associated with the intense political moments that produce political oppression.

There are two types of situations in which the *Charter of Rights* seems a positive constitutional instrument. One is when legislatures neglect to calculate the extraordinary impact of legislative measures on particular individuals. Another is when they know full well the impact on certain people but do not care enough about the problem (or do not have the time or skill to cope with the problem) to tailor the measure to avoid the injury to constitutional rights. Courts applying the terms of the *Charter of Rights* can give to individuals and groups both a forum to explain the precise nature of the disadvantage, and relief from undue burdens.

The other scenario that impels the entrenchment of rights is one in which fear and distaste by the majority for certain people leads to the oppression of those people. The Canadian historical record reveals a number of instances of political passion directed against conspicuous minorities—Japanese Canadians, Hutterites, Doukhobors, aboriginal peoples, Jehovah's Witnesses, the Acadians, Metis, Roman Catholics, communists, and separatists.[21] All of these groups have, at some point, been seen as producing more social disruption and risk than society has been able to bear and all of these groups have been governmentally burdened in order to reduce the fear that has surrounded their presence. In all of these cases the governmental assessment of risk has been facile and overstated. In all of these cases the governmental response has been more than merely disadvantageous to members of these groups. It has been brutal, community crushing, and life destroying. Political passion that is generated by the fear that there are communities within whose practices subvert the fabric of our society is powerful and terrifying.

In a recent article, Professor Andrew Petter quotes the famous observation of Judge Learned Hand: "Liberty lies in the hearts of men and women; when it dies there, no constitution, no law, no court can save it; no constitution, no law, no court can even do much to help it."[22] To the extent that this is accepted the moments of political anger and passion that I fear—the moments of political reaction that we invariably come later to regret—will not be forestalled by the removal of the override powers. There are, however,

19  Bill 144, 4th Sess., 20th Leg. Saskatchewan, 1985–86.

20  "It would not be consistent with the Canadian experience for Canada's constitution to be based on the whole-hearted adoption of a single political idea." From R. Romanow, J. Whyte, and H. Leeson, *supra*, note 15 at 259.

A similar claim on behalf of ideological modesty is made in B. Schwartz, *First Principles, Second Thoughts* (Montreal: Institute for Research on Public Policy, 1986) at 18.

21  See, T. Berger, *Fragile Freedoms: Human Rights and Dissent in Canada* (Toronto: Clarke Irwin, 1981).

22  L. Hand. "The Contribution of an Independent Judiciary to Civilization" in *The Spirit of Liberty and Other Writings* (1953) at 144 quoted in A. Petter, "Canada's Charter Flight: Soaring Backwards into the Future" (1989) 16 Jo. of Law & Society 151.

two ways in which Learned Hand's assessment of the role of courts in applying constitutionalized human rights is unduly pessimistic.

First, the terms of the *Charter of Rights* are not totally indeterminate. Judges are not free to reflect the dominant political winds in interpreting rights. The systematic destruction of a group's expression and practices cannot easily be denied as a *Charter* violation. Judges are, of course, aware of the political passion that is around them, but the values of independence and discipline that we seek to vindicate in appointments, do frequently shine through both in this country and in the brave judgments of courts in nations with a longer record of repression than ours.

The claim that is most commonly made about the political values that are represented in judging are the values of class and wealth.[23] Even if one were to accept the impossibility of understanding the life experiences of the poor and dispossessed, this claim has much more salience in cases of ordinary infringement, for instance, in cases of equality claims based on the differential impact of a regulation on marginalized members of society. Even those who have enjoyed a life of privilege know both the social impact of radical political control and exclusion, and the legal rights that have been placed in jeopardy by such controls. In other words, the moments of extreme political reaction that are likely to generate use of the legislative override power are the moments of serious political repression; cultural blindness to disadvantage is much less possible with respect to the elements of this sort of oppression.

Of course, it must be admitted that if the override clause were not available, governments engaged in oppression would argue that a loss of rights was reasonable in view of the dire social condition. With the *Charter's* section 1 formula available to justify the deprivation of rights it is easier to see the possibility of judges becoming caught up in the political impetus for control. This concern gives credibility to Learned Hand's doubts about judicial effectiveness. The answer is, again, to point to the judges comparatively advantageous position to measure the legality of legislated repression. They are disciplined by the legal text and legalism. They are committed to due process in assessing competing claims. They are politically indifferent, at least at a structural level. They are distanced from the popular expression of political will.

The second claim to make for the benefit of judicial supervision in moments of oppression is that the calling into play of Charter claims reminds the political community of the costs to fundamental values of political desperation. For the political process, for the people whose rights are being abridged and for the future political environment, the process of identifying carefully and calmly the precise loss of freedoms and rights is a process to be valued above all others in extreme political moments.

It is my view that the *Charter*, in its normal course, does not substantially rearrange society. In the normal course the *Charter's* benefits are, in any event, distributed in the same manner as legal services—preponderantly to the wealthy. It seems perverse to advocate the retention of a provision which is most likely to be used to preclude judicial intervention when that process has its strongest moral claim, and when the radically dispossessed will have no route for salvation other than appealing to courts to intervene on behalf of the *Charter* values of liberty, equality, and due process.

23  "There are few public institutions whose composition more poorly reflects, and whose members have less direct exposure to, the interests of the economically and socially disadvantaged.... In short, there is nothing about the Canadian judiciary to suggest that they possess the background, the experience, or the training to comprehend the social impact of Claims made to them under the Charter, let alone to resolve those claims in ways that promote, or even protect, the interests of disadvantaged Canadians." A. Petter, *ibid.* at 157.

32

## Author's Introduction

The inclusion of a clause in the Canadian Charter of Rights and Freedoms that allows federal or provincial legislatures to immunize a piece of legislation from Charter review by the courts for five years set up a rousing debate. That debate goes to the very heart of one's ideal of constitutionalism. For those such as John Whyte who oppose the notwithstanding clause, constitutional rights only have force and meaning when the judiciary has the exclusive and final voice in interpreting what they mean. The article that follows responds to this view by arguing that the meaning of constitutionally enshrined rights is a matter of judgment in which judges should certainly play a leading role. But in a constitutional democracy, I argue, resolving questions about the meaning of rights and freedoms is too important a responsibility to be given exclusively to any branch of government, including the judiciary.

Source: Peter H. Russell, "Standing Up for Notwithstanding," *Alberta Law Review* 29(2) (1991): 293–309.

Peter H. Russell*

# Standing Up for Notwithstanding

## I. INTRODUCTION

[The *Alberta Law Review*]'s first annual supplement on constitutional issues includes an essay by Professor John Whyte putting the case against the notwithstanding clause in the *Canadian Charter of Rights and Freedoms*.[1] Whyte's article is the most fully reasoned attack we have had on the *Charter's* override clause. It is an important contribution to our constitutional debate which certainly deserves a reply from one of those singled out, quite rightly, by Professor Whyte as a defender of the override.

Although I readily confess to being a supporter of the override clause, I am not at all satisfied with Professor Whyte's understanding of the rationale for such a clause. Unfortunately, instead of carefully examining the scholarly writings of those who have defended the override, he cites only a portion of one sentence from an "opinion piece" in the *Toronto Star* by Professor Paul Weiler and myself and a few words from a passage in Professor Hogg's book on the *Constitutional Law of Canada*. The words quoted and the arguments he proceeds to knock down do not

come close to providing an acceptable justification of the *Charter's* notwithstanding clause.

## II. BAD REASONS FOR THE NOTWITHSTANDING CLAUSE

The passage quoted from our *Toronto Star* piece draws attention to the distinctively Canadian manner in which the notwithstanding clause balances the British tradition of responsible democratic government with the American tradition of judicially enforced constitutional rights. I would certainly agree with Professor Whyte in dismissing arguments for the override clause that depend primarily on showing that it is distinctively Canadian. I am sure there are plenty of things that are distinctively Canadian that are perfectly dreadful. The point we were making is that the override gives Canada an opportunity to get the best out of British and American constitutionalism, the two traditions which have profoundly influenced our constitutional development. Professor Whyte, unhappily, may be right, and as English Canada moves ever closer to *Charter* worship, it may no longer be distinctively Canadian to try to strike a shrewd balance between the wisdom derived from these two parts of our heritage.

* Dept. of Political Science, University of Toronto.
1 J.D. Whyte, "On Not Standing for Notwithstanding" (1990) 28 Alta. L. Rev. 347.

It may well be true, as the quotation from Professor Hogg suggests, that political defenders of the override have most often couched their arguments in terms of the need to preserve the principle of parliamentary sovereignty. Again, I am in agreement with Professor Whyte that the case for the override cannot rest on a simple invocation of that principle. Even if one were to accept, as I do not, a purely Burkean standard for constitutional development and insist that our constitutional future never break from inherited tradition, it simply is not true that the Canadian constitution historically has been based on the principle of parliamentary sovereignty. No Canadian legislature or parliament has ever been sovereign and I hope none ever shall be.[2] Legislatures in colonial Canada were subject to important controls, and since 1867, Canadian legislatures have been subject to judicially enforceable limitations, limitations based on more than preserving the federal division of powers.

Equally unacceptable as a defence of the override is an appeal to simple majoritarianism. The crude utilitarian standard of "the greatest happiness of the greatest number" is an unacceptable ethical foundation for a constitutional democracy. *Liberal* democracy requires much more than giving free play to the preferences of the majority. Professor Whyte delineates a number of the "deeper conditions" of democratic government: "political participation, equality, autonomy, and personal liberty."[3] Professor Ronald Dworkin in his contribution to the same issue of the review cogently argues that democratic government should not be founded on a statistical, head-counting conception of political equality but on a communal understanding in which citizens share equally the responsibilities of determining what is right for their political community.[4]

With all of this I whole-heartedly agree. The override should not be defended on the grounds that appointed judges must never be able to thwart the will of a body elected by the majority. Such an argument

would rest on the most simplistic and illiberal conception of democracy, a conception oblivious to the need for checks and balances as a condition of liberty and oblivious to the injustices which a majority may wish to inflict on a minority. Such a simplistic and morally shallow theory of democracy is not held by this defender of the notwithstanding clause, nor, I suspect, by most others who see its merits.

Now, having cleared away the underbrush of unacceptable arguments for the override, I shall attempt to put forward what I regard as the strongest grounds for retaining this provision in the *Canadian Charter of Rights and Freedoms*. These are the arguments which Professor Whyte does not address.

## III. THE CASE FOR THE OVERRIDE

The major arguments in support of a legislative override turn on considerations about the substantive outcome of decision-making and about the process of decision-making in a liberal democracy. Let me deal first with substantive considerations.

### A. Substantive Considerations
In a nutshell, the argument about the substance of decision-making is as follows. Judges are not infallible. They may make decisions about the limits and nature of rights and freedoms which are extremely questionable. There should be some process, more reasoned than court-packing and more accessible than constitutional amendment, through which the justice and wisdom of these decisions can be publicly discussed and possibly rejected. A legislative override clause provides such a process. At the core of this argument is recognition of the kind of questions courts typically deal with in interpreting and applying a constitutional charter of rights. These are questions not about the validity of the core values enshrined in the general language of the *Charter*—freedom of speech, fundamental justice, equality—but about the proper limits of rights based on these values.[5] It is a truism that no single right should be treated as an absolute.

2  Although, collectively, the federal parliament and the provincial legislatures might now be considered "sovereign" in Canada since under Part V of the *Constitution Act, 1982*, in various combinations these legislatures have the power to amend the Constitution of Canada.

3  *Supra*, note 1 at 352.

4  R. Dworkin, "Equality, Democracy and Constitution: We The People in Court" (1990) 28 Alta. L. Rev. 324.

5  I have developed this point more fully in "The Political Purposes of the Canadian Charter of Rights and Freedoms" (1983) 61 Can. Bar Rev. 30.

This truism is recognized in section 1 of the *Charter* which states that all the rights in the *Charter* are "subject to reasonable limits prescribed by law as can be demonstrably justified in a free and democratic society." It is also recognized in decisions of the Supreme Court of Canada eliminating certain kinds of claims from the definition of the entrenched right or freedom.[6] Thus, it is quite misleading to describe what the courts are doing in deciding *Charter* cases as "guaranteeing" that citizens enjoy the rights entrenched in the *Charter*. What judicial review under the *Charter* guarantees is careful consideration by the judiciary of a citizen's claim that a *Charter* right or freedom has been unreasonably encroached upon by a law or executive act of government. In dealing with such a claim the court must decide whether it should be upheld or whether it should give way to other important rights or interests with which it conflicts.

Consider the Supreme Court of Canada's decisions on claims based on section 2(b), the freedom of expression section of the Charter. In these cases the Court has determined whether the following were reasonable limits on the constitutional right to freedom of expression:

- a Criminal Code provision requiring that a trial judge, on the request of a complainant in a sexual assault case, ban publication of information identifying the complainant,[7]
- an injunction issued by a judge, ex parte, prohibiting striking court workers from picketing courthouses,[8]
- a law prohibiting commercials directed at children under 13,[9]
- an order from a labour relations board requiring an employer to write a letter of recommendation about a wrongfully dismissed employee;[10]

- a law requiring French-only commercial signs and firm names,[11]
- a law prohibiting publication of the details of evidence adduced in matrimonial proceedings.[12]

In the first four of these cases the Supreme Court decided that the limit on free speech was justified and in the latter two that it was not. One does not find in these cases the Court defending citizens against government attacks on what is fundamental to the right of free speech in a democracy, the right to criticize the government and advocate opposition to it. Instead, in each case the Court dealt with an issue at the margin, not at the core, of free speech and whether such a marginal claim should give way to some other value. In effect, in these cases, the Court was making decisions about the policy of free speech—how far this essential democratic right should be extended and under what circumstances and for what purposes it should be subject to restrictions.

In making the case for a legislative override in the Charter, one need not, and indeed should not, argue that the judiciary should play no part in policy decisions such as these. I agree with Professor Whyte that "Canada, in enacting the Charter of Rights, accepted that some political problems were capable of adjudication…."[13] But Professor Weiler and I and other defenders of the notwithstanding clause part company with Whyte when he contends that these issues must be *"ultimately* adjudicable,"[14] that once the judiciary has spoken there must be closure on these issues.

Far from its being the case, as Professor Whyte claims, that we Canadians in adopting the *Charter* committed ourselves to having questions about the limits of rights and freedoms ultimately determined by the courts, our constitution-makers in 1982, through the override clause, provided for a partnership between legislatures and courts. In Professor Weiler's words:[15]

6 See, for example, Justice Wilson's restrictive interpretation of the right to security of the person in *Operation Dismantle Inc.* v. *R.* [1985] 1 S.C.R. 441, and Chief Justice Dickson's denial of corporate economic claims as part of the right to liberty in *Irwin Toy Limited* v. *A.G. Quebec*, [1989] 1 S.C.R. 927.
7 *R.* v. *Canadian Newspapers Company*, [1988] 2 S.C.R. 122.
8 *British Columbia Government Employees' Union* v. *A.G. British Columbia*, [1988] 2 S.C.R. 214.
9 *Irwin Toy Limited* v. *A.G. Quebec*, [1989] 1 S.C.R. 927.
10 *Slaight Communications Incorporated* v. *Davidson*, [1989] 1 S.C.R. 1038.
11 *Ford* v. *A.G. Quebec*, [1988] 2 S.C.R. 712.
12 *Edmonton Journal* v. *A.G. Alberta*, [1989] 2 S.C.R. 1326.
13 *Supra*, note 1 at 351.
14 *Ibid.*
15 P.C. Weiler, "Rights and Judges in a Democracy: A New Canadian Version" (1984) 18 University of Michigan Journal of Law Reform, 51 at 84.

Under this approach judges will be on the front lines; they will possess both the responsibility and the legal clout necessary to tackle "rights" issues as they regularly arise. At the same time, however, the *Charter* reserves for the legislature a final say to be used sparingly in the exceptional case where the judiciary has gone awry.

Under the *Charter* we can certainly benefit, in ways described by Professor Whyte, by having "rights" issues systematically ventilated in the courts. Most often we will accept the decisions of the courts on these rights issues. But occasionally situations will arise in which the citizenry through a responsible and accountable process concludes that a judicial resolution of a rights issue is seriously flawed and seeks to reverse it. These are the situations in which we should enjoy the benefit of the legislative override.

For anyone familiar with the history of judicial review in the United States or in our own country, it is difficult to believe in the infallibility of judges. In American history, the decisions of the Supreme Court in *Lochner* and other early twentieth century cases denying state legislatures the power to ensure vulnerable workers decent conditions of employment are reminders of the injustice and harm that can flow from judicial decisions interpreting constitutional guarantees.[16] Already under the *Charter*, several judicial decisions vetoing legislation might be questioned for the harm they inflict on vulnerable groups in Canadian society. One example is the decision of the Ontario Court of Appeal that in certain circumstances it would be an unreasonable limitation on an accused's *Charter* rights to give effect to the recent amendment of the Criminal Code protecting complainants in sexual assault cases from being forced to give evidence on their prior sexual conduct.[17] Another is the decision of the British Columbia Court of Appeal overturning provincial regulations designed to channel the influx of new doctors to areas of the province where they are most urgently needed,[18] a decision from which the Supreme Court of Canada has denied leave to appeal.

Countries without legislative overrides in their constitutional bills of rights have other means of reversing judicial decisions. In no constitutional democracy is there absolute closure on rights issues once they have been pronounced upon by the judicial branch. The most direct method of reversal is constitutional amendment. But in most constitutional democracies (and certainly in Canada), amending the constitution is an extraordinarily difficult process which may leave decision-making power in the hands of a small group of people who are indifferent to or beneficiaries of the injustice resulting from a judicial decision. The more usual method of reversing constitutional decisions of the courts, at least in the United States, is to change or threaten to change the composition of the judicial bodies most influential in interpreting the constitution.[19]

Absent a Canadian-style legislative override, court-packing or court-bashing are the devices to which democratic leaders are most likely to resort when faced with judicial interpretations of the constitution they consider to be seriously unjust and harmful. These devices may yield relatively quick results as was the case with Roosevelt's threat to pack the U.S. Supreme Court, or they may work much more slowly, as has been the case with the efforts of Republican Presidents to reverse certain decisions of the Warren Court. In either case court-packing or court-bashing, involving as they do the application of raw majoritarian power to the judicial branch, would seem less appropriate devices than legislative debate and discussion for challenging judicial decisions. The legislative override has the merit, when properly used, of applying reasoned discussion in a publicly accountable forum to the great issues of justice and public well-being at stake.

Now it will be noticed that I have qualified my support of the legislative override by arguing for its superiority "when proper used." By "properly used" I mean when it is invoked only after a reasoned debate in the legislature. This is precisely the point about the

---

16   There are of course many accounts, but for a brief discussion of these cases see A.T. Mason and W.M. Beaney, *The Supreme Court in Free Society* (Prentice-Hall, 1959) c. 11.

17   *Seaboyer v. R.* (1987), 37 C.C.C. (3d) 53.

18   *Wilson v. Medical Services Commission of British Columbia* (1988),

53 D.L.R. (4th) 171. But see Justice Lamer's condemnation of Wilson in Reference Re Criminal Code, ss. 193 & 195.1(l)(c) (1990), 77 C.R. (3d) 1 (S.C.C.).

19   For an overview of political constraints on the U.S. Supreme Court see W. Lasser, *The Limits of Judicial Power: The Supreme Court in American Politics* (Chapel Hill: University of North Carolina Press, 1988).

override which the Supreme Court of Canada failed to grasp in *Ford*[20] when it upheld Quebec's blanket use of the override. The Court held that legislatures are not even required to name the rights or freedoms which are to be restricted. By insisting on an entirely formal approach to the override clause, as Professor Lorraine Weinrib has put it,[21]

> The Court thereby defers to a legislative process devoid of its legitimating qualities of reasoned and focused debate by the people's representatives.

The Supreme Court's approach to the notwithstanding clause, unfortunately and ironically, is a departure from the purposive approach applied to other sections of the *Charter*. The primary purpose of the override is to provide an opportunity for responsible and accountable public discussion of rights issues, a purpose that may be seriously undermined if legislatures are free to use the override without discussion and deliberation.

At this point it is essential to turn to the second wing of the argument for the *Charter*, the argument that focuses on the process advantages of the override. It is only when we recognize the contribution an override can make to the quality of democratic government that the inadequacy of the Supreme Court's ruling on section 33 can be fully understood and the merits of the notwithstanding clause fully appreciated.

## B. Process Considerations

A legislative override does not guarantee that we will arrive at the right answers to the questions of political and social justice raised by the *Charter*. What it can do is subject these questions to a process of wide public discussion so that the politically active citizenry participate in and share responsibility for the outcome.

The advantage of retaining a role for legislatures in the determination of rights issues is not to ensure that the will of the majority prevails. Even if one accepted a simplistic majority rule conception of democracy (which this writer does not), the decisions of legislatures can rarely be realistically equated with the will

of the majority. This is especially true of legislative decisions on the issues of moral conscience and justice raised by questions about the appropriate limits of rights and freedoms. The point of maintaining parliamentary bodies in a democracy is not to ensure that majority preference gets its way on all public issues. Given the wonders of modern electronics, we do not need legislative chambers to register citizens' preferences. No, the fundamental purpose of parliamentary bodies is to facilitate the democratic ideal of government by discussion. A parliament must above all be a "talking place"—that is, after all, the root meaning of the term. Through media coverage of legislative debates, citizens are engaged in deliberating on public issues. It is through parliamentary institutions that we move closer to experiencing a form of democratic government that is not simply rule of the greater number but that, in the words of Ernest Barker,[22]

> … elicits and enlists—or at any rate is calculated to elicit and enlist, so far as is humanly possible the thought, the will, and the general capacity of every member … a government depending on mutual interchange of ideas, on mutual criticism of the ideas interchanged, and the general capacity of every member.

Much the same democratic ideal is put forward by Professor Dworkin in his recent contribution to [the *Alberta Law Review*]. Dworkin rejects what he calls a "statistical democracy" whose institutions are designed simply to ensure that political decisions match the will of the majority. Instead he argues for a "communal democracy" in which[23]

> each citizen insists that his political convictions are in every important sense his business, that it is his independent responsibility to decide what is required of the nation to do well, and whether or how far it has succeeded.

We have much less chance of realizing Barker's or Dworkin's democratic ideal, if, as Professor Whyte

---

20  *Supra*, note 11.
21  L. Weinrib, "Learning to Live with the Override" (1990) 35 McGill L.J. 541 at 570.

22  E. Barker, *Reflections on Government* (New York: Oxford University Press, 1958) at 36.
23  *Supra*, note 4 at 337.

insists, we give judges the last word, the ultimate say, on rights issues raised by the *Charter*. To exclude citizens and their elected legislators from the ultimate determination of these issues is to exclude them from resolving questions of justice which should be at the very heart of political life. As Aristotle taught so long ago,[24]

> It is the peculiarity of man, in comparison with the rest of the animal world, that he alone possesses a perception of good and evil, of the just and the unjust, and of similar qualities; and it is association in a common perception of these things which makes a family and a polis.

Giving judges the last word, the definitive say, on issues of social and political justice is to exclude citizens from participation in the essential activity of a political community.

In making this point I do not mean to denigrate the contribution judicial decisions can make to public discussion and consideration of rights issues. Some *Charter* critics, in my view, have gone too far in denouncing judicial review under the *Charter* as excessively elitist and undemocratic. These critics tend to underestimate the extent to which legal aid and the organization of advocacy groups have made litigation much more accessible than in the past, as well as the extent to which *Charter* litigation generates action on law reform issues which are neglected or ignored by legislatures. Also, I would acknowledge that both the presentation of *Charter* issues before judges and their reasoned decisions on those issues can contribute significantly to public understanding. But I am not persuaded that these benefits are so great as to justify making adjudication always the ultimate means of resolving rights issues. Court decisions on whether restricting where new doctors supported by public medicare can practice is a justifiable restriction of individual freedom, or on whether a French-only sign law is needed to preserve the predominantly French character of Quebec, may well have helped the public understand those issues. But in a democracy that aspires to government by discussion and full participation of its citizens in questions of social and political

justice, court decisions should not close off further debate and decision-making in elected and publicly accountable legislatures.

Legislatures, it is true, may act precipitately and make questionable decisions. On occasion their consideration of rights issues may, to use Professor Whyte's phrase, be unduly influenced by "the dominant political winds."[25] But it is a dreadful distortion to suggest that such impassioned and inconsiderate behaviour is the norm in Canadian legislatures. A reading of legislative debates on justice issues such as capital punishment, criminal procedure, aboriginal rights, and language rights does not find legislators simply pandering for popularity. At the same time we should recognize that, while judges are free from any pressure to curry favour with the public, they are not altogether free from other institutional biases. The Supreme Court's curt opinion in *B.C.G.E.U.* v. *British Columbia* upholding the power of a judge to restrict the free speech rights of workers does not shine out as a carefully reasoned and balanced consideration of that issue.[26] Professor Dale Gibson's article ... reveals other instances of judicial bias and self-interest.[27]

In designing the institutional matrix for making decisions on rights issues it is a mistake to look for an error-proof solution. Both courts and legislatures are capable of being unreasonable and, in their different ways, self-interested. By providing a legislative counter-weight to judicial power the Canadian *Charter* establishes a prudent system of checks and balances which recognizes the fallibility of both courts and legislatures and gives closure to the decisions of neither. A legislature's decision to use the override, it must be remembered, is not ultimate. It is good for only five years. After five years it can be reviewed but not without re-opening the issue for public debate and discussion.

If we do anything to section 33 of the *Charter*, we should reform it, not abolish it. There is need to overcome by constitutional amendment that part of the Supreme Court's decision in *Ford* which permits standard-form overrides without any obligation on the legislature to identify the specific legislative provision

24  *The Politics of Aristotle*, trans. E. Barker (Oxford: Claredon Press, 1948) at 6.

25  *Supra*, note 1 at 356.
26  *Supra*, note 8.
27  D. Gibson, "The Real Laws of the Constitution" (1990) 28 Alta. L. Rev. 358.

which in its judgment needs protection or the right or freedom which it in its view should not be given priority. Professor Weiler and I have advocated a further amendment which would require that any use of the override be subject to two enactments, one before and one after an election.[28] This would ensure a cooling off period and time for second thoughts. What is even more important, it would also ensure broad citizen involvement, thus contributing to the fundamental process value of the override.

## IV. TWO TEST CASES

Discussion of the merits of the override might be more focused by considering two test cases: one in which I think the override should have been used but wasn't, and one in which it was used but a lot of people think it shouldn't have been.

### A. The Elections Act Case

In 1983, the federal Parliament amended the Elections Act to effectively prohibit private interest groups from funding opposition to candidates or parties during election campaigns. In June 1984, Mr. Justice Medhurst of the Alberta Court of Queen's Bench ruled that this legislation was an unreasonable restriction on the right to freedom of expression. The federal government, with an election pending, decided not to appeal this decision. The federal Elections Commissioner, in order to maintain uniform election rules across the country, applied Justice Medhurst's ruling nation wide, in effect rendering the Elections Act amendment null and void.

It is important to recognize that what is at stake in this case is nothing less than the integrity and fairness of our election process in Canada—no small issue for a democracy! But Justice Medhurst's decision striking down the legislation shows little sensitivity to the complexity or importance of working out an appropriate legislative scheme for democratic elections. His decision fails to address the fairness or effectiveness of imposing spending limits on political parties which

do not apply to private interest groups. For Justice Medhurst, such limits can be justified only through "actual demonstration of harm or a real likelihood of harm to a society value...."[29] He does not carefully examine the evidence presented to him by the federal government showing actual harm. Nor does he provide any indication of the degree or nature of the harm which could justify a limitation.[30]

Professor Whyte has attacked Professor Weiler and me for endorsing the use of the override to reverse Justice Medhurst's decision.[31] In doing so he states that we[32]

> seem to believe restrictions on political participation is an appropriate policy to adopt in the context of elections and argue that the override should be used to counteract *any* court decision that protected political participation on the basis of freedom of speech or equal protection of the laws. (Emphasis added.)

Professor Whyte's statement is a grave distortion of our position. Support for one particular restriction on election spending obviously does not entail support for any and all restrictions on participation in elections. I would surmise that Professor Whyte himself favours some legislative regulation of the election process and would not welcome judicial decisions overturning any and all regulations that he favoured.

It is important to understand why Whyte advances such an erroneous and illogical interpretation of our position. He does so, I believe, because he has wrongly dichotomized our institutional choice in making decisions about the proper limits of rights and freedoms: either we accept legislative determinations of these issues as ultimate, or we accept judicial determinations as ultimate. If we accept one legislative determination of such an issue, then we must be prepared to accept any and all legislative determinations, no

---

28  P.H. Russell and P. Weiler, "Don't Scrap Override Clause—It's a Very Canadian Solution," *The Toronto Star* (4 June 1989) B3. A more extensive discussion of this proposal is contained in Professor Weiler's 1984 article, *supra*, note 15.

29  *National Citizens' Coalition Inc.* v. *A G. Canada*, [1984] 5 W.W.R. 436 at 453.

30  For an extensive critique of this decision see Janet Hiebert, "Fair Elections and Freedom of Expression Under the *Charter*" (1990) 24 Journal of Canadian Studies 72.

31  I advocated this use of the override earlier in Peter H. Russell, "The First Three Years in Charterland" (1985) 28 Canadian Public Administration 367, at 377–8.

32  *Supra*, note 1 at 352, note 9.

matter how appallingly illiberal and undemocratic we may find them, as unquestionable and ultimate. It is precisely the override's genius that by providing a basis for a shared responsibility between legislatures and courts in deciding rights issues it enables us to avoid such a drastic either/or choice. It would be most unwise to give the judiciary the ultimate say on how to regulate the electoral process. One inherent weakness of the judiciary's treatment of rights issues under the *Charter* is a tendency to overlook or give insufficient weight to the ways in which private, non-governmental centres of power can adversely affect the freedom and equality of citizens. Judicially mandated deregulation of the election process could lead to a situation in which large accumulations of private wealth can unduly effect election outcomes. We should not declare closure on legislative discussion and re-consideration of these issues just because a judge has spoken.

## B. *The Quebec Signs Case*

In December 1988 the Quebec National Assembly used the notwithstanding clause to overcome the Supreme Court of Canada's decision striking down the French-only signs provisions of Quebec's Bill 101.[33] This use of the notwithstanding clause provoked the sharpest outcry to date against the clause. Much of this outrage came from outside Quebec, but not all of it. The Bourassa government's decision to enact Bill 178,[34] the legislation invoking the override and requiring French-only outside signs, led to the resignation of four of Bourassa's English-speaking ministers. It prompted Prime Minister Mulroney, whose government enjoyed a strong Quebec base, to declare that the Canadian Constitution was "not worth the paper it was printed on."[35] And, of course, I should add that the Premier of Manitoba, Gary Filmon, responded to this use of the override by withdrawing the Meech Lake Constitutional Accord from the Manitoba legislature. Many would regard Quebec's enactment of Bill 178 as the decisive turning point in the failure of Meech Lake.

So this use of the override appears to be a "hard" case for supporters of the notwithstanding clause, particularly one, like the present writer, who was an ardent advocate of the Meech Lake Accord. But it is essential to understand that support for a constitutional procedure does not require supporting each and every use of that procedure. Those who believe in judicial interpretation of constitutional guarantees are not necessarily in favour of every judicial interpretation of constitutional rights. No more are supporters of a legislative override logically committed to favouring every use of this power. The key question to ask in the contest of the *Quebec Signs* case is not whether the Supreme Court or the Quebec National Assembly reached the right decision on the issue at stake, but whether this type of question is one on which the judiciary ought to have the last word.

What Prime Minister Mulroney's rhetoric and the shrill outrage of many others who attacked this use of the override seriously distorted was the nature of the question at issue. To hear them, one would think that what was at stake was nothing less than the essential core of freedom of speech and minority rights. But the central issue in this case was much tougher: to what extent does the need to preserve the predominantly French character of Quebec justify limiting the right to advertise in the language of one's choice?

The Supreme Court, like Quebec's National Assembly, regarded the preservation of the predominance of the French language in Quebec as a "serious and legitimate"[36] legislative objective, one that would justify limiting the right to advertise in the language of one's choice. In *Allan Singer Ltd.* v. *A.G. Quebec*,[37] decided at the same time as *Ford*, the Court upheld provisions of Bill 101 which for some commercial purposes required the use of French but permitted the use of a second language. In *Ford*, the Court's only difference with the Quebec legislature was that while the Court was prepared to justify legislation requiring that signs in Quebec be predominantly in French, it had not been demonstrated that signs exclusively in French were necessary to maintain a French *"visage linguistique"* in Quebec. According to the Court, the specific question of whether a French-only sign law as

---

33   *Supra*, note 11.
34   An Act to Amend the Charter of the French Language, S.Q. 1988, c. 54.
35   *The [Toronto] Globe and Mail* (8 April 1989).
36   *Supra*, note 11 at 778.
37   [1988] 2 S.C.R. 790.

opposed to a French-predominance sign law was necessary to preserve the predominantly French character of Quebec was "simply not addressed by the materials" before the Court.[38] In response to this decision, the Quebec legislature after several days of debate and public discussion passed Bill 178, which at least its members regarded as a compromise between the Supreme Court's decision and the overturned provisions of Bill 101: French-only signs outdoors, predominantly French signs indoors.

It is certainly arguable that Bill 178 is an unsuccessful compromise and that from both a political and administrative point of view it would have been better for those who believe a French-only sign law to be essential for the survival of a predominantly French Quebec to have simply re-enacted the provisions of Bill 101. But that's not the point on which the override's legitimacy should depend. The legitimacy of the override in the context of this case depends on whether or not one believes that Quebec's National Assembly should continue to have any decision-making role on the question of what kind of sign is required after the Supreme Court has spoken on the matter.

In my view this question should be answered in the affirmative. The sign case poses a fundamental issue of political justice concerning the relationship of the rights and interests of two minorities. On the one hand there is the minority of Quebeckers who are not French and their right to express themselves in their own language, and on the other the Francophone Quebeckers who are a vulnerable cultural minority in North America and their right to preserve their distinctive culture. Working out an appropriate balance between these two concerns about minority rights is a profound challenge not only for Quebeckers but for all Canadians. This is not an issue which we Canadians either have withdrawn or should withdraw from consideration by Quebec's legislature for *ultimate* determination by the Supreme Court. To do so would be to detract too much from the responsibility of Quebeckers and other Canadians for participating in the resolution of a question fundamental to the political justice of the political community they share. I would add that it is extremely doubtful that the unity of Canada could survive an insistence by the rest of Canada that Quebec's legislature be denied a continuing role in deciding what is necessary to preserve Quebec's French character.

## V. THE PERSPECTIVE OF PRINCIPLE

At the beginning of his article Professor Whyte argues that the future of the override cannot be settled by resort to principle. By this he means that the case for the override cannot be a logical deduction from the "basic constitutional principles" he perceives to be at work in the "formal structure of the Canadian state"— namely, "legalism, democracy, and federalism."[39] The elimination of the override, he argues, is at least as consistent with these principles as its retention. Given that the established principles of our constitution cannot settle the issue, the merits of the override should be assessed on a more prudential basis in terms of "the actual social goods and bads" it is likely to produce and "what will produce the soundest government and fairest society."[40]

As I have earlier indicated, I have no difficulty accepting Whyte's suggestion that we not try to judge the override entirely on the basis of our constitutional antecedents. And I agree with him that the override should be judged in terms of what will produce a sound and fair polity for Canadians. But I do take issue with his treatment of what he regards as Canada's basic constitutional principles and their bearing on the override issue.

I have the least quarrel with Whyte's treatment of the federal principle. He is right in viewing federalism as a check on national majoritarianism and pointing out that judicial decisions enforcing the federal division of powers have significantly constrained Canadian legislatures in the past. But he overlooks an important difference between judicial review based on federalism and judicial review based on a bill of rights. Also, he underestimates the impact of the *Charter* on the workings of Canadian federalism and on the unity of the country.

When courts strike down legislation on federalism grounds, normally this means that one level

---

38  *Supra*, note 11 at 779.

39  *Supra*, note 1 at 349.
40  *Ibid.*

of government, but not the other, is precluded from implementing a policy. This is a less drastic result than when legislation is struck down on *Charter* grounds, for then the judicially vetoed policy, absent the override, is placed beyond both levels of government. It is in this sense that removing the override from the *Charter* would, contrary to Whyte's assertion, entail a greater shift in the balance of power between legislatures and courts than is inherent in the judicial enforcement of federal limits. Secondly, the *Charter* does have a centralizing effect on Canadian federalism. The article by Morton et al., also in the most recent issue of this supplement, tracking the judicial nullification of statutes begins to take the measure of the Supreme Court's capacity under the *Charter* to impose uniform policies on the Provinces.[41] This centralization of policy-making power, from a normative perspective, may at times have clear benefits for Canadian society. At the same time it may reduce the policy pluralism and diversity that many of us value in federalism. Finally, and from the perspective of national unity, most seriously, as I have already suggested, it is most unlikely that we could retain Quebec as a member of the Canadian federation if we were now to insist on removing the override from the *Charter*. This is not because the majority of Quebeckers are opposed to rights and freedoms but because they want to keep a reasonable measure of control over their cultural security in their own hands.

But Professor Whyte's elucidation of the principle of legalism gives me much more difficulty than his discussion of federalism. For it is here that he seems to slide into the very mode of analysis he has cautioned us to eschew and to argue, in effect, that regardless of "the goods and bads that are likely to be produced" we must be bound by the implications of his principle of legalism.

Whyte's initial formulation of what he calls legalism—namely, "the notion that there are adjudicable public issues"[42]—is not problematic. But then he goes on to assert that "we have come to terms with these issues being *ultimately* adjudicable—not subject to legislative review and revision." Here he seems to be

saying that having accepted through adoption of the Charter that a great many public issues which were heretofore dealt with by the "political branches" are now to be subject to adjudication, we are ineluctably committed to giving the judiciary ultimate control of these issues. But that surely isn't so. Certainly when the *Charter* was adopted with an override we Canadians made no such commitment. The question now before us, using Whyte's own criteria, is whether making *Charter* issues "ultimately adjudicable" will lead to the soundest and fairest system of government.

For reasons already advanced in this article I believe that in terms of both the substance of rights policy and its process it would not be sound even to try to let all the public issues which may be adjudicated under the *Charter* be ultimately settled by judges. I say "try" because that is the closest we can come to realizing Whyte's ideal of forever removing the *Charter* from what he calls "a purely political process." The experience of the United States shows what an illusion it is to think that without the possibility of a legislative override, rights issues dealt with by the judiciary are forever withdrawn from the political process. School desegregation was not withdrawn from the American political process after the Supreme Court in *Plessy* v. *Ferguson*[43] gave its blessing to "separate but equal," any more than Roosevelt's New Deal legislation was removed from the political agenda after being vetoed by the Supreme Court.

But it is difficult to see why even trying to remove rights issues *entirely* from the political process should result in "sounder" or "fairer" laws. Professor Whyte asserts that "the capacity of governments to regulate society for the public good has not, yet, been fundamentally hampered by *Charter* decisions."[44] Some might consider the damage done in Wilson to government's capacity to provide for an equitable distribution of publicly funded medical services, or in *National Citizens' Coalition* to government's freedom to follow an election commission's advice on how best to provide fair and effective election laws, as already a refutation of Whyte's dictum. But, let us concede that these decisions have not *fundamentally* hampered government from "regulating for the public good." The

---

41   F.L. Morton, G. Solomon, I. McNish, and D.W. Poulton, "Judicial Nullification of Statutes Under the *Charter* of Rights and Freedoms, 1982–1988" (1990) 28 Alta. L. Rev. 396.

42   *Supra*, note 1 at 351.

43   (1896), 163 U.S. 537.

44   *Supra*, note 1 at 353.

question remains: why is it sound and fair to accept this much judicial damage to effective, socially responsible regulation without the possibility of legislative review and, indeed, risk the possibility that judicial decisions might go further and fundamentally cripple government's effectiveness in providing for the public good? Are the judiciary and the judicial process so inherently superior to the legislature and the processes of ordinary politics that we are justified in running these risks?

Professor Whyte apparently thinks they are. The problem with legislatures, he tells us, is that sometimes they "neglect to calculate the extraordinary impact of legislative measures on particular individuals."[45] Sometimes too, he says, they simply do not care enough about the injury to some persons' right to tailor measures which will minimize the damage. I agree with Whyte that legislatures certainly do these things, and these are precisely the situations in which we may be well served by *Charter*-based judicial review. But I would submit that judicial review of legislation under the *Charter*, in turn, has its own limitations and blind spots. Judges often fail to take into account, and indeed sometimes are exposed to the scantiest of submissions on, the relationship of a challenged law to its total social or policy context.[46] In *Wilson*, for example, the British Columbia Court of Appeal, in upholding the "liberty" of new doctors to practice their profession at public expense wherever they wish in the province, did not consider the possible inequity in not extending a similar liberty to other newly graduated professionals in that province or the impact of this decision on the financing of other social programs.[47] Judges considering *Charter* challenges to legislation and government regulation may minimize the damage which can be inflicted by private centres of social and economic power on the freedom and equality of the most vulnerable groups in a market economy. It is to his credit

that Chief Justice Dickson warned against this possibility.[48] But we cannot always count on such enlightened judicial leadership or on its being followed.

The art of living with the *Charter* and with its override is to get the best out of both the judicial and the legislative process in making decisions on rights issues. However, according to Whyte's principle of legalism, we must now put all our eggs in the judicial basket. A legislative back-up, in his view, is too apt to plunge rights issues back into the grubby, unprincipled, partisan realm of "pure politics." It is here that we encounter what I find most unacceptable in Whyte's argument, his disdain for democratic politics.

In his discussion of the democratic principle Whyte rejects, as I would, a simplistic majoritarian conception of democracy. I agree with him that a liberal democracy requires checks and balances and that judicial review based on a constitutional bill of rights is not inherently undemocratic. Where I differ with him on the democratic principle is on how best to enhance and develop our capacity for democratic citizenship. The attempt to remove rights issues, irretrievably, from the arena of popular politics is to give up on what democratic politics at its best should be—the resolution of questions of political justice through a process of public discussion. As I have written before, it "represents a further flight from politics, a deepening disillusionment with the procedures of representative government and government by discussion as a means of resolving fundamental questions of political justice."[49] For me, the legislative override clause is a way of countering this flight from democratic politics. It is a signal that we Canadians have not yet given up on our capacity for debating and deciding great issues of political justice in a popular political forum.

In the concluding paragraphs of his article Professor Whyte turns to what for many may be the clinching argument against the override—the need for

---

45  *Ibid.* at 355.
46  For a discussion of the institutional weaknesses of the judiciary in deciding policy issues related to constitutional rights, see D.L. Horowitz, *The Courts and Social Policy* (Washington: Brookings Institution, 1977).
47  For a discussion of this case and of the judiciary's limitations in dealing with labour relations and employment policy issues, see P.C. Weiler, "The *Charter* at Work: Reflections on the Constitutionalizing of Labour and Employment Law" (1990) 40 U.T.L.J. 117.

48  "… the courts must be cautious to ensure that it [the Charter] does not simply become an instrument of better situated individuals to roll back legislation which has as its object the improvement of the condition of less advantaged person." *Edwards Books and Art Limited* v. R., [1986] 2 S.C.R. 713 at 779.
49  P.H. Russell, "The Effect of a Charter of Rights on the Policy-Making Role of Canadian Courts" (1982) 33 Canadian Public Administration 1 at 32.

a judicial check against "extreme political reaction."[50] It is in moments of "serious political repression," he contends, that we are most in need of cool judicial guardians to check the passions of democracy. Now, I have no doubt that legislative bodies can act unreasonably and fall under the sway of very repressive forces. In the 1950s we witnessed just that when McCarthyism held sway in the United States. We also witnessed then how ineffective that country's judicial guardians were in checking that repression. But more fundamentally, I would argue that a democracy which puts its faith as much in its politically active citizenry as in its judges to be the guardians of liberty is stronger than one that would endeavour to vest ultimate responsibility for liberty and fundamental rights exclusively in its judiciary.

---

50    *Supra*, note 1 at 356.

# 33

## *Author's Introduction*

When the Canadian Constitution was "patriated" in 1982, it included an entrenched Charter of Rights and Freedoms. This was new to Canadian politics, and not entirely welcomed by all concerned. Politicians on both the left and the right of the political spectrum raised concerns about how the Charter would change Canadian politics. In the decade following entrenchment, academic commentators on both sides of the ideological divide took up these arguments and anaylzed early Supreme Court decisions to try to find proof of their predictions. I found this convergence of left- and right-wing critics curious and wanted to lay out what the issues were and what to make of them.

Source: Richard Sigurdson, "Left- and Right-Wing Charterphobia in Canada: A Critique of the Critics," *International Journal of Canadian Studies* (1993): 95–117.

Richard Sigurdson

# Left- and Right-Wing Charterphobia in Canada: A Critique of the Critics[*]

ONE REASON FOR the failure of the Charlottetown Accord that was often cited by its critics was the alleged damage it would do to the Canadian Charter of Rights and Freedoms. There were those, of course, who insisted that such fears were unfounded, that the Accord would do no harm to the precious Charter. Seldom did we hear from anyone who might say that the Charter is not worth protecting, that it was a mistake to enter into Charterland in the first place. For these sorts of arguments, one has to turn to academics, many of whom are highly critical, not just of the Canadian Charter of Rights and Freedoms specifically but of the constitutional entrenchment and codification of rights in general.

Various writers have long suggested that the Charter's "importance in terms of Canada's constitutional future is that it is centralizing, legalizing and Americanizing" (Cheffins and Johnson, 1986: 148). And many leading scholars have been critical, or at least sceptical, of these tendencies right from the start. For instance, Donald Smiley (1983) worried that the attempt to achieve national unity by means of a centralizing, entrenched charter would have precisely the opposite effect to the one desired. Peter Russell

---

*    An earlier version of this paper was delivered at the annual meetings of the Canadian Political Science Association in Charlottetown, PEI, June 1992. The author would like to thank Ted Morton and Rainer Knopff for helpful comments on the text.

(1983) told us that the principal impact of the Charter would be to "judicialize politics and politicize the judiciary" and that the danger of this would lie not so much in the fact that non-elected judges would impose their will in an undemocratic fashion, but that social and political questions would become transformed into abstract, technical ones that the bulk of the citizenry will feel incompetent to debate and attempt to resolve. And William Christian and Colin Campbell (1983) warned that the adoption of a charter would shift Canadian political culture away from its tory and collectivist past towards a much more individualistic, Lockean liberal focus. In other words, that the Canadian Charter of Rights and Freedoms would exacerbate the trend which George Grant (1965) so eloquently lamented.

In this paper I wish to take a closer look at a more recent trend in Charter scholarship—one that has produced a highly normative literature, often on the basis of the observations noted above. My intention, then, is to outline and discuss this new, more ideological, academic attack upon the Canadian Charter of Rights and Freedoms. I will refer to this anti-Charter position as "Charterphobia" because I see in it not just a scepticism about our specific Charter but a more generalized fear of, and antipathy towards, any constitutionally entrenched bill or charter of human rights in a modern, liberal, democratic state. I think that this anti-Charter attitude is unnecessarily alarmist—that is, I can find little concrete evidence to support the Charterphobic account of what is going on in Charterland. I will argue, as well, that the Charterphobes are largely unable to provide appropriate alternative methods for addressing the major social and economic concerns of a modern and diverse liberal democracy. My main strategy, however, is not to counterattack with discussions of specific provisions and cases and their interpretation. Rather, I am concerned with the rhetorical significance of recent anti-Charter scholarship and will discuss its effects on our political discourse.

In particular, I will identify two fundamental strains of Charterphobia—left-wing Charterphobia and right-wing Charterphobia—that rely upon curiously similar arguments about the impact of the Charter and the perils of judicial review. In fact, both left- and right-wing Charterphobes assail the Charter in the way best calculated to evoke shock and horror in a society like ours—that is, they accuse it of generating anti-democratic political consequences. As we will see, there are some interesting points of overlap between these two types of Charterphobia and it is worth pondering just what this tells us about the persistence of certain Canadian intellectual traditions. Of course, there are significant differences, too, and we will have to explore the arguments used to portray the Charter as an instrument of anti-democracy and what each side means by "democratic."

My discussion will be presented in three parts. First, I will outline and explain the major objections to the Charter put forward by leading, leftist, legal scholars. Second, I will look at the critique of Charter politics by conservatives, mainly in the discipline of political science. In the third section, I will review the arguments, try to show that the Charterphobes have not made a convincing case, and sketch a defence—albeit a qualified one—of the Charter, warts and all.

## LEFT-WING CHARTERPHOBIA

I shall begin with a discussion of the left-wing fear of the Charter. This was evident during the 1981 constitutional negotiations in the position taken by Saskatchewan Premier Alan Blakeney, who feared, among other things, that the Charter would have a centralizing influence on Canadian federalism. Still smarting from recent Supreme Court decisions against his province in CIGOL (1978) and Potash (1979), Blakeney did not relish the prospect of federally-appointed courts setting uniform national standards, often in policy areas of exclusive provincial jurisdiction.

What is more, Blakeney was certain that the Charter would constitute a threat to the interests of organized labour. He based this opinion, in part, on his critical observations of the American experience, where the Bill of Rights has been used to strike down laws setting minimum wages, minimum hours of work, etc. (Greunding, 1990: 192). Blakeney was convinced, moreover, that his province's progressive social programs, such as medicare, might have been struck down by a conservative court. Since he considered the state as an instrument for providing important public services while pursuing greater equity for all citizens, Blakeney could see no benefit in a charter that would restrain government in order to protect the rights of citizens to be free from state interference in their economic or social lives. Indeed, he was "aghast that any social democratic party would be in favour of transferring power from legislatures to courts" (Greunding, 1990: 196).

An additional, more personal, dimension to Blakeney's opposition to the Charter links him to a significant British-tory streak within the tradition of English-Canadian social democracy. That is, Blakeney simply preferred the tory-collectivist features of the British parliamentary tradition over the liberal individualism of the US model and its rights-based constitution. The son of a traditional Tory family in Nova Scotia, product of a Loyalist legal education at Dalhousie and a British one at Oxford, Blakeney defined himself as a "British constitutional lawyer type" who believes that rights are best protected by Parliament and not by a constitution which is interpreted by the courts. After all, he said, "the British Parliament has worked not all that badly" (Greunding, 1990: 192). Not surprisingly, then, Blakeney was an adamant champion of parliamentary sovereignty throughout the constitutional negotiations, reluctantly giving in to the pressure to accept an entrenched charter only once he was assured that there would be a clause allowing legislatures to make laws "notwithstanding" certain rights. And even on this matter he proved to be a tenacious Charterphobe, demanding for longer than anyone else that both the gender equality provision in Section 28 and the aboriginal rights clause in Section 35 should remain within the jurisdiction of the provincial override.

It must be noted, of course, that Blakeney's position was far from being the majority one within his own party, especially at the national level. Indeed, support for an entrenched charter had been party policy since the days when M.J. Coldwell was leader of the CCF. What is more, Blakeney's opposition to the Charter put him in direct and public conflict with the national party leader, Ed Broadbent, with party elders Tommy Douglas, David Lewis, and Stanley Knowles, and with several groups usually supportive of the party, including civil libertarian and feminist organizations. In the end, the national party backed the Charter. In fact,

the only NDP MP to vote against the Charter, Svend Robinson, did so not because it undermined parliamentary sovereignty but because it included a legislative override clause. Since then, leftist politicians have rarely been vocal in their opposition to the Charter and lately prefer a strategy of attempting to increase the list of constitutionally protected rights to include, for example, social and economic entitlements to be set out in some sort of social charter.

Nowadays, then, pure left-wing Charterphobia is most evident in the academy, most notably in writings by Canadian legal scholars (rather than political scientists). The most thorough example of this can be found in Michael Mandel's book, *The Charter of Rights and the Legalization of Politics in Canada* (1989). Excellent examples can also be found in articles by Joel Bakan (1991) and Robert Martin (1991). But perhaps the most vociferous leftist assaults on the Charter have been launched by Andrew Petter, who is now British Columbia's Aboriginal Affairs Minister, and Osgoode Hall Law School's Alan Hutchinson (Petter, 1986, 1987, 1989; Petter and Hutchinson, 1988, 1989, 1990; and Hutchinson, 1989, 1991).

Simply put, these scholars argue that despite its marketing as part of a "people's package" the Charter is yet another tool for the advancement of the private interests of corporations, professionals, and other privileged groups at the expense of workers, the unemployed, women, aboriginals, racial minorities, and other socially and economically disadvantaged Canadians. The principal lines of argument advanced to support this conclusion involve discussions of (1) the nature of rights; (2) the nature of the judicial process itself, including problems with access to the judicial system and concerns with the composition of the judiciary; and (3) the Americanizing influence of the Charter. First, left-wing Charter critics suggest that all those who supported the Charter because they saw it as a means of advancing the interests of disadvantaged Canadians failed to understand the true nature of rights, i.e., that "the conferral of rights under a charter is a zero-sum rather than a positive-sum game" (Petter, 1986: 474). Hence, expanding rights for some groups will result in the loss of entitlements for others. Moreover, the disadvantaged will not be on the winning side of these disputes because of the ideological nature of the rights enshrined in our Charter. As Andrew Petter puts it, the Charter is "a 19th century document let loose on a 20th century welfare state. The rights in the Charter are founded on the belief that the main enemies of freedom are not disparities in wealth nor concentrations of private power, but the state" (Petter, 1987: 857).

In other words, the rights conferred in the Charter are largely negative rights aimed at protecting individuals from state interference rather than positive rights or entitlements to, say, employment, shelter, or health care services. And since Charter politics is a zero-sum game, private rights are given to individuals only insofar as they are taken away from governments and public institutions. This explains why the judicial activism of the courts has so far been confined to cases dealing with the Charter's legal rights provision (e.g., procedural rights of accused persons, prisoners, and immigrants). Individuals and groups without much social power are sometimes beneficiaries of these legal rights decisions; but, from the perspective of the legal left, the real winners are criminal lawyers and the system itself—the former benefits from more money and prestige, the latter benefits from much needed legitimation services (Mandel, 1989: 128–83).

Petter and his colleagues see it as ironic that the groups who supported the Charter as a means of aiding the socially and economically disadvantaged are those who insist most forcefully upon the need for greater positive intervention by government. This is ironic since it is these very groups who are likely to suffer the loss of hard-won entitlements as courts inhibit governmental ability to implement measures aimed at achieving greater social justice. Like Blakeney before him, then, Petter fears that the power of governments to provide social services, to attempt to redistribute economic resources, and to regulate private conduct will be successfully attacked in the courts (Petter, 1989: 152). Indeed, there is already a body of evidence to suggest that some of this is now occurring—e.g., corporations are using the Charter to protect themselves against governmental regulation and control (Mandel, 1989: 217–38; Martin, 1991: 124–25).

In their second line of attack on the Charter, leftist legal scholars argue that its supporters who see it as a distributive instrument are wrong because they fail to understand the ideological nature of the judicial framework in which Charter rights operate. "In

a word," explains Michael Mandel, "the Charter has *legalized* our politics. But legalized politics is the quintessential conservative politics" (1989: 4). There are two interrelated dimensions to this analysis of the adjudicative process: the first concerns the unequal access to the judicial process and the other concerns the composition of the judiciary and the biases of the courts.

On the former matter, critics observe that access to the courts is extremely unequal. Although the formal equality provisions that govern the legal system entitle all to litigate, litigation is very expensive. Consequently, "oppressed and disempowered groups who are the supposed beneficiaries of progressive Charter litigation will, because of their lack of resources, be the least likely to have genuine access to the courts" (Bakan, 1991: 318). And even if these groups are able to muster enough cash to get into court in the first place, they are likely to be at a competitive disadvantage since the lawyers on the other side, representing business or government, will have greater resources to fight the case. Groups representing left-wing causes are thus in a no-win situation when it comes to the Charter: if they resist Charter litigation they may risk the eradication of legislation beneficial to their interests; but if they do succumb to the pressure to defend or promote their causes in court, that will mean that money, time, and energy will be taken away from lobbying and other forms of political action (Petter, 1987: 859; Mandel, 1989: 70).

As well as these worries about unequal access, leftist scholars have raised concerns about the unrepresentativeness of the judiciary and the ideological biases within the judicial system. Judges in Canada are for the most part white, male, and wealthy. Moreover, the legal training and work experience of judges tends to encourage affinities between the attitudes and beliefs of those on the bench and the interests of litigants who represent the social and economic elite. Thus there exists an inevitable set of judicial biases against the economically and socially disadvantaged. By legalizing politics, then, the Charter has vastly enhanced the political power of lawyers and judges who possess neither the "background, the experience, [n]or the training to comprehend the social impact of claims made to them under the Charter, let alone to resolve those claims in ways that promote, or even protect, the interests of disadvantaged Canadians" (Petter, 1989: 157).

Finally, left-wing Charterphobes have noted that the Charter has effected a shift from a British to an American conception of the appropriate relations between the legal profession and representative institutions. In particular, the Charter has promoted a redefinition of the judicial role along American lines. Unelected and unaccountable judges increasingly see the Supreme Court as the guardian of the Constitution rather than simply as an adjudicator of disputes between parties. For many left-wing Charterphobes this is an anti-democratic departure from our traditions of parliamentary supremacy. No one is more upset about this than Robert Martin, who complains that "Parliamentary government was the democratic heart of our political system. To subvert parliamentary government in Canada is, then, to subvert democracy" (1991: 123).

Martin goes on to discuss three ways in which the Charter has been used in the process of the Americanization of Canada. First, the Charter undermines the sense of Canadian uniqueness. Now that we have a Charter similar in most respects to the US Bill of Rights, we are quickly forgetting that we once had our own values, institutions, and practices. And it does not help that Canadian courts, in the absence of any significant history of home-grown civil liberties case law, have relied upon American precedents to determine solutions to Canadian legal problems. This underlines the fact that large numbers of Canadians, especially students, now believe that prior to the enactment of the Charter in 1982 Canadians enjoyed virtually no rights.

Second, Martin complains that Canadian judges have taken to proclaiming the social and political primacy of the individual. Not only is this contrary to our tory past, but it undermines the potential legitimacy of collectivist public policy. We are being taught to conceptualize our needs, desires, and whims as rights. This rights-thinking, by its nature, is alienating and socially divisive. Michael Mandel (1989: 239) agrees, adding that the individualism of the Charter can be damaging to subordinate groups, such as women and aboriginals, who see their interests best served by the protection of their collective rights rather than the individual rights of their members. And Petter and Hutchinson (1988: 292) point out that the individualizing thrust of Charter rights has allowed judges to

support a mythical public/private distinction that limits the Charter's applicability to legislative or governmental action while excluding from Charter scrutiny the major source of inequality within our society—the maldistribution of private property entitlements among individuals.

Third, Martin argues that the Charter has encouraged the contemporary process of delegitimizing politics and worshipping economics. It does so because the negative nature of rights means that Charter cases almost inevitably involve an individual seeking protection against the strong arm of the state. So, Martin assumes, if rights are seen as "good," then the state will be seen as "bad." This process is especially insidious in Canada, Martin worries, since here there has traditionally been a higher acceptance rate for positive state action than in the USA. In some ways, Canadian society has been a virtual creation of state action, and state institutions have played a decisive role in the development of a unique Canadian identity. Hence, "to put the legitimacy of the state in doubt is to put the legitimacy of Canada in doubt" (Martin, 1991: 130).

It is interesting to note, in conclusion, that the left-wing attack on the Charter concerns almost exclusively its promise to better protect fundamental rights and freedoms. Leftist legal scholars are largely silent on the other primary political purpose of the Charter, as identified by Peter Russell, which "has to do with national unity and the Charter's capacity to offset, if not reverse, the centrifugal forces which some believe threaten the survival of Canada as a unified country" (1983: 30). Nor do they raise any concerns about the process that Alan Cairns has traced. In his writings, Cairns has shown how a Charter that emphasizes the rights of citizens rather than the powers of governments tends to transform, in his words, a "Government's Constitution" to a "Citizens' Constitution" (1991: 108–38, 199–222).

Why is it that the leftist fear of the Charter is not so great when it comes to its centralizing influence? One reason might be that socialists and social democrats in Canada have historically believed that a strong central government is necessary in order to redistribute wealth and income, to provide social security and to constrain the power of big business. To the extent that the Charter actually works as a nationalizing force, then, it is consistent with social democratic purposes. Moreover, the left is not about to lament the demise of elite accommodation ("eleven men in suits deciding the nation's future") if the result is an increased role in the decision-making process for representatives of various citizens' groups—e.g., women's groups, aboriginal groups, and minority groups. To the extent that the Charter really works to make ours more of a citizens' constitution, then, it is again consistent with social democratic principles.

## RIGHT-WING CHARTERPHOBIA

Turning next to right-wing Charterphobia, we should note that it, too, was present during the 1981 negotiations in the person of Manitoba Premier Sterling Lyon—"the stubby, irascible, Praetorian guardsman of a vanishing British Canada" (Sheppard and Valpy, 1982: 10–11). Premier Lyon expressed concerns that the Charter would undermine the role of the monarchy in Canada and that it would dictate the behaviour of provincial governments in relation to their religious, ethnic, and ideological minorities. Most importantly, however, he saw entrenched rights as a threat to the doctrine of parliamentary supremacy. In the end, these views held even less sway than did Blakeney's. As we know, Lyon, who had returned to Manitoba to fight a provincial election, suffered the indignity of being shut out, along with Quebec's representatives, of the all-night negotiations that produced a draft agreement for the patriation of the Constitution with a Charter of Rights of Freedoms. Lyon himself went down to electoral defeat and, since then, conservative politicians, like their leftist brethren, have ceased to play leading roles in the anti-Charter movement.

Nowadays one has to look to representatives of right-wing interest groups to find a concerted political attack on the Charter and its values. For example, REAL Women argues that the Charter is being used by feminist group elites promoting their own personal extremist views to force governments to allow abortion, extend rights to same sex couples, provide universal subsidized childcare, and implement pay equity and affirmative action schemes. Many concerns have been raised in the conservative media as well—i.e., that expensive social programs will be forced on governments by courts sympathetic to the needs of various equality-seeking groups (Simpson, 1992). Another fear

is that the "substantive equality" (equality of results) sought by these groups will have to come at public expense and at the costs of the idea that formal rights must be enjoyed equally by all members of society—as Clifford Lincoln would say, that "rights are rights are rights" (Simpson, 1992: 14A).

Of course, many conservative politicians have raised similar concerns about the dangers of an overtly activist court. For instance, Justice Minister Kim Campbell worried that activist Supreme Court justices might force elected politicians to spend public money against their wishes. She fears, moreover, that if courts become unduly activist, and parliaments lose their ability to make key decisions, then politicians will use this as an excuse to abdicate their policy-making responsibilities and leave all difficult or controversial decisions to the courts (Campbell, 1992). Other conservative politicians, especially in the West, adopt the position most forcefully advanced by Reform Party Leader Preston Manning that Canada should have, like the USA, a concept of rights that makes no mention of race, gender, or language. In addition, many right-wing politicians in Canada wish to emulate the American model of individualism and free-enterprise by including a provision for property rights in the Canadian Charter of Rights and Freedoms.

Nevertheless, most conservative politicians today appear to accept the notion that rights and freedoms should be guaranteed and the integrity of the Charter defended. Indeed, Conservative Prime Minister Brian Mulroney has gone on record saying that "the constitution is not worth the paper it is written on"—but not because the Charter places unnecessary limits on the power of elected parliamentarians. On the contrary, the reason for the Prime Minister's outrage is that the Charter goes too far in accommodating the supremacy of Parliament (especially of provincial parliaments) since its infamous "notwithstanding clause" allows for the override of Charter provisions.

Quite the opposite view is expressed by those academics I will call "right-wing Charterphobes." The most powerful figures in this movement are political scientists rather than lawyers, and the most prominent among them are University of Calgary professors Rainer Knopff and F.L. Morton. These two have espoused their views on the Charter separately, collectively, and with other collaborators in recent books, articles, and conference papers (Knopff, 1988, 1989; Morton, 1990, 1991, 1992; Morton, et al., 1990; Morton and Knopff, 1990, 1992); but perhaps the most accessible single source is their new book, *Charter Politics* (1992). It must be noted, however, that in *Charter Politics* Knopff and Morton take considerable pains to subordinate their own views to the general task of clarifying the debates about the Charter. Thus they portray these quarrels in terms of the opposition between "Charterphiles" and "Charter sceptics" (of both the left and right), not between Charterphiles and Knopff and Morton. Nevertheless, they are themselves key participants in the debate they are attempting to clarify, and there can be no doubt that their work should be identified as a Charter critique from the political right.

Knopff and Morton argue that the Charter is neither democratic nor consistent with the traditional liberal respect for the private sphere and limited government. Their principal lines of argument include (1) the idea that the Charter promotes equality at the expense of private liberty and individual rights, and that its implementation involves a massive and unwelcome exercise in "social technology"; (2) the notion that the judiciary has neither the democratic legitimacy nor the political competence to justify its transformation since the introduction of the Charter from an adjudicative body to a policy-making one; and (3) the claim that a "court party" of feminists, civil libertarians, environmentalists, and racial and ethnic minorities have, with the aid of their left-liberal lawyers, used the Charter to advance their own narrow ("special") interests over and against the wishes of the majority and its duly elected servants.

First, the right-wing critique of the Charter is grounded on a theoretical analysis of the shifting meanings of democracy and rights from their classical liberal roots to the present. That is, the original idea of democratic government emphasized political rights and formal equality of individuals, while today's rights advocates have in mind social rights and the equality of group results. In the earlier view, rights would secure a sphere of private liberty invaded only by the few limits on personal action that could be consented to by self-interested individuals in order for them to live as safely as possible. According to this line of thought, inequality of political or legal rights would be prohibited but other forms of inequality

were expected to flourish. Indeed, as the greatest liberal theorists all seemed to agree, the very purpose of government was not to make individuals better or to force them to live in equal conditions, but rather to protect their unequal capacities of acquiring and enjoying property (Knopff, 1989: 17–31).

In contemporary rights theory and practice, however, the terms of the classical liberal equation are reversed—individual liberty is restricted in the name of social equality and the private domain is whittled away in favour of increased public authority. In what Knopff calls "the new war on discrimination," the systemic deficiencies of existing society are attacked by a set of rationalist rules designed to achieve the intellectually derived criteria of "individual treatment" and "equality of result." For Knopff, the irony of the situation is that the language of human rights, originally a bulwark of individual liberty and democracy, has been appropriated by the foes of liberal democracy who use it to deny personal freedom and to suppress democratic decision making (Knopff, 1989: 213).

The argument runs that today's rights enthusiast wish to subject essentially unplanned social processes to a variety of unrealistic and illiberal policy initiatives—e.g., anti-discrimination legislation enforced by human rights commissions, equality provisions entrenched in the Charter, and affirmative action programs. The shared characteristic of these policy developments is their attempt to remake human beings by changing the social environment. According to Knopff, these exercises at "constructivist social technology" are bound to fail since the anti-social tendencies they seek to eradicate are rooted in nature. Consequently, "such projects in social engineering are fundamentally misconceived and the suppression of freedom they require will be permanent, not temporary" (Knopff, 1989: 22).

Moreover, the principal result of entrenching the Charter has been to transfer political power from more accountable democratic institutions to relatively unaccountable judicial and quasi-judicial agencies that are under the sway of a leftist and partisan intellectual elite. That is why Morton and Knopff argue that the Charter is both undemocratic and illiberal. It is undemocratic because it results in a legalized politics that by passes the traditional democratic processes of collective self-government through popular elections and responsible parliamentary government. And it is illiberal to the extent that its "most ardent partisans and practitioners are imbued with an 'unconstrained' vision of politics that is antithetical to the respect for the private sphere and limited government that informs the tradition of constitutionalism" (Morton and Knopff, 1992: 2).

This underpins Knopff's and Morton's second main line of criticism of the Charter—that the triumph of legalized politics means that the courtroom is now more than ever a political arena and that judges are, at least potentially, "politicians in robes." Whether judges will exercise this power to its full potential depends upon how they view their role in the political process. Hence the crucial importance of the debates discussed in *Charter Politics*, i.e., those over the proper balance between judicial "activism" and "self-restraint," as well as over the merits of the leading theories of constitutional interpretation—"interpretivism" and "noninterpretivism."

Although they are not always dogmatic on this point, Knopff and Morton tend to side with restrained interpretivism over noninterpretivist activism. That is, they prefer a court limited to enforcing original or traditional understandings in a restrained manner rather to one that boldly exerts its policy influence in order to keep political institutions relevant in rapidly changing times. It is generally felt that this sort of judicial self-restraint should impede radical policy initiatives or, at least, reduce the possibility that radical policies will be generated by a judiciary itself over-anxious to prescribe political remedies for legal problems. The usual defence of this view is a separation of power argument: there is a division of responsibilities between the executive and legislative branches on the one hand, and the judicial branch on the other; to the extent that judges allow themselves to engage in courtroom politics, they have overstepped their proper authority and become instruments of anti-democratic forces.

Knopff and Morton suggest that violations by the courts of this separation of powers doctrine have been vastly multiplied since the introduction of an entrenched charter. With its vaguely worded provisions, generally open to a variety of interpretations, the Charter rarely involves judges in simply enforcing law-like rights against insensitive governments. Rather,

the judges are now actively involved in making laws, in creating new rights. Hence the Charter has been a catalyst for an unprecedented style of activist judicial review. Courts are no longer content with simply invalidating, and hence delaying (perhaps temporarily), policy decisions by elected representatives. They now feel emboldened to tell the other branches of government what they have to do and how they have to do it. This is problematic for reasons the leftist critics might have advanced themselves: (1) it is undemocratic to have appointed judges trespassing on the policy-making jurisdiction of duly elected politicians, and (2) the judges doing the trespassing have no special competence in resolving difficult social, moral, and political problems.

Knopff and Morton object to both the consequences of an increasingly noninterpretivist activism among judges and to the general belief that helps sustain this practice—i.e., that judges and not politicians are the best oracles of what the law requires. In *Charter Politics*, therefore, Knopff and Morton ponder alternatives to the politics of the oracular courtroom. One possibility would be to restrict judicial decisions to the immediate adjudicative context. Under this scheme, judicial opinions would be persuasive but not binding on other branches of government (Knopff and Morton, 1992: 178–79). Another proposal, one which they seem to endorse more heartily, would see the policy opinions of the judiciary fully integrated into an overtly political system of checks and balances. In this way, one could reject judicial finality without rejecting judicial review (even noninterpretivist activism). One way in which judicial policy-making can be integrated into a system of checks and balances involves what Peter Russell (1982: 32) has called "the legislative review of judicial review." Although a version of this already exists in the override clause (at least for provision in Sections 2 and 7–15), Knopff and Morton point out that the existing Canadian legislative and executive institutions would have to be reformed before they enjoyed the legitimacy necessary for them to act as effective counterweights for the courts (1992: 232–33).

In any case, replacing oracular legalism with a healthy system of checks and balances would have the special merit of discouraging interest groups from using the courtroom as a political arena. If decisions by the courts are no longer final, then interest groups will be less likely to attempt to use the Charter and the courts to circumvent the traditional channels of policy making. Indeed, the fact that so many organized interest have succeeded in doing just this is the third major feature of the right-wing argument against the Charter.

Knopff and Morton argue that "the Charter's main beneficiaries are special interest groups, who invoke it to persuade appointed judges to reverse the decisions of democratically elected representatives" (Knopff and Morton, 1992: 28). In other words, these groups turn to an undemocratic institution to seek victories that eluded them in the normal arena of free and open democratic competition. The Charter, then, rewards losers who whine loudly enough about the importance of their specific rights and entitlements to get a sympathetic hearing in court. Activist judges, meanwhile, will open wide their courtroom doors to these interest group litigants, even those who have no more direct stake in the outcome of the case than the ordinary citizen generally. What is more, courts will hear moot cases when interest groups convince them that the issues posed are of sufficient public importance (Knopff and Morton, 1992: 193).

For Knopff and Morton, the introduction of the Charter has not made ours a more democratic "Citizens' Constitution" but a constitution of special interests. The argument runs that the transfer of power from the legislatures to the courts has promoted the growth of a "court party" in Canadian politics that consists of new citizens' interest groups, state bureaucracies, academics, and media elites (Knopff and Morton, 1992: 79–80; Morton and Knopff, 1992: 6–21). Unlike political parties that participate in elections, the "court party" is a new social movement that prefers the policy-making power of the courts to the democratic world of polling booths and legislatures. The Charter provides the foundation for this "court party" to the extent that it officially recognizes a number of specific groups and interests. Women receive explicit recognition in Sections 15 and 28; racial and ethnic minorities are included in Sections 15 and 27; Section 15 also bestows official status on age-based groups, and on those representing the interest of the mentally or physically handicapped; the rights of minority language groups are enshrined in Sections 16 to 23; and aboriginal interests are recognized in Sections 25 and 35.

The politics of the "court party" involves the calculated attempts by these groups to maintain and expand their visibility and status. The key currency here is explicit recognition as a constitutional category: "Constitutional status gives a group official public status of the highest order, and groups who enjoy it have an advantage impressing their claims against government over groups who do not" (Knopff and Morton, 1992: 82). The self-interest of those groups demands that any who are already in the "Charter club" must seek to exclude other entrants, no matter how politically relevant. And the club members constantly fight amongst themselves for relative power, attempting to construct pecking-orders or hierarchies of constitutionally protected interest that are to their own particular advantage.

Needless to say, this is not a flattering picture of the role in Charter politics played by contemporary citizens' groups. Indeed, they are portrayed as a divisive and potentially undemocratic element in our public life. Yet even right-wing Charterphobes recognize that the formalism of legalized politics and the biases of the judicial process have so far combined to limit the legal victories of feminist, aboriginal, social action, or ethnocultural groups. Still, as Alan Cairns and other have shown, the greatest influence of such groups has been realized in constitutional politics. This, too, is a result of their official recognition as Charter club members—that is, as potentially affected groups they demand involvement in any process that might be consequential for their constitutional fate. According to many right-wing Charter critics, this has a divisive rather than a unifying influence. Thus, in this area at least, the dreams of Charter supporters to forge a national consensus around shared Charter rights is unrealized. Indeed, it may be argued that the very multiplicity of group concerns works against the Charter's intended success at creating a single, unifying Canadian identity.

## REVIEW AND CRITICISM

As we have seen, both left- and right-wing Charterphobes condemn the rise of legalized politics and bemoan the undemocratic consequences of judicial review of the Charter. But as is the case in interpretations of legal decisions, the important part is less the verdict than the reasons behind it. It is here that we find considerable tension between the philosophies underlying these majority concurring decisions.

The bottom line for the legal left is that the Charter is a disaster because it is a liberal document. For these critics, "Liberalism is a failure: it cannot pass conceptual, social, legal, or political muster. A continued reliance on its intellectual assumptions and ideological prescriptions is indefensible" (Petter and Hutchinson, 1988: 295). The immediate need is to abandon liberal individualism and to replace it with some form of social democracy that might be capable of responding to the inequalities of economic and political power that liberalism and its disciples permit and condone. This would entail a real redistribution of power in ways contradicting the logic of the marketplace. It would mean, at a minimum, a significant expansion of the public sector and a contraction of the private sphere (Mandel, 1989: 267).

Needless to say, this is not a prospect to which right-wing Charterphobes look forward with great joys of anticipation. They are more likely to respond, in the spirit of Adam Smith, that a system of private property rights is the best way to channel natural human selfishness into socially useful projects. What is more, intervention by the state on the behalf of groups who are disproportionately at the lower levels of status and class hierarchies is seen by most on the right as a violation of the democratic idea of the formal equality of rights. It should be condemned, as well, for strictly practical reasons: human nature being what it is, success in planning the lives of other people or of society as a whole is likely to be limited.

In any event, the eradication of free market capitalism in Canada does not seem immanent. Hence, right-wing Charterphobes are willing to take their chances that the ideas of Mandel, Petter, and others on the anti-Charter left will fail to capture much of a market share in any free and open democratic competition. What is more troublesome, from their point of view, is the ascendancy of a pro-Charter, left-liberal egalitarian democracy. It is this ideology that Knopff and Morton fear has taken over the legal profession and justified the granting of an unfair advantage to "special" interest groups—groups based more on gender, race, and ethnicity than on class.

But is there any concrete evidence to support these claims? I think not. First, right-wing Charterphobes can point to few cases where their fears have been realized concerning activist judicial review of the Charter forcing governments to spend money against their wishes. Second, recent evidence suggests that we should not exaggerate the audacity of the courts, except perhaps in legal rights cases. After an original spurt of judicial activism, the Supreme Court seems to have settled back to a more comfortable role of simply ensuring that Charter rights are not violated flagrantly. The Court has rather tired of actively challenging governments' decision-making prerogatives. One indication of this is the steep drop in the rate at which the Court has been striking down legislation. It is often pointed out that in its first fifteen Charter decisions the Supreme Court upheld the Charter claim in a staggering nine cases—a 60% success rate for Charter claimants. According to one recent count, however, the Charter success rate fell to 17.5% in 1989–90 (7 out of 40 cases), and to a miniscule 11.8% (2 out of 17) in cases outside criminal law (Eliott: 1992). There might be several reasons for this: the changing nature of cases coming forward; the conservative influence of recent judicial appointments; or a rethinking by the justices themselves of their role in the political process. In any event, the evidence seems to point to a greater acceptance of judicial self-restraint, at least since the *Edwards Books* decision in 1986.

Of course, the numbers may not tell the whole story. The very possibility of negative judicial decisions may be forcing governments to make corrections or assessments prior to the enactment of legislation. Since politicians would inevitable rely upon lawyers within their Justice Departments to carry out these assessments—to make sure that legislation is "Charterproof," to use Patrick Monahan's phrase (1992)—political power may have gravitated towards the technical, legal experts and away from the elected politicians. This means another triumph for legalized politics and raises alarms about democratic legitimacy and policy-making competence similar to those sounded by left- and right-wing Charterphobes.

But is it necessarily a bad thing that governments have learned to double-check their plans against the prevailing values and standards of Charter provisions? Indeed, if politicians cannot convince their own bureaucrats that their policies and programs are sensible, necessary, or otherwise "demonstrably justifiable in a free and democratic society," then perhaps they have no business enacting them, after all. And anyway, the courts are only assessing legislation according to provisions placed in a charter only recently by duly elected governments, governments that have the power to amend those provisions (or to override most of them) in the event of overwhelming popular evidence that this is necessary. Yet Canadian governments have still failed to demonstrate that, when left to themselves, they can be trusted to make sure that their legislation passes Charter standards. This was proved during the three years allotted to them to clean up statutes that might violate Section 15. Few governments made wise use of that time and many found themselves having to react in a near panic situation.

Moreover, even the most progressive gains that have been made in the courts against the will of governments by certain individuals and groups have not, in my mind, come at the expense of any fundamental principles of Canadian democracy. Voting rights for people with disabilities, new rules about sentencing individuals found not guilty by reason of insanity, expansion of the due process rights of alleged perpetrators or incarcerated persons, decriminalization of abortion, rollbacks of pay equity caps, rights to UIC benefits for those over sixty-five, limited expansion of benefits to same sex couples, abolition of discriminatory "spouse in the house rules" for social services—all of these victories for underprivileged individuals and groups enhance, rather than undermine, the democratic character of our society. The fact that they were won in the courts rather than in the legislative arena does not make them any less democratic.

And what about the central component to the right-wing Charterphobic attack—the rise of a "court party"? Here, too, I see little evidence that feminists, anti-racists, multicultural activists, or any other special groups have pursued their social policy agendas in the courts to the disregard of other, more direct, forms of democratic politics. And even if they did, would this not be more of a condemnation of our system of party politics that has shut them out rather than of our legalized Charter politics?

Indeed, the very assumption that there are "special" interest groups that somehow shun the open glare of

the public stage to pursue their narrow interests behind the closed doors of the courtrooms conveys a distorted image of reality. First, it ignores the fact that representatives of disadvantaged individuals and groups have been extremely active for generations in a variety of political forums, though not always successfully. The advent of the Charter has simply increased access to the courts of Canada for a wider range of groups. This only means that now they, too, can approach the courts as a supplement to their other forms of activity, in the exact same way more institutionalized groups—largely business-oriented ones—have done for years. What seems to disturb right-wing Charterphobes most, then, is the types of groups that have now gained access. Yet groups with "special" interests—those from specific provinces or regions—have always been recognized players within federal-provincial relations or federalism jurisprudence. On this score, I fail to see why the narrow focus of regional interest is proper and legitimate, while the same is not true of the shared interest of women or people of colour.

More important philosophically is the argument that special-interest group activity violates democratic ideals. This is said to be so because group or collective rights contradict the formal logic of free competition between equally rights-empowered individuals, and this makes it impossible for the majority will to have the final say on all public issues. Political scientist Iris Young shows how this view assumes the intrinsic value of attaining some sort of "universality of a general will that leaves difference, particularity, and the body behind in the private realms of family and civil life" (Young, 1990: 97). Young demonstrates that this idea of an "impartial general will" is a myth that serves ideological functions by masking the ways in which the particular perspectives of dominant groups claim universality, thus justifying hierarchical decision-making structures. Hence, she argues that the full inclusion and participation of everyone in public discussion requires more than a formally equal right for individual participation—it requires mechanisms for group representation. Social justice and equality for members of disadvantaged groups will only be had, she says, if difference is recognized and affirmed. And this sometimes means the accommodation of special rights that attend to specific group differences in order to undermine oppression and disadvantage (Young, 1989: 117–41). Our Charter certainly does not guarantee that less advantaged groups will be given the means to overcome oppression and inequality. But by recognizing the special needs of those who have historically been targets for discrimination, the Charter helps to prevent at least the worst rights abuses and announces our society's commitment to a certain standard of decency and respect for others. And contrary to the suspicions of some right-wing Charterphobes, it does so without harming unnecessarily the privileges of those already relatively well off in terms of social and economic power.

For the anti-Charter left, of course, the fact that some fundamental rights are protected is not enough. The Charter, they say, recognizes only negative and not positive rights, and its formalism demands that rights protection be applied equally to everyone. Furthermore, whatever marginal utility is derived from rights discourse is perceived by the legal left as being had at the expense of agendas for social reform. So concerned are these scholars that some imaginary future government's progressive social or economic policies might be overturned by conservative judges, that they are willing to allow existing governments to do what ever they want.

This left-wing Charterphobic argument exaggerates, in my view, the disutility of rights in political advancement for disadvantaged groups. It ignores (or at least downplays) the fact of a long history of Canadian legislation against the interest of women, the poor, aboriginals, and racial and ethnic minorities. And its argument that negative rights are disutile, even harmful, trivializes the lived experience of any person or group whose vulnerability has been truly protected by rights. As Patricia Williams, an African American legal scholar, explains: "For the historically disempowered, the conferring of rights is symbolic of all the denied aspects of their humanity: rights imply a respect that places one in the referential range of self and others, that elevates one's status from human body to social being. For blacks, then, the attainment of rights signifies the respectful behaviour, the collective responsibility, properly owed by a society to one of its own" (1991: 153). Williams reminds us that one's sense of empowerment defines one's relation to the law and to rights. Hence, the male white left, already rights-empowered, may feel that rights discourse should be replaced by some

sort of needs discourse that would justify positive state action on behalf of the truly needy. But those who have been historically disempowered may not trust that the replacement of a formal legal rights system by a more informal political one will lead to better outcomes.

A case in point is the debate within aboriginal communities over the utility of Charter rights. Male Native leaders tend to want aboriginal self-governments to be exempt from the Canadian Charter. Representatives of Native women's associations see things differently: "Native women and children need a safeguard against the abuse of power by male leaders and," Gail Stacey Moore says, "until an acceptable alternative is put in place, we insist on having the safeguard of the Charter" (*Globe & Mail* [Toronto], 29 May 1992: A6). One cannot assume that the accommodation of collective or group aspirations will include the protection of significant individual rights. Nor should we assume that the majority of citizens out in the larger world want to overcome sexism, racism, and alienation rather that heartily embrace them. This underscores Williams' sense of the importance of rights: "rights are to law what conscious commitments are to the psyche. This country's worst historical moments have not been attributable to rights *assertion* but to a failure of rights commitment" (1991: 159).

On a more empirical level, as well, the left-wing Charterphobic argument is a poor guide to life in Charterland. As many have pointed out since 1982, the Canadian Charter of Rights and Freedoms includes not just negative individual rights but also a long list of collective rights and some exemptions from rights (Elkins, 1989: 699–716). Without exhausting the list, one could mention "society's rights" as conferred in Section 1; linguistic and minority language education rights; aboriginal and treaty rights; multicultural rights; affirmative action provisions in Sections 6(4) and 15(2); provincial group rights in Sections 38(2) and (3); and the override provision in Section 33. Moreover, the Charter lacks some of the more individualistic concepts found in the American Bill of Rights, most importantly property rights. Consequently, the Charter is not as liberalizing, individualizing, and Americanizing as some critics would suggest.

Still, left-wing Charterphobes have been right to point out that the introduction of the Charter has highlighted some real problems in our legal system: e.g., access to the courts is unequal and judges are unrepresentative of the general population. But is this the fault of the Charter or are these structures the products of social forces and of individuals who want them this way? It is certainly true, for instance, that by making it difficult for all but the economically powerful to access the courts, high litigation costs help to determine how Charter guarantees will be interpreted. This is because vague Charter provisions will only be clarified through a process of judicial interpretation. If the issues and concerns of the wealthy and powerful are given disproportionate attention in the courts, then that will shape and influence the authoritative decisions about the nature and scope of various rights in ways that reflect these vested interests (Petter, 1989: 156–57). Yet governments can make policy decisions that would equalize access either by changing the rules to reduce litigation costs or by providing public funds to allow economically disadvantaged groups to participate in Charter cases as litigants or as interveners. The Court Challenges Program, recently terminated by the Mulroney government, is a very modest example of the latter approach. The crucial point, however, is that decisions about the creation, expansion, and demise of this program were made by elected politicians, the representatives of the many, and not by the few who are judges or lawyers.

What is more, discussions about the high costs of litigation should not overlook the fact that there is also an extremely high cost associated with electoral participation or with non-judicial, interest-group activity. This works to exclude socially and economically disadvantaged individuals and groups from democratic politics just as surely as it does from legalized politics. Likewise, one should not dismiss judicial review because of the unrepresentativeness of judges without looking at the reality of representation in the other two branches of government. In fact, there are more reasons to be optimistic about the possibility of greater representativeness in the judiciary than in Parliament, where the party-centred system continues to create obstacles for the advancement of females and other disadvantaged individuals. For instance, the composition of the judiciary is closely tied to law school populations, and there have been dramatic changes in these institutions: in 1971, only nine percent of law school graduates were women; by 1991, however, a full 51 percent of law students were women. This expanding pool

of female lawyers will no doubt have its effect on the composition of the judiciary in a few years. Moreover, the very fact that so many leftist and feminist scholars are now teaching in law schools bodes well for the future development of a progressive left-liberal orientation in the legal profession.

This brings us to a paradoxical feature of left-wing Charterphobia—it is in many ways the more "conservative" of the two approaches. Left-wing Charterphobes want to "conserve" or "preserve" the parliamentary status quo, partly in order to help protect those practices and attitudes that distinguish Canadian from American political culture. Yet can we assume, as Blakeney and Martin do, that our British-style, parliamentary democratic institutions work well enough as it is? A brief glance at the historical record should dispel any notions that freedom was better protected in the past by parliamentary governments that we can expect it to be by the courts in the future.

The Charter of Rights and Freedoms joins four other instruments that have long been part of our constitutional system: (1) the rule of law; (2) the division of jurisdiction; (3) statutory bills of rights; and (4) the institutions of Parliament. But how effective have these been as rights protectors? The idea that the rule of law is the bulwark that protects us from arbitrary treatment from the executive was brought home dramatically by the case of *Roncarelli* v. *Duplessis* in 1959. But there are few other such dramatic cases. *Reference re Alberta Statutes* (1937) and *Switzman* v. *Elbling* (1957) prove that when courts decide on jurisdictional matters they can also protect rights and freedoms. But these cases were rare and they do not demonstrate that the violation of democratic freedoms would be beyond all legislatures, only provincial ones. Moreover, the federal government's passage of the Canadian Bill of Rights in 1960 did not usher in a bright new dawn of rights enjoyment in this country. Aside from *Drybones* v. *the Queen* (1970), the Supreme Court was notoriously unwilling to strike down legislation even when it was clear that rights or freedoms mentioned in the Bill were being denied. Finally, there is little evidence to suggest that the institutions of Parliament also serve to protect the rights and freedoms of individuals. The party system and the rules of the House of Commons help to make sure that the opposition has little weight as an important sanction against repressive laws, even if it is opposed to them.

## CONCLUSION

In conclusion, then, I remain unconvinced by the recent crop of anti-Charter writers that we have taken the wrong path by adopting an entrenched charter. This does not mean that I think the Charter is perfect, that it cannot be improved upon. Indeed, the response from citizens and interested parties during the so-called "Canada Round" of constitutional negotiations demonstrates that the Charter suffers from several serious omissions. Most importantly, there is a lack of a better recognition that, as self-governing, majority cultures, aboriginals, and Quebeckers have claims to distinct rights that are different in status to claims made by, say, religious or ethnic minorities. The Charlottetown Accord would have addressed some of these concerns by entrenching into the Constitution an inherent right to aboriginal self-government and by recognizing Quebec as a distinct society within Canada. What is more, there has been a concerted effort in recent years to expand the existing list of rights to include some social or economic rights as well. It was more difficult for governments to agree to this change, however, and the Charlottetown Accord included only an unjusticiable provision committing governments to the principle of preserving and developing Canada's social and economic union.

What is more, there are still concerns with the incompatibility between an entrenched charter and a legislative override provision. In fact, the notwithstanding clause—the only Charter provision applauded by both right- and left-wing Charterphobes—remains the most unpopular element of the Charter. Consequently, the Special Joint Committee on a Renewed Canada, the Beaudoin-Dobbie Committee, heard pleas for the dismantling of Section 33 in every city where hearings were held. Representatives from minority groups, in particular, urged that at least Section 15 (1) should be exempted from the clause. With the legislative override still in place, they argued, minorities and other less advantaged Canadians remain inadequately protected from rights abuses. Any changes to this provision would require unanimous provincial consent, however, and knowing that this would be impossible, the drafters of our various constitutional reform packages since 1982 have consistently left out any such change.

In the end, of course, the Charlottetown Accord was rejected in the October 1992 referendum. Crucial to its defeat were the lobbying efforts made by various pro-Charter constituencies, including women's groups, social justice advocates, and groups representing ethnic and racial minorities. Governments that supported the constitutional reforms were consistently put on the defensive, forced to insist that the rights recognized and protected under the Charter would not be infringed or denied by any of the new provisions. Canadians, it would seem, have not only become used to life after the Charter, but recognize the Charter as a valuable and authoritative symbol of this country's commitment to freedom, equality, and human dignity.

I would add, nevertheless, that in spite of all the ink spilled over it, the Charter is only a part of our political system as a whole and its nature and function will be shaped and formed within the same matrix of social and economic forces that influence the other parts of the system. As a result, the Charter has not had a dramatic effect on the distribution of wealth and power or on the lever of social justice in Canadian society, nor should it have been expected to on its own. As Shelagh Day notes: "It doesn't mean that women aren't still being beaten, it doesn't mean that women aren't still earning less than men" (*Victoria Times-Colonist* [Victoria], 12 April 1992: A5). Of course, she is right: we still have children living in poverty; we have rampant racism and homophobia; and we have people with disabilities who are prevented from achieving their full potential or who are not institutionalized when they ought to be.

Still, the constitutional guarantees in the Charter have altered the way Canadians view their relationship with government and the way they argue for change. In my view, this has been for the better. Not only has the Charter given women and other disadvantaged groups access to an additional arena of democratic participation, it has also signalled to those who resist progressive change that they cannot so easily ignore the claims of Charter rights-holders. In this sense, the Charter, by holding out the prospect of attainment of equality or fairness under the law, has been a fiercely motivational force for those who have not always enjoyed much hope. It is for this reason that we must be warned against debasing rights or abandoning the project of rights protection under a charter. "In discarding rights altogether," as Williams points out, "one discards a symbol too deeply enmeshed in the psyche of the oppressed to lose without trauma and much resistance" (1991: 165).

## BIBLIOGRAPHY

Bakan, Joel (1991). "Constitutional Interpretation and Social Change: You Can't Always Get What You Want." In *The Canadian Bar Review*, 70: 307–328.

Cairns, Alan C. (1991). *Disruptions: Constitutional Struggles, from the Charter to Meech Lake*. Ed. Douglas E. Williams. Toronto: McClelland and Stewart.

Campbell, Kim (1992). "Opening Remarks" to the conference "The Charter: Ten Years After." May 15–16. Simon Fraser University at Harbour Centre, Vancouver, BC. In P. Bryden, S. Davis, and J. Russell (eds.), *The Charter: Ten Years After. Essays on the Charter's Place in Canada's Political, Legal and Intellectual Life*. Toronto: University of Toronto Press.

Cheffins, Ronald I. and Patricia A. Johnson (1986). *The Revised Canadian Constitution: Politics as Law*. Toronto: McGraw-Hill Ryerson.

Christian, William and Colin Campbell (1983). *Political Parties and Ideologies in Canada*. 3rd ed. Toronto: McGraw-Hill Ryerson.

Eliott, Robin (1993). "The Effect of the Charter on the Role of the Courts." In P. Bryden, S. Davis, and J. Russell (eds.), *The Charter: Ten Years After. Essays on the Charter's Place in Canada's Political, Legal and Intellectual Life*. Toronto: University of Toronto Press.

Elkins, David J. (1989). "Facing our Destiny: Rights and Canadian Distinctiveness." *Canadian Journal of Political Science* 22: 699–716.

Grant, George (1965). *Lament for a Nation*. Toronto: The Carleton Library No. 50, McClelland and Stewart.

Greunding, Dennis (1990). *Promises to Keep: A Political Biography of Alan Blakeney*. Saskatoon: Western Producer Prairie Books.

Hutchinson, Alan C. (1989). "Determinacy and Democracy: An Essay on Legal Interpretation." In *University of Miami Law Journal* 43: 541–76.

Hutchinson, Alan C. (1991). "Waiting for Coraf (Or the Beatification of the Charter)." In *University of Toronto Law Journal* 41: 332–56.

Knopff, Rainer and F.L. Morton (1992). *Charter Politics*. Scarborough: Nelson.

Knopff, Rainer (1987). "What do Constitutional Equality Rights Protect Canadians Against?" In *The Canadian Journal of Political Science* 20: 265–86.

Knopff, Rainer (1988). "Parliament vs. the Courts: Making Sense of the Bill of Rights Debate." In *Legislative Studies* 3: 2.

Knopff, Rainer (1989). *Human Rights & Social Technology: The New War on Discrimination*. Ottawa: Carleton University Press.

Mandel, Michael (1989). *The Charter of Rights and the Legalization of Politics in Canada*. Toronto: Wall and Thompson.

Martin, Robert (1991). "The Charter and the Crisis in Canada." In *After Meech Lake: Lessons for the Future*. Ed. David E. Smith, Peter MacKinnon, and John C. Courtney. Saskatoon: Fifth House.

Monahan, Patrick (1993). "The Impact of the Charter on Government Policy-Making." In P. Bryden, S. Davis, and J. Russell (eds.), *The Charter: Ten Years After. Essays on the Charter's Place in Canada's Political, Legal and Intellectual Life*. Toronto: University of Toronto Press.

Morton, F.L. (1987). "The Political Impact of the Canadian Charter of Rights and Freedoms." In *The Canadian Journal of Political Science* 20: 31–55.

Morton, F.L. (1990). "Morgantaler vs. The Queen: A Political Analysis." In *A Time for Life, Abortion and Human Rights*. Ed. Ian Gentles. Toronto: Stoddart.

Morton, F.L. (1991). "The Charter Revolution and the Court Party." Paper prepared for "Roundtable Conference on the Impact of the Charter on the Public Policy Process." Centre for Public Law and Public Policy. November 15–16. York University, Toronto Ontario.

Morton, F.L. (1992). "Institutional Retooling: The Evolution of the Supreme Court of Canada from Adjudicator to Policy-Maker." Paper prepared for the Annual Meeting of the Canadian Political Science Association. May 31. University of Prince Edward Island, Charlottetown PEI.

Morton, F.L. and Rainer Knopff (1990). "Permanence and Change in the Written Constitution: The 'Living Tree' Doctrine and the Charter of Rights." In *Supreme Court Law Review*, Second Series 1: 533–46.

Morton, F.L. and Rainer Knopff (1992). "The Supreme Court as the Vanguard of the Intelligentsia: The Charter Movement as Postmaterialist Politics." Research Study 8.1, Occasional Papers Series, Research Unit for Socio-Legal Studies. University of Calgary.

Morton, F.L., G. Soloman, I. McNish, and D.W. Poulton (1990). "Judicial Nullification of Statutes Under the Canadian Charter of Rights and Freedoms." In *Alberta Law Review* 28: 396–425.

Petter, Andrew (1986). "The Politics of the Charter." In *Supreme Court Law Review* 8: 473–505.

Petter, Andrew (1987). "Immaculate Deception: The Charter's Hidden Agenda." In *The Advocate* 45: 857–66.

Petter, Andrew (1989). "Canada's Charter Flight: Soaring Backwards into the Future." In *Journal of Law and Society* 16: 151–65.

Petter, Andrew and Alan C. Hutchinson (1988). "Private Rights/Public Wrongs: The Liberal Lie of the Charter." In *University of Toronto Law Journal* 38: 278–97.

Petter, Andrew and Alan C. Hutchinson (1989). "Rights in Conflict: The Dilemma of Charter Legitimacy." In *UBC Law Review* 23: 531–48.

Petter, Andrew and Alan C. Hutchinson (1990). "Daydream Believing: Visionary Formalism and the Constitution." In *Ottawa Law Review* 22: 365–85.

Russell, Peter H. (1982). "The Effect of the Charter of Rights and Freedoms on the Policy-Making Role of Canadian Courts." In *Canadian Public Administration* 25: 1–33.

Russell, Peter H. (1983). "The Political Purposes of the Canadian Charter of Rights and Freedoms." In *The Canadian Bar Review* 61: 30–54.

Sheppard, Robert and Michael Valpy (1982). *The National Deal: The Fight for the Constitution*. Toronto: Fleet Books.

Simpson, Jeffrey (1993). "Rights Talk: The Discourse of the 1990s." In P. Bryden, S. Davis, and J. Russell (eds.), *The Charter: Ten Years After. Essays on the Charter's Place in Canada's Political, Legal and Intellectual Life*. Toronto: University of Toronto Press.

Smiley, Donald (1983). "A Dangerous Deed: The Constitution Act, 1982." In *And No One Cheered: Federalism, Democracy and the Constitution Act*. Ed. Keith Banting and Richard Simeon. Toronto: Methuen.

Williams, Patricia J. (1991*). The Alchemy of Race and Rights*. Cambridge: Harvard University Press.

Young, Iris Marion (1989). "Polity and Group Differences: A Critique of the Ideal of Universal Citizenship." In *Feminism and Political Theory*. Ed. Cass R. Sunstein. Chicago & London: University of Chicago Press.

Young, Iris Marion (1990). *Justice and the Politics of Difference*. Princeton: Princeton University Press.

## Part Seven
# Minority Rights and Constitutional Renewal

MINORITIES CAN BE construed in different ways be they territorial or non-territorial. The last forty years, but the last two decades especially, have been shaped by the rise of the West. The excerpt by Roger Gibbins and Loleen Berdahl is the starting point for the final section of the book. Although only a few pages in length, this selection offers significant insights not only into Western perspectives but also into issues concerning municipalities, which have been the subject of a great deal of attention in recent years. As it turns out, different regions of Canada commiserate in feeling marginalized and misunderstood by the Rest of Canada. Gibbins and Berdahl explain both "why the West wants in" and "what the West wants." In the process, they discuss the significance of cities both to the West and to Canadian federalism. For anyone who has ever wondered why the North is dotted with territories rather than provinces, Robertson explains the rationale and actually cautions against provincehood for the Northern Territories. To those who wonder how the *Constitution Act, 1982* could possibly have been so profoundly alienating for Quebec, Rémillard explains Quebec's version of events in a way that only someone who was as intimately involved with renegotiating the Constitution on Quebec's behalf, as he was, can. With the Meech and Charlottetown Accords having failed, is there more mega-constitution making yet to come? Roderick Macdonald posits a tentative yet reasoned answer to this enduring question in his essay included here.

If, for now at least, Canada is done with mega-constitutional politics, that does not mean that all grievances have been settled; far from it. Time and again the Supreme Court of Canada has emerged as the final arbiter on fundamental constitutional disputes. Conscious of the divisive nature of these disputes and with a keen eye on the need for their decisions to be deemed legitimate by the parties involved, Sujit Choudhry and Robert Howse examine how Canadian judges strike a balance between competing imperatives. The Supreme Court has made a significant contribution to clarifying and enunciating Canada's key constitutional principles. The selection by John Borrows reflects on similar concerns, but does so from an Aboriginal legal perspective. Aboriginal perspectives on the constitution are explored further with a piece that situates Aboriginal communities' greatest single ongoing grievance within the constitutional debate: treaty rights. As Brian Slattery explains, the legal landscape in this area is extremely complex, given the variety of agreements between First Nations and Indigenous peoples on the one hand, and the Crown on the other hand.

The reader concludes with a reflection by Peter H. Russell on how and why Canada continues to succeed where so many other countries fail. His conclusion is that Canada successfully reconciles different and competing constitutional demands in a deeply diverse society. After all, Canadian constitutional politics does not just inform Canadian students; it has attracted the attention of scholars and practitioners from around the world who are interested in learning from the Canadian constitutional experience.

## 34

### Authors' Introduction

In the early 2000s, many Western Canadians and their provincial politicians were expressing strong discontent with the federal government. As Roger Gibbins and I wrote in the introduction to *Western Visions, Western Futures*, "In 2001, the West saw the establishment of the Alberta Independence Party, public arguments for provincial 'firewalls,' and a seemingly endless number of radio programs, editorial commentary and newspaper opinion pieces voicing feelings of regional discontent with the federal system and the federal government" (2003, 4).

Regional discontent in Western Canada was certainly not a new phenomenon; indeed, Western Canadian grievance with the federal government has a long history. But this outpouring of grievance in the early 2000s was striking given the relative success and prosperity of the region. Thus, in our book we asked, "What does the West want?"

A persistent theme emerging from Western Canadian discussions about the federal government has been the desire for institutional reform. Over the decades, Western Canadian voices have floated a number of reform options, including increased direct democracy, reduced federal encroachment on areas of provincial jurisdiction, and Senate reform. In the following excerpt, Roger Gibbins and I consider institutional reform in light of the political realities of policy interdependence and multilevel governance in the twenty-first century.

Source: Roger Gibbins, and Loleen Berdahl, "Western Canadian Perspectives on Institutional Reform: Introduction and Context," in *Western Visions, Western Futures: Perspectives on the West in Canada* (Toronto: University of Toronto Press, 2003), 191–201.

Roger Gibbins and Loleen Berdahl

# Western Canadian Perspectives on Institutional Reform: Introduction and Context

## INSTITUTIONAL REFORM

If the Government of Canada is to function effectively in an environment of multi-level governance and policy interdependence, it needs political and institutional sensitivity to regional, provincial, and municipal interests. The existing government is ill-equipped in this respect, and the shortcomings are multitudinous: an antiquated Senate shorn of any legitimacy as a regional chamber, the lack of a cabinet or bureaucratic interface with municipal governments, regionally unbalanced political parties, party discipline that inhibits the expression of regional interests, and a parliamentary system that increasingly concentrates political power in the hands of the prime minister. In short, the federal government is not prepared for the new governance environment; it lacks the institutional dexterity and agility that federalism should instill.

Any discussion of regional prosperity in an interdependent world, therefore, inevitably loops back to the thorny issue of institutional reform. Certainly this is the case in western Canada where a lack of confidence in the neutrality of the federal government continually threatens to derail effective multi-level governance. It is difficult to move ahead when confidence in both parties is absent.

Western Canadian discussions of institutional reform generally start, and unfortunately often end, with Senate reform. How do we explain this fixation? Why not tackle the dominant parliamentary institution, the House of Commons? Why not concentrate on party discipline within the House, on the closed nature of decision-making in national institutions, on the growing concentration of power in the hands of the prime minister? Part of the answer is that the Canadian Senate is such a clear exception among federal systems across the world; no other democratic federal state has an upper house staffed by federal government appointees—actually prime ministerial appointees—with no input from the governments or citizens of the provinces they are deemed to represent. (Senators are appointed by the prime minister of the day and serve until age 75.) Other federal states use their upper chambers to articulate rather than ignore federal principles, to provide territorial representation that complements and supplements representation by population in the lower house. The Canadian Senate is all but impossible to explain, much less defend, to international or, for that matter, national audiences.

Perhaps a large part of the answer for the concentration of the reform impetus on the Senate is that the Senate is a relatively easy target. Senators lack much in the way of public credibility; they are seen, not without reason, as individuals reaping the financial rewards for service to the governing party of the day they were appointed. No one will come to the defense of the Senate, whereas the House has proven to be a very effective defender of institutional arrangements that often seem out of date. Moreover, as we will see in the conclusion to this section, Senate reform is the best trigger to pull in order to initiate other forms of parliamentary reform.

What, then, are the principles that western Canadians would like to see embedded within a reformed Senate? The following reflect a strong regional consensus:

1. Senators should be elected. Western Canadians display no enthusiasm whatsoever for the present method of Senators appointed by the prime minister and have expressed little more enthusiasm for Senators appointed by provincial governments. Election is a consensual value, one very much in step with the democratic spirit of the times and the democratic face that Canada tries to project to the international community. There is, however, no consensus on, and little public discussion of, the specific means by which Senators might be elected.

2. The Senate should have some autonomous field of action, some policy leverage that is not subject to override by the House of Commons.

3. This said, western Canadians would also prefer a parliamentary order in which the House of Commons was the primary legislative assembly.

4. The Senate should provide some counterweight to the principle of representation by population in the House of Commons.

These conditions could be met by the Triple E model that dominates Senate reform discussions in the West—a Senate based on direct popular election, equality of representation for the provinces, and some significant measure of legislative influence. However,

## Interstate and Intrastate Federalism

Political scientists draw a useful distinction between *interstate* and *intrastate* federalism, terms that refer to different ways in which provincial residents connect to their federal government. Interstate representation refers to indirect methods of representation that take place through provincial governments. A resident of Saskatoon, for example, may count on the Saskatchewan government to represent, advance, and protect her interests through the intergovernmental forums in which the Government of Saskatchewan participates. (Interstate federalism can also refer to the constitutional division of powers, which can shield provincial residents from the actions of the national government, but this meaning is less relevant here.) In other words, she channels her representation through the provincial government, which speaks on her behalf and can be held accountable for so doing. In the future, cities such as Saskatoon may also play a role in this respect. Intrastate representation refers to representation that takes place directly through federal politicians rather than indirectly through provincial (or municipal) politicians. MPs and Senators are the primary routes for intrastate federalism. Most of the institutional reform debate in western Canada focuses on the inadequacies of intrastate federalism—on the failure of MPs, Senators, and cabinet representatives to provide effective and transparent channels for regional representation.

it is not clear that strict provincial equality would serve western Canadian interests well. It would provide tremendous leverage for Atlantic Canada's four provinces, home to only 7.6 per cent (and falling) of the national population; Atlantic Canada would have a slightly smaller proportion of the new Senators, but those individuals would yield much more clout than do their existing counterparts. However, an equal Senate would do less for Alberta, with 9.9 per cent of the national population, and British Columbia with 13.0 per cent.[1] There is, then, some room for negotiation with respect to provincial equality, whereas there is no room on the principle of direct popular election.

Senate reform is important in its own right as it would provide a check on the power of the prime minister and cabinet, and a counterweight to representation by population. A reformed Senate would add some badly needed institutional muscle to the federal nature of Canada. Senate reform, however, could also trigger other much-needed reforms. A different election format for the Senate might stimulate interest in electoral reform for the House of Commons. A reformed Senate might lead to parliamentary reforms designed to enhance the status of MPs and reduce the weight of party discipline in the House. As William Thorsell argues:

> Whatever the odds of success, the next great Canadian cause should be reform of our electoral and parliamentary systems to require much more negotiation among political persuasions and regions through the life of any parliament. Our zero-sum democracy needs to move to a 60-40 democracy, where majorities prevail only after having to respond to other interests and opinions. The process of politics between elections must be meaningful if the elections are to be meaningful—and if Canada is to be claimed by all its people. Through its direct spending power, meanwhile, the federal government should assume a much higher profile in the lives of ordinary Canadians where they live—in cities and suburbs in every region, even the prosperous ones. Calgary won't mind.[2]

The point to stress is that the higher federal government profile that Thorsell recommends can be brought about only if it is wedded to, in fact preceded by, meaningful institutional reform.

At first glance, and indeed at second and third glance, the prospects for institutional change appear to be bleak. There is apparently little appetite in the country for constitutional change, and it is difficult to go very far down the institutional reform path without running up against the need for constitutional change. However, the prospects may not be as remote as is often assumed. The institutional reform debate could break open for a number of reasons:

1. The independence movement could rise again in Quebec. Perhaps more likely, the election of a federalist government in Quebec could re-open the debate about a renewed federalism.

2. Debates about continental integration could bring institutional reform into play.

3. We could confront a democratic crisis in the Senate, perhaps where an incoming Canadian Alliance government confronts a Senate in which it has no representation. In such a scenario, it would be foolish to expect the Liberal-dominated Senate to acquiesce to the legislative agenda brought forward by an Alliance government. At some point we will see a change of government in Ottawa, and at that point the new government will confront a Senate in which the Liberal majority will have been entrenched for a generation.

4. We may have constitutional change forced upon us by developments with respect to Aboriginal self-government, by the northern territories' quest for provincial recognition, by the push from the cities for constitutional recognition, or by a crisis with the Royal Family in Britain.

5. Continuing regional cleavages within the party system may impede effective government in Canada to the point where the risks of undertaking constitutional change become tolerable.

6. Senate reform may reappear on the agenda of national political parties.

7. Canadians at large, and western Canadian in particular, may grow to be fed up with political institutions that are so badly out of step with our understanding of democracy in the twenty-first century.

It would be foolish, therefore, to dismiss the long term prospects for fundamental constitutional and

## Paradox of Constitutional Change

Canada's troubled history with constitutional reform carries two important messages. The first is that western Canadian discontent is not sufficient to ignite or drive constitutional change. Perhaps because that discontent is never linked to a credible separatist threat, it is neither a necessary nor sufficient condition for a national debate on constitutional reform. Witness, for example, the lack of any progress on the Senate reform file. The constitutional reform process is driven by discontent in Quebec, which is a necessary and, when linked to a credible separatism threat, a sufficient condition. However, the second message is that although Quebec rather than the West drives the process, the *results* do not necessarily reflect the constitutional aspirations or even interests of Quebec. The 1982 Constitution Act bears a much closer resemblance to western Canadian constitutional visions than it does to the constitutional visions in Quebec, federalist or sovereigntist, that prevailed in the late 1970s and early 1980s. Western Canadians never speak of the "betrayal" of the 1982 Constitution Act.

institutional reform even though at present there appears to be little public appetite. Such reform has been accomplished by other countries, and there is no reason to believe that Canada will remain forever a backwater with respect to the currents of democratic reform found throughout the western world. For example, Australia, Britain, and New Zealand have all achieved, or are contemplating, institutional reforms equal in magnitude to Senate reform in Canada. It is important, therefore, to have an understanding of what might be done should the opportunity arise. History tells us that it is unlikely that the West could create or drive a national institutional reform agenda—the impetus, as always, is more likely to come from Quebec—but western Canadians should be ready when opportunity next presents itself. Although any drive for constitutional change is more likely to focus on democratic reform than on enhancing regional representation—such as reigning in the powers of the prime minister and the Prime Minister's Office and addressing the election of unchecked majority governments by a minority of the electorate—there is no reason why issues of regional representation could not be included in the reform agenda.

It is also important that regional discussions of institutional and constitution reform look forward as well as back. While the flaws of existing parliamentary institutions should be addressed, attention must be paid to the effective incorporation of Aboriginal peoples and the northern territories. Perhaps of even greater importance, Canadians must address the constitutional and institutional standing of the metropolitan centres that are increasingly dominating Canadian life.

### URBAN SITES FOR MULTI-LEVEL GOVERNANCE

It is difficult to go very far in any discussion of policy interdependence and multi-level governance without running smack into Canadian cities. Canada is a highly urbanized country, and nowhere is this more true than in the West. Calgary's population, for example, now exceeds that of any of the Atlantic provinces, and the population of metropolitan Vancouver at the time of the 2001 Census was equivalent to 86 per cent of the total Atlantic population. The cities, it should be stressed, carry more than numerical clout. They are widely recognized as the primary drivers of the new, knowledge-based economy, the incubators for human capital, centres for the arts, and magnets for international immigration. The health and vitality of Canada's major metropolitan areas will be a key determinant of our success in global competition. As a consequence, urban affairs can only climb on the nation's political agenda in the years to come, something that has been recognized by the Prime Minister's Caucus Task Force on Urban Affairs and by the prominence of urban affairs within the platforms of federal parties, with the Canadian Alliance being a puzzling exception.

## A Parliament for Western Canada?

One of the more creative—and radical—proposals for constitutional change has come from Wayne Eyre, a Saskatoon writer and editor.[3] Eyre has proposed a "loose east-west confederation within the larger Canadian dominion with one Parliament in Ottawa, another in the West." The existing Parliament in Ottawa would continue to exercise jurisdiction over such matters as defence, foreign policy, and macro-economic policy, while provincial governments in the West would be folded into the regional parliament, modeled in principle along the lines of the new legislative assemblies in Scotland and Wales. As Eyre suggests, "Western Canada would become analogous to Scotland; Ottawa, to Westminster; Canada, to the U.K." Home rule for the West would facilitate legislation that would "better reflect western sensibilities and priorities." As a consequence, "western alienation would evaporate; easterners would continue on, happy in Ottawa-land."

At the very least, a western Parliament would provide an institutional vehicle for addressing pan-regional issues. However, the abolition of existing provincial governments would certainly be seen by most western Canadians as a step too far.

The emerging urban agenda is both large and complex. It embraces financial resources and taxation tools, urban infrastructure, the continued vitality of the arts communities, immigrant absorption, and multiculturalism. At times, it embraces a robust debate on the potential constitutional recognition of cities. In the context of the present discussion, however, the important point to note is that cities already are sites for multi-level governance. The programs of not only municipal governments but also the provincial and federal governments have an immediate impact on the health and international competitiveness of Canadian cities. Municipal governments are necessarily engaged with their provincial and federal counterparts, and the intensity of this engagement will increase. Whether this will necessitate some adjustment in the constitutional and institutional configuration of the Canadian federal state is still open to question.[4] However, what is not open to question is that the cities will provide the primary test in the years ahead for Canada's capacity to handle policy interdependence and multi-level governance.

The emergence of an urban agenda poses some significant challenges for western Canada. It cannot be assured, for example, that a national urban strategy articulated through the existing political parties and parliamentary institutions will give full weight to the urban character of western Canada. There is a risk it may boil down to a Montreal/Toronto strategy, one that equates the renewal of the Toronto waterfront and the

economic competitiveness of Montreal as synonymous with the national interest. An urban agenda could also become entangled with the east/west divide within the West, with most of the urban growth occurring in Alberta and British Columbia. Finally, and by no means least, the urban agenda brings into bold relief the more precarious demographic, economic, and social status of the rural West. As George Melnyk explains, cities were seen as a blight on traditional images of the West:

> The attempt to exclude urban life from the image of the West is rooted in a deep anti-urban bias that runs through our heritage and has its roots as far back as Roman times, when the city was portrayed as a source of intrigue, decadence and indulgence, while the countryside was heralded as the home of virtue. Christian religious fundamentalism enhanced this attitude by denouncing cities as the sources of sin, where temptation and vice lurked for the unwary innocents from the countryside. This bias imprinted itself on the prairie mind. Not only were prairie cities full of dangers, but they were also derivative, nothing more than the re-creations of nineteenth-century Eastern Canadian cities. There was nothing original here, just a carbon copy of what was already established elsewhere. The soul of the West was in the countryside.[5]

While this may not be an easy orientation to shake, shake it we must, for as Melnyk concludes, "the city

## Urban Aboriginal Policy

An excellent example of the complexities of multi-level governance and the realities of policy interdependence comes from the set of policies and programs now in place for Aboriginal peoples living in western Canada's major urban centers. Both the federal and provincial governments are active with programs of universal application but of direct relevance for Aboriginal residents, with general programs whose delivery is tailored in part for Aboriginal peoples, and with programs designed explicitly for Aboriginal peoples.[6] Municipal governments are also active with respect to policing, cultural policies, recreational activities, and homeless shelters. School boards may have special programs and facilities, and regional health authorities attempt to respond to the particular dynamics of Aboriginal health. In some cases, neighbouring First Nations governments provide outreach services for their residents living in urban environments. And, as a final complication, many government programs are delivered through Aboriginal and non-Aboriginal not-for-profit organizations. To say that the maze of policies, programs, responsibilities, and funding is complex only begins to capture the labyrinth within which urban Aboriginal Canadians function. At the same time, to argue that only one government should handle this difficult file is to ignore the realities of policy interdependence. All governments *are* involved whether they like it or not.

is the technological hub of cyberspace, the new geography of the twenty-first century, and it is this geography that is transforming who and what we are."[7] It is more than time for the "soul of the West" to move to the urban heartland.

## NOTES

1 Equality of representation would make no sense for the northern territories. Nonetheless, these rapidly evolving political communities would have to be incorporated in a reformed Senate.

2 William Thorsell, "It's time to tackle the next great Canadian cause," *The Globe and Mail* 25 March 2002: A15.

3 Wayne Eyre, "A bonnie West awaits," *The Vancouver Sun* 16 May 2001: A15.

4 For a detailed discussion of this point, see Denis Wong, *Toward Urban Renaissance: Addressing Intergovernmental Structures for Western Canada's Cities* (Calgary, AB: Canada West Foundation, 2002).

5 George Melnyk, *New Moon at Batoche: Reflections on the Urban Prairie* (Banff, AB: The Banff Centre Press, 1999) 89.

6 Calvin Hanselmann, *Urban Aboriginal People in Western Canada: Realities and Policies* (Calgary, AB: Canada West Foundation, 2001); Calvin Hanselmann, *Enhanced Urban Aboriginal Programming in Western Canada* (Calgary, AB: Canada West Foundation, 2002).

7 Melnyk 101.

# 35

## Editor's Introduction

Many people wonder why the territories are not provinces and why Canada has territories to begin with. In this chapter from a long out-of-print book, Gordon Robertson explains that territorial aspirations for province-hood are born out of a profound misunderstanding of the difference between provinces and territories. The piece proceeds to spell out those differences. Robertson should know. He was, after all, one of Canada's most distinguished and decorated civil servants with a career in public service spanning more than half a century, including his close involvement in constitutional politics throughout the 1960s and 1970s in senior federal civil service positions, including as Clerk of the Privy Council and Secretary to Cabinet, and Secretary to Cabinet for Federal–Provincial Relations. Prior to these appointments, he had spent ten years as Commissioner of the Northwest Territories. Robertson's long-time expertise in federal–provincial relations and his extensive first-hand experience of the North give him privileged insights into governance in this remote part of the country.

Source: Gordon Robertson, "The Holy Grail," in *Northern Provinces: A Mistaken Goal* (Montreal: Institute for Research on Public Policy, 1985), 21–40.

Gordon Robertson

# The Holy Grail: Provincial Status

THE COMMON ASSUMPTION that provincial status should be the objective for the territories ignores the problems which the attainment of that status would almost certainly create. Such problems would become apparent at once if provincial status were to be sought at an early date. Even if that status is not pursued in the near future, its retention as the preferred objective is likely to impose serious constraints on innovative and unusual political structures that might best suit the circumstances of a territory. Such structures, reflecting the particular ethnic, cultural, or economic conditions of areas that are unique in Canada, are not likely to conform to our conventional provincial patterns of government.

In general, provincial status seems to have been accepted as the objective simply because it has been the normal means by which self-government has been established and authenticated in Canada in the past. The status as such has rarely been analysed to determine just what it involves, what the problem of attainment might be, and whether it would in fact fit the special conditions that prevail in the North. Moreover, it seems that no comprehensive examinations exist of the alternative possibility: that everything important for the North, including full self-government and a share in the control over and revenues from resource development, could be achieved without provincial status.

What does provincial status involve?

From a long association with federal-provincial relations I would suggest that it involves three things: a constitutional regime, a financial regime, and "membership in a club"—the federal-provincial club.

## THE CONSTITUTIONAL REGIME

The constitutional regime for provinces comprises two elements: status and powers.

The status is the essence of federalism—the existence of two orders of government, one central and the other state or provincial, each government with its own basis in a written constitution, with a constitutionally defined role and with protection for its authority and powers guaranteed by an independent judicial authority. The powers of the two orders are laid down in the constitution of the federation, in our case largely in Sections 91 and 92 of the British North America Act, now called the Constitution Act, 1867. Other sections, and a new Section 92A enacted in the Constitution Act, 1982 confirming resource jurisdiction for the provinces, round out the lists. Clashes over which government has the power to legislate in particular circumstances have been frequent. The Judicial Committee of the Privy Council before 1949 and the Supreme Court of Canada since 1949 have had the final word.

What is the difference between the constitutional regime for the provinces and the one that applies to our two present territories? The difference today is more in status than in powers.

The powers of the two territories are not set out in the Constitution. They are set out in two federal statutes: the Yukon Act and the Northwest Territories Act. In substance, those powers are very much the same as the powers of a province under Section 92 of the Constitution Act, 1867, with one major and a few minor exceptions. The greatest difference, as indicated earlier, is in the ownership of Crown lands and the control over natural resources. These belong to the federal government and are administered by it. In all provinces the Crown lands are the property of the province. Each province has jurisdiction over the resources within its territory.

No other difference in powers looms large. The Attorney General of Canada directs criminal proceedings in the territories; provincial attorneys general do so in the provinces. A few other differences of detail relate to health services, specific roads, and other matters. None is significant.

In the exercise of powers, changes in the past fifteen years have made the territorial governments operate very like those in the provinces. The commissioner is almost indistinguishable from a lieutenant governor in Yukon and nearly so in the Northwest Territories. The Legislative Assemblies are composed entirely of elected representatives of the people—sixteen in Yukon and twenty-four in the Northwest Territories. The assemblies elect the commissioners' advisers—the Executive Councils, on which the commissioner does not sit in Yukon but on which he does in the Northwest Territories. Those executive bodies must have the confidence of their Legislative Assemblies to continue in office. They are essentially like provincial cabinets, although in the Northwest Territories the absence of a system of political parties at the territorial level removes the element of party discipline that makes for cohesion within the provincial bodies. There is no premier, but rather a Leader of the

Government in each territory. The system is largely the kind of responsible parliamentary government that is traditional and familiar in Canada.

On the question of status the position is vastly different. Neither the powers of the governments nor their methods of operation have a constitutional base. The federal enactments that list the powers are out of date. They set out a system of administering the powers that is totally different from the one described above. The Yukon Act and the Northwest Territories Act legally vest the powers of government in the commissioners, say nothing of an Executive Council whose advice must be taken, and suggest comprehensive ministerial control from Ottawa. It is on that power of control that the whole system rests today. Instructions from the minister to the commissioners, and nothing more formal or more enduring, have changed the systems from those of undemocratic colonies to the parliamentary democracies of today. Neither constitution nor law provides any guarantee or protection for the status that now exists.

## THE FINANCIAL REGIME

At Confederation in 1867 the financial regime that was established for the provinces was quite simple, which is not surprising since government then was so limited in scale. The new federal government created in 1867 took over the debts of the federating colonies. The colonies became provinces, and they were to finance their operations by direct taxation plus some grants from the federal government. Those grants were spelled out, for purposes of finality, in the Constitution itself.

With superb optimism the constitutional provision stated, "Such grants shall be in full Settlement of all future Demands on Canada." As the Rowell-Sirois Report put it, "great efforts were made to freeze them [i.e., the provincial subsidies] at the 1867 amounts."[1] The effort was futile. In fact, the first adjustment came only two years later, in 1869, to help quell dissatisfaction in Nova Scotia. An amendment of the British North America Act in 1907 and several other revisions in the following years adjusted the grants. They had initially provided a substantial part of provincial revenues—over 50 per cent in 1868 and still nearly 40 per cent in 1890—because other provincial revenue sources were then so limited. As the provinces developed new methods of raising money, however, their dependence on federal transfers diminished. By 1930 only 10 per cent of their funds came from the federal government. That reliance on what the provinces could raise by themselves was satisfactory as long as their economies were buoyant, but the depression of the 1930s and the disastrous drought of those years in the Prairies made clear the inadequacies in the system. The near bankruptcy of some provinces led to the appointment of the Royal Commission on Dominion-Provincial Relations (the Rowell-Sirois Commission). Its report in 1940 is the intellectual basis of the very different financial regime of today. The commission's essential recommendation was for a system of "national adjustment grants" to make it purpose [sic] transfers and equalization transfers.

Specific purpose transfers to the provinces pay a substantial part of the costs of social security programs, most of them established since the Second World War. The programs include health and hospital insurance, post-secondary education, welfare under the Canada Assistance Plan, and other matters much smaller in scale. These transfers go to all provinces. In fiscal year 1985–1986 they amount to $20.9 billion.

The principle enunciated by the Rowell-Sirois Commission has gone through intense scrutiny, repeated negotiation, and the most meticulous refinement every five years since it was put into practice in 1957. The importance of the concept of equalization is reflected in the fact that it is now entrenched in our Constitution.

Section 36(2) of the Constitution Act, 1982, commits the federal Parliament and government "to the principle of making equalization payments to ensure that provincial governments have sufficient revenues *to provide reasonably comparable levels of public services at reasonably comparable levels of taxation*" (emphasis added).

The virtue of the concept is equalled only by the difficulty of the task. It would be extraordinarily difficult to achieve any objective or measurable comparison of "levels of public services." It would be even more difficult to get any agreement as to whether the administration in a specific province is efficient and economical or whether unduly high costs are the result of waste or extravagance. Such questions and judgements would be essential if payments depended directly on the extent of services in different provinces or on what those services appeared to cost. As a result, no attempt has ever been made to compare standards of service, to investigate the true cost of services under any provincial administration, or to focus on the "needs" of a government.

What one *can* measure objectively without becoming involved in the auditing of provincial accounts or in the assessment of their administrations is *how much a given level of taxation yields* in a province as compared with other provinces or with some national average. In other words, it is possible to determine how much money a tax on a person in, say, Newfoundland will provide to the provincial government there as compared with the amount the same tax would provide, per person, in Canada as a whole. If the tax yields less in Newfoundland (as it does), the taxpayers of that province would have to be taxed more heavily to make the same amount of money available for their public services than would the taxpayers of, say, Ontario or Alberta. They could not, on their own, have "comparable levels of public services" available to them "at reasonably comparable levels of taxation." This is accordingly the basis on which equalization has always worked. The key question is the *tax yield per capita* in a province, not the cost of services.

The per capita tax yield of twenty-nine revenue sources in each province is now the calculation that determines whether a province receives equalization. The yield in each province is compared with what is called the "representative average standard." If the yield in a province is *less* than that "average," the province receives equalization to bring it up to the average. At present six provinces receive these transfers: the four Atlantic provinces, Quebec, and Manitoba. In the current fiscal year, 1985–1986, the total amount to be provided comes to $5.1 billion.[2]

In addition to equalization a few other general purpose transfers will provide another $827 million to the provinces in 1985–1986.

The equalization part of the federal-provincial regime constitutes the big difference between the financial system that applies to the provinces and that which applies to the two territories. The territories have, in general, the same powers to raise revenues as the provinces do. The main exception is that, because they do not own the resources of their region, they cannot now impose taxes or royalties on resource development or production. The territories also receive specific purpose transfers from the federal government on much the same basis as the provinces do. The estimate of these transfers for 1985–1986 is $105.2 million. The territories *do not*, however, receive equalization. Indeed, if the equalization standard now used were applied to the territories *they would not qualify to receive it at all.*

Instead of equalization, each territory has thus far received from the federal government a grant to make up the difference between, on the one hand, the total of the revenues it could raise itself, plus federal transfers for specific programs, and, on the other hand, the total expenditures budgeted for the following fiscal year. Because the grant is designed to cover the difference between revenues and expenditures—the prospective deficit—it has usually been referred to as a "deficit grant." It has covered, year by year, inadequacies of revenue to meet expenditures both for operations and for capital purposes. No such deficit grant exists for any province.

The deficit grant brought the federal government into an examination of territorial affairs in order to get agreement on the program of expenditure for each territory in each year. It also operated as a deterrent to territorial efforts to increase their revenues by their own efforts since whatever they raised in additional tax revenue they would lose from their deficit grant. Because of these two problems the report of the Honourable C.M. Drury in January 1980 recommended a new method of calculating the grant. This recommendation has, in its essentials, been accepted. Instead of being determined a year at a time, the grant for each territory, starting with the fiscal year 1985–1986, will rely on a base year in which a deficit grant was established in the old manner. The total revenues of each territory in the base year will be adjusted by means of an "escalator" related to changes in the level of provincial and municipal expenditures in the country as a whole.[3] This will eliminate both of the problems in the old system. Although the method of calculation is new, the basis of the grant remains

the amount needed to cover the territorial deficit at a point of time with annual, but now arithmetically objective, adjustment. It is still a deficit grant, and still something no province receives.

### The Extent of the Difference

The profound difference between the results of the equalization plan for the provinces and the deficit grant system for the territories is indicated in the following table, which shows the amount of the respective grants received as a percentage of the total revenues of the six provinces receiving equalization and of the corresponding revenues of the two territories:[4]

*Equalization Payments as a Percentage of Provincial Gross General Revenues*

|  | 1982–1983 | 1983–1984 | 1984–1985 |
|---|---|---|---|
| Newfoundland | 29.8% | 25.9% | 26.2% |
| Prince Edward Island | 30.5 | 28.9 | 28.5 |
| Nova Scotia | 26.5 | 23.4 | 22.3 |
| New Brunswick | 27.7 | 22.7 | 22.0 |
| Quebec | 14.2 | 13.5 | 12.4 |
| Manitoba | 16.0 | 14.5 | 13.3 |

*Deficit Grants as a Percentage of Territorial Gross General Revenues*

|  | 1982–1983 | 1983–1984 | 1984–1985 |
|---|---|---|---|
| Yukon | 41.6% | 54.1% | 54.8% |
| NWT | 62.6 | 66.4 | 68.3 |

Newfoundland and Prince Edward Island receive the highest proportion of total revenue from equalization, but in none of the recent years has that exceeded 30.5 per cent. The other receiving provinces are substantially lower in their proportions. In contrast, the Yukon Territory has received from 41.6 to 54.8 per cent of its revenues from its deficit grant, and the Northwest Territories from 62.6 to 68.3 per cent.

Per capita, the difference in federal revenue made available is much more striking. In 1982–1983, for the two territories together, taking a population of 70,000 (in 1981 it was 68,611), the deficit grants amounted to $5,371 per capita. For the six provinces receiving equalization in that year the per capita figures were: Prince Edward Island, $953; Newfoundland, $906; New Brunswick, $702; Nova Scotia, $675; Manitoba, $414; and Quebec, $407. The two territories received, per capita, 5.6 times as much in federal transfers as the province with the largest equalization transfers.

Differences of this kind do not reflect wanton extravagance by the territorial administrations. They are the financial reflection of what everyone familiar with the North knows: costs of virtually everything are much higher than in the South. Distances are enormous, population is sparse, the country is at an early stage of development with great need for economic and social infrastructure, the climate is cruel, building conditions are difficult, and commodities from "outside" must come long distances at high cost.

The Drury report found the average per capita expenditures of the government of the Yukon Territory in 1978–1979, $4,742, to be more than twice as high as the national per capita average of all of Canada for provincial and territorial expenditures, $2,054. Expenditures of the Northwest Territories, $5,933 per capita, were almost three times the average for all Canada. Undoubtedly, more revenue could be raised in the North itself to meet these very high costs. The cost burden for its citizens and for businessmen and companies operating there is, however, already far heavier than in the South. The simple truth is that the need of governments in the North is much greater than of those in the South because every kind of cost is greater. Such are the facts of the North.

The financial regime of the provinces does not remotely fit the North. As has been mentioned, if the territories were to be treated like provinces, they would not even qualify to receive equalization. As measured by the formula for tax yield, the territorial taxes show a per capita capacity to derive revenues that is slightly *above* the national average. The tax yield is high in relation to a national average. It is, however, desperately low in relation to the costs of government that must be met in the North. As Drury says in his report: "The equalization formula was never intended to be used as a basis for making comparisons between jurisdictions that have widely differing costs of providing public services." To put the matter another way, the financial regime that applies to the provinces is based

on the assumption that their expenditure needs for services to their populations are comparable from province to province. That assumption does not hold in the circumstances of the territories. As a result the financial regime that well suits the needs of the present provinces would not meet those of provinces north of sixty degrees.

## MEMBERSHIP IN A CLUB

The association of federal and provincial governments undoubtedly constitutes the most exclusive "club" in Canada. Starting with five "members" in 1867, the club today comprises eleven. Because some provinces thought there might be risk of some new candidates being brought in under the old "rules" that could affect their interests, they managed to tighten them up in the Constitution Act, 1982.

From participation in countless federal-provincial conferences and meetings over a period of thirty years, and from a fascinated observation of the conduct of a wide variety of participants in this privileged club, I would say there are six important rules:

1. Membership is restricted to independent governments, with their status guaranteed by the Constitution. Cities may have—and do have—populations ten or twenty-five times that of a province, but they need not apply; they cannot be members. Population or wealth provides no entrée to the magic circle.
2. The federal government is different, but it is not superior. Its representative is normally chairman of the club meetings, and the difference in the role and responsibility of the federal government is recognized. It will usually, however, pay a high price if it tries to dominate. A "co-operative" demeanour is favoured and is, on the whole, the most productive.
3. All provincial members are equal in formal status. To paraphrase the report of the Royal Commission on Taxation of some twenty years ago, "a province is a province is a province." The realities of size are not ignored, but the dignity and the form of equality are important. Special status is fiercely resisted. Governments of Quebec found this out over many years of discussion of ways to recognize the distinctive

character of Quebec as the heartland of French culture in Canada. Every effort foundered on the rock of equality.

4. To ensure that rules 1, 2, and 3 are not impaired, arrangements for fiscal transfers from the federal government must be under a formula that is open to all provinces. They may not all qualify, as four (Ontario, Alberta, British Columbia, and Saskatchewan) now do not for equalization, but the formula is open to all and the rules are clear. No province can be given a special "deal."

5. The status of members of the club cannot be changed except under strict procedures now laid down in the amending clauses of the Constitution Act, 1982.

6. No new member can be admitted to the club except after consultation with all and agreement of eight of the present eleven. Until 1982 that was not so: the federal government alone could admit new members, as it did for Manitoba in 1870 and for all other additions to the club up to and including Newfoundland in 1949. That is no longer the case. Sections 42(1) (f) and 38(1) of the Constitution Act, 1982, provide "black ball" rules as effective as any club could want. They will be used with a hard eye in the interest of the present members.

These propositions are not laid down as club rules, but I do not state them in jest. I think they represent a reality that should be understood, with all its implications, by anyone who advocates provincial status as an option or as an objective for the political development of the northern territories.

The reality underlying the rules is not simply a desire on the part of existing provincial governments to be exclusive or restrictive. Genuine and important provincial and regional interests are involved. Awareness of those interests led to the successful pressure to have the new amending procedures for the Constitution require the approval of two thirds of the provinces with at least 50 per cent of the population of all the provinces (Section 38 [l]) before a new province could be established.

That provision, which is the general amending procedure for the Constitution, reflects one of the most important of Canadian realities—our deep regional differences and regional interests. Under the amending procedure no amendment can carry if any four provinces are opposed, which means that both the West and the Atlantic region, each of which has four provinces, can veto any change that either region perceives to be against its own interest.

The arithmetic that produces four as the magic number with power to block an amendment was no accident. It was the mathematical alternative to the specific recognition of regionalism that was provided in the "Victoria amending formula." That formula, providing vetoes in clear words for Quebec, for Ontario, for the West, and for the Atlantic was too direct. What was worse, it conferred "special status" on Ontario and Quebec as specific provinces and so infringed the club rule that all provincial members are equal. Still, regionalism is too deep to be ignored. The arithmetic of the amending formula protects it for the vulnerable areas of East and West without referring to it.

The establishment of one new province would not upset the arithmetic that produces the "blocking four." With eleven provinces, the approval of eight would be required for an amendment, so four could block. The West and the Atlantic region would still be protected. If two territories or three were to become provinces, however, making twelve or thirteen provinces in total, the mathematics so carefully designed to protect regionalism would be destroyed. In either case the requirement for two thirds of the provinces to pass an amendment would mean that eight out of twelve or nine out of thirteen could do it. It would thus require five provinces to block an amendment. In short, the amending procedure itself, effective in 1982, has created a new interest by the existing provinces in the possible establishment of any new ones.

A special relevance of these realities for any desire in the North to see new provinces there is that, as described above, the financial regime for the provinces would not fit northern conditions. If, as suggested by the Honourable David Crombie in an address to the Legislative Assembly of the Northwest Territories in Yellowknife on 6 February 1985, a plan could be worked out for "joint federal-territorial natural resource management and the sharing of revenues derived from development" of minerals, oil, and gas, there would in time be added revenues for the territories or for some of them. It would, however, require great confidence in future oil prices or in the competitive position of northern resources to assume that the rate of development, and the amount of tax that development could stand, would move northern governments from a position of needing 50 to 60 per cent of revenue in deficit grants to one where 28 or 30 per cent would suffice—assuming some new basis of equalization that would make equalization payments available at all.

A territorial candidate for admission to the provincial club would be seeking either a major change in the basis of equalization, now established for nearly thirty years with new constitutional sanctity given to it in 1982, or a special financial regime for its own needs. It would be a very large order indeed to expect that the former would or could be done. The latter would be quite contrary to the rules.

A transitional arrangement could provide additional funds for a new province during some brief period. Newfoundland was accorded twelve years "to facilitate the adjustment of Newfoundland to the status of a province of Canada" under Article 28 of the Terms of Union of December 1948. There was provision for possible limited extension if necessary under Article 29, which was in fact provided. But that was all. Newfoundland then became a province like the others. A northern province could probably expect something comparable, but, after a short transition period such as fifteen or twenty years, it would have to be able to finance under the general provincial fiscal regime. The other club members would almost certainly go no further. They would have the constitutional power to impose their views, even if a federal government was prepared to establish a new and more generous regime for a northern province with all the leverage that would provide at a later date to force up the payments to other "have not" provinces.

## NOTES

1  *Report of the Royal Commission on Dominion-Provincial Relations* (the Rowell-Sirois Commission), 1940, Book 11, p. 126.
2  *Treasury Board News Release*, 26 February 1985, Fact Sheet No. 5. This figure may be subject to adjustment since it is an estimate and, to some degree, subject to agreement on the several elements going into it.
3  The new "Fixed Tax Rate Formula" provides that the federal grant paid to each territorial government in any given year will be the difference between two amounts designated as A and B. A is the prospective expenditure side. It is defined as the gross expenditures of each territory in the base period (the fiscal year 1982–1983) escalated by a three-year moving average of the rate of growth in provincial plus local expenditures for Canada as a whole. B is the prospective revenue side calculated on the basis of "eligible revenues." Eligible revenue for each territory includes federal transfer payments under the specific purpose transfers plus the revenues the territory can raise for itself, also related to the 1982–1983 base year. That calculation is the yield (the 1982–1983 tax rates and other financial recovery rates applied to the value of retail sales, personal incomes, and other revenue sources in the territory for the year in question.
4  Department of Finance, Ottawa. The 1984–1985 figures were not final but were the most complete available when the table was prepared in April 1985.

# 36

## Editor's Introduction

Gil Rémillard is among the most important figures in Quebec constitutional politics. His two volumes on *Le Fédéralisme canadien* are anchors of Quebec scholarship on the subject. He wrote the first volume while advising the Parti québécois government of Réné Lévesque in the late 1970s; the second volume analyzes shortcomings of the constitutional compromise that followed. In an effort to affect change, he subsequently consulted the federal government, including the minister of justice. Upon becoming Quebec's minister of justice, he wrote and became the first to present Quebec's five minimum requests to the Rest of Canada that ended up laying the foundation for the Meech Lake Accord. He subsequently was intimately involved in the negotiations of both the Meech Lake and Charlottetown constitutional accords. Yet he wrote almost exclusively in French. This selection thus provides a uniquely incisive critique of the *Constitution Act, 1982*, from the perspective of a judge, a scholar, and a politician who, over a crucial period of almost twenty years, left Quebec's unmistakable imprint on constitutional negotiations.

Source: Gil Rémillard, "The Constitution Act, 1982: An Unfinished Compromise," *American Journal of Comparative Law* 32 (1984): 269–81.

Gil Rémillard[1]

# The Constitution Act, 1982: An Unfinished Compromise

ON 15 MAY 1980, in Montreal, Prime Minister Pierre-Elliot Trudeau addressed an enthusiastic crowd of citizens favouring a rejection by Quebec of the sovereignty-association option which was to be decided by referendum five days later:

> It is to the undecided that I speak. We all recognize that a rejection will be interpreted as a mandate to change the Constitution and to renew federalism. I am not the only one to say it, but am joined by 74 liberal deputies at Ottawa and the Prime Ministers of the nine other provinces.[2]

The referendum of 20 May returned a strong rejection by the people of Quebec of the sovereignty-association option, with about 60% of the votes cast. Prime Minister Trudeau, along with his Minister of Justice, Jean Chretien, and several other officials immediately met to establish a plan for renewing the Canadian Constitution as it had been promised during the referendum campaign. Trudeau then called together the provincial Premiers to an initial meeting to discuss a project for constitutional reform, based on the following subjects:

1) That where their numbers warrant, French minorities outside Quebec and English minorities inside Quebec be guaranteed the right to education in their own language;

2) That Canada have its own constitution written and adopted by Canadians, rather than continue to use the British North America Act of 1867;

3) That the constitution guarantee basic human rights to all Canadian citizens;

4) That Canadians in all provinces agree to share their economic opportunities by means of the richer provinces helping the poorer ones;

5) That Canadians agree to retain the parliamentary system of government both for the provinces and the federal government;

6) That the Queen continue as the Head of State of Canada.

Thus began an intensive period of constitutional discussions without precedent in the history of

---

1   Gil Rémillard is Professor of Law at the University of Laval, Quebec. The French text was translated by Nancy Jackson, Boalt class of '86.

2   Barbeau, "Trudeau s'engage a renouveler immediatement le federalisme," *Le Devoir*, Montreal, Thursday, 15 May 1980, at 12.

Canadian federalism, culminating in the Constitutional Conference of 2 November 1981. This "last chance" conference, as it was called, was convened by Trudeau to achieve a compromise necessitated by the Supreme Court Opinion of 28 September. In this historic opinion, the Supreme Court had concluded that the federal government could, in a strict legal sense, proceed with its contemplated patriation of the Constitution with the consent of only two provinces, Ontario and New Brunswick. The Court added, however, that such a patriation would be illegitimate because it would violate a constitutional convention requiring patriation to be undertaken with the agreement of a substantial number of provinces. It was thus necessary for Trudeau to build support for his patriation proposal among the provinces at the Constitutional Conference in order to give it the legitimacy it lacked.

The result was a compromise between the federal government and the provinces, with the exception of Quebec. In his inaugural address to the Quebec National Assembly on 9 November, Prime Minister René Levesque declared that his province had been shamefully betrayed and that he would never permit Quebec's legislative powers to be tampered with without his consent. Unfortunately for Quebec, her disapproval had no legal significance, since legitimacy of the Compromise Agreement was only a political concept, supported by constitutional convention. Nevertheless, the question whether Quebec could veto the Compromise Agreement now that nine provinces had agreed to it had important political consequences.

History supported Quebec's contention that it had such a right. The Fulton-Favreau patriation formula of 1964–65, the Victoria formula of 1971, and the Trudeau resolution of 1980 all provided for a veto right for Quebec. On the other hand, the procedure for amending the Constitution adopted by the provinces and the federal government in the Compromise Agreement did not provide for a veto right for Quebec or for any other province. The right of veto had been abandoned in favour of the right of a province to opt out of any amendment "that derogates from the legislative powers, proprietary rights, or any other right or privilege of the legislature or government of a province."

The major error of the Levesque government was not to have asked the Supreme Court, immediately after its decision of 28 September 1981, to explain

whether the expression "a substantial number of provinces" necessarily included Quebec—in effect giving it a veto right. To be sure, the decision would have been solely political, since based upon a convention, but it still could have delayed the Constitutional Conference of 2 November and perhaps permitted the negotiation of a more favorable compromise for Quebec. Unfortunately, it was not until February 1982 that the Quebec government submitted the question to the courts. The Quebec Court of Appeals held that there did not exist any constitutional convention guaranteeing Quebec a veto right. The Supreme Court of Canada confirmed the lower court's opinion on 6 December 1982, eight months after passage of the Constitution Act.

This Supreme Court opinion put an end to the legal patriation battle, but did nothing to resolve the political problem caused by Quebec's refusal to accept the second federative compromise of Canadian constitutional history. Quebec's dissent is easily understood upon reading the Constitution Act, 1982: both the Charter of Rights and Freedoms and the amendment procedure create serious difficulties for Quebec.

## THE CHARTER OF RIGHTS AND FREEDOMS

Since 17 April 1982, the Canadian Constitution has included a Charter of Rights and Freedoms. Under the Constitution Act, 1982 Canadians now enjoy certain rights and freedoms which have a supra-legislative force, since Art. 52 establishes for the first time the primacy of our Constitution over all legislation.

Actually the Charter of Rights and Freedoms sets down few new social, political, or economic guarantees for Canadians. In certain respects it is less extensive than the Parliament's Canadian Bill of Rights, or the Provincial Charters already existing, particularly that of Quebec. But it is in the area of legal guarantees that change is most evident. Before the passage of the new Charter, rights and freedoms were set forth in simple federal or provincial legislation, thus subject to modification by the government at both levels. Today these rights and freedoms are part of our Constitution and are binding on the Canadian Parliament as well as on the provincial legislatures. Furthermore, modification is possible only under the general amendment procedure established in the Constitution Act, whereby a resolution must have the support of the Canadian Parliament and seven provinces, totalling at least 50% of the aggregate population of all the provinces.

It is clear that the Charter represents an important guarantee of the rights of Canadian citizens. It has certain less desirable consequences, however, for Quebec: the linguistic rights set forth therein directly challenge the legislative authority of the Quebec National Assembly in matters of language and education.

In a previous constitutional proposal, the Task Force on National Unity (the Pépin-Robarts Commission), created by the Trudeau government, had recommended in 1979 that fundamental rights be introduced into the Constitution, but with the exception of linguistic rights. The Commission believed that the respect of minorities would be better achieved at the provincial level, and not imposed from above, in order to avoid possible friction among Canada's mixed population. The protection of minority linguistic rights could only become a reality, according to the Commission, if the provinces developed a consensus among themselves that could eventually be incorporated into the Constitution. It was also felt that there must be no constitutional obstacles hindering the development of Quebec's French character. The Pépin-Robarts Commission's recommendation was not adopted by the Constitution Act, which reads as follows:

> Art. 23(1) Citizens of Canada
> (a) whose first language learned and still understood is that of the English or French linguistic minority population of the province in which they reside, or
> (b) who have received their primary school instruction in Canada in English or French and reside in a province where the language in which they received that instruction is the language of the English or French linguistic minority population of the province, have the right to have their children receive primary and secondary school instruction in that language in that province.
> (2) Citizens of Canada of whom any child has received or is receiving primary or secondary school instruction in English or French in Canada, have the

> right to have all their children receive primary and secondary school instruction in the same language.
> (3) The right of citizens of Canada under subsections (1) and (2) to have their children receive primary and secondary school instruction in the language of the English or French linguistic minority population of a province
> (a) applies wherever in the province the number of children of citizens who have such a right is sufficient to warrant the provision to them out of public funds of minority language instruction; and
> (b) includes, where the number of those children so warrants, the right to have them receive that instruction in minority language educational facilities provided out of public funds.

Under Art. 23, the right of members of either a French- or English-speaking minority in a given province to have their children educated in their own language is determined by the following three criteria:

(1) Mother Tongue

If, for example, the mother tongue (first language learned and still understood) of a Canadian is English, and if he lives in Quebec, he will have the right under the Constitution to have his children educated in English.

This mother tongue criterion was hotly debated, since the verification of a person's true native language is almost impossible. What is the native language of someone whose mother is English-speaking, whose father is French-speaking, and who lives in a French neighborhood of Montreal (as is the case with Prime Minister Trudeau himself)? Because of such difficulties the Charter provides that the mother tongue criterion is not to be applied in Quebec until authorized by Proclamation of the Legislative Assembly or the Quebec Government.[3] Thus, for example, an English-speaking immigrant of the United Kingdom has no constitutional right to send his children to an English school in Quebec.

---

3   The Quebec Government succeeded in getting a law passed by the National Assembly saying that only the National Assembly could authorize such a proclamation.

(2) Language of Parents' Education (in Canada)

If, for example, a Canadian was educated in English in Canada and resides in Quebec, he will have the right to send his children to an English school in Quebec, under what is known as the "Canada clause" of the Charter. A similar "Quebec clause" was recently held to be unconstitutional by the Superior Court of Quebec, a decision upheld by the Court of Appeal.[4] Art. 73 of the Quebec French Language Charter of September 1983 provided that only those children whose parents had been educated [in English] in Quebec could attend an English school, a requirement clearly in conflict with the "Canada clause" of the Charter of Rights and Freedoms. In rejecting the "Quebec clause," the courts cited Art. 1 of the Charter of Rights and Freedoms, which provides that a rule of law may only restrict a right or a liberty in a reasonable way, as that expression is understood in a free and democratic society.

(3) The Language of Instruction of One Child in the Family

Finally, if one child in a family has received or is receiving his primary or secondary education in French or in English in Canada, parents have the right to have all their children educated in that language.

These three criteria give children of a linguistic minority the right to be educated in their own language. Art. 23(3), however, provides that they may exercise this right only when justified by the number of eligible children. The difficult question of what number is sufficient to warrant providing either courses in the minority language or entire schools in that language will be for the courts to decide, based on an evaluation of political, economic, and social factors.

Although Art. 23 of the Charter has clearly limited the legislative authority of Quebec in the area of language and education, its real consequences remain to be seen. The "Canada clause" (Art. 23(1) (b)) is not so critical in and of itself: assuming one accepts federalism, minority linguistic rights, whether French or

English, go without saying. But it is the inclusion of the third criterion, giving all children of a family the right to study in a minority language if one child does, which could produce some serious consequences. Consider, for example, a Greek family who come to live in Toronto, and upon arrival immediately send the oldest child to an English school. Three years later, the parents become Canadian citizens and decide to settle in Montreal. It follows that all their children will have the right to attend an English school. The third criterion of Art. 23 would also permit parents living in Quebec near the border of another province, like the citizens of Hull for instance, to send one child for a short time to an English school in Ottawa, Ontario, and afterwards to send all their children to an English school in Hull.

What will be the consequences of such an extended "Canada clause" for the linguistic equilibrium of Quebec? It is too early to tell, since demographic evolution cannot be foreseen. The true application of Art. 23 will depend on the interpretation given it by the courts.[5]

The limits placed on Quebec's authority in matters of language and education also apply to the other provinces, although it is difficult to compare the situation of the English-speaking population of Quebec with that of the French-speaking population outside Quebec. For instance, a somewhat different problem presents itself in Ontario, where it is not access to French education that is at issue, but rather the right of French-speakers to control the management of the French schools. Although this right is not spelled out in Art. 23, the French-Canadian Association of Ontario (FCAO) has recently decided to go to the courts to seek it. Again, the difficult question will arise as to what number of children is sufficient to justify public funds being spent on an educational institution completely managed by the minority population. The answer given to these questions will be determinative of the future of French-speakers outside Quebec. The right to receive a French education is of questionable value when it is only a special curriculum of a school otherwise organized for English-speakers, in which English is spoken in the library and in the

---

4   *Quebec Association of Protestant School Boards v. P.G. an Québec et al* (1982) C.S. 673.

5   Henripin and Larochelle, *La situation demolinguistique au Canada; evolution passée et prospective* 250, 287 (1980).

playground. As Maxwell Yalden, Commissioner of Official Languages recently stated, "mixed schools are like assimilation factories."

From now on it will be the courts, and in the final analysis the Canadian Supreme Court, which will for all practical purposes determine the linguistic policies of Canada. If along with the dismemberment of the Quebec French Language Charter comes the establishment of those rights for which French-speakers outside Quebec have been fighting for so long, the Charter of Rights and Freedoms could represent the beginning of a new era of Canadian federalism for French-speaking minorities. This is especially true since the institutional bilingualism of Manitoba, New Brunswick, Quebec, and the federal government, expressly guaranteed by the Constitution, would reinforce national bilingualism.[6]

Bilingualism at the federal level, however, poses further problems. The courts will have to determine the significance of such vague notions as "significant demand" and "nature of the office," the two requirements for the use of French or English in communications with the federal administration.[7] If they are interpreted broadly, bilingualism could, at least in theory, become a reality of Canadian federalism. There would still remain a significant obstacle, though: Ontario's refusal to accept institutional bilingualism. Ontario, like other provinces, is bound by the minority language educational provision, but it has never agreed to be bound by an express constitutional provision concerning its bilingualism, as have Manitoba, New Brunswick, Quebec, and the federal government. Ontario's rationale is that it alone is capable of perceiving and evaluating its own population's gradual acceptance of bilingualism. Recent legislation has, in fact, demonstrated such an on-going policy by granting certain desired rights to the French-speakers of Ontario, particularly in the area of the administration

of justice. These rights, however, are based on nothing more than ordinary legislation, without constitutional guarantees.

The next ten years will reveal the success or failure of the Charter of Rights and Freedoms, and in particular the sections dealing with linguistic rights. This is the minimum time necessary for the Supreme Court to make fundamental decisions concerning the interpretation and application of this important addition to our Constitution and to create a new approach regarding national bilingualism.

## AMENDMENT PROCEDURE

Despite the limits placed on Quebec's legislative authority by Art. 23 of the Charter, these linguistic provisions still leave room for optimism. The same cannot be said for the Constitution's amendment procedure, which is completely unacceptable to Quebec in its present form.

Art. 38(1) of the Constitution Act, 1982 provides that the Canadian Constitution can be amended with the consent of the Senate, the House of Commons, and at least two-thirds of the provinces whose aggregate population represents at least 50% of the national population. The procedure also permits a province to opt out of a given amendment if it affects the province's legislative authority, property rights, or any other right or privilege. The province must in this case express its dissent by a resolution adopted by the majority of its legislative deputies (Art. 38(3)). If the amendment from which the province withdraws pertains to education or culture, "Canada shall provide reasonable compensation to any province to which the amendment does not apply" (Art. 40).

The government of Quebec was right to denounce this compromise as completely unsatisfactory. It is of course an improvement over previous provisions which, while seemingly giving Quebec a veto right over proposed constitutional modifications, in fact simply afforded Quebec a political tool with no legal significance. (It is what the Supreme Court of Canada has decided in its Advice on the Quebec Veto on 6 Dec. 1982.) In this sense the right to opt out of an amendment is a significant constitutional gain, since it implicitly

---

6   The bilingual character of Manitoba was confirmed in the well-known case, *Le Procureur general du Manitoba* v. *Forest* (1979) 2 R.C.S. 1032. In this case, the Canadian Supreme Court held that the Official Act of 1890, which abolished French as an official language of Manitoba, was unconstitutional, since Art. 23 of the Manitoba Act of 1870 established as a constitutional matter the bilingualism of this province, just as Art. 133 of the Constitution Act of 1867 did so for Quebec.

7   Constitution Act, 1982, Art. 29(1).

recognizes Quebec's uniqueness by granting financial compensation in the areas of culture and education.

On the other hand, the right to opt out is incomplete, in that it does not grant financial compensation in all cases of withdrawal from an amendment. Consider, for example, environmental protection, which falls under both federal and provincial jurisdiction. If the other provinces agreed to hand over all authority in this area to Ottawa, Quebec could express its disagreement and withdraw from such a constitutional amendment; it would not, however, have a constitutional right to receive any federal funding for environmental projects, since they would fall outside the areas of education and culture. The citizens of Quebec, by paying federal taxes, would be paying for the environmental protection of all the provinces while at the same time taking on the expense of their own protection system. In other words, except for matters of culture and education, a province choosing to opt out of a particular amendment would see its citizens doubly taxed.

Furthermore, even if financial compensation were granted in all cases of opting out, the present amendment procedure would still be unacceptable to Quebec. Art. 42 provides that the general amendment procedure will apply to the following areas:

42(1) An amendment to the Constitution of Canada in relation to the following matters may be made only in accordance with subsection 38(1):
(a) the principle of proportionate representation of the provinces in the House of Commons prescribed by the Constitution of Canada;
(b) the powers of the Senate and the method of selecting Senators;
(c) the number of members by which a province is entitled to be represented in the Senate and the residence qualifications of Senators;
(d) subject to paragraph 41(d), the Supreme Court of Canada;
(e) the extension of existing provinces into the territories; and
(f) notwithstanding any other law or practice, the establishment of new provinces.

This article means that certain fundamental rules of Canadian federalism could be modified against the wishes of Quebec, which accounts for only 25% of the Canadian population. The problem is all the more critical since the federal government expressed its intention to reform the Canadian Senate on the basis of Art. 42 and set up a joint House/Senate committee to study the matter.

Art. 42 does not contemplate a right to opt out, and it is easy to understand why. A province could hardly withdraw from an amendment, let alone receive financial compensation, in cases where such basic institutions as the House of Commons, the Senate, or the Supreme Court are involved. Nevertheless, the subjects of Art. 42 are among the most fundamental of our federalism. How could one accept the principle that the proportional representation of the House of Commons could be modified without the consent of Quebec? Or that the Senate, cornerstone of the federal/provincial balance and guarantor of Quebec's uniqueness, could be reformed? The possibilities of fundamental change against Quebec's will abound, from modification of the powers of the Supreme Court to the acceptance by Canada of new provinces.

Quebec must demand a veto right in these areas, just as the English-speaking provinces demanded and obtained two important rights during the constitutional discussions: a veto right on "the office of the Queen" and the right of a province to have at least as many deputies in the House of Commons as it has Senators in the Senate (Art. 41).

Thus, in addition to extending the right to opt out of an amendment with financial compensation to areas besides education and language, it is also necessary to modify Art. 42 to read as follows:

42(1) Any modification of the Canadian Constitution concerning the following subjects must be made as provided in 42(2):
a) the principle of proportionate representation of the provinces in the House of Commons prescribed by the Constitution of Canada;
b) the powers of the Senate and the method of selecting Senators;
c) the number of members by which a province is entitled to be represented in the Senate and the residence qualifications of Senators;
d) subject to paragraph 41(d), the Supreme Court of Canada;

e) the extension of existing provinces into the territories; and

f) notwithstanding any other law or practice, the establishment of new provinces.

42(2) The subjects listed in paragraph 42(1) may be modified:

a) by resolution of the Senate and the Chamber of Commons; and

b) by resolution of the legislative assemblies of a majority of the provinces; this majority must include:

    i)  every province whose population, at the date of the declaration of the present amendment, represents at least 20% of the Canadian population, according to any recent census,

    ii)  at least two Atlantic provinces, of which the combined population represents at least 50% of the total population of these provinces according to the most recent census available,

    iii) at least two Western provinces, of which the combined population represents at least 50% of the total population of these provinces according to the most recent census available,

42(3) The following definitions shall apply for the purposes of this Article:

    "Atlantic provinces": Nova Scotia, New Brunswick, Prince Edward Island, and Newfoundland.

    "Western provinces": Manitoba, British Columbia, Saskatchewan, and Alberta.

Such an amended Art. 42 reflects a greater respect for Canadian dualism and regionalism. Along with financial compensation in all cases of opting out, this modification would make the amendment procedure acceptable to Quebec.

## CONCLUSION

17 April 1982 will certainly remain one of the most important dates in the history of Canadian federalism. On that date, the Canada Bill, voted on several days before by the Parliament of Westminster, became the Constitution Act, 1982.

The Constitution Act 1982 has had two major legal consequences:

1) It severed Canada's last colonial link to the United Kingdom by establishing a completely Canadian amendment procedure.

2) It amended the original federative compromise of 1867 by incorporating a Charter of Rights and Freedoms, an amendment procedure, an equalization principle and regional disparities, a recognition of aboriginal rights, and amendments concerning the division of legislative authority in the area of natural resources.

There is little to say about the fact that Constitution Act 1982 put an end to the last vestiges of Canada's colonial past. Although Canada became a sovereign state by the Statute of Westminster 1931, authority to amend the Constitution remained in London due to an inability of the provinces to agree on a Canadian alternative. London's role, however, proved to be formal only, since the Parliament at Westminster has always acted according to the desires of Canada.

In a strict legal sense, London could rescind its decision and make Canada a colony again by amending the Westminster Statute 1931 and the Canada Act 1982. This is an obviously far-fetched thought but is legally possible, since Canada chose to proceed by way of the Parliament of Westminster rather than by Canadian proclamation. Canada was in no way obliged to choose this course: the Canadian Parliament and the provinces could have unilaterally proclaimed their independence and the modifications they intended to incorporate into the Constitution.

In having recourse one last time to the old colonial mechanism, Canada was able to overlook both the fact that Quebec was dissenting and the fact that the Canadian people were being completely ignored in the process of Constitutional revision. Not one government involved, whether at the federal or provincial level, had received a specific mandate from its electorate to proceed with such constitutional amendments. It is hard to understand why a democratic country like Canada would amend its constitution so substantially without consulting its population.

The Constitution Act, 1982 is an unfinished compromise which must some day be completed. The consequences of the Charter of Rights and Freedoms are presently uncertain: its limiting and derogatory clauses, its sole application to public institutions, its omission of certain rights, and its vague and ambiguous terms can only leave us perplexed as to the protection the Charter affords to Canadians in general, and to Canadian duality in particular.

The answers will come from the courts, which have become the principal interpreters of our society. They will have to settle the age-old dilemma of the proper balance between fundamental individual rights and collective rights. Art. 1 of the Charter implicitly recognizes this dilemma, by providing that a federal or provincial rule of law may restrict fundamental rights only within reasonable limits prescribed by a free democratic society. The courts will also have to state more precisely the rules governing the application of linguistic rights, by defining terms such as "sufficient number," "significant demand," and "office use."

As for the amendment procedure, the issue was resolved when the Supreme Court on 6 December 1982 held that Quebec never had a veto right, since the precedents suggested by the Fulton-Favreau Formula and the Victoria Formula were found to have only political significance.[8] The major mistake of the Quebec government was not to have requested an opinion of the Supreme Court before patriation was completed. If such an opinion had been requested following the 21 September 1981 patriation decision, the political consequences might have been substantial.

The amendment procedure, in its present form, is unacceptable to Quebec but could become acceptable with necessary modifications. First, financial compensation should be granted to provinces upon opting out of any amendment, not only those dealing with language and education. Second, some provinces, including Quebec, should be granted a veto right in areas where opting out is unrealistic, but where the issues at stake are fundamental to the future of Quebec in a federal system. With these important modifications the Constitution Act 1982 could become a first step to the constitutional reform Canada needs with respect to the joint issues of regionalism and dualism.

---

8    In both situations, Quebec's refusal stopped Ottawa's procedure of patriation.

37

## Author's Introduction

Constitutions are meant to serve people. They are at once the *generators* of institutions, practices, aspirations, identities, and communities and the *consequence* of institutions, practices, aspirations, identities, and communities. Often they conceal the forces that give rise to them; sometimes they provide a label that enables such forces to be mediated and channelled. Written constitutions are properly read like a musical theme upon which citizens and political actors compose variations; but sometimes they are reduced to list of unchanging formulae. The unwritten constitution has a particular role: many scholars naively conceive it as providing magic answers to momentarily vexing political and legal conflicts; others laud an implicit constitutional inheritance for its role in framing the questions through which citizens of a polity grapple with existential issues on a daily basis.

For the last half of the twentieth century in Canada, explicit constitutional reform was a preoccupation. Because Quebec personalities—Lesage, Trudeau, Lévesque, Mulroney, Parizeau, and Chrétien—loomed so large in ongoing debate, many other dimensions of Canadian constitutionalism were neglected. The historical antecedents and earlier paired iterations of the explicit Constitution—1774–1791; 1841–1867—received little attention in the dynamic of 1982 and Meech Lake. Neither did the influence of "new players"—loyalists in 1791, Maritimers in 1867, Westerners and First Nations in the 1980s. Nor finally, did the significant shifts in the policy objectives and the deployment of tools of governance from Macdonald's initial National Policy of 1878, through the second National Policy consequent upon the Rowell-Sirois Commission, to the third National Policy reflected in the Charter, the North American Free-Trade Agreement, and the use of the federal spending power.

Written in the aftermath of the second Quebec secession referendum, the following essay draws four lessons from Canada's near-death experience: the constitutional conversation is (and should be) perennial; constitutionalism in Canada runs in paired cycles of unity (centralization, homogeneity) and plurality (decentralization, heterogeneity); the policy constitution is as important as the legal constitution; and the primary challenge for the future is to find institutions and processes to recognize diversity and to empower citizens as agents.

Source: Roderick A. Macdonald, "Three Centuries of Constitution Making in Canada: Will There Be a Fourth?" *University of British Columbia Law Review* 30(2) (1996): 211–34.

Roderick A. Macdonald

# Three Centuries of Constitution Making in Canada: Will There Be a Fourth?

## INTRODUCTION

There is, one supposes, something inevitable about the fact that a public lecture delivered in a Faculty of Law by a legal academic from Quebec should deal with the Canadian Constitution. Yet mere inevitability is not sufficient justification for selecting any particular topic. I have chosen to speak about the Constitution for both practical and personal reasons. The former require no great elaboration. Last fall's referendum outcome was a sobering, if cathartic, reminder of just how fragile political arrangements can be. As for the latter I need mention only one idea. Holding the Douglas McK. Brown Visiting Professorship has given me the occasion to spend a semester in British Columbia and to experience first hand the aspirations and frustrations of British Columbians with Canadian constitutional politics. These aspirations and frustrations, I have learned, are every bit as genuine and deeply felt as those held in that part of Canada where I live.

No thoughtful assessment of Canada's constitutional conundrums can leave them unaddressed.

This lecture is my effort, however incomplete and however inadequate it may be, to repay the benefit this Chair has bestowed on me. I would like to offer a perspective on Canadian constitutional politics that originates in the aspirations and frustrations of someone from Quebec. But let me immediately enter two caveats. Most importantly, my perspective originates in the understandings of a member of a very special subset of the Quebec population: its English-speaking community. And even then, I cannot claim to reflect the diversity of opinion present within Quebec's various English-speaking communities. Just as we err in thinking that francophone Quebeckers have a single voice on constitutional matters, so too we err in thinking that English-speaking Quebeckers are constitutionally univocal. Part of my message here is that heterogeneity and multiplicity increasingly characterize how constitutional questions in Canada are framed and debated.

My second caveat relates to my authority to be giving a lecture on this theme at all. My perspective is that of a non-specialist and I speak neither as a politician, nor as a member of a political elite. Moreover, even though I occupy the F. R. Scott Chair of Constitutional and Public Law at McGill University, I do not hold myself out to be, and I am not generally perceived as, a constitutional expert in the normal sense of the term. My opinion is rarely sought by politicians and the media. The philosophy, history, politics and sociology of law are my principal research fields. As applied to the Canadian Constitution, these concerns are my animating themes this evening.

I have divided this lecture into four sections. I begin with philosophy: what questions should define constitutionalism in a liberal democracy and what questions and issues actually do define constitutionalism in Canada today? I then consider history: what have been, over three centuries, the different approaches we have taken to asking and answering these questions? Constitutional politics is the theme of my third section: what do we want from our Constitution? "What processes and institutions do we have for realizing our objectives? My fourth section is about sociology, or what has been labelled as "the Quebec question": is partition—of Canada, of Quebec—our only option for

recognizing and accommodating geographic, ethnic, cultural and linguistic diversity? I conclude by suggesting how we might recast the form of our defining constitutional questions in a way that allows us to come to workable answers for the twenty-first century and beyond.

It goes without saying that I do not for a minute believe that we can put the constitutional issue to bed once and for all. No matter the outcome of any referendum or any process of constitutional amendment, we will never "solve" our constitutional conundrums. To borrow a metaphor, a constitutional arrangement is somewhat like a marriage: the only time the various tensions, conflicts and upsets of a normal, healthy relationship between two people are solved is when the marriage ends. And if it ends in divorce, we all know that the decree *nisi* rarely produces closure on the previous relationship. Politicians, professors and pundits who promise a quick fix that will lead to constitutional closure are either wilfully blind about Canadian constitutional philosophy, ill-informed about Canadian constitutional history, duplicitous about Canadian constitutional politics, naive about Canadian constitutional sociology, or all four at once. As I hope to illustrate, constitutional debate about the extent of federal and provincial legislative authority and about the make-up of institutions of national governance is our one truly national symbol. We disparage this constitutional debate at our peril.

When I was a young boy, I first heard a joke that I now realize perfectly captures the Canadian situation:

Once upon a time there was an international essay writing competition in which teenagers from the G-7 countries participated. The topic was "the elephant." The student from the U.K. wrote an essay entitled "The Elephant and the Monarchy." The French student wrote "The Gourmet Guide to the Elephant." The Italian wrote "The Love Life of the Elephant." The German submission was "Are Elephants Well-organized and Efficient?" The Japanese student wrote "The Elephant and the Export Trade." The student from the U.S. wrote "The Elephant and the Market Economy." And the Canadian student entitled the essay "The Elephant, a Federal or a Provincial Responsibility?"

## PLUS CA CHANGE, PLUS C'EST PAREIL: HAVEN'T WE BEEN HERE BEFORE?

Federal-provincial constitutional politics do, at first glance, seem to be Canada's albatross. Why are we and our politicians so preoccupied with this aspect of the Constitution? If we have to debate the Constitution, why can't we be like the United States, where important matters such as the Bill of Rights attract attention? Moreover, why is it that when the economy is in need of attention and public finances are in shambles, the division of constitutional powers continues to occupy such an important place in Canadian political life? Why can't we settle the Quebec issue once and for all? And why has everyone else—from the premiers of Alberta and British Columbia, to equality seekers under the *Canadian Charter of Rights and Freedoms*, to aboriginal peoples claiming an inherent right to self-government—caught the Quebec disease of turning every conceivable issue and grievance into a constitutional conflict?

Some commentators see these preoccupations as evidence of a deep malaise in the country. They ask why our politicians don't get the message the way Bill Clinton got it four years ago: "It's the economy, stupid!" My view is just the opposite. Far from deflecting us from our true agenda as a polity and far from being destructive of the fabric of the country—that is, far from being an inappropriate surrogate for public policy issues that really matter—asking and answering these types of questions are in fact what defines Canada. Not just today, not just over the past fifty years, not just since the confederal period of 1867–1873 and not just from the time of the British conquest of New France in 1759 and 1760 have these issues been a concern. In fact, they have dominated since the first contacts between Europeans and aboriginal peoples in the sixteenth and seventeenth centuries. Just as the fictional American student essayist correctly saw concern with the market economy as reflecting a recurring, rock-bottom theme in U.S. political self-definition, so too the fictional Canadian student essayist correctly saw concern with the institutions of governance and with the allocation of political authority (and since 1867, with the management of federal and provincial jurisdictional conflict) as a recurring, rock-bottom theme in Canadian political self-definition.

I acknowledge that it is unusual to phrase the *telos* of a country in terms of arguments about governance. Usually journalists, scholars and politicians take the position that what defines a country is its commitment to a relatively limited set of goals. This commitment is said to permit citizens to describe their patriotism by reference to core values that are broadly shared regardless of geography or gender, religion or race, culture or class. We are all familiar with such expressions of patriotism; they seem to enamour our neighbours to the south. One can be American or one can be un-American. And if one is American, one can be as American as apple pie, or baseball or, more recently and thanks to Madison Avenue, Chevrolet.

But can one be either Canadian or un-Canadian? The very expression "un-Canadian" rings false. And because it rings false it is also very difficult to imagine a noun to describe what being Canadian entails. Some years ago, a CBC radio contest was held on this theme. Contestants were asked to complete the phrase "as Canadian as…." The winning entry struck me as uncannily accurate. It was: "as Canadian as … it is possible to be under the circumstances."

This winning entry provides the key to a tremendously important point of constitutional philosophy that is underappreciated by political theorists, probably because of the overwhelming dominance of the American model of civic republican virtue. What defines a modern liberal, pluralistic state is not a common set of values to which all citizens subscribe. It is neither an exclusionary ethnic nationalism nor a shared set of beliefs about the purposes of the state, the functioning of the society and the economy sustaining an exclusionary civic culture. When Lucien Bouchard says that Canada is not a *real* country he is making a fundamental mistake about the character of a liberal-democratic polity. For Bouchard, Canada is not a real country because it does not have a particular set of shared values and shared purposes: it does not have what American political theorists like to call an ideological mission and what separatists in Quebec like to call a *projet de société* (a blueprint for a society). What he means to say, and what misguided federalist politicians who constantly harp on the theme of national unity by proclaiming flag days and promoting national anthems and pledges of allegiance mean to say, is that they want a country where there can be a specific and uniform predicate to the phrase "as Canadian as...."

Yet to imagine such a predicate requires one first to imagine that there can be a congruence of *état* (political state) and *nation* (be this defined as civic culture or as ethnicity). It presupposes that a modern state depends on positing an exact fit between linguistic-cultural-ethnic character and political organization. Such a congruence is a virtual impossibility in modern heterogeneous countries like Canada. It was, nonetheless, the founding fiction of the nation-state. The state was conceived as the highest expression of the general public will of a people—its *volksgeist*. This same assumption is the founding fiction of multi-ethnic, democratic, jacobin territorial states such as, for example, France and the United States. There is said to be a civic culture—a non-ethnic civic patriotism—that is unique to each state and by reference to which the ideological boundaries of the state may be drawn. Whether explicitly ethno-cultural or linguistic, or whether grounded in the invocation of a distinctive civic culture, all nationalist movements in modern democratic states appeal to the homogenizing imagination that, if transposed to Canada, would require a relatively precise definition of Canadian.

Let there be no doubt about my own position. I categorically reject all attempts to control membership in any political unit by reference either to ethnicity, language, religion, culture or to some set of common obligatory values of civic virtue. It is not the content of the definition that is troubling, for it matters not at all whether the values are propounded by Lucien Bouchard, Sheila Copps or Glen Clark. Of course, I acknowledge the temptation to frame debates about society in such substantive terms. So, for example, in the United States politicians seek to appropriate a position on issues such as freedom of speech, the right to bear arms, capital punishment, abortion and family values as being the American way. They castigate adversaries as un-American. Again, in Quebec there is an industry that seeks to define its *projet de société* as to distinguish between real Quebeckers *(nous)* and others *(les autres)*. And, unfortunately, in Canada today there is a growing gaggle of well-meaning but misguided powdermonkeys who seek to define what it means to be Canadian in terms of substantive shared values: medicare, regional equalization payments, social programs, bilingualism and so on are said to differentiate Canada from the United States. Commitment to these so-called shared values is held out as a litmus test for identifying true Canadians. These values are then deployed to proclaim that, for example, the Reform Party is not simply wrong on certain of its policies, but is in fact un-Canadian. Even though I do not personally support the Reform Party, I find this exclusionary conception of citizenship and social definition distasteful.

I believe, rather, that what genuinely characterizes a polity and what differentiates one polity from another are the questions that are understood as framing political debate. How do citizens understand basic issues of public policy? How do they structure these issues for discussion? Of course, the specific answers one gives to these questions, and to a lesser degree even the questions themselves, are not etched in stone: they will change over time. But even in the divergent ways in which they have been formulated over time, and even in the multiple ways in which they might presently be formulated, they will have a continuity and a commonality.

Part of my purpose is to suggest that what many denigrate as constitutional wrangling is a central component of our shared framing of questions. In Canada, we debate foundational questions about the kind of society we wish to build and maintain—questions about equality, poverty, liberty and personal security—by reference to the organization of constitutional authority. These debates are engaged through questions about the character of membership in the Canadian political community: how should we recognize and accommodate ethnic, cultural and linguistic diversity? They recur in questions about the locus of sovereignty: does ultimate political authority reside in the Queen, in Parliament, in the courts, in the Constitution or in the people? And they are worked out in questions of institutional design: what is the relative political presence that should be afforded, for example, to provinces and regions that have traditionally been more industrialized, and to provinces and regions that have traditionally been more agricultural and resource based?

To be blunt about the matter, politicians, professors and pundits who want us to solve our constitutional conundrums once and for all are engaged in a risky business. To solve the constitutional issue is not to solve the basic socio-economic problems and political concerns that have historically generated constitutional debate as a means for their expression. These prognosticators had better have some replacement issues handy as a vehicle for framing our deepest questions about the kind of society in which we want to live. Furthermore, these replacement issues had better be ones that do not lead us down the path of exclusionary nationalism that is characteristic of both the *Parti québécois* and over-zealous American patriots like Pat Buchanan.

## JAMAIS DEUX SANS TROIS: TO FORGET HISTORY IS TO BE CONDEMNED TO RELIVE IT

I have just tried to argue that as a matter of legal and political philosophy we should not be troubled by our apparent preoccupation with constitutional matters. In this section, I would like to make a parallel plea from the perspective of legal history. Here I retrace the steps by which the polity now called Canada has, over the past three centuries, previously worked through analogous conundrums to those it now confronts. However much we may believe our current situation to be unique and unprecedented, it is not. Our constitutional history has much to teach, if only we would listen.

As a matter of legal continuity, European politico-legal traditions that have become established in Canada trace their origins to the founding of Quebec in 1608. Earlier European settlements, by the Vikings at Anse-aux-Meadows in the tenth to twelfth centuries and by Sir Humphrey Gilbert in Newfoundland at the end of the sixteenth century, have simply left no continuing legal deposit. Viewed as a matter of constitutional law, and excepting those small parts of the maritime provinces transferred to the United Kingdom under the *Treaty of Utrecht of 1713*, the Canada of 1996 finds its origins in two events of 1763: the *Treaty of Paris*, by which the French Crown formally ceded *quelques arpents de neige* (a few acres of snow) to the British Crown, preferring to retain islands in the Caribbean as a more valuable colony; and the English *Royal Proclamation of 1763*, by which certain aboriginal claims were recognized.

During the first decade following the capitulation of New France much confusion reigned as to the nature of the political regime, the institutions of governance and the rules of law applicable to the conquered territory. Sovereignty passed from the French Crown to the British Crown, yet doubt remained about the status of the French-speaking Roman Catholic population. At the same time, a contest for control of government broke out between those English, Scottish and Irish settlers and officials who were more or less sympathetic to the conquered *habitants* and those who were not. Recently arrived English-speaking merchants of Montreal and Quebec, as well as British soldiers, sought to replace the existing civil law with the common law, especially in connection with matters of trade and commerce, land tenure and successions. Finally, the local inhabitants engaged in a form of passive resistance by boycotting the newly established English courts.

The threat of unrest from the Thirteen Colonies to the south and the desire of colonial authorities to maintain the fidelity of the population of New France led to both military rule being lifted from the conquered colony and to the passage of the *Quebec Act* in 1774. This statute recognized French civil law, afforded full civil and political rights to Roman Catholics and established the first institutions of colonial government. It was a constitutional document intended to produce both unity and coherence in the political administration of the colony. While the *Quebec Act* was cited in the American *Declaration of Independence* as one of the grievances justifying rebellion, it achieved its domestic purposes and the population of Quebec resisted both the blandishments of Benjamin Franklin and the army of Benedict Arnold in 1775. Nevertheless, despite the efforts of the colonial governor, Sir Guy Carleton, to maintain a conciliatory policy towards the *habitants*, an influx of large numbers of American Loyalists after the British surrender in 1783 radically changed the demography of the new colony. Before long, Canada's first separatist movement arose. Following an investigation by the British colonial secretary, a pluralizing and diversifying constitutional arrangement was proposed. Under the *Constitutional Act* of 1791, Ontario was formally separated from Quebec. Two new colonies—Upper Canada and Lower Canada—emerged from the partition.

Over the course of this thirty-year period, what have since become Canada's dominant constitutional themes made their first appearance on the political landscape. These constitutional themes include the tension between English-speaking and French-speaking inhabitants, the disruptive effect of new players (in these circumstances, loyalist immigrants) on existing constitutional arrangements, the economic conflict between commercial interests and agricultural and resource-based economic interests, the allure of the United States, the desire to maintain an evolutionary rather than a revolutionary constitutional tradition, and a willingness to fundamentally reorganize the organic framework and institutions of government. Twice more—once in the nineteenth century and once in the twentieth—these themes repeated themselves over a similar thirty-year period.

The nineteenth century equivalent of the pattern first played out between 1763 and 1791 took place from the 1830s through the 1860s. Political conflict in Upper and Lower Canada culminated in the rebellions of 1837 and 1838 and was followed by a commission of inquiry that gave rise to what is now known as the *Durham Report*. This report, which also considered the situation in Nova Scotia and New Brunswick, made two recommendations of present interest. To begin, the report proposed the gradual establishment of responsible government within all the colonies of British North America. Secondly, it proposed the reunification of Upper and Lower Canada in a new political arrangement, the express purpose being to assimilate the French-speaking population of the latter. Following a three-year period of military government, the 1841 *Act of Union* was proclaimed. The new Constitution accomplished both of these institutional goals, although the substantive goal of assimilation did not follow. As in 1774, the solution to socioeconomic conflict and political instability was thought to lie in a political structure that emphasized unity and coherence in colonial governance.

Nevertheless, the turmoil did not abate significantly. In 1849, the Montreal commercial bourgeoisie produced an Annexation Manifesto in which it sought to join the United States. It felt that its trading interests were being sacrificed on the altar of politics and that politics also precipitated a general economic depression. That same year, the English-speaking loyalist rabble of Montreal torched the parliament buildings in Montreal as a protest against conciliatory policies towards the French-speaking population of Lower Canada: conciliatory policies that came in the form of the *Rebellion Losses Bill*. Finally, the legislative assembly of Canada became hopelessly deadlocked on political matters, and governments constantly rose and fell. The conflicts were numerous. They existed between Roman Catholics and Protestants, between commercial interests and the landed classes, between the Tory and ecclesiastical establishment (in Quebec, the *bleus*) and the reformers and clear Grits (in Quebec, the *rouges)*, and most notably, between political *élites* in Upper Canada and Lower Canada. Durham's plan to assimilate French-speaking Quebeckers rested on giving equal representation to the more sparsely populated Upper Canada of 1841; by the mid-1850s immigration to Ontario meant that the concept of equal representation of Upper and Lower Canada undervalued the voice of Upper Canada in the governing process.

Two decades of political disruption, social conflict and economic hardship produced further inquiry into revising constitutional arrangements. Moreover, as in the 1780s, new players—New Brunswick, Nova Scotia, Newfoundland and Prince Edward Island at the table, with the Red River Colony, British Columbia and Vancouver Island not far from view—shaped the new design. The threat of another U.S. invasion became increasingly real as the U.S. Civil War was winding down. The mercantile classes of Montreal and, to a lesser extent, those of Toronto, sought out a new hinterland for their respective commercial empires. The clamour for greater colonial self-government and decolonialization was raised by most political groups and factions in Canada. Not surprisingly, a socio-economic and political context like that of the 1780s generated a constitutional solution like that of 1791. Just as the constitutions of 1841 and 1774 were initiatives that promoted unity, coherence and homogeneity, the *British North America Act* of 1867 (as completed by later enactments embracing Manitoba in 1870, British Columbia in 1871 and Prince Edward Island in 1873), like the *Constitutional Act* of 1791, was a reconfiguration aimed at plurality, diversity and heterogeneity. But this time, instead of a strict political separation, a federal structure was included in the new constitutional arrangement.

This thirty-year pattern seems to be in the course of repeating itself once more in the twentieth century. The 1960s witnessed violent civil unrest in Quebec, and in 1970 the *War Measures Act* was invoked to deal with the F.L.Q. kidnappings. Canada also experienced significant socio-demographic change, especially after modifications to immigration policy in 1968. These produced not one, but two, Royal Commissions of Inquiry: these were the Dunton-Laurendeau Commission on Bilingualism and Biculturalism in the 1960s and the Pepin-Robarts Commission of the late 1970s. Following the election of the separatist *Parti quebecois* in 1976 and Quebec's first sovereignty referendum in 1980, the federal government promoted a new constitutional pattern that resulted in the enactment of the *Constitution Act, 1982*. As in 1774 and 1841, two main organic purposes were pursued: decolonialization and unity. The former was accomplished through patriation of the amending formula, a step intended to finally sever the imperial link. However, unlike the unification of executive and parliamentary institutions previously pursued, coherence in 1982 was sought symbolically: the *Charter* was intended to galvanize a new unifying view of Canadianism and national citizenship.

As in the previous two centuries, this constitutional renovation did not actually calm political turbulence. Once again there were new players who contested their place in the newly-ordained structure. The multicultural constituency, *Charter* patriots and aboriginal peoples all came to advance claims for constitutional recognition. Changing population and changing economic patterns put the legitimacy of existing institutions and patterns of governance into question: cabinet representation, the conditions of senate membership and resource ownership became key points of conflict. There was a renewed threat from the United States. This time the threat was neither military nor political but, as a result of changes to the Canadian economy that were later reflected in the Free Trade Agreement of the late 1980s, economic. And of course, the country has lived through yet another decade of political stalemate over negotiating Quebec's place in the federation. When these are taken together, it is no surprise that contemporary constitutional politics, most notably those reflected in the politics of the failed Meech Lake and Charlottetown Accords, bear an uncanny resemblance to the politics of the old Province of Quebec in the 1780s and to the politics of the United Canadas in the 1850s.

This series of thirty-year cycles, the third of which is now nearing completion, might suggest an inexorable logic to Canadian constitutional reform. But it is important not to overstate the lessons of history. First, these cycles have been cast primarily as cycles of unity and plurality, of coherence and diversity, and of homogeneity and heterogeneity. But they are much more than that; they are also cycles of progressive decolonialization and progressive political democratization, as well as cycles of accommodating new territories and new groups of citizens. On the first point, the gradual achievement of political sovereignty has already been noted. But it is also worth observing how the management of constitutional politics has become more democratic. Between 1774 and 1791, Canadian constitutional politics were managed primarily by the governor general with minimal input from his advisors, even though the input increased throughout the period. Between 1841 and 1867 Canadian constitutional politics were managed primarily by the elected executive with minimal input from parliamentary political *élites*, also with that input increasing throughout the period. Between 1982 and 1996 Canadian constitutional politics have been managed by political *élites* with minimal input from extra-parliamentary interest groups and coalitions. However, once again the input from such groups has increased throughout the period.

Second, these cycles have been cast using the language of unity and plurality, of coherence and diversity, and of homogeneity and heterogeneity. Recently, at the urging of politicians in Quebec, aided and abetted by the premiers of Alberta and British Columbia, it has become common to describe them in terms of centralization and decentralization. This is much too unidimensional a characterization because it suggests, ahistorically, that the only issue in question is the relative jurisdictional authority of the provincial and federal Parliaments. The above discussion reveals that these cycles of formal constitutional reconfiguration also relate to the loci of executive and legislative authority, to the character of the dominant structures of governance, to the spirit of political participation and to the criteria for membership in the polity. The objects and purposes of these paired attempts to maintain constitutional equilibrium simply cannot be captured in the unsubtle structuralist language of centralization and decentralization.

Third, it is misleading to see each of these swings of the governance pendulum as uniquely homogenizing or heterogenizing. However much the *Quebec Act* of 1774 was a constitution promoting unity and coherence, by legitimating the Roman Catholic church in the new colony it also worked to pluralize and diversify political authority. However much the *Constitutional Act* of 1791 was a pluralizing constitution, it maintained a unitary executive in the person of the Governor-General of Canada, and by so doing it protected the transportation, financial and trading infrastructure of the commercial empire of the St. Lawrence. However much the *Act of Union* of 1841 was a constitution promoting unity and coherence in colonial governance, the legal, municipal and educational institutions of Upper and Lower Canada retained their diversity. However much the *British North America Act* of 1867 was a pluralizing and diversifying constitution, the vesting of the principal trade and financial powers in the federal government operated an important unification of the new country's economic institutions. Finally, however much the *Constitution Act*, 1987 was cast in the genre of unity and coherence, the accompanying s.92A of the renamed *Constitution Act*, 1867 on non-renewable natural resources, and the various formulae for constitutional amendments, including the unanimity formula for significant changes, effected at least some pluralization of political power. Failed attempts at amendment since 1982 clearly reveal this pluralization.

What emerges from this review is the sense that Canadian constitutional renovation invariably occurs in two formal stages, however multiple its informal stages may have been. Thirty years of attempted unity and coherence as a response to civic turbulence (1763 to 1791) were followed by 50 years of relative plurality and diversity (1791 to 1841). Then 30 years of attempted unity and coherence as a response to civic turbulence (1841 to 1867) were followed by 115 years of relative plurality and diversity (1867 to 1982). Given the continuing political contestation of the *Constitution Act*, 1982, one might well conclude that the pattern seems to be repeating itself. On three different occasions over three consecutive centuries the strategy of unity,

coherence and homogeneity as a response to socioeconomic change and political conflict has not produced a lasting constitutional equilibrium. It remains to be seen whether Canadians are capable of imagining, within the next few years, a constitutional reconfiguration that parallels those of 1791 and 1867 or whether, in the absence of achieving a new equilibrium, the break up of the country is inevitable. This is the issue to which I now turn.

## L'ÉTAT, C'EST MOI: WHAT DO WE WANT FROM OUR CONSTITUTION?

To present Canadian constitutional history as I have, implies that the domain of constitutional politics will be our most important challenge in the immediate future. Within this domain, questions of constitutional design will predominate over those of constitutional practice. The challenge is to imagine the contours of the constitutional text that completes the 1982 initiative. Our previous institutional arrangements and our previous self-understandings suggest that this challenge will have three quintessentially Canadian dimensions.

First, there is the dimension of membership. We need to consider who will take up the destabilizing role that new constitutional players typically fill. How shall we deal with the aspirations of aboriginal peoples and how shall we accommodate the changing sociodemographic and population patterns that result from migration and immigration and that affect the whole country? Second, there is the dimension of constitutional continuity and adaptability. We need to consider how the country will maintain its political and economic sovereignty in a world economy. Is there a way to conceive our political and economic future without simply substituting economic colonialism in a global marketplace for our previous political colonialism in the British Empire? Third, there is the dimension of framework and institutions of governance. We need to consider the substance of a compensating constitutional adjustment that will counterpoint the patriation exercise. What will it comprise? Can we find political structures and processes of governance within which the Canadian constitutional conversation will continue, even if these are as different from the federal strategy of 1867 as the strategy of 1867 was from the separatist strategy of 1791?

At a higher level of abstraction there is nothing especially unique to Canada about these questions; they reflect themes that underpin liberal constitutionalism itself. Nonetheless, they have a particular timbre in Canadian constitutional politics. It is this particularity that provides clues as to where our answers may lie and as to how these answers may help us address concerns emanating from Quebec.

Consider first the idea of membership. Modern constitutions usually prescribe who is establishing the constitutional order by a formula such as "We the People." These formulae serve to enumerate which groups and which individuals are to form part of the political community. But the formulae themselves remain without content. Whether any particular constitution takes adequate account of aboriginal or indigenous peoples, whether it entrenches slavery, whether it distinguishes between the political rights of men and women, whether it gives adequate voice to newer arrivals such as immigrants or whether it adequately reflects population transfers within a polity, are matters of practical politics that can only be answered by reference to specific cases.

Even when implicit, as in Canada, a "We the People" formula for membership typically does not speak to the possibility of, and the need for, future inclusion of the presently excluded. The *Quebec Act* of 1774 did not envision, and was not designed to reconcile, the linguistic, religious and cultural tensions generated by the massive migration of United Empire Loyalists in the 1780s. A new design—that of the *Constitutional Act* of 1791—was required for this. Again, the *Act of Union* of 1841 simply did not offer adequate institutional structures to respond to the demographic shift during the 1850s. It could not accommodate the shift between a previously less populated Upper Canada and a previously more populated Lower Canada, and it also could not accommodate other political units like Nova Scotia and New Brunswick in the 1860s. For this, a new design, that of the *British North America Act* of 1867, was required. Today we can see that the *Constitution Act*, 1982 did not adequately anticipate various institutional adjustments. These adjustments relate to the amending formula, the character and make-up of the Senate, and interprovincial equalization required by

changing population patterns in, for example, the maritime provinces and British Columbia. Despite some acknowledgment of the fact, the 1982 Act also failed to elaborate a constitutional structure within which new political units—be they new territories such as Nunavut or areas of self-government created through the land claims settlement process—giving voice to aboriginal peoples could be easily recognized.

Without a careful rethinking of these membership issues, Canada will not survive the twentieth century. The means for readjusting our responses to the aspirations of francophone citizens in Quebec are held within the very rethinking that seeks to accommodate the aspirations of Canada's aboriginal peoples and those of citizens of provinces like Alberta and British Columbia. Remembering that the real constitutional issue has historically been one of membership also reminds us that concerns emanating from Quebec have played a key role in creating the heterogeneous polity called Canada that is now celebrated around the world.

A second recurrent theme of modern constitutions is their attempt to trace the conditions of their own continuity and adaptability. A constitution typically asserts its supremacy over all other law and provides an exclusive amendment procedure for accommodating change. A national constitution rests on the belief that the tangled web of attachments and commitments of the past can be transformed in such a way that they do not impede the full exercise of political autonomy. However much the new state must reconcile itself in practice to a world of economic and social interconnectedness, the proclamation of sovereignty permits this *de facto* dependence to be asserted as volitional, rather than as historically required. In addition, constitutions usually provide for complex processes to govern their amendment. These processes may be uniform, or they may be variable, depending on the amendment in question. They may sometimes require only ratification by legislatures or they may require ratification by the electorate. They may sometimes provide for a veto power for certain constituencies and may sometimes elaborate principles that may not be amended, even by unanimous consent. Necessarily, the scope of political independence and the content of a domestic amending formula are also questions of practical politics that can only be answered by reference to specific cases.

In the Canadian context the question of sovereignty has had, and still has, several dimensions. The *Quebec Act* of 1774 did not contemplate that the first colonial assemblies would mature into the full-blown Legislative Assemblies that were central features of the *Constitutional Act* of 1791. The *Act of Union* of 1841 did not really imagine that its bow to responsible government would lead to the establishment of colonial self-government in the *British North America Act* of 1867. Today, however, the issue is less one of political independence—should Canada discard the monarchy and become a republic?—than it is one of economics. The *Constitution Act*, 1982 simply does not speak to how the country might further extract itself from overdependence on one trading partner through an enhanced federally-managed economic union, and through active participation in multilateral trade agreements like the GATT and the now expanding NAFTA. What is more, far from facilitating constitutional amendment, the *Constitution Act*, 1982 has made it practically unachievable. By a perverse logic, the harder that explicit amendment is made, the more it becomes desirable. That which is designed to ensure the stability and continuity of a constitutional order may, by its very myths of stability and continuity, generate a rhetoric that all politics are constitutional.

Without carefully rethinking the rationales for any given framework of internal and international trade or for any given amending formula, Canada will not survive the twentieth century. But again, in this very rethinking to accommodate a changed dynamic of economic interdependence lies the means for readjusting our responses to Quebec's concern about protecting its socio-cultural specificity through a selective constitutional veto. Remembering that the real constitutional issue has historically been one of adaptation—an evolutionary rather than a revolutionary constitutionalism—also reminds us of the key role that Quebec's concerns have played in creating the 233-year-old governance structure that has been justly celebrated around the world for its continuity and adaptability.

The third constant in contemporary liberal constitutionalism is the shifting balance between the authority of central and state governments and in the practical allocation of control over the institutions of governance. Modern constitutions typically express a choice about the allocation of political sovereignty by establishing either a unitary, federal or confederal system. If federal or confederal systems, these allocations will necessarily rest either on a mythology of symmetry or a reality of asymmetry. A constitution will speak to the intra-state institutions, mechanisms and procedures that are to be adopted, the powers that should be allocated to each of the governmental agencies or constituent parts, and the rationales for allocational differences (be these grounded in material factors such as a natural resource base, political factors such as a large slave population or linguistic-cultural-ethnic factors). Similarly, the allocational challenge bears on the getting and giving of revenue: ownership of public property, taxation, borrowing and spending (including transfer payments to states and individuals), equalization and the division of the public debt. Once again, these allocations are questions of practical politics that can only be answered by reference to specific cases.

The Canadian constitutional arrangement, whatever its form, has never been symmetrical. In the *Constitution Act* of 1791, Upper and Lower Canada had different structures of governance, different provisions relating to established religions and different legal systems. In the *Act of Union* of 1841, many of these were maintained and Upper Canada was given an equal number of seats in the Parliament of the United Canadas, notwithstanding a significantly smaller population. In the *British North America Act* of 1867 and its complementary constitutional documents of 1870, 1871 and 1873, given the diversity of the provinces comprising the federation, these asymmetries were myriad. They touched the distribution of legislative jurisdiction, the ownership of non-renewable and offshore resources, implicit understandings about the location of federal defence, prison or departmental facilities, and the dispensing of governmental largesse. Quebec has always been required to be bilingual and initially had a bicameral legislature with guaranteed minority representation. Prince Edward Island and British Columbia received promises of ferries and railways respectively. Newfoundland and Nova Scotia have different rights to the offshore fishery. Moreover, in practice, through regionally-targeted expenditure programs such as unemployment insurance or through federal equalization payments,

Canada's several provinces have never actually been symmetrically treated.

Without carefully rethinking the character of and justification for these asymmetries in legislative authority and federal spending, and without an effort to balance them against mythical assertions that the country is a compact between ten equal provinces, Canada will not survive the twentieth century. But in this very rethinking—within a general context of reconfiguring institutions of governance—lies the means for readjusting our responses to the desire of Quebec's government to achieve recognition of the province's distinctiveness. Remembering that the real constitutional issue has historically been one of assessing the limits of asymmetry also reminds us that Quebec's concerns have played a key role in creating a federal constitution that can successfully accommodate a province with almost 40 percent of the country's population (Ontario) alongside a province that has less than one percent (P.E.I.).

Explicit constitutional provisions that relate to membership, sovereignty and governance have a particularity because of the context of their elaboration, the conventions of drafting and the accidents of history. But they also have a particularity because the written constitution of any country must always be read against its unwritten constitution: its constitutional inheritance and constitutional practices. The claims of history are such that there can be no easily importable constitutional solution that reflects the distilled and abstract wisdom of another polity. Moreover, every constitution, however revolutionary, is tributary to the day-to-day practices of the political community to which it bears witness. Nonetheless, acknowledging history does not mean that the implicit constitution will have a fixed political content, and recognizing practices does not mean that these conventions will be immunized from evolution. Every constitutional order mediates the claims of history and the claims of practice through its explicit text. Thus, however much the advent of the *Charter* may have made some forms of Canadian constitutionalism more similar to those found in the United States, Canadian political and legal culture is largely resistant to framing its substantive questions as they are framed in the United States.

The politics of constitutionalism in Canada are driven by the unique manner in which it seeks a reconciliation of history and practice. Whatever the historical grounding of Quebec's claim to cultural distinctiveness, this claim is mediated by the practical claim of, for example, British Columbia to greater constitutional influence. Whatever the historical grounding of Quebec's claim that Canada is comprised of two founding peoples, this claim is mediated by the practical claim of, for example, aboriginal peoples for analogous constitutional recognition. And whatever the historical grounding of Quebec's claim that the final colonial link should be cut through a declaration that Canada is a republic, this claim is mediated by the practical claim from the rest of the country for cultural and social policies to palliate its threatened economic colonization by the United States. Recognizing the importance of achieving this reconciliation through a constitutional text brings me to my fourth theme—the sociology of the Constitution.

## VIVE LA DIFFERENCE: HOW SHOULD WE DEAL WITH DIFFERENCE?

In the past, the question of political difference (including linguistic, religious, ethnic, cultural and geographic difference) in Canada has most often been posed as the question "What does Quebec want?" Today, by contrast, this question is explored through the metaphor of partition: can we partition Canada? If so, can we partition Quebec? In the language of constitutional sociology all these several questions may be recast as one: "Must nations become states?" Phrased in this way, the issue is not just a Quebec question because it applies equally to aboriginal peoples. What is more, as Canada's various provinces become more visible as the culturally heterogeneous societies they always were, the question can now be seen as one that affects all Canadians.

It has never been possible to argue that Canada is a homogenous ethnic nation-state. Largely because of Quebec, heterogeneity has been an inescapable feature of Canadian political life from the beginning. Even if Quebec were now to separate, given continuing patterns of immigration and the belated recognition of aboriginal peoples, heterogeneity would be inescapably with the country for the conceivable future. How, then, should a political state recognize and accommodate the kind of linguistic, religious, ethnic and cultural diversity that is characteristic of Canada?

This question may be best approached by standing the problem on its head: what types of responses are open to linguistic, cultural, religious and ethnic minorities who feel marginalized by political majorities? While secession is that which now comes immediately to mind, it is in fact only one of at least five possible responses. These five are secession, emigration, participation, assimilation and suicide. From the perception of the majority, there is a mirror image to each of these. They are territorial expulsion, deportation, recognition, co-optation and genocide. The fifth possibility should be summarily left aside since collective suicide is not a response that ensures the continuing survival of the minority; and of course, its mirror—genocide—is not a morally defensible approach to the issue of diversity. Nevertheless, various twentieth century experiments in ethnic cleansing suggest that moral repugnance is no bar to a political leadership bent on recovering some lost empire.

Secession, emigration and assimilation, like suicide, do not really address the issue of recognizing and accommodating difference. Consider secession. If the minority in question succeeds in engineering a definitive territorial rupture of the state, whether accomplished by constitutional means such as a negotiated partition or whether accomplished by non-constitutional means such as a unilateral declaration of independence, the partitioned political state ceases to exist as a linguistically, culturally and ethnically diverse entity because the relevant elements of diversity are no longer present. That is also the case for emigration. If all members of a linguistic, cultural or ethnic community emigrate, the prior state ceases to exist as a polylinguistic, polycultural or polyethnic entity. The situation is likewise for assimilation. Whether this is accomplished voluntarily or whether it is coerced by the political majority, the assimilation of a minority means that the prior state ceases to exist as a polylinguistic, polycultural or polyethnic entity. In each of these three cases (assuming the secession, emigration or assimilation is total) the sociological result is the same: linguistic, cultural and ethnic homogeneity. Of course, from the perspective of the minority, what distinguishes secession and emigration from

assimilation and suicide is that in the former cases, the minority survives intact.

The challenge for modern heterogeneous liberal democratic states, therefore, is to understand the conditions under which minorities will choose the third possible response—participation—over secession, emigration, assimilation and suicide. The question is this: when will a minority bent on survival resist the siren-song of personal or collective self-determination in favour of membership in a larger heterogeneous political state? Its answer demands consideration of what makes political participation meaningful. Not surprisingly, much depends on the attitude taken by majorities. In order for members of a minority to feel that their membership in a larger society is possible without their assimilation, they must believe that their participation as a minority is welcome and that their voice is being heard. The central issue for minorities is recognition: are they afforded recognition by the majority and do they recognize themselves in that recognition?

The problem in Quebec today is that many francophones have concluded that their full participation as francophones in the Canadian political community is no longer possible. They believe that they are viewed by the majority as just another immigrant group that will be assimilated over time, like the cajuns of Louisiana. Even more, they believe that it is more possible to elaborate a comprehensive *projet de societe* that ensures their survival outside the framework of the Canadian federation than within it. But even among those Quebec nationalists who voted *oui* in the sovereignty referendum, about one-half still entertain the hope that meaningful participation in the Canadian political community is possible. They believe that other Canadians do wish to "hear their voice" in the sense of accepting that they may have different political and constitutional beliefs, faiths, convictions, interests and preoccupations. And they do at least partly recognize themselves in the idea of Canada, even if they feel that the recognition is currently imperfect. For francophone Quebeckers, the emotional struggle is for a recognition that makes a meaningful participatory voice possible.

But *nota bene*: participation is a perception of the minority speaker, not the majority listener. However much the federal government does in fact promote and buttress the French language across Canada, this is less important than the perception of non-recognition within Quebec. How well francophones in Quebec feel that their voice is being heard cannot be measured by assessing how much hostility is provoked in other parts of Canada when Ottawa makes efforts to listen. Federal policies of bilingualism outside Quebec may serve the interests of francophone provincial minorities such as Acadians, franco-Ontarians, franco-Manitobans and the like. In Quebec, however, they work to opposite effect: they serve the interests of the English-speaking minority. This explains the ambivalence that many francophone Quebeckers hold towards official bilingualism in Ottawa. It also explains why the provisions of the Meech Lake Accord that sought to afford Quebec recognition as a distinct society and to enshrine a veto on constitutional amendments had such an importance.

The symbolism of *société distincte* has become the litmus test of recognition for most francophones in Quebec, be they nationalists or federalists. It is, of course, significant that the Prime Minister and the leader of the opposition are both francophones from Quebec, and that between them they dominate the federal constitutional agenda. Recognition certainly involves meaningful input into federal institutions (cabinet representation, influence on Bank of Canada decisions, adequate representation in the Senate, a seat on the Supreme Court of Canada and so on) of the very kind that many in British Columbia, with some reason, feel is denied to them.

But recognition also involves acknowledging the special role that the government of Quebec has in fostering the French language in Canada. The whole idea of a federal system is itself one mark of such recognition. Nonetheless, since Confederation in 1867, the development of telecommunications and transportation technology, changes to the social program expectations visited upon governments, and especially since the *Charter of Rights and Freedoms* in 1982, modifications to the role of the courts have significantly altered the initial federal design as it plays out in Quebec. Today, meaningful recognition requires explicit (and not just, as in the *British North America Act* of 1867, implicit) acknowledgment that even though every province has its distinctiveness, Quebec is truly a province unlike all the others.

The above understanding of when participation will be preferred to secession, emigration, assimilation and suicide applies equally to minorities within provinces. Aboriginal peoples across Canada, francophones in provinces other than Quebec and in particular, English-speakers in Quebec, have come to perceive their destinies in these same terms. Faced with the possibility of Quebec secession, the situation of aboriginal peoples and of the diverse English-speaking communities in Quebec is more or less analogous to that of Quebec francophones within Canada. All perceive that territorial separation is a viable option; once one boundary is up for grabs, all boundaries are up for grabs. But there is this difference. The answer to the question, "What does Quebec want?" will invariably be couched primarily in the language of recognition rather than in the demand for special powers. The answer to the question, "What do English-speaking Montrealers want?" will invariably be couched primarily in the language of special powers rather than in the language of recognition. In this difference it is possible to see why cartesian claims of principle formulated in Quebec are not adequately addressed by responses grounded in Lockian pragmatic experimentalism formulated elsewhere in Canada.

As a matter of constitutional sociology, the lesson of the independence movement in Quebec over the past thirty years would seem to be this: recognition—both symbolically through the distinct society clause and institutionally through a constitutional veto—is the *sine qua non* for a perception of meaningful participation. However much other political units in Canada may feel that the current institutions of federal governance are ill-adapted and non-responsive to their aspirations, this lack of responsiveness does not amount, in its political logic, to a denial of recognition. As a matter of symbolic recognition, what matters most in Quebec is the acknowledgment of its specificity, and this acknowledgment is grounded in exactly the same perception as the claim of aboriginal peoples for recognition of their inherent right to self-government.

As a matter of institutional legitimacy, the rationale for a constitutional veto is intimately connected to the loss of *defacto* political power. With a domestic amending formula that denied *de jure* what the government of Quebec previously could claim *de facto*, the establishment of a division-of-powers veto assumes a key place in achieving recognition. Paradoxically, the more British Columbia achieves such *de facto* power and the more its political importance in Canada comes to approximate that of Ontario, the less it genuinely needs any such formal veto.

Finally, as a matter of practical politics, there is little transfer of constitutional jurisdiction that differentiates the position of the Quebec government from that of British Columbia's government. After all, it is the federal power to tax, spend and redistribute—much more than any head of federal legislative authority—that undermines meaningful federalism in Canada.

## CONCLUSION

In concluding this peroration on the possible constitutional futures of Canada, four points strike me as worthy of reiteration.

First of all, our constant preoccupation with the Constitution—with institutions of governance and the allocation of authority between Ottawa and the provinces—is not the unmitigated evil it is portrayed to be. Failure does not lie in our inability to solve this problem once and for all. It consists, rather, of our inability to convince the international money markets that the Constitution is our question, in exactly the same way that bickering about how liberals in Washington are destroying the economy is the American question. Political instability may be our albatross, but our ongoing constitutional conversation is not. This reminds me of the joke with which my professor of Wills and Estates opened his course in 1971:

After two decades of hard work that generated the revenue to finance his child's legal education, a small-town sole practitioner took his first vacation when that child graduated and joined the office as a junior. When he returned from vacation some four weeks later, the child proudly announced: "Father, you know that Macdonald estate on which you were working these past twenty years? Well, I finally wound it up while you were gone." At this news the father became apoplectic. "You imbecile," he said. "It was billing on that file that put you through law school."

Let us not forget that federal-provincial constitutional negotiation is how we debate the kind of society we wish to have. It is our question—the question that keeps concern alive for those issues that make Canada the most admired (although, let us acknowledge, nonetheless imperfect) polity in the world today. We settle it conclusively at our peril.

Second, our formal constitutional history has typically run in cycles of unity and plurality, of coherence and diversity, of homogeneity and heterogeneity. We are currently between the pairs of a twentieth century version of constitutional renovation that will lead to a new equilibrium. These pairs have, in their slightly different eighteenth and nineteenth century manifestations, ensured the continuity of this polity—whatever its formal name and complexion. Canada has previously achieved equilibrium through both separation and federalism. It may be that our future holds forth an equilibrium operated by means of a true confederation. However much we may be attached to our current structures of governance, we need not atavistically hold to them when they can no longer serve our purposes:

In Tom Sawyer there is a story of Tom and Huck trying to dig up buried treasure. Even though there is a shovel nearby, Tom starts digging with his penknife. Huck keeps trying to give him the shovel but Tom replies: "Everyone says this is a job for a penknife." After twenty or so futile minutes, Tom turns to Huck, pointing at the shovel and says, "Pass that penknife over there."

Let us recognize that, even though we have recently been engaged in a particular constitutional discourse, we have not always deployed this discourse and the language we use has not always meant the same thing. We have the power to change the content we give to our treasured formulae; we even have the power to change the formulae themselves.

Third, our constitutional politics are not static. We cannot imagine that the specific components of our constitutional conversation will remain constant. Our issues and our interests—about membership, continuity and governance—have retained a permanency. But we should acknowledge the likely transformations of each that will be brought about by the recognition of aboriginal peoples, by an internation-alized trading context, and by alternative conceptions of constitutional asymmetry. The constant reminder provided by disquiet in Quebec will help us to better understand the character of our contemporary challenges. What we must do, as we work through the adjustments that these socio-economic transformations suggest, is keep the wisdom of the law reformer clearly in view. Law reform rarely provides solutions to the social problems that the law is trying to regulate. It usually only solves existing legal problems by giving ongoing social problems a new expression and a new form. Our task as Canadians is to make certain that when we modify our Constitution, we trade in our old class of constitutional problems for a better class of problems that allows us to address our genuine political concerns more effectively:

> As a child I remember a story about a sick man who enters the hospital for a serious operation. Following the operation, the patient's spouse inquired as to her husband's health. She was told that the operation was a complete success. When she asked to see her husband, the doctor informed her that he had died as a result of the operation. But, he added, that as his widow she at least had the satisfaction of knowing that he had died cured.

Let us acknowledge that now is the time to complete the process of constitutional renovation that was begun in 1982. This should be done by seeking ways of expressing our fundamental questions that will engage the imagination and fidelity of all Canadians. But let us also not be so keen to change our entire Constitution with one big round of textual reform that we wind up killing the country in the process.

Fourth, the principal challenge confronting Canada today is the challenge of recognition. In slightly different ways, it is a challenge that speaks to all of us. It is a challenge that speaks to the aspirations of francophone Quebeckers, it is a challenge that speaks to the claims of aboriginal peoples, it is a challenge that speaks to the ambitions of equality seekers under the *Charter* and it is a challenge that speaks to the frustrations of British Columbians. Finding the metaphors and the vehicles for acknowledging and accommodating these diverse needs for recognition is the key to moving constitutionalism forward. Just as Quebec's fundamental interest in recognition is a constitutional constant—although its particular negotiating position as reflected in the expression *societe distincte* may need to be recast or abandoned—so too is our fundamental interest in the continuity of a Canada whose questions we know need not commit us to any particular position as to how that interest is maintained in the years ahead. However much our federal constitution in 1867 was preferable to our separatist constitution in 1791, and however much it may be preferable to a separatist constitution parading as *souvereineté-association* in 1996, it is not ineluctably preferable to any other model for continuing Canada's constitutional conversation into the twenty-first century.

I began this lecture with a rhetorical question: "Three Centuries of Constitution Making in Canada: Will There Be a Fourth?" I now conclude with the hope that the analysis presented here leads you to agree with me that an affirmative answer is indicated.

# 38

## Editor's Introduction

Sujit Choudhry and Robert Howse provide an unparalleled critique of the Supreme Court of Canada's *Quebec Secession Reference*. They draw attention to the lack of systematic reflection from the perspective of constitutional theory on the relationship between constitutional adjudication and democratic politics. This article raises several interesting concerns about the use of principle and reason in legitimizing constitutional adjudication that is by its very nature highly politicized when the Court is called upon to balance competing and largely irreconcilable constitutional visions. The article provides insights into the Court's cognizance of having to trade off a limited versus expansive view of legal sources, exclusive and supreme versus less robust interpretive responsibility, and interpretive style that distinguishes adjudication from normative reasoning writ-large when engaging in judicial review that is bound to be controversial yet needs to be accepted as valid by the contending parties. The authors' findings have broader implications for areas where the Court steps into the fold to fill up vessels left empty by political discord.

Source: Sujit Choudhry and Robert Howse, "Constitutional Theory and the Quebec Secession Reference," *Canadian Journal of Law and Jurisprudence* 13(2) (2000): 143–69.

## Sujit Choudhry and Robert Howse

# Constitutional Theory and the Quebec Secession Reference

### 1. INTRODUCTION: THE *QUEBEC SECESSION REFERENCE* AND THE POVERTY OF THEORY IN CANADIAN CONSTITUTIONAL DISCOURSE

From the moment that it was handed down, the judgment of the Supreme Court of Canada in the *Quebec Secession Reference* produced a torrent of public commentary.[1] Journalists, politicians, and legal academics

have debated the consequences, and the merits and demerits of the result. The judgment has been read as a statute that lays down the roadmap to referendum and secession. If one of the Court's goals was to secure a central place for the judgment in the ongoing debate over the future of the country, that goal has surely been met.

Remarkable as the decision is, however, and given the fundamental issues about the relationship between

---

1   *Reference re Secession of Quebec*, [1998] 2 S.C.R. 217 [hereinafter *Quebec Secession Reference*]; A.C. Cairns, "The Quebec Secession Reference: The Constitutional Obligation to Negotiate" (1998) 10:1 Constitutional Forum 26; Editorial, "Court Answers Succeed," *The Kitchener-Waterloo Record* (25 August 1998) A6; D. Greschner, "The Quebec Secession Reference: Goodbye to Part V?" (1998) 10:1 Constitutional Forum 19; P. Joffe, "Quebec's Sovereignty Project and Aboriginal Rights" (1999) 7 Canada Watch 6; J. Legault, "How to deny Quebec's right to self-determination: With the Supreme Court's opinion, we have entered the realm of colonial federalism," *The Globe and Mail* (21 August 1998) A19; P.J. Monahan, "Doing the Rules: An Assessment of the Federal Clarity Act in Light of the Quebec Secession Reference" (2000) 135 C.D. Howe Institute Commentary 3; P.J. Monahan, "The Public Policy Role of the Supreme Court of Canada in the Secession Reference" (1999) 11 N.J.C.L. 65; J. Morin, "L'avis de la Cour supreme: Une sécession légitime et réalisable... en théorie," *Le Devoir* (31 August 1998)

A7; T. Morton, "A ticket to separate: Has the Supreme Court curbed separatism? No, says Ted Morton," *Ottawa Citizen* (22 August 1998) B7; P. Oliver, "Canada's Two Solitudes: Constitutional and International Law in Reference re Secession of Quebec" (1999) 6:1 Int'l J. on Minority and Group Rights 65; C. Ryan, "What if Quebeckers voted clearly for secession? While the Supreme Court did a good job of defining broad principles, it left a great contradiction hanging in the air," *The Globe and Mail* (27 August 1998) A19; J. Simpson, "Court finds the right tradeoff," *The Globe and Mail* (25 August 1998) A12; D. Turp, "Globalizing Sovereignty" (1999) 7 Canada Watch 4; W. Walker, "Difficult Questions Remain for the Politicians to Resolve," *The Toronto Star* (21 August 1998) A9; J.D. Whyte, "The Secession Reference and Constitutional Paradox" in D. Schneiderman, ed., *The Quebec Decision: Perspectives on the Supreme Court Ruling on Secession* (Toronto, ON: Lorimer, 1999) 130; J. Woehrling, "Unexpected Consequences of Constitutional First Principles" (1999) 7:1–2 Canada Watch 18; R.A. Young, "A Most Politic Judgment" (1998) 10:1 Constitutional Forum 14.

law and politics that it raises, the discussion in question has remained almost entirely in what we describe as the pragmatic perspective, which asks how positive politics entered into the motivations and justifications of the Court, and looks at the results in terms of their political consequences, without deep or sustained reflection on the ultimate grounds for the role the Court took upon itself, or on the normative sources of its reasoning. The preoccupations of this perspective are along the following lines:

- What were the political origins of the judgment? More specifically, what circumstances led the Court to be thrust into the political morass of constitutional reform, and how did the Court respond? It is fairly clear that the reference to the Supreme Court was a centre-piece of the federal government's strategy to get tough with Quebec—widely known as "Plan B." Moreover, rather than shying away from the task thrust upon it, the Court interposed itself into the political thicket, and fundamentally altered the rules of the game.
- What were the political effects of the judgment? On this point, there seems to be a consensus that the judgment was a success. It has been widely accepted by political actors across the political spectrum. Moreover, it has shaped the terms of debate in a stability-promoting way. It has eliminated extreme opinions—that a yes vote would effect a unilateral secession, or could be ignored by the federal government with impunity. Additionally, it has focused debate over certain issues, such as what constitutes a clear majority and a clear question.
- Who were the political winners and losers? Here, the picture is mixed. As expected, the Court summarily rejected arguments made on Quebec's behalf that it would be legal for Quebec to unilaterally secede from Canada, decisively refuting the claim that Quebec possessed a right to self-determination cognizable in Canadian constitutional law. Contrary to expectations, though, the Court decided that in the event of a yes vote, the federal government would be under a

constitutional duty to negotiate in good faith. The uncertainty of the federal response to a positive referendum result—a source of strategic power for the federal government in the past—has been eliminated. Moreover, Quebec nationalists now have an incentive to hold referenda repeatedly until they achieve a positive result.

- What political issues remain unresolved? The Court left many questions unanswered, creating ongoing uncertainty—the borders of an independent Quebec, the division of the national debt, citizenship, and the rights of aboriginal peoples in northern Quebec, to name a few. More accurately, the Court relegated these issues to constitutional negotiations, and steadfastly refused to speculate on the implications of a breakdown in those discussions.

The domination of the pragmatic perspective in public discourse about the judgment is perhaps understandable, given the political context in which the Court was asked to decide and the obviously high stakes in Canadian constitutional politics. But this dominance also reflects an abdication of intellectual responsibility on the part of the Canadian academy, and the traditional poverty of theory in Canadian constitutional law. Apart from some rather crude attacks on the "politicization of the law" through activist judicial review,[2] with some important exceptions,[3] analysis

2   The foremost work here is F.L. Morton & R. Knopff, *The Charter Revolution and the Court Party* (Peterborough, ON: Broadview Press, 2000).
3   Some notable exceptions are: J. Bakan, *Just Words: Constitutional Rights and Social Wrongs* (Toronto, ON: University of Toronto Press, 1997); D. Beatty, *Constitutional Law in Theory and Practice* (Toronto, ON: University of Toronto Press, 1995); R.F. Devlin, ed., *Canadian Perspectives on Legal Theory* (Toronto, ON: E. Montgomery Publications, 1991); R.F. Devlin, "Some Recent Developments in Canadian Constitutional Theory with Particular Reference to Beatty and Hutchinson" (1996) 22:1 Queen's L.J. 81; D. Dyzenhaus, "The New Positivists" (1989) 39 U.T.L.J. 361; J. Fudge, "The Public/Private Distinction: The Possibilities of and the Limits of the Use of Charter Litigation to Further Feminist Struggles" (1987) 25:3 Osgoode Hall L.J. 485; P. Horwitz, "The Sources and Limits of Freedom of Religion in a Liberal Democracy: Section 2(a) and Beyond" (1996) 54:1 U.T. Fac. L. Rev. 1; A. Hutchinson & A. Petter, "Private Rights/Public Wrongs: The Liberal Lie of the Charter" (1988) 38:3 U.T.L.J. 288; A.C. Hutchinson, *Waiting for Coraf: A Critique of Law and Rights* (Toronto, ON: University

of Canadian constitutional law and jurisprudence based on systematic reflection concerning the relationship between constitutional adjudication and democratic politics has been, for the most part, sorely lacking. While some of the crucial elements of the judgment beg for adequate theorization—especially the reliance on unwritten constitutional principles and the Court's self-limitation of its judicial review function with respect to the application of the law by the political actors—it has of course been possible either to embrace or reject these features of the decision, understanding them cynically as the Court seeking an "old-fashioned" Canadian compromise, or getting itself out of a political bind into which the government awkwardly and unjustifiably put it.

Yet the respect of citizens for the Court depends importantly on their view of it as a forum of principle and of reason. Indeed, absent such a belief, it is doubtful that the judgment of the Court could play any role whatever in restraining or informing political behaviour in the circumstances of the secession, where hateful passion and prejudice are likely to be running at their highest, and the potential "end game" nature of the situation removes many of the usual pragmatic constraints on the degeneration of political action into force and fraud. Thus, even from a pragmatic perspective dominated by a concern with political effects, the question of the legitimacy of the Court's decision, the "compliance pull" of its reasons even and especially in the presence of potentially overmastering passion, deserves serious attention. And this question, especially given the apparent novelty and anomaly of some of the Court's holdings in this

case, can only be answered through an excursion into constitutional theory of the kind dreaded by many Canadian legal academics.

The premise of this paper is that for constitutional adjudication to be a legitimate practice, it must be supported by reasons that justify the judicial role. Although courts may not be forthright in providing these reasons, the task of the constitutional theorist is to identify whatever justifications the courts may provide, and to weave those justifications into coherent accounts. Constitutional theories emerge from and seek to justify our interpretive practice. Only then can we examine the ability of that theory to provide satisfactory explanations of the salient features of particular constitutional decisions, such as the *Quebec Secession Reference*. Practically, a theoretical account is valuable for two reasons: it helps us to better identify in what respects the Court owes us more detail on the legal framework governing secession, and more generally, it helps us to grasp the Court's understanding of its own role in the Canadian constitutional scheme.

## 2. THE THEORETICAL CONTEXT

Our excursus into constitutional theory takes place against the background of a voluminous critical literature. Not surprisingly given what we have already said about the relative poverty of theory in Canadian constitutional scholarship, much of that literature is American, and is framed around that nation's constitutional practice. Nevertheless, that literature is general in aspiration, and accordingly may be of relevance to other jurisdictions, including Canada. What we do here is to briefly mention some of the relevant debates in American constitutional theory. In section 3, we develop an analytical framework to organize these debates; in sections 4 and 5, we examine the *Quebec Secession Reference* in the light of that framework.

*The Political Questions Doctrine*: A long-standing dispute among American constitutional scholars is the question of whether some constitutional provisions, or some constitutional disputes, are by their very nature non-justiciable and hence beyond the ambit of constitutional adjudication, because they are perceived as being fundamentally political in nature. Well-known examples of such political questions are impeachment

---

of Toronto Press, 1995); P. Macklem, "Constitutional Ideologies" (1988) 20:1 Ottawa L. Rev. 117; P. Macklem, "Normative Dimensions of an Aboriginal Right of Self-Government" (1995) 21:1 Queen's L.J. 173; P.J. Monahan & A. Petter, "Developments in Constitutional Law: the 1985–86 Term" (1987) 9 Supreme Court L. R. 69; P. Monahan, *Politics and the Constitution: The Charter, Federalism and the Supreme Court of Canada* (Scarborough, ON: Carswell, 1987); D. Réaume & L. Green, "Education and Linguistic Security in the Charter" (1989) 34:4 McGill L.J. 777; B. Ryder, "The Demise and Rise of the Classical Paradigm in Canadian Federalism: Promoting Autonomy for the Provinces and First Nations" (1991) 36:2 McGill L.J. 309; D. Schneiderman, "Economic Citizenship and Deliberative Democracy: An Inquiry Into Constitutional Limitations on Economic Regulation" (1995) 21:1 Queen's L.J. 125; B. Slattery, "A Theory of the Charter" (1987) 25:4 Osgoode Hall L.J. 701; L. Weinrib, "Limitations on Rights in a Constitutional Democracy" (1996) 6 Caribbean L. Rev. 428.

trials by the Senate and House of Representatives, and the interpretation of the Guarantee Clause (Article IV, section 4) and the Privileges and Immunities Clause (Amendment XIV, section 1).[4]

Although there is general agreement that such a doctrine—known as the political questions doctrine—exists, scholars and courts are divided over its rationale and scope. Some scholars ground the political questions doctrine in constitutional text, claiming that some provisions of the U.S. Constitution commit an issue to the legislative and executive branches for their final determination.[5] Given that constitutional texts are rarely so explicit or unambiguous, though, other scholars have turned instead to the apparent lack of judicially manageable standards for interpreting open-ended constitutional language as a rationale for the doctrine.[6] However, in the face of the development of large and complex bodies of jurisprudence to implement open-ended guarantees such as "equal protection" and "due process" in the U.S. Constitution, defenders of the political questions doctrine have been pushed back to prudential concerns regarding the legitimate scope of judicial review. At this level, critics of the political questions doctrine raise the stakes by arguing that a commitment to judicial review is logically incompatible with the political questions doctrine, because the legitimacy concerns that drive the latter in fact undermine the justification of the former.[7] Proponents of the political questions doctrine respond in two different ways—that a political questions doctrine protects the legitimacy of judicial review by avoiding disputes that would undermine it; and that the political questions doctrine acknowledges that constitutional supremacy does not necessarily lead to an exclusive power for courts to interpret and apply the constitution.[8]

*The Judicial Supremacy & Exclusivity Debate*: Related to the political questions doctrine is the issue of the proper scope of the power of judicial

review first asserted by the U.S. Supreme Court in *Marbury* v. *Madison*.[9] *Marbury* stands for the proposition that the power of courts to interpret constitutional provisions, and to give them priority over conflicting legislation, follows from the combination of (i) the notion of constitutional supremacy (i.e. that the constitution is supreme law), and (ii) the power of the courts to resolve legal disputes before them on the basis of the relevant legal materials, including the Constitution. *Marbury* is the source of on-going controversy, because it infers that courts are competent to interpret and enforce written constitutions (point (ii)) from the very idea of a written constitution that creates institutions and confers limited powers upon them (point (i)). The notion of constitutional supremacy, though, is agnostic on the practical question of which institution is best suited to enforce constitutional provisions.[10] Driven by the suspicion that *Marbury* may have amounted to a judicial usurpation of constitutional power, critics of the decision read it narrowly, by highlighting that it is ambiguous on two critical questions. The first is whether judicial competence implies judicial *supremacy*, i.e. whether judicial interpretations of the Constitution bind other institutions whose own interpretations of the Constitution may differ. The second is whether judicial competence implies judicial exclusivity, i.e. whether only the courts have the power to interpret the Constitution.

Debate on the first issue has revolved around the relationship between the doctrine of precedent and the separation of powers. Proponents of a narrow reading of *Marbury* have suggested that court decisions only bind the parties to a lawsuit (Jefferson), or both the parties and the executive with respect to the enforcement of that decision (Lincoln). However, they stress that precedent does not operate to preclude independent executive or legislative consideration of a constitutional issue.[11] Proponents of a broad reading of *Marbury* argue that judicial supremacy is important because it settles legal disputes with finality, and

4   *Baker* v. *Carr*, 369 U.S. 186 (1962).

5   H. Wechsler, "Toward Neutral Principles of Constitutional Law" (1959) 73:1 Harv. L. Rev. 1.

6   A.M. Bickel, *The Least Dangerous Branch: The Supreme Court at the Bar of Politics* (Indianapolis, IN: Bobbs-Merrill, 1962).

7   M.H. Redish, "Judicial Review and the 'Political Question'" (1984) 79 Nw. U.L. Rev. 1031.

8   M. Tushnet, "Principles, Politics, and Constitutional Law" (1989) 88:1 Mich. L. Rev. 49.

9   5 U.S. (1 Cranch) 137 (1803), 31 U.S. (6 Pet.) 515 (1832) [hereinafter *Marbury*].

10   R.M. Dworkin, *Freedom's Law: The Moral Reading of the American Constitution* (Cambridge, MA: Harvard University Press, 1996) at 33–34.

11   See generally, G. Gunther & K. Sullivan, *Constitutional Law*, 13th ed. (Westbury, NY: Foundation Press, 1997) at 20–27.

hence argue that judgments in constitutional cases establish precedents binding on the other branches of government.[12] Debate on the second issue is focused on whether courts are uniquely qualified to interpret the Constitution. Proponents of exclusivity have argued that certain institutional features of courts (judicial independence and impartiality, the requirement of reasoned decisions) give them a comparative advantage in matters of constitutional adjudication.[13] Critics of exclusivity argue both empirically, positing that non-judicial actors are capable of constitutional interpretation, and normatively, asserting that constitutional discourse should not be confined to legal fora.[14]

12  L. Alexander & F. Schauer, "On Extrajudicial Constitutional Interpretation" (1997) 110:7 Harv. L. Rev. 1359.

13  O.M. Fiss, "Foreword: The Forms of Justice" (1979) 93:1 Harv. L. Rev. 1.

14  M.V. Tushnet, "The Hardest Question in Constitutional Law" (1996) 81:1 Minn. L. Rev. 1; N. Devins & L. Fisher, "Judicial Exclusivity and Political Instability" (1998) 84:1 Va. L. Rev. 83. To some extent, the American debate over the scope and extent of *Marbury* is inapplicable to Canada, because there is clear support in both the constitutional text and in the Canadian constitutional tradition, for the practice of judicial review. Section 52(1) declares the *Constitution Act, 1982* to be the supreme law of Canada, and provides that laws inconsistent with it are of no force or effect; moreover, the status of the *Constitution Acts* as enactments of the Imperial Parliament justifies judicial review as a means to pursuing the traditional goals of parliamentary supremacy and legislative intent. By contrast, since Alexander Bickel's examination of the question in the *Least Dangerous Branch*, there is a broad consensus that neither the text of the U.S. Constitution nor the intent of the framers expressly or impliedly authorizes judicial review. Judicial review must therefore be justified as a matter of first principle. Nevertheless, the institutional questions raised by *Marbury* with respect to the interpretive responsibility of courts are relevant to the Canadian context, because the scope and extent of judicial review are open to differing interpretations.

In this connection, we mention the important work of Brian Slattery. In "A Theory of the Charter," *supra* note 3, Slattery argues for a theory of judicial review in Canada in which courts, executives and legislatures all share the responsibility of interpreting the *Canadian Charter of Rights and Freedoms*. Moreover, he suggests, barring exceptional circumstances, that judicial interpretations of the *Charter* may not even be supreme. Slattery in effect resists a conception of judicial review in Canada that would be identical to a broad reading of *Marbury* in the United States. Slattery's argument is novel, because it is premised not only on the institutional considerations at play in the American discourse, but on the nature of law itself. For Slattery, the very idea of law is that it possesses a normative force that makes it a guide for conduct, a standard for evaluation, and a reason for compliance, in the minds of the persons to whom it is addressed. The role of coercive sanctions to ensure compliance with the law is secondary, or parasitic. In the constitutional context, this means that the rules of constitutional

*The Theory vs. Anti-Theory Debate:*[15] The last debate of relevance revolves around the role of normative political, social, and economic theory in adjudication. Over the course of the last half-century, the most imaginative and influential legal scholarship has applied normative theories to the analysis of legal doctrine, statutes and institutions. Normative law and economics is a prominent example;[16] another is scholarship that relies on the liberal tradition defined by Kant and Rawls[17] or Locke and Nozick.[18] The rise of normative theory in law can in part be understood as a response to an intellectual movement known as Legal Realism. Put simply, the Realists proposed that formal sources of law—legal texts and precedents—did not contain within them the resources to provide "the sort of determinate and defensible answers to concrete and controverted normative questions required by the very idea of law and its rule."[19] Realists attributed this deficiency to the vagueness, abstractness or indeterminacy of legal terms and categories. These features of legal language served as a cloak for judges to implement their own preferences through adjudication, often at the price of important rule of law values such as consistency. In response, scholars invoked normative theories as a means to constrain judicial discretion, to pursue important social goals, and to protect important values.[20]

law are addressed primarily not to the courts that enforce them, but to political institutions that are bound by them. Inasmuch as coming to terms with constitutional norms is an inherently interpretive act, Slattery accordingly argues that executives and legislatures have an important role to play in constitutional interpretation, and that the power of courts to interpret the Constitution is not exclusive. Moreover, since political institutions are presumed to give due consideration to constitutional questions in arriving at their decisions, Slattery suggests that their constitutional interpretations be given deference in certain circumstances defined by relative institutional competence.

15  We draw this account from F. Michelman, "Normative Theory in Legal Scholarship: Moral and Related Political Philosophy" [unpublished].

16  E.g., R.A. Posner, *The Economics of Justice* (Cambridge, MA: Harvard University Press, 1981).

17  E.g., R.M. Dworkin, *Taking Rights Seriously* (Cambridge, MA: Harvard University Press, 1978); F. Michelman, "Constitutional Welfare Rights and A Theory of Justice" in N. Daniels, ed., *Reading Rawls: Critical Studies on Rawls' A Theory of Justice* (Oxford: Basil Blackwell, 1975).

18  R.A. Epstein, *Takings: Private Property and the Power of Eminent Domain* (Cambridge, MA: Harvard University Press, 1985).

19  Michelman, *supra* note 17, section 2 at 2.

20  Set against this background, the debate between non-interpretivists and interpretivists—between scholars who endorsed the reliance

In recent years, though, scholars have begun to question the appropriate role of normative theory in legal interpretation generally, and constitutional interpretation in particular. There are two versions of this criticism. Strong critics argue that moral theories do not and should not play a role in adjudication.[21] Instead, adjudication should be conceived of pragmatically, relying not on moral theory but on common sense, professionalism, and a sense of people's needs, wants, and expectations. Weak critics argue that given the fact of reasonable pluralism in modern societies, adjudicating on the basis of particular moral theories lacks legitimacy.[22] Courts should resist the tendency to ascend to abstract normativity, and instead ground their judgments on "incompletely theorized agreements" that can secure the consent of persons holding divergent and mutually irreconcilable conceptions of the good.

The relevance of these debates among American constitutional theorists to an analysis of the *Quebec Secession Reference* is clear. The judgment, for example, vests primary responsibility for contextualizing the constitutional rules governing secession with the political organs of the Constitution, and eschews any supervisory role for the courts. This part of the judgment is reminiscent of the political questions doctrine, and therefore implicates issues regarding that doctrine's scope and rationale. Similarly, by dividing interpretive responsibility for the norms of the Canadian Constitution between the judicial and political branches, the judgment invites an examination of the issues of interpretive supremacy and exclusivity. This is an issue with far broader implications than

the constitutional framework governing the secession of Quebec.

Finally, the Court's reliance on abstract, unwritten constitutional principles implicates the place of normative political theory in its crafting of the decision. It may be that the intuitively plausible appeal of these principles in the context of secession comes not so much from their implicit source in the constitutional text taken as a whole—the constitution that is being *rejected* by one of the parties in this dispute—but from their place in a certain kind of regime, a liberal democratic one, which the majority of both federalists and secessionists are compelled to accept as legitimate. Here, it may be that one of the most important lessons of the *Reference* for debates in constitutional theory about the role of abstract argument in the presence of normative controversy, is that there are some situations where the problem of agreement under conditions of normative dissensus actually points to a solution at a higher rather than lower level of abstraction. Because of historical disagreements and grievances about Quebec's acceptance of the written constitutional text, including and especially an amending formula that did not give it a veto over most constitutional changes, reliance on the text would have accentuated normative dissensus, while reliance on basic liberal democratic principles did not.

## 3. A FRAMEWORK FOR ANALYSIS

We propose to examine these questions by using the following analytical framework. Our claim is that despite fundamental differences in methodology and outlook, every theory of constitutional interpretation has the following three components. First, a theory of constitutional interpretation must contain an account of *sources*; that is, it must specify criteria for the identification of the constitutional norms which are the objects of constitutional interpretation. Although an emphasis on sources is a prominent feature of positivist jurisprudence,[23] any theory of legal interpretation must address the issue of which materials may

in adjudication on substantive principles of political morality not expressed in the written text of the Constitution (T.C. Grey, "Do We Have an Unwritten Constitution?" (1975) 27:3 Stan. L. Rev. 703) and those who did not (Justice H.L. Black, "The Bill of Rights" (1990) 35 N.Y.U. L. Rev. 865) can easily be seen as part of the larger debate over Legal Realism.

21   R.A. Posner, "The Problematics of Moral and Legal Theory" (1998) 111:7 Harv. L. Rev. 1637. Also see the following commentaries on Posner's lecture in the same issue of the Harvard Law Review: R.M. Dworkin, "Darwin's New Bulldog" (1998) 111:7 Harv. L. Rev. 1718 [hereinafter *Darwin's New Bulldog*]; C. Fried, "Philosophy Matters" (1998) 111:7 Harv. L. Rev. 1739; M.C. Nussbaum, "Still Worthy of Praise" (1998) 111:7 Harv. L. Rev. 1776.

22   C.R. Sunstein, "Incompletely Theorized Agreements" (1995) 108:7 Harv. L. Rev. 1733; C.R. Sunstein, *Legal Reasoning & Political Conflict* (New York: Oxford University Press, 1996) [hereinafter *Legal Reasoning*]; R.H. Fallon, Jr., "Foreword: Implementing the Constitution" (1997) 111:1 Harv. L. Rev. 54.

23   E.g., H.L.A. Hart, *The Concept of Law* (Oxford: Clarendon Press, 1961) (the rule of recognition); H. Kelsen, *General Theory of Law and State*, trans. A. Wedberg (Cambridge, MA: Harvard University Press, 1945) (the grundnorm).

properly figure into interpretation, even if the criteria so specified do not sharply distinguish between the law and normativity more generally.[24] An account of sources, in turn, will usually contain a theory of *amendment*, which specifies criteria for the adoption of new constitutional norms, or the removal of existing ones. Again, it may be that a particular theory denies the possibility of amendment[25] but nevertheless in so stating touches on the issue.

Second, a theory of constitutional interpretation must also contain an account of *interpretive responsibility*, which specifies which institutions are charged with the task of constitutional interpretation. Interpretive responsibility can be understood in two different but equally important senses. It can be understood as *jurisdiction*, that is, whether interpretive responsibility for constitutional norms is exclusive to, divided among, or shared by certain institutions. But interpretive responsibility can also be understood as *supremacy*, which addresses the question of whether the constitutional interpretations of an institution or of institutions vested with interpretive jurisdiction bind other institutions. Although jurisdiction and supremacy are different dimensions of interpretive responsibility, jurisdiction is of primary importance, because exclusive jurisdiction over constitutional interpretation obviates an assessment of which competing interpretation is supreme.

Third, a theory of constitutional interpretation must contain an account of *interpretive style*. Given the identification of constitutional norms, and the allocation of interpretive responsibility, the question which remains is how those norms are to be interpreted and applied. For most of the last half century, American constitutionalists have hotly debated whether the text, original intent, or various versions of substantive political morality should be given pride of place in constitutional interpretation. It is important to recognize that interpretive methodology or style is to a large extent indissociable from the first two features of theories of constitutional interpretation. Debates over style,

in essence, have revolved around the identification of the sources of constitutional norms, and the relative importance of these various sources. Similarly, style may be driven by the institutional allocation of interpretive responsibility, so that, for example, a court may decline to articulate a complete theory of a constitutional provision in order to prompt a political actor to do so.[26]

## 4. THE POSITIVIST UNDERSTANDING OF CONSTITUTIONAL INTERPRETATION

Utilizing this framework, we now detail what we call the *positivist account* of constitutional interpretation. This account cannot be found in any canonical texts or judicial decisions. Rather, it is a composite that we have constructed on the basis of our understanding of Canadian constitutional culture. The positivist account, in other words, articulates many of the intuitions held by the various actors in the Canadian constitutional scheme, but in a systematic way. Although this account is descriptively inaccurate of actual Canadian constitutional practice, the enterprise is nevertheless valuable because it serves to highlight the distinctive features of the judgment in the *Quebec Secession Reference*. In important ways, although not more than crudely theorized, this account is *presupposed* in the attack on "activist" judicial review by right-wing scholars such as Morton and Knopf, who adopt a conservative variation of the positivist account, in which ambiguous constitutional language is construed by reference to original intent, or failing that, the "traditional understanding" of the concepts invoked by constitutional provisions, as revealed by political practice.[27]

*Sources*: According to the positivist account, the sources of constitutional norms in Canada are limited to the express provisions of the *Constitution Acts* (this account has, of course, to deal in some way with important rules of Canadian constitutional law, for example concerning the prerogative powers of the Crown and the doctrine of parliamentary privilege, that are not specified in the constitutional text; this

---

24  E.g., *Taking Rights Seriously, supra* note 17 at 344; R.M. Dworkin, *Law's Empire* (Cambridge, MA: Belknap Press, 1986).

25  E.g., the view of the German Constitutional Court that certain articles of the German Basic Law are unamendable (see D.P. Kommers, *The Constitutional Jurisprudence of the Federal Republic of Germany* (Durham, NC: Duke University Press, 1989) at 76).

26  N.K. Katyal, "Judges as Advicegivers" (1998) 50:6 Stan. L. Rev. 1709.

27  R. Knopff & F.L. Morton, *Charter Politics* (Scarborough, ON: Nelson Canada, 1992) at 130.

element in the Canadian constitutional system drives something of a wedge, however narrow, between positivism and textualism tout court). One textual basis for the textualism of the positivists is s. 52(2) of the *Constitution Act, 1982*,[28] which lists the legal documents that together make up the Constitution of Canada.[29] This is not to say that the *Constitution Acts* are exhaustive of constitutional law; the positivist account also gives an important place to past interpretations of those provisions, which have precedential force. However, those precedents derive their legitimacy from the fact that they represent authoritative interpretations of the constitutional text, and applications of the constitutional text to the facts of particular cases.

The centrality of text to the positivist account of constitutional interpretation has three important implications for the relationship between the norms of constitutional law, and normativity at large. First, it suggests a sharp distinction between the former and the latter. The latter lies outside the law; in constitutional terms, it lies in the world of politics. The former, by contrast, lies within and defines the boundaries of the world of the Constitution. Secondly, positivism has to cope with the possibility that no written text can explicitly contain rules for all those situations in which it would be desirable for the text to be governing of the controversy. One answer to this dilemma is to revert to original intent, asking how the framers would have wished a controversy to be resolved given what *is* explicitly specified in the text. An alternative answer, more characteristic of Canadian than

American constitutionalism, is to simply say that, after a point, the law runs out. The constitutional order contains gaps, in which the law is silent, and politics reigns supreme, absent an explicit choice to amend the Constitution to deal explicitly with that situation. Thus, amendment to the Constitution requires express additions to the constitutional text, themselves the product of textually specified processes of amendment. As it turns out, Part V of the *Constitution Act, 1982* contains a variety of procedures to amend the Constitution. The relevant point for our discussion is that amendment is exclusively the domain of the political institutions (Parliament and the provincial legislatures).

*Interpretive Responsibility*: The positivist account is clear on the allocation of interpretive responsibility, in both of its senses. The task of constitutional interpretation is vested with the judiciary, and, ultimately, the Supreme Court of Canada. Moreover, the responsibility of the Supreme Court is both exclusive and supreme. It has exclusive jurisdiction over constitutional interpretation because no other actors in the constitutional scheme—neither executives nor legislatures at the provincial or federal level—have any kind of interpretive responsibility with respect to constitutional norms. To adapt a distinction most famously made by Ronald Dworkin, the political organs are uniquely qualified and hence confined to examine considerations of policy, whereas courts are expert in and limited to examining questions of constitutional principle.[30] Because the Supreme Court has exclusive jurisdiction over constitutional interpretation, its interpretations also enjoy supremacy; more accurately, the issue of supremacy among competing interpretations does not really arise, because the Court's jurisdiction is exclusive.[31]

*Interpretive Style*: Finally, the positivist account contains a view of interpretive style. Legal interpretation is delimited by the text of the Constitution, so that the beginning and ending points of constitutional interpretation are the express terms of individual constitutional provisions. This is not to say that principles of substantive political morality should not play a role in constitutional interpretation. As Fred Schauer

---

28  *Constitution Act, 1982*, being Schedule B to the *Canada Act 1982* (U.K.), 1982, c. 11 [hereinafter *Constitution Act, 1982*].

29  Section 52(2) of the *Constitution Act, 1982*, provides that:
The Constitution of Canada includes:
(a) the *Canada Act 1982*, including this Act;
(b) the Acts and orders referred to in the schedule; and
(c) any amendment to any Act or order referred to in paragraph (a) or (b). Note, though, that the Supreme Court of Canada held in *New Brunswick Broadcasting Co.* v. *Nova Scotia*, [1993] 1 S.C.R. 319 that s. 52(2) should not be read exhaustively (i.e., that "includes" is not synonymous with "means"), and as a consequence, that the doctrine of parliamentary privilege constituted part of the Constitution of Canada. The source of this unwritten rule was the preamble to the *Constitution Act, 1867* (U.K), 20 & 31 Vict., c. 3, which states that the Constitution of Canada is "a Constitution similar in Principle to that of the United Kingdom."

30  *Taking Rights Seriously, supra* note 17 at ch. 4.

31  For a similar account, see "A Theory of the Charter," *supra* note 3.

persuasively argues, some constitutional provisions appear to incorporate principles of political morality "by reference," and therefore invite (but do not compel) courts to engage in the type of normative reasoning characteristic of moral and political philosophy.[32] Schauer's point, though, is that not all provisions are worded in this way. Setting to one side the inherent limitations of legal language to address factual situations that were unanticipated when that language was framed (the problem of open-texturedness), some provisions are relatively specific and precise, and admit of a narrower range of interpretive choices. The interpretive frames surrounding such terms is narrow enough to create a strong presumption against the recourse to normative reasoning.[33] Given the primacy of text in signaling the appropriate style of interpretation, the positivist account defends the possibility of distinguishing the construction of constitutional provisions from moral reasoning writ-large.

The positivist account has a number of important features worth emphasizing because of their relevance to our analysis of the *Quebec Secession Reference*. First, a central tenet of legal positivism is a sharp distinction between legality and legitimacy. A legal regime may conform with legality if it complies with the formal rules and procedures laid down in the constitution. But such a legal regime may nonetheless lack legitimacy if it fails to accord with principles of political justice that can justify the coercive use of state power. Legitimacy and legality may coincide; indeed, it is the ambition of liberal democracy to make the latter a condition of the former.[34] However, in cases where they diverge (as occurred in the *Quebec Secession Reference*), the positivist account denies courts the power to draw them together.

Second, the special role of the Supreme Court in constitutional interpretation yields a view on justiciability. Since the interpretive responsibility of the Court is both exclusive and supreme, every rule of constitutional law in principle can be the subject of

adjudication. As a consequence, every rule of constitutional law is justiciable, and a dispute that is non-justiciable lies outside the bounds of constitutional law.

Finally, the positivist account, by implication, suggests what inappropriate judicial behaviour consists of. Courts that look beyond the text of the Constitution as a source of constitutional norms, that engage in amendment under the guise of interpretation, that surrender interpretive authority to other organs of government, or that engage in grand theorizing in a manner not invited by the constitutional text, have contravened the constitutional norms defining the judicial role.

## 5. PARTNERSHIP AND INSTITUTIONAL DIALOGUE

*Sources*: What is particularly striking about the *Quebec Secession Reference* is that it rejects each of the features of the positivist account. Consider the judgment's conception of sources. The Court considered and rejected the notion that the text of the *Constitution Acts* were exhaustive of Canadian constitutional law. Rather, at the outset of its answer to the reference questions, the Court stated:

> The "Constitution of Canada" certainly includes the constitutional texts enumerated in s. 52(2) of the *Constitution Act, 1982*. Although these texts have a primary place in determining constitutional rules, they are not exhaustive. The Constitution also "embraces unwritten, as well as written rules"....[35]

The Court's assertion that the Canadian Constitution contains unwritten rules or "principles" (terms which the Court used interchangeably, without reference to the technical distinction between the two drawn by legal theorists)[36] required some sort of justification. Indeed, given the Court's statements in a recent judgment that written constitutions ground the legitimacy

---

32  F. Schauer, "Constitutional Invocations" (1997) 65:4 Fordham L. Rev. 1295.

33  F. Schauer, "Easy Cases" (1985) 58:1 S. Cal. L. Rev. 399.

34  J. Habermas, *Between Facts and Norms: Contributions to a Discourse Theory of Law and Democracy* (Cambridge, MA: MIT Press, 1996); D. Dyzenhaus, "The Legitimacy of Legality" (1996) 46:1 U.T.L.J. 129.

35  *Quebec Secession Reference, supra* note 1 at para. 32, quoting s. 52(2) of the *Constitution Act, 1982, supra* note 28 and *Reference re Remuneration of Judges of the Provincial Court of Prince Edward Island*, [1997] 3 S.C.R. 3 [hereinafter *Provincial Judges Reference*] at para. 92.

36  E.g., *Taking Rights Seriously, supra* note 17 at ch. 2.

of judicial review in liberal democracies, and promote legal certainty and predictability[37]—elements of the positivist account—the Court needed to explain why the conventional account was inadequate. Unless, of course, what it meant by "unwritten rules" was confined to those rules that have long existed as part of Canadian constitutional law, concerning, for example, the prerogative powers of the Crown and the doctrine of parliamentary privilege, and which were not extinguished by the creation of the Constitution Act, 1982.[38]

In its defense of the presence of unwritten rules or principles in the Canadian constitutional scheme, though, it is clear that the Court had in mind much more than these well-established rules. Upon close reading, it appears that the Court offered two different defenses. The first justification attempted to tie the written text and the unwritten *principles* of the Constitution together. According to the Court, the unwritten principles "inform and sustain the constitutional text: they are the vital unstated assumptions upon which the text is based."[39] This formulation suggests that the principles are general or abstract in nature, and the specific provisions of the constitutional text implement or actualize them. Indeed, the unwritten norms identified by the Court—federalism, democracy, constitutionalism and the rule of law, and respect for minority rights—*were* general or abstract. These principles, in the Court's words, formed the Constitution's "internal architecture" or "basic constitutional structure," around which the specific provisions of the Constitution were framed.[40] This justification of unwritten constitutional principles also suggests that they play a rather limited practical role—as aids to the construction of ambiguous constitutional provisions or the harmonious interpretation of different and perhaps apparently divergent or conflicting constitutional provisions. Again, the Court said as much, when it stated that these principles "assist in the interpretation of the text and the delineation of spheres of jurisdiction, the scope of

rights and obligations, and the role of our political institutions."[41]

The difficulty with the first justification is that it cannot explain the Court's judgment, for the Court went far beyond using unwritten principles to construe ambiguous constitutional provisions or reconcile provisions that were in conflict. In fact, the constitutional text contains no references, explicit or implicit, to the legal principles governing secession. Moreover, in contrast to the generality or abstractness of the unwritten norms of federalism, the rule of law, etc., the rules governing secession laid down by the Court are rather specific. What must be acknowledged is that the Court engaged in a style of constitutional interpretation which on any positivist account would be characterized as making constitutional rules, as opposed to merely applying them. In effect, the Court wove a secession clause into the Constitution through the use of unwritten constitutional norms. It seems that the Court acknowledged this, when it quoted, with approval, a statement in an earlier judgment that the unwritten principles could be used to fill the "gaps in the express terms of the constitutional text."[42]

Faced with the inadequacy of its first justification to make sense of its judgment, the Court offered another. It defended the use of unwritten rules to not only clarify the written Constitution, but also to augment it. This argument was functional. In the Court's words, the unwritten rules of Canadian constitutional law exist:

> because problems or situations may arise which are not expressly dealt with by the text of the Constitution. In order to endure over time, a constitution must contain a comprehensive set of rules and principles which are capable of providing an exhaustive legal framework for our system of government.[43]

The Court's argument appeared to be that the written text of the Constitution cannot possibly specify in advance adequate rules to govern all the situations that may arise in the future in which the constitutional order has a stake or interest. The difficulty with this

37  *Provincial Judges Reference, supra* note 35 at para. 93.
38  P.W. Hogg, *Constitutional Law of Canada*, Student ed. (Scarborough, ON: Carswell, 2000) at c. 1.7 and 1.9.
39  *Quebec Secession Reference, supra* note 1 at para. 49.
40  *Ibid.* at para. 50; the second quotation is from *OPSEU v. Ontario (A.G.)*, [1987] 2 S.C.R. 2 at 57.
41  *Quebec Secession Reference, supra* note 1 at para. 52.
42  *Ibid.* at para. 53, citing *Provincial Judges Reference, supra* note 35 at para. 104.
43  *Ibid.* at para. 32.

argument, though, is that it appears to beg the question as to why the appropriate solution to this in a given case would be to evolve the Constitution through judicial interpretation of the underlying principles at its foundation, rather than to turn responsibility over to the political actors to effect an amendment of the Constitution, pursuant to the procedures provided in Part V of the *Constitution Act, 1982*. Here one kind of institutional answer that might have at least limited theoretical force is that the practice reference of questions from the political branch to the Court gives it a place, where invited by the political branch to do so, in charting the future influence of the Constitution on political events that the court might not possess when deciding cases and controversies. It should be noted that, in the *Secession Reference*, the very constitutional basis for references was challenged, and the Court had to provide an explicit affirmation of the legitimacy of the institutional role thrust upon it through the practice of the reference. Yet, in that part of the judgment as well, the Court remained largely unforthcoming with any general theory about the significance of the reference for the balance of judicial and political action in charting the future evolution of constitutional law and politics.

Thus, what the Court required, but what its judgment did not provide, is an account of sources that justifies the recourse to unwritten constitutional norms. In our view, the theory that best justifies the judgment is one we call dualist interpretation.[44] The dualist scheme comprehends two different interpretive roles for courts. First, there is the task of *ordinary interpretation*, whereby courts interpret and apply the constitutional text in the fashion suggested by the conventional account. The existence of unwritten norms is acknowledged here; however, their role is limited to resolving textual ambiguities and reconciling conflicting provisions. Ordinary interpretation covers day-to-day matters in the life-cycle of modern constitutions—specifically, the resolution of concrete legal disputes before courts of law where the parties do not challenge the very legitimacy of the constitutional order itself.

However, at exceptional moments, a court may engage in *extra-ordinary interpretation*, in which the text assumes secondary importance. Here, the Constitution is comprehended as a scheme of principle organized around unwritten norms that explain, and are implemented by, the constitutional text. These norms are regarded as providing "an exhaustive legal framework for our system of government," and as a consequence, invite the courts to interpret them in a manner that, in positivist eyes, would resemble amendment, and lead to the fashioning of new constitutional rules. We would classify the Court's judgment in the *Quebec Secession Reference* as a paradigmatic case of extra-ordinary interpretation.

The dualist scheme raises a number of questions that revolve around the relationship between the power of the courts to engage in extra-ordinary interpretation, and the power of political institutions to alter the Constitution through formal amendment. The first concerns the respective roles of extra-ordinary interpretation and formal amendment: has extra-ordinary interpretation displaced the need for ordinary amendment, and if not, how do we determine which one applies? The second question raised by the dualist scheme concerns the distinction between extra-ordinary interpretation and formal amendment: are extra-ordinary interpretations of the Constitution equivalent to amendments, or are they something different? Again, the Court was woefully unclear, in large part because while at some points it recognizes the extra-ordinary nature of the context, in many other places it seeks to present its judgment as quite ordinary, rather than acknowledging that it had shifted gears into an extra-ordinary mode. Thus, for example, at one point it stated that the duty to negotiate flowed not from a positive referendum result that amounted to a repudiation of the existing constitutional order, but rather from any proposals for constitutional amendment.[45]

Nonetheless, some points are clear. Extra-ordinary interpretations, in strictly legal terms, are not formal amendments to the constitutional text. But extra-ordinary interpretation does force the positivist distinction between amendment and interpretation, and replaces it with a broader notion of constitutional

---

44  As will became apparent, our account of dualist interpretation differs sharply from Bruce Ackerman's account of dualist democracy in *We the People, Vol. 1: Foundations* (Cambridge, MA: Belknap Press of Harvard University Press, 1991).

45  *Quebec Secession Reference, supra* note 1 at para. 69.

evolution. Instead of imagining the Constitution as bounded or as containing gaps, that must be added to by constitutional amendment, dualist interpretation views the Constitution as a dynamic entity that aspires to exhaustiveness. In one narrow sense, the written Constitution does "run out," because the textual provisions may not address a particular scenario. But in a more fundamental sense, it does not, because the internal logic of the constitutional document is capable of governing those situations. The extension of the internal logic of the Constitution occurs either through formal amendment or extra-ordinary interpretation.[46]

*Interpretive Responsibility*: Another distinctive feature of the judgment is that it vests substantial, if not exclusive, responsibility for interpreting the constitutional rules on secession in particular situations or contexts with political organs, not the courts. This is a break with the Canadian constitutional tradition, which, as the Court itself noted, has hitherto drawn a distinction between the law of the Constitution, which was judicially enforceable, and the political conventions of the Constitution, which were only subject to political sanctions. Indeed, given that the operation of the unwritten rules on secession was held to impose binding legal obligations on the federal and provincial governments, one might have expected the Court to hold that the application of those rules to particular situations related to secession would be a matter of judicial interpretive responsibility. However, the Court noted "that judicial intervention, even in relation to the *law* of the Constitution, is subject to the Court's appreciation of its proper role in the constitutional scheme."[47]

The Court then went to hold that its role was "limited to the identification of the relevant aspects of the Constitution in their broadest sense."[48] The relevant constitutional rules—defined in earlier passages—fell into two categories. First, there were the pre-requisites to the duty to engage in constitutional negotiations: a referendum vote by "a clear majority [of the population of Quebec] on a clear question" that evinced their intention to secede from Canada. Second, there

were the rules governing both the process and outcome of the negotiations themselves. The Court's governing premise appeared to be that those negotiations must be conducted "in accordance with the underlying constitutional principles already discussed," such as democracy.[49] This premise led the Court to reject the view that a positive referendum would impose a "legal obligation on the other provinces and federal government to accede to the secession of a province."[50] But it also rejected the "the reverse proposition, that a clear expression of self-determination by the people of Quebec would impose *no* obligations upon the other provinces or the federal government."[51] Instead, the Court held that a positive referendum vote for secession triggers "a reciprocal obligation on all parties to Confederation to negotiate constitutional changes to respond to that desire," which seems to amount to an obligation not only to negotiate, but to negotiate in good faith.[52] Moreover, the judgment seemed to suggest that the substantive outcome of any agreement must show adequate respect for the unwritten constitutional principles. Thus, the Court stated that

46 Compare this account with Ackerman's in *We the People, supra* note 44—ours is almost a mirror image of his dualist account.
47 *Quebec Secession Reference, supra* note 1 at para. 98 [emphasis in original].
48 *Ibid.* at para. 100.
49 *Ibid.* at para. 88. Also see *ibid.* at para. 90: "The conduct of the parties in such negotiations would be governed by the same constitutional principles which give rise to the duty to negotiate: federalism, democracy, constitutionalism and the rule of law, and the protection of minorities."
50 *Ibid.* at para. 90.
51 *Ibid.* at para. 92 [emphasis in original]. The Court went on to say (in *ibid.* at para. 92) that "[t]he continued existence and operation of the Canadian constitutional order cannot remain indifferent to the clear expression of a clear majority of Quebecers that they no longer wish to remain in Canada."
52 *Ibid.* at para. 88. It is noteworthy that "[w]hile the negotiators would have to contemplate the possibility of secession," the Court clearly envisions that the negotiations may not reach agreement (*ibid.* at para. 97). Also see *ibid.* at para. 96: "No one can predict that course that such negotiations might take. The possibility that they might not lead to an agreement amongst the parties must be recognized." Thus, the Court never endorses the proposition that, at the end of the day, good faith in negotiation extends to actually offering or acceding to secession. The possibility of impasse, even in the case that the constitutional principles are respected by all parties to the negotiations, clearly implies that these principles do not contain a decision-rule able to break such an impasse. An example of such a decision-rule would be that Quebec must be offered secession if it agrees to terms consistent with the four principles. But the Court clearly preferred to accept the possibility of an impasse, with a judgment on the responsibility for the impasse to be left to the world community, than to tilt even that far in implying a right to secede. On these points, see *Special Senate Committee on Bill C-20 Debates*, (8 June 2000) (R. Howse), online: Proceedings of the Special Committee on Bill C-20 <http://www.parl.gc.ca/36/2/parlbus/commbus/senate/com-e/clar-e/04ev-e.htm>.

"[t]he negotiation process must be conducted with an eye to the constitutional principles we have outlined, which must inform the actions of *all* the participants in the negotiation process."[53] Beyond specifying these constitutional rules, the Court stated that it had "no supervisory role."[54]

Given this radical departure from normal constitutional practice, the Court owed us an account of how it understood its role in the Canadian constitutional scheme. The Court offered two such explanations. The first, oddly enough, reverted to the traditional distinction between the law of the Constitution and "the workings of the political process."[55] The former defines the constitutional framework within which the latter sorts of non-constitutional decisions are made. Moreover, because those latter decisions are non-constitutional, they are beyond the scope of judicial review and non-justiciable. As the Court stated:

> The Court has no supervisory role over the *political aspects* of constitutional negotiations. Equally, the initial impetus for negotiation, namely a clear majority on a clear question in favour of secession, is subject only to *political evaluation*, and properly so.[56]

A few sentences later, the Court re-iterated the distinction between the legal framework governing secession and the non-justiciability of the political judgments that must be made within that framework, when it added, "[t]o the extent that the questions are political in nature, it is not the role of the judiciary to interpose its own views on the different negotiating positions of the parties."[57] Finally, the Court clarified that non-legal was synonymous with non-justiciable, when it referred to "[t]he non-justiciability of political issues that lack a legal component."[58]

The difficulty with this justification is that it does not yield the Court's innovative holding that the rules governing secession are at once legally binding and non-justiciable. Rather, the Court appears to have regressed to the standard view that the law of

the Constitution is the business of the Courts, and defines the decisional space within which the political process can proceed unimpeded aside from those constraints. Judicial interpretation of the Constitution, in other words, is both exclusive and supreme. This sort of analysis suggests the following *ratio*—that the legal rules governing secession are fully justiciable, but that beyond those legal requirements, political actors may act unconstrained. The Court, though, held exactly the opposite—that the legal rules governing secession are non-justiciable (or at least not fully justiciable), but that those rules are legally binding on all parties to the negotiating process and must guide their deliberations. In other words, the Court's judgment modified the traditional approach to interpretive responsibility in two different respects. First, it replaced exclusive with shared interpretive jurisdiction, giving the political actors a role in constitutional interpretation. Moreover, by eschewing a "supervisory role," the Court may have even divided interpretive supremacy over the Constitution, at least with respect to the rules governing secession.

The Court's second justification spoke directly to these novel aspects of its judgment. Instead of sharply distinguishing between law and politics, the Court relied on the comparative institutional advantage of the political actors in this area of constitutional interpretation, stating that the Court itself lacked the requisite "information and expertise."[59] Elaborating upon the informational limitations of the litigation process, the Court explained that "the methods appropriate for the search for truth in a court of law are ill-suited to getting to the bottom of constitutional negotiations."[60] Clarifying the limitations of its expertise, the Court reasoned that "the strong defence of legitimate interests and the taking of positions which, in fact, ignore the legitimate interests of others is one that also defies legal analysis."[61] In other words, judicially enforceable standards are absent. Presumably, shared jurisdiction and divided supremacy are suitable responses to these institutional considerations.

Unfortunately, the Court's second justification is problematic as well. It is not at all clear, for example,

---

53  *Ibid.* at para. 94 [emphasis in original].
54  *Ibid.* at para. 100.
55  *Ibid.*
56  *Ibid.* [emphasis added].
57  *Ibid.* at para. 101.
58  *Ibid.* at para. 102.

59  *Ibid.* at para. 100.
60  *Ibid.* at para. 101.
61  *Ibid.*

that the Court is incapable of adjudicating upon both the pre-conditions to, and the process and outcome of, constitutional negotiations. The interpretation of the terms "clear majority" and "clear question," the enforcement of the obligation to negotiate in good faith, and even the compliance of a negotiated agreement with certain basic constitutional principles, are not totally beyond the realm of judicial competence.[62] As the debate over the political questions doctrine illustrates, judicially enforceable standards can always be developed. Moreover, assuming these institutional considerations to be valid, they fail to define the Court's role. Although the Court has eschewed the prospect of supervision, it nevertheless articulated the justifications behind the rules governing secession. Although this feature of the judgment may be necessary in cases of extra-ordinary interpretation, one gets the sense that the Court would have offered these justifications regardless.

The account which best explains the Court's judgment is one we call the model of *joint constitutional responsibility*. It is inspired by Lawrence Sager's theory of the underenforced constitutional norm. Sager's basic claim is that there are situations where the U.S. Supreme Court, "because of institutional concerns, has failed to enforce a provision of the Constitution to its full conceptual boundaries."[63] That norm is legally valid to its full conceptual limits. Judicial decisions only demarcate the limits of its judicial enforcement, and reflect the practical limitations on the ability of courts to translate abstract constitutional ideals into judicially enforceable standards. Beyond the boundaries of judicial competence, then, it is for the political organs of the Constitution to frame their own interpretations of those norms and assess their own compliance with them. Thus, interpretive responsibility for particular constitutional norms is both shared and divided. It is shared to the extent that courts are responsible for articulating constitutional norms in their conceptually abstract form. But interpretive

responsibility is divided because beyond the limits of doctrine, constitutional interpretation is left to the political organs. The image which emerges is one of "judicial and legislative cooperation in the molding of concrete standards through which elusive and complex constitutional norms … come to be applied."[64]

The model of joint constitutional responsibility also draws a distinction between the full conceptual limits of a constitutional norm and the boundaries of judicial enforceability. The limits of justiciability, though, turn not on competence but on legitimacy. Vesting the courts with exclusive and supreme interpretive responsibility creates the danger of marginalizing the Constitution in public discourse. By denying democratic institutions any role in constitutional interpretation, those institutions may fail to examine constitutional considerations at all in the legislative process. As a consequence, the Constitution may recede from importance in public life. This is a particular problem for liberal democracies like Canada, for which constitutions are a central component of national self-understanding. We adopt here the (admittedly simplifying) distinction between civic nations, which are founded on the basis of a shared commitment to principles of political justice, and ethnic nations, that are viewed as instruments to ensure the survival and flourishing of a particular people or Volk. In civic nations like Canada, the principles of political justice often take the form of written constitutions. Written constitutions, then, serve as the cement of social solidarity, and can give rise to a constitutional patriotism. However, for that constitutional patriotism to be sustained, it is imperative that constitutional discourse take place not just in the courts, but in democratic institutions, giving a concrete political existence to the common values and principles that underpin such constitutional patriotism.[65]

---

62  For example, see the judgment of the Constitutional Court of South Africa in *Certification of the Constitution of South Africa, 1996 (Re)*, [1996] S.A.J. No. 19, where that court measured the compliance of the Final South African Constitution with a list of "constitutional principles" spelled out in the Interim Constitution.

63  L.G. Sager, "Fair Measure: The Legal Status of Underenforced Constitutional Norms" (1978) 91:6 Harv. L. Rev. 1212 at 1213.

64  *Ibid.* at 1240.

65  This understanding of the importance of constitutional politics—by necessity, a politics of principle—amounts to a rejection of the view that politics is merely about registering and aggregating the preferences of citizens. See generally, J. Cohen, "Deliberation and Democratic Legitimacy" in A. Hamlin & P. Pettit, eds., *The Good Polity: Normative Analysis of the State* (New York: Basil Blackwell, 1989); J. Cohen, "Procedure and Substance in Deliberative Democracy" in S. Benhabib, ed., *Democracy and Difference: Contesting the Boundaries of the Political* (Princeton, NJ: Princeton University Press, 1996); J. Elster, "The Market and the Forum" in J. Elster & A. Hylland, eds., *Foundations of Social Choice Theory*

The model of joint constitutional responsibility raises a number of difficult questions. The first is the question of *which* constitutional norms should be subject to this shared and divided jurisdiction, as opposed to exclusive judicial interpretation. The judgment itself offers little assistance in this regard. By focusing on institutional considerations, to the exclusion of the larger issues of political legitimacy raised by involving the courts in the future of the federation, the Court deprived itself of the opportunity to address this issue. It may be that what drove the Court was a sense that the judicial interpretation of the rules governing secession would have failed to generate widespread acceptance in the political community. This is yet another part of the judgment where the Court owed us a better explanation than it provided.

The second question raised by the model of joint constitutional responsibility concerns the interpretive responsibility of political institutions.[66] That responsibility entails an obligation for the political organs to lay down relatively concrete principles that interpret and apply the constitutional rules governing secession. This obligation follows from the general principle that rules of constitutional law often must be interpreted and specified to be fully implemented. Courts do this through the development of doctrine. Political institutions, by contrast, may do this through statutes, resolutions, or declarations. In the wake of the *Quebec Secession Reference*, for example, political institutions must now define what a clear majority and a clear question mean. These terms are not self-defining, and require elaboration. This, of course, is the best way to understand the proposed *Clarity Act* (Bill C-20), the long title of which is "An Act *to give effect* to the requirement for clarity as set out in the opinion of the Supreme Court of Canada in the *Quebec Secession Reference*."[67] Indeed, one effect of

the judgment has been to force these issues onto the forefront of the political agenda. Bill C-20 takes up this challenge, by spelling out procedures and criteria according to which the House of Commons will determine whether a clear majority has voted in favour of a clear question in favour of secession. The more general point is that the vesting of interpretive responsibility with political institutions enhances political accountability. The Court's simultaneous statement that it lacked the power to interpret the rules governing secession, but that the political institutions *were* charged with this task, had the effect of clarifying the lines of responsibility.[68] Thus, coupled with a much clearer legal framework governing secession, the judgment means that political institutions can no longer avoid difficult questions on the pretext that they are clouded in constitutional uncertainty. Indeed, there is no doubt that *Quebec Secession Reference* gave rise to a political dynamic that made the enactment of Bill C-20 both politically inevitable and constitutionally required.

A further perspective on the Court's view of interpretative responsibility is provided by Sunstein's observation that certain judicial outcomes can be understood as democracy-promoting, or even democracy-forcing.[69] The Court may further a conception of deliberative democracy by deciding in such a way as to require democratic deliberation, or to improve its quality. In some instances, where positions are entrenched and common ground elusive, there may be not be an evident starting point or even rules of the game for democratic deliberation, the idea of a "clear background" against which democratic institutions can work. By specifying some general rules or norms that can constitute legitimate common ground on which deliberation might occur, but by refusing to decide in such a way as to foreclose the possible outcomes of deliberation, the Court promotes democracy. In fact, the duty to negotiate—the most striking unwritten rule elaborated by the Court in this decision—could well be described as "democracy-forcing." The democratic angle is useful, particularly, in pointing out the oversimplification in the positivist account

---

(New York: Cambridge University Press, 1986); C.R. Sunstein, "Preferences and Politics" (1991) 20 Phil. & Publ. Affairs 3 at 20.

66  For interesting discussions of this issue in the American context, see D.A. Strauss, "Presidential Interpretation of the Constitution" (1993) 15 Cardozo L. Rev. 113; P. Brest, "The Conscientious Legislator's Guide to Constitutional Interpretation" (1975) 27:3 Stan. L. Rev. 585.

67  Bill C-20, *An Act to give effect to the requirement for clarity as set out in the opinion of the Supreme Court of Canada in the Quebec Secession Reference*, 2d Sess., 36th Parl., 1999 (as passed by the House of Commons 15 March 2000) [emphasis added].

68  Katyal, *supra* note 26.

69  C.R. Sunstein, *One Case at a Time: Judicial Minimalism on the Supreme Court* (Cambridge, MA: Harvard University Press, 1999).

that suggests the appropriate posture for the Court, where the existing law "runs out," is to leave matters to the political process or constitutional amendment. But by failing to act at all, the Court may, in certain situations, actually worsen, or increase the transaction costs, of the political actors resolving the controversy, or agreeing to new explicit constitutional rules for future resolution of this kind of controversy by the judiciary.

The final question is whether the model of joint constitutional responsibility excludes the possibility of judicial review entirely. Recall that constitutional rules are valid to their conceptual limits, but are underenforced for reasons of legitimacy. It is not inconceivable, then, that a situation might arise where an interpretation put on an underenforced constitutional rule by a political institution might be conceptually invalid. This is a hard case, because the courts defer matters to the political institutions precisely because a judicial decision would lack the requisite legitimacy. But if a political institution's interpretation is conceptually flawed, then its decision may lack legitimacy as well. It may be in these exceptional cases that the courts would retain the power to strike down political decisions. Indeed, one of the justifications for allowing courts to articulate a theory underlying a provision may be to put political institutions on notice that such judicial review is still available. What this suggests is that the model of joint responsibility is ultimately founded on judicial self-restraint, rather than the abdication of the power of judicial review in deference to the prerogatives of the other branches of government. Thus, we are somewhat skeptical that the Court has washed its hands entirely of the rules governing secession.[70] In this regard, the enactment

of Bill C-20 may rather unexpectedly give the courts an opening to re-enter the legal fray over the constitutional framework regarding secession, because it provides a statutory basis for judicial intervention.[71] Indeed, interpreting the Court to have closed off further *dialogue ex ante* with the political branches by permanently renouncing interpretive responsibility over certain subject-matter—pre-judging its competence, as it were, without being willing to consider, based on the issues that emerge, which have sufficient legal elements to warrant further intervention—would suggest not joint responsibility, but abdication of responsibility, at odds with the Court's own substantive criteria for sharing.[72]

*Interpretive Style*: The final issue we address in this section is the Court's interpretive methodology. Instead of sticking closely to the constitutional text, as the conventional account urges courts to do, the Court articulated a normative vision of the Canadian constitutional order. This is evident from the outset of the judgment, where the Court stated that this case presented "momentous questions that go to the heart of our system of constitutional government."[73] After dealing with some preliminary objections to its reference jurisdiction, the Court then turned not to the text of the *Constitution Acts*, but to the unwritten principles of constitutional law that lay at the foundation of the Canadian constitutional order. The Court then went on to discuss each principle in considerable detail, both at the level of theory and practice. Thus, the Court took pains to distinguish constitutional democracy subject to the rule of law from simple

---

70  Compare *Nixon* v. *United States*, 506 U.S. 224 (1993) (various justices expressing the view that Congressional interpretation of the term "trial" in the Impeachment Clause are subject to judicial review in extreme circumstances, such as the adoption of Senate rules providing for automatic convictions without any formal proceedings).

The question of whether the Court will second-guess interpretations of the rules governing secession adopted by the political actors is distinct from another issue—whether the Court will enforce the provisions of Part V of the *Constitution Act, 1982* to ensure that the correct amending formulas are applied to effectuate constitutional change. Unfortunately, the judgment is extremely ambiguous on this point. On the one hand, the failure of the Court to mention the amending procedures in Part V, coupled with its

disavowal of any supervisory role in constitutional negotiations, suggests that unwritten norms subject to political interpretation alone will guide the process of secession. The centrality of referenda to constitutional change, despite the lack of any textual support for that view, also lends support to this interpretation. On the other hand, the Court does consider constitutional changes as drastic as secession to still fall within the definition of a constitutional amendment (*Quebec Secession Reference, supra* note 1 at para. 84), and emphasizes that secession will require an amendment (*Ibid.* at para. 97). Coupled with the Court's reference to "the applicability of various procedures to achieve lawful secession" (*Ibid.* at para. 105), the Court might be suggesting that Part V will be engaged. However, even here, the Court does not identify the relevant amending formula, or even refer to Part V explicitly, suggesting that the existing formulas may be inadequate.

71  We owe this point to Amir Sperling.

72  This point was suggested to us by Annalise Acorn.

73  *Quebec Secession Reference, supra* note 1 at para. 1.

majority rule. Out of these principles, the Court then fashioned the constitutional rules governing secession.

The Court offered little in the way of justification for its ascent to abstract normativity. This is rather unfortunate, given its departure from its normal practice—to begin with the relevant provisions of the Constitution. The Court came closest to providing a justification, though, in its scattered references to the relationship between legality and legitimacy. To the Court, legality stood for the compliance of public decision-making with the institutional formalities and procedures laid down by the constitutional text. Legitimacy, by contrast, referred to the justness or rightness of a constitutional regime. A constitution is legitimate if it reflects "the aspirations of the people," suggesting that a democratic pedigree is one condition of legitimacy.[74] Another condition of legitimacy, though, is compliance with "moral values, many of which are imbedded in our constitutional structure," including values which presumably do not merely reflect majority preferences.[75]

The Court's statements on the relationship between legality and legitimacy are hard to interpret, because they point to two rather different conceptions of that relationship. At times, the Court argued that legality and legitimacy are both necessary, but not sufficient, criteria for the survival of a constitutional system. On this account, legitimacy and legality are analytically distinct. Thus, the Court was careful to point out that the patriation of the Constitution in 1982 complied both with requirements of legality (adoption by the Imperial Parliament) and legitimacy (the conventions governing constitutional amendments); by implication, had either been absent, the 1982 amendments might not have taken hold. At other times, though, the Court seemed to suggest that legality is a necessary means to securing legitimacy. As we noted earlier, this is the aspiration of liberal democracy. We take this to be the meaning of the Court's obscure statement that in the Canadian constitutional tradition "legality and legitimacy are linked."[76]

The Court's apparently contradictory statements on the relationship between legitimacy and legality can be reconciled in the following way. On most occasions—in the day-to-day operations of the state—legality is sufficient to secure the legitimacy of liberal democratic regimes. However, in exceptional circumstances, legality and legitimacy may come apart, so that the issue of legitimacy must be addressed directly. It is readily apparent from the judgment that a positive referendum vote in favour of secession would force apart legitimacy and legality in this manner. Thus, while the Court noted that "the results of a referendum have no direct role or legal effect," it also noted that the "continued existence and operation of the Canadian constitutional order cannot remain indifferent to the clear expression of a clear majority of Quebecois that they no longer wish to remain in Canada," because the latter amounted to a "clear repudiation of the existing constitutional order."[77]

The coming apart of legality and legitimacy in exceptional circumstances raises the question of how the legitimacy of a constitutional order could be restored. The positivist account, for example, suggests that the express exclusion of the courts from the amending procedures reflects an institutional division of labour between the courts and the political organs of the Constitution in the protection of legality and legitimacy. Courts ensure fidelity to legality through judicial review; Parliament and the provincial legislatures use the amending power to ensure that the constitutional scheme as a whole is legitimate. The special role of institutions that are politically accountable in constitutional change might in fact render judicial amendment illegitimate. What the Court had to explain, then, is why it did not allow the normal processes of constitutional politics and amendment to operate, and instead took on the task of restoring the legitimacy of the Canadian Constitution itself. Indeed, how could the principles of the Canadian constitutional order legitimately govern or structure a process whose starting premise was, in the Court's own admission, a clear repudiation of that order? It

---

74   *Ibid.* at para. 67.

75   *Ibid.*

76   *Quebec Secession Reference, supra* note 1 at para. 33.

---

77   *Ibid.* at paras. 87, 92, 88. For a discussion of the challenge for constitutional interpretation posed by the coming apart of legitimacy and legality, and the need to have recourse to an adjudicative approach of the kind we describe in in this article, see R.J. Howse & A. Malkin, "Canadians are a sovereign people: how the Supreme Court should approach the reference on Quebec secession" (1997) 76 Can. Bar Rev. 186.

would seem that only constitutional amendment by the political actors could reconcile the repudiation of the constitutional order by one province with the overall legality and integrity of that order, through formalizing the response to repudiation in a constitutional amendment.

However, once we examine the political context surrounding the *Quebec Secession Reference*, it becomes evident that the Court acted in the face of the failure of federal political institutions to face the challenge posed by the referendum process in Quebec to the legitimacy of the Canadian constitutional order, and the comparable failure of the Quebec separatists to even engage the issue of the legitimacy of secession in terms of Canadian constitutional principles, rights, and interests, claiming that the choice to make a state is a matter of the will of a Volk, impervious to any effects on "others" who are not members of the Volk. Before the reference questions had been issued, it was entirely open to the federal government to lay down principles governing referenda and secession. To do so, however, would have been to confront the Schmittean extra-legalism of the Quebec separatists with a unilateral claim of the "enemy" (the federal authorities) about legitimacy. This would have reinforced the notion, propounded by separatists, that what was at stake was merely a clash of wills, unresolvable by any agreed or shared legal principles or conception of legitimacy.

In thus referring the matter to the Supreme Court, the federal government made a brilliant institutional wager—that the Court would not simply be identified by those whom it sought to persuade of the illegitimacy of unilateral secession, with the federal authorities *and* with one side in a boundless political struggle. The Court could effectively play a political role that the federal government would fail at precisely because of the Court's observance, historically and in this very case, of institutional constraints on its interpretive authority that would allow it to be fairly perceived as not "politicized" in the sense that separatists initially *claimed* that it would inevitably be if it chose to adjudicate the matter. In sum, the Court had to play a political role, which it could only legitimately and effectively do through setting institutional bounds around its engagement with the political choices of political actors.

The political context, and the Court's response to it, explains the shift to extraordinary interpretation. Moreover, the challenge to the legitimacy of the Canadian Constitution raised by the case also makes sense of the Court's ascent to abstract normativity. In the submissions of the parties, the Court was presented with two dramatically different and mutually incompatible accounts of the legitimacy of the Canadian constitutional order. On the one hand, the federal government took the position that democratic expressions of the will of the people of a province in themselves were of no significance to the legitimacy of the constitutional scheme. Rather, what was dispositive was adherence to legality, which, in the case of secession, was adherence to the amending procedures laid down in Part V of the *Constitution Act, 1982*. On the other hand, the amicus curiae took exactly the opposite position—that the legitimacy of the Canadian constitutional order was entirely dependent on expressions of democratic will, and that constitutional procedures could not fetter the right of Quebec to self-determination.

This clash of constitutional visions placed the Court in an extraordinarily difficult position. Choosing one position by necessity entailed the rejection of the other. Had the Court sided with one of the parties, its judgment would have, in effect, rendered the Constitution illegitimate in the eyes of a large segment of Canadians. But nor was it open to the Court to avoid the abstract normative dispute at the heart of the litigation, in a manner akin to that suggested by Cass Sunstein. Sunstein proposes that, in normal cases, courts should be averse to grounding their decisions in controversial moral or political theories, because those theories are unlikely to secure wide agreement in liberal societies characterized by the fact of reasonable pluralism. He argues, though, that it may be possible that persons who disagree on a fundamental level may nevertheless agree on particular results, and on reasons that operate at a relatively low level of abstraction to justify them. Sunstein also acknowledges, however, that there are other cases, rather atypical of the daily fare of public law litigation, where it is inappropriate, or unrealistic, to seek low-level, untheorized or undertheorized agreement. He remarks that there are occasions where deciding cases on the basis of abstract, "relatively large-scale principles" is "legitimate and even glorious," referring to "rare occasions when more ambitious thinking becomes necessary to resolve a case or when the case for ambitious theory is so insistent that a range of judges can converge on it."[78]

The limitation of Sunstein's account (as he himself acknowledges) is that low-level agreement may not always be possible, especially when disagreements on fundamental questions of principle produce disagreements on specific outcomes. In the *Quebec Secession Reference*, for example, the normative dispute was of this nature, because the competing constitutional visions of the parties dictated dramatically different positions on the question of unilateral secession. Indeed, had the Court tried to follow Sunstein's advice on how *normal* cases should be adjudicated, it would have courted disaster. Justifying its decision on the basis of a theoretical account that was obscure and underdeveloped might have created the misunderstanding that it was applying one party's view by stealth, throwing into question the very legitimacy of its judgment. In fact, in a more recent articulation of his theory of adjudication, Sunstein actually raises the possibility that higher level agreement about general norms may exactly be what is required, where sharp divergences of perspective exist at a more concrete level. However, Sunstein identifies this situation strongly with constitution-making, not interpretation.[79] Yet, while this observation may be sound, there is no intrinsic reason why the only situation where agreement is easier with respect to abstract principles and harder with respect to particulars is that of constitution-making.

If one understands the Court's task as to provide a judgment that is legitimate in the eyes of Canadians on both sides of the secession debate, then we can see clearly why it resorted to general principles to craft its ruling. In the perspective of the divide between federalists and secessionists, these principles could enjoy the reasonable assent of everyone, whereas at the core of the debate over secession is in fact the moral bindingness of the constitutional *text* on Quebec, given the secessionist historical narrative of Quebec's "exclusion" in the creation of a self-standing written constitution in 1982, and the failure to remedy this exclusion

in subsequent rounds of constitutional negotiations (Meech Lake, Charlottetown). Indeed, one could even say that in appealing to the four principles, the Supreme Court was appealing to the pride of the separatists that, contrary to the suspicions of many of their opponents, their movement is entirely liberal democratic. How then could they really repudiate the principles in question? And if they could not repudiate the principles, then how could they not accept the proposition that secession itself must take place in accordance with those principles? Thus, while in this case the Court's formal legitimacy was weak, given the secessionist repudiation of the formal text of the Constitution as a basis for deciding Quebec's future in relation to Canada, its substantive legitimacy was strong. Yet the Court apparently saw how easily this substantive legitimacy would slip away, were it required to apply in detail the abstract principles upon which it relied, and therefore enunciated its refusal to do so.

The judgment in the *Quebec Secession Reference* accordingly suggests the possibility of a dynamic interaction between sources, interpretive responsibility, and interpretive style. The idea is that only particular combinations of conceptions of sources, interpretive responsibility, and interpretive style will together secure the legitimacy of judicial review. These different components balance each other, together constituting a theory of constitutional interpretation. Moreover, altering a conception of one element in this package necessitates the modification of the others. The positivist account, for example, balances a robust notion of interpretive responsibility—judicial interpretation of the Constitution is both exclusive and supreme—against a view of interpretive style that sharply distinguishes adjudication from normative reasoning writ-large, and a narrow view of legal sources. The ascent to abstract normativity in the *Quebec Secession Reference*, along with an expansive view of sources, accordingly required an adjustment in the Court's conception of interpretive responsibility, to one where interpretive jurisdiction is both shared and divided.

The resort to abstract normativity in the *Quebec Secession Reference* raises the interesting question of *when* such a shift is justified. In this judgment, for example, the ascent to abstract normativity went hand-in-hand with extra-ordinary adjudication. In this judgment, the two were part and parcel of the

78  *Legal Reasoning, supra* note 22 at 46.
79  *One Case at a Time, supra* note 69 at 11–12.

same phenomenon. But one could imagine situations where the sort of institutional failure that gave rise to extra-ordinary interpretation here did not exist, but the Court nevertheless ascended to abstract normativity. Novel cases, cases where there are conflicting lines of authority, or cases where the established case-law seems to run counter to widely held moral and political values—different varieties of hard cases—all might invite the court to engage in what Ronald Dworkin calls a process of "justificatory assent."[80]

Another question which emerges is whether the phenomenon of institutional failure explains some of the more dramatic judicial decisions in Canadian constitutional history. The failure of the Trudeau government and the provinces to agree on a set of principles regarding provincial participation in the patriation of the Canadian Constitution may account for the holding on constitutional conventions in the *Patriation Reference*. The goal of relying on conventions was

to combine an ambitious normative account of the Canadian federation with institutional self-restraints in the enforcement of those norms, albeit in a different manner from the *Quebec Secession Reference*. However, the use of conventions created serious problems of its own, because it conferred constitutional significance and normative force on mere political practice and tradition without any further considerations. Likewise, the inability of the federal and provincial governments to strengthen the economic union may have motivated the Court to step into the breach, with a series of ambitious judgments on the federal trade and commerce power, federal jurisdiction over peace, order and good government, mobility rights, and the constitutional aspects of conflicts of laws.[81] This suggestion is speculative, but we raise it for discussion.

---

80  *Darwin's New Bulldog, supra* note 21.

81  *General Motors of Canada Ltd.* v. *City National Leasing Ltd.*, [1989] 1 S.C.R. 641; *R.* v. *Crown Zellerbach Canada Ltd.*, [1988] 1 S.C.R. 401; *Black* v. *Law Society of Alberta*, [1989] 1 S.C.R. 591; *De Savoye* v. *Morguard Investments Ltd.*, [1990] 3 S.C.R. 1077; *Hunt* v. *T & N Plc*, [1993] 4 S.C.R. 289.

## 39

### Editor's Introduction

John Borrows is so well regarded within the Aboriginal law community that his scholarship has been cited in Supreme Court cases. The book from which this selection is drawn received the Donald Smiley Prize for best book in Canadian political science. Instead of conceptualizing Canadian and Aboriginal legal traditions as juxtaposed, the essence of Borrows's position is that Canadian law stands to benefit from Aboriginal traditions, culture, and legal concepts. This excerpt provides a valuable commentary from that perspective on Canada's core constitutional principles as enunciated by the Supreme Court of Canada in paragraphs 49–82 of its *Quebec Secession Reference* (1998).

Source: John Borrows, *Recovering Canada: The Resurgence of Indigenous Law* (Toronto: University of Toronto Press, 2002), 124–37.

### John Borrows

# Recovering Canada: The Resurgence of Indigenous Law

THE UNSTATED PRECEPTS that "inform and sustain the [Canadian] constitutional text" in relation to Aboriginal peoples are two-pronged. They can be drawn from the oral traditions of Aboriginal peoples throughout this country,[1] and they can be sourced in the unwritten traditions of the West.[2]

The courts should examine how Aboriginal oral traditions, laws, and perspectives could inform and sustain Canada's constitutional text,[3] just as they have explored the influences of Western law on the constitution. Comparing the Supreme Court's principles in the *Quebec Secession Reference* with

Aboriginal reflections on Canadian constitutionalism, like those told to me by my Aunt Irene, demonstrates the potential interaction of the two traditions.

In the *Quebec Secession Reference*, the Supreme Court of Canada identified the fundamental traditions influencing the interpretation of Canada's constitutional text as federalism, democracy, constitutionalism and the rule of law,[4] and the protection of minorities. The court described these precepts as "underlying constitutional principles" that "may in certain circumstances give rise to substantive legal obligations which constitute substantive limitations upon government action."[5] What can these four constitutional principles, considered together,[6] tell us about the legality and legitimacy of the extinguishment of Aboriginal rights prior to 1982, and their justifiable infringement subsequent to 1982? A brief examination of each doctrine reveals that Aboriginal peoples can interrogate and overturn assertions of Crown sovereignty that permit the unilateral extinguishment and diminishment of Aboriginal rights.

## A. FEDERALISM

The first principle the Supreme Court considered in the *Quebec Secession Reference* was federalism. The court wrote that the federal system is only partially complete "according to the precise terms of the *Constitution Act, 1867*"[7] because the "federal government retained sweeping powers that threatened to undermine the autonomy of the provinces."[8] A simple reading of the Constitution Act, 1867 would seem to confirm the notion that the federal government secured the paramount legislative authority over the provinces in Canada.[9] The court observed that the structure of the document was unbalanced: since "the written provisions of the Constitution do not provide the entire picture" of the Canadian federal structure, the courts have had to "control the limits of the respective sovereignties."[10] This interpretation was necessary to facilitate "democratic participation by distributing power to the government thought to be most suited to achieving the particular societal objective," with regard to the diversity of the component parts of Confederation.[11] It limited the power of the federal government relative

to provincial governments and resulted in a more appropriate sharing of political power between the two orders.[12] Provincial power has been significantly strengthened under this interpretation.[13]

Applying these principles to the treatment of Aboriginal peoples, would it not also be possible to regard the federal system as only partially complete?[14] It could similarly be argued that the "federal government retained sweeping powers" relative to Aboriginal peoples "which threatened to undermine the autonomy" of these groups.[15] Furthermore, since the "written provisions of the Constitution does [*sic*] not provide the entire picture" in relation to Aboriginal peoples, the courts could also "control the limits of the respective sovereignties" by distributing power to the Aboriginal government "thought to be most suited to achieving [a] particular societal objective." If the courts can draw on unwritten principles of federalism to fill in the "gaps in the express terms of the constitutional text"[16] to strengthen provincial powers, could they not apply the same principles to facilitate "the pursuit of collective goals by [the] cultural and linguistic minorities"[17] that comprise Aboriginal nations? Following the court's reasoning, the principle of federalism could be applied to question assertions of sovereignty that purportedly diminish Aboriginal powers. Federal power over Aboriginal peoples would thereby be circumscribed, allowing Aboriginal people to function as an equal integral part of the federal structure in Canada.

Significantly, Anishinabek traditions would be consistent with principles of Canadian federalism and they provide clues as to how this system could be rebalanced to incorporate Anishinabek interests. Anishinabek law contains "an historical lineage stretching back through the ages, which aids in the consideration of the underlying constitutional principles"[18] in Crown/Aboriginal relations. Some of the stories told by Aunt Irene illustrate this legal genealogy. For instance, in 1763, the generation of my great-great-great-grandparents, First Nations leaders in the Great Lakes and upper Ohio river valley were invited to attend a conference at Niagara with William Johnson, the Crown's chief representative for Indian Affairs, to discuss principles that would govern their relationship.[19] This was the first such meeting of Anishinabek peoples with representatives of the Crown, who had previously been their enemies on the battlefield.[20] The gathering was thus significant in setting the framework by which the parties would relate to one another. Through participation and consent, the Anishinabek and the Crown representatives created a pattern to follow in "constituting" their relations. The principles agreed to at this inaugural meeting therefore provide pointed guidance for those concerned with Aboriginal peoples' place within Canadian federalism. Those principles include, among others, the recognition of Aboriginal governance,[21] free trade, open migration, respect for Aboriginal land holdings, affirmation of Aboriginal permission and consent in treaty matters, criminal justice protections, military assistance,[22] respect for hunting and fishing rights, and adherence to principles of peace and friendship.[23] The principles elaborated at Niagara have never been entirely abrogated and they underpin Canada's legal structure. Other treaty nations can point to similar promises recognizing their place in Canada's political structures,[24] as such meetings generally involved the negotiation of principles to govern their relationship with the Crown. These agreements have formed the implied term and condition of subsequent treaties[25] and could inform contemporary interpretations of Canada's federal relationship with First Nations throughout the country.

The treaty at Niagara,[26] negotiated through July and August of 1764, was at the time regarded as "the most widely representative gathering of American Indians ever assembled,"[27] as approximately two thousand chiefs and representatives were in attendance.[28] At least twenty-four nations[29] had gathered with "representative nations as far east as Nova Scotia, and as far west as the Mississippi, and as far north as Hudson Bay."[30] The assembled nations included peoples from the great western and eastern Indian confederacies of the day: the Algonquins, Chippewas (Anishinabek), Crees, Fox, Hurons, Pawnees, Menominees, Nippisings, Odawas, Sacs, Toughkamiwons, Potawatomies, Cannesandagas, Caughnawagas, Cayugas, Conoys, Mohicans, Mohawks, Nanticokes, Onondagas, and Senacas.[31] Aboriginal people throughout the Great Lakes and northern, eastern, and western colonial regions travelled for months and weeks to attend this meeting.[32]

When everyone was assembled,[33] Sir William Johnson presented "the terms of what he hoped would prove a Pax Britannica for North America."[34] On behalf of the Crown he read the terms of the Royal Proclamation, gave gifts,[35] and presented two different wampum belts to the gathered Indians. In turn, Aboriginal representatives accepted the belts, made speeches, and promised peace to establish a state of mutual respect between the parties.[36] One belt Johnson passed, the Gus Wen Tah or Two-Row wampum, has been described as follows: "There is a bed of white wampum which symbolizes the purity of the agreement. There are two rows of purple, and those two rows have the spirit of your ancestors and mine. There are three beads of wampum separating the two rows and they symbolize peace, friendship and respect. These two rows will symbolize two paths or two vessels, travelling down the same river together. One, a birch bark canoe, will be for the Indian people, their laws, their customs and their ways. The other, a ship, will be for the white people and their laws, their customs and their ways. We shall each travel the river together, side by side, but in our own boat. Neither of us will try to steer the other's vessel."[37] The two-row wampum has important implications for federalism because it reflects a conception of governance that recognizes the simultaneous interaction and separation of settler and First Nations societies. An agreement to this effect was first struck by the Haudonosaunee upon contact with Europeans; the principles it represents were renewed by them in 1764 and received for the first time by the Anishinabek in the same year.[38] The two-row wampum belt illustrates a First Nation/ Crown relationship founded on peace, friendship, and respect; neither nation will interfere with the internal affairs of the other. The belt contemplates interaction and sharing between First Nations and the Crown, as demonstrated by the three rows of white beads. But it also envisions separation and autonomy between the two governments, as represented by the two parallel rows of purple beads. The twin principles of separation and integration are a recurring theme in Crown–First Nations relations, and they are consistent with a notion of Canadian federalism that respects the need to distribute power to the government thought to be best suited to achieving the particular societal objective, having regard to the diversity of the component parts of Confederation.[39]

The second belt Sir William Johnson presented, which was accepted by the assembled group, also displays themes consistent with Canadian federalism. After referencing the two-row wampum,[40] Thomas Anderson, a Superintendent of Indian Affairs in 1845, described the second belt as follows: "On the other wampum belt is marked at one end a hieroglyphic denoting Quebec on this continent, on the other, is a ship with its bow towards Quebec; betwixt those two objects are wove 24 Indians, one holding the cable of the vessel with his right, and so on, until the figure on the extreme left rests his foot on the land at Quebec. Their traditional account of this is, that at the time it was delivered to them (1764) Sir William Johnson promised, in the name of the Government, that those Tribes should continue to receive presents as long as the sun would shine … and if ever the ship came across the Great salt lake without a full cargo, these tribes should pull lustily at the cable until they brought her over full of presents."[41] The principles found in this belt similarly envision a political relationship that incorporates autonomy and integration. The Indians and Crown are clearly separate from one another, yet they are connected in important physical ways. The offer of mutual support and assistance (the cable can be pulled from either end) that also respects the independent nature of each party is a powerful archetype for Canada's federal relationships. Sir William Johnson himself, in introducing this belt at Niagara in 1764, captured the mutuality and diversity embedded in this agreement:

> Brothers of the Western Nations, Sachems, Chiefs and Warriors; You have now been here for several days, during which time we have frequently met to renew and Strengthen our Engagements and you have made so many Promises of your Friendship and Attachment to the English that there now remains for us only to exchange the great Belt of the Covenant Chain that we may not forget our mutual Engagements.
>
> I now therefore present you the great Belt by which I bind all your Western Nations together with the English, and I desire that you will take fast hold of the same, and never let it slip, to which end

> I desire that after you have shewn this belt to all Nations you will fix one end of it to the Chipeweighs at St. Mary's whilst the other end remains at my house, and moreover I desire that you will never listen to any news which comes to any other Quarter. If you do it, it may shake the Belt.[42]

The principles symbolized in this belt, together with Johnson's speech and the two-row wampum, are important because they testify to the foundational treaty of alliance and peace between First Nations and the Crown in Canada. Through the exchange of promises, presents, and wampum the parties agreed to subsequently adhere to principles that incorporated two jurisprudential worlds. While these principles find partial expression in the written text of the constitution and the Royal Proclamation, they are given much fuller exposition through the oral and documentary law and history that underlies Canada's constitutional text.[43] Recognition of the Indigenous lineage in Canada's constitutionalism would contribute to working out the legality and legitimacy of Canadian law, consistent with the principles in the *Quebec Secession Reference*.

## B. DEMOCRACY

The second principle considered by the Supreme Court in the *Quebec Secession Reference* was democracy. The court held that "democracy has always informed the design of our constitutional structure, and continues to act as an essential interpretive consideration to this day." According to the court, democracy "can best be understood as a sort of baseline against which the framers of our Constitution, and subsequently, our elected representatives under it, have always operated."[44] The court's notion of democracy[45] embraces ideas of majority rule, the promotion of self-government and the accommodation of cultural and group identities, the popular franchise, and the consent of the governed. Despite the promises made at Niagara, Canada has rarely followed through with these principles in its dealings with Aboriginal peoples.

Applying the Supreme Court's framework, Canada's unilateral attempts to extinguish Aboriginal rights and repeated denials of the legal right to question this treatment undermine majority rule. Aboriginal peoples were in the majority in most parts of the country at the time their rights were purportedly extinguished, and they were later denied the political and legal means to challenge the Crown's actions.[46] Furthermore, as discussed in the last chapter, the Crown's assumption of overarching sovereignty does not promote community self-government, nor does it accommodate Aboriginal identities. Aboriginal governments were overlaid by elected Indian Act governments, and Aboriginal individuals were subjected to ruthless assimilation policies.[47] Finally, denial of underlying Aboriginal title and the equality of Aboriginal sovereignty does not secure the consent of the governed. Aboriginal peoples in every province and community have consistently resisted the unilateral extinguishment and diminishment of their rights by the Crown.[48] In fact, as Aunt Irene told me, the lives of my great-great-grandparents were strongly influenced by their attempts to resist the contraction of their participation with the land and those who were newly settling on it. Their efforts, and those of others like them, should become more visible in Canada's constitutional structure. Otherwise, Canada will continue to fail to abide by and apply the democratic ideals underlying its constitution.

My great-great-grandparents lived during a time of unparalleled transition in Anishinabek communities, and their response to these changes contains important lessons for Canadian democracy. They maintained a belief in and practice of consent and participation in government, despite the arrival of hundreds of thousands of settlers who strained their traditional economic, social, and spiritual relationships. Peter Kegedonce Jones, my great-great-grandfather, was chief of the Nawash band in this period and his behaviour exemplified this strong democratic tradition.[49] In 1837, when he was twenty years of age, Peter attended school at Beaverton, Ontario, on the shores of Lake Simcoe, two hours north of Toronto. While he was in school the Rebellion of Upper Canada took place, led by William Lyon Mackenzie. Peter became involved in the Rebellion and his participation was recounted by his grandson: "I can still recollect hearing him tell me the story of his experiences at this time—how he was recruited as one of Mackenzie's supporters, given a blanket, a musket, powder horn and shot, and after months of weary waiting, was finally taken with others, to the vicinity of Toronto and York, as it was then

called. Here they waited, but never had the chance to get into action."[50] Oral tradition recalls with pride Peter's association with a cause that sought to extend citizen involvement in Canadian politics in community with other Canadians.

Peter's partner, Margaret, also exemplified ideals consistent with Canada's democratic principles. She was born around 1820 in the place now known as Alberta, the child of an Ojibway mother and a Scottish father. Her father, Joseph McLeod, was a fur trader in the Northwest in the early 1800s. When his fur trading days were over, he deserted his Native family and returned to Scotland to live on the Isle of Skye. Margaret's Anishinabek mother, Teresa Riel, raised her daughter in the traditional Ojibway manner. The family eventually migrated from the prairies and settled at La Cloche, on the north shore of Lake Huron. When they heard that Peter was taking people into his community, the McLeods moved from La Cloche to settle at Nawash.[51] Margaret married Peter in the 1840s, when she was in her early twenties.

Margaret developed skills throughout her life that indicate the importance accorded by Anishinabek people to participation in public affairs. She was a midwife and medicine woman who possessed a vast knowledge of herbal remedies for curing various ailments. She would selflessly spend her time gathering the natural harvest of flora, fauna, herbs, and roots from the shores of the lakes, the grasslands, and the forest for the benefit of the community.[52] Margaret shared these medicines and her healing skills freely, without thought of payment or monetary reward. She was also a teacher and educator who spoke three languages: Ojibway, French, and English. French was spoken in the home, Ojibway in the community, and English when she went off the reserve. As Margaret grew older she became a repository of the traditions, myths, parables, fables, allegories, legends, and stories of our people,[53] and thus greatly assisted in the maintenance of community values and the ancient ethics of participation. In fact, many of the stories recounted in these pages echo her words and themes. They contain strong messages about the importance of participation and consent—principles that are central to democratic thought and could be considered an integral part of Canada's unwritten constitutional heritage.

Unless Aboriginal peoples and perspectives are included in Canada's governing institutions, the country will not create a legitimate framework or legal foundation upon which to build an appropriate political relationship. Despite the strong democratic traditions characteristic of many First Nations, Canadian courts and politicians have not identified and implemented a system that reflects the legal heritage and aspirations of Aboriginal peoples. The political exclusion of Aboriginal people represents a failure of democracy. As the Supreme Court observed in the *Quebec Secession Reference*,

> It is the law that creates the framework within which the "sovereign will" is to be ascertained and implemented. To be accorded legitimacy, democratic institutions must rest, ultimately, on a legal foundation. That is, they must allow for the participation of, and accountability to, the people, through public institutions created under the Constitution. Equally, however, a system of government cannot survive through adherence to the law alone. A political system must also possess legitimacy, and in our political culture, that requires an interaction between the rule of law and the democratic principle. The system must be capable of reflecting the aspirations of the people. But there is more. Our law's claim to legitimacy also rests on an appeal to moral values, many of which are embedded in our constitutional structure.[54]

The court here suggests that the Canadian constitution must create a "framework" and a "legal foundation" for people's participation in federal structures. Aboriginal peoples throughout Canada have never received an unencumbered opportunity to participate as traditional or effective governments within the federal structure. They have not been a part of the Canadian "framework," and thus have been virtually prevented from officially promoting and implementing normative values consistent with their vision of Canadian democracy. Legally, their exclusion is most telling when it includes the Crown's extinguishment and infringement of Aboriginal rights without requisite participation or consent. Morally, the exclusion from democratic participation is most repugnant when the assumption of extinguishment and infringement

leads to forced integration, assimilation, and cultural eradication. Though such labelling may not be completely consistent with usage in international law and treaties, for many Aboriginal peoples, extinguishment is reminiscent of genocide.[55] The principle of democracy, from both the Canadian Supreme Court and Aboriginal legal perspectives, cannot sanction such treatment.

## C. THE RULE OF LAW

The third principle examined by the Supreme Court in the *Quebec Secession Reference* is the rule of law. While this principle has been discussed in some detail above, it is worth observing that the rule of law must be placed beside federalism and democracy when considering the dispossession Aboriginal people face as a result of the Crown's assertion of underlying title and overarching sovereignty. In the *Quebec Secession Reference*, the court observed that "at its most basic level, the rule of law vouchsafes to the citizens and residents of the country a stable, predictable and ordered society in which to conduct their affairs."[56] The unilateral extinguishment of Aboriginal rights before 1982, coupled with the infringement of those rights since 1982, does not ensure a predictable and ordered society: it severely disrupts Aboriginal nations and causes deeply rooted resentment of the federal government.[57] This resentment translates into strained, adversarial relations, periodic blockades, and endless litigation. It tears apart the fabric of Aboriginal communities[58] and leads to instability within the larger population by reducing investment, creating social tension, and causing uncertainty.[59] The consequences of this resentment could further escalate and lead to dissension and violence if left unattended. If relations between Aboriginal peoples and others ever degenerate to the point of frequent, chronic violence, the legal doctrines allowing for non-consensual Crown derogation from Aboriginal rights might be one of the underlying causes of such distress. Such a situation would be partially attributable to the failure of the Canadian state to fully extend the rule of law to Aboriginal peoples.

The failure of the Crown and the courts to protect Aboriginal peoples from arbitrary power has already affected First Nations in at least three profound ways. First, there were few safeguards to protect the fundamental human rights and individual freedoms of Aboriginal peoples throughout most of Canada's history.[60] As a result, their individual and collective lives were unduly "susceptible to government interference."[61] Governmental interference is evidenced through the suppression of Aboriginal institutions of government,[62] the denial of land,[63] the forced taking of children,[64] the criminalization of economic pursuits,[65] and the negation of the rights of religious freedom,[66] association,[67] due process,[68] and equality.[69] A second manifestation of the lack of protection for Aboriginal peoples under the rule of law is that the parties to the creation of Canada did not ensure that, as a vulnerable group, Aboriginal peoples were "endowed with institutions and rights necessary to maintain and promote their identities against the assimilative pressures of the majority."[70] This lack of cultural protection led to further vulnerability and violence, as Aboriginal peoples were not extended the institutional means to resist the violation of their rights. A final consequence of the failure to extend the rule of law to Aboriginal peoples is that the political organization of Canada did not "provide for a division of political power"[71] that would prevent the provincial and federal governments from usurping the powers of Aboriginal governments. Non-Aboriginal governments usurped Aboriginal authority "simply by exercising their legislative power to allocate additional political power to [themselves] unilaterally."[72] Consequently, these governments have been unjustly enriched at the expense of Aboriginal peoples. These various transgressions of the rule of law illustrate the problems of founding a country without incorporating the legal perspectives and ideas of all of its inhabitants. They do not produce a stable, ordered, and predictable society. For all these reasons, the courts must not sanction the continued violation of the rule of law with respect to Aboriginal peoples.

Perhaps nothing is more illustrative of Canada's violation of the rule of law with respect to Aboriginal peoples than the Indian Act, first passed in 1876.[73] My great-grandfather, Charles Kegedonce Jones, was the first chief of the Chippewas of the Nawash elected under the Indian Act's provisions. He worked for over fifty years in this position and struggled to make it relevant to the values and activities of the people he served. The Act imposed a normative structure on Aboriginal communities that was largely inconsistent with their own legal and political systems. Charles found it difficult to integrate the statute's authoritarian proscriptions with the consensual approach to governance found within Anishinabek political and legal thought. His successes in responding to community needs were most often achieved in spite of the Indian Act, and he had to take great steps to preserve the rule of law at Cape Croker, which that statute undermined.

For example, Charles had to overcome threats to Anishinabek normative order and the rule of law in the areas of property law, governance, family relations, education, freedom to contract, and religious freedom. The Indian Act contained provisions that forcibly prohibited or restricted Anishinabek order in all these areas. While Charles and his councils did the best they could to maintain their means of subsistence (for example through Band resolutions dealing with sales of timber on our lands,[74] the lease and pasture of farm land,[75] the acquisition of seeds for cultivation,[76] the purchase of livestock,[77] and the harvesting of their fisheries)[78] the Indian Act's provisions largely prevented them from making the rule of law effective within their community.[79] The Indian Act is an affront to the rule of law throughout Canada. It stands as evidence of the arbitrary nature of Canada's political order relative to Aboriginal peoples. It must be repealed and replaced by a document that facilitates the recreation of normative order in Aboriginal communities.

The rule of law has also suffered in the community's relations with its non-Native neighbours. Charles's father Peter had signed two treaties in 1854[80] and 1857[81] that promised many material goods and services in return for non-Native people settling on Anishinabek territory. In fact, Peter's signature was the first one on the 1857 treaty. These treaties covered over 500,000 acres of prime land in southwestern Ontario, extending east from Goderich on Lake Huron to Arthur in central- southwestern Ontario, and then north to Owen Sound on Lake Huron. Anishinabek people felt (and still feel) deeply for their lands, and making the decision to share them with others was not easy. Yet Peter and his people signed the treaty as an exercise

of governance, to obtain promises that would peren-
nially compensate for their loss. The promises secured
for sharing the land included, among others, increasing capital payments through trust funds deposits and
payments, perpetual medical assistance, the provision
of education, the building of infastructure (such as
roads, public buildings, and docks), housing, hunting,
fishing, and timber rights. The Anishinabek were told
"that from the sale of the land [they] would soon have
a large income, would all be able to ride in carriages,
roll in wealth and fare sumptuously every day."[82] The
government's promises were not fulfilled, despite
Anishinabek adherence to the treaty's terms. Among
other problems there were issues with reserve size,[83]
non-native settlement,[84] the development of agricultural lots,[85] the building of schools,[86] the provision of
funds,[87] and official sanction for acts undertaken by
the Band Council.[88]

Charles and others of his generation repeatedly
petitioned Canada to respect the rule of law and
adhere to its treaty promises. Canada did not respond
to these appeals, and to this day it has not lived up to
its commitments. The Nawash have even had to pursue litigation to compel the government to abide by
its covenants. The violation of basic legal principles
of offer, agreement, and consideration does not bode
well for the rule of law in Canada. While Canadians
enjoy the material wealth and political benefits that
derive from access to such a large piece of land, the
Anishinabek are criticized for wanting to enjoy the
contemporary benefits that flow from their side of
the bargain. Canadians are quite happy to uphold
the right for non-Native people to perpetually live
on treaty lands but often blanche when Native people
assert perpetual rights to housing, education, medical care, or federal transfers of money. The rule of law
should not sanction such uneven and arbitrary applications of normative order. The principles embedded
in the *Quebec Secession Reference* direct us otherwise.

## D. THE PROTECTION OF MINORITIES

Fourth, and finally, in considering the legality and
legitimacy of constitutional principles that relate
to the diminishment of Aboriginal rights it should
be recalled that the Supreme Court in the *Quebec
Secession Reference* held that "the protection of minority rights is itself an independent principle underlying
our constitutional order."[89] To return to the arguments
made at the beginning of this chapter, Aboriginal title
and sovereignty must not be unilaterally subject to
Crown title and sovereignty because this would fail
to protect Aboriginal peoples from the majority in
Canada. Aunt Irene's stories, and those of countless
thousands of Elders throughout this country, must be
incorporated into our understanding of Canadian constitutionalism. Failure to abide by their views would,
in the words of the *Quebec Secession Reference*, defeat
the "promise" of section 35, which "recognized not
only the ancient occupation of land by [A]borigi-
nal peoples, but their contributions to the building
of Canada, and the special commitments made to
them by successive governments."[90] The Crown's claim
that it can define and adjudge Aboriginal rights on
its authority alone does not seem consistent with the
court's observation that "the protection of minority
rights was clearly an essential consideration in the
design of our constitutional structure."[91] One wonders how Canadians would respond if the positions
were reversed and Aboriginal peoples were vested
with the exclusive power to interpret and circum-
scribe non-Aboriginal rights. They would likely want
to be protected in such circumstances and insist on
the application of principles similar to those outlined
in this chapter. The courts, in one of their roles, are a
counter-majoritarian body; they should be ever-mind-
ful of the challenges faced by peoples in a minority situation in Canada and act to protect their rights from
unfair occlusion.

The courts must combine the principles of federalism, democracy, the rule of law, and the protection
of minorities to assess the legality and legitimacy of
Canada's assertions with respect to Aboriginal peoples. If the courts agree with the conclusions suggested in this chapter, then Canada's laws should be
declared invalid, though enforceable, by the application of the rule of law until the parties resolve this
situation through negotiation, participation and consent. Until this negotiation occurs, Aboriginal peoples will continue to protest the unjust application
of Canadian law to their societies. If the relationship
between Crown and Aboriginal sovereignties is not
resolved through law and negotiation, Aboriginal

peoples may one day claim a right to be released from a situation that denies them the fundamental guarantees of a free and democratic society. They may claim they are not subject to Canada's jurisdiction, because Canada's claims over them are not legal or legitimate. As both an Anishinabek and Canadian citizen, I look forward to the day when Aboriginal peoples will be able to claim the benefits of the rule of law— both their own and Canada's. I sincerely hope that the day will never come when rights to live according to Canadian constitutionalism are unalterably withdrawn, and Aboriginal peoples must rely on a declaration of external self-determination to sustain their communities.

## CONCLUSION: THE RULE OF LAW AND SELF-DETERMINATION

This chapter has illustrated that the Crown's assertion and the courts' acceptance of a subsequent claimant's non-consensual assertion of rights over another legal ordering is not consistent with the law's highest principles. Any judicial or other sanction of the colonization, subjugation, domination, and exploitation of Aboriginal peoples in Canada is not a "morally and politically morally defensible conception of Aboriginal rights."[92] It "perpetuat[es] historical injustice suffered by Aboriginal peoples at the hands of [the] colonizers;"[93] it is illegitimate and illegal. In the absence of negotiation and reconciliation, this treatment may ultimately result in a claim of a legal right to self-determination for those who suffer such abuses. Ideally, Aboriginal self-determination should receive negotiated expression within Canada through an appropriate extension of the rule of law in matters of federalism, democracy, and minority protection. Otherwise, we might properly regard the Crown's treatment of Aboriginal peoples as "colonial rule" that leads to their "subjugation, domination and exploitation" and blocks their "meaningful exercise of self-determination."[94]

Under international law, people who are prevented from exercising self-determination within a nation state may have a right of "external self-determination": a right to secede from the country in which they live. In commenting on the implications of obstructing self-determination, the Supreme Court in the *Quebec*

*Secession Reference* observed that external self-determination can be claimed in three circumstances: "the international law right to self-determination only generates, at best, a right to external self-determination in situations of former colonies; where a people is oppressed, as for example under foreign military occupation; or where a definable group is denied meaningful access to government to pursue their political, economic, social and cultural development. In all three situations, the people in question are entitled to a right to external self-determination because they have been denied the ability to exert internally their right to self-determination."[95] Aboriginal peoples may have an argument for self-determination on the authority of these principles if the Crown's assertions of sovereignty are not tempered in ways suggested in this chapter. If negotiated settlement does not occur, and the principles outlined in the *Quebec Secession Reference* are not extended to them, Aboriginal peoples may be able to argue that they are colonial peoples with a right to external self-determination. They could say in such circumstances that they are "inherently distinct from the colonialist Power and the occupant Power and that their 'territorial integrity,' all but destroyed by the colonialist or occupying Power, should be fully restored."[96] Furthermore, Aboriginal peoples may be able to claim the legal right to self-determination by arguing that Canada's diminishment and extinguishment of their rights has not "promote[d] ... [the] realization of the principle[s] of equal rights and self-determination of peoples ... bearing in mind that subjection of peoples to alien subjugation, domination and exploitation constitutes a violation of the principle [of friendly relations], as well as a denial of fundamental human rights, and is contrary to the [Charter of the United Nations]."[97]

## NOTES

1  See John Borrows, "'Constitutional Law from a First Nations Perspective': Self-Government and the Royal Proclamation" (1994) 28 *University of British Columbia Law Review* 1.
2  See Brian Slattery, "The Organic Constitution: Aboriginal Peoples and the Evolution of Canada" (1996) 34 *Osgoode Hall Law Journal* 101.
3  Though the court has written of the importance of Aboriginal oral traditions (*Delgamuukwat* 1064–79 (S.C.C.), law *(VanderPeet* at 545), and perspectives (*Sparrow* at 1112). For academic

commentary on the implications of Aboriginal normative values for constitutional law see John Borrows and Len Rotman, "The Sui Generis Nature of Aboriginal Rights: Does it Make a Difference?" (1977) 36 *Alberta Law Review* 9; Sakej Henderson, "Empowering Treaty Federalism" (1995) 58 *Saskatchewan Law Review* 241; Brian Slattery, "Understanding Aboriginal Rights" (1987) 66 *Canadian Bar Review* 727; James Tully, *Strange Multiplicity: Constitutionalism in an Age of Diversity* (Cambridge: Cambridge University Press, 1995); Jeremy Webber, "Relations of Force and Relations of Justice: The Emergence of Normative Community Between Colonies and Aboriginal Peoples" (1995) 33 *Osgoode Hall Law Journal* 623; Mark Walters, "The Golden Thread of Continuity: Aboriginal Customs at Common Law and Under the Constitution Act, 1982" (1999) 44 *McGill Law Journal* 711.

4  *Reference Re Secession of Quebec* at 240.

5  Ibid, at 249.

6  See ibid, at 248, where Lamer C.J.C. wrote: "These defining principles function in symbiosis. No single principle can be defined in isolation from the others, nor does any one principle trump or exclude the operation of any other."

7  Ibid, at 250.

8  Ibid.

9  For a discussion of the centralist orientation of the Constitution Act, 1867, see Donald Creighton, *Confederation: Essays* (Toronto: University of Toronto Press, 1967).

10  *Reference Re Secession of Quebec* [1998] 2 S.C.R. 217 at 250, citing *Northern Telecom Canada Ltd. v. Communication Workers of Canada*, [1983] 1 S.C.R. 733 at 741.

11  *Reference Re Secession of Quebec* at 251.

12  Alan Cairns, "The Judicial Committee and its Critics" (1971) 4 *Canadian Journal of Political Science* 301; Murray Greenwood, "Lord Watson, Institutional Self-interest, and the Decentralization of Canadian Federalism in the 1890's" (1974) 9 *University of British Columbia Law Review* 244; Richard Risk, "Constitutional Scholarship in the Late Nineteenth Century: Making Federalism Work" (1996) 46 *University of Toronto Law Journal* 427.

13  See *Citizens Insurance Company v. Parsons* (1881), 7 A.C. 96 (J.C.P.C.); *Hodge v. The Queen* (1883), 9 A.C. 117 (J.C.P.C.); *A.G. Ontario v. A.G. Canada* (The Local Prohibition Reference), [1896] A.C. 348 (J.C.P.C.); *Montreal v. Montreal Street Railway*, [1912] A.C. 333 (J.C.P.C.); *A.G. Canada v. A.G. Alberta* (The Insurance Reference), [1916] 1 A.C. 598 (J.C.P.C.); *Reference Re the Board of Commerce Act 1919 and the Combines and Fair Prices Act, 1919*, [1922] 1 A.C. 191 (J.C.P.C.); *King v. Eastern Terminal Elevator Co.*, [1925] S.C.R. 434; *A.G. Canada v. A.G. Ontario* (Labour Conventions), [1937] A.C. 326 (J.C.P.C.); *A.G. Canada v. A.G. Ontario* (the Employment and Social Insurance Act), [1937] A.C. 355 (J.C.P.C.); *A.G. British Columbia v. A.G. Canada* (the Natural Products Marketing Act), [1937] A.C. 377 (J.C.P.C.). For further discussion of the strengthening of provincial powers under the constitution through judicial interpretation see Gerald P. Browne, *The Judicial Committee and the British North American Act* (Toronto: University of Toronto Press, 1967).

14  See Bruce Ryder, "The Demise and Rise of the Classical Paradigm in Canadian Federalism: Promoting Autonomy for the Provinces and First Nations" (1991) 36 *McGill Law Journal* 308.

15  Dominion jurisdiction in relation to Aboriginal peoples is found in s. 91(24) of the Constitution Act, 1867, which provides federal power in matters of "Indians and Lands reserved for the Indians." Problems of application of s. 91 (24) which "threaten to undermine the autonomy of Aboriginal Peoples" are discussed in Menno Boldt

and J. Anthony Long, *Governments in Conflict* (Toronto: University of Toronto Press, 1985).

16  *Reference Re Secession of Quebec* at 249, citing *Reference Re Remuneration of Judges of the Provincial Court of Prince Edward Island*, [ 1997] 3 S.C.R. 3 at 75.

17  *Reference Re Secession of Quebec* at 252.

18  Ibid, at 247.

19  Johnson persuaded the Algonquin and Nippising Nations of the Ottawa and French River valleys to be messengers in inviting other Nations to attend a peace council at Niagara in the summer of 1764. Representatives of these two Nations travelled throughout the winter of 1763–4 with a printed copy of King George Ill's Royal Proclamation, and with various strings of wampum, in order to request the various First Nations to this council. Public Archives of Canada (PAC), Sulpician Documents, M. 1644, No. 70.

20  In the early 1760s Minavavana, an Ojibway Chief from west of Manitoulin at Michilimackinac, declared:

> Englishman, although you have conquered the French you have not yet conquered us! We are not your slaves. These lakes, these woods and mountains, were left to us by our ancestors. They are our inheritance; and we will part with them to none. Your nation supposes that we, like the white people, cannot live without bread, and pork and beef. But, you ought to know, that He, the Great Spirit and Master of Life, has provided food for us, in these spacious lakes, and on these woody mountains.
>
> Englishman, our Father, the king of France, employed our young men to make war upon your nation. In this warfare, many of them have been killed; and it is our custom to retaliate, until such time as the spirits of the slain are satisfied. But, the spirits of the slain are to be satisfied in either of two ways; the first is the spilling of the blood of the nation by which they fell; the other, by covering the bodies of the dead, and thus allaying the resentment of their relations. This is done by making presents.
>
> Englishman, your king has never sent us any presents, nor entered into any treaty with us, wherefore he and we are still at war; and, until he does these things, we must consider that we have no other father or friend among the white man, than the king of France … you have ventured your life among us, in the expectation that we should not molest you. You do not come armed, with an intention to make war, you come in peace, to trade with us, to supply us with necessities, of which we are in much want. We shall regard you therefore as a brother; and you may sleep tranquilly, without fear of the Chipeways. As a token of our friendship we present you with this pipe, to smoke.

Quoted in Wilbur R. Jacobs, *Wilderness Politics and Indian Gifts: The Northern Colonial Frontier, 1748–1763* (Lincoln: University of Nebraska Press, 1966), at 75.

21  Sir William Johnson noted regarding Aboriginal governance "… I am well convinced, they never mean or intend anything like it, and that they cannot be brought under our laws, for some Centuries, neither have they any word which can convey the most distant idea of subjection, and it should be fully explained to them, and the nature of subordination punishment ettc [*sic*], defined, it might produce infinite harm … and I dread its consequences, as I recollect that some attempts towards Sovereignty not long ago, was one of the principal causes of all our troubles…." See Paul

Williams, "The Chain" (LL.M. thesis, York University, 1982), at 83, quoting Sir William Johnson.

22 The purpose of the meeting was to create a political relationship that would, in Johnson's words, ensure a "Treaty of Offensive and Defensive Alliance" that would include promises to "assure them of a Free Fair & open trade, at the principal Posts, & a free intercourse & passage into our Country, That we will make no Settlements or Encroachments contrary to Treaty, or without their permission. That we will bring to justice any persons who commit Robberys or Murders on them & that we will protect and aid them against their and our Enemys & duly observe our engagements with them." C. Flick, ed., *The Papers of Sir William Johnson*, vol. 4 (Albany: State University of New York Press, 1925), at 328.

23 Transcripts of a meeting at Drummond Island in Lake Huron to the west of Manitoulin on July 1818 between Anishnabe peoples and representatives of the British Crown contain articulate references to the Treaty of Niagara. An account of the meeting is as follows:

> The Chiefs did de camp [sic], laying down a broad Wampum Belt, made in 1764; one made in 1786; and one marked Lieutenant M'Dowal, Commanding Michilimackinac, with the pipe of peace marked on it.
>
> Orcarta [Anishnabe] speaker:
>
> Father, Your children now seated round you, salute you sincerely, they intend to talk to you a great deal, and beg you will listen to them with patience, for they intend to open their hearts to you …
>
> Holding the Belt of 1764 in his hand he said:
>
> Father, This my ancestors received from our Father, Sir W. Johnson. You sent word to all your red children to assemble at the crooked place (Niagara). They heard your voice—obeyed the message—and the next summer met you at the place. You then laid this belt on a mat, and said—"Children, you must all touch this Belt of Peace. I touch it myself, that we may all be brethren united, and hope our friendship will never cease. I will call you my children; will send warmth (presents) to your country; and your families shall never be in want. Look towards the rising sun. My Nation is as brilliant as it is, and its word cannot be violated."
>
> Father, Your words were true—all you promised came to pass. On giving us the Belt of Peace, you said—"If you should ever require my assistance, send this Belt, and my hand will be immediately stretched forth to assist you."
>
> Here the speaker laid down the Belt.

Cptn. T.G. Anderson, "Report on the Affairs of the Indians of Canada, Section III," Appendix No. 95 in App. T of the *Journals of the Legislative Assembly of Canada*, vol. 6.

24 For example, see Arthur Ray, J.R. Miller, and Frank Tough, *Bounty and Benevolence: A History of Saskatchewan Treaties* (Montreal: McGill-Queen's University Press, 2000); Harold Cardinal and Walter Hildebrandt, *Treaty Elders of Saskatchewan: Our Dream is That Our People Will One Day be Clearly Recognized as Nations* (Calgary: University of Calgary Press, 2000).

25 For example, this is evidenced in a treaty on Manitoulin Island in 1836 where Sir Francis Bond Head, lieutenant governor of Upper Canada, started negotiations with the Anishinabek by noting "Seventy snow seasons have now passed away since we met in council at the crooked place (Niagara) at which time your Great Father, the King and the Indians of North America tied their hands together by the wampum of friendship." Canada, *Indian Treaties and Surrenders, from 1680–1890* (Ottawa: Printer to the Queen's Most Excellent Majesty, 1891–1912 [Toronto: Coles, 1971]), at 112.

26 Johnson proposed, on behalf of the British, that, "at this treaty … we should tie them down (in the Peace) according to their own forms of which they take the most notice, for example, by exchanging a very large belt with some remarkable & intelligible figures thereon. Expressive of the occasion which should always be shown to remind them of their promises." Ibid, at 329.

27 Donald Braider, *The Niagara* (New York: Holt, Rinehart and Winston, 1972), at 137.

28 William G. Godfrey, *Pursuit of Profit and Preferment in Colonial North America: John Bradstreet's Quest* (Waterloo: Wilfrid Laurier University Press, 1982), at 197.

29 William Warren, an Ojibway writer, records that "twenty-two different tribes were represented" at the council at Niagara. William Warren, *History of the Ojibway of Lake Superior* (St Paul: Minnesota Historical Society, 1885; repr. Minneapolis: Ross and Haines, 1970), at 219.

30 Williams, "The Chain," at 79.

31 Flick, ed., *The Papers of Sir William Johnson*, vol. 2, at 278–81, 481, 511–14.

32 Alexander Henry, *Travels and Adventures in Canada and the Indian Territories between the Years 1760–1776* (Toronto: Morang, 1901), at 157–74.

33 Another author has recorded the attendance at the treaty: "Deputys from almost every nation to the Westward viz Hurons, Ottawaes, Chippawaes, Meynomineys or Folles avoins, Foxes, Sakis, Puans, ettc.[sic] with some from the north side of Lake Superior and the neighbourhood of Hudson's Bay." The Delawares and Shawnees were not in attendance at the treaty. William Johnson to the Lords of Trade, 8 October 1764, in E.B. O'Callaghan, ed., *Documents Relative to the Colonial History of the State of New York*, vol. 7 (Albany: Weed, Parsons, 1856), at 648.

34 G.Johnson to T. Faye, 16 March 1764, in Flick, ed., *The Papers of Sir William Johnson*, vol. 2, at 487.

35 Presents were exchanged to certify the binding nature of the promises being exchanged. The expenditure for the provisions and presents at Niagara were enormous for that day and age, and signify that the assembly was an unique and extraordinary meeting. Johnson's papers lists "Expence [sic] of provisions for Indians only … £25,000 New York Currency Besides the Presents … £38,000 Sterling." Williams, "The Chain," at 82. Johnson's generous bestowal of presents demonstrates that he followed the principles of First Nations diplomacy in ratifying their agreement. Furthermore, the extravagance and value of these presents illustrates that he did not want the Indians to soon forget the treaty.

36 Braider, *The Niagara*, at 137.

37 Robert A. Williams, Jr., "The Algebra of Federal Indian Law: The Hard Trail of Decolonizing and Americanizing the White Man's Indian Jurisprudence" (1986) *Wisconsin Law Review* 219 at 291.

38 F.W. Major, *Manitoulin: Isle of the Ottawas* (Gore Bay: Recorder Press, 1974), at 11–15 ("An Indian Council").

39 *Reference Re Secession of Quebec* at 251.

40 "… the two memoranda (wampum) which they hold; the one being a pledge of perpetual friendship between the NA Indians, and the British Nations, and was delivered to the Tribe at a Council convened for that purpose, by Sir William Johnson, at Niagara in 1764." Thomas G. Anderson, Superintendent of Indian Affairs at Manitoulin Island, Indian Department Report, *Report of Indian Affairs* (1845), at 269.

41 Ibid.

42 Flick, ed., *The Papers of Sir William Johnson*, vol. 2, at 309–10.

43 John Borrows, "Wampum at Niagara: The Royal Proclamation, Canadian Legal History and Self-Government," in Michael Asch,

ed., *Aboriginal and Treaty Rights in Canada: Essays in Law, Equality and Respect for Difference* (Vancouver: UBC Press, 1997), at 155.

44 Ibid, at 253.

45 Ibid, at 253–6.

46 For example, see the discussion in Harris, *The Resettlement of British Columbia*, at 68–102; and Tennant, *Aboriginal Peoples and Politics*, at 39–52, 96–113.

47 Ian Getty and Antoine Lussier, *As Long as the Sun Shines and the Water Flows: A Reader in Canadian Native Studies* (Vancouver: UBC Press, 1983), at 29–190 (development of the Indian Act); James R. Miller, *Shingwauk's Visions: A History of Native Residential Schools* (Toronto: University of Toronto Press, 1996), at 151–216 (assimilation through residential school policy).

48 See the voluminous transcripts from the Royal Commission on Aboriginal Peoples, where these viewpoints were continuously expressed, recorded on CD-ROM, The Royal Commission on Aboriginal Peoples, *For Seven Generations: Report of the Royal Commission on Aboriginal Peoples* (Montreal: Libraxus, 1997).

49 Peter was the hereditary chief of the Nawash but had also to maintain his position through the consent of the people. While George Copway noted: "The rulers of the Ojibway were inheritors of the power they held…." at 140, this statement should be compared with the following quotation, which indicates that hereditary power was not always the means for a person to become a chief: "leadership was not always offered to those who trained for it or to those who were born into the leadership totem. Merit was the criteria for assessing the quality of the candidate. Thus, if a person, born of another totemic group were deemed to possess a greater capacity for leadership than one so prepared, he would be preferred." Basil Johnston, *Ojibway Heritage* (Toronto: McClelland and Stewart, 1976), at 63.

50 Lawrence A. Keeshig, "Historical Sketches of the Cape Croker Indians" *CanadianEcho* [Newspaper, Wiarton, Ont.] (8 January, 1931).

51 Margaret arrived at Nawash with her mother, brother, and sister.

52 A collection of recipes for traditional Native medicines compiled at the turn of the twentieth century preserves many of these remedies. It was written by a Christian missionary living among our people but taken from interviews with Native women and the ingredients are written in the Ojibway language. See Ontario Provincial Archives, OPA Box 103, Cape Croker Reserve Papers, MS 108.

53 Verna Patronella Johnston, *Tale of Nokomis* (Toronto: Musson Book Company, 1975); see Preface (Nokomis translated means "grandmother"). The book consists of stories remembered by Verna and told to her by Margaret McLeod, who heard them from her great-grandparents (36).

54 *Reference Re Secession of Quebec* at 256.

55 George Watts, Chairman of the Nuu-Chah-Nulth Nation on Vancouver Island said: "There is this term being tossed around about aboriginal title. Well, I even disagree with this term…. What we have in our area is the Ha Houlthee, which is not aboriginal title. Ha Houlthee is very different from the legal term of aboriginal title. And you can't extinguish my title because it comes from my chief. You have to destroy us as a people if you want to extinguish our title. That is the only possible way to extinguish our title, to get rid of us as a people." Frank Cassidy, ed., *Reachingjust Settlements: Land Claims in British Columbia* (Lantzville, BC: Oolichan Press, 1991), at 22.

56 *Reference Re Secession of Quebec* at 257.

57 A paradigmatic expression of Aboriginal resentment towards Canadian law and policy relative to Aboriginal peoples is Cardinal, *The Unjust Society*. This book continues to have great

relevance, although it was written over thirty years ago, because many of the issues identified have not been resolved, but instead have grown worse.

58 Anne McGillivray and Brenda Comaskey, *Black Eyes All of the Time* (Toronto: University of Toronto Press, 1999), 22–52; Dara Culhane Speck, *An Error in Judgement* (Vancouver: Talonbooks, 1987).

59 For treatment of these issues see, generally, Cassidy, *Reaching Just Settlements*.

60 *Reference Re Secession of Quebec*.

61 *Reference Re Quebec Secession*, [1998] 2 S.C.R at para. 74.

62 *Logan v. Styres* (1959), 20 D.L.R. (2d) 416 (Ont. H.C.) (upholding forceable eviction of traditional Haudenosaunee government).

63 For example, Joseph Trutch, in denying Aboriginal title in British Columbia observed: "The title of the Indians in the fee of the public lands, or any portion thereof, has never been acknowledged by Government, but, on the contrary, is distinctly denied." *British Columbia, Papers Connected with the Indian Land Question, 1850–1875* (Victoria: Government Printer, 1875), at appendix, 11.

64 John S. Milloy, *A National Crime: The Canadian Government and the Residential School System, 1879–1986* (Winnipeg: University of Manitoba Press, 1999).

65 Aborignal people are constantly charged with criminal offences for hunting and fishing in traditional economic pursuits. Some high-profile cases are *R. v. Syliboy*, [1929] 1 D.L.R. 307 (N.S. Co. CL); *R v. Simon* (1985), 24 D.L.R. (4th) 390 (S.C.C.); *R v. Horseman*, [1990] 1 S.C.R. 901; *R v. Cote* (1996), 138 D.L.R. (4th) 185 (S.C.C.); *R v. Badger* (1996), 133 D.L.R. (4th) 324 (S.C.C.); *R. v. Marshall*, [1999] 2 S.C.R. 456.

66 *Thomas v. Noms*, [1992] 2 C.N.L.R. 139 (B.C.S.C.) (Aboriginal spirit dancing not protected by Charter); *Jack and Charlie v. The Queen* (1986), 21 D.L.R. (4th) 641 (S.C.C.) (taking fresh deer meat for Aboriginal death ceremony not protected).

67 Many bands were kept apart or relocated to prevent their association because of a government fear they would organize to resist impingements of their rights.

68 A Crown fiduciary duty has recently been articulated in an attempt to cure violations of Aboriginal rights stemming from differences in the way Aboriginal people hold and access their rights. Significant cases in this regard are *Guerin v. The Queen* (1984), 13 D.L.R. (4th) 321 (S.C.C.); *Kruger v. The Queen* (1985), 17 D.L.R. (4th) 591 (F.C.A.); *Blueberry River Indian Bandv. Canada* (1995), 130 D.L.R. (4th) 193 (S.C.C.). For a fuller discussion see Len Rotman, *Parallel Paths: Fiduciary Doctrine and the Crown-Native Relationship in Canada* (Toronto: University of Toronto Press, 1996).

69 *Canada (A.G.) v. Lavell*, [1974] S.C.R. 1349 (invidious distinctions in the Indian Act on the basis of sex upheld).

70 *Reference Re Secession of Quebec* at 259.

71 Ibid.

72 Ibid.

73 The Indian Act, S.C. 39 Vict., c. 18., now as amended, R.S.C. 1985, c. 1–5.

74 "This band requests the Indian department to pay expenses incurred by Peter Nadjiwan and Chief Jones to Walkerton in regard to timber carried." 20 July 1914, motion 7, Reserve Records.

75 "That hand bills be printed and circulated announcing the willingness of the band to open the pasture cattle in the vacant land of the reserve at the rate of fifty cents pr month pr head … that any cattle trespassing on the reserve shall be put in the pound when it is ascertained that the fees required has not been paid." 2 June 1902, 267. Reserve Records.

76 "That owing to some of our people being in want of seed and no means to obtain it the Department is asked if they would be

willing to grant a sum of money out of our funds not to exceed one thousand dollars to be given to those who would make good use of same and paying it back with interest out of their shares if interest money in two payments...." 5 March 1900, Reserve Records.

77   "That with a view to encourage the pursuit of agriculture and make use of the vast area of pasture lands in the reserve & assisting in making the homes industrious Indians more comfortable and attractive We ask the department to allow our agent to obtain good stock, in cows, sheep & pigs or even horses etc. and have it so arranged that they cannot sell the same for a certain time, this privilege to be given to those deserving of help and to those who attain a proficiency in economy or may be helped to get lumber in the same way." Dec. 1898, Reserve Records.

78   "That we appoint Ed Johnston to act as fishery overseer on the north westerly side of Cape Croker & on the Easterly side Paul Johnson to act & see that no white man nor a french man to fish on Indian fishing grounds. Carried." 7 October 1907, Reserve Records.

79   For a detailed and extensive record of community decisions relative to our community maintenance and development one should refer to the Cape Croker Reserve Records, MS 108, microfilmed and preserved at the Ontario Archives.

80   For the text of Treaty 72 see Canada, *Canada: Indian Treaties and Surrenders* (Ottawa: Queen's Printer, 1891–1912), at 195–6.

81   For text, see ibid, at 213.

82   Enemikeese (Conrad Van Dusen), *The Indian Chief: An Account of the Labours, Losses, Sufferings and Oppressions of Ke-zigJio-e-ne-ne (David Sawyer), A Chief of the Indians of Canada West* (London: William Nichols Printer, 1867), at 51.

83   "When we surrendered our land, and made a treaty with Mr. Oliphant in October last, Mr. Oliphant, with ourselves, walked upon a road open from our village (Saugeeng) about one mile in a straight line to the shore of Lake Huron. This road, we supposed, ran northward; and was to be the boundary between the land we surrendered, and that which we reserved adjoining Saugeeng village. But when the surveyors commenced their work, it was found that a line running due north from the village, does not reach the shore of Lake Huron till it extends about five miles and a half from the boundary agreed on by Mr. Oliphant and ourselves. By this survey we are shut out from the water of the Lake, greatly to our inconvenience and damage." Ibid, at 84–6.

84   "In a former Treaty made with Captain Anderson last summer, it was fully expressed and understood that when our land would be sold, actual settlement should be required; and we thought the same condition was implied in the Treaty made with Mr. Oliphant last October." Ibid. Notice that the Indians felt the negotiations with Anderson and Oliphant constituted the same treaty.

85   "Having no more hunting ground, from choice, as well as from necessity, we wish to turn our attention, more than ever before, to the cultivation of our land; and therefore hope our great father will encourage us in this, by giving to each in our tribe a title deed of one hundred acres of land, as prayed for in our memorial of last April." Ibid.

86   "We also beg the privilege of speaking to our great father about the propriety of taking steps towards establishing at Saugeeng, and at Newash, 'manual schools' for the benefit of our youth." Ibid.

87   "We also wish to present a 'requisition' for one hundred pounds, for the payment of our expenses and c., according to the decision of our General Council held at Saugeeng on the 5th inst., a copy of the proceedings which we have to present." Ibid. Note the exercise of self-government in holding meetings to decide how to allocate funds from their interest.

88   "We also wish to make some statements to our great father, setting forth our wishes to secure his sanction to the acts of our General Councils from time to time, when considered by the Governor in Council, calculated to secure the harmony, and promote the interest, of our tribe." Ibid.

89   Ibid, at 261–2.

90   Ibid, at 262.

91   Ibid.

92   *Van derPeet* at 547, citing Mark Walters, "British Imperial Constitutional Law, and Aboriginal Rights: A Comment on *Delgamuukw v. B.C.*" (1992) 17 *Queen's Law Journal* 350 at 413.

93   *Cote* at 407.

94   For the Supreme Court's discussion of similar issues in Quebec's claim of the right to secede on the principles of self-determination see *Reference Re Secession of Quebec* at 284–6. The exploitation and colonization of Aboriginal peoples occurred through, inter alia: the imposition of band councils over hereditary governments; the criminalization of their social, economic, and spiritual relations through the enactment of the laws against potlach; the fragmentation of their territorial integrity through the denial and/or infringement of land rights and the creation of small inadequate reserves; the century-long denial of the right to vote in federal and provincial elections; the traumatic removal of whole generations of children through residential schools and insensitive child welfare laws; and the restricted access to their traditional food sources through the imposition of discriminatory fishing and hunting licences.

95   *Reference Re Secession of Quebec* at 287.

96   Ibid, at 284–5, citing Antonio Cassese, *Self-Determination of Peoples: A Legal Reappraisal* (Cambridge: Cambridge University Press, 1995), at 334.

97   *Reference Re Secession of Quebec* at 285, citing the *Declaration on Principles of International Law concerning Friendly Relations and Co-operation among States in accordance with the Charter of the United Nations*, GA Res. 2625 (XXV), UN GAOB, 25th Sess., Supp. No. 28, UN Doc. A/8082 (1970) 121 at 123–4.

# 40

## Author's Introduction

This selection proposes a basic framework for understanding the decisions of the Supreme Court of Canada relating to Aboriginal and treaty rights. It argues that the foundations of these rights lie in the common law doctrine of Aboriginal rights, which originated in ancient custom generated by historical relations between the Crown and Indigenous peoples, as informed by basic principles of justice. This sui generis doctrine is part of the common law of Canada and operates uniformly across the country; it also provides the context for interpreting section 35(1) of the *Constitution Act, 1982*. The doctrine of Aboriginal rights has a number of distinct branches. One branch governs treaties between Indigenous peoples and the Crown, and determines their basic status, existence, interpretation and effects. Another branch deals with the various types of Aboriginal rights, including Aboriginal title and the right of self-government. Here, the doctrine distinguishes between generic and specific rights, exclusive and non-exclusive rights, and depletable and non-depletable rights. Still other branches of the doctrine articulate the principles governing the operation of Aboriginal customary law and the fiduciary role of the Crown.

Source: Brian Slattery, "Making Sense of Aboriginal and Treaty Rights," *Canadian Bar Review* 79 (2000): 196–224.

Brian Slattery

# Making Sense of Aboriginal and Treaty Rights

## I. INTRODUCTION

Over the past thirty years, the Supreme Court of Canada has begun remapping the neglected territory of aboriginal and treaty rights. It has done so piecemeal, in a series of important decisions extending from *Calder*[1] in 1973 to the recent *Marshall* case.[2] When it started, the Court had little to go on. The results of previous forays into this territory had been uncertain at best and misleading at worst. The leading authority on the subject, the Privy Council decision in *St. Catherine's Milling and Lumber Company*,[3] was replete with dubious assumptions and obscure terminology. In effect, the Supreme Court inherited a sketch map of shadowy coasts and fabulous isles, with monsters at every turn.

Let it be said that the Supreme Court has fared well in its initial ventures. Little-known areas have been brought to light and apocryphal seas dispelled.

We now know broadly what is *terrafirma* and what is not, and the monsters have been largely tamed or banished to the decorative margins. Nevertheless, the first fruits of the Court's labours amount to a series of explorer's charts, enlightening so far as they go, but covering different areas, drawn in varying projections, and sometimes bearing an uncertain relation to one another. We lack a reliable *mappamundi*. The purpose of this paper is to attempt such a map—one that surveys the subject as a whole and displays the various parts in their proper dimensions and inter-relationships.

We start with the common law doctrine of aboriginal rights and examine its two major sources: ancient custom and basic principles of justice. We then consider treaties between indigenous peoples and the Crown and discuss their status and effects. We conclude with a review of the various types of aboriginal rights, focussing on the distinctions between generic and specific rights, exclusive and non-exclusive rights, and depletable and non-depletable rights.

---

1   *Calder v. British Columbia (A.G.)*, [1973] S.C.R. 313.
2   *R. v. Marshall*, [1999] 4 C.N.L.R. 161 (S.C.C.).
3   *St. Catherine's Milling and Lumber Co. v. The Queen* (1888), 14 A.C. 46 (P.C.).

## II. THE COMMON LAW DOCTRINE OF ABORIGINAL RIGHTS

The indigenous peoples of Canada originally had the status of independent entities in international law, holding title to their territories and ruling themselves under their own laws.[4] However, by a variety of historical processes spread over several centuries, their position changed and they became protected nations, connected by binding links to the Crown, which assumed the role of overall suzerain.[5] The relationship between indigenous peoples and the Crown is governed by a distinct branch of law known as the *doctrine of aboriginal rights.*

In a nutshell, the doctrine of aboriginal rights is a body of Canadian common law[6] that defines the constitutional links between aboriginal peoples and the Crown and governs the interplay between indigenous systems of law, rights and government (based on aboriginal customary law) and standard systems of law, rights and government (based on English and French law). The doctrine of aboriginal rights is a form of "inter-societal" law, in the sense that it regulates the relations between aboriginal communities and the other communities that make up Canada and determines the way in which their respective legal institutions interact.[7]

The doctrine of aboriginal rights has two main sources. The first source is a distinctive body of custom generated by the intensive relations between indigenous peoples and the British Crown in the seventeenth and eighteenth centuries. This body of custom coalesced into a branch of British imperial law, as the Crown gradually extended its protective sphere in North America. Upon the emergence of Canada as an independent federation, it became part of the fundamental Canadian common law that underpins the Constitution.

The second source of the doctrine of aboriginal rights consists of basic principles of justice. These principles have broad philosophical foundations, which do not depend on historical practice or the actual tenor of Crown relations with aboriginal peoples. They provide the doctrine of aboriginal rights with its inner core of values and mitigate the rigours of a strictly positivistic approach to law. Basic principles of justice have always informed the common law doctrine of aboriginal rights to some extent. However, in modern times, their influence has been enhanced by the entrenchment of aboriginal and treaty rights in s. 35(1) of the *Constitution Act, 1982*.[8] These two sources—historical and philosophical—operate in tandem to support and nourish the doctrine of aboriginal rights in Canadian law. The two sources are not completely distinct but interact in myriad and complex ways: correcting, completing and reinforcing each other.

As fundamental law, the doctrine of aboriginal rights operates uniformly throughout Canada. This holds true despite the fact that the various territories comprising Canada have distinctive histories and laws and were acquired by the Crown in different ways. So,

---

4   *Calder* v. *British Columbia (A.G.), supra* note 1, per Hall J. at 383, quoting *Worcester* v. *Georgia*, 6 Peters 515 (U.S.S.C. 1832), at 542–43; R v. *Sioui*, [1990] 1 S.C.R. 1025 at 1053; B. Slattery, "Aboriginal Sovereignty and Imperial Claims" (1991) 29 Osg. Hall L.J. 681. The terms "indigenous peoples", "aboriginal peoples", and "Indian peoples" will be used interchangeably in this paper. In ordinary discourse, the term "Indian" usually has a narrower meaning, which excludes Inuit and Metis peoples, however in Canadian legal usage it often refers to indigenous peoples generally.

5   This distinctive status is reflected in the *Royal Proclamation of 1763*, which speaks of "the several Nations or Tribes of Indians, with whom We are connected, and who live under Our Protection ..."; *Royal Proclamation of 7 October 1763*, in C.S. Brigham, ed., *British Royal Proclamations Relating to America* (Worcester, Mass.: American Antiquarian Society, 1911), 212. The term "suzerain" is more apt than "sovereign" in this context because it accommodates the existence of protected political entities that retain their collective identities and some measure of internal autonomy.

6   By "Canadian common law", I mean simply the unwritten law applied by Canadian courts, whether in "common law" or "civil law" jurisdictions. I do not mean English common law, as received in certain parts of Canada. In certain spheres (notably that of aboriginal rights), Canadian common law operates uniformly across the country.

7   The concept that the law of aboriginal rights is "inter-societal" was

endorsed in *R.* v. *Van der Peet*, [1996] 2 S.C.R. 507 at 547, citing M. Walters, "British Imperial Constitutional Law and Aboriginal Rights: A Comment on *Delgamuukw* v. *British Columbia*" (1992) 17 Queen's L.J. 350, at 412–13; B. Slattery, "The Legal Basis of Aboriginal Title", in F. Cassidy, ed., *Aboriginal Title in British Columbia: Delgamuukw* v. *The Queen* (Lantzville, B.C.: Oolichan Books, 1992), at 120–21; and B. Slattery, "Understanding Aboriginal Rights" (1987) 66 Can. Bar Rev. 727, at 737. See also: J. Borrows & L. I. Rotman, "The *Sui Generis* Nature of Aboriginal Rights: Does It Make a Difference?" (1997) 36 Alta. L. Rev. 9. Of course, the various communities that make up Canada overlap; an individual may be a member of an aboriginal nation, a Nova Scotian and a Canadian simultaneously.

8   *Constitution Act, 1982*, being Schedule B to the *Canada Act 1982* (U.K.), 1982, c. 11.

the operation of the doctrine of aboriginal rights is not affected by the fact that French civil law is the basis of private law in Quebec while English common law is the foundational law in the rest of Canada. This uniformity is explained by the distinctive origins of the doctrine and its status as federal common law.[9] The following sections explore these points in greater detail.

## A. Ancient Custom[10]

The principal source of the doctrine of aboriginal rights is an ancient body of inter-societal custom that emerged from relations between British colonies and neighbouring Indian nations in eastern North America.[11] The principles informing this body of custom were suggested by the actual circumstances of life in America, the laws and practices of indigenous societies, imperial law and policy, and broad considerations of comity and justice. As early as the seventeenth century, certain elements of these principles can be discerned in aboriginal-British practice emanating from New England, New York, Virginia, and other English settlements along the Atlantic seaboard. They assumed more definite forms during the eighteenth century and were reflected in numerous Anglo-Indian treaties and Crown instruments.[12] By the time the *Royal Proclamation of 1763*[13] was issued, they had coalesced into a distinct branch of common law now known as the doctrine of aboriginal rights. This doctrine formed part of the special body of British law dealing with the Crown's overseas dominions—"imperial constitutional law", or "imperial law" for short.[14]

The doctrine of aboriginal rights developed at the same time as other basic doctrines of British imperial law and shared essentially the same juridical character. Just as imperial law governed such matters as the status of colonies and their lands, the application of English law, and the relative powers of local assemblies and the Imperial Parliament, it also harboured rules concerning the status of indigenous peoples and their lands, the operation of their laws, and the relationship between aboriginal and colonial institutions.

The doctrine of aboriginal rights, like other doctrines of imperial law, applied automatically to a new colony when it was acquired.[15] As such, the doctrine furnished the presumptive legal structure governing the position of indigenous peoples throughout British territories in North America. The doctrine applied, then, to every former British territory now incorporated in Canada, from Newfoundland to British Columbia, and from Quebec in the south to Rupert's Land in the north. Although the doctrine was a species of unwritten British law, it was not English common law in the narrow sense, and its application to a colony did not depend on whether or not English law was imported en bloc. It was part of a larger body of fundamental constitutional law that governed a colony regardless whether the local law was English, French, aboriginal, or some other type. Thus, the doctrine of aboriginal rights automatically

9   In *R. v. Cote,* [1996] 3 S.C.R. 139, at 173, the Court stated that the law of aboriginal title "represents a distinct species of federal common law rather than a simple subset of the common or civil law or property law operating within the province ...", citing *Roberts* v. *Canada,* [1989] 1 S.C.R. 322 (S.C.C.), at 340, and Royal Commission on Aboriginal Peoples, *Partners in Confederation: Aboriginal Peoples, Self-Government, and the Constitution* (Ottawa: Minister of Supply and Services Canada; 1993), at 20. For discussion, see J. M. Evans & B. Slattery, "Case Note: Federal Jurisdiction—Pendent Parties—Aboriginal Title and Federal Common Law—Charter Challenges—Reform Proposals: *Roberts* v. *Canada*" (1989) 68 Can. Bar Rev. 817, at 829–32.

10  This section draws on B. Slattery, "Understanding Aboriginal Rights", *supra* note 7 at 728–29, 736–41.

11  The process is well-described by Strong J. in *St. Catharine's Milling and Lumber Co.* v. *The Queen* (1887), 13 S.C.R. 577, at 607–16, quoted with approval by Hall J. in *Calder* v. *British Columbia (A. G.), supra* note 1 at 376–79. See also B. Slattery, *Ancestral Lands, Alien Laws: Judicial Perspectives on Aboriginal Title* (Saskatoon: University of Saskatchewan Native Law Centre, 1983), at 17–38; B. Slattery, "Understanding Aboriginal Rights", *supra* note 7 at 732–41; B. Slattery, "The Legal Basis of Aboriginal Title", *supra* note 7 at 113–21; J. Webber, "Relations of Force and Relations of Justice: The Emergence of Normative Community between Colonists and Aboriginal Peoples" (1995) 33 Osgoode Hall L.J. 623; J. Borrows, "With or Without You: First Nations Law (in Canada)" (1996) 41 McGill L.J. 629.

12  See M.D. Walters, *"Mohegan Indians* v. *Connecticut* (1705–1773) and the Legal Status of Aboriginal Customary Laws and Government in British North America" (1995) 33 Osgoode Hall L.J. 785; B. Slattery, *The Land Rights of Indigenous Canadian Peoples* (D.Phil. Thesis, Oxford University, 1979; reprint, Saskatoon: University of Saskatchewan Native Law Centre, 1979), at 95–282.

13  *Royal Proclamation of 7 October 1763,* in C.S. Brigham, ed., *British Royal Proclamations Relating to America, supra* at 212. For the Proclamation's meaning and effects, see J. Borrows, "Constitutional Law from a First Nation Perspective: Self-Government and the Royal Proclamation" (1994) 28 U.B.C.L. Rev. 1; B. Slattery, *The Land Rights of Indigenous Canadian Peoples, supra* note 12 at 191–349.

14  For the status of imperial law, see B. Slattery, "The Independence of Canada" (1983) 5 Supreme Court L.R. 369, at 375–84. In older usage, imperial law is often described as "colonial law".

15  See *R. v. Cote, supra* note 9 at 173; citing B. Slattery, "Understanding Aboriginal Rights", *supra* note 7 at 737–38.

extended to New France when Great Britain acquired the territory in 1760–63, and the doctrine was not affected by the subsequent confirmation of local French law in the *Quebec Act* of 1774.[16] As such, the doctrine limits the extent to which French civil law applies to indigenous peoples in Quebec, just as it curtails the application of English common law in the rest of Canada.

This consideration explains the continuance of indigenous customary law in Canada, a phenomenon long recognized in our courts (if not always well-understood).[17] When the Crown gained suzerainty over a North American territory, the doctrine of aboriginal rights provided that the local customs of the indigenous peoples would presumptively continue in force, except insofar as they were unconscionable or incompatible with the Crown's suzerainty. This provision resembles the imperial rule governing conquered and ceded colonies, which holds that the local law of the colony remains in force, subject to similar exceptions. However, the doctrine of aboriginal rights has a broader application than the imperial rule regarding conquests and takes effect regardless whether the territory was acquired by conquest, cession, settlement, annexation, tacit acquiescence, or some other method. It should be stressed that the doctrine is distinct from the rule governing the survival of local custom in England and is animated by different considerations. It would be as inappropriate to apply the tests governing English local custom to aboriginal peoples as it would be to saddle them with the rule against perpetuities.

The Québec case of *Connolly v. Woolrich* (1867)[18] provides an interesting example of the doctrine's operation. In that case, the courts considered the validity of a marriage contracted in the Canadian North-West under Cree customary law between an Indian woman and a man of European descent. The courts upheld the marriage, notwithstanding the fact that the man had later purported to marry another woman in a Christian ceremony under Quebec law. In attempting to discredit the first marriage, the second wife argued that English common law had been introduced into the North-West before the marriage took place, thus invalidating Indian custom. In any case, she said, the marriage customs of the Cree could not be recognized by the courts, even as among the Cree themselves. These arguments did not persuade the trial judge. He noted that the first English and French settlers in the North-West found the country in the possession of numerous and powerful Indian tribes. Even if the settlers brought with them the laws of their mother countries,

> yet, will it be contended that the territorial rights, political organization, such as it was, or the laws and usages of the Indian tribes, were abrogated; that they ceased to exist, when these two European nations began to trade with the aboriginal occupants? In my opinion, it is beyond controversy that they did not, that so far from being abolished, they were left in full force, and were not even modified in the slightest degree, in regard to the civil rights of the natives.[19]

From its origins in British imperial law, the doctrine of aboriginal rights has passed into Canadian common law and operates uniformly across Canada.[20] The doctrine was inherited not only by Canada but also by the United States after the American Revolution. A series of early decisions written by Chief Justice Marshall of the United States Supreme Court review the history of British dealings with indigenous peoples in America and identify certain principles implicit in those dealings.[21] These decisions perform for the doctrine of aboriginal rights what Lord Mansfield's celebrated decision in *Campbell v. Hall*[22] performs for other principles of imperial law, providing structure and coherence to an untidy and diffuse body of common law based on official practice.[23] While the

---

16  14 Geo. III, c. 83 (U.K.).

17  See, e.g., *Re Noah Estate* (1961), 32 D.L.R. 185 (N.W.T.T.C.), and N. K. Zlotkin, "Judicial Recognition of Aboriginal Customary Law in Canada: Selected Marriage and Adoption Cases" [1984] 4 C.N.L.R. 1.

18  *Connolly v. Woolrich* (1867), 17 R.J.R.Q.75 (Que. S.C.); reproduced in 1 C.N.L.C. 70. The decision was upheld on appeal *sub nom. Johnstone v. Connolly* (1869), 17 R J.R.Q. 266 (Que. Q.B.); 1 C.N.L.C. 151.

19  *Connolly* v. *Woolrich*, ibid, at 84.

20  The transformation of imperial legal principles into rules of Canadian common law is examined in B. Slattery, "The Independence of Canada", *supra* note 14 at 390–92.

21  See esp. *Johnson v. M'Intosh*, 8 Wheaton 543 (U.S.S.C. 1823); *Worcester v. Georgia*, 6 Peters 515 (U.S.S.C. 1832).

22  (1774), Lofft 655 (K.B.).

23  *R. v. Van derPeet, supra* note 7 at 541, citing an earlier version of this passage in B. Slattery, "Understanding Aboriginal Rights",

Marshall decisions deal with the distinctive situation of the United States, they identify a number of basic principles that have an obvious relevance to Canada and have won the approval of our courts.

The recent decisions of the Supreme Court of Canada testify to the common law foundations of aboriginal rights.[24] In dealing with such subjects as the existence and nature of aboriginal title, the character of customary rights, the fiduciary obligations of the Crown, and the effects of Indian treaties, the Court treats them as matters of Canadian common law, which exists independently of statute or executive order. The Court clearly assumes that the common law governing these subjects is uniform and does not vary from place to place. There is no suggestion that the law is unique to the specific provinces under consideration. This uniformity means that for many purposes there is no need to determine precisely which territories are covered by the Indian provisions of the *Royal Proclamation of 1763*. While there is reason to think that the *Proclamation's* basic provisions apply across Canada,[25] the question is rendered moot by the fact that the common law principles reflected in the Proclamation are in force throughout the entire country.

The fruits of this approach are evident in the *Guerin* case,[26] which involved an action by the Musqueam band of British Columbia against the federal government. The band possessed valuable reserve lands in the City of Vancouver. They alleged that, in 1957, the government induced them to surrender part of their reserve to the Crown for leasing to a golf club, with the rent to be applied to the band's account. After obtaining the surrender from the band, the government leased the land to the golf club for seventy-five years on terms much less favourable than the band had agreed to and did not even give them a copy of the lease until twelve years later. Evidence showed that the lands were potentially among the most valuable in Vancouver and could have commanded a much higher rent. The band argued that the government was guilty of a breach of trust, and asked for damages. The government responded that it was not legally responsible to the band for what it did with the lands after the surrender. In effect, it might have leased the lands on whatever terms it saw fit, regardless of what it had told the band earlier. The government's only responsibility to the band was political rather than legal.

The Supreme Court unanimously rejected the government's arguments and held it legally accountable for its actions, awarding the band ten million dollars in damages. The principal opinion was written by Dickson J., who based his decision squarely on the concept of aboriginal land rights. He held that aboriginal title is a legal right derived from the indigenous peoples' historic occupation of their lands. That title both pre-dated and survived the claims to sovereignty made by European nations in colonizing North America. Although aboriginal title was recognized in the *Royal Proclamation of 1763*, it has an independent basis in Canadian common law. It entitles indigenous peoples to possess their homelands until their title is extinguished by a voluntary cession to the Crown or by legislation. As provided in the Proclamation, aboriginal peoples have a special relationship with the Crown whereby they cannot dispose of their lands to third parties but may only cede them to the Crown. As such, the Crown serves as an intermediary between aboriginal peoples and individuals wishing to purchase or lease their lands. This relationship gives rise to a distinctive fiduciary obligation on the part of the Crown to deal with ceded lands for the benefit of the aboriginal peoples. If the Crown fails in the performance of its fiduciary duties, it is liable in damages.

In *Guerin*, then, the Court treats a rule embodied in the *Royal Proclamation of 1763* as operable in British Columbia, without entering into the question whether the Proclamation as such applies there.[27] *Guerin* also stands for the proposition that statutes

---

*supra* note 7 at 739.

24  See esp. *Roberts* v. *Canada, supra* note 9 at 340; *R.* v. *Van der Peet, supra* note 7 at 538; *R.* v. *Cote, supra* note 9 at 173–74; J. M. Evans & B. Slattery, "Case Note: Federal Jurisdiction—Pendent Parties—Aboriginal Title and Federal Common Law—Charter Challenges—Reform Proposals: *Roberts* v. *Canada", supra* note 9 at 829–32; Royal Commission on Aboriginal Peoples, *Partners in Confederation: Aboriginal Peoples, Self-Government, and the Constitution* (Ottawa: Minister of Supply and Services Canada, 1993), *supra* note 9 at 20.

25  See K.M. Narvey, "The Royal Proclamation of 7 October 1763. The Common Law, and Native Rights to Land within the Territory Granted to the Hudson's Bay Company" (1973–74) 38 Sask. L. Rev. 123; B. Slattery, *The Land Rights of Indigenous Canadian Peoples, supra* note 12 at 175–282; B. Slattery, "The Legal Basis of Aboriginal Title", *supra* note 7 at 121–29.

26  *Guerin* v. *The Queen,* [1984] 2 S.C.R. 335.

27  *Ibid.* Dickson J. at 376–79, 383–84, Estey J. at 392.

and other acts concerning aboriginal people should be read in the light of the common law of aboriginal rights, and the Court adopts this approach in interpreting the provisions of the Indian Act.[28] By implication, the common law also provides the context for understanding treaties signed with Indian nations, as well as such important constitutional provisions as s. 91(24) of the *Constitution Act, 1867*,[29] and ss. 25 and 35 of the *Constitution Act, 1982*.

As a common law doctrine, albeit a fundamental one, the doctrine of aboriginal rights could in principle be overridden or modified by legislation passed by a competent legislature, in the absence of constitutional barriers such as those embodied in the *Royal Proclamation of 1763* and s. 35(1) of the *Constitution Act, 1982*. This conclusion flows from a standard doctrine of British law attributing paramountcy to Acts of Parliament.[30] It seems doubtful whether aboriginal peoples initially understood or accepted the principle that their basic rights could be unilaterally altered by statute, and Crown agents were often less than candid on this point when they negotiated treaties with Indian nations. Nevertheless, in practice, the impact of the doctrine of Parliamentary sovereignty has been muted by the fact that, throughout much of Canadian history, the powers of local Canadian legislatures to affect aboriginal rights have been subject to certain constitutional restrictions.[31]

The doctrine of aboriginal rights has a number of distinct branches. The part dealing specifically with aboriginal lands is called the doctrine of aboriginal title.[32] Other branches of the doctrine deal with such matters as customary rights, powers of self-government, the fiduciary role of the Crown, and the status and effects of treaties. Here we can only sketch the outlines of these subjects and indicate their inter-relationships.

## B. Basic Principles of Justice
As just seen, the origins of the doctrine of aboriginal rights can be traced to the customary *modus vivendi*

reached between aboriginal peoples and the British Crown during the seventeenth and eighteenth centuries, as reflected in the *Royal Proclamation of 1763*. However, the doctrine's inner dynamic has always been linked to fundamental principles of justice, as expressed in the distinctive fiduciary role assumed by the Crown as the protector of aboriginal peoples—a role encapsulated in the phrase "the honour of the Crown".[33] These basic principles of justice constitute the second major source of the doctrine of aboriginal rights.

In recent years, the influence of this source has been enhanced by the enactment of s. 35(1), *Constitution Act, 1982*, which recognizes and affirms existing aboriginal and treaty rights. The broad significance of this provision was underlined by the Supreme Court in the landmark *Sparrow* decision.[34] The Court indicated that s. 35(1) places aboriginal and treaty rights on a new footing and infuses them with the fundamental values and principles that pervade the Constitution of Canada as a whole. So doing, it renounces the old colonial framework, which at times arguably recognized aboriginal and treaty rights only in partial and attenuated forms and subordinated them to the will of Parliament. At the same time, s. 35(1) indicates that the past cannot be entirely reversed. It limits the scope of the section to the "existing" rights of the aboriginal peoples. This word serves to indicate that certain rights originally held by aboriginal peoples were extinguished prior to 1982 and cannot be revived without injustice to third parties or serious disruption of the social order. Such rights do not qualify as "existing" rights and do not gain the protection of the section.

The concrete implications of this approach were spelled out in the *Côté* case.[35] The appellants, who were members of the Algonquin people, were convicted of regulatory offences arising from an expedition to a wilderness zone in the Outaouais region of Québec. The purpose of the expedition was to teach traditional hunting and fishing techniques to young aboriginal students. The appellants asserted that they were exercising aboriginal rights under s. 35(1). The Crown replied that no aboriginal rights could have

28  *Ibid.* esp. Dickson J. at 383–87, Wilson J. at 348–50.

29  *Constitution Act, 1867* (U.K.), 30 & 31 Vict., c. 3.

30  For the genesis of this doctrine in the colonial context, see B. Slattery, *The Land Rights of Indigenous Canadian Peoples, supra* note 12 at 384–90.

31  See B. Slattery, "Understanding Aboriginal Rights", *supra* note 7 at 774–82.

32  *R. v. Van derPeet, supra* note 7 at 540.

33  See *R. v. Sparrow*, [1990] 1 S.C.R. 1075, at 1107–10; *R. v. Van der Peet, supra* note 7 at 536–37.

34  *R. v. Sparrow, ibid.* esp. at 1091, 1103–06.

35  *R. v. Côté, supra* note 9 at 168–75, See also *R. v. Adams*, [1996] 3 S.C.R. 101, at 120–22.

survived the French assertion of sovereignty over New France because under French colonial law the Crown assumed full ownership of all lands in the territory. In deciding the case, the Supreme Court expressed its scepticism of the Crown's account of the status of aboriginal rights under the French legal regime. However, it held that the case could be resolved simply on the basis of s. 35(1), which "changed the landscape of aboriginal rights in Canada". The advent of French sovereignty did not negate the potential existence of aboriginal rights in New France for the purposes of s. 35(1). If practices, customs and traditions central to aboriginal societies continued after European contact, they were entitled to constitutional protection under s. 35(1) unless specifically extinguished. The absence of formal recognition in French colonial law should not undermine that protection. The French regime's failure to recognize legally a specific aboriginal practice cannot be equated with a "clear and plain" intention to extinguish the practice, as s. 35(1) requires.

The Court observed that the Crown's argument would create an awkward patchwork of constitutional protection for aboriginal rights across Canada, depending on the distinctive historical patterns of colonization prevailing in different regions. Such a "static and retrospective" interpretation of s. 35(1) could not be reconciled with the noble and prospective purpose of constitutional entrenchment. It would risk undermining the very rationale of the section, by "perpetuating the historical injustice suffered by aboriginal peoples at the hands of colonizers who failed to respect the distinctive cultures of pre-existing aboriginal societies." So, even assuming that the French Crown did not recognize any aboriginal rights in New France, an aboriginal group could still possess aboriginal rights within those territories for the purposes of s. 35(1).

Here the Supreme Court indicates that, in ascertaining the existence of aboriginal rights under s. 35(1), it will not blindly endorse the tenets of colonial legal regimes but will ensure that the inquiry is informed by basic considerations of justice. It will not allow s. 35(1) to be interpreted in a manner that simply perpetuates historical injustices visited on aboriginal people in colonial times. In particular, the Court rejects the view that the advent of French sovereignty or general principles of French colonial law were capable in themselves of extinguishing aboriginal rights for the

purposes of s. 35(1). However, at the same time the Court acknowledges that aboriginal rights could be extinguished by specific Crown acts that were sufficiently clear and plain.

## III. HISTORIC TREATIES

From an early period in the European penetration of North America, it became customary for relations between the Crown and Indian nations to be conducted by means of publicly negotiated agreements styled "treaties". This practice, which was well-established by the close of the seventeenth century, continued into the early years of the twentieth century and more recently has been revived as a mode of settling aboriginal claims. The contemporary pattern of treaty-making has changed significantly from the model of earlier eras and so is governed by somewhat different considerations. Here, we will confine our discussion to "historic treaties".[36]

In this context, the term "treaty" has been interpreted broadly as encompassing all engagements made to aboriginal peoples by representatives of the Crown or other persons in authority.[37] As consensual agreements, historic treaties vary widely in their terms.[38] However, just as ordinary contracts are governed by uniform principles embodied in the overarching law of contract, treaties are necessarily governed by a uniform body of law, which determines their existence, legal character, interpretation and effects. Which body of law governs historic treaties between the Crown and aboriginal peoples? Is it English common law, or the customary law of the aboriginal people in question? Or is it perhaps international law?

This inquiry touches on the much-debated question whether Indian treaties, considered as a class, are international agreements or domestic agreements governed by Canadian law.[39] However, as traditionally framed, this question poses false alternatives. It

---

36 We also leave aside inter-state treaties which contain undertakings regarding indigenous peoples.

37 *Simon v. The Queen*, [1985] 2 S.C.R. 387, at 408–09; *R. v. Sioui, supra* note 4 at 1035–45.

38 *R. v. Sundown*, [1999] 1 S.C.R. 393, at para. 25.

39 See, e.g., *Simon v. The Queen, supra* note 37 at 398–401; *R. v. Sioui, supra* note 4 at 1038, 1052–56.

seems unlikely that all agreements styled "Indian trea-ties" share exactly the same legal character. A different conclusion is suggested by the widely varying circum-stances in which historic treaties were concluded and the disparate purposes they served. In any case, there is reason to think that some treaties constitute *both* international and domestic instruments, produc-ing legal effects at both levels. International law and Canadian law are distinct and potentially overlapping systems of rules. On occasion, both systems may rec-ognize certain transactions as valid and attach legal consequences to them, each within its proper sphere.

Here we will not be able to examine the interna-tional status of Indian treaties and will confine our attention to their position in Canadian law. Viewed in this context, it seems clear that historic treaties are governed, neither by English common law nor abo-riginal customary law, but by a unique body of treaty law that forms a branch of the doctrine of aborigi-nal rights. As with other facets of the doctrine, this body of treaty law was generated by long-standing customary relations between aboriginal peoples and the Crown and is informed by basic principles of jus-tice which engage the Crown's honour. So, the law of Indian treaties is *sui generis* and does not necessarily conform with international law, English contract law or aboriginal custom.[40] For example, ancient practice attests that Indian treaties bind (and benefit) not only the individuals who were members of the aboriginal group at the time the treaty was concluded, but also individuals born into that group at later periods. This rule holds true even assuming that it violates English rules regarding third party beneficiaries of a contract.

Historic treaties were profoundly influenced by Indian concepts, procedures and ceremonial and dif-fered in a number of ways from treaties typical among European states. The outstanding difference for our purposes is the fact that normally they were oral rather than written agreements.[41] An Indian treaty typically took the form of a spoken exchange of proposals and responses, often marked by special rituals, and usu-ally taking place in several sessions extending over

a number of days, leading to a firm understanding between the parties on certain matters. In principle, the content of such a treaty can be discovered only by consulting the oral exchanges to see which proposals were ultimately accepted by the parties, with what var-iations, and under what conditions. For this reason, detailed written transcripts of the entire proceedings of a treaty were sometimes kept by the English parties, while the Aboriginal parties would commit to memory the main terms of the oral agreement, using a variety of memory-aids, including beaded belts.

At times, the English parties recorded some of the treaty terms in a concise written document that the Indian parties would be asked to "sign". Such a doc-ument has sometimes come to be regarded as the "treaty". However, this conclusion is usually unwar-ranted. In most cases, the treaty was the oral agree-ment, and the written document just a memorial of that agreement, similar in status to the belts used by some Indian parties. Many such documents have proven to be unreliable guides to the oral compacts. They often record only matters of particular interest to the English parties and omit certain terms of significance to the Indian parties. Even the recorded terms may not represent an accurate or balanced account of the true oral bargain. The written documents were often translated to the Indian parties in a manner allowing ample opportunity for misunderstanding and distor-tion. Marks on a printed sheet of paper had about as much significance for many aboriginal peoples as the colours and patterns of a treaty belt had for many English. The treaty was neither the written memorial nor the belt but the agreement reached by the par-ties during the oral exchanges. In the absence of com-plete transcripts of those proceedings, the true content of a treaty can be determined only by a comprehen-sive assessment of all available sources of information, including any written memorials or accounts, but also oral tradition, the broader social and political objec-tives of the parties, and the history of their relationship.

Treaties served a broad range of purposes. In early years, they were often used to establish or confirm peace and friendship between the parties, to regulate matters of trade, to cement military and political alli-ances against other nations, or to resolve particular disputes or grievances. On other occasions, they were used to cede aboriginal lands to the Crown in return

---

40  *Simon v. The Queen, supra* note 37 at 404; *R. v. Sioui, supra* note 4 at 1038, 1043, 1056; *R. v. Marshall,* [1999] 4 C.N.L.R. 161 (S.C.C.), at para. 44.

41  *R. v. Badger,* [1996] 1 S.C.R., 771, at 798–99, 800–03; *R. v. Sundown, supra* note 38 at para.24; *R. v. Marshall, ibid.* at paras. 14, 19, 40.

for stated benefits, to draw boundaries between aboriginal territories and areas open to settlement, or to describe in detail the limits of lands reserved for indigenous peoples within larger tracts ceded to the Crown.

Despite these differences, many historic treaties are best understood as *constitutional agreements,* which establish or reaffirm a fundamental and enduring relationship between the Crown and an aboriginal people, and which evolve over time in response to new conditions. True, not all historic treaties fit this mould. Each treaty must be assessed in its own terms. But many historic treaties cannot readily be understood apart from the fact that the parties occupied a unique position vis-à-vis each other in Canadian law—the Crown as ultimate suzerain and protector, holding certain juduciary obligations, and the aboriginal party as a protected and partially autonomous entity, owing ultimate allegiance to the Crown, but capable of acting independently within its own sphere of authority.

Are the terms of an historic treaty limited to those explicitly articulated by the parties, whether in the oral negotiations or the written memorial? Or do they also include certain *implied terms* based on the customary relations between the parties and any underlying assumptions? In the *Marshall* case,[42] the Supreme Court took the latter view. Justice Binnie noted that, even under general contract law, it is recognized that when parties enter into agreements they make certain assumptions that give their arrangements efficacy. In such instances, courts will read an implied term into the contract on the basis of the presumed intentions of the parties where it is necessary to ensure the contract's efficacy, that is, where it meets the "officious bystander test". Binnie J. went on to hold:

> If the law is prepared to supply the deficiencies of written contracts prepared by sophisticated parties and their legal advisors in order to produce a sensible result that accords with the intent of both parties, though unexpressed, the law cannot ask less of the honour and dignity of the Crown in its dealings with First Nations.

Problems have arisen in the interpretation of many historic treaties. In light of the fiduciary obligations owed by the Crown to aboriginal peoples, the Supreme Court has held that treaty terms, both oral and written, should be interpreted generously, in a manner that is favourable to the aboriginal parties and takes full account of their concerns and perspectives in entering into the treaty.[43] Moreover, treaty provisions are not "frozen-in-time" but should be interpreted in a flexible and evolutionary manner that is sensitive to changing conditions and practices.[44]

Questions have also arisen as to the enforceability of Indian treaties against the Crown. It now seems clear that, under Canadian common law, historic treaties are binding on the Crown and enforceable in its courts.[45] This conclusion is supported by a number of considerations. It would be incongruous if the Crown could now deny that it is bound by such treaties after consistently representing the contrary to aboriginal peoples over a period of several centuries. In equity, the Crown cannot be permitted to impugn the binding force of statements that have induced another party to surrender certain rights or otherwise alter its position to its detriment, as by accepting the suzerainty of the Crown or ceding tracts of aboriginal lands.[46]

Prior to 1982, treaties were subject to the doctrine of Parliamentary sovereignty, which held that a competent legislature might enact statutes infringing the terms of an Indian treaty.[47] Nevertheless, courts should hold legislatures to a high standard of clarity in this area.[48] It cannot be lightly presumed that the Crown in Parliament would disregard promises

---

42  *R. v. Marshall, supra* note 40 at para. 43.

43  *Simon v. The Queen, supra* note 37 at 402; *R. v. Sioui, supra* note 4 at 1035–36; *R. v. Badger, supra* note 41 at 794, 798–99.

44  *Simon v. The Queen, supra* note 37 at 402–03; *R. v. Sundown, supra* note 38 at Para. 32; *R v. Marshall, supra* note 40 at para. 53.

45  *Simon v. The Queen, supra* note 37 at 408–09; *R. v. Sioui, supra* note 4 at 1063; *R. v. Badger, supra* note 41 at 793–94.

46  *Guerin v. The Queen, supra* note 26 at 388–89; *R. v. Marshall, supra* note 40 at para. 12.

47  *Simon v. The Queen, supra* note 37 at 411; *R. v. Marshall, supra* note 40 at para. 48.

48  *Simon v. The Queen, supra* note 37 at 405–06; *R. v. Sioui, supra* note 4 at 1061; *R. v. Badger, supra* note 41 at 794. In *R. v. Marshall, supra* note 40 at para. 48, Binnie J. states that prior to the enactment of the Constitution Act, 1982, "the treaty rights of aboriginal peoples could be overridden by competent legislation as easily as could the rights and liberties of other inhabitants." However, in light of his subsequent discussion of the strict interpretive principles flowing from the "honour of the Crown" (in paras. 49–52), this statement should be understood as referring simply to the question of Parliamentary *competence,* rather than the applicable standards of interpretation.

made to an aboriginal group to which it owes fiduciary obligations. Of course, since 1982, a court may strike down legislation inconsistent with the terms of Indian treaties, under section 35(1) of the *Constitution Act, 1982.*[49]

What is the relationship between treaty rights and aboriginal rights? Clearly, the relationship may vary, depending on the precise terms of the treaty and the overall context. In some cases, the treaty may recognize and guarantee certain existing aboriginal rights. In other instances, it may alter aboriginal rights, as by consolidating them, redefining them, sharing them, ceding them, or reshaping them in some other fashion. Where a treaty recognizes and guarantees aboriginal rights, it does not convert them into treaty rights, in the absence of very clear language to that effect. Treaty rights throw a protective mantle over aboriginal rights, providing an extra layer of security.[50] The latter become "treaty-protected" aboriginal rights.

What does this additional layer of protection entail? First, where the Crown guarantees certain aboriginal rights in a treaty, it forfeits any asserted power to alter those rights by a *unilateral prerogative act*—that is, a Crown act not supported by legislation enacted in Parliament or by a treaty with the affected aboriginal group. According to some views, the Crown held special prerogative powers to deal with aboriginal peoples, which it could exercise by simple royal act, such as letters-patent or order-in-council. Whatever the accuracy of these Views, it is submitted that the Crown cannot exercise unilaterally any residual prerogative powers in a manner inconsistent with an historic treaty.

Second, treaty undertakings made by the Crown to aboriginal peoples give rise to particular fiduciary obligations to honour those undertakings—obligations that represent concrete instances of the Crown's more general fiduciary duties. So, as noted above, legislation passed by the Crown in Parliament should be construed as respecting the Crown's treaty undertakings, in the absence of language that specifically overrides the treaty provision. It is submitted that the requisite degree of legislative clarity is significantly higher in

relation to treaty rights than it is to aboriginal rights, otherwise the treaty undertakings would not have the effect of *reinforcing* aboriginal rights, which are already protected by a rule of interpretation requiring "clear and plain" legislation.

## IV. CLASSES OF ABORIGINAL RIGHTS

Aboriginal rights take many forms; however they also share certain general characteristics and so fall naturally into a number of classes, which we will now review. While our discussion focuses on aboriginal rights, some of our observations apply by extension to treaty rights, and we will draw several examples from that area. The links between aboriginal and treaty rights are not surprising because, as just noted, many treaty provisions reflect pre-existing aboriginal rights.

### A. Generic and Specific Rights[51]
Aboriginal rights fall into two broad categories, which for convenience we may call *generic rights* and *specific rights.*[52] A *generic* aboriginal right is a right of a standardized character held by all aboriginal groups that satisfy certain criteria. The basic contours of a generic right are determined by general principles of law rather than aboriginal practices, customs and traditions. So the broad dimensions of the right are identical in all groups where the right arises, even if certain concrete features of the right may vary somewhat from group to group. By contrast, a *specific* aboriginal right is a right distinctive to a particular aboriginal group. The overall dimensions of the right are determined by the historical practices, customs and traditions of the group in question. So, specific rights may differ substantially in form and content from group to group.

Aboriginal title provides a good example of a generic right. In the *Delgamuukw* case, Chief Justice Lamer holds that aboriginal title is governed by two principles.[53] First, title gives an aboriginal group the

49  R. v. *Badger, supra* note 41 at 812–16; R. v. *Marshall, supra* note 40 at para. 48.

50  *Simon* v. *The Queen, supra* note 37 at 401–02; see also R. v. *Marshall, supra* note 40 at para. 47.

51  This section draws on B. Slattery, "Varieties of Aboriginal Rights" (1998) 6 Canada Watch 71.

52  Lamer C.J.C. tacitly recognizes a distinction of this kind in *Delgamuukw* v. *British Columbia*, [1997] 3 S.C.R. 1010, at 1095–97; see also the remarks of La Forest J. at 1126–27.

53  *Delgamuukw* v. *British Columbia, ibid*, at 1083–91. For discussion, see K. McNeil, "Aboriginal Rights in Canada: From Title to Land to Territorial Sovereignty" (1998) 5 Tulsa J. Comp. & Int'l L. 253. The

right to the exclusive use and occupation of the land for a broad variety of purposes. These purposes do not need to be grounded in the historical practices, customs and traditions of the group. So, the group is free to use its lands in ways that differ from the ways in which the land was traditionally used. A group that lived mainly by hunting, fishing and gathering at the time of European sovereignty is free to farm the land, to ranch on it, to use it for eco-tourism or to exploit its natural resources. Second, lands held under aboriginal title cannot be used in a manner that is irreconcilable with the fundamental nature of the group's attachment to the land, so that the land may be preserved for use by future generations. In other words, the group may not ruin the land or render it unusable for its original purposes. These two principles define the basic contours of aboriginal title in all cases. As such, aboriginal title qualifies as a generic right. Nevertheless, it can be seen that the concrete application of the second principle is partly governed by a factor particular to the group—the nature of the group's original attachment to the land. So, while aboriginal title is basically a generic right, in one aspect it resembles a specific right.

Aboriginal title is not the only example of a generic right. For instance, an aboriginal right to speak an indigenous language would likely also be generic, because the basic structure of the right would presumably be identical in all groups where it arises, even though the specific languages protected would vary from group to group. As we will see later, the aboriginal right of self-government is probably also a generic right, because the powers of aboriginal governments and their place in the Canadian federal scheme are governed by uniform legal principles, even if the concrete forms that aboriginal governments take may often diverge.

By contrast, as stated in the *Van der Peet* case,[54] the character of a *specific* aboriginal right is determined by the historical practices, customs and traditions of the

particular group in question and so differ from group to group. Specific aboriginal rights may be classified in three groups, according to their degree of connection with the land.[55] The *first* group comprises *site-specific* rights—rights that relate to a definite tract of land but do not amount to aboriginal title.

For example, where an aboriginal people regularly hunted on certain lands adjoining its ancestral territory but never occupied them on a permanent basis, it may nevertheless hold a site-specific hunting right in those lands.[56]

The *second* group of specific aboriginal rights consists of land-based rights that are not tied to any *particular* tract of land—what may be called *floating rights*. A floating right is the right to engage in certain land-related activities on any lands to which members of the group have access, whether as aboriginal people or as ordinary members of the public. Consider the case where an aboriginal group has traditionally gathered wild plants for medicinal purposes. Let us suppose that these plants are not found in any particular place but grow freely in various locations, which change from year to year. It happens that the active ingredients in some of these plants are listed as "restricted drugs" in the *Food and Drugs Act*.[57] If members of the group were charged with possession of restricted drugs under the Act, they might be able to defeat the charge by establishing an aboriginal right to gather the plants for medicinal purposes. Here the aboriginal right would be a "floating right" because, although it involves a use of land, it is not tied to any specific tract of land.

In the *third* group we find specific aboriginal rights that are not necessarily linked with the land at all—*cultural rights* for short. Like other specific rights, cultural rights are grounded in the historical practices, customs and traditions of a particular aboriginal group. Their distinguishing characteristic is the fact they do not involve any particular use of the land. For example, a group might have an aboriginal right to perform certain traditional dances that are not connected with any particular location and do not involve

concept of aboriginal title is analysed in K. McNeil, *Common Law Aboriginal Title* (Oxford: Clarendon Press, 1989); K. McNeil, "The Meaning of Aboriginal Title", in M. Asch, ed., *Aboriginal and Treaty Rights in Canada* (Vancouver: University of British Columbia Press, 1997); P. Macklem, "What's Law Got to Do With It? The Protection of Aboriginal Title in Canada" (1997) 35 Osg. Hall L.J. 125.

54  *R. v. Van der Peet, supra* note 7. See also *R. v. N.T.C. Smokehouse Ltd.*, [1996] 2 S.C.R. 672; *R. v. Gladstone*, [1996] 2 S.C.R. 723.

55  This classification was suggested by the Court's observations in *Delgamuukw v. British Columbia, supra* note 52 at 1094–95. Note that a similar classification could be applied to generic rights.

56  *Delgamuukw v. British Columbia, ibid,* at 1094–95.

57  R.S.C. 1985, c. F-27, s. 46, and Schedule H.

"using" the land in a way that transcends the normal effects of human activity.

Although the distinction between generic and specific rights is clear in principle, it is less sharp in practice. What the courts initially regard as a specific right, distinctive to a particular group, may later prove to be a concrete instance of a generic right, if rights sharing the same basic structure are found to exist in a substantial number of aboriginal societies. For example, a specific right to perform certain religious rites might constitute the concrete manifestation of a generic right to practice indigenous religions. In short, as the jurisprudence of aboriginal rights evolves, specific rights may gradually be subsumed under general headings relating to generic rights.

Is the right of self-government a generic or a specific aboriginal right? In the *Pamajewon* case,[58] the Court viewed the question of self-government through the lens of specific rights, as provided by the *Van der Peet* decision, and held that the right of self-government would have to be proved as an element of specific practices, customs and traditions integral to the particular aboriginal society in question. According to this approach, the right of self-government would consist of a bundle of specific rights to govern particular activities rather than a generic right to deal with a range of more abstract subject-matters. However, *Pamajewon* was decided before the Court's holding in *Delgamuukw*, which significantly broadened our understanding of aboriginal rights and furnished us with the alternative category of generic rights.

In the light of *Delgamuukw*, it now seems preferable to treat the right of self-government as a generic aboriginal right rather than as a bundle of specific rights. On this view, the right of self-government is governed by uniform principles laid down by Canadian common law. The basic structure of the right does not vary from group to group; however its application to a particular group may differ depending on the local circumstances. This is the approach to the right of self-government taken in the Report of the Royal Commission on Aboriginal Peoples, which the Supreme Court cites in its brief comments on self-government in *Delgamuukw*.[59]

However, it could be argued that certain observations in *Delgamuukw* rule out this approach. In declining to be drawn into an analysis of self-government, the Court reiterates its holding in *Pamajewon* that rights to self-government cannot be framed in "excessively general terms". It notes that in the current case the aboriginal parties advanced the right to self-government "in very broad terms, and therefore in a manner not cognizable under s. 35(1)."[60] On one interpretation, these remarks support the view that the right of self-government is a bundle of specific rights, governed by the criteria laid down in *Van derPeet*. However, I suggest that these comments are better read simply as a warning against over-ambitious litigation, which attempts to induce the courts to settle very abstract and difficult questions without an appropriate factual or argumentative context.[61]

Elsewhere in *Delgamuukw*, the Court indicates an approach to the question of self-government that builds on the concept of aboriginal title. In discussing the communal nature of the title, Lamer C.J. states:

> Aboriginal title cannot be held by individual aboriginal persons; it is a collective right to land held by all members of an aboriginal nation. *Decisions with respect to that land are also made by that community.*[62]

This point has two important ramifications.[63] First, the manner in which the members of the group use their aboriginal lands is presumptively governed by

---

58  *R. v. Pamajewon*, [1996] 2 S.C.R. 821, at 832–33.

59  *Delgamuukw* v. *British Columbia*, *supra* note 52 at 1115; see Canada,

*Report of the Royal Commission on Aboriginal Peoples* (Ottawa: Canada Communication Group, 1996), Vol. 2, Part 1, especially at 163–280. On the right of self-government, see P. Macklem, "First Nations Self-Government and the Borders of the Canadian Legal Imagination" (1991) 36 McGill L.J. 382; B. Slattery, "First Nations and the Constitution: A Question of Trust" (1992) 71 Can. Bar Rev. 261; P. Macklem, "Distributing Sovereignty: Indian Nations and Equality of Peoples" (1993) 45 Stanf. L. Rev. 1311.

60  *Delgamuukw* v. *British Columbia*, *supra* note 52 at 1114–15.

61  As the Court states: "The broad nature of the claim [of self-government] at trial also led to a failure by the parties to address many of the difficult conceptual issues which surround the recognition of aboriginal self-government…. We received little in the way of submissions that would help us to grapple with these difficult and central issues. Without assistance from the parties, it would be imprudent for the Court to step into the breach."; *ibid*, at 1115.

62  *Ibid.* at 1082–83; emphasis added.

63  See discussion in K. McNeil, "Aboriginal Rights in Canada: From Title to Land to Territorial Sovereignty", *supra* note 53.

the internal law of the group. So, in effect, the concept of aboriginal title supplies a protective legal umbrella, in the shelter of which customary land law may develop and flourish. Second, since decisions with respect to the lands must be made by the community, there must be some internal structure for communal decision-making.

The need for a decision-making structure provides an important cornerstone for the right of aboriginal self-government. At a minimum, an aboriginal group has the inherent right to make communal decisions about how its lands are to be used. In particular, the group may determine how to apportion the lands among group members, make grants and other dispositions of the communal property, lay down laws and regulations governing land-use, impose taxes relating to the land, determine how any land-based revenues are to be expended, and so on. Since aboriginal title is itself a generic right, it follows that the right to make communal decisions about aboriginal lands is also a generic right whose basic legal contours do not vary from group to group. Nevertheless, the precise application of this right and the particular modalities of self-government that it supports will clearly be governed by factors specific to the group.

Our discussion is summarized in the following diagram:

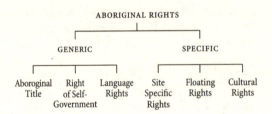

## B. Proving Specific Rights

In *Van der Peet*, the Supreme Court holds that, in order to qualify as a specific aboriginal right, an activity must be based on a practice, custom or tradition that was integral to the distinctive culture of the specific aboriginal group prior to European contact.[64] This criterion has two basic facets. First, the practice, custom or tradition must have been *integral* to the culture of the

aboriginal group; that is, it must have been a "central and significant" part of the culture, one of the things that made the society what it was. So aspects of an aboriginal society that were only "incidental or occasional" do not qualify; they need to have been "defining and central attributes" of the society.[65] A practice must have constituted a distinctive or characteristic element of the society; however, there is no need to show that the practice was unique to the group or different from the practices of other societies.[66]

Second, the practice, custom or tradition must have been integral to the aboriginal society *in the period prior to European contact*.[67] For a modern activity to qualify as an aboriginal right, it must have continuity with pre-contact practices, customs or traditions. Nevertheless, aboriginal rights are not frozen in the form that they assumed in pre-contact times but may evolve into modern forms that represent an adaptation to new conditions.[68] The fact that a pre-contact practice, custom or tradition has changed in response to the arrival of Europeans does not necessarily break the chain of continuity. However, a practice, custom or tradition that arose solely or primarily as a response to European influences will not meet the required standard.[69]

In effect, the second requirement holds that specific aboriginal rights must be of a certain vintage. They must find their origins in a stock of practices, customs and traditions that existed at a particular *threshold date*. In *Van der Peet*, Lamer C.J. holds that the appropriate threshold date is the time of "contact", when the particular aboriginal people first encountered Europeans. He rejects alternative threshold dates such as the time that a European state first asserted sovereignty over the aboriginal people in question, or the time that the Crown established effective governmental authority in the area.

The significance of this approach is demonstrated by the facts in *Van der Peet*. The appellant, a member of the Sto:lo nation, was charged with selling fish caught

---

64   *R. v. Van der Peet, supra* note 7 at 549, 554–55.

65   *Ibid,* at 553.
66   *Ibid,* at 560–61.
67   *Ibid,* at 554–55.
68   *Ibid,* at 556–67.
69   *Ibid,* at 561–62, 570. The Court uses the term "solely" at 562 but adopts the term "primarily" in applying the criterion to the facts at 570.

under an Indian food fishing licence. The applicable regulations prohibited the sale of fish caught under such a licence. The appellant argued that the regulations infringed her aboriginal right to sell fish and were invalid under s. 35(1), *Constitution Act, 1982*. At trial, the court found that prior to European contact the Sto:lo had traded fish only casually or for ceremonial purposes; however, once Europeans established themselves in the region, the Sto:lo developed a well-defined trade in fish with the Hudson's Bay Company. On these facts, the Supreme Court ruled that the appellant had failed to show the existence of an aboriginal right, since the evidence was insufficient to establish that the trade in fish was an integral part of Sto:lo society at the time of European contact. The trade with the Hudson's Bay Company was qualitatively different from that existing on contact and arose primarily as a result of European influence; as such, it could not help the appellant's case.[70] However, the Court's ruling might well have been different had it chosen the time of Crown sovereignty as the threshold date, since the trade with the Hudson's Bay Company had emerged by that date.[71]

We may observe that the Court's choice of threshold date is somewhat puzzling.[72] In British imperial law, the simple fact of "contact" between the Crown and indigenous peoples had no legal significance. Contact did not give indigenous peoples any rights in British law, nor did it have any legal impact on indigenous systems of law and rights. Contact was a legally innocent event. It was only when the Crown acquired jurisdiction over a territory that the issue of the rights of the local inhabitants arose in British law. Only at this point could the doctrine of aboriginal rights come into play. So, while it would not be *impossible* for the doctrine to recognize only customary rights that existed at some prior date of "contact", in practice this would be a strange and inconvenient way for the doctrine to operate. It would have made it virtually impossible for British officials on the spot at the time to know which asserted aboriginal rights

they should respect, without a battery of historians and anthropologists at their elbows. Not surprisingly, there seems to be no historical evidence that imperial law actually functioned in this manner.

In the subsequent case of *Delgamuukw*, the Court ruled that the threshold date for aboriginal title was the time of *Crown sovereignty* rather than *contact*.[73] The Court aptly observed that, since aboriginal title was a burden on the Crown's underlying title, it did not make sense to speak of its existence prior to the date of sovereignty. However, the Court did not overrule the *Van der Peet* criterion as it applies to specific rights. This gives rise to an odd discrepancy. Suppose that an aboriginal group of hunters moved into a certain area *after* the date of contact but substantially *before* the date of Crown sovereignty.[74] Under current law, the group would apparently be precluded from showing an aboriginal right to hunt in the area; however, paradoxically, it might be able to establish aboriginal title there, despite the fact that aboriginal title would include hunting rights. In effect, the test for the lesser right is more onerous than for the greater right. The anomaly is compounded where Group A occupied the area at the time of contact but had been displaced by Group B by the time of sovereignty. Here, Group A could show a specific aboriginal right to hunt in the area but not aboriginal title. By contrast, Group B could show aboriginal title but not a specific right to hunt. Such complications suggest the need [for] a *common historical baseline* for establishing both aboriginal title and specific aboriginal rights.

Of course, the Court's approach to specific rights in *Van der Peet* has a plausible explanation. The aboriginal right asserted there involved the exploitation of limited fishing resources—resources that the aboriginal group likely shared with other user groups, including commercial and sports fishers, as well as other aboriginal groups. No doubt, the Court was concerned about the impact of a favourable ruling on

---

70  *Ibid*, at 564–71.

71  *Ibid*, at 532.

72  For discussion, see K. McNeil, "Aboriginal Title and Aboriginal Rights: What's the Connection?" (1997) 36 Alta. L. Rev. 117, at 118,128–33; J. Borrows, "The Trickster: Integral to a Distinctive Culture" (1997) 8:2 Constitutional Forum 27.

73  *Delgamuukw v. British Columbia, supra* note 52 at 1098–99. For discussion, see K. McNeil, "Aboriginal Rights in Canada: From Title to Land to Territorial Sovereignty", *supra* note 53.

74  In some parts of Canada, contact took place long before the date that sovereignty was asserted or achieved. In the interval, there was often considerable movement among aboriginal groups, as people migrated from one area to another in response to such factors as war, internal strife, trade opportunities, and changing ecological conditions.

other user groups. However, it seems doubtful whether adopting an artificial threshold date is the best way to solve this problem. In the end, the equitable sharing of resources is better attained through governmental regulations that meet the standards of section 35(1), coupled with agreements with the groups concerned.

What is the alternative to the *Van der Peet* approach? We suggest that specific aboriginal rights may be proven in either of two ways:

1. Historical evidence showing that the right was a recognized strand in the fiduciary relationship established at the time when the Crown assumed governmental responsibility for the particular aboriginal people in question (the "transition date"). The evidence could consist of official practice, legislation, negotiations or treaties, and it could emanate either from the era when the Crown assumed responsibility, or from periods before or after that era, so long as it tended to show the basic terms of the relationship at the transition date.
2. Proof that the right is grounded in practices, customs or traditions that were integral to the distinctive culture of the specific aboriginal group at the transition date.

The second criterion can be linked to the first in the following way. If it can be proven that an activity was integral to the culture of the aboriginal group, it is presumed to have formed an incident in the fiduciary burden assumed by the Crown, even in the absence of specific historical evidence to this effect.

## C. Exclusive and Non-Exclusive Rights

Some aboriginal rights are *exclusive*. They give an aboriginal group the sole right to engage in certain activities, to use and occupy a tract of land, to exploit particular resources, and so on. The holders of the right are the only ones entitled to exercise it, and they can maintain the right against the entire world. For example, where a group has aboriginal title to a certain tract of land, it generally has the sole right to occupy and use the land and exploit its resources.[75] No one outside the group is entitled to occupy the land, and the group has the right to expel trespassers. For most practical purposes, the aboriginal group "owns" the land.

Aboriginal title is perhaps the clearest example of an exclusive aboriginal right. However, it is not necessarily the only one. For example, an aboriginal group might have exclusive rights to certain songs and stories that are a central part of the group's cultural heritage. Since the right is exclusive, persons outside the group would not be able to reproduce those songs and stories without the group's permission. The group would have a kind of aboriginal "copyright" to them.

Other aboriginal rights are *non-exclusive*. While they give an aboriginal group the right to engage in certain activities—such as to use a tract of land or to exploit a resource—they do not give the group sole benefit of the right or the capacity to prevent others from exercising corresponding rights. Suppose, for example, that a certain group has an aboriginal right to hold potlatches as a central part of its cultural heritage; however, at common law, the general public are also free to hold potlatches if they want to. Here the group's aboriginal right does not entitle it to prevent others from engaging in the same activity. It is a non-exclusive right.

What, then, is the legal status of a non-exclusive aboriginal right? Clearly it does not carry the same legal clout as an exclusive right. Nevertheless, in some contexts, a non-exclusive aboriginal right will have greater weight than a corresponding common law right. This difference flows from the distinctive origins and character of the aboriginal right: Aboriginal rights are governed by a unique fiduciary relationship between the Crown and aboriginal peoples.[76] Under this relationship, the Crown has the duty to protect the basic rights and interests of the aboriginal peoples. One effect of this duty is to restrain the hand of the Crown itself in its dealings with aboriginal peoples and their rights. So, legislation should generally be interpreted in a manner favourable to aboriginal

---

75  Nevertheless, two or more aboriginal groups may hold overlapping aboriginal titles to the same tract of land; *Delgamuukw* v. *British Columbia, supra* note 52 at 1105–06.

76  *R.* v. *Sparrow, supra* note 33 at 1107–10; *R.* v. *Van der Peet, supra* note 7 at 536–37.

and treaty rights. By contrast, rights held by the general public do not generally benefit from a similar rule of statutory interpretation.

Non-exclusive aboriginal rights may also furnish the policy basis for statutory differentiations between the rights of aboriginal peoples and those of the general public. For example, a non-exclusive aboriginal right to fish may provide the rationale for statutory provisions granting special fishing privileges to aboriginal peoples, beyond those held by the public. This sort of statutory differentiation may be shielded from Charter scrutiny by s. 25 of the *Constitution Act, 1982*, which provides that the Charter shall not be construed so as to derogate from the aboriginal, treaty and other rights held by the aboriginal peoples of Canada. Where a statute differentiates between an aboriginal group and the general public, it may be immune to challenge under the Charter if the purpose of the differentiation is [to] protect aboriginal rights, even where those rights are non-exclusive in character.

In other cases, legislative provisions may give special protection to aboriginal or treaty rights on a global basis. For example, s. 88 of the *Indian Act* states that all provincial laws of general application are applicable to Indians, subject to "the terms of any treaty".[77] The effect of the latter qualification is to shield treaty rights (both exclusive and non-exclusive) from restrictions imposed by general provincial legislation—restrictions that would apply to comparable rights held by the general public. So, for example, a non-exclusive hunting right enshrined in a treaty would be protected from provincial legislation under s. 88. Of course, the prime instance of such protective legislation is s. 35(1) of the *Constitution Act, 1982*, which recognizes and affirms "existing aboriginal and treaty rights" and shelters them from governmental limitation and infringement.

## D. The Coexistence of Exclusive and Non-Exclusive Rights

Some exclusive aboriginal rights, although in principle held against the whole world, may coexist with the exclusive rights of other parties. Conversely, some non-exclusive aboriginal rights may qualify the exclusive rights of other parties in unexpected ways. These complications merit a closer look.

In principle an exclusive right takes effect against the entire world. Nevertheless, in practice such a right sometimes overlaps with exclusive rights held by other parties. For example, where a group has an exclusive aboriginal right to pick berries in a certain area, in principle the only persons entitled to pick berries there are group members. Suppose however that the area encompasses a tract of land owned by a private individual. So long as the tract is not actually occupied by the owner in a manner that effectively precludes berry-picking, it seems that in some cases the aboriginal right may apply to the tract and co-exist with the private owner's rights.[78] Here the rights of the aboriginal group and the private owner are both exclusive; in principle they both take effect against the entire world. However, in practice the rights co-exist and overlap; neither operates to the complete exclusion of the other. In effect, both the aboriginal group and the private owner are entitled to pick berries in the tract. Again, consider a situation where two distinct indigenous groups have aboriginal rights to fish at the same location on a river bank. In each case, the aboriginal right is exclusive and holds good against the entire world. Since both rights are held in respect of the same fishing station, neither aboriginal group has the right to prevent the other from fishing there. Here, the two groups have shared exclusive rights, which co-exist and overlap.[79]

So far we have considered only exclusive rights. However, non-exclusive rights may also overlap with other rights. Consider the case where an aboriginal group holds a non-exclusive treaty right to hunt in an area that comprises some privately-owned land. This non-exclusive right may co-exist with the exclusive rights of the private owners, so long as the private land is not occupied in a manner that precludes the exercise of the hunting right. For example, in the *Badger* case,[80] the Supreme Court considered the effect of a clause in the *Natural Resources Transfer Agreement, 1930*, which provides that Indians have the right of hunting, trapping and fishing for food on unoccupied Crown lands and on any other lands to which they

---

77  R.S.C. 1985, c. 1–5.

78  This result appears to follow from the ruling in *R. v. Badger, supra* note 41 at 790–809, discussed below.

79  The concept of "shared exclusivity" is discussed in *Delgamuukw v. British Columbia, supra* note 52 at 1105–06.

80  *R. v. Badger, supra* note 41 at 790–809.

have a "right of access". The Court held that this provision should be read in the light of Treaty No. 8 of 1899, which undertakes that the Indian parties have the right to hunt, trap and fish throughout the territory surrendered in the Treaty, excepting such tracts taken up "for settlement, mining, lumbering, trading or other purposes". We may note that this right appears to be non-exclusive, in the sense that it does not preclude others from hunting in the same territory. The Court ruled that under these provisions the Indians were entitled to hunt on privately-owned land, so long as the lands were not put to visible use that was incompatible with hunting. In effect, a non-exclusive hunting right co-exists with the otherwise exclusive rights of private land-owners.

These distinctions are complicated by the fact that aboriginal rights and treaty rights—exclusive and non-exclusive alike—enjoy the protection of s. 35(1) of the *Constitution Act, 1982*. So, even where a non-exclusive aboriginal or treaty right replicates a common law right held by the general public, the aboriginal or treaty right will have the benefit of a constitutional shield not enjoyed by the common law right. For example, in the *Marshall* case,[81] the Supreme Court considered a situation where a Mi'kmaq group held treaty rights to hunt, fish and trade that arguably replicated rights held by the general public at common law. Justice Binnie held that a general right enjoyed by all citizens could nevertheless be made the subject of an enforceable treaty promise. The effect of the treaty promise was not necessarily to confer *preferential* rights on the aboriginal parties. However, even if the treaty did not enhance the *content* of the rights, it affected the level of legal protection they enjoyed. Where a statute imposes restrictions on the exercise of the treaty rights, the restrictions will not take effect unless justified under s. 35(1), *Constitution Act, 1982*. Justice Binnie observed that the fact that the content of Mi'kmaq rights under the treaty was no greater than that enjoyed by the general public did not detract from the higher protection the treaty afforded the Mi'kmaq people under s. 35(1).

By implication, the *Marshall* case supports the parallel proposition that the enactment of s. 35(1) did not normally convert non-exclusive rights into exclusive rights. Suppose that prior to 1982 a group had an aboriginal right to fish in a certain area. The right was non-exclusive and replicated the fishing rights of the general public at common law. Absent unusual circumstances, it seems that s. 35(1) would not transform this non-exclusive right into an exclusive one. After 1982, the general public would still be free to fish in the area at common law. Nevertheless, under s. 35(1), the aboriginal right would gain a measure of constitutional protection from statutory infringement that the common law right would not possess.

### E. Depletable and Non-Depletable Rights

Aboriginal rights may also be classified as *depletable* and *non-depletable*. *Depletable rights* are rights whose exercise tends to use up some portion of a finite material resource—whether renewable (like fish and trees) or non-renewable (like minerals). By contrast, the exercise of *non-depletable rights* does not involve the consumption of a finite material resource. This distinction is a practical one, which does not pretend to absolute analytical rigour. Obviously, any human activity involves the use of certain finite resources (such as space and energy). So, in this broad sense, virtually every right has resource implications because certain amounts of space and energy are needed to exercise it. When we speak of depletable rights, we have something more specific in mind—rights whose resource implications significantly transcend the routine effects of human activity.

Where a depletable right is *non-exclusive*, the exercise of the right will obviously affect the amount of the resource available to other user-groups—whether temporarily or permanently. For example, if an aboriginal group exercises its non-exclusive right to fish in certain waters, its activities will diminish the stock of fish available that season for other users and may also have long-term effects on the stock's capacity to reproduce itself. Even where a depletable right is *exclusive*, it may affect the rights of others. For example, the exercise of an exclusive aboriginal right to fish in certain waters will often affect the rights of user-groups in other waters, since fish are a mobile resource and migrate from area to area.

By contrast, non-depletable rights do not have significant resource implications. The right to speak an aboriginal language is a good example. When members of the Cree nation exercise their right to speak

---

81   R. v. *Marshall, supra* note 40 at paras. 45–48.

their ancestral tongue, they do not lessen the capacity of non-Cree people to speak the language. Rather, by keeping their language alive and flourishing, native Cree speakers enhance the opportunity of outsiders to learn and enjoy the language. In other words, when people speak their mother tongue, they do not make "withdrawals" from a finite account in a language bank. They contribute to the language bank and enrich its resources—which in principle are available to the entire world.

Depletable rights may be further sub-divided into *limited* and *unlimited* rights. *Limited* depletable rights have built-in legal restrictions that help to conserve the material resource or to safeguard the rights of other user-groups. In some cases, the scope of the right may be determined by the *amount of the resource* available at any given time. For example, a group might have the aboriginal right to fish in a certain area, subject to a built-in limit that ensures that enough fish remain for the stock to reproduce itself. In other cases, the scope of the right may be limited internally by *the purpose* that it serves—such as a right to fish for food, social and ceremonial purposes but not for commercial purposes,[82] or the right to trade the products of fishing and hunting so as to support a "moderate livelihood" but not the "accumulation of wealth".[83]

By contrast, *unlimited* depletable rights do not have built-in legal restrictions and so in principle may be exercised so as to exhaust the material resource in question. So, for example, an aboriginal group might have the exclusive right to exploit a mineral resource found on certain lands. Here the right could well be unlimited, in that it does not prevent the entire mineral resource from being used up. Of course, the fact that an aboriginal or treaty right is unlimited as a matter of internal definition does not necessarily prevent it from being regulated by aboriginal governments or by public legislation that satisfies the standards laid down under s. 35(1), *Constitution Act, 1982*.

The main significance of the distinction between depletable and non-depletable rights lies in the constitutional arena. The entrenchment of aboriginal and treaty rights in s. 35(1) has greater implications for depletable rights than non-depletable rights, because it may affect the distribution of the resource among the various user-groups. By contrast, the entrenchment of a non-depletable right does not have this effect, because the exercise of such a right does not diminish the capacity of others to exercise equivalent rights. So, in applying s. 35(1), there is good reason to distinguish between depletable and non-depletable rights and to apply different standards to them.

## CONCLUSION

We have argued that the foundations of aboriginal and treaty rights lie in the common law doctrine of aboriginal rights, which originated in ancient inter-societal custom generated by interaction between the Crown and indigenous peoples, as informed by basic principles of justice. This *sui generis* doctrine is part of the common law of Canada and operates uniformly across the country; it also provides the context for interpreting section 35(1) of the *Constitution Act, 1982*. The doctrine of aboriginal rights has a number of distinct branches. One branch governs treaties between indigenous peoples and the Crown, and determines their basic status, existence, interpretation and effects. Another branch deals with the various types of aboriginal rights, including aboriginal title and the right of self-government. So doing, the doctrine distinguishes between generic and specific rights, exclusive and non-exclusive rights, and depletable and non-depletable rights. Still other branches of the doctrine articulate the principles governing the operation of aboriginal customary law and the fiduciary role of the Crown. In brief, the common law doctrine of aboriginal rights provides the basic frame within which particular aboriginal and treaty rights may be identified. It is our *mappamundi*.

---

82    See *R. v. Sparrow, supra* note 33 at 1099–1101.
83    *R. v. Marshall, supra* note 40 at paras. 57–61.

# 41

## Author's Introduction

This article looks at Canada's lengthy engagement in constitutional politics from the perspective of Canada being a multi-national society. Most countries in the world are in some sense multi-ethnic or multicultural but far fewer are multi-national. Multi-nationalism within a country goes deeper than multiculturalism or ethnic diversity. A country is multi-national when it has societies within it that claim national status. Canada is such a society primarily because the English-speaking people that came to dominate it did not complete their conquest of the Canadiens, the French-speaking inhabitants of New France, nor of the many North American Indigenous nations. Instead, the British North Americans tried to accommodate the nationalist aspirations of the Québécois through the agreement that resulted in Confederation and the vital interests of the Indigenous nations through treaties with Indian nations. The constitutional politics of accommodating nations within becomes ever more difficult when it must respond to a new country-wide Canadian nationalism with which a majority of Canadians who are neither francophone nor Aboriginal strongly identify. This article argues that the main lesson to be learned from Canada's recent engagement in constitutional politics is to avoid trying to accommodate these competing nationalisms through one grand mega-effort at constitutional change.

Source: Peter H. Russell, "Canada: A Pioneer in the Management of Constitutional Politics in a Multi-National Society," in *The Politics of Constitutional Reform in North America: Coping with New Challenges*, ed. Rainer-Olaf Schultze and Roland Sturm (Opladen: Leske + Budrich, 2000), 227–34.

Peter H. Russell

# Canada: A Pioneer in the Management of Constitutional Politics in a Multi-National Society

IT IS CANADA'S fate to have become a pioneer in managing a very challenging type of constitutional politics. This is the constitutional politics of a democratic political community among whose people there are very different senses of national allegiance and identity. In such a society the big background issue of constitutional politics always is: can these people or peoples constitute a political community?

Canada's engagement in this kind of constitutional politics has come about not through rational choice or abstract philosophy. We have stumbled into this situation without fully realizing what we were doing. Even now many Canadians, perhaps even a majority—especially in "English Canada" and among new immigrants—would not accept my characterization of Canada as a multi-national society. They yearn for a Canada with a single sense of national identity. In effect, they yearn for a different Canada than the one in which they find themselves. Indeed, their very sense of unease about our disunity is an important element in Canada's constitutional restlessness.

In large measure we Canadians stumbled into the situation we find ourselves in through incomplete conquests. In the eighteenth century, the British did not complete their conquest of New France by expelling the Canadiens as they had earlier done with the Acadians. Nor did they carry through with a program of forced assimilation of French Catholics into their English/Protestant culture. Within 15 years of the conquest they recognized the conquered people's religion and civil law. The British did not do this out of any profound philosophical commitment to political or cultural pluralism. They did it mainly as a strategy for securing the loyalty of the Canadiens at a time when the Empire was threatened with rebellion in the American colonies to the south. Nonetheless it was a decisive move towards a deeply pluralist Canada and Empire.

The absence of any commitment to cultural pluralism was evident again in the nineteenth century when British constitutionalists responded to rebellions in their two Canadian provinces. Lord Durham's plan was to assimilate the French Canadians into the English culture which he believed would soon dominate a reunited Canada. But the Québécois defeated this effort by surviving with their own sense of identity and forcing a federal constitutional solution with a province in which they as a majority would have enough political power to secure the essential elements of their distinct society.

The other incomplete conquest concerns the Indigenous peoples. In the seventeenth and eighteenth centuries the British (like the French) for military and commercial reasons entered into treaty-like agreements with Aboriginal nations. The Royal Proclamation of 1763 which set out British policy for governing the lands ceded by France at the end of the Seven Years War recognized the Indian nations' possession of territory outside the settled British colonies and laid down that settlement in this territory could take place only on lands that were sold or ceded by the Indians to the Crown. The Royal Proclamation, though often ignored in the nineteenth and twentieth centuries, survives as part of Canada's constitutional law. In 1982 its primacy was acknowledged in section 25 of the new Canadian Charter of Rights and Freedoms.

In Canada as in the United States once the settlers clearly had the upper hand militarily and demographically, treaty-like relations with Indigenous peoples gave way to colonial domination. Still there is an important difference between the two countries. In Canada right up into the twentieth century, treaties were the principal means for acquiring new lands from the Indians for settlement and economic development in much of Ontario, the western prairies, north-eastern British Columbia and part of the Northwest Territories. While the practical impact of these treaties was massive dispossession, nonetheless they did entail recognition by the incoming settler state of the Aboriginal signatories' nationhood and their collective ownership of traditional lands. The United States also made hundreds of treaties with Indian nations and through Chief Justice John Marshall's jurisprudence accorded Indian peoples the status of "domestic, dependent nations." However,

soon after the Civil War, Congress abolished all future treaty-making. The American west was won from the Indians through brutal warfare rather than duplicitous treaties.

The continuity of treaty relationships with Aboriginal peoples in Canada has had important consequences for the present day. In the 1960s and 70s, a resurgence of Aboriginal nationalism induced the federal government to abandon its program of assimilation and resume the process of making agreements with native peoples who continue to occupy their traditional lands. Taking advantage of the constitutional restructuring brought on by Québec nationalism, Aboriginal peoples were able to have their rights, including treaty rights, recognized in the Constitution Act of 1982. Federal and provincial governments in Canada now recognize Aboriginal peoples as "First Nations" and are engaged, all across the country, in a process of negotiating self-government agreements with them, as well as with the Metis nation and Inuit peoples.

It is the persistence over centuries of the Québécois and the Indigenous peoples of Canada in insisting on their recognition as distinct peoples or nations that obliges Canada, if it is to survive with its present borders and population, to manage the constitutional affairs of a multi-national community. Let us be clear that what is at issue here is not simply a multi-cultural state but a multi-national state. Virtually every state in the world is in fact multi-cultural and acknowledges this, in varying degrees, in its laws and policies. Canada goes much further with multi-culturalism than most, extending financial support and encouragement to many ethnic minorities besides French-speaking Canadians and Aboriginal peoples. Functioning as a multi-national political community means something much more difficult and problematic than multi-culturalism. It means, in the Canadian case, acknowledging that two groups, French Canadians and Indigenous peoples, are not just cultural minorities but political societies with the special rights of homeland peoples to maintain political jurisdictions in which they can ensure their survival as distinct peoples.

Most of the Canadian citizens who belong to these "nations within" have a dual sense of national identity. In varying degrees most Aboriginal Canadians and French-speaking Québecers identify with Canada as well as with their own historic nations—though they may be reluctant to recognize Canada as "their nation." Alongside them, the majority of Canadians acknowledge Canada as their nation—their only nation—and in varying degrees despair of accommodating the "nations within." Managing the constitutional affairs of a population with such conflicting and incoherent notions of national identity is not just Canada's challenge but the challenge of many areas in the world today where some kind of national autonomy within a larger political community is the main alternative to the splintering of states or international conflict. That is why Canada's fortunes in dealing with this challenge bear watching.

Throughout its first century the Canadian federation had very few constitutional affairs to manage. The Confederation Constitution was based on an agreement between English and French Canadian politicians laden with ambiguity and conflicting expectations about the future of the federation. Indigenous peoples were included only as mute subjects of the new central government. Constitutional sovereignty—the power to amend the constitutional text—remained in the hands of the British Parliament. The federation grew and its structure evolved without any grand attempts to settle or accommodate constitutional differences. The main developments were the strengthening of provincial rights, a very strong commitment to a federal ethic, the confining of French Canada primarily to Québec, and concerted efforts by the federal government, despite the treaty process, to assimilate native peoples into what was fervently believed to be the superior culture of the Europeans.

Canadians did not become embroiled in constitutional politics until after World War II when federal politicians—French as well as English—moved by a sense of Canadian nationalism became determined to terminate Canada's constitutional colonialism and "patriate" the country's Constitution. They then confronted the unresolved ambiguities and differences about the nature of Canada as a political community. For transferring the power to amend the Constitution from Britain to Canada meant deciding who or what in Canada—which government or governments, which people or peoples—would be constitutionally sovereign. By the mid-1960s it was becoming clear that this grand issue—a mega issue in constitutional politics if ever there was one—would not be easy to resolve. A secular nationalism was also now moving many French Québecers to insist that patriation, the fulfillment of Canadian nationhood, should take place only if the position of Québec as the homeland of a nation within Canada was more strongly and explicity secured in the Canadian Constitution. The result, of course, of this collision of nationalisms and constitutional visions was an entire generation of very heavy constitutional politics—what I have called "mega constitutional politics."

Fear not—I am not about to take you through the many chapters of this seemingly endless constitutional struggle—the Victoria Charter, Trudeau's initiatives, the 1980 Québec referendum, Patriation, the conferences with Aboriginal peoples, Meech Lake, the Charlottetown Accord, the 1995 Québec referendum and all of that. If you want details, there are many books written about all of these events, including one of my own (Russell 1993). (Indeed, I am in no position to complain about the struggle as I have truly dined out on it—in Canada and around the world). But I do wish to reflect on its outcome, and what we can learn from the experience about constitutionalism in societies that are deeply divided in a multi-national sense.

The first thing to observe is that after a generation of constitutional wrangling Canadians are no closer to resolving explicitly in formal constitutional terms the big issues that divide them. Important constitutional changes were made in 1982—patriation, a constitutional bill of rights and constitutional recognition of Aboriginal rights. But Prime Minister Trudeau's government forced these changes through over the opposition of Québec's provincial government and most of Canada's Aboriginal leaders. This led to the subsequent constitutional efforts—the inconclusive First Ministers' Conferences with Aboriginal leaders, the defeat of the Meech Lake Accord designed to accommodate Québec and the referendum defeat of the Charlottetown Accord designed to accommodate everyone. The miracle is not that this latter effort failed but that it came so close to succeeding!

At the end of all this, many observers of our constitutional scene would conclude that the Canadian political community is more deeply divided than it was at the beginning of this constitutional struggle. In the light of the nearly 50-50 split in the 1995 Québec referendum, the same might be said of Québec as a political community. And, as the Nisga'a Treaty with its provision for an Aboriginal nation to exercise a real share of law-making sovereignty in Canada runs into stiff opposition among non-Aboriginal Canadians, there is no sign of a clear consensus on the future of Aboriginal peoples in Canada. The one point on which Canadians are now constitutionally united is their exhaustion with contesting constitutional issues. It is this feeling of constitutional exhaustion that may in the end persuade Québec sovereignists not to proceed with yet another referendum. These failed efforts at reaching a constitutional consensus in Canada did succeed in changing one important feature of Canada's constitutional culture: they democratized it. Making the written Constitution the most important political issue in the country for a generation, talking about the Constitution as ideally a vision of our society, a mirror in which all Canadians can see themselves, a document inscribing what we are all about—all of this convinced the Canadian public that they must have a crucial say in making any important changes in the Constitution. Political elites may still play the lead role in negotiating and drafting constitutional proposals—that much of consociational democracy remains intact. But for proposals for fundamental constitutional change to be legitimate in Canada they must now be ratified by the people voting in referendums.

This democratization of Canada's constitutional process has not been written into the country's Constitution—though it has been incorporated into the constitutional systems of Québec, the three western-most provinces and several Aboriginal nations. Nonetheless, I believe that for major constitutional changes in the structure of our federal institutions or the structure of the federation, in the status of Indigenous peoples, or in the Charter of Rights and Freedoms, a Canadian wide referendum would be a political imperative for all. For this reason Bruce Ryder and I in a paper on "Ratifying a Post-referendum Agreement on Québec Sovereignty" (Ryder/Russell 1997) argued that, if after a sovereignist win in a Québec referendum, federal, provincial and Aboriginal leaders negotiated an agreement on a fundamental change in Québec's constitutional status, their agreement would have to be submitted to a Canada-wide referendum.

At a very abstract philosophical level, a compelling case can be made for this democratization of the constitutional process: in a constitutional democracy, after all, shouldn't the people be sovereign and have the final

say on their highest law, the Constitution? The trouble with applying this simple principle of popular sovereignty to a multi-national society like Canada is the absence of an agreement on who the sovereign people are or on how that will can be identified. Québec sovereignists would say the people of Québec are sovereign and a majority of them express the people's will. This view is repudiated by federalists within and outside Québec, many of whom would argue that some majority of Canadians—simple or extraordinary— is sovereign in Canada. Most Aboriginal people do not believe their nations ever surrendered their sovereignty—though they might have difficulty agreeing on how that sovereignty is expressed in the present context.

Thus in the Canadian case—and I would submit in other multi-national communities—that first step in the Lockean social contract whereby all consent to form a single sovereign people to be governed by an agreed upon political authority has not and may never be taken. In a setting such as this attempts at grand constitutional settlements are much more likely to exacerbate than to resolve societal conflict.

The recipe for managing constitutional affairs that this analysis yields is not one of constitutional immobilisme. One of the worst myths haunting Canada's constitutional affairs is that the only alternative to a grand resolution of constitutional issues is a constitutional deep-freeze. Through the 1990s since the demise of the Charlottetown Accord important changes have been taking place in the operation of our constitution. Changes in the roles and responsibilities of government in our federal system have occurred without formal constitutional amendment. Some of this was consolidated in a political agreement on the Social Union (see Lazar/McLean: this volume). The parties to this agreement were the federal government and all of the Canadian provinces except Québec. In this agreement, the provinces for the first time acknowledge the legitimacy of the federal government using its spending power to support initiatives in areas of exclusive provincial jurisdiction, and in exchange the federal government agrees to launch such shared-cost or block-funded programs only with the agreement of a majority of provincial governments.

Québec's non-participation in the Social Union agreement demonstrates the strength and limitation of this kind of change. In effect it underlines

Québec's special status in the Canadian federation without requiring that Canadians agree on explicit recognition of this special status in the constitutional text—an agreement that would probably be impossible to secure.

Progress has also been made in reforming Aboriginal relations. The Royal Commission on Aboriginal Peoples—the first collaborative inquiry in world history of indigenous and non-indigenous people into the past, present and future of their mutual relationship—has mapped out the path to a post-colonial relationship through treaty-like agreements on land and governance. Through such an agreement, Nunavut, the homeland of the Eastern Arctic Inuit, is now up and running as a new self-governing territory of Canada. Treaty negotiations on land and governance issues are currently under way at approximately 80 different "tables" in every part of Canada. The Supreme Court of Canada's 1997 decision in *Delgamuukw* confirming Aboriginal peoples' ownership and control of their traditional, unsurrendered lands gave strong legal backing to this modern treaty process.

Popular support for this process of recognizing Aboriginal nations as self-governing nations within Canada is, however, shaky. Many non-Aboriginal commentators in the popular media are shocked to learn that under the Nisga'a Agreement the Nisga'a people besides being citizens of Canada will be recognized as citizens of the Nisga'a nation and that the Nisga'a government will have supreme law-making authority on matters such as their own constitution, language and culture, the education of their children and the management of the 10% of their traditional lands and resources recognized in the Agreement as belonging to them. Similar provisions are contained in other agreements now being negotiated across the country. The Nisga'a people have ratified the agreement and a very unpopular British Columbian government has pushed it through the British Columbia legislature. It is now before the federal parliament which must also approve it before it becomes law. The Chretien government having been a party to the treaty and with a majority in the House of Commons will ensure its safe passage, but not without an acrimonious political debate. If, as the opposition urged, the Nisga'a Agreement had been put to a referendum in B.C., it would very likely have been rejected. The Nisga'a Agreement, the product of over twenty years of negotiations, is inevitably a compromise. It is bitterly attacked by native critics as giving up too much land and self-government, just as many non-Aboriginal Canadians question it for going too far the other way. In constitutional referendum campaigns fought through the mass media nay-sayers have an easier time standing on the high ground of pure principle and scaremongering about change than do the defenders of grubby compromise.

Thus we Canadians limp along adjusting constitutional relationships in our multi-national political community without definitively settling the question of who or what we are, and without any clear popular consensus on the nature of the country expressed in the text of our constitution. The lesson we may have taught ourselves, and perhaps other deeply divided political communities, is that it is best not to try reaching a grand and explicit popular agreement on fundamental constitutional principles. As a number of our constitutional commentators have observed, abeyance and avoidance of intractable abstract questions such as the locus of sovereignty and the identity of the nation are conditions of constitutional peace in Canada. Of course, there are some who do not want peace. The most militant of these are the Québec sovereignists. They, by definition, do not accept that sovereignty should be shared. And despite constitutional exhaustion, they may yet force the issue. If they do have another referendum, and if they win it (whatever "winning" means), I am not sure what the final outcome will be—a totally independent Québec, a Québec in some new partnership relation with Canada or the status quo. However, I am fairly certain of one thing which is that in a newly configured Canada or an independent Québec with its present borders, as in Canada as it now is, sovereignty will in fact be shared among peoples, and there will once again be a need to practice the quiet and delicate constitutional arts of sharing sovereignty in a multi-national society.

## REFERENCES

Russell, Peter H. 1993: *Constitutional Odyssey. Can Canadians Be a Sovereign People?* Toronto: University of Toronto Press.
Ryder, Bruce/Russell, Peter H. 1997: "Ratifying a Post-referendum Agreement on Québec Sovereignty," in *The Secession Papers*, Toronto: C.D. Howe Institute.

# Credits

1

MacGregor Dawson, Robert. "The Constitution." In *Democratic Government in Canada,* 6th ed., rev. by Norman Ward (Toronto: University of Toronto Press, 1989), 86–94. Reproduced with permission of the publisher. © University of Toronto Press 1989.

2

Mallory, James R. "The Pattern of the Constitution," from *The Structure of Canadian Government,* rev. ed. (Toronto: Gage Publishing, 1984), 1–26. Rights unattributable.

3

Mallory, James R. "Responsive and Responsible Government." *Transactions of the Royal Society of Canada* 12 (1974): 210. Public domain.

4

Forsey, Eugene, and G.C. Eglinton. *The Question of Confidence in Responsible Government* (Ottawa: Special Committee on the Reform of the House of Commons, 1985), 1–20, 119. Public domain.

5

Smith, David E. "The Canadian Senate: What Is To Be Done?" In *The Canadian Senate in Bicameral Perspective* (Toronto: University of Toronto Press, 2003), 149–175, footnotes pp. 219–223. Reproduced with permission of the publisher. © University of Toronto Press 2003.

6

Watts, Ronald L. "The Federative Superstructure." In *Options for a New Canada* (Kingston: Institute of Intergovernmental Relations, 1991), 309–336. Reprinted with permission from the Institute of Intergovernmental Relations.

7

Stanley, George. "A Short History of the Constitution." In *The Birth of Western Canada* (Toronto: Ryerson Press, 1969), 71–80. Reproduced with permission from the author's estate.

8

Rawlyk, George A. "The Historical Framework of the Maritimes and the Problems of Confederation." In *The Atlantic Provinces and the Problems of Confederation* (St. John's, NL: Breakwater, 1979), 8–18. Reproduced with permission from Breakwater Books and the author's estate.

9

Silver, A.I. "Confederation and Quebec." In *The French-Canadian Idea of Confederation: 1864–1900,* 2nd ed. (Toronto: University of Toronto Press, 1997), 33–50. Reproduced with permission of the publisher. © University of Toronto Press Incorporated 1997.

10

Creighton, Donald G. "The Division of Economic Powers at Confederation." In *British North America at Confederation.* A Study Prepared for the Royal Commission on Dominion-Provincial Relations (Ottawa: 1939), section IX, pp. 49–58. Public domain.

11

LaSelva, Samuel V. "Confederation and the Beginnings of Canadian Federalist Theory." In *The Moral Foundations of Canadian Federalism: Paradoxes, Achievements, and Tragedies of Nationhood* (Montreal: McGill-Queen's University Press, 1996), 31–48. Reproduced with permission from McGill-Queen's University Press.

12

Smiley, Donald V., ed. *The Rowell-Sirois Report: An abridgement of Book 1 of the Royal Commission Report on Dominion-Provincial Relations,* Carleton Library No. 5 (Toronto: McClelland and Stewart, 1940), 30–43, 70–81. Rights unattributable.

13

Simeon, Richard. "The Social and Institutional Context." In *Federal-Provincial Diplomacy: The Making of Recent Policy in Canada* (1972; repr., Toronto: University of Toronto Press, 2006), 20–42. Reproduced with permission of the publisher. © University of Toronto Press Incorporated 2006.

14

Russell, Peter H. "Provincial Rights." In *Constitutional Odyssey,* 3rd ed. (Toronto: University of Toronto Press, 2004), 34–52, footnotes pp. 307–311. Reproduced with permission of the publisher. © University of Toronto Press Incorporated 2004.

15

Armstrong, Christopher. "The Mowat Heritage in Federal-Provincial Relations." In *Oliver Mowat's Ontario,* ed. Donald Swainson (Toronto: Macmillan, 1972), 93–118. Rights unattributable.

16

Russell, Peter H. "The Supreme Court and Federal-Provincial Relations: The Political Use of Legal Resources." *Canadian Public Policy* 11(2) (1985): 161–170. Article reproduced with permission from *Canadian Public Policy.*

17

Smith, Jennifer. "The Origins of Judicial Review in Canada." In *Law, Politics, and the Judicial Process in Canada,* ed. Ted Morton (Calgary: University of Calgary Press, 1987), 433–441. Reproduced with permission from University of Calgary Press and Ted Morton.

18

Cairns, Alan C. "The Judicial Committee and Its Critics." In *Constitution, Government and Society in Canada: Selected Essays by Alan C. Cairns,* ed. Douglas E. Williams. (Toronto: McClelland and Stewart, 1988) 43–85, footnotes 261–81. Reprinted with permission from the author.

19

Saywell, John. "The Watson Era, 1889–1912." In *The Lawmakers: Judicial Power and the Shaping of Canadian Federalism* (Toronto: Osgoode Society for Canadian Legal History and University of Toronto Press, 2002), 114–149. Reprinted by permission of the Osgoode Society for Canadian Legal History and the author.

20

Scott, Frank R. "Some Privy Counsel." *Canadian Bar Review* 28 (1950): 780. Reproduced with permission from the *Canadian Bar Review.*

21

Cairns, Alan C. "The Living Canadian Constitution." *Queen's Quarterly* 77(4) (1970): 1–16. Reprinted with permission.

22

Lederman, William R. "The Independence of the Judiciary." In *Law, Politics, and the Judicial Process,* ed. F.L. Morton (Calgary: University of Calgary Press, 2002) 183–88. Reproduced with permission from the University of Calgary Press and F.L. Morton.

23

Hogg, Peter W. "Is the Supreme Court of Canada Biased in Constitutional Cases?" *Canadian Bar Review* 57 (1979): 721–739. Reproduced with permission from the *Canadian Bar Review* and the author.

24

Silver, A.I. "Manitoba Schools and the Rise of Bilingualism." In *The French-Canadian Idea of Confederation, 1864–1900,* 2nd ed. (Toronto: University of Toronto Press, 1982), 180–217. Reproduced with permission of the publisher. © University of Toronto Press Incorporated 1997.

**25**

Dafoe, J.W. "The Tactics of Victory." In *Laurier: A Study in Canadian Politics* (Toronto: McClelland and Stewart, 1968), 34–39. Rights unattributable.

**26**

Pigeon, Louis-Philippe. "The Meaning of Provincial Autonomy." *Canadian Bar Review* 29 (1951): 1126–1135. Reproduced with permission from the *Canadian Bar Review.*

**27**

Brady, Alexander. "Quebec and Canadian Federalism." *Canadian Journal of Economics and Political Science* 25(3) (1959): 259–270. Reprinted with permission from Cambridge University Press. *The Canadian Journal of Economics and Political Science / Revue canadienne d'Economique et de Science politique* © 1959.

**28**

Trudeau, Pierre Elliott. "Quebec and the Constitutional Problem." In *Federalism and the French Canadians* (Toronto: Macmillan, 1968), 3–51. Reprinted by permission of Marc Lalonde, Literary Executor of the Trudeau Estate.

**29**

Laforest, Guy. "Lord Durham, French Canada and Quebec: Remembering the Past, Debating the Future." In *Lord Durham's Report: A Re-Edition*, ed. J. Azjenstat (Montreal: McGill-Queen's University Press, 2007), 177–203. Reproduced with permission from McGill-Queen's University Press.

**30**

Cairns, Alan C. "Reflections on the Political Purposes of the Charter: The First Decade." In *Reconfigurations: Canadian Citizenship & Constitutional Change*, Alan C. Cairns, ed. Douglas E. Williams (Toronto: McClelland and Stewart, 1995), 197–199. Reproduced with permission from the author.

**31**

Whyte, John. "On Not Standing for Notwithstanding." *Alberta Law Review* 28 (1990): 347–357. Reproduced with permission from the *Alberta Law Review* and the author.

**32**

Russell, Peter H. "Standing Up for Notwithstanding." *Alberta Law Review* 29(2) (1991): 293–309. Article reproduced with permission from the *Alberta Law Review* and the author.

**33**

Sigurdson, Richard. "Left- and Right-Wing Charter-phobia in Canada: A Critique of the Critics." *International Journal of Canadian Studies* (1993): 95–117. Reprinted with permission from the *International Journal of Canadian Studies.*

**34**

Gibbins, Roger, and Loleen Berdahl. "Western Canadian Perspectives on Institutional Reform: Introduction and Context." In *Western Visions, Western Futures: Perspectives on the West in Canada*, Roger Gibbins and Loleen Berdahl (Toronto: University of Toronto Press, 2003), 191–201. Reproduced with permission of the publisher. © 2003 Roger Gibbins and Loleen Berdahl.

**35**

Robertson, Gordon. "The Holy Grail." In *Northern Provinces: A Mistaken Goal*, Gordon Robertson (Montreal: Institute for Research on Public Policy, 1985), 21–40. Reproduced with permission from the Institute for Research on Public Policy, www.irpp.org.

**36**

Rémillard, Gil. "The Constitution Act, 1982: An Unfinished Compromise." *American Journal of Comparative Law* 32 (1984): 269–281. Reproduced with permission from the *American Journal of Comparative Law.*

**37**

Macdonald, Roderick A. "Three Centuries of Constitution Making in Canada: Will There Be a Fourth?" *University of British Columbia Law Review* 30(2) (1996): 211–234. Article reproduced with permission from the *University of British Columbia Law Review.*

502

### 38

Choudhry, Sujit, and Robert Howse. "Constitutional Theory and the Quebec Secession Reference." *Canadian Journal of Law and Jurisprudence* 13(2) (2000): 143–169. Reproduced with permission from the *Canadian Journal of Law and Jurisprudence*.

### 39

Borrows, John. *Recovering Canada: The Resurgence of Indigenous Law* (Toronto: University of Toronto Press, 2002), 124–137, footnotes pp. 250–260. Reproduced with permission of the publisher.

### 40

Slattery, Brian. "Making Sense of Aboriginal and Treaty Rights." *Canadian Bar Review* 79 (2000): 196–224. Reproduced with permission from the *Canadian Bar Review* and the author.

### 41

Russell, Peter H. "Canada: A Pioneer in the Management of Constitutional Politics in a Multi-national Society." In *The Politics of Constitutional Reform in North America: Coping with New Challenges*, eds. Rainer-Olaf Schultze and Roland Sturm (Opladen: Leske + Budrich, 2000), 227–234. Reproduced with permission from Springer Publications.